ISBN 978-0-260-01783-3
PIBN 11110959

Forgotten Books is a registered trademark of FB &c Ltd.
Copyright © 2018 FB &c Ltd.
FB &c Ltd, Dalton House, 60 Windsor Avenue, London, SW19 2RR.
Company number 08720141. Registered in England and Wales.

For support please visit www.forgottenbooks.com

1 MONTH OF
FREE
READING

at

www.ForgottenBooks.com

By purchasing this book you are eligible for one month membership to ForgottenBooks.com, giving you unlimited access to our entire collection of over 1,000,000 titles via our web site and mobile apps.

To claim your free month visit:

www.forgottenbooks.com/free1110959

Ontario, Legisla... Ass...bly.

SESSIONAL PAPERS

.11

VOLUME XXXIX.—PART I.

Third Session of Eleventh Legislature

OF THE

PROVINCE OF ONTARIO

SESSION 1907

TORONTO:

Printed and Published by L. K. CAMERON, Printer to the King's Most Excellent Majesty

1907.

Printed by WARWICK BRO'S & RUTTER Limited, Printers,
TORONTO.

LIST OF SESSIONAL PAPERS.

4

Title.	No.	Remarks.
Horticultural Societies, Report......................	27	*Printed.*
Hospitals, Charities and Refuges, Report............	43	"
Hydro-Electric Power Commission, Report............	48	"
Industries, Report	28	*Printed.*
Insurance, Report................................	10	"
Judicature Act, Orders-in-Council	56	*Not printed.*
Jury Selection. Alternative method, etc.............	68	"
Justices of the Peace, Commissions.................	67	"
Justices of the Peace in Essex.....................	54	"
Labour, Report..................................	30	*Printed.*
Lands, Forests and Mines, Report	3	"
Legal Offices, Report	38	"
Library, Report	47	*Not printed.*
License Inspectors, appointments..................	51	"
Liquor License Acts, Report	44	*Printed.*
Liquor Licenses, Fort Frances	61	*Not printed.*
Live Stock Associations, Report	22	*Printed.*
Livingstone and Davis Estate, protest..............	64	*Not printed.*
Loan Corporations, Statements....................	11	*Printed.*
Mines, Report...................................	4	*Printed.*
Mining Companies, incorporated	66	*Not printed.*
Municipal Act, Report *re* Conmee clauses............	62	"
Municipal Auditor, Report	45	*Printed.*
Nipissing Mines Company, correspondence	74	*Not printed.*
Ontario Railway and Municipal Board, Report........	9	*Printed.*
Ontario Railway and Municipal Board, Report on Conmee clauses of Municipal Act..................	62	*Not printed.*
Petawawa Camp, Documents and correspondence......	71	*Printed.*
Police Magistrates in Essex	54	*Not printed.*
Poultry Institute, Report..........................	23	*Printed.*
Prisons and Reformatories, Report.................	42	"
Provincial Municipal Auditor, Report	45	"
Public Accounts, 1906	1	"
Public Works, Report	6	"
Queen Victoria Niagara Falls Park, Report..........	5	"
Queen Victoria Niagara Falls Park, protest of C. Livingstone and Davis Estate....................	64	*Not printed.*
Railway and Municipal Board, Report..............	9	*Printed.*
Railway and Municipal Board, Report on the Conmee clauses of Municipal Act	62	*Not printed.*
Registry Offices, Report of Inspector	39	*Printed.*

TITLE.	No.	REMARKS.
Saint Joseph Island, kinds of Patents issued to locatees	57	*Not printed.*
Secretary and Registrar, Report	40	*Printed.*
Statutes, Distribution of	72	*Not printed.*
Succession Duties, Estates unsettled	58	"
Supplementary Revenue, amounts credited to cities, towns, etc......................................	59	"
Surrogate Courts, Orders-in-Council	56	"
Temiskaming and N. O. Railway, Report	8	*Printed.*
Temiskaming and N. O. Railway, cash expenditure on construction	60	"
Text-book Commission, Report	49	"
Titles, Fees received by Master of	55	*Not printed.*
Toronto Electric Light Company, date of incorporation, etc............	52	"
Toronto University, Auditor's Report................	13	*Printed.*
Vegetable Growers' Association, Report..............	18	*Printed.*
Women's Institutes, Report..	24	*Printed.*

LIST OF SESSIONAL PAPERS.

Arranged in Numerical Order with their Titles at full length; the dates when Ordered and when presented to the Legislature; the name of the Member who moved the same, and whether Ordered to be Printed or not.

CONTENTS OF VOL. I.

No. 1.. | Public Accounts of the Province for the year 1906. Presented to the Legislature, February 26th, 1907. *Printed.*

No. 2.. | Estimates for the service of the Province until the Estimates of the year are finally passed. Presented to the Legislature 25th January, 1907. *Not printed.* Estimates for the service of the Province, until the Estimates for the year are finally passed. Presented to the Legislature 14th February, 1907. *Not printed.* Estimates for the year 1907. Presented to the Legislature, 26th February, 1907. *Printed.* Estimates (Supplementary). for the year 1907. Presented to the Legislature, 9th April, 1907. *Printed.* Estimates (Supplementary), for the year 1907. Presented to the Legislature, 15th April, 1907. *Printed.*

No. 3.. | Report of the Minister of Lands, Forests and Mines for the year 1906. Presented to the Legislature 14th February, 1907. *Printed.*

CONTENTS OF VOL II.

No. 4.. | Report of the Bureau of Mines for the year 1906. Presented to the Legislature, 20th March, 1907. *Printed.*

No. 5.. | Report of the Commissioners of the Queen Victoria Niagara Falls Park, for the year 1906. Presented to the Legislature, 19th February, 1907. *Printed.*

No. 6.. | Report of the Minister of Public Works for the year 1906. Presented to the Legislature, 8th March, 1907. *Printed.*

No. 7.. | Report relating to the Registration of Births, Marriages and Deaths during the year 1906. Presented to the Legislature, 30th January, 1907. *Printed.*

No. 8.. | Report of the Temiskaming and Northern Ontario Railway Commission, for the year 1906. Presented to the Legislature, 15th March, 1907. *Printed.*

No. 9.. | Report of the Ontario Railway and Municipal Board, for the year 1906. Presented to the Legislature, 31st January, 1907. *Printed.*

CONTENTS OF VOL. III.

No. 10.. | Report of the Inspector of Insurance for the year 1906. Presented to the Legislature, 30th March, 1907. *Printed.*

No. 11.. | Loan Corporations, Statements by Building Societies, Loan and other Companies, for the year 1906. Presented to the Legislature, 7th March, 1907. *Printed.*

CONTENTS OF VOL. IV.

No. 12.. | Report of the Minister of Education, for the year 1906, with the Statistics of 1905. Presented to the Legislature, 27th February, 1907. *Printed.*

No. 13.. | Auditors' Report to the Board of Governors University of Toronto, on Capital and Income Accounts, for the year ending 30th June, 1906. Presented to the Legislature, 30th January, 1907. *Printed.*

No. 14.. | Report of the Ontario Agricultural College and Experimental Farm, for the year 1906. Presented to the Legislature, 21st March, 1907. *Printed.*

CONTENTS OF VOL. V.

No, 15.. | Report of the Ontario Agricultural and Experimental Union of the Province, for the year 1906. Presented to the Legislature, 21st March, 1907. *Printed.*

No. 16.. | Report of the Fruit Growers' Associations of the Province, for the year 1906. Presented to the Legislature, 21st March, 1907. *Printed.*

No. 17.. | Report of the Fruit Experimental Stations of the Province, for the year 1906. Presented to the Legislature, 21st March, 1907. *Printed.*

No. 18.. | Report of the Vegetable Growers' Association for the year 1906. Presented to the Legislature, 21st March, 1907. *Printed.*

No. 19.. | Report of the Entomological Society. for the year 1906. Presented to the Legislature, 21st March, 1907. *Printed.*

No. 20.. | Report of the Bee-Keepers' Association of the Province, for the year 1906. Presented to the Legislature 21st March, 1907. *Printed.*

No. 21.. | Report of the Dairymen's Associations of the Province, for the year 1906. Presented to the Legislature, 21st March, 1907. *Printed.*

No. 22.. | Report of the Live Stock Associations of the Province, for the year 1906. Presented to the Legislature, 21st March, 1907. *Printed.*

CONTENTS OF VOL. VI.

CONTENTS OF VOL. VII.

CONTENTS OF VOL. VIII.

CONTENTS OF VOL. IX.

No. 51.. | Return to an Order of the House of the sixteenth day of March, 1906, for a Return shewing the names of all License Inspectors appointed since the first day of February, 1905, together with their addresses and the dates of their appointment; the business or occupation of each Inspector prior to his appointment and the present occupation or business, other than their official business, of each such Inspector. Presented to the Legislature, 11th February, 1907. Mr. *McMillan*. *Not printed*.

No. 52.. | Return to an Order of the House, of the thirtieth day of January 1907, for a Return giving the following information regarding the Toronto Electric Light Company, Limited. 1. Date of incorporation. 2. Applicants for Incorporation. 3. Objects of the Company. 4. Names of the Provisional Directors. 5. Amount of Capital. 6. Increase of Capital Stock. 7. Names of the Directors and Shareholders of the Company, according to the last Return to the Government. Presented to the Legislature, 11th February, 1907. Mr. *Hoyle*. *Not printed*.

No. 53.. | Return to an Order of the House of the nineteenth day of February, 1907, for a Return of copies of all correspondence between the Government, or any member or official thereof, and any other person or persons, with reference to the dismissal of James Gillespie, of Picton, from the office of Sheriff of the County of Prince Edward. Presented to the Legislature, 26th February, 1907, Mr. *Currie*. *Not printed*.

No. 54.. | Return to an Order of the House of the seventh day of February, 1907, for a Return shewing :—(1) List of names of Police Magistrates and Justices of the Peace in and for the County of Essex, on the 31st January, 1905. (2) List of names of Police Magistrates and Justices of the Peace in and for the County of Essex, appointed since February 1st, 1905. (3) Names of those who have qualified as Police Magistrates, or Justices of the Peace, in the County of Essex. Presented to the Legislature, 27th February, 1907. Mr. *Auld*. *Not printed*.

No. 55.. | Return of all Fees received by the Master of Titles under Rule 77 of the Land Titles Act, for the year 1906. Presented to the Legislature, 5th March, 1907. *Not printed*.

No. 56.. | Copies of Orders-in-Council commuting the Fees payable to His Honour Judge Finkle and increasing the commutations paid to His Honour Judge Benson, His Honour Judge McDonald, His Honour Judge Hardy and His Honour Judge Snider, under Section 187 of the Judicature Act and Subsection 2 of Section 84 of the Surrogate Courts Act. Presented to the Legislature, 5th March, 1907. *Not printed*.

No. 57.. | Return to an Order of the House of the thirteenth day of February, 1907, for a Return shewing the various kinds of Patents issued to Locatees on St. Joseph Island. Presented to the Legislature, 5th March, 1907. Mr. *Smith* (*Sault Ste. Marie*). *Not printed*.

No. 58.. | Return to an Order of the House of the twenty-fifth day of February, 1907, for a Return shewing all Estates now unsettled upon which Succession Duty was claimed by the Treasury Department where the due date was on or before the first day of January, 1905, and the estimated amount of duty due and the reasons why unsettled. Presented to the Legislature, 7th March, 1907. Mr. *Kerr   Not printed.*

No. 59.. | Return to an Order of the House of the eighth day of March, 1907, for a Return shewing the amounts credited to the cities, towns, villages and organized townships in the Province of Ontario, from the sum received under Section 2, Subsection 5, of the Supplementary Revenue Act, 1899, as amended from time to time, and also the amount charged against each such city, town, village or organized township, respectively, for the maintenance of inmates of lunatic or other asylums in the Province under the provisions of Subsection 2, of Section 4, of Chapter 9 of the Statutes of 1906. Presented to the Legislature, 11th March, 1907. Mr. *Hislop. Not printed.*

No. 60 . | Statement shewing cash expenditure on construction of the Temiskaming and Northern Ontario Railway, as of December 31st, 1906. Presented to the Legislature, 14th March, 1907. *Printed.*

No. 61.. | Return to an Order of the House of the sixth day of March, 1907, for a Return of:—1. Copies of all correspondence between the Government, or any Member or Official thereof and any person or persons, relating to the cancellation or granting of a liquor license to the Palace Hotel, at Fort Frances. 2. Copies of all correspondence between the Government, or any Member or Official thereof and any person or persons, relating to the cancellation or granting of a liquor license to one Thomas Wilson, at Fort Frances 3. Copies of all correspondence between the Government, or any Member or Official thereof and any person or persons, relating to the resignation or dismissal of the License Inspector or any member of the Board of License Commissioners at Fort 'Frances. Presented to the Legislature, 20th March, 1907. Mr *McDougal. Not printed.*

No. 62.. | Report of the Ontario Railway and Municipal Board upon certain Bills amending the Municipal Act *in re* the Conmee clauses, referred to the Board by the Standing Committee on Municipal Law, in the Session of 1906. Presented to the Legislature, 19th March, 1907. *Not printed.*

No. 63.. | Report upon the Feeble-minded in Ontario. Presented to the Legisture, 15th April, 1907. *Printed.*

No. 64.. | Return to an Order of the House of the eighth day of March, 1907. for a Return of copies of all correspondence and papers relating to or in the matter of the protest of Mr. Chisholm Livingstone and the Davis Estate, against the purchase price awarded them by the arbitrators for their property for the Queen Victoria Niagara Falls Park. Presented to the Legislature, 20th March, 1907. Mr. *Fraser. Not printed.*

No. 65.. | Report upon the Horse Industry of Ontario, for the year 1906. Presented to the Legislature, 21st March, 1907. *Printed.*

No. 66.. | Return to an Order of the House, of the first day of March, 1907, for a Return shewing the number of Mining Companies incorporated in the year 1906, also total amount paid into the Treasury Department from incorporation of Mining Companies in 1906, including licenses to companies previously incorporated. Presented to the Legislature, 21st March, 1907. Mr. *Pearce. Not printed.*

No. 67.. | Return to an Order of the House, of· the twenty-seventh day of February, 1906, for a Return shewing, according to Counties— 1. How many persons held Commissions and were qualified as Justices of the Peace, within the Province, on the 7th day of February, 1905. 2. How many persons held Commissions on the 7th day of February, 1906. 3. How many persons were included in the General Commission of the Peace, issued by the present Government. 4. How many of the persons named in such General Commission were continued in office from previous Commissions. Presented to the Legislature, 21st March, 1907. Mr. *Ross. Not printed.* •

No. 68.. | Return to an Order of the House, of the seventh day of February, 1907, for a Return shewing:—1. The names of Counties which have adopted the "Alternative Method" of selecting Jurors under the Amendment of 1902 to the Jurors' Act. 2. For a Comparative Statement shewing the expenses incurred under the old and new system in said Counties from the years 1902 to 1906, both inclusive. 3. The Counties (if any) in which the "Alternative Method" has been repealed and have returned to the old system of selecting Jurors. Presented to the Legislature, 22nd March, 1907. Mr. *Hoyle. Not printed.*

No. 69. | Return to an Order of the House, of the sixth day of March, 1907, for a Return of copies of all correspondence between the Government and the Northumberland-Durham Power Company, with respect to a lease of water power at Healey Falls. Presented to the Legislature, 3rd April, 1907. Mr. *Pense. Not printed.*

No. 70., | Return to an Order of the House, of the seventh day of February, 1907, for a Return, shewing the number and names of the settlers located in the Township of Gaudette and Hodgins in the District of Algoma, since the year 1906. Presented to the Legislature, 5th April, 1907. Mr. *Smith (Sault Ste. Marie). Not printed.*

No. 71.. | Documents and correspondence regarding Petawawa Camp. Presented to the Legislature, 15th April, 1907. *Printed.*

No. 72.. | Statement of distribution of Revised and Sessional Statutes. Presented to the Legislature, 17th April, 1907. *Not printed.*

No. 73. . | Copy of a letter from His Honour A Constantineau, Judge of the
Counties of Prescott and Russell, addressed to the Attorney-
General of Ontario in the matter of the case Chatillon *vs.* Bertrand. Presented to the Legislature, 18th April, 1907. *Not
printed.*

No. 74. . | Return to an Order of the House of the twenty-second day of March,
1907, for a return of copies of all correspondence between the
Nipissing Mines Company, or any Official thereof and the Government, or any Member thereof, relating to the property, or title
thereto, of the said company, or any part or or parcel thereof,
situated in the Cobalt District; or to any application relating
to the same; its title, or to the operation of the mines of the
company, made by or on behalf of the company, or any of
its Directors or Officers. Presented to the Legislature, 18th
April, 1907. Mr. *McMillan, Not printed.*

PUBLIC ACCOUNTS

OF THE

PROVINCE OF ONTARIO

FOR THE

YEAR ENDED 31ST DECEMBER,

1906.

TORONTO:
Printed and Published by L. K. CAMERON, Printer to the King's Most Excellent Majesty
1907

WARWICK BRO'S & RUTTER, Limited, Printers,
TORONTO.

a P.A.

To His Honour WILLIAM MORTIMER CLARK, K.C.,

Lieutenant-Governor of Ontario.

MAY IT PLEASE YOUR HONOUR:

The undersigned has the honour to present to Your Honour the PUBLIC ACCOUNTS of the Province of Ontario for the year ended 31st December, 1906.

Respectfully submitted,

A. J. MATHESON,

Treasurer.

TREASURY DEPARTMENT, ONTARIO,

TORONTO, Feb. 20th, 1907.

AUDIT OFFICE,
Feb. 20th, 1907.

Hon. A. J. MATHESON,
Provincial Treasurer,
Toronto.

SIR,—I have the honour to submit to you the Public Accounts for the year ended 31st December, 1906.

I have the honour to be,

Sir,

Your obedient servant,

J. CLANCY,
Provincial Auditor.

Treasury Board Orders

JAMES CLANCY, ESQ.,
Provincial Auditor.

The undersigned respectfully recommends that the following payments be made in connection with the special examination and audit of the books, accounts and securities of the York County Loan and Savings Company, and the inquiry into the conduct of the business of the company, held under the provisions of section 118 (a) of "The Loan Corporations Act," namely,—

W. H. Cross, services as Special Examiner.	$1,000	00
" a/c Stenographer's fees	157	50
" a/c Registration fees re Titles	37	40
	$1,194	90
C. A. Masten, services as Counsel	725	63
A. W. Briggs, services as Assistant Counsel	100	00
G. F. Clarkson, services as Accountant	375	00

(Sgd.) J. J. FOY,
Attorney-General.

Copy of a Minute of the Treasury Board, dated the 8th day of August, A.D. 1906.

Upon consideration of the report of the Honourable the Attorney-General, dated the 8th day of August, A.D. 1906, the Treasury Board doth hereby order, pursuant to the provisions of section 20, cap. 23, R.S.O. 1897, that the sum of One thousand four hundred and two dollars and forty-four cents ($1,402.44) be placed to the credit of the Honourable the Treasurer to cover overdraft necessary for the payment of expenditures in connection with the special examination and audit of the books, accounts and vouchers of the York County Loan and Savings Company and the inquiry into the conduct of the business of the company, held under the provisions of section 118 (a) of The Loan Corporations Act.

Certified,
J. LONSDALE CAPREOL,
Clerk, Treasury Board.

To the Provincial Auditor:

The undersigned has the honour to report that the appropriation for $5,000 for "Commissions re Sundry Investigations" has become exhausted, and that the sum of $565 is required to pay the account of Mr. Joseph C. Judd, the Commissioner appointed to inquire into the charges against Mr. Samuel T. Bastedo, Deputy Commissioner of Fisheries, and Mr. James S. Webster, Chief Clerk of the Fisheries Department, the undersigned therefore respectfully recommends that pursuant to the provisions of section 20, Cap. 23, R.S.O. 1897, the said sum of $565 be placed to the credit of the Honourable the Treasurer for the payment of the said account.

(Sgd.) J. J. FOY,
Attorney-General.

Copy of a Minute of the Treasury Board, dated the 16th day of August, A.D. 1906.

Upon consideration of the report of the Honourable the Attorney-General, dated the 14th day of August, A.D. 1906, the Treasury Board doth hereby order, pursuant to the provisions of section 20, Cap. 23, R.S.O. 1897, that the sum of Five hundred and sixty-five dollars ($565) be placed to the credit of the Honourable the Treasurer for the payment of the account of Mr. Joseph C. Judd, the Commissioner appointed to inquire into the charges against Samuel T. Bastedo, Deputy Commissioner of Fisheries, and Mr. James S. Webster, Chief Clerk of the Fisheries Department, the appropriation for "Commissions re Sundry Investigations," to which said account is chargeable, having become exhausted.

Certified,
J. LONSDALE CAPREOL,
Clerk, Treasury Board.

TORONTO, 22nd October, 1906.

JAMES CLANCY, ESQ.,
　　　　Provincial Auditor.

The undersigned begs leave to report that on account of the extra travelling expenses the sum appropriated at the last Session of the Legislature for "Travelling Expenses and Contingencies of the Office of the Inspector of Division Courts" has become exhausted.

The undersigned therefore begs to recommend that pursuant to the provisions of section 20, Cap. 23, R.S.O. 1897, the sum of Four hundred dollars ($400) be placed to the credit of the Honourable the Treasurer to cover payments on account of Travelling expenses and Contingencies of the said Office for the balance of the current year.

(Sgd.) J. J. FOY,
Attorney-General.

Copy of a Minute of the Treasury Board, dated the 23rd October, A.D. 1906.

Upon consideration of the report of the Honourable the Attorney-General, dated the 22nd day of October, A.D. 1906, the Treasury Board doth hereby order that pursuant to the provisions of section 20, Cap. 23, R.S.O. 1897, the sum of Four hundred dollars ($400) be placed to the credit of the Honourable the Treasurer, to cover payments on account of travelling expenses and contingencies of the office of the Inspector of Division Courts for the balance of the current year, the appropriation for said service having become exhausted.

Certified,

J. LONSDALE CAPREOL,
Clerk, Treasury Board.

JAMES CLANCY, ESQ.,
> Provincial Auditor,
> Toronto.

Referring to the Order-in-Council of 16th November, 1906, authorizing the payment over to James Shappee of the sum of $192, being the amount of the fine less four per cent. commission paid over to the Province in the case of The King *vs.* Wesley Duschane. It appears that the appropriation for refunds, "Miscellaneous," has become exhausted. Under the circumstances the undersigned recommends that under the provisions of section 20, Cap. 23, R.S.O. 1897, the said sum of One hundred and ninety-two dollars ($192) be placed to the credit of the Honourable the Treasurer, so that a cheque may issue for the payment of the same to Mr. Shappee.

(Sgd.) J. J. FOY,
Attorney-General.

19th November, 1906.

Copy of a Minute of the Treasury Board, dated the 22nd day of November, A.D. 1906.

Upon consideration of the report of the Honourable the Attorney-General, dated the 19th day of November, 1906, the Treasury Board doth hereby order that pursuant to the provisions of section 20, Cap. 23, R.S.O. 1897, the sum of One hundred and ninety-two dollars ($192) be plced to the credit of the Honourable the Treasurer to cover the payment to James Shappee of the fine imposed in the case of The King *v.* Wesley Deshane, the appropriation for refunds Miscellaneous having become exhausted.

Certified,

J. LONSDALE CAPREOL,
Clerk, Treasury Board.

JAMES CLANCY, ESQ.,
      Provincial Auditor.

The undersigned begs to report that the appropriation for expenses in connection with the arbitration, "Canada, Ontario and Quebec," has become exhausted, and an account for $638.45, for which there are no funds available, has been presented for payment by Messrs. Warwick Bros. & Rutter, for printing the factum and appeal case in Ontario *v.* The Dominion of Canada, being an appeal by the Province from the decision of the Exchequer Court of Canada to the Supreme Court of Canada in the matter of the Common School Fund.

The undersigned therefore respectfully recommends that under the provisions of section 20, Cap. 23, R.S.O. 1897, a further appropriation of $638.45 be placed to the credit of the Honourable the Treasurer to cover the payment of the said account.

           (Sgd.) J. J. FOY,
                Attorney-General.

21st November, 1906.

Copy of a Minute of the Treasury Board, dated 22nd November, A.D. 1906.

Upon consideration of the report of the Honourable the Attorney-General, dated the 21st day of November, 1906, the Treasury Board doth hereby order that pursuant to the provisions of section 20, Cap. 23, R.S.O. 1897, the sum of Six hundred and thirty-eight dollars and forty-five cents ($638.45) be placed to the credit of the Honourable the Treasurer to cover the payment of the account of Messrs. Warwick Bros. & Rutter for printing the Factum and Appeal case in Ontario *vs.* The Dominion of Canada, being an appeal by the Province from the decision of the Exchequer Court of Canada to the Supreme Court of Canada in the matter of the Common School Fund, the appropriation for the expenses of the arbitration, Canada, Ontario and Quebec having become exhausted. '

          Certified,
        J. LONSDALE CAPREOL,
             Clerk, Treasury Board.

JAMES CLANCY, ESQ.,
      Provincial Auditor.

The undersigned begs to report that owing to extra expenditure for printing, postage and stationery the appropriation for contingencies of the Office of the Inspector of Legal Offices has become exhausted and that an additional sum of Fifty dollars ($50) will be required for printing and stationery during the months of November and December and the settlement of some small accounts.

The undersigned therefore respectfully recommends that under the provisions of section 20, Cap. 23 R.S.O., 1897, a further appropriation of fifty dollars be made to cover the said increased expenditure.

(Sgd.) J. J. FOY,
Attorney-General.

28th November, 1906.

Copy of a Minute of the Treasury Board dated the 29th day of November, A.D., 1906.

Upon consideration of the report of the Honourable the Attorney-General, dated the 28th day of November, A.D. 1906, the Treasury Board doth hereby order that pursuant to the provisions of section 20, Cap. 23, R.S.O., 1897, the sum of Fifty dollars ($50) be placed to the credit of the Honourable the Treasurer to meet the requirements of the Office of the Inspector of Legal Offices for Contingencies, for the balance of the current year, the appropriation for said service having become exhausted.

Certified,
J. LONSDALE CAPREOL,
Clerk, Treasury Board.

JAMES CLANCY, ESQ.,
Provincial Auditor.

The undersigned begs to report that the appropriation for Contingencies of the Registrar's Office, High Court of Justice, has become exhausted, and it is estimated that the sum of Four Hundred dollars ($400) will be required to meet further payments on this account for the balance of the current year. The undersigned therefore recommends that under the provisions of Section 20, Cap. 23, R.S.O., 1897, a further appropriation of Four Hundred dollars ($400) be made accordingly.

(Sgd.) J. J. FOY,
Attorney-General.

4th December, 1906.

Copy of a Minute of the Treasury Board, dated the 5th day of December, A.D. 1906.

Upon consideration of the report of the Honourable the Attorney-General, dated the 4th day of December, A.D. 1906, the Treasury Board doth hereby order that pursuant to the provisions of section 20, Cap. 23, R.S.O., 1897, the sum of Four Hundred dollars ($400) be placed to the credit of the Honourable the Treasurer, to meet further payments on account of Contingencies of the Registrar's Office, High Court of Justice, the appropriation for said service having become exhausted.

Certified,

J. LONSDALE CAPREOL,

Clerk, Executive Council.

JAMES CLANCY, ESQ.,
   Provincial Auditor.

The undersigned begs to report that the appropriation for salaries of the Referees, etc., under the Drainage Trials' Act has become exhausted and that the sum of Three hundred and four dollars and twenty-three cents ($304.23) is required to meet the salary of Mr. Geo. F. Henderson, Drainage Referee, for the balance of the year. The undersigned therefore recommends that under the provisions of section 20, Cap. 23, R.S.O., 1897, a further appropriation of the said sum of Three hundred and four dollars and twenty-three cents ($304.23) be made to cover the payment of the said salary.

(Sgd.) J. J. FOY,

Attorney-General.

5th December, 1906.

Copy of a Minute of the Treasury Board, dated the 5th day of December, A.D. 1906.

Upon consideration of the report of the Honourable the Attorney-General, dated the 5th day of December, A.D. 1906, the Treasury Board doth hereby order that pursuant to the provisions of section 20, Cap. 23, R.S.O., 1897, the sum of Three hundred and four dollars and twenty-three cents ($304.23) be placed to the credit of the Honourable the Treasurer to cover the payment of the salary of Mr. George F. Henderson, Drainage Referee, for the balance of the year, the appropriation for salaries, etc., under the Drainage Trials' Act having become exhausted.

Certified,

J. LONSDALE CAPREOL,

Clerk, Executive Council.

JAMES CLANCY, ESQ.,
 Provincial Auditor.

Referring to the Order-in-Council of 5th December, 1906, authorizing the payment of the sum of Two thousand five hundred dollars ($2,500) on account of the charges and disbursement of the Counsel and the Actuary retained by the Government on behalf of the Policy Holders of the Province of Ontario in connection with the Royal Commission of Insurance, the undersigned begs to report that the appropriation for "Commissions re Sundry Investigations" is exhausted and there are no funds available out of which the said payment may be made. Under the circumstances the undersigned respectfully recommends that under section 20, Cap. 23, R.S.O., 1897, a further appropriation of Two thousand five hundred dollars ($2,500) be made to cover the payment of the said charges and disbursements.

(Sgd.) J. J. FOY,
 Attorney-General

11th December, 1906.

Copy of a Minute of the Treasury Board, dated the 11th day of December, A.D. 1906.

Upon consideration of the report of the Honourable the Attorney-General, dated the 11th day of December, A.D. 1906, the Treasury Board doth hereby order pursuant to the provisions of section 20, Cap. 23, R.S.O., 1897, that the sum of Two thousand five hundred dollars ($2,500) be placed to the credit of the Honourable the Treasurer, for the payment of the charges and disbursements of the Counsel and the Actuary retained by the Government on behalf of the Policy Holders of the Province of Ontario in connection with the Royal Commission on Insurance, the appropriation for Commissions re Sundry Investigations having become exhausted.

Certified,
 J. LONSDALE CAPREOL,
 Clerk, Treasury Board.

JAMES CLANCY, ESQ.,
 Provincial Auditor.

The undersigned begs to report that the appropriation for contingencies for shorthand reporters at the Assizes and Election Courts has become exhausted owing to the purchase of a new typewriter and increased travelling expenses. There is now at the credit of this appropriation Twenty-three dollars

and fifteen cents ($23.15) and accounts outstanding amounting
to One hundred and ninety-six dollars and thirty cents ($196.30).
The undersigned therefore recommends that under the provisions of section 20, Cap. 23, R.S.O., 1897, a further appropriation of one hundred and seventy-three dollars and fifteen cents
($173.15) be made to cover the payment of these accounts.

(Sgd.) J. J. FOY,
Attorney-General.

27th December, 1906.

Copy of a Minute of the Treasury Board, dated the 27th
day of December, 1906.

Upon consideration of the report of the Honourable the
Attorney-General, dated the 27th day of December, A.D. 1906,
the Treasury Board doth hereby order that pursuant to the provisions of section 20, Cap. 23, R.S.O., 1897, the sum of One
hundred and seventy-three dollars and fifteen cents ($173.15)
be placed to the credit of the Honourable the Treasurer to
cover the payment of certain outstanding accounts chargeable
to contingencies for shorthand reporters at the Assizes and
Election Courts, the appropriation for said service having become exhausted.

Certified,
J. LONSDALE CAPREOL,
Clerk, Treasury Board.

JAMES CLANCY, ESQ.,
    Provincial Auditor.

The undersigned begs to report that the appropriation for
contingencies of the Referees, etc., under the Drainage Trials
Act has become exhausted, and that the sum of One hundred
and eighty dollars ($180) is required to meet the salary of Miss
L. M. Sager, shorthand reporter, for the balance of the year.
The undersigned therefore recommends that under the provisions of section 20, Cap. 23, R.S.O. 1897, a further appropriation of the sum of One hundred and eighty dollars ($180)
be made to cover the payment of the said salary.

(Sgd.) J. J. FOY,
Attorney-General.

27th December, 1906.

Copy of a Minute of the Treasury Board, dated the 27th day of December, A.D. 1906.

Upon consideration of the report of the Honourable the Attorney-General, dated the 27th day of December, A.D. 1906, the Treasury Board doth hereby order that pursuant to the provisions of section 20, Cap. 23, R.S.O. 1897, the sum of One hundred and eighty dollars ($180) be placed to the credit of the Honourable the Treasurer to cover the salary of Miss L. M. Sager, stenographer to the Drainage Court of Eastern Ontario, for the balance of the year, the appropriation for contingencies of the Referee, etc., under the Drainage Trials Act having become exhausted.

Certified,

J. LONSDALE CAPREOL,

Clerk, Treasury Board.

TORONTO, 29th December, 1906.

JAMES CLANCY, ESQ.,
            Provincial Auditor.

SIR,—I have the honour to inform you that the sum appropriated at the last Session of the Legislature for maintenance and travelling expenses of the Office of the Provincial Municipal Auditor is insufficient by the sum of Twenty-five dollars ($25), which is principally due to the placing of a telephone for the use of the Whips and others temporarily occupying the office of the Provincial Municipal Auditor, during the session of 1906. I therefore beg to recommend that authority be given under R.S.O. 1897, Cap. 23, sec. 20, for the payment of the said amount of $25.

I am, sir,

Yours respectfully,

J. R. CARTWRIGHT,

Deputy Attorney-General.

Copy of a Minute of the Treasury Board, dated the 9th day of January, A.D. 1907.

Upon consideration of the report of the Deputy Attorney-General, dated the 27th day of December, A.D. 1906, the Treasury Board doth hereby order that pursuant to the provisions of section 20, Cap. 23, R.S.O. 1897, the sum of Twenty-five dollars ($25) be placed to the credit of the Honourable the Treasurer, to cover the payment of maintenance and travelling expenses in connection with the office of the Provincial Municipal Auditor for the balance of the year 1906, the appropriation for said service having become exhausted.

Certified,

J. LONSDALE CAPREOL,

Clerk, Treasury Board.

JAMES CLANCY, ESQ.,
      Provincial Auditor.

The undersigned has the honour to report that the appropriation for the expenses of the Arbitration for the settlement of Accounts between the Dominion of Canada and the Provinces of Ontario and Quebec is almost exhausted, there remaining only the sum of $236.03 at the credit of the said appropriation, and that the further sum of $1,007.26 is required to meet the payment of the following accounts for professional services in the matter of the appeal to the Supreme Court in the suit of the Province of Ontario *vs*. The Dominion of Canada to recover interst on trust funds of the Province, short paid by the Dominion, namely:

Æmilius Irving, Esq., K.C., Toronto $650 00
W. Assheton Smith, Esq., Barrister 593 29

                                     $1,243 .29

The undersigned therefore respectfully recommends that under the provisions of section 20, Cap. 23, R.S.O. 1897, a further appropriation of $1,007.26 be made for the payment of the above accounts.

(Sgd.) J. J. FOY,

Attorney-General.

4th January, 1906.

Copy of a Minute of the Treasury Board, dated the 9th day of January, A.D. 1907.

Upon consideration of the report of the Honourable the Attorney-General, dated the 4th day of January, A.D. 1907, the Treasury Board doth hereby order that pursuant to the provisions of section 20, Cap. 23, R.S.O. 1897, the sum of One thousand and seven dollars and twenty-six cents ($1,007.26) be placed to the credit of the Honourable the Treasurer to meet the payment of the following accounts for professional services in the matter of the appeal to the Supreme Court in the suit of

the Province of Ontario *vs.* the Dominion of Canada to recover
interest on Trust funds of the Province, short paid by the Dominion, the appropriation for the expenses of the Arbitration
for the settlement of accounts between the Dominion of Canada
and the Provinces of Ontario and Quebec being insufficient for
the purpose, namely:

Æmilius Irving, Esq., K.C., Toronto $650 00
W. Assheton Smith, Esq., Barrister, Toronto 593 29

Certified,

J. LONSDALE CAPREOL,
Clerk, Treasury Board.

JAMES CLANCY, ESQ.,
　　Provincial Auditor.

The undersigned has the honour to report that an Order-
in-Council was passed on the 24th day of April, 1906, directing
that the sum of Thirty-two dollars and fifty cents ($32.50) be
refunded to the estate of the late Harrison Carey, being excess
of surrogate fees charged on the realty of the deceased devised
to be sold, the Judge having commuted his fees and said excess
having come to the Province, and that a warrant for the said
sum was issued in favour of Messrs. Lewis and Richards, Chatham, the Solicitors for the said Estate. That the said amount
was by mistake charged to "Refunds Succession Duty," whereas
the same should have been charged to the appropriation for
"Refunds Miscellaneous," which latter appropriation has become exhausted.

Under the circumstances the undersigned respectfully
recommends that under the provisions of section 20, Cap. 23,
R.S.O., 1897, a further appropriation of $32.50 be made to
cover the payment of the said refund.

(Sgd.) J. J. FOY,
Attorney-General.

4th January, 1906.

Copy of a Minute of the Treasury Board, dated the 9th
day of January, A.D. 1907.

Upon consideration of the report of the Honourable the
Attorney-General, dated the 4th day of January, A.D. 1907, the
Treasury Board doth hereby order that pursuant to the provisions of section 20, Cap. 23, R.S.O., 1897, the sum of Thirty-
two dollars and fifty cents be placed to the credit of the

2* P.A.

Honourable the Treasurer to cover the payment of a refund
of said amount to the estate of the late Harrison Carey, being
excess of surrogate fees charged on the realty of the deceased,
devised to be sold, the Judge having commuted his fees and
said excess having come to the Province, the appropriation
for "Refunds Miscellaneous" having become exhausted.

Certified,

J. LONSDALE CAPREOL,
Clerk, Treasury Board.

James Clancy, Esq.,
       Provincial Auditor.

The undersigned has the honour to report that the appropriation for the expenses of the Arbitration for the settlement
of Accounts between the Dominion of Canada and the Provinces
of Ontario and Quebec is exhausted and that the further sum
of $336.42 is required to meet the account of Mr. H. S. White,
Barrister, Toronto, for professional services in assisting Mr.
Aemilius Irving, K.C., in the preparation of the case and proceedings in the suit in the Court of Exchequer of the Dominion
of Canada vs. the Province of Ontario in respect of claim for
payments to Indians on North-west Angle Treaty No. 3.

The undersigned respectfully recommends that under section 20, Cap. 23, R.S.O., 1897, a further appropriation of the
said sum of Three hundred and thirty-six dollars and forty-
two cents ($336.42) be made to cover the payment of the said
account.

(Sgd.) J. J. FOY,
Attorney-General.

8th January, 1907.

Copy of a Minute of the Treasury Board, dated the 9th
day of January, A.D. 1907.

Under consideration of the report of the Honourable the
Attorney-General, dated the 8th day of January, A.D. 1907,
the Treasury Board doth hereby order that pursuant to the
provisions of section 20, Cap. 23, R.S.O., 1897, the sum of
Three hundred and thirty-six dollars and forty-two cents
($336.42) be placed to the credit of the Honourable the Treas-
urer to cover the payment of the account of Mr. H. S. White,
Barrister, Toronto, for professional services in assisting Mr.
AEmilius Irving, K.C., in the preparation of the case and
proceedings in the suit in the Court of Exchequer of the Domi-

2a* P.A.

nion of Canada vs. the Province of Ontario in respect of Claim
for payments to Indians on the North-West Angle Treaty No.
3, the appropriation re Arbitration Canada, Ontario and Quebec having become exhausted.

Certified,

J. LONSDALE CAPREOL,

Clerk, Treasury Board.

JAMES CLANCY, ESQ.,
      Provincial Auditor.

The undersigned has the honour to report that the appropriation for the expenses of the arbitration for the setlement
of Accounts betwen the Dominion of Canada and the Provinces of Ontario and Quebec is exhausted, and that the further
sum of $86.72 is required to meet the payment of the account
of Messrs. Ewart, Osler, Burbidge and Maclaren, for professional services in the matter of the appeal to the Supreme Court
in the suit of the Province of Ontario vs. the Dominion of
Canada to recover interest on trust funds of the Province short
paid by the Dominion.

The undersigned therefore respectfully recommends that
under the provisions of section 20, Cap. 23, R.S.O., 1897, the
further appropriation of the said sum of Eighty-six dollars and
seventy-two cents ($86.72) be made to cover the payment of the
above account.

(Sgd.) J. J. FOY,

Attorney-General.

January, 1907.

Copy of a Minute of the Treasury Board, dated the 15th
day of January, A.D. 1907.

Upon consideration of the report of the Honourable the
Attorney-General, dated the 14th day of January, A.D. 1907,
tthe Treasury Board doth hereby order that pursuant to the
provisions of section 20, Cap. 23, R.S.O., 1897, the sum of
Eighty-six dollars and seventy-two cents ($86.72) be placed to
the credit of the Honourable the Treasurer to cover the payment of the account of Messrs. Ewart, Osler, Burbidge and
Maclaren, for professional services in the matter of the appeal
to the Supreme Court in the suit of the Province of Ontario
vs. the Dominion of Canada to recover interest on trust funds

of the Province short paid by the Dominion, the appropriation for the expenses of the arbitration for the settlement of Accounts between the Dominion of Canada and the Provinces of Ontario and Quebec having become exhausted.

Certified,

J. LONSDALE CAPREOL.
Clerk, Treasury Board.

TORONTO, 19th July, 1906.

The undersigned begs to report to the Provincial Auditor that the sum appropriated at the last session of the Legislature for "Clearing along the Temiskaming Railway, has become exhausted, together with ten thousand dollars placed to the credit of the Honourable the Treasurer of Ontario, per Minutes of Treasury Board of 22nd June, 1906, and recommends that a further sum of Ten thousand dollars be granted under authority of section 20, Cap. 23, R.S.O., 1897, for the continuance of the work.

(Sgd.) F. COCHRANE,
Minister of Lands, Forests and Mines.

J. CLANCY, ESQ.,
Provincial Auditor.

Copy of a Minute of the Treasury Board, dated the 25th day of July, A.D. 1906.

Upon consideration of the report of the Honourable the Minister of Lands, Forests and Mines, dated the 19th day of July, A.D. 1906, the Treasury Board doth hereby order that pursuant to the provisions of section 20, Cap. 23, R.S.O. 1897, the sum of Ten thousand dollars ($10,000) be placed to the credit of the Honourable the Treasurer for the purpose of the continuation of the work of clearing along the line of "The Temiskaming and Northern Ontario Railway, the appropriation for said service having become exhausted.

Certified,

J. LONSDALE CAPREOL.
Clerk, Executive Council.

TORONTO, August 23rd, 1906.

The undersigned begs to report to the Provincial Auditor that the sum appropriated at the last session of the Legislature for "Clearing along the Temiskaming Railway, has become exhausted, together with Twenty thousand dollars placed to the credit of the Honourable the Treasurer of Ontario per minutes of Treasury Board of 22nd of June and 19th of July, 1906, and recommends that a further sum of Ten thousand dollars be granted under authority of section 20, Cap. 23, R.S.O. 1897, for the continuance of the work.

(Sgd.) F. COCHRANE,
Minister of Lands, Forests and Mines.

J. CLANCY, ESQ.,
Provincial Auditor.

———

Copy of a Minute of the Treasury Board, dated the 18th day of December, A.D. 1906.

Upon consideration of the report of the Honourable the Minister of Lands, Forests and Mines, dated the 15th day of December, A.D. 1906, the Treasury Board hereby order that pursuant to the provisions of section 20, Cap. 23, R.S.O. 1897, the sum of Ten thousand dollars ($10,000) be placed to the credit of the Honourable the Treasurer, to meet the requirements of clearing along the line of The Temiskaming and Northern Ontario Railway for the balance of the current year, the appropriation for said service having become exhausted.

Certified,

J. LONSDALE CAPREOL.
Clerk, Treasury Board.

———

TORONTO, 20th September, 1906.

J. CLANCY, ESQ.,
Provincial Auditor.

The undersigned has the honour to report to the Provincial Auditor, that the amount appropriated for contingencies in the forests and lands section of his department has become exhausted, owing chiefly to increased expenditure through the employment of extra clerks required, in order to secure efficient services in the various branches.

The undersigned recommends that a further appropriation of $5,000 be granted under authority of R.S.O. 1897, Cap. 23, section 20, to meet the claims of the service.

(Sgd.) F. COCHRANE,
Minister of Lands, Forests and Mines.

Copy of a Minute of the Treasury Board dated the 25th day of September, A.D. 1906.

Upon consideration of the report of the Honourable the Minister of Lands, Forests and Mines, dated the 20th day of September, A.D. 1906, the Treasury Board doth hereby pursuant to the provisions of section 20, Cap. 23, R.S.O. 1897, order that the sum of Five thousand dollars be placed to the credit of the Honourable the Treasurer to meet the requirements of the Department of Lands and Forests Contingencies for the balance of the current year, the appropriation for the same having been exhausted.

Certified,

J. LONSDALE CAPREOL.
Clerk, Treasury Board.

TORONTO, Sept. 27th, 1906.

The undersigned begs to report to the Provincial Auditor that the sum appropriated at the last Session of the Legislature for "Clearing along the Temiskaming Railway," has become exhausted, together with Thirty Thousand dollars, placed to the credit of the Honourable the Treasurer of Ontario, per Minutes of Treasury Board of 22nd June, 19th of July and 23rd August, 1906, and recommends that a further sum of Ten thousand dollars be granted under authority of section 20, Cap. 23, R.S.O. 1897, for the continuance of the work.

(Sgd.) F. COCHRANE,
Minister of Lands, Forests and Mines.

J CLANCY, ESQ.,
Provincial Auditor.

Copy of a Minute of the Treasury Board, dated 27th September, A.D. 1906.

Upon consideration of the report of the Honourable the Minister of Lands, Forests and Mines, dated the 27th day of

September, A.D. 1906, the Treasury Board doth hereby order that pursuant to the provisions of section 20, Cap. 23, R.S.O. 1897, the sum of Ten thousand dollars ($10,000) be placed to the credit of the Honourable the Treasurer for the purpose of the continuation of the work of clearing along the line of The Temiskaming and Northern Ontario Railway, the appropriation for said service having become exhausted.

Certified,

J. LONSDALE CAPREOL.
Clerk, Treasury Board.

TORONTO, 16th October, 1906.

JAMES CLANCY, ESQ.,
Provincial Auditor.

The undersigned respectfully recommends that authority be given under R.S.O. 1897, Cap. 23, section 20, for the issue of a warrant to the Honourable the Treasurer for the sum of $4,000 to provide for the necessary and unavoidable expense of the Bureau of Mines for the remainder of the year, the Legislature's appropriation of $6,000 for such service having been exhausted.

(Sgd.) F. COCHRANE,
Minister of Lands, Forests and Mines.

Copy of a Minute of the Treasury Board, dated the 16th day of October, A.D. 1906.

Upon consideration of the report of the Honourable the Minister of Lands, Forests and Mines, dated the 16th day of October, A.D. 1906, the Treasury Board doth hereby order that pursuant to the provisions of section 20, Cap. 23, R.S.O. 1897, the sum of Four thousand dollars ($4,000) be placed to the credit of the Honourable the Treasurer to cover the necessary and unavoidable expenses of the Bureau of Mines for the balance of the current year, the appropriation for "Contingencies" having become exhausted.

Certified,

J. LONSDALE CAPREOL,
Clerk, Executive Council.

ToRONTO, Oct. 27th, 1906.

The undersigned begs to report to the Provincial Auditor that the sum appropriated at the last session of the Legislature towards commutation of Volunteer Veterans' Land Grants has become exhausted.

As there are yet to be paid a large number of applicants who wish to avail themselves of the privilege, the undersigned recommends that a further sum of Twenty-five thousand dollars ($25,000) be granted under authority of section 20, Cap. 23, R.S.O. 1897, to meet requirements.

(Sgd.) F. COCHRANE,
Minister of Lands, Forests and Mines.

J. CLANCY, ESQ.,
Provincial Auditor.

Copy of a Minute of the Treasury Board, dated the 30th day of October, A.D. 1906.

Upon consideration of the report of the Honourable the Minister of Lands, Forests and Mines, dated the 27th day of October, A.D. 1906, the Treasury Board doth hereby order that pursuant to the provisions of section 20, Cap. 23, R.S.O. 1897, the sum of Twenty-five thousand dollars be placed to the credit of the Honourable the Treasurer to cover the payments of commutations in connection with the Volunteer Veterans' Land Grants, for the balance of the current year, the appropriation for said service having become exhausted.

Certified,

J. LONSDALE CAPREOL.
Clerk, Executive Council.

ToRONTO, 7th November, 1906.

SIR,—The undersigned begs to report to the Provincial Auditor that the amount hitherto appropriated for contingencies of his Department has been spent, and that a further sum will be required to meet liabilities already incurred, and for the payment of the services of extra clerks for the balance of the year. The undersigned recommends that the further sum of $4,000 be granted under the provisions of section 20, Cap. 23, R.S.O. 1897, to meet requisite payments.

Extra Clerks	$2,300
Printing and Stationery	1,000
Advertising	300
Postage	300
Sundries	100
	$4,000

(Sgd.) F. COCHRANE,
Minister of Lands, Forests and Mines.

J. CLANCY, ESQ.,
    Provincial Auditor,
        Toronto.

Copy of a Minute of the Treasury Board, dated the 9th day of November, A.D. 1906.

Upon consideration of the report of the Honourable the Minister of Lands, Forests and Mines, dated the 7th day of November, A.D. 1906, the Treasury Board doth hereby order that pursuant to the provisions of section 20, Cap. 23, R.S.O. 1897, the sum of Four thousand dollars ($4,000) be placed to the credit of the Honourable the Treasurer to meet liabilities already incurred, and the payment of the services of extra Clerks for the balance of the current year, the appropriation for "Contingencies" having become exhausted.

Certified,

J. LONSDALE CAPREOL.
Clerk, Treasury Board.

TORONTO, December 10th, 1906.

SIR,—As the amount appropriated for expenditure in Forest Reserves is insufficient to meet the requisite payments, I would beg to recommend that a further sum of Three Thousand five hundred dollars be granted for that purpose under authority of R.S.O. 1897, Cap. 20, section 23.

It was found necessary in order to efficiently protect the reserves to appoint a larger number of rangers than was anticipated when the estimate of the expenditure on this service was made.

The amount applied for is required to pay outstanding accounts.

(Sgd.) F. COCHRANE,
Minister of Lands, Forests and Mines.

J. CLANCY, ESQ.,
Provincial Auditor,
Toronto.

Copy of a Minute of the Treasury Board, dated the 12th day of December, A.D. 1906.

Upon consideration of the report of the Honourable the Minister of Lands, Forests and Mines, dated the 10th day of December, A.D. 1906, the Treasury Board doth hereby order that pursuant to the provisions of section 20, Cap. 23, R.S.O. 1897, the sum of Three thousand five hundred dollars ($3,500) be placed to the credit of the Honourable the Treasurer to meet the requirements of expenditure in connection with Forest Reserves for the balance of the current year, the appropriation for said service having become exhausted.

Certified,

J. LONSDALE CAPREOL,
Clerk, Executive Council.

TORONTO, December 15th, 1906.

SIR,—As the unexpended balance of the appropriation for Agents' salaries will not be sufficient to meet the amount of the December pay list owing largely to the extension of the system of Homestead Inspection during the year, I beg to recommend that authority be given under the Act, R.S.O. 1897, Cap. 23, section 20, for the appropriation of a further sum of Two thousand five hundred dollars ($2,500) to complete the payments requisite under this service.

Yours truly,

(Sgd.) F. COCHRANE,
Minister of Lands, Forests and Mines.

J. CLANCY, ESQ.,
Provincial Auditor,
Parliament Buildings.

Copy of a Minute of the Treasury Board, dated the 18th day of December, A.D. 1906.

Upon consideration of the report of the Honourable the Minister of Lands, Forests and Mines, dated the 15th day of December, A.D. 1906, the Treasury Board doth hereby order that pursuant to the provisions of section 20, Cap. 23, R.S.O. 1897, the sum of Two thousand five hundred dollars ($2,500) be placed to the credit of the Honourable the Treasurer to meet the requirements of Crown Lands Agents' salaries for the balance of the current year, the appropriation for said service being insufficient.

Certified,

J. LONSDALE CAPREOL,
Clerk, Treasury Board.

TORONTO, July 12th, 1906.

The undersigned reports for the information of the Provincial Auditor.

That the appropriation for the payment of special services of the Hamilton Collegiate Masters as Lecturers in the Normal College for the session 1905-1906 is insufficient to meet the necessary expenditure.

The undersigned therefore recommends that under authority of R.S.O. 1897, Cap. 23, section 20, a further sum of Ninety-five dollars ($95) be made to meet the additional expenditure required as per accompanying schedule.

(Sgd.) R. A. PYNE,
Minister of Education.

J. CLANCY, ESQ.,
Provincial Auditor,
Parliament Buildings, Toronto.

Schedule of further amount required to meet the payment of special services of the Hamilton Collegiate Masters as Lecturers in the Normal College for the Session 1905-1906:

S. A. Morgan, arrears 1905 as Acting Lecturer in Psychology, etc., during Dr. McLellan's illness paid per Certificate 411, May 7th, 1906.............. $500.00

S. A. Morgan, services January to June, 1906, as
Acting Lecturer in Psychology, etc., during Dr.
McLellan's illness, payable as per Certificate
799, July 10th... 500.00
J B. Turner, J. T. Crawford, A. M. Logan, E. S. Ho-
garth, F. F. Macpherson, A. Paterson, J. Gill,
S. A. Morgan and G. J. Johnson, for special services as Lecturers for Session 1905-1906 at $121.67
each ....: 1,095.00

Payable for certificates 800, of July 10th..............$2,095.00
Amount of appropriation per Vote 17, page 26........$2,000.00

Estimates 1906. Additional Amount required ....$ 95.00

H. M. WILKINSON,
Accountant.

EDUCATION DEPARTMENT,
July 12th, 1906.

Copy of a Minute of the Treasury Board, dated the 13th
day of July, A.D. 1906.

Upon consideration of the report of the Honourable the
Minister of Education, dated the 12th day of July, A.D. 1906,
the Treasury Board doth hereby, pursuant to the provisions of
section 20, Cap. 23, R.S.O. 1897, order that the sum of Ninety-
five dollars ($95) be placed to the credit of the Honourable the
Treasurer, to meet the additional expenditure required for the
payment of special services of the Hamilton Collegiate Masters
as Lecturers in the Normal College for the session of 1905-1906,
the appropriation for said service having become exhausted.

Certified,

J. LONSDALE CAPREOL,
Clerk, Executive Council.

TORONTO, July 12th, 1906.

The undersigned reports for the information of the Provincial Auditor,—

That the appropriation for the payment of the allowances
to Superannuated Teachers for the current year is exhausted,

and that an additional sum will be required to pay the balance of such claims to date.

The undersigned therefore recommends that under authority of R.S.O. 1897, Cap. 23, section 20, a further appropriation of One hundred and sixty-two dollars ($162.00) be made to meet the additional expenditure as per the accompanying schedule.

(Sgd.) R. A. PYNE,
Minister of Education.

J. CLANCY, ESQ.,
> Provincial Auditor,
> > Parliament Buildings.

———

Schedule of further amount required to meet payment of allowances to Superannuated Teachers to date for current year:

Allowances paid to June 30..............................$ 63,027.50
Allowance to be paid as per Certificate No. 668
    herewith 134.50

                                       $ 63,162.00
Amount of Legislative Appropriation 63,000.00

             Balance required........................:........ $ 162.00

H. M. WILKINSON,
Accountant.

EDUCATION DEPARTMENT,
> July 12th, 1906.

———

Copy of a Minute of the Treasury Board, dated the 13th day of July, A.D. 1906.

Upon consideration of the report of the Honourable the Minister of Education, dated the 12th day of July, A.D. 1906, the Treasury Board doth hereby order pursuant to the provisions of section 20, Cap. 23, R.S.O. 1897, that the sum of One hundred and sixty-two dollars ($162) be placed to the credit of the Honourable the Treasurer for the payment to date of the allowances to Superannuated Teachers, the appropriation for said service having become exhausted.

Certified,

J. LONSDALE CAPREOL,
Clerk, Treasury Board.

Additional amount required by Education Department for the following services:

Furniture and Furnishings.

Accounts for furnishing of Superintendent's office	153.35
Other accounts for purchases made or to be made before end of year..................	346.65
	$500.00

Expenses of Grounds.

Pay lists and wages of extra men on grounds to end of year	600.00
Further purchases, bulbs, seeds, tools, manure cartage, etc.	200.00
	$ 800.00

Additional amount required............... $1,300.00

(Sgd.) R. A. PYNE,
Minister of Education.

J. CLANCY, ESQ.,
    Provincial Auditor,

Copy of a Minute of the Treasury Board, dated 11th day of September, 1906.

Upon consideration of the report of the Honourable Mr. Foy, acting for the Minister of Education, dated the 31st day day of August, A.D. 1906, the Treasury Board doth hereby order pursuant to the provisions of section 20, Cap. 23, R.S.O. 1897, that the sum of One thousand three hundred dollars ($1,300) be placed to the credit of the Honourable the Treasurer to meet the requirements of the Education Department to the end of the year in connection with the sub-services of "Furniture and Furnishings" and "Expenses of Grounds," as per the annexed statement, the appropriation for said services having become exhausted.

Certified,

M. CURREY,
Ass't. Clerk Executive Council.

TORONTO, 27th September, 1906.

SIR,—The undersigned reports for the information of the Provincial Auditor, that the appropriation for the "Costs of Investigations" under Vote 24, Education Department, "Miscellaneous," is insufficient to meet the claims upon the fund for the current year. The undersigned therefore recommends that under authority of the Act, a further appropriation of One thousand and forty-six dollars and sixty-eight cents ($1,046.68) be made to meet the further expenditure required in the matter of payments in connection with the investigation into certain irregularities in examinations at the Strathroy High School, as approved by Order-in-Council of 26th September, 1906.

(Sgd.) R. A. PYNE,
Minister of Education.

J. CLANCY, ESQ.,
Provincial Auditor,
Toronto.

———

Copy of a Minute of the Treasury Board, dated the 27th day of September, A.D. 1906.

Upon consideration of the report of the Honourable the Minister of Education, dated the 27th day of September, A.D. 1906, the Treasury Board doth hereby order that pursuant to the provsions of section 20, Cap. 23, R.S.O. 1897, the sum of One thousand and forty-six dollars and sixty-eight cents ($1,046.68) be placed to the credit of the Honourable the Treasurer to meet the requirement of "Costs of Investigations" under Vote 24, Education Department (Miscellaneous).

Certified,

M. CURREY,
Clerk, Treasury Board.

———

TORONTO, 1st October, 1906.

SIR,—The undersigned reports for the information of the Provincial Auditor.

That the appropriations for the sub-items of "Examiners for Departmental Examinations" and "Paper, Postage and Supplies for Examiners and Services and Expenses of Assistants" under Vote 16, Estimates, for the current year are exhausted, and paysheets, accounts, etc., to the amount of $1,382.07 are now waiting for payment, while further pay lists

Four hundred dollars ($400) provided for the "Expenses Advisory Council" under Vote No. 75 of the estimates of 1906, is exhausted, and a further sum of One thousand dollars ($1,000) will be required to meet the further necessary expenses of the service for the current year.

The undersigned therefore recommends that a further sum of One thousand dollars be granted under authority of the Act R.S.O. 1897, Cap. 23, section 20, to meet the claims enumerated as per schedule attached hereto, and that payment of the same be made as usual upon the certificate of the Education Department or King's Printer's Department, as the audit office may require.

(Sgd.) R. A. PYNE,
Minister of Education.

James Clancy, Esq.,
    Provincial Auditor,
      Toronto.

Schedule of further amounts required for the sub-service of Election and Expenses of the Advisory Council of Education, 1906.

Services of Registrar, Scrutineers and Assistant as per Order-in-Council of November 30, 1906......$ 700.00
Printing and Advertising, Travelling Expenses of Members of Council for December, and Incidentals 300.00

$1,000.00

H. M. WILKINSON,
Accountant Education Department.

Toronto, December 5th, 1906.

Copy of a Minute of the Treasury Board, dated 7th December, 1906.

Upon consideration of the report of the Honourable the Minister of Education, dated the 5th day of December, A.D. 1906, the Treasury Board doth hereby order that pursuant to the provisions of section 20, Cap. 23, R.S.O. 1897, the sum of

3*a P.A.

One thousand dollars ($1,000) be placed to the credit of the Honourable the Treasurer to cover the claims mentioned in the annexed schedule in connection with the election and expenses of the Advisory Council of Education, the appropriation for said service having become exhausted.

Certified,

J. LONSDALE CAPREOL,
Clerk, Treasury Board.

TORONTO, December 5th, 1906

DEAR SIR,—The undersigned reports for the information of the Provincial Auditor that the sum of Five thousand dollars ($5,000) provided under Vote No. 70 of this year's estimates for "Commissions for Sundry Investigations" is exhausted, and the approximate sum of One thousand dollars ($1,000) is required to be provided, to be charged against as needed for expenses and servces, *re* the investigation into the management of the Institution for the Deaf and Dumb, Belleville.

The undersigned therefore recommends that under the authority of the Act, R.S.O. 1897, Cap. 23, section 20, a further sum of One thousand dollars be provided subject to payment certificates to be issued under the authority of the Department of Education.

(Sgd.) R. A. PYNE,
Minister of Education.

JAMES CLANCY, ESQ.,
Provincial Auditor,
Toronto.

Copy of a Minute of the Treasury Board, dated the 7th day of December, A.D. 1906.

Upon consideration of the report of the Honourable the Minister of Education, dated on the 5th day of December, A.D. 1906, the Treasury Board doth hereby order that pursuant to the provisions of section 20, Cap. 23, R.S.O. 1897, the sum of One thousand dollars ($1,000) be placed at the credit of the Honourable the Treasurer to meet payments for services and expenses in connection with the investigation into the management of the Institution for the Deaf and Dumb at Belleville, the appropriation for "Commissions re Sundry Investigations" having become exhausted, such payments to be made upon the usual certificates of the Education Department.

Certified,

J. LONSDALE CAPREOL,
Clerk, Treasury Board.

SIR,—The undersigned has the honour to report for the information of the Provincial Auditor that the sum appropriated at the last session of the Legislature for butcher's meat, fish and fowl for the Institution for the Blind at Brantford, is insufficient to pay the December accounts by the sum of Eighty-two dollars ($82.00).

Also that the appropriation for butter and lard is insufficient to pay the December accounts by the sum of $37.68, the deficiency in each case being due to the increase in the contract prices for these commodities.

The undersigned therefore recommends that authority be given under the act for a further appropriation of One hundred and nineteen dollars and sixty-eight cents ($119.68) to meet the accounts to be presented in December for these services.

(Sgd.) R. A. PYNE,
Minister of Education.

JAMES CLANCY, ESQ.,
Provincial Auditor,
Toronto.

EDUCATION DEPARTMENT,
TORONTO, November 29th, 1906.

Copy of a Minute of the Treasury Board, dated the 5th day of December, A.D. 1906.

Upon consideration of the report of the Honourable the Minister of Education, dated the 29th day of November, A.D. 1906, the Treasury Board doth hereby order that pursuant to the provisions of section 20, Cap. 23, R.S.O. 1897, the sum of One hundred and nineteen dollars and sixty-eight cents ($119.68) be placed to the credit of the Honourable the Treasurer to cover the payment of accounts for butcher's meat, fish and fowl, and for butter and lard during the month of December in connection with the Institution for the Blind at Brantford, the appropriation for said service having become·exhausted.

Certified,

J. LONSDALE CAPREOL,
Clerk, Executive Council.

The undersigned has the honour to report for the information of the Provincial Auditor

That whereas under the authority of Orders-in-Council of July 13th, 1907, and December 10th, 1907, certain payments amounting to $937.50 are now due the acting Principal and certain Lecturers on the Staff of the Ontario Normal College for services to the end of the current year.

And whereas under authority of the first named Order-in-Council, such salaries are to be charged to any balance remaining in the appropriation for the Normal College.

But whereas after providing for sundry maintenance and other accounts of the Normal College now on hand, or yet to be presented to the end of the year, the available balance in the Normal College appropriation for this purpose will be only $600.00,

The undersigned therefore recommends that authority be given under the Act R.S.O. 1897, Cap. 23, section 20, for the issue of a warrant for Three hundred and thirty-seven dollars and fifty cents ($337.50) to meet the deficiency.

(Sgd.) R. A. PYNE,
Minister of Education.

JAMES CLANCY, Esq.,
Provincial Auditor,
Toronto.

TORONTO, December 12th, 1906.

Copy of a Minute of the Treasury Board, dated the 20th day of December, A.D. 1906.

Upon consideration of the report of the Honourable the Minister of Education, dated the 12th day of December, A.D. 1906, the Treasury Board doth hereby order that pursuant to the provisions of section 20, Cap. 23, R.S.O. 1897, the sum of Three hundred and thirty-seven dollars and fifty cents ($337.50) be placed to the credit of the Honourable the Treasurer, to cover the payment of the salaries of the Acting Principal and certain Lecturers on the Staff of the Ontario Normal College to the end of the current year, the appropriation for said Institution being insufficient for the purpose.

Certified,

J. LONSDALE CAPREOL,
Clerk, Executive Council.

The undersigned reports for the ·information of the Provincial Auditor.

That the appropriation for the sub-service of Departmental Examinations under Vote 16 is exhausted, as well as the additional provision of $3,000.00 made under Minute of the Treasury Board of the 6th October, 1906.

That as certain pay lists for examiners and assistants are yet unpaid, covering the services of scholarships and other examiners, the additional amount of $1,700 is needed. This increased amount is owing to the heavier examination work of the year and the extra clerical assistance required owing to the long and serious illness of the registrar.

The undersigned therefore recommends that under the authority of the Act a further appropriation of $1,700 be made to meet the further expenditure required.

(Sgd.) R. A. PYNE,
Minister of Education.

JAMES CLANCY, ESQ.,
Provincial Auditor,
Toronto.
TORONTO, December 14th, 1906.

Copy of a Minute of the Treasury Board, dated the 20th day of December, A.D. 1906.

Upon consideration· of the report of the Honourable the Minister of Education, dated the 14th day of December, A.D. 1906, the Treasury Board doth hereby order that pursuant to the provisions of section 20, Cap. 23, R.S.O. 1897, the sum of One thousand seven hundred dollars be placed to the credit of the Honourable the Treasurer to meet further expenditure required for the balance of the current year in connection with departmental examinations the appropriation for said service having become exhausted.

Certified,

J. LONSDALE CAPREOL,
Clerk, Treasury Board.

———

I have the honour to inform you that the appropriation for Commissions *re* Sundry Investigations is exhausted, as well as the amount of Fifteen hundred dollars provided by Order on the Treasury Board of 20th October last for expenses of the Text Book Commission, and a further sum of Twelve hundred dollars ($1,200) is required to meet subsequent expenditures on account of salaries, travelling, office and other expenses of the said Commission.

The undersigned therefore recommends that authority be given under the Act for an appropriation of Twelve hundred dollars ($1,200) for this purpose, and that an accountable for this amount be issued in favor of Mr. A. C. Casselman, Secretary of the said Commission.

(Sgd.) R. A. PYNE,
Minister of Education.

JAMES CLANCY, ESQ.,
Provincial Auditor,
Toronto.

———

Toronto, December 14th, 1906.

Copy of a Minute of the Treasury Board, dated the 27th day of December, A.D. 1906.

Upon consideration of the report of the Honourable the Minister of Education, dated the 26th day of December, A.D. 1906, the Treasury Board doth hereby order that pursuant to the provisions of section 20, Cap. 23, R.S.O. 1897, the sum of One thousand two hundred dollars ($1,200) be placed to the credit of the Honourable the Treasurer to cover expenditures on account of salaries, travelling, office and other expenses of the Text Book Commission for the balance of the current year, the appropriations for "Commissions *re* Sundry Investigations" having become exhausted.

Certified,

J. LONSDALE CAPREOL,
Clerk, Treasury Board.

The undersigned reports for the information òf the Provincial Auditor that the amounts voted for the following sub-services of Education are exhausted, and that a few more payments are urgently needed to close the transactions of the year for these sub-services. These amounts are as follows:

1. Teachers' Associations.
   Grants of $25 each to Teachers' Institutes South
   Wellington, Frontenac and Carleton, total...$75
2. Maintenance Toronto Normal and Model Schools
   Buildings.
   Amount required for scrubbing and cleaning and·
   supplies for work done and to be done to 31st
   December inst.   50
3. Maintenance London Normal School Buildings.
   Scrubbing and cleaning, cartage and supplies to
   31st December inst.   75

The undersigned therefore recommends that a further appropriation of Two hundred dollars ($200) be made under the Act to cover the above expenditure and that payments be made upon the presentation of the usual certificates, or pay lists, by the Department of Education.

(Sgd.) R. A. PYNE,
Minister of Education.

JAMES CLANCY, ESQ.,
        Provincial Auditor,
            Toronto.

Toronto, December 27th, 1906.

Copy of a Minute of the Treasury Board, dated the 2nd day of January, A.D. 1907.

Upon consideration of the report of the Honourable the Minister of Education, dated the 27th day of December, A.D. 1906, the Treasury Board doth hereby order that pursuant to the provisions of section 20, Cap. 23, R.S.O. 1897, the sum of Two hundred dollars ($200) be placed to the credit of the Honourable the Provincial Treasurer to meet the requirements of "Teachers' Associations," "Maintenance Toronto Normal and Model School Buildings,'.' and "Maintenance London Normal School Buildings" for the balance of the current year, the appropriations for said services having become exhausted.

Certified,

J. LONSDALE CAPREOL,
Clerk, Treasury Board.

TORONTO, Oct. 2nd, 1906.

SIR,—I have the honour to report that the sum appropriated at the last session of the Legislature for Legislation expenses will not be sufficient to meet the expenditures.

The following accounts remain unpaid on account of the appropriation being exhausted :

Armour and Mickle, prof. services *re* Mines Act	$100.00
Annual Review Pub. Co., 100 copies Can. American Review	227.50
Biographical Pub. Co., 100 copies Life Sir Oliver Mowat	500.00
Houston's Standard Pubns., 100 copies Financial Review	250.00
A. B. Gillies, services in Post Office	184.00
F. M. Campbell, Services in Law Clerk's Office	40.00
S. I. Dunn, Services King's Printer's Office	168.00
Bell Tel. Co., Messages and Rent of 'Phones	291.85
D. F. Tolchard, Meals to Operators during session	52.50
Might's Directories, Directory	7.50
Dom. Express Co., charges	89.50
Can. Express Co., charges	61.93
G T. Ry. Co., freight charges	24.45
National Typewriter Co., rent of Typewriters	35.00
United Typewriter Co., do	62.00
Remington Typewriter Co., do	32.00
John Nunn, Books	15.00
C. N. Bastedo, Papers	5.00
Sundry Newspapers	11.30
King's Printer, Stationery	60x.94

$2,762.47

The undersigned therefore recommends that a further appropriation of $3,000 be granted under authority of R.S.O. 1897, Cap. 23, section 20, for the balance of the current year.

(Sgd.) A. J. MATHESON,
Provincial Treasurer.

JAMES CLANCY, ESQ.,
Provincial Auditor.

———

Copy of a Minute of the Treasury Board, dated the 4th day of October, A.D. 1906.

Upon consideration of the report of the Honourable the Treasurer, dated the 2nd day of October, A.D. 1906, the Treasury Board doth hereby order that pursuant to the provisions of section 20, Cap. 23, R.S.O. 1897, the sum of Three thousand dollars ($3,000) be placed to the credit of the Honourable the Treasurer to meet the expenses of legislation for the balance of the current year, the appropriation for said service having become exhausted.

Certified,

J. LONSDALE CAPREOL,
Clerk, Executive Council.

TORONTO, 21st November, 1906.

DEAR SIR,—The appropriation for contingencies and extra assistance for the Succession Duty Branch of the Treasury Department has been exhausted, and I therefore request that pursuant to section 20, Cap. 23, R.S.O. 1897, that you will recommend that a Treasury Board warrant be issued for the sum of Two hundred and fifty dollars ($250) for payment of these services.

(Sgd.) A. J. MATHESON,
Provincial Treasurer.

JAMES CLANCY, ESQ.,
    Provincial Auditor,
        Toronto.

Copy of a Minute of the Treasury Board, dated the 27th day of November, A.D. 1906.

Upon consideration of the report of the Honourable the Treasurer, dated 21st November, A.D. 1906, the Treasury Board doth hereby order that pursuant to the provisions of section 20, Cap. 23, R.S.O. 1897, the sum of Two hundred and fifty dollars be placed to his credit to meet the requirements of Contingencies and extra assistance of Succession Duty Branch for the balance of the current year, the appropriation for said service having become exhausted.

Certified,

J. LONSDALE CAPREOL,
Clerk, Treasury Board

TORONTO, November 21st, 1906.

HON. A. J. MATHESON,
Provincial Treasurer.

DEAR SIR,—I beg to inform you that the Library appropriation of $4,000 for purchase of books has been exhausted by the accounts sent in up to this date. Before the end of the year there will be a few other accounts becoming due, and I therefore respectfully recommend that a Treasury Board warrant for $150 to meet such accounts be issued.

Yours faithfully,

AVERN PARDOE,
Librarian.

JAMES CLANCY, ESQ.,
Provincial Auditor,
Toronto.

DEAR SIR,—The undersigned respectfully recommends that authority be given pursuant to the provisions of section 20, Cap. 23, R.S.O. 1897, for the issue of a Treasury Board warrant in favour of the Honourable the Provincial Treasurer for the sum of $150 to meet the requirements as stated above.

(Sgd.) A. J. MATHESON,
Provincial Treasurer.
Toronto, November 21st, 1906.

Copy of a Minute of the Treasury Board, dated the 22nd day of November, A.D. 1906.

Upon consideration of the report of the Honourable the Treasurer, dated the 21st day of November, 1906, the Treasury Board doth hereby order that pursuant to the provisions of section 20, Cap. 23, R.S.O. 1897, the sum of One Hundred and fifty dollars ($150) be placed to his credit to meet the requirements of the Legislative Library for the balance of the current year, the appropriation for said service having become exhausted.

Certified,

J. LONSDALE CAPREOL,
Clerk, Treasury Board.

The undersigned begs to report that the provision made in the current year's estimates for Incidentals under Miscellaneous is about exhausted, owing principally to large expenditures for legal services and for advertising the Provincial Loan, and a further sum of $2,500 will be required to meet expenses for the balance of the current year.

The amount at present required to be paid is as follows:

To American Bank Note Company, engraving and furnishing bonds ....:........................$2,600.00

The undersigned therefore recommends that authority be given pursuant to the provisions of section 20, Cap. 23, R.S. O. 1897, for the issue of a Treasury Board warrant in favor of the Provincial Treasurer for the sum of $2,500.00.

(Sgd.) A. J. MATHESON,
Provincial Treasurer.

JAMES CLANCY, ESQ.,
       Provincial Auditor,
           Toronto.
           7th December, 1906.

Copy of a Minute of the Treasury Board, dated the 11th day of December, A.D. 1906.

Upon consideration of the report of the Honourable the Treasurer, dated the 7th day of December, A.D. 1906, the Treasury Board doth hereby order that pursuant to the provisions of section 20, Cap. 23, R.S.O. 1897, the sum of Two thousand five hundred dollars ($2,500) be placed to the credit of the Honourable the Treasurer to cover the payment of accounts for the balance of the year chargeable to the appropriation for "Incidentals" in the current year's estimates, the said appropriation being almost exhausted.

Certified,

J. LONSDALE CAPREOL,
Clerk, Treasury Board.

12th December, 1906.

The undersigned begs to report that the provision made in the current year's estimates for Hydro-Electric Power Commission is exhausted, owing principally to large expenditures for engineering research, travelling and general office expenses, and a further sum of $2,000 will be required to meet the expenses for the balance of the current year.

The undersigned therefore recommends that authority be given pursuant to the provisions of section 20, Cap. 23, R.S.O. 1897, for the issue of a Treasury Board warrant in favour of the Provincial Treasurer for the sum of Two thousand dollars ($2,000).

(Sgd.) A. J. MATHESON,
Provincial Treasurer.

JAMES CLANCY, ESQ.,
     Provincial Auditor,
       Toronto.

———

Copy of a Minute of the Treasury Board, dated the 12th day of December, A.D. 1906.

Upon consideration of the report of the Honourable the Treasurer, dated the 12th day of December, A.D. 1906, the Treasury Board doth hereby order that pursuant to the provisions of section 20, Cap. 23, R.S.O. 1897, the sum of Two thousand dollars ($2,000) be placed to the Treasurer's credit to meet travelling and general office expenses in connection with the Hydro-Electric Power Commission for the balance of the current year, the appropriations for said service having become exhausted.

Certified,

J. LONSDALE CAPREOL,
Clerk, Treasury Board.

———

The undersigned begs to report that in addition to the amount granted by the Treasury Board Order of the 12th instant, further provision will require to be made to meet necessary expenses for the current year of the Hydro-Electric Power Commission.

The undersigned therefore recommends that authority be given pursuant to the provisions of section 20, Cap. 23, R.S.O. 1897, for the issue of a Treasury Board warrant in favour of the Provincial Treasurer for the sum of One thousand dollars ($1,000).

A. J. MATHESON,
Provincial Treasurer.

JAMES CLANCY, ESQ.,
     Provincial Auditor.
       December 26th, 1906.

Copy of a Minute of the Treasury Board, dated the 28th day of December, A.D. 1906.

Upon consideration of the report of the Honourable the Provincial Treasurer, dated the 26th day of December, A.D. 1906, the Treasury Board doth hereby order that pursuant to the provisions of section 20, Cap. 23, R.S.O. 1897, the sum of One thousand dollars ($1,000) be placed to his credit .o meet necessary expenses for the current year of the Hydro-Electric Power Commission, the appropriation for said service having become exhausted.

Certified,

M. CURREY,
for Clerk, Treasury Board.

The undersigned begs to report that the provision in the estimates for the current year to meet Premiums on Fidelity Bonds has been exhausted owing to payments made for accounts held over from 1905 and additional new premiums incurred during 1906.

The undersigned therefore recommends that authority be given pursuant to the provisions of section 20, Cap. 23, R.S.O. 1897, for the issue of a Treasury Board warrant in favour of the Provincial Treasurer for the sum of $2,686.14.

A. J. MATHESON,
Provincial Treasurer.

JAMES CLANCY, ESQ.,
    Provincial Auditor.
        December 27th, 1906.

Copy of a Minute of the Treasury Board, dated the 28th day of December, A.D. 1906.

Upon consideration of the report of the Honourable the Provincial Treasurer, dated the 27th day of December, A.D. 1906, the Treasury Board doth hereby order that pursuant to the provisions of secton 20, Cap. 23, R.S.O. 1897, the sum of Two thousand six hundred and eighty-six dollars and fourteen cents be placed to his credit to meet Premiums on Fidelity Bonds, the appropriation for said service having become exhausted.

Certified,

M. CURREY,
for Clerk, Treasury Board.

TORONTO, December 27th, 1906.

SIR,—I have the honour to report that the sum appropriated at the last session of the Legislature for Legislation Contingencies will not be sufficient to meet expenses for the balance of the current year owing to unexpected expenditures in connection with that service.

There are at present accounts unpaid, on account of the appropriation being exhausted, to the amount of $2,489. There will be required to pay present accounts unpaid, and for the balance of the current year, the sum of Three thousand dollars ($3,000). The undersigned therefore recommends that a further appropriation of Three thousand dollars ($3,000) be granted under authority of R.S.O. 1897, Cap. 23, sec. 20, for the balance of the current year.

A. J. MATHESON,
Provincial Treausrer.

JAMES CLANCY, ESQ.,
Provincial Auditor.

Copy of a Minute of the Treasury Board, dated the 4th day of January, A.D. 1907.

Upon consideration of the report of the Honourable the Treasurer, dated the 27th day of December, A.D. 1906, the Treasury Board doth hereby order that pursuant to the provisions of section 20, Cap. 23, R.S.O. 1897, the sum of Three thousand dollars ($3,000) be placed to his credit to cover the payment of unpaid accounts for the balance of the year 1906 in connection with Legislation Contingencies, the appropriation for said service having become exhausted.

Certified,

J. LONSDALE CAPREOL,
Clerk, Treasury Board.

TORONTO, January 3rd, 1907.

The provision in the estimates for Miscellaneous Refunds having been exhausted, the undersigned begs to recommend that authority be given under 49 Victoria, Chapter 4, section

20, for refunding the sum of $246.53 to Mr. Joseph Pim, being an overpayment by him on account of Algoma Taxes.

A. J. MATHESON,
Provincial Treausrer.

JAMES CLANCY, ESQ.,
Provincial Auditor,
Toronto.

———

Copy of a Minute of the Treasury Board, dated the 9th day of January, A.D. 1907.

Upon consideration of the report of the Honourable the Treasurer, dated the 3rd day of January, A.D. 1907, the Treasury Board doth hereby order that pursuant to the provisions of section 20, Cap. 23, R.S.O. 1897, the sum of Two hundred and forty-six dollars and fifty-three cents ($246.53) be placed to his credit to meet a refund of said amount to Mr. Joseph Pim, being an overpayment by him on account of Algoma Taxes, the appropriation for "Refunds Miscellaneous" having become exhausted.

Certified,

J. LONSDALE CAPREOL,
Clerk, Treasury Board.

———

TORONTO, 17th January, 1907.

SIR,—The undersigned has the honour to report for the information of the Provincial Auditor, that the amount appropriated for the payment of gratuities and annuities to Indians of Ontario under Treaty No. 9, payable through the Government of the Dominion, is insufficient to make the payments for 1906 by the sum of $6,124.

The undersigned therefore respectfully recommends that a further appropriation of $6,124 be granted under the authority of R.S.O. 1897, Cap. 23, sec. 20, to meet balance of payments for the year 1906 on the above account.

A. J. MATHESON,
Provincial Treausrer.

JAMES CLANCY, ESQ.,
Provincial Auditor.

Copy of a Minute of the Treasury Department, dated the 18th day of January, A.D. 1907.

Upon consideration of the report of the Honourable the Treasurer, dated the 18th day of January, A.D. 1907, the Treasury Board doth hereby order that pursuant to the provisions of section 20, Cap. 23, R.S.O. 1897, the sum of Six thousand one hundred and twenty-four dollars ($6,124) be placed to the Treasurer's credit to cover the payment of gratuities and annuities to Indians of Ontario under Treaty No. 9, through the Government of the Dominion, the appropriation for said service being insufficient for the purpose.

Certified,

J. LONSDALE CAPREOL,
Clerk, Treasury Board.

TORONTO, Ont., October 3rd, 1906.
JAMES CLANCY, ESQ.,
Provincial Auditor.

The undersigned respectfully reports to the Provincial Auditor:—

That the sum appropriated by the last Legislature for Special Investigations is insufficient by the sum of One hundred and twenty-eight dollars;

That this deficiency arises through an allowance of One hundred and twenty-eight dollars for fees as stenographer to Miss Minnie N. Jarrett in reporting the "Bastedo-Webster Investigation."

I therefore beg to recommend that authority be given under R.S.O. 1897, Chapter 23, section 20, for the payment of the said amount of One hundred and twenty-eight dollars.

Respectfully submitted,

(Sgd.) J. O. REAUME,
Minister of Public Works.

Copy of a Minute of the Treasury Board, dated the 5th day of October, A.D. 1906.

Upon consideration of the report of the Honourable the Minister of Public Works, dated the 3rd day of October, A.D.

4* P.A.

1906, the Treasury Board doth hereby order, pursuant to the provisions of section 20, Cap. 23, R.S.O. 1897, that the sum of One hundred and twenty-eight dollars ($128) be placed to the credit of the Honourable the Treasurer to cover the allowance to Miss Minnie N. Jarrett for services in reporting the "Bastedo-Webster Investigation," the appropriation for Special Investigations having become exhausted.

Certified,

J. LONSDALE CAPREOL,
Clerk, Treasury Board.

TORONTO, Ont., October 24th, 1906.

JAMES CLANCY, ESQ.,
Provincial Auditor,

SIR,—I beg to report that the cost of L'Amable Bridge, in the Township of Dungannon, owing to increased cost of materials and labour, has exceeded the estimated cost.

The sum provided by the estimates, together with the grants made by the Municipalities of the County of Hastings, the Township of Dungannon, and the Township of Farraday, is inadequate to pay the outstanding accounts. The total cost of the Bridge is $1,734.73, and the balance of unpaid accounts not provided for $571.43.

I therefore beg leave to recommend that authority be given under R.S.O. sec. 20, Cap. 23, for payment of the above sum of Five hundred and seventy-one dollars and forty-three cents ($571.43).

I have the honour to be,
Sir,
Your obedient servant,

(Sgd.) A. W. CAMPBELL,
Deputy Minister of Public Works.

Approved.
J. O. REAUME,
Minister of Public Works.

Copy of a Minute of the Treasury Board, dated the 1st day of November, A.D. 1906.

Upon consideration of the report of the Honourable the Minister of Public Works, dated the 24th day of October, A.D.

4a* P.A.

1906, the Treasury Board doth hereby order that pursuant to the provisions of section 20, Cap. 23, R.S.O. 1897, the sum of Five hundred and seventy-one dollars and forty-three cents ($571.43) be placed to the credit of the Honourable the Treasurer for the payment of outstanding accounts in connection with the construction of the L'Amable Bridge in the Township of Dungannon, the appropriation for same having become exhausted.

Certified,

J. LONSDALE CAPREOL,
Clerk, Treasury Board.

To the Provincial Auditor :

The undersigned has the honour to report that the Legislative appropriation to pay stationery, postage and other contingencies in the Fisheries Department is exhausted, and that it is necessary provision shall be made for the payment of these services for the balance of the current year. He would therefore respectfully recommend that authority be given under the Act, R.S.O. 1897, Cap. 23, sec. 20, for the issue of a warrant for the sum of Four hundred dollars for that purpose.

J. O. REAUME,
Commissioner of Fisheries.

1st November, 1906.

Copy of a Minute of the Treasury Board, dated the 6th day of November, A.D. 1906.

Upon consideration of the report of the Honourable the Commissioner of Fisheries, dated the 1st day of November, A.D. 1906, the Treasury Board doth hereby order that pursuant to the provisions of section 20, Cap. 23, R.S.O. 1897, the sum of Four hundred dollars ($400) be placed to the credit of the Honourable the Treasurer to meet the requirements of the Fisheries Department "Contingencies" for the balance of the current year, the appropriation for said service having become exhausted.

Certified,

J. LONSDALE CAPREOL,
Clerk, Treasury Board.

DEPARTMENT OF PUBLIC WORKS, ONTARIO,

TORONTO, November 8th, 1906.

JAMES CLANCY, ESQ.,
  Provincial Auditor,

SIR,—I beg to report that the appropriation for Capital
Account, Algoma District, General repairs, etc., Gaoler's residence, Sault Ste. Marie, is exhausted, and would therefore recommend that authority be given under Act R.S.O. 1897, Cap.
23, section 20, to issue a warrant for the sum of One hundred
and five dollars and thirty-one cents ($105.31) to cover the fol-
lowing:—

Wm. Hallam, Contract ptg. and papering, bal. of acct. $16 73
D. P. McPhail,   do.   shingling house, etc. 88 58
                                                           ————
                                                           $105 31

A. W. CAMPBELL,
Deputy Minister of Public Works.

Approved.
J. O. REAUME.

Copy of a Minute of the Treasury Board, dated the 14th
day of November, A.D. 1906.

Upon consideration of the report of the Honourable the
Minister of Public Works, dated the 8th day of November,
A.D. 1906, the Treasury Board doth hereby order that pursuant
to the provisions of section 20, Cap. 23, R.S.O. 1897, the sum
of One hundred and five dollars and thirty-one cents ($105.31)
be placed to the credit of the Honourable the Treasurer to cover
the payment of accounts in connection with repairs to the Gaoler's residence, Sault Ste. Marie, the appropriation for capital
account, Algoma District, General repairs, etc., having become exhausted.

Certified,

J. LONSDALE CAPREOL,
Clerk, Treasury Board.

DEPARTMENT OF PUBLIC WORKS, ONTARIO.

TORONTO, November 12th, 1906.

JAMES CLANCY, ESQ.,
  Provincial Auditor.

SIR,—I beg to report that the appropriation for Nipissing
District Lock-up at Cobalt is exhausted, and would recommend

that a further sum of Five hundred and eighty-seven dollars and five cents ($587.05) be granted under R.S.O. 1897, Cap. 23, section 20, for the following:

E. D. Pittam, balance of contract building
Lock-up $227 08
 do Chimney stacks 25 00
 do Coal and Wood shed 230 00
          ————— $482 08
The N. L. Piper Ry. Supply Co., pails......................4 50
R. H. Elliott, furnishings 37 27
A. S. Galoska Co. do 9 30
Dreaney Bros. do 53 90

    Total $587 05

     (Sgd.) A. W. CAMPBELL,
     Deputy Minister of Public Works.

Copy of a Minute of the Treasury Board, dated the 14th day of November, AD. 1906.

Upon consideration of the report of the Deputy Minister of Public Works, dated the 12th day of November, A.D. 1906, the Treasury Board doth hereby order that pursuant to the provisions of section 20, Cap. 23, R.S.O. 1897, the sum of Five hundred and eighty-seven dollars and five cents be placed to the credit of the Honourable the Treasurer for the payment of certain accounts in connection with the construction of the Lock-up at Cobalt, District of Nipissing, the appropriation for said services having become exhausted.

    Certified,

     J. LONSDALE CAPREOL,
     Clerk, Treasury Board.

   DEPARTMENT OF PUBLIC WORKS, ONTARIO.

      TORONTO, November 12th, 1906.
JAMES CLANCY, ESQ.,
  Provincial Auditor.

SIR,—I beg to report that the appropriation for "General Repairs Maintenance" Parliament Buildings is exhausted, and

would recommend that a further sum of Five thousand five
hundred dollars be granted under R.S.O. 1897, Cap. 23, section
20 for as follows:

M. Thomas, Gravel ....$ 117 00
A. Muirhead, Brooms, Mops, etc.,........................   18 00
Townley and London, Painting Kitchen..................   43 90
Pay List of Men, Grounds, etc............ .... 3,331 55
Pay Lists of Charwomen cleaning buildings............ 1,266 75
To meet sundry accounts, repairs to elevators, sup-
    plies, soaps, etc., to end of year....................   722 80
                                                   $5,500 00

The increased expenditure is due to an insufficient amount
being appropriated to meet pay lists of men and charwomen
and provide for additions to the staff and increases in wages
during the year.

(Sgd.) A. W. CAMPBELL,
Deputy Minister of Public Works.

Copy of a Minute of the Treasury Board, dated the 14th
day of November, AD. 1906.

Upon consideration of the report of the Deputy Minister
of Public Works, dated the 12th day of November, A.D. 1906,
the Treasury Board doth hereby order that pursuant to the provisions of section 20, Cap. 23, R.S.O. 1897, the sum of Five
thousand five hundred dollars be placed to the credit of the
Honourable the Treasurer to meet the requirements for general
repairs and maintenance of the Parliament Buildings for the
balance of the current year, the appropriation for said service
having become exhausted.

Certified,

J. LONSDALE CAPREOL,
Clerk, Treasury Board.

JAMES CLANCY, ESQ.,
    Provincial Auditor,

SIR,—I beg to report that there is not sufficient of the
appropriation left for "Root and Boiler House" and for "Re-

construction of Laundry" at the Kingston Asylum to wholly meet the Contractors' certificates as follows:

Root and Boiler House.

R. F. N. McFarlane 1,452 00
Amount of Appropriation 1,200 00

.........Balance required.................... $252 00

Reconstruction of Laundry.

R. F. N. McFarlane 1,123 44
Balance to credit of appropriation 581 72

Balance required 541 72

       793 72

I therefore recommend that authority be given under section 20, Cap. 23, R.S.O. 1897, for the issue of a warrant in favour of the Provincial Treasurer for the sum of $793.72 for the payment of said balances.

       (Sgd.) A. W. CAMPBELL,
            Deputy Minister of Public Works.

Approved J. O. R.,
     Minister of Public Works.
Toronto, December 1st, 1906.

———

Copy of a Minute of the Treasury Board, dated the 27th day of December, A.D. 1906.

Upon consideration of the report of the Honourable the Minister of Public Works, dated the First day of December, A.D. 1906, the Treasury Board doth hereby order that pursuant to the provisions of section 20, Cap. 23, R.S.O. 1897, the sum of Seven hundred and ninety three dollars and seventy-two cents ($793.72) be placed to the credit of the Honourable the Treasurer to cover the payment of the Contractors' certificates in connection with the "Root and Boiler House" and "Construction of Laundry" at the Kingston Asylum, the appropriation for said services having become exhausted.

       Certified,

       J. LONSDALE CAPREOL,
            Clerk Treasury Board.

James Clancy, Esq.,
     Provincial Auditor,

TORONTO, 10th December, 1906.

SIR,—The undersigned begs to report that the sum voted for Contingencies for the Public Works Department is exhausted, and for the purpose of paying the following an additional amount of seven hundred and sixty-five dollars ($765) is required, viz.:

Salaries of extra clerks, draughtsmen, etc.	$232 00
Postage	50 00
Car Tickets	50 00
Sundry Accounts	20 00
Stationery for October and November	188 00
Telephone service for half-year	225 00
	$765 00

The undersigned therefore respectfully recommends that authority be given under the Act, R.S.O. 1897, Cap. 23, section 20, for the issue of a warrant for $765 in favor of the Honourable the Treasurer.

(Sgd.) A. W. CAMPBELL,
Deputy Minister of Public Works.
Approved J. O. Reaume,
Minister of Public Works.

Copy of a Minute of the Treasury Board, dated the 27th day of December, A.D. 1906.

Upon consideration of the report of the Honourable the Minister of Public Works, dated the 10th day of December, A.D. 1906, the Treasury Board doth hereby order that pursuant to the provisions of section 20, Cap. 23, R.S.O. 1897, the sum of Seven hundred and sixty-five dollars ($765) be placed to the credit of the Honourable the Treasurer to meet the requirements of "Contingencies" of the Public Works Department for the balance of the current year, the appropriation for said service having become exhausted.

Certified,

J. LONSDALE CAPREOL,
Clerk, Treasury Board.

JAMES CLANCY, ESQ.,
Provincial Auditor.

SIR,—I beg to report that the maintenance appropriation
for repairs and alterations and for furnishings at Osgoode
Hall is exhausted, and would recommend that under R.S.O.
1897, Cap. 23, section 20, the sum of Twelve hundred and ninety-three dollars ($1,293) be placed to the credit of the said ap-
propriation for the purposes of paying the following:

Sundry approved accounts in hand	$504 30
Pay lists for wages balance of year	150 00
Repairs to roof	100 00
Alterations to Surrogate Clerk's office	400 00
W. A. Murray, account furnishings, bal. of	138 70
	$1,293 00

(Sgd.) A. W. CAMPBELL,
Deputy Minister of Public Works.

J O. R.

Toronto, December 11th, 1906.

———

Copy of a Minute of the Treasury Board, dated the 18th
day of December, A.D. 1906.

Upon consideration of the report of the Honourable the
Minister of Public Works, dated the 11th day of December,
A.D. 1906,the Treasury Board doth hereby order that pursuant
to the provisions of section 20, Cap. 23, R.S.O. 1897, the sum
of One thousand two hundred and ninety-three dollars ($1,293)
be placed to the credit of the Honourable the Treasurer to
cover the payment of accounts for the balance of the current
year in connection with repairs and alterations and furnishings
at Osgoode Hall, the appropriation for said service having become exhausted.

Certified,

J. LONSDALE CAPREOL,
Clerk, Treasury Board.

TORONTO, December 29th, 1906.

Mr. James Clancy,
         Provincial Auditor,
               Parliament Buildings.
               Toronto.

SIR,—The undersigned begs to report that in cases where specific sums were voted at the last Session of the Legislature for Colonization Roads a number of the Overseers exceeded their instructions and made small over-expenditures, as shown in the attached memorandum, aggregating $1,349.81. The total expenditure on Colonization Roads, however, is about $9,000 less than the amounts appropriated.

I would recommend that authority be given under the Act, R.S.O. 1897, Cap. 23, sectios 20, for the said sum of $1,349.81 in order that the said balances may be paid, and the accounts closed.

                     Yours respectfully,

                         J. O. REAUME,
                  Minister of Public Works.

Copy of a Minute of the Treasury Board, dated the 4th day of January, A.D. 1907.

Upon consideration of the report of the Honourable the Minister of Public Works, dated the 29th day of December, A.D. 1906,the Treasury Board doth hereby order that pursuant to the provisions of section 20, Cap. 23, R.S.O. 1897, the sum of One thousand three hundred and forty-nine dollars and eight-one cents ($1,349.81) be placed to the credit of the Honourable the Treasurer to meet the requirements of Colonization Roads for the balance of the year 1906, the appropriations for certain roads having become exhausted.

                     Certified,

                    J. LONSDALE CAPREOL,
                     Clerk, Treasury Board.

JAMES CLANCY, ESQ.,
         Provincial Auditor.

SIR,—The undersigned begs leave to report that the sum appropriated at the last session of the Legislature for Contingencies for the Fisheries Branch of the Public Works Department is deficient by $300.

This is caused by the allowance to Edwin Tinsley, Chief Game Warden, for services as Deputy Commissioner of Fisheries, these being in addition to his ordinary duties.

The undersigned therefore begs to recommend that authority under R.S.O. 1897, Cap. 23, sec. 20, for the payment of the above amount be given.

J. O. REAUME,

Minister of Public Works and Commissioner of Fisheries.
Toronto, January 3rd, 1907.

Copy of a Minute of the Treasury Board, dated the 4th day of January, A.D. 1907.

Upon consideration of the report of the Honourable the Minister of Public Works and Commissioner of Fisheries, dated the 3rd day of January, A.D. 1907, the Treasury Board doth hereby order that pursuant to the provisions of section 20, Cap. 23, R.S.O. 1897, the sum of Three hundred dollars be placed to the credit of the Honourable the Treasurer to cover the payment of the allowance to Edwin Tinsley, Chief Game Warden, for services as Deputy Commissioner of Fisheries, the appropriation for contingencies of the Fisheries Branch of the Public Works Department having become exhausted.

Certified,

J. LONSDALE CAPREOL,
Clerk, Treasury Board.

Toronto, January 3rd, 1907.

James Clancy, Esq.,
Provincial Auditor,
Toronto.

Dear Sir,—I beg to inform you that the appropriations voted at the last session of the Legislature are insufficient to meet the pay lists and accounts due on the following works, viz.:—

Bala Bridge—

Balance of pay list, Dec. 1st to 21st............$91 05
Accounts for cement piers and abutments......346 80
————— $437 85

North River, removing rock—
Balance due Overseer 28 01

$465 86

I therefore recommend that authority be given under section 20, Cap. 23, R.S.O. 1897, for the issue of a warrant in favour of the Honourable the Provincial Treasurer for the sum of Four hundred and sixty-five dollars and eighty-six cents ($465.86) for the payment of the said accounts.

A. W. CAMPBELL,
Deputy Minister of Public Works.

Approved.
    J. O. REAUME,
      Minister.

Copy of a Minute of the Treasury Board, dated the 4th day of January, A.D. 1907.

Upon consideration of the report of the Honourable the Minister of Public Works, dated the 3rd day of January, A.D. 1907, the Treasury Board doth hereby order that pursuant to the provisions of section 20, Cap. 23, R.S.O. 1897, the sum of Four hundred and sixty-five dollars and eighty-six cents ($465.86) be placed to the credit of the Honourable the Treasurer to meet pay lists and accounts due on the following works, the appropriation for same having become exhausted, namely:
Bala Bridge—

Balance of pay list, Dec. 1st to 21st $91 05
Accounts for cement piers and abutments ... 346 80
                                    ————— 437 85
North River, removing rock—
Balance due Overseer .... 28 01.

                                        $465 86.

Certified,

J. LONSDALE CAPREOL,
Clerk, Treasury Board.

TORONTO, Jan. 9th, 1907.

JAMES CLANCY, ESQ.,
    Provincial Auditor,
        Province of Ontario.

SIR,—I beg to report that the appropriation for the Burnt River Bridge made at the last session of the Legislature is insufficient to pay the account of James A. Vance for the steel superstructure.

The increased expenditure was caused by the extra costs of concrete foundations.

I would therefore recommend that authority be given under the Act, R.S.O., Cap. 23, sec. 20, for the issue of a warrant for the sum of Two hundred and seventeen dollars and eleven cents ($217.11) for the payment of said account.

I have the honour to be,
Sir,
Your obedient servant,

A. W. CAMPBELL,
Deputy Minister of Public Works.

Approved.
    J. O. R.,
        Minister.

Copy of a Minute of the Treasury Board, dated the 15th day of January, A.D. 1907.

Upon consideration of the report of the Honourable the Minister of Public Works, dated the 9th day of January, A.D. 1907, the Treasury Board doth hereby order that pursuant to the provisions of section 20, Cap. 23, R.S.O. 1897, the sum of Two hundred and seventeen dollars and eleven cents ($217.11) be placed to the credit of the Honourable the Treasurer to cover the payment of the account of James A. Vance for the steel superstructure of the Burnt River Bridge, the appropriation for said work having become exhausted.

Certified,

J. LONSDALE CAPREOL,
Clerk, Treasury Board.

The undersigned begs to report to the Provincial Auditor:
That the Chief Officer of the License Branch has reported that the Legislative appropriation to pay stationery, postage and contingencies in the License Branch for the current year is exhausted owing to the fact that the salary of a Clerk and Messenger has, in the absence of an Order-in-Council, been charged to this fund instead of to another item in the estimates, as anticipated by the Chief Officer at the time the estimate was prepared, and the cost of a typewriter has also been charged to this fund; and as it is necessary to make up the deficiency thus created, the undersigned respectfully re-

commends that authority be given under the Act, R.S.O. 1897.
Cap. 23, sec. 20, for the issue of a warrant for the sum of
Four hundred dollars ($400) for that purpose.

(Sgd.) W. J. HANNA,
Provincial Secretary.

PROVINCIAL SECRETARY'S OFFICE,
Toronto, August 16th, 1906.

———

Copy of a Minute of the Treasury Board, dated the 16th
day of August, A.D. 1906.

Upon consideration of the report of the Honourable the
Provincial Secretary, dated the 16th day of August, A.D. 1906,
the Treasury Board doth hereby order, pursuant to the provisions of section 20, Cap. 23, R.S.O. 1897, that the sum of
Four hundred dollars ($400) be placed to the credit of the
Honourable the Treasurer to meet the Requirements of "Contingencies" in the License Branch, the appropriation for said
service for the current year having for the reasons set forth
in the Minister's report become exhausted.

Certified,

J. LONSDALE CAPREOL,
Clerk, Treasury Board.

———

TORONTO, 21st September, 1906.

SIR,—I have the honour to inform you that the sum appropriated at the last session of the Legislature for expenses
in the office of the Inspector of Prisons and Public Charities is
insufficient by the sum of $5,000.

The estimate was deficient for the following reasons: Salaries appropriated under the estimates have been unexpended
to the extent of $1,925 owing to your ruling that payments may
not be made to temporary clerks out of moneys appropriated by
the Legislature for special service. The amount appropriated
for travelling expenses of the Inspectors was, on account of the
large amount of travelling done, under-estimated. Unfore-
seen expenditure on account of postage, printing and supplies
ncessitated by the Act of last session under which the cost of
maintenance of lunatics is charged upon the municipalities,
has caused an over-expenditure in contingencies. The amount

required owing to changes in the bookkeeping and books necessitated by the method of accounting in the public institutions recently adopted, has been in excess of what was estimated
to the extent of $1,400.

The items which it is now necessary to cover are as follows:

Salaries for employees	$1,500
Travelling expenses for Inspectors	500
Printing, Stationery, Postage and contingencies	1,600
Changes re bookkeeping, including new books	1,400
	$5,000

I therefore beg leave to recommend that authority be given
under R.S.O. 1897, section 20, Cap. 23, for the payment of
the said amount, $5,000.

I have the honour to be, Sir,
Your obedient servant,

(Sgd.) THOMAS MULVEY,
Assistant Provincial Secretary.

Approved.

W. J. HANNA,
Provincial Secretary.

Copy of a Minute of the Treasury Board. dated the 5th
day of October, A.D. 1906.

Upon consideration of the report of the Honourable the
Provincial Secretary, dated the 21st day of September, 1906,
the Treasury Board doth hereby order that pursuant to the
provisions of section 20, Cap. 23, R.S.O. 1897, the sum of Five
thousand dollars ($5,000) be placed to the credit of the Honour-
able the Treasurer to cover expenses of Prisons and Public
Charities Branch of the Provincial Secretary's Department, as
indicated by the Minister's report. the appropriation for said
service having become exhausted.

Certified,

J. LONSDALE CAPREOL,
Clerk, Treasury Board.

The undersigned begs to report to the Provincial Auditor:
That the Legislative appropriation to pay expenses of
enforcing Liquor License Law being exhausted, a further sum

of $2,500 will be required to pay salaries and expenses of officers and detectives up to the 31st of December next.

The undersigned respectfully recommends that authority be given under the Act, R.S.O. 1897, Cap. 23, sec. 20, for the issue of a warrant for the sum of $2,500 for that purpose.

(Sgd.) W. J. HANNA.
Provincial Secretary.

THE PROVINCIAL SECRETARY'S DEPARTMENT,
October 4th. 1906.

Copy of a Minute of the Treasury Board, dated the 5th day of October, A.D. 1906.

Upon consideration of the report of the Honourable the Provincial Secretary, dated the 4th day of October, A.D. 1906, the Treasury Board doth hereby order that pursuant to the provisions of section 20, Cap. 23, R.S.O. 1897, the sum of Two thousand five hundred dollars ($2,500) be placed to the credit of the Honourable the Treasurer to cover the expenses of enforcing the Liquor License Law during the balance of the current year, the appropriation for said service having become exhausted.

Certified,

J. LONSDALE CAPREOL,
Clerk, Executive Council.

The undersigned begs to report to the Provincial Auditor.

That the legislative appropriation to pay contingencies in the License Branch being exhausted, the undersigned respectfully recommends that authority be given under the Act, R. S.O., Cap 23, section 20, for the issue of a warrant for the sum of Three hundred dollars to cover Contingencies up to tne 31st day of December next.

(Sgd.) W. J. HANNA,
Provincial Secretary.

PROVINCIAL SECRETARY'S DEPARTMENT,
October 4th, 1906.

Copy of a Minute of the Treasury Board, dated the 5th day of October, A.D. 1906.

Upon consideration of the report of the Honourable the Provincial Secretary, dated the 4th day of October, A.D. 1906, the Treasury Board doth hereby order that pursuant to the provisions of section 20, Cap. 23, R.S.O. 1897, the sum of Three hundred dollars ($300) be placed to the credit of the Honourable the Treasurer to cover the payment of contingencies in the License Branch for the balance of the current year, the appropriation for said service having become exhausted.

Certified,

J. LONSDALE CAPREOL,

. Clerk, Treasury Board.

PROVINCIAL SECRETARY'S OFFICE,

TORONTO, November 1st, 1906.

The undersigned respectfully reports that the appropriation to meet the general expenses of the Administration of Justice within the Provisional Judicial District of Thunder Bay is practically exhausted, and that the least possible sum required to meet the necessary disbursements connected with the sittings of the High Court of Justice and other courts to be held within the district, and other necessary expenditures, including the sum of $2,448.38 for September Quarter's accounts now here and properly vouched for is $3,248.38.

The undersigned therefore respectfully recommends that authority be given under R.S.O. 1897, Cap. 23, section 20, for the issue of a warrant for the above named sum·of $3,248.38 to cover the balance of the year.

(Sgd.) W. J. HANNA,

Provincial Secretary.

JAMES CLANCY, ESQ.,

Provincial Auditor,

Toronto.

Copy of a Minute of the Treasury Board, dated the 6th day of November, A.D. 1906.

Upon consideration of the report of the Honourable the Provincial Secretary, dated the First day of November, A.D. 1906, the Treasury Board doth hereby order that pursuant to the provisions of section 20, Cap. 23, R.S.O. 1897, the sum of Three thousand two hundred and forty-eight dollars and thirty-eight cents ($3,248.38) be placed to the credit of the Honourable the Treasurer to meet the general expenses of the Administration of Justice within the Provisional Judicial District of Thunder Bay for the balance of the current year, the appropriation for said service having become exhausted.

Certified,

J. LONSDALE CAPREOL,

Clerk, Treasury Board.

5* P.A.

PROVINCIAL SECRETARY'S OFFICE,
TORONTO, Nov. 13th, 1906.

The undersigned respectfully reports that the appropriation to meet the general expenses of the Administration of Justice within the Provisional Judicial District of Nipissing is
practically exhausted, owing chiefly to the large increase in
the number of persons arrested, commiteed to and maintained
in gaols during the current year, as compared with the year
1905, and that the probable sum required to meet the necessary
disbursements of the sittings of the Courts and other necessary
expenditures, including the sum of $2,974.73 for September
Quarter's Accounts, now here and properly vouched for, is
$3,500.

The undersigned therefore respectfully recommends that
authority be given under R.S.O. 1897, Cap. 23, section 20,
for the issue of a warrant for the above named sum of $3,500
to cover the balance of the year.

(Sgd.) W. J. HANNA,
Provincial Secretary.

JAMES CLANCY, ESQ.,
Provincial Auditor.

Copy of a Minute of the Treasury Board, dated the 15th
day of November, A.D. 1906.

Upon consideration of the report of the Honourable the
Provincial Secretary, dated the 13th day of November, A.D.
1906, the Treasury Board doth hereby order that pursuant to
the provisions of section 20, Cap. 23, R.S.O. 1897, the sum of
Three thousand five hundred dollars ($3,500) be placed to the
credit of the Honourable the Treasurer to meet the requirements of expenses in connection with the Administration of Justice within the Provisional District of Nipissing for the balance
of the current year, the appropriation for said service having
become exhausted.

Certified,
J. LONSDALE CAPREOL,
Clerk, Treasury Board.

PROVINCIAL SECRETARY'S OFFICE,
TORONTO, November 16th, 1906.

The undersigned respectfully reports that the appropriation to meet the general expenses of the Administration of Justice with the Provisional Judicial District of Muskoka is ex-

hausted, owing chiefly to an increase in the number of prisoners maintained in the Gaol during the current year and the salary and travelling expenses of an additional Constable, and that the probable sum required to meet the necessary disbursements of the Sittings of the Courts and other expenditures is $1,000.

The undersigned therefore respectfully recommends that authority be given under R.S.O. 1897, Cap. 23, section 20, for the issue of a warrant for the above named sum of $1,000 to cover the balance of the year.

(Sgd.) W. J. HANNA,
Provincial Secretary.

JAMES CLANCY, ESQ.,
    Provincial Auditor.

Copy of a Minute of the Treasury Board, dated the 21st day of November, A.D. 1906.

Upon consideration of the report of the Honourable the Provincial Secretary, dated 16th day of November, 1906, the Treasury Board doth hereby order that pursuant to the provisions of section 20, Cap. 23, R.S.O. 1897, the sum of One thousand dollars ($1,000) be placed to the credit of the Honourable the Treasurer to meet the requirements of the general expenses of the Administration of Justice within the Provisional Judicial District of Muskoka for the balance of the current year, the appropriation for said service having become exhausted.

Certified,

J. LONSDALE CAPREOL,
Clerk, Treasury Board.

TORONTO, 21st November, 1906.

SIR,—I have the honour to inform you that the sum appropriated at the last session of the Legislature for contingencies, etc., of this Department has been found to be insufficient by the sum of $1,500. This has been owing to the unexpectedly heavy pressure of the work on the Department, entailing the employment of extra clerks, the purchase of extra quantities of supplies, etc., and an increased expenditure for postage.

I therefore beg leave to recommend that authority be given under R.S.O. 1897, Cap. 23, section 20, for payment of the said sum of $1,500.

I have the honour to be,

Sir,

Your obedient servant,

(Sgd.) THOMAS MULVEY,

Assistant Provincial Secretary.

Approved,

    W. J. H.

        Provincial Secretary.

THE PROVINCIAL AUDITOR,

        Parliament Buildings.

        Toronto.

Copy of a Minute of the Treasury Board, dated the 27th day of November, A.D. 1906.

Upon consideration of the report of the Honourable the Provincial Secretary, dated the 23rd day of November, A.D. 1906, the Treasury Board doth hereby order that pursuant to the provisions of section 20, Cap. 23, R.S.O. 1897, the sum of One thousand five hundred dollars ($1,500) be placed to the credit of the Honourable the Treasurer to meet the requirements of "Contingencies," etc., of the Provincial Secretary's Department for the balance of the current year, the appropriation for said services having become exhausted.

Certified,

J. LONSDALE CAPREOL,

Clerk, Treasury Board.

27th November, 1906.

SIR,—The undersigned begs to report that the appropriation for the general office expenses of the Children's Branch will be exceeded and that it will be necessary to have Four hundred dollars more to pay all accounts to the end of the year. The chief items of increase are extra office help, printing and postage.

The undersigned would recommend that a Treasury Order for the sum of Four hundred dollars be passed.

(Sgd.) W. J. HANNA,

Provincial Secretary.

JAMES CLANCY, ESQ.,

    Provincial Auditor.

Copy of a Minute of the Treasury Board, dated the 29th day of November, A.D. 1906   .

Upon consideration of the report of the Honourable the Provincial Secretary, dated the 27th day of November, A.D. 1906, the Treasury Board doth hereby order that pursuant to the provisions of section 20, Cap. 23, R.S.O. 1897, the sum of Four hundred dollars be placed to the credit of the Honourable the Treasurer to meet the requirements of the Children's Branch of the Department for General Office expenses for the balance of the current year, the appropriation for said service having become exhausted.

Certified,

J. LONSDALE CAPREOL,
Clerk, Treasury Board.

———

TORONTO, December 11th, 1906·

JAMES CLANCY, ESQ.,
Provincial Auditor,
Toronto.

DEAR SIR,—Having had under consideration the annexed report of the Chief Officer of the License Branch, I recommend that authority be given, under section 20, Chapter 23, of the Revised Statutes of Ontario, 1897, for the issue of a warrant for the sum of $1,000 for the purposes therein mentioned.

(Sgd.) W. J. HANNA,
Provincial Secretary.

The undersigned begs to draw the attention of the Minister to the fact that the appropriation amounting to the sum of $10,000 for the enforcement of the Liquor License Act is about exhausted, owing to increased expenditure incurred in the employment of a larger staff than was at first contemplated, which was rendered necessary in order to enable this Branch to enforce the provisions of the Act in Local Option municipalities, and especially in the Districts known as New Ontario.

The further sum of One thousand dollars ($1,000) will be required to meet the expenditure for this Branch of the work for the next month.

The principal officer employed in enforcing the Liquor License Laws in the outlying districts is Mr. George E. Morrison, who has secured 112 convictions since January 1st, and the sum of $4,540 has been collected in fines as the result of these convictions.

(Sgd.) E. SAUNDERS,
Chief Officer.

To the Honourable the Provincial Secretary.
LICENSE BRANCH,
    TORONTO, December 11th, 1906.

Copy of a Minute of the Treasury Board, dated the 13th day of December, A.D. 1906.

Upon consideration of the report of the Honourable the Provincial Secretary, dated the 11th day of December, A.D. 1906, the Treasury Board doth hereby order that pursuant to the provisions of section 20, Cap. 23, R.S.O. 1897, the sum of One thousand dollars ($1,000) be placed to the credit of the Honourable the Treasurer to cover expenditure in connection with the enforcement of the Liquor License Act for the balance of the current year, the appropriation for said service having become exhausted.

Certified,

J. LONSDALE CAPREOL,
Clerk, Treasury Board.

PROVINCIAL SECRETARY'S OFFICE,

TORONTO, December 17th, 1906.

The undersigned respectfully reports that the appropriation to pay Sheriffs, Criers and Constables in attending Courts of Assize, Chancery and County Courts, Deputy Clerks of the Crown and Pleas attending Assizes, and their postage, etc., is exhausted, the only reason which can be assigned for the over-draft is the greater volume of business before the courts, necessitating more prolonged and frequent sittings, the approximate sum of $600 will be required to cover these services for the balance of the year. The undersigned therefore respectfully recommends that authority be given under R.S.O. 1897, Cap. 23, sec. 20, for the issue of a warrant for $600 to cover the above services.

(Sgd.) W. J. HANNA,
Provincial Secretary.

JAMES CLANCY, ESQ.,
    Provincial Auditor.

Copy of a Minute of the Treasury Board, dated the 18th day of December, A.D. 1906.

Upon consideration of the report of the Honourable the Provincial Secretary, dated 17th December, A.D. 1906, the Treasury Board doth hereby order that pursuant to the provisions of section 20, Chapter 23, R.S.O. 1897, the sum of Six hundred dollars be placed to the credit of the Honourable the Treasurer to pay Sheriffs, Criers and Constables in attending Courts of Assize, Chancery and County Courts, Deputy Clerks of the Crown and Pleas attending Assizes, and their postage, etc., for the balance of the current year, the appropriation for said service having become exhausted.

Certified,

J. LONSDALE CAPREOL,
Clerk, Treasury Board.

TORONTO, December 27th, 1906.

SIR,—I have the honour to inform you that the sum appropriated at the last session of the Legislature for the administration of the Act relating to automobiles is insufficient by the sum of $1,294.34, the extra expenditure having been required in order to pay the salaries of the special constables employed by the Government during the summer months.

I have therefore the honour to recommend that authority be given under R.S.O. 1897, Cap. 23, sec. 20, for the payment of the said amount, $1,294.34.

I have the honour to be,
Sir,
Your obedient servant,

THOMAS MULVEY,
Assistant Provincial Secretary.

The Provincial Auditor,
Parliament Buildings,
Toronto.

Copy of a Minute of the Treasury Board, dated the 9th day of January, A.D. 1907.

Upon consideration of the report of the Honourable the Provincial Secretary, dated 5th January, A.D. 1907, the Treasury Board doth hereby order that pursuant to the provisions of section 20, Cap. 23, R.S.O. 1897, the sum of One thousand two hundred and ninety-four dollars and thirty-four cents ($1,-294.34) be placed to the credit of the Honourable the Treasurer to cover the expenses of Automobile law enforcement for the balance of the year 1906, the appropriation for said service having become exhausted.

Certified,

J. LONSDALE CAPREOL,
Clerk, Treasury Board.

TORONTO, December 27th, 1906.

SIR,—I have the honour to inform you that the sum appropriated at the last session of the Legislature for maintenance and repairs at the Asylum for the Insane at Kingston is insufficient by the sum of $10,000, made up as follows:—

Heat and light	$1,200
Clothing	2,500
Repairs	3,000
Farm	2,000
Laundry	1,300
	$10,000

I therefore beg leave to recommend that authority be given under R.S.O. 1897, Cap. 23, sec. 20, for the payment of the said sum of $10,000.

I have the honour to be,
Sir,
Your obedient servant,

THOMAS MULVEY.
Assistant Provincial Secretary.

The Provincial Secretary,
    Parliament Buildings,
       Toronto.

Copy of a Minute of the Treasury Board, dated the 15th day of January, A.D. 1907.

Upon consideration of the report of the Honourable the Provincial Secretary, dated the 27th day of December, A.D. 1906, the Treasury Board doth hereby, pursuant to the provisions of section 20, Cap. 23, R.S.O. 1897, order that the sum of Ten thousand dollars ($10,000) be placed to the credit of the Honourable the Treasurer to cover the payment of accounts for the balance of the year ending 31st December, 1906, in connection with the maintenance and repairs at the Asylum for the Insane, Kingston, the appropriation for said service having become exhausted.

Certified,
J. LONSDALE CAPREOL,
Clerk, Treasury Board.

TORONTO, December 27th, 1906.

SIR,—I have the honour to inform you that the sum appropriated at the last session of the Legislature for Maintenance and Repairs in connection with this Department is insufficient by the sum of $150. The above amount is required for the balance of the current year, and is owing to the necessity of increased facilities for dealing with the large increase of work in the Department.

I beg leave to recommend, therefore, that authority be given under R.S.O. 1897, Cap. 23, sec. 20, for payment of the said sum of $150.

I have the honour to be,
Sir,
Your obedient servant,
THOMAS MULVEY,
Assistant Provincial Secretary.

The Provincial Auditor,
Parliament Buildings,
Toronto.

Copy of a Minute of the Treasury Board, dated the 9th day of January, A.D. 1907.

Upon consideration of the report of the Honourable the Provincial Secretary, dated the 27th day of December, A.D. 1906, the Treasury Board doth hereby order that pursuant to the provisions of section 20, Cap. 23, R.S.O. 1897, the sum of One hundred and fifty dollars ($150) be placed to the credit of the Honourable the Treasurer to meet the requirements of Repairs and Maintenance of the Provincial Secretary's Department for the balance of the year 1906, the appropriation for said service having become exhausted.

Certified,
J. LONSDALE CAPREOL,
Clerk, Treasury Board.

TORONTO, December 27th, 1906.

SIR,—I have the honour to inform you that the sum appropriated at the last session of the Legislature for Miscellaneous Refunds is insufficient by the sum of $682.50.

I may explain that refunds to this amount are owing by the Department to certain persons as amounts paid in on applications for incorporation in excess of the proper fees, or on applications which have since been withdrawn.

I therefore beg leave to recommend that authority be given under R.S.O. 1897, Cap. 23, sec. 20, for payment of the said amount of $682.50.

I have the honour to be,
Sir,
Your obedient servant,

THOMAS MULVEY,
Assistant Provincial Secretary.

The Provincial Auditor,
Parliament Buildings.

Copy of a Minute of the Treasury Board, dated the 9th day of January, A.D. 1907.

Upon consideration of the report of the Honourable the Provincial Secretary, dated the 27th day of December, A.D. 1906, the Treasury Board doth hereby order that pursuant to the provisions of section 20, Cap. 23, R.S.O. 1897, the sum of Six hundred and eighty-two dollars and fifty cents ($682.50) be placed to the credit of the Honourable the Treasurer to cover the payment of refunds to certain persons as amounts paid in on applications for incorporation in excess of the proper fees or on applications which have since been withdrawn, the appropriation for Refunds Miscellaneous having become exhausted.

Certified,

J. LONSDALE CAPREOL,
Clerk, Treasury Board.

TORONTO, December 29th, 1906.

SIR,—I have the honour to inform you that the sum appropriated at the last session of the Legislature for mainten-

ance and repairs at the Asylum for the Insane at Penetanguishene is insufficient by the sum of $3,100, made up as follows:

Heat and light $2,200
Clothing 500
Repairs 300
Farm and garden 100
                                                                    ———
                                                                  $3,100

    I therefore beg leave to recommend that authority be given.
under R.S.O. 1897, Cap. 23, sec. 20, for payment of the said
sum of $3,100.

I have the honour to be,
Sir,
Your obedient servant,

THOMAS MULVEY,
Assistant Provincial Secretary.

The Provincial Auditor,
  Parliament Buildings,
    Toronto.

———

    Copy of a Minute of the Treasury Board, dated the 15th
day of January, A.D. 1907.

    Upon consideration of the report of the Honourable the
Provincial Secretary, dated the 29th day of December, A.D.
1906, the Treasury Board doth hereby order that pursuant to
the provisions of section 20, Cap. 23, R.S.O. 1897, the sum of
Three thousand one hundred dollars ($3,100) be placed to the
credit of the Honourable the Treasurer for the payment of accounts for the balance of the year ending 31st December, 1906,
in connection with the maintenance and repairs at the Asylum
for the Insane, Penetanguishene, the appropriation for said
service having become exhausted.

Certified,

J. LONSDALE CAPREOL,
Clerk, Treasury Board.

———

TORONTO, 29th December, 1906.

    SIR,—I have the honour to inform you that the sum ap-
propriated at the last session of the Legislature for Contingencies, etc., of the Prisons and Public Charities Branch of

this Department is insufficient by the sum of $1,500. This is owing to the heavy pressure of work on the Branch, entailing the employment of extra clerks, purchase of extra quantities of supplies, etc., and an increased expenditure for postage.

I have, therefore, the honour to recommend that authority be given under R.S.O. 1897, Cap. 23, sec. 20, for the payment of the said sum of $1,500.

I have the honour to be,

Sir,

Your obedient servant,

THOMAS MULVEY,

Assistant Provincial Secretary.

The Provincial Auditor,
    Parliament Buildings,
        Toronto.

Copy of a Minute of the Treasury Board, dated the 2nd day of January, A.D. 1907.

Upon consideration of the report of the Assistant Provincial Secretary, dated the 29th day of December, A.D. 1906. the Treasury Board doth hereby order that pursuant to the provisions of section 20, Cap. 23, R.S.O. 1897, the sum of One thousand five hundred dollars ($1,500) be placed to the credit of the Honourable the Treasurer to meet the requirements of Contingencies of the Prisons and Public Charities Branch of the Provincial Secretary's Department, the appropriation for said service having become exhausted.

Certified,

J. LONSDALE CAPREOL,

Clerk, Treasury Board.

Toronto, January 2nd, 1907.

Sir,—I have the honour to inform you that the sum appropriated at the last session of the Legislature for the maintenance of this Department is insufficient by the sum of $200. additional expenditures having become necessary owing to the unusual press of work on the Department, entailing an extra supply of stationery, forms, general office supplies, etc.

I therefore beg leave to recommend that authority be given under R.S.O., Cap. 23, sec. 20, for the payment of the said amount of $200.

I have the honour to be,
Sir,
Your obedient servant,

THOMAS MULVEY,
Assistant Provincial Secretary.

Approved.
W. J. HANNA,
Provincial Secretary.

The Provincial Auditor,
Parliament Buildings,
Toronto.

Copy of a Minute of the Treasury Board, dated the 9th day of January, A.D. 1907.

Upon consideration of the report of the Honourable the Provincial Secretary, dated the 2nd day of January, A.D. 1907, the Treasury Board doth hereby order that pursuant to the provisions of section 20, Cap. 23, R.S.O. 1897, the sum of Two hundred dollars ($200) be placed to the credit of the Honourable the Treasurer to cover additional expenditure in connection with the maintenance of the Provincial Secretary's Department for the balance of the year 1906, the appropriation for said service having become exhausted.

Certified,

J. LONSDALE CAPREOL,
Clerk, Treasury Board.

PROVINCIAL SECRETARY'S OFFICE,
TORONTO, 3rd January, 1907.

The undersigned respectfully reports that the appropriation of $600 provided under Treasury Board order of the 18th in attending Courts of Assize, Chancery and County Courts. day of December, 1906, to pay Sheriffs, Criers and Constables Deputy Clerks of the Crown and Pleas and their postage, etc., is about exhausted, and that a further sum of Five hundred is required to pay accounts received up to the closing of the Treasury Books for the year 1906.

The undersigned therefore respectfully recommends that authority be given under R.S.O. 1897, Cap. 23, sec. 20, for the issue of a warrant for $500 to cover the above services.

W. J. HANNA,

Provincial Secretary.

JAMES CLANCY, ESQ.,
    Provincial Auditor.

Copy of a Minute of the Treasury Board, dated the 4th day of January, A.D. 1907.

Upon consideration of the report of the Honourable the Provincial Secretary, dated the 3rd day of January, A.D. 1907, the Treasury Board doth hereby order that pursuant to the provisions of section 20, Cap. 23, R.S.O. 1897, the sum of Five hundred dollars ($500) be placed to the credit of the Honourable the Treasurer for the payment of accounts to the end of the year 1906 of Sheriffs, Criers and Constables in attending Courts of Assize, Chancery and County Courts, Deputy Clerks of the Crown and Pleas, and their postage, etc., the appropriation for said service having become exhausted.

Certified,

J. LONSDALE CAPREOL,

Clerk, Treasury Board.

PROVINCIAL SECRETARY'S OFFICE,

TORONTO, January 4th, 1907.

The undersigned respectfully reports that the appropriations for the Administration of Criminal Justice within the Districts of Rainy River, Parry Sound, Manitoulin and Thunder Bay are exhausted, and that the further sums required to meet accounts now received and due for the year ending 31st December, 1906, for these respective districts are:—

Rainy River	$400
Parry Sound	200
Manitoulin	150
Thunder Bay	200
	$950

The undersigned therefore respectfully recommends that authority be given under R.S.O. 1897, Cap. 23, sec. 20, for the issue of warrants for the sums named above for the respective Provisional Judicial Districts of Rainy River, Parry Sound, Manitoulin and Thunder Bay.

W. J. HANNA,
Provincial Secretary.

JAMES CLANCY, ESQ.,
Provincial Auditor.

Copy of a Minute of the Treasury Board, dated the 9th day of January, A.D. 1907.

Upon consideration of the report of the Honourable the Provincial Secretary, dated the 4th day of January, A.D. 1907, the Treasury Board doth hereby order that pursuant to the provisions of section 20, Cap. 23, R.S.O. 1897, the sum of Nine hundred and fifty dollars be placed to the credit of the Honourable the Treasurer to cover the payment of accounts now received and due for the year ending 31st December, 1906, in connection with the Administration of Criminal Justice within the following Districts, the appropriations for said services having become exhausted.

Rainy River	$400
Parry Sound	200
Manitoulin	150
Thunder Bay	200

Certified,

J. LONSDALE CAPREOL,
Clerk, Treasury Board.

January 4th, 1907.

JAMES CLANCY, ESQ.,
Provincial Auditor,

SIR,—I beg to report that the appropriation under Hospitals and Charities for the Industrial Schools for maintenance of pupils is insufficient to meet the required expenditure to the amount of $2,272.81. The reason for this over-expenditure was the committal to these institutions of more pupils than were expected. The undersigned would therefore recommend that a Treasury Board warrant be issued for the said sum of $2,272.81.

W. J. HANNA,
Provincial Secretary.

Copy of a Minute of the Treasury Board, dated the 9th day of January, A.D. 1907.

Upon consideration of the report of the Honourable the Provincial Secretary, dated the 4th day of January, A.D. 1907, the Treasury Board doth hereby order that pursuant to the provisions of section 20, Cap. 23, R.S.O. 1897, the sum of Two thousand two hundred and seventy-two dollars and eighty-one cents ($2,272.81) be placed to the credit of the Honourable the Treasurer to meet the requirements of Industrial Schools for maintenance of pupils for the balance of the year 1906, the appropriation for said service under Hospitals and Charities having become exhausted.

Certified,
J. LONSDALE CAPREOL,
Clerk, Treasury Board.

January 4th, 1907.

James Clancy, Esq.,
        Provincial Auditor,

Sir,--I beg to report that under date of November 29th, 1906, a Treasury warrant for $400 was issued to meet the additional expenses in the Children's Branch, caused by illness of a stenographer and extra postage and printing. This sum has proven inadequate to meet all the expenses, and the undersigned would therefore recommend that a Treasury Board warrant for the further sum of $200 be issued to cover the deficit.

(Sgd.) W. J. HANNA,   .
Provincial Secretary.

Copy of a Minute of the Treasury Board, dated the 9th day of January, A.D. 1907.

Upon consideration of the report of the Honourable the Provincial Secretary, dated the 4th day of January, A.D. 1907, the Treasury Board doth hereby order that pursuant to the provisions of section 20, Cap. 23, R.S.O. 1897, the further sum of Two hundred dollars ($200) be placed to the credit of the Honourable the Treasurer to meet additional expenses in the Children's Branch of the Provincial Secretary's Department caused by the illness of a stenographer and extra postage and printing, the appropriation for said Children's Branch having become exhausted.

Certified,
J. LONSDALE CAPREOL,
Clerk, Treasury Board.

The undersigned having had under his consideration the report hereto attached, of the Chief officer of the License Branch with reference to the amout required for refunds of License Duties authorized by Orders-in-Council as stated therein, he begs to recommend that a Treasury Board Order be issued for the sum of $297.50 to cover the same under the authority of section 20, Cap. 23, R.S.O. 1897.

(Sgd.) W. J. HANNA,
Provincial Secretary.

JAMES CLANCY, ESQ.,
Provincial Auditor.

PROVINCIAL SECRETARY'S OFFICE,
Toronto, January 9th, 1907.

———

The License Branch having been informed that ..1e appropriation made by the Legislature for Miscellaneous Refunds has been exhausted, the undersigned begs to report that a Treasury Board Order will be required to cover the refunds authorized by Orders-in-Council to Philip Tennyson, of Underwood, $30; P. Hansen, Cobalt, $100; D. H. McRae, Strathburn, $25; and Sheriff Geo. A. Dana, Brockville, Assignee, for Oscar J). Brooks and Co., $142.50; in all $297.50.

EUDO SAUNDERS,
Chief Officer.
To the Hon. the Provincial Secretary.

LICENSE BRANCH,
TORONTO, Jan. 9, 1907.

———

Copy of a Minute of the Treasury Board, dated the 15th day of January, A.D. 1907.

Upon consideration of the report of the Honourable the Provincial Secretary, dated the 9th day of January, A.D. 1907, the Treasury Board doth hereby order that pursuant to the provisions of section 20, Cap. 23, R.S.O. 1897, the sum of Two hundred and ninety-seven dollars and fifty cents ($297.50) be placed to the credit of the Honourable the Treasurer to cover the paymet of certain refunds of License Duties, the appropriation for Refunds Miscellaneous having become exhausted.

Certified,
J. LONSDALE CAPREOL,
Clerk, Treasury Board.

6* P.A.

PROVINCIAL SECRETARY'S OFFICE,
TORONTO, January 10th, 1907.

The undersigned respectfully reports that the appropriation as well as the sums provided under Treasury Board Orders to pay Sheriffs, Criers and Constables in attending Courts of Assize, Chancery and County Courts, Deputy Clerks of the Crown and Pleas and their postage, etc., is exhausted, and that a further sum of Eight hundred dollars is required to pay accounts received and due for the year ending 31st December, 1906.

The undersigned therefore respectfully recommends that authority be given under R.S.O., Cap. 23, section 20, for the issue of a warrant for $800 to cover the above services.

(Sgd.) W. J. HANNA,
Provincial Secretary.

JAMES CLANCY, ESQ.,
Provincial Auditor.

Copy of a Minute of the Treasury Board, dated the 15th day of January, A.D. 1907.

Upon consideration of the report of the Honourable the Provincial Secretary, dated the 10th day of January, A.D. 1907, the Treasury Board doth hereby order that pursuant to the provisions of section 20, Cap. 23, R.S.O. 1897, the sum of Eight hundred dollars ($800) be placed to the credit of the Honourable the Treasurer to meet the payment of accounts received and due for the year ending December 31st, 1906, of Sheriffs, Criers and Constables in attending Courts of Assize, Chancery and County Courts, Deputy Clerks of the Crown and Pleas, and their postage, the appropriation for said service having become exhausted.

Certified,
J. LONSDALE CAPREOL,
Clerk, Treasury Board.

TORONTO, January 11th, 1907.

SIR,—I have the honour to inform you that the sum appropriated at the last session of the Legislature for exterior repairs to buildings and alterations, etc., and improvement in water supply at Mimico Asylum, is insufficient by the sum of Two thousand dollars, the improvements in the water supply having exceeded the appropriation by that amount.

6a* PA.

I beg leave therefore to recommend that authority be given under R.S.O. 1897, Cap. 23, section 20, for the payment of the said sum of $2,000.

I have the honour to be,
Sir,
Your obedient servant,
THOMAS MULVEY,
Assistant Provincial Secretary.

Approved,
W. J. H.

Copy of a Minute of the Treasury Board, dated the 15th day of January, A.D. 1907.

Upon consideration of the report of the Honourable the Provincial Secretary, dated the 11th day of January, A.D. 1907, the Treasury Board doth hereby order that pursuant to the provisions of section 20, Cap. 23, R.S.O. 1897, the sum of Two thousand dollars be placed to the credit of the Honourable the Treasurer to cover the payment of accounts for the balance of the year 1906 in connection with exterior repairs to buildings and alterations at Mimico Asylum and improvement in water supply for the said Institution, the appropriation for said Institution having become exhausted.

Certified,
J. LONSDALE CAPREOL,
Clerk, Treasury Board.

TORONTO, January 11th, 1907.

SIR,—I have the honour to inform you that the sum appropriated at the last session of the Legislature for the maintenance of Orillia, Mimico, Hamilton and Toronto Asylums is insufficient by the sum of $24,320.02.

Orillia Asylum.
Provisions .... $ 744 54
Farm 885 88
                                              $1,730 42
Mimico Asylum.
Provisions 373 63
Clothing 1,232 26
Heat and Light 217 69
Farm 929 13
                                              $2,752 71

Hamilton Asylum.

Provisions	2,356	ᴐ5
Clothing	1,831	75
Laundry	ყᴛ	74
Farm	6ᴛᴛ	37
Miscellaneous	2,338	ყᴢ

$7,287	33

Toronto Asylum.

ᴘrovisions	3,419	40
Heat and Light	1,878	32
Clothing	3,066	56
Laundry	521	95
Repairs	1,899	81
Farm	1,418	97
Miscellaneous	344	55

$12,549	ᴐᴜ

I therefore beg leave to recommend that authority be given under R.S.O. 1897, Cap. 23, section 20, for the payment of the said sum of $24,320.02.

I have the honour to be,

Sir,

Your obedient servant,

THOMAS MULVEY,

Assistant Provincial Secretary.

THE PROVINCIAL AUDITOR,
      Parliament Buildings,
          Toronto.

———

Copy of a Minute of the Treasury Board, dated the 15th day of January, A.D. 1907.

Upon consideration of the report of the Honourable the Provincial Secretary, dated the 11th day of January, A.D. 1907, the Treasury Board doth hereby order that pursuant to tne provsisions of section 20, Cap. 23, R.S.O. 18ყ7, the sum of Twenty-four thousand three hundred and twenty dollars and two cents ($24,320.02) be placed to the credit of the Honourable the Treasurer to meet the requirements of maintenance of the Orillia, Hamilton, Mimico, and Toronto Asylums for the balance of the year 1906, the appropriations for said services having become exhausted.

Certified,

J. LONSDALE CAPREOL,

Clerk, Treasury Board.

PROVINCIAL SECRETARY'S OFFICE,
TORONTO, January 11th, 1907.

The undersigned respectfully reports that the appropriation
for the Administration of Criminal Justice within the Districts
of Parry Sound and Manitoulin are exhausted, and that the
further sums required to meet accounts received and now due
for the year ending 31st December, 1906, for these respective
districts are, Parry Sound $300, Manitoulin $450.

The undersigned respectfully recommends that authority be
given under R.S.O. 1897, Cap. 23, sec. 20, for the issue of warrants for the sums named above for the respective provisional
Judicial Districts of Parry Sound and Manitoulin.

W. J. HANNA,
Provincial Secretary.

JAMES CLANCY, ESQ.,
Provincial Auditor.

———

Copy of a Minute of the Treasury Board, dated the 15th
day of January, A.D. 1907.

Upon consideration of the report of the Honourable the
Provincial Secretary, dated the 11th day of January, A.D.
1907, the Treasury Board doth hereby order that pursuant to
the provisions of section 20, Cap. 23, R.S.O. 1897, the sum of
Seven hundred and fifty dollars ($750) be placed to the credit of
the Honourable the Treasurer, to meet accounts now received
and due for the year ending 31st December, 1906, in connection with the Administration of Criminal Justice within the
Districts of Parry Sound and Manitoulin, the appropriation
for said service having become exhausted.

Certified,

J. LONSDALE CAPREOL,
Clerk, Treasury Board.

———

PROVINCIAL SECRETARY'S OFFICE,
TORONTO, January 11th, 1907.

The undersigned respectfully reports that the appropriation for the General Administration of Criminal Justice in
Counties for the year 1906 is practicaly exhausted, owing chiefly
to the very heavy business at the sittings of the High Court, and
that the sum of $15,000 is required to pay accounts now received
and due for the year ending 31st December, 1906.

The undersigned therefore respectfully recommends that authority be given under R.S.O. 1897, Cap. 23, sec. 20, for the issue of a warrant for the sum of $15,000 to cover the above service.

W. J. HANNA,
Provincial Secretary.

JAMES CLANCY, ESQ.,
Provincial Auditor.

—————

Copy of a Minute of the Treasury Board, dated the 15th day of January, A.D. 1907.

Upon consideration of the report of the Honourable the Provincial Secretary, dated the 11th day of January, A.D. 1907, the Treasury Board doth hereby order that pursuant to the provisions of section 20, Cap. 23, R.S.O. 1897, the sum of Fifteen thousand dollars ($15,000) be placed to the credit of the Honourable the Treasurer to meet the payment of accounts now received and due for the year ending 31st December, 1906, in connection with the general Administration of Criminal Justice in Counties, the appropriation for said service having become exhausted.

Certified,
J. LONSDALE CAPREOL,
Clerk, Treasury Board.

—————

TORONTO, January 14th, 1907.

SIR,—I have the honour to inform you that the sum appropriated at the last session of the Legislature for maintenance and repairs at the Central Prison and at Toronto, Mimico, Brockville, London, and Kingston Asylums, is insufficient by the sum of $6,810.07, made up as follows:—

Central Prison—

Turn table	$44 26	
Fencing	186 14	
		$230 40
Toronto Asylum—		
Interior repairs $2,468 11		
		2,468 11
Mimico Asylum—		
Exterior repairs $1,834 79		
Fire protection	25 00	
		1,859 79
Brockville Asylum—		
Engineer's Sunpplies	$18 92	
Exterior repairs	162 21	
		181 13

London Asylum—

Railway switch	$37 00	
		37 00

Kingston Asylum—

Interior repairs, etc.	$958 70	
Machinery repairs, etc.	632 69	
Surgical appliances	233 00	
Nurses' Home, etc.	7 25	
Replacing laundry machinery	202 00	
		2,033 64

Total	$6,810 07

I therefore beg leave to recommend that authority be given under R.S.O. 1897, Cap. 23, sec. 20, for payment of the said sum of $6,810.07.

I have the honour to be,

Sir,

Your obedient servant,

(Sgd.) W. J. HANNA,

Provincial Secretary.

The Provincial Auditor,
   Parliament Buildings,
     Toronto.

Copy of a Minute of the Treasury Board, dated the 15th day of January, A.D. 1907.

Upon consideration of the report of the Honourable the Provincial Secretary, dated the 14th day of January, A.D. 1907, the Treasury Board doth hereby order that pursuant to the provisions of section 20, Cap. 23, R.S.O. 1897, the sum of Six thousand eight hundred and ten dollars and seven cents ($6,810.07) be placed to the credit of the Treasurer to meet the requirements of maintenance and repairs of the Central Prison and the Toronto, Mimico, Brockville, London and Kingston Asylums for the balance of the year 1906, the appropriations for said services having become exhausted.

Certified,

J. LONSDALE CAPREOL,

Clerk, Treasury Board.

PROVINCIAL SECRETARY'S OFFICE,
TORONTO, January 16th, 1906.

The undersigned respectfully reports that the appropriation to pay the Judges' travelling expenses in connection with
the revision of Voters' Lists is exhausted, and that the further
sum of $300 is required to pay accounts now received and due
for the year ending December 31st, 1906.

The undersigned therefore respectfully recommends that
authority be given under R.S.O. 1897, Cap. 23, sec. 20, for
the issue of a warrant for the sum of $300 to cover the above
sum.

W. J. HANNA,
Provincial Secretarv

JAMES CLANCY, ESQ.,
Provincial Auditor.

Copy of a Minute of the Treasury Board, dated the 17th
day of January, A.D. 1907.

Upon consideration of the report of the Honourable the
Provincial Secretary, dated the 16th day of January, A.D.
1907, the Treasury Board doth hereby order that pursuant to
the provisions of section 20, Cap. 23, R.S.O. 1897, the sum of
Three nundred dollars ($300) be placed to the credit of the
Honourable the Treasurer to cover the payment of accounts now
received and due for the year ending 31st December, 1906, in
connection with the Judges' travelling expenses in revising
voters' lists, the appropriation for said service having become
exhausted.

Certified,

J. LONSDALE CAPREOL,
Clerk, Treasury Board.

TORONTO, 10th October, 1906.

The undersigned begs to report that the sum appropriated
under Civil Government at the last session of the Legislature
for Colonization and Forestry Contingencies having proved insufficient to meet the expenditure incurred, has been over-
drawn, and it is estimated that, including the present over-
draft, the sum of Nine hundred dollars ($900) will be required
to meet accounts for wages, postage, office supplies, and printing for the remainder of the current year.

The undersigned further reports that the sum appropriated for the maintenance of the colonization office at the Union Station, Toronto, has been found insufficient on account of the expansion that has taken place in immigration work, and it is estimated that the further sum of $200 will be required to meet expenditures under this head for the balance of the year.

The undersigned therefore recommends that, under the provisions of section 20, Cap. 23, R.S.O. 1897, authority be given for the appropriation of the further sum of Nine hundred dollars ($900) on account of Colonization and Forestry Contingencies and of Two hundred dollars ($200) on account of Office rent and Maintenance, Union Station.

(Sgd.) NELSON MONTEITH,
Minister of Agriculture.

JAMES CLANCY, ESQ.,
    Provincial Auditor.

Copy of a Minute of the Treasury Board, dated the 16th day of October, A.D. 1906.

Upon consideration of the report of the Honourable the Minister of Agriculture, dated the 10th day of October, A.D. 1906, the Treasury Board doth hereby order that pursuant to the provisions of section 20, Cap. 23, R.S.O. 1897, the sum of One thousand one hundred dollars be placed to the credit of the Honourable the Treasurer, to meet the requirements of Colonization and Forestry "Contingencies" and "Maintenance of Office, Union Station," for the balance of the current year, the appropriation for said service having become exhausted.

Certified,

J. LONSDALE CAPREOL,
Clerk, Treasury Board.

TORONTO, 26th November, 1906.

JAMES CLANCY, ESQ.,
    Provincial Auditor.

The undersigned begs to report that, under the vote for Colonization and Immigration, the amount appropriated for contingencies of the Liverpool office has been exhausted, and that the further sum of Five hundred dollars $500) will be required for the expenses in Great Britain of James Thompson as Special Agent in the interest of immigration.

The undersigned begs, therefore, to recommend that under the provisions of section 20, Cap. 23, R.S.O. 1897, the authority of the Treasury Board be obtained for the payment of the said sum, $500.

                              (Sgd.) NELSON MONTEITH,
                                    Minister of Agriculture.

———

Copy of a Minute of the Treasury Board, dated the 27th day of November, A.D. 1906.

Upon consideration of the report of the Honourable the Minister of Agriculture, dated the 26th day of November, A.D. 1906, the Treasury Board doth hereby order that pursuant to the provisions of section 20, Cap. 23, R.S.O. 1897, the sum of Five hundred dollars be placed to the credit of the Honourable the Treasurer to cover the expenses of James Thompson in Great Britain as special agent in the interest of immigration, the appropriation for Contingencies of the Liverpool office under the vote for Colonization and Immigration having become exhausted.

                              Certified,

                    J. LONSDALE CAPREOL,
                              Clerk, Treasury Board.

———

                              TORONTO, Dec. 11th, 1906.

DEAR SIR,—The appropriation of $600 for the inspection of apiaries will be insufficient to meet the expenditure. Accounts amounting to $320.85 have already been paid. We have on hand further accounts for work authorized by this Department as follows: Balance of services of Inspector, $291.50, and expenses of Inspector, $59.70. To meet these is required $72.05 in addition to the unexpended balance on hand.

I therefore request that pursuant to section 20, Cap. 23, R.S.O. 1897, a Treasury Board warrant be issued for the sum of One hundred dollars ($100) to meet accounts now on hand and for contingencies in connection with the inspection of apiaries, vote No. 47.

                              Yours truly,

                    NELSON MONTEITH,
                              Minister of Agriculture.

JAMES CLANCY, ESQ.,
          Provincial Auditor,
                    Parliament Buildings.

Copy of a Minute of the Treasury Board, dated the 18th day of December, A.D. 1906.

Upon consideration of the report of the Honourable the Minister of Agriculture, dated the 11th day of December, 1906, the Treasury Board doth hereby order that pursuant to the provisions of section 20, Cap. 23, R.S.O. 1897, the sum of One hundred dollars ($100) be placed to the credit of the Honourable the Treasurer to meet the requirements of the Inspection of Apiaries for the balance of the current year, the appropriation for said service having become exhausted.

Certified,

J. LONSDALE CAPREOL,
Clerk, Treasury Board.

TORONTO, December 27th, 1906.

The appropriation for $3,000 for advertising, printing, postage and stationery in connection with the Agricultural College and Experimental Farm has become exhausted. The vote is therefore insufficient to pay the account of the Farmer's Advocate for special advertising of the College in the Christmas issue. I have therefore respectfully to recommend that authority be given under the Act, R.S.O. 1897, Cap. 23, section 20, for the issue of a warrant for six hundred dollars ($600) to meet this deficiency.

Respectfully submitted,

NELSON MONTEITH,
Minister of Agriculture.

JAMES CLANCY, ESQ.,
Provincial Auditor,
Toronto.

Copy of a Minute of the Treasury Board, dated the 28th day of December, A.D. 1906.

Upon consideration of the report of the Honourable the Minister of Agriculture, dated the 27th day of December, A.D. 1906, the Treasury Board doth hereby order that pursuant to the provisions of section 20, Cap. 23, R.S.O. 1897, the sum of Six hundred dollars be placed to the credit of the Honourable the Treasurer to cover the account of the Farmer's Advocate for special advertising of the Agricultural College and Experimental Farm in the Christmas issue, the appropriation for advertising, printing, postage and stationery for the said Institution having become exhausted.

Certified,

M. CURREY,
Clerk, Treasury Board.

Toronto, December 27th, 1906.

The appropriation of $6,000 taken at the last session of the Legislature for Spring Stallion Shows and Investigations (Vote No. 43) has been found insufficient to meet the requirements. Eight hundred and seventy-five dollars of this vote was used for Spring Stallion Shows, leaving Five thousand one hundred and twenty-five dollars available for the investigations of the horse industry.

The work of carrying on the investigation into the horse industry of the Province has been found to be more extensive and more onerous than had been calculated upon. The expenses and allowance for services have exceeded our estimates. Accounts chargeable against this appropriation have been paid or recommended for payment as follows:

Travelling expenses of Commissioners	$1,721 95
Library accounts	804 15
Services of Commission	3,378 00
Local officers' expenses (in some cases including livery)	322 72
	$6,226 82

There are accounts now in hand and being adjusted to the amount of $1,824.48. It is desirable and in the interest of this work that all the accounts in connection with this investigation be paid and charged to the accounts of this year. I have therefore respectfully to recommend that under the Act, R.S.O. 1897, Cap. 23, section 20, a further appropriation of Three thousand dollars ($3,000) be made to meet the requirements of this service.

NELSON MONTEITH,
Minister of Agriculture.

James Clancy, Esq.,
Provincial Auditor.

———

Copy of a Minute of the Treasury Board, dated the 28th day of December, A.D. 1906.

Upon consideration of the report of the Honourable the Minister of Agriculture, dated the 27th day of December, A.D. the provsisions of section 20, Cap. 23, R.S.O. 1897, the sum of Three thousand dollars ($3,000) be placed to the credit of the Honourable the Treasurer to cover the payment of accounts for the balance of the current year in connection with the work of carrying on the investigation into the horse industry of the Province, the appropriation for Spring Stallion Shows and Investigation (Vote No. 43) being insufficient for the purpose.

Certified,

M. CURREY,
for Clerk, Treasury Board.

Toronto, December 27th, 1906.

The appropriation for Furniture and Furnishings, cleaning and care of rooms in conection with this Department under Vote 53 is inadequate to meet our requirements. The increase of work, the fitting up of new offices and the replacing of worn-out carpets have necessitated the purchase of material beyond our calculations. The vote is exhausted, and the following accounts are on hand:

United Typewriter Company	$25 00
Library Bureau	21 50
L. Rawlinson	133 00
	$179 50

It is desirable that these accounts be paid at once. I have therefore to request that under the Act, R.S.O. 1897, Cap 23, section 20, authority be given for the issue of a warrant for the sum of One hundred and seventy-nine dollars and fifty cents ($179.50) to pay the above accounts.

NELSON MONTEITH,
Minister of Agriculture.

James Clancy, Esq.,
Provincial Auditor,
Toronto.

Copy of a Minute of the Treasury Board, dated the 28th day of December, A.D. 1906.

Upon consideration of the report of the Honourable the Minister of Agriculture, dated the 27th day of December, A.D. 1906, the Treasury Board doth hereby order that pursuant to the provisions of section 20, Cap. 23, R.S.O. 1897, the sum of One hundred and seventy-nine dollars and fifty cents ($179.50) be placed to the credit of the Honourable the Treasurer for the

payment of the following accounts for furniture and furnishings in connection with the Department of Agriculture, the
appropriation for said service having become exhausted.

United Typewriter Company	$25 00
Library Burean	21 50
L. Rawlinson	133 00

$179 50

Certified,

M. CURREY,
for Clerk, Treasury Board.

———

TORONTO, January 11th, 1907.

SIR,—I beg to report that the appropriation for Experimental Fruit Farm is exhausted, and the following accounts
in connection with the same are on hand, and it is desirable
in the public interest that they be paid, viz.:

J. B. Reynolds, Expenses ....¿. $	6 70
R. J. Moyer, Implements	22 50
T. Schaefer, Tile	96 30
Watts and Bate, Tools	27.41

$152 91

I beg to recommend that a warrant be issued for the sum
of One hundred and fifty-two dollars and ninety-one cents for
the payment of these accounts, under the Act, R.S.O. 1897,
Cap. 23, section 20.

Yours truly,

NELSON MONTEITH,
Minister of Agriculture.

JAMES CLANCY, ESQ.,
        Provincial Auditor.

———

Copy of a Minute of the Treasury Board, dated the 15th
day of January, A.D. 1907.

Upon consideration of the report of the Honourable the
Minister of Agriculture, dated the 11th day of January, A.D.
1907, the Treasury Board doth hereby order that pursuant to
the provisions of section 20, Cap. 23, R.S.O. 1897, the sum of
One hundred and fifty-two dollars and ninety-one cents ($152.91)

be placed to the credit of the Treasurer to cover the payment
of the following accounts in connection with the Experimental
Fruit Farm, the appropriation for said service having become
exhausted.

J. B. Reynolds, Expenses .... $	6 70
R. J. Moyer, Implements	22 50
T. Schaefer, Tile	96 30
Watts and Bate, Tools	27 41
	$152 91

J. LONSDALE CAPREOL,
Clerk, Treasury Board.

TOTAL TREASURY BOARD ORDERS ($238,157.87.)

Service.	Appropriation.	Expended.	Treasury Board Orders.
Civil Government......................	428,330 00	428,280 46	25,140 00
Legislation	214,850 00	215,195 36	6,150 00
Administration of Justice............. ..	564,844 93	544,826 60	29,148 76
Education	1,381,456 64	1,320,921 71	8,960,86
Public Institutions Maintenance	1,042,451 58	1,016,252 37	37,420 02
Colonization and Immigration............	38,565 00	35,350 86	700 00
Agriculture........	460,556 95	432,296 90	7,079 73
Hospitals and Charities...................	340,799 40	334,169 56	2,272 81
Repairs and Maintenance................	89,710 00	76,488 22	5,829 50
Public Works...........................	117,010 00	85,117 29	1,254 40
Public Buildings	556,748 00	368,846 75	10,296 15
Colonization Roads......................	235,010 00	219,559 37	1,349 81
Charges Crown Lands	492,225 00	476,660 81	46,000 00
Refunds................................	47,628 92	48,241 48	1,451 03
Miscellaneous..........................	261,207 19	285,972 53	55.104 80

SPECIAL WARRANTS ISSUED UNDER ORDER OF HIS HONOR THE LIEUTENANT-GOVERNOR.

The undersigned begs to report to His Honour the Lieutenant-Governor in Council.

That the amount appropriated for the cutting and clearing of the forest on each side of The Temiskaming and Northern Ontario Railway, where it extends through the Temagami Forest Reserve, which was authorized by Order-in-Council of 14th August, 1905, has been expended.

The undersigned has the honour to recommend that a further sum of Eleven thousand dollars be granted to meet the present requirements of the work, and that a special warrant issue in favor of the Honourable the Treasurer of Ontario pursuant to the provisions of sub-section 2 of section 9, Cap. 23, R.S.O. of 1897.

(Sgd.) F. COCHRANE,
Minister of Lands and Mines.

Toronto, Feby. 16th, 1906.

The undersigned has the honour to report that there is no legislative provision for the above expenditure, and that it is necessary to issue a special warrant for the sum, and recommends that such special warrant be issued under the provisions of R.S.O., Cap. 23,, s. 9, ss. 2.

(Sgd.) A. J. MATHESON,
Provincial Treasurer.

Copy of an Order-inCouncil approved by His Honour the Lieutenant-Governor, the 17th day of February, A.D. 1906.

Referring to the Order-in-Council of 14th August, 1905, authorizing the cutting and clearing of the forest on each side of The Temiskaming and Northern Ontario Railway where it extends through the Temagami Forest Reserve, a sufficient distance back from the railway to protect from destruction by fire the valuable pine timber which exists in great quantities in said reserve, and upon the recommendation of the Honourable the Minister of Lands and Mines, the Committee of Council advise that a further sum of Eleven thousand dollars ($11,000) be appropriated under the provisions of sub-section 2, section 9, Cap. 23, R.S.O. 1897, to carry out the work now in operation. and that a special warrant for the said sum be issued in favour of the Honourable the Treasurer to be placed by him to a special account against which cheques may issue from time to time in the usual form as they may be required.

Certified,

J. LONSDALE CAPREOL,
Clerk, Executive Council.

To His Honour
THE LIEUTENANT-GOVERNOR-IN-COUNCIL.

The undersigned has the honour to report that the sum of Five hundred dollars ($500) is required for the expenses in connection with the Inter-Provincial Conference at Ottawa, for which there is no appropriation.

The undersigned has, therefore, the honour to recommend that a special warrant be issued to Horace Wallis, Secretary to the Prime Minister to the amount of Five hundred dollars ($500) for the payment of the above mentioned expenses.

(Sgd.) A. J. MATHESON,
Provincial Treasurer.

Toronto, Sept. 27, 1906.

The undersigned has the honour to report that there is no legislative provision for the above expenditure, and that it is necessary to issue a special warrant for the sum, and recommends that such special warrant be issued under the provisions of R.S.O., Cap. 23, s. 9, ss. 2.

(Sgd.) A. J. MATHESON,
Provincial Treasurer.

Copy of an Order-in-Council approved by His Honour the Lieutenant-Governor, the 28th day of September, A.D. 1906

Upon the recommendation of the Honourable the Treasurer the Committee of Council advise that a special warrant for the sum of Five hundred dollars ($500) be issued in favor of Horace Wallis, Secretary to the Prime Minister, to pay expenses in connection with the Inter-Provincial Conference at Ottawa.

Certified,

M. CURREY,
Asst. Clerk, Executive Council.

To His Honour
> THE LIEUTENANT-GOVERNOR-IN-COUNCIL.

The undersigned has the honour to report that by section 16 of Cap. 19, 6 Edward VII. (The Statute Law Amendment Act, 1906) it is provided that each District Court Judge shall receive for all work done in connection with "The Surrogate Courts Act," "Mechanics' and Wage Earners' Lien Act," "Woodmen's Lien for Wages Act," and "The Act for protecting the Public Interest in Rivers, Streams and Creeks," the sum of $500 per annum in lieu of all fees heretofore payable to them under any of the said Acts and the said fees shall be payable hereafter in stamps and form part of the Consolidated Revenue Fund of the Province. It appears that no appropriation was made in the estimates for the current year to cover the payment of such remuneration and as the necessity for the expenditure for said purpose is urgent the undersigned respectfully recommends that in order to meet the same a special warrant for the sum of Two thousand eight hundred and forty dollars ($2,840) be issued in favor of the Honourable the Treasurer to be placed by him to a special account against which cheques may issue from time to time in the usual form as they may be required.

> (Sgd.) J. J. FOY,
> Attorney-General.

31st August, 1906.

The undersigned has the honour to report that there is no legislative provision for the above expenditure, and that it is necessary to issue a special warrant for the sum, and recommends that such special warrant be issued under the provisions of R.S.O., Cap. 23, s. 9, ss. 2.

> A. J. MATHESON,
> Provincial Treasurer.

Copy of an Order-in-Council approved by His Honour the Lieutenant-Governor, the 7th September, 1906.

Upon the recommendation of the Honourable the Attorney-General the Commtitee of Council advise that a special warrant for the sum of $2,840 be issued in favor of the Honourable the Treasurer to be placed by him to a special account against which cheques may issue from time to time in the usual form as they may be required to cover the payments to be made to the various District Judges for services in connection with The Surrogate Courts Act, Mechanics' and Wage Earners' Lien Act,

7a* P.A.

Woodmen's Lien for Wages Act, and the Act for protecting the Public Interest in Rivers, Streams and Creeks, as provided by section 16 of Cap. 19, 6 Edward VII.

Certified,

M. CURREY,
Asst. Clerk, Executive Council.

———

TORONTO, 1st November, 1906.

To HIS HONOUR
THE LIEUTENANT-GOVERNOR-IN-COUNCIL.

The undersigned begs to state that it is very desirable that some arrangement other than that now existing be made for the housing of immigrants on their arrival in Toronto before being distributed to various situations. It is very necessary that some lodging house that can be absolutely controlled by the Government should be provided for immigrants as they arrive.

The undersigned has succeeded in finding a residential building which it is believed will answer the purpose, the location of which at the south-east corner of Peter and Wellington Streets, is convenient to the immigration offices at the Union Station and is capable with slight alterations of accommodating one hundred to one hundred and fifty. An offer has been received of this building for the sum of Twelve thousand dollars ($12,000) which in the opinion of the undersigned is a very reasonable price.

It is urgent that some building should be provided and fitted for this purpose before the rush of immigration begins. The offer for this building must be accepted immediately in order to secure the property which appears to be the most desirable for the purpose in the vicinity of the Union Station where the Immigration Distributing Office is situated.

No appropriation for such an expenditure was made at the last session of the Legislature, as it was not foreseen that this urgency would arise.

The undersigned would therefore respectfully recommend that in view of the facts above set forth a special warrant be issued under the authority of R.S.O. 1897, Cap. 23, section 9, subsection 2, for the above mentioned sum.

(Sgd.) NELSON MONTEITH,
Minister of Agriculture.

TORONTO, 1st November, 1906.

To His Honour
    THE LIEUTENANT-GOVERNOR-IN-COUNCIL.

The undersigned has the honour to report that there is no Legislative provision for the above expenditure, and that it is necessary to issue a special warrant for the sum of Twelve thousand dollars ($12,000), and recommends that such special warrant be issued under the provisions of R.S.O., Cap. 23, ss. 2. s. 9.

(Sgd.) A. J. MATHESON,
Provincial Treasurer.

Copy of an Order-in-Council approved by His Honour the Lieutenant-Governor, the 2nd day of November, A.D. 1906.

The Committee of Council have had under consideration the annexed report of the Honourable the Minister of Agriculture with reference to the purchase of certain property on the south-east corner of Peter and Wellington Streets in the City of Toronto for the purpose of providing accommodation for immigrants on their arrival in Toronto, and advise that a special warrant for the sum of Twelve thousand dollars ($12,000.00) the amount of the purchase money for the said property be issued in favor of the Honourable the Treasurer under the provisions of sub-section 2, section 9, Cap. 23, R.S.O. 1897.

Certified, .

J. LONSDALE CAPREOL,
Clerk, Executive Council.

To His Honour
    THE LIEUTENANT-GOVERNOR-IN-COUNCIL.

The undersigned has the honour to report that there is due the amount of $13,262.75 to the Bank of Toronto for hemp purchased by the Colonial Cordage Company and interest, and the amount of $9,830.66 to the Independent Cordage Company and interest, for both of which there is no legislative provision.

The undersigned has, therefore, the honour to recommend that a special warrant be issued under authority of R.S.O. 1897, cap. 23, s. 9, ss. 2, for the above mentioned sums.

W. .J. HANNA,
Provincial Secretary.

Toronto, 18th January, 1907.

The undersigned has the honour to report that there is no legislative provision for the above expenditures, and that it is necessary to issue a special warrant for the sum of $23,093.41, and recommends that such special warrant be issued under the provisions of R.S.O., Cap. 23, s. 9, ss. 2.

·A. J. MATHESON,
Provincial Treasurer.

Toronto, 18th January, 1907.

Copy of an Order-in-Council approved by His Honour the Lieutenant-Governor, the 18th day of January, A.D. 1907.

The Committee of Council have had under consideration the report of the Honourable the Provincial Secretary, dated 18th January, 1907, wherein he states that there is due the sum of Thirteen thousand two hundred and sixty-two dollars and seventy-five cents ($13,262.75) to the Bank of Toronto for hemp purchased by the Colonial Cordage Company and interest, and the sum of Nine thousand eight hundred and thirty dollars and sixty-six cents ($9,830.66) to the Independent Cordage Company and interest, for both of which there is no legislative provision. The Minister recommends that in view of the fact that the payment of the said sums is urgent and necessary in the public interest, a special warrant for the sum of Twenty-three thousand and ninety-three dollars and forty-one cents ($23,093.41) be issued in favor of the Honourable the Treasurer under the provisions of R.S.O. 1897, Cap. 23, section 9, sub-section 2.

The Committee concur in the recommendation of the Minister and advise that the same be acted on.

Certified,

J. LONSDALE CAPREOL,
Clerk, Executive Council.

MISCELLANEOUS STATEMENTS.

No. 1.

Balance Sheet showing the Receipts and Payments of the Treasurer of Ontario during the year 1906, with the Cash Balances on the 1st of January and the 31st December.

Receipts

Receipts.	$ c.	$ c.	$ c.
Balances as per Public Accounts, 1905.			
Amount at Special Deposit 31st December, 1905.	1,570,642 27		
Amount at Current Account 31st December, 1905	368,937 69		1,939,579 96
CONSOLIDATED REVENUE FUND.			
From Dominion of Canada:			
Subsidy on population	1,116,872 80		
" 47 Vic, c. 4	142,414 48		
Special grant	80,000 00		
Interest paid by Dominion see Statement No. 5		149,933 64	
Less interest paid by Ontario for twelve months ended 31st December, 1906, on balance of account current with Dominion from Confederation to date as finally adjusted		69,487 60	
	80,446 04		1,339,287 28
Interest on investments	80,689 90	161,135 94	
Department Lands, Forests and Mines:			
Crown Lands			
Agricultural	83,846 64		
Mining	118,243 62	202,090 26	
Grammar School Lands		2,669 52	

Payments

Payments.	$ c.	$ c.	$ c.
CONSOLIDATED REVENUE FUND.			
For Civil Government		428,280 46	
" Legislation		215,195 36	
" Administration of Justice		544,828 60	
" Education		1,270,921 71	
" Public Institutions Maintenance		957,347 35	
" Central Prison Industries		58,905 02	
" Colonization and Immigration		35,350 86	
" Agriculture		432,296 90	
" Hospitals and Charities		334,169 56	
" Repairs and Maintenance Parliament Buildings, etc.		76,488 22	
" Locks, Dams, etc.		14,725 99	
" Colonization Roads		219,559 37	
" Charges, Crown Lands		476,660 81	
" Surveys, Inspections, etc.		663 82	
" Refunds re Crown Lands	32,844 62		
" Education	1,932 87		
" Miscellaneous	11,309 36	46,086 85	
" Miscellaneous Services		214,172 53	
" Inter-Provincial Conference, Ottawa		435 50	
" Provincial Boundaries Conference, Ottawa		73 65	
" Grant to Sick Children's Hospital (6 Edw. VII. Cap. 5).		2,000 00	
" Medical Faculty of Queen's College for promotion of Medical Education.			5,328,160 56
OPEN ACCOUNTS.			
" Commutation Volunteer Veterans Land Grants			50,000 00
For Asylum for Insane, Toronto		11,060 17	71,800 00
" " Mimico		22,572 10	

University Lands		1,082 40		London	9,074 06
Railway Lands		22 25		Hamilton	9,761 75
Rent:				Kingston	27,369 80
Mining Leases	46,618 69				11,684 70
Crown "	3,372 83	49,991 52		Cobourg	3,412 37
Woods and Forests:					68,405 48
Bonus	535,970 57			Penetang	10,664 86
Timber dues	1,295,378 53			Idiots, Orillia	3,159 78
Ground Rent	66,118 47			Ref'y for Females	2,608 86
Transfer Fees	3,447 05	1,900,914 62		Central Prison	23,005 49
Cull Fees	652 83			Normal School, Toronto	5,207 59
Cullers' Fees	348 00			" Ottawa	3,809 31
Guides' Fees	132 00			" London	3,668 15
Assay Fees	1,655 20			Additional Normal Schools	4,618 33
Rondeau Park	189 00			School of Practical Science	70,080 00
"	296 50	3,273 53		Agric'l College	55,140 20
Mining Licenses and Fees	70,256 06			Deaf and Dumb Inst., Belleville	3,700 86
Royalty on Mines	15,000 00	85,256 06		Blind Institute, Brantford	4,112 20
Refunds:				Dist'rt of Alta	93 99
Temagami Timber cutting	3,531 54			" Parry Sound	4,165 53
Forest Reserves	1,221 50			" Nipissing	3,627 50
Fire Ranging	83 90			" Algoma	320 31
Mining Inspection	21 75			" ...er Bay	1,016 16
Bureau of Mines	53			" Rainy River	517 20
Inspection Fees	12 00			Muskoka Lakes Wks	2,580 47
Agents' Salaries	172 87			Mary and Fairy Lake Wks	3,964 29
Diamond Drill	2,855 37	7,899 46		Neighick Lake Wks	898 15
				LaVase and Boon Creek Im-	
		2,263,199 62		Keewatin Bridge	804 22
Licenses		579,207 10			200 00
Law Stamps		85,945 60		Rainy River Bridge	1,990 52
Algoma Taxes		9,099 33		Sleeman's Bridge	1,044 80
Education Department		64,545 85		Vermilion River Bridge	662 75
Secretary's Department		208,023 59		Goulais River Bridge	1,892 58
Fisheries		63,998 57		...th River Wks	986 07
Agriculture		86,224 16		Sauble River Bridge	3,561 55
Supplementary Revenue Act		614,201 99		Spanish River Bridge	5,560 37
62, 63 Vic. and 4 Edw. VII				Veuve River Bridge	4,487 17
Succession Duty		1,015,713 24		Wrights Creek Bridge	1,059 95
				...th Road Bridge	1,877 24
				...wa Bridge	3,815 40
				...ne ...dge	1,395 22
				Manitowaba Bridge	798 51
				Bala Bridge	3,277 76
		1,939,579 96			409,703 77
	6,510,582 27				5,449,960 56

No. 1.—Concluded.

Balance sheet showing the Receipts and Payments of the Treasurer of Ontario during the year 1906, with the Cash Balances on the 1st of January and the 31st of December.—Concluded.

Receipts

Receipts	$	c.	$	c.
Brought forward			6,510,582	27	1,939,579	96
From Casual Revenue	173,819	50		
" Public Institutions:				
Toronto Lunatic Asylum	50,281	64		
London "	42,715	26		
Hamilton "	31,529	61		
Kingston "	10,067	82		
Mimico "	16,264	54		
Brockville "	11,866	84		
Orillia "	11,787	70		
Cobourg "	911	17		
Penetang "	2,440	11		
Woodstock "	3,532	33		
Reformatory for Females	3,569	96		
Central Prison Industries	92,474	68	277,441	66
			6,961,843	43
OPEN ACCOUNTS				
From Department of Lands, Forests and Mines:				
Clergy Lands	3,969	71		
Common School Lands	9,218	61		
Drainage Debentures, Municipal	8,517	17		
Drainage Debentures, Tile	7,775	00	29,480	49

Payments

Payments	$	c.	$	c.	$	c.
Brought forward			409,703	77	5,449,960	56
For Canard River Bridge			1,000	00		
" Big East River Bridge			800	00		
" La Mable Bridge			1,271	43		
" Beaver Creek Bridge			996	77		
" Madawaska River Bridge			3,000	00		
" Sturgeon River Bridge						
" South River and Eagle Lake Bridges			267	75		
" Black Duck and Indian River Bridge			673	13		
" Woleley River Bridge			809	48		
" Axe Creek, Houseys Outlet and Kashee Bridges			974	20		
" Katrine Bridge			1,221	57		
" Burnt River Bridge			1,257	23		
" La Blanche River Bridge			2,017	11		
" Drainage Works			511	79		
" Refund re Land Improvement Fund			14,010	00		
" do re Municipalities Fund			1,911	31		
" Widows' Pensions			243	32		
For Statutory Expenditure:						
Good Roads (1 Edw. VII. Cap. 32)	95,141	89				
Sugar Beet Industry (1 Edw. VII. Cap. 44)	75,000	00				
University of Toronto (5 Edw. VII. Cap. 37)	30,000	00				
University of Toronto (6 Edw. VII. Cap. 55)	86,629	00				
Distribution to Municipalities from Railway Tax (6 Edw. VII. Cap. 9)	81,060	99	367,831	88		

For Aid to Railways	130,860 68	
" Annuities	102,900 00	
" Drainage Debentures, Municipal	37,307 18	
" Drainage Debentures, Tile	1,800 00	
" Common School Land	6,038 73	
" Purchase of Property for Immigration Purposes	12,000 00	
" Purchase of Hemp from the Independent Cordage Co'y	12,596 71	
" Interest, Charges and Sinking Fund for 1906 on Ontario Government Inscribed Stock (5 Edw. VII, cap. 2 and 3) £1,200,000	158,154 47	1,270,218 51
Total Expenditure		6,720,179 07
" Advance to the Temiskaming & Northern Ontario Railway		1,872,286 53
For Ontario Government Treasury Bills falling due May 15th, 1906 ......£1,200,000		5,840,004 00
Amount at Special Deposit 31st December, 1906	3,310,636 79	
Amount at Current Account 31st December, 1906	186,602 83	3,497,239 62
		17,929,709 22

Temiskaming and Northern Ontario Railway: From Earnings	158,154 47	
Total Receipts		7,149,478.39
Stationery Account, excess of distribution over purchases		646 87
Proceeds of sale of Ontario Government Inscribed Stock (English Loan) 5 Edw. VII, cap. 2 & 3 ....£1,152,000		
Temiskaming and Northern Ontario Railway, included in advance. See Statement No. 18. £48,000 ...£1,200,000		5,840,004 00
Proceeds of sale of Ontario Government Bonds and Stock (Canadian Loan), (5 Edw. VII, cap. 2 & 6 Edw. VII, cap. 4)		3,000,000 00
		17,929,709 22

No. 2.

STATEMENT OF BANK BALANCES, 31ST DECEMBER, 1906.

		$ c.	$ c.
Current Balance,	Imperial Bank	4,809 03	
	Bank of Commerce	25,136 02	
	Crown Bank	13,157 06	
	Dominion Bank	14,068 07	
	Bank of Hamilton	8,251 25	
	Bank of Ottawa	4,410 20	
	Bank of Montreal	22,332 80	
	Bank of Montreal, Wellington St. Branch	11,299 72	
	Sovereign Bank	1,064 81	
	Union Bank	2,548 84	
	Bank of Nova Scotia	11,033 70	
	Quebec Bank	4,961 94	
	Traders Bank	18,105 87	
	Molsons Bank	858 42	
	Standard Bank	6,788 37	
	Home Bank	4,347 51	
	Bank of Toronto	7,082 86	
	Royal Bank	7,046 86	
	United Empire Bank	7,203 67	
	Merchants Bank	2,984 55	
	Metropolitan Bank	6,635 57	
	Bank of B. N. A.	2,475 71	
			186,602 83
Special Deposits,	Imperial Bank	170,000 00	
	Bank of Commerce	10,000 00	
	Crown Bank	478,000 00	
	Dominion Bank	150,000 00	
	Bank of Hamilton	115,000 00	
	Bank of Ottawa	410,000 00	
	Bank of Montreal	240,000 00	
	Bank of Montreal, Wellington St. Branch	40,000 00	
	Sovereign Bank	177,358 79	
	Union Bank	60,000 00	
	Bank of Nova Scotia	20,000 00	
	Quebec Bank	10,550 00	
	Traders Bank	78,800 00	
	Molsons Bank	125,000 00	
	Standard Bank	70,000 00	
	Home Bank	20,800 00	
	Bank of Toronto	498,028 00	
	Royal Bank	80,000 00	
	United Empire Bank	350,000 00	
	Merchants Bank	206,000 00	
	Bank of B. N. A.	1,100 00	
			3,310,636 79

No. 3.

STATEMENT of the Consolidated Revenue Fund, 31st December, 1906.

	$ c.	$ c.		$ c.	$ c.
To expenditure as per Statement No. 1......	5,449,960 56		By balance, as per Statement No. 3, 1905..	19,142,722 01	
To Land Improvement Fund.....	1,911 31		By receipts, as per Statement No. 1.......	6,961,843 43	
		5,451,871 87			26,104,565 44
			By Temiskaming and Northern Ontario Railway, from earnings.......	......	158,154 47
			By Municipalities Fund: Twenty per cent. on amount collected during the year for cost of management........	......	793 94
To Balance..	......	20,813,252 57	By Municipalities Fund: Receipts from Clergy Lands added to the grant to Public and Separate Schools, 1906 (see 50 Vic. cap. 5).	......	1,610 59
		26,265,124 44			26,265,124 44

No. 4.
INVESTMENT ACCOUNT.

To whom paid.	Nature of Investment,	Amount. $ c.	Amount. $ c.	Amount.	Amount.
Sundry banks.	Amount of special deposits, 31st December, 1905		1,570,642 27		
Imperial Bank.	Special deposits made up to 31st ?ber, 1906	345,850 00			
Bank of Commerce.	do	80,000 00			
Crown Bank.	do	503,000 00			
Dominion Bank.	do	300,000 00			
Bank of Hamilton.	do	245,000 00			
Bank or Ottawa.	do	550,000 00			
Bank of Montreal.	do	880,000 00			
Bank of Montreal, Wellington St. Branch.	do	40,000 00			
Ontario Bank.	do	131,577 83			
Sovereign Bank.	do	421,908 75			
Union Bank.	do	135,000 00			
Bank of Nova Scotia.	do	20,000 00			
Quebec Bank.	do	10,550 00			
Traders Bank.	do	85,500 00			
Molsons Bank.	do	160,000 00			
Standard Bank.	do	110,000 00			
Home Bank.	do	20,800 00			
Bank of Toronto.	do	730,000 00			
Royal Bank.	do	100,000 00			
United Empire Bank.	do	350,000 00			
Metropolitan Bank.	do	646,000 00			
?? Bank	00	75,000 00			
Bank of British North America.	do	1,100 00			
			5,941,286 62		
	Less amount drawn to meet current expenditure		7,511,928 89		
Imperial Bank		340,925 00			
Bank of Commerce		164,500 00			
Crown Bank		60,000 00			
Dominion Bank		280,900 00			
Bank of Hamilton		230,000 00			
Bank of Ottawa		241,600 00			
Bank of Montreal		740,000 00			

No. 4.—*Concluded.*

To whom paid.	Nature of Investment.	Amount.	Amount.	Amount.	Amount.
		$ c.	$ c.	$ c.	$ c.
	Ontario Bank	230,277 83			
	Sovereign Bank	293,000 00			
	Union Bank	155,000 00			
	Bank of Nova Scotia	50,000 00			
	... Bank	35,000 00			
	Traders ... Bank	122,769 11			
	... Bank	141,220 16			
	Standard Bank	135,000 00			
	Bank of Toronto	346,200 00			
	Royal Bank	20,000 00			
	Merchants Bank	521,000 00			
	Metropolitan ... Bank	114,000 00			
			4,201,292 10		
	Interest bearing securities held by the Province:				
	Drainage debentures			3,310,636 79	
	Tile drainage debentures			85,779 50	
	(Sault Ste. Marie) Municipal debentures			62,645 85	
	Temiskaming & Northern Ontario Railway Loan			25,572 50	
				3,408,450 80	
					6,893,085 44

No. 5.
INTEREST ACCOUNT.

Statement of interest received during the year ended 31st December, 1906.

From whom received.	Nature of Investment	Amount.	Total.
		$	$
Hon. Minister of Finance, Canada..	Interest on Trust Funds:		
	U. C. Grammar School Fund ...... $ 312,769.04 at 4 % for 12 months	12,510 76	
	U. C. Building Fund ...... 1,472,391.41 do	58,895 66	
	Land Improvement Fund ...... 124,685.18 do	4,987 40	
	Common School Fund:		
	$1,469,561.73 at 5 % for 12 months $73,478.08		
	3,440.17 do 131 days interest on Ontario's proportion of collections 1905 paid over in 1906 ...... 61.74	73,539 82	149,933 64
Sundry municipalities	Interest on drainage debentures		5,760 53
Sundry subscribers	do re Provincial bonds		12,292 54
A. E. Long & Co.	do one year on mortgage School of Medicine Building		410 63
University of Toronto	do re pre-payment		162 74
Sundry estate	do re succession duty		3,848 09
Landed B. & L. Co.	do re debenture re Blind Institution		17 00
Binder Twine Contract	do on deposit as security		194 38
Canadian Bank of Commerce	do on special deposits	1,702 37	
Crown Bank	do do	2,302 58	
Dominion Bank	do do	3,375 75	
Home Bank	do do	243 28	
Bank of Hamilton	do do	3,510 34	
Imperial Bank	do do	4,200 70	
Merchants Bank	do do	6,704 30	
Metropolitan Bank	do do	1,134 47	
Molson's Bank	do do	2,724 47	
Bank of Montreal	do do	7,590 57	
do Wellington street branch	do do	236 68	
Bank of Nova Scotia	do do	749 57	
Ontario Bank	do do	1,971 71	
Bank of Ottawa	do do	4,785 81	

No 5.

INTEREST ACCOUNT.—*Continued.*

Statement of interest received during the year ended 31st December, 1906.

From whom received.	Nature of Investment.	Amount.	Total.
		$	$
Quebec Bank	Interest on special deposits	539 99	
Royal Bank	do	1,106 28	
Sovereign Bank	do	6,536 49	
Standard Bank	do	2,286 83	
Bank of Toronto	do	4,285 23	
Traders Bank	do	1,472 65	
Union Bank	do	2,217 48	
United Empire Bank	do	904 09	60,591 64
			233,211 19
	Deduct payments and refunds:		
	Refund of interest, over-payment on special deposit, Molson's Bank	1 64	
	Allowance for interest on funds deposited with Provincial Treasurer in lieu of bond for payment of succession duty	1,919 97	
	Interest on balance of account current with Dominion from Confederation to date as finally adjusted	69,487 60	
	Interest paid on hemp purchased by the Colonial Cordage Co.	666 04	72,075 25
			161,135 94

8* P.A.

No. 6.

Statement of Receipts of the Education Department during twelve months ended December 31st, 1906.

	Particulars.	Amount.	Total.
		$	$
Normal and Model Schools, Toronto	Fees from Normal, Model and Kindergarten students and pupils	13,022 00	
do do Ottawa	do do	8,242 00	
do London	do School students	1,352 00	22,616 00
Normal College, Hamilton	Fees from students		3,505 00
Departmental Examinations	Examination fees and appeals		18,502 00
Superannuated Teachers	Subscriptions, 1906		687 00
Miscellaneous	Sale of School Acts, waste paper, etc	501 43	
	Publishers' payments for extension of term of right to publish Readers to end of 1906	300 00	
	Refund from School Section No. 3, Township of Draper	50 00	
	do do No. 9, do	50 00	
	do estate late D. McCaig, balance of accountable warrant for travelling expenses	25 85	927 28
Institution for the Education of the Blind, Brantford	Fees from pupils, sales, etc		838 62
Institution for the Education of the Deaf and Dumb, Belleville	do do		2,158 65
School of Practical Science	Students fees for half year to 1st July, 1906		15,331 30
			64,545 85

8a* P.A.

No. 7.

STATEMENT OF REVENUE from Agriculture during twelve months ended 31st December, 1906.

	$ c.	$ c.	$ c.
AGRICULTURAL COLLEGE :—			
College :—			
Tuition and laboratory fees	5,651 50		
Board.......................................	16,728 77		
Supplemental examinations.....................	54 00		
Rent of post office boxes	39 00		
Fines and breakages............................	337 41		
Analysis of water (chemical laboratory).........	26 00		
Rent of cottages..............................	220 00		
Sale of brushwood	2 00		
do old range...............................	2 00		
do old mare...............................	89 00		
do old refrigerator	7 00		
do windmill top	4 00		
Rent of rooms	76 00		
Sale of scrap iron.............................	10 00		
		23,246 68	
Macdonald Institute and Hall :—			
Tuition and laboratory fees	4,243 50		
Board	11,412 55		
Sale of supplies to nature study students..........	25 13		
Fines and breakages...........................	207 90		
		15,889 08	
Farm and Feeding :			
Sale of cattle :—			
32 steers, 43145 lbs. @ from 4c. to 5c...........	2,112 30		
13 do for................................	545 00		
2 bulls for	95 00		
2 cows, 2 heifers, and 1 calf..................	305 00		
		3,057 30	
Sale of pigs :—			
122 hogs, 24,478 lbs., @ from 4.70 to 7.75 cwt....	1,615 74		
16 hogs for	174 50		
		1,790 24	
Sale of sheep :—			
5 sheep....................................	21 00		
10 lambs	40 00		
		61 00	
Sale of carcases used at short courses:—			
4 beef, 4,010 lbs., @ 7c.......$280 70			
4 hides 32 60			
$313 30			
Less killing.............. 14 65	....	298 65	
Service of animals.............................		123 50	
Sale of wool, 353 lbs., @ from 15½c to 19c........		62 60	
do hides 2 for............................		7 16	
do old team		85 00	
do old iron..............................		1 50	
do grain:			
188 bus. barley @ 75c	141 00		
157 bus. wheat @ 70c	110 30		
24 bus. oats @ 50c	12 00		
2 bus. corn @ $1.00...................	2 00		
		265 30	
do potatoes:			
96 bags @ 90c.........................	86 40		
8⅝ bags @ 75c.........................	5 15		
		91 55	
do bags, 85 @ 20c..........................	....	17 00	
Dairy:—			
Sale of butter, 39,113 lbs. @ from 15c to 30c		9,129 13	
do cheese, 12,958 lbs. @ from 8c to 15c		1,597 60	
do milk, 6,145 qts. @ 4c...................	245 80		
do milk, 21,982 lbs. @ 1.60 cwt..............	350 26		
		596 06	

No 7.—*Continued.*

STATEMENT OF REVENUE from Agriculture.—*Concluded.*

		\$ c.	\$ c.	\$ c.
Dairy.—*Continued.*				
Sale of skim milk and whey, 64,000 lbs. @ 10c cwt.		64 00		
do skim milk and whey, 8,150 lbs. @ 20c cwt.		16 30		
do season's whey		20 00		
			100 30	
do cream, 1,083 qts. @ from 15c to 40c			210 88	
do cattle:				
11 calves		21 50		
3 bull calves		110 00		
9 cows		245 00		
			376 50	
Sundries :—Rennet 60c; milk tested \$1.25; 3 butter boxes 60c; 1 bottle 25c; old pump \$5.00; old rope 40c; refund express 30c; rent of house \$16.00			25 40	
Dairy School :—				
Fees		70 00		
Breakages		3 75		
Sale of butter, 11,742 lbs. @ from 15c to 30c		3,034 39		
do cheese, 2,445 lbs. @ from 5c to 13c		261 02		
do milk, 1,625 qts.@ 4c; 9,481 lbs. @ \$1.60 cwt.		216 60		
do cream, 452 qts. @ 20c		90 40		
Sundries :—Milk tested 10c ; refund freight \$1.25 ; old iron 20c		1 55		
			3,677 80	
Poultry :—				
Sale of eggs, for hatching, 1,092 @ 5c		54 60		
do eggs, do 107¾ sets @ from 75c to \$2.50.		128 75		
			183 35	
do eggs, for domestic use, 1,072 doz. @ from 10c to 35c			208 77	
do live poultry, 127 birds @ from \$1.00 to \$50.00			307 60	
do dressed poultry, 4,440 lbs. @ from 10c to 44c.		604 35		
do 106 ducks		66 40		
do 2 geese @ \$1.00		2 00		
do 8 squabs at 25c		2 00		
			674 75	
do feathers, 5 lbs. @ 25c			1 25	
do beef scrap, 100 lbs			3 00	
Horticultural :—				
Sale of strawberries, 60½ crates @ \$1.00		60 50		
do cabbage, 12¼ doz. @ 40c		4 90		
do onions, 4½ bags @ \$1.00		4 50		
do squash		25		
			70 15	
				62,159 10
Eastern Dairy School :—				
Sale of butter, 5,933¼ lbs. @ from			1,543 14	
do cheese, 7,589¼ lbs. @ from 6c to 13c			913 59	
do cream			156 48	
do skim milk			49 78	
Fees			103 00	
				2,765 99
Western Dairy School :—				
Fees, etc				56 80
Miscellaneous :—				
For services of Instructors to cheese factories and creameries			12,299 00	
Agricultural societies *re* expert judges at fairs			3,635 20	
Institutes, for services of Lecturers at meetings			920 63	
Pioneer Dairy Farm, sale of farm stock and implements			3,937 70	
Fruit Growers, for chemicals supplied and work done *re* spraying			215 32	
Sundry persons, refunds travelling expenses (1905)			234 42	
				21,242 27
				\$ 86,224 16

No. 8.

Statement of Revenue received from Fisheries Branch of Public Works Department during the year ended 31st December, 1906.

District.	Name of Overseer.	Amount.	Total.
		$ c.	$ c.
Lake of the Woods and Rainy River District.	Nash, John..............	1,166 00	.
	Perry, John	30 00	
			1,196 00
River Nepigon.....................	Leitch, P. A............	....	1,595 00
Lake Superior	Ashforth. J. G...........	4,046 00	
	Van Norman, R. M	1,768 00	
			5,814 00
Lake Huron (North Channel)	Henbruff, Joseph	22 00	
	Hunter, William........	5 00	
	Oliver, R. C	5,589 00	
			5,616 00
Georgian Bay	Bettes, A. L	85 15	
	Dusang, B. A	260 00	
	France, William, Jr.....	131 00	
	Free, John	74 00	
	Hewitt, James.........	11 00	
	Jermyn, J. W...........	638 00	
	Kennedy, John.........	890 00	
	Laughington, Henry	1,129 00	
	Robinson, Thomas W....	485 00	
	Williams, J. T..........	220 00	
			3,923 15
Lake Huron (proper) and River St. Clair.	Blundin, H. A	3,696 00	
	Kehoe, Daniel	127 00	
	McMurray, Robert......	683 00	
	Robertson, David	864 20	
			5,370 20
Lake St. Clair, River Thames and Detroit River.	Crotty, John...........	67 00	
	Drouillard, Arzas.	1,146 52	
	Laframboise, Remi......	195 00	
	Little, Richard.........	527 00	
	Osborne, Henry........	45 50	
	Pettier, Theodore	407 00	
			2,388 02
Lake Erie and Grand River.............	Briggs, T. J	24 00	
	Farrell, John	571 00	
	Fitzpatrick, Jerome.....	5,530 00	
	Freedenburg, D........	57 00	
	Henderson, H. A	1,727 00	
	Johnson, Henry........	30 50	
	Krait, Samuel	204 00	
	Lee, Edward	1,255 00	
	McCall, George D......	285 00	
	McEwan, Archibald.....	2,725 00	
	McClellan, Kenneth	3,375 00	
	Pierce, J. P	2,162 84	
	Vokes, James...........	1,805 00	
	Shelley, George........	634 90	
	Proceeds from sale of fish.		
	Wigle, Lewis	3,297 50	
			23,683 74
Lake Ontario and Bay of Quinte	Brickwood, J. H........	571 04	
	Buckley, George A......	1,455 00	
	Clark Marshall.........	533 00	
	Covell, John.....	105 00	
	Gault, Thomas.........	396 00	
	Carried forward	3,060 04	49,586 11

No. 8.

Statement of Revenue.—*Continued.*

District.	Name of Overseer.	Amount.	Total.
		$ c.	
	Brought forward	3,060 04	49,586 11
Lake Ontario and Bay of Quinte.—*Con*....	Glass, Irving............	40 00	
	Hayes, H. W............	55 00	
	Holliday, Henry........	230 00	
	Huffman, E. M.........	45 00	
	Kerr, C. J..............	292 00	
	May, J. C..............	397 00	
	Murdock, John.........	228 50	
	Sargent, William	70 00	
	Walker, R. J...........	55 00	
	Willis, J. M	36 00	
	Wood, W. R............	168 08	
	Boyd, J. H	19 00	
			4,695 62
Counties Frontenac, Leeds, Prescott, Russell, Carleton, Renfrew, Lanark, Grenville.	Bourgon, J. B	76 00	
	Birch, W. J	107 00	
	Covell, H. N...........	5 00	
	Christink, Erwin	19 00	
	Davis, J. W	32 00	
	Drew, Henry	30 00	
	Deacon, Ephriam......	10 00	
	Esford, Henry.........	97 00	
	Hull, Charles...........	243 00	
	Knight, N. R..........	200 00	
	Loveday, E. T	34 25	
	McGuire, John.........	323 00	
	Phillips, Herbert.......	256 00	
	Spence, William........	209 00	
	Shillington, Nathaniel...	66 00	
	Stewart, James.........	5 00	
	Taylor, Charles	3 00	
	Townsend, James......	126 00	
			1,841 25
Peterborough, Northumberland, Victoria and other inland counties.	Blais, D................	· 4 00	
	Bradshaw, A............	58 75	
	Cassan, C. H	78 00	
	Clarkson, William	86 00	
	Green, John............	34 00	
	Hess, J. H.............	39 00	
	Irish, John	3 00	
	Johnston, David.......	39 90	
	Johnston, T. H	11 00	
	Johnston, W. H	2 00	
	Langton, Newton	4 00	
	Lean, Wellington	24 00	
	McAlister, J. R........	70 00	
	Merriam, D. E....	16 00	
	Merriman, Enoch......	77 00	
	Moore, F. J............	275 00	
	Morton, J. W...........	5 00	
	Nicholls, Garner	436 00	
	Purcill, H. R...........	31 00	
	Smith, William	10 00	
	Toole, Ira	26 00	
	Watson, John	31 00	
	Watt, John.............	6 00	
	Willmott, J. H	171 00	
	Worden, Frank........	5 00	
			1,542 65
	Carried forward.....	....	57,665 63

No. 8.

Statement of Revenue.—*Continued.*

District.	Name of Overseer.	Amount.	Total.
		$ c.	$ c.
	Brought forward	....	57,665 63
River St. Lawrence	Acton, Nassau	20 00	•
	Cox, Matthew	20 00	
	Fraser, J. A	10 00	
			50 00
Lakes Simcoe, Couchiching and Sparrow..	Dodds, W. T...........	26 00	
	Doolittle, Herbert.......	260 00	
	McGinn, William.......	14 00	
	McPhee, Donald	12 00	
	MacDonald, Hector	5 00	
	Mayor, Harry	10 00	
	Tillett, Robert.........	4 00	
			331 00
Nipissing	Baechler, Fred.........	2 00	
	Cartier, Alfred.........	2,654 00	
	Huntington, S. A........	262 00	
	McKelvie, Daniel	50 00	
	MacDonald, S. C........	978 00	
			3,946 00
Unclassified	Licenses issued from Office	352 00	
	Fines, etc	8 00	
	Balance account 1905....	5 00	
	Sale of Gilphie..........	1,600 00	
	Rebate on insurance policy.................	40 94	
			2,005 94
			$63,998 57

No. 9.

Statement of Receipts of the Secretary's Department during twelve months ended 31st December, 1906.

From Whom Received.	Service.	$ c.	$ c.
Provincial Secretary's Department....	Letters Patent, Licenses, etc	181,854 11	
	Companies Returns	12,590 20	
	Automobile Licenses and Renewals ...	5,523 15	
	Marriage Act Forms	3,878 45	
	Commission under Great and Privy Seal	1,996 95	
	Certificates	110 00	
	By-laws, Copies and Searches........	957 18	206,909 84
Provincial Registrar's Office....	7 Exemplications of Patent.........	66 50	
	80 Certified Copies Patent	200 00	
	280 Searches.......................	70 00	
	3 Special Certificates..............	1 50	338 00
Registrar General's Branch....	359 Certificates of Birth	179 50	
	146 do Marriage	73 00	
	291 do Death..................	145 50	
	1,511 Searches	377 75	775 75
			$208,023 59

No. 10,

ALGOMA TAXES REVENUE.

Statement showing the several amounts received by the Treasurer of Ontario on account of TAXES ON PATENTED LANDS in the Districts of Algoma, Thunder Bay and Rainy River during the year ended 31st December, 1906.

From whom Received.	Service.		Amount.	Total.
			$ c.	
Arpen, Rev. L	On account of taxes	....	26 08	
Adams, Cuyler	do	....	7 26	
Allan, W. A	do	....	100 38	
Allan & Fleming	do	....	70 90	
Andrew, G. H	do	....	11 42	
Allison, Mrs. Isabella	do	....	1 38	
Allison, D. W	do	....	55 55	
Armour & Mickle	do	....	2 00	
Allan, J. A	do	....	10 17	
Abell Estate, John and C. J. Agar	do	....	6 40	
Abrey, W. R	do	....	2 93	
Atikokan Iron Co.	do	....	2 10	
Austin, Mrs. W. A	do	....	2 00	
Bradford, I. H	do		80	
Bird, John P	do	....	1 72	
Bradley, H. M	do	....	1 35	
Burton, James L	do	....	1 82	
Bank of Hamilton	do	....	105 72	
Bliss, Aaron P	do	....	5 24	
Barker, F. J	do		70	
Bearinger Estate, Isaac	do	....	7 91	
Brydges, John	do		81	
Binswanger, H. P	do	....	1 60	
Bowser, Thomas	do	....	45	
Browne, J. C	do	....	1 90	
Bruce, Mary M	do	....	16 05	
Butler, Notman & Co	do	....	65	
Birdsall, W. W	do	....	6 44	
Block, D. Allan	do	....	6 08	
Brewster, C. E	do	....	3 42	
Bielli, John	do	...	80	
Bate Estate, Co.	do	....	1 70	
Best, Eugene N	do	....	5 09	
Brady, N.	do	....	2 72	
Baker, Alfred	do	....	6 26	
Brady, J. C	do	....	15 98	
Banks, G	do		25	
Barwick, Aylesworth & Co	do	....	1 60	
Brown, S. L	do	....	4 79	
Belmore Bay, G. M. Co	do	....	23 31	
Brady, G. N	do	....	6 80	
Croze, Joseph	do	....	9 36	
Crotby & Love	do	....	11 93	
Cowan, William	do	....	3 18	
Crompton, R. W	do	....	158 31	
Carmichael, A	do	....	54 20	
Craig, J. W	do	....	9 78	
Coveney, Charles A	do	....	1 05	
Campbell, A. G	do	....	4 13	
Carried forward			782 47	

No. 10.

ALGOMA TAXES REVENUE.—*Continued.*

From whom Received.	Service.	Amount.	Total.
		$ c.	
Brought forward...............	....	782 47	
Climax, G. M. & Co..................	On account of taxes	2 53	
Crofts, F. F...........................	do	7 14	
Cassils, Charles.......................	do	2 30	
Cochrane, J. B., Executor	do	5 61	
Campbell, The Messrs.................	do	1 10	
Conlon, J. and D. Kelly..............	do	24 70	
Call, Byron N.........................	do	54	
Colvin, W. W.........................	do	11 72	
Cracker Jack G. M. Co...............	do	3 36	
Chandler, H. & J.....................	do	3 08	
Cockburn, Alicia......................	do	76	
C. P. Railway.........................	do	20 70	
Crompton Corset Co...................	do	2 01	
Craig, J. W	do ...	2 15	
Canadian Copper Co	do	48 00	
Cressey, Mrs. E. H...................	do	71	
Coronation, G. M. Co.................	do	1 20	
Cummins, A. C........................	do	4 68	
Cassels, Brock & Co..................	do ...	105 40	
Campbell, Alex........................	do	4 47	
Campbell, James B....................	do	2 14	
Clarke, H. C..........................	do	2 41	
Doyle, Benjamin	do	5 00	
De Lamorandiere Dominic.............	do	16 78	
Draper, G. H..........................	do	79 37	
Dobie, J. C	do	8 68	
Donaldson, J. T.......................	do	62 37	
Dobie & Co............................	do	161 22	
Deachman, A. F.......................	do ...	1 60	
Debernardi, Jos. E....................	do	22 28	
Dunn, B. W...........................	do ..	2 02	
Danforth, Mrs. G.....................	do	1 60	
Dohman, F. Co........................	do	9 87	
Delaney, Estate Thomas...............	do	15 66	
Dominion S. & L. Co.	do ..	16 80	
Deschamps, P..........................	do	1 32	
Day, Alvin W..........................	do	80	
Evans, B. H	do	14 30	
Edwards, N. M........................	do	4 02	
Elliott & Hume........................	do	234 16	
Edmesin, A. H........................	do	37 88	
Eschweiler, F. C......................	do	68 27	
Eastwood, James......................	do	1 00	
Franklin Investment Co.	do	1 60	
Fulton, Robert M......................	do	46 00	
Frood, Thomas.....	do	47 68	
Ferguson, P............................	do	20	
Frees, H. J............................	do	1 60	
Fletcher Bros..........................	do	6 01	
Fabian, W. J	do	1 57	
Falk, C................................	do	2 00	
Fisher, J. P............................	do	7 33	
G. N. W. Mining Co..................	do	1 26	
Carried forward	....	1,919 43	

No. 10.

ALGOMA TAXES REVENUE.—*Continued*.

From whom Received.	Service.	Amount.	Total.
		$ c.	
Brought forward...............	....	1,919 43	
Graham, H. R.........................	On account of taxes	56	
Ganley, Joseph.	do	18 81	
Gage, J. Walter	do	2 43	
Gilman, C. A........................	do	1 50	
Gibbons, W. & Co., Ltd	do	48 15	
Gibbons, W. F.......................	do	29	
Gay, J. E...........................	do	6 28	
Griswold, F. A	do	40	
Goodell, R. R....	do	85	
Goetz, Alvis.......................	do	7 08	
Great West Life Ass'ce Co..............	do	1 66	
George, J...........................	do	12 73	
G. T. Pacific Railway.................	do	1 04	
Hearst, McKay & Darling	do	3 47	
Hamilton, H. C	do	13 21	
Humble, J. W.......................	do ...	23 01	
Hime, H. L. & Co	do	138 11	
Hille, Charles F	do	42 93	
Hays, W. P........	do	89	
Hamilton. C. W	do	1 73	
Hunter, J. H........................	do	6 12	
Hanson, C. L........................	do	597 47	
Healy, M.............	do	6 52	
Horlick, William....	do	2 54	
Hallinbeck, A. F	do	1 60	
Hamm, William......................	do	3 62	
Hartford G. M. & D. Co.................	do	1 10	
Hicks, Frank........................	do	1 13	
Harris, T. S	do	66	
Heck, Mrs. J. M.	do	10 63	
Hill, John H........................	do	2 76	
Hough, J. S.........................	do	1 68	
Harvey, John	do	2 62	
Harris, Harold.......................	do	3 95	
Hesson, W. H.......................	do	39 47	
Ionson, Mrs. William	do	1 60	
Independent Order Foresters...........	do	90 01	
Jenkins, Thomas.....................	do	42	
Jenkins, Charles.....................	do	8 90	
Jeffers, E. B........................	do	1 60	
Jones, Albert E......................	do	15 41	
Josselyn, H. S.......................	do	3 39	
Jenke, Russ S.......................	do	6 90	
King, Mrs. Myrtle.......	do	1 60	
Klock, R. H. & Co....................	do	3 40	
Kittermaster & Gurd..................	do	6 74	
Keating, W. J.......................	do •	23 81	
Kansas City Hay Press Co..............	do	19 45	
Kidd, J. J..........................	do	3 94	
Keefer, T. H........................	do	102 76	
Kerr, Bull & Shaw...................	do	38 09	
Krause, C. A........................	do	1 80	
Krause, C. H........................	do	2 90	
Ketchum, C. V......................	do	88	
Lougheed, A	do	26 50	
Carried forward................	....	3,286 53	

No. 10.

ALGOMA TAXES REVENUE.—*Continued*.

From whom Received.	Service.	Amount.	Total.
		$ c.	
Brought forward..................	....	3,286 53	
Leech, Harlan E........................	On account of taxes	2 00	
Lee, O'Donoghue & O'Connor	do	6 28	
Lee, W. T. J...........................	do	40	
Lamplough, F. W	do	1 44	
Lye, Henry............................	do	15 30	
Murphy & Fisher.......................	do	11 60	
Mutchmor, B. F........................	do	29 66	
Murphy, John L........................	do	31 24	
Mitchell, W. S.........................	do	75	
Morley, M. A..........................	do	1 60	
Margach. J. A..........................	do	24 71	
Morris, C. S...........................	do	30 00	
Moore, C. H...........................	do	116 96	
Maxwell, Ellen D.......................	do	1 66	
Messer, A	do	80	
Moore, Gardner S......................	do	5 49	
Mingaye, W. R........................	do	7 02	
Murdock, Mrs. F.......................	do	8 24	
Machell, H. T.........................	do	7 66	
Miller, J. W..........................	do	2 03	
McArthur, C...........................	do	2 00	
McFadden & McFadden.................	do	10 41	
McCulloch, M..........................	do	3 53	
McLennan, Allan	do	8 69	
McLennan, A. N. & Co.................	do	65 31	
McCahill, James	do	8 72	
McBrady, W...........................	do	51 36	
McKinnon, Angus	do	5 33	
McLean, F. N..........................	do	8 46	
McArthur Bros. Co.....................	do	13 40	
McGill, E..............................	do	4 94	
McKinlay, Alice S......................	do	4 08	
McNaughton, John.....................	do	90	
McLeod, A. A..........................	do	18 87	
McIntosh, Anselm	do	6 01	
McCabe, Exrs. Estate William...........	do	31 64	
McGee, J. C...........................	do	15 33	
Nelson. Arnt J.........................	do	1 00	
Nairn, J. J............................	do	12 12	
Nairn, Robert	do	3 40	
National Trust Co......................	do	24 07	
Nepigon Pulp Co.......................	do	48 50	
Nason, Joseph	do	4 80	
Northern Lights Mines Co...............	do	3 04	
O'Flynn & Goodwin	do	24 50	
Osborne, Chase S......................	do	54	
Pumpelly, R., and H. L. Smith*.........	do	99 80	
Price, Richard	do	3 27	
Perry, Frank	do	69 04	
Paterson, N. H........................	do	1 50	
Pardee & Burnham.....................	do	27 12	
Phoenix, G. M. Co.....................	do	11 82	
Partington, J. A.	do	2 37	
Plummer, H...........................	do	2,494 81	
Carried forward..................	....	6,681 85	

No. 10.

ALGOMA TAXES REVENUE.—*Continued.*

From whom Received.	Service.	Amount.	Total.
		$ c.	
Brought forward..............................	....	6,681 85	
Princess G. M. Co............................	On account of taxes	13 77	
Proctor, J. A., and W. Harty............	do	19 92	
Paine, F. W..............................	do	2 52	
Parsons, G. O.........................	do	1 71	
Palmer, Mrs. J. C.......................	do	2 51	
Page, John W. B..........................	do	10	
Petrie, A. B	do	2 10	
Parsons, Elizabeth	do	80	
Piper, E. S..............................	do	1 60	
Priester, William ...	do	6 42	
Peden, William...	do	97	
Perley, G. H............................	do	6 61	
Queen of the Lakes G. M. & D. Co.....	do	9 79	
Quebec Bank	do	6 63	
Quackenbush, Mrs. V..................	do	2 77	
Ross, Walter.............................	do	4 17	
Robinson, William...	do	16 05	
Rowland, P. T.......................	do	10 99	
Reading Mining Co	do	13 18	
Richardson, G. H.....................	do	4 29	
Richardson & Day	do	125 87	
Roach, W. J.............................	do	21 27	
Rogers, F	do	1 74	
Rowell, Reid & Co.....................	do	27 27	
Rowell, N. W., Trustee..................	do	14 79	
Ripley, M. T..........................	do	6 78	
Ross, A. G.............................	do	1 75	
Reynolds, F. R	do	70	
Riopelle, Joseph......................	do	85	
Reikel, J. G	do	1 60	
Robinson, G. H......................	do	2 33	
Reesor, H. A	do	7 74	
Rat Portage M. & D. Co.............	do	4 29	
Ramage, A. T	do	1 35	
Rogers, Fred. W......................	do	25 09	
Ray, Charles A	do	8 50	
Roedel, John and Theo. Frytag..........	do	6 80	
Roberts, D. E.........................	do	2 45	
Ritchie, C. H.........................	do	355 64	
St. Anthony G. M. Co.................	do	7 93	
Schneidler, A........................	do	1 89	
Sweeney, J. M........................	do	65	
Smith, F. H..........................	do	80	
Spencer, H. R	do	3 28	
Stinson, John	do	1 43	
Shaw, Geo. A.........................	do	6 38	
Sangster, F. H........................	do	3 48	
Seegmiller, M	do	48 26	
Scranton, G. G.......................	do	13 49	
Smith, A. H..........................	do	2 17	
Sibley, H. F....	do	16 79	
Scott, J. C..........................	do	1 00	
Savage, J. M...:	do ..	1 63	
Seuter John..........................	do	8 99	
Carried forward..................	....	7,543 73	

No. 10.

ALGOMA TAXES REVENUE.—*Continued*.

From whom Received.	Service.	Amount.	Total.
		$ c.	$ c.
Brought forward.....................	....	7,543 73	
Sloan, H. C............................	On account of taxes	36	
Sanford, W. E. Mfg. Co	do	2 19	
Stephens, Henry........................	do	11 17	
Smith, Rae & Greer.....................	do	6 40	
Sunderland, C. H.......................	do ....,	5 10	
Saltonstall, F. G	do	9 56	
Stinson, John..........................	do	03	
Silver Lake Mining Co	do	7 63	
Smith. A. H............................	do	4 94	
Spragge, A.............................	do	40	
Southard & Southard....................	do	1 05	
Thorpe, R. J...........................	do	50	
Turner, W.............................	do	24 69	
Totten, O. Dr.........................	do	645 66	
Tough, R. J	do	9 60	
Thompson, A. J	do	159 34	
Thurston, C. B	do	1 60	
Tupper, Galt & Co..	do	4 82	
Tanbush, H. L..........................	do	6 57	
Torrance, Mrs. C. M	do	3 81	
Thomas, A. J..........................	do	43	
Tisdale, D.............................	do	15 44	
Taylor Copper Mines Co.................	do	39 33	
Turner, William.......................	do	225 25	
Upham, N. J. & Co	do	2 60	
Wood, William.........................	do	12 00	
Watzke, Anton	do	66	
Weir, W. A	do	37 77	
Washington & Beasley..................	do	55	
White, J. L	do	4 56	
Webber, R. H	do	4 36	
Williams, T. E......	do	31 05	
Whittaker, William....................	do	50	
Wiegand, Thomas.......................	do	39 25	
Weadock, Purcell & Weadock	do	17 62	
Williams, H...........................	do	25 80	
Wideman, A. E.........................	do	3 20	
Walton, C. W	do	1 90	
Wirth, Max	do	90	
Wright, A. W	do	1 60	
Walker, J. M..........................	do	3 72	
Weir, Chas	do	7 25	
Walsh, M	do	1 60	
Wright, W. C	do	71	
Wells, W. H...........................	do	7 91	
Welch, Henry W	do . ..	10 93	
Young, A. H	do	3 29	
Yawkey, W. H	do	150 00	
		————	9,099 33

No· 11.

Statement of Revenue received on account of Law Stamps during the year ended 31st December, 1906.

County.	Distributor.	Amount.
		$ c.
Brant	A. J. Wilkes	1,361 10
Bruce	Thos. Dixon	812 00
Carleton	J. A. Ritchie	2,025 00
Dufferin	T. Bowles	376 25
Elgin	Jno. Farley	1,106 00
Essex	Francis Cleary	960 00
Frontenac	J. L. Whiting	1,500 00
Grey	Jno. Armstrong	875 00
Haldimand	J. A. Murphy	300 00
Hastings	P. J. M. Anderson	2,045 00
Huron	D. McDonald	2,285 00
Halton	W. J. Dick	557 00
Kent	Jas. Holmes	1,117 00
Lambton	J. P. Bucke	2,156 25
Lanark	W. P. McEwen	550 00
Lennox and Addington	H. M. Deroche	320 00
Leeds and Grenville	O. K. Frazer	1,439 00
Lincoln	M. Brennan	560 00
Middlesex	J. B. McKillop	1,900 00
Northumberland and Durham	W. F. Kerr	2,115 00
Norfolk	C. C. Rapelji	400 00
Ontario	J. E. Farewell	450 00
Oxford	F. R. Ball	950 00
Peterborough	R. E. Wood	650 00
Prescott and Russell	J. Belanger	300 00
Prince Edward	J. R. Brown	291 50
Peel	W. H. McFadden	400 00
Perth	G. F. McPherson	2,100 00
Renfrew	J. R. Metcalfe	650 00
Simcoe	J. R. Cotter	2,020 00
Stormont, Dundas and Glengary	Jas. Dingwall	900 00
Victoria	J. R. McNeillie	300 00
Waterloo	M. H. Bowlby	845 00
Welland	T. D. Cowper	862 00
Wellington	H. W. Peterson	1,300 00
Wentworth	S. F. Washington	3,776 50
York	Jas. McMahon	27,000 00
Toronto	Joseph Tait	15,350 00
Algoma District	S. A Marks	380 00
Manitoulin "	A. G. Murray	80 00
Muskoka "	Thos. Johnson	250 00
Nipissing "	A. G. Browning	1,482 00
Parry Sound "	E. Jordan	234 00
Rainy River · "	J. W. Humble	180 00
Thunder Bay "	A. W. Thompson	435 00
		85,945 60

No. 12.

STATEMENT OF SUCCESSION DUTY FOR THE YEAR ENDED 31st DECEMBER, 1906

County and Estate.	$ c.	$ c.
BRANT—		
E. R. Cockshutt........................	2,715 94	
George Foster.....................	2,938 78	
M. P. Harris.........................	1,576 54	
J. B. Henderson.....................	10,094 23	
L. R. Latshaw.....	1,016 25	
Wilson Robertson...................	184 29	
		18,526 03
BRUCE—		
Andrew Griffith	307 20	
Robert Young	416 20	
		723 40
CARLETON—		
H. F. Brading.....................	500 00	
John Caldwell	646 72	
Peter Dunne	20 00	
F. E. W. Eliot.....................	13,272 49	
E. M. Fowler.....................	9,995 00	
C. Gairdner	69 40	
Neil McDiarmid.....................	593 35	
S. J. Major.....................	1,692 12	
James Pyper.....................	603 42	
R. J. H. Reiffenstein.................	481 52	
Robert Sedgewick..................	132 00	
H. A. Wicksteed	1,250 85	
		29,256 87
DUFFERIN—		
H. Ferns.........................	....	117 23
ELGIN—		
Leonard Cline	100 00	
John Rundle	25 00	
R. Simmonds.....................	812 37	
R. J. Wilson.....................	121 51	
John Wise.....................	150 00	
		1,208 88
ESSEX—		
J. H. Beattie.....................	229 86	
Jane E. Benjamin	482 82	
L. R. Medbury.....................	7,240 00	
A. W. Nelson.....................	1,759 97	
Mary Scotten	318 70	
		10,031 35
FRONTENAC—		
N. M. Auchinvole..................	638 49	
Edwin Chown.....................	50 00	
D. C. Hickey.....................	27 80	
J. B. McIver..:...................	376 71	
O. S. Strange.....................	458 25	
Robert Waddell....................	495 93	
		2,047 18
GREY—		
Thomas Campbell..................	2,113 70	
W. J. Earley.....................	53 30	
Henry Parker.....................	2,930 64	
		5,097 64
Carried forward	....	67,008 58

No. 12.

STATEMENT OF SUCCESSION DUTY, 1906.—*Continued.*

County and Estate.	$ c.	$ c.
Brought forward	....	67,008 58
HALDIMAND—		
Andrew Murray	....	1,044 18
HALTON—		
Amando Baxter......	47 80	
J. W. Bowes	2,200 00	
		2,247 80
HASTINGS—		
C. L. Bell...	3,801 83	
W. B. Curry	28 88	
E. J. Johnson..	560 38	
E. D. O'Flynn...	73 85	
H. P. O'Horo	1,019 25	
E. W. Rathbun...	10,756 13	
		16,240 32
HURON—		
Neil McGill...	964 55	
John Scott...	119 79	
		1,084 34
KENT—		
Joseph Coatsworth...	539 75	
Alex. Cumming...	607 51	
S. J. Johnston	700 00	
James McKinlay..	42 40	
James Scarlett	527 51	
John Serson	621 11	
		3,038 28
LAMBTON—		
Wm. Kells...	276 00	
Robert McKenzie	808 29	
J. S. Scott...	634 74	
David Thom...	119 38	
		1,838 41
LANARK—		
Thomas Arthur..	501 12	
A. C. Burgess...........	2,306 75	
J. M. Moag...	558 36	
James Moir..	540 63	
		3,906 86
LEEDS AND GRENVILLE—		
Wm. Bulloch....................................	1,935 88	
C. W. Dickinson	412 64	
Janet Forgie...	1,153 44	
J. N. Poole	100 00	
		3,601 96
LENNOX AND ADDINGTON—		
F. H. Amey..	700 00	
T. W. Martin..	369 18	
D. H. Miller	840 00	
		1,909 18
LINCOLN—		
J. A. Carroll	958 39	
O. Collver...	34 39	
J. McCalla.........	110 00	
T. R. Merritt	29,000 00	30,102 78
Carried Forward..		132,022 69

9* P.A.

No. 12.

STATEMENT OF SUCCESSION DUTY, 1906.—*Continued.*

County and Estate.	$ c.	$ c.
Brought forward	....	132,022 69
MIDDLESEX—		
C. Alexander............................	164 16	
A. W. Bailey...........................	2.424 24	
H. C. Burrows..........................	742 30	
Joseph Campbell........................	438 07	
Malcolm Campbell.......................	470 01	
A. D. Gillies...........................	58 00	
John Gilmour...........................	259 46	
Wm. McDonough........................	3,898 62	
P. McPhillips...........................	603 31	
M. A. Manson...........................	2,138 91	
C. A. Morley...........................	315 74	
S. S. Ogden	57 90	
T. G. Pulford...........................	1,164 08	
S. Stewart	4,640 14	
N. Tackaberry..........................	1,146 00	
M. Timmis.............................	82 33	
Hugh Wiley	1,386 70	
		19,989 97
NORFOLK—		
E. G. Charlton	....	5.764 09
NORTHUMBERLAND AND DURHAM—		
Thomas Bassett.........................	15 11	
G. M. Clark............................	855 65	
Mary Giles	816 07	
Thomas Hoar...........................	16 24	
Franklin House.........................	2,980 33	
G. S. Miller............................	1,531 78	
A. F. Wallbridge.......................	1,231 13	
H. J. D. Williams	4,000 00	
		11,446 31
ONTARIO—		
James Coombe..........................	842 50	
F. Gardineer	50 00	
Jeremiah Long..........................	1,306 62	
		2,199 12
OXFORD—		
James Duffy............................	521 74	
George Gordon	518 78	
Ruth Hadcock..........................	85 75	
E. J. Hall.............................	202 10	
James Sutherland.....	12,655 51	
E. D. Tillson..........................	2,166 53	
		16,150 41
PEEL—		
J. F. Neelands..........................	317 20	
George Russell..........................	444 60	
		761 80
PERTH—		
R. Ballantyne..........................	768 30	
Martha Hall............................	172 88	
W. V. Hutton..........................	3,796 49	
Robert Knott...........................	126 10	
	4,863 77	
Carried forward	....	188,334 39

No. 12.

STATEMENT OF SUCCESSION DUTY, 1906.—*Continued.*

County and Estate.	$ c.	$ c.
Brought forward	....	188,334 39
PERTH— *Continued.*	4,863 77	
F. Strasser............................	200 00	
Thos. Wood	681 30	
		5,745 07
PETERBORO—		
J. C. Campbell	650 23	
Edward Cooney	375 90	
A. C. Dunlop...........................	3,185 28	
Wm. Walsh	250 00	
		4,461 41
PRESCOTT AND RUSSELL—		
C. H. Cushing	255 38	
John Hunter.............................	1,445 94	
G. A. McBean..........................	131 97	
Wm. McDermid...........................	824 88	
M. A. Millar............................	976 38	
		3,634 55
PRINCE EDWARD—		
H. M. D. Low.........................	549 40	
Davidson Macdonald	300 00	
		849 40
RAINY RIVER—		
E. B. Kenrick.........................	....	75 50
RENFREW—		
Peter Comrie	12 00	
Richard Dulmage	5,015 44	
Mary Lacey............................	15 00	
C. McLachlin...........................	19,255 55	
Mary Moles............................	29 00	
A. Smallfield...........................	23 65	
		24,350 64
SIMCOE—		
Thos. Black	1,741 00	
James Johnson	616 00	
W. P. Laverock.........................	421 85	
		2,778 85
STORMONT, DUNDAS AND GLENGARRY—		
E. Gibson	861 97	
J. Hesson.............................	350 00	
A. McArthur	1,620 00	
Wm. McWalters	335 28	
A. Stewart............................	8 21	
		3,175 46
THUNDER BAY—		
A. Crysler............................	....	8 17
VICTORIA—		
Joseph Beckett	832 18	
B. J. Spurr............................	79· 68	
		911 86
WATERLOO—		
James Bailey	47 75	
M. A. Clark	15 25	....
	63 00	
Carried forward	....	234,325 30

No. 12.

STATEMENT OF SUCCESSION DUTY, 1906.--*Continued.*

County and Estate.	$ c.	$ c.
Brought forward	63 00	234,325 30
WATERLOO—*Continued*		
Adam Doering	330 00	
Samuel Kingsburgh	548 90	
		941 90
WELLAND--		
Peter Barrick	687 08	
C. F. Dunbar	722 21	
John McDonagh	50 00	
J. C. M. F. McRae	500 05	
		1,959 34
WELLINGTON—		
R. M. Boswell	1,827 52	
John Davidson	40 00	
E. F. Heath	131 48	
A. A. MacDonald	300 00	
		2,299 00
WENTWORTH—		
Elizabeth Brown	894 58	
H. A. Brown	8,485 70	
Elizabeth Carse	95 50	
Michael Doran	1,032 45	
Robert Ferris	600 00	
A. W. H. Gibb	47 82	
W. H. Gillard	36 52	
J. S. Grafton	1,325 54	
E. E. E Gourlay	21 14	
W. J. Harris	3,287 75	
A. T. Hazell	211 26	
Agnes Irvine	300 00	
H J. Long	1,210 11	
Henry McLaren	5,769 53	
Margaret McCall	25 16	
A, A. Sawyer	80 27	
Jacob Smith	562 50	
G. B. Spriggs	4,749 28	
J. W. Sutherland	1,061 77	
T. C. Watkins	227 02	
J. D. Wilson	1,999 38	
		32,023 28
YORK—		
Thos. Alison	1,738 80	
James Allan	712 45	
W. N. Anderson	622 38	
J. A. Angus	.1 00	
John Badgerow	50 00	
T. D. Bell	235 90	
John Bertram	10,000 00	
Simon Blight	311 88	
Alex. Brown	2,925 00	
M. Brummitt	1,745 47	
James Butt	626 91	
Henry Cawthra	520 60	
Margaret Cox	29,112 21	
James Crane	1,650 00	
James Crocker	13,750 00	
	64,002 60	
Carried Forward		271,548 82

No. 12.

STATEMENT OF SUCCESSION DUTY, 1906.—*Continued.*

County and Estate.	$	c.	$	c.
Brought forward...............................			271,548	82
YORK—*Continued*................................	64,002	60		
Emma Davies..................................	10,000	00		
J. M. Douglas................................	512	92		
Michael Dwyer	589	90		
George Evans.................................	2,495	74		
Wm. Farley	143	65		
Jesse H. Farwell.............................	208	78		
Wm. Faulkner.................................	300	00		
Edson Fitch	586	93		
John Foote	2,032	00		
C. Fullerton	1,138	32		
Alfred Gibb..................................	13	25		
C. H. Gooderham.............................	8,397	95		
George Gooderham............................	519,676	43		
Margaret Hartney............................	35	00		
Thos. Hetherington	5,029	10		
L. Heyden	6,404	70		
G. W. Hives..................................	501	28		
John Irwin...................................	25	20		
Sarah Jaffray	1,867	19		
S. P. Jarvis	970	60		
Wm. Johnston.................................	1,131	75		
Mary Keliher.................................	1,387	32		
J. H. Kerr	182	65		
G. W. Kiely..................................	2,000	00		
E. A. King	1,881	80		
Edouard Lacroix..............................	515	12		
Duncan Laurie	550	60		
Mary Lloyd	48	10		
C. E. S. Major...............................	310	37		
John Miller..................................	740	80		
F. J. Munro	929	81		
J. W. Murray.................................	146	87		
J. A. Nesbitt................................	1,954	05		
R. W. Norman.................................	2,222	15		
E. C. Orkney	6,933	38		
M. McD. Paxton	579	56		
James H. Peck................................	1,025	45		
Mary Percy...................................	617	43		
Henry Phillips...............................	279	36		
Margaret Pollock.............................	419	35		
W. B. Rankine................................	1,210	20		
Barbara Reford	144	06		
Sarah Robinson...............................	3,061	35		
A. E. Ross...................................	35,767	22		
Robinson Sawer...............................	480	23		
Sarah Seymour................................	7	32		
H. F. Sharpe.................................	371	12		
F. C. Sibbald	1,507	35		
John Simons..................................	90	27		
Wm. Spry.....................................	1,497	37		
T. S. Stayner	9,678	69		
John Swain...................................	10	00		
J. H. Tait	703	48		
Robert Thomson	5,154	87		
	708,470	99		
Carried Forward............................			271,548	82

No. 12.

STATEMENT OF SUCCESSION DUTY, 1906.—*Concluded*.

County and Estate.	$ c.	$ c.
Brought forward.................................	....	271,548 82
YORK—*Continued*..	708,470 99	
S. M. Toy	52 67	
T. J. Tracy	600 37	
David Walker...	4,483 22	
Joseph Widdifield......................................	4,344 51	
G. H. Winter...	23 18	
T. R. Wood........	33,954 80	
W. W. Wood	239 05	
J. J. Woodhouse.......................................	23 10	
C. F. Worthington	2,222 53	
		754,414 42
Refunds.		1,025,963 24
H. C. Biggar (Welland) (1905).........................	75 00	
L. Bolster (York) (1904)	450 00	
E. Fenlon (Simcoe) (1905).............................	478 59	
Wm. Fleming (York) (1905)...........................	419 80	
Wm. Graham (Waterloo) (1905)........................	2,235 85	
J. D. Ham (Lennox and Addington) (1905)	80 81	
H. H. Harris (Carleton) (1900)	3,000 00	
Wm. Hendra (Middlesex) (1905)	108 31	
A. S. Irving (York) (1904)............................	2,389 52	
A. McAllister (N. and D.) (1902)......................	46 31	
E. McWhinnie (York) (1905)..........................	99 38	
R. Shaw Wood (Middlesex) (1905)	3,027 50	
John Shields (York) (1898)..........................	203 56	
W. A. Sutherland (Victoria) (1905)........	315 15	
R. H. Warden (York) (1905)..........................	970 22	
		13,900 00
Funds deposited in lieu of Bond for payment of Succession Duty.		1,012,063 24
BRUCE—		
Alex. Patton	1,000 00	
PEEL—		
Alex. Lamont...	350 00	
WELLINGTON—		
S. E. Wadel	400 00	
WENTWORTH—		
H. E. Davis	1,100 00	
YORK—		
M. I. Ryan...	800 00	
		3,650 00
		1,015,713 24

No. 13.

STATEMENT OF REVENUE.

Under 62 Vic. Cap. 8 ; 63 Vic. Cap. 6 ; 6 Edwd. VII, Cap. 9.

From whom received.	———	$ c.	$ c.
Life Insurance Cos....	Ætna Life Insurance Co.................	1,546 11	
	Canada Life Assurance Co................	12,770 44	
	Confederation Life Association	6,524 53	
	Commercial Union Assurance Co...........	57 54	
	Continental Life Insurance Co.............	1,216 50	
	Crown Life Insurance Co.................	454 78	
	Dominion Life Assurance Co.............	1,519 01	
	Equitable Life Assurance Society of the U.S.	1,973 75	
	Edinburgh Life Assurance Co.............	107 48	
	Excelsior Life Insurance Co..............	1,482 41	
	Federal Life Assurance Co................	2,645 36	
	Great West Life Assurance Co............	1,808 43	
	Home Life Association of Canada..........	888 99	
	Imperial Life Assurance Co. of Canada	3,527 45	
	London and Lancashire Life Assurance Co..	1,189 46	
	London Life Insurance Co................	2,581 58	
	Liverpool & London & Globe Insurance Co.	19 70	
	Mutual Reserve Fund Life Association	620 03	
	Mutual Life Insurance Co. of New York	2,384 71	
	Mutual Life Assurance Co. of Canada......	8,835 99	
	Manufacturers' Life Insurance Co..........	5,131 72	
	Metropolitan Life Insurance Co............	5,053 71	
	National Life Assurance Co. of Canada	635 14	
	Northern Life Assurance Co. of Canada.....	· 1,031 23	
	North British & Mercantile Insurance Co ..	79 40	
	New York Life Insurance Co.............	4,099 87	
	North American Life Assurance Co........	6,509 46	
	Pelican & British Empire Life Office	656 78	
	Provident Savings Life Assurance Society of		
	New York	342 05	
	Royal Victoria Life Insurance Co..........	358 58	
	Royal Insurance Co......................	96 90	
	Sovereign Life Insurance Co. of Canada.....	408 67	
	Sun Life Assurance Co. of Canada	6,796 12	
	Star Life Assurance Society	183 85	
	Standard Life Assurance Society...........	3,540 15	
	Scottish Amicable Life Assurance Co.......	27 82	
	Travellers' Insurance Co. of Hartford, Conn.	1,309 66	
	United States Life Insurance Co...........	217 19	
	Union Mutual Life Insurance Co	297 32	
	Union Life Ansurance Co. of Toronto......	655 11	
	State Life Insurance Co..................	158 45	
			89,743 43
Fire Insurance Cos...	Ætna Insurance Co. of Hartford	530 19	
	Alliance Assurance Co	428 21	
	Atlas Assurance Co......................	1,040 46	
	Anglo-American Fire Insurance Co.........	1,522 80	
	British American Assurance Co............	1,917 20	
	Canadian Fire Insurance Co..............	332 92	
	Caledonian Insurance Co.................	854 05	
	Commercial Union Assurance Co	1,277 86	
	Connecticut Fire Insurance Co............	187 88	
	Equity Fire Insurance Co	689 38	
	German-American Fire Insurance Co.......	196 85	
	Carried forward.....................	8,977 80	89,743 43

No. 13.

STATEMENT OF REVENUE.— *Continued.*

Under 62 Vic. Cap. 8 ; 63 Vic. Cap. 6 ; 6 Edwd. VII Cap. 9.

From whom received.	——	$ c.	$ c.
	Brought forward	8,977 80	89,743 43
Fire Insurance Co's.. (*Continued*).	Guardian Fire & Life Assurance Co.........	1,151 56	
	Hartford Fire Insurance Co...............	1,384 18	
	Home Insurance Co	1,110 89	
	Insurance Co. of North America...........	709 70	
	London & Lancashire Fire Insurance Co....	870 38	
	London Assurance Corporation...:........	320 99	
	London Mutual Fire Insurance Co.........	1,396 03	
	Law Union & Crown Insurance Co.........	219 52	
	Liverpool & London & Globe Insurance Co..	2,480 84	
	Mercantile Fire Insurance Co	456 12	
	Manitoba Fire Insurance Co...............	400 77	
	Montreal-Canada Fire Assurance	469 68	
	Norwich Union Fire Insurance Society......	1,521 36	
	North British & Mercantile Insurance Co..	1,643 33	
	Northern Assurance Co...................	1,397 96	
	Ottawa Fire Insurance Co................	519 13	
	Phenix Insurance Co. of Brooklyn, N.Y....	335 45	
	Phœnix Assurance Co. of London	1,604 46	
	Phœnix Insurance Co. of Hartford, Conn....	292 .17	
	Queen Insurance Co. of America...........	1,347 65	
	Quebec Fire Insurance Co	201 84	
	Royal Insurance Co	3,270 78	
	Scottish Union & National Insurance Co	527 18	
	Sun Insurance Office.....................	769 91	
	Union Assurance Society of London	923 43	
	Western Assurance Co	2,304 45	
	Rochester German Fire Insurance Co......	7 24	36,614 80
Sundry Insurance Cos paying also an assessment under the Ontario Insurance Co's Act......	Central Life Insurance Co	186 82	
	Canadian Casualty & Boiler Insurance Co...	203 72	
	Economical Mutual Fire Insurance Co. of Berlin................................	269 94	
	Fire Insurance Exchange Corporation.......	114 60	
	Gore District Mutual Fire Insurance Co.....	207 73	
	Hand in Hand Insurance Co..............	191 90	
	Merchants' Fire Insurance Co.............	336 01	
	Metropolitan Fire Insurance Co	390 62	
	Millers' & Manufacturers' Insurance	99 05	
	Monarch Cash Mutual Fire Insurance Co....	447 25	
	Perth Mutual Fire Insurance Co...........	202 42	
	Queen City Fire Insurance Co.............	265 54	
	Standard Fire Insurance Co...............	695 16	
	Traders Fire Insurance Co................	310 75	
	Toronto Life Insurance Co...............	716 58	
	Waterloo Mutual Fire Insurance Co.......	292 63	
	Wellington Mutual Fire Insurance Co......	268 78	
	York Mutual Fire Insurance Co...........	360 63	
	Equity Life Insurance Co	111 87	
	Independent Fire Insurance Co............	265 62	
	Independent C. M. Fire Insurance Co.....	207 19	6,144 81
	Carried forward		132,503 04

No· 13.

STATEMENT OF REVENUE.—*Continued.*

Under 62 Vic. Cap. 8 ; 63 Vic. Cap. 6 ; 6 Edwd. VII. Cap. 9.

From whom received.	—	$ c.	$ c.
	Brought forward......................		132,503 04
Miscellaneous........	American Surety Co. of New York........	32 54	
	Accident and Guarantee Co. of Canada.....	76 50	
	Boiler Inspection and Insurance Co. of Can..	' 129 82	
	British and Foreign Marine Insurance Co...	12 11	
	Canada Accident Assurance Co...........	156 52	
	Canadian Railway Accident Insurance Co...	713 11	
	Dominion Plate Glass Insurance Co........	73 21	
	Dominion of Canada Guarantee and Accident Insurance Co........................	608 98	
	Dominion Guarantee Co..................	27 08	
	Employers Liability Assurance Corporation.	953 94	
	Empire Accident and Surety Co............	81 57	
	Fidelity and Casualty Co. of New York....	23 72	
	Fireman's Fund Insurance Co..............	80 22	
	Guarantee Co of North America...........	73 00	
	Imperial Guarantee and Accident Insurance Co......	75 67	
	International Fidelity Insurance Co........	9 33	
	London Guarantee and Accident Co......	457 55	
	Lloyds Plate Glass Insurance Co...........	186 30	
	Mannheim Insurance Co	46 49	
	Maryland Casualty Co....................	114 01	
	New York Plate Glass Insurance Co	25 12	
	Ontario Accident Insurance Co............	722 16	
	Ocean Accident and Guarantee Corporation.	519 66	
	Reliance Marine Insurance Co.............	4 48	
	Railway Passengers Assurance Co	74 84	
	Travellers' Insurance Co. of Hartford.......	367 22	
	Thames and Mersea Marine Insurance Co...	96 17	
	Union Marine Insurance Co..............	36 17	
	United States Fidelity & Guarantee Co.....	110 23	
			5,887 72
Loan Companies......	Acme Loan & Savings Co..................	119 60	
	Agricultural Savings & Loan Co	410 15	
	British Canadian Loan & Investment Co....	259 35	
	British Mortgage Loan Co. of Ontario......	290 55	
	Brockville Loan & Savings Co.............	131 30	
	Canada Landed & National Investment Co...	652 60	
	Canada Permanent Mortgage Corporation...	3,900 00	
	Canadian Birkbeck Investment & Savings Co.	643 50	
	Canadian Savings Loan & Building Association..................................	373 75	
	Central Canada Loan & Savings Co..........	975 00	
	Chatham Loan & Savings Co...............	200 20	
	Colonial Investment & Loan Co............	1,582 75	
	Credit Foncier Franco Canadien for Ontario.	632 23	
	Crown Savings & Loan Co.................	129 35	
	Dyment Securities, Loan & Savings Co......	423 80	
	Dominion Permanent Loan Co.............	698 10	
	Dominion Savings & Investment Society.....	607 75	
		12,029 98	
	Carried Forward..........................		138,390 76

No. 13.

STATEMENT OF REVENUE.—*Continued.*

Under 62 Vic. Cap. 8 ; 63 Vic. Cap. 6 ; 6 Edwd. VII., Cap. 9.¶

From whom received.	——	$ c.	$ c.
	Brought forward......................	12,029 98	138,390 76
Loan Companies.....	East Lambton Farmers' Loan & Savings Co..	117 00	
	Essex County Savings & Loan Co...........	65 00	
	Frontenac Loan & Investment Society	130 00	
	Grey & Bruce Loan Co....................	169 00	
	Guelph & Ontario Investment & Savings Society....................:.........	288 60	
	Hamilton Mutual Building Society	65 00	
	Hamilton Provident & Loan Society	715 00	
	Home Savings & Loan Co...........	130 00	
	Huron & Erie Loan & Savings Co..........	1,235 00	
	Huron & Lambton Loan & Savings Co......	244 55	
	Imperial Loan & Investment Co...........	478 40	
	Industrial Mortgage & Savings Co..........	290 55	
	Lambton Loan & Investment Co...........	325 00	
	Landed Banking & Loan Co...............	455 00	
	London & Canadian Loan & Agency Co.....	650 00	
	London Loan & Savings Co................	442 00	
	Midland Loan & Savings Co.......	234 00	
	North British Canadian Investment Co.....	250 90	
	Ontario Loan & Debenture Co.............	780 00	
	Ontario Loan & Savings Co............... .'	195 00	
	Owen Sound Building & Savings Society....	65 00	
	Oxford Permanent Loan & Savings Co......	179 40	
	People's Building & Loan Association......	200 20	
	Provident Investment Co.................	65 00	
	Real Estate Loan Co. of Canada	243 10	
	Reliance Loan & Savings Co. of Ontario.....	633 75	
	Royal Loan & Savings Co................	325 00	
	Security Loan & Savings Co..............	178 75	
	Simcoe Loan & Savings Co....	68 90	
	Southern Loan & Savings Co..............	586 30	
	Standard Loan Co........................	308 75	
	Stratford Building & Savings Society.......	86 45	
	Sun & Hastings Savings & Loan Co........	533 65	
	Toronto Mortgage Co.....................	471 25	
	Toronto Savings & Loan Co..............	650 00	
	Victoria Loan & Savings Co..............	92 95	
	Walkerville Land & Building Co..........	325 00	
	Scottish-American Investment Co..........	108 55	
	Scottish-Ontario & Manitoba Land Co......	109 85	
	North of Scotland Canadian Mortgage Co....	· 474 50	
	Trust and Loan Co. of Canada	136 50	
	Dovercourt Land, Building & Savings Co....	65 00	
			25,197 83
Banks..............	Bank of British North America.............	3,200 00	
	Canadian Bank of Commerce.............	4,350 00	
	Crown Bank	1,187 28	
	Dominion Bank ....•.........	3,075 00	
	Banque d'Hochelaga......................	1,100 00	
	Imperial Bank of Canada	3,275 00	
	Merchants Bank of Canada...........	4,650 00	
	Carried forward	20,837 28	163,588 59

No. 13.

STATEMENT OF REVENUE.—*Continued.*

Under 62 Vic. Cap. 8 ; 63 Vic. Cap. 6 ; 6 Edwd. VII, Cap. 9.

From whom received.	——	$ c.	$ c.
	Brought forword......................	20,837 28	163,588 59
	Metropolitan Bank	1,450 00	
	Bank of Montreal	3,775 00	
	Molsons Bank	3,250 00	
	Banque Nationale	850 00	
	Bank of Nova Scotia..................... ..	2,375 00	
	Ontario Bank	2,175 00	
	Bank of Ottawa	3,200 00	
	Quebec Bank.............................	1,450 00	
	Royal Bank of Canada	1,675 00	
	Standard Bank...........................	1,875 00	
	Sovereign Bank of Canada.................	2,842 32	
	Traders Bank of Canada	3,750 00	
	Bank of Toronto..........................	3,400 00	
	Union Bank of Canada....................	3,250 00	
	Western Bank of Canada.................	1,000 00	
	Bank of Hamilton	3,350 00	
			60,504 60
Trusts Companies	National Trust Co. of Ontario	1,335 00	
	Imperial Trust Co. of Canada..............	250 00	
	London & Western Trusts Corporation......	315 00	
	Toronto General Trusts Corporation........	1,335 00	
	Trusts & Guarantee Co....................	900 00	
	Canada Trust Co..........................	315 00	
	Union Trust Co...........................	1,810 00	
	Royal Trust Co...........................	510 00	
			6,770 00
Street Railways	Brantford Street Pailway Co. for 1905.......	154 40	
	Guelph Radial Railway Co.................	120 00	
	Galt, Preston & Hespeler Street Railway Co.	92 00	
	Hamilton, Grimsby & Beamsville Electric Railway...............................	97 50	
	Hamilton Street Railway Co................	405 54	
	Hamilton & Dundas Street Railway Co......	42 42	
	Hamilton Radial Electric Railway..........	136 44	
	International Railway Co..................	341 90	
	Kingston, Portsmouth & Cataraqui Electric Railway........	120 21	
	London Street Railway Co.................	394 30	
	Oshawa Railway Co.......................	67 50	
	Ottawa Electric Street Railway Co.........	887 40	
	Preston & Berlin Street Railway Co........	103 75	
	Port Dalhousie, St. Catharines & Thorold Electric Railway Co.....................	92 00	
	Sandwich, Windsor & Amherstburg Railway Co......................................	300 00	
	Toronto Railway Co......................	5,114 44	
	Toronto & York Radial Railway Co........	396 60	
	Niagara Falls, Wesley Park & Clifton Tramway Co...............................	78 10	
			8,944 50
	Carried forward.......................		239,807 69

No. 13.

STATEMENT OF REVENUE.—*Concluded*

Under 62 Vic., Cap. 8 ; 63 Vic., Cap. 6 ; 6 Edw. VII., Cap, 9.

From whom received.		$ c.	$ c.
	Brought forward.....................		239,807 69
Railways	Bay of Quinte Railway......	1,405 12	
	Brockville, Westport & Northwestern Railway	675 00	
	do for 1905	675 00	
	Canada Atlantic Railway...................	20,840 08	
	Canadian Pacific Railway	124,686 84	
	Canadian Northern Railway...............	14,140 00	
	Canada Southern Railway.................	25,940 80	
	Central Ontario Railway..................	2,019 00	
	Grand Trunk Railway	168,535 60	
	Kingston & Pembroke Railway.............	1,546 50	
	Lake Erie & Detroit River Railway	13,348 20	
	Niagara, St. Catharines & Toronto Railway..	285 00	
	Nosbonsing & Nipissing Railway...........	82 50	
	Ottawa & New York Railway..............	825 00	
	Thousand Islands Railway	94 95	
	Toronto, Hamilton & Buffalo Railway.......	1,265 25	
			376,364 84
Gas and Electric Light Cos.	Brantford Gas Co., Limited................	61 40	
	Brantford Electric & Operating Co., Limited.	131 30	
	City Gas Co. of London...................	240 00	
	Consumers' Gas Co. Toronto................	2,250 00	
	Dundas Electric Co.................. ..	60	
	Hamilton Electric Light & Power Co.......	250 00	
	Hamilton Gas Light Co...................	300 00	
	Incandescent Light Co. of Toronto.........	619 35	
	London Electric Co., Limited..............	392 50	
	Lincoln Light & Power Co.................	150 00	
	Ottawa Electric Co.......................	994 00	
	Ottawa Gas Co........................	453 20	
	Stratford Gas Co.......	70 26	
	Toronto Electric Light Co.................	2,991 91	
	Trenton Electric & Water Co., Limited	150 60	
	Woodstock Gas Co.........................	75 00	
	Windsor Gas Co...........................	200 00	
	Chatham Gas Co., Limited	116 22	
			9,446 34
Parlor Car Co	Pullman Palace Car Co.....................		1,748 33
Telephone Cos	Bell Telephone Co. of Canada	6,250 00	
	Haileybury, Cobalt Telephone Co..........	3 62	
	North American Telegraph Co..............	100 00	
	Temiskaming Telephone Co............ ...	7 51	
			6,361 13
Natural Gas Co.......	Provincial Natural Gas & Fuel Co. of Ontario.		3,831 42
Telegraph Cos	North American Telegraph Co.............	125 00	
	Dominion Telegraph Co....................	475 00	
	Montreal and G.N.W. Telegraph Co........	717 24	
			1,317 24
Express Cos	American Express Co......................	925 00	
	Canadian Express Co	1,800 00	
	Dominion Express Co......................	1,800 00	
	United States Express....................	800 00	
			5325 00
	Total......|............		644,201 99

No. 14.

CASUAL REVENUE.

From whom received.	Service.	$ c.	$ c.
Clerks of the Peace—			
Algoma	Fines and Forfeitures	53 08	
Brant.................	do	29 51	
Bruce.................	do	19 20	
Carleton	do	1,586 83	
Essex	do	916 80	
Frontenac............	do	31 35	
Grey.................	do	34 82	
Haldimand	do	51 15	
Halton	do	31 68	
Hastings	do	305 76	
Huron	do	217 53	
Kent.................	do	89 13	
Lanark...............	do	52 80	
Leeds and Grenville	do	576 00	
Lincoln	do	40 30	
Middlesex.............	do	675 78	
Manitoulin............	do	106 41	
Muskoka..............	do	151 68	
Nipissing.............	do	1,546 56	
Northumberland and Durham.............	do	22 08	
Ontario	do	24 00	
Oxford	do	1,954 48	
Perth	do	56 00	
Peterborough..........	do	76 80	
Renfrew	do	2 72	
Stormont, Dundas and Glengarry............	do	647 29	
Thunder Bay..........	do	4 80	
Toronto..............	do	11,574 59	
Welland	do	923 52	
Wellington............	do	96 00	
Wentworth............	do	472 00	
York	do	16 00	
C. J. Hollands, P.M.....	do	120 00	
W. A. Quibell, P.M......	do	95 00	
Andrew More, P.M......	do	2,545 00	
T. E. Williams, P.M.....	do	11 00	
E. Cruickshank..........	do	25 00	
J. J. A. Weir, P.M.......	do	65 00	
G. F. Jelfs, P.M.........	do	28 00	
M. Elliott, P.M..........	do	63 00	
M. Smith, P.M..........	do	6 00	
T. P. Morton, P.M.......	do	70 00	
W. J. Conn, J.P.........	do	3 75	
A. Love, J.P...........	do	12 85	
S. Fournier, J.P.........	do	53 00	
John Rutherford. J.P.....	do	5 00	
F. J. Quinn, J.P........	do	20 00	
G. H. Hornibrook, J.P...	do	8 00	
Geo. Menzies, P.C.C......	do	77 50	
Bursar Central Prison.....	do	62 03	
Thos. Penfold	do	36 20	
T. C. Dawson, Sheriff.....	do	456 00	
J. T. Middleton, Sheriff...	do	23 75	
J. Flintoft, Sheriff.......	do	284 64	
Warren Manufacturing Co.	do	200 00	
	Carried Forward......................		26,657 37

No. 14.

CASUAL REVENUE.—*Continued.*

From whom received.	Service.	$ c.	$ c.
	Brought forward..............		26,657 37
W. H. Carney.............	Jury fees.............................	24 00	
T. J. Bourke..............	do	83 00	
C. C. Platt...............	do	7 50	
James Meek..............	do	27 00	
E. Jordan................	do	12 00	
			153 50
Counties Crown Attorney.	Surplus fees, 57 Vic.. cap 9, Secs. 8-9....	1,119 26	
Clerks County Court......	do 57 Vic., cap 9, Sec. 4......	105 54	
Deputy Clerks Crown.....	do do	2,086 70	
Local Registrars, H. C. J..	do do	2,398 33	
Surrogate Registrars	do do	2,792 55	
Registrars' Deeds.........	do do	4,108 37	
Clerks Division Court.....	do do	3,567 93	
Surrogate Court Judges...	do do	2,171 00	
			18,349 68
Insurance Branch........	Ontario Insurance Act—		
	Insurance Registers..................	19,932 50	
	Friendly Society Registers	783 00	
	Miscellaneous......................	442 80	
			21,158 30
	Loan Corporations Act		
	Loan Companies' Register..........	6,062 50	
	Trust do do	1,525 00	
	Loaning Land Companies Register ...	500 00	
	Miscellaneous......................	1,335 80	
			9,423 30
Provincial Game Warden.	Deer hunters' licenses, 1905...........	39 60	
	do do 1906...........	11,378 34	
	Non-resident do 1905...........	49 00	
	do do 1906...........	10,783 50	
	Moose hunters' do 1905...........	43 35	
	do do 1906...........	1,366 50	
	Game dealers' do	480 00	
	Cold storage do	50 00	
	Hotel and restaurant licenses	142 00	
	Fines and confiscations	1,287 78	
			25,620 07
Sundry Persons...........	Circus licenses		2,817 00
Counties Treasurer........	Removal of lunatics....................		3,368 50
Clerk Legislative Assembly	Private bills		11,366 55
King's Printer............	Sale of Statutes.......................	1,272 74	
	do Rules of Practice............	13 20	
			1,285 94
Carswell Co.............	do B. N. A. Act Cases...........		10 50
Warwick Bros. & Rutter..	Ontario Gazette........................		7,340 04
Librarian L. A...........	Sundry persons—lost books...........		3 93
Grand Trunk R.R........	Rent of land—old Parliament Buildings		6,000 00
Sheriff Varin.............	Maintenance prisoners who paid their		
	fines.................................		184 00
Treasurer Nipissing.......	do		15 80
Thos. Penfold............	do		26 00
Escheated Estates.........	*re* James Cragill......................	1,488 83	
	re Stewart *vs.* Walker.................	213 97	
	re Lillian Richardson..................	223 64	
			1,926 44
Intestate's Estates........	*re* James Sparks......................	5,611 98	
	re Charles Andrews...................	1,610 61	
	re Anastasia Huron...............	798 45	
		8,021 04	
	Carried forward..................	....	135,706 92

No. 14.

CASUAL REVENUE.—*Continued.*

From whom received.	Service.	$ c.	$ c.
Intestate's Estates—*Cont.*	*Brought forward*	8,021 04	135,706 92
	re A. Maxwell....................	487 20	
	re Margaret Hall...................	313 40	
	re John Carroll................. ..	208 56	
	re David Borland....................	394 08	
	re Julia Lynch.....................	1,521 21	
	re Alice M. Stewart.............	1,199 65	
			12,145 14
Unclaimed Money Div.	W. F. Kerr, Crown Attorney.........	13 99	
Court.................	John Armstrong do	24 98	
	J. A. Richie do	4 23	
	A. J. Wilkes do	4 80	
	E. G. Mallock do	24 06	
	J. R. Metcalfe do	9 23	
			81 29
Dominion Life Ins. Co....	Insurance re A. McDougall...........	2,067 23	
Mutual Reserve Fund Life			
Insurance Co...........	do	6,908 79	
Mutual Life Ins. Co......	do	1,857 77	
			10,833 79
W. E. Genno.............	Rent land cor. Queen, Shaw and Massey		50 00
Fred Train...............	Refund accountable warrant...........		75 00
Northern Assurance Co....	Rebate re cancelled policy re "Gilphie"		46 85
Estate R. B. Miles........	Bequest to Blind Institution...........		500 00
Estate John Foote........	" Mercer Reformatory........		1,000 00
T. D. Cowper, C. P........	re Rex v. Hunt.....................		700 00
Colonial Cordage Co.....	Two bales hemp.....................		51 30
Inspector Prisons.........	Sale soft coal, Muskoka gaol and court-house........................		141 30
Supreme Court Judicature.	re Gamey charges....................		2,000 00
Provincial Board of Health	Analysis water......................		5 00
Attorney General.........	re Attorney General v. Hargraves......		1,577 38
L. M. T., Sault Ste. Marie	Sale of stove.......................		5 00
Public Works Department.	Sale scrap iron, etc., Lindsay lock and bridges........................		90 65
Sherriff Middleton.......	Refund re election trials..		26 25
City of Toronto	Purchase part Block E, cor. Queen and Lisgar streets		7,640 00
A. E. Long & Co.........	Payment on mortgage re cor. Gerrard and Sackville.....................		500 00
Refund	V 4,585 of '05 cap. acct, Toronto La, V 4,321		37 40
do	Admin. Jus., March Qtr.,'04, A. Racine, $1, W. Falona, 50c................		1 50
Treas., fyle 393............	W. O. Robson, Sup. Sec., Sup. Court, Royal Arcanum...................		25 00
Refund	R. Simpson Co., V. 4,321, '05........		60 80
do	Burk's Falls, Admin. Jus., Treas. fyle, 1,194.........................		6 00
Cook & Bros. Lumber Co..	One-half salary, constable at Spragge...		182 00
Refund, J. G. Scott.......	V. 2,570, '05....................		3 50
Department Justice, Ottawa	Refund Rex v. Tushenegeh............		271 90
A. Bartlett, P.M..........	Refund...........		100 00
John Douglas.............	do		50 00
University Commission ...	do		88 47
Attorney General	Copies of extracts and evidence........		207 35
Inspector of Prisons.......	Sale of Huntsville lock-up............		150 00
G. W. Brown.............	Purchase, West Fort William gaol property........................		945 31
Grand and Toy...........	Refund, Vr. 2,123....................		14 40
	Carried forward		175,319 50

No. 14.

CASUAL REVENUE.—*Concluded.*

From whom received.	Service.	$ c.	$ c.
	Brought forward................		175,319 50
Less.........	Invested in Ontario Government Stock (Canadian Loan)—		
	Robt. B. Miles, bequest to Blind Institute.........................	500 00	
	John Foote, bequest to Mercer Reformatory	1,000 00	
			1,500 00
			173,819 50

No. 15.

GOVERNMENT STATIONERY OFFICE

		$	c.	$	c.	$	c.
	Balance ... ... December, 1905 ...			12,781	36		
Allen-Macdonell Co	Strawboard	5	25				
Bouvier, L. P.	Envelopes	1,350	44				
Brown Bros	Stationery, note books, ink, etc	365	19				
Buntin, Reid & Co	Paper	44	00				
Barber & Ellis Co	Envelopes	176	55				
Buntin, Gillies & Co	do stationery, pads, etc	2,646	87				
Bain & Cubitt	Registers, note ? ?, envelopes, etc						
Brown, E. W.	Copy-holder	2,936	98				
Cairns, Bernard	Stamps, pads, dies, etc	3	00				
Canadian Typewriter Co	Paper, ? ? stationery, etc	306	45				
Canada Stationery Co	?	398	65				
Canada Tag and Label Co	Seals and ?	1,349	47				
? Paper ?	typewriter ribbons	110	91				
Copeland-Chatterson Co	? fees and binder	6	75				
? law Book ?	Municipal manual	63	82				
Carswell Co	Law reports	10	00				
Cameron, F. R.	Document cases		40				
? Legal Pub'g Co	Law list	30	00				
Canadian Express Co	Express ?	3	00				
C. P. ? ?	Freight charges	1	25				
? Tire Co	? bands	4	52				
Doust, ?	?	480	92				
Foster, J	Magnifier	1	00				
Grand and Toy	Stationery, etc	2	50				
Grand Trunk Railway	Freight charges	3,287	14				
Hart & Riddell	Paper, embossing, cheque books, etc	2	86				
Harcourt, E. H. Co	Paper, maps, files, etc	3,525	29				
Hamilton Steamboat Co	Freight charges	1,952	21				
Jones, J. L. Engraving Co	Zinc cuts	12	04				
Kilgour Bros	Fire bags	89	55				
Littlejohn & Vaughan	Zinc cuts	5	10				

Distribution for twelve months ended October 31st, 1906:

Civil Government :

	$	c.
Premier and Pres. Ex. Council, stationery	433	13
do paper	f	56
? General's Department, stationery	435	84
do paper	29	79
Education Department, stationery	632	04
do paper	8	97
Department of Lands and ?, stationery	4,007	22
do paper	265	58
Bureau of ?, stationery	2,369	20
do paper	76	05
? and Forestry, stationery	212	20
do paper	3	22
Public ? Department, stationery	742	31
do paper	47	48
? Branch, ?	280	94
do paper	29	79
? Protection, stationery	52	85
do paper	13	67
Labor ? ?, ?	94	87
do paper	6	12
? Department, stationery	926	71
do paper	49	12
Succession Duty ?, stationery	249	34
do paper	13	87
Provincial Audit ?, stationery	117	59
do paper	63	29
Provincial Secretary's Dept., stationery	1,742	62
do ?	36	18
Prisons Office, stationery	1,013	71
do paper	164	91
License ?, stationery	358	80
do paper	56	86

No. 15.—GOVERNMENT STATIONERY OFFICE.—Continued.

		$ c.
Lockhart Photo Supply Co.	Photo materials, tracing linen, etc.	601 76
Library Bureau of Canada	Folders and cards	49 47
Lawson & Jones	Envelopes	16 25
Lloyd, H. S.	Ink	13 77
Lyon & James, Limited	Embossing	118 54
Litke, F. E.	Magnifying glass	1 75
Musson Book Co.	Paper, scrap books, etc.	3,723 70
Nay, W. A. & G.	Bags and ...	217 50
Murray, W. A. & Co.	Suit cases and hand bags	255 25
Monarch ... Co.	Supplies	217 00
Muirhead, A. ...	Dusters	2 16
National Stationery Co.	Document cases, stationery, etc.	528 78
Newsome, W. H.	Supplies and rubber sheets	546 05
National Typewriter Co.	Supplies	603 49
... Specialty Mfg. Co.	Document ...	75 72
Perine, M. B. & Co.	Twine	153 47
Pears, Geo. Jr.	Carbon paper	36 00
... Engravers Ltd	Halftones	1 50
Rolph & ... Co.	Engraving and embossing	515 35
Rice ... wis & Son	Knives, scissors, etc.	785 60
Remington Typewriter Co.	Supplies	3 00
Roelofson and Roelofson.	Ink	3 00
Stanton, O. B.	Baskets, pads, stati'n'ry, etc	350 75
Stanton, O. B. & Wilson Co.	Stationery	56 39
Toronto Engraving Co.	Supplies	3 50
The Art Metropole	Supplies	87 33
...Flinn, C. and Co.	Mounting maps	225 65
Thomson Engraving Co.	Zinc cuts	9 54
Tolton and McIntosh	Box openers	16 50
Toronto Lithographing Co.	Maps	958 68
Thorne, A. M. and Co.	Paper	72 60
United Typewriter Co.	Supplies	214 60
Wilson, The H.A. Co.	Rubber sheets, erasers, toilet paper, etc.	397 70
Williams, N	Cartage	35
Warwick, Bros. & Rutter.	Paper and stationery	1,694 21

	$ c.	$ c.
Civil Government —*Continued.*		
Audit Criminal Justice ..., stationery	62 27	
do do paper	3 58	
Register— ... Branch, stationery	1,068 06	
do do paper	41 15	
Board of ..., stationery	376 86	
do paper	9 70	
Department of Agriculture, stationery	332 47	
do paper	36 48	
Factory Inspection, stationery	46 25	
do paper	128 15	
... ..., stationery	5 43	
Neglected Children's ..., stationery	160 42	
do paper	3 56	
King's Printer's Office, stationery	11 80	
do paper	24	
Municipal Auditor, stationery	8 85	
... Registry Offices, stationery	59 70	
Colonization Roads Office, do	257 77	
Highways do do	47 40	17,195 97
Legislation—		
Stationery, printing & binding, stationery	1,639 64	
Sessional Writers, Clerks of Committees, etc., stationery	327 19	
Expenses, stationery	1,642 05	
do paper	1 76	
Postage and Cost of House Post Offices, stationery	52 03	
Library, stationery	69 80	
Archives, do	104 49	
do paper	8 10	
Administration of Justice—		
Supreme Court, stationery	292 46	
do paper	70	
Appeal Court, stationery	66 82	3,845 06

PUBLIC ACCOUNTS.
cxlvi

Description	$	c.
Young, J.B.	Stationery and pens	13	80
Younger, Wm.	Baskets	23	50
		31,766	67
Less received from sales of stationery		15	70
*Accumulated profits on stock			
*Accumulated profits on stock distributed to Departments now appears in the shape of stock on hand			

	31,750	97
	3,568	40

Description	$	c.
Appeal Court, paper	11	89
High Court, stationery	14	90
do paper	37	85
Central office, salary	7	35
do paper	318	13
Registrar's Office, stationery	618	58
do paper	6	64
Taxing Office, stationery	26	55
Weekly Court, do	12	05
Surrogate Office, do	62	94
Inspection Division Courts, stationery	67	73
do paper	15	64
Local Master of Titles, stationery	495	85
do paper	10	80
Land Titles Office, stationery	152	70
do paper	61	03
Drainage Trials Act stationery	151	71
District No., do	170	70
do Thunder Bay, do	159	50
do Rainy River, do	41	00
do Nipissing do	70	25
do Parry Sound do	16	75
Inspection Legal Office do	83	90
do paper	9	23
Seals, stationery	43	00
Revision of Statutes, stationery	22	60
	3,049	25
Education—		
School of Practical Science, stationery	678	76
do paper	19	81
District Schools, paper		86
Inspection of do S., stationery	356	34
do paper	56	48
Inspection Separate Schools, stationery	26	47
Deaf and Dumb Inst., stationery	231	60
do paper	5	13
Poor Schools, paper	2	04
City Model Schs, stationery	7	75
do paper	2	21
Ontario Normal College, stationery	1	35
do paper	1	40
Inspection High Schools, stationery	79	00
do paper	7	88
High Schools, stationery	46	61
Normal School, London, stationery		90

No. 15.—GOVERNMENT STATIONERY OFFICE.—*Continued.*

	$ c.	$ c.
Education.—*Cont'd.*		
Normal School, do	450 97	
do do, paper	36 47	
do do, stationery	176 69	
do do paper	5 14	
Public Libraries, stationery	117 37	
do paper	24 19	
Travelling Lib, stationery	14 40	
Library and Museum, do	208 90	
do paper	4 34	
Department Exams, stationery	976 63	
do paper	121 11	
Kindergarten Schools, do	2 58	
Teachers' Associations, do	70	
Technical Education, stationery	85 88	
Continuation Classes, do	10 05	
do paper	1 37	
Blind Institution, stationery	41 80	
Miscellaneous, do	545 44	
do paper	9 30	4,357 92
Public Institutions, Maintenance—		
Asylum for Insane, Toronto, stationery	2 35 05	
do do paper	31 21	
do London, do	25 85	
do Mimico, do	15 05	
do do paper	15 80	
do Woodstock, stationery	4 80	
do do paper	5 41	
Asylum for Idiots, do	40 50	
Central Prison, do, stationery	149 45	
do do paper	16 74	
Mer Reformatory, Toronto, stationery	75 00	
do do paper	13 04	627 90
Agriculture—		
Fairs Branch stationery	60 24	
do paper	2 25	
Dairy Instruction stationery	9 00	

Farmers' Institutes	do	297 15	
do	paper	27 73	
Live Stock Branch	stationery	135 66	
Bureau of Industries	do	339 65	
do	paper	50 55	
Agricultural Societies	stationery	60	
Incidentals	do	295 63	
do	paper	10 74	1,229 20
Colonization and Immigration—			
Maintenance Office, Union Station	stationery	53 07	
do	paper	2 62	
General Colonization Purposes	stationery	40 25	95 94
Repairs and Maintenance—			
Public Works Department — document boxes for Game Branch		21 00	
Parliament Buildings	toilet paper	29 00	50 00
Charges Crown Lands—			
Algonquin Park	stationery	17 95	
do	paper	17 60	
Agents Salaries	stationery	10 00	
Mining Inspection	do	570 50	
do	paper	6 43	
Surveys	stationery	331 00	963 48
Miscellaneous—			
Railway Board	stationery	342 09	
Elections	do	95 52	
	paper	13 00	
Enforcement of Liquor Act	stationery	30 90	
University Commission	do	13 37	
Auto Tags	do	6 00	
Fisheries	do	310 14	
Licenses	do	182 10	993 12
Balance Stock on hand			32,397 84
			15,702 89
Total			48,100 73

Total.... 48,100 73

Total....

No. 16.

Statement showing amounts payable annually for certificates issued by the Treasurer of the Province for " Aid to Railways " and Annuities.

Year.	Railway Aid Certificates.	Annuities.	Year.	Railway Aid Certificates.	Annuities.
	$ c.	$ c.		$ c.	$ c.
			Forward....	2,417,213 60	1,997,350 00
1907...........	120,860 68	102,900 00	1927	120,860 68	56,950 00
1908...........	120,860 68	102,900 00	1928	120,860 68	50,700 00
1909...........	120,860 68	102,900 00	1929	120,860 68	50,700 00
1910...........	120,860 68	102,900 00	1930	120,161 08	50,700 00
1911...........	120,860 68	102,900 00	1931	116,663 08	43,700 00
1912...........	120,860 68	102,900 00	1932	109,667 08	32,700 00
1913...........	120,860 68	102,900 00	1933	106,868 68	28,700 00
1914...........	120,860 68	102,900 00	1934	104,769 88	28,700 00
1915...........	120,860 68	102,900 00	1935	92,876 68	24,700 00
1916...........	120,860 68	102,900 00	1936	86,838 15	16,700 00
1917...........	120,860 68	102,900 00	1937	76,207 94	9,200 00
1918...........	120,860 68	102,900 00	1938	72,709 94	2,850 00
1919...........	120,860 68	102,900 00	1939	67,870 49	....
1920...........	120,860 68	102,900 00	1940	63,987 16	....
1921...........	120,860 68	102,900 00	1941	49,691 89	....
1922...........	120,860 68	102,900 00	1942	13,566 54	....
1923...........	120,860 68	102,900 00	1943	6,668 65	....
1924	120,860 68	96,200 00	1944	4,443 22	....
1925...........	120,860 68	82,500 00	....	....	....
1926...........	120,860 68	69,350 00	....	....	....
Forward......	2,417,213 60	1,997,350 00	Totals......	3,872,786 10	2,393,650 00

NOTE.—Present value of Railway Certificates (interest 1¾ per cent. half yearly)...$2,306,822.69
do   Annuities   1¼   do   ... 1,610,200.59

No. 17.

CASH AND DEBENTURE ASSETS OF THE PROVINCE.

Bank Balances :—
Current account... 186,602 83
Special deposits bearing interest........................... 3,310,636 79
                                                                              3,497,239 62

Sinking Fund :—
Re Ontario Government inscribed stock, 5 Edward VII., cap. 2
  and 3, £1,200,000, one half of one per cent per annum on the
  principal.
Amount of stock purchased for the Province for sinking fund by
  the Bank of Montreal, Fiscal Agents, to the 31st December, 1906,
  £6,294 9s. 7d., at par of exchange............................. 30,591 17

Debentures —:
Drainage Debentures.. 85,779 50
Tile Drainage Coupons.. 62,645 85
Sault Ste. Marie Debentures 25,572 50
                                                                              173,997 85

                                                                              3,701,828 64

TRUST FUNDS OF THE PROVINCE HELD BY THE DOMINION.

Upper Canada Grammar School Fund, 2 Vic., cap, 10, and 250,000
  acres of land allotted to it 312,769 04
Upper Canada Building Fund (under the 18th section, Act 1854)
Seignorial Tenure set apart for local purposes in Upper Canada....... 1,472,391 41
Land Improvement Fund, being one-fourth of the collection on
  account of Common School Lands sold between the 14th day of
  March, 1853, and the 6th day of June, 1861, as per award......... 124,685 18
Common School Fund (see Consolidated Statutes, c. 26) 1,000,000
  acres set apart (proceeds realized to 31st December 1905), after
  deducting Land Improvement Fund, $2,585,639 99, portion
  belonging to Ontario as per population of 1901.................... 1,473,001 90
                                                                              3,382,847 53

NOTE.—See Awards, sessional papers, 1900 and 1901.

LIABILITIES OF THE PROVINCE.

(1) Debts due to Dominion as settled by arbitration, with the
    exception of claim as under Indian Treaty No. 3, in dispute.... 1,737,190 72

   NOTE.—17th Award, see Sessional Paper No. 58, 1901. Payments
have since been made to Dominion on account of C. S. Fund,
reducing amount mentioned in award.

(2) Ontario Government Inscribed Stock (London, Eng., loan) 5
    Edward VII., cap. 2 and 3, issued to redeem Treasury Bills
    falling due May 15, 1906, £1,200,000 at par of exchange....... 5,840,004 00

(3) Ontario Government Bonds and Stock, 5 Edward VII, cap. 2
    and 6 Edward VII. cap. 4 (Canadian Loan) issued for construc-
    tion of Temiskaming and Northern Ontario Railway.......... 3,000,000 00
                                                                              8,840,004 00

NOTE.—Against these liabilities the Province has an asset, the Temiskaming and Northern Ontario Railway, now under construction, the amount expended on which to 31st December, 1906, is $408,450 80 in excess of the above loans.

(4) Railway Certificates, present value, outstanding on 31st December, 1906 .... 2,306,822 69
Annuity Certificates, present value, outstanding on 31st December, 1906 .... 1,610,200 59
                                                                                                3,917,023 28

(5) Common School Fund collections by Ontario from 1st January, 1906, payable to the Dominion, in trust, for both Provinces...   6,694 91
          In trust for Ontario..................... 3,813 99
          In trust for Quebec..................... 2,880 92

(6) University of Toronto Certificates $30,000 per annum for 29 years, 5 Edward VII., Cap. 37.
          Present value at 3½ per cent. per annum....................   541,073 10

          Total direct liabilities 15,041,986 01

INDIRECT LIABILITIES OF THE PROVINCE AND GUARANTEES.

(1) Algoma Central and Hudson Bay Railway and Associated Industries Guarantee Loan, payable 1st April, 1907, (4 Edward VII., Cap. 19) $1,000,000 00

NOTE.—The Government has as security for this guarantee certain first mortgage bonds, income bonds and stock of the Lake Superior Corporation, and the stock and bonds of the Algoma Central and Hudson Bay Railway Company, and of the Manitoulin and North Shore Railway Co., and a promissory note for $725,000, secured by mortgage on certain steamships and vessels of the Algoma Central Railway Company.

(2) Niagara Falls Park Bonds—(50 Vic. c. 13).......... 525,000 00
                              (57 Vic. c. 13).......... 75,000 00
                                                        600,000 00
                                                                    1,600,000 00

NOTE. — The income of the Park Commission from lease of power, etc., was sufficient to pay all maintenance and interest charges and leave a balance available for capital expenditures, which balance will be much exceeded in future, and available as a source of Provincial revenue.

(3) The Canadian Northern Ontario Railway Company (formerly the James Bay Railway Company.)
Guarantee by the Province of Ontario under authority of 4 Edward VII., c. 20, of principal and interest at 3½ per cent. per annum, Debenture Stock of above Railway payable in 30 years from 10th July, 1906. £1,101,369 17s. sterling...................   5,360,000 00

No. 18.

TEMISKAMING AND NORTHERN ONTARIO RAILWAY.

EXPENDITURE TO 31ST DECEMBER, 1906.

Ontario Government inscribed stock, 5 Edw. VII. Cap. 2 and 3, issued
to redeem Treasury Bills falling due May·15th, 1906, £1,200,000 at
par of exchange... 5,840,004 00
Advanced by the Province to Railway Commission in 1905, 1,536,164 27
     "   "   "   in 1906, 1,872.286 53
                                   ——   —— 3,408,450 80
                                                          ———— 9,248,454 80

NOTE.—The above expenditure includes costs of sale of Ontario
Government inscribed stock, £1,200,000, as per the following
statement :
Statement of costs of sale of Ontario Government inscribed
stock, £1,200,000.
Discount 1½ per cent............................. .... £18,000
Bank of Montreal, Fiscal Agents, charges for underwriting,
. etc., 1⅞ per cent.................................... 22,500
Imperial Government stamp charges ⅝ per cent........... 7,500
                                                             ———— £48,000

      £48,000 at 9 $\frac{1}{16}$ = \$232,666.66.

No. 19.

ONTARIO GOVERNMENT INSCRIBED STOCK (LONDON, ENGLAND LOAN) 3½ PER
CENT., £1,200,000 STG. 5 EWD. VII. CAP. 2 AND 3................$5,840,004.00

Principal due 1st January, 1946.

Issued to redeem Treasury Bills falling due May 15, 1906.

Proceeds of sale £1,152,000
Costs and discount included in advances to Temiskaming and Northern
   Ontario Railway.   See Statement 18.............................   £48,000
                                        £1,200,000

STATEMENT OF COSTS.

Discount, 1½ per cent.. £18,000
Bank of Montreal, Fiscal Agents charges for underwriting, etc.,
   1⅞ per cent.. 22,500
Imperial Government, stamp charges, ⅝ per cent.............. 7,500
                                  £48,000

No. 20.

PROVINCE OF ONTARIO LOAN (CANADIAN),
5 Edw. VII. Cap. 2 and 6 Edw. VII. Cap. 4..

$3,000,000 issued at par, Bonds and Stock 3½ per cent.

RECEIPTS.

Bond subscription	$2,280,500 00	
Stock "	719,500 00	
		$3,000,000 00

EXPENDITURE.

Advertising, sundry newspapers	4,770 26	
Printing stock certificates	25 00	
Engraving and printing book bonds and coupons	2,600 00	
		$7,395 26
NOTE.—Accrued interest paid by bond subscribers after 31st July, 1906. (This amount is included in Interest Statement No. 5.)	$12,292 54	
Deduction in interest from stock subscription after 31st July, 1906...	346 34	
		$12,638 88

EXPENDITURE STATEMENT

STATEMENT OF THE EXPENDITURE by the Treasurer of Ontario During the Year
Ended 31st December, 1906.

CIVIL GOVERNMENT.

LIEUTENANT-GOVERNOR'S OFFICE.

SALARIES ($2,600.00).

Jas. Fraser Macdonald:	Twelve months' salary	as Official Secretary	1,400 00
D. D. Young:	do	A.D.C. to Lieut.-Governor	600 00
Thos. Lymer:	do	Messenger	600 00

EXPENSES ($1,700.00).

Hon. Wm. Mortimer Clark, To pay sundries	1,700 00

OFFICE OF THE PRIME MINISTER AND PRESIDENT OF THE COUNCIL.

SALARIES ($11,200.00).

Hon. J. P. Whitney:	Twelve months' salary as	Prime Minister and President of the Council	7,000 00
Horace Wallis:	do	Chief Clerk and Prime Minister's Secretary	2,000 00
C. J. Jeffrey:	do	Clerk	700 00
Isobel Clarke:	do	do	500 00
C. H. Chase:	do	Messenger Ex. Council and Caretaker	1,000 00

EXPENSES ($2,127.23).

Alexander & Cable, engraving cards and ptg., 5.00; Barnes, J., cab hire, 9.50	14 50
Biographical Pub. Co., sketch of Sir Oliver Mowat, 7.50; Bell Telephone Co., rent of instruments, 111.83; messages, 39.90	159 23
Bond, R., cab hire, 182.00; Banks, W. Jr., typewriting 175 folios at 20c, 35.00	217 00
Can. Law Book Co., law books, 19.00; Ont. Digest, 3.75	22 75
Can. Legal. Pub. Co., law lists, 3.00; C.P.R. Tel. Co., telegrams, 125.17; Can. Stat'y Co., typewriter, 115.00	243 17
Carswell Co., Digest & Law Journal reports, 3.50; Doane Bros., cab hire, 2.00	5 50
Dom. Express Co., charges, 1.85; G. N. W. Tel. Co., telegrams, 59.74; Gripton, C., rubber stamps and repairs, 60c	62 19
Hendrie, Hon. Jno. S., trav. expenses, 200; Hubertus, Mrs., postage stamps, 148.00	348 00
King's Printer, stationery, 410.68; paper, 1.56	412 24
Library Bureau of Canada, rubber roller, labels, etc.	5 75
Might Directories, directory, 6.00; National Typewriter Co., rep. machine, 9.00	15 00
Newspapers, sundry, subscriptions, 78.50; Toronto Ry. Co., car tickets, 135.00	213 50
Toronto Ry. and Steamboat Guide, subscns, 10.00. Whitney, Hon. J. P., trav. expenses, 85.25	95 25
Willoughby, Hon. W. A., trav. expenses, 300.00; Warwick Bros. & Rutter, printing and binding, 13.15	313 15

ATTORNEY-GENERAL'S DEPARTMENT.

SALARIES ($15,800.00).

Hon. J. J. Foy:	Twelve months' salary as	Attorney-General	4,000 00
J. R. Cartwright:	do	Deputy Attorney-General	3,500 00
J. Lonsdale Capreol:	do	Clerk Executive Council	1,950 00
M. Curry:	do	Asst. Clerk Ex. Council and Atty-General's Secretary	1,650 00
A. Mennie:	do	Stenographer and Assistant	500 00
A. M. Dymond:	do	Law Secretary	800 00
C. A. Fitch:	do	First Class Clerk	1,300 00
Wm. Marseilles:	do	Second do	1,100 00
C. F. Bulmer:	do	do do	1,000 00

CIVIL GOVERNMENT.—*Continued.*

ATTORNEY-GENERAL'S DEPARTMENT.—*Continued.*

EXPENSES ($2,055.32).

Bell Telephone Co., rent of instruments, 169.45; messages, 25.00...............	194 45
Bulmer, C. F., trav. expenses, 1.40; Can. Express Co., charges, 2.95.........	4 35
Can. Law Book Co., law books and reports, 65.00; Can. Legal Pub. Co., legal chart and law list, 13.50	78 50
Carswell Co., law books, reports, etc., 112.20; Chase, C. H., trav. expenses, 15.90	128 10
Circuit Guide Pub. Co., copies of guide, 3.00; C.P.R. Tel. Co., telegrams, 70.17	73 17
Doane Bros., cab hire, 8.25; Dom. Express Co., charges, 3.44	11 69
Fitch, C. A., petty office expenses, 5.00; G.N.W. Tel. Co., telegrams, 47.00	52 00
Hubertus, Mrs., postage stamps	290 00
King's Printer, stationery, 458.29; paper, 29.79	488 08
Library Bureau of Canada, roller, copier, guides, etc., 132.25; Law Society Secretary, annual fees Deputy Attorney-General, 17.00	149 25
Might Directories, directory, 6.00; National Typewriter Co., cleaning typewriter, etc., 10.00	16 00
Newspapers, sundry, subscriptions, 161.20; Pears, Geo. J., book typewriter, 190.00	351 20
Postmaster, unpaid postage, 2.39; Thompson, Ed. Co., encyclopædias of law, 22.50	24 89
Tangent Cycle Co., repairs to messenger's wheel, 75c.; Tolchard, D., lunches for assistant secretary, 3.75	4 50
Toronto Ry. Co., car tickets, 28.00; Toronto Ry. & Steamboat Guide, subscriptions, 10.00	38 00
United Typewriter Co., typewriter, 120.00; Warwick Bros. & Rutter, ptg. and binding, 27.64	147 64
Wilson, Wm., cab hire	3 50

AUDIT OF CRIMINAL JUSTICE ACCOUNTS.

SALARIES ($2,300.00).

E. A. Maclaurin:	Twelve months' salary as Inspector Criminal Justice Accounts		1,800 00
Ruby J. Moore:	do	Stenographer	500 00

EXPENSES ($161.84).

Can. Legal Pub. Co., law list, 3.00; Circuit Guide Pub. Co., copies guide, 50c.	3 50
C. P. R. Tel. Co., telegrams, 50c.; Gripton, C., stamp, ink, etc., 1.35	1 85
International Ry. Guide, subscription	3 00
King's Printer, stationery, 62.27, paper, 3.58	65 85
McIntyre, H. M., postage stamps, 48.00; Warwick Bros. & Rutter, printing, 39.64	87 64

INSURANCE BRANCH.

SALARIES ($7,000.00).

J. Howard Hunter:	Twelve months' salary as Inspector of Insurance and Regr. Friendly Societies		3,000 00
W. J. Vale:	do	Assistant Regr. of Friendly Societies	1,400 00
K. A. Chisholm:	do	Clerk	1,000 00
H. P. Royal:	do	do	950 00
Alice C. Lynch:	do	Stenographer	650 00

EXPENSES ($2,330.93).

Barnes, C. C., map of Canada and World, 1.90; Bulletin Pub. Co., subscription, 2.00	3 90
Bell Telephone Co., moving 'phone, 8.80; rent of instruments, 45.78	54 58
Can. Law Book Co., law books and binding, 72.90; Can. Legal Pub. Co., legal chart and law list, 4.50	77 40

CIVIL GOVERNMENT.—*Continued.*

INSURANCE BRANCH.—*Continued.*

EXPENSES.—*Continued.*

Carswell Co., law books and reports, 64.60; Chisholm, K., trav. expenses, 31.90	96	50
Circuit Guide Pub. Co., copies guide, 2.00; C. P. R. Tel. Co., telegrams, .72	2	72
Fraternal Monitor, books, 3.65; subscription, 1.00	4	65
G.N.W. Tel. Co., telegrams, .88; Gripton, C., rubber stamps and repairs, 7.50	8	38
Heaton's Agency, Commercial Handbook, 1.00; Hubertus, Mrs., postage, stamps and cards, 126.00	127	00
Hunter, J. H., trav. expenses, 19.70; duty on book, 1.60	21	30
Insurance Financial Review, subscription (2 years), 4.00; Insurance Finance Chronicle, subscription, 4.00	8	00
Insurance Monitor, subscription, 3.00; International Ry. Guide, subscription, 2.00	5	00
Journal of Commerce, subscription	2	00
King's Printer, stationery, 128.15; paper, 5.43	133	58
Landis, A., book, 5.00; Legislative Library, book, .49; Monetary Times, subscription, 2.00	7	49
Newspapers and periodicals, subscriptions, 7.00; Poole, Arthur & Co., law books, 16.00	23	00
Postmaster, unpaid postage, 2.00; Riordon Paper Mills, paper for reports, 462.70	464	70
Spectator Pub. Co., books, 40.10. Toronto Ry. and Steamboat Guide, subscriptions, 12.50	52	60
United Typewriter Co., cleaning and repairing typewriter, 14.50;. Vale, W. J., trav. expenses, 182.70	197	20
Warwick Bros. & Rutter, printing and binding	1,040	93

EDUCATION DEPARTMENT.

SALARIES ($22,016.65).

Hon. R. A. Pyne: Twelve months' salary as		Minister of Education		4,000 00
Jno. Seath: Seven	do	Supt. of Education		2,079 30
A. H. U. Colquhoun: Ten	do	Deputy Minister of Education		2,705 35
C. W. James: Twelve	do	cmfwy shrdl cmfwy vbgk		
H. M. Wilkinson:	do	Senior Clerk and Accountant		1,650 00
A. C. Paull:	do	Clerk of Records		1,500 00
T. F. Callaghan:	do	do Correspondence		1,350 00
S. A. May:	do	Asst. Clerk of Correspondence		900 00
T. J. Greene:	do	do Records		1,000 00
E. A. Faulds:	do	Clerk of Statistics		1,000 00
F. Woodley:	do	do and Asst. Accountant		900 00
Allen Ker:	do	do and Stenographer...		900 00
N. A. Brown:	do	Junior Clerk		600 00
M. A. Ashall: Six	do	Stenographer		250 00
S. B. Shields:	do	do		275 00
E. Dennis: Eight	do	do		400 00
M. Gregg: Seven	do	do		381 00
L. McCorkindale: Twelve	do	Caretaker		600 00
Geo. Lyons: Eight and one-half do		Messenger		226 00

EXPENSES ($2,763.45).

Atkinson, J. H., services as attendant Minister's reception to Members L.A.		75
Bell Telephone Co., rent of instruments, 84.39; messages, 5.70	90	09
Brandon & Gilbert, cartage, 1.75; Cairns, B., rubber stamps, etc., 13.40...	15	15
Can. Express Co., charges, 1.40; Can. Legal Pub. Co., law lists, 9.00	10	40
Can. Stationery Co., embossing, stationery, etc., 39.15; Carleton St. Post Office, postage stamps, 1.00	31	15
Clark, Jno., services, messenger at 5.00 a week, 20.84; C.P.R. Tel. Co., telegrams, 17.00	37	84
Colquhoun, A. H. U., trav. expenses, 47.25; to pay telegrams, .31	47	56
Crawford, W. C., services attendant Minister's reception to Members L. A.		75

CIVIL GOVERNMENT.—*Continued.*

EDUCATION DEPARTMENT.—*Continued.*

Expenses.—*Continued.*

Dept. Pub. Ptg., postal guides, 2.43; Doane Bros., cab hire, 1.75	4 18
Dom. Express Co., charges, 3.40; Dom. School Supply Co., map, labels, etc., 4.50	7 90
East & Co., repairing document bag, .40; Farmer Bros., photos, 50.00........	50 40
G. N. W. Tel. Co., telegrams, 52.02; Graham, T., cartage, 1.75	53 77
Grand & Toy stationery rack, blank books, etc., 14.50; Gregg, M., services as Stenog. at 9.00 per week, 195.50	210 00
James, C. W., trav. expenses	28 20
King's Printer, stationery, 591.17; paper, 49.84	641 01
Lyons, Geo., services messenger, at 5.00 per week, 85.84; McCorkindale, L., weighing waste paper, .40	86 24
McMaster, M., postage stamps, 510.00; Meredith, Thos. & Co., paste pail, etc., 1.35	511 35
Mescall, J., short cuts in figures, 5.00; Might Directories, directories, 18.00	23 00
National Typewriter Co., typewriter, 110.25; supplies, 18.45	128 70
Newell, R., cab hire, 87.25. newsboys' Xmas gratuities, 1.50..................	88 75
Newspapers and periodicals, advertising, 33.00; subscriptions, 24.00........	57 00
News Publishing Co., refund charges from C. P. R. Tel. Co.	25
Office Specialty Co., loose leaf indexes, 3.50; Phillips, L. M., services as stenog. at 12.00 per week, 40.00	43 50
Post Office, special delivery stamps, 1.00; Riordon Paper Mills, paper, .47	1 47
Robinson & Heath, brokerage, freight, etc., 1.12; Seath, Jno., trav. expenses, 222.15	223 27
Scott, J. L., unpaid postage, 10.23; Thompson, G., services clerk at 12.00 per week, 30.00	40 23
Simpson, G. J., services of orchestra, Minister's reception to members L. A.	25 00
Titus, Ethel, attendant in waiting rooms Minister's reception to L. A., 1.00; Toronto Ry. Co., car tickets, 162.00	163 00
United Typewriter Co., rent of typewriter, 36.00; Warwick Bros. & Rutter, printing and binding, 104.29	140 29
Williams, N. & Co., cartage	2 25

DEPARTMENT OF LANDS, FORESTS AND MINES.

Salaries ($54,024.56).

Hon. F. Cochrane:	Twelve months' salary as	Minister	4,000 00
Aubrey White:	do	Deputy Minister	3,500 00
Geo. Kennedy:	do	Law Clerk	2,400 00
Geo. W. Yates:	do	Minister's Secretary	1,600 00
E. S. Williamson:	do	Secretary to Department......	1,500 00
J. Garvie:	do	Stenographer	600 00

Land Sales and Free Grants.

J. J. Murphy:	Twelve months' salary as	Chief Clerk	2,000 00
Selby Draper:	do	Clerk	1,050 00
W. R. Ledger:	do	do	1,000 00
Walter Cain:	do	do	1,000 00
W. A. Collins: Six	do	do	400 00
M. Bengough: Twelve	do	Stenographer	600 00
M. C. Jaffray: Nine	do	do	375 00

Military Grants.

R. H. Browne:	Twelve months' salary as	Chief Clerk	1,500 00
R. L. Winter:	do	Clerk	700 00
E. F. O'Neill:	do	Stenographer	500 00

CIVIL GOVERNMENT.—*Continued.*

DEPARTMENT OF LANDS, FORESTS AND MINES.—*Continued.*

SALARIES.—*Continued.*

SURVEYS AND PATENTS.

Geo. B. Kirkpatrick:	Twelve months' salary as	Director	2,300
J. F. Whitson:	do	Surveyor and Draughtsman	1,750 00
D. G. Boyd: Eleven	do	Draughtsman	1,145 86
C. S. Jones: Twelve	do	Clerk of Patents and Inspector of Agencies	1,750 00
W. S. Sutherland:	do	Clerk	1,050 00
W. F. Lewis:	do	do	1,100 00
E. M. Jarvis:	do	do	900 00
J. B. Proctor:	do	do	900 00
C. E. Burns:	do	do	900 00
W. Carrell:	do	do	950 00
H. Treeby:	do	do	900 00
M. H. W. Kirkland:	do	Stenographer	500 00

WOODS AND FORESTS BRANCH.

J. A. G. Crozier:	Twelve months' salary as Chief Clerk		2,000 00
K. Miller:	do	Clerk	1,150 00
J. B. Cook:	do	do	1,300 00
H. D. Gillard:	do	do	1,000 00
F. J. Niven:	do	do	900 00
W. F. Trivett:	do	do	850 00
R. H. Hodgson:	do	do	800 00

ACCOUNTS BRANCH.

D. G. Ross:	Twelve months' salary as Accountant		2,000 00
E. Leigh:	do	Clerk	1,200 00
M. J. Ferris:	do	do	1,150 00
H. M. Lount:	do	do	1,000 00
A. E. Robillard: Nine	do	do	553 73
F. Yeigh: Twelve	do	Registrar	1,500 00
H. Cartwright:	do	Clerk	1,100 00
H. Brophy:	do	Messenger	650 00

EXPENSES ($25,852.82).

Arnoldi, Frank, legal services *re* burnt timber sale, 200.00; Art Metropole, supplies, 7.05	207 05
Bell Telephone Co., rent of instruments, 309.89; messages, 12.05	321 94
Biographical Pub. Co., book, 6.00; Blanchett. F. .C., draughtsman, at 2.00 per day, 400.00	406 00
Brown, E. M., services at 10.00 per week	521 66
Bryan. E. B., do do do	521 66
Can. Forestry Asso. fees, 1.00; Can. Express Co., charges, 22.78	23 78
C.P.R. Telegraph Co., telegrams, 407.15; Can. Law Book Co., law books, etc., 9.00	416 15
Can. Legal Pub. Co.. legal charts and law lists, 18.00; Circuit Guide Pub. Co., copies guide, 2.00	20 00
Clarke, W. K., services as messenger	15 00
Clarke, C. J., services. at 12.00 per week	626 00
Collins, Wm. A., do do	312 00
Collison. B. W., do 2.00 per day	108 00
Crane, G. A., services, at 12.00 per week, 596.00; Crain, The Rolla Co., indexes, etc., 8.25	604 25
Cunningham, Stella, services, at 10.00 per week	215 00
Doane Bros., cab hire. 7.75; Dies. Chester. services, at 14.00 per week, 682.00	689 75
Dominion Express Co. charges	256 05

CIVIL GOVERNMENT.—*Continued.*

DEPARTMENT OF LANDS, FORESTS AND MINES.—*Continued.*

EXPENSES.—*Continued.*

Farmer Bros., photos and frames, 20.00; Foster, Jas., level rod, etc., 9.00...	29 00
G. N. W. Telegraph Co., telegrams	62 68
Harris, Geo., services at 2.00 per day, 208.00; Harris Exp. Co., cartage, .25	208 25
Harris, H. G., do at 12.00 per week, 626.00; Hall, T. H., services as stenog., 30.00	656 00
Heaton's Agency, commercial handbook, 1.00; Houser, Jno., services at 14.00 per week, 682.00	683 00
Ireland, L. G., services at 12.00 per week, 276.00; Jennings, J. E., services at 2.00 per day, 6.00	282 00
Johnston, R. A., services at 2.00 per day, 134.00; Johnston, H. E., services at 14.00 per week, 376.00	510 00
Kelly, J. J., services at 2.50 per day, 127.50; King's Printer, stationery, 3,745.92; paper, 265.58	4,139 00
Kirkpatrick, G. B., travelling expenses, 86.20; Lamb, A. J., services at 2.00 per day, 224.00	310 20
Loscombe, N. W., services at 10.00 per week, 165.00; Lovell, John & Son, copy legal compendium, 3.00	168 00
Lucas, F., services at 2.00 per day, 24.00; Lennon, F., services at 10.00 per week, 521.66	545 66
McCrea, M., services at 10.00 per week, 478.66; McKillop, Kate, services at 10.00 per week, 10.50	489 16
McMaster, M. H., postage stamps, 1,840.40; Maher, P., cab hire, 1.00	1,841 40
Might Directories, Ltd., directories, 16.00; Molson's Bank, protest charges, 1.58	17 58
Morrow, C., cab hire, 12.00; National Typewriter Co., rent of machine, 12.00; supplies, 24.25	43 25
Newspapers sundry, advertising *re* land for settlement, 62.00; *re* pulpwood, 2,238.66; general, 861.80; *re* timber, 864.62; *re* sale of islands Lake Temagami, 32.50. *re* survey road allowance twp. Ops, 11.40; subscriptions, 121.05	4,192 03
Newsome, W. H. Co., typewriters, 220.00; O'Neill, A. H., services at 2.00 per day 284.00	504 00
Ontario Land Surveyors' Asso., annual fees, 8.00; Gram, Jean, services as Stenog. at 10.00 per week, 280.00	288 00
Patterson, J. H., services at 12.00 per week, 436.00; Platt, S. A., services at 14.00 per week, 682.00	1,118 00
Postmaster, unpaid postage, 18.28, Remington Typewriter Co., repairs, 3.00	21 28
Renouf Pub. Co., book, 4.00; Riordon Paper Mills, paper, 73.91	77 91
Richardson, E. F., services at 12.00 per week, 280.00; Roe, A., services at 14.00 per week, 132.00	412 00
Rouillard, E., book, 1.00; Ross, Donald, services at 2.00 per day, 626.00	627 00
	405 00
Samuels, F., services at 8.00 per week	
Toronto Ry. Co., car tickets, 60.00; Toronto Ry. & Steamboat Guide, copies of guide, 10.00	70 00
United Typewriter Co., rent of machine, 20.00; new machine, 119.00; repairs, 21.50	160 50
Warwick Bros. & Rutter, printing and binding, 2,273.18; White, Aubrey, travelling expenses, 386.50	2,659 68
Yates, G. W., travelling expenses of Minister and party to Temiskaming District	62 95

BUREAU OF MINES.

SALARIES ($4,473.99).

Thos. W. Gibson:	Twelve months' salary as Deputy Minister			3,000 00
A. Moffatt:	do	Clerk		700 00
W. H. Morris: Seven	do	do		440 02
E. Craig:	do	do	and Stenographer	333 97

CIVIL GOVERNMENT.—*Continued.*

BUREAU OF MINES.—*Continued.*

EXPENSES ($9,101.55).

American Inst. of Mining Engineers, dues, 11.00; Art Metropole, supplies 4.00	15 00
Barr, D. H., services at 2.00 per day, 252.00; Beck, Jos., services as 2.00 per day, 276.00	528 00
Bell Telephone Co., rent of instrument, 23.76; Browning, A. G., copy of deposition *re* inquest, Kusta Stanos, 1.50	25 26
Can. P. Ry. Tel. Co., messages, 118.11; Can P. Ry. Co., freight charges, 3.67	121 78
Can. Express Co., charges, 13.20; Can. Legal Pub. Co., law lists, 3.00......	16 20
Can. Inst. Mining Engineers, dues	10 00
Copp, Clark Co., printing maps Nickel Basin, 26.00; Stobie, 58.00; Copper Cliff, 80.00; electros, 1.50	165 50
Craig, E., services at 10.00 per week, 216.00; Cray & Gerlach, books, 29.11	245 11
Dennis, E., services copying, 15.00; Dom. Express Co., charges, 75.62......	90 62
Engineering and Mining Journal, book	10 00
Fisher, R. D., services at 14.00 per week	682 00
Gibson, T. W., trav. expenses ,45.50; Gillespie, G., views of Cobalt, 3.50	49 00
Gould, Annie J., services at 10.00 per week, 21.66; G. N. W. Tel. Co., messages, 34.08	55 74
G. T. Ry. Co., freight charges, 2.02; Griffin, Chas. & Co., books, 3.63 ...	5 65
Harris, J., cartage	50
Johnston, H. E., services at 14.00 per week	306 00
King, P. S. & Son, Parliamentary papers, 5.83; King's Printer, stationery, 1,965.39; paper, 73.85; maps, 95.34	2,140 41
London Ptg. and Litho. Co., lithographing maps Julia River and Scott's Camp	92 63
McDougall, F., services as Stenog. at 10.00 per week	231 66
McFadden, M., copy of deposition *re* death Jas. Newall, 2.00; McMaster, M. H., postage stamps, 367.60	369 60
Marks, M. L., services at 2.00 per day, 170.00; Maher, P., cab hire, 2.50...	172 50
Micklethwaite, F. W., photo supplies, 3.06; Might Directories, directory, 6.00	9 06
Morris, W. H., services at 12.00 per week ·..	260 00
National Typewriter Co., repairs, 9.25; newspapers, advertising, 262.80; subscriptions, 200.18	472 23
Oliver, Thos., copy of deposition and verdict *re* inquest Kusta Stanos ...	1 50
Renouf Pub. Co., book, 11.00; Riordon Paper Mills, paper, 396.94	407 94
St. John, W. C., services at 2.00 per day	302 00
Sinclair, R. A., services at 12.00 per week	528 00
Thompson, Phillips, indexing report	32 00
United Typewriter Co., typewriter, 115.00; supplies and repairs, 8.00	123 00
Warwick Bros. & Rutter, printing and binding, 1,629.32; Weg Max. book, 3.34	1,632 66

PUBLIC WORKS DEPARTMENT.

SALARIES ($20,130.16).

Hon. J. O. Reaume: Twelve months' salary as		Minister	4,000 00
A. W. Campbell:	do	Deputy Minister	3,000 00
H. C. Maisonville:	do	Clerk and Minister's Secretary	1,500 00
J. P. Edwards:	do	Accountant and Law Clerk.	1,450 00
F. R. Heakes:	do	Architect	2,000 00
R. P. Fairbairn:	do	Engineer	2,000 00
A. J. Halford: Seven and two-thirds months' salary as Assistant Engineer			766 66
H. F. McNaughton: Twelve months' salary as		Secretary Public Works	1,250 00
H. E. Moore: Eight	do	Assistant Architect	866 00
M. C. O'Donnell: Twelve	do	Clerk and Paymaster	1,200 00
M. N. Jarrett:	do	do and Stenographer ...	600 00
C. O'Grady:	do	Clerk of Files	600 00
M. E. McLeister: Six	do	Stenographer	247 50
G. Forester: Twelve	do	Messenger and Caretaker ...	650 00

CIVIL GOVERNMENT.—*Continued.*

PUBLIC WORKS DEPARTMENT.—*Continued.*

EXPENSES ($5,385.16).

Am. Technical Soc., books, 12.50; Art Metropole, blue print paper, 12.95	25 45
Bell Telephone Co., rent of instruments, 201.60; messages, 143.30; Brandon & Gilbert, cartage, 1.00	345 90
Bennett, W. E., photo. for report	2 75
Carswell Co., book. 5.00; Cairns, L. L., stenog. at 2.00 per day, 5.00; Campbell, A. W., trav. expenses, 192.55	202 55
Can. Legal Pub. Co., law lists, 9.00; C. P. Ry. Telegraph Co., telegrams, 76.08; Can. Exp. Co., charges, 3.60	88 68
Can. P. Ry. Co., freight charges	72
Dom. Express Co., charges, 14.80; Doane Bros., cab hire, 29.50; Dunn, Wm. K. & Co., folders, guides, etc., 10.97	55 27
Dunbar, Wilfred, services as messenger at 7.00 per week	21 00
Foster, Jas., repairing level, etc.	9 75
G. N. W. Tel. Co., messages, 78.38; Gripton, C., rubber stamps, etc, 13.20	91 58
Halford, A. J., services as draughtsman at 3.00 per day, 339.00; Heaton's Agency, commercial handbook, 1.00; Henry, Thos., blue print paper, 4.00; Hubertus, Mrs., postage stamps, 275.00	619 00
Kentleton, C., services as clerk, 48.00. King's Printer, stationery, 742.31; paper, 47.48	837 79
Lamarche, C., abstract of titles, 4.08; Lewis Rice & Son, steel tape and hammer, 8.70	12 78
McLean, J. G., services as draugthsman at 20.00 per week, 833.33; trav. expenses, 30.10	863 43
McLeister, Edith, services as stenog. at 9.00 per week	213 00
Maisonville, H. C., travelling expenses, 106.85; Medcalf, D. M., trav. expenses, 20.20; Might Directories, directory, 6.00	133 05
National Typewriter Co., repairs, 2.50; newspapers and periodicals, subs., 98.35	100 85
Ontario Land Surveyors' Association, dues	4 00
Postmaster, unpaid postage, 5.40; Potter, Chas., levelling rod, 18.00	23 40
Ramsey, J. G. & Co., photo supplies, 5.52; Reaume, Hon. J. O., travelling expenses, 137.24	142 76
Remington Typewriter Co., repairs, 23.40; Riordon Paper Mills, paper, 66.90	90 30
Rolph, Clark & Co., Ltd., engraving cards	4 50
Sparling, W. F., services as draughtsman at 20.00 per week, 400.00; Spinks, W. H., photo, for report 6.00	406 00
Tarling, C. & Co., mounting maps, 5.00; Thomson Engraving Co., cuts for report, 47.00	52 00
Toronto Ry. Co., car tickets, 181.00; Toronto Ry. and Steamboat Guide, subscription, 10.00	191 00
United Typewriter Co., inspection of machines	3 00
Warwick Bros. & Rutter, printing and binding, 188.65; Webster, T. N., services clerk at 2.00 per day, 626.00	814 65
Whitehead, W. E., time stamp	30 00

HIGHWAYS BRANCH.

SALARIES ($1,950.00).

W. A. McLean:	Twelve months' salary as Clerk		1,000 00
M. St. Charles:	do	Stenographer	500 00
E. Purvis:	do	do	450 00

EXPENSES ($1,455.64).

Art Metropole, instruments, 11.25: Bell, J. A., photo for report, 1.50	12 75
Bell Telephone Co., moving phone, .60; messages. 2.40	3 00
Bengough, T. & Son, transcript proceeding Good Roads Convention, 10.00; Bickmore, J. M.. photo for report, 3.00	13 00
Can. Society Civil Engineers. dues. 8.00. C.P.R. Tel. Co.. telegrams, 1.27	9 27
Engineers' Club, dues. 5.00; Hubertus. Mrs., postage stamps, 150.00	155 00

CIVIL GOVERNMENT.—*Continued.*

HIGHWAYS BRANCH.—*Continued.*

EXPENSES.—*Continued.*

King's Printer, stationery, 47.40. McLean, W. A., trav. expenses, 79.55...	126 95
Newspapers, magazines and journals, sundry, subscriptions, 68.04; Ramsey, J. G. & Co., photo supplies, 7.20	75 24
Riordon Paper Mills, paper, 535.28; Tarling, C. & Co., mounting maps, 2.25	537 53
Toronto Railway Co., car tickets, 1.00; Vannevar & Co., books, 31.00......	32 00
Wadsworth, Jno. A., services clerk at 14.00 per week, 100.00; Warwick Bro's & Rutter, printing and binding, 390.90	490 90

COLONIZATION ROADS' BRANCH.

SALARIES ($4,050.00).

Henry Smith, Twelve months' salary as Superintendent			1,900 00
M. P. Doherty	do	Accountant	1,200 00
J. H. Bradshaw	do	Clerk	950 00

EXPENSES ($417.21).

Art Metropole, blue prints, 2.50; Campbell, A. W., trav. expenses for self and Minister, 74.46	76 96
C. P. R. Tel. Co., telegrams, 24.15; G. N. W. Tel. Co., telegrams, 4.08; Gripton, C., stamps and supplies, 6.75	34 98
Hubertus, Mrs., postage stamps, 135.00; King's Printer, stationery, 110.94	245 94
Newspapers, sundry, advertising, 13.84; Riordon Paper Mills, paper, .34...	14 18
Smith, Henry, trav. expenses, 23.20; Warwick Bros. & Rutter, printing, and binding, 21.95	45 15

FISHERIES BRANCH.

SALARIES ($5,150.50).

S. T. Bastedo, Seven months' salary as Deputy Commissioner			1,283 00
J. S. Webster, Twelve	do	Chief Clerk	1,400 00
H. G. Cox	do	do	950 00
A. B. Wallace	do	do and Stenographer	600 00
A. J. McNeill	do	do	550 00
N. Lynch, Nine and two-thirds months' salary as Clerk			367 50

EXPENSES ($2,069.14).

American Fisheries Society, dues, 2.00; Bastedo, S. T., trav. expenses, 14.70	16 70
Bell Telephone Co., rent of instruments, 60.78; messages, 18.75..............	79 53
Brandon & Gilbert, cartage, .50; Can. Legal Pub. Co., law list, 3.00.........	3 50
Can. Express Co., charges, 29.01; Cox, H. G., trav. expenses, 9.15..........	38 16
C. P. R. Tel. Co., telegrams, 37.69; Doane Bros., cab hire, .75; Dom. Express Co., charges, 2.80	41 24
G. N. W. Tel. Co., telegrams, 57.76; Harris, Edward, 3,000 copies pamphlet on fisheries, 150.00	207 76
Hypson, M. L., services stenog. at 10.00 per week	6 70
King's Printer, stationery, 280.94; paper, 29.79	310 73
McHugh, T. G., services at 14.00 per week, 238.00. McMaster, M. H., postage stamps, 300.00	538 00
Maisonville. H. C., trav. expenses, 61.89; newspapers and periodicals, sundry. subscriptions, 32.12	94 01
North America Fish & Game Assn., dues, 6.00; Postmaster, unpaid postage, 8.14	14 14
Riordon Paper Mills. paper, 97.57; Tinsley, E., services Acting Deputy Commissioner, 300.00	397 57
Toronto Railway Co., car tickets, 15.00; Toronto Ry. & Steamboat Guide, subscriptions, 10.00	25 00
Warwick Bros. & Rutter, printing and binding, 277.10; Webster, J. S., trav. expenses, 19.00	296 10

CIVIL GOVERNMENT.—*Continued.*

GAME PROTECTION.

SALARIES ($2,400.00).

E. Tinsley, Twelve months' salary as Chief Warden	1,500 00
J. H. Pegg do Clerk...	900 00

EXPENSES ($563.86).

Bell Telephone Co., rent of instruments, 22.01; Can. Express Co., charges, 6.15	28 16
C. P. R. Tel. Co., telegrams, 10.12; Dom. Express Co., charges, 1.25........	11 37
G. N. W. Tel. Co., telegrams, 10.84; Harris, Edward, 4,000 copies pamphlet on quail, 100.00	110 84
King's Printer, stationery, 52.85; paper, 13.67	66 52
McMaster, M. H., postage stamps, 130.00; Riordon Paper Mills, paper, 17.97	147 97
Tinsley, E., trav. expenses, 6.35; Toronto Railway Co., car tickets, 15.00...	21 35
Warwick Bros. & Rutter, printing and binding	177 65

BUREAU OF LABOR.

SALARIES ($2,100.00).

Robert Glockling: Nine months' salary as Secretary	1,125 00
Jno. A. Armstrong: Three do do	375 00
M. I. Nolan: do Clerk and Stenographer............	600 00

EXPENSES ($929.43).

Armstrong, Jno., trav. expenses	18 80
Bell Telephone Co., rent of instrument, 23.76; messages, 1.20..................	24 96
Bureau of Labor Statistics of America, 50 copies of proceedings of convention, 10.00; dues, 10.00	20 00
Canada Legal Pub. Co., law lists, 3.00; Glockling, R., trav. expenses, 133.40	136 40
Gripton, C., stamps and repairs, 2.50; Hubertus, Mrs. postage stamps, 40.00	42 50
King's Printer, stationery, 94.87; paper, 6.12	100 99
Newspapers and periodicals, susbcriptions, 7.00; advertising, 45.00	52 00
Riordon Paper Mills, paper, 269.58; Toronto Railway Co., car tickets, 11.00	280 58
Warwick Bros. & Rutter, printing and binding	253 25

TREASURY DEPARTMENT.

SALARIES ($17,004.16).

Hon. A. J. Matheson: Twelve months' salary as		Treasurer...........	4,000 00
C. H. Sproule	do	Assistant Treasurer	3,000 00
W. N. Douglas:	do	Chief Clerk and Account't	1,600 00
L. V. Percival:	do	Clerk of Bonds and Algoma Taxes	1,800 00
C. A. Matthews, Jr.:	do	Clerk and Minister's Secretary	1,000 00
G. W. Duncan:	do	Cashier	1,300 00
D. R. Mackenzie	do	Second Class Clerk	1,000 00
W. A. P. Byrch:	do	do and Bookkeeper	850 00
N. H. Crow:	do	Clerk (law stamps, etc.)...	850 00
W. W. McKinlay: Two	do	Second Class Clerk	116 66
A. Gayfer: Twelve	do	Clerk and Bank Messenger	800 00
E Cosgrove:	do	Clerk	500 00
Geo. J. L. Jones: Five	do	Junior Clerk and Messenger	187 50

CIVIL GOVERNMENT.—*Continued.*

TREASURY DEPARTMENT.—*Continued.*

EXPENSES ($4,572.25).

Bank of Hamilton, to pay telegram, .25. Bond, R., cab hire, .75...............	1 00
Bell Telephone Co., rent of instruments, 88.15; messages, 11.10............	99 25
Byrch, W. A. P., meals *re* estimates, 3.50; Can. Legal Pub. Co., law lists, 6.00	9 50
Cashier, postage stamps, 92.12; Circuit Guide Co., copy of guide, .25......	92 37
Cole, N. J., services at 14.00 per week, 182.00; C.P.R. Tel. Co., telegrams, 89.48	271 48
Crain, Rolla L. Co., ledger leaves, tabs, etc., 16.20; Doane Bros., cab hire, 1.75	17 95
Dominion Express Co., charges, 9.33; Farmer Bros., portrait of Hon. J. P. Whitney, 10.00	19 33
G. N. W. Tel. Co., telegrams, 25.63; Gripton, C., stamps and repairs, 30.15	55 78
Heaton's Agency, copy hand book, 1.00; Hubertus, Mrs., postage stamps, 1,072.00	1,073 00
Jones, G. J. L., services Junior Clerk and Messenger at 8.00 per week ...	84 00
King's Printer, stationery, 742.21; paper, 49.12; cheque books, 184.50.........	975 83
McKinlay, W. W., services at 2.00 per diem, 52.00; Matheson, Hon. A. J., trav. expenses, 80.00	132 00
Messcall, J., book, 1.00; Might Directories, directories, 12.00	13 00
Newspapers, periodicals, etc., subscriptions, 188.75; National Typewriter Co., repairs, 12.50	201 25
Office Specialty Mfg. Co., trays, cards, etc., 3.75; Postmaster, unpaid postage, 7.85	11 60
Riordon Paper Mills, paper, 354.43; Taylor, N. B., services at 14.00 per week, 268.00	622 43
Toronto Railway Co., car tickets, 30.00; Toronto Railway and Steamboat Guide, subscription, 5.00	35 00
Truslove & Hansen, books, 4.24; United Typewriter Co., repairs, etc., 9.00	13 24
Warwick Bros. & Rutter, printing and binding, 644.24; Wood, W. W., extra work, preparing estimates, 1903-4-5, 200.00	844 24

SUCCESSION DUTIES BRANCH.

SALARIES ($5,329.43).

J. B. McLeod: Twelve months' salary as	Solictor		2,400 00
R. E. M. Meighen:	do	Assistant Solicitor	1,100 00
J. S. Rowland:	do	Second Class Clerk	1,000 00
M. O. Norris:	do	Stenographer	550 00
W. M. Morrow: Seven and one-half do	do	....	279 43

EXPENSES ($1,696.28).

Bell Telephone Co., rent of instrument, 23.76; messages, 2.25	26 01
Canada Law Book Co., law books, etc., 24.75; subscription to English law reports, 21.00	45 75
Can. Legal Pub. Co., law list, 6.00; Circuit Guide Co., copy of guide, .25	6 25
Clarke, B. S., services at 3.00 per day, 933.00; C. P. R. Tel. Co., telegrams, 6.70	939 70
G. N. W. Tel. Co., telegrams, 4.53; Heaton's Agency, copy of hand book, 1.00	5 53
King's Printer, stationery, 249.34; paper, 13.87	263 21
Law Society, Treasurer, dues, 34.00; McLeod, J. B., to pay duty, .50	34 50
Manual of Statistics, copy of statistics, 5.00; Morrow, W. M., services as stenog. at 1.50 per day, 84.00	89 00
National Typewriter Co., repairs, 10.00; newspapers, periodicals, etc., subscriptions, 8.35	18 35
Stevenson, M. M., services as stenog. at 8.00 per week	65 33
United Typewriter Co., typewriter, 110.00; repairs, etc., 6.00	116 00
Warwick Bros. & Rutter, printing and binding	86 65

CIVIL GOVERNMENT.—*Continued.*

PROVINCIAL AUDIT OFFICE.

SALARIES ($11,427.68).

James Clancy: Twelve months' salary as Provincial Auditor........			3,000 00
W. W. Wood:	do	Assistant Auditor	1,800 00
A. J. Rattray:	do	Chief Clerk ....^..........	1,700 00
T. P. Stewart: Ten	do	Clerk	1,203 34
G. A. Brown: Twelve	do	do	1,200 00
C. O. Brimer: do	do	do.	1,050 00
W. A. Glockling: do	do	do	600 00
W. H. Hewitt: Seven and one-half	do	do	434 67
F. J. Coles: do	do	do	434 67

EXPENSES ($1,515.44).

Bell, A. W., services at 14.00 per week, 56.00; Bell Telephone Co., rent of instruments, 45.78; messages, 1.70	103 48
Brown, G. A., travelling expenses, 13.60; Burritt, D. H., services at 14.00 per week, 78.00 ....;...:	91 60
Can. P. Ry. Tel. Co., telegram, .27; Clancy, J., travelling expenses, 6.65	6 92
Coles, F. J., services at 14.00 per week, 274.00; Crain, Rolla, L. Co., ledger leaves, etc., 37.66	311 66
Deacon, A. T., services at 14.00 per week	38 00
Gripton, C., rubber stamp repairs	40
Hewitt, W. H., services at 14.00 per week, 274.00; Heaton's Agency, copy hand book, 1.00	275 00
Hubertus, Mrs., postage stamps	25 00
International Ry. Guide, subscription	2 00
Jennings, T. R., services at 14.00 per week	40 00
King's Printer, stationery, 117.59; paper, 63.29	180 88
Might Directories, Ltd., directory	6 00
Newspapers and periodicals, 12.00; Nott, Percy, services messenger at 8.00 per week, 72.00	84 00
Patterson, J. H., services at 14.00 per week, 56.00. Penman & Sprang, refilling dupligraph, 8.00	64 00
Reid, G. S., services at 14.00 per week	138 00
Stewart, T. P., to pay cab hire	1 50
Toronto Ry. Co., car tickets, 20.00; Toronto Ry. & Steamboat Guide, subscription, 5.00	25 00
Warwick Bros. & Rutter, printing and binding, 99.60; Wood, W. W., travelling expenses, 22.40	122 00

PROVINCIAL SECRETARY'S DEPARTMENT.

SALARIES ($21,103.32).

Hon. W. J. Hanna: Twelve months' salary as Secretary and Registrar......			4,000 00
Thos. Mulvey:	do	Assistant Secretary	3,000 00
J. F. C. Usaher:	do	Deputy Registrar	1,550 00
L. Homfray Irving:	do	Assistant do	1,350 00
A. E. Semple:	do	First Class Clerk and Minister's Secretary	1,600 00
J. B. McLachlan:	do	First Class Clerk	1,500 00
J. D. Warde:	do	do	1,450 00
E. Jenkinson:	do	Second Class Clerk	1,200 00
R. A Eaton:	do	Junior Second Class Clerk...	900 00
F. Costello:	do	do do ...	900 00
E. A. Dent:	do	Clerk	700 00
M. M. Durkin:	do	Stenographer	600 00
L. C. Morrow:	do	do	600 00
Geo. O'Leary:	do	Junior Clerk	600 00
Irene L. Hoag: Eight	do	do	333 32
Edwin Woods: Six	do	Messenger	175 00
W. F. Lillico: Twelve	do	Messenger and Caretaker....	650 00

CIVIL GOVERNMENT.—*Continued.*

PROVINCIAL SECRETARY'S DEPARTMENT.—*Continued.*

EXPENSES ($7,290.94).

Bell Tel. Co., rent of instruments, 112.46; messages, 11.45	123 91
Britnell A., book, 3.25; Cairns, B., rubber stamps, .25	3 50
Can. Express Co., charges, 9.22; Can. Legal Pub. Co., law lists, 15.00	24 22
Can. Railway News Co., books, 8.40; Circuit Guide Co., copies of guide, 2.00	10 40
Carswell Co., law books, etc., 31.25; C.P.R. Tel. Co., telegrams, 36.80.....	68 05
Doane Bros., cab hire, 25.00; Dom. Express Co,, charges, 6.25	31 25
Eaton, T. Co., ribbon for documents, 1.44; Elliott, W. M. book, 7.50	8 94
G. N. W. Tel. Co., telegrams, 32.89; Graham, A., services as engrosser at 10.00 per week, 118.58	151 47
Gripton, C., stamps and repairs, 14.30; Hanna, Hon. W. J., trav. expenses, 250.00	264 30
Heaton's Agency, copy of handbook, 1.00; Hoag, Irene L., services as stenog. at 10.00 per week, 171.67	172 67
Jacobs, A. L., services as stenog. at 10.00 per week, 520.00; Jenkinson, E., trav. expenses, 5.30	525 30
Jordan, A. A., services as stenog. at 10.00 per week	175 00
King's Printer, stationery, 1,703.99; paper, 74.81	1,778 80
Law Society of Upper Canada, dues, 17.00; McCutcheon, Wm., services as extra clerk at 14.00 per week, 232.00	249 00
McIntyre, H. M., postage stamps, 715.00; McLachlan, J. B., trav. expenses, 10.00	725 00
McMaster, M H., postage stamps, 535.00; Maher, P., cab hire, 1.50	536 50
Might Directories, directories, 12.00; Mitchell, A., sealing Marriage Act forms, .50	12 50
Mulvey, T., trav. expenses, 16.60. newspapers, periodicals, etc., subscriptions, 18.00	34 60
National Typewriter Co.. repairs, etc., 9.00; Osborne, Kate E., services at 10.00 per week, 75.00	84 00
Postmaster, unpaid postage, 24.08; Remington Typewriter Co., typewriter, repairs, etc., 181.95	206 0?
Riordon Paper Mills, 34.00; Rolph & Clark, Ltd., engraving charters. 315.00	349 00
Ryan, M., services as clerk at 400.00 per annum, 274.99; Toronto Railway Co., car tickets, 30.00	304 99
Toronto Railway & Steamboat Guide, subscriptions, 20.00; Twomey, M., services as stenog. at 10.00 per week, 526.67	546 67
Tyrrell, Wm. & Co., books, 2.25; Warwick Bros. & Rutter, printing, 815.68	817 93
Williams, R. M.. engrossing charters, 19.25; Woods, Edwin, services as messenger at 7.00 per week, 67.66	86 9?

INSPECTION PUBLIC INSTITUTIONS.

SALARIES ($18,275.00).

Dr. R. W. Bruce Smith:	Twelve months' salary	as Inspector Hospitals and Charities	2,600 00
S. A. Armstrong:	do	Inspector of Asylums...	2,500 00
E. R. Rogers:	do	Inspector of Asylums and Prisons	2,500 00
Jas. Mann:	do	First Class Clerk........	1,450 00
F. M. Nicholson:	do	do	1,350 00
W. A. Kavanagh:	do	do	1,350 00
I. R. Aikens:	do	do	1,350 00
F. C. Williams:	do	do	1,300 00
F. O. Loft:	do	Second Class Clerk......	1,100 00
C. Le Brun:	do	Junior do	850 00
Edith C. Fleming: Six	do	do do	275 00
A. A. Jordan: do	do	do do	250 00
N. E. Flannigan: Twelve	do	Stenographer	500 00
E. C. Jury: do	do	Clerk	900 00

CIVIL GOVERNMENT.—*Continued.*

INSPECTION PUBLIC INSTITUTIONS.—*Continued.*

´EXPENSES ($16,852.73).

Armstrong, S. A., trav. expenses, 161.29; Aikens, I. R., to pay for law stamps re E. Booth estate, .30; trav. expenses, 27.95	189 54
Asling, Ethel M. M., services as stenog. at 10.00 per week	109 98
Bell Telephone Co., rent of instruments, 140.38; messages, 107.40; moving 'phones, 4.00	251 78
Boggey, E. Rose, services as stenog. at 450.00 per annum, 117.50; Brandon & Gilbert, cartage, .75	118 25
Cairns, B., rubber stamp and repairs, 8.90; C.P.R. Tel. Co., telegrams, 15.53	24 43
Can. Express Co., charges, 7.05; Can. Printing Co., printing blank forms, 114.75	121 80
Can. Legal Pub. Co., law lists, 6.00; Canada Law Book Co., law books, 31.50	37 50
Canada Cabinet Co., folders, etc., 11.90; Carveth, T. A. & Co., book, 2.00	13 90
Carscallen & Cahill, legal services re Isabella Little, 4.64; Chadwick, H. A., services as clerk at 50.00 per month, 140.00	144 64
Circuit Guide Co., copies of guide, .50; Chisholm, R. A., services at 550.00 per annum, 550 03	550 53
Cross, W..H., services revision of accounts of returns of Prisons and Asylums	500 00
Dominion Express Co., charges	15 50
Fee, W. G., services, 51.98. Fleming, E. .E., services at 550.00 per annum, 275.00	**326 98**
Gale. V. V., services as stenog. at 450.00 per annum, 248.75; G.N.W. Tel. Co., telegrams, 16.56	265 31
Green, Thomas, services at 15.00 per week	235 00
Hallam, R., messenger service, .15; Harcourt, E. H. Co., printing and ruling, 18.00	18 15·
Hosking, A. W., services at 40.00 per month, 404.00; Hubertus, Mrs., postage stamps, 1,282.70	1,686 70
Jordan, A. A., services as stenog. at 10.00 per week, 85.72; John Hopkins Press, sub. Am. Journal of Insanity, 5.03	90 75
King's Printer, stationery, 1,013.71; paper, 164.91	1,178 62
Law Society, dues, 17.00: Le Brun, C., special services re change in bookkeeping system, 250.00	267 00
Leng, W. E., services as clerk at 83.33 per month	220 42
Library Bureau of Canada, index, guides, etc.	48 95
McCarthy, L. M., services as stenog. at 10.00 per week	282 83
Murdock, W., services as stenog. at 37.50 per month	453 42
Monarch Typewriter Co., typewriters	225 00
National Typewriter Co., typewriter, 127.00; Noble's Dom. Detective Agency, services and expenses, 89.80	216 80
Newspapers, periodicals, etc., subscriptions	60 75
Patton, Pauline, services as stenog. at 450.00 per annum, 379.91; Perry, John, cartage, .45	398 36
Peacock, A. A., services at 60.00 per month, 446.61; trav. expenses, 351.29; To pay: Hanna, Le Seur & Price, services re Menton property, 5.00; Wilson, Pike & Gundy, services re Wilson lot, Wallaceburg, 5.00...	807 90
Peters, L. V., services at 60.00 per month, 120.00; travelling expenses, 142.40	262 40
Postmaster, unpaid postage	13 46
Riordon Paper Mills, paper, 55.45; Rogers, E. R., travelling expenses. 300.00	355 45
Shaw, J. Morgan, services as special agent at 75.00 per month, 858.87; trav. expenses, 697.71	1,556 58
Smith, R. W. B., travelling expenses	523 45
Thorne, L. E. C., services as accountant at 200.00 per month, 2,350.00; travelling expenses, 48.65	2,398 65
Toronto Ry. Co., car tickets, 145.00; Toronto Ry. & Steamboat Guide, subscription, 10.00	155 00
Trunk & Leather Goods Co., bag, box and case, 13.00; Tyrrell, Wm. & Co., books, etc., 5.50	13 50
United Typewriter Co., rent of machines, repairs, etc.	60 15
Watson. Mary A., travelling expenses	139 14
Warwick Bros. & Rutter. printing and binding, 1,206.27; binders, sheets, forms, etc., 1,239.09	2,445 36
Williams F. C., travelling expenses	48 80

CIVIL GOVERNMENT.—*Continued.*

LICENSE BRANCH.

SALARIES ($9,000.00).

E. Saunders: Twelve months' salary as	Chief Officer		2,200	00
J. W. Gordon:	do	Provincial Inspector	2,000	00
Jos. F. Mowat:	do	First Class Clerk	1,800	00
S. J. Crosby:	do	Second do	1,100	00
J. J. Mulligan:	do	Junior Second Class Clerk	800	00
W. Sailsbury:	do	do do	800	00
Tura Moore: Eight	do	Stenographer	300	00

EXPENSES ($1,367.23).

Baker, H. W., services at 14.00 per week	266	00
Bell Telephone Co., rent of instrument, 37.46; messages, 24.95	62	41
Brandon & Gilbert, cartage		50
Canada Law Book Co., law journal, 5.00; Canada Legal Pub. Co., legal charts, etc., 4.50	9	50
Can. P. R. Tel. Co., telegrams, 28.50; Can. Exp. Co., charges, 2.75	31	25
Carswell Co., subscription *Ont. Weekly Reporter,*	6	50
Circuit Guide Pub. Co., copies of guide		75
Devitt, G. W., services at 1.00 per day, 214.00; Dominion Exp. Co., charges, 10.50	224	50
G. N. W. Tel. Co., telegrams, 16.25; Gripton, C., stamps and repairs, 12.90	29	15
Hoag, E. C., services at 10.00 per week, 37.15; Hubertus, Mrs., postage stamps, 50.00	87	15
King's Printer, stationery, 214.19; paper, 57.78	271	97
Might Directories, Ltd., directory, 6.00; Moore, T., services at 7.00 per week, 149.00	155	00
Monarch Typewriter Co., exchange on typewriter, ...	92	50
Newspapers and periodicals, etc., advertising, 4.75; subscriptions, 12.00...	16	75
National Typewriter Co., supplies	5	75
Percy, J. G., services at 9.00 per week, 36.00; Postmaster, unpaid postage, 6.95	42	95
Remington Typewriter Co., repairs	18	15
St. John, W. E., services at 2.00 per day, 10.00; Souch, W. J., services at 2.00 per day, 10.00	20	00
Toronto Ry. and Steamboat Guide, subscription, 12.30; Townsend Livery, cab hire, 3.00	15	30
Warwick Bros. & Rutter, printing	11	15

REGISTRAR-GENERAL'S BRANCH.

SALARIES ($12,200:00).

Dr. Chas. A. Hodgetts: Twelve months' salary as	Dep. Reg.-General and Secretary Board of Health...		2,750	00
George Wheler:	do	Chief Clerk	1,200	00
Jas. McG. Ridley:	do	Second Class Clerk	1,150	00
Frank Jones:	do	do	950	00
C. S. Horrocks:	do	do	1,050	00
T. K. Rogers:	do	do	1,050	00
S. J. Manchester:	do	do	900	00
E. V. Donnelly:	do	do	1,050	00
W. F. Jones:	do	do	900	00
H. J. Scobie:	do	Stenographer	600	00
J. H. Latimer:	do	Messenger	600	00

EXPENSES ($3,576.34).

Bell Telephone Co., rent of instrument, 23.76; Beresford, Wm., services at 2.00 per day, 178.00	201	76
Can. Express Co., charges, .50; Canada Law Book Co., encyclopedia, 4.00	4	50
Dominion Express Co., charges		30

CIVIL GOVERNMENT.—*Continued.*

REGISTRAR-GENERAL'S BRANCH.—*Continued.*

EXPENSES.—*Continued.*

Foster, Jas., barometer, hydrometer, etc.	25	65
G. N. W. Telegraph Co., telegrams		33
Hodgetts, Dr. C. A., travelling expenses, 100.65; Hart & Riddell, marriage registers, 12.00	112	65
King's Printer, stationery, 1,068.06; paper, 41.15	1,109	21
Might Directories, Ltd., directory, 7.50; McMaster, M. H., postage stamps, 150.00	157	50
Pears, Geo., Jr., typewriters, 380.00; Postmaster, unpaid postage, .50	380	50
Riordon Paper Mills, paper	82	01
Toronto Ry. Co., car tickets	10	00
United Typewriter Co., repairs	3	00
Warwick Bros. & Rutter, printing and binding, 1,254.48; William, N. Co., cartage, .25	1,254	73

Services as Registrar in unorganized districts:

Armstrong, Jno., 6.00; Aldbright, Jno. M.. 2.40; Annis, A. E., 1.40...
Beatty. Alex., 4.40; Brett, R. H., 3.80; Cole, R., 3.80; Davies, John, 2.60; Deveney, J. A., 19.00
Deacon, F., 2.40; Guy. H. C. .60; Harris, W., 10.80
Kinney, J. W., 3.60; Kelcey, E. H.. 5.00; Lefebore, A. P., 3.40. Lowrie, Miss Maggie. 7.00
Lafrance, O.. 22.20; McAulay, A., 2.40; McArthur, Geo. J., 20.80
McDougall, W. D., 3.40; Martin, E. B., 1.80; Maw, Miss Lottie, 3.60; Miller, R. E., 4.00
Nichol, J. A., 15.00; Nichols. W. L., 12.20; Patterson. Miss O., 9.20.
Rumsey. Wm., 9.80; Sims, C. L. D., 38.60. Salt. Charles, 2.80; Stoddart. Thos.. 6.80

Walford, A. J.	234	20

PROVINCIAL BOARD OF HEALTH.

SALARIES ($8,050.66).

E. E. Kitchen, M.D. :	Eight months' salary as	Chairman		266 00
Chas. Sheard, M.D. :	Two	do	do	66 66
R. W. Bell, M.D. :	Twelve		Medical Inspector	2,050 00
J. A. Amyot, M.D. :	do		Provincial Analyst	1,600 00
G. G. Nasmith :	Eight	do	Provincial Chemist	734 00
W. T. Connell :	do	do	Asst. Bacteriologist	334 00
G. B. Lindsay :	Twelve	do	Chief Clerk	1,100 00
Geo. W. Jones :	do	do	Clerk	700 00
L. F. Young :	do	do	Messenger	650 00
J. Benning :	do	do	Stenographer	550 00

EXPENSES ($6,804.77).

Amyot. Dr. J. A., trav. expenses, 184.90; Bursar, Toronto University, rent of laboratory. 500.00	684	90
Beeman, Dr. M. J., services. 50.00; trav. expenses. 37.75	87	75
Bell Telephone Co.. rent of instruments, 86.27; messages, 23.90	110	17
Boucher, R. P.. M.D., attendance at Board meetings, 170.00; trav. expenses, 93.40	263	40
Brandon & Gilbert, cartage, 1.25; British Medical Ass'n., dues. 6.20	7	45
Britnell. J., books, 32.45; Burroughes, Williams & Co., water analysis case, 31.28	63	73
Can. Express Co., charges, 2.36; Can. Law Book Co., books. 20.00	22	36
Can. Legal Pub. Co., law list, 3.00; Cairns, B., sheet of rubber, stamps, etc., 4.85	7	85
Cassidy, J. J.. M. D., attendance at Board meetings, 145.00; trav. expenses. 6.37	151	37
Chandler, Ingram & Bell, laboratory supplies, 156.85; Carveth, J. A., books and microscopic slides, 80.60	237	45

2 P.A.

CIVIL GOVERNMENT.—*Continued.*

PROVINCIAL BOARD OF HEALTH.—*Continued.*

EXPENSES.—*Continued.*

Clark, C., washing towels, 2.00; C. P. R. Tel. Co., telegrams, 16.10	18 10
Connell, W. T., services at 500.00 per annum	166 00
Coughlin, Dr. C. B., services, 30.00; trav. expenses, 11.90	41 90
Doane Bros., cab hire, 32.50; DeLeury, Ralph, special laboratory work on sewage, 80.00	112 50
Dominion Express Co., charges, 7.20; Dunning. C. A., food for animals, 8.16	15 36
Douglas, W. J.. M.D., attendance at Board meetings, 70.00; trav. expenses, 39.60; Douglas, W. J., M.D., Estate of, services, 20.00; trav. expenses, 11.20	140 80
Fletcher Mfg. Co., laboratory supplies, 19.50; G. N. W. Tel. Co., telegrams, 11.71	31 21
Graham, D. L., services at 50.00 per month	400 00
Hall, Dr. H. B., services, 80.00; trav. expenses, 46.85	126 85
Hartz, J. F. Co., laboratory supplies, 5.74; Hodgett's, Dr. C. A., trav. expenses, 403.95	409 69
Hookway, C. W., services calculating statistics, 10.00; Irwin, C. W., brokerage charges, 10.11	20 11
King's Printer, stationery, 376.86; paper, 9.70	386 56
King, P. S. & Sons, books, etc., 23.76; Kitchen, E. E., M.D., trav. expenses, 75.19	98 95
Lake Simcoe Ice Co., ice, 30.00; Lewis, H. K., books, 70.31	100 31
Lindsay, G. B., trav. expenses, 21.80; McMaster, M. H., postage stamps, 165.00	186 80
McCullough, Dr. J. W., services, 60.00; trav. expenses, 18.95	78 95
Motton; T., food and care of animals, 221.70; Murray, G. & J., light, taps, etc., 4.20	225 90
Nasmith, G. G., services at 1,100.00 per annum, 366.00; National Ass'n. Study Tuberculosis, photos, 23.47	389 47
Newspapers, periodicals, etc., subscriptions	84 40
Oldright, W., M.D., attendance at Board meetings, 105.00; trav. expenses, 5.80	110 80
Parke Bros., photo supplies, 23.00; Parke, Davis & Co., laboratory supplies, 137.31	160 31
Patents, Commissioner of, copies of patent *re* sewage and sewage disposal	39 05
Pathalogical Dept. of Toronto General Hospital, laboratory supplies, 34.00; Pollock, J. S., iron and plate, fitting up freezer, etc., 27.15	61 15
Rawlinson, M., cartage, .50; Riordon Paper Mills, paper, 180.30	· 180 80
Robinson, Dr. W. J., services, 60.00; trav. expenses, 18.60	78 60
Roberts & Son, photos, 31.20; Thibeaudeau, A., services at 50.00 per month, 200.00	231 20
Thompson, A., M.D., attendance at Board meetings, 40.00. trav. expenses, 20.70; Thompson, A., M.D., Estate of, services, 20.00; expenses, 20.25	100 95
Toronto Ferry Co., charter of steamer to collect samples of water in lake......	90 00
Toronto Railway Co., car tickets, 7.00; Toronto Liquid Carbonate Co., laboratory supplies, 2.50	9 50
United Typewriter Co., supplies, repairs, etc., 12.00; Victor Varnish Co., oil soap, 7.00	19 00
Vereinigte Fabriken für Laboratoriums bedarf, apparatus	517 65
Warwick Bros. & Rutter, printing and binding, 532.47; Wood, W. Lloyd, · laboratory supplies, 3.00	535 47

NEGLECTED CHILDREN'S BRANCH.

SALARIES ($5,700.00).

J. J. Kelso:	Twelve months' salary as	Superintendent and Inspector	2,100 00
Wm. O'Connor:	do	Inspector	1,200 00
L. J. Harvie:	do	Children's Visitor	750 00
L. McMahon:	do	Clerk and Stenographer	600 00
B. Dewar:	do	Clerk	450 00
D. C. Cunningham:	do	Children's Caretaker	600 00

CIVIL GOVERNMENT.—*Continued.*

NEGLECTED CHILDREN'S BRANCH.—*Continued.*

EXPENSES ($3,007.81).

Advertising Novelty Mfg. Co., services and expenses *re* illustrated lectures	12	75
Bell Telephone Co., messages, 11.25; rent of instrument, 23.76	35	01
Business Systems, Ltd., binders, sheets, etc.	23	00
Can. P. Ry. Tel. Co., telegrams, 3.68; Can. Express Co., charges, .60	4	28
Can. Newspaper Co. copies of paper, 3.78; Coleman, J. S, photos of children, 10.01	13	79
Cunningham, D. C., services (1905)	50	00
Doane Bros., cab hire, 1.00; Dominion Express Co., charges, 2.30	3	30
Donohoe, T., horse hire and negatives	5	00
G. N. W. Tel. Co., telegrams, 10.36; Gripton, C., rubber stamp and repairs, 1.20	11	56
Harvie, Mrs. L. J., travelling expenses, 530.19; Hubertus, Mrs., postage stamps, 186.00	716	19
Kelso, J. J., travelling expenses, 422.80; King's Printer, stationery, 160.42; paper, 3.56	586	78
Maher, P., cab hire, 15.00; Methodist Book Room, books, 1.80; Morris, Winnifred, services as Stenog. at 12.00 per week, 120.00	136	80
Newspapers, periodicals, etc. subscriptions, 15.32; advertising, 5.00	20	32
Office Specialty Co., index cards, 1.75; O'Connor, W., travelling expenses, 513.30	515	05
Postmaster, unpaid postage		82
Reading, A. J., lantern slides, etc.	35	70
Riordon Paper Mills, paper, 168.24; Ramsey, J. G. & Co., photo supplies, 13.35	181	59
Sallows, R. R., photos, etc., 2.50; Staunton, O. B. & Co., fountain pen, 4.25	6	75
Toronto Ry. and Steamboat Guide, subscription, 10.00; Toronto Ry. Co., car tickets, 20.00	30	00
Toronto Working Boys' Union, members' fees	5	00
United Typewriter Co., repairs, etc.	6	00
Varley, H., addressing reports at 1.00 per day	10	00
Warwick Bros. & Rutter, printing and binding, 270.87; Wilson, Wm., cab hire, 2.25	273	12
Willson, W., services as Stenog. at 6.00 per week, 62.00; Wren, F., services at 6.00 per week, 258.00	320	00

DEPARTMENT OF AGRICULTURE.

SALARIES ($23,128.00).

Hon. Nelson Monteith :	Twelve months' salary as	Minister	4,000 00
C. C. James :	do	Deputy Minister and Sec. Bureau of Industries....	3,000 00
W. F. McMaster :	do	Assistant Secretary	1,800 00
W. B. Varley :	do	First Class Clerk and Minister's Secretary	1,600 00
W. O. Galloway :	do	Chief Clerk	1,750 00
N. J. Clark :	do	Second Class Clerk	1,200 00
Thos. McGillicuddy :	do	do	1,200 00
W. J. Gray :	do	do	1,200 00
Jno. Darrach :	do	do (Municipal Statistics)	1,200 00
A. G. Henderson :	do	Second Class Clerk	1,200 00
P. W. Hodgetts :	do	do and Accountant...	1,200 00
M. J. Malone :	do	do Class Clerk	1,050 00
D. F. Cashman :	do	Junior Second Class Clerk	700 00
M. J. O'Driscoll :	do	do and Messenger	700 00
Thos. Lynch :	do	Messenger	600 00
Robt. J. Dawson ·	do	Junior Messenger	260 00
Irene Webb :	do	Stenographer	468 00

CIVIL GOVERNMENT.—*Continued.*

DEPARTMENT OF AGRICULTURE.—*Continued.*

EXPENSES ($1,682.78).

Adams Furniture Co., desk fyle, 1.35; American Asso. for advancement of Science, dues, 3.00	4 35
Bell Telephone Co., messages, 36.05; rent of instruments, 132.08; Briggs, Wm., books, 4.60	172 73
Can. P. R. Telegraph Co., telegrams, 24.60; Can. Express Co., charges, 39.34	63 94
Can. Legal Pub. Co., law lists, 6.00; Circuit Guide Pub. Co., copies of guide, .50	6 50
Coo, W. C., reporting Minister's address at Dairymen's Association	3 00
Doane Bros., cab hire, 30.25; Dominion Express Co., charges, 25.12	55 37
Elliott & Co., supplies for addressing machine	3 10
G. N. W. Tel. Co., telegrams, 12.69. Gazette Printing Co., copies of paper, 20.00	32 69
Gripton, C., rubber stamps and repairs, 6.50; Heaton's Agency, copy hand-book, 1.00	7 50
Hubertus, Mrs., postage stamps	25 00
Irwin, C. W., duty, express and brokerage charges, 1.40; James, C. C., travelling expenses, 12.15	13 55
King's Printer, stationery, 332.47; paper, 36.43	368 95
Le Drew, H. H., book, 1.25; Lynch, Thos., paste, 6.00; McMaster, M. H., postage stamps, 275.00	282 25
Maher, P., cab hire, .75; Mack, C. W., rubber stamp, 2.20	2 95
Might Directories, Ltd., directory, 6.00; Monteith, Hon. N., travelling expenses, 200.00	206 00
Municipal World, Assessors' guide	50
Newspapers, periodicals, etc., subscriptions	317 41
Office Specialty Mfg. Co., ruled cards	1 03
Petersen, A., estate of, framing photo, 2.25; Postmaster, unpaid postage, 5.86	8 11
Reading, A. J., photo Massey Hall, Guelph	1 75
Toronto Ry. Co., car tickets, 20.00; Toronto Ry. and Steamboat Guide, subscriptions, 20.00	40 00
United Typewriter Co., repairs, etc.	18 10
Warwick Bros. & Rutter, printing and binding, 42.00; Wilson, Harold A. Co., postal guides, 6.00	48 00

COLONIZATION AND FORESTRY BRANCH.

SALARIES ($6,679.88).

Thos. Southworth: Twelve months' salary	as	Director	2,000 00
J. F. Clark:	do	Forester	1,463 88
N. McLeod:	do	Stenographer	600 00
A. Robertson:	do	Clerk	1,000 00
W. G. Lindsay: Eight and one-half	do	do	565 00
J. Cadieux: Twelve	do	do	800 00
H. J. Tutt: Three	do	Clerk at Station	251 00

EXPENSES ($3,881.35).

Acheson, B., services as Stenog. at 10.00 per week, 521.67; American Forestry Ass'n, dues, 2.00	523 67
American Lumberman, book	3 50
Bell Telephone Co., rent of instruments, 60.78; messages, 16.90	77 68
Bretono's, book, 1.76; Brandon & Gilbert, cartage, 2.00	3 76
Britnell, A., books, 15.75; Brown, J. P., book, 2.80	18 55
Cadieux, J., trav. expenses. 55.00; Can. Express Co., charges, 1.35	56 35
Can. Forestry Ass'n., fees, 2.00; Can. Legal Pub. Co., law list, 3.00	5 00
Clark, J. F., trav. expenses, 339.75; C. P. R. Tel Co., messages, 22.35	362 10
Detroit *Free Press,* copies of paper, 15.00. Detroit *Journal,* copies of paper, 6.00	21 00
Doane Bros., cab hire. 11.25; Dom. Express Co., charges, 4.90	16 15
Duggan, R., services as stenog. at 10.00 per week	521 67

CIVIL GOVERNMENT.—*Concluded.*

COLONIZATION AND FORESTRY BRANCH.—*Continued.*

EXPENSES.—*Continued.*

Forestry, Quarterly, subscription, vols. 3 and 4, 4.00; G. N. W. Tel. Co., telegrams, 40.17	44	17
Galbraith Photo Co., photo supplies, 1.00; Gripton, C., rubber stamps, 7.85	8	85
Howie, R. G., to pay expenses re Minister's trip, 52.00; Hubertus, Mrs., postage stamps, 770.00	822	00
International Railway Guide, subscription	2	00
Irwin, C. W., duty on book, .70; brokerage charges, .25		95
King's Printer, stationery, 359.03; paper, 3.22	362	25
Library Bureau of Canada, cabinet, cards, etc.	21	60
Lindsay, W. G., services as Clerk at 2.00 per day	188	50
Lockhart Photo Supply Co., photo supplies, 3.76;. Morang & Co., subscription to *Monthly Review*, 5.00	8	76
Massachusetts Forestry Ass'n, dues	2	00
Might Directories, directory, 7.50; Morris, W., services as stenog., at 10.00 per week, 341.34	348	84
Mountain Lumber Manufacturers' Ass'n., copy of grading rules	1	00
Newspapers, periodicals, etc., subscriptions, 17.38; Niblick, O. K., book, 1.50	18	88
O'Leary, J. J., cab hire, 2.50; Pennsylvania Forestry Ass'n, dues, 2.00...	4	50
Photo Mounts, Ltd., photo supplies, 8.90; Potter, C., photo supplies, 4.60	13	50
Ramsey, J. G. & Co., photo supplies, 64.95; Reading, A. J., lantern slides, etc., 15.10	80	05
Riordon Paper Mills, paper, 38.22; Southworth, Thos., trav. expenses, 200.00	238	22
Steinberger, Hendry Co., map of Ontario, 5.00; United Typewriter Co., repairs, etc., 8.50	13	50
Weichert, S., translating German letters, 5.00; Warwick Bros. & Rutter, printing and binding, 87.85	92	85

FACTORY INSPECTION.

SALARIES ($6,400.00).

J. T. Burke:	Twelve months' salary as	Inspector		1,150 00
Thos. Keilty:	do	do		1,150 00
A. W. Holmes:	do	do		1,100 00
Jno. Argue:	do	do		1,100 00
Margaret Carlyle:	do	Female Inspector		700 00
Annie Brown:	do	do		650 00
E. Conlin:	do	Stenographer		550 00

EXPENSES ($4,040.16).

Argue, J., travelling expenses, 744.63; Bell Telephone Co., messages, 2.15; rent of instrument, 22.01	768	84
Brown, Mrs. A., travelling expenses, 469.48; Burke, Jno. T., travelling expenses, 500.43	969	91
Can. Express Co., charges, 1.80; C. P. R. Telegraph Co., messages, .55	2	35
Carlyle, M., travelling expenses, 330.04; East & Co., suit case, 15.00	345	04
Galbraith Photo Co. photo of soap machine, 3.00; G. N. W. Tel. Co., telegrams, .50	3	50
Holmes, A. W., travelling expenses	499	04
International Ass'n of Factory Inspectors, dues, 20.00; copies of report, 10.00	30	00
Keilty, T., travelling expenses, 845.21; King's Printer, stationery, 46.25...	891	46
Landers, S. L., translating regulations re bake shops	10	00
McCrimmon, A., legal services, Rex v. Ferguson, 46.00; McMaster, M. H., postage stamps, 85.00	131	00
Newspapers, periodicals, etc., advertising, 124.00; subscriptions, 8.50	132	50
Office Specialty Co., binding cases and indexes	2	47
Queen Printing Co., printing regulations re bake shops in Yiddish	8	00
Riordon Paper Mills, paper, 54.82; Robb, Annie, transcribing reports, 120.73	175	55
United Typewriter Co., repairs, etc., 12.00; Warwick Bros. & Rutter, printing and binding, 58.50	70	50

MISCELLANEOUS.

KING'S PRINTER.

SALARIES ($4,600.00).

L. K. Cameron: Twelve months' salary as King's Printer			1,600 00
S. P. Grant:	do	Assistant King's Printer	1,100 00
W. H. Clarke:	do	Chief Clerk	1,000 00
W. H. Sutherland:	do	Clerk	900 00

EXPENSES ($171.87).

Bell Telephone Co., rent of instruments, 45.78; messages, 10.80	56 58
Can. Leg. Pub. Co., law list, 4.50; Charles, D. J. H., services, taking stock, 50.00	54 50
Dominion Express Co., charges	75
King's Printer, stationery, 11.80; paper, .24	12 04
Might Directories, directory, 6.00; newspapers, periodicals, etc., subscriptions, 12.00	18 00
Toronto Railway Co., car tickets, 20.00; Toronto Ry. and Steamboat Guide, subscriptions, 10.00	30 00

OFFICIAL GAZETTE ($5,843.67).

Warwick Bros & Rutter, printing	5,843 67

INSPECTION OF REGISTRY OFFICES ($2,250.00).

D. Guthrie, Twelve months' salary as Inspector	1,750 00
do travelling expenses	496 15
Can. Express Co., charges, .40; Dom. Express Co., charges, .30	70
Warwick Bros. & Rutter, printing	3 15

MUNICIPAL AUDITOR ($2,713.72).

J. B. Laing, Twelve months' salary as Auditor	2,100 00
do travelling expenses	450 00
Bell Telephone Co., rent of instrument, 7.05; messages, .60	7 65
C.P.R. Tel. Co., messages, .70; G.N.W. Tel. Co., messages, 1.18	1 88
Hubertus, Mrs., postage stamps, 20.00; King's Printer, stationery, 8.85	28 85
Riordon Paper Mills, paper, 73.89; Warwick Bros. & Rutter, printing, 51.45	125.34
Total Civil Government	$428,280 46

LEGISLATION.

SALARIES ($25,050.00).

Hon. J. W. St. John: Twelve months' salary as Speaker			2,500 00
Hon. Chas. Clarke:	do	Clerk of the House	2,000 00
A. H. Sydere:	do	Clerk's Assistant and Clerk of Routine	1,800 00
F. J. Glackmeyer:	do	Sergeant-at-arms	1,400 00
A. M. Dymond:	do	Law Clerk	1,500 00
W. B. Wilkinson:	do	Assistant Law Clerk	1,500 00
C. S. Berthon:	do	Stenographer	600 00
J. M. Delamere:	do	Postmaster	1,500 00
J. W. Dill:	do	Assistant Postmaster	950 00
Avern Pardoe:	do	Librarian	2,000 00
M. Wilson:	do	Assistant Librarian	1,100 00
E. J. O'Neill:	do	Assistant Librarian (Annex)	650 00

LEGISLATION.—*Continued.*

SALARIES.—*Continued.*

Alexander Fraser:	Twelve months' salary as	Archivist	1,500 00
J. N. Belanger:	do	Clerk	800 00
Muriel Merrill:	do	Stenographer	550 00
L. K. Cameron:	do	Accountant of the House	400 00
F. G. Lee:	do	Housekeeper and Chief Messenger	1,000 00
M. J. Collier:	do	Assistant Housekeeper.	900 00
M. Bailey:	do	House Messenger	700 00
V. P. Fayle:	do	do	650 00
D. F. Tolchard:	do	do	500 00
D. Keenan:	do	do	550 00

CLERKS OF COMMITTEES ($3,279.00).

Bartlett, P. H., Services as Clerk to Municipal Committee	850 00
Robinson, Napier, do do Public Accounts Committee	250 00
Carter, W.; do Secretary to Mr. Speaker	264 00
Jennings, John, do Secretary to Leader of Opposition	1,000 00
Kent, R. H., do Clerk of Committees	850 00
Banks, Wm. Jr., services reporting financial statement, 40.00; Boultbee, H., Reporter Public Accounts Committee, 25.00	65 00

SESSIONAL CLERKS, WRITERS, MESSENGERS, PAGES, ETC. ($15,890.00).

Writers at 3.00 per day:

Burritt, D. H., 258.00; Harper, Richard, 258.00; Cutten, W. E., 300.00; Lilley, F. G., 279.00; Tooley, R., 216.00..	1,311 00

Writers at 2.50 per day:

Bennett, J. M.	215 00

Writers at 2.00 per day:

Beresford, Wm., 170.00: Bateson, G. A., 146.00; Badger, A. L., 88.00; Brown, John, 170.00; Carmichael, D., 150.00; Caswell, Jas., 12.00; Carroll, G. H., 142.00: Gifford, F. M., 170.00: Hawkins. D., 170.00; Hugill, W. M., 160.00; Knight, E. J., 48.00; Lillle, Jno., 122.00; Matson, Robt., 120.00; Maude, Wm., 170.00; Morris, W. J., 170.00; McCutcheon, Wm., 170.00; McBride, W. G., 130.00; McIntyre, J. A., 148.00; Peer, M. E., 130.00: St. John, Wm. C., 150.00 Souch, W. J., 122.00; Wilmott, J. E., 170.00.................................	3,028 00

Stenographers at 3.00 per day:

Jennings, Thos. R.	268 00

Stenographers at 2.00 per day:

Banford, E. Blanche, 178.00: Boyd, Elena, 150.00; Brownlee, Louise J., 178.00; Campbell, Florence M., 182.00: Frazer, Edith, 178.00: Irving, Grace, 178.00: King, M. D., 144.00 Kinnear, Mabel E., 172.00; Leitch, T., 122.00; McLachlan, E. M., 144.00; McMartin, Lily L., 158.00; Macpherson, Agnes, 178.00; Phillips, L. M., 170.00; Wells, Francis, 178.00.............................	2,310 00

Pages at 1.00 per day:

Burns, W., 86.00; Cameron, R., 85.00; Campaign, A., 86.00; Clarke, R. R., 86.00: Clarke, W. K., 86.00: Cuthbert. John, 86.00: Fitzgerald, Thos., 86.00: Fox. Fred. C., 86.00: Greer. Douglas, 86.00: Jennings, Douglas, 86.00; Kaiser, Brock, 86.00; Kinney, J. H., 86.00; Lucas, Fred., 86.00; McBride, Sidney H., 86.00; Rutherford, E. H., 86.00; Steele, Fred., 86.00; Thompson, P. H., 86.00; Watts. J. W., 86.00	1,547 00

LEGISLATION.—*Continued.*

SESSIONAL CLERKS, WRITERS ,MESSENGERS, PAGES, ETC.—*Continued.*

Messengers at 3.00 per day:
Beck, Joseph, 261.00; Harris, Edward, 258.00 .... 519 00

Messengers at 2.00 per day:
Ball, Richard, 172.00; Blanchett, F. E., 170.00; Brethour, Jas., 170.00;
Brown, Robt., 170.00; Burns, Hubert, 190.00; Cordingly, W. W., 178.00;
Craig, Wm., 176.00; Daville, E. M., 164.00; Dunn, S. Irving, 172.00;
Delmage, R. D., 188.00; Dunn, Wm., 174.00; Fraser, Allan M., 172.00;
Greer, Jas., 172.00; Huyck, Bruce, 184.00; Jones, Geo. J. L., 176.00;
Lambe, Jno., 170.00; Lowe, A., 178.00; McConnell, A. H., 128.00;
McClure, John. 172.00; McMillan, J., 170.00; McNeish, Jno., 174.00;
Magee, Jas., 172.00; Mills, R. Wesley, 178.00; Parry, Jno. J., 172.00;
Powers, Jas., 172.00; Ross, David, 170.00; Scott, George, 122.00;
Scovill, A. G., 192.00; Shier, Jesse, 170.00; Thompson, Jos., 172.00;
Towers, Jno. W., 138.00; Umphrey, N., 172.00; Wilson, W. L., 170.00;
Wadsworth, Jno. A., 172.00;   Williams, Geo., 122.00.................. 5,914 00

Messengers at 1.50 per day:
Hesketh, Angus, 129.00; Swanton, Robt., 129.00............................. 258 00

Mesesngers at 1.00 per day:
Davidson, W. D. 96 00

Messengers at .50 per day:
Horn, H., 21.00; Kesteven, John, 15.50 .... 36 50

Charwomen at 1.25 per day:
Carr, Mrs. A., 83.75;   Currie, Mrs. Isabella, 103.75;
Craik, Mrs. Elizabeth, 105.00;   Reid, Mrs. Mary J., 85.00;
McCann, Bella, 10.00 .... 387 50

POSTAGE AND COST OF HOUSE POST OFFICE ($1,842.03).

Cairns, B., stamps and repairs 4 85
King's Printer, document boxes, 31.80; McIntyre, M., postage stamps,
1,300.00 .... 1,331 80
Postmaster, carriage of mails, 500.00; Postmaster, unpaid postage, 5.38... 505 38

STATIONERY, PRINTING AND BINDING ($52,339.93).

Bain & Cubitt, book, paper, etc., 1,058.58; Beck, C., Mfg. Co., boxes,
30.60 .... 1,089 18
Bouvier, L. P., envelopes for members 175.00; Brandon & Gilbert, cart-
age, 1.00 .... 176 00
Cairns, B., rubber stamps, 1.10; Can. Express Co., charges, 214.18......... 215 28
Can. Law Book Co., delivering statutes, 4.55; Canada Stationery Co.,
filing boxes, 35.00 .... 39 55
Copp, Clark Co., engraving maps. etc. 606 00
Dom. Express Co., charges, 439.44; Firstbrook Box Co., boxes, 102.08... 541 52
Grand & Toy, stationery for members, 1,400.00; Grip, Limited, half tones,
etc., 24.55 .... 1,424 55
G. T. Railway Co., freight charges, .92; Harcourt, E. H. Co., half tones.
etchings. lithographing, etc., 698.61 .... 699 53
Hart & Riddell, paper, 496.00; Hopkins, F., cartage, 6.25 .... 502 25
Hubertus, Mrs., postage stamps, 80.00; Jones, J. L., Engraving Co., half
tones, 220.66 .... 300 66
King's Printer, stationery, etc., 1,795.93; Ontario Engraving Co., half
tones for reports, 87.58 .... 1,883 51
Photo Engravers, Ltd., half tones for reports, 177.52; Riordon Paper
Mills, paper, 18,294.51 .... 18,472 03
Rolph & Clark. cheque book, etc., 13.50; Tarling. C. & Co., mounting
maps, 100.00 .... 113 50
Thomson Engraving Co., engravings for reports. etc. 422 73
Toronto Engraving Co., engraving diagrams, etc., for reports 105 12

LEGISLATION.—*Continued.*

STATIONERY, PRINTING AND BINDING.—*Continued.*

Toronto Lithographing Co., extra engraving and colors, 150.00; 2,000 maps Sudbury nickel region, 450.00; 2,000 maps of Windy Ann Lake and Murray Mine. 115.00	715 00
Toronto Railway Co., car tickets, 10.00; Warwick Bros. & Rutter, printing and binding, 37,048.00	37,058 00
Williams, N. & Co., cartage	2 10
	64,373 51
Less paper transferred to Departments	12,033 58
	52,339 93

LIBRARY ($4,055.00).

Annual Dues:

American Dialect Society, 1.00; American Economic Association, 4.00; American Forestry Association, 2.00; American Political Science Association, 3.00; National Geographic Society, 2.00 .... 12 00

Books ·

Allen, E. G. & Son, 589.01; Annual Review Pub. Co., 3.50; Baker, Taylor & Co., 20.81; Barry, J. W., 3.00; Biographical Pub. Co.. 15.00; Boston, H. C. Bros., 36.85; Briggs, W., 51.27; Britnell, A., 9.90; Britnell, J., 8.85; Brough. Wm., Sons. 14.07; Butterworth & Co., 10.91; Cadby, J. W., 3.18; Can. Law Book Co., 111.20; Can. Ry. News Co., 3.00; Carswell Co., 289.51; Carveth. J. A. & Co., 24.35; Chapman, A. T., 1.00; Chicago University Press. 6.69; Clark, Arthur H. & Co., 18.80; Clarke, Robt. Co.. 1.48; Copp Clark Co., 92.40; Dana, W. B. Co., 2.00; Davis, T. A. & Co., 4.00; Desbarats Advertising Co., 2.50; Diome, Dr. N. E.. 3.00; Dodd. Mead & Co., 16.46; Dussaulte & Proulx. 1.13; Emerson, G. D., 1.10; Edwards, Francis, 17.13; Falcain Society, .89; Foote, A. R., 3.60; Forestry & Irrigation Pub. Co., 6.30; Foster, J. G. & Co., 3.00; Gagnon, E., .82; Girouard. Hon. Justice, 10.00; Goodspeed's Bookshop, 17.00; Gosselin, Rev. A. H., .82; Grant, Jno., 9.43; Gray, Henry, 4.22; Harding, Geo.. 286.19; Harper Bros., 6.87; Heaton's Agency, .60; Hicks, M. & Co., 5.30; Historical Pub. Co., 1.50; Hitchman, J., 13.38; Holt, Henry & Co., 15.75; Hopkin's Press. John, 3.00; Houghton. Mifflin & Co., 23.81; Houston, W. R., 3.00; Houston's Standard Publications, 5.00; Jack, D. R., 3.50; Keith. M. S., 2.00; Kelly Law Book Co., 42.56; Kelly Pub. Co., 5.00; Kimball Bros., 17.59; King, P. S. & Son, 141.37; La Patrie Pub. Co., .55; Lauriat, Chas. E. Co., 10.50; Leslie, F. H., .50; Leslie, J., 10.00; Librairie, Beauchemin, 5.00; Lippincott, J. B. & Co., 8.70; Little, Brown & Co., 5.32; Longmans, Green & Co., 6.12; Lovell, J. & Son, 7.96; Lyon, J. B., & Co., 2.50; McAnish & Co., 20.00; McDonough, J., 15.67; McGraw Pub. Co., 7.65; Macmillan & Co.. 5.20; Moody Corporation, 7.50; Morang & Co., 86.19; Morrison, N. F.. .68; Morton, J. P., & Co.. 4.00; Mudie's Select Library, 119.84; Museum Book Store, 27.30; National Conference of Charities, 1.25; New York State Library. .25; New York Tribune Association, 1.50; Niel, Morrow. Dodd Book Co.. 4.18; Nunn, John, 2.00; Pickering & Chatto, 1.07; Pierre, Georges Roy, 2.00; Publisher's History of Royal N. W. Mounted Police, 5.00; Poole, Arthur & Co.. 13.50; Publisher's Weekly. 21.12; Putnam, G. P. Sons, 28.30; Quebec Daily Telegraph. 1.67; Renault, R.. 32.64; Rouillard. E.. 3.00; Roy, P. G., 12.00; Scribner's, Chas. Sons, 2.00; Scientific American Compiling Dept, 68.64; Seers, R., 2.01; Small, Maynard & Co., 2.90; Smith, W. H. & Son, 14.50; Statute Law Book Co., 50.50; Street, G. & Co.. 3.75; Sutton, Alfred. 7.65; Sweet & Maxwell, 17.87; Theoret, C., 5.00; Thomas, Cyrus, 1.50; Thompson, E. & Co., 30.00;

LEGISLATION.—*Continued.*

LIBRARY.—*Continued.*

Toronto Antiquarian Book Co., 28.00; Tyrrell, Wm. & Co., 176.22; Union Pub. Co., 5.00; Van Nostrand, D. Co., 15.11; Viscount de Fronsac, 1.00; Westmount Co., 2.00; Wilson, H. W. Co., 22.70	2,931	61
Bartlett & Co., dictionaries, 5.15; Boston Book Co., copies Can. Monthly, 1.60	6	75
Can. Express Co., charges, 14.68; Can. Legal Pub. Co., legal charts and law lists, 7.50	22	18
Carswell Co., Law Journal reports, 300.00; binding, 9.90	309	90
Circuit Guide Pub. Co., copies of guide, .50; C. P. Ry. Co., freight charges, 2.29	2	79
Curry, A., material for repairing books, 5.69; Dom. Express Co., charges, 26.75	32	44
G. T. Railway Co., freight charges, 1.58; Irwin, C. W., brokerage charges, 20.40	21	98
Magazines and periodicals: *American Academy Political Science*, 5.00; *Revue Canadienne*, 3.00; Tyrrell, Wm & Co., 288.05	296	05
Might Directories, directory, 6.00; Tarling, C. & Co., mounting maps, 62.40	68	40
Warwick Bros. & Rutter, printing and binding	350	65
Woodbridge, T. & Co., punches		25

INDEMNITY TO MEMBERS ($100,901.40).

Accountant of the House, to pay indemnity and mileage to members	100,901	40

EXPENSES ($11,833.00).

Annual Review Pub. Co., 100 copies *Review*, 227.50; Armour & Mickle, services *re* Mines Amendment, 100.00	327	50
Beck, Jos., services in reading room at 3.00 per diem	51	00
Bell Telephone Co., rent of instruments, 262.67; messages, 56.00	318	67
Biographical Pub. Co., 100 copies *Sir Oliver Mowat*	500	00
Brandon & Gilbert, cartage, 5.75; Bruce, J., group picture members L. A., 100.00	105	75
Burritt, D. H., services in Law Clerk's office at 3.00 per diem	90	00
Campbell, F. M., services in Law Clerk's Office at 2.00 per diem	100	00
Can. Express Co., charges. 113.34; Can. Law Book Co., 100 copies Weir's Assessment Law, 450.00	563	34
Can. Legal Pub. Co., law lists, 10.50; Carswell Co., books, 20.00	30	50
Can. Printing Co., 25,000 copies Hon. Provincial Secretary's speech *re* Liquor License Act	600	00
C. P. R. Tel. Co., telegrams, 5.47; Cutten, W. E., services proofreading, etc., 200.00	205	47
Dominion Express Co., charges	125	17
Dunn, S. J., services in King's Printer's office at 2.00 per diem	418	00
Fraser, Edith S., services Stenog. in Speaker's office at 6.50 per week	68	50
Gilbert, Dunn & Woodland, typewriter supplies	15	00
Gillies, A. B., services in Post Office at 2.00 per diem	730	00
G. N. W. Tel. Co., telegrams, 21.15; Gripton, C., stamps and repairs, .80	21	95
Heaton's Agency, copy of handbook, 1.00; Hewitt, Alfred, 150 copies Can. Year Book, 25.00	26	00
Houston's Standard Publications, 100 copies of Annual Financial Review	250	00
International Railway Guide, subscriptions	9	00
Kent, R. A., services *re* Ontario Railway Act	150	00
King's Printer, stationery, 1,811.72; paper, 1.76; 4,000 copies of Premier's speech on University Bill. 91.26	1,904	74
Librarian University of Toronto, 150 copies "Historical Publications"	112	50
Lovell, Jno. & Son, index to Dominion and Provincial Statutes, 2.50; copy of compendium, 3.00	5	50
McEachern's Cleaning and Pressing Co., cleaning and pressing official suits	2	55
McCutcheon, Thos., Messenger, at 2.00 per diem	30	00
McLean, Starr & Spencer, legal services *re* bill inspecting prospectuses	100	00

LEGISLATION.—*Concluded.*

EXPENSES.—*Continued.*

McPherson, W. D., legal services *re* Mines Act	1,000 00
Might Directories, directories, 43.50; Mills, R. W., services at 2.00 per day, 34.00	77 50
Munro, R. H. R., services in library at 2.00 per day	134 00
Murray, W. A. & Co., supplies for Mr. Speaker	33 00
National Typewriter Co., rent of machines	35 00
Newspapers and periodicals, advertising, 92.20; subscriptions, 704.63	796 83
Nunn, Jno., engraving and books	12 50
Police, Chief of, services of force at opening of Legislature	40 00
Remington Typewriter Co., Ltd., rent of machines	32 00
Robertson, N., 100 copies History County of Bruce	250 00
Robinson, C. C., services as Counsel, Railway Committee	600 00
Score, R. & Son, clothing for pages, 316.15; Stewart, A. M., legal services, 50.00	366 15
Star Cleaning and Pressing Co., cleaning and pressing official suits	1 00
Tolchard, D. F., meals for telegraph operators during session	52 50
Toronto Railway Co., car tickets, 120.00; Toronto Railway and Steamboat Guide, subscriptions, 10.00	130 00
United Typewriter Co., rent of machines, 62.00; Williams, N. & Co., cartage, .90	62 90
Wyant, Geo. V., services *re* Assessment Act, 16.00; trav. expenses, 18.25	34 25
Archivist:	
Annual Review Pub. Co., review	20 25
Bastedo, C. N., historical papers, books, etc.	33 69
Bell Tel. Co., messages, 3.35; Brandon & Gilbert, cartage, 16.75	20 10
Briggs, Wm., book, 7.00; Britnell, A., book, 6.95	13 95
Britnell, J., books, 137.50; Bruce Photo Art Studio, photo, .50	138 00
Can. Express Co., charges, 3.35; Can. Legal Pub. Co., law lists, 3.00	6 35
Carter, J. Smith, books, 4.00; C. P. Railway Co., freight charges, 1.46	5 46
C. P. R. Tel. Co., telegrams, 1.08; Dominion Book Store, book, 1.50	2 58
Dominion Typewriter Exchange, rent of typewriter	17 50
Educational Review, book, 2.00; Fraser, Alex. trav. expenses, 88.46	90 46
G. T. Railway Co., freight charges, 27.76; Irwin, C. W., brokerage, 2.75	30 51
Jones, Rev. Arthur E., Jones' collection of manuscripts *re* early Ontario	500 00
Killaly, R. F., photo, 10.00; Kimble Bros., books, 31.84	41 84
King's Printer, paper, 24.10; stationery, 88.49	112 59
Leslie, F. H., book, .50; newspapers and periodicals, subscriptions, 27.50	28 00
Nunn, Jno., books, photos, etc., 22.75; Potter, Chas., reading glass, 1.60	24 35
Rawlinson Express Co., cartage. .75; Renault. R., books, 25.10	25 85
Riordon Paper Mills, paper, .68; Rouillard. E., book, 2.00	2 68
Sober, M. G., books, 71.50; Trott, W. D., photo, 1.07	72 57
United Typewriter Co., typewriter, 120.00; Warwick Bros. & Rutter. printing, 11.50	131 50
Williams, N. & Co., cartage	1 00
Total Legislation	$215.195 36

ADMINISTRATION OF JUSTICE

SUPREME COURT OF JUDICATURE ($36,874.65).

Hon. Chas. Moss	Chief Justice of Ontario,	Allowance	1,000 00
Hon. F. Osler	Justice of Appeal,	do	1,000 00
Hon. J. T. Garrow	do	do	1,000 00
Hon. J. J. Maclaren	do	do	1,000 00
Hon. Sir J. A. Boyd	Chancellor of Ontario,	do	1,000 00
Hon. Jas. Magee	Justice, Chancery,	do	1,000 00
Hon. R. M. Meredith	do	do	1,000 00
Hon. J. P. Mabee	do	do	1,000 00

ADMINISTRATION OF JUSTICE.—*Continued.*

SUPREME COURT OF JUDICATURE.—*Continued.*

Hon. W. G. Falconbridge.....Chief Justice, King's Bench, Allowance			1,000 00
Hon. W. P. R. Street.........Justice, do do			500 00
Hon. B. M. Britten............. do do do			1,000 00
Hon. W. R. Riddell............. do do do			224 65
Hon. Sir W. R. Meredith.....Chief Justice, Common Pleas, do			1,000 00
Hon. Hugh McMahon.........Justice, Common Pleas, do			1,000 00
Hon. J. V. Teetzel............. do do do			1,000 00
Hon. Sir Wm. Mulock.........Chief Justice, Exchequer, do			1,000 00
Hon. R. C. Clute.................Justice do do			1,000 00
Hon. F. A. Anglin............. do do do			1,000 00
J. A. McAndrew: Twelve months' salary as Registrar			2,000 00
Jas. S. Cartwright: do Master-in-Chambers			3,200 00
Fulford Arnoldi: do Clerk			1,850 00
Clarence Bell: do Assistant Clerk			1,100 00
A. B. G. Cull: do Entering Clerk			700 00
Thos. Hodgins: do Master-in-Ordinary			4,000 00
Neil McLean: do Chief Clerk and Accountant			2,000 00
A. E. Bastedo: do Clerk and Stenographer			1,300 00
Jno. H. Thom: do Senior Taxing Officer			2,200 00
M. J. McNamara: do Junior do			1,800 00

REGISTRAR SUPREME COURT AND COURT OF APPEAL.

EXPENSES ($10.50).

Canada Legal Pub. Co., legal chart and law list, 4.50; Might Directories, Ltd., directory, 6.00	10 50

MASTER-IN-CHAMBERS.

EXPENSES ($314.67).

Brandon & Gilbert, cartage, .75; Can. Legal Pub. Co., legal charts and law lists, 9.00	9 75
Can. Law Book Co., law books, 9.00; Can. Stamp and Stencil Co., stamps and repairs, 1.00	10 00
Carswell Co., law books and reports, 16.10; Circuit Guide Pub. Co., copies of guide, 4.00	20 10
Hubertus, Mrs., postage stamps, 75.00; King's Printer, stationery, 197.32	272 32
Warwick Bros. & Rutter, printing, 2.00; Williams, N. & Co., cartage, .50	2 50

MASTER-IN-ORDINARY.

EXPENSES ($177.04).

Brandon & Gilbert, cartage, 1.25; Can. Legal Pub. Co., legal chart and law lists, 7.50	8 75
Can. Law Book Co., law books, 8.50; Can. Stamp and Stencil Co., stamps and repairs, 1.75	10 25
Carswell & Co., law books and reports, 32.50; Circuit Guide Pub. Co., copies of guide, 1.00	33 50
Hubertus, Mrs., postage stamps, 13.00; King's Printer, stationery, 95.14; paper, .70	108 84
National Typewriter Co., repairs, 2.50; Remington Typewriter Co., supplies, .95	3 45
Warwick Bros. & Rutter, binding, 12.00; Williams Express Co., cartage, .25	12 25

TAXING OFFICERS.

EXPENSES ($46.80).

Brandon & Gilbert, cartage, 75c.; Can. Legal Pub. Co., legal charts and law lists, 9.00	9 75
Carswell & Co., law books and reports, 6.50; Gripton, C., repairs to stamp, etc., 4.00	10 50
King's Printer, stationery	26 55

ADMINISTRATION OF JUSTICE.—*Continued.*

JUDGES' LIBRARY AND COPIES JUDICATURE ACT.
EXPENSES ($944.80).

Boyd, Hon. Chancellor, grant to library	200 00
Carswell & Co., 17 copies Judicature Act	244 80
Osler, Hon. Justice, grant to library	500 00

COURT OF APPEAL.
SALARIES ($3,200.00).

C. S. Grant : Twelve months' salary as Assistant Clerk and Clerk of Election Court			1,500 00
Eli Oliver:	do	Usher and Messenger	800 00
W. M. Winterberry :	do	Secretary to Judges	900 00

EXPENSES ($1,011.06).

Bell Telephone Co., rent of instrument, 22.50; Brandon & Gilbert, cartage, .75	23 25
Canada Law Book Co., law books and reports, 5.00; printing catalogue, 124.40	129 40
Circuit Guide Pub. Co., copies of guide, 1.00; Hubertus, Mrs., postage stamps, 35.00	36 00
King's Printer, stationery, 66.82; paper, 11.89	78 71
Might Directories, Ltd., directories, 12.00; Moss, Hon. Chief Justice, allowance, petty expense fund, 550.00	562 00
Oliver, Eli, special services *re* Judges' Library catalogue	100 00
Remington Typewriter Co., repairs, 19.85; Toronto Ry. Co., car tickets, 3.00	22 85
Warwick Bros. & Rutter, printing and binding, 58.60; Williams, N., cartage, .25	58 85

HIGH COURT.
SALARIES ($2,800.00).

G. B. Nicol : Twelve months' salary as Clerk of Assize			1,400 00
A. E. Trow :	do	Clerk of Process.......................	1,400 00

EXPENSES ($132.55).

Brandon & Gilbert, cartage, .25; Can. Legal Pub. Co., legal chart and law lists, 7.50	7 75
Hubertus, Mrs., postage stamps, 16.50; King's Printer, paper, 37.85; stationery, 14.90	69 25
Might Directories, Ltd., directory, 6.00; Nicol, G. B., allowance for rent of office, 25.00	31 00
Warwick Bros. & Rutter, printing	24 55

CENTRAL OFFICE.
SALARIES ($14,094.00).

M. B. Jackson : Twelve months' salary as Clerk of the Crown			2,500 00
Edmund Harley :	do	Clerk of Records and Writs...	1,550 00
D'Arcy Hinds :	do	Judgment Clerk	1,150 00
A. J. Elliott :	do	Clerk	1,100 00
Wm. MacTavish :	do	do	1,100 00
F. W. Scott :	do	do	900 00
R. F. Killaly :	do	do	900 00
M. B. Black :	do	do	850 00
R. W. Ralfe :	do	do	750 00
Geo. Hilliar :	do	Housekeeper and Messenger......	700 00
J. Gorrie :	do	Messenger	650 00
G. Crawford :	do	do	400 00
C. Sutherland :	do	Housekeeper	400 00
G. Smith :	do	Assistant Housekeeper	400 00
N. J. Harrison :	do	Assistant to do	480 00
M. Hilliar :	do	do do	264 00

ADMINISTRATION OF JUSTICE.—*Continued.*

CENTRAL OFFICE.—*Continued.*

EXPENSES ($736.53).

Arthurs & Cox, artificial feet for G. Smith, 130.00; Brandon & Gilbert, cartage, 1.25	131 25
Can. Law Book Co., law books, 5.00; Can. Legal Pub. Co., legal charts and law lists, 13.50	18 50
Carswell & Co., law books, 6.50; Circuit Guide Pub. Co., copies of guide, .75	7 25
Hubertus, Mrs.; postage stamps, 17.00; International Ry. Pub. Co., subscription to guide, 2.25	19 25
King's Printer, stationery, 318.13; paper, 7.35; Might Directories, Ltd., directory, 6.00	331 48
United Typewriter Co., repairs, 3.00; Warwick Bros. & Rutter, printing and binding, 225.55	228 55
Williams, N. & Co., cartage	25

REGISTRAR'S OFFICE.

SALARIES ($10,400.00).

Geo. S. Holmsted:	Twelve months' salary as	Senior Registrar and Referee of Titles	3,000 00
A. F. Maclean:	do	Junior Registrar	2,200 00
C. O. Strange:	do	Clerk	1,200 00
A. Y. Blain:	do	do	1,500 00
W. W. Perry:	do	Usher and Stenographer to Judges	900 00
R. Lawson:	do	Usher and Stenographer ...	700 00
R. A. Walker:	do	do ...	900 00

EXPENSES ($882.66).

Bell Telephone Co., rent of instruments, 12.50; Brandon & Gilbert, cartage, 1.00	13 50
Canada Law Book Co., law books, 5.00; Canada Legal Pub. Co., legal charts and law lists, 9.00	14 00
Canadian Express Co.. charges, .50; C.P.R. Telegraph Co., telegrams, 19.16	19 66
Circuit Guide Pub. Co., copies of guide, 22.00; Dominion Express Co., charges, .65	22 65
G.N.W. Telegraph Co., telegrams, 23.38; Gripton, C., stamps and repairs, 1.75	25 13
Holmsted. G. S. sundry disbursements, 2.85; Hubertus. Mrs.. postage stamps, 49.00	51 85
King's Printer, stationery, 613.58; paper, 6.64; Might Directories, Ltd., directories, 12.00	637 22
Remington Typewriter Co., repairs, etc., 14.50; Riordon Paper Mills, paper, .17	14 67
Warwick Bros. & Rutter, printing and binding, 82.98; Williams, N. & Co.. cartage, 1.00	83 98

WEEKLY COURT ($1,637.05).

Geo. M. Lee: Twelve months' salary as Registrar and Clerk	1,600 00
Canada Legal Pub. Co., law list. 3.00; Carswell Co., law books and reports, 16.00	19 00
King's Printer, stationery, 12.05; Might Directories, Ltd., directory, 6.00	18 05

EXCHEQUER DIVISION ($750.00).

Geo. L. Crooks: Twelve months' salary as Usher and Stenographer	750 00

ADMINISTRATION OF JUSTICE.—*Continued.*

SURROGATE COURT

SALARIES ($3,025.00).

C. J. McCabe : Twelve months' salary as Surrogate Clerk		2,000 00
W. S. Anderson : do Clerk		800 00
F. B. Reade : do Stenographer (part time)		225 00

EXPENSES ($122.24).

Brandon & Gilbert, cartage, .25; Can. Legal Pub. Co., legal charts and law lists, 9.00	9 25
Gripton, C., repairing stamps, 14.50; King's Printer, stationery, 62.94...	8 44
Might Directories, Ltd., directory, 6.00; Warwick Bros. & Rutter, printing and binding, 29.55	35 55

COMMUTATIONS *re* SURROGATE JUDGES, LOCAL MASTERS, ETC. ($28,428.57).

His Honor Judge Ardagh : Twelve months' commutation as Surrogate Judge						585 00
do	McDonald :		do			690 00
do	Benson :		do			880 00
do	Winchester :		do			2,600 00
do	Morgan :		do			1,600 00
do			do			1,500 00
do	Price :		do			752 00
do	Hardy :		do			611 50
do	McCarthy : Six months'		do			84 00
do	Doyle : Twelve months'		do			1,000 00
do	McWatt :		do			1,000 00
do	Barron :		do			873 00
do	Barron : Twelve months' commutation as Local Master...					850 00
do	Klein :		do		...	400 00
J. E. O'Reilly :			do		...	3,500 00
S. S. Lazier :			do		...	3,000 00
A. M. McKinnon :			do		...	2,000 00
J. W. Curry : Four months' salary as Crown Attorney, Toronto						1,166 00
J. W. Seymour Corley : Eight do do						2,334 00
His Honor Judge Reynolds : Allowance out of surplus Surrogate fees, 1905						666 00
do	Jamieson :	do	do	do		108 75
do	Deacon :	do	do	do		666 00
do	Edward Elliott :	do	do	do		657 25
do	Ketchum :	do	do	do		112 70
do	Ketchum :	do	do	do	1906	126 37
do	Edward Elliott :	do	do	do		666 00

INSPECTION OF LEGAL OFFICES.

SALARIES ($3,500.00).

J. W. Mallon : Twelve months' salary as Inspector	2,200 00
J. F. Grant do do Clerk	1,300 00

EXPENSES ($718.30).

Brandon & Gilbert, cartage, .75; Canada Legal Pub. Co., legal chart and law list, 4.50	5 25
Carswell Co., law books, 5.75; Circuit Guide Pub. Co., copies of guide, 1.00	6 75
Hubertus, Mrs., postage stamps, 50.00; King's Printer, stationery, 59.90; paper, 9.23	119 13
Mallon, J. W., travelling expenses, 500.00; Might Directories, Ltd., directory, 7.50	507 50
Riordon Paper Mills, paper, 7.42; Warwick Bros. & Rutter, printing and binding, 72.25	79 67

ADMINISTRATION OF JUSTICE.—*Continued.*

INSPECTION DIVISION COURTS.

SALARIES ($5,000.00).

J. Dickey: Twelve months' salary as Inspector			1,800 00
J. B. Macdonald:	do	Assistant Inspector	1,400 00
W. W. Ellis:	do	Clerk	1,050 00
H. A. Locke:	do	do	750 00

EXPENSES ($1,744.30).

Bell Telephone Co., rent of instrument, 22.01; messages, .40	22 41
Canada Law Book Co., law reports, 5.00; C.P.R. Telegraph Co., telegrams. 5.54	10 54
Canada Legal Pub. Co., law list	3 00
Dickey, J., trav. expenses, 613.50; Ellis, W. W., trav. expenses, 846.35...	1,459 85
G.N.W. Telegraph Co., messages, 6.53; Gripton, C., stamps and repairs, 1.85	8 38
Hart & Riddell, blank books, 7.25; Heaton's Agency, copy of handbook, 1.00	8 25
Hubertus, Mrs., postage stamps, 56.00; International Ry. Guide, subscription, 2.00	58 00
King's Printer, stationery, 63.33; paper, 20.04; Might Directories, Ltd., directory, 7.50	90 87
Newspapers, subscriptions, 5.00; Riordon Paper Mills, paper, 14.85	19 85
United Typewriter Co., repairs, 13.00; Warwick Bros. & Rutter, printing and binding, 50.15	63 15

LAND TITLES OFFICE.

SALARIES ($6,650.00).

J. G. Scott: Twelve months' salary as Master of Titles				3,500 00
H. D. Sinclair: Five and one-half	do	Chief Clerk		457 00
W. J. Lander: Seven	do	do	do	674 00
H. C. Russell: Twelve	do	do	Clerk	900 00
W. G. Yelland: do	do	do	do	800 00
E. G. R. Clarke: Five	do	do	do	121 46
Kenneth Wright: Five and one half do	do	do		197 54

EXPENSES ($648.99).

Art Metropole, brushes, etc., .89; Brandon & Gilbert, cartage, .75	1 64
Can. Legal Pub. Co., law list, 3.00; Gripton, C., stamps and repairs, 11.34	14 34
King's Printer, paper, 61.03; stationery, 152.70	213 73
McMahon, Jas., postage stamps, 13.00; Might Directories, directory, 6.00	19 00
Office Specialty Mfg. Co., steel document boxes, etc.	177 50
Scott, J. G., trav. expenses, 98.25; Stephenson, T. M., Canadian almanac, .75	99 00
Wynne, Miss, typewriting	65
Warwick Bros. & Rutter, printing and binding, 91.19; Williams, N. & Co., cartage, 1.00	92 19
Wright, K. W., services as Clerk	30 94

LOCAL MASTERS OF TITLES IN THE DISTRICTS ($5,366.62).

J. E. Lount: Allowances as Local Master, Bracebridge			300 00
H. J. F. Sissons:	do	Fort Frances	300 00
R. E. Preston:	do	Kenora	300 00
Chas. Lamarche:	do	North Bay	400 00
P. McCurry:	do	Parry Sound	300 00
J. M. Munro:	do	Port Arthur	160 00
V. McNamara	do	Sault Ste. Marie	400 00

ADMINISTRATION OF JUSTICE.—*Continued.*

LOCAL MASTERS OF TITLES IN THE DISTRICTS.—*Continued.*

Bracebridge:
Can. Express Co., charges, 1.15; Gripton, C., pad and ink, .80......	1 95
King's Printer, stationery	6 00
Lount, J. E., services *re* registration of patents, 1905	127 10

Fort Frances:
Dom. Express Co., charges, 8.45; King's Printer, stationery, 80.00......	88 45
Sissons, H. J. F., services *re* registration of patents, 1905	148 98
Warwick Bros. & Rutter, printing	1 50

Kenora:
Dom. Express Co., charges, 2.00; Electric Light, Telephone and Water Dept., light, 27.32	29 32
Gripton, C., rubber stamp	1 85
King's Printer, paper, 10.80; stationery, 40.50	51 30
McDermott, Jno., services as caretaker (two and one-half months)...	25 00
Preston, R. E., services as registrar of patents, 1905	6 05
Sinnott, J., services as caretaker (one and one-half months)	95 00

North Bay:
Can. Express Co., charges, 1.55; King's Printer, stationery, 94.40......	95 95
Lamarche, C., services *re* registration of patents, 1905	197 30
Loughrin, Jno., do do	521 00
Richardson, J. W., filing boxes, 10.80; Warwick Bros. & Rutter, printing, 3.00	13 80

Parry Sound:
Can. Express Co., charges, .55; King's Printer, stationery, 43.25......	43 80
McCurry, P., services *re* registration of patents, 1905	349 50
Office Specialty Mfg. Co., vault fittings	496 00
Warwick Bros. & Rutter, printing	1 80

Port Arthur:
Dom. Express Co., charges, .70; King's Printer, stationery, ·12.50...	13 20
Munro, J. M., services *re* registration of patents, 1905	50

Sault Ste. Marie:
Dom. Express Co., charges, 1.55; Farwell, C. F., rent of office, 260.42	261 97
Hamilton, H. C., services *re* registration of patents, 1905	58 04
King's Printer, stationery	92 05
McNamara, V., services *re* registration of patents, 1905	88 56
Office Specialty Mfg. Co., vault fittings, 336.00; Togona Water & Light Co., light, 13.25	349 25
Templeton, A.. cartage, 3.00; Woolrich, Geo., work of men re-placing vault, 6.00	9 00

General:
Can. Express Co., charges, 1.40; Dom. Express Co., charges, 1.10...	2 50
Scott, J. G., trav. expenses, 21.95; Warwick Bros. & Rutter, printing; 7.95	29 90

DRAINAGE TRIALS ACT.

SALARIES ($5,954.23).

J. B. Rankin: Twelve months' salary as Referee	3,500 00
G. F. Henderson: Seven and one half months' salary as Referee	1,554 23
E. I. Scully: Twelve do Stenographer ...	900 00

EXPENSES ($665.84).

Can. Express Co., charges, 2.00; Dom. Express Co., charges, 1.88	3 88
Hart & Riddell, engraving and embossing, 9.00; Henderson, G. F., travelling expenses, 12.65	21 65
King's Printer, stationery, 151.71; Rankin, J. B., travelling expenses, 183.85	335 56
Scully, E. I., travelling expenses, 120.05; Sager, L. M., travelling expenses, 4.70	124 75
Sager, L. M., services as stenog. at 600.00 per annum	180 00

3 P.A.

ADMINISTRATION OF JUSTICE.—*Continued.*

DEPUTY CLERKS OF THE CROWN AND PLEAS ($16,438.03).

J. T. Hewitt:	Salary as Deputy Clerk of the Crown and Pleas,		Brant	450 00
Matthew Goetz:	do	do	Bruce	450 00
J. P. Featherstone:	do	do	Carleton	450 00
W. J. L. McKay (acting):	do	do	Dufferin	32 25
Jno. McLaren:	do	do	do	61 92
Jno. A. V. Preston:	do	do	do	355 83
D. McLaws:	do	do	Elgin	450 00
Francis Cleary:	do	do	Essex	450 00
T. M. Asselstine:	do	do	Frontenac	450 00
S. C. Macdonald:	do	do	Haldimand	400 00
W. A. Bishop:	do	do	Grey	500 00
W. A. Lawrence:	do	do	Halton	400 00
John Williams:	do	do	Hastings	450 00
D. McDonald:	do	do	Huron	500 00
James Holmes:	do	do	Kent	450 00
Alex. Saunders:	do	do	Lambton	450 00
W. P. McEwen:	do	do	Lanark	450 00
O. K. Fraser:	do	do	Leeds and Grenville	500 00
W. P. Deroche:	do	do	Lennox and Addington	400 00
J. Clench:	do	do	Lincoln	450 00
J. Macbeth:	do	do	Middlesex	500 00
C. C. Rapelje:	do	do	Norfolk	450 00
Jno. T. Field:	do	do	Northumberland and Durham..	500 00
L. T. Barclay:	do	do	Ontario	450 00
J. Canfield:	do	do	Oxford	450 00
J. B. Dixon:	do	do	Peel	400 00
N. Gilbert:	do	do	Prince Edward.	400 00
W. C. Moscrip:	do	do	Perth	450 00
J. Moloney:	do	do	Peterborough	450 00
J. Belanger:	do	do	Prescott and Russell	450 00
J. A. McDougald:	do	do	Stormont, Dundas and Glengarry	500 00
J. R. Cotter (acting):	do	do	Simcoe	61 50
J. McL. Stevenson:	do	do	do	214 05
E. A. Little:	do	do	do	230 48
H. W. Perrett:	do	do	Renfrew	400 00
D. R. Anderson:	do	do	Victoria	450 00
J. McDougall:	do	do	Waterloo	450 00
J. E. Cohoe:	do	do	Welland	532 00
T. H. A. Begue:	do	do	Wentworth	500 00
S. A. Marks:	do	do	Algoma	100 00
J. Meek:	do	do	Thunder Bay....	100 00
E. Jordan:	do	do	Parry Sound....	100 00
I. Huber:	do	do	Muskoka	100 00
T. J. Bourke:	do	do	Nipissing	100 00

DEPUTY CLERKS OF THE CROWN AS LOCAL REGISTRARS ($6,793.00).

J. T. Hewitt:	Salary as Registrar,	Brant	225 00
Matthew Goetz:	do	Bruce	225 00
W. J. L. McKay:	do	Dufferin	13 77
Jno. McLaren:	do	do	28 89
Jno. A. V. Preston:	do	do	182 34
D. McLaws:	do	Elgin	225 00
Francis Cleary:	do	Essex	225 00
T. M. Asselstine:	do	Frontenac	225 00
S. C. Macdonald:	do	Haldimand	200 00
W. A. Bishop:	do	Grey	250 00

ADMINISTRATION OF JUSTICE.—*Continued.*

DEPUTY CLERKS OF THE CROWN AS LOCAL REGISTRARS.—*Continued.*

W. A. Lawrence:	Salary. as Registrar,	Halton	200 00
D. McDonald:	do	Huron	250 00
James Holmes:	do	Kent	225 00
Alex. Saunders:	do	Lambton	225 00
W. P. McEwen:	do	Lanark	225 00
O. K. Fraser:	do	Leeds and Grenville	250 00
W. P. Deroche:	do	Lennox and Addington	200 00
J. Clench:	do	Lincoln	225 00
C. C. Rapelje:	do	Norfolk	225 00
J. T. Field:	do	Northumberland and Durham	250 00
L. T. Barclay:	do	Ontario	225 00
J. B. Dixon:	do	Peel	200 00
N. Gilbert:	do	Prince Edward	200 00
W. C. Moscrip:	do	Perth	225 00
J. Moloney:	do	Peterborough	225 00
J. Belanger:	do	Prescott and Russell	225 00
J. A. McDougald:	do	Stormont, Dundas and Glengarry....	250 00
H. W. Perrett:	do	Renfrew	200 00
D. R. Anderson:	do	Victoria	225 00
J. McDougall:	do	Waterloo	225 00
J. E. Cohoe:	do	Welland	268 00
S. A. Marks:	do	Algoma	50 00
J. Meek:	do	Thunder Bay	50 00
E. Jordan:	do	Parry Sound	50 00
I. Huber:	do	Muskoka	50 00
I. J. Bourke:	do	Nipissing	50 00

CROWN COUNSEL PROSECUTIONS ($10,423.00).

Services, Fall Assizes, 1905:—
Carleton, Frank Arnoldie	361.00
Hastings, E. Meredith, 200.00; Peterboro, E. Meredith, 250.00	450 00
Thunder Bay, F. H. Keeler, 56.00; York, J. W. Curry, 550.00; E. E. A. DuVernet, 319.00	925 00

Services, Winter Assizes:—
Carleton, Frank Arnoldi, 205.00; Lambton, G. L. Staunton, 159.00...	364 00
Middlesex, M. Wilson, 101.00; Stormont, Dundas and Glengarry, Jas. Leitch, 20.00	121 00
Wentworth, S. F. Washington, 10.00; York, H. H. Strathy, 292.00; E. E. A. DuVernet, 1,200.00	1,502 00

Services Spring Assizes:—
Brant, J. W. Elliott, 120.00; Bruce, Hugh Morrison, 20.00	140 00
Carleton, James Leitch, 186.00; Dufferin, F. J. Roche, 20.00	206 00
Essex, H. B. Elliott	62 00
Frontenac, Jno. McIntyre, 62.00; Grey, A. J. Russell Snow, 20.00	82 00
Halton, J. H. McGhie, 48.00; Haldimand, Harrison Arrell, 20.00	68 00
Hastings, E. Meredith, 750.00; Huron, J. C. Makins, 20.00	770 00
Kent, W. M. Reade	78 00
Lanark, J. M. Rogers, 20.00; Leeds & Grenville, F. J. French, 26.00	46 00
Lennox and Addington, D. A. Givens, 20.00; Lincoln, N. F. Patterson, 78.00	98 00
Middlesex, H. B. Elliott, 20.00; Muskoka, W. A. Boys, 20.00	40 00
Northumberland and Durham, F. E. Hodgins, 20.00; Nipissing, M. J. O'Connor, 140.00	160 00
Norfolk, Frank Reid, 20.00; Ontario, A. J. Russell Snow, 20.00	40 00
Oxford, Frank Arnoldi, 31.00; Peel, W. G. Fisher, 37.00	68 00
Perth, J. W. Logan, 20.00; Peterboro, E. Meredith, 200.00	220 00
Prince Edward, W. C. Mikel, 26.00; Prescott and Russell, C. G. O'Brien, 20.00	46 00
Parry Sound, F. R. Purcell, 20.00; Simcoe, W. A. Boys, 20.00	40 00
Stormont, Dundas and Glengarry, G. E. Tripp	51 00
Victoria, F. D. Moore, 20.00; Waterloo, E. L. Essery, 32 00	52 00
Welland, J. M. Pike, 20.00; Wellington, Frank Arnoldi, 186.00	206 00
Wentworth, E. E. A. DuVernet, 400.00; York, N. F. Patterson, 126.00	526 00

ADMINISTRATION OF JUSTICE.—*Continued.*

CROWN COUNSEL PROSECUTIONS.—*Continued.*

Services, Summer Assizes:—

Algoma, F. H. Keefer, 20.00; Manitoulin, H. H. Strathy, 231.50...   251 50
Rainy River, F. H. Keefer, 293.00; Thunder Bay, M. McFadden, 20.00   313 00

Services, Fall Assizes:—

Algoma, M. McFadden. 58.00; Brant, C. R. McKeown, 36.00 ....   94 00
Bruce, J. W. Hanna, 287.00; Carleton, S. H., Bradford, 175.00........   462 00
Dufferin, F. J. Roche, 20.00; Dundas and Glengarry, J. R. Lovell, 20.00   40 00
Elgin, W. S. Brewster, 132.00; Essex, W. M. Ready, 58.00 ....   190 00
Frontenac, Jno. McIntyre, 106.00; Grey, N. F. Patterson, 20.00 ....   126 00
Hastings, Frank Arnoldi, 200.00; Haldimand, Harrison Arrell, 20.00...   220 00
Halton, J. C. Makins, 36.00; Huron, F. J. Roche, 20.00 ....   56 00
Kent, H. B. Elliott, 82.00; Lambton, F. W. Wilson, 57.00 ....   139 00
Lanark, D. H. Preston, 58.00; Lennox and Addington, A. M. Wilson,
  20.00 ....   78 00
Lincoln, J. M. Pike, 26.00; Manitoulin, M. J. O'Connor, 81.00 ....   107 00
Middlesex, H. B. Elliott, 20.00; Muskoka, D. W. Bruce, 40.00 ....   60 00
Nipissing, A. Abbott, 40.00; Norfolk, F. W. Casey, 20.00 ....   60 00
Northumberland and Durham, W. C. Mikel, 47.00; Ontario, F. D.
  Moore, 52.00 ....   99 00
Oxford, J. G., Wallace, 20.00; Parry Sound, F. R. Powell, 22.00......   42 00
Perth. J. J. Drew, 114.00; Prescott and Russell. C. G. O'Brien, 20.00   134 00
Peterboro, F. D. Moore. 52.00; Prince Edward. R. H. Hubbs. 20.00.....   72 00
Rainy River. T. H. Keefer, 181.50; Renfrew, W. H. Williams, 20.00......   201 50
Simcoe, T. E. Godson, 62.00; Stormont. Dundas and Glengarry, J.
  Dingwall, 10.00 ....   72 00
Thunder Bay, F. H. Keefer. 263.00; Victoria, F. E. Hodgins, 106.00......   369 00
Waterloo, W. M. Reade. 20.00; Wellington. E. S. Smith, 93.00 ....   113 00
Wentworth. H. C. Gwyn, 62.00; York, H. H. Strathy, 360.00...........   422 00

GENERAL ADMINISTRATION OF JUSTICE IN COUNTIES ($191,551.45).

Expenditure as Treasurer:—

Brant, A. Foster, December quarter, 1,652.19; March quarter, 895.17;
  June quarter. 680.30; September quarter, 440.46 ....   3,668 12
Bruce. N. Robertson, December quarter, 1,220.03; March quarter,
  698.68; June quarter, 677.24 ....   2,595 95
Carleton, H. Reilly, December quarter, 3,050.44; March quarter,
  1,373.53; June quarter. 1,737.53; September quarter, 1,723.08...   7,884 58
Dufferin, C. R. Wheelock, December quarter, 456.17; March quarter,
  291.65; June quarter, 512.20; September quarter, 227.49..........   1,487 51
Elgin, J. McCausland, September quarter, 831.39; December quarter,
  1,358.86; March quarter, 1,550.54; June quarter, 753.72; Septem-
  ber quarter, 1,282.30 ....   5,776 51
Essex, G. A. Wintermute, December quarter, 1,434.67; March quarter,
  1,523.00; June quarter, 604.16; September quarter, 972.96 ......   4,534 79
Frontenac. D. Purdy, December quarter, 824.65;   March quarter,
  432.78; June quarter, 946.47; September quarter, 841.30.........   3,045 20
Grey, S. J. Parker, December quarter, 1,363.32; March quarter,
  805.78; June quarter, 1,020.50; September quarter, 912.79......   4,102 39
Haldimand, M. McConnell, September quarter, 799.50; December
  quarter, 487.56; March quarter, 288.18; June quarter, 501.37;
  September quarter, 932.12 ....   3,008 73
Halton, G. Andrew, December quarter, 673.89; March quarter, 171.30;
  June quarter, 548.41; September quarter, 203.02 ....   1,596 62
Hastings, B. Mallory, March quarter, 1,580.24; June quarter, 809.42;
  September quarter, 1,293.13; December quarter, 2,622.00; March
  quarter, 1,649.18; June quarter, 1,808.67 ....   9,762 64
Huron. W. Holmes, December quarter, 1,073.14; March quarter,
  1,081.31; June quarter, 1,159.51 ....   3,313 96
Kent, J. C. Fleming, December quarter, 1,210.61; March quarter,
  1,334.89; June quarter, 1,407.65; September quarter, 1,234.75...   5,187 90

ADMINISTRATION OF JUSTICE.—*Continued*.

GENERAL ADMINISTRATION OF JUSTICE IN COUNTIES.—*Continued*.

Expenditure as Treasurer.—*Continued*.

Lambton, H. Ingram, December quarter, 1,300.64; March quarter, 703.11 June quarter, 555.08; September quarter, 797.34.........	3,356 17
Lanark, Jno. Code, December quarter, 634.19; March quarter, 325.51; June quarter, 372.29; September quarter, 402.51	1,734 50
Leeds and Grenville, R. J. Jelly, December quarter, 1,226.53; March quarter, 845.23; June quarter, 800.86; September quarter, 545.04	3,417 66
Lennox and Addington, I. Parks, December quarter, 388.16; March quarter, 524.85; June quarter, 452.75; September quarter, 464.73	1,830 49
Lincoln, Ira F. Culp, September quarter, 314.45; December quarter, 1,082.99; March quarter, 542.56; June quarter, 961.30; September quarter, 690.32 ....:.....	3,591 62
Middlesex, A. M. McEvoy, September quarter, 1,277.63; December quarter, 2,910.98; March quarter, 1,667.79; June quarter, 2,081.97; September quarter, 2,000.50	9,938 87
Norfolk, R. Crysler, December quarter, 850.37; March quarter, 119.00; June quarter, 186.34; September quarter, 309.93	1,465 64
Northumberland and Durham, N. MacNachtan, December quarter, 874.35; March quarter, 584.82; June quarter, 755.51; September quarter, 575.16 ...:	2,789 84
Ontario, D. Mackay, September quarter, 426.01; December quarter, 615.74; March quarter, 383.51; June quarter, 379.19	1,804 45
Oxford, R. McIntosh, December quarter, 1,874.06; March quarter, 721.18; June quarter, 545.66; September quarter, 915.17............	4,056 07
Peel, R. Crawford, December quarter, 496.58; March quarter, 488.09; June quarter, 862.56; September quarter, 661.63	2,508 86
Perth, G. Hamilton, December quarter, 1,034.72; March quarter, 879.27; June quarter, 718.24; September quarter, 869.65	3,501 88
Peterborough, December quarter, 1,307.63; March quarter, 404.94; June quarter, 918.54; September quarter, 660.62	3,291 73
Prescott and Russell, J. Belanger, June quarter, 479.96; September quarter, 238.50; December quarter, 292.36; March quarter, 231.51; June quarter, 287.06: September quarter, 362.35	1,891 74
Prince Edward, D. L. Bongard, December quarter, 368.49; March quarter, 451.62; June quarter, 347.07; September quarter, 140.00	1,307 18
Renfrew, A. Morris, September quarter, 375.66; December quarter, 709.42; March quarter, 247.46; June quarter, 503.55; September quarter, 515.58	2,351 67
Simcoe, D. Quinlan, June quarter, 1,339.38; September quarter, 1,001.86; December quarter, 1,657.31; March quarter, 1,050.69; June quarter, 778.42; September quarter, 983.61	6,811 27
Stormont, Dundas and Glengarry, Geo. Stacey, December quarter, 709.52; March quarter, 956.22; June quarter, 467.36; September quarter, 502.35	2,635 45
Victoria, J. R. McNeillie, December quarter, 311.57; March quarter, 300.57; June quarter, 635.18; September quarter, 626.54	1,873 86
Waterloo, H. J. Bowman, December quarter, 1,099.20; March quarter, 450.72; June quarter, 381.59; September quarter, 741.58	2,673 09
Welland, W. H. Gainer, December quarter, 906.32; March quarter, 254.72; June quarter, 803.14; September quarter, 657.18	2,621 36
Wellington, Wm. Reynolds, December quarter, 1,342.16; March quarter, 1,066.26; June quarter, 1,391.71; September quarter, 1,002.61...	4,802 74
Wentworth, A. Cochrane, December quarter, 2,446.58; March quarter, 1,788.45; June quarter, 1,227.43; September quarter, 1,225.96...	6,688 42
Hamilton, A. Stuart, December quarter, 778.29:	
do W. R. Leckie (acting) March quarter, 337.92; June quarter, 348.80: September quarter, 370.80	1,835 81
Toronto, R. T. Coady, December quarter, 6,221.31; March quarter, 3,273.34; June quarter, 4,007.51; September quarter, 2,186.27...	15,688 43
Toronto and York, R. T. Coady, September quarter, 4,202.94; December quarter, 9,180.37; March quarter, 30.40; June quarter, 4,739.88	18,153 59
York, J. K. Macdonald, September quarter, 558.52; December and March quarters, 931.20; June and September quarters, 450.21...	1,939 93

ADMINISTRATION OF JUSTICE.—*Continued.*

GENERAL ADMINISTRATION OF JUSTICE IN COUNTIES.—*Continued.*

Expenses and disbursements, Provincial Detectives, etc.:—

Bruce, Greer Wm., 24.50; Murray, J. W., 97.10	121 60
Essex, Finney, J. W., legal services re extradition of Wm. and Walter Mitchell	468 60
Carleton, Harman, G., copy of judgment Rex. v. Lacelle	2 00
Dundas, Murray, J. W.	28 75
Durham, Reburn, H., services, 93.00; trav. expenses and disbursements, 59.85	152 85
Elgin, Hansen, Christian, trav. expenses, 46.50; McCrimmon, A., legal services Rex v. Ferguson, 25.50; Reburn, H., services, 24.00; trav. expenses, 23.10	119 10
Dufferin, Reburn, H., services, 24.00; trav. expenses, 22.10; Rogers, J. E., trav. expenses, 235.25	281 35
Essex, Rogers, J. E.	54 65
Grenville, Rogers, J. E.	15 00
Glengarry, Greer, Wm., 36.10; Phelan, R., salary as constable, 233.00	269 10
Grey, Murray, J. W., 89.70; Reburn, H., services and expenses re Thornbury fire, 29.95; Rogers, J. E., 57.10	176 75
Hastings, Murray, J. W.	98 60
Halton, Reburn, H., services re dynamite outrage, 12.00; expenses, 15.60; Rogers, J. E., 5.30	32 90
Kent, Rogers, J. E.	266 11
Lambton, Rogers, J. E.	43 75
Lanark, Rogers, J. E.	27 65
Leeds, Rogers, J. E.	22 95
Middlesex, Angus, Geo., services as reporter King v. O'Gorman, 612.20; Armour, Eric, witness fees, expenses, etc., 1,473.00; Judd, J. G., accountable warrant, 1,000.00; Murray, J. W., 22.30; Reburn, H., services, 156.00; trav. expenses, 280.25; Rogers, J. E., 29.80	3,573 55
Northumberland and Durham, Murray, J. W. (bal. 1905), 10.80; 1906, 17.00	27 80
Ontario, Rogers, J. E.	18 00
Oxford, Greer, Wm.	41 70
Peel, Greer, Wm., 65.05; Rogers, J. E., 22.75	87 80
Peterboro', Murray, J. W., 11.80; Reburn, H., services re shooting and stealing cattle, 6.00; expenses, 9.25; Wells, W. J., services, 135.00; trav. expenses, 43.55; Rogers, J. E., trav. expenses, 20.95	226 55
Renfrew, Irving, W. C., services as auditor, 50.00; postage, 2.00	52 00
Simcoe, Murray, J. W., 6.50; Rogers, J. E., 13.75	20 25
Toronto, Grasett, H. J., Chief Constable, expenses of detective Mackie, arrest and bringing back from England Christopher Holland, 553.59; Greer, Wm., 38.40; High Commissioner for Canada, expenses Metropolitan Police re Holland case, 64,20	656 19
Victoria, Greer, Wm.	15 35
Waterloo, Rogers, J. E.	20 85
Welland, Greer, Wm., 274.85; to pay: Stokes, R. A., 82.75; Rogers, J. E., 11.80; Thiel Detective Agency, services and expenses re operatives lottery case, 266.26; Watts, W. H. and T. S., services and expenses re lottery case, 356.01	991 67
Wellington, Greer, Wm.	41 95
Wentworth, Durand Sir Mortimer, expenses re extradition L. N. McCauley, 2.80; Greer, Wm., 79.34; to pay: Nobles Detective Agency, 33.14; Pinkerton's National Detective Agency, services and expenses re murder case, 58.57; Wells, W. J., services and expenses re Barton murder, 111.00	284 85
York, Durand, Sir Mortimer, expenses re extradition of Edward Baskin, 44.14	
Durand, Sir Mortimer, expenses re extradition of Albin Adamy, 149.19	
Gibbs, Clinton B., legal services re extradition of Albin Adamy, 150.00	
Greer, Wm., 11.30; Neild, E., Copies of evidence Rex v. McMichael, 75.00	

ADMINISTRATION OF JUSTICE.—*Continued.*

GENERAL ADMINISTRATION OF JUSTICE IN COUNTIES.—*Continued.*

Expenses, etc.—*Continued.*

Murray, J. W., 13,25 ....

Reburn, H., services and expenses *re* assault case, 27.50; services and expenses *re* incendiary, 12.50; Rogers, J. E., trav. expenses, 200.45 ....

Stonehouse, R. S., copy of evidence Miller v. Beck, 22.50...........

Thiel Detective Agency, services and expenses *re* bookies, 1,411.63. 2,117 46

Circuit Guide Pub. Co., copies distributed to Local Registrars and D.C.C. 21 50

Clothing for discharged prisoners and Bailiffs:—

Applegath, Jess, 3.00;   Bourdon, N. J., 40.00;   Brock, W. R. Co., 324.77; C. P. Industries, 2,061.68; Fairweather, J. W. T. & Co., 3.00; Guinane, Jno., 8.00; Murray, W. A. & Co., 15.00; Simpson, R. Co., 58.80 .... 2,514 25

Edmison and Laidlaw, Drs., medical attendance on Bailiff Ryan 50 00

King Edward Hotel, Kenora, expenses of Bailiff Ryan 8 50

Lyons, F. W., trav. expenses *re* transfer of prisoners 116 25

Murphy, N., services Asstg. Crown Attorney 1 week, 60.00; services *re* combine case, 180.00 .... 240 00

Rogers, J. E., accountable warrant, 50.00 ....

To pay: battery for light, .35; Fletcher Hardware, revolvers, etc., 12.90; lock for leg irons, 1.00; postage (1905), 5.03; telegrams, 6.45 75 73

Ryan, J. J., Twelve months' salary as Bailiff, 1,200.00; trav. expenses and disbursements *re* transfer of prisoners, 1,072.45 .... 2,272 45

Simser, Philip, trav. expenses and disbursements *re* transfer of prisoners, 3,018.05; expenses *re* transfer of Bailiff Ryan, Kenora to Toronto, 94.45 .... 3,112 50

Sisters of Providence, maintenance and attendance of Bailiff Ryan while in hospital 47 00

To pay carriage of discharged prisoners: Jaffray, Alex., 2,125.73; Laird, R. W., 50.00; McKenzie, Thos., 32.64 .... 2,208 37

INSPECTORS OF CRIMINAL INVESTIGATION ($4,180.00).

J. W. Murray: Six months' salary as Chief Detective 950 00

J. E. Rogers: Twelve   do   Detective 1,600 00

W. Greer: do   do   do 1,500 00

Bell Telephone Co., rent of instrument 25 00

Employees' Liability Corporation, premium on accident policy Chief Detective 35 00

London Guarantee and Accident Co., premiums on accident policies Greer and Rogers 70 00

SHERIFFS' FEES. ETC., ($12,255.30).

Attendance at Court as Sheriff:

Brant, Wm. Watt, 50.50; Bruce, C. V. Parks, 106.50 .... 157 00

Carleton, J. Sweetland, 675.70; Elgin, D. McColl, 49.00 .... 724 70

Essex, J. C. Iler, 315.75; Frontenac, T. Dawson, 46.25 .... 362 00

Grey, C. H. Moore, 90.75; Haldimand, R. H. Davis, 20.00 .... 110 75

Hastings, Geo. F. Hope, 175.25; Huron, R. J. Reynolds. 181.00 .... 356 25

Kent, J. R. Gemmill, 149.00; Lambton, J. Flintoft, 118.50............... 267 50

Lanark, W. McGarry, 5.00; Lincoln, T. C. Dawson, 117.75 .... 122 75

Lennox and Addington, G. D. Hawley, 9.50; Leeds and Grenville, Geo. A. Dana, 166.50 .... 176 00

Middlesex, D. M. Cameron, 359.00; Norfolk, Jos. Jackson, 34.50 .... 393 50

Northumberland and Durham, J. O. Proctor, 70.25; Ontario, J. F. Paxton, 53.50 .... 128 75

Oxford, J. Brady, 49.75; Peel. R. Broddy, 26.75 .... 76 50

Perth, J. Hossie, 104.00; Peterborough; J. A. Hall, 47.25 .... 151 25

Prescott and Russell, A. Hagar, 24.00; Prince Edward, J. Gillespie, 15.00 .... 39 00

Renfrew, Wm. Moffat, 18.00; Simcoe, Wm. Harvey, 145.50 .... 163 50

Stormont, Dundas and Glengarry, W. R. Mack, 43.00; Victoria, J. McLennan, 52.50 .... 95 50

ADMINISTRATION OF JUSTICE.—*Continued.*
SHERIFFS' FEES, ETC.—*Continued.*

Attendance at Court as Sheriff.—*Continued.*

Waterloo, J. Motz, 71.00; Welland, Jas. Smith, 17.50	88 50
Wellington, A. S. Allan, 66.00; Wentworth, J. T. Middleton, 180.75 ...	246 75
York, J. H. Widdifield, 1,424.75; A. Sutherland (acting), 96.25; J. T. Daville, 866.50	2,387 50
Toronto, Fred. Mowat	1,301 50

Allowance to Sheriffs to make up income, 2 Edward VII., cap. 12, sec. 5:

Dufferin, T. Bowles, 256.39; Halton, M. Clements, 325.84	582 23
Lanark, Wm. McGarry, 263.94; Norfolk, J. Jackson, 322.28	586 22
Peel, R. Brady, 84.45; Peterborough, J. A. Hall, 157.17	241 62
Prescott and Russell, A. Hagar, 209.56; Prince Edward, J. Gillespie, 734.06	943 62

Attendance at Courts as D.C.C. and Pleas:

Brant, J. T. Hewitt, 48.09; Bruce, M. Goetz, 64.40	112 49
Carleton, J. P. Featherston, 148.75; W. L. Scott (acting), 24.00	172 75
Dufferin, J. A. V. Preston, 40.06; Agnes McLaren, Estate of late Jno. McLaren, 8.00	48 06
Elgin, D. McLaws, 96.35; Essex, F. Cleary, 60.08	156 43
Frontenac, T. Asselstine, 44.47; Grey, W. A. Bishop, 80.00	124 47
Haldimand, G. C. Macdonald, 32.08; Halton, W. A. Lawrence, 28.16..	60 24
Hastings, J. Williams, 84.60; Huron, D. McDonald, 76.65	161 25
Kent, J. Holmes, 88.31; Lambton, A. Saunders, 56.50	144 81
Lanark, W. P. McEwen, 32.17; Leeds and Grenville, O. K. Fraser, 68.24	100 41
Lennox and Addington, W. P. Deroche, 20.16; Lincoln, J. Clench, 44.14	64 30
Middlesex, Jno. Macbeth, 104.10; R. K. Cowan, 28.00	132 10
Norfolk, C. C. Rapelje, 32.21; Northumberland and Durham, J. T. Field, 44.16	76 37
Oxford, J. Canfield, 56.14; W. T. Mullen, 12.00	68 14
Ontario, L. T. Barclay, 44.14; Parry Sound, E. Jordan, 36.18	80 32
Peel, J. B., Dixon, 28.08; Perth, W. C. Moscrip, 60.10	88 18
Peterborough, J. Moloney, 48.31; Prince Edward, N., Gilbert, 24.02...	72 33
Prescott and Russell, J. Belanger, 12.12; Renfrew, H. W. Perrett, 20.00	32 12
Simcoe, J. R. Cotter, 52.00; J. Stevenson, 20.00; E. A. Little, 16.00...	88 00
Stormont, Dundas and Glengarry, J. A. McDougald	96 18
Victoria, W. R. Anderson, 36.00; Waterloo, J. McDougall, 36.06	72 06
Welland, J. E. Cohoe, 32.34; Wellington, A. McKinnon, 48.28	80 62
Wentworth, T. H. A. Begue, 104.72; York, J. Henderson (crier), 200.00	304 72
Algoma, N. Simpson, 16.00; Manitoulin, C. C. Platt, 16.00	32 00
Muskoka, Isaac Huber, 16.00; Nipissing, T. J. Bourke, 140.00	156 00
Thunder Bay, Jas. Meek	28 06

SEALS AND OTHER CONTINGENCIES ($179.88).

Armstrong, Jno., taking over 6 Division Court Grey	5 70
Can. Express Co., charges, 4.80; Dominion Express Co., charges, 2.20...	7 00
Dixon, Thos., taking over 7 Division Court, "C. Bruce," 5.00; travelling expenses, 4.65	9 65
Gripton, C., seal and press 1 Division Court, Lambton, 6.00; 3 Division Court, Grey, 6.00	12 00
2 Division Court, Lanark, 6.00; 2 Division Court, Ontario, 6.00	12 00
2 do do Stormont, Dundas and Glengarry	6 00
12 do do do	6 00
12 do do Frontenac, 6.00; 1 Division Court Prescott and Russell, 6.00	12 00
1 do do Nipissing	6 00
King's Printer, stationery, 1.00; seal High Court Huron, 6.00	7 00
Seal County Court, Huron, 6.00; seal Surrogate Court, Huron, 6.00...	12 00
do High Court, Welland, 6.00; seal Surrogate Court, Kenora, 6.00...	12 00
do District Court, Kenora, 6.00; seal Local Registrar's Office, Kenora, 6.00	12 00
do County Court Clerk, York, 6.00; seal Local Master's Office, Belleville, 6.00	12 00
do Local Master, Napanee, 6.00; seal Deputy Registrar, Belleville, 6.00	12 00
Seager, C., services and expenses taking over 4 Division Court, Huron ...	33 53

ADMINISTRATION OF JUSTICE.—*Continued.*

LITIGATION OF CONSTITUTIONAL QUESTIONS ($5,377.91).

Armour & Mickle, legal services *re* International Railway Co.		250 00
Belcourt, N. A., do Appeal to Privy Council *re* right of members of certain religious communities to be considered qualified teachers for purposes of Separate School Act		800 00
Blake, Lash & Cassels, do International Railway Co.		250 00
Butcher, N. R. & Co., typewriting, Dominion *vs.* Ontario		93 87
Code, R. G., legal services *re* do Legislation		750 00
Ewart, Osler, Burbidge & Maclaren, legal services *re* Niagara Power Co.		4 04
Hearst, W. H., legal services *re* location of Thunder Bay branch of G. T. P. Ry.		310 00
do do Keewatin Power Co. *vs.* Kenora, and Thunder Bay Co. *vs.* Kenora.........		600 00
Henderson, Geo. F., do Appeal to Privy Council *re* right of members of certain religious communities to be considered qualified teachers for purposes of Separate School Act		800 00
McCarthy, D. D., do Water lots and water power, Ottawa River		500 00
McPherson, W. D., do Appeal to Privy Council *re* right of members of certain religious communities to be considered qualified teachers for purposes of Separate School Act		800 00
Macdonald, Shepley, Middleton & Donald, legal services *re* qualification of teachers in Separate Schools		100 00
Robinson, C. C., legal services *re* Appeal to Privy Council *re* railway protection on level crossings		120 00

GROUPED COUNTIES ($444.70).

His Honor Judge Madden, services and expenses			257 80
do Price do			186 90

SHORTHAND REPORTERS.

SALARIES ($13,600.00).

Alex. H. Crawford; Twelve months' salary as Reporter			1 800 00
A. J. Henderson: do do			1,800 00
R. Tyson: do do			1,800 00
E. E. Horton: do do			1,800 00
F. V. Dickson: do do			1,600 00
N. R. Butcher: do do			1,600 00
H. J. Emerson: do do			1,600 00
J. Agnew: do do			1,600 00

EXPENSES ($1,372 85).

Agnew, J., allowance for stationery to December 31st, 1906	100 00
do travelling expenses reporting assizes, Stormont, D. & G......	28 00
Butcher, N. R., allowance for stationery to December 31st, 1906	100 00
do travelling expenses reporting assizes, Northern Circuit	201 35
Canadian Typewriter Co., exchange on typewriter	96 50
Crawford, A. H., allowance for stationery to December 31st, 1906	100 00
Dickson, F. V., do do	100 00
do travelling expenses reporting Northern Circuit	42 10
Emerson, H. J., allowance for stationery to December 31st, 1906	100 00
do travelling expenses, reporting assizes Northern Circuit...	66 00
Ferguson, E., reporting evidence, Morris *v.* Stewart, Grey Co..................	9 85
Johnston, W. F., reporting High Court, Ottawa	10 00
Horton, E. E., allowance for stationery to December 31st, 1906	100 00
do travelling expenses	32 00

ADMINISTRATION OF JUSTICE.—*Continued.*

SHORTHAND REPORTERS.—*Continued.*

EXPENSES.—*Continued.*

Henderson, A. J., allowance for stationery to December 31st, 1906	100 00
do travelling expenses reporting assizes, Nipissing.........	43 30
Maxwell, C. F., travelling expenses reporting assizes, Elgin	5 00
Sager, L. M., travelling expenses reporting winter assizes, Stormont, D. & G.	5 00
Sanderson, L., services reporting assizes, Perth	10 00
Tyson, R., allowance for stationery to December 31st, 1906	100 00
do travelling expenses reporting assizes, Manitoulin	23 75

COUNTY LAW LIBRARIES ($1,200.00).

Treasurer of Ontario to pay Library:— Brant, 39.91; Bruce, 36.19; Carleton, 54.17; Elgin, 39.29; Essex, 39.29; Frontenac, 39.91; Grey, 38.05; Hamilton, 54.79; Hastings 38.67; Huron, 41.77; Kent, 40.53; Lambton, 40.22; Leeds, 43.01; Lindsay, 39.91; Middlesex, 52.31; Norfolk, 35.57; Ontario, 37.75; Oxford (1905 and 1906), 71.09; Perth, 38.69; Peterborough, 40.86; Rainy River (1904-1905 and 1906), 101.63; Simcoe, 44.89; Stormont, 38.07; Waterloo, 42.41; Welland, 38.07; Wellington (1905 and 1906), 72.95	1,200 00

MAINTENANCE OSGOODE HALL.

Fuel, light and water ($3,489.08).

Burns, P. & Co., 60.970 tons soft coal at 4.10 per ton, 247.99; 2.1900 tons Briar Hill coal at 6.50 per ton, 19.17	267 16
Consumers' Gas Co., gas, 1,022.72; Fayle, V. P., expenses weighing coal, 6.30	1,029 02
Grenadier Ice Co., ice	32 00
McGill, Wm. & Co., 3 tons stove coal at 6.00, 18.00; 4 tons stove coal at 5.61, 22.44; 112.1100 tons grate coal at 5.80, 653.08; 399.875 tons grate coal at 5.41, 2,160.96; 1 cord wood, 5.00; cutting, .50.....................	2,859 98
Newspapers, advertising *re* fuel, 9.15; Water Works Dept., water, 181.77	190 92
	4,379 08
Less refund by Law Society for heating and lighting............	890 00
	3,489 08

Salaries of Engineer, Fireman and Caretaker ($1,810.00).

T. Cunerty: Twelve months' salary as Engineer			1,000 00
C. Sendall:	do	Fireman	460 00
K. McKenna:	do	Caretaker................................	350 00

Furniture and incidentals ($1,372.06).

Armstrong, Fred., changing and insulating electric wiring system, 91.55; chandelier, etc., 9.60	101 15
Alexander, Wm., cleaning and repairing clocks, 25.00; Coyell, Alf., bookshelves, 25.50	50 50
Davis Mary, cleaning, 84.00; allowance for meals, 21.00	105 00
Eaton, T. Co., awning, etc., 4.30; Ellis, P. W. & Co., care of clocks, 22.50	26 80
Geroghty, Jane, cleaning at 1.00 per day, 101.50; Godden, C. P., carpet sweepers, etc., 52.25	153 75
Hilliar, Geo., to pay for jugs, etc., .75; Hargrave Bros., chemicals, 4.00	4 75
Hopkins, T. N., cleaning chimneys, 11.35; Jennings, C. B., repairing furniture, cleaning carpets, etc., 370.31	381 66
Kay, Jno., Son & Co., furniture, 15.62; Matthews, A., ventilator, register, etc., 45.65	61 27
Michie & Co., soap and candles, 7.30; Murray, W. A. & Co., carpets, rug, etc., 296.43	303 73
Sutherland, Mrs. C., cleaning at 1.25 per day, 177.00; Wanty, Wm., putting in register in Land Titles Office, 6.45	183 45

ADMINISTRATION OF JUSTICE.—*Continued.*

MAINTENANCE OSGOODE HALL.—*Continued.*

Appliances for fire protection, hose, etc. ($1,252.90).

Alert Fire Appliance Co., 25 Alert fire extinguishers	275 00
Durham Rubber Co., hose, couplings, racks, etc.	977 90

General repairs, drains, etc. ($2,294.86).

Armstrong, Fred., mantles, globes, etc	98 91
Dinnis, R. & Son, lumber, deflectors, etc., 58.26; Dorrien Plating Co., bolts, 2.50	60 76
Gander, Thos. & Son, plastering, etc., 15.05; Hamblin, Wm., bricklaying cement, 5.85	20 90
Inglis, Jno. & Co., repairing boilers, 12.50; Lyon, Jas. D., clearing snow from roofs, 127.90; repairing roofs, pipes, troughs, etc., 255.74	396 14
Morrison, Jas., Brass Mfg. Co., gate valves, etc., 6.74; Ontario Lead and Wire Co., closet, etc., 33.85	40 59
Pike, D. & Co., repairing awnings, 8.00; pay lists, wages of carpenters, bricklayers, plumbers, laborers, etc., 1,503.79	1,511 79
Robertson, Jas., Co., castings, 3.29;Shipway Iron Bell & Wire Mfg. Co., locksmithing, 4.55	7 84
Stewart, Jno., painting, glazing etc., 136.17; Townley & London, painting and varnishing, 6.40	142 57
Vokes Hardware Co., castings, etc., 12.36; Wanty, Wm., mortar, 3.00	15 36

New telephones ($172.00).

Dominion Phone Co., desk and ball phones	172 00

Painting walls, etc., court room ($820.03).

Browne, A. M., contract painting Court Room, 273.00; painting and cleaning, etc., 126.83	399 83
Stewart, Jno., painting, papering, etc.	420 20

Telephone and telegraph service ($175.00).

Macbeth, H., Secy. Law Society, grant towards expense of service	175 00

DISTRICT OF ALGOMA ($18,422.55).

W. A. Quibell: Two months' salary as Police Magistrate	104 95
D. M. Brodie: Twelve do do	1,000 00
T. E. Williams: do do	1,000 00
W. H. Carney: do Sheriff	1,400 00
N. Simpson: Eight months' salary (including rent allowance) Clerk of the Peace and District Attorney	342 00
G. H. Hayward: One-third month's salary as Clerk of the Peace (acting)	16 50
Moses McFadden: Three and one-third months' salary do	141 50
S. A. Marks: Twelve months' salary (including rent allowance), Clerk of the District Court	750 00
R. Rush: Twelve months' salary as Constable	600 00
A. E. Storie: do do	500 00
John Graham: do do	483 33
Henry Jourdin: do do	200 00
Robt. Pirie: do do	150 00
A. W. Gummerson: do do	250 00
J. H. Martin: Six and two-thirds months' salary as Constable	432 63
A. McKellar: Nine do Gaoler, Sault Ste. Marie	450 00
John Hurst: Six do do do	300 00
Isabella McKellar: Nine do Matron do	150 00
Katherine Hurst: Six do do do	100 00
C. B. Harris: Twelve do Turnkey do	550 00
Ernest Taylor: do do Assistant Turnkey, Sault Ste. Marie	400 00
S. E. Fleming, M.D.: Twelve do Gaol Surgeon do	200 00
A. E. Storie: do Gaoler, Webbwood	150 00
J. M. Bayes: do Matron, do	75 00

ADMINISTRATION OF JUSTICE.—*Continued.*

DISTRICT OF ALGOMA.—*Continued.*

Brown, J. F., furniture	79	77
Brodie, D. M., travelling expenses, 125.95; Bull & Baker, alabastine, 7.25	133	20
Carney, W. H., Treasurer to pay Administration of Justice accounts: December quarter, 1905, 2,457.36; March quarter, 1906, 1,866.46; June quarter, 1,814.64; September quarter, 1,104.56; December quarter, (accountable), 700.00	7,943	02
Calbeck, A., vault key, 5.00, Can. Pacific Ry. Co., freight charges, 5.23...	10	23
Cowick, J. C., legal services *re* extradition of Carl Christopherson	53	50
Dominion Express Co., charges, .85; Gummerson, A. W., arrears of salary 1905, 24.34	26	19
Hart & Riddell, Bailiff's fee books, 23.88; Hinds, O., paints and brushes, 12.30	36	18
Irving, J. C. & Co., wall paper, shades, etc., 4.60; Jackson Bros., linoleum, 11.00	15	60
Kennedy, Mrs. C., 4 days' work cleaning, 5.00; King's Printer, stationery, 37.50	42	50
Martin, J. H., allowance for board, 6.28; travelling expenses, 34.80	41	08
Moore & Brown, hardware, paint and glass, 3.49; Quibell, W. A., arrears of salary late P. M., 266.00	269	49
Thorburn, W. A., work at .30 per hour, 14.70; Tucker, W. J., paints, brushes, etc., 4.25	18	95
Warren Sporting Goods Co., revolver, etc., for Constable Martin..............	6	93

DISTRICT OF THUNDER BAY ($16,090.14).

W. C. Dobie:	Twelve months' salary as	Police Magistrate	1,000	00
Wm. Newcombe:	Three	do	do	....	250	00
Wm. Palling:	Seven and one-half	do	do	....	624	00
A. W. Thompson:	Twelve	do	Sheriff and Treasurer	1,200	00
J. Meek:		do	Clerk of the District Court ...	450	00
W. F. Longworthy:		do	Clerk of the Peace and District Attorney	250	00
W. R. Stretton:		do	Constable	400	00
Thos. Penfold:		do	Gaoler, Port Arthur	800	00
Nettie Penfold:		do	Matron, do	175	00
C. J. H. Chipman, M.D.		do	Gaol Surgeon, Port Arthur.....	150	00
Robert Poulin:		do	Gaoler, Nepigon	200	00

Dominion Express Co., charges, 5.13; Hart & Riddell, bailiffs' fee books, 2.70	7	83
King's Printer, stationery, 187.00; McRae, J. C., services *re* arrest of Mike Jovina, charged with murder, 175.00	362	00
Lewis, Rice & Son, revolver, handcuffs, etc., for Constable Stretton........	13	55
Moore, D. J., repairing window and door, gaol Port Arthur	8	85
Port Arthur, Town of, laying and cartage iron pipe water service, 14.03; laying tile pipe for sewer, 16.27	30	30
Thompson, A. W., Treasurer, to pay Administration of Justice accounts: December quarter, 1905, 1,804.83; March quarter, 1906, 1,608.68; June quarter, 2,679.60; September quarter, 2,448.38; December quarter, (accountable), 1,600.00	10,141	49
Wells & Emmerson, castings	27	12

DISTRICT OF RAINY RIVER ($16,211.29).

Andrew More:	Twelve months' salary as	Police Magistrate	1,000	00
Thos. P. Morton:	Seven and one-half do	do	....	375	00
C. J. Hollands:	Twelve months' do	do	....	400	00
J. W. Humble:		do	Sheriff	1,000	00
Chas. W. Chadwick:		do	Registrar and Clerk of District Court	700	00
P. E. Mackenzie:		do	Clerk of Peace and District Attorney	250	00
M. Emmons:		do	Constable	600	00

ADMINISTRATION OF JUSTICE.—*Continued.*

DISTRICT OF RAINY RIVER.—*Continued.*

Robert Nairn:	Twelve months' salary as	Treasurer			150 00
W. H. McKay:	Eleven	do	Gaoler, Kenora		500 00
D. J. McKinnon:	One	do	do	do	100 00
Christian I. McKay:	Eleven	do	Matron,	do	166 67
Christina McKinnon:	One	do	do	do	33 33
J. A. Martin:	Twelve	do	Turnkey,	do	744 00
S. S. Scovil, M.D.:		do	Gaol Surgeon, Kenora		200 00
John Perry:		do	Gaoler, Fort Frances..............		450 00
H. McDonald:		do	do	Atikokan	150 00
J. R. Gilbert:		do	do	Mine Centre	300 00

Cotter, A., repairing closets lock-up, Kenora, 2.75; Dominion Exp. Co., charges, 6.03	8 78
Graham & Co., linoleum and laying same Court House, Kenora	49 50
Hollands, C. J., Local Treasurer, expenditure: December quarter, 1905, 44.00; March quarter, 1906, 180.45; September quarter, 116.90; October and November, 56.85	398 20
Hose & Canniff, tinsmithing, .95; Judge Chapple, services hearing assessment appeals, 18.80	19 75
King's Printer, stationery	84 15
Nairn, Robert, Treasurer, to pay Administration of Justice accounts: December quarter, 1905, 1,626.82; March quarter, 1906, 849.06; June quarter, 2,333.70; September quarter, 1,272.33; December quarter, (accountable), 1,550.00	7,631 91
Robertson, D., arrears of salary late P. M. Town Rainy River	900 00

DISTRICT OF NIPISSING ($26,502.87).

Henry Hartman:	Twelve months' salary as	Police Magistrate		1,100 00
H. C. Varin:		do	Sheriff and Treasurer	950 00
A. G. Browning:		do	Clerk of Peace and District Attorney	250 00
T. J. Bourke:		do	Clerk of District Court	450 00
A. Thompson:		do	Constable	300 00
Geo. Caldbick:	Ten	do	Chief Constable	1,200 00
Archie Fortin:	Nine	do	Constable	375 00
T. Keaney:	Twelve	do	Gaoler, Sudbury	500 00
Bridget A. Keaney:		do	Matron, do	150 00
W. H. Howey:		do	Gaol Surgeon, Sudbury	150 00
S. A. Huntington:		do	Gaoler, North Bay	600 00
Julia G. Huntington:		do	Matron, do	175 00
E. F. Huntington:		do	Turnkey, do	400 00
Arthur E. Ranney:		do	Gaol Surgeon, North Bay	150 00
John McMeekin:		do	Gaoler, Mattawa	300 00
M. E. McMeekin:		do	Matron, do	100 00
Chas. W. Haentschel:		do	Gaol Surgeon, Mattawa	100 00
Jos. Riviat:		do	Gaoler, Sturgeon Falls	125 00
John Harteau:	Four	do	Constable	258 00
W. J. Mills:	Nine	do	do	802 00
R. Mutten:	Three	do	do	220 00
John McKay:	Nine	do	do	764 00
S. Wood:	do	do	do	764 00
John E. Thurlow:	Four	do	do	323 00

Browning & McConachie, legal services *re* mining leases, 9.64; Caldbick, J., travelling expenses, 17.25	26 89
Can. Exp. Co., charges, 2.65; Connelly, Jno., repairing radiator, lock-up, Gore Bay, 2.75	5 40
Carter & Cote, pipe and tape, 3.50; Dominion Exp. Co., charges, 4.80	8 30
Ellis, W. H., M.D., analysis of viscera, 50.00; Farrell, J. E. & Co., plumbing, etc., 8.52	58 52
Gagne, F., services and expenses *re* drowning accident, 18.00; Greer Bros., clothing for police, 225.90	243 90

ADMINISTRATION OF JUSTICE.—*Continued.*

DISTRICT OF NIPISSING.—*Continued.*

Greer, Wm., balance 1905 *re* tres ass 30.46; *re* arson, 41.50; Gauthier, T., repairing furnace, etc., 5.50 P.	77 46
Hart & Riddell, bailiff's books, 12.87; Horne, Robert, pipe, bolts, etc., 14.22	27 09
King's Printer, stationery	80 25
Labreche, F., cell doors, gaol North Bay, 15.75; McDonald, A., table, 10.50	26 25
McKay, Jno., D., trav. expenses, 17.90; McDonald & Hay, stove repairs, etc., 18.35	36 25
Mack, C. W., badges for constables	3 00
Murselles, S. B., repairing vault, Registry Office, North Bay	12 00
Mutten, R. B., travelling expenses, 3.10; Purvis Bros., repairing furnace, etc., 40.00	43 10
Richardson, J. W., repairing range Gaol, etc., North Bay	13 60
Rice Lewis & Son, revolvers, handcuffs, etc., for Constables Mills and Hurtea, 23.90; Rice Lewis & Son, revolvers, handcuffs, etc., for Constables McKay and Mutten, 27.40; Rice Lewis & Son, revolver, handcuffs, etc., for Constable Wood, 13.70	65 00
Rogers, J. E., fire inquest Haileybury, 69.40; alleged murder and arson, 35.30	104 70
Sturgeon Falls Lumber Co., lumber, 6.05; Thiel Detective Service Co., services and expenses *re* Haileybury fire inquest, 97.43	103 48
Tindall, R., repairing cell doors	8 00
Varin, H. C., Treasurer, to pay Administration of Justice accounts: December quarter, 1905; 2,957.96; March quarter, 1906, 3,430.81; June quarter, 4,172.68; September quarter, 2,970.23; December, quarter, 1,500.00	15,031 68
Villeneuve, L., lime, etc., 7.75; Woods, S., travelling expenses, 12.45	20 20
Warwick Bros. & Rutter, printing	1 80

DISTRICT OF MUSKOKA.

SALARIES ($9,307.43).

W. H. Spencer: Twelve months' salary as			Police Magistrate	500 00
H. B. Bridgland: Four		do	Sheriff	166 66
D. E. Bastedo: Seven		do	do	333 34
Thos. Johnson:	Twelve	do	Clerk of Peace and District Attorney	250 00
I. Huber:		do	Clerk of District Court	450 00
S. C. McElwain:		do	Constable	739 92
Richard Mills:		do	Gaoler, Bracebridge,	500 00
Rebecca Mills:		do	Matron, do	100 00
O. W. Calbeck, M.D.:		do	Gaol Surgeon, Bracebridge	150 00
Brandon & Gilbert, cartage				50
Burgess, A. M., M.D., medical attendance, Constable McElwain				50 00
Canadian Express Co., charges				3 10
Calvert, A., services as Nurse, Constable McElwain				30 00
Ecclestone, Geo. W., electric bells, etc., 20.31; Fenn, J. L., Sons & Co., ink, brush, etc., .45				20 76
Fish, W. S., glazing, etc., 8.00; Hart & Riddell, clerk's fee books, etc., 9.34				17 34
King's Printer, stationery				230 40
Lount, J. E., Treasurer, to pay Administration of Justice accounts: December quarter, 1905, 999.96; March quarter, 479.14; June quarter, 766.69; September quarter, 637.37; December quarter, 2,850.00				5,733 16
Rogers, J. E., expenses *re* arson case				14 95
Warwick Bros. & Rutter, printing				15 80
Whitten, Jas., repairing flush tank Court House, Bracebridge				1 50

ADMINISTRATION OF JUSTICE.—*Continued.*

DISTRICT OF PARRY SOUND ($13,671.72).

J. Farrer: Twelve months' salary as Police Magistrate			600 00
S. Armstrong:	do	Sheriff	500 00
W. L. Haight:	do	Clerk of Peace and District Attorney and Treasurer	500 00
E. Jordan:	do	Clerk of District Court	450 00
John Duke:	do	Police Magistrate	250 00
John Free: Seven	do	Constable	175 00
Chas. H. Knight: Three and one-half months' salary as Constable			95 00
John Moore: Twelve months' salary as Constable			500 00
D. McRae:	do	do	400 00
James Manson:	do	Gaoler, Parry Sound	550 00
Martha Manson:	do	Matron, do	100 00
Dr. Hugh McLean: Five	do	Gaol Surgeon, do	62 50
Dr. A. E. Burrows: Seven	do	do do	87 50
Thos. Daniels: Twelve	do	Gaoler, Burk's Falls	250 00
Mary F. Daniels:	do	Matron, do	50 00
Jno. Free: Nine	do	Gaoler, Byng Inlet	225 00
C. H. Knight: Three	do	do do	75 00
John Moore: Twelve	do	do French River	75 00
Can. Express Co., charges, 1.20; Clark, C. W., repairing furnace and cistern, 15.10			16 30
Fenn, A. N., pipe, etc., 13.53; Greer, Wm., expenses *re* murder case, 52.25			65 78
Hart & Riddell, bailiff's books			20 90
Haight, W. L., Treasurer to pay Administration of Justice accounts: December quarter, 1905, 1,164.61; March quarter, 1,413.55; June quarter, 2,104.34; September quarter, 2,286.79; December quarter, 1,300.00			8,269 29
Hilliar, Jos., tile, padlocks, etc., 10.25; King's Printer, stationery, 16.75			27 00
Moore, Jno., arrears of salary, 1905, 241.30; Murray, J. W., trav. expenses *re* arson case, 42.90			284 20
Poitress, A., metalling light in basement, Court House			1 50
Riddell, J. D., storm sash, 3.25; Rogers, J. E., expenses *re* cattle poisoning 37.75			41 00
Wolton, H. D., frosting sash			75

DISTRICT OF MANITOULIN ($10,533.13).

Wm. H. Price: Twelve months' salary as Stipendiary Magistrate			1,000 00
E. H. Jackson:	do	Sheriff	500 00
R. R. McKessock:	do	Treasurer	150 00
A. G. Murray:	do	Clerk of the Peace and District Attorney	250 00
"'. R. Abrey:	do	Registrar of Deeds and Master of Titles	600 00
Chas. C. Peatt:	do	Clerk of District Court	450 00
John A. Shields:	do	Constable	350 00
John Ramsbottom:	do	do	400 00
Thos. Ellis:	do	do	97 84
Thos. Griffith:	do	do	245 03
Dominic Solomon:	do	do	600 00
Geo. Meredith: Nine	do	do	110 34
A. Thorburn: Twelve months' salary as Gaoler, Gore Bay			300 00
Margt. Thorburn:	do	Matron, do	100 00
Dominie de Lamorandiere:	do	Gaoler, Killarney	100 00
Samuel Walker:	do	do Manitowaning	200 00
Dominion Express Co., charges, .55; Griffith, Thos., investigation theft of timber, 70.00			70 55
Hart & Riddell, bailiff's fee books, 16.59; King's Printer, stationery, 9.00.			25 59
McKessock, R. R., Treasurer, to pay Administration of Justice accounts:— December quarter, 1905, 475.24; March quarter, 1906, 861.15; June quarter, 1,853.39; September quarter, 1,044.00; December quarter (accountable), 750.00			4,983 78

ADMINISTRATION OF JUSTICE. —*Continued.*

PROVISIONAL COUNTY OF HALIBURTON ($1,426.35).

W. Fielding, Twelve months' salary as Police Magistrate	800 00
Judge Harding, allowance for travelling expenses	37 77
Judge McMillan, do do	362 23
E. C. Young, salary as Registrar of Deeds	200 00
J. E. Rogers, expenses *re* cattle poisoning case	26 35

ALLOWANCE TO DISTRICT JUDGES ($2,840.00).

(6 Edward VII., Cap. 19, Sec. 60).

Judge	Chapple:	Allowance	315 55
do	Johnston:	do	315 56
do	Leask:	do	315 55
do	Mahaffey:	do	315 56
do	McCallum:	do	315 56
do	McCurry:	do	315 55
do	O'Connor:	do	315 56
do	O'Leary:	do	315 55
do	Valin:	do	315 56

PROVINCIAL POLICE, NIAGARA AND DETROIT RIVERS.

Salaries and Expenses ($13,756.13).

W. H. Mains:	Twelve months' salary as Chief Constable, Niagara Falls...				1,150 00
J. W. R. Kee:	do	do	do	...	1,050 00
Patrick Kelly:	do	Constable,	do	...	700 00
Wm. McHattie:	do	do	do	...	700 00
M. McNamara:	do	do	do	...	700 00
T. D. Greenwood:	do	do	do	...	700 00
John Pay:	do	do	do	...	700 00
J. J. Moriarty:	do	do	do	...	700 00
John R. Dowd:	do	do	do	...	700 00
W. J. Sheppard: Six	do	do	do	...	300 00
Wm. Scott: Four	do	do	do	...	200 00
C. Wadsworth:	do	do	do	...	225 00
Oliver Taylor:	do	do	do	...	200 00

Alex. Bartlet: Allowance as Police Magistrate Detroit River	100 00
A. F. Campeau: Twelve months' salary as Chief Constable, Detroit River	1,000 00
Chas. Mahoney: Twelve months' salary as Constable, Detroit River	900 00
Andrew Murray: Eleven do Constable, Sarnia	685 00
A. E. Sarvis: One do do do	62 50
J. G. Ruthven: Twelve do (arrears 1905, 13.70), Magistrate, Bridgeburg	513 70
J. T. James: Arrears salary, Police Magistrate, Bridgeburg	475 00

Niagara River:—

Baldry, C., meals for prisoners	97 75
Bell Telephone Co., rent of instruments and messages	236 79
Buckley, W. H., stationery, etc.	5 85
Cole & McMurray, handcuffs, etc., 34.00; Cruickshanks, E., trav. expenses, .65	34 65 ·
Dowd, J. R., trav. expenses, 40.65; G.N.W. Tel. Co., telegrams, 15.11	55 76
Greenwood, T. D., trav. expenses, 24.75; Kee, J. W. R., trav. expenses, 8.90	33 65
Kelly, P., trav. expenses, 23.45; McHattie, W., trav. expenses, 22.75	46 20
McNamara, M., trav. expenses, 13.70; Mains, W. H., trav. expenses, 34.10	47 80
Moriarty, J. J., trav. expenses, 38.65; Murdock, W. G., trav. expenses. 10.00	48 65
Murray Bros., clothing for police; 602.00; Niagara Falls Ptg. Co., printing and stationery, 9.50	611 50

Andrew Murray: Eleven months' salary as Constable, Sarnia	685 00

ADMINISTRATION OF JUSTICE.—*Concluded.*

PROVINCIAL POLICE, NIAGARA AND DETROIT RIVERS.—*Continued.*

Pay, Jno., trav. expenses, 14.95; Postal Photo Co., photos, 1.25	16 20
Postmaster, postage stamps, 16.50; Quagleoriello, Jno., interpreter, 1.00	17 50
Scott, Wm., trav. expenses, 4.20; Welland *Tribune*, printing and stationery, 1.20	5 40
Wilson Photo Studio, photos	3 00

Detroit River :—

Bell Telephone Co., rent of instruments, 58.91; messages, 40.88	99 79
Cairns, T. A., photos of prisoner, 2.50; Campeau, A. F., trav. expenses, 24.55	27 05
Chicago *Detective*, subscription, 1.00; C.P.R. Tel. Co., messages, .93...	1 93
Davis, Jno., rent of office, 50.00; G.N.W. Tel. Co., messages, 1.85...	51 85
Gordon & Griffith, clothing for police	125 00
Livery hire: Janesse, C. D., 2.50; Kitchen, W. J., 2.50; Kemp, J. G., 3.50; Kercher, A. M., 1.50; Kerrigan, J. J., 2.00; Knight, J., 3.00; McFee, C., 69.50; Montgomery, J. D., 5.00; Moore Bros., 25.50; Overholdt, W., 3.50; Renaud, J. D., 1.50; Townsend, T. B., 3.00	123 00
Mahoney, C., trav. expenses, 59.55; Marentette, V. E., stationery, 2.15	61 70
Murray, A., trav. expenses, 144.96; Oldham, W., police clothing, 75.00	219 96
Postmaster, postage stamps, 7.00; Sarnia *Observer*, printing circulars, 3.00	10 00
Standard Printing Co., printing, etc., 7.95; Thom, J. S., photographing, 1.00	8 95
Union Pub. Co., directories	5 00

REVISION OF STATUTES ($5,026.54).

Berthon, C., services at 7.00 per week	343 00
Campbell, Florence, M., services as stenog. at 12.00 per week, 304.29; Canadian Express Co., charges, 2.05	306 34
Dymond, A. M., services, 1,250.00; travelling expenses, 89.60...............	1,339 60
King's Printer, stationery, 22.60; Mulvey, Thos., special services *re* Ontario Companies' Act, 300.00	322 60
Perry, W. W., extra services as reporter, 25.00; Robinson, C. C., legal services, 1,400.00	1,425 00
Robinson, N., services *re* Railway Act, 150.00; Saunders, Eudo, special services *re* Liquor License Act, 300.00	450 00
Wilkinson, W. M., services	840 00

Total Administration of Justice................................ $544,826 60

EDUCATION.

PUBLIC SCHOOLS ($213,193.25).

Treasurer County of :—

Brant, 1,533.00;	Bruce, 3,670.00;	Carleton, 2,808.00;	
Dufferin, 1,732.00;	Elgin, 2,897.00;	Essex, 2,824.00;	
Frontenac, 2,211.00;	Grey, 5,353.00;	Haldimand, 1,582.00;	
Haliburton, 693.00;	Halton, 1,313.00;	Hastings, 3,746.00;	
Huron, 4,498.00;	Kent, 3,454.00;	Lambton, 3,689.00;	
Lanark, 2,071.00;	Leeds and Grenville, 3,662.00;		
Lennox and Addington, 1,985.00;		Lincoln, 1,593.00;	
Middlesex, 4,756.00;	Northumberland and Durham, 4,460.00;		
Norfolk, 2,316.00;	Ontario, 3,075.00;	Oxford, 3,181.00;	
Peel, 1,712.00;	Perth, 3,107.00;	Peterboro, 2,095.00;	
Prescott and Russell, 1,928.00;		Prince Edw., 1,365.00;	
Renfrew, 3,750.00;		Simcoe, 5,815.00;	
Stormont, Dundas and Glengarry, 5,204.00;		Victoria, 2,150.00;	
Waterloo, 2,321.00;	Welland, 1,952.00;	Wellington, 3,302.00;	
Wentworth, 2,579.00; York, 4,971.00			111,353 00

4 P.A.

EDUCATION.—*Continued.*

PUBLIC SCHOOLS.—*Continued.*

Treasurer City of :—

Belleville, 791.00;	Brantford, 2,058.00;	Chatham, 934.00;
Guelph, 1,164.00;	Hamilton, 5,838.00;	Kingston, 1,611.00;
London, 4,435.00;	Niagara Falls, 805.00;	Ottawa, 3,584.00;
Peterboro, 1,171.00;	St. Catharines, 1,053.00;	St. Thomas, 1,374.00;
Stratford, 1,227.00;	Toronto, 24,156.00;	Windsor, 1,109.00;
Woodstock, 1,033.00		

52,343 00

Treasurer Town of :—

Alexandria, 36.00;	Allison, 146.00;	Almonte, 277.00;
Amherstburg, 121.00;	Arnprior, 284.00;	Aurora, 193.00;
Aylmer, 252.00;	Barrie, 687.00;	Berlin, 1,053.00;
Blenheim, 180.00;	Bothwell, 107.00;	Bowmanville, 329.00;
Bracebridge, 344.00;	Brampton, 315.00;	Brockville, 859.00;
Bruce Mines, 84.00;	Cache Bay, 85.00;	Carleton Place, 469.00;
Clinton, 248.00;	Cobourg, 355.00;	Collingwood, 815.00;
Copper Cliff, 239.00;	Cornwall, 320.00;	Deseronto, 389.00;
Dresden, 207.00;	Dundas, 329.00;	Dunnville, 277.00;
Durham, 213.00;	East Toronto, 379.00;	Essex, 170.00;
Forest, 190.00;	Fort Frances, 69.00;	Fort William, 706.00;
Galt, 944.00;	Gananoque, 453.00;	Goderich, 450.00;
Gore Bay, 96.00;	Gravenhurst, 294.00;	Haileybury, 55.00;
Hanover, 240.00;	Harriston, 205.00;	Hawkesbury, 59.00;
Hespeler, 260.00;	Huntsville, 266.00;	Ingersoll, 435.00;
Kenora, 448.00;	Kincardine, 283.00;	Kingsville, 185.00;
Leamington, 323.00;	Lindsay, 625.00;	Listowel, 247.00;
Little Current, 86.00;	Massey, 38.00;	Mattawa, 27.00;
Meaford, 245.00;	Midland, 457.00;	Milton, 185.00:
Mitchell, 226.00;	Mount Forest, 234.00;	Napanee, 402.00;
New Liskeard, 114.00;	Newmarket, 279.00;	Niagara, 169.00;
North Bay, 292.00;	North Toronto, 271.00;	Oakville, 191.00;
Orangeville, 318.00;	Orillia, 461.00;	Oshawa, 545.00;
Owen Sound, 1,128.00;	Palmerston, 240.00;	Parkhill, 147.00;
Paris, 388.00;	Parry Sound, 337.00;	Pembroke, 385.00;
Penetanguishene, 314.00;	Perth, 267.00;	Petrolia, 471.00;
Picton, 403.00;	Port Arthur, 624.00;	Port Hope, 516.00;
Powassan, 72.00;	Prescott, 261.00;	Preston. 246.00;
Rainy River, 96.00;	Renfrew, 215.00;	Ridgetown, 264.00;
Sandwich, 110.00;	Sarnia, 907.00;	Sault Ste. Marie, 701.00;
Seaforth, 210.00;	Simcoe, 364.00;	Smith's Falls, 593.00;
Southampton, 216.00;	St. Mary's, 361.00;	Stayner, 139.00;
Steelton, 179.00;	Strathroy, 342.00;	Sturgeon Falls, 107.00;
Sudbury, 146.00;	Thessalon, 130.00;	Thornbury, 95.00;
Thorold, 180.00;	Tillsonburg, 260.00;	Toronto Jct., 1,013.00;
Trenton, 318.00;	Uxbridge, 194.00;	Vankleek Hill, 71.00;
Walkerton, 242.00;	Walkerville, 221.00;	Wallaceburg, 307.00;
Waterloo, 376.00;	Welland, 213.00;	Whitby, 233.00;
Wiarton, 298.00;	Wingham, 262.00	

86,297 00

Treasurer Village of :—

Acton, 183.00;	Ailsa Craig, 80.00;	Alvinston, 93.00;
Arkoua, 57.00;	Arthur, 83.00;	Athens, 106.00;
Ayr, 105.00;	Bancroft, 69.00;	Bath, 45.00;
Bayfield, 61.00;	Beamsville, 94.00;	Beaverton, 100.00;
Beeton, 86.00;	Blyth. 117.00;	Bobcaygeon, 108.00;
Bolton, 57.00;	Bradford, 118.00;	Bridgeburg, 144.00;
Brighton, 155.00;	Brussels, 137.00;	Burk's Falls, 92.00;
Burlington, 159.00;	Caledonia, 95.00;	Campbellford, 298.00;
Cannington. 119.00;	Cardinal, 141.00;	Casselman, 10.00;
Cayuga, 115.00;	Chatsworth, 48.00;	Chesley. 238.00;
Chesterville, 81.00;	Chippewa, 93.00;	Clifford, 68.00;
Cobden, 90.00;	Colborne, 122.00;	Creemore, 80.00;
Delhi, 86.00;	Drayton. 95.00;	Dundalk, 98.00;
Dutton, 103.00;	Eganville, 68.00;	Elmira, 160.00;

EDUCATION.—*Continued.*

PUBLIC SCHOOLS.—*Continued.*

Treasurer Village of :—

Elora, 127.00; Embro, 67.00; Erin, 60.00; Exeter, 187.00; Fenelon Falls, 142.00; Fergus, 168.00; Fort Erie, 118.00; Garden Island, 28.00; Georgetown, 166.00; Glencoe, 97.00; Grand Valley, 101.00; Grimsby, 111.00; Hagersville, 115.00; Hastings, 53.00; Havelock, 121.00; Hensall, 107.00; Hintonburg, 146.00; Holland Landing, 48.00; Iroquois, 122.00; Kemptville, 157.00; Lakefield, 149.00; Lanark, 97.00; Lancaster, 61.00; L'Orignal, 117.00; Lucan, 95.00; Lucknow, 120.00; Madoc, 121.00; Markdale, 110.00; Markham, 113.00; Marmora, 69.00; Maxville, 97.00; Merrickville, 112.00; Merritton, 150.00; Millbrook, 103.00; Milverton, 93.00; Morrisburg, 178.00; Newboro, 51.00; Newburg, 57.00; Newbury, 44.00; Newcastle, 77.00; New Hamburg, 149.00; Norwich, 150.00; Norwood, 104.00; Oil Springs, 100.00; Omemee, 79.00; Ottawa, E., 80.00; Paisley, 108.00; Point Edward, 115.00; Port Carling, 32.00; Port Colborne, 146.00; Port Dalhouse, 67.00; Port Dover, 124.00; Port Elgin, 157.00; Port Perry, 146.00; Port Rowan, 75.00; Portsmouth, 53.00; Port Stanley, 68.00; Richmond, 57.00; Richmond Hill, 73.00; Rockland, 27.00; Shelbourne, 139.00; Springfield, 51.00; Sterling, 62.00; Stouffville, 142.00; Streetsville, 64.00; Sundridge, 47.00; Sutton, 72.00; Tara, 73.00; Teeswater, 102.00; Thamesville, 73.00; Thedford, 71.00; Tilbury, 67.00; Tiverton, 60.00; Tottenham, 64.00; Tweed, 128.00; Vienna, 39.00; Wardsville, 37.00; Waterdown, 79.00; Waterford, 126.00; Watford, 149.00; Wellington, 75.00; Weston, 149.00; Westport, 41.00; Winchester, 138.00; Woodbridge, 71.00; Woodville, 51.00; Wroxeter, 49.00;

Wyoming, 79.00 .... 12,920 00

Treasurer Tp. Pelee Island 76 00

Educational Pub. Co., 2,000 copies *School Trustee*, for School Boards......... 200 00

Riordon Paper Mills, paper 4 25

SEPARATE SCHOOLS ($28,279.00).

Trustees R. C. S. S. Section :—

10 Adjala, 30.00; 4 Admaston, 15.00; 3 Alfred, 21.00; 6 Alfred, 21.00; 7 Alfred, 24.00; 8 Alfred, 54.00; 9 Alfred, 25.00; 10 Alfred, 80.00; 11 Alfred, 19.00; 12 Alfred, 28.00; 13 Alfred, 26.00; 14 Alfred, 13.00; 15 Alfred, 24.00; U. 7 Alfred with 8 Plantagenet, 10.00; 2-5-8 Anderson with 6-9 Sandwich W., 25.00; 3-4 Anderson, 13.00; 11 Anderson and Maiden, 15.00; 6 Arthur, 25.00; 3 Arthur, 22.00; 10 Arthur, 30.00; 2 Ashfield, 50.00; 4 Asphodel, 20.00; 15 Augusta, 11.00; 3 Biddulph, 6.00; 4 Biddulph, 32.00; 6 Biddulph, 13.00; 9 Biddulph with McGillivray, 12.00; 2 U. Brant with 3 Greenock, 11.00; 1 (15) Brighton, 16.00; 4 Bromley, 17.00; 6 Bromley, 25.00; 7 Bromley, 42.00; 1 Brougham, 7.00; 2 N. Burgess, 27.00; 4 N. Burgess, 8.00; 6 N. Burgess, 8.00; 3-4-10 Caledonia, 16.00; 10 Caledonia, 15.00; 12 Caledonia, 34.00; 13 Caledonia, 15.00; 6 Caledonia with 7 Plantagenet, 13.00; 3 Cambridge, 32.00; 4 Cambridge, 28.00; 5 Cambridge, 45.00; 6 Cambridge, 18.00; 6-7 Cambridge, 58.00; 14 P. Cambridge, 27.00; 15 Cambridge, 16.00; 1 Carrick, 25.00; 2 Carrick, 19.00; 4 Carrick, 30.00; 14 Garrick, 98.00; 1 U. Carrick with 1 Culross, 53.00; 2 U. Carrick with 2 Culross, 11.00; 15 Charlottenburg, 50.00; 3 Clarence, 27.00; 5 Clarence, 105.00; 6 Clarence, 73.00; 8 Clarence, 43.00; 11 Clarence, 30.00; 12 Clarence, 19.00; 13 Clarence, 12.00; 14 Clarence, 25.00; 16 Clarence, 26.00; 17 Clarence, 21.00; 18 Clarence, 17.00; 19 Clarence, 26.00; 20 Clarence, 18.00; 21 Clarence, 31.00; 1 Cornwall, 15.00; 16 Cornwall, 71.00; 17 Cornwall, 18.00; 1 U. Culross with 1 Carrick, 59.00;

EDUCATION.—*Continued.*

SEPARATE SCHOOLS.—*Continued.*

Trustees R. C. S. S. Section :—

2 U. Culross with 2 Carrick, 11.00;   10 Cumberland, 7.00;
11 Cumberland, 16.00;   13 Cumberland, 22.00;   14 Cumberland, 29.00;
3 Dover, 72.00;   .   7 Dover, 25.00;   9 Dover, 28.00;
9 Downie, 38.00;   2 Edwardsburg, 2.00;   1 Ellice, 16.00;
6 Ellice, 36.00;   7 Ellice, 20.00;   4 Emily, 37.00;
6 Emily, 22.00;   5 Finch, 68.00;   5 Glenelg, 17.00;
7 Glenelg, 26.00;   4-5-12 Gloucester, 7.00;   14 Gloucester, 51.00;
15 Gloucester, 60.00;   17 Gloucester, 17.00;   20 Gloucester, 11.00;
22 Gloucester, 10.00;   25 Gloucester, 105.00;   26 Gloucester, 25.00;
1 Gloucester with 3 Osgoode, 10.00;   3 Greenock, 59.00;
3 Greenock with Brant, 17.00;   3 Griffith, 17.00;   4 Hagarty, 45.00;
12 Hagarty, 59.00;   2 Haldimand, 37.00;   14 Haldimand, 11.00;
9 Harwich, 19.00;   2 Hawkesbury E., 58.00;   4 Hawkesbury, 15.00;
6 Hawkesbury, 13.00; 7 Hawkesbury E., 90.00; 10 Hawkesbury, 46.00;
11 Hawkesbury, 24.00; 12 Hawkesbury E., 6.00; 15 Hawkesbury, 17.00;
16 Hawkesbury, 9.00;   19 Hawkesbury E., 15.00;   1 Hay, 27.00;
11 Hay, 20.00;   3 (1) Hibbert, 23.00;
2 Hibbert, Logan and McKillop 45.00;
3   do   do 3.00;
3 Holland, 7.00;   1 Howe Island, 8.00;   2 Howe Island, 15.00;
3 Howe Island, 16.00;   2 Hullett, 18.00;   14 Hungerford, 8.00;
14 Hungerford, arrears, 5.00;   8 Kingston, 20.00;   12 Kenyon, 9.00;
11 Lochiel, 15.00;   12 A. Lochiel, 37.00;   12 B. Lochiel, 76.00;
2 W. Longueil, 23.00;   4 A. Longueil, 24.00;   7 Longueil, 23.00;
2 Loughboro, 9.00;   10 Loughboro, 13.00;   1 Maidstone, 24.00;
2 Maidstone, 26.00;   4 Maidstone with 2 Rochester, 16.00;
8 Maidstone with 5 Sandwich, 24.00;   3 A. Malden, 33.00;
3 B. Malden, 24.00;   3 Mara, 50.00;   3 March, 42.00;
1 Marmora and Lake, 72.00; 3 Matawatchan, 17.00; 3-4-5 Moore, 8.00;
4 Mornington, 32.00;   1 McGillivray with 9 Biddulph, 10.00;
1 McKillop, 27.00;   U. 3 McKillop with 1 Hibbert, 7.00;
7 Nepean, 19.00;   15 Nepean, 93.00;   1 Nichol, 11.00;
5 Normanby, 14.00;   10 Normanby, 21.00;   1 Osgoode, 13.00;
2 (15) Osgoode, 11.00;   3 Osgoode with 1 Gloucester, 11.00;
8 Peel, 17.00;   12 Peel, 13.00;   5 Percy, 13.00;
12 Percy with 12 Seymour; 9.00;   4 Plantagenet N., 21.00;
7 Plantagenet N., 18.00;   8 Plantagenet N., 58.00;
9 Plantagenet N., 31.00;   12 Plantagenet N., 15.00;
4 Plantagenet S., 57.00;   7 Plantagenet S., 53.00;
8 Plantagenet S., 9.00;   11 Plantagenet S., 40.00;
12 Plantagenet S., 13.00; U. 7 Plantagenet S. with 6 Caledonia, 14.00;
U. 8 Plantagenet S. with 7 Alfred, 8.00;   11 Portland, 20.00;
6 Proton, 22.00;   5 Raleigh, 21.00;   6 Raleigh, 18.00;
10-17 Richmond, 13.00;   2 Rochester with 4 Maidstone, 21.00;
3 Rochester, 29.00;   6 Rochester, 27.00;   7 Rochester, 30.00;
9-14 Rochester 17.00;
8 Rochester with 11 Tilbury W. and 11 Tilbury N.......................8.00;
11 Rochester with 10 Tilbury N., 4.00;   12 Roxboro, 79.00;
16 Roxboro, 11.00;   4 Russell, 19.00;   6 Russell, 114.00;
7 Russell, 20.00;   8 Russell, 39.00;   13 Russell, 20.00;
14 Russell, 19.00;   1 Russell with 12 Winchester, 12.00;
1 Sandwich E., 86.00; 2 Sandwich E., 17.00; 3 Sandwich E., 31.00;
4 Sandwich E., 104.00;   5 Sandwich S. with 8 Maidstone, 23.00;
7 Sandwich S., 27.00; 1 Sandwich W., 51.00; 4 Sandwich W., 19.00;
6-9 Sandwich W. with 2-5-3 Anderdon 24.00;
12 Seymour with 12 Percy, 12.00;   5 Sheffield, 28.00;
6 Sherwood, 59.00;   2 Stafford, 29.00;   1 Stanley, 22.00;
6 Stephen. 35.00;   5 Sombra, 19.00;   7 Sydenham, 9.00;
1 Tilbury E., 8.00;   3 Tilbury E., 16.00;   1 Tilbury N., 71.00;
2 Tilbury N., 28.00;   6 Tilbury N., 21.00;   7 Tilbury N., 35.00;
10 Tilbury N. with 11 Rochester 15.00;
11 Tilbury N. with 11 Tilbury W. and 8 Rochester..................8.00;
11 Tilbury W. with 11 Tilbury N. and 8 Rochester..................14.00;
2 Tiny, 98.00;   6 Toronto Gore, 13.00;   18 Tyendinaga, 11.00;

EDUCATION.—*Continued.*

SEPARATE SCHOOLS.—*Continued.*

Trustees R. C. S. S. Section ·— .
14 Tyendinaga, arrears, 23.00;   20 Tyendinaga, 19.00;
24 Tyendinaga, 19.00; 28 Tyendinaga, 11.00; 30 Tyendinaga, 14.00;
3 Waterloo, 64.00;   1 Wawanosh W., 18.00;   5 Wellesley, 22.00;
9-10 Wellesley, 31.00;   11 Wellesley, 77.00;   12 Wellesley, 4.00;
10 Williams W., 13.00;   15½ Wilmot, 53.00;   8 Windham, 55.00;
12 Winchester with 1 Russell, 13.00;   1 Wolfe Island, 7.00;
2 Wolfe Island, 11.00; 4 Wolfe Island, 36.00; 7 Wolfe Island, 13.00;
10 Woolwich, 34.00; 4 Yonge and Escott, rear, 7.00; 1 York, 43.00   6,930 00

Treasurer R. C. S. S. City of:—
Belleville, 230.00;   Brantford, 278.00;   Chatham, 205.00;
Guelph, 284.00;   Hamilton, 1,206.00;   Kingston, 543.00;
London, 670.00;   Niagara Falls, 104.00; .   Ottawa, 4,120.00;
Peterboro, 506.00;   St. Catharines, 270.00;   St. Thomas, 171.00;
Stratford, 290.00;   Toronto, 4,075.00;   Windsor, 548.00;
Woodstock, 56.00 .... 13,556 00

Treasurer R. C. S. S. Town of:—
Alexandria, 232.00;   Almonte, 69.00;   Amherstburg, 142.00;
Arnprior, 178.00;   Barrie, 104.00;   Berlin, 333.00;
Bonfield, 100.00;   Brockville, 266.00;   Cobourg, 150.00;
Cornwall, 406.00;   Dundas, 73.00;   Fort Frances, 23.00;
Fort William, 204.00;   Galt, 68.00;   Goderich, 58.00;
Hawkesbury, 479.00;   Kenora, 94.00;   Ingersoll, 53.00;
Lindsay, 216.00;   Massey, 30.00;   Mattawa, 144.00;
Mount Forest, 34.00;   Newmarket, 28.00;   North Bay, 159.00;
Oakville, 20.00;   Orillia, 122.00;   Oshawa, 60.00;
Owen Sound, 78.00;   Paris, 48.00;   Parkhill, 30.00;
Pembroke, 251.00;   Perth, 128.00;   Picton, 37.00;
Port Arthur, 195.00;   Prescott, 110.00;   Preston, 67.00;
Rainy River, 28.00;   Renfrew, 163.00;   Sandwich, 127.00;
Sarnia, 160.00;   Sault Ste. Marie, 147.00;   Seaforth, 52.00;
Steelton, 99.00:   St. Mary's, 44.00;   Sturgeon Falls, 159.00;
Sudbury, 234.00;   Thorold, 68.00;   Trenton, 98.00;
Vankleek Hill, 95.00:   Walkerton, 116.00;   Walkerville, 66.00;
Wallaceburg, 64.00; Waterloo, 93.00; Whitby, 32.00 .... 6,634 00

Treasurer R. C. S. S. Village of:—
Arthur, 63.00;   Belle River, 69.00;   Casselman, 72.00;
Chesterville, 29.00;   East Rockland, 40.00;   Eganville, 60.00;
Elora, 26.00;   Fergus, 7.00;   Hastings, 42.00;
Hintonburg, 204.00;   L'Orignal, 32.00;   Merritton, 43.00;
Ottawa E., 105.00;   Port Dalhousie, 30.00;   Portsmouth, 22.00;
Rockland, 157.00:   Tilbury, 75.00;   Tweed, 28.00;
Weston, 11.00; Westport, 44.00 .... 1,159 00

POOR SCHOOLS ($17,332.63).

Trustees R. C. S. S. Section:—
4 Admaston, 40.00;   10 Alfred, 50.00;   14 Alfred, 40.00;
15 Augusta, 50.00;   2-5-8 Anderdon with 6-9 Sandwich, 40.00;
15 Brighton, 40.00;   6 Bromley, 40.00;   7 Bromley, 40.00;
1 Brougham, 60.00;   2 Burgess, N., 50.00;   4 Burgess, 50.00;
6 Burgess, 50.00;   13 Caledonia, 50.00:   4 Cambridge, 40.00;
15 Charlottenburg, 50.00;   6 Clarence, 90.00;   5 Clarence, 50.00;
1 Cornwall, 50.00;   7 N. Crosby, 50.00;   14 Cumberland, 50.00;
4-5-12 Gloucester, 50.00;   17 Gloucester, 50.00;   22 Gloucester, 60.00;
25 Gloucester, 50.00;   3 Griffith, 75.00;   4 Hagarty, 50.00;
12 Hagarty, 60.00;   14 Haldimand, 40.00;   12 E. Hawesbury, 40.00;
19 E. Hawkesbury, 40.00;   12 Kenyon, 50.00;   1 Howe Island, 40.00;
2 Howe Island, 40.00;   14 Hungerford, 25.00;   11 Lochiel, 50.00;
12 A. Lochiel, 50.00;   4 Longueil, 40.00;   10 Loughboro, 40.00;
3 March, 50.00:   3 Matawatchan, 75.00;   1 Osgoode, 40.00;
2 Osgoode, 40.00;   5 Percy, 40.00;   4 Plantagenet, S., 50.00;

EDUCATION.—*Continued.*

POOR SCHOOLS.—*Continued.*

12 Percy and Seymour, 75.00;   11 Portland, 60.00;
10-17 Richmond, 60.00;   8 Rochester, 40.00;   12 Roxborough, 50.00;
4 Russell, 40.00;   6 Russell, 40.00;   1 Sandwich, E., 50.00;
4 Sandwich, E., 50.00;   1 Sandwich, W., 50.00;   6 Sherwood, 60.00;
1 Tilbury, E., 40.00;   1 Tilbury, N., 50.00;   2 Tiny, 40.00;
6 Toronto Gore, 40.00;   28 Tyendinaga, 30.00;   30 Tyendinaga, 50.00;
4 Yonge and Escott, rear, 50.00..   3,000 00

Treasurer County of, Special Aid to:—
   Bruce, 570.00;   Carleton, 300.00;   Elgin, 40.00;
   Essex, 150.00;   Frontenac, 1,437.00;   Grey, 170.00;
   Haliburton, 3.705;   Hastings, 290.00;   Kent, 100.00;
   Lanark, 625.00;   Leeds and Grenville, 450.00;
   Lennox and Addington, 665.00;   Ontario, 180.00;
   Peterboro, 940.00;   Renfrew, 1,300.00;   Simcoe, 100.00;
   Stormont, D. & G., 50.00;   Wellington (17 Arthur and Minto), 100.00;
   Victoria 975.00;

Treasurer, Tp. of, Special Aid to:—
   Bangor, McClure and Wicklow, 330.00;   Carlow, 170.00;
   Dungannon, 200.00;   23 Edwardsburg, 25.00;
   Elzevir and Grimsthorpe, 150.00;   Faraday, 210.00;
   Herschel and Monteagle, 403.00;   Huntington, 50.00;   Limerick, 65.00;
   Madoc, 30.00;   Marmora, 35.00;   Mayo, 220.00;   2 Oxford, 50.00;
   Tudor and Cashel, 155.00; Wollaston, 82.00....................................   14,322 00
G. T. Ry. Co., freight charges 1 68
King's Printer, paper 2 90
Warwick Bros. & Rutter, printing 6 05

DISTRICT SCHOOLS ($59,665.00).

Albany, James Bay District 100 00
Algoma, Trustees Public School:—
   1 Aberdeen, 80.00;   2 Aberdeen, 130.00;   1 Balfour, 135;
   3 Balfour, 115.00;   4 Balfour, 115.00;   1 Biscotasing, 85.00;
   1 Bright and Gladstone, 115.00;   3 Bright, 75.00;   1 Cartier, 115.00;
   1 Chapleau, 115.00;   1 Cobden, 50.00;   1 Day and Gladstone, 65.00;
   1 Denison, Drury&Graham, 115.00; 2 Denison, Drury&Graham,115.00;
   2 Denison, Drury and Graham 115.00;
   3 Denison, Drury and Graham 115.00;
   3   do'   do   Mines School 115.00;
   5   do   do   Graham 170.00;
   6   do   and Louise, 170.00; 1 Fenwick, 115.00; 2 Fenwick, 90.00;
   1 Gaudette and Hodgins, 90.00; 1 Galbraith, 130.00; 1 Hallam, 50.00;
   2-6 Hallam and May, 90.00; 1 Johnston. 115.00; 2 Johnston, 105.00;
   3 Johnston, 130.00;   4 Johnston, 115.00;   1 Korah, 115.00;
   2 Korah, 75.00; 3 Korah, 115.00; 4 Korah, 115.00; 1 Laird, 115.00;
   3 Laird, 65.00;   2 Laird and Tarbutt, 90.00;   1 Lefroy, 100.00;
   3 Laird and Tarbutt, 50.00;   3 Lefroy, 115.00;
   2 Lefroy, Thessalon and Kirkwood, 130.00; 1 Lefroy and Plummer, 15.00;
   1 Lewis, 115.00; 1 Long, 130.00; 5 May, 85.00; 3 Michipicoten, 130.00;
   1 Merritt and Baldwin, 105.00;   1 Missanabie, 65.00;
   2   do   do   25.00;   1 McDonald and Meredith, 115.00;
   2 McDonald and Meredith, 115.00; 3 do   do   130.00;
   4   do   do 115.00;
   3   do   do   and Aberdeen 125.00;
   1 Nairn and Lorne. 115.00;   2 Parkinson, 130.00;
   3 Parkinson and Grissette, 30.00;   1 Patton, 80.00;
   1 Plummer and Rose, Addtl., 65.00;   1 Plummer, 90.00;
   1   do   addtl., 50.00;   2 Plummer and Rose, 115.00;
   1 Prince, 65.00; 2 Prince, 75.00; 2 Rayside, 130.00; 3 Rayside, 100.00;
   4 Rayside, 90.00;   1 Salter, 100.00;   3 Salter, 115.00;
   3 Salter and May, etc., 105.00; 1 Shedden, 115.00; 2 Shedden, 160.00;

EDUCATION.—*Continued.*

DISTRICT SCHOOLS.—*Continued.*

1 Snider and Creighton, 100.00;   1 Snider and Waters, 130.00;
1 Spragge, 115.00;   1 Tarbutt, 115.00;   2 Tarbutt, 115.00,
1 Tarentorus, 115.00;   2 Tarentorus, 115.00;   2 Thessalon, 115.00;
3 Thessalon, 115.00;   1 Thompson, 130.00;   2 Thompson, 105.00;
1 Victoria, 90.00; 2 Victoria, 80.00; 1 Wells, 105.00; 3 Wells, 105.00;
1 White River, 115.00 .... - 8,875.00

Trustees, R. C. S. S. Section:—
   2 Balfour, 115.00;   1 Balfour and Rayside, 130.00;   6 Dilke, 125.00;
   1 Keewatin, 115.00; 3 McIntyre, 125.00; 2 Rayside, 135.00...............   745 00

Manitoulin, Trustees Public Schools:—
   1 Aird Island, 115.00;   2 Allen, 115.00;   3 Allen, 125.00;
   1 Assignack, 115.00;   2 Assignack, 115.00;   3 Assignack, 115.00;
   5   do   130.00;   6   do   115.00;   7   do   115.00;
   1 Barrie Island, 115.00;   4 Bidwell, 115.00;   5 Bidwell, 115.00;
   6 Bidwell, 125.00;   1 Billings and Allen, 115.00;
   2 Billings and Allen, 115.00;   1 Burpee, 115.00;   2 Burpee, 120.00;
   1 Campbell, 155.00;   2 Campbell, 155.00;   3 Campbell, 115.00;
   4   do   155.00;   1 Carlyle, 55.00;   1 Carnarvon, 115.00;
   2 Carnarvon, 115.00;   3 Carnarvon, 115.00;   6 Carnarvon, 115.00;
   1 Cockburn Island, 115.00;   2 Cockburn Island, 115.00;
   1 Dawson, 140.00;   1 Duck Island, 55.00;   1 Gordon, 115.00;
   4 Gordon, 115.00;   5 Gordon, 125.00;   1 Hilton, 115.00;
   6 Hilton, 165.00;   2 Howland, 115.00;   3 Howland, 115.00;
   7 Howland, 115.00;   8 Howland, 115.00;   1 Jocelyn, 115.00;
   2 Jocelyn, 115.00;   3 Jocelyn, 115.00;   4   do   115.00;
   1 John Island, 115.00;   1 Mills, 115.00;   1 Robinson, 140.00;
   1 Rutherlord, 115.00;   1 St. Joseph, 115.00;   2 St. Joseph, 115.00;
   3 St. Joseph, 115.00;   4   do   115.00;   5   do   115.00;
   1 Sandfield, 115.00;   2 Sandfield, 125.00;
   3   do   and Tehkummah 115.00;
   4   do   do 130.00;
   5   do   do   50.00;   4 Shequiandah, 115.00;
   1 Tehkummah, 115.00; 4 Tehkummah, 130.00; 5 Tehkummah, 40.00;   7,065 00

Muskoka, Trustees Public Schools:—
   U 1 Baxter, with 9 Tay, 100.00; 1 Brunell, 115.00; 2 Brunell, 120.00;
   3 Brunell, 120.00;   4 Brunell, 120.00;   5   do   120.00;
   6   do   120.00;   7   do   95.00;   1 Cardwell, 130.00;
   2 Cardwell, 115.00;   4 Cardwell, 130.00;   5 Cardwell, 130.00;
   1 Chaffey, 120.00;   3 Chaffey, 95.00;
   5 Chaffey, 120.00;   6 Chaffey, 120.00;   7 Chaffey, 110.00;
   8 Chaffey, 120.00;   9 Chaffey, 100.00;   10 Chaffey, 110.00;
   U. 1 Draper, 120.00;   2 Draper, 125.00;   3 Draper, 120.00;
   4 Draper, 130.00;   5 Draper, 125.00;   U. 6 Draper, 125.00;
   7 Draper, 130.00;   U. 8 Draper, 120.00;   U. 9 Draper, 125.00;
   2 Franklin, 110.00;   3 Franklin, 120.00;   4 Franklin, 95.00;
   5 Franklin, 70.00;   6 Franklin, 120.00;   McLean, 100.00;
   1 McLean and Ridout, 15.00;   1 Macaulay, 120.00;
   2 McLean and Ridout, 25.00;   U. 2 Macaulay, 120.00;
   3 McLean and Ridout, 25.00;   3 Macaulay, 125.00;
   5 McLean and Ridout, 25.00;   4 Macaulay, 125.00;
   5 Macaulay, 100.00;   6 Macaulay, 105.00;   7 Macaulay, 105.00;
   8 Macaulay, 130.00;   2 Medora, 115.00;   3 Medora, 115.00;
   4 Medora, 115.00;   5 Medora, 115.00;   6 Medora, 65.00;
   8 Medora, 115.00;   10 Medora, 115.00;   2 Monck, 115.00;
   3 Monck, 85.00;   4 Monck, 115.00;   6 Monck, 115.00;
   7 Monck, 115.00;   8 Monck (2 Schools), 230.00;   Morrison, 150.00;
   2 Muskoka, 115.00;   3 Muskoka. 115.00;   5 Muskoka, 105.00;
   6 Muskoka (2 Schools), 245.00; 1 Oakley, 120.00; 2 Oakley, 80.00;
   U. 4 Oakley, 120.00;   1 Ryde, 120.00;   2 Ryde, 120.00;
   U. 5 Ryde, 100.00;   5 Ryde, 25.00;   7 Ryde, 130.00;
   2 Ridout, 100.00;   3 Ridout, 100.00;   1 Stephenson, 115.00;

EDUCATION.—*Continued.*

DISTRICT SCHOOLS.—*Continued.*

2 Stephenson, 130.00;   3 Stephenson, 115.00;
U. 4 Stephenson (2 schools), 245.00;   5 Stephenson, 115.00;
7 Stephenson, 130.00;   8 Stephenson, 130.00;   9 Stephenson, 115.00;
1 Sinclair, 120.00;   U. 2 Stisted, 95.00;   2 Stisted, 120.00;
3 Stisted, 115.00;   4 Stisted, 120.00;   5 Stisted, 120.00;
6 Stisted, 120.00;   7 Stisted, 120.00;   1 Watt, 115.00;
2 Watt, 130.00;   3 Watt, 115.00;   4 Watt, 115.00;
5 Watt, 116.00;   7 Watt, 115.00;   1 Wood, 115.00;
2 Wood, 105.00; 3 Wood, 130.00; 4 Wood, 130.00; 5 Wood, 30.00......   11,590 00
Treasurer, School Board Tp. Morrison for Sec. Nos. 1-2-3-4-5..............   500 00

Nipissing, Trustees Public Schools:—

1 Airy, 95.00;   2 Airy, 100.00;   1 Appleby, 110.00;
2 Badgerow, 85.00;   1 Blezard, 115.00;   2 Blezard, 115.00;
1 Bonfield, 130.00;   2 Bonfield, 115.00;   1 Broder, 175.00;
1 Caldwell, 125.00;   2 Caldwell, 115.00;   3 Caldwell, 115.00;
4 Caldwell, 95.00;   5 Caldwell, 125.00;   1 Calvin, 115.00;
2 Calvin, 125.00;   3 Calvin, 115.00;   4 Calvin, 115.00;
1 Cameron, 115.00;   1 Capreol, 125.00;   2 Capreol, 165.00;
1 Cassimir, 125.00;   1 Chisholm, 120.00;   2 Chisholm, 125.00;
3 Chisholm, 75.00;   4 Chisholm, 145.00;   5 Chisholm, 25.00;
1 Dryden, 115.00;   1 Dunnett, 115.00;   2 Dunnett, 130.00;
3 Dunnett, 115.00;   4 Dunnett, 115.00;   1 Ferris, 115.00;
2 Ferris, 85.00;   3 Ferris, 80.00;   1 Field, 130.00;
2 Field, 90.00;   2 Gibbons, 120.00;   1 Hager, 115.00;
1 Hanmer, 115.00;   2 Hanmer, 115.00;   1 Hugel, 125.00;
2 Hugel, 125.00;   1 Hunter, 120.00;   1 Jennings, 130.00;
1 Kirkpatrick, 80.00;   2 Kirkpatrick, 115.00;   3 Kirkpatrick, 115.00;
4 Kirkpatrick, 15.00;   5 Kirkpatrick, 130.00;
1 Lyell and Murchison, 150.00;   2 Lyell and Murchison, 120.00;
1 McCraney, 70.00;   4 McKim, 65.00;   1 Martland, 115.00;
1 Mattawan, 115.00;   1 Neelon, 105.00;   2 Neelon, 175.00;
3 Neelon, 175.00;   2 Papineau, 100.00;   4 Springer, 105.00;
2 Widdifield, 115.00;   3 Widdifield, 25.00;   4 Widdifield, 90.00;
5 Widdifield, 125.00; 6 Widdifield, 140.00 ....   7,405 00

Treasurer, R. C. S. S. Section:—

1 Appleby, Cassimir and Dunnett, 95.00;   1 A. Bonfield, 50.00;
1 B. Bonfield, 50.00;   1 Bonfield, 15.00;   2 Bonfield, 115.00;
4 Bonfield, 115.00;   5 Bonfield, 125.00;   1 Caldwell, 70.00;
2 Chisholm, 125.00; 1 Chisholm and Boulter, 125.00; 1 Cosby, 75.00;
Dunnett and Rutter, 130.00;   2 Ferris, 115.00;   3 Ferris, 125.00;
4 Ferris, 125.00;   1 Gibbon, 65.00;   1 Grant, 105.00;
1 McCraney, 50.00;   1 McPherson and Kirkpatrick, 105.00;
1 Mason, 85.00;   1 Papineau, 130.00;   2 A. Papineau, 115.00;
2 B. Paninean, 115.00;   1 Springer, 115.00;   2 Springer, 115.00;
3 Springer, 115.00;   5 Springer, 115.00;   2 Widdifield, 115.00;
3 Widdifield, 50.00 ....   2,850 00

Parry Sound, Trustees Public Schools:—

U. 1 Armour, 115.00;   3 Armour, 115.00;   4 Armour, 95.00;
5 Armour, 95.00;   6 Armour, 115.00;   2 Bethune, 90.00;
U. 1 Carling, 110.00;   2 Carling, 115.00;   3 Carling, 90.00;
4 Carling, 110.00;   8 Carling, 130.00;   U. 1 Chapman, 115.00;
2 Chapman, 115.00;   3 Chapman, 130.00;   4 Chapman, 115.00;
5 Chapman, 135.00;   1 Christie, 115.00;   2 Christie, 115.00;
3 Christie, 110.00;   U. 5 Christie, 115.00;   1 Croft, 115.00;
2 Croft, 130.00;   3 Croft, 95.00;   1 Ferguson, 135.00;
U. 1 Ferris, 115.00;   2 Foley, 115.00;   3 Foley, 115.00;
4 Foley, 115.00;   1 Gurd, 100.00;   2 Gurd, 120.00;
1 Hardy, 40.00;   1 U. Hagerman, 110.00;   2 Hagerman, 110.00;
4 Foley, 115.00; 1 Gurd, 100.00; 2 Gurd, 120.00; 3 Gurd, 120.00;
3 Hagerman, 115.00;   4 U. Hagerman, 140.00;   5 Hagerman, 115.00;

EDUCATION.—*Continued.*

DISTRICT SCHOOLS.—*Continued.*

3 Himsworth N., 120.00; 4 Himsworth N., 115.00; 1 Himsworth S., 120.00;
2 Himsworth S., 120.00; 3 Himsworth S., 70.00; 4 Himsworth S., 110.00
5 Himsworth S., 120.00; 6 Himsworth S., 115.00; 9 Himsworth S., 90.00;
1 Humphrey, 2 schools, 230.00; 2 Humphrey, 85.00; 4 Humphrey, 90.00;
6 Humphrey, 125.00; 4 U. Humphrey, 30.00; 1 Joly, 120.00;
1 Laurier, 90.00; 2 Laurier, 110.00; 3 Laurier, 120.00;
1 Lount, 95.00; 2 Lount, 115.00; 1 Machar, 120.00;
2 Machar, 115.00; 3 Machar, 120.00; 4 Machar, 95.00;
5 Machar, 115.00; 6 Machar, 90.00; 7 Machar, 120.00;
1 Mills, 115.00; 1 Monteith, 115.00; 2 Monteith, 100 00;
3 Monteith, 90.00; 4 Monteith, 95.00; 1 Mowat, 115.00;
2 McDougall, 110.00; 3 McDougall, 115.00; 4 U. McDougall, 105.00;
5 McDougall, 95.00; 6 McDougall, 100.00; 1 McKellar, 115.00;
3 McKellar, 125.00; 4 McKellar, 115.00; 5 McKellar, 90.00;
6 McKellar, 125.00; 1 McKenzie, 95.00; 1 U. McMurrich, 115.00
2 U. McMurrich, 115.00; 3 McMurrich, 115.00; 4 McMurrich, 110.00;
5 McMurrich, 135.00; 1 Nipissing, 120.00; 2 Nipissing, 120.00;
3 Nipissing, 120.00; 5 Nipissing, 120.00; 1 U. Patterson, 115.00;
1 Perry, 65.00; 2 Perry, 115.00; 3 U. Perry, 115.00;
4 Perry, 130.00; 5 Perry, 140.00; 6 Perry, 115.00;
7 U. Perry, 115.00; 8 Perry, 115.00; 9 U. Perry, 115.00;
2 U. Pringle, 115.00; 3 U. Pringle, 40.00; 1 Proudfoot, 120.00;
1 Ryerson, 115.00; 2 Ryerson, 115.00; 3 Ryerson, 115.00;
4 Ryerson, 115.00; 5 Ryerson, 115.00; 1 U. Spence, 135.00;
2 Spence, 115.00; 4 Spence, 65.00; 1 Strong, 110.00;
2 Strong, 115.00; 3 Strong, 115.00; 5 U. Strong, 115.00;
6 Strong, 130.00; · 1 Wallbridge, 115.00; 2 Wallbridge, 115.00;
1 U. Wilson, 115.00; 2 U. Wilson, 85.00 .... 13,325 00

Rainy River, Trustees Public Schools:—
1 Aubrey and Eton, 125.00; 1 Aylesworth, 115.00; 1 Burriss, 115.00;•
2 Burriss, 80.00; 1 Carpenter, 115.00; 2 Carpenter, 85.00;
3 Carpenter, 130.00; 3 Chapple, 110.00; 7 Chapple, 100.00;
2 Crozier, 95.00; 3 Crozier, 65.00; 1 Devlin, 115.00;
2 Devlin, 115.00; 3 Devlin, 115.00; 6 Dilke, 115.00;
2 Dobie, 80.00; 4 Dobie, 115.00; 1 Gold Rock, 75.00;
1 Ignace, 115.00; 1 Keewatin, 115.00; 5 Lash, 115.00;
10 Lash, 125.00; 1 McCrossen, 30.00; 1 U. Morley and Pattullo, 125.00;
7 Morley, 65.00; 7 Morley and Pattullo, 50.00;
9 Morley and Dilke, 90.00; 1 Sandford and Aubrey. 105.00;
1 Shenstone, 115.00; 5 Shenstone, 115.0; 1 Southworth, 90.00;
1 Vanhorne and Wainwright, 115.00; 1 Wabigoon, 115.00;
1 Wainwright. 30.00; 1 Woodyatt, 115.00; 1 Worthington, 115.00;
2 Zealand, 110.00 .... 3,720 00

Temiskaming, Trustees Public Schools:—
1 Armstrong, 115.00; 1 Brethour, 115.00; 1 Coleman, 95.00;
2 Coleman, 40.00; 1 Casey, 25.00; 2 Casey, 15.00;
2 Casey and Harris, 50.00; 1 Dack, 85.00; 2 Dymond, 115.00;
3 Dymond, 115.00; 4 Dymond, 115.00; 1 Evanturel. 115.00;
1 Harley. 115.00; 1 Harris, 115.00; 1 Hilliard, 15.00;
2 Hilliard, 65.00; 3 Hilliard, 15.00; 1 Hudson, 115.00;
1 Kearns, 115.00; 2 Kearns, 65.00; Latchford, 50.00 .... 1,670 00

Trustees R. C. S. S. Section:—
Coleman 75 00

Thunder Bay, Trustees Public Schools:—
1 Dorion, 105.00; 2 Dorion, 90.00; 1 Gillies, 100.00;
2 Gillies and O'Connor, 115.00; 3 McIntyre. 135.00; 1 Nepigon, 115.00;
1 O'Connor, 90.00; 1 Oliver, 85.00; 2 Oliver, 115.00;
3 Oliver, 115.00; 1 Paipoonge, 115.00; 2 Paipoonge, 115.00;
3 Paipoonge, 115.00; 1 Rossport, 115.00; 1 Savanne, 105.00;
1 Schreiber, 115.00 .... 1,745 00

EDUCATION.—*Continued.*

SPECIAL GRANTS.

PUBLIC AND SEPARATE RURAL SCHOOLS ($59,982.72).

Treasurer County of:—

Brant, 776.00; Bruce, 1,862.00; Carleton, 1,423.00;
Dufferin, 878.00; Elgin, 1,468.00; Essex, 1,432.00;
Frontenac, 1,120.00; Grey, 2,711.00; Haldimand, 801.00;
Haliburton, 351.00; Halton, 665.00; Hastings, 1,898.00;
Huron, 2,279.00; Kent, 1,750; Lambton, 1,869.00;
Lanark, 1,050.00; Leeds and Grenville, 1,855.00;
Lennox and Addington, 1,006; Lincoln, 807.00; Middlesex, 2,409.00;
Northumberland and Durham, 2,262.00; Norfolk, 1,174.00;
Ontario, 1,558.00; Oxford, 1,612.00; Perth, 1,575.53;
Peterboro, 1,062.00; Peel, 868.00; Prescott and Russell, 977.00;
Prince Edward, 692.00; Renfrew, 1,900; Simcoe, 2,948.00;
Stormont, D. and G., 2,636.00; Victoria, 1,090.00;
Waterloo, 1,176.00; Welland, 991.00; Wellington, 1,676.00;
Wentworth, 1,308.00; York, 2,520.00; Treas. Twp. Pelee Island, 38.00   56,473 53

Trustees R. C. S. S. Section:—

10 Adjala, 15.00; 4 Admaston, 7.00; 3 Alfred, 15.22;
6 Alfred, 15.22; U. 7 Alfred with 8 Plantagenet S., 7.61;
7 Alfred, 15.22; 8 Alfred, 15.22; 9 Alfred, 15.22;
10 Alfred, 15.22; 11 Alfred, 15.22; 12 Alfred, 15.22;
13 Alfred, 15.21; 14 Alfred, 15.21; 15 Alfred, 15.21;
2-5-8 Anderdon with 6-9 Sandwich W., 5.66; 3-4 Anderdon, 11.30;
11 Anderdon and Malden, 11.67; 3 Arthur, 12.66;
6 Arthur, 12.67; 10 Arthur, 12.67; 2 Ashfield, 25.00;
4 Asphodel, 10.00; 15 Augusta, 6.00; 3 Biddulph, 9.43;
4 Biddulph, 9.43; 6 Biddulph, 9.43;
U. 9 Biddulph with 1 McGillivray, 4.71; U. 2 Brant with 3 Greenock, 3.09;
1 Brighton, 8.00; 4 Bromley, 14.34; 6 Bromley 14.33;
7 Bromley, 14.33; 1 Brougham, 4.00; 2 Burgess N., 7.00;
4 Burgess, 7.00; 6 Burgess, 7.00; 3-4-10 Caledonia 10.67;
10 Caledonia, 10.67; 6 Caledonia with 7 Plantagenet S, 5.33;
12 Caledonia, 10.67; 13 Caledonia, 10.66; 3 Cambridge, 17.50;
4 Cambridge, 17.50; 5 Cambridge, 17.50; 6-7 Cambridge, 17.50;
6 Cambridge, 17.50; 14 P. Cambridge, 17.50; 1 Carrick, 22.60;
2 Carrick, 23.60; U. 1 Carrick with 1 Culross, 11.80;
4 Carrick, 23.60; . U. 2 Carrick with 2 Culross, 11.80;
14 Carrick, 23.60; 15 Charlottenburg, 26.00; 3 Clarence, 17.80;
5 Clarence, 17.08; 6 Clarence, 17.07; 8 Clarence, 17.07;
11 Clarence, 17.07; 12 Clarence, 17.07; 13 Clarence, 17.07;
14 Clarence, 17.07; 16 Clarence, 17.07; 17 Clarence, 17.07; 18 Clarence, 17.07;
19 Clarence, 17.07; 20 Clarence, 17.07; 21 Clarence, 17.07;
1 Cornwall, 17.67; 16 Cornwall, 17.67; 17 Cornwall, 17.66;
U. 1 Culross, with 1 Carrick, 23.39; 2 Culross, with 2 Carrick, 11.61;
10 Cumberland, 9.50; 11 Cumberland, 9.50; 13 Cumberland, 9.50;
14 Cumberland, 9.50; 3 Dover, 21.34; 7 Dover, 21.33; 9 Dover, 21.33;
9 Downie, 19.00; 2 Edwardsburgh, 1.00; 1 Ellice, 11.77;
6 Ellice, 12.34; 7 Ellice, 11.77; 4 Emily, 15.00;
6 Emily, 15.00; 5 Finch, 34.00; 5 Glenelg, 11.00;
7 Glenelg, 11.00; 1 Gloucester with 3 Osgoode, 8.82;
4-5-12 Gloucester, 17.65; 14 Gloucester, 17.65; 15 Gloucester, 17.65;
17 Gloucester, 17.65; 20 Gloucester, 17.65; 22 Gloucester, 17.65;
25 Gloucester, 17.64; 26 Gloucester, 17.64; 3 Greenock, 19.00;
4 Greenock with Brant, 21.91; 3 Griffith, 9.00;
4 Hagarty, 27.33; 12 Hagarty, 27.33; 2 Haldimand, 12.00;
14 Haldimand, 12.00; 9 Harwich, 9.00; 2 Hawkesbury E., 15.00;
4 Hawkesbury, 15.00; 6 Hawkesbury, 15.00; 7 Hawkesbury E., 15.00;
10 Hawkesbury, 15.00; 11 Hawkesbury, 15.00; 12 Hawkesbury E., 15.00;
15 Hawkesbury, 15.00; 16 Hawkesbury, 15.00; 19 Hawkesbury E., 15.00;
1 Hay, 12.00; 19 Hay, 12.00; 1 Hibbert (3), 16.43;
U. 2 Hibbert with McKilIop, 16.19; U. 3 Hibbert with McKillop, 5.97;
3 Holland, 4.00; 1 Howe Island, 6.67; 2 Howe Island, 6.67;

EDUCATION.—*Continued.*

SPECIAL GRANTS.— *Continued.*

3 Howe Island, 6.66 ; 2 Hullett, 9.00 ; 14 Hungerford, 5.00 ; Kenyon, 4.00 ;
Kingtson, 10.00 ;   11 Lochiel, 21.67 ;   12 A. Lochiel, 21.67 ;
12 B. Lochiel, 21.66 ;   2 W. Longueil, 11.67 ;   4 A. Longueil, 11.67 ;
7 Longueil, 11.66 ;   2 Loughboro, 5.50 ;   10 Loughboro, 5.50 ;
1 Maidstone, 16.00 ;   2 Maidstone, 16.00 ;
4 Maidstone with 2 Rochester, 8.00 ; 8 Maidstone with 5 Sandwich. 8.00 ;
3 A. Malden, 13.19 ;   3 B. Malden, 13.18 ;   3 Mara, 26.00 ;
3 March, 22.00 ; 1 Marmora and Lake, 11.00 ; 3 Mattawachan, 9.00 ;
1 McGillivray with 9 Biddulph, 5.00 ;   1 McKillop, 12.84 ;
U. 3 McKillop with 1 Hibbert, 8.16 ;   3-4-5 Moore, 4.00 ;
4 Mornington, 16.00 ;   7 Nepean, 28.50 ;   15 Nepean, 28.50 ;
1 Nichol, 5.00 ;   5 Normanby, 8.50 ;   10 Normanby, 8.50 ;
1 Osgoode, 6.80 ;   2 (15) Osgoode, 6.80 ;
3 Osgoode with Gloucester, 3.40 ;
8 Peel, 7.50 ;   12 Peel, 7.50 ;   5 Percy, 7.33 ;
12 Percy, 3.67 ;   4 Plantagenet N., 14.60 ;   7 Plantagenet N., 14.60 ;
8 Plantagenet, 14.60 ; 9 Plantagenet N., 14.60 ; 12 Plantagenet N., 14.60 ;
4 Plantagenet S.,16.34 ; 7 Plantagenet S.,16.33 ; 8 Plantagenet S.,16.33 ;
U. 7 Plantagenet S. with 6 Caledonia, 8.17 ; 11 Plantagenet S., 16.33 ;
U. 8 Plantagenet S. with 7 Alfred, 8.17 ;   12 Plantagenet S., 16.33 ;
11 Portland, 10.00 ;   6 Proton, 12.00 ;   5 Raleigh, 10.00 ;
6 Raleigh, 10.00 ;   10-17 Richmond, 6.00 ;
2 Rochester with 4 Maidstone, 9.54 ;   3 Rochester, 19.07 ;
6 Rochester, 19.07 ;   7 Rochester, 19.07 ;
8 Rochester with 11 Tilbury W. and 11 Tilbury N., 3.82 ;
9-14 Rochester, 19.07 ;   11 Rochester with 10 Tilbury N., 6.36 ;
12 Roxboro, 23.00 ;   16 Roxboro, 23.00 ;
1 Russell with 12 Winchester, 9.54 ;   4 Russell, 19.08 ;
6 Russell, 19.08 ;   7 Russell, 19.08 ;   8 Russell, 19.08 ;
13 Russell, 19.07 ;   14 Russell, 19.07 ;   1 Sandwich W., 19.20 ;
4 Sandwich W., 19.20 ; U. 6-9 Sandwich W. with 2-5-8 Anderson, 9.60 ;
1 Sandwich E., 30.25 ;   2 Sandwich E., 30.25 ;   3 Sandwich E., 30.25 ;
4 Sandwich E., 30.25 ;   5 Sandwich S. with 8 Maidstone, 8.34 ;
7 Sandwich S., 16.66 ;   12 Seymour with 12 Percy, 6.00 ;
5 Sheffield, 14.00 ;   6 Sherwood, 27.34 ;   5 Sombra, 10.00 ;
2 Stafford, 15.00 ;   1 Stanley. 11.00 ;   6 Stephen. 18.00 ;
7 Sydenham, 5.00 ;   1 Tilbury E., 6.00 ;   3 Tilbury E., 6.00 ;
1 Tilbury N., 19.53 ;   2 Tilbury N., 19.53 ;   6 Tilbury N., 19.53 ;
7 Tilbury N., 19.52 ;   10 Tilbury N. with 11 Rochester, 13.01 ;
11 Tilbury N. with 11 Tilbury W. and 8 Rochester, 4.88 ;
11 Tilbury W. with 11 Tilbury N. and 8 Rochester, 7.00 ;
2 Tiny, 50.00 ;   6 Toronto Gore, 7.00 ;   18 Tyendinaga, 7.40 ;
20 Tyendinaga, 7.40 ;   24 Tyendinaga. 7.40 ;   28 Tyendinaga, 7.40 ;
30 Tyendinaga, 7.40 ;   13 Waterloo, 33.00 ;   1 Wawanosh W. 9.00 ;
5 Wellesley, 17.00 ;   9-10 Wellesley. 17.00 ;   11 Wellesley, 17.00 ;
12 Wellesley, 17.00 ;   10 Williams W., 7.00 ;   15½ Wilmot, 27.00 ;
12 Winchester. 7.00 ;   8 Windham, 28.00 ;   I Wolfe Island, 3.50 ;
2 Wolfe Island. 8.50 ;   4 Wolfe Island, 8.50 ;   7 Wolfe Island, 8.50 ;
Woolwich, 17.00 ; 4 Yonge and Escott rear, 4.00 ; York, 22.00 ....   3,509 19

MILITARY INSTRUCTION.

PUBLIC SCHOOL CADET CORPS ($300.00).

Treasurer Board of Education, Toronto :
    Grant to six Public School Cadet Corps : Parkdale. Givens, Wellesley,
      Dufferin, Jesse Ketchum and Ryerson Schools 300 00

KINDERGARTEN SCHOOLS ($3,463.20).

Treasurer Public School, City of :
    Brantford. 140.14 ; Chatham, 98.67 ; Guelph. 26.46 ....   265 27
    Hamilton. 347.49 ; Kingston, 91.52 ; London, 323.18 ....   762 19
    Ottawa, 348.20 ; Stratford, 90.81 ; Toronto. 1;349.20 ....   1,788 21

EDUCATION.—*Continued.*

KINDERGARTEN SCHOOLS.—*Continued.*

Treasurer Public School, Town of:

Aylmer, 23.60; Berlin, 131.56; Cobourg, 21.45	176 61
Galt, 29.32; Hespeler, 34.32; Ingersoll, 17.87	81 51
Listowel, 21.45; Owen Sound, 65.78; Peterboro, 72.93	160 16
Picton, 22.16; Preston, 27.89; Simcoe, 21.45	71 50
Tilsonburg, 22.16; Toronto Junction, 72.21; Waterloo, 35.75............	130 12
Welland	16 45
Educational Pub. Co., advertising, 1.00; King's Printer, paper, 2.58........	3 58
Queen's Quarterly, advertising, 3.00; *Varsity,* advertising, 1.00	4 00
Warwick Bros. & Rutter, printing	3 60

NIGHT SCHOOLS ($249.35).

Treasurer P. S. Board, City of:

St. Catharines, 5.40; Toronto, 225.45; advertising, *Acta Victorian,* 1.50	232 35
Educational Pub. Co., 2.00; *Queen's Quarterly,* 4.00; University Co., 2.00	8 00
Varsity, 1.00; McMaster, M. H., postage stamps, 8.00	9 00

INSTRUCTION IN AGRICULTURE AND HORTICULTURE IN GROUPED RURAL SCHOOLS ($124.50).

Treas. Co. Lincoln for Clinton, U. S. S. No. 1 with 2 Louth, Grant	100 00
Warwick Bros. & Rutter, printing	24 50

CONTINUATION CLASSES ($31,785.33).

Treasurer, County of:—

	Special grant.	Regular grant.		Special grant.	Regular grant.
Brant..............	95 00	190 00	Bruce............	100 00	200 00
Carleton............	562 50	1,140 00	Dufferin............	20 00	40 00
Elgin......	222 50	445 00	Essex..............	137 50	275 00
Frontenac.........	22 50	45 00	Grey..............	92 50	185 00
Haldimand.........	95 00	190 00	Halton.............	7 50	15 00
Haliburton.........	15 00	30 00	Hastings........	60 00	120 00
Huron......	242 50	500 00	Kent..............	540 00	1,080 00
Lambton............	15 00	45 00	Lanark..........	57 50	115 00
6 Lanark...........	7 50	15 00	Leeds and Grenville	67 50	135 00
Lennox and Adding-					
ton..............	15 00	30 00	Lincoln............	7 50	15 00
Middlesex..........	105 00	210 00	Norfolk............	22 50	45 00
Northumberland and					
Durham........	120 00	240 00	Ontario............	47 50	95 00
Ontario, S..........	15 00	30 00	Oxford............	292 50	585 00
Perth......	85 00	170 00	Peterboro.........	57 50	115 00
Prescott and Russell.	40 00	80 00	Prince Edward.....	52 50	105 00
Renfrew............	72 50	145 00	Simcoe.............	402 50	805 00
Stormont, Dundas					
and Glengarry ..	242 50	485 00	Victoria............	15 00	30 00
Waterloo...........	7 50	15 00	Welland............	62 50	125 00
Wellington.........	100 00	200 00	Wentworth.........	60 00	120 00
York..............	127 50	280 00			13,000 00

Board, Public School Trustees, Town of:—

	Special grant.	Regular grant.		Special grant.	Regular grant.
Alliston....	100 00	200 00	Amherstburg....... ...	100 00	200 00
Blenheim......	100 00	200 00	Blind River.........	15 00	30 00
Bothwell...........	100 00	200 00	Bracebridge........ ...	200 00	400 00
Bruce Mines........	100 00	200 00	Copper Cliff........ ..	15 00	30 00
Dresden............	100 00	200 00	Fort Frances........	100 00	200 00
Gore Bay...........	100 00	500·00	Huntsville..........	100 00	200 00

EDUCATION.—*Continued.*

CONTINUATION CLASSES.—*Continued.*

Board, Public School Trustees, Town of :

	Special grant.	Regular grant.		Special grant.	Regular grant.	
Little Current........	25 00	50 00	Milton..............	100 00	200 00	
Palmerston	100 00	200 00	Parry Sound........	100 00	400 00	
Penetanguishene....	100 00	200 00	Powassan..........	50 00	100 00	
Rainy River........	15 00	30 00	Stayner............	100 00	200 00	
Southampton........	50 00	100 00	Sturgeon Falls......	25 00	50 00	
Sudbury............	100 00	200 00	Thessalon..........	50 00	100 00	
Toronto, North.....	28 75	57 50	Wingham...........	100 00	200 00	
Wallaceburg........	100 00	200 00	Walkerville.........	25 00	50 00	7,096 25

Board, Public School Trustees, Village of :—

	Special grant.	Regular grant.		Special grant.	Regular grant.	
Acton	100 00	200 00	Ailsa Craig.........	7 50	15 00	
Alvinston	100 00	200 00	Arkona............	12 50	25 00	
Ayr.................	25 00	50 00	Bath...............	50 00	100 00	
Bayfield............	12 50	25 00	Beaverton..........	25 00	50 00	
Beeton.............	100 00	200 00	Blyth..............	50 00	100 00	
Bobcaygeon	37 50	75 00	Bolton	50 00	100 00	
Bridgeburg	25 00	50 00	Brussels............	100 00	200 00	
Burk's Falls........	100 00	400 00	Burlington	12 50	25 00	
Cannington	12 50	25 00	Cardinal...........	25 00	50 00	
Chatsworth.........	12 50	25 00	Chesterville........	50 00	100 00	
Clifford	7 50	15 00	Cobden............	7 50	15 00	
Creemore...........	50 00	100 00	Delhi..............	12 50	25 00	
Drayton	100 00	200 00	Dundalk	25 00	50 00	
Durham............	150 00	300 00	Eganville	12 50	25 00	
Embro.............	12 50	25 00	Erin...............	50 00	100 00	
Exeter	150 00	300 00	Fenelon Falls.......	100 00	50 00	
Fort Erie..........	25 00	50 00	Grand Valley.......	50 00	100 00	
Havelock...........	25 00	50 00	Hanover............	50 00	100 00	
Hensall............	12 50	25 00	Hespeler	7 50	15 00	
Hintonburg.........	25 00	50 00	Kingsville..........	25 00	50 00	
Lanark.............	50 00	100 00	Lucknow	25 00	50 00	
Markdale	25 00	50 00	Marmora...........	25 00	50 00	
Maxville	50 00	100 00	Merrickville........	50 00	100 00	
Millbrook..........	50 00	100 00	Milverton	12 50	25 00	
Newboro'..........	7 50	15 00	New Hamburgh	7 50	15 00	
Norwich...........	100 00	200 00	Oil Springs.........	50 00	200 00	
Ottawa, East.......	25 00	50 00	Paisley.............	75 00	200 00	
Port Carling........	15 00	30 00	Port Colborne.......	25 00	50 00	
Port Stanley.......	25 00	50 00	Richmond..........	50 00	100 00	
Shelburne..........	100 00	200 00	Springfield.........	25 00	50 00	
Sundridge..........	15 00	30 00	Thamesville........	50 00	100 00	
Teeswater	50 00	100 00	Tiverton	7 50	15 00	
Thornbury	12 50	25 00	Tottingham........	100 00	200 00	
Tilbury	12 50	25 00	Wellington	25 00	50 00	
Tweed.............	50 00	100 00	Winchester.........	50 00	100 00	
Westport...........	50 00	100 00	Wroxeter..........	12 50	25 00	
Woodbridge	50 00	100 00				9,447 50

Board, Public School Trustees :—

	Special grant.	Regular grant.		Special grant.	Regular grant.	
2 Assiginack.......	50 00	100 00	2 Christie..........	15 00	30 00	
1 Hallam..........	15 00	30 00	6 Himsworth, S. ...	25 00	50 00	
1 Hilton...........	15 00	30 00	1 Keewatin........	100 00	200 00	
2 Machar..........	25 00	50 00	3 Medora..........	15 00	30 00	
6 McKellar........	15 00	30 00	6 Muskoka........	15 00	30 00	
8 Perry	15 00	30 00	1 Schreiber........	25 00	50 00	
2 Stephenson......	25 00	50 00	1 St. Joseph.......	15 00	30 00	1,110 00

Board R. C. S. S. Trustees, Town of :—

	Special grant.	Regular grant.		Special grant.	Regular grant.	
Amherstburg.......	50 00	100 00	Mattawa...........	25 00	50 00	
Sudbury...........	15 00	30 00				270 00

EDUCATION.—*Continued.*

CONTINUATION CLASSES—*Continued.*

Board R. C. S. S. Trustees, Village of :—

	Special grant.	Regular grant.		Special grant.	Regular grant.	
Eganville	50 00	100 00	Chesterville	7 50	15 00	
Westport	50 00	100 00				322 50

Board R. C. S. S. Section :—

	Special grant.	Regular grant.		Special grant.	Regular grant.	
2 Ashfield	25 00	50 00	2 Wolfe Island	7 50	15 00	
9 Biddulph with 3			10 Adjala	7 50	15 00	
McGillivray	7 50	15 00	U 1 Carrick & Culross	12 50	25 00	
15 Gloucester	12 50	25 00	12 Hagarty	7 50	15 00	
9 Harwich	7 50	15 00	Hastings	7 50	15 00	
6 Raleigh	7 50	15 00	1 W. Wawanosh	7 50	15 00	
						330 00

Educational Pub. Co., advertising	4 00
King's Printer, stationery, 10.05 ; paper, 1.37	11 42
McMaster, M., postage stamps, 125.00 ; Riordon Paper Mills, paper 1.70	126 70
Warwick Bros. & Rutter, printing, etc	66 96

COUNTY MODEL SCHOOLS ($10,168.31).

Public School Board Trustees :—

Athens, 150.00 ;	Barrie, 150.00 ;	Beamsville, 150.00 ;
Berlin, 150.00 ;	Bracebridge, 150.00 ;	Bradford, 150.00 ;
Brampton, 150.00 ;	Caledonia, 150.00 ;	Chatham, 150.00 ;
Clinton, 150.00 ;	Cornwall, 150.00 ;	Durham, 150.00 ;
Elora, 150.00 ;	Forest, 150.00 ;	Gananoque, 150.00 ;
Goderich, 150.00 ;	Gore Bay, 300.00 ;	Hamilton, 150.00 ;
Ingersoll, 150.00 ;	Kincardine, 150.00 ;	Kingston, 150.00 ;
Lindsay, 150.00 ;	London, 150.00 ;	Madoc, 150.00 ;
Meaford, 150.00 ;	Milton, 150.00 ;	Minden, 150.00 ;
Morrisburg, 150.00 ;	Mt. Forest, 150.00 ;	Napanee, 150.00 ;
Newmarket, 150.00 ;	Norwood, 150.00 ;	Orangeville, 150.00 ;
Owen Sound, 150.00 ;	Parry Sound, 150.00 ;	Perth, 150.00 ;
Picton, 150.00 ;	Port Arthur, 150.00 ;	Port Hope, 150.00 ;
Port Perry, 150.00 ;	Prescott, 150.00 ;	Renfrew, 150.00 ;
Sarnia, 150.00 ;	Sault Ste. Marie, 150.00 ;	Simcoe, 150.00 ;
Stratford, 150.00 ;	Strathroy, 150.00 ;	St. Thomas, 150.00 ;
Toronto, 150.00 ;	Toronto Junction, 150.00 ;	Vankleek Hill, 150.00 ;
Walkerton, 150.00 ;	Welland, 150.00 ;	Whitby, 150.00 ;
Windsor, 150.00 ;	Woodstock, 150.00	8,550 00

Special Grants :—

Berlin, 150.00 ;	Bracebridge, 150.00 ;	Gore Bay, 300.00 ;
Parry Sound, 150.00 ;		Porth Arthur, 150.00 ;
Sault Ste. Marie, 150.00		1,050 00

Canadian Express Co., charges, .75 ; Educational Pub. Co., advertising, 10.00	10 75
King's Printer, stationery, 7.75 ; paper, 2.21	9 96
McLaughlin, Jno., special services, re Model School term for teachers, Gore Bay	500 00
McMaster, M., postage stamps, 25.00 ; O. A. C. Review, advertising, 2.00	27 00
Queen's Quarterly, advertising	2 00
University Co., advertising in Educational Monthly	3 00
Warwick Bros. & Rutter, printing	15 60

FRENCH-ENGLISH TRAINING SCHOOL ($405.09).

Board of High School Trustees, grant Plantagent bi-lingual school	405 09

EDUCATION.—*Continued.*

TEACHERS' ASSOCIATIONS ($3,068.25).

Treasurer, Teachers' Association:—
Brant, 25.00; Bruce, E., 25.00; Bruce, W., 25.00; Carleton, 25.00; Dufferin, 25.00; Dundas, 25.00; Durham (arrears, 1905), 25.00; Durham, 25.00; Essex, N., 25.00; Essex, S., 25.00; Frontenac, 25.00; Glengarry, 25.00; Grey, E., 25.00; Grey, S., 25.00; Grey, W., 25.00; Haliburton, 25.00; Haldimand, 25.00; Halton, 25.00; Hastings, N., 25.00; Hastings, S., 25.00; Huron, E., 25.00; Huron W., 25.00; Kent, E., 25.00; Kent, W., 25.00; Lambton, E., 25.00; Lambton, W., 25.00; Lanark, 25.00; Leeds, 1, 25.00; Leeds, 3 and Grenville, 25.00; Leeds, 2, 25.00; Lennox and Addington, 25.00; Lincoln, 25.00; Manitoulin, 25.00; Middlesex, E., 25.00; Middlesex, W., 25.00; Muskoka, S. & E. 25.00; Norfolk, 25.00; Northumberland, 25.00; Nipissing, 25.00; Nipissing, N., 25.00; Ontario, N., 25.00; Ontario, S., 25.00; Ontario, E., 25.00; Oxford, 25.00; Parry Sound, W., 25.00; Parry Sound, E., and N. Muskoka, 50.00; Perth, 25.00; Peterboro', 25.00; Prescott and Russell, 25.00; Prince Edward, 25.00; Rainy River District, 25.00; Renfrew, 25.00; Simcoe, N., 25.00; Simcoe E., and Muskoka, W., 25.00; Simcoe, S.W., 25.00; Stormont, 25.00; Thunder Bay District, 25.00; Victoria, E., 25.00; Victoria, W., 25.00; Waterloo, 25.00; Welland, 25.00; Wellington, N., 25.00; Wellington, S., 25.00; Wentworth, 25.00; York, N., 25.00; York, S., 25.00 .... 1,675 00

Treasurer, Teachers' Association, City of:—
Brantford, 25.00; Brockville, 25.00; Guelph, 25.00; Hamilton, 25.00; Kingston, 25.00; London, 25.00; Ottawa, 25.00; Peterboro, 25.00; St. Catharines, 25.00; St. Thomas, 25.00; Stratford, 25.00; Toronto, 25.00; Windsor and Walkerville, 25.00 .... 325 00
Acta Victoriana, advertising 2 00
Educational Pub. Co., advertising, 4.00; King's Printer, paper, .70......... 4 70
R. C. S. S. Board, London, grant in aid of the convention Separate School teachers of the Sisters of Sacred Heart 25 00
McMaster, M., postage stamps, 25.00; O. A. C. Review, advertising, 1.00. 26 00
Ontario Educational Association, grant 1,000 00
Queen's Quarterly, advertising, 4.00; Varsity, advertising, 1.00............. 5 00
Warwick Bros. & Rutter, printing 5 55

INSPECTION OF PUBLIC, SEPARATE AND DISTRICT SCHOOLS ($80,456.28).

J. J. Tilley : Twelve months' salary as Inspector of Model Schools............. 2,000 00
do Travelling expenses.................... 459 80
R. H. Cowley: Four do Inspector Public Schools................ 666 66
do Travelling expenses................. 322 80
J. F. Power: Twelve months' salary as Inspector Separate Schools 1,700 00
do Travelling expenses.................... 472 55
Wm. Prendergast : do Inspector Separate Schools 1,700 00
do Travelling expenses.................... 395 30
Michael O'Brien : do Inspector Separate Schools 1,700 00
do Travelling expenses.................... 513 30
Telesphore Rochon : do Inspector Bi-lingual Schools........... 1,700 00
do Travelling expenses 208 10
Rev. Geo. Grant: do Inspector District Schools 1,500 00
do Travelling expenses.................... 248 46
J. McLaughlin : do Inspector District Schools.............. 1,700 00
do Travelling expenses.................... 175 40
do Services *re* Model School work, Manitoulin, 1905 .... 250 00
L. A. Green: Twelve months' salary as Inspector District Schools 1,700 00
do Travelling expenses.................... 80 20
Jno. Ritchie: do Inspector District Schools 1,700 00
do Travelling expenses.................... 44 00
J. B. McDougall : do Inspector District Schools 1,700 00
do Travelling expenses.................... 93 95

EDUCATION.—*Continued.*

INSPECTION OF PUBLIC, SEPARATE AND DISTRICT SCHOOLS.—*Continued.*

A. H. Leake: Twelve months' salary as Inspector Technical Schools............   1,900 00
do   Travelling expenses...................   725 10

Public School Inspectors:—

Atkin, W., 770.00; Ball, J. H., 758.75; Barnes, C. A., 770 00; Brown, A., 740.75; Brown, J. C., 636.12; Burgess, H. H., 747.50; Burrows, F., 770.00; Campbell, N. W., 770.00; Carlyle, W., 801.25; Chenay, D., 1,083.25; Chislom, W. J., 770.00; Clendenning, W. S., 180.00; Colles, Rev. W. H. G., 701.75; Cowley, R. H., 503.34; Craig, J. J., 692.00; Cook, H. F., 770.00; Craig, T. A., 691.25; Davidson, A. B., 334.75; Day Isaac, 1,564.00; Deacon, J. S., 702.50; Embury, A., 720.50; Fotheringham, D., 770.00; Galbraith, R., 743.75; Gordon, N., 765.50; Huff, S., 664.25; Ireland, W. W., 695.75; Irwin, W., 770.00; Jamieson Thomas, 266.67; Johnston, H. D., 737.00; Johnston, J. J., 738.50; Johnston, Wm., 725.00; Kinney, R. M. D., 704.75; Knight, J. H., 659.75; Lees, R., 636.12; McBrien, J., 689.00; McCool, J., 590.00; McDiarmid, D., 693.50; McKee, Rev. Thos. 768.50; McLaughlin, John, 339.35; McNaughton, A., 728.75; Macintosh, Wm., 770.00; Maxwell, D. A., 758.75; Mitchell, F. L., 811.25; Mills, G. K., 754.25; Moses, C, 727.25; Moshier, D. D., 770.00; Mulloy, G. W., 400.00; Odell, A, 770.00; Park, R., 717.50; Pearce, Thos., 763.25; Phillips, S., 1,608.75; Platt, G. D., 707.00; Robb, D., 770.00; Scott, R. G., 850.62; Sheppard, F., 702.50; Smith, J. H., 737.00; Spankie, Wm., M.D., 789.37; Standing, Thos. W., 680.00; Stevens, W. H., 1,346.75; Summerby, 767.75; Thompson, P. J. 753.50; Tilley, W. E., 770.00; Tom, J. E., 770.00; Waugh, J., 695.75............   47,355 09

Travelling Expenses *re* meeting District Inspectors:—

Day Isaac, 10.60; Stevens W. H., 8.75...   19 35

Treasurer, Board Public School Trustees, City of:—

Belleville, 105.00; Brantford, 250.00; Brockville, 120.00; Chatham, 150.00; Guelph, 172.50; Hamilton, 830.00; Kingston, 260.00; London, 640.00; Niagara Falls, 90.00; Ottawa, 570.00; Peterboro, 190.00; St. Catharines, 125.00; St. Thomas, 205.00; Stratford, 175.00; Windsor, 205.00; Woodstock, 150.00 ....   4,237 50

Treasurer, Board of Education. Toronto .... -   2,940 00

Treasurer, Board of Public School Trustees, Town of:—

North Toronto, 45.00; Prescott, 35.00; St. Mary's, 50.00; Smith's Falls, 95.00; Toronto Junction, 155.00; Trenton, 45.00; Walkerville, 40.00   465 00
Acta Victoriana, advertising, 2.00; Aikens, Thos., services at 12.00 per week, 38.00 ....   40 00
Brandon and Gilbert, cartage, .25; Canadian Express Co., charges, 5.00...   5 25
Clarke, Jno., clerical, services at 8.00 per week, 217.34; Dominion Express Co., charges, 6.36 ....   223 70
Educational Publishing Co., advertising, 44.00; Educational Monthly, advertising, 9.00 ....   53 00
King's Printer, stationery, 381.54; King's Printer, paper, 57.75 ....   439 29
McMaster, M., postage stamps, 305.00; O. A. C. Review, advertising, 12.00   317 00
Phillips, L. M., services as stenographer, at 12.00 per week...............   362 00
Queen's Quarterly, advertising, 17.00; Riordon Paper Mills, paper, 24.75.   41 75
Toronto Railway Co., car tickets, 3.00; Varsity, advertising, 7.50........   10 50
Williams, N. & Co., cartage, .25; Warwick Bros. and Rutter, printing, and binding, 290.98 ....   291 23

EDUCATION.— *Continued.*

DEPARTMENTAL EXAMINATIONS ($35,538.69).

W. W. Jenkins, Twelve Month's Salary as Registrar			2,000 00
F. N. Nudel,	do	Clerk and Secretary Board of Examiners	1,750 00
W. W. Teffers,	do	Clerk of Examinations	1,100 00
R. J. Bryce,	do	Assistant Clerk of Examinations	1,000 00
Bruce Leadbetter,	do	Printer	1,000 00

Services and expenses as examiners:—

	Services.	Expenses.		Services.	Expenses.
Anderson, W. J	98 44	13 00	Anderson, F. C	95 38	7 00
Andras, J. W. G	181 98		Andrews, David	84 00	6 80
Andrews, R. T	97 56		Archer, Mary A	96 69	5 75
Armstrong, F. G	84 00	4 95	Asselstine, R. W	83 13	9 00
Arthur, C. C	89 25	3 95	Auld, Chas	76 13	6 70
Bain, A. R	201 31	12 80	Bale, Geo. S	84 88	9 20
Ballard, W. H	188 50	17 79	Barnes, Chas. S	95 38	
Barron, Robt. A	78 75	7 45	Bell, John J	94 06	8 70
Bellwood, W. A. M		1 00	Bradley, W. M	24 33	
Bennett, A. Maud	76 13	11 65	Brethour, J. H	98 88	4 20
Bigg, E. M	84 00	17 20	Brown, C. L	76 13	4 35
Brunt, R. A	89 25	11 50	Bryan, Hugh W	100 63	12 10
Burnham, A. M	100 19	8 85	Burt, Arthur W	78 75	3 25
Cameron, J. S	77 88	5 85	Cameron, J. H	35 00	
Carscadden, Thos	81 38	3 55	Case, H. J	3 33	
Chenay, D	58 10		Closs, Frank D	84 00	10 70
Coates, Don H	81 38	3 75	Cole, J. M	84 88	5 35
Cohoe, W. P	84 00		Colling, James	81 38	3 45
Conlin, Evelyn E	74 38	5 6	Conn, H	89 25	3 50
Cook, Margaret	100 19	6 9	Coombs, A. E	91 00	2 00
Corkill, E J	84 00	6 7	Cornish, G. A	84 88	3 95
Cornwall, J. L	76 13	5 8	Courtice, S. J	81 38	8 10
Coutts, R. D	99 31	2 20	Cranston, David L	77 88	6 70
Crawford, J. T	81 38	2 00	Crockett, R. W. E	10 00	4 25
Currie, A. M	37 50		Dales, J. N	85 75	9 00
Davidson, S. K	42 00	21 09	Davidson, John H	81 38	9 95
Day, A. E	100 19	6 25	Day, Isaac	16 00	
De Guerre Ambrose	77 00	3 55	De Lury, Ralph E	84 00	
Devan, I. M	25 00	7 59	Dickson, J. E	77 44	4 30
Dickenson, E. W	77 88	10 25	Dickson, J. D	76 56	4 20
Dickinson, J. A	38 15	6 70	Dearnes, J	30 00	8 20
Doidge, T. C	81 38	6 35	Dolan, Geo. R	84 88	4 00
Dolan, John H	78 75	7 40	Dowsley, W. C	78 75	12 80
Dunkley, A. W	78 75	2 00	Dunsmore, T	60 38	6 70
Edgar, P	94 15		Eldon, R. H	38 60	
Ellis, Wm. S	92 31	9 00	Elliott, T. W	84 88	9 00
Elliott, John	76 13	10 80	Emery, J. W	84 88	11 60
Ewing, W. C	89 25	13 80	Fairchild, A. H	84 00	7 30
Ferguson, W. C	84 88	5 70	Findlay, W	81 38	
Findley, W. A	95 38		Fleming, Ethel C	100 19	4 25
Fleming, Ethel M	77 44	8 30	Fleming, R. D	12 00	1 45
Forrest, Wm	87 94	15 45	Faucar, W. K	79 63	7 70
French, F. W	84 88	10	Froats, J	60 38	13 95
Freeman, J. A	78 75	3 20	Galbraith, R	82 25	4 45
Galbraith. W	100 19	2 10	Gavin, F. P	89 25	11 50
Gillespie, J. H	10 33		Girdwood, A. P	77 88	11 45
Girdwood, A. R	18 00		Glossev, David A	81 38	2 50
Gourlay, Richard	84 88		Govenlock, W. M	76 13	5 70
Graham, R. G	84 00	10 95	Grainger, H. A	86 63	8 00
Grant, David M	94 06	8 35	Grant, Christine C	125 69	5 35
Grant, R.W.G	93 80	65	Gray, Robt. A	80 06	
Green, L.A	44 00	73	Guillett, Cephas	87 06	
Gundy, A.P	84 00	4 25	Gundy, H. M	98 44	12 66
Hamilton, Robert S	82 25	3 45	Hannahoe, Miss L.K	16 33	
Hardie, W	86 63	13 10	Hardy, A. E	247 05	
Hayes, C. F		1 75	Hill, Ethelbert L	92 31	2 50

5 P.A

EDUCATION.—*Continued.*

DEPARTMENTAL EXAMINATIONS —*Continued.*

Services and expenses as examiners :—

Name	Services.	Expenses.	Name	Services.	Expenses.
Hill, Minnie........	84 00	9 20	Hoag, J. P.........	78 75	3 75
Hobbs, T	84 00	5 75	Hogarth, E. S......	86 63	2 00
Hogarth, G........	77 88	2 00	Horton, Chas. W....	84 88	
Houston, Jessie.....	100 19	14 10	Houston, J.........	79 63	6 20
Houston, John A....	76 13	11 00	Howard, Ed. S.....	82 69	7 35
Henry, Thos. M.....	84 00	10 00	Jamieson, J. S......	83 13	13 60
Jamieson, Thos.....	84 00	16 70	Jeffries, John......	77 44	3 85
Jennings, E. W.....	77 44	8 85	Jermyn, P. T.......	78 75	6 70
Johnston, G. W.....	267 01		Jones, E	24 33	
Keith, J	81 38	6 20	Kelley, H. H.......	81 38	8 10
Kemp, W	90 13	9 25	Kennedy, L. A.....	83 13	
Kennedy, G. W. E.	84 88	6 50	Kennedy, T.........	76 13	
Kenrick, F. B.......	165 06		Kent, Eleanor......	95 38	6 70
Kerfoot. H. W......	60 38	13 20	Kerr, Chas. S......	96 69	4 35
Keys, S. J..........	39 38	14 10	Longford, T. E.....	84 00	3 75
Lawlor, Gertrude...	79 63		Leake, A. H........	64 00	
Leighton, R. H......	60 38	5 25	Lennox, Thos. H...	79 19	4 70
Lewis, T. N.........	61 25	14 00	Lick, Addie........	81 38	3 85
Little, James G.....	76 13	8 75	Little, Robt. A......	81 38	5 70
Lowe, J. G..	7 00		McCuaig, H. M....	83 13	4 50
McDonald, James...	77 44	15 50	McDougall, J. B....	96 02	35 55
McKay, D. A......	84 00	3 75	McKellar, H. S.....	86 63	6 10
McKinley, J. M.....	116 00	11 45	McKinnon, C.......	76 13	6 20
McLaughlin, Jno....	68 00	5 25	McLay, W. S. W....	284 62	16 50
McLennan, J. C.....	234 36		McManus, Emily ...	84 00	7 10
McRae, Donella.....	83 13	11 05	McQueen, J.........	83 13	3 20
Mabee, Geo. E.....	78 75	12 20	MacDonald, John F.	100 63	12 00
MacMurchy, Norman	79 19	3 45	MacNaughton, J....	75 00	32 40
Macpherson, Fred ..	90 13	2 20	Madill, A. J........	89 25	4 85
Magee, J. A........	57 75	5 85	Malcolm, Geo.......	83 13	4 60
Matheson, J.	200 64	49 00	Maxwell, Jno.......	16 20	
Mayberry, Charles ..	99 31	4 60	Meesmore, J. F.....	99 75	11 40
Might, L...........	84 88	5 25	Milburn, E. F......	77 44	6 25
Mills, G. K.	83 13	4 75	Miller, G. A........	57 75	9 85
Montizambert, J. R.	84 00	13 10	Morgan, Sidney A...	84 00	2 00
Moore, J. R........	89 25		Morrow, J. D.......	98 44	5 20
Mowat, A..........	77 44	12 60	Murray, R. W......	57 75	
Munro, P. F.	96 69	5 90	Moshier, D. D......	25 00	11 05
Nesbit, David A.....	87 06	8 00	Newman, Geo. E...	83 13	5 20
Norris, James......	81 38	6 35	Packham, J. H.....	39 20	14 40
Passmore, Samuel F.	81 38	3 75	Pattee, Ada.........	83 13	5 70
Patterson, Andrew..	78 75	2 00	Patterson, David....	84 88	8 85
Patterson, W. J.....	81 38		Perry, Samuel W...	69 13	7 50
Phillips, Sylvanus...		4 00	Piersol, W. H.......	184 26	
Potter, Chas.	81 38	7 80	Prendergast, W.....	259 52	34 40
Preston, T..........	89 25	10 95	Price, W. H........		5 00
Pugsley, E.	82 25	5 50	Race, M. B........	76 56	24 45
Radcliffe, Stephen J.	74 38	5 70	Redditt, Thos. H...	84 88	4 95
Reed, Geo. H.......	90 13	1 10	Reid, Robert	77 44	8 45
Rennie, W..........	12 00		Richardson, Kate...	77 88	11 60
Robb, D...........	58 00	25 85	Robertson, J C. ...	260 04	29 95
Robertson, Hugh S..	76 13	4 70	Robinson, J B.....	61 25	2 50
Rutherford, W. H...	81 38		Rutherford, W. W..	15 00	12 15
Sait, E. M..........	94 06		Sanders, Charlotte...	89 25	6 00
Saunders, R. W.....	84 00	2 25	Saunders, W. J.....	84 88	13 60
Sealey, Ethel May ..	80 94	7 20	Seaton, E. T........	81 38	3 25
Scott, R. G.	30 00	12 95	Shaw, R............	81 38	70
Shepherd, M. W....	84 88	17 35	Sinclair, S. B.......	20 00	20 30
Smeaton, W........	89 25	13 30	Smith, A. W.	9 00	
Smith, R. Wilson ...	97 56		Smith, Lyman C. ..	81 38	1 95
Smith, T. C.........	84 00	11 30	Somerville, T. C....	84 88	3 10
Squair, J...........	139 68		Stevenson, L.	84 88	1 95
Stevenson, O. J.	98 00	7 10	Stevens, W. H......	44 00	5 90

5a P.A.

EDUCATION.—*Continued.*

DEPARTMENTAL EXAMINATIONS.—*Continued.*

Services and expenses as examiners :

	Services.	Expenses.		Services.	Expenses.
Stevenson, A.	77 44	4 60	Stewart, J. B.	4 33	
Strong, H. I.	45 00	21 75	Story, Selina G.	84 00	6 60
Tamblyn, W. F.	100 19	5 70	Taylor, J. G.	84 00	11 00
Tennant, Isabella	77 44		Teskey, Edith A	99 31	12 00
Tremeer, J.	97 56	1 10	Trenaman, Mabel N.	100 19	17 20
Voaden, J.	89 25	2 40	Walker, D.	25 00	7 95
Watson, A. H.	83 13	7 60	Watterworth, Grace		
Waugh, J.	20 00	3 20	M.	100 19	6 20
White, E. T.	77 88	16 45	Wilkinson, J. H.	10 00	
Woren, J. S.	81 38		Wilson, W. J.	84 00	
Young, Rev. A. J.	10 00	1 80	Wright, W. J.	100 63	2 25
					22,822 79

Clerical assistance :

	Services.	Expenses.		Services.	Expenses.
Adams, W. A.	33 84	4 60	Adamson, J.	33 84	
Aikens, T.	116 00		Ashall, F. M.	120 00	
Buckingham, G. S.	37 88	5 35	Clark, John	16 00	
Coatsworth, E. T.	128 00		Crawford, C. S.	42 42	
Fennell, A. B.	161 25	9 00	Firth, Thomas	67 84	6 30
Fleming, A. G.	212 79		Gilchrist, L.	4 50	
Hamilton, D.	31 65		Hodgson, J. E. J.	65 48	
Hooper, A. G.	101 46	3 85	McDonald, Kate	66 00	7 60
McPherson, Agnes	302 00		Meacham, J.	31 82	1 95
Morgan, E. A.	164 25	9 10	Murton, J. S.	45 96	3 80
Norris, D. A.	32 66	7 20	Park, W.	97 50	3 20
Rankin, M. D.	87 00		Rollings, W.	84 00	
Shaver, G.	127 00		Shaver, G. N.	167 00	
Slaughter, G. W.	33 84	4 60	Stuart, H. J.	60 94	
Thompson, G.	379 00		Thompson, Joseph.	56 00	
Woodhouse, J.	42 93				3,017 40

Educational Council, travelling expenses :—

Knight, A. P., 106.85; Plewes. J. W., 123.95; Wetherell, J. E., 42.10	272 90
Acta Victoriana, advertising, 5.00; Bell, Jno. J., trav. expenses *re* Strathroy investigation, 16.30	21 30
Bell Tel. Co., messages, 5.10; Brandon & Gilbert, cartage, .75	5 85
Briggs, W., Text books, .94; Brock, W. A., lead seals and wire, 10.00	10 94
Cairns, B., stamps and repairs. 12.15; Can. Express Co., charges, 20.09	32 24
Clark, J., services assisting printer, six weeks	42 00
Davis, C., cartage, .25; Doane Bros., cab hire, 2.50	2 75
Dom. Express Co.. charges, 13.10; Dunkley A. H., trav. expenses, 1.50	14 60
Educational Pub Co., advertising, 20.00; Farmer Bros. photos, 15.00	35 00
Fuller, F. W., messenger service, .10; Graham, Thomas, cartage, 25.50	25 60
Grand & Toy, shelf boxes, etc., 250.40; G. T. Railway Co., freight charges, .60	251 00
Harris, E., Co., modelling clay, 2.00 : Hale, E. B., cartage, .25	2 25
Henry, W.. cartage, .25; Hogarth, Thos., cartage, 1.00	1 25
Jenkins, W. H., trav. expenses, 4.60; Johnson, W. D., trav. expenses *re* Strathroy investigation, 10.05	14 65
King's Printer, stationery, 976.63; paper. 121.11	1,097 74
Knickerbocker Ice Co., ice, 8.20; Leake. J. H., models for exams. 1.85	10 05
McMaster. M., postage stamps, 295.00; Methodist Book Room, books, 1.43	296 43
Manitoulin *Guide*, advertising Model School notice	1 00
Newell, R., cab hire, 8.00; Nudel, F. N., trav. expenses, 32.90	40 90
O. A. C. *Review*. advertising	4 00
Piersol, W. H., services collecting science material	45 25
Pride, A., services collecting science material, 56.00; expenses, 6.80	62 80
Pritchard, F., cartage, .15 : Queen City Oil Co., printers' supplies, 1.53	1 68
Queen's Quarterly, advertising, 12.00; Remington Typewriter Co., rep. machine, .50	12 50
Rawlinson, M., cartage, .25; Richardson, S., cartage, .50	75
Rickaby & Son, advertising Model School notice	1 00
Riordon Paper Mills, paper, 15.27; Skeen, F., cartage, .20	15 47

EDUCATION.—*Continued.*

DEPARTMENTAL EXAMINATIONS.—*Continued.*

Steen, Wm., services as pressman at 10.00 per week	40 00
Steinberger, Hendry Co., crayons, etc., 3.25; Sutherland, W., books, 1.80...	5 05
Thomas Co., stationery Muskoka School Exams...................................	6 00
Toronto Electric Light Co., power for press, 17.85; Toronto Railway Co., car tickets, 22.00	39 85
Toronto Type Foundry, printers' supplies, 2.10; Townson, H., grinding scissors, .15	2 25
University, advertising, 7.00; Warwick Bros. & Rutter, printing and binding, 407.20	414 20
Williamson, G., drawing model, 1.00; Williamson, T., services as janitor, 18.00	19 00
Yates, G. W., cartage	25

NORMAL AND MODEL SCHOOLS, TORONTO.

SALARIES ($29,350.00).

Wm. Scott:	Twelve months' salary as	Principal		2,600 00
W. H. Elliott:		do	Vice-Principal	2,100 00
A. C. Casselman:		do	Drawing Master	1,200 00
Guy de Lestard:		do	French Master....:............	300 00
A. T. Cringan:		do	Music Master	1,050 00
James H. Wilkinson:		do	Instructor Manual Training...,...	1,200 00
David Borland:		do	Drill Master	250 00
Grace C. Leroy:		do	Clerk and Stenographer........	500 00
Emma Macbeth:		do	Instructor in Sewing............	550 00
Meta Macbeth:		do	Pianist.........................	150 00
Anna A. Ewing:		do	Instructor of Household Science..	750 00
M. W. Brown:		do	Instructor in Reading...........	500 00
Angus McIntosh:		do	Head Master Model School	1,800 00
R. W. Murray:		do	Assistant Boys' Model School....	1,300 00
T. M. Porter		do	do	1,300 00
M. A. Sorsoliel:		do	do	1,125 00
F. M. Taylor:		do	do	950 00
M. Meehan:		do	Head Mistress Girls' Model School	1,100 00
M. K. Caulfield:		do	Assistant do	950 00
A. E. G. Wilson:		do	do do	900 00
Mary H. Merritt:		do	do do	800 00
A. F. Laven:		do	do do	850 00
Jean Somers:		do	Instructor in Calisthenics for Girls' Model School	550 00
Mary Macintyre:		do	Director of Kindergarten........	1,100 00
Ellen Cody:		do	Assistant Director do	650 00
George Vair:		do	Head Gardener	650 00
J. Boasi:		do	Assistant do	500 00
Patrick Gafney:	Four	do	Engineer	250 00
Thomas Mannell:	Twelve	do	do	550 00
John Moore:		do	Laborer on Grounds............	500 00
H. Blunt:		do	do	500 00
R. Gilpin:		do	Janitor Normal School	550 00
E. Knox:		do	Janitress do	400 00
Thos. Williamson:		do	Janitor Boys' Model School......	525 00
Bella Simpson:		do	Janitress Girls' Model School....	400 00

EXPENSES ($3,055.43.

Art Metropole, blotting paper	35
Bell Telephone Co., messages, 3.25; rent of instruments, 87.93..............	91 18
Briggs, W., to reference books, 9.50; Brown Bros., record books, etc., 9.75	19 25
Brandon & Gilbert, cartage, 4.00; City Dairy Co., milk *re* Domestic Science, 6.00	10 00
Cody, Ellen, decorating and sundries for Xmas Kindergarten..................	5 00
Consolidated Electric Co.. Ltd., repairing rheostat, 1.20; Copp, Clark Co.. stationery, 215.94	217 14
Dean, Jos., Bird seed and food, .70; Defender Photo Supply Co., photo paper, 3.42	4 12

EDUCATION.—*Continued.*

NORMAL AND MODEL SCHOOLS, TORONTO.—*Continued.*

EXPENSES.—*Continued.*

Duggan, J., supplies, 1.22; Dominion School Supply Co., chemicals, etc., 35.71	36 93
Eaton, T., Co., cotton and cord, .35; Elliott, W. H., travelling expenses. 28.10	28 45
Ellis, P. W. & Co., supplies, etc., 1.20; Farmer Bros., photos, 95.00	96 20
Flint, B., services as substitute teacher, 8.00; Galbraith Photo Co., photo supplies, 12.20	20 20
Gafney, P., salary as engineer, 93.75; Gage, W. J. & Co., text and blank books, etc., 383.86	477 61
Godden, C. P., hardware, 2.75; Graham, C. W., blackboard drawings, 1.10	3 85
Harris, E., Co., modelling clay, 15.00; Harcourt, E. H., Co., paper labels, etc., 35.10	50 10
Holman, J. W., supplies, 18.29 Jarvis, A. H., supplies, 6.20	24 49
King's Printer, paper, 36.47; stationery, 450.97; Keystone View Co., stereographs, etc., 125.00	612 44
McCarthy, M., services as pianist, 5.00; McIntyre, M.E., kindergarten supplies, 15.28	20 28
McIntosh, A., grant in aid of Model School games, 45.00; McMaster, M., postage stamps, 40.00	85 00
Manton, T., Xmas tree, 5.00; Marshall, Geo., chemicals, .57	5 57
Might Directories, directory, 6.00; Mills, Mrs. M. B., services as copyist, 15.00	21 00
Millar & Richard, card cutter, 54.51; Meredith, Thos. & Co., hardware. etc., 32.64	87 15
Methodist Book Room, books, 25.29; Murray, W. A. & Co., flannel, linen, etc., 62.70	87 99
Newell, R., cab hire, 9.00; National Oil Co., linseed oil, .85	9 85
Newspapers and periodicals, advertising, 46.74; Noble, Jas., insect cases, etc., 8.25	54 99
Nordheimer Piano Co., rent of organs, 18.00; Oldright, Dr. Wm., lecturing on hygiene, 200.00	218 00
Painter, A. J., collection of seeds, .35; Poole Publishing Co., reference books, 28.99	29 34
Potter, C., lantern slides, 20.45; Reid & Co., lumber 164.16; Riordon Paper Mills, paper, 18.55	203 16
Scott, J. L., unpaid postage, .69; Simpson, R. Co., chemicals, etc., 84.10; frames, 12.00	96 79
Simmers, J. A., holly and evergreen, 2.50; Stewart, R. H., supplies, 39.86	42 36
Stated Relief Map Co., maps, 10.00; Standard Paste Co., paste, .35	10 35
Steinberger, Hendry Co., raffia, reeds, needles, etc., 154.49; University of Toronto, Student's Book Dept., books, 3.75	158 24
Toronto Railway Co., car tickets, 27.00; United Typewriter Co., supplies, 20.00	47 00
Warwick Bros. & Rutter, printing & binding, 142.54; Williams, R. S. and Sons Co., rent of piano, 3.00	145 54
Wilkinson, J. H., supplies, 3.29; Yorkville Laundry Co., laundrying, 32.22	35 51

NORMAL AND MODEL SCHOOLS, OTTAWA.

SALARIES ($23,552.33).

J. F. White :	Twelve months' salary as Principal				2,500 00
S. B. Sinclair :	do	Vice-Principal			2,100 00
J. A. Dobbie :	do	Drawing Master			1,100 00
J. Fleury :	do	French Master			650 00
T. A. Brown :	do	Music Master			1,050 00
J. H. Putman :	do	Head Master Boys' Model School			1,700 00
J. F. Sullivan :	do	Assistant	do		1,250 00
F. A. Jones :	do	do	do		1,200 00
F. A. Jones :	do	Drill Instructor	do		200 00
M. E. Butterworth :	do	Head Mistress Girls'	do		1,100 00
E. H. Weir :	do	Assistant	do	do	700 00
A. G. Hanahoe :	do	do	do	do	800 00
Jennie Foster :	do	do	do	do	750 00

EDUCATION.—*Continued.*

NORMAL AND MODEL SCHOOLS, OTTAWA.—*Continued.*

SALARIES.—*Continued.*

E. H. Keyes: Twelve months' salary as Instructor in Calisthenics	800 00
A. E. Robertson : Eleven do do Household Science	733 33
L. Cumming : One do do Sewing	43 00
Eliza Bolton : Twelve do Director of Kindergarten	1,100 00
A. H. Baker : do Assistant do	550 00
Arthur Heeney : do First Engineer and Gardener	700 00
James Mooney : do Second do	550 00
Oliver Macdonald : do Janitor and Caretaker Normal School	1,260 00
E. Murphy : do Night Watchman and Fireman	500 00
J. S. Harterre : do Instructor of Manual Training	1,100 00
A. M. Delaney : do Secretary and Librarian	450 00
Jennie Hilliard : Ten and one-half do Assistant Boys' Model School	590 00
M. R. Elliott : One do do do do	76 00

EXPENSES ($1,457.10).

American Express Co., charges	1 18
American Entomological Co., pins, .53; Arcade, The, canvass, etc., 3.56	4 09
Bell Telephone Co., rent of instruments, 45.00; Birks, Henry & Sons, spoons, 2.50	47 50
Bishop, A. F. & Co., cups, etc., 2.10; Black, C. A., ink, 3.00	5 10
Brown, L. A., trav. expenses	15 10
Bryson, Graham & Co., tape, damask, etc., 19.55; Kindergarten supplies, 10.03	29 58
Bysche, Herbert & Co., tools, 2.00; Can. Express Co., charges, 3.19	5 19
C. P. Railway Co., freight charges, 4.93; Copp, Clark Co., text books, 6.21	11 14
De Wolfe & Fiske Co., books, 2.57;; Dom. Express Co., charges, 3.95	6 52
Edwards, W. C. & Co., lumber, 1.97; Esmondes, J. P. & F. W., pans, dishes, etc., 10.41	12 38
Foster, R., Xmas tree	4 00
G.N.W. Telegraph Co., telegram, .27; Govt. Postoffice, bulletins, 1.38	1 65
G. T. Railway Co., freight charges, 16.33; Graham Bros., kindergarten supplies, .95	17 28
Hind & Co., meat, Domestic Science, .10; Hope, Jas. & Sons, books, etc., 231.04	231 14
Imperial Foundry Co., castings	65
Irwin, Gladys H., copy "The Empire and the Century"	2 00
Jarman, Frank, engraving, etc., 5.43; Jarvis, A. H., kindergarten supplies, .25	5 68
Jones, H. L., repairing brackets, .40; Kavanagh Bros., supplies, 68.45	68 85
Ketchum & Co., foot-balls, etc.	7 35
King's Printer, stationery, 176.69; paper, 5.14	181 83
Lavis, J. R., polish, 1.00; Lee, S. W., supplies, 8.02	9 02
Library Bureau of Canada, lumber, 78.77; McGee Bros., meat Domestic Science, .30	79 07
McKinley & Northwood, lantern globe, .10; McMaster, M., postage stamps, 40.00	40 10
MacMillan & Co., books	3 26
Methodist Book Room, books, 31.13; Might Directories, directory, 4.00	35 13
Miller, H. H., collection of weeds, 3.50; Morang Educational Co., text books, 30.00	33 50
Mortimer, Co., 1,000 "Certificates of honor" cards	18 50
Newspapers and Periodicals, advertising. 21.00; subscriptions, 55.30	76 30
Ogilvie, Jas., stationery, music readers, etc., 50.16; postage stamps, 29.00	79 16
Ottawa Drug Co., chemicals, 7.63; Perkins. R. M., kindergarten supplies, .20	7 83
Pewry Picture Co., colored pictures, 1.78; Pittway, A. G., photos, 4.00	5 78
Poole Pub. Co., books, 149.72; Poulin, L. N., kindergarten supplies, 5.17	154 89
Pulsometer Engineering Co., vacuum pump. plate. etc.	44 69
Putman, J. H., repairing foot-ball, .10; Ross, C., Co., prints needles, etc., 4.10	4 20
Sisters of Our Lady of Charity, washing towels	21 72
Scrim, Chas., flowers, 1.15; Slattery. B., supplies, 11.00	12 15
Steinberger, Hendry, Co., slated cloth, 53.03; Storey, D., lumber, 2.71	55 74

EDUCATION.—*Continued.*

NORMAL AND MODEL SCHOOLS, OTTAWA.—*Continued.*

EXPENSES.—*Continued.*

Steiger, E. & Co., supplies	1	14
Students' Book Dept., University of Toronto, book	1	88
Superintendent of Documents, Washington, bulletins	1	35
Thorburn, C. H., books, 5.38; Tobin Tent and Awning Co., canvas cover, 1.85	7	23
Topley Studio, lantern slides, etc., 5.00; Troy, J. P., lantern slides, 11.00	16	00
Warwick Bros. & Rutter, printing	27	30
White, J. F., trav. expenses, 26.85; grant in aid Model School games, 35.00	61	85
Wright, R. H., flowers	1	10

MAINTENANCE.

Expenses of grounds ($88.20).

Graham Bros., seeds, bulbs, etc., 20.05; Kileen, G. F., cartage earth, 3.75	23	80
McConnell, R., mowing school field, 8.00; McKinley & Northwood, axe and handle, 1.25	9	25
Mahon, Geo., manure, 1.00; Murray, Levi, cutting down and removing tree, 1.80	2	80
Scrim, C., plants, 50.85; Simmers, J. A., plants, 1.50	52	35

Fuel, light, water, etc. ($2,386.74).

Butterworth, J. J. & Co., 15 cords, hard wood at 5.59 per cord, 83.85; 10 cords slabs at 2.10 per cord, 21.00	104	85
Charlebois, J. O., ice, 2.50; Corporation City of Ottawa, water, 352.50...	355	00
McKinley & Northwood, coal oil, 1.25; Ottawa Electric Co., light, 23.07	24	32
Ottawa Gas Co., gas, 143.67; lamp, .75	144	42
Ray, C. C. Co., 300 tons egg coal at 5.83 per ton, 1,749.00; sundry newspapers, advertising *re* fuel, 9.15	1,758	15

Furniture, incidentals, etc. ($735.14).

Blais, A., tinting and repairing, 7.75; Blais, Mrs., hemming towels, 1.00...	8	75
Bryson, Graham & Co., burlap, candles, soda, etc., 19.36; Butterworth & Co., hardware, etc., 38.43	57	79
Bsyche, Herbert & Co., keys, .15; Currier, L. W. & Co., school desks and table, 29.75	29	90
Davies, S. J., carpentering, etc., 30.80; Edwards, W. C. & Co., lumber, etc., 15.13	45	93
Gillis. B., clearing snow from walks, 10.08; G. T. Railway Co., freight charges, 2.68	12	76
Howe, Wm., floor oil, etc., 5.48; Library Bureau of Canada, cleaning and repairing school desks, 12.35	17	83
Lindsay, T., oilcloth	3	50
McKinley & Northwood, plumbing, locks, etc., 96.02; clearing snow from roofs, 112.40	208	42
McDonald, O. K., care of clocks, 60.00; Medcalf, D. M., trav. expenses, 36.35	96	35
Mason & Risch Piano Co., repairing piano, 55.00; Mitchell, A., repairing wall, 5.00	60	00
Mooney. Jas., carting ashes, 42.50; Mooney, T., clearing snow from walks, 1.62	44	12
Moore. Wm., racks for rubbers, etc., 37.10; Office Specialty Mfg. Co., library cabinet, 29.20	66	30
Ottawa Electric Co., repairing fuse, .25; Ottawa Fireproof Supply Co., asbestos cement, 2.00	2	25
Ottawa Gas Co.. lamp. 10.00; Orme, J. L. & Son, tuning pianos, 10.00...	20	00
Perry, J., sod. 3.00; Poulin, L. N., toilet set and jug, 2.30	5	30
Queen City Oil Co., supplies, 2.25; Ross. C. & Co., towels, etc., 19.07	21	32
Shore, T. A., rubber racks, etc., 15.50; Stacy, Harry, painting rubber racks, 9.00	24	50
Stewart, P., re-glazing, paint, etc., 9.51; Storey, D., lumber, .61	10	12

EDUCATION.—*Continued.*

NORMAL SCHOOL, LONDON.

SALARIES ($9,156.00).

F. W. Merchant :	Twelve months' salary as	Principal	2,600 00
John Dearness :	do	Vice-Principal	2,100 00
S. K. Davidson :	do	Drawing and Writing Master	275 00
F. L. Evans :	do	Music Master	275 00
Geo. McLaren : Eight	do	Drill, Gymnastics and Calisthenics	117 00
Albert Slatter : One	do	do do ...	14 00
Jean Laidlaw : Twelve	do	Kindergarten Teacher	125 00
Nellie Heffernan :	do	Stenographer and Clerk	500 00
Andrew Templeton :	do	Engineer	650 00
Wm. Casey :	do	Gardener	550 00
Ada Butchart :	do	Instructor Household Science	400 00
Sugden Pickles :	do	Instructor Manual Training	1,100 00
W. C. Robertson :	do	Caretaker	450 00

EXPENSES ($2,688.71).

Back, J. H. & Co., photo supplies, 20.05; Bell Telephone Co., rent of instruments, 104.15	124 20
Brock, W. A., electric supplies, .25; Bausch & Lomb, optical apparatus, 30.77	31 02
Board of Education, annual grant providing Public School for practical teaching to students	1,500 00
Boyd, H. J., set of sad irons, etc., 4.20; Campbell, T., lecture on sanitary science, 100.00	104 20
City Sash & Door Co., lumber, 125.08; Carson, D. H., lecture on life saving, 15.00	140 08
Can. Express Co., charges, 7.73; Can. Chemical Mfg. Co., chemicals, 1.65	9 33
Can. Furniture Mfg. Co., rattan, 5.56; Central Electric & School Supply Co., thermometer, 2.50	8 06
Coo, Wm. C., stencil paper, etc., 15.75; Carrie, W. L., Stationery Co., books, etc., 59.32	75 07
Chapman, Chas. & Co., stationery, 19.50; Dom. Express Co., charges, 2.41...	21 91
Emmerson, N. W., chemicals, 3.15; Electrical Construction Co., wire, tape, etc., 2.29	5 44
Janes, T. H., supplies	56 69
Kingsmill, T. F., napkins, 6.07; London Street Ry. Co., car tickets, 5.00	11 07
London Brass Works Co., castings, 2.97; London Printing & Litho. Co., stationery, etc., 38.01	40 98
London Electric Co., power and current, 80.00; McLean, G., tools, screws, etc., 87.44	167 44
McKenzie, D. & Co., shafting, cases, etc., 20.20; McMaster, M., postage stamps, 60.00	80 20
Merchant, F. W., travelling expenses, 10.20; Mills, Jno., stationery, 18.28	28 48
Meek & Vining, chemicals, etc., 10.40; Methodist Book Room, books, 30.93	41 33
Newspapers, subscriptions, 127.75; Nix, E. S., cartage, .50	128 25
King's Printer, stationery, .90; Potter, C., gas and tanks, 14.17	15 07
Readhead, R. H., clay, 2.00; Scott, P. S., cartage, 5.00; Scott, E. W. & Son, centre for lathe, 8.50	15 50
Steinberger, Hendry Co., reeds, raffia, etc., 33.35; Treblecock, H., supplies, .96	34 31
University of Toronto, book, 1.87; United Typewriter Co., supplies, 9.25...	11 12
Westman, A., hardware, etc., 15.13; Weldon, W. & Co., binding, 3.20	18 33
Warwick Bros. & Rutter, printing, .30; Wright, Wm., express charges, .30	60
Westland, M., nature study appliances, 2.75; Young, R. J. & Co., supplies, 17.23	19 98

MAINTENANCE.

Fuel, light and water ($1,361.04).

Chantler Bros., 162.580 tons egg coal at 6.75 per ton	1,095 46
City Gas Co., gas, 22.64; London Electric Co., light current, 89.68	112 32
Mann, Jno. & Son, 4 cords of slabs at 4.00 per cord	16 00
National Oil Co., coal oil, 1.75; newspapers, advertising *re* fuel, 9.15	10 90
Water Commissioners, water	126 36

EDUCATION.—*Continued.*

NORMAL SCHOOL, LONDON.—*Continued.*

Furniture, incidentals, etc., ($89.32).

Aikenhead Hardware Co., hardware, etc., 2.25; Abram, R. S., taking down storm windows, 31.50	33	75
Colerick, H. & Co., painting, glazing, etc., 24.75; Johnston, Alex., repairing boiler, 1.50	26	25
London Brass Co., repairs, .52; McLean, G., sash cord, 1.20	1	72
Skelly, Wm. S., plumbing, 25.16; Stenberger, Hendry Co., liquoid staining, 2.44	27	60

Grounds, trees, etc. ($285.73).

Brock, W. A., repairing lawn mower, 2.80; Canada Floral Co., planting beds, 150.00	152	80
Dunn, Jas., repairing tools, 2.25; Dunn, Chas., manure, 1.50	3	75
Gladwell, W., cartage, 1.00; Johnson, E. G., work on grounds, 31.50	32	50
McLean, G., manure fork, 1.00; Morgan, A. J., bulbs, 27.93	28	93
Maddeford, W., repairing mower, .25; Reidy, Jno., cutting lawn, 67.50	67	75

Scrubbing, cleaning, cartage, etc. ($521.69).

Adams, Edw. & Co., soap, etc., 12.05; Berry, W. J. T., washing windows, 64.12; cartage, 4.50	80	67
McGee, Mrs. B., cleaning 20.00, washing towels 1.64; Macfee, Mrs. R., washing and cleaning, 80.25	101	89
Perry, Norris, cartage, 18.00; Perry, Mrs. R., cleaning, etc., 307.19	325	19
Pope, Mrs., cleaning storm windows. 5.94; World's Only Dustless Brush Co., brushes, 8.00	13	94

HIGH SCHOOLS AND COLLEGIATE INSTITUTES ($120.954.18).

J. E. Hodgson : Eight and one-half months' salary as Inspector	2,011	00
do Travelling expenses	258	25
do do (balance 1905)	2	60
J. E. Wetherell : Three and one half months' salary as Inspector	803	00
do Travelling expenses	242	85
H. B. Spotton : Three and one-half months' salary as Inspector	803	00
do Travelling expenses	216	90
John Seath : Five months' salary as Inspector	1,156	86
do Traveling expenses	130	75

Treasurer, Board High Schools and Collegiate Institutes:

Alexandria. 652.37 ;	Almonte. 734.32 ;	Arnprior, 627.54 ;
Arthur, 631.84 ;	Athens. 744.12 ;	Aurora, 605.71 ;
Aylmer, 879.93 ;	Barrie, 1,131.56 ;	Beamsville, 482.66 ;
Belleville, 841.25 ;	Berlin. 1,290.76 ;	Bowmanville, 841.65 ;
Bradford, 611.87 ;	Brampton, 871.67 ;	Brantford, 1.271.48 ;
Brighton, 476.31 ;	Brockville, 1.232.34 ;	Caledonia, 599.59 ;
Campbellford. 716.28 ;	Carleton Place. 723.43 ;	Cayuga, 589.13 ;
Chatham, 1,222.06 ;	Chesley. 535.25 ;	Clinton, 920 40 ;
Cobourg. 1.100.81 ;	Colborne. 495.69 ;	Collingwood, 935.62 ;
Cornwall. 922.66 ;	Deseronto. 669.32 ;	Dundas, 657.67 ;
Dunnville. 703.21 ;	Dutton. 653.09 ;	East Toronto, 535.68 ;
Elora, 549.88 ;	Essex. 698.45 ;	Fergus, 612.19 ;
Forest, 627.33 ;	Fort William, 585.59 ;	Galt, 1.193 42 ;
Gananoque. 811.09 ;	Georgetown, 701.83 ;	Glencoe. 625.21 ;
Goderich. 1.116.08 ;	Gravenhurst. 498.19 ;	Grimsby. 476 17 ;
Guelph. 1,322 84 ;	Hagersville. 618 57 ;	Hamilton. 1.457.73 ;
Harriston, 639.22 ;	Hawkesbury. 572.84 ;	Ingersoll, 1.162.48 ;
Iroquois, 774.50 ;	Kemptville. 736.66 ;	Kincardine, 789.17 ;
Kenora ; 622.45 ;	Kingston. 1,274.47 ;	Leamington, 705.67 ;

EDUCATION.—*Continued.*

HIGH SCHOOLS AND COLLEGIATE INSTITUTES.—*Continued.*

Lindsay, 1,282.37; Listowel, 689.54; London, 1,448.52; Lucan, 664.13; Madoc, 604.30; Markham, 741.45; Meaford, 869.78; Midland, 569.63; Mitchell, 624.31; Morrisburg, 1,032.03; Mt. Forest,, 722.81; .Napanee, 1,091.84; Newburgh, 584.87; Newcastle, 485.39; Newmarket, 718.69; Niagara, 443.57; Niagara Falls, 1,207.88; Niagara Falls South, 501.51; North Bay, 644.59; Norwood, 602.84; Oakville, 655.26; Omemee, 428.19; Orangeville, 841.25; Orillia, 1,192.83; Oshawa, 830.53; Ottawa, 1,298.45; Owen Sound, 1,239.14; Paris, 718.11; Parkhill, 698.73; Pembroke, 749.47; Perth, 961.56; . Peterboro, 1,248.00; Petrolea, 797.30; Picton, 867.13; Plantagenet, 394.91; Port Arthur, 681.61; Port Dover, 467.48; Port Elgin, 567.70; Port Hope, 920.57; Port Perry, 696.35; Port Rowan, 427.99; Prescott, 644.77; Renfrew, 983.85; Richmond Hill, 563.44; Ridgetown, 951.85; Rockland, 381.68; Sault Ste. Marie, 610.67; Sarnia, 1,300.58; Seaforth, 978.24; Simcoe, 819.77; . Smithville, 457.92; Smith's Falls, 744.01; Stirling, 540.06; Stratford, 1,231.57; Strathroy, 929.49; Streetsville, 473.22; St. Catharines, 1,243.27; St. Mary's, 907.47; St. Thomas, 1,277.28; Sydenham, 614.40; Toronto (Harbord), 1,379.93; Toronto (Jamieson Ave.), 1,330.80; Toronto (Jarvis St.), 1,328.54; Toronto Junction, 1,245.71; Thorold, 515.91: Tillsonburg, 626.75; Trenton, 731.85; Uxbridge, 654.79; VanKleek Hill, 995.22; Vienna, 447.73; Walkerton, 786.04; Wardsville, 437.77; Waterdown, 504.07; Waterford, 638.49; Watford, 674.17; Welland, 637.65; Weston, 614.51; Whitby, 830.23; Wiarton, 630.49; Williamstown, 674.24; Windsor, 1,350.49; Woodstock, 1,158.17...... 111,349 00

Special Grants, Treasurer High School Board:
Fort William. 585.59: Gravenhurst, 498.19; Kenora, 622.45;
North Bay, 644.59: Port Arthur, 681.61; Sault Ste. Marie, 610.67... 3,643 10
Acta Victoriana, advertising, 2.00; Brandon & Gilbert, cartage, .25......... 2 25
Educational Pub. Co., advertising 17 00
King's Printer, stationery, 125.61: paper, 7.88 .... 133 49
McMaster, M., postage stamps, 115.00: O. A. C. Review, advertising, 8.00 123 00
Queen's Quarterly, advertising, 5.00: University Co., advertising. 4.00...... 9 00
Varsity, advertising, 2.00; Warwick Bros. & Rutter, printing and binding,
50.13 .... 52 13

ᴎ MILITARY INSTRUCTION.

HIGH SCHOOL CADET CORPS ($1,600.00).

Treasurer, High School Board and Collegiate Institutes:
.Arthur. 50.00: Barrie. 50.00; Brantford, 50.00; Brockville. 50.00; Cobourg. 50.00; Collingwood, 50.00; Galt, 50.00; Guelph, 50.00; Hamilton, 100.00; Ingersoll, 50.00; London, 50.00; Lindsay, 50.00; Morrisburg. 50.00; Mount Forest. 50.00; Napanee. 50.00; Norwood, 50.00: Ottawa. 50.00: Owen Sound, 50.00; Peterborough. 50.00; Port Perry. 50.00; Ridgetown, 50.00; Sarnia, 50.00; Seaforth, 50.00; St. Thomas, 50.00; Strathroy. 50.00; Toronto (Harbord St.), 50.00; Toronto (Jamieson Ave.). 50.00: Toronto (Jarvis St.). 50.00; Uxbridge, 50.00: Vankleek Hill. 50.00; Woodstock, 50.00......... 1,600 00

SUB-TARGETS FOR CADET CORPS ($12,500.00).

Sub-target Gun Co., 50 sub-target gun machines 12,500 00

EDUCATION.—*Continued.*

ONTARIO NORMAL COLLEGE.

SALARIES ($6,450.00).

J. A. McLellan :	Twelve months' salary as		Principal	3,000 00
R. A. Thompson :	do		Vice-Principal	500 00
do	Six	do	Acting Principal (1905)	500 00
do	do	do	do (1906)	500 00
Wm. Bailey :	Twelve	do	Instructor, Manual Training	1,100 00
M. C. McPherson :		do	do Household Science	400 00
E. M. McPherson :		do	Clerk	450 00

EXPENSES ($8,282.49).

Aitchison, D., basswood, etc., 21.10; Abbott, A. H., services as lecturer, 375.00; travelling expenses, 68.25	464 35
Bell Telephone Co., rent of instrument, 12.50; Can. Exp. Co., charges, .30	12 80
Can. Westinghouse Co., time of engineer *re* motor	7 00
Cunningham, A. M., seeds, plants, etc., 2.25; Cloke & Sons, stationery, etc., 66.35	68 60
Crawford, J. T., special services lecturing, 121.67; Corson, G. H., lecture on "Life-saving," 10.00	131 67
Dom. Exp. Co., charges, .25; Electric Supply Co., wiring for arc light, etc., 10.30	10 55
Fidelity Trustee & Receivers Co., one set of natural history	12 00
Gill, J., special services lecturing, 121.66; Hamilton Cataract Power, Light & Traction Co., power, 51.60	173 26
Hamilton Gas Light Co., gas for cooking, domestic sc., 25.40; Hogarth, E. S., special services lecturing, 121.67	147 07
Johnson, G. J., special services lecturing	121 66
Junor, R., glassware, 2.30; King's Printer, paper, 1.40, stationery, 1.35....	5 05
Logan, W. M., special services lecturing, 121.67; McCabe, Dr., lecture on sanitary science, 100.00	221 67
McPherson, F. F., services as lecturer, etc., 221.67; McMaster, M., postage stamps, 40.00	261 67
Murray, W. A. & Co., screen, 2.75; Methodist Book & Pub. Co., 35.54	38 29
Morang & Co., books, 25.00; Milner, W. S., lecturing, 50.00	75 00
Morgan, S. A., special services lecturing, 121.66, arrears as acting lecturer during illness of Principal McLellan, 1,000.00	1,121 66
Newspapers, subscriptions, 9.00, advertising, 14.00	23 00
Ontario Normal College Literary Society, annual grant	25 00
Paterson, A., special services lecturing, 121.67; Parisian Laundry Co., laundrying, 4.69	126 36
Peeble, Hobson & Co., supplies, 27.70; Souter, A. M. & Co., shades, 38.75.	66 45
Smye, Wm., Jr., supplies, 95.72; Secy. Bd. of Education, grant, 4,500.00. -	4,595 72
Tracy, F., services as lecturer, 375.00, travelling expenses, 44.49	419 49
Turner, J. B., special services lecturing, 121.67; Vernon, H., Hamilton directory, 3.00	124 67
Warwick Bros. & Rutter, printing, 13.30; Wood Vallance & Co., screw eyes, etc., 16.20	29 50

LIBRARY AND MUSEUM.

SALARIES ($8,307.33).

J. Geo. Hodgins :	Twelve month's salary as		Historiographer	2,200 00
H. R. Alley :	do		Librarian	1,600 00
D. Boyle :	do		Superintendent of Museum	1,600 00
W. H. C. Phillips :	do		Clerk in Museum	1,000 33
W. A. Poole :	Eight	do	do	494 00
F. F. Evans :	Twelve	do	do	900 00
E. Dennie :	Four	do	Stenographer	150 00
E. King :	Eight	do	do	363 00

EDUCATION.—*Continued.*

LIBRARY AND MUSEUM.—*Continued.*

EXPENSES ($7,029.59).

Library:—

Alley, H. R., arrears of salary for (1905)	300 00
Annual Review Pub. Co., book, 3.25; Bates & Guild Co., books, 21.45.	24 70
Butter, W., book	1 50
Can. Express Co., charges, 5.20; Cairns, B., stamps and repairs, 3.00...	8 20
Can. Pub. Co., books, 1.13; Carter, J. S., book, 2.00	3 13
Chamberlain Argus, book, 2.00; Dane, Jno. & Co., books, 3.03.........	5 03
Davis Press. school art books, 10.00; Dom. Express Co., charges, 3.24...	13 24
Ethical Addresses, books, 12.50; Fridenker Pub. Co., book, 1.00.........	13 50
Goode, W. J., book, 3.50; Graham, Thos., cartage, 11.75	15 25
G. T. R. Co., freight charges, .74; Historical Pub. Co., books, 1.50......	2 24
Irwin, C. W., brokerage & freight, .77; King, E., services in library, 137.34	138 11
King's Printer, paper, 4.34, stationery, 24.25; Library Supply Co., books, 175.68	204 27
McMillan & Co., books, 19.12; McMaster, M., postage stamps, 35.00.	54 12
Mail & Empire, book, 3.00; Manual Arts Press, book, 2.00	5 00
Morang & Co., books, 20.00; Might Directories, directory, 7.50	27 50
Methodist Book Room, books, 327.83; Nash, C. W., books, .90	328 73
Nature Study Review, books 1.53; Newell, Robt., cab hire, 1.00.........	2 53
Newspapers, Magazines, and periodicals, subscriptions	354 20
North Am. Review, copies, .50; National Typewriter Co., repairs, .50.	1 00
Palmer Co., books, 10.35; Phillips, L. M., services, 80.00	90 35
Pope, James, book, 2.50; Reynolds, G. W., index cabinet, etc., 12.05...	14 55
Scribner. Chas. & Sons, books, 52.35; Smith, J. H., books, 2.00.........	54 35
Smith, Briggs, & Howe, books, 7.76; Stickley, Gustave, book, 1.00......	8 76
Toronto Ry. Co., car tickets, 12.00; Tyrrell, Wm. & Co., books. etc., 16.97	28 97
Viscount, de Fronsac, book, 1.00; Warwick, Bros. & Rutter, printing and binding. 82.95	83 95
Wilson, H. H., book	6 25

Museum:—

American Anthropological Association, annual dues, 6.00, subscription, 1.56 ....,...................	7 56
Am. Folk Lore Socy., subscription, 3.03; Allward, W.S., bust of Goldwin Smith, 25.00	28 03
Art Metropole, supplies, 5.40; Bastedo, C. N., Indian relics. 7.00......	12 40
Brodie, Dr. Wm., services, 1,000.00; Boasi, J., services, musical entertainment, 1.00	1,001 00
Bay, John, Indian relics, 20.00; Bull, Miss L. A., tear bottles, 25.00...	45 00
Brown, L. B., collection of Indian corals, 40.00; Boyle, D., travelling expenses, 355.90	395 90
Cockburn. N., services as attendant, 450.00; Cairns, B., stamps and supplies, 1.10	451 10
C. P. R. Co., freight charges, 25.32; Can. Ex. Co., charges, 8.44......	83 76
Cox, Geo. B., model of steam ship, 75.00; Carter, Geo. & Co., Persian armour. 35.00	110 00
Dom. Ex. Co., charges, 11.80; Doble, Arthur, bronze medal, 1.00......	12 80
Elliot & Co. chemicals. 2.55; Farmer Bros., portraits, 60.00	62 55
Florentine Statuary Co., repairing and painting groups, 15.05; G. T. Ry. Co., freight charges, 2.18.	17 23
Gearing. Thos. & Co., tables, cases, etc., 159.75; Glassford, R., box opener. 1.50	161 25
Graham. Thos., cartage, 4.50; Granner, A., cartage, .25	4 75
Greer Bros., uniform for attendant, 28.00; Haskett, Edna, services at 1.50 per day, 18.00...	46 00
Hooper Co., chemicals, 11.00; Hammond, J. H., manuscript, 6.00......	17 00
Hutchinson. M., tables, etc., 23.00; Haynes, Wm. J., repairing bust, 3.00	26 00
Irwin. C W., brokerage. 1.75 · Jarratt A., specimen of sea horse, .75.	2 50
King's Printer. stationery, 184.65; Lyon, W. A. & Co., photo supplies, 10.08	194 73

EDUCATION.—*Continued.*

LIBRARY AND MUSEUM.—*Continued.*

EXPENSES.—*Continued.*

Leavy, Mrs., wood carving, 100.00; Mackenzie & Co., frames, tables, etc., 12.75	112 75
Maughan, Jno., Jr., photos, cartage, etc., 10.60; services, articulating moose, 85.50	96 10
National Drug Co., chemicals, 4.45; Nash, C. W., services on catalogue, 200.00	204 45
Neate, Wm., indian relics	1 50
Ontario Society of Artists, five paintings, entitled: "Men may come and men may go;" "A quiet Old Road;" "The Vale of Tinturn;" "In the Laurentians;" "Solitude in the Moors."	800 00
Poole, W. A., services as attendant, 206.00; Phillips, W. H. C., travelling expenses, 24.40	230 40
Pilkey, P. T., use of steam launch visiting Serpent Mound, 3.00; Rawlinson, M., cartage, .75	3 75
Riordon Paper Mills, paper, 397.50; Sherwood, W. A., oil painting, 150.00	547 50
Simpson, Robt. Co., cork carpet, 3.75; Spanner, O., mounting birds, 6.00	9 75
Stewart, Jno., show cases, 65.55; Toronto Ry. Co., car tickets, 8.00	73 55
Usborne, Gordon, busts of Indians, 100.00; Van Wickel, H. A., Indian relics, 45.00	145 00
Ward, Chas. H., busts, etc., 4.50; Wintemberg, W. J., article on use of harpoons, etc., 39.75	44 25
Warwick Bros. & Rutter, printing and binding, 327.10; Willimas, J. B., tables for specimens, 14.00	341 10
Yates, T. W., cartage	50

SCHOOL OF PRACTICAL SCIENCE.

SALARIES ($58,747.00).

J. Galbraith :	Six months' salary as Professor of Engineering and Principal		2,134 00
A. P. Coleman :	do	Geology	1,467 00
W. H. Ellis :	do	Applied Chemistry	1,400 00
L. B. Stewart :	do	Surveying	1,467 00
C. H. C. Wright :	do	Architecture	1,467 00
G. R. Rosebrugh :	do	Electrical Engineering	1,467 00
G. R. Mickle :	do	Mining	1,267 00
R. W. Angus :	do	Mechanical Engineering	1,200 00
I. McGowan :	do	Lecturer in Applied Mechanics	1,000 00
J. W. Bain :	do	Applied Chemistry	1,000 00
G. R. Anderson :	do	on Physics (Optics)	867 00
H. M. Price :	do	Electrical Engineering	867 00
P. Gillespie :	do	Theory of construction	867 00
J. R. Cockburn :	do	Descriptive Geometry	867 00
E. G. R. Ardagh :	do	Demonstrator in Chemistry	534 00
H. G. Smith :	do	Engineering	534 00
J. G. McMillan :	do	Mining and Engineering	534 00
M. C. Boswell :	do	Chemistry	467 00
S. Dushman :	do	Drawing	468 00
J. Park :	do	Fellow in Chemistry	334 00
L. W. Morden :	do	do	334 00
L. E. McGorman :	do	Mechanical Engineering	334 00
W. W. Gray :	do	Mining Engineering	468 00
E. Wade :	do	Chemistry	334 00
E. W. Walker :	do	Metallurgy and Assaying	334 00
Chas. M. Teasdale :	do	Surveying	334 00
J. D. Shepley :	do	do	334 00
R. H. Armour :	do	Electrical Engineering	334 00
R. B. Ross :	do	do	334 00

EDUCATION.—*Continued.*

SCHOOL OF PRACTICAL SCIENCE.—*Continued.*

SALARIES.—*Continued.*

C. B. Aylesworth : Six months' salary as Fellow in Civil Engineering			334 00
L. R. Crearer :	do	Drawing	334 00
D. T. Townsend :	do	do	334 00
W. E. Douglas :	do	do	334 00
W. M. Bristol :	do	do	334 00
A. T. Laing :	do	Registrar and Librarian	1,068 00
A. J. Rickard :	do	Stenographer	300 00
Jean Weir : One and one-third months' salary as Stenographer			113 15
V. R. Ardagh : Six months' salary as Messenger			90 00
D. Hamilton :	do	do	90 00
David Sinclair :	do	Attendant in Chemistry	400 00
J. Deacon :	do	Metallurgy	175 00
D. K. Ambrust :	do	Draughting Room	200 00
Ernest Thompson :	do	Electrical Laboratory	200 00
Edward Tozer :	do	Mining	200 00
James Carson : Five and one-fourth months' salary as Attendant in Chemical Laboratory			79 00
W. J. Graham : Six month's salary as Caretaker Engineering Building			450 00
E. A. Allen :	do	Aest. do	do	213 00
E. A. Bishop :	do	Caretaker Chemistry & Mining Building	400 00
W. Simpson :	do	Engineer & Machinist (Eng. & Min. B'ld'g.)	600 00
Robert Fullerton :	do	Assistant in Mechanical Laboratory	250 00
John Cowan :	do	Fireman & Stoker Experimental Steam Plant	300 00
Jas. Kerr :	do	do (Eng. B'ld'g.)	300 00
Arthur Lepper :	do .	do	200 00
M. McBrearty : Four	do	Chief Engineer Chemical & Mining B'ld'g.	400 00
Samuel Hunter : Six	do	do	467 00
J. Kennedy :	do	Night Fireman	do	30? 00
Jno. Sherridan . Five	do	do	do	250 00
William Foggett : Four	do	Fireman Chemistry & Mining B'ld'g	200 00
J. S. McCracken : Six	do	Carpenter	376 00
University of Toronto, Balance of appropriation, 1906			26,107 85

EXPENSES ($10,075.00).

Apparatus, repairs and supplies for laboratories:

Alexander Engraving Co., 2.00; American Tent and Awning Co., 3.60; Art Metropole, 52.84; Beaver Glass Co., 4.95; Bennett & Wright Co., 11.50; Booth Copper Co., 4.60; Bookes, Roberts & Co., 9.41; Can. Heine Safety Boiler Co., 27.50; Can. General Electric Co., 411.36; Can. Chemical Mfg. Co., 47.49; Can. Foundry Co., 5.16; Cameron & Campbell, 27.50; Can. Westinghouse Co., 2.56; Chandler, Ingram & Bell, 10.00; Central Electric School Supply Co., 7.35; Coyell, Alf., 285.26; Dean Bros., 7.97; Dodge Mfg. Co., 24.17; Ehrhardt & Metzer, 11.20; Ernicke, Ferdinand, 5.49; Eimer & Amend, 165.15; Farthing, R., 8.60; Fletcher Mfg. Co., 288.18; Foster. Jas., 31.00; Goddard, J. A., 8.00; Gowans, Kent & Co., 4.50; Grip, Ltd., 4.38; Harris, E. & Co., 7.90; Hamilton Steel & Iron Co., 6.84; Herman Boker & Co., 37.37; Inglis, Jno. & Co., .60; Kay, Jno., Son & Co., 27.23; Keith & Fitzsimons Co., 1.50; Kirby, R. G., 4.40; Lake Simcoe Ice Co., 6.40; . Lucas, Jno. & Co., 2.00; Lyman Bros. & Co., 182.79; McDonald & Willson, 5.00; McGuire, W. J., 6.15; National Oil Co., 64.35; Ont. Lime Assn., 27.03; Ontario Rubber Co., 75.89; Paterson, A., Estate, 18.41; Pearsall, G., .90; Potter, Chas., 11.25; Reynolds, G. N. & Co., 5.50; Rhodes Metallic Packing Co., 7.20; Rice Lewis & Son, 388.77; Royal Eng. Co., 8.19; Sharpe, H. F. Co., 380.60; Sandusky Portland Cement Co., 1.60; Standard White Lime Co., 1.25; Thompson. A. L. & Co., 5.00; Tolton & McIntosh, 3.00; Treloar, Blashford & Co., 22.39; Tretheway, W. G., 10.50;

EDUCATION.—*Continued.*

SCHOOL OF PRACTICAL SCIENCE.—*Continued.*

EXPENSES.—*Continued.*

Vivian, G. L., .35; Vokes Hardware Co., 67.50;
Volta Electric Repair Works, 2.00; Wanty, W., 8.80;
Weston Elec. Inst. Co., 4.41; Woods Natural Sc. Establishment, 7.50;
Whitfield, Jno. Co., 31.64; Williams, A. R., Machy. Co., 2.53;
Woodburys Co., .50; Yeomans, R. M., 2.00;
Crosby Steam Gauge & Valve Co., 40.00 .... 2,938 83
Books, Examination Papers and Reports:
Beasley, Jeffries. 4.00; Cornell University, 2.00;
Engineering and Mining Journal, 4.50; Friedlander & Sohn, R., 11.41;
Guild, Wm. H. & Co., 39.94; Henry, Thos., 9.75;
Institute of Mining and Metallurgy, 2.66; Iron and Steel Inst., 2.05;
Leimcke & Beuchner, 19.63; Might Directories, directory, 12.00;
Students' Book Dept., Univ. of Toronto, 1.30; Tyrrell, Wm. & Co., 8.00;
University Press, 288.02; Van Nostrand, D. & Co., 3.60 .... 408 86
American Chemical Socy., dues, 10.00; American Soc'y for testing materials,
dues, 5.50; Bell Telephone Co., rent of instruments, 76.58;
messages, 2.20; Brandon & Gilbert, cartage, 1.25;
C.P.R. Tel. Co., messages, .27; C.P.R. Rwy. Co., freight charges, 1.83 97 63
Canadian Express Co., charges, 2.85; Chemical Soc'y. of England, dues, 9.84;
Coyell, Alf., removing desks, 91.45 .... 104 14
Dominion Express Co., charges, 1.30; Engineering Soc'y., grant, 75.00;
G. T. Rwy. Co., freight charges, 6.23; G.N.W. Tel. Co., messages, 2.18;
Guild, Wm. H. & Co., subscriptions to magazines. journals, etc., 100.15;
German Chemical Soc'y., dues, 7.28; Grand & Toy, stationery, 33.30... 225 44
Harper, W., duty charges on apparatus, 10.05; Hamilton Steamboat Co.,
freight charges, .35; Humphrey Bicycle & Hardware Co., replating
instrument fronts, .75; Jepson, W. C., services as asst. Librarian,
session 1905-06, 25.00 .... 36 15
King's Printer, stationery, 678.76; paper, 19.81; Laing, A. T., to pay
postage, .96; McMaster, M., postage stamps, 65.00 .... 764 53
Mickle, G. R., trav. expenses, 31.35; Murray, W. A. & Co., linoleum for
laboratory, 12.84; Mons, D. F., pulley sets, .29 .... 44 48
Newspapers and periodicals, advertising, 322.36; subscriptions, 12.00;
Robinson & Heath, freight, express and brokerage charges, 28.46 ...... 362 82
Starr, E. E., filling in diplomas, etc.. 10.95; United Typewriter Co.,
repairs, 7.50; Warwick Bros. & Rutter, printing, 287.45 .... 305 90
Wi'liams, N. & Co., cartage, .85; Wright, C. H. C.. trav. expenses, 105.85 106 70
University of Toronto, balance of appropriation, 1906 .... 4.679 52

MAINTENANCE.

Gas, fuel, water and electrical current ($9,500.00).

Consumers' Coal Co.. 1 cord slabs. 4.00; Consumers' Gas Co., gas, 618.88... 622 88
Fayle, V. P., exp. weighing coal, 11.40; Hammill, G. H. & Co., 2½ cords
slabs at 4.00 per cord, 10.00 .... 21 40
Lake Simcoe Ice Co., ice 7 30
McGill, Wm. & Co., 751.1780 tons soft screenings at 2.96 per ton, 2,225.71;
20.1650 tons egg coal at 6.00. per ton. 124.95; 2 tons coke at 6.00 per
ton. 12.60; 500 lbs. bloss coal. 1.75; 2.925 tons grate coal at 5.80 ton,
14.29; 1 cord pine wood at 7.00; ½ cord, 3.50; ½ cord cut wood at 8.00,
4.00 .... 2.393 80
Milnes Coal Co.. 1 cord wood 4 85
Toronto Electric Light Co.. light. 266.30; power current. 101.56; Water
Works Dept., water. 379.57 .... 747 43
University of Toronto, balance of appropriation, 1906 .... 5.702 34

Ground rent ($925.00).

University of Toronto. appropriation, 1906 .... 925 00

EDUCATION.—*Continued.*

SCHOOL OF PRACTICAL SCIENCE.—*Continued.*

MAINTENANCE.—*Continued.*

General repairs, drains, walks, furniture, incidentals, etc. ($4,500.00).

Armstrong, Fred Co., electric supplies, 17.30; Coyell, Alf., lumber, etc., 1,055.40	1,072 70
Dinnis, R. & Son, sawdust, 1.95; Eaton, T. Co., 2 clocks, 6.00	7 95
Gearing, Thos. V., repairing windows, lumber, 513.47; Godden, C. P., furnishings, 20.28; Gillett, E. W., lye, 1.80	535 55
Hamblin, Wm., bricklaying, 9.30; Imperial Chemical Co., engine and cyl. oil, 8.25	17 55
Inglis, Jno. & Co., repairing boiler, 15.80; Indian Alkali Works, savogran, 8.18	23 98
McGuire, W. J. & Co., repairing valves, 5.60; Morrison, Jas., Brass Co., pipe, etc., 19.84	25 44
Murray, W. A. & Co., cheese cloth, mat, etc., 6.75; National Oil Co., oil, soap, etc., 224.20	230 95
Ontario Lead & Wire Co., bolts, pipes, etc., 46.24; Qtis Fensom Elevator Co., repairs, 8.30; Ovens, L. A., oiling, painting, etc., 163.29	217 83
Power Bros., lowering flag pole, 5.00; pay lists, wages of carpenters, laborers and plumber, 1,347.71; Purdy, Mansell & Co., steamfitting, etc., 34.20	1,386 91
Queen City Concrete & Paving Co., sand, 2.50; Roberts, E. H., locksmithing, etc., 22.50	25 00
Robertson, Jas. Co., castings, etc., 41.07; Rice Lewis & Son, rope, 1.79; Rodgers, R. & G. & Co., cement and sand, 22.50	65 36
Smith, J. B. & Sons, repairing roof, 39.20; Simmers, J. A., seeds, 9.00; Stewart. Jno., painting, etc., 50.17; Stewart, W. L. & Co., repairing roofs, 96.36	194 73
Toronto Electric Light Co., lamps, 37.50; Townley & London, painting and glazing, 18.60; Thomas, M., gravel for walks, 9.75	65 85
Vokes Hardware Co., hardware, etc., 10.49; Wanty, Wm., repairing ventilators, 1.70	12 19
University of Toronto, balance of appropriation, 1906	618 01

Temporary help ($3,600.00).

Clark, J., services as asst. caretaker at 2.00 per day, 325.00; Cross, R., services on grounds, 58.45	383 45
Mintern, C., clearing snow, 2.00; Neal, Wm., clearing snow, 6.00	8 00
Passmore, J. J., services as night watchman at 2.00 per day	332 00
Scrubbing, cleaning, etc.:—	
Hamilton, Mrs., at 1.00 per day, 2.50; Laballister, Mrs., at 1.00 per day, 3.50;	6 00
McCann, Bella, at 1.25 per day, 135.00; O'Brien, Mrs. E., at 1.25 per day, 178.75	313 75
Pilch, Mrs. M., at 1.25 per day, 178.75; Poole; W. S., at 2.00 per day, 325.00	503 75
Stephens, Mrs. A., at 1.00 per day, 3.50; Winters, Jane, washing towels, 32.25	35 75
Weir, Jane, services as office assistant, 28.20; Soady, C., services on grounds, 350.00	378 20
University of Toronto, balance of appropriation, 1906	1,639 10

PUBLIC LIBRARIES ($30,951.12).

T. W. H. Leavitt: Twelve months' salary as Superintendent		$1 700 00
Wm. Lemon: do Clerk		950 00
Treasurer, Public Library:—		

Abingdon. 10.77;	Acton, 54.30;	Addison, 17.37;
Ailsa Craig. 62.59;	Allen's Mills. 4.50;	Alliston, 8.01;
Alma, 35.85;	Almonte. 45.88;	Alton, 55.55;
Amherstburg. 120.19;	Arkona, 19.57;	Arnprior, 23.79;
Arthur, 54.14;	Auburn, 14.86;	Aurora, 46.59;

EDUCATION.—*Continued.*

PUBLIC LIBRARIES.—*Continued.*

Avonmore, 32.79; Aylmer, 106.16; Ayr, 45.34;
Barrie, 42.20; Beachville, 37.27; Beamsville, 43.39;
Beaverton, 63.60; Belleville, 250.00; Bellwood, 39.39;
Berlin, 250.00; Blenheim, 48.06; Blyth, 10.16;
Bobcaygeon, 53.70; Bagnor, 20.42; Bolton, 53.33;
Bothwell, 69.10; Bowmanville, 63.79; Bracebridge, 147.30;
Bracondale, 98.44; Bradford, 11.15; Brampton, 148.34;
Brantford, 244.66; Bridgeburg, 10.23; Brigden, 38.38;
Brighton, 24.95; Brockville, 177.94; Brooklin, 46.97;
Brucefield, 48.14; Brussels, 95.18; Bunyan, 15.55;
Burk's Falls, 94.46; Burlington, 47.29; Burnstown, 16.86;
Caledon, 24.72; Caledonia, 79.90; Cambray, 36.29;
Camden, E., 33.07; Campbellford, 102.20; Canfield, 9.88;
Cannington, 26.78; Cardinal, 30.12; Cargill, 70.09;
Carleton Place, 111.76; Carp, .75; Cayuga, 19.25;
Chapleau, 7.87; Chatham, 114.05; Chatsworth, 36.70;
Cheapside, 26.68; Chesley, 73.84; Chesterville, 50.56;
Claremont, 39.32; Clifford, 73.23; Clinton, 156.83;
Cobden, 10.64; Cobourg, 146.17; Coldwater, 22.71;
Cookstown, 80.02; Collingwood, 147.95; Comber, 68.92;
Cornwall, 100.93; Creemore, 11.68; Deer Park, 200.00;
Delhi, 32.92; Deseronto, 125.06; Don, 25.09;
Drayton, 26.38; Drumbo, 67.73; Dundas, 129.26;
Dungannon, 44.54; Dunnville, 24.06; Durham, 46.91;
Dutton, 43.18; East Toronto, 101.57; Easton's Corners, 21.75;
Elmira, 43.08; Elmwood, 29.69; Elora, 69.60;
Embro, 69.53; Ennotville, 60.00; Erin, 25.71;
Essex, 59.33; Ethel, 7.54; Exeter, 111.15;
Fenelon Falls, 43.74; Fergus, 54.46; Fonthill, 33.61;
Forest, 70.55; Forrester's Falls, 25.38; Fort Erie, 21.67;
Fort Frances, 50.39; Frankford, 82.27; Galt, 250.00;
Gananoque, 147.39; Garden Island, 119.21; Georgetown, 77.37;
Glenmorris, 33.81; Goderich, 96.97; Gore's Landing, 20.31;
Grand Valley, 47.30; Grantham, 48.22; Gravenhurst, 37.35;
Grimsby, 84.08; Guelph, 250.00; Hagersville, 14.95;
Haliburton, 34.94; Hamilton, 250.00; Hanover, 12.22;
Harrington, 25.62; Harriston, 83.45; Hawkesbury, 38.39;
Hespeler, 99.97; Highland Creek, 21.42; Hillsdale, 37.37;
Holstein, 51.24; Honeywood, 29.80; Huntsville, 66.85;
Ingersoll, 110.28; Islington, 40.55; Jarvis, 28.40;
Kemptville, 72.19; Kenora, 123.04; Kincardine, 54.36;
Kingston, 107.44; Kingsville, 107.95; Kinmont, 44.74;
Kirkfield, 42.34; Komoka, 34.43; Lakefield, 53.54;
Lancaster, 53.62; Leamington, 109.05; Lefroy, 42.69;
Lindsay, 249.66; Listowel, 67.65; Little Britain, 48.10;
Little Current, 8.89; London, 250.00; Lucknow, 36.51;
Madoc, 108.77; Manilla, 61.65; Manotick, 19.22;
Maple, 33.15; Markdale, 70.18; Markham, 57.74;
Marlbank, 39.15; Matilda, 19.05; Meaford, 53.66;
Merrickville, 49.79; Merriton, 27.19; Midland, 82.16;
Millbrook, 66.84; Mildmay, 28.35; Millgrove, 13.25;
Milton, 32.20; Milverton, 46.59; Minden, 30.64;
Mitchell, 89.26; Mono Road, 11.14; Morrisburg, 79.43;
Morriston, 8.50; Mt. Forest, 44.20; New Durham, 14.39;
New Durham (arrears, grant 1903), 57.98; New Hamburg, 29.07;
Napanee, 210.43; New Liskeard, 53.68; Newburg, 18 22;
Newmarket, 47.78; Niagara, 96.31; Niagara Falls, 184.21;
North Bay, 40.23; North Gower, 25.64; Norwich, 55.33; Norwood, 12.97;
Oak Grove, 9.99; Oakville, 42.83; Oakwood, 27.45;
Odessa, 31.07; Omemee, 34.41; Ont. Library Association, 200.00;
Orangeville, 123.03; Orillia, 104.34; Orono, 31.73;
Oshawa, 117.53; Owen Sound, 79.03; Oxford Mills, 8.01;
Paisley, 72.93; Paris, 125.82; Parkhill, 41.40;
Parry Sound, 19.42; Pembroke, 217.09; Penetanguishene, 104.16;

6 P.A.

EDUCATION.—*Continued.*

PUBLIC LIBRARIES.—*Continued.*

Peterboro, 211.31;   Petrolea, 18.41;   Pickering, 25.90;
Picton, 215.56;   Pinkerton, 21.08;   Plattsville, 31.04;
Port Arthur, 139.89;   Port Carling, 27.44;   Port Colborne, 50.91;
Port Credit, 17.74;   Port Elgin, 23.28;   Port Hope, 77.76;
Port Perry, 59.40;   Port Stanley, 22.95;   Port Rowan, 67.51;
Prescott, 127.16;   Preston, 129.30;   Princeton, 22.43;
Queensville, 27.50;   Renfrew, 20.46;   Richmond, 18.18;
Richmond Hill, 47.88;   Ridgetown, 61.47;   Ridgeway, 38.46;
Riverdale, 18.58;   Rockwood, 40.78;   Rodney, 33.55;
Romney, 40.12;   Russell, 46.65;   Saltfleet, 55.53;
Sarnia, 250.00;   Sault Ste. Marie, 153.88;   Scarboro, 57.14;
Schomberg, 50.00;   Scotland, 26.28;   Seaforth, 94.13;
Shedden, 29.38;   Shelbourne, 75.14;   Simcoe, 250.00;
Smith's Falls, 191.69:   Smithville, 9.30;   Southampton, 28.58;
South Mountain, 75.99;   Sparta, 23.18;   Speedside, 59.79;
Stayner, 31.18;   Stirling, 17.65;   Stratford, 238.47;
Strathroy, 133.65;   Streetsville, 53.91:   Stouffville, 75.49;
St. Catharines, 250.00;   St. George, 20.83;   St. Helens, 21.10;
St. Mary's 116.28;   St. Thomas, 209.98;   Sturgeon Falls, 75.27;
Sunderland, 73.05;   Sunnidale, 42.47;   Sydenham, 56.72;
Tara, 32.56;   Tavistock, 122.69;   Teeswater, 94.84;
Thamesford, 10.08;   Thamesville, 27.38;   Thedford, 39.34;
Thessalon, 34.16;   Thornbury, 19.11;   Thornhill, 1.00;
Thorold, 65.09;   Tilbury, 42.37;   Tilsonburg, 65.99;
Toronto, 250.00;   Toronto Junction, 87.34;   Underwood, 40.12;
Unionville, 40.15;   Uxbridge, 76.65;   Vankleek Hill, 43.58;
Victoria Mines, 59.41;   Walkerton, 78.60;   Walkerville, 228.87;
Wallaceburg, 141.60;   Walton, 13.45;   Waterdown, 30.88;
Waterford, 27.82;   Waterloo, 172.96;   Watford, 68.71;
Welland, 92.19;   Wellesley, 45.78;   Westford, 25.85;
Weston, 71.64;   Wheatley, 14.04;   Whitby, 62.25;
Wiarton, 13.55;   Williamstown, 29.51;   Winchester, 55.72;
Windsor, 250.00;   Wingham, 121.50;   Woodbridge, 29.86;
Woodstock, 250.00;   Woodville, 27.77;   Wroxeter, 42.78;
Zephyr, 1.15; Special Grant to Huron Institute, 300.00 .... 21,381 91

Treasurer County of:—
 Brant (11 schools), 100.95;   Bruce (13 schools in W. B.), 86.32;
 Carleton (23 schools), 153.07;   Dufferin (4 schools), 32.50;
 Elgin (52 schools), 196.35;   Elgin (aid to Dunwich), 9.75;
 Essex (5 schools) 48.55;
 Essex (aid to No. 3 Gosfield S. and No. 2 Mersea) 15.51;
 Frontenac (9 schools), 87.50;   Grey (26 schools), 208.07;
 Haldimand (3 schools), 19.00;   Haliburton (6 schools), 49.00;
 Halton (10 schools), 86.90;   Hastings (24 schools), 201.31;
 Huron (15 schools), 110.38;   Kent (24 schools), 194.43;
 Lambton (11 schools), 74.30;   Lanark (16 schools), 110.50;
 Leeds and Grenville (6 schools) 45.00;
 Lennox and Addington (2 schools) 16.25;
 Lincoln (28 schools), 280.00;   Middlesex (27 schools), 208.25;
 Norfolk (15 schools), 86.29; Northumberland & Durham (8 schools), 90.07;
 Ontario (16 schools), 145.00;   Oxford (6 schools), 60.00;
 Peel (4 schools), 40.00;   Perth (20 schools), 178.73;
 Prescott & Russell (12 schools), 87.23; Peterborough (3 schools), 20.00;
 Prince Edward (15 schools), 123.26;   Renfrew (11 schools), 81.04;
 Simcoe (22 schools), 186.75; Stor. Dun. & Glengarry (25 schools), 225.12;
 Victoria (9 schools), 51.11;   Waterloo (6 schools), 55.00;
 Wellington, 118.35;
 York (17 schools), 106.57 .... 4,069 40

Trustees, Public Schools in District of W. Parry Sound:—
 8 Carling, 3.00; 1 Croft, 7.88; 1 Ferrie, 5.52; 2 Hagerman, 10.00;
 5 Hagerman, 7.50; 1 Humphrey, 10.00; U. 4 Humphrey, 5.00;
 U. 2 McDougall, 10.00 .... 58 90

6a P.A.

EDUCATION.—*Continued.*

PUBLIC LIBRARIES.—*Continued.*

District of Muskoka:—
2 Laurier, 4.12;   5 Machar, 10.00;   8 Macaulay, 5.00;
1 McLean, 7.50;   2 Medora, 10.00;   3 Nipissing, 10.00;
7 Ryde, 5.00;   2 Stisted, 10.00;   4 Watt, 10.00;   1 Wood, 10.00;
2 Wood, 10.00 ....   91 62

District of Rainy River:—
3 Crozier, 2.50;   2 Dobie, 10.00;   2 Devlin, 10.00;
1 Morley and Pattullo, 10.00; 1 Nepigon, 10.00 ....   42 50

Trustees R. C. Separate Schools:—
2 Ashfield, 5.70;   6 Arthur, 10.00;   6 Biddulph, 1.98;
1 Carrick and Culross, 10.00; 2 Maidstone, 6.24; 5 Sandwich S., 5.47;
7 Sandwich S., 5.93;   5 Sombra, 8.00;   13 Waterloo, 7.50;
11 Wellesley, 10.00; 1 York, 10.00 ....   80 82

American Library Association, books, 2.61; *Annual Review*, copies, 16.00   18 61
Brandon & Gilbert, cartage, .25; Brown & Nolan, books, 7.71 ....   7 96
Cairns, B., rubber stamps and pad, 6.36; Can. Express Co., charges, 2.35   8 71
C. P. Railway Co., freight charges, 1.01; Dom. Express Co., charges, 9.17   10 18
Farmer Bros., photos, 10.00; Gearing, Thos. V., book cases, 93.85.........   103 85
Harcourt, E. H., half tones, 51.98; Hynes, Lillian, services 3 weeks 5 days
at 2.00 per day, 46.00 ....   97 98
King's Printer, paper and stationery, 141.56; Leavitt, T. W. H., travelling
expenses, 275.81 ....   417 37
Longman's, Green & Co., books, maps, etc., 48.04; McMaster, M., postage
stamps, 327.00 ....   375 04
McMillan Co., books, 14.60; Methodist Book Room, dictionary, 1.60.........   16 20
Musson Book Co., books, 13.50; National Typewriter Co., rent of type-
writer, supplies, repairs, etc., 23.25 ....   36 75
National Typewriter Co., typewriter and tabulator, 139.50; Poole Pub.
Co., books, 10.00 ....   149 50
Potter, Chas., gas, cartage, etc., 3.90; Publisher's Weekly, subscription
to *Library Journal*, 1906, 4.00 ....   7 90
Post, W. L., catalogue, .53; Reading Camp Association, Rev. A. Fitz-
patrick, grant, 1,000 ....   1,000 53
Riordon Paper Mills, paper, 57.94; Toronto Ry. Co., car tickets, 13.00...   70 94
Warwick Bros. & Rutter, printing, etc. 170 32

Travelling Libraries:—
Briggs, Wm., books, 1.28; C. P. Railway Co., freight charges, .47;
Canadian Express Co., charges, 1.00; Dom. Express Co., charges,
10.73; G. T. Railway Co., freight charges, .62; King's Printer, stationery, 14.40; Meredith, Thos. & Co., brackets, staples, etc., 1.63; Mc-
Master, M., postage stamps, 50.00; Stewart, Jno., lettering boxes,
4.00 ....   84 13

ART SCHOOLS AND ART MUSEUM, ETC. ($4,260.85).

Grants:—
Hamilton Art School, 2,400.00; Ontario Society of Arts, 500.00; To-
ronto Art School, 400.00 ....   3,300.00
Clark, C. A. H., labelling specimens, 657.00; Meredith, Thos. & Co., escut-
cheon pins, 1.55 ....   658 55
McMaster, M., postage stamps, 50.00; Murray, W. A. & Co., carpets, etc.,
163.65 ....   213 65
Reynolds, G. N. & Co., desk, cabinet, etc., 83.60; Rowland, H. A., chemi-
cals, 5.05 ....   88 65

LITERARY AND SCIENTIFIC ($4,200.00).

Canadian Institute,	Legislative grant............................	1,500 00
Hamilton Scientific Society,	do	400 00
Institut Canadien,	do	400 00
Ottawa Field Naturalists' Club,	do	300 00
Ottawa Literary and Scientific Association,	do	400 00
Ottawa University and Scientific Society,	do	100 00
Royal Astronomical Society,	do	600 00
Society of Chemical Industry,	do	200 00
St. Patrick's Literary Association,	do	200 00
Wellington Field Naturalists' Club,	do	100 00

EDUCATION.—*Continued.*

HISTORICAL SOCIETIES ($1,900.00).

Essex Historical Society,	Legislative grant	100 00
Lundy's Lane Historical Society,	do	200 00
Middlesex and London Historical Society,	do	100 00
Niagara Historical Society,	do	600 00
Ontario Historical Society,	do	600 00
Wentworth Historical Society,	do	100 00
Women's Canadian Historical Society	do	100 00
Women's Wentworth Historical Society	do	100 00

TECHNICAL EDUCATION ($26.798.50).

Grants:—

Alvinston Public School Board, Manual Training	388 80
Belleville High School Board, Household Science,	80 00
Berlin Collegiate Institute Board, Manual Training, 580.00; Household Science, 340.00; Special Technical Instruction, 750.00	1,670 00
Brantford Technical School Board, Manual Training, 510.00; Special Instruction, 400.00	910 00
Brantford Young Men's Christian Association, Household Science	260 00
Broadview Boys' Institute, Technical and Industrial Classes	294 00
Brockville Public School Board, Household Science, 126.66; Manual Training, 462.50	589 16
Cobourg Collegiate Institute Board, Manual Training	198 00
Cornwall Public School Board, Manual Training	268 00
Essex High School Board, Manual Training	184 00
Guelph Consolidated School Board. Household Science, 160.00; Manual Training, 330.00	490 00
Guelph Public School Board, Household Science, 368.00; Manual Training, 505.00	873 00
Hamilton Board of Education, Household Science	532 00
Hamilton School of Art	500 00
Ingersoll Board of Education, Household Science, 180.00; Manual Training, 310.00	490 00
Kingston Board of Education, Household Science, 96.00; Manual Training, 435.00; Special Technical Instruction, 600.00	1,131 00
London Collegiate Institute Board, Household Science, 200.00; Manual Training, 175.00	375 00
Ottawa Public School Board, Manual Training: Bolton St., 198.00; Cartier St., 226.00; Cambridge St., 331.00; Elgin St., 219.00; First Ave.. 254 00; George St., 321.00; Glashan St., 293.00; Slater St., 525.00; Wellington St., 212.00	2,579 00
Renfrew Board of Education, Household Science. 100.00; Manual Training, 102.04	202 04
Stratford Collegiate Institute Board. Manual Training. 455.00; Special Technical Instruction, 600.00	1,055 00
Stratford Public School Board. Household Science	280 00
St. Thomas Public School Board, Manual Training	227 00
Toronto Board of Education (arrears grant. 1905) 1.620.00; 1906, 1,670.00; Household Science: King Edward Public School, 331.00; Queen Alexandra, 300.00; Queen Victoria. 300.00; Wellesley. 300.00: Winchester St., 300.00. Manual Training: Dufferin Public School. 535.00; Givens St., 535.00; Lansdowne Ave.. 545.00; Queen Alexandra. 525.00; Wellesley, 535.00	7,496 00
Woodstock Collegiate Institute Board. Manual Training. 395.00; Special Technical Instruction, 400.00	795 00
Woodstock Public School Board. Household Science	260 00

Scholarships:—

Anderson, Geo. J.. 75.00; Bartley. Annie. 50.00; Buckle, Mabel C.. 50.00; Burnette. Jessie. 50 00; Evans, Kate A., 50.00; Hawkin. Lizzie, 50.00; Hocken. Muriel J.. 50.00; Keays, J. A.. 75.00; Legge. A. Maude, 50.00; McDiarmid Bella. 50.00; MacIntyre. Maud, 50.00; Metcalfe, W. H., 75.00; Newhouse. F. J.. 75.00; Patton. J.. 75.00; Thorburn. Aggie, 50.00; Stewart. Kate M.. 50.00; Stinson. Mary E., 50.00	975 00

EDUCATION.—*Continued.*

TECHNICAL EDUCATION.—*Continued.*

Summer Schools: sundry persons' services lecturing:

Attwood, A. E., 25.00;	Bailey, W., 125.00, expenses, 95c.:
Butchart, A., 75.00;	Casselman, A. C., 110.00;
Davidson, Alexander, 10.00;	Davidson, S. K., 110.00;
Dearness, Jno., 140.00; Dobbie, J. A., 100.00; Elliott, W. H., 140.00;	
Fletcher, Dr. Jas., 25.00; Gallop, M. E., 75.00; Harterre, J. S., 100.00;	
Heffernan, N., 50.00;	Johnston, G. L., 125.00, expenses, 60c.;
Macdonald, O., 16.00; MacPherson, M., 125.00; McPherson, E., 10.00;	
Merchant, F. W., 165.00; Macbeth, Mrs. E., 75.00; Perney, F. E., 35.00:	
Pickles, S., 110.00;	Putman, J. H., 175.00; Scott, Wm. 165.00;
Sullivan, J. F., 50.00;	Turner, J. B., 150.00;

Wilkinson, Jas. H., 100.00; White, J. F., 50.00 .... 2,437 55
Grace LeRoy, services as stenographer 50 00
Mrs. E. Knox, do attendant 10 00
Aikenhead Hardware, Ltd., glue, .85; Aitcheson, D. & Co., lumber, etc., 10.80 11 65
American Civil Assn., pamphlets, .20; Brandon & Gilbert, cartage, .50... 70
Britnell, A., book, 1.00; Brown Bros., cardboard, etc., 5.05 .... 6 05
Can. Express Co., duty and charges, 13.48; Cloke & Son, stationery, etc., 20.59 .... 34 07
Council of Supervisors, year books, 12.00; Coyell, Alf., box for lanterns, etc., 18.02 .... 30 02
Derby Collard Co., books, 2.00; Dom. Express Co., charges, 2.76 .... 4 76
Errett, C. W., negatives for lantern slides, 4.75; Graham, Thos., cartage, 13.50 .... 18 25
Hoodless, Mrs. Adelaide, services, 600.00; trav. expenses, 143.19 .... 743 19
Hope, Jas. & Sons, pads, 1.80; King's Printer, stationery, 85.88............. 87 68
Leake, A. H., to pay sundries, 3.15; Lennox, T. H., lantern slides, 3.50 6 65
McMaster, M., postage stamps, 25.00; Office Specialty Mfg. Co., cards, etc., 4.00 .... 29 00
Potter, Chas., lantern slides, etc., 54.05; Rice Lewis & Son, sash cord, 79 54 84
Riordon Paper Mills, paper, 38.45; Siche Gas Co., machine and carbide, 18.75 .... 57 20
Smye, Wm., Jr., supplies, 8.99; Staunton, O. B., & Co., stationery, .30... 9 29
Steinberger, Hendry Co., reeds, raffia, etc., 14.35; Topley Studio, lantern slides, 2.70 .... 17 05
United Typewriter Co., supplies, 1.00; Warwick Bros. & Rutter, printing and binding, 78.85 .... 79 85
Wilkinson, J. H., trav. expenses 8 70

SUPERANNUATED TEACHERS ($63,190.00).

Acres, Jno. W., 276.00; Adair, C. F., 158.00; Adams, Adam, 80.00; Alexander, Robt., 335.50; Allan James, 122.00; Allison, Andrew, 131.00; Amos, Thos., 199.00; Anderson, John. 151.50; Anderson, Edward, 234.00; Anderson, Wm., 206.00; Anderson, Jane. 237.50; Andrews, Adolphus, 129 00; Andrew, Arch., 158.00; Armstrong, J. W., 171.00; Armstrong, Thos., 152.00; Ash, Geo. Hy., 181.50; Aylesworth, Lucinda. 179.00: Banks, R. H., 91.00; Banks. Maltimore, 172.00; Barber, Albert, 192.00; Bates, I., 87.00; Bell, Wm., 251.50; Bell, L. C., 215.50; Bell, Helen. 122.00; Bell, David, 122.00; Beatty, W. H., 98.00; Bigg, W. R., 259.00; Biggar, Mrs. P. W., 86.00; Bigelow, Geo., 184.00; Birch, James, 261.50; Blackman, Theo., 232.00; Blackwood, R., 132.50; Boal, Wm., 62.50; Bodaly, John, 83.00; Bowes, Ellen. 125.00; Bradley, Jno. H., 254.50; Bradley, Wm. E., 157.00: Brackin, James. 203.50; Bradley, Wm., 101.00; Breman, Jno., 65.50; Bridge. Amos. 200.50; Brown. Clara L., 86.00; Brueckner, Julius O., 176.00; Bowerman. Jas., 181.50; Bulmer, H. S., 173.50; Cameron, Peter. 71.00; Cameron. Hugh, 133.00; Campbell, J. C., 203.50; Campbell. Wm., 125.50; Campbell. Alex., 283.00; Carley, Abram. 185.00; Capsey, Mrs. M., 147.00; Carpenter, G., 56.00; Carnochan, Janet, 269.00; Carroll, Wm., 255.00; Casewell, Thos. B., 255.00; Chaplin, Thos., 98.00; Chislett. T., 136.50; Chaisgreen. Chas., 185.00; Clarke, J., 47.00; Clapp, David P., 237.50; Clendenning. Wm Scott. 301 50; Coates, Robt., 178.00; Cochrane. Jno. G., 241.00; Courtney, Mrs. P. S., 98.00; Courtlandt. H. N., 235.00; Connor. Jas. W., 276.00; Cook, S. G., 246.50;

EDUCATION.—*Continued.*

SUPERANNUATED TEACHERS.—*Continued.*

Cooke, Jas., 100.50;　Calhoun, C. B., 123.00;　Costello Catharine, 128.00;
Coyne, M. H., 279.50;　　Crane, Geo., 209.50;　　Crisp, R., 68.00;
Crawford, Peter, 205.50;　　　Croll, Eliz. (for late David), 217.00;
Cull, F. A., 200.00;　　　　　　　　Cullen, Helen, 134.00;
Curry, Wm., 92.00;　Currie, Malcolm, 120.00;　Cundal, Jno., 200.00;
Dafoe, Jno. W., 277.00;　Dalgish, Jno., 95.00; Davidson, Wm., 234.00;
Davis, Flavelle, 246.00; Davis, Jas. Alf., 162.00; Deachman, R., 107.00;
DeCow, Rebecca, 327.00; Derby, Samuel, 128.00; Dimsdale, Alf. W., 113.00;
Dochstader, J. N., 158.00;　　　　　Drummond, Jos., 200.00;
Dulmage, G. W., 128.00; Duncan, James, 295.00; Dunn, Hannah O., 290.00;
Duff, Andrew, 136.00; Eckardt, Tobias, 194.50; Eckert, W. D., 375.50;
Eden, W., 109.00;　　Ellis, F. L., 134.00;　　Elliott, J. C., 293.00;
Elliott, Mrs. C., 68.00; Elmslie, Wm., 109.00; Evans, Ed. Thos., 143.00;
Faltou, Jas. J., 68.00; Ferguson, Jno., 176.00; Ferguson, Rod'k, 176.00;
Fetterley, Julia A., 80.00;　　　　Flavelle, Dorothea, 77.00;
Fletcher, Robert, 143.00;　　　　Flynn, Mrs. Susan, 266.00;
Fraser, Alex., 153.50;　French, Gilbert, 151.50;　Fulton, Jas., 185.00;
Froats, Luther S., 214.00;　　　　Gamble, Mrs. Ann, 98.00;
Garrett, Glenholme, 215.50; Gill, Martin, 192.50; Gilbert, A. B., 151.50;
Gibson, James, 87.00; Godwin, W. H., 253.50; Goodbody, Wm., 182.00;
Gould, A. A., 206.00;　Graham, T. C., 65.00;　Grandy, Robert, 115.00;
Gray, Jno., 55.50;　Gray, Wm., 212.00;　Gregory, Thos., 162.00;
Green, P. H., 174.50; Grenier, Isaac, 176.00; Graham, Harriet, 155.00;
Grey, Jas. B., 367.00; Haight, Mrs. M. J., 131.00; Hankison, D. L., 101.00;
Hanson, M. E. F., 227.00; Hall, R. D., 279.50;　Hanna, Jno., 179.00;
Hamilton, Sarah M., 153.50;　　　　Hamilton, R. E., 78.00;
Hamilton Robert, 172.00;　　　　Hamilton, Susan M., 262.00;
Hamilton, Geo., 231.50; Hammond, Thos., 129.00; Harrison, E. B., 252.50;
Henry, H. C., 146.00;　Henry, P. D., 98.00;　Henstridge, J. W., 229.00;
Henderson Geo. F., 224.00;　　　Henderson, Anson Gains, 139.50;
Hewson, E. T., 142.00; Hewson, Alf. Jno., 160.50; Heydon, Wm. H., 146.00;
Hickey, A., 223.50;　Hindson, Wm., 220.50;　Hickson, Wm., 169.00;
Hobbs, Wm. B., 45.00; Holmes, N. L., 164.00; Hopkins Mrs. Eliza, 147.50;
Hovenden, Sarah, 153.00; Hobbs, J. H., 119.00; Horne, A. F., 122.00;
Hunt, Mrs. F. S., 168.00;　　　　　Husband, Hy., 293.50;
Herrick, A. C. (Ex Est.). 176.00;　　Ireland, Jno., 171.00;
Ireland, Mrs. Irene, 50.00;　　Jackson, Bertha, 153.50;
Jarvis, Nicholas, 205.00;　　　Johnson, Mrs. R. A., 86.00;
Johnston, D. J., 182.00;　　　　Johnson, Geo. W., 213.00;
Keatley, James, 90.50;　Kearney, Jas., 56.00;　Kelly, Jas., 167.50;
Kennedy, Eliz. E., 241.00; Kennedy, A. E., 92.00; Kennedy, Alex., 199.00;
Keenan, D. D., 185.00; Kessack, Jane, 192.00; Keirman, W. M., 122.50;
Kilman, A. H., 149.50;　　　　Kilpatrick, Samuel Jas., 114.00;
Knowles, Richard H., 203.00;　Kyle, Jos., 147.50;　Latter, Jos., 234.00;
Langdon, Jno., 217.00;　Lee. A. H., 116.00;　Leighton, S. H., 142.00;
Leitch, Alex. L., 130.00;　Lee, Fred., 92.00;　Leith, Wm., 164.00;
Lemery, Anthime, 158.00;　　　　Lindsay, Geo., 152.50;
Levergood, Mary H., 122.00; Laughlin, Wm., 175.00; LeRiche, P. F., 128.00;
Lusk, Chas. H., 272.50; Ludlow, John, 164.00;　Logan, S. M., 119.00;
Mackie, Vina L., 74.00;　　　　MacDonald. Adam F., 332.50;
MacKenzie, Wm. F., 276.00; Morton, J. B., 227.50; Martin, Samuel, 188.50;
Masales, Geo. W., 97.50; Matthews, Jno., 100.00; Matthewson, Wm., 146.00;
Maynard, R., 262.00; Maxwell, Jas., 107.00; Metzdorf, C. F. H., 104.00;
Mills, David, 216.50; Minchins, W. H., 219.00; Mitchell, Jno., 143.50;
Middleton, Geo., 152.50; Monkman, J. M., 157.00; Monds, Wm., 148.00;
Moore, Thos. T., 280.00; Morton, Adam, 234.00; Morgan, Jas. Wm., 234.00;
Morrison, Adam, 281.00;　　　　Mover, Freeman H., 218.00;
Murray, Eliz., 122.00;　　　　　McAlpine, Mrs. M., 146.00;
McArtney, Chas., 104.00;　　　McAulay, Donald, 173.00;
McBain, J. W., 116.00; McBrien, A. B., 78.50; McBride, G. D., 95.00;
McCall, Wm., C., 182.00;　　　　McClinton, Jno., 212.00;
McColl, D., 129. 50;　　　McDonald, Mrs. R. R., 119.00;
McDonald, Donald, 178.00;　　　McGeehan, M. E., 140.00;
McGregory, Alex., 167.00;　　McGregory, Robert C., 127.50;

EDUCATION.—*Continued.*

SUPERANNUATED TEACHERS.—*Continued.*

McGoey, T. Q., 159.00; McGrath, Jno., 150.50; McEachern, W. C., 229.00;
McEwan, Robert, 206.00; McIntyre, Geo. A., 181.50; McKay, Jno., 164.00;
McKerrall, T., 153.50; McKeown, Wm., 260.00; McKinnell, Geo., 176.00;
McKinnon D. C., 167.00; McKinnon, A. J., 131.00; McLaren, Peter, 196.00;
McLean, Jno. (Galt), 208.50;   McLean, Jno. (Hamilton), 66.00;
McLeay, Donald, 169.00;   McLim, W. A., 186.00;   McLean, Jas., 89.50;
McLean, D. N., 116.00;   McMillan, R., 77.00;
McMahon, M. A., 95.00;   McNamara, Jno., 98.00;
McNeilie, J. R., 170.00;   McPhee, Hugh, 202.00;
McQueen, Mrs. Isabella, 92.00;   McQueen, Robert, 220.00;
McFaul, L. L., 209.50;   McPherson, Crawford, 266.50;
McFarlane, David, 182.00; Nisbet, N. R., 200.00; Nicholson, W. J., 41.00;
Nolan, A. C., 164.00;   Norton, Theophilius, 188.50;
O'Connor, Anthony, 98.00; O'Meara, Jas., 110.00; Osborne, A. C., 193.50;
Ouelette, Anthony, 149.00;   Payne, G. F. B., 170.00;
Page, Otway, 218.50;   Patterson, Alex., 167.50;   Pegg, J. P., 76.50;
Pegg, Wm. W., 218.00;   Peters, Geo., 129.00;   Perry, S. T., 189.50;
Phillips, Jno., 190.00; Plunkett, Wm., 203.00; Powell, F. C., 264.50;
Pollock, J. E., 24.00; Prouty, Chester, 164.00; Quinn, Andrew, 156.50;
Rabb, John, 215.50;   Rannie, Wm., 220.00;   Read, H. H., 200.50;
Reid, Wm. Kirk, 244.00; Reid, J. C., 156.00; Redmond, J., 140.50;
Regan, M. L., 95.00; Regan, Emma R., 185.00; Reynolds, Rose B., 197.00;
Richardson, Mrs. M. Y., 183.50;   Ritchie, D. S. F., 252.50;
Robertson, Duncan, 207.00;   Robertson, C. M., 166.00;
Robertson Dorcas D., 174.50;   Robertson, W. P., 258.00;
Robertson, G. E., 97.50; Robbs, Jno., 204.00; Rose, Jno. George, 136.00;
Ross, John, 325.00;   Rothwell, A. T., 125.00;
Rothwell, Benj. (Listowel), 287.50; Rothwell, Benj. (Chatham), 240.50;
Round, George, 176.50; Ryerson, Jesse, 27.50; Sanderson, Robert, 213.00;
Scott. W. H., 181.50;   Shaw. Pringle, 194.00;   Shaw, J., 275.00;
Settell, Jas. J., 180.50; Shanks. Robert P., 206.00; Sharman, Geo., 232.00;
Sheehan, Jno., 122.50; Shirreff. Ben., 193.00; Shoemaker Eliz., 155.00;
Sinclair, Wm., 213.50; Sinclair. Arch., 187.00; Sinclair. Jno., 134.00;
Simpson, E. M., 149.00; Sine, Geo. Wm., 155.50; Smith, Jas., 213.00;
Smith, Abram B.. 278.50; Smith. David, 167.50; Slaven, Annie, 152.00;
Stewart, Alex., 74.00; Sullivan, Daniel, 131.00; Sullivan, C. F., 66.00;
Sutherland, Philip, 107.00;   Styles, Wm., 290.00;
Spillett, Stanley. 172.00; Tasker, R.. 160.50; Telfer. John, 61.50;
Thornhill, Wm.. 116.00; Todd, Alex., 150.00; Torrence. Rev. Robt., 255.00;
Tomlinson, Jordan. 212.00: Treadgold, Carey. 98.00; Trovell. Wm., 139.50;
Unsworth. R.. 173.00; Vandewater, S., 112.50; Vandeburgh, Harvey, 157.50;
Varcoe, J., 128.00;   Wallace. Jas., 83.00;   Walker, J. W., 83.00;
Warburton, Lucd'a. 245.50; Ward, J. G.. 164.50; Ward. Henry, 220.00;
Watts, Mary, 128.00; Watson. Thos., 194.00; Waterson. John A., 160.50;
Washburn, Saxon. 107.00;   Waugh. Thos., 146.00;
Weatherston, Mary. 157.00; Weighill, Jno., 185.00; Wells. Eliz. C., 262.00;
Westervelt, Samuel B.. 226.00;   Williams. D. L., 188.50;
Wilson, Abraham. 92.00;   Wilkins. Eliz. A.. 239.00;
Wightman, Geo. F., 244.50;   Winterbottom, A. C., 209.00;
Wood, Jno., 232.00;   Work. Alex., 323.00;   Wright. Justus, 150.50;
Wright. M. N., 175.00;   Wright. A. W., 155.50:   Yates. J. F., 176.00;
Young, L. G., 74.00 ....

PROVINCIAL UNIVERSITY ($123.837.91).

Bursar University of Toronto:
  Agricultural examinations University degree B.S.A........................... 425 00
  Statutory grant (60 Vict.. Chap. 59) 7,000 00
    do   (1 Edw. VII.. Sec. 16. Cap. 41) 53,460 67
    do   Domestic Science Department 700 00
  Grant from sale of lands (60 Vict.. Chap. 59. Sec. 5)...................... 1,186 06
  Actual deficit 60,953 68
Librarian Universiay of Toronto. 150 copies of Historical Publications
  of Canada 112 50

EDUCATION.—Continued.

SCHOOL OF MINING, KINGSTON ($37,000.00).

G. Y. Chown, Treasurer, Legislative grant 37,000 00

MEDICAL FACULTY OF QUEEN'S COLLEGE, FOR PROMOTION OF MEDICAL EDUCATION ($50,000.00).

J. C. Connell, Dean, and W. T. Connell, Secretary-Treasurer, Legislative
grant 50,000 00

MAINTENANCE EDUCATIONAL BUILDINGS.

Furniture and furnishings ($1,174.19).

Ashall, W., attending clocks, 18.00; Armstrong, Fred., chandeliers, 67.50...   85 50
Coatsworth, E. E., mats, glassware,, etc., 19.20; Dominion School Supply
Co., stationery, blackboards, etc., 146.72 ....   165 92
Eaton, T. Co., mirror, pail, etc., 7.00; Godden, C. P., lamps, etc., 7.50...   14 50
Gourlay, Winter & Leming, tuning pianos, 10.00; Hutchinson, M., oak
panels, drawers, etc., 18.25 ....   28 25
Lloyd Automatic Wire Weaving Co., wire mat, 5.10; Murray, W. A. & Co.,
carpets, rugs, etc., 314.40 ....   319 50
Nerlich & Co., flags, 6.20; National Typewriter Co., chairs, etc., 40.00...   46 20
Nordheimer Piano Co., rent of organ, 24.00; Office Specialty Mfg. Co.,
cabinet, 27.00 ....   51 00
Reid & Co., lumber, 9.57; Rice Lewis & Son, stone filter, 5.00 ....   14 57
Reynolds, G. N. & Co., desks, chairs, etc., 388.30; Simpson, Robert Co.,
furnishings, 25.45 ....   413 75
United Typewriter Co., chair, 7.50; Whale, Albert, cushions and repg.
furniture, 14.50 ....   22 00
Williams, R. S. & Sons, cartage and rent of pianos 13 00

Scrubbing, cleaning and supplies, Night Fireman, etc. ($1,222.78).

Coatsworth, C. E., soap, mops, etc., 30.51; Gilpin, R., allowance for sup-
plies, 25.00 ....   55 51
Godden, C. P., pails, etc., 5.00; Hill, Gertie, scrubbing and cleaning, 2.50   7 50
Knox, Mrs. Emma, allowance for supplies, 25.00; Lyon, J. D., galv'd iron,
glass, etc., 12.69 ....   37 69
McCorkindale, L., to pay charwomen, 282.50; washing towels, 13.23 ......   295 76
Melrose, Mrs. Ada, scrubbing and cleaning, 2.50; Meredith, Thos. & Co.,
pails, etc., 3.00 ....   5 50
Noble, Wm., services as night fireman, 600.00; National Oil Co., turpen-
tine, varnish, etc. 15.60, soap 28.20 ....   643 80
Nicholson, Mrs. E., scrubbing and cleaning, 2.50; Pethick, J., cleaning
windows, 7.00 ....   9 50
Simpson, Mrs. Bella, allowance for supplies, 25.00; sundry women, scrub-
bing and cleaning, 22.50 ....   47 50
Stirling, Mrs. A., scrubbing and cleaning, 9.50; Simpson, Robert Co.,
towelling, soap, etc., 25.87 ....   35 37
Stanley, Annie, scrubbing and cleaning, 10.50; Villiers, A., cleaning win-
dows, 8.00 ....   18 50
Williamson, T., allowance for supplies, 25.00; Whale, Albert, cleaning
carpets, etc., 41.15 ....   66 15

Expenses of grounds ($1,793.07).

Arnott Chemical Co., horticulture manure, 27.00; Apted, S., work on
grounds at 1.50 per day, 86 00 ....   113 00
Chapman, Geo., wages, 19.50; City Treasurer, garbage tickets, 45.00...   64 50
Cotterell, Jno., plants, etc., 306.45; Feigehen, Jas., manure, 2.75 ....   309 20
Fogarty, P., plants, 4.50; Godden, C. P., snow shovels, etc., 6.00 ....   10 50
Lepper, A., work on grounds at 1.50 per day 198 00

EDUCATION.—*Continued.*

MAINTENANCE EDUCATIONAL BUILDINGS.—*Continued.*

Expenses of grounds.—Continued.

McDonald, C. D., trees, 17.00; Marchmont, S. W., manure, 1.50............	18 50
Moore, J. O. L., work on grounds at 1.50 per day, 397.50; Meredith, Thos. & Co., garden tools, etc., 4.65	402 15
Pay lists—wages men employed on grounds, 144.00; Pearsall, Geo., repairing mower, etc., 26.00	170 00
Rowley, Mrs., T. L., plants, 10.00; Simmers, J. A., seeds, etc., 11.47...	21 47
Secombe, J., sod, 3.50; Walton, Geo., work on grounds, 397.50	401 00
White, Geo., plants, loam, etc...	84 75

Fuel, light and water ($3,232.99).

Burns, P. & Co., 20.1040 tons soft coal at 4.10 per ton	84 13
Consumers' Gas Co., gas, 100.48; Godden, C. P., coal oil and candles, 1.65.	102 13
Hammill, J. H. & Co., 7 cords of edgings at 4.00 per cord	28 00
Knickerbocker Ice Co., Ice	6 00
McGill, Wm., & Co., 6.1075 tons stove coal at 6.00 per ton, 39.23; extra for bagging, .56; 7,1009 tons nut coal at 6.00 per ton, 45.00; extra for bagging, .63; 320.1725 tons egg coal at 6.00 per ton, 1,883.85; 12.0125 tons grate coal at 5.80 per ton, 65.86; 2.1650 tons soft coal at 6.50 per ton, 18.37	2,053 50
Newspapers, sundry advertising *re* fuel, 9.15; Toronto Electric Light Co., light, 641.05	650 20
Water Works Dept., water	309 03

Repairs, etc., including carpentry work ($2,852.84).

Ashall, Wm., care of clocks, 60.93; Apted, S., services, at 2.00 per day, 10.00	70 93
Armstrong, Fred, packing, bolts, etc., 55.52; Clappison Packing and Covering Co., covering boilers, 18.00	73 52
Eaton, T., Co., repairing flag, etc., 1.75; Fiddes, Hogarth & Co., putting in sink, etc., 29.45	31 20
Frame, J. A., repairing electric bells, etc., 94.45; Gourlay, Winter and Leeming, tuning pianos, 5.00	99 45
Gander, Thos. & Son, plastering, etc., 4.70; Godden, C. P., boiler compound, 45.84	50 54
Hutchinson, M., lumber, 31.04; Hamblin, Wm., cement, sand, etc., 10.00.	41 04
Kent, A. & Sons, repairing and regulating clocks, 60.00; Lyon, Jas. D., galv'd. iron work, etc., 84.97	144 97
McCorkindale, L., services as caretaker at evening entertainments............	24 00
Morrison, Jas., Brass Mfg. Co., repairing closet levers, 15.05; Meredith. Thos. & Co., hardware, 54.67	69 72
National Oil Co., turpentine, oil, boiler compound, etc., 103.99; Otis-Fensom Elevator Co., repairing ash lifts, 6.40	110 39
Ontario Lead and Wire Co., chain stays, plugs, etc., 14.85; W. J. McCleary, twelve months' salary as carpenter, 650.00	664 85
Pay lists:—wages, men, 618.37; Pearsall, Geo., sharpening saws, tools, etc., .1.80	620 17
Roberts, E. H. repairing locks, etc., 8.85; Rice Lewis & Son, hardware, and etc., 2.58	11 43
Reid & Co., lumber, 106.95; Robertson, Jas., Co., repairing ball cocks, .25	107 20
Stewart, Jno., painting, graining, etc., 543.48, contract painting Drill Hall floor, 122.43	665 91
Smith, C. T., decorating hall, 28.50; Smith & Frame, repairing bells, etc., 34.45	62 95
Simpson, R., Co., repairing blind, .80; Worrell & Keates, putting light in boiler room, 3.77	4 57

Fire appliances ($143.00).

Alert Fire Appliance Co., 13 fire extinguishers, at 11.00	143 00

Painting fences ($400.00).

Stewart, Jno., painting, scraping and cleaning fences	400 00

EDUCATION.—*Continued.*

MISCELLANEOUS ($10,458.71).

Angus, Geo., services as reporter, Strathroy investigation	273 75
Baird, Jas., services and expenses as Commissioner, do	517 10
Brown, Katie E., travelling expenses witness, do	14 40
Bain & Bicknell, legal services, do	443 98
Bell, J. J., services and expenses as examiner, do	38 45
Crawford, H. J., services examining papers, and giving expert testimony, Strathroy investigation	15 00
Dominion Express Co., charges	1 35
Free Text Books, Treasurer, Co.: Huron, 5.87; Lanark, 14.15; Middlesex, 14.69; Wentworth, 12.62, Perth, 1.34	48 67
Harcourt, E. H. & Co., etching and stereo	5 56
Kingston, W. H., legal services, re S. S., 12 and 13 Minto and U. S. S. 17	119 00
King's Printer, stationery and paper	554 74
Jackson, W. S., services, examining papers and giving expert testimony, Strathroy investigation	15 00
McMaster, M., postage stamps	25 00
Milner, W. S., services examining papers, and giving expert testimony, Strathroy investigaton	15 00
Neville, R. S., legal services, revision and consolidation Public and High School Acts	1,500 00
Robertson, J. C., services examining papers, and giving expert testimony, Strathroy investigation	75 00
Ross, N. W., copying re Documentary History, 1.13; Riordon Paper Mills, paper, 727.41	728 54
Seath, Jno., special services preparing supplementary catalogue of reference books for High School libraries and teachers	875 00
Spotton, A., services and expenses re S. S. 12 and 13 Minto	20 00
Warwick Bros. & Rutter, P. S. registers, printing, binding, etc.	5,173 17

ELECTION EXPENSES ADVISORY COUNCIL ($1,240.09).

Brandon & Gilbert, cartage, .50; Church, Thos. L., services as scrutineer, 150.00	150 50
Farmer Bros., photos, 10.00; Greene, T. J., services as scrutineer, 100.00	110 00
Hales, Jas., services as scrutineer, 150.00; Ker, Allan, services as asst. 100.00	250 00
McMaster, M., postage stamps, 200.00; Newspapers, advertising, 255.39	455 39
Nudel, F. N., services as registrar, 200.00; Warwick Bros. & Rutter, printing and binding, 74.20	274 20

INSTITUTION FOR THE DEAF AND DUMB, BELLEVILLE.

SALARIES ($25,783.01).

R. Mathison: Eleven months' salary as Superintendent				2,187 00
C. B. Coughlin: One and one-half do	do			250 50
P. D. Goldsmith, M.D.: Nine	do	Physician		450 00
W. W. Boyce, M.D.: Three	do	do		150 00
W. Cochrane:	Twelve	do	Bursar	1,000 00
M. Ross		do	Matron and Housekeeper	500 00
D. R. Coleman:		do	Teacher	1,200 00
Paul Denys:		do	do	1,000 00
J. C. Baylis:		do	do	1,000 00
G. F. Stewart:		do	do	1,000 00
W. J. Campbell:		do	do	1,000 00
H. L. Ingram:		do	do	750 00
Effie Terrill:		do	do	650 00
Sarah Templeton:		do	do	700 00
F. Croes:		do	do	600 00
Thos. C. Forrester:	Eight	do	Instructor Manual Training and Teacher	433 00
Mary Bull:	Twelve	do	Teacher	350 00
Sylvia L. Balis:		do	do	650 00
Georgina Linn:		do	do	450 00

EDUCATION.—*Continued.*

INSTITUTION FOR THE DEAF AND DUMB, BELLEVILLE.—*Continued.*

SALARIES.—*Continued.*

Ada James : Eleven months' salary as Teacher				300 00
Agnes A. Gibson :		do	do	425 00
Annetta Johnston :	Three	do	Teacher and Monitor	51 00
H. M. Gowsall :	Twelve	do	Teacher Domestic Science	400 00
A. G. Chisholm :		do	Stenographer and Clerk	400 00
Wm. Nurse :		do	Storekeeper and Asst. Supervisor	600 00
W. S. Minns :		do	Supervisor of Boys	450 00
M. Dempsey :		do	Seamstress and Girls' Supervisor	350 00
F. M. Bates :		do	Trained Nurse	400 00
Jno. Dawrie :		do	Carpenter	550 00
Wm. Langmuir :		do	Asst. Carpenter	250 00
A. Morrice :		do	Shoemaker	500 00
J. T. Burns :		do	Printing Instructor	550 00
C. J. Peppin :		do	Engineer	650 00
D. Cunningham :		do	Baker	450 00
James Forge :		do	Farmer and Gardener	425 00
Henry McIllhaw	Ten	do	Stoker and Night Watchman	320 00
Wm. Wilkins :	Two	do	do	64 00
C. Lloyd :	Twelve	do	do	384 00
J. Juby :		do	Teamster	288 00
P. Shane :	Ten	do	Sewage man	304 00
H. Jackson :	Two	do	do	50 00
S. Richett :	Twelve	do	Messenger	264 00
Cooks (2)		do		370 00
Maids (10)		do		1,401 25
Laundresses (3)		do		566 81
Nurse Maids (2)		do		345 00
Helen B. Palen : Thirty-four days		do	Temporary Stenographer	34 00
H. Jackson : Five months ten days		do	do Laborer	127 75
Lena Mallory : Three weeks		do	do Stenographer	15 00
Sarah Sheridan : Thirty-nine days		do	do Trained Nurse	92 80
Jennie McShea : Thirty-two days		do	do do	71 40
Edna Johnson :				
Nine and one-quarter days		do	do do	18 50

EXPENSES ($23,197.09).

Advocate, The, advertising, 9.00 ; American Ass'n to promote speech to Deaf, annual dues, 2.00	11 00
Allen, Norman, coal, 943.1180 tons at 5.39 ; 139.10 tons at 5.65 ; 15 tons at 6.00	5,904 82
American Annals of the Deaf. subscription, 30 copies, 60.00 ; Arnott, A. B., berries, 464 qts. at .08, 37.12	97 12
Armstrong, Fred, lamps, 3 only at 3.75, 1 only at 6.00, 17.25 ; Asselstine, A., use of van, 2.50	19 75
Atteaux Dyeing & Finishing Co., ammonia powder, 200 lbs. at 4½	9 00
Bates. F. E., travelling expenses, 3.95 ; Bell Telephone Co., messages, 15.20, repairs. 39.90 ; exchange service, 114.00, 169.10	173 05
Belleville Canning Co., canned vegetables, 4 doz. at .70, 10 doz. at .77, 110 doz. at .85, 50 doz. at 1.05. 16 doz. at 1.15 ; can fruit, 20 doz. at 1.50, 26 doz. at 2.00, 10 doz. at 2.50, less discount, 4.22	277 68
Belleville Cemetery Co., care of lot, .50 ; Belleville Water Works, water rates, 900.00	900 50
Belleville Gas Works. gas, 88.16 ; Belleville Pottery Co., earthen pots. 2 doz. at 2.00. 4.00	92 16
Bishop, C. E., seeds. 44.48 : Balis, S. C., travelling expenses. 11.00	55 48
Black. Wm. & Son, fish. 90 lbs. at .07, 186 lbs. at .08. 1,145½ lbs. at .11, 18¾ lbs. at 12 ; ham, 126 lbs. at .14, 62¼ lbs. at .15 ; bacon. 159¼ lbs. at .14, 10½ lbs. at .15, 73¼ lbs. at .16 ; lard, 40 lbs. at .11½, 200 lbs. at .12 ; sundries, .36	211 05
Blackburn, T., repairs to clock, 1.50 ; Boyd, Jas., milk. 9.225 quts. at 3½, 4.960 qts. at .04, 521.28	522 78

EDUCATION.—*Continued.*

INSTITUTION FOR THE DEAF AND DUMB, BELLEVILLE.—*Continued.*

Expenses.—*Continued.*

Boyle, Geo., rolled oats, 3 bbls. at 5.50; mop sticks, 1 doz. at 1.50; oranges, 30 doz. at 30c., 5½ doz. at 40c., 1 crate at 11.75; gold dust meal, 100 lbs. at 2.25 cwt.; flour, 525 lbs. at 2.50 cwt., 100 lbs. at 3.00 cwt.; figs, 60 lbs. at 5c.; almonds, 20 lbs. at 17c., 25 lbs. at 18c; walnuts, 45 lbs. at 18c; salmon, 20 doz. at 1.70, 12 doz. at 1.75, 72 doz. at 1.80; fish, 20 lbs. at 9c.; sugar, 4,500 lbs. at 4.40 cwt.; cheese, 87 lbs. at 14½c.; salt, 1 bbl. at 1.65; soap, 7 boxes at 4.00; evaporated peaches, 32 lbs. at 14c.; prunes, 75 lbs. at 5c., 30 lbs. at 11½c.; raisins, 56 lbs. at 5½c., 54½ lbs. at 7c., 2 boxes at 3.40, 3 boxes at 3.75; apricots, 9 lbs. 15c.; peanuts. 25 lbs. at 16c., 25 lbs. at 17c.; cocoa, 6 lbs. at 45c.; currants, 72 lbs. at 8c.; canned vegetables, 6 doz. at 85c., 6 doz. at 90c., 6 doz. at 1.10; candies, 60 lbs. at 9c.; sundries, 13.31 .... 595 48
Brandon & Gilbert, cartage, 50c.; Briggs, Wm., books, 67.26 .... 67 76
Brown, T. P., wall paper, 22 rolls at 50c.; border, 85 yds. at 10c., 28 yds. at 15c.; shades, 12 only at 65c., 2 only at 85c., 2 only at 1.75, 5 only at 1.25; holland, 61 yds. at 27½c.; carpet, 18 1-3 yds. at 1.35; tops, 2 only at 35c., 2 only at 50c.; sundries, 60c. 86 78
Burns, J. T., travelling expenses, 9.40; Bursar, to pay sundries, 1.57; travelling expenses, 6.25, 7.82 .... 17 22
Campbell, W. J., travelling expenses, 28.58; C.P.R. Tel. Co., messages, 14.64 .... 43 22
Canadian Mute Acct., postage stamps, 8.10; Canadian Express Co., charges, 15.55 .... 23 65
Canadian Weaving Co., wipers, 1 gro. at 10.50; Canning & Zufelt, horse-shoeing, 56.45; repairs, 40c., 56.85 .... 67 35
Canniff, P. F., repairs to typewriter, 3.32; Carman, T. S., advertising, 3.30 .... 6 62
Carter, W. J., double sockets, 2 only at 1.00; wire, 200 ft. at 1½c.; sundries, 1.43 .... 5 93
Casey, P. J., hay, 1.800 ton at 8.00, 11.20; Central Prison Industries, bed castors, 25 sets at 25c., 6.25 .... 17 45
Chisholm, C. F., honey, 510 lbs. at 8c., 40.80; Clark, Wm., meat contract, 2,476 lbs. at 5.70 cwt., 35,090 lbs. at 6.20; pork, 110 at 10c., 210 lbs. at 12c.; sausage, 490 lbs. at 9c., 70 lbs. at 10c.; spare ribs, 10 lbs. at 7c., 2,404.69 .... 2,445 49
Clarke, F. C., gasoline, 4 gals. at 25c.; coal oil, 20 gals. at 23c.; turpentine, 5 gals. at 1.20; paint, oils, etc., 25.30; vanilla, 2 qts. at 2.00; fly paper, 3 boxes at 50c.; aluminum, 6 pts. at 50c.; floor wax, 6 tins at 50c.; soap, 400 lbs. at 7c., 4 doz. at 1.50, 1 doz. at 50c.; sponges, 6 only at 20c., 6 only at 22½c.; glue, 10 lbs. at 25c.; putty, 102 lbs. at 3c.; yankee cleaner, 6 tins at 25c.; drugs, chemicals, etc., 24.15; sundries, 14.00 ... 130 66
Cochrane, W., travelling expenses, 1.25; Coleman, D. R., trav. expenses... 22 75
Collip, J. D., potatoes, 189 11-90 bags at 1.00, 4 20-90 bags at 1.25; cabbage, 200 only at 4c.; celery, 300 only at 2c.; holly, 1.00 .... 208 75
Common Sense Mfg. Co., roach exterminator, 6 tins at 1.00, 6.00; Connecti-cut Magazine Co., booklet, 14.00 .... 20 00
Convention American Instructors of Deaf, annual subscription 1 00
Cook, D. C. Pub. Co., Sunday School magazines, 28.75; Cornelius, Jno., painting signs, 3.00 .... 31 75
Coulson, Jas., tar felt, 43 lbs. at 2½c., 1.08; Cronk, Ida, stabling privileges, 6 months, 7.50 .... 8 58
Crown Oil Refining Co., metal polish, 1 gal. at 2.00; Cummins, Jas., repairs to harness, etc., 24.75 .... 26 75
Cummins, M., painting motto for chapel, 45.00; Custom House, duty on buttons, 2.45 .... 47 45
Davies, Wm. Co., Ltd., pickled pork, 270 lbs. at 10c., 290 lbs. at 11c., 58.90; Dempsey, M., travelling expenses, 10.40 .... 69 30
Denys, P., travelling expenses, 18.40; Dolan, F., removing sidewalk, 15.00 .. 33 40
Dominion Express Co., charges, 6.92; Doyle, J. V., drugs, chemicals, etc., 5.25 .... 12 17
Duckworth & Brough, repairs to vehicles, etc. 68 45
Eaton, T. Co., Ltd., curtain stretcher, 1 only at 2.00; Emmerson, T., services cutting corn, 4.00 .... 6 00
Fairbairn, F. E., anti-friction oil, 55 gals. at 60c.; cylinder oil, 54 gals. at 85c. 78 90

EDUCATION.—*Continued.*

INSTITUTION FOR THE DEAF AND DUMB, BELLEVILLE.—*Continued.*

EXPENSES.—*Continued.*

Feeney, P., services cutting grain, 16.00; Forge, Geo., seed potatoes, 15 bags at 1.00; seeds, 1.60, 16.60 ....   32 60

Foster, Chas., ice 95 00

Geen, A. L., drugs, chemicals, etc., 79.68; sundries, 3.25, 82.93; Grafton, T. E. & Sons, books, 22.40 ....   105 33

Graham, R. J., evaporated apples, 100 lbs. at 10c., 50 lbs. at 11c.; dried apples, 75 lbs. at 7c.; maple syrup, 40 gals. at 1.00; maple sugar, 70 lbs. at 12c., 69.15; Graham, A., livery hire, 50c. 69 65

Grand Trunk Ry., freight, 2.39; G.N.W. Tel. Co., messages, 1.36 ....   3 75

Greenleaf & Son, keys, 4 doz. at 50c.; wire, 4 lbs. at 30c.; sundries, 2.85...   6 05

Gunn, Donald, 3.1600 tons at 9.00, 34.20; Gillette, E. W. Co., Ltd., perfumed lye, 6 cases for 19.38 ....   53 58

Hall, W. A., potatoes, 5 25-90 bags at 1.25, 6.60; Hall, P., report books, 2 only at 2.00, 4.00 ....   10 60

Hamm & Fairfield, bran, 1.500 tons at 20.00, 1 ton at 20.00, 1,300 lbs. at 22.00 ton; chop feed, ½ ton at 26.00; onions, 5 bags at 1.15. 10 bus. at 42c.; linseed, 4 lbs. at 5c. 83 45

Hamilton Engine Packing Co., indrubestos, 4 lbs. at 1.25; spiral packing, 1 lb. at 1.57 ....   6 57

Harker & Pearson, fish, 60 lbs. at 8c., 7 lbs. at 10c., 2 doz. at 35c., 2 doz. at 40c.; rolled oats, 1 bag at 2.75, 2 bags at 2.50; tea, 5 lbs. at 28c.; gelatine, 1 doz. at 1.50; figs, 66 lbs. at 5½c.; cheese, 176 lbs. at 15c.; oranges, 4 doz. at 40c.; raisins, 56 lbs. at 9c.; pepper, 38 lbs. at 35c.; oysters, 5 qts. at 50c.; flour, 400 lbs. at 3.00 cwt., 200 lbs. at 2.75 cwt.; prunes, 100 lbs. at 11c.; sapolio, 3 doz. at 1.00; soap, 17 boxes at 4.00, 2 boxes at 4.30; sugar, 100 lbs. at 4.20 cwt.; salt, 1 bbl. at 3.50; lemons, 3½ doz. at 30c.; fruit, sundries, etc., 45.37 ....   232 35

Hartz., J. F. Co., Ltd., medical appliances, 29.22; Hodge, Jas., repairs to pump, 11.00 ....   40 22

Holton, C. P., sawdust, 2.00; Hunt Bros., flour contract, 215 bbls. at 3.80, 817.00 ....   819 00

Hudson Hardware Co., thermometer, 1 only at 1.25; washing machine, 1 only at 5.00; clothes wringer, 1 only at 3.00; harness dressing, 6 bottles at 25c.; latch, 1 only at 2.00; spikes, 100 lbs. at 2½c.; scoops, 1 only at 1.10, 3 only at 1.00; axes, 3 only at 1.00, 1 only at 1.25; axe handles, 1 only at 30c., 3 only at 35c., 6 only at 40c.; rakes, 2 only at 65c.; paints, oils, etc., 7.15; glue, 15 lbs. at 25c.; rugs, 2 only at 2.00; whips, 1 only at 1.50, 1 only at 1.75; screwdrivers, 2 only at 2.00; spoons, 2 doz. at 3.00; locks, 1 only at 1.00, 1 doz. at 1.20, 1½ doz. at 2.40, 2 only at 2.25; cotton hose, 150 ft. for 22.50; screen cloth, 5 yds. at 20c.; man-jack, 1½ doz. at 3.00; glass, 1 case at 6.22, 1 case at 6.44, 1 case at 8.00, 1 case at 6.00, 1 case at 6.38, 4 cases at 5.35, 4 cases at 5.85; japan, 1 gal. at 1.00; binder twine, 50 lbs. at 13c.; cleaner, 3 tins at 50c.; belt laces, 3 lbs. at 90c.; rope, 20 lbs. at 17c., 52¼ lbs. at 15c., 25¼ ft. for 3.83; bolts, 24 only at 6c.; hoes, 2 only at 45c.; putty, 210 lbs. at 4c.; sash cord, 10 lbs. at 40c.; knives, 6 doz. at 1.50; carvers, 12 prs. at 1.75; keys, 4 doz. at 65c., 2 doz. at 1.00, 2 doz. at 1.75; paris green, 5 lbs. at 25c.; tacks, 10 lbs. at 10c., 10 lbs. at 15c.; forks, 2 only at 50c., 1 only at 55c.; files, ½ doz. at 2.20; nails, 1 keg at 2.50; shovels, ½ doz. at 9.00; glass cutter, 1 only at 4.25; door mats, 3 only at 2.00; iron hardware, etc., 52.63 ....   328 83

Intelligencer, The, subscription, 1 year, 3.00; advertising, 22.70; paper tubes, 50 only at 7c., 25 only at 5c. 30 45

Jeffery, F., threshing oats, 541 tons at .02; use of engine and help cutting corn, 8.00 ....   18 82

Johnston, W., inspecting scales 3 00

Kenny, Walmsley & Co., pails, 1 doz. at 2.40; sugar, 1 bag at 3.93, 20 bags at 4.05, 30 bags at 4.13, 10 bags at 4.25, 25 bags at 4.33; vinegar, 60 gals. at 20c., 30 gals. at 25c.; salt, 1 bbl. at 3.00; rice, 224 lbs. at 5½c.; brooms, 28 doz. at 2.55; Gilletts lye, 6 cases at 3.60; starch, 100 lbs. at 5½c., 100 lbs. at 7c.; paper bags, 500 only for 1.35; raisins, 56 lbs. at 7c. ...   507 32

King's Printer, paper, 5.13; stationery, 231.60 ....   236 73

Lafferty, Jno., livery hire, 2.00; Lambert, W., livery hire, 2.25 ....   4 25

EDUCATION.—*Continued.*

INSTITUTION FOR THE DEAF AND DUMB, BELLEVILLE.—*Continued.*

EXPENSES.—*Continued.*

Laidlaw & Ketcheson, tape, 48 pcs. at 5c., 1 doz. yds. at 84., 7 doz. yds. at 60c.; sheeting. 512½ yds. at 40c.; serge, 5 yds. at 50c.; thread, 6 gro. at 5.35 elastic, 4 doz. yds. at 1.20; 3 doz. yds. at 50c.; table linen, 9 yds. at 1.25; buttons, 1 gro. at 30c., 1⅓ gro. at 1.25, 1 gro. at 1.50, 1½ gro. at 1.75, 1 gro. at 1.80; needles, 22 pkgs. at 5c., 3 pkgs. at 20c.; muslin, 12 yds. at 25c., 10 yds. at 30c.; table napkins, 1 doz. at 3.25, 1 doz. at 3.50; sundries, 6.49 .... 129 24

Lewis, Jno. & Co., solder, 5 lbs. at 25c.; pans, 6 only for 3.40; repairs to tinware, etc., 17.70; putz cream, 1 qt. at 1.00; lantern, 1 only at 1.40; Jenkins' discs, 24 only at 7c., 24 only at 8c.; soil pipe, 1 only at 1.00; valves, 2 only at 75c.; water cans, 6 only for 5.50; dust pans, 6 only for 3.50; sauce pans, 1 only at 4.00; dish pans, 1 only at 1.35; oil cans, 2 only at 1.50; copper starch kettle, 1 only at 55.00; castings, 46⅓ lbs. for 3.72; iron sink, 1 only at 4.75; basin cocks, 2 only at 1.75; lead trap, 1 only at 1.50; closet spud, 1 only at 1.00; lead bend, 1 only at 1.00; granite boiler, 1 only at 1.00; tea pots, 2 only at 1.85; roasting pans. 6 only for 4.95; water coolers, 3 only at 4.50; butcher steels, 2 only at 1.50; radiator wrenches, 5 only at 40c.; iron hardware, etc., 22.97 ...... 169 79

Lockwood, S. A., potato digger, 1 only at 13.00; London, J. W., stationery, 259.09; subscriptions to *Globe* and *Mail*, 8.00, 267.09 .... 280 09

Madoc *Review*, advertising, 1.00; Manley, Thos., repairs, mason work and plastering, 10.25 .... 11 25

Marmora *Herald*. advertising, 1.00; Marshall, O. A., dental services, 45.00 46 00

Massey, Harris Co., repairs to implements, 3.90; Mathison, R., travelling expenses 66 65

Meincke, C. A. & Co., duck. 29 yds. at 85c., 24.65; Meyer Bros., repairs to laundry machinery, 17.60 .... 42 25

Medcalf, D. M., travelling expenses, 35.35; Moon, Chas., wheelbarrow, 1 only at 5.00 .... 40 35

Morang & Co., books, 35.00 .... 35 00

McCoy. Robt., livery hire, 23.00; McCormick, R., photographs. 35.70 ...... 58 70

McCrodan, A. J., prunes, 200 lbs. at 8c., 125 lbs. at 9½c., 75 lbs. at 10c., 50 lbs. at 11c., 25 lbs. at 12c.; oranges. 3½ doz. at 30c., 7¼ doz. at 40c.; flour. 600 lbs. at 2.50 cwt., 300 lbs. at 2.60 cwt., 1,300 lbs. at 3.00 cwt.; figs, 65 lbs. at 6c., 31 lbs. at 6¼c., 62 lbs. at 6¼c.. 6 lbs. at 20c.; ammonia, 1 case at 3.25; raisins, 84 lbs. at 7c.; sardines. 3 doz. tins at 1.75; cheese, 90 lbs. at 14½. 254 lbs. at 15c.; mops, 1 doz. at 1.50; baking powder, 18 lbs. at 45c.; currants, 80 lbs. at 7c., 150 lbs. at 8c.; almonds, 3 lbs. at 35c.: pickles, 15 bottles at 20c.. 2 doz. at 4.80, 1 doz. at 3.50; rolled oats. 50 lbs. at 3.10 cwt., 50 lbs. at 3.50 cwt., 1 bbl. at 5.50. 2 bbls. at 5.25; canned fish, 4 doz. at 1.75; Keen's blue, 12 lbs. at 20c.; barley, 50 lbs. at 4c.: cloves, 4 lbs. at 40c.; bath brick. 2 boxes at 1.00; shoe polish. 3 doz. at 1.08 1-3; soap, 12 boxes at 4.00. 1 box at 4.50. 3 boxes at 4.25, 1 pkg. at 65c., 5 doz. at 50c.; salt,. 2 bbls. at 1.50, 1 bbl. at 3.25, 1 bag at 85c.; cocoa, 48 lbs. at 45c., tapioca. 30 lbs. at 5c.. 25 lbs. at 10c.; corn starch, 40 lbs. at 7c., 160 lbs. at 8c.: brushes, 2 doz., 2.25; lard, 40 lbs. at 12c., 40 lbs. at 14c.; gelatine, 2 doz. at 1.50, 3 doz. at 1.75; walnuts, 3 lbs. at 35c.; chow chow, 15 btls. at 20c.: mustard, 6 lbs. at 45c.; cranberries, 55 lbs. at 12c.: berries, 8 boxes at 10c., 68 boxes at 12½c.; shredded wheat, 18 boxes at 12½c.; spice, 4 lbs. at 30c.; cinnamon, 3 lbs. at 40c.; pears, 1 bbl. at 3.00; sundries, 38.81 477 11

McFee, A., knives, 2 only at 62½c.. 1 doz. at 3.75. 1 doz. at 4.00: forks. 1 doz. at 4.00, 1 doz. at 4.25; spoons. 2 doz. at 3.25, 1 doz. at 4.75, ½ doz. at 6.00; alarm clock. 1 only at 1.50 .... 33 00

McGie, Wm.. repairs to boilers, 35.00; McInnich. H., repairs to implements, etc., 28.10 .... 63 10

McIntosh Bros.. object lessons. 1.20; McKeown, J. S., drugs, chemicals, etc., 99.63 .... 100 83

McKeown, Jno.. rubber boots, 1 pr. at 4.00, 1 pr. at 6.00, 10.00; McMurray, B.. repairs to telephones, 16.55 .... 26 55

Napanee *Beaver*. advertising. 1.00; Nasmith, The Co., pupils' lunches, 15.40; Naylor, F.. horseshoeing, 33.00 .... 49 40

EDUCATION.—*Continued.*

INSTITUTION FOR THE DEAF AND DUMB, BELLEVILLE.—*Continued.*

EXPENSES.—*Continued.*

Panter, Jno. & Son, flour, 300 lbs. at 2.40 cwt., 475 lbs. at 3.00 cwt.; ham, 43½ lbs. at 15c.; eggs, 150 doz. at 23c., 60 doz. at 24c., 95 doz. at 25c., 120 doz. at 26c., 90 doz. at 22c., 60 doz. at 21c., 125 doz. at 18c., 367 doz. at 16c., 315 doz. at 15c., 30 doz. at 15½c., 120 doz. at 17c., 10 doz. at 19c., 30 doz. at 20c.; beans, 3 50-60 bus. at 1.50, 2 bus. at 2.10, 50 lbs. at 3½c.; cheese, 83 lbs. at 13½c.; lard, 40 lbs. at 12c.; fowl, 1½ pr. at 1.00, 6 prs. at 88 1-3c., 3 prs. at 90c., 5 prs. at 95c., 3 prs. at 1.25, 3 prs. at 1.03 1-3, 2 prs. at 1.02½, 44 prs. at 65c., 6 prs. at 80c., 2 prs. at 85c., 2 prs. at 70c., 7 prs. at 75c., 1 pr. at 55c., 8½ lbs. at 10c., 37 5-8 lbs. at 11c., 63¾ lbs. at 12c., 18¾ lbs. at 12½c., 11½ lbs. at 18½c.; bacon, 9¾ lbs. at 15c.; rolled oats, 1 bbl. at 4.50, 3 bbls. at 4.75; sundries, 1.28	460 89
Paterson, D., elastic, 3 doz. yds. at 1.00, 20½ yds. at 12½c.; cotton, 50 yds. at 9c.; towels, 5 prs. at 50c.; canvas, 10 yds. at 10c.; broadcloth, 5 yds. at 50c.; dress goods, 7 yds. at 50c.; butter cloth, 25 yds. at 5c.; percaline, 25 yds. at 15c.; table oil, 8½ yds. at .25; cashmere, 6 yds. at 50c.; sateen, 10 yds. at 14c.; sundries, 6.92	38 01
Peck & Wills, lumber, 15.81; Pepper, Jno., repairs to flag pole, 3.00	18 81
Perry, Geo., rubber stamps, 1 only at 25c., 1 only at 85c., 1 only at 2.00	3 10
Postmaster, postage stamps and post cards, 154.60; rent of P.O. box, 4.00	158 60
Potter, Chas., rent of lantern slides, 1.53; Purdy, T. H., apples, 1 bbl. at 2.50	4 03
Reid, W. C., apples, 2 bbls. at 3.00, 2 bbls. at 3.50, 13.00; Reid, W .W., turkey, 277½ lbs. at 17c.; chickens, 6 prs. at 65, 51.08	64 08
Ritchie, The. Co., duck, 25 yds. at 25c.; mitts, 2 prs. at 50c.; muslin, 22 yds. at 25c.; chambray, 12 yds. at 15c.; dress goods, 6½ yds. at 50; linen, 267 yds. at 12½c., 88½ yds. at 15c., 30 yds. at 17c.; yarn, 7 lbs. at 1.50; hooks and eyes, 1 gro. at 6.00; towelling, 214½ yds. at 15c.; flannel, 2 yds. at 20c.; sateen, 25 yds. at 20c., 10 yds. at 21c.; gingham, 12 yds. at 15c., 11 yds. at 20c.; madras, 6½ yds. at 50c.; cotton, 50 yds. at 5c., 30 yds. 8c., 20 yds. at 12½c.; lining, 10 yds. at 25c., 50 yds. at 12½c.; sheeting, 5 yds. at 45c., 359½ yds. at 48c., 120½ yds. at 60c.; table linen, 208 yds. at 50c., 6 yds. at 75c.; suits, 2 only at 3.50; serge, 2 yds. at 75c.; canvas, 10 yds. at 15c.; cotton, 10 yds. at 10c., 25 yds. at 9c., 25 yds. at 5c.; pants, 2 prs. at 85c.; ticking, 30 yds. at 23c.; sundries, 3.95	531 75
Riggs, W. B., pupils entertainment, 6.30; Roblin, G. E., honey, 130 lbs., at 10c., 13.00	19 30
Ryrie Bros., medals, 3 only at 5.00	15 00
Sanford, N., cleaning flues, 12.00; Scanlon, M., stereoscopic views, 34.60; stereoscopes, 2 only at 90c., 36.40	48 40
Schuster, The Co., lumber, 11.70; Shane, Peter, services on sewage works, 16.00	27 70
Shoe Shop Acct., shoes, 1 pr. at 1.75, 7 prs. at 2.00, 1 pr. at 2.25, 1 pr. at 2.50, 7 prs. at 2.75; laces, 235 prs. at 4½c.; repairs to shoes, 43.95	94 28
Sills, S. G., apples, 1 bbl. at 2.50; Sills, G. L., clipping horses, 2.00; stabling privileges, 15.00; livery hire, 10.50, 27.50	30 00
Singer Sewing Machine Co., needles, 12 doz. at 20c., 2.40; Sloan, Jno. & Co., fish, 20 doz. at 1.57½; pails, ½ doz. at 1.85; mop sticks, 1 doz. at 1.25; tea, 208 lbs. at 16½c., 60 lbs. at 19c.; starch, 100 lbs. at 5½c.; jam, 360 lbs. at 6¾c.; syrup, 3.525 lbs. at 3c., 1,891 lbs. at 3¼c.; brooms, 12 doz. at 2.35; mustard, 24 doz. at 40c.; rice, 133¾ lbs. at 6 3-8c.; raisins, 112 lbs. at 10½c.; less barrels returned, 1.75, 332.75	335 15
Spankie, Wm., conducting examinations, 50.00; travelling expenses, 3.25	53 25
Sprague, Mark, butter contract, 611 lbs. at 23c., 7,534 lbs. at 25c.	2,036 53
Stewart, Geo. F., travelling expenses, 14.60; Sundry newspapers, advertising *re* fuel, 9.15	23 75
Sulman, C. N., plates, 20 doz. at 80c., 1 doz. at 1.50., 1 doz. at 1.20., 1½ doz. at 1.35, 1 doz. at 1.75; saucers, 20 doz. at 30c.; soup casserole and ladle, 1 only at 2.50; ewers, 9 only at 45c.; sauce dishes, 1½ doz. at 75c.; cups, 16 doz. at 60c., 5 doz. at 80c., 1½ doz. at 1.75, ½ doz. at 1.20, 11 doz. at 85c.; peppers and salts, 1 7-12 doz. at 1.00; vinegar bottles, 2 doz. at 3.60; scallops, 4 doz. at 2.50; basins, 9 only at 45c., ¼ gal measures, 4 doz. at 1.25; glass dishes, 2 only at 60c.; jars, 3 doz. at 1.25; pitchers,	

EDUCATION.—*Continued.*

INSTITUTION FOR THE DEAF AND DUMB, BELLEVILLE.—*Continued.*

EXPENSES.—*Continued.*

6 only at 40c.; baskets, 1 doz. at 8.00, 1 doz. at 9.60; brushes, 12 only at 65c., 6 only at 75c., 2 doz. at 1.20; polish, 2 doz. at 95c.; toilet paper, 2 cases at 8.25, 1 case at 8.50; paper, 8 rolls at 25c., 17 rolls at 40c.; moulding, 70 ft. at 5c.; door mats, 4 only at 5.00; soap, 2,408 lbs. at 5½c.; Jap napkins, 100 doz. for 3.70; bonami, 1 doz. at 1.40; linen floss, 6 doz. at 40c.; collars, 20 only at 10c., 20 only at 11¼c.; pins, 30 papers at 5c., 2 doz. at 55c., 2 doz. at 60c.; elastic, 2 doz. yds. at 85c.; combs, 2 doz. at 90c., 2 doz. at 1.40, 4 doz. at 1.50; laces, 1 gro. at 1.00, 4 gro. at 1.10, 2 gro. at 1.20; buttons, 1 grt. gro. at 45c., 1 grt. gro. at 1.00; sundries, 27.48 .... 386 06

Taylor, Clark, repairs to flag pole, 6.00; Thompson, D., yeast, 167 lbs. at 30, 50.10 .... 56 10

Thompson, N., cartage, 29.50; Tickell & Sons Co., repairs to furniture, 67.95 97 45

Toronto *World*, 200 copies at 5c., 10.00; Trenton *Advocate*, advertising, 1.00 11 00

Trenton Electric & Water Co., electric light 938 73

Walton, Geo. & Co., lumber, 62.62; cartage, 1.00, 63.62; Walker, The, Foundry, repairs to implements, 40.97 .... 104 59

Wallace, Jas. & Co., grapes, 16 bas. at 30c., 35 bas. at 35c., 31 bas. at 40c.; oranges, 4½ doz. at 40c.; lemons, 8¼ doz. at 20c., 3 doz. at 25c., 2 doz. at 30c.; currants, 5 bas. at 1.25; peaches, 1 bas. at 40c., 2 bas. at 60c., 1 bas. at 80c., 26 bas. at 85c., 3 bas. at 1.00; plums, 12 bas. at 1.00; bannanas, 25 doz. at 20c., 2 doz. at 30c., 2 doz. at 25c.; pine apples, 26½ doz. at 1.50, 1 only at 20c., 2 only at 25c.; berries, 452 boxes at 10c., 122 boxes at 12½c.; bread, 84 loaves at 10c.; sundries, 12.55 .... 171 50

Wallbridge & Clarke, biscuits, 24 tins at 30c., 18 lbs. at 20c., 825¾ lbs. at 14c., 18 tins at 25c., 564 lbs. at 8c., 16¾ lbs. at 18c., 2 lbs. at 12½c.; cocoa, 24 lbs. at 45c.; prunes, 50 lbs. at 7¼c., 10 lbs. at 12c.; figs, 65¼ lbs. at 5c., 31 lbs. at 5¾c., 4 lbs. at 12½c., 6 lbs. at 20c., 2 lbs. at 25c.; dates, 13 lbs. at 15c.; baking powder, 9 doz. at 4.80, 1 doz. at 5.40; herring, 1 keg at 1.35; sardines, 6 tins at 45c., 2 doz. tins at 2.25; candies, 55 lbs. at 9c.; oranges, 29 doz. at 25c., 6 doz. at 30c., 9 doz. at 35c., 18 doz. at 40c.; oysters, 16 qts. at 50c.; cheese, 83 lbs. at 14½c.; soap, 2 doz. at 40c., 1 doz. at 1.50, 5 cases at 4.00, 1 case at 4.25; chocolate, 6 lbs. at 45c.; coffee, 360 lbs. at 25c.; ox tongues, 2 tins at 75c.; ham, 11 7-8 lbs. at 16c.; gelatine, 1 doz. at 1.50; tea, 80 lbs. at 25c., 140 lbs. at 39c.; shoe polish, 5 doz. at 90c., 1 doz. at 95c.; cherries, 6 bas. at 1.50; sapolio, 3 doz. at 1.50; sundries, 33.77 .... 556 43

Warwick Bros. & Rutter, printing, etc., 35.05; Waters, D. M., drugs, chemicals, etc., 100.79 .... 135 84

Whitehead & Hoag Co., buttons, 7.00 .... 7 00

REPAIRS TO BUILDINGS, FURNITURE, ETC

Adjustable Desks ($240.50).

Canada Office School Furniture Co., desks 240 50

Cement floor, metal ceilings, etc. ($289.77).

Alford, W., cement floor, boys' playroom, 166.00; new floor, engineer's room, 42.12; new frame and lintel, cellar door, 11.65 .... 219 77

Lewis, Jno. & Co., metal ceiling, boys' playroom 70 00

Furniture and furnishings ($397.25).

Brown, T. P., linoleum, 12.67; Johnson, T. J., carpet and making, 146.60... 159 27

Laidlaw & Ketcheson, rug, 25.00; Lewis, Jno. & Co., hot water boiler, range, etc., 180.00 .... 205 00

Ritchie & Co., rug and paper 32 98

EDUCATION.—*Continued.*

INSTITUTION FOR THE DEAF AND DUMB, BELLEVILLE.—*Continued.*

EXPENSES.—*Continued.*

Metal sheeting for school rooms ($906.88).

Cummins, M., painting and decorating ceilings	95 38
Lewis, Jno., metal ceilings as per contract	747 00
do do old Hospital room	64 50

Maple floors in girls' sitting room, etc. ($345.00).

Crowe, Geo. & Sons, hardwood floors and laying	245 00
Gill and Fortune, lumber	100 00

Lumber for boys to make table scats, etc. ($322.50).

Gill and Fortune, lumber	322 50

Chapel repairs, metal sheeting, etc. ($450.00).

Cummins, M., painting and decorating, 50.00; Lewis, Jno. & Co., metal ceilings, 400.00	450 00

Lumber, hardware, plaster, oil, etc. ($348.23).

Green, A. L., White lead, 35.00; Lewis, Jno. & Co., closets, taps, valves, etc., 54.98	89 98
McIntosh, H., Window screens, etc., 28.50; McKeown, J., turpentine, etc., 9.15	37 65
McKeown, J. S., paints, oils, etc., 120.05; Waters, D. M., paint, varnish, etc., 100.55	220 60

Wages of extra carpenters, painters, etc. ($400.00).

Pay lists, wages carpenters, painters, etc.	400 00

INSTITUTION FOR THE BLIND, BRANTFORD.

SALARIES ($17,989.64).

H. F. Gardiner :	Twelve months' salary as	Principal	2,400 00
W. B. Wickens :	do	Assistant Principal	1,200 00
W. N. Hossie :	do	Bursar and Storekeeper	1,100 00
J. A. Marquis, M.D. :	do	Physician	500 00
A. M. Rice :	do	Matron	450 00
M. E. Walsh :	do	Teacher	500 00
C. Gillin :	do	do	500 00
Emma Moore :	do	do	500 00
E. Lee :	do	do	400 00
E. A. Harrington :	do	do	400 00
E. Loveys :	do	do	350 00
L. H. Haycock :	do	do	350 00
K. Burke : Nine	do	do	150 00
P. J. Roney : Twelve	do	do	500 00
E. A. Humphries :	do	do	800 00
T. S. Usher :	do	do	500 00
Geo. A. Ramsay :	do	Supervisor of Boys	400 00
M. J. Cronk : Nine	do	Visitors' Attendant	180 00
J. Kirk : Twelve	do	Nurse	290 00
M. Stewart :	do	do	260 00
Geo. G. Lambden :	do	Carpenter	548 00
Jas. B. Wilson :	do	Engineer	600 00
A. L. McIntyre :	do	Assistant Engineer	475 00
Chas. F. Lewis :	do	Fireman and Farmhand	375 00
David Willits :	do	Farmer and Gardener	500 00

7 PA.

EDUCATION.—*Continued.*

INSTITUTION FOR THE BLIND, BRANTFORD.—*Continued.*

SALARIES.—*Continued.*

P. Berney : Twelve months' salary as	Teamster		350 00
F. R. Osborne : Four	do	Messenger	86 00
Leslie Mnill : Eight	do	do	173 00
Geo. Grierson : Twelve	do	Baker	425 00
Cooks (3) :	do		345 29
Maids (10) :	do		1,173 40
Laundresses (3) :	do		488 65
Robt. Guillie :	do	Night Watchman	370 00
Jno. Daly :	do	Temporary Laborer	350 30

EXPENSES ($14,242.92).

Agnew, Jno., shoes, 1 pr. at 1.00, 4 pr. at 1.50, 2 pr. at 2.00; laces, 1 gro. at 1.00, ½ gro. at 1.20, ¼ gro. at 2.80; sundries, .50	14 50
American Felt Co., tuning hammers, 2 only, at 10.25, 1 only, at 8.25; nippers, 1 only, at 1.70; brace, 1 only, at 1.70; sundries, .36	32 51
American Express Co., charges, 19.61; Ashdown's Music Store, sheet music, 2.96	22 57
American Printing House for Blind, school books, 68.75; writing cards, 8.00; freight, .50	77 25
Ballantyne, R. G. & Son, painting, 31.60; kalsomining, 86.40; paints, oils, etc., 16.43; alabastine, 10.80; lettering six benches, 4.00	149 23
Bauslaugh, T., photos, 9.00; Beasley, T. S., drugs, chemicals, etc., 43.70; sundries, 13.38, 57.08	66 08
Bell, Dr. B. C., professional services, 69.00; examinations and report, 25.00	94 00
Bell Telephone Co., exchange service, 69.00; messages, 2.55, 71.55; Boucher, J. A., sheet music, 10.45	82 00
Bowers, F. J., milk, 165 qts, at .5, 8.25; Brant Ave. Methodist Church, pupils sittings, 48.00	56 25
Brant Milling Co., flour contract, 87 bbls. at 3.85, 334.95; Brantford Gas Co., gas, 76.51	411 46
Brantford Water Commission, rent of hydrants, 160.00; water supply, 277.75	437 75
Brantford Electric and Operating Co., light and power	595 42
Brantford Street Ry. Co., car tickets, 21.00; Brantford, City of, arc lamps, 227.60; sewer on St. Paul's Ave., 100 ft., at 79 1-10, 306.70	327 70
Britnell. A., books, 28.20; Brown, Edman, repairs to pianos and organ, 14.00	42 20
Burrill, W. B. & Co., bench castings, 60 only, at 1.50, 90.00; Bursar, to pay sundries, 4.48; railway fares for pupils, 37.65; travelling expenses, 3.10, 45.23	135 23
Buskard, Jno., repairs to typewriters	16 40
Calbeck & Barber, shoes, 4 pr. at .65, 6 pr. at .75, 7.10; C.P.R. Telegraph Co., messages, 1.00	8 10
Canadian Express Co., charges, 8.65; Casavant Bros., repairs to organ, 13.00	21 65
Caudwell Bros., wool, 1 lb. at 1.12; huckaback, 167½ yds. at .25; sheeting, 123 yds. at .35; tray cloths, 2 only, at 1.00; centre pieces, 2 only, at 1.00; blankets, 25 pr. at 4.00; towelling, 45 yds. at .15; buttons, 3 doz. at .5; pillow cotton, 54 yds. at .25; counterpanes, 6 only, at 2.50; oil cloth, 24 yds. at .25; napkins, 1 doz. at 3.50; crash, 100 yds at .25, 150 yds. at .18; damask, 15 yds. at .75; sundries, 8.15	306 29
Cockshutt, W. F. & Co., seeds, 37.26; Cockshutt Plow Co., repairs to implements, 1.70; Cole, S. R., making cider, 1.20	40 16
Corey, Fred., kippered herring, 1 doz. tins at 1.10; biscuit, 39 lbs. at .7; lard, 40 lbs. at .14; rice, 100 lbs. at .6; raisins, 28 lbs. at .7, 27 lbs. at .8; figs, 33 lbs. at .5; syrup, 2 gals. at .60; gelatine, 1 doz. at 1.80; soap, 170 lbs. at 5½; sugar, 100 lbs. at 4.10 cwt., 631 lbs. at 4.60 cwt.; bacon, 24 lbs. at .17; breakfast food, 1 doz. at 1.68; cheese, 8½ lbs. at .15, 8½ lbs. at .17; salmon, 4 doz. at 1.80; salt, 1 bbl. at 1.40; starch, 39 lbs. at .6; sundries, 3.23	89.28

7a F.A.

EDUCATION.—*Continued.*

INSTITUTION FOR THE BLIND, BRANTFORD.—*Continued.*

EXPENSES.—*Continued.*

Coulbeck, A., eggs, 15 doz. at .18, 10 doz. at .22, 28 doz. at .23, 34 doz. at .25; bread, 44 loaves at .5; lard, 80 lbs. at .13½; salt, 1 bbl. at 1.35; bacon, 10 lbs. at .19, 10 lbs. at .18; rice, 100 lbs. at .5½; biscuits, 30 lbs. at .7½; beans, 2 bush. at 2.90; soap, 60 lbs. at .4¾, 1 box at .4½; candy. 37 lbs. at .8; baskets, 3 only at .25, 2 only at .10; raisins, 25½ lbs. at .9½, 28 lbs. at .10½, 23 lbs. at .11½; tea, 15 lbs. at .45; sugar, 100 lbs. at 4.40, 661 lbs. at 4.65; cheese, 16 lbs. at .16; cream tartar, 5 lbs. at .30; starch, 50 lbs. at .9; cranberries, ½ bush. at 4.00; salmon, 1 doz. at 2.00; sundries, 17.74 .... 140 85
Cutcliffe, A. B., veterinary services 2 50
Darwen's Orchestra, music, 14.00; Dominion Express Co., charges, 2.05 .... 16 05
Ellis, W. Hodgson, analyzing flour 20 00
Darwen's Orchestra, music. 14.00; Dominion Express Co., charges, 2.05...... 16 05
motor, 1 only, at 102.00; men's time, 17 hours at .35; sundries, 2.69, 110.65 .... 111 90
Ferguson, Jno., travelling expenses, 1.50; First Baptist Church pupils' sittings, 10.00 .... 11 50
Forde, J. Co., yeast, 35½ lbs. at .30; currants. 40 lbs. at .8; cocoa, 1 doz. tins at 2.70; cann. vegetables, 2 doz. at 1.10; soap, 2 boxes at 2.85, 1 box at 4.25, 1.918 lbs. at .5½; cann. fruit, 1 doz. at 2.25; evaporated apples, 50 lbs. at .13, 100 lbs. at .14; cheese, 16 lbs. at .16; maple syrup, 5 gals. at 1.30; biscuit, 29 lbs. at .8; bacon, 18½ lbs. at .19; lard, 80 lbs. at 12½; eggs, 92 doz. at .18, 8 doz. at 15; brooms, 1 doz. at 3.60; soda, 280 lbs. at 2¾; sugar, 598 lbs. at 4.50 cwt., 100 lbs. at 4.10 cwt.; jam, 3 pails at .55; cann. fish, 1 doz. at 1.80; apricots, 25 lbs. at .16; rice, 100 lbs. at .6½; sundries, 8.34 .... 259 37
Foster, Jas., watchman's dials 7 50
Gardiner, H. F., travelling expenses, 27.05; books, 1.28, 28.33; Gardiner, M. E., travelling expenses, 5.30 .... 33 63
Gibbins, C., travelling expenses, 9.95; Ginn, A., plants, 15.15 .... 25 10
G.N.W. Telegraph Co., messages, 2.21; Grand Trunk Railway, freight, 13.50 .... 15 71
Grace Anglican Church, pupils' sittings, 56.00; Grafton & Co., clothing, 1 suit at 6.95; underwear, 2 suits, at .75, 8.51 .... 64.51
Grierson, G., eggs, 60 doz. at .27 .... 16 20
Harp, F. C., cann vegetables, 2 doz. at 1.15, 4 doz. at .95; orange meat, 1 doz. at 2.64; lard, 60 lbs. at .12; prunes, 25 lbs. at .8; salt, 1 bbl. at 1.40; sugar, 614 lbs. at 4.45 cwt., 100 lbs. at 4.20 cwt.; jam, 7 lbs. at .55; finnan haddie, 1 doz. tins at 1.10; cocoanut, 10 lbs. at .20; oil of lemon, ½ lb. at 2.00; gelatine, 1 doz. at 1.70; salmon, 1 doz. tins at 1.70, 1 doz. at 1.90; eggs, 30 doz. at .14, 30 doz. at .16½, 4 doz. at .17; starch. 50 lbs. at .8, 41 lbs. at .6; cheese, 16 lbs. at .16; bacon, 10¾ lbs. at .18; currants, 30 lbs. at 7½; biscuits, 27 lbs. at 7½; brooms, 1 doz. at 3.25; beans, 30 lbs. at .4; potatoes, 5 bags at 1.25; seeds, 1.10; sundries, 5.84 .... 104 62
Harrington, Edith A.. travelling expenses, 2.60; Haycock, L. H., travelling expenses, 15.50 .... 18 10
Hepburn, Alice, services polishing pupils' shoes, 2.00; Hext, Geo., repairs to vehicles. 9.35 .... 11 35
Howie & Fealey. wire cloth, 6 yds. at .20; repairs, 11.88; rope, 39 lbs. at .17; brush, 1 only, at 1.25; pans, 2 only, at 1.30; fire pots, 2 sets at 7.75; cement. 15 lbs. at .10; brass taps. 2 only, at .65; monkey wrench, 1 only, at .85; paris green, 10 lbs. at .17; steel drums, 2 only, at 1.12½; castings. 214 lbs. at .10; iron hardware, etc., 9.05 .... 77 12
Howey, J. R., 5 loads manure at .50, 2.50; Humphries, E. A., travelling expenses, 21.10 .... 23 60
Hunt & Colter, teaming 5 00
Jaffray Bros., advertising 7 20
Kelly, Wm., services, 17.06; King's Printer, stationery, 41.80 .... 58 86
Kinney, Jas., hay, 1 ton at 9.00; Kirk, Mrs. Jas., Christmas presents to pupils, 10.00; travelling expenses, 4.60, 14.60 .... 23 60

EDUCATION.—*Continued.*

INSTITUTION FOR THE BLIND, BRANTFORD.—*Continued.*

EXPENSES.—*Continued.*

Lambden, G. G., travelling expenses, 3.55; Lawton, C. W., advertising, 7.50	11 05
Lee, E., travelling expenses, 10.85; Lyons Electric Co., auer lights, 8 only, at .75; key sockets, 3 only, at .25; electrical repairs, 5.38; sundries, 5.75, 17.88	28 73
Malcolm, J. & Son, butter contract, 4,370 lbs. at .24, 1,048.80; Mann, Jno. & Sons, wood, 1½ cords at 7.50; repairs, 5.37, 16.62	1,065 42
Massey, Harris Co., Ltd., repairs to implements, 1.26; Medcalf, D. M., trav. expenses, 3.55; Miller & Millan, wood, 1½ cords at 7.50, 11.25	16 06
Minnes, T. J. & Co., plumbing repairs, 3.63; Minnes, W. J., horse-shoeing, 44.28; general repairs, 10.00, 54.28	57 91
Mintern, M., meat contract, 15,880 lbs. at .8, 762 lbs. at 6.40 cwt.; sausage, 40 lbs. at .10	1,323 17
Mitchell, C. J., repairs to implements, 5.40; Moffatt, Jno., livery hire, 1.00	6 40
Montgomery, J. D., filling ice house, 171.50; Muil, Wm., hay, 1.1840 tons at 8.00, 15.36	186 86
National Horse Food Co., horse food, 200 lbs. at .10½	21 00
Ogilvie, Lochead & Co., elastic, 2 doz. yds. at .85; towelling, 12 yds. at .10, 40 yds. at .14, 15 yds. at .50; lining, 14 yds. at .15; print, 14 yds. at .12½; hosiery, 4 pr. at .39, 2 pr. at .25; muslin, 8 yds. at .12½; sheeting, 36 yds. at .50, 49½ yds. at .25; pillow cotton, 25 yds. at 30; hats, 1 only, at 2.00; blankets, 25 pr. at 4.00; braid, 3 doz. yds. at .50; cheese cloth, 12 yds. at .5; dress goods, 16 yds. at .35, 13 yds. at .50; lustre, 2½ yds. at .35; corsets, 3 pr. at .50; collars, 10 only, at .10; towels, 2 doz. at 3.00; napkins, 1 doz. at 3.00; table cloths, 1 only, at 4.75, 1 only at 8.75; awning cloth, 12 yds. at .25; sundries, 10.03	215 81
Oliver, T. C., manure, 1.00; Orr, Jos., harness repairs, 34.70	35 70
Osborne, Wm., hay, 2.1240 ton at 7.50, 19.65; O'Neil, J. F., shorts, 500 lbs. at .95 cwt., 500 lbs. at 1.00 cwt., 500 lbs. at 1.10 cwt.; bran, 1½ ton at 18.00, 1,500 lbs. for 13.25; chop feed, 1 ton at 24.00, 1½ ton at 25.00; oats, 30 bush. at .42, 123.35	143 00
Park & Co., books, 1.05; Passmore, F. S., services as examiner, 50.00	51 05
Pearce, W. T., eggs, 30 doz. at .18, 14 doz. at .19, 20 doz. at .20; brushes, ½ doz. at 1.50; bacon, 10 lbs. at .17, 6½ lbs. at .20; salmon, 3 doz. tins at 1.75; lard, 20 lbs. at .13, 20 lbs. at .14; prunes, 25 lbs. at .8; cann. vegetables, 2 doz. at 1.10; ham, 18½ lbs. at .15; biscuits, 16 lbs. at .14; rice, 50 lbs. at .6; coffee, 12 lbs. at .35; soap, 1 box at 2.75, 1 box at 4.50; vanilla, 1 bottle at 1.25; cheese, 9½ lbs. at .14, 5 lbs. at 15.; sugar, 318 lbs. at 4.50 cwt., 650 lbs. at 4.40 cwt.; raisins, 31 lbs. at .10; molasses, 3 gals. at .40; currants, 10 lbs. at .8; vinegar, 30½ gals. at .30; pepper, 5 lbs. at .25; tapicoa, 50 lbs. at .8; sundries, 6.15; sugar, 640 lbs. at 4.50 cwt	150 74
Pitcher, A. S., rice, 100 lbs. at .5½; tapicoa, 100 lbs. at .6; starch, 41 lbs. at .5½, 60 lbs. at .8; bacon, 33 1-3 lbs. at .18; mustard, 4 lbs. at .25; gelatine, 1 doz. at 1.75; cheese, 18½ lbs. at .14½; lard, 60 lbs. at .12½; figs, 30½ lbs. at .5; sausage, 10 lbs. at .10; cann. vegetables, 2 doz. at 1.00, 2 doz. at 1.10; salt, 2 doz. bags at 1.00, 1 bbl. at 1.50; biscuits, 47 lbs. at .8; apricots, 25 lbs. at .11½; coffee, 12 lbs. at .35; cream tartar, 5 lbs. at .30; cann. fish, 1 doz. at 1.20; currants, 30 lbs. at .8; sugar, 627 lbs. at 4.70 cwt., 200 lbs. at 4.30; eggs, 19 doz. at .28, 30 doz. at .24; sundries, 5.15, 119.35	148 15
Pollock, Jas., manure, 8 loads at .50, 4.00; Postmaster, stamps and postcards, 107.00; P. O. drawer rent, 6.00, 113.00	117 00
Porter, S., potatoes, 3 bags at 1.25, 3.75; Portell, M., hay, 1.200 ton at 9.00, 9.90	13 65
Preston, T. H., advertising, 7.28; subscription to *Expositor*, 3 copies, 9.00	16 28
Ramsey, Geo. A., travelling expenses, 12.65; Ratcliffe, W. A., tea, 325 lbs. at .25; coffee, 165 lbs. at .25, 122.50	135 15
Reid, Robt., kindergarten chairs, 6 only, at .75; rubber screw tips, 10 doz. at .40; mirror, 1 only, at 7.50; kindergarten tables, 2 only, at 2.25; couch, 1 only, at 11.50; mattrasses, 7 only, at 5.50; repairing mattrass, 10.00	80 50

EDUCATION.—*Continued.*

INSTITUTION FOR THE BLIND, BRANTFORD.—*Continued.*

EXPENSES.—*Continued.*

Reville Bros., printing, 83.22; advertising, .60, 83.82; Ritzer, M. G., coffee, 190 lbs. at .25; tea, 20 lbs. at .45, 56.50 .... | 140 32

Robson, R. C., bran, 1 ton at 16.00, 2¼ tons at 18.00, ¼ ton at 17.00; chop feed, 2 tons, at 24.00, ¼ ton at 25.00, ¼ ton at 26.00; shorts, 3,000 lbs. at 1.00 cwt.; roll oats, 5 sacks at 2.45, 6 sacks at 2.10, 5 sacks at 2.25; oats, 35 bush. at .40; seed oats, 16 bush. at .50; paris green, 15 lbs. at .25; sundries, .88 .... | 204 73

Roe, J., subscription to *Musical Opinion*, 1.00; Ryerson, T. E. & Co., fowl, 1 pr. at 1.00, 4 pr. at 1.10, 1 pr. at 1.15, 5 pr. at 1.20, 6 pr. at 1.25, 4½ pr. at 1.30, 8½ pr. at 1.40, 15½ pr. at 1.50, 1 only at .45, 3 only at .62 2-3, 146¼ lbs. at .17; fish, 4 tins at .17½, 4 tins at .12½, 4 tins at .15, 2 tins at .20, 1 doz. at .75, 1 doz. at 1.80, 11½ lbs. at 10½; oysters, 2½ qts. at .50, 9 qts. at .40; grapes, 8 lbs. at .20; oranges, 32½ doz. at .40, 2 doz. at .25, 5 doz. at .15, 2 doz. at .30; raisins, 1 box at 1.10; honey, 2.22; pine apples, 2 doz. at 2.50; plums, 5 baskets at .75; peaches, 6 baskets at .75; cranberries, 36 qts. at .15; celery, 3.53; lemons, 11½ doz. at .20; candy, 25 lbs. at .12½, 3 lbs. at .30, 1 lb. at .45; berries, 54 boxes at .7, 108 boxes at .8, 9 boxes at 8 1-3, 8 boxes at .8½, 108 boxes at .9, 41 boxes at .10, 10 boxes at .12½; cherries, 2 baskets at 1.00, 4 baskets at 1.25; currants, 1 bush. at 3.84, 40 qts. at .8; sundries, 36.96, 228.73 .... | 229 73

Sayles & Carson, fish, 1,440 lbs. at .10, 144.00; Schultz Mnfg. Co., maple wands, 2.00 .... | 146 00

Secord, P. H. & Son, repairs to buildings, 468.67; hinges, 12 pr. at .75; bolts, 75 only, at .2½; sundries, .15 .... | 479 70

Series, Geo. W., twine, 3 balls at .35; currants, 10 lbs. at .7, 20 lbs. at .8; prunes, 50 lbs. at .8; rice, 100 lbs. at .5 4-5; canned vegetables, 1 case at 1.90, 1 case at 2.00, 1 case at 2.20; cheese, 20 7-16 lbs. at .16; L. and P. sauce, 1 doz. at 3.60; soap, 1 box at 4.25; cocoanut, 10 lbs. at .25; eggs, 30 doz. at .24; beans, 100 lbs. at .3½; sausage, 10 lbs. at .10; raisins, 34 lbs. at .10; sugar, 610 lbs. at 4.70 cwt.; matches, 1 doz. boxes at 1.75; bacon, 8½ lbs. at .20, 18 7-8 lbs. at .17; lard, 60 lbs. at .12½; brooms, 1 doz. at 3.25; tea, 2 lbs. at .50; pepper, 10 lbs. at .30; biscuit, 17¼ lbs. at .8; jam, 3 pails at .55; plates, 2 doz. at .65, 2 doz. at .75, 1 doz. at .60; glasses, 1 doz. at 1.00; cups and saucers, 2 doz. at 1.00, 1½ doz. at .75; sundries, 10.11 .... | 118 65

Sheppard, F. F., manure, 4 loads at .50, 2.00; Simpson, I., Mnfg. Co., repairs to vehicles, 51.38 .... | 53 38

Singer Sewing Machine Co., oil, 1 qt. at .50; Smiley, A. W., drugs and chemicals, 49.59 .... | 50 09

Smith, A. J., brooms, 1 doz. at 3.00; blue, 12 lbs. at .18; corn starch, 40 pkgs. at .6; sugar, 100 lbs. at .4½; soap, 1 box at 1.20, 1 box at 2.60; eggs, 22 doz. at .18, 10 doz. at .19, 14 doz. at .20, 16 doz. at .22; lard, 20 lbs. at .14, 20 lbs. at .14½; jars, 2 doz. at .70, 6 doz. at .76, 2 doz. at .90, 3 doz. at 1.00, 2 doz. at 1.20; starch, 42 lbs. at 6¼; sundries, 24.38 | 73 88

Spicknell, Mrs. S., board and care of pupil 14 weeks at 1.50, 21.00; *Star Printing Co.*, advertising, 9.00 .... | 30 00

St. Basil's Roman Catholic Church, pupils' sittings, 42.00; St. Andrew's Presbyterian Church, pupils' sittings, 44.00 .... | 86 00

Stedman Bros., toilet paper, 9 cases at 5.00; stationery, 130.71; books, 8.75. .... | 184 46

Stratford, Jno. H., Hospital, care and attendance of pupils .... | 11 50

Suddaby, S., cheese, 26¾ lbs. at 15c., 18 lbs. at 16c.; sausage, 15 lbs. at 10c; lard, 60 lbs. at 12½c., 60 lbs. at 15c.; prunes, 50 lbs. at 8c.; tea, 3 lbs. at 48c., 2 lbs. at 50c.; fish, 1 case at 7.00; tapioca, 100 lbs. at 8c.; brooms, 1 doz. at 3.00; canned vegetables, 1 case at 2.00, 1 case at 1.90; rice, 100 lbs. at 5½; gelatine, 1 doz. at 1.60; cocoanut, 10 lbs. at 25c.; soap, 1 doz. at 1.00, 1 doz. at 1.20; 1 box, at 3.00; currants, 43 lbs. at 8c.; sugar, 608 lbs. at 4.70, 100 lbs. at 4.30 cwt, 100 lbs. at 4.25 cwt., 341 lbs. at 4.40 cwt., 20 lbs. at 8c.; coffee, 20 lbs. at 37½c.; raisins, 25 lbs at 14. 31 lbs. at 8c.; biscuits, 20 lbs. at 7½c.; canned salmon, 4 doz. at 1.90; corn starch, 1 case at 3.00; bacon, 10 lbs. at

EDUCATION.—*Continued.*

INSTITUTION FOR THE BLIND, BRANTFORD.—*Continued.*

EXPENSES.—*Continued.*

17c., 4 lbs. at 20; eggs, 47 doz. at 28; starch, 40 lbs. at 6¼c.; oat meal, 1 doz. at 3.00; vanilla, 1 lb. at 1.25; sundries, 13.88 .... 187 67
Sundry Newspapers, advertising, 14.40; Sur-Coat Mfg. Co., boiler covering, 100 lbs. at 15c., 15.00 .... 29 40
Taylor, Chas. & Co., repairs to plumbing, 115.37; Tapscott, S. & Co., drugs and chemicals, 75c 116 12
Thomas, J. S., inspection of scales, 6.60; Tipper, Wm. & Sons, repairs to plumbing, 1.09 .... 7 69
Toronto College of Music, examinations in music 38 50
Turbull, Howard & Co., feather duster, 1 only at 1.40; hinges, 1 pr. at 2.00; rakes, 2 only at 65c.; spade, 1 only at 1.15; paints, oils, etc., 38.30; glass, 12 panes at 20c., 4 panes at 35c., 4 panes at 45c., 2 panes at 50c.; kettles, 1 only at 2.00, 1 only at 3.50; brushes, 1 only at 75c., 1 only at 1.25, 1 only at 1.75; spoons, 1 doz. at 1.00, ½ doz. at 2.75, ½ doz. at 5.00; strainers, 1 only at 25c., 1 only at 50c.; vegetable dishes, 2 only at 1.50; boiler, 1 only at 3.00; repairs to tinware, 1.00; cocoa mats, 2 only at 2.75; tea pot, 1 only at 1.25; hoes, 3 only, at 50; axe, 1 only at 1.25; nails, 25 lbs. at 5; 1 keg at 2.35; rim locks, 1 only at 1.00; knives and forks, 1 doz. at 1.25, 1 doz. at 3.50; saucepans, 1 only at 45, 1 only at 75c.; pails, 3 only at 65c.; cullendor, 1 only at 1.50; dish pans, 1 only at 1.50;; sundries, 47.63.................... 145 26
Union Publishing Co., city director 2 copies at 2.50, 5.00; Usher, Thos., travelling expenses, 3.60 .... 8 60
Vanstone, A. L., plates, 1 doz. at 75c., 1 doz. at 1.00; fruit dishes, 1 doz. at 60c., 2.35; Virtue & Co., books, 39.50 .... 41 85
Wade, B. J., moving pianos, 18.00; Walsh, F. H., coal, 77.1475 tons at 4.32, 474.1690 tons at 5.74, slabs, 1 cord at 5.00, 1 cord at 5.50, 1-8 cord at 10.80, 3,073.24 .... 3,091 24
Warden, King & Son, Limited, washers for heater, 1 set at 1.80; Warwick Bros. & Rutter, printing, 36.30 .... 38 10
Waterous Engine, Works Co., engine oil, 6 gals. at 56c.; cotton waste, 25 lbs. at 13c.; repairs, 1.90 .... 8 51
Watt & Squire, shears, 1 pr., at 1.75; glass, 6 panes at 20c., screen windows. 5 only at 30c., 1 only at 25c.; paints, oils, etc., 7.88; nails, 50 lbs. 2½c.; bits, 1 set at 7.50, 1 set at 3.00; saw, 1 only at 2.00; snips, 1 pr. at 1.50; paper racks, 2 only at 75; mitts, 1 pr. at 75c., hose, 100 ft. at 13c.; yale locks, 1 only at 1.75; chisels. 1 set at 6.00; planes, 1 only at 1.50, 1 only at 2.00, 1 only at 2.50; oil stove, 1 only at 1.50; polish, 1 1/6 doz. at 2.40; diamonds, 1 only at 10.00; sundries, 22.59. 93 72
Wenger, Aaron, butter, 32 lbs. at 21½c.; eggs, 30 doz. at 16c., 30 doz. at 21c., 30 doz. at 23c. 24 86
Westminster, The, Co., subscription, 1.50; Wickens, W. B., travelling expenses, 33.40 .... 34 90
Wilks, R. F. repairing pianos, 482.00; Willits. D., pressing apples, 1.20... 483 20
Wilson, Harold, A. Co., foot ball, 1 only at 2.98; Winter, O. W., books, 13.50 .... 16 48
Workshop, Acct., repairs to chairs, 4.75; Wright, Jas., repairs to furnace, 81.85 .... 86 60
Young, J. M., & Co., lace. 4 yds. at 25c.; carpet, 58½ yds. at 1.00; 28½ yds. at 1.30; making and laying carpet, 87 yds. at 10c.; sundries, 1.38...... 106 63

School desks ($46.80).

Can. Office and School Furniture Co., desks... 46 80

New lavatory for hospital ($87.00).

Taylor, Chas. & Co., contract closet, bath and basin 87 00

Hardware, paints, oils, glass, etc. ($4.45).

Medcalf, D. M., travelling expenses, boiler inspection 4 45

Total Education $1,320,921 71

PUBLIC INSTITUTIONS MAINTENANCE.

ASYLUM FOR INSANE, TORONTO.

SALARIES ($39,624.81).

C. K. Clarke, M.D:	Twelve months' salary as	Medical Superintendent	2,600 00
W. K. Ross, M.D.:	do	Assistant do	1,400 00
W. J. Harris, M.D.:	do	Assistant Physician	1,050 00
Josephine Wells: Six	do	Dentist	150 00
James Corcoran: Twelve	do	Bursar	1,700 00
J. F. Dwyer :	do	Storekeeper	900 00
B. Winnifrith :	do	Steward	850 00
James Barrie :	do	Trades Instructor	600 00
Alex. Mackenzie :	do	Tailor	600 00
Robert McCammon	do	Baker	525 00
Thos. Hughes:	do	Carpenter ....•....	600 00
James Anthony:	do	Carpenter ......:	550 00
John Simons	do	Painter	600 00
John Daly: ble	do	Bricklayer and Mason.........	625 00
James E. No· :	do	Engineer	850 00
James Young:	do	Assistant Engineer............	450 00
C. F. Arnott|	do	Gardener	600 00
W. P. Strick and:	do	Assistant Gardener............	525 00
F. J. Dundas:	do	Engine Driver	400 00
George Maguire: Eight and half	do	Porter........................	216 00
Edward Maguire: Twelve	do	Chief Attendant	450 00
Richard McCreary: Nine	do	Chief Supervisor..............	300 00
R. Anderson: Five	do	Messenger ....•......	110 00
Eliza M. Corley: Twelve	do	Matron	500 00
May McKinley: do	do	Assistant Matron.	300 00
Marion Bethune: do	do	Trained Nurse	400 00
M. J. Howie: Seven	do	Musical Instructress	140 00
Eva M. Cuthbertson: Twelve	do	Stenographer	250 00
Annie McWilliams:	do	Seamstress...................	216 00
Male Supervisors (8)	do	....	2,796 00
Male Attendants (22)	do	....	7,422 03
Female Supervisors (9)	do	....	2,014 60
Female Attendants (24)	do	....	4,731 61
Laundresses (7)	do	....	1,356 00
Cooks (6)	do	....	1,420 98
Housemaids (6)	do	....	625 47
Stokers (5)	do	....	534 45
J. B. Fowler: Three	do	Temp. services, Bursar's clerk..	156 00
W. F. Knight: One	do	do knittting machine	28 00
F. Stephens: do	do	do baker	34 67
A. Mckay: do	do	do do	30 00

EXPENSES ($86,803.63).

Adamson & Dobbin, 1 directory, 6.00; American Medico Psychological Assn. subn., 5.00	11 00
Atteaux Dye, Stuff & Chemical Co., ammonia powder. 1,181 lbs. at 4½c., 53.14; 813 lbs. at 4½c., 36.59; washing soda, 6,750 lbs. at 80c., 2.225 lbs. at 80c	161 53
Abbot's Heat Market, lamb, 13¼ at 1.75, 1¼ at 1.60, 1¼ at 1.45 25.80; potatoes, 75 bus. at 65c., 75 bus. at 68c., 74¾ bus. at 70., 152.23........	178 03
Adams Furniture Co., curled hair, 600 lbs. at 39c., 234.00; Arnott Bros., plants, 8.00 ....:........	242 00
Andrew, C. H., hay, 3.470 tons at 13.50	43 66
Brock, W. R. Co., cotton, 129¾ yds. at 10c., 791 yds. at 6c., 1,325¼ yds. at 9c., 351¾ at 8c., 161¾ at 11c., 325½ at 11½c., 610 yds. at 12½c., 308¾ at 13c.; thimbles, 9 doz. at 1.00; safety pins, 10 doz. at 25c., tape, 30, doz. at 10c., 60 doz. at 10c.; laces, 5 gross at 80c., 5 gross at 1.30; matting, 27½ yds. at 18½c.; table napkins. 6 doz. at 1.50, 18 doz. at 2.00; pique. 41 yds. at 18½; sundries, 47.29; italian, 27¾ yds. at 65c., 79 yds. at 37½; canvas, 100 yds. at 16½c.; silesia, 66½ yds. at 19½c., 69½	

PUBLIC INSTITUTIONS MAINTENANCE.—*Continued.*

ASYLUM FOR INSANE, TORONTO.—*Continued.*

EXPENSES.—*Continued.*

yds. at 16c., 50½ yds. at 18½; holland, 46 yds. at 17½c., haircloth, 48½ yds. at 27½c.; dress goods, 199½ yds. at 37½c., 50½ yds. at 42½c.; silence cloth, 15 yds. at 75c.; hosiery, 3 doz. at 1.25, 12 doz. at 1.25; fingering, 35 spools at 3.75, 1 at 8.00; sateen, 134½ yds. at 15c., 77½ yds. at 17½; muslin, 296 yds. at 14c., 405 yds. at 25c., 24 yds., at 13½c., 169 yds. at 8c., 161 yds. at 15c.; print, 542 yds., at 10c., 320 yds. at 10c.; Melton, 562¼ yds. at 12c.; flannelette, 1,212 yds. at 10c., 299 yds. 10½c., 554¼ yds. at 12½c.; sheeting, 899 yds. at 18c., 313¼ at 18½c., 1,067 yds. at 18½c., 1,033 yds. at 19c., 312¾ at 25½c., 1,139¾ at 25c.; shirting, 2,234¾ yds. at 12½c., 306½ yds. at 7c.; ticking, 551¼ yds. at 18c., 338 yds. at 17½c.; Denim, 338½ yds. at 19½c., 554 yds. at 16c.; plush, 50⅛ yds. at 1.00; hessian, 322 yds. at 11c., 108 yds. at 12c.; rugs, 3 at 4.00, 3 at 9.00; towels, 32 doz. at 2.25; 6 doz. at 4.50, 12 doz. at 1.40; scrim, 2.95½ yds. at 8c., 123 yds. at 15c.; butter cloth, 616¼ yds. a 4½c.; quilts, 48 at 78c., 50 at 1.00, 36 at 1.15, 22 at 1.35, 24 at 1.50; carpet, 49 5/8 yds. at 95c., 86½ at 1.00; corduroy, 30 yds. at 60c., hooks and eyes, 1 gross at 3.00; table napkin, 23 doz at 2.00; linoleum, 28 yds. at 75c.; lace edge canvas, 76 yds., at 10c.; point lace, 440½ yds., at 10c.; percoline, 105 yds. at 11½c.; ladies' vests, 1/6 doz. at 8.50; mats, 1/3 doz. at 8.40, 3 at 1.35; crash, 271½ yds. at 10c.; linen, 298½ yds. at 37½c.; yarn, 204 lbs. at 45c.; mitts, 3 doz. at 4.50, 12 doz. at 2.70; hoods, 20 doz. at 3.00; serge, 106¼ yds. at 2.25; bats, 4 bales at 6.00; shirts and drawers, 8 doz. at 7.00, 8 doz. at 7.25	4,875 57
Big Four Cap Co., caps, 10 doz. at 4.50; Brown, Jno., cotton, 12 pkgs. at 50c.; sundries, 1.65; braid, 12 doz. yds. at 20c	65 05
Beal Bros., leather, 150½ ft. at 9c., 103 lbs. at 15c., 65 lbs. at 17c., 43¼ ft. 17c., 222 lbs. at 28c., 61½ lbs. at 28c., 19¼ at 35c., 28 lbs. at 40c., 27 lbs. at 47c, sundries	161 81
Boncock, Bert, hay, 1.1230 tons at 12.50; Brown Bros., stationery, 17.75 ...	37 93
17.75	37 93
Bowden, Frank A., lumber, 165.51; Bethune, R., coffee, 117 lbs. at 19½c., 22.78	188 29
Bursar, to pay sundries, 21.58; Burns, P. & Co., coal, 403.1290 tons at 4.50, 76.690 at 2.00, 120.1900 at 5.00, 502.690 at 5.23, 352.1710 at 5.45	7,145 74
Bell Telephone Co., messages, 3.86, telephone service, 97.25	101 11
Bowden, F. A., lumber, 67.15; Bedson, Geo. E., interments, 24.00	91 15
Cairns, B., signature stamp, 1 at 35c.; indelible ink, 2 qts., 14.00; ink pad, 25c	14 60
Cruickshank, J. L., inspection of scales, 3.87; Canadian Shipbuilding Co., castings, 83.27	87 14
Croil, Jas., tweed, 46 3/8 yds. at 1.90, 88.11; Cairo Bros., apples, 10 lbs. at 1.50, 15 bbls. at 1.65; 10 bbls at 2.00, 5 bbls. at 2.50	160 36
Conger Coal Co., coal, 74 tons at 3.69, 66.1466 at 3.60, 208.1240 at 4.63, 15 tons at 6.25	1,578 95
Carveth, J. A., medical books, 5.50; Cluff Bros., grate bars, 1 set at 4.39	9 89
Cotterill, Jno., plants and seeds, 22.93; Caslor, Jno., repairing lawn mowers, 7.00	29 93
Clarke, Dr., travelling expenses, 67.64; Cannington *Gleaner*, advertis'g, 1.00	68 64
Canadian Pacific Railway, freight, 3.62; Cairns, Bernard, indelible ink, 7.00	10 62
Common Sense Mfg. Co., rat exterminator, 18 tins at 1.00, 18.00; Coleman, C. W., repairing clocks, 5.75	23 75
Central Prison Industries, beds repaired and painted, 23 at 3.25; blankets, 140 lbs. at 45c.; packing 50c.; tweed, 314 yds. at 55c.	310 95
Consumers' Gas Co., gas, 1,742.73; Catholic Register Pub. Co., subscription 1 year, 1.50	1,744 23
Chandler, Ingram & Bell, medical appliances, drugs, etc., 198.13; Canada Paint Co., oils, etc., 473.35; sand paper, 1 rm. 9.75	681 23
Canadian Rubber Co., rubber boots, 1 pr. at 3.35, 1 pr. at 3.50; fireman's coat, 4.25; rubber hose, 6.81; hose covers, 2 at 2.80, 5.60	23 51
Clark Bros., advertising, 1.56; Crawford, Jas., potatoes, 3,077 bus. at 63c., 1,939.04, less freight 23.59	1,917 01
Clare, Dr., travelling expenses, 6.25; City Dairy Co., ice cream, 12.45...	18 70

PUBLIC INSTITUTIONS MAINTENANCE.—*Continued.*

ASYLUM FOR INSANE, TORONTO.—*Continued.*

Expenses.—*Continued.*

Cowan, J. G., sweeping chimneys, 25.00; Cass, H. & Son, rubbers, 1 pr. at 1.00 .... 26 00

Canadian Express Co., charges, 3.15; Canadian General Electric Co., 3 lt. pendant, 1 at 6.00; lamps, 2 only at 1.67 3.34, 2 at 2.50 5.00; 1 bracket at 1.67, 6 at 2.75, 16.50; shades, 1-12 doz. at 5.34, 5.79, 1 7-12 at 2.16, 3.42; sundries, 43.16 .... 63 86

Canada Brokerage Co., rice, 1,120 lbs. at 4½c., 42.60; evap. apples, 500 lbs. at 10½c., 500 lbs. at 10½c.; tobacco, 72 lbs. at 46c., 24 lbs., at 44c.; corn starch, 200 lbs. at 7c.; sundries, 4.80; prunes, 625 lbs. at 7½c.; cocoanut, 20 lbs. at 15c.; sage, 86 lbs. at 5½c.; ginger, 10 lbs. at 26c.; marmalade, 210 lbs. at 6¾c.; pepper, 50 lbs. at 20c.; flavoring extract. 6 doz. at 2.25; fruit sugar, 50 lbs. at 4.43; sugar, 2,500 lbs. at 4.18, 30 bags at 4.38½ 545 42

Clubb Coffee Co., coffee, 100 lbs. at 20c., 20.00; Cusack, H. M., repairs to instruments, 10.50 .... 30 50

C. P. R. Telegraph Co., telegrams, 10.24; *Canadian Grocer*, subscription 1 yr., 2.00 .... 12 24

Canadian Practitioner and Review. subscription. 8.00; Canadian Oil Co., engine oil, 46 gals. at 45c., 20.70; belt dressing, 10 lbs. at 20c., 2.00; benzine, 1 bbl. at 7.54; wax, 100 lbs. at 8c.; boiler compound, 473 lbs. at 10c. 93 54

Cohen Bros., spectacles, 9 doz. at 2.25, 20.25; Canadian Printing Co., advertising, 1.50 .... 21 75

Davidson & Hay, biscuits, 24 lbs. at 21c., 5.04; sundries, 8.55; fish, 4 kegs at 3.00; sugar, 3,047 lbs. at 4.13; currants, 208 lbs. at 5½c.; canned vegetables, 50 doz. at 77½c., 30 doz. at 85c.; barley, 8 at 4.90, 980 lbs. at 2½c.; pearline, 5 boxes at 3.90; blacking, 6 doz. at 40c.; marmalade, 210 lbs. at 6¾c.; mustard. 50 jars at 25c., 12 jars at 75c.; tea, 475 lbs. at 24c.; jelly, 3 doz. at 90c.; corn starch, 200 lbs. at 7c.; raisins, 140 lbs. at 6½c.; syrup, 5 pails at 90c.; onions. 1 doz. at 1.75 .... 477 30

Duck, R. F., bay. 1 670/2000 tons at 10.50, 7 320/2000 at 13.50; Donnelly, M., 4 590/2000 tons at 11.00 .... 156 56

Dineen, W. & D. Co., Ltd., hats, 12 doz. at 3.00, 3 doz. at 2.00................. 42 00

Dodge Mfg. Co., sundry merchandise 1 98

Davies, Wm. Co.. Ltd.. sausages, 1.600 lbs. at 8c., 500 lbs. at 7½c. 165 50

Doyle. M. Fish Co., 26.610 lbs. at 8c., 15 lbs. at 20c., 2,131.80; Dominion Radiator Co., grate box, 1.20 .... 2,133 00

Dalton Bros., pepper, 50 lbs. at 18c. 9 00

Evans, J. D., beeswax, 202 lbs. at 35c., 70.70; Elliott & Son, wall paper, 42 yds. at 15c., 92 yds. at 20c., 24.70 .... 95 40

Edgar, J. F., services as notary 1 00

Eaton. T. Co.. Ltd.. cushion slips, 3 at 59c.; cushion tops. 4 at 25c., 9 at 35c.; cushion backs. 12 at 15c.; girdles. 2 at 49c.; cords. 8 at 49c., 3 at 75c.; cushion. 1 at 59c.; sundries. 94c.; silk. 14½ doz. at 45c....... 22 93

Fairles, G. H.. roll oats, 55 lbs. at 5.20; split peas, 20 lbs. at 4.50; roll wheat. 5 lbs. at 2.40. 25 lbs. at 2.50 .... 450 50

Foy, Geo. J., spirits for medicinal purposes, 20 gals. at 2.90 .... 58 00

Fleischmann & Co., yeast, 367 lbs. at 30c. 110 25

Fairles Milling Co., split peas, 5 bbls. at 4.50; roll wheat, 10 bbls. at 2.50; roll oats, 15 bbls. at 5.35, 15 bbls. at 5.20 .... 205 75

Godden. C. P.. castor oil, 2 gals. at 1.50; axle grease, 1 pail at 1.00; discs, 50 at 8c., 26 at 7c., 12 at 15c., 12 at 12c.; padlocks, 2 doz. at 1.25; padlock keys, 4 doz. at 75c., 3 doz. at 50c.; glass, 2 cases at 4.50, 2 cases at 4.75; putty, 100 lbs. at 2½c.; shellac, 1 gal. at 4.00; twine, 7½ lbs. at 30c.; sundries, 1.60; plates, 6 doz. at 50c.; oxalic acid, 20 lbs. at 15c.; bolts, 1 doz. at 2.25; porcelain knobs, 1 gro. at 2.50; knives, 2 at 1.15; saw blades, 1 at 1.25 .... 63 21

Gallagher & Co., pears, 102 bush. at 60c.; mush melon, 155 at 10c.; water mellon, 50 at 30c.; peaches, 110 bush. at 70c.; grapes, 110 baskets at 55c., 10 lbs. at 20c.; apples, 5 bbls. at 4.25; cranberries, 1 bbl. at 10.00; oranges, 6 doz. at 35c., 2 doz. at 45c., 2 doz. at 30c., 8 cases at 3.40;

PUBLIC INSTITUTIONS MAINTENANCE.—*Continued.*

ASYLUM FOR INSANE, TORONTO.—*Continued.*

Expenses.—*Continued.*

bananas, 6 doz. for 1.09, 7 doz. at 20c., 2 doz. at 17½c., 5 bun. at 1.60; lemons, 1 case at 4.00, 1 case at 6.00, 6 doz. at 40c., 6 doz. at 25c., 1 case at 3.75; pineapples, 2 at 20c.; berries, 343 boxes at 11c., 2,062 boxes at 10c., 40 bas. at 1.30, 767 boxes at 10c.; currants, 30 bas. at 1.00; plums, 100 bas. at 95c. 820 32

Golden's Livery, livery hire, 6.00; Greer, B. J., gas radiator, 1 at 5.50; gas tube, 12 ft. at 7c. 12 34

Glassford, R., nail puller, 1.50; Graham, Jas. A., hay, 2 tons at 13.00, 9 426/2000 at 13.50, 3 780/2000 at 14.00, 5 1110/2000 at 10.00, 4 400/2000 at 10.00, 1 360/2000 at 13.50 .... 312 79

Gowans, Kent & Co., crockery, 5.98; spades, 2 doz. at 2.50; lindsay lights, 1 doz. at 7.80; lindsay mantles, 1 doz. at 2.10; cups and saucers, 25 doz. at 65c., 1 doz. at 4.50, 50 doz. at 65c.; jugs, 9 doz. at 1.40, 2 doz. at 2.40, 5 doz. at 3.60; ewers, 2¼ doz. at 3.80, 1 doz. at 3.80; basins, 5 doz. at 3.80; sundries, 24.13; tumblers, 37 doz. at 50c., 8 1-3 doz. at 45c., 3 2-3 at 45c.; egg cups, 1 gross at 5.40; dishes, 3 1-3 doz. at 4.80, 1 2-3 for 7.84, 1 2-3 at 10.60, 4 at 4.20, 1 at 1.25, 1 at 2.00, 1 1-3 at 6.40; plates, 25 doz. at 60c., 25 doz. at 80c.; dinner set, 1 at 15.00; oblong bakers, ½ doz. at 90c.; bowls, 12 doz. at 80c., 50 doz. at 80c.; butters, 3 doz. at 2.25; mustards, 3 doz. at 85c.; salts, ½ gro. at 3.00, ¼ doz. at 6.00; oval bakers, 6 doz. at 76c.; glass cruet bottles, 3 doz. at 90c.; toilet jar, 1 at 6.25; sugar bowls, 2 doz. at 2.40; 1 doz. at 2.40; slop jar, 1 at 1.60 .... 402 98

Gutta Percha Rubber Co., packing, 10 1-8 lbs. at 70c., 11 10-16 lbs. for 7.33; hospital sheets, 48 at 2.25, 48 at 2.00; fire hose washers, 1-8 lb. for 1.53; gaskets, 5¼ lbs. at 70c., 8¾ lbs. at 70c.; sundries, 31.57; hose, 50 ft. for 6.41, 100 ft. for 12.00; compression waders, 60 at 6½c., 60 at 8c. 272 48

Great North Western Telegraph Co., telegrams, .25; Graham Ice Co., ice, 88.50 .... 88 75

Gurney Foundry Co., repairs to stoves, 4.25; Gripton, C., indelible ink, 8.80; pneumatic stamp, 1 at 85c. 13 90

Gray, F. A., drugs and chemicals, 173.96; Grant, Jas., keys, 1.00 .... 174 96

Grenadier Ice Co., ice, 460.08; Gaughan, J., keys, 1.00 .... 461 08

Grand Trunk Railway, freight, 10.34; Globe Printing Co., subscription 2 copies, 10.00 .... 20 34

Humphrey, F. W., sugar, 2,084 lbs. at 4.18 cwt., 3.924 at 4.28, 2,955 at 4.48, 2,987 at 4.38; pot barley, 5 lbs. at 4.35; tobacco, 56 lbs. at 45c., 90 lbs. at 46c.; biscuits, 72 lbs. at 21c.; pickles, 12 doz. at 1.50, 14 doz. at 1.50; cornmeal, 2 bbls. at 3.60, 3 bbls. at 3.50; marmalade, 630 lbs. at 7c.; currants, 259 lbs. at 6½c., 250 lbs. at 7¼c.; sundries, 11.33; can vegetables, 40 doz. at 85c., 20 doz. at 92½c.; corn starch, 600 lbs. at 7c.; pearline, 5 cases at 3.80; matches, 1 case at 3.10; evaporated apples, 500 lbs. at 7½c., 500 lbs. at 8c.; rice, 1,120 lbs. at 4¼c.; starch, 200 lbs. at 5¼c.; cassia, 10 lbs. at 23c.; flavoring extracts, 3 doz. at 2.00, 3 doz. at 2.25; raisins, 94 lbs. at 12c.; L. & P. sauce, 3 doz. at 6.50; blacking, 2 doz. at 1.05 .... 1,072 38

Hobbs, Samuel, stove pipe, 200 lengths at 11c.; micas, 2 doz. at 1.00; iron handles, 2 doz. at 1.00; repairs to range, 11.45; dippers, 1 doz. at 1.50, 1 doz. at 2.00; dust pans, 2 doz. at 1.80; stone crocks, 2 at 75c., 1.50; elbows, 8 at 15c.; iron handles, 3 doz. at 1.00; flesh forks, 6 at 1.00... 56 25

Hubbard, C. H. & Co., dentist chair, 1 at 15.00; Harvey, Jno. G., disinfectant, 55 gals. at 1.25, 68.75 .... 83 75

Hedley, Shaw Milling Co., 70 bbls. at 3.75; 30 bbls. at 3.80, 20 bbls. at 3.90 454 50

Halliday, Jas., difference in exchange of cows, 625.47; purchase of meat, 12,744.63 .... 13,370 10

Hurlbut, J. J., repairs to vehicles, 1.00; Harris, E. Co., Ltd., beeswax, 50 lbs. at 38c., 19.00 .... 20 00

Hamilton Dental Depot, dental supplies, 56.60; Hind, J. W., horseshoeing, 64.19; repairs, etc., 39.00 .... 159 79

Hamilton *Times*, subscription, 2.00; Haselden, G., keys, 1.00 .... 3 00

PUBLIC INSTITUTIONS MAINTENANCE.—*Continued.*

ASYLUM FOR INSANE, TORONTO.—*Continued.*

EXPENSES.—*Continued.*

Hurd, H. E., V.S., professional services, 36.75; Harcourt, E. H. & Co., Ltd., stationery, 20.29 .... 57 04

Harris Abattoir Co., pork, 6,457 lbs. at 9c., 2,075 lbs. at 9¼c., 5,325 at 9½c., 5,219 at 9¾c. 1,787 81

Hughes, H. L., subscription to *Alienist and Neurologist*, 5.00; Heintzman, Gerhard, tuning piano, 3.50 .... 8 50

Hartz, J. F. Co., Ltd., medical supplies, 34.76; Hutchinson, M., lumber, 163.80 .... 198 56

Hunt Bros., flour, 941 bbls. at 3.74, 3,520.30; Hopkins, Jno. Press, *American Journal of Insanity*, 1 year's subscription, 5.00 .... 3,525 30

Inglis, Jno. Co., repairs, 141.18; Imperial Varnish Co., floor finish, 3 gals. at 2.50, 7.50; paint, oils, etc., 194.40 .... 343 08

Imperial Chemical Co., oil, paints, etc. 73 65

Johnston, R., keys, 1.00; Johnson, D., keys, 1 doz. at 3.50 .... 4 50

Jaynes Electrical Co., station dials, 3 boxes at 2.50, 7.50; Johnson, Wm.; repairs to carriage, 3.50; horseshoeing, 6.50 .... 17 50

Jennings, C. B., repairs to furniture, upholstering, etc., 77.00; Kemp Mfg. Co., tinware, etc., 20.42 .... 97 42

Kingston Asylum, brushes, 6 doz. at 2.30, 13.80, 3 doz. at 2.84 1-3, 8.53... 22 33

Kirkpatrick, W. A. & Son, harness, 1 set at 35 00

Kingsbury, Wm., hay, 3 6/2000 tons at 10.00, 30.30, 2 1150/2000 at 10.00, 26.38 .... 56 68

Kenny, T. & Co., tea, 795 lbs. at 21 1-3c. 169 65

King's Printer, paper, 31.21; stationery, 235.05 .... 266 26

Kinnear, T. & Co., syrup, 80 lbs. at 35c.; corn meal, 2 bbls. at 3.70; sal soda, 1,875 lbs. at 85c.; corn starch, 200 lbs. at 6c., 200 lbs. at 7c.; force, 1 case at 4.50; fish, 288 lbs. at 7½c.; mustard, 12 jars at 75c.; 12 jars at 42c.; tapioca, 454 lbs. at 5½c., 463 lbs. at 6½c.; baking powder, 120 lbs. at 25c.; chicken soup, 6 doz. at 2.05; sauce, 2 doz. at 2.40; sundries, 9.40; evaporated apples, 500 lbs. at 11½c.; marmalade, 416 lbs. at 6½c.; pearline, 6 doz. at 3.90; Gillard's relish, 3 doz. at 2.00; shoe polish, ½ gro. at 10.80; pickles, 12 doz. at 1.50, 6 doz. at 1.75; catsup, 2 doz. at 2.00, 16 doz. at 77½c.; cornmeal, 2 bbls. at 3.75; corn starch, 600 lbs. at 7c., 200 lbs. at 5½c., 400 lbs. at 7c.; biscuits, 43 lbs. at 21c.; tobacco, 89 lbs. at 46c.; sugar, 3,014 lbs. at 4.18, 4,433 lbs. at 4.08, 504 lbs. at 3.50, 50 lbs. at 5½c.; can vegetables, 20 doz. at 85c., 20 doz. at 62½c., 20 doz. at 1.25; salt, 10 bbls. at 1.50; barley, 10 bags at 2.50; matches, 1 case at 3.10; hominy, 100 lbs. at 3½c.; sago, 148 lbs. at 6½c.; 300 lbs. at 6½c.; starch, 200 lbs. at 5½c., 195 lbs. at 5c.; tea, 450 lbs. at 25c. 1,123 64

Lewis, Rice & Son, mouse traps, 3 doz. at 60c.; rat traps, 1 1-3 doz. at 8.25; Boston guard, 1 at 2.50; trimmer, 1 at 5.10; barber's clippers, 8 prs. at 1.90; coal hods, 1 doz. at 5.00; harness paste, 1 doz. at 2.50; keys, 16 at 15c.; harness dressing, 1 doz. at 2.20; mythelated spirits, 1 gal. at 2.00; steel trays, 2 doz. at 3.75; cuspidors, 2½ doz. at 2.25; duplex batteries, 3 at 50c.; wrench, 1 at 1.00; alabastine, 200 lbs. at 7.25, 2 boxes at 3.00, 1 box at 6.00, 200 lbs. at 6.00; nails, 2 kegs at 2.60, 3 at 2.20, 3 at 2.10, 3 at 2.25, 1 at 2.15; bathroom shower, 1 at 2.00; sash weights, 364 lbs., at 13.75 cwt.; refrigerator, 1 at 15.75; palmetta twist, 3 lbs. at 1.25; metallic scale, 1 at 1.50; jelly moulds, 2 at 75c.; garnet paper, 17 doz. at 8.50 ream. 1 ream at 9.75; steel rules, ¼ doz. at 4.05; forks, 12 doz. at 5.10; knives, 12 doz. at 4.50; brass keys, 3 doz. at 3.50; spoons, 12 doz. at 1.00; Italian hemp, 136¼ lbs. for 19.79; glass, 71.52; water barrel, 1 at 8.82; fish knife and fork, 1 at 5.00; Jenkin's steam trap, 2 at 5.50; night latch, 1 at 1.35; trays, ½ doz. at 6.90, 3 at 35c.; pulls, 1 doz. at 2.50; glue, ½ gal. at 2.54; catches, 1 doz. at 3.20; leather belting, 100 for 16.07; 1 brace at 2.25; bits in case, 1 set at 5.00; cooper's shaves, 1 at 2.70, 1 at 1.43, 1 at 1.50; chisels, 1 set at 5.75; hood clamps, 4 sets at 1.05; drills in case, 1 set at 1.50, 1 at 4.25; screw drivers, 2 at 70c., 2 at 85c.; plane, 1 at 1.75. 2 at 3.65, 2 at 1.00, 2 at 90c.; saws, 3 at 1.95, 1 at 1.50; grindstone, 1 at 5.40; tin, 1 box at 10.90. 41 lbs. for 3.20; locks, 3 doz. at 85c.,

PUBLIC INSTITUTIONS MAINTENANCE.—*Continued.*

ASYLUM FOR INSANE, TORONTO.—*Continued.*

Expenses.—*Continued.*

48 only at 2.60;. asbestos paper, 430 lbs. at 6.35; carpet felt, 277 lbs.
at 2.60 cwt.; irons, 8 sets at 75c.; meat chopper, 1. at 1.50, 1 at 4.10;
slicer, 1 at 2.00; shears, 2 prs. at 6.00, 1 doz. at 4.56, 1
doz. at 5.32; pails, ½ doz. at 5.40, ¼ doz. at 6.00, ½ doz. at 6.24; rice
boiler, ½ doz. at 13.40; kettles, ½ doz. at 8.40, ⅔ doz. at 8.64; bushings,
castings, etc., 39.57; carpet sweepers, 1 doz. at 27.00; flue cleaner, 2 at
2.67; sash cord, 40 lbs. at 32c.; scrapers, 1 at 1.20, 1 at 1.60, 1 at 2.45;
brass chair nails, 4,000 at 50c. M.; asbestos paper, 220 lbs. at 4.50;
screw drivers, ¼ doz. at 10.00, 1 at 1.40, ½ doz. at 5.18; spiral chairs, 2
doz. at 2.55; force cups, 5 at 75c.; cold chisels, 1 doz. at 2.40; belt laces,
5 doz. at 80c.; leather belting, 50 ft. 3 in. for 12.92; boiler tin, 86 lbs.
at 7c.; galv. iron, 500 lbs. at 3.50; putty, 206 lbs. at 1.90; solder, 25
lbs. at 22c., 10¼ lbs. at 28c., 20 lbs. at 25c., 20 lbs. at 25½c.; steel, 277
lbs. at 3.50 cwt.; iron handles, 2 1-3 doz. at 75c.; spoons, 10 doz. at
70c., 1 at 1.50, 12 doz. at 1.78¾; valves, ½ doz. for 5.52, 1 at 12.65, 15
for 21.10; gas tips, 1 gro. at 1.50; warding files, 1 doz. at 1.80;
carpet sweepers, 1 doz., at 24.00; castors, 12 set at 34c., 12 set at 43c.;
curry combs, 1 doz. at 1.50; sundries, 113.68; rat traps, 3 doz. at 1.25,
2-3 doz. at 8.25; horse clipper, 1 pr. at 2.50; picture hooks, 1 gro. at
2.00; packing, 27 lbs. at 12½c., 1 pkg. at 8.00, 1 at 6.25, 261 lbs. at 14½c.;
beeswax, 100 lbs. at 38c., 100 lbs. at 40c.; auto pump, 1 at 3.25; netting, 33 1-3 yds. at 9c., 16 2-3 at 10c.; padlocks, 2 doz. at 1.15, ½ doz.
at 14.85; basin cocks, ¼ doz. at 14.00; stock drills, 1¼ doz. at 1.68 2-3;
hoop iron, 120 lbs. at 2.70 cwt.; gem freezer, 1 at 3.20; lawn mowers, 2 at
17.00, 3 at 5.00, 1 at 2.31, 3 at 6.00; twine, 3 pkgs. at 1.20; fly screen,
1 roll at 3.63; tennis marker, 1 at 3.00; brass screen, 6 ft. at 25c.; brass
handles, ¼ doz. at 2.40; wire cloth, 1 roll at 1.45; putty paste, 2 doz.
at 4.25; razors, 2 doz. at 7.45½; glue, 25 lbs. at 12½c. 1,464 38
Lumbers, Jas., sugar, 3,058 lbs. at 3.98 cwt., 900 lbs. at 3.63, 3,193 lbs. at 4.28,
3,224 lbs. at 4.48, 3,274 at 4.40; barley, 5 bbls. at 5.00; biscuits, 24 lbs.
at 21c.; sapolio, 3 doz. at 2.85; salt, 10 bbls. at 1.40, 2 bbls. at 3.00,
10 bbls. at 1.50; pails, 3 doz. at 3.50; pepper, 50 lbs. at 20c.; sago, 633
lbs. at 7c.; tobacco, 45 lbs. at 36c., 4 lbs. at 45c.; sundries, 12.60;
codfish, 1 case at 4.50; herring, 2 bbls. at 5.75; pearline, 5 cases at
3.90; syrup, 88 gals. at 32c.; prunes, 100 lbs. at 9c.; matches, 1 case
at 3.00; paper bags, 3,000 at 1.10, 1 M at 1.50, 1 M at 1.90, 1 M at
2.70, 1 M at 7.00; marmalade, 210 lbs. at 7c. 871 70
Lynn, H., hay, 1 290/2000 tons at 11.00 .... 12 59
Lyons, Geo. A., hay, 754 lbs. at 14.00 ton; chop oats, 2 tons at 22.50, 6 tons at
23.00, 2 710/2000 at 24.00. 12 327/2000 at 23.00; bran, 24,070 at 1.75,
10 tons at 19.00, 4 600/1700 at 20.00, 9 1950/2000, at 20.00; straw,
1 540/2000 tons at 6.50. 8 1590/2000 tons at 6.50; pea meal, 1,200 lbs.
at 26.00; oats. 20 bus. 7.80, 20 bus. at 39c., 30 bus. at 40c.; *Leader,*
advertising, 90c. 1,337 22
Lockhart Photo Supply Co., chemicals. etc., 14.53; Lawson, Ernest H., subscriptions various magazines. 50.90 .... 65 43
Lippincott. J. & B. Co., books, 15.25; Lawton, C. W.. advertising. 1.00...... 16 25
Leader Pharmacy Co., drugs, chemicals, etc., 163.29; Lavery, M., books,
4.40 .... 167 69
Muldoon, J., lime. 1,000 lbs. for 4.00. 3,000 for 3.50; gravel, 3 loads at
3.25, 1 at 2.25, 3 at 2.25; cement. 17 bbls. at 2.15; hair 1 bag at 1.00;
elbows, pipe, etc., 7.72; lath, 1,000 ft. for 4.50; fire brick, 500 at 35.00
per M; fire clay, 100 lbs. for 6.00; sand, 4 loads at 2.00; plaster, 160
lbs. for 2.00 .... 116 52
Matthews. F., smoking hams, 231 at 5c., 11.55; Moore & Hortopp, oats,
104½ bus. at 41½c.. 43.37 .... 54 92
Moore, Jas., hay, 2 1230/2000 tons at 13.50, 5 1150/2000 at 13.50 .... 97 05
Maguire. E. A., travelling expenses 11 70
Moore, Wm. & Son, prunes, 1.000 lbs. at 8.60 cwt.. 1.250 lbs. at 8.85;
oranges, 4 boxes at 3.65, 1 box at 3.00. 1 box at 3.75; jelly powder. 3
doz. at 1.00; lemons. 1 box at 2.50. 1 box at 2.60, 1 box at 3.00;
sundries, 30c. 229 38

PUBLIC INSTITUTIONS MAINTENANCE.—*Continued.*

ASYLUM FOR INSANE, TORONTO.—*Continued.*

Expenses.—*Continued.*

Medcalf, D. M., travelling expenses *re* boiler inspection, 3.75; May, Samuel & Co., repairing bowling alleys, 30.00	33 75
Mulholland, D., hay, 2 1420/2000 tons at 11.00	29 80
Meakins & Sons, Ltd., brushes, 2 doz. at 14.40, ½ doz. at 1.93, ½ doz. 2.30, ½ doz. 2.64, 3 doz. at 1.50, 1 at 33c.	37 09
Malkin, A., return of keys, 1.00; Morton, Miss, refund on keys, 1.00	2 00
Meadows, Geo. B., spark guards, 3 at 12.00; wire guards, 1 at 3.75; wire door with Yale lock, 1 at 50.00; Yale keys, 9 at 50c.	98 25
Matthews, F. W. C., interments, 16.00; Matthews Bros., glass, 18.00	34 00
Matthews, Geo. Co., Ltd., lard, 240 lbs. at 11¾c.; pork, 985 lbs. at 9c., 1,042 lbs. at 8¾c., 1,033 lbs. at 9¼c., 1,060 lbs. at 9.40 cwt.	403 22
Murray, W. A. & Co., costume chambray, 1,556 yds. at 22c.; cretonne, 13½ yds. at 35c.; flannel, 70½ yds. at 12½c.; denim, 53½ yds. at 15c., 128 yds. at 35c.; collars, 13½ doz. at 1.40, 4 at 1.35; white vesting, 30 yds. at 30c.; sundries, 15.66; gingham, 202¼ yds. at 20c., 251 yds. at 20c.; embroidery, 26½ yds. at 15c.; spun glass, 6 yds. at 20c.; thread, 2 doz. at 1.40; sateen, 6 yds. at 20c.; cushion check, 84 yds. at 15c.; gimp, 1 pc. at 1.25	570 99
Mackenzie & Co., picture frames, 2.00; Might Directories, city directory, 1 copy at 6.00	8 00
Morrison, Jas. Brass Mfg. Co., white oval hopper, 1 at 3.60; reading lamp, 1 at 5.68; porcelain shades, 4 at 50c.; castings, etc., 137.16; valves, 3 at 50c., 2 at 2.55; self-closing stops, ½ doz. at 25.20; Lindsay lights, 4 doz. at 8.40; globes, 2 doz. at 3.00; repairs, 57.15	264 39
Monetary Times, subn. 2.00; Morrow, C., livery hire, 1.00	3 00
Markham *Sun*, advtg.	1 82
Morton, David & Sons, soap, 5,315 lbs. at 4½c., 6,900 lbs. at 4c., 135 doz. at 45c.	575 94
Mail Printing Co., subsu., 2 copies	8 00
Macdonald, Jno. & Co., thread, 3 gro. at 1.45; cotton, 608½ yds. at 9½c., 434½ at 7½c., 1,020 at 13½c.; flannellette, 1,023½ yds. at 11c.; linen, 603½ yds. at 19½c., 327¾ yds. at 12½c.; ticking, 287½ yds. at 16½c.; wraperette, 183 yds. at 11½c.; buttons, 14 gro. at 90c., 9 5-6 gro. at 75c., 6 gro. at 65c., 10 8-12 gro. at 85c., 15 8-12 gro. at 1.00, 6 gro. at 55c., 1 gro. at 60c., 1 gro. at 55c.; bath robes, 2 at 7.00; pipes, 3 at 1.50; handerchiefs, 12 doz. at 90c., 12 doz. at 2.25, 12 doz. at 25c.; braces, 3 doz. at 2.25; collars, 11 11-12 doz. at 60c.; chairs, 1 at 2.00; bags, ¼ doz. at 2.25, ½ doz. at 6.50, ¼ doz. at 9.00; sundries, 2.25; lace, 2 doz. yds. at 1.00, 2 doz. yds. at 2.50, 3 doz. yds. at 90c., 3 doz. yds. at 45c.; ribbon, 2 yds. at 75c., 30 yds. at 15c.; muslin, 24 yds. at 25c.; allover lace, 12¾ yds. at 30c.; broaches, 1 doz. at 2.00; shawls, 4-12 doz. at 9.00, ½ doz. at 7.25	741 77
McWilliam & Everist, oranges, 1 bo[illegible] 3.75; McCormick, W. J., medical books, 6.00	9 75
McPherson, W., keys, 1.00; McDonald, A. G., sharpening instruments, 1.50	2 50
McMillan & Co., cartage	12 00
McDonald, Jno., 17.1510 tons hay at 9.50; 4.840 tons at 14.00; 1.470 at 12.00; 1.670 at 13.00; 1.670 at 13.00	280 05
McDonald & Willson, repairs, 1.44	1 44
McCann, Wm. Milling Co., chop feed, 13.1350 tons at 23.50; 8,890 at 23.90; oats, 2,270 lbs. at 38c. bus., 3,420 lbs. at 39½c.; pea meal, 4.200 tons at 24.40, 1.70 at 26.90, 2½ at 25.90; oil cake, 1.500 tons at 32.50; straw, 9.1300 tons at 6.50	884 33
McLennon, Miss, refund on book, 2.00; McMahon, Miss, refund on keys, 1.00	3 00
Nerlich & Co., combs, 11½ doz. at 2.75, 12 doz. at 85c., 3 doz. at 85 2-3, 12 doz. at 3.75	89 40
Nordheimer Piano Co., violincello, 1 at 45.00; 1 cornet at 35.00; clarionets, 2 at 18.00; cello strings, 85c.; sheet music, 19.07	139 97
Nelson, W. H. & Co., combs, 1 gro. at 24.00, 1 gro. at 9.60; sundries, 4.14	37 74
Noble, C., hay, 14.1390 tons at 9.50, 10 tons 290 lbs. at 10.00	236 05
North Ontario *Times*, advertising, 2.00; *News Record*, advertising, 1.00	3 00
Ontario Rubber Co., pneumatic mattress, 1 at 27.00; peg leg boots, 1 pr. at 2.50	29 50

PUBLIC INSTITUTIONS MAINTENANCE.—*Continued.*

ASYLUM FOR INSANE, TORONTO.—*Continued.*

Expenses.—*Continued.*

Ontario Reformatory for Females, potatoes, 107 bus. at 60c.; coal, 15.775 tons at 5.45 .... 150 98

Ontario Lead & Wire Co., bath, 1 at 20.65; fuller cock, 1 at 2.35; closet, 1 at 16.00; double hubs, 2 at 1.82; sheet lead, 5 lbs. for 1.28; solder, 10¾ lbs. at 22c.; caulking lead, 25 lbs. for 1.20; sundries, 11.13 .... 58 62

Ogilvie, Thos. & Sons, French canvas, 75 yds. at 16½c., 75 yds. at 16c.; silesia, 54¾ yds. at 14c.; holland, 49 yds. at 15½c.; linen thread, 5 lbs. at 2.05; buttons, 1 gro. at 1.75; sundries, 2.21 .... 55 90

Parsons, Chas. & Sons, leather, 196 lbs. at 12c., 225 at 18c., 815¼ at 20c., 67½ at 22c., 199 at 28c., 282¾ at 29c., 65¼ at 30c, 137 lbs. at 50c., 17¼ at 85c.; dressing, 1 gal. at 1.25; sundries, 14.53 .... 414 03

Piper, N. L., Rlwy Supply Co., lanterns, 2 doz. at 9.00, 18.00; lantern globes, 2 doz. at 90c., 1.80; sundries, 2.66 .... 22 46

Perkins, Ince & Co., jelly, 3 doz. at 90c.; baking powder, 80 lbs. at 25c.; flavoring extract. 2 doz. at 2.00, 2 doz. at 2.25; canned vegetables, 16 doz. at 80c.; shelled almonds, 10 lbs. at 35c.; barley, 980 lbs. at 2.25; salt, 3 bbls. at 3.00, 10 bbls. at 1.50; canned vegetables, 20 doz. at 92½c.; candies, 200 lbs. at 14c.; tea, 2,878 lbs. at 25c.; coffee, 212 lbs. at 20c.; blacking, 1 gro. at 1.00; vinegar, 633 gals. at 28c., 1,200 gals. at 23c., 209 gals for 59.48, 123.6 gals. at 25c.; pickles, 2 doz. at 3.10; dome lead, 1 gro. at 2.40; baking powder, 80 lbs. at 25c.; currants, 233 lbs. at 8c.; corn starch, 200 lbs. at 7c., 200 lbs. at 5½c.; corn meal, 4 bags at 1.75; prunes, 750 lbs. at 8c.; raisins, 280 lbs. at 9¾c., 500 lbs. at 8½c.; rice, 1,250 lbs. at 4¼c., 1,125 lbs. at 4¼c.; cassia, 10 lbs. at 20c.; ginger, 10 lbs. at 20c.; sapolio, 2 boxes at 2.85; tobacco, 60 lbs. at 45c., 45 lbs. at 36c., 98 lbs. at 46c., 48 lbs. at 53c.; Perrin's sauce, 3 doz. at 6.00; matches, 1 case at 3.10, 1 case at 3.00; herring, 4½ bbls. at 3.50, 2 bbls at 6.00; tapioca, 45 lbs. at 6½c., 906 lbs. at 7¼c.; sundries, 25.61; wheat starch, 200 lbs. at 7c.; chicory, 25 lbs. at 8½c., 25 lbs. at 9½c.; mustard, 12 jars at 75c.; cod, 96 lbs. at 7c.; jam, 30 lbs. at 6½c.; ideal blue, 100 doz. at 13½c.; sugar, 4,455 lbs. at 4.28, 3,026 at 4.38; soda, 50 lbs. at 2½c.; biscuits, 24 lbs. at 21c.; blacking, 2 doz. at 37½c., 6 doz. at 90c.; marmalade, 714 lbs. at 7c.; fruit peels, 42 lbs. at 11c., 7 lbs. at 19c. ... 2,122 03

Price, S. & Sons., milk, 690 gals. at 18c., 240 gals. at 22c., 177.00; Park. Andrew, keys, 1.00 .... 178 00

Postmaster, stamps, 159.00; postal notes, 24c. 159 24

Pugsley, Dingman & Co., soap, 1,200 lbs. at 4c. 48 00

Perrin, Fred. J., coffee, 700 lbs. at 20c.; tea, 1,250 lbs. at 25c.; chicory, 50 lbs. at 9c., 50 lbs. at 10c. 462 00

Phillips Mfg. Co., moulding, 29.98; mirrors, 12.53 .... 42 51

Pike, D. & Co., tent hooks and eyes, 4 doz. at 25c.; awnings, 6 at 5.00; tents, 2 at 15.00 .... 61 00

Patterson, Bertha, return of text book and keys 4 50

Reid & Co., lumber, 8.00; Ross, W. K., expenses capturing eloper, 2.00 .... 10 00

Rowland, H. R., drugs and chemicals 233 25

Rooney, N., sheeting, 62 yds. at 27½c.; towels, 6 doz. at 4.00, 6 doz. at 2.50. 2 doz. at 75c., 2 doz. at 1.00; napkins, 4 doz. at 4.00, 2 doz. at 3.75, 2 at 5.00; tabling, 50 yds. at 70c., 86 at 45c., 164½ at 50c.; linen, 130¼ yds. at 27½c., 116½ at 50c., 518¼ at 16c., 73½ at 45c., crash, 91½ yds. at 15c.; towelling, 200¼ yds. at 9½c.; table cloths, 3 at 6.75 .... 511 90

Ritchie, R., hay, 2.1730 tons, 2.760 tons at 12.00; Rogers Hardware store. Souvenir range, 41.50; stove board. 1.45 .... 108 29

Rice, T. G., Wire Mfg. Co., altering wire window guard 1 50

Richelieu & Ontario Navigation Co., freight, 7.74; Rathbone, G., lumber. 237.05 .... 244 79

Ramsey, J. G. & Co., photographic supplies 6 00

Rogers, Elias & Co., coal. 752.160 tons at 5.23; Rennie, Wm. Co., Ltd., farming implements, 1.60 .... 3,934 97

Smith & Carmichael, beans, 17.29 bus. at 1.65; sundries, 1.50; eggs, 180 doz. at 16½c.; lard. 150 lbs. at 11½c. 77 30

Sundry newspapers, advtg. *re* supplies, 120.00; advtg. *re* fuel, 24.50 .... 144 50

Standard Fuel Co., grate coal, 46.1850 tons at 5.95 .... 279 21

PUBLIC INSTITUTIONS MAINTENANCE.—*Continued.*

ASYLUM FOR INSANE, TORONTO.—*Continued.*

EXPENSES.—*Continued.*

Sparrow, Geo. & Co., ring and lid for range, 1.50; trimmings for jacket and kettles	32 70
Sheen, J., hay, 5 tons at 10.00; Sparrow, Geo. & Co., repairing copper boiler, etc., 37.33; repairing fire boxes of range, 11.90	99 23
Sanderson & Rossiter, brushes, 2 doz. at 2.00; Simmers, J. A., seeds, 38.56	42 56
Star Printing Co., advtg., 3.00; Stevens, Miss, refund on book, 2.00; refund on keys, 1.00	6 00
Smith, Geo., hay, 1.370 tons at 15.00; Smith, E. D., jam, 6 pails at 67c., 1 doz. qts. at 4.00, 1 doz. at 6.00, 1 doz. at 5.00	36 79
Simpson, R. Co., Ltd., wall paper, 15 rolls at 75c., 5 rolls at 25c., 22 rolls at 25c., 30 rolls at 30c., 26 rolls at 25c., 29 rolls at 12½c.; border, 12 rolls at 25c.; shades, 1 at 2.05, 2 at 70c.; silkoline, 35 yds. at 15c., 120 yds. at 15c.; braid, 6 doz. at 20c.; fringe, 39 yds. at 5c.; stretchers, 1 pr. at 2.50; lace, 58¾ yds. at 10c., 13 yds. at 15c., 17 yds. at 8c.; shoes, 6 prs. at 2.00; wall paper, 30 rolls at 35c., 14 rolls at 75c., 12 rolls at 65c.; gimp, 50 yds. at 15c.; border, 75 yds. at 20c.; burlap, 40 yds. at 40c., 8 yds. at 1.00; cushions, 100 at 39c.; sundries, 2.90	210 87
St. Michael's Cathedral, livery hire *re* religious services	112 50
Stewart, Wm., hay, 1 ton 1,700 lbs. at 14.00; Strong, L. B., hay, 1.150 at 15.00	35 44
Steele, Briggs Seed Co., oil cake, 1 ton at 34.00, 1 ton at 32.00; seeds, 46.45; shears, 1 pr. at 1.50; wreathing, 50 yds. at 3½c.; holly, 5 lbs. at 20c.	117 90
Sloan, Jno. & Co., sugar, 3,947 lbs. at 4.08, 100 at 5½c., 3,014 at 4.23, 3,241 at 4.28, 3,241 at 4.48; biscuits, 96 lbs. at 21c.; sundries, 1.17; syrup, 5 gals. at 40c., 1,463 at 33c.; capers, 2 doz. at 2.00; tobacco, 60 lbs. at 45c., 30 lbs. at 46c.; chloride of lime, 25 lbs. at 8c.; twine, 5 lbs. at 30c.; rice, 1,120 lbs. at 4 5-8c.; pails, 3 doz. at 3.50; tapioca, 446 lbs. at 7c.; paper, 248 lbs. at 3c.; force, 1 case at 4.50; allspice, 10 lbs. at 15c.; pepper, 10 lbs. at 22c.; cloves, 10 lbs. at 25c.; prunes, 500 lbs. at 9½c.; tea, 509 lbs. at 25c.	1,000 98
Smith, T. H., eggs, 390 doz. at 25c., 90 doz. at 23c., 750 doz. at 26c., 150 doz. at 28c., 950 at 21c., 300 at 19c., 546 at 18c., 330 at 17c., 180 at 16c., 390 at 18c.; cheese, 414 lbs. at 13½c., 205 lbs. at 13½c., 215 at 12c., 226 at 12¾c., 251 lbs. at 13c.; turkey, 9 lbs. at 16c., 10¾ at 15c.; sundries, 22.00; lard, 440 lbs. at 11½c., 208 at 12c., 270 lbs. at 12½c.; bacon, 37½ lbs. at 15c., 130½ at 16c.; cider, 15 gals. at 35c.; ham, 485 lbs. at 16c.	1,374 37
Simpson, Geo., expenses capturing eloper	3 00
Singer Sewing Machine Co., needles, 1.05; oil, 90c.; repairs, 4.25; machines, 1 at 27.20, 1 at 35.20	68 60
Telegram, Evening, advertisements, 1.60; Turner, J. J. & Sons., hospital tent complete, 1 at 90.00	91 60
Toronto Water Works, water, 1,637.01; Timpson, G. J., music for dances, 131.00	1,768 01
Taylor, Forbes & Co., grate bars for boiler, 2 at 2.35, set at 10.24	14 94
Toronto Hardware Mfg. Co.. basket grates, 18 at 2.00	36 00
Toronto Laundry Machine Co., repairing washer, 6.00; extractor rubbers, 3 at 1.50, 4.50	10 50
Temple, A., hay, 2 tons 770 lbs. at 14.00, 1,930 lbs. at 14.00	46 89
Toronto Street Railway Co.. car tickets	163 44
Taylor, Jno. & Co., soap, 2,439 lbs. at 4½c., 1,727 lbs. at 5c., 906 lbs. at 5c., 822 at 5½c., 6½ gro. at 5.40	341 74
Toronto Electric Light Co., electric current, 2,346.34; arc lights, 182.25; lamps, 144 at 25c.. 36.00	2,564 59
Toronto Silver Plate Co., replating knives and forks	8 00
United Factories, brooms, 34 doz. at 3.01½, 10 doz. at 3.06, 10 doz. at 3.18 1-5, 2 doz. at 4.86; baskets, ¼ doz. at 9.00; brushes, 2 doz. at 2.07, 2 doz. at 2.18, 3 doz. at 1.35, 2 doz. at 5.70, 1 at 9.00, 3 at 2.68, 12 for 38.19, 3 doz. at 2.34, 6 doz. at 1.80; whisks, 6 doz. at 1.50	285 15
Vokes Hardware Co., butcher block, 1 at 24.75; picture books, 6 doz. at 20c.; sundries, 96c.	26 91

PUBLIC INSTITUTIONS MAINTENANCE.—*Continued.*

ASYLUM FOR INSANE, TORONTO.—*Continued.*

EXPENSES.—*Continued.*

Willard & Co., butter, 3,187 lbs. at 19c., 30,823 at 22½c., 6,473 at 22½c., chickens, 10½ lbs. at 18c., 17 lbs. at 12c., 14½ at 15c., 13 lbs. at 14c., 14 at 11c., 23 at 18c., 36 at 17c., 21 at 15c., 18 at 13c., 18 at 12c., 40 at 14c., 304 at 12c.; ducks, 35½ lbs. at 13c., 43½ at 14c., 17 at 15c.; beans, 1.70; eggs, 90 doz. at 24c., 480 doz. at 16c., 750 at 19c., 300 at 20c., 450 at 21c., cheese, 246 lbs. at 13¾c., 485 lbs. at 14½c., 233 at 12½c., 241 at 12c., 233 at 13½c., 253 at 14c., geese, 815 lbs. at 12c.; lard, 150 lbs. at 11½c.; salt, 10 lbs. at 1.60; turkey, 1,011 lbs. at 16c.; tierces, 2 only at 2.00, 2 at 37½c.; bacon, 21 lbs. at 16c.		8,671 31
Western Planing Mill Co., shavings, 9 loads at 90c.		8 10
Wolfe, S., hay, 1.620 tons at 10.50, 1.1720 at 11.00, 6.1300 at 15.00, 6.30 at 15.00, 7.1060 at 15.00; straw, 1,890 lbs. at 6.50		343 28
Watson, Jos., hay, 2.1630 tons at 14.00; Wright, R. J., inspection of weights and measures, 6.70		46 11
Winnifrith, B., keys, 1.00; Weatherburn & Glidden, sheet music, 16.43		17 43
Whillans, R. & Co., sand, 5 loads at 1.40; lime, 1,030 lbs. at 45c. cwt., 960 lbs. at 45c. cwt.; plaster, 1 bbl. at 2.00; coke, 20 bus. at 12c.		20 36
Whaley, Royce & Co., music stands, 3 for 2.98; Winnifrith, B., expenses of patients to circus, 34.00		36 98
Wicks, E. & Son, hay, 16 tons, 910 lbs. at 13.50		222 14
Wright, S., 95 10-90 bags at 90c.		85 60
West, Taylor, Bickle & Co., brushes, 5¼ doz. at 1.70, 2 doz. at 2.65; sundries, 82c.		15 05
Warwick Bros. & Rutter, printing, 104.50; Wheler, G., inspecting flour, 1.50		106 00
York Mfg. Co., Ltd., mangle felt, 102 lbs. at 65c.		66 30

ASYLUM FOR INSANE, LONDON.

SALARIES ($46,660.34).

G. A. McCallum, M.D.:	Twelve months' salary as	Medical Superintendent		2,600 00
H, E. Buchan, M.D.:	do	1st Assistant Physician		1,300 00
P. McNaughton, M.D.:	do	2nd do do		1,100 00
George McNeil, M.D.:	Eleven do	3rd do do		825 00
Chas. A. Sippi:	Five do	Bursar		583 33
John C. Hazard:	Six do	do		833 33
David Rodger:	Twelve do	Bursar's Clerk		800 00
John C. Hazard:	Four do	Storekeeper		333 33
Norval K. Wanless:	Twelve do	Assistant Storekeeper		600 00
James B. Duff:	do	Baker		450 00
J. C. Richardson:	do	Butcher		425 00
Alex. Macfie:	do	Engineer		800 00
Geo. Ross:	do	First Assistant Engineer		450 00
A. A. Boston:	do	Engineer (infirmary)		360 00
Wm. England:	do	Laundryman		360 00
John A. Stewart:	do	Carpenter		600 00
Fred McVein:	do	Assistant Carpenter		500 00
T. Westcott	do	Plasterer and Bricklayer		600 00
G. A. Armis:	Eleven do	Mason		458 33
Edward Blake:	Twelve do	Tailor		560 00
S. W. Scott:	do	Shoemaker		350 00
K. Errington:	Seven do	Painter		265 00
Samuel Roberts:	Three do	do		112 50
William Murdock:	Twelve do	Farmer		800 00
John Gall:	do	Assistant Farmer		450 00
Farm Hands (3):				392 00
John Munn:	Twelve do	Yardman		288 00
George W. Rennie:	Three do	Gardener and Steward		188 00
W. H. K. Talbot:	Nine do	Gardener		488 00
James Gall:	Twelve do	Assistant Gardener		300 00
Amos Duval:	do	Second Gardener		300 00
Richard Flynn:	do	Sewageman		500 00

PUBLIC INSTITUTIONS MAINTENANCE.—*Continued.*

ASYLUM FOR INSANE, LONDON.—*Continued.*

SALARIES.—*Continued.*

M. A. Pope:	Four months' salary as	Matron......................	167	00
Lilly Jones:	Eight	do	do	333	00
Jean Whitton:	Eleven	do	Trained Nurse	385	00
Cooks (7):		do	....	1,424	24
Maids (8):		do	....	1,089	15
Laundresses (4):		do	....	824	18
L. Quirie:	Four	do	Preserver....................	43	54
M. O'Loughlin:	Twelve	do	Tailoress	240	00
F. Norton:		do	Seamstress..................	204	00
Penelope Gall:		do	Stenographer	250	00
Maggie Dwyer:		do	Portress....................	168	00
Chief Male Attendants (3):		do	....	1,200	00
Male Supervisors (8):		do	....	2,670	00
M. A. Meehan:		do	Chief Female Attendant......	250	00
Male Attendants (31):		do	....	8,547	18
Female Supervisors (9):		do	....	1,835	88
Female Attendants (34):		do	....	5,629	95
E. T. Angus:		do	Organist....................	112	57
Wm. E. Leng, Temporary services Bursar's office			....	351	43
Stokers			....	1,963	40

EXPENSES ($93,443.28).

Adams, Edward & Co., tea, 4,287 lbs at 22c.; rice, 2,016 lbs. at 3¾c.; blue, 324 lbs. at 17c.; starch, 200 lbs. at 6¼c., 100 lbs. at 6½c.; currants, 625 lbs. at 6c.; blacking, 1 gro. at 9.00; mops, 4 doz. at 1.25; raisins, 560 lbs. at 5c., 560 lbs. at 9c., 336 lbs. at 10c.; syrup, 232 gals. at 32c.; sal. soda, 1,125 lbs. at 87½c. cwt.; pipes, 6 boxes at 90c, 13 7-12 doz. at 2.25; sugar, 6,000 lbs. at 4.37 cwt., 7,500 lbs. at 4.17 cwt., 12,500 lbs. at 4.27 cwt., 2,000 lbs. at 4.47 cwt., 941 lbs. at 4.12; matches, 6 cases at 2.20, 7 cases at 3.00; tapioca, 138 lbs. at 5c., 177 lbs. at 6½c., 168 lbs. at 7c., 150 lbs. at 7½c.; prunes, 625 lbs. at 7c., 1,500 lbs. at 7½c., 850 lbs. at 8c.; washing crystal, 6,300 lbs. at 3c.; pails, 4 doz. at 1.85, 2 doz. at 2.00; soap, 172 lbs. at 8c., 244 lbs. at 8½c.; baking powder, 10 11-12 doz. at 3.00; canned vegetables, 12 doz. at 85c., 6 doz. at 1.00, 12 doz. at 1.17½, 6 doz. at 1.40; sago, 153 lbs. at 6c., 141 lbs. at 6½c.; canned fruit, 6 doz. at 1.67½; 6 doz. at 2.60; 6 doz. at 2.85; evaporated apples, 200 lbs. at 12c.; corn starch. 80 lbs. at 7c.; pot barley, 98 lbs. at 2½c.; malta vita, 1 doz. at 95c.: tanglefoot, 2 cases at 3.75; fruit peol, 35 lbs. at 12½c., 14 lbs. at 22c.; rat traps, 1 doz. at 1.00; chocolate, 10 lbs. at 30c.; tobacco, 105 lbs. at 47c.; mustard, 1 doz. jars at 9.00; twine, 10 lbs. at 25c., 10 lbs. at 30c.; sundries, 18.93 .... 3.414 90

Adams & Panton, wheat, 5,700 lbs. at 1.40 cwt., 400 lbs. at 1.45 cwt., 1,500 lbs. at 1.50 cwt.; kaffir corn, 100 lbs. at 1.80 cwt.. 600 lbs. at 1.85 cwt.; seeds, 46.05; oats, 1,600 lbs. at 1.30 cwt.; crack wheat, 50 lbs. at 1.60 cwt., 100 lbs. at 1.75 cwt.; pot barley. 1 bag at 2.00; Hungarian corn, 1 bush. at 1.00; oyster shell, 200 lbs. at 80c. cwt., 100 lbs. at 75c. cwt.; crack corn, 700 lbs. at 1.15 cwt., 400 lbs. at 1.20 cwt., 300 lbs. at 1.25 cwt.; mullett, 1½ bush. at 1.00; oat meal, 50 lbs. at 3c.; corn meal, 24 bags at 1.70; beans, 12 bush. at 2.00............ 280 15

Allison & Element, printing, 4.50; American Medico Psychological Association, annual dues, 5.00 .... 9 50

Anderson. J. W., unloading coal, 32.00; Armstrong, W. P., milch cow, 1 only, at 45.00 .... 77 00

Barnard, John S., spectacles, 10½ doz. at 1.75, 18.38; Bayley, A., milch cow, 1 only, at 52.50 .... 70 88

Beaton, Jno. A., travelling expenses, 4.00; Bell Telephone Co., rent of instruments, 110.50; messages, 10.60 .... 125 10

Beresford Oil Co., paints, oils, etc., 107.88; Bott & Brown, cover cloth, 15.50; mattress, 1 only, at 13.50; gimp, 15 yds. at 5c.; pillows, 1 pr. at 6.50; buttons, 17½ doz. at 10c.; seats, 12.00, 50.00 .... 157 88

8 PA.

PUBLIC INSTITUTIONS MAINTENANCE.—*Continued.*

ASYLUM FOR INSANE, LONDON.—*Continued.*

EXPENSES.—*Continued.*

Boyd, H. J., enamelled pot, 1 only at 3.75; coffee pots, 1 doz. at 9.00; cereal cooker, 1 only, at 1.25; kettles, 2 only, at 2.00; fish boiler, 1 only at 5.25; tea boiler, 1 only at 6.50; plates, 2 doz. at 2.04; boilers, 3 only, at 1.25; bread box, 1 only, at 10.70; bake pans, 6 only at 1.10; potato boiler, 1 only, at 17.25; scoops. 3 only, at 1.16 2-3; sundries, 7.95 .... 83 58

Brick Mnfg. & Supply Co., brick, 9,550 at 7.50 per m.; cement. 8 bbls. at 2.10, 70 bbls. at 2.20; fire clay, 2,100 at 60c. cwt.; lime, 45 bbls. at 80c.; elbows, 4 only, at 25c. 292 03

Brock, G. S., moss, 965 lbs. at 10c., 96.50; Brooks, R., lamps, 15 only. at 6.50; mutton, 95 lbs. at 9c.; veal, 893 lbs. at 8c., 578 lbs. at 9c., 229.51 ... 326 01

Brownlee, J. A., charcoal, 25 bush. at 25c.; mugs, 6 doz. at 1.80; dust pans, 1 doz. at 4.00; ladles, 12 only, at 10c.; candle wick, 10 lbs. at 28c.; teapot, 1 only, at 2.00; ash buckets, 6 only, at 1.25; lantern globes, 3 doz. at 1.15; douche cans, 3 only, at 50c.; chambers, 6 doz. at 6.00; preserving kettles, 2 only, at 1.00, 3 only, at 1.25. 3 only, at 2.25; cuspidors, 1 doz. at 4.20; repairs, 66.70; sundries, 10.44, 169.34; Bursar, to pay sundries, 21.03 .... 190 37

Cahoon & Patterson, turkey, 303 lbs. at 16c.; geese, 102 lbs. at 11c. 59 70

Cairns, Bernard, rubber stamps, 3.95; Cambridge, J. & Son, fish, 3,788 lbs. at 10c., 378.80 .... 382 75

C. P. R. Telegraph Co., messages, 76c.; Canada Customs, customs duties, 5.95 .... 6 71

Canadian Oil Co., wax, 667 lbs. at 8c., 226 lbs. at 8½c.; engine oil, 76.84 gals. at 28c.; coal oil, 128.17 gals. at 16c.; shafting oil, 37.32 gals. at 29c.; cylinder oil, 83 gals. at 60c.; benzine, 45.45 gals. at 17¼c.; less discount, 1.07 .... 182 10

Canada Spice and Grocery Co., vanilla, 6 gals. at 10.00; chicory. 340 lbs. at 12c.; cinnamon, 10 lbs. at 20c.; pepper, 200 lbs. at .19, 50 lbs. at 20c.; nutmegs, 10 lbs. at 50c.; cloves, 5 lbs. at 25c., 20 lbs. at 28c., 5 lbs. at 30c.; pickling spice, 10 lbs. at 17c.; coffee, 1,864 lbs. at 18c., 2.008 lbs. at 27c.; roasted rye, 680 lbs. at 3c.; lemon, 3 gals. at 10.00; ginger, 15 lbs. at 20c., 5 lbs. at 23c.; cassia, 5 lbs. at 20c., 20 lbs. at 25c.; cocoanut, 20 lbs. at 17c.; allspice, 50 lbs. at 17c.; sundries. 1.49 .... 1,117 47

Canada Floral Co., plants, 172.45; wheel hoe, 1 only, at 3.50; hand weeders, 9 only, at 25c.; bug finish, 32 only. at 4.50 .... 322 20

Canada Brass & Supply Co., valve washers, 8 only, at 75c.; gauge cocks, 12 only, at 50c.; traps for closet range, 2 only, at 1.15; hydrant plug. 1 only, at 5.00; castings, etc., 47.05 .... 66 35

Canadian Express Co., charges. 10.35; Canadian Pacific Railway, freight, 21.77; rent of sidings, 114.80, 136.57 .... 146 92

Canadian Packing Co., lard, 400 lbs. at 11½c., 200 lbs. at 12c., 700 lbs. at 12¼c., 600 lbs. at 12¾c., 400 lbs. at 13c., 100 lbs. at 13 1-10c., 100 lbs. at 13¼c.; bacon, 72 lbs. at 12c., 91 lbs. at 14c., 273 lbs. at 15c., 100 lbs. at 15½c., 192¼ lbs. at 16c.; pork, 989 lbs. at 8.85 cwt.. 645 lbs. at 9.50 cwt.; brawn, 1,169 lbs. at 8c.; ham, 35¼ lbs. at 13c., 70¾ lbs. at 14½c., 108 lbs. at 15c., 93 lbs. at 15½c., 147 lbs. at 16c., 52 lbs. at 16¼c.; fertilizer, 44 loads at 50c. 762 91

Carrie. W. L. Stationery Co., stationery, 51.21; sheet music. 11.70...... 62 91

Catholic Record. subscription 2 copies 1 year, 8.00; candles, 6 lbs. at 50c.; floats, 1 box at 2.00; candle sticks, 1 pr. at 50c., 13.50; Caughlin. D., inspecting scales, 6.00 .... 19 50

Chandler, Ingram & Bell, medical appliances, 51.11; Chapman, Chas. & Co., stationery and printing, 81.00 .... 132 11

Chapman, Jno. & Co., cups, 3 doz. at 75c., 20 doz. at 50c.; white cotton. 118¼ yds. at 10c.; blankets, 2 pr. at 5.00; curtains, 3 pr. at 2.75, 4 pr. at 4.00; rug. 1 only, at 6.75; silkaline, 25 yds. at 15c.; sheeting, 22¾ yds. at 30c.; frilling, 30 7-8 yds. at 15c.; towels. 6 only, at 75c., 1 doz. at 2.15, 1 doz. at 2.75; shawls, 1 doz. at 2.50, 4 doz. at 2.75, 1 doz. at 3.00; towelling, 219 yds. at 9c., 106¾ yds. at 12½c., 141¼ yds. at 15c., 2 doz. at 2.90; print, 424 3-8 yds. at 10c.; silk tapestry,

8a P.A.

PUBLIC INSTITUTIONS MAINTENANCE.—*Continued.*

ASYLUM FOR INSANE, LONDON.—*Continued.*

EXPENSES.—*Continued.*

3¼ yds. at 2.50; silk, 5 yds. at 75c.; muslin, 76¼ yds. at 25c.; quilts, 2 only, at 2.50; linen, 6 yds. at 20c.; sundries, 11.95	258 46
Central Prison Industries, tweed, 1,654½ yds. at 55c.; shoes, 18 pr. at 1.20, 18 prs. at 1.40, 84 prs. at 1.80, 1 pr. at 2.30; flannel, 284¼ yds. at 25c., 284½ yds. at 50c.; petticoating, 299½ yds. at 50c.; blankets, 1,336 lbs. at 45c.; yarn, 7 lbs. at 45c.; binder twine, 150 lbs. at 11½c.; bed fabrics, 5 only, at 2.00; packing, 10.85	2,205 80
Childs, H. J., drugs, chemicals, etc., 80.25; Christersen, Mrs., eggs, 5 doz. for 1.00	81 25
City Gas Co., gas, 3,375.94; Citizen's, The, Gas Control Co., one year's rental of gas governors, 200.00	3,575 94
Clare, Robt., gravel, 4¼ cord at 3.50, 14.88; Columbia Handle & Lumber Co., sawdust, 1 load at 1.00	15 88
Colerick, H. C., glass, 112.85; paint, oils, etc., 144.25; moulding, 106 ft at 3½c., 68 ft. at 4c.; wall paper, 16 yds. at 15c., 2.40, 10 roll at 90c.	274 93
Coursey, Jas., expenses recovering eloper, 1.00; Crosbie, Peter, evergreens, 5 loads at 1.00, 5.00	6 00
Croil, Jas., tweeds, 135½ yds. at 1.90	257 69
Darch & Hunter Seed Co., seeds, 265.25; implements, 17.25; cultivator, 1 ton at 10.75; dessicated bone and potash, 1 ton at 35.00; tree oil, 1 pkge. at 1.25; berry boxes, 500 at 40c	331 50
Davies, Wm., Co., Ltd., butter, 36.815 lbs. at 22c., 8,099.30; Dawson, Jos., milch cow, 1 only, at 45.00	8,144 30
Dayman, W. H., baskets, ½ doz. at 4.80, 2½ doz. at 7.20; 2 doz. at 10.00	40 40
Dennis Iron & Wire Works Co., Ltd., wire cylinder, 1 only, at 3.90; repairing screens, 8.25; railing elbows, 12 only, at 20c	14 55
Doan, Herbert, services as constable 6 nights at 1.00, 6.00; Dominion Expres Co., charges, 4.25	10 25
Douglas, Jno. S., bull, 1 only, at 50.00; Down Bros., medical appliances, 16.56	66 56
Dreaney, H., manure, 10 loads at 50c., 5.00; Dufhow & Co., tweed, 271¾ yds. at 50c.; packing, 25c., 136.13	141 13
Dufton, Jno., tweed, 272¼ yds. at 50c.; less freight, 50c., 135.63; Dunn, Jas., repairs to harness, 11.00	146 63
Dyer Bros., manure, 12.50; stabling privileges, 24.00	36 50
Electric Boiler Compound Co., boiler compound, 3,854 lbs. at 4c., less freight, 7.07	147 09
Elliott & Olmstead, interments, 12.00; Ellsworth, Jas. W. & Co., coal, 536.1300 tons at 3.66, 1,964.14	1,976 14
Elviage, Henry, expenses recovering eloper, 5.39; Emerson, N. W., drugs, chemicals, etc., 27.00	32 39
Empire Mnfg. Co., steam pipe, 6.24; hydrant brasses, 1 set at 2.00; packing, 4½ lbs. at 1.00; bibb cocks, 6 only, at 55c.; cement, 4 sacks at 2.75; valves, 23.38; com'p. bibbs, 3 only, at 65c., 3 only at 95c.; lead pipe, 42 lbs. at 7c.; sink, 1 only, at 3.21; lead trap, 1 only, at 83c.; lever pet cocks, 1 doz. at 2.76; stop cocks, ½ doz. at 11.70; compression bibbs, 1 doz. at 6.60; valves bushings, etc., 13.10; sundries, 3.22	93 73
Farmers' Advocate, advertising, 1.00; Fitzgerald, R., hay, 5.290 tons at 8.00, 43.68	44 68
Fitzgerald & Duncan, drugs, chemicals, etc., 34.39; Fitzgerald, Thos. J., brooms, 40 doz. at 2.40, 10 doz. at 2.50, 121.00	155 39
Flannigan, Geo., milch cow, 1 only, at 48.00; Flock, Jas. K., leather belting, 60¼ ft. at 20 1-5c., 100 ft. at 15 3-10c., 120 ft. for 18.36, 43.76	91 76
Ford, R. S., ticking, 218 yds. at 18c.; towelling, 530½ yds. at 12½c., 308 yds. at 15c.; print, 321 yds. at 10¾c.; cotton, 1,081¼ yds. at 9½c., 700 yds. at 7½c.; table linen, 306¼ yds. at 45c., 22 yds. at 55c., 36 yds. at 90c.	523 78
Foster, J. G., London directory, 3 copies at 3.00, 9.00; Fraser, D., horseshoeing, 61.03	70 03
Free Press Printing Co., subscription, 5 copies for 1 year, 30.00; advertising, 3.59	33 59

PUBLIC INSTITUTIONS MAINTANCE.—*Continued.*

ASYLUM FOR INSANE, LONDON.—*Continued.*

EXPENSES.—*Continued.*

Frost & Wood Co., repairs to implements, 4.20; Gall, Jno, chickens, 5 only for 1.75	5 95
Gallard & McLachlan, drugs, chemicals, etc., 86.84; Galpin & Barr, pipes, ½ doz. at 9.00; walking stick, 1 only, at 1.25, 5.75	92 59
Garner, R., vinegar, 248½ gals. at 25c., 62.12; Gas Appliance Co., zena chimneys, 2 doz. at 1.50; hall fixture, 1 only, at 5.00; globes, 2 only, at 40c., 4 only at 50c.; sundries, 1.35, 12.15	74 27
Globe Printing Co., advertising, 39c.; Grand Trunk Ry. Co., freight, 55.02	55 41
Graham Bros., straw hats, 12 doz. at 2.00; felt hats, 2 only, at 2.00	28 00
G.N.W. Telegraph Co., messages, 4.01; Gutta Percha & Rubber Mnfg. Co., Ltd., hospital sheets, 72 only, at 2.00, 144.00	148 01
Gurd, Wm. & Co., billiard tips, 1 box at 1.50; cement, 1 bottle at 25c.; sundries, 65c.	2 40
Hagen, A. T. & Co., canvass for mangle, 2 sets at 7.10; bed canvas, 1 set at 3.20	17 40
Hagerman, W. A., manure, 6.00; Halliday, Jas., purchase of meat, 14,275.49	14,281 49
Harris, W. J., travelling expenses, 7.50; Hartz, J. F. Co., Ltd., medical appliances, 2.42	9 92
Hamilton, Jas. R., poultry, 10.00; Harvey, Jno. G., disinfectant, 5 gals. at 1.25; powdered ammonia, 90 lbs. at 4½c., 10.30	20 30
Haskett Bros., geese, 206 lbs. at 11c.; turkey, 305½ lbs. at 16c., 71.54; Heaman, W. A., travelling expenses, 9.30	80 84
Heighway, R. J., admission of patients to circus, 33.00; Higby, W., cab hire *re* religious services, 44.00	77 00
Hiscott, Thos., violin strings, etc., 13.47; cymbols, 1 pr. at 10.00	23 47
Hookway, R. & Son., beans, 10 bush. at 1.90, 22 bush. at 2.00, 3 bags at 3.80; barley, 2 bags at 2.75; split peas, 15 bags. at 2.75; corn meal, 6 bbls. at 3.60, 23 bbls. at 3.75; flour, 1 bbl. at 4.00	233 00
Hopkins, Jno., Press, subscription to *American Journal of Insanity*	5 00
Howie, Wm., lumber, 545.01; Howe, Geo. & Son, wall paper, 29 yds. at 12c. 3.48	548 49
Howard, C. E., repairs to vehicles, 42.35; repairs to implements, 11.50; sleighs, 1 pr. at 25.00	78 85
Howden, D. H. & Co., glass, 4 lights at 75c., 4 cases at 4.15, 4 cases at 6.65, 1 case at 12.40; tacks, 6 m. at 70c.; fork handles, 2 doz. at 1.95; diamond, 1 only, at 8.00; rule, 1 only, at 1.25; hinges, 1 doz. at 1.00, 1 doz. at 2.35, 2½ doz.—147 lbs. at 6½c.; rim knobs, 2 doz. at 1.30; sofa springs, 25 lbs. at 8c.; washers, 10 lbs. at 9c., 20 lbs. at 10c.; wire nails, 1 keg at 2.25, 2 kegs at 2.30, 1 keg at 2.35, 3 kegs at 2.40, 2 kegs at 2.45, 3 kegs at 2.50, 2 kegs at 2.55, 1 keg at 2.65, 1 keg at 2.90; rubber hose, 50 ft. at 8c., 25 ft. at 12c.; jack screws, 4 only, at 3.60; trowel, 1 only, at 1.35; knives, ½ doz. at 2.00, 1 doz. at 3.25, 1-6 doz. at 10.50, 1 only at 5.50; castors, 12 set at 14c., 12 set at 17c., 6 set at 35c., 6 set at 45c., 6 set at 50c., 6 set at 70c.; fox scale, 1 only, at 18.50; hay forks, 2 doz. at 5.75; tool baskets, ½ doz. at 4.75; drawer pulls, 3 doz. at 75c.; padlocks, 1 doz. at 2.25, 2 doz. at 2.50, 1 doz. at 3.25, 2 doz. at 3.50, 1 doz. at 4.00, ½ doz. at 15.10; castings, 24.16; rope, 20 lbs. at 16c.; glass cutters, 6 only, at 25c.; files, 1 doz. at 1.75; rim locks, 1 doz. at 2.75; rasps, ½ doz. at 3.50; wire cloth, 9 rolls at 2.95½; Yale latch, 1 only, at 2.00; paint, oils, etc., 246.59; hoes, 1 doz. at 5.25; hatchets, 1 only, at 1.00; forks, 1 doz. at 2.15; scythes, ½ doz. at 11.50; snaths, ½ doz. at 9.50; repairing mower, 6.00; whiffletrees, 4 only, at 1.00, 2 only at 1.50; staples, 1 keg at 3.00; kegs, 1 doz. at 2.00; knives for bell cut box, 1 set at 6.00; hemp packing, 25 lbs. at 18c.; lawn mower, 1 only, at 6.80, 1 only at 7.25; lawn mower parts, 38 pcs. for 87.53; spoons, ½ gro. at 7.50, ½ gro. at 17.25; chisels, ½ doz. at 5.40, ½ doz. at 5.65; door springs, 1 doz. at 2.00; steels, 1 doz. at 7.75; snow shovels, ½ doz. at 13.50; netting, 8 rolls at 4.65, 7 rolls at 5.40, 4 rolls at 7.20; trays, ½ doz. at 6.75, ½ doz. at 7.50, ½ doz. at 8.00; coal scoops, 1½ doz. at 13.23; throat plates, 2 only, at 1.00; shovels, ½ doz. at 13.50; screws, 4 gro. at 35c.; lawn rakes, 1 doz. at 6.50; mugs, 5 doz. at 1.05, 5 doz. at 1.20; kettles, 1 only, at 5.15, ½ doz. at 15.25; tailors' shears, 1 pr at 8.75; axes, ½ doz. at 12.00; ice saws, 9 ft. at 80c.; sundries, 83.99	1,014 06

PUBLIC INSTITUTIONS MAINTENANCE.—*Continued.*

ASYLUM FOR INSANE, LONDON.—*Continued.*

Expenses.—*Continued.*

Hueston, Robt. & Sons, manure, 25.00; Hunter & Son. manure, 18.00 ...	43 00
Hunt Bros., coal, 872.730 tons at 4.34, 1,344.500 tons at 4.38, 38.500 tons at 4.75, 13.1,760 tons at 4.78, 28.650 tons at 5.00	10,063 51
Hunt Bros., bran, 1¼ tons at 17.00, 5 tons at 18.00, 1½ tons at 19.00, 3 tons at 20.00, 7¼ tons at 21.00; shorts, 5 tons at 21.00, 2 tons at 22.00, 2¼ tons at 23.00; flour, 1,728¼ bbls. at 3.79 .....:	7,083 78
Imperial Oil Co., Ltd., oils, etc., 36.31; Ingles, Jas., hogs, 9 only for 52.00	88 31
Irwin, J. C., street car tickets, 75c.; Isaac, J. R., cheese, 624 lbs. at-11¼c., 69.42	70 17
Jenkins, Thos., tobacco, 256 lbs. at 45c., 408 lbs. at 46c.	302 88
Johnston, W. J., gas mantles, 1 doz. at 1.80, 3 doz. at 3.00, 4 doz. at 2.50, 1 doz. at 4.20	25 00
Jones, A., cleaning sewage tank, 35.00; cleaning flues and pipes, 47.25; cleaning closet vaults, 52.50	134 75
Jones, Jno., horse collars, 1 pr. at 6.00; repairing harness, 31.20, 37.20; Jones, L., travelling expenses, 13.40	50 60
Kernohan, Geo. N., lumber, 263.05; Kernohan, H. R., milch cow, 1 only at 42.68	305 73
Kincaid, W. R., veterinary services, 28.75; King's Printer, stationery, 25.85	54 60
Kingsmill. T. F., shirting, 230¼ yds. at 10c., 451½ yds. at 12c.; towelling, 318 yds. at 10c., 215 yds. at 12c.; scrim, 108 yds. at 10c., 184½ yds. at 12½c.; fringe, 100 yds. at 10c.; linoleum, 32 yds. at 55c.; rollers, 6 only, at 25c.; tapestry covering, 5 1-6 yds. at 75c.; curtains, 2 pr. at 2.50, 2 pr. at 3.00, 2 pr. at 4.50; tabling, 263¾ yds. at 42½c., 28¾ yds. at 47½c.; huck., 95 yds. at 12c., 191½ yds. at 25c.; muslin, 36 yds. at 25c., 6 yds. at 35c.; carpet, 119½ yds. at 75c.; blind cloth, 38¼ yds. at 35c.; print, 92¾ yds. at 10c., 156 yds. at 11¾c.; rubber, 6 2-3 lbs. at 3.00; blankets, 2 pr. at 3.00, 2 pr. at 4.80; sundries, 4.53	588 12
Kingston Asylum, brushes. 36 doz. at 2.00, 22 doz. at 2.50, 12 doz. at 3.00	163 00
Kitchen, W. J., music furnished, 14.00; Labatt Mnfg. Co., repairing hydrants, 24.98; pipe nipple, 1 only, at 1.00; sink, 1 only, at 2.45; hydrant valve seat, 1 only, at 6.00; iron pipe, 29.69; closet bowl, 1 only, at 4.50; turning crank shaft, 8.40; sundries, 8.23, 85.25	99 25
Ladell, A. E., tobacco, 412 lbs. at 45c., 570 lbs. at 46c., 447.60; Land, Wm., livery hire, 26.00	473 60
Langford, A. A., Co., Ltd., stationery. 54.83; toilet paper, 3 cases at 6.00	72 83
Langford, E., oats, 179 bush. for 69.98; Lawson & Jones, stationery, embossing, etc., 53.50	123 48
Lawrason, S. F.. soap. 966 lbs. at 2½c., 742 lbs. at 4½c., 22,823 lbs. at 4¾c., 50 boxes at 2.40: soda ash. 737 lbs. at 2¼c., 754 lbs. at 2½c.	1,297 04
Leng, W. E., travelling expenses, 3.90; Leonard, E. & Sons, coal grates, 620 lbs. at 3¼c., 20.15	24 05
Line, McDonald & Co., cigars. 100 only at 5.50, 100 only at 3.50	9 00
London, Stencil & Stamp Works, rubber stamps, 2.05; London Advertiser, advertising, 2.19	4 24
London Street Ry. Co., car tickets, 80.25; carrying mail from post office, 58.33	138 58
London Electric Co., pencil zines, 48 only at 5c., wire 10 10/16 lbs. at 40c.; sundries, 40c.	7 08
London Engine Supply Co., leather, 6 lbs. at 70; pipe cutter, 1 only at 2.00; hemp packing. 25 lbs. at 15c.; 25 lbs. for 1.25, 11.20; London Printing and Lithographing Co,, printing, 29.50	40 70
London Crockery Co., dishes, ¼ doz. at 9.00; cups, 10 doz. at 60c. spittoons. 5 only at 1.00; ewers, 2 doz. at 6.00; gas globes, 13 doz. at 3.00; 3 only at 65c.: soup plates. 12 doz. at 80c., 10 doz. at 85c.; jugs, 3 doz. at 1.20, 2 doz. at 2.00, 1½ doz. at 3.60, plates, 20 doz. at 60c.; bowls. 5 doz. at 90c., 5 doz. at 1.20; soup tureen. 1 only at 3.50; lantern globes, 2 11/12 doz. at 1.20; tumblers, 44 doz. at 50c., 1 doz. at 1.50; jars, 1 gross at 12.00; toilet sets. 1 only at 3.50; sundries, 8.00	176 05
Macklin. H.. cloth caps. 15 doz. at 3.25, 48.75; Macfie, A., travelling expenses, 2.10	50 85

PUBLIC INSTITUTIONS MAINTENANCE.—*Continued.*

ASYLUM FOR INSANE, LONDON.—*Continued.*

EXPENSES.—*Continued.*

Maker, Tom, livery hire, 78.00; Mallock, Wm. & Co., pinion wheel, 1 only at 4.25; castings, 302 lbs. at 3½c.; boring, facing gear and sprocket, 2.75, 17.58 .... 95 58

Mammoth, The Livery, stabling privileges, 24.00; manure, 12.50 .... 36 50

Mann, Jno. & Sons., cement, 40 bbls. at 2.25; 10 bbls. at 2.40, 5 bbls. at 2.65, 10 bbls. at 2.70; trap, 1 only at 2.90; lime, 47 bbls. at 95c.; plaster, 5 bbls. at 2.25; fire brick, 500 at 32.00, 2,000 at 33.00; sewer pipe, 100 ft. at 8c., 50 ft at 9c., 100 ft. at 12c., 100 ft. at 20c.; sundries, 12.90 .... 352 45

Maple Leaf Automobile & Electric Mfg. Co., steel cable, 120 ft. at 9c...... 10 80

Mara, T. E., hoods, 6 only at 65c., dress goods, 32 yds. at 25c., 11.90; Massey Harris Co., Ltd., repairs to implements, 13.70 .... 25 60

Matthews & Granger, shoes, 1 pr. at 1.00, 1 pr. at 1.25, 57 pr. at 2.00, 30 pr. at 2.25; rubbers, 20 pr. at 60c.; overshoes, 6 pr. at 1.75......... 206 25

Matheson, N., yarn, 720½ lbs. at 50c., 360.25; May, Wm., horseshoeing, 45.28 .... 405 53

Medcalf, D. M., travelling expenses, re boiler inspection, 37.25; Meek, A. J., tuning pianos, 7.30 .... 44 55

Michigan Central Ry., freight, 2.70; Mills, J., veal, 178 lbs. at 8c., fertilizer, 14 loads at 50c., 21.24 .... 23 94

Mitchell, B. A., drugs chemicals. etc. 130 76

Mountjoy, R. & Son, lemons, 39 doz. at 25c., 19 doz. at 30c., 3 doz. at 40c., 3 doz. at 45c., 13 doz. at 50c.; pineapples, 6 only at 20c.; grapes, 2 bas. at 50c.; oranges, 2 doz. at 40c.; bananas, 2 doz. at 20c.; peaches. 1 bas. at 55c., 1 bas. at 65c., 2 bas. at 70c., 2 bas. at 85c., 2 bas. at 90c.; 2 bas. at 95c 35 90

Murdock, Wm., entry fee for sows at exhibition, 3.00; travelling expenses, 5.00 .... 8 00

MacCallum, G. A., M.D., travelling expenses, 51.50; MacVoy, L., expenses capturing eloper, 4.40 .... 55 90

McAinsh, D. T. & Co., medical books, 15.00; McCallum, C. & Co., drugs, chemicals, etc., 71.22; chamois skins, ¼ doz. at 7.90; sponges, ½ doz. at 10.80; soap, 1 doz. at 60c., 1 doz. at 1.20; baking powder, 46 doz. at 3.00, 220.37 .... 235 37

McCartney, Jas., livery hire, 16.00; McClary, Mfg. Co., repairs to furnace. 26.43; cast iron kettle, 1 only at 20.28; cast iron table, 1 only at 18.28; castings, 336 lbs. at 6c.; patterns for grates, 9.00; sundries, 4.66, 98.81 114 81

McClellan, D. A., horse, 1 only at 205.00; McCormick, Geo., manure, 2.00 207 00

McCormick, C. J., cheese, 315 lbs. at 13½c., 1,099 lbs. at 14c., 761 lbs. at 14½c.; eggs, 30 doz. at 15, 180 doz. at 18c., 300 doz. at 19c., 360 doz. at 20c., 60 doz. at 21c., 14 doz. at 22c., 150 doz. at 23c., 70 doz. at 24c., 60 doz. at 25c., 230 doz. at 26c., 90 doz. at 27c., 300 doz. at 28c.; chickens, 27½ lbs. at 12½c., 3 pr. at 1.10, 3 pr. at 1.20; rabbits, 16 only at 25c.; potatoes, 400.50 bags at 85c., 335.50 bags at 1.00, 31.10 bags. at 1.40 .... 1,456 63

McCormick, A. & Son, cheese, 485 lbs. at 11½c., 603 lbs. at 14c.; fish, 300 lbs. at 7c., 120 lbs. at 8c., 330 lbs. at 9c.; oranges, 2 cases, at 3.50; turkey, 322 lbs. at 15c., 29 lbs. at 18c 261 02

McGibbon's Drug Store, drugs, chemicals etc., 80.00; McIntosh, P. & Son, roll oats. 10 bbls. at 5.15, 90 bbls. at 5.25. less cartage, 10.00, 514.00 ... 594 00

McLean, Gillian, spoons, 6 doz. at 1.00, 1 doz. at 4.75; knives, 6 doz. at 2.00; ½ doz. at 3.00, 1/6 doz. at 12.00; solarine, 1 doz. at 9.00; sifters, 3 only at 25c.; barley forks, ¼ doz. at 15.00; razors, 1 only at 1.50; pulleys, 1 only at 1.25. 1 only at 2.25; nail brushes, 1 doz. at 1.00; car bits, 2 only at 65c.; shovels. ½ doz. at 12.00, ½ doz. at 18.00; rope, 42 ft for 2.00; curtain rings, 1 doz. at 50c., 3 doz. at 90c.; lawn rakes. ½ doz. at 7.20; carvers 1 pr. at 1.50, 1 pr. at 2.00, wrench 1 only at 7.50; sundries. 1.95 .... 82 90

McMahon, Granger & Co., yarn, 24 lbs. at 42½c., 6 lbs., at 45c., 6 lbs. at 50c.; cotton. 631½ yds. at 6½c., 1,302 yds. at 7c., 646½ yds. at 7½c., 678½ yds. at 8c., 659 yds. at 8½c. 4,585½ yds. at 9c., 476½ yds. at 10c.; cheese cloth, 110 yds. at 3¾c.; ticking, 658½ yds. at 17c., 554½ yds. at 17½c., 192 yds. at 18; thimbles. 2 gross at 1.25; braces, 28 doz. at 2.25,

PUBLIC INSTITUTIONS MAINTENANCE.—*Continued.*

ASYLUM FOR INSANE, LONDON.—*Continued.*

EXPENSES.—*Continued.*

1 7/12 doz. at 3.00, 5½ doz. at 3.50, 3 doz. at 3.75, 1 doz. at 4.00, 1 1/12 doz. at 4.50; thread, 8 lbs. at 58c., 2 doz. at 80c., 4 doz. at 1.10, 31 doz. at 2.60, 22¼ gross at 5.40; denim, 62 yds. at 16½, 231¼ yds. at 18½c.; silesia, 66 yds. at 15c.; machine silk, 1 lb. at 8.00; quilts, 604 only at 95c.; duck, 54 yds. at 16c., 60 yds. at 17c.; sheeting, 588 yds. at 17c., 3,259¾ yds. at 17½ c., warp, 100 lbs. at 23c.; shirting, 587¼ yds. at 8c., 82 yds. at 8½c., 223¼ yds. at 9½c., 2,170¼ yds. at 10c., 3,829¼ yds. at 12c.; combs, 12 doz. at 42½c.; 21 doz. at 75c., 6 doz. at 85c., 36 doz. at 90c., 12 doz. at 1.00, 12 doz. at 1.15, 3 doz. at 1.25, 1 gross at 12.00; buttons, 4 doz. at 50c., 4 gross at 65c., 9 gross at 75c., 2 gross at 1.00, 6 doz. at 75c.; pins, 6 doz. at 18c., 9 doz. at 30c., cottonade, 369¾ yds. at 15c., 288¼ yds. at 16c., 328¾ yds. at 18½c.; canvas, 162 yds. at 8c., 64 yds. at 10c., 195 yds. at 11c., 127 yds. at 12c., 127¼ yds. at 12½c., 60 yds. at 14½c.; tweed, 49¾ yds. at 47½c., 328 yds. at 50c.; pocketing, 118 yds. at 9½c., handkerchiefs, 6 doz. at 58c., 5 doz. at 60c., 5 doz. at 65c., 5 doz. at 75c., 10 doz. at 85c.; batts, 2 bales at 6.50; shoe laces, 4 doz. at 60c., 3 gross at 2.50; towelling, 1,303 yds. at 8c., 560¾ yds. at 10c., 392 yds. at 15c.; linen, 501 yds. at 27½c.; umbrellas, ¾ doz. at 12.00; golfers, 6 only at 1.25; sweaters, 2 doz. at 6.75; 4¼ doz. at 9.00; frilling, 12 doz. at 1.50; mitts, 1 doz. at 2.25, 10 1/6 doz. at 4.50; muslin, 373¼ yds. at 8c., 154 yds. at 9½c., 143¼ yds. at 12½c.; comb sets, 2 sets at 2.50; 3 sets at 3.00; turkey red, 1 pc. at 75c., 2 pcs. at 85c., 2 pcs. at 1.00; collars, 2 doz. at 1.00, 2 doz. at 1.75; ladies' vests, ½ doz. at 6.50, ½ doz. at 10.50; dress goods, 40¼ yds. at 19½c., 33¼ yds. at 20., 168 yds. at 37½c.; gloves, 1 doz. at 2.25; corsets, ¼ doz. at 6.50, 1/12 doz. at 9.00; pique, 41½ yds, at 17½c., needles, 2 m. at 1.00; pillow cotton, 171 yds. at 14c., 481 yds. at 15c.; flannelette, 1,203¼ yds. at 8c., 226¼ yds. at 9c., 1,157½ yds. at 10c.; shirts, ½ doz. at 8.40, 1 doz. at 9.00; ties, 1 doz. at 1.80, 6 doz. at 2.25, ½ doz. at 4.50; table linen, 303 yds. at 40c., 182 yds. at 45c.; india linen, 135 yds. at 18½c.; nett, 198½ yds. at 7½c.; lace, 12 doz yds. at 25c., 14 doz. yds. at 35c., 6 doz. yds. at 37½c., 9 doz. yds. at 65c., 3 doz. yds. at 1.15; shawls, 1 5/12 doz. at 4.50, 3 1/6 doz. at 6.50, ½ doz. at 9.00; ribbons, 90 yds. at 7½c., 54 yds. at 11c.; mufflers, 2½ doz. at 4.50, 2 doz. at 6.00, 1½ doz. at 9.00; hose, 4 doz. at 2.25, 2½ doz. at 3.25; lining, 103¾ yds. at 9½c.; sundries, 64.82	5,435 29
McMillan, N., splicing steel cable, 2.50; McMullen Printing Co., printing, 10.00	12 50
McNeil, Geo., street car tickets	1 75
National Drug & Chemical Co., drugs, chemicals, etc., 88.53; sponges, 6 only at 11c., 2 only at 40c.; tubing, 2 lbs. at 90c	91 79
Nerlich & Co., tennis nets, 1/6 doz. at 36.00; tennis racquets, 1-3 doz. at 21.00; tennis balls, 1 doz. at 4.00	17 00
Onn, F. S., fish, 8,150 lbs. at 10c., 815.00; Ontario Rubber Co., hospital sheets, 8 doz. at 18.00; rubber ice caps, ¼ doz. at 9.00; express charges, 21c., 146.46	961 46
Perrin, D. L. & Co., biscuits, 1,279½ lbs. at 7c., 53½ lbs. at 6c., 18 lbs. at 12c., 629½ lbs. at 12½c., 46¼ lb., at 13c., 57½ lbs. at 13½., 26½ lbs. at 14c., 19 lbs. at 14½c., 21½ lbs. at 16c.; pop corn, 2 gross at 1.00	199 30
Percival, Henry, cartage, 16.00; Platt, J. E., marking ink, 4 qts. at 6.25; baking powder, 120 lbs. at 25c.; jeyes fluid, 44 gals. at 1.00; sponges, ½ doz. at 2.00; soap, 6 doz. at 1.10; laundry wax, 10 lbs. at 18c.; rat poison, 1 doz. at 2.50; drugs, chemicals, etc., 95.55, 206.45	222 45
Pocock, Bros., shoes, 37 pr. at 2.25; valise, 1 only at 5.25	88 50
Post Master, postage stamps, 180.00; Post Office, box rent, 5.50	185 50
Queen City Oil Co., coal oil, 46 gals. at 16; wax, 240 lbs. at 8c	26 56
Red Star News Co., subscriptions to sundry magazines, 73.45, brooches, 5 doz. at 3.00; mouth organs, ½ doz. at 3.00; delivering mail bag, 16 months at 2.00 per month; Christmas decorations, 4.90; Canadian Almanac, 6 only at 75c.; subscription to daily journal, 24 copies, 30.00.	161 35
Reid, W. J. Co., tumblers, 41¾ doz. at 40c., 52 doz. at 75c., 2 doz. at 1.50, plates, 37 doz. at 60c., 10 doz. at 80c., 6 doz. at 85c., 1 doz. at 90c.,	

PUBLIC INSTITUTIONS MAINTENANCE.—*Continued.*

ASYLUM FOR INSANE, LONDON.—*Continued.*

EXPENSES.—*Continued.*

1 doz. at 2.00, 1 doz. at 5.75; basins, 1 doz. at 4.80; bowls, 13 doz. at 1.00, 19 doz. at 1.10, 13 doz. at 1.20, 1 doz. at 4.80; block soap, 1 doz. at 1.20; salt cellars, 3 doz. at 1.50; chambers, 6 doz. at 4.00; globes, 3 doz. at 65c., 6 only at 83c., covered dishes, 1 doz. at 6.00; cups and saucers, 40 doz. at 50c., 20 doz. at 55c., 36 doz. at 60c., 20 doz. at 70c., 6 doz. at 80c., 12 doz. at 85c., 6 doz. at 90c., 1 doz. at 2.50, 1 doz. at 4.80; ewers, 2½ doz. at 4.80; vegetable dishes, 2 doz. at 6.00; toilet sets, 3 only at 3.50; gravy boats, 1 doz. at 2.40; sugar bowls, ½ doz. at 3.00; vases, 1 doz. at 5.00; jardiniers, 3 only at 33c., 3 only at 40c., 3 only at 50c., 3 only at 80c., 1 only at 1.50; jars, 7-12 gross at 10.50 cuspidors, ½ doz. at 10.00; sundries, 1.05	361 85
Rice Lewis & Son, knives, 1 doz. at 2.15, 1 doz. at 3.75, 1 doz. at 7.05; spoons 1 doz. at 4.25; 1 doz. at 7.50, 1 doz. at 8.50	33 20
Richardson, Jno., expenses capturing eloper, 3.95; services as constable, 5 nights at 1.00	8 95
Richard, Pure Soap Co., soap, 1 gross at 8.00, 1,196 lbs. at 4½c	61 82
Roberts, Wm., splicing cable, 5.00; Rooney, N., quilts, 6 only at 2.25; linen towels, 2 doz. at 3.50; lace curtains, 6 pr. at 2.50; table cloths, 6 only at 4.50; napkins, 2 doz. at 3.00; sheeting, 62 yds. at 31½c., 88.03	93 03
Rumble, J., expenses recovering eloper, 3.00; Saunders, W. E. & Co., drugs, chemicals, etc., 22.87; medical appliances, 46.21, 69.08	72 08
Scandrett Bros., yeast, 106½ lbs. at 35c.; spirits for medical use, 79.95; starch, 766 lbs. at 6¾c., 40 lbs. at 7c., 40 lbs., at 7½c.; canned vegetables, 6 doz. at 82½c., 2 doz. at 85c., 6 doz. at 90c., 6 doz. at 95c.; fish, 2 doz. at 1.50., 2 doz. at 1.57½, 2 doz. at 1.58, 2 doz. at 1.65, 2 doz. at 2.65, 2 doz. at 3.75; prunes, 250 lbs. at 7c., 250 lbs. at 7½c., 975 lbs. at 8c.; sugar, 916 lbs. at 3.92, 902 lbs. at 4.02, 1,500 lbs. at 4.17., 1,000 lbs., at 4.27, 3,000 lbs. at 4.47, cwt.; sago, 337 lbs. at 6½c.; malta vita, 4½ doz. at 1.00; alcohol, 2 gals, at 4.50; rice, 1,344 lbs, at 3¾c.; twine, 10 lbs. at 20c.; quaker oats, 1 case at 3.00; syrup, 1,356 lbs. at 2¾c.; chocolate, 12 lbs. at 38c.; mustard, 22 jars at 75c.; canned fruit, 6 doz. at 1.50, 6 doz. at 2.82½., 4 doz. at 2.85; tea, 665 lbs. at 22c.; currants, 206 lbs. at 6¼c.; 381 lbs. at 6½c., 325 lbs. at 7¾c.; raisins, 336 lbs. at 5c., 280 lbs. at 5½c., 280 lbs. at 6¼, 56 lbs. at 7¼c., 30 lbs. at 10c., 3 cases at 2.40; tubs, 1-6 doz. at 85c., 1-3 doz. at 9.00; soap, 105 lbs. at 8c., 110 lbs. at 8½c.; tapico, 344 lbs. at 6½c.; pickles, 2 doz. at 2.25. 1 doz. at 3.60; Gillet's lye, 4 doz. at 95c.; gelatine, 2 doz. at 1.25; cocoanut, 50 lbs. at 18c.; vinegar, 148 gals. at 25c.; almonds, 324 lbs. at 16½c.; pecans, 25 lbs. at 16c.; walnuts, 108 lbs. at 12½c.; filberts, 100 lbs. at 10c.; pails, 2 doz. at 1.85; sundries, 7.90	1,295 33
Scott, H. H., repairs to vehicles, 55.50; Sharpe, J. F., pillow sham patterns, 5.10	60 60
Shoebotham & Coote, polishing knives, 6.25; surgical instruments, 2.00, 8.25; Short & Stewart, manure, 5.45	13 70
Smallman & Ingram, sheeting, 555¼ yds. at 15½c., 42 yds. at 30c.: flannel, 53½ yds., at 30c.; mull, 192 yds. at 14½c.; hosiery, 5 doz. at 1.00, 2 doz. at 1.25, 1 doz. at 2.75; pillow covers, 7 only at 25c., velour, 5½ yds. at 2.50; art silk, 19½ yds. at 75c.: linen, 79 yds. at 45c.; print, 1,165¼ yds. at 10¾c.; cotton, 72 yds. at 8½c., 141½ yds. at 9½, 276 yds. at 10c.; napkins, 2 doz. at 2.80: nett, 24¾ yds. at 22c.; lace, 18 doz. yds. at 50c.; quilts, 2 only at 2.75: elastic, 3 doz. yds. at 33 1-3c.; cord, 8½ yds. at 25c.; frilling, 11¾ yds. at 15c.; corsets, 1 pr. at 50c., 1 pr. at 1.25; sundries, 11.82	434 93
Smith, A. M. & Co., tea, 2,098 lbs. at 22c.; evaporated apples, 434 lbs. at 8c., 200 lbs. at 9¾c., 527 lbs. at 10c.; sugar, 50 lbs. at 5½c., 655 lbs. at 3.82 cwt., 2,141 lbs. at 3.92 cwt., 904 lbs. at 4.02 cwt., 3,000 lbs. at 4.07 cwt., 4,500 lbs. at 4.17 cwt., 6,000 lbs. at 4.27 cwt., 7,000 lbs. at 4.37 cwt., 1,000 lbs. at 4.39 cwt., 3,000 lbs. at 4.47 cwt., 50 lbs. at 5.20 cwt.; pails, 2 doz. at 1.85; corn starch, 280 lbs. at 7c.; sapolio, 3 doz. at 94c.; rice, 1,344 lbs. at 3½c.; matches, 7 cases at 3.10; salmon,	

PUBLIC INSTITUTIONS MAINTENANCE.—*Continued.*

ASYLUM FOR INSANE, LONDON.—*Continued.*

Expenses.—*Continued.*

2 doz. at 1.45; pickles, 1 doz. at 3.25; macaroni, 5 lbs. at 10c.; sardines, 24 boxes at 10c.; soap, 109 lbs. at 7¼c.; candles, 6 lbs. at 12c.; paper, 35 lbs., at 3c.; tapioca, 136 lbs. at 7c.; chocolate, 12 lbs. at 30c.; syrup, 28 gals. at 32c.; vinegar, 204.8 galls, at 21c.; starch, 500 lbs. at 5c., 200 lbs., at 5¼c.; prunes, 165 lbs. at 5¼c., 200 lbs. at 6½c., 700 lbs. at 7½c., 50 lbs. at 9c.; canned fruit, 4 doz. at 1.27½, 10 doz. at 1.65; 4 doz. at 1.75, 10 doz. at 2.20, 4 doz. at 2.25, 6 doz. at 2.82½, 4 doz. at 2.85, 4 doz. at 2.87½; whisks, 1 doz. at 1.20; blue, 132 lbs. at 17c.; lobster, 2 doz. at 3.85; gelatine, 1 doz. at 1.45; L. and P. sauce, 1 doz. at 3.70; currants, 600 lbs. at 6½c., 314 lbs. at 7½c.; pipes, 2 cases at 75c.; wash boards, 1 doz. at 2.25; barley, 100 lbs. at 2¼c.; tanglefoot, 2 cases at 3.75; sundries, 35.53 .... - 2,309 70

Smith, The Plumbing Co., gas pillars, 21 only at 2c.; globe holders, 18 only at 8c 1 86

Smith Bros. & Co., cylinder, 1 only at 1.50; brancheader, 1 only at 1.50— 3.00; Smith, L. C., & Bro., repairs to typewriter, 2.00 .... 5 00

Smith, A., teaming coal, 7.05; Smith, Jno., milch cow, 1 only at 45.00...... 52 05

Smith, Tretheway & Co., shoes, 280 prs. at 1.35, 1 pr. at 1.45, 168 prs. at 1.50; rubbers, 20 pr. at 60c.; long boots, 100 pr. at 3.00 .... 943 45

Smith Son & Clarke, interments, 99.00; Smith, Hugh, expenses capturing elopers, 11.55 .... 110 55

Smith, F. & Co., rubber boots, 1 pr. at 6.00; Somerville & Co. turkey, 308 lbs. at 16c.; geese, 200 lbs. at 11c., 71.28 .... 77 28

Southam Printing Co., printing, 19.00; Sterling, Bros., shoes, 101 prs. at 1.25, 126.25 .... 145 25

Stevenson, Jno., suit case, 1 only at 3.00, 1 only at 3.50; curry combs, 6 only at 25c.; horse blankets, 3 pr. at 5.00; horse brushes, 2 only at 35c., 2 only at 75c., 2 only at 1.25; harness repairs, 2.65; sundries, 9.25 .... 39 60

Stevens Mfg. Co., castings, 13.49; Stevens, J. & Son, Co., Ltd., medical appliances, 71.92 .... 85 41

Stroyan, A. G., manure, 41.70; Sumner, T. N., drugs, chemicals, etc., 5.71. 47 41

Summers, Wm., veal 105 lbs. at 9c.; cows, 2 only at 43.50, 2 only at 44.65. 185 75

Sundry Newspapers, advertising re supplies, 137.50; advertising re fuel, 24.50 .... 162 00

Sur-Coat Mfg. Co., boiler compound, 200 lbs. at 15c............................ 30 00

Sutherland Bros., lampwick, 2 gross at 65c., 3 gross at 1.00; pitchers, 1 doz. at 7.20; boilers, 2 only at 1.25, 1 only at 5.50; milk pans, 1 doz. at 1.45; wash bowls, 1 doz. at 6.60; tea kettles, 1 only at 1.15; lamp burners, 2 doz. at 1.75, ½ doz. at 2.00; registers, 2 only at 1.75; dust pans, 1 doz. at 4.80; pails, 6 only at 20c., 2. doz at 5.20; sauce pans, 2 only at 55c., 2 only at 75c., 2 only at 1.00; chambers, 5 doz. at 4.80; lanterns, 1 doz. at 12.00; burners, 3 doz. at 1.75, 2¼ doz. at 2.00; lantern globes, 3 doz. at 1.25; sundries, 4.19 .... 112 39

Tackaberry & Co., harness repairs, 21.40; circingles, 6 pr. at 50c., 6 pr. at 65c.; horse blankets, 2 pr. at 4.00; 1 pr. at 5.50 .... 41 80

Tanton, J. & Son, roll wheat, 143 bbls. at 2.62; pot barley, 2 bags at 2.50; timothy, 14½ bus. at 2.25; binder twine, 40 lbs. at 14c.; cheese, 497 lbs. at 12½c., 1,263 lbs. at 13½; corn meal, 12 bags at 1.75; salt, 40 bags at 90c., 10 bags at 95c., 51 bbls. at 1.25, 2 bbls. at 2.75; land salt, 20 ton at 4.75; split peas, 2 bags at 2.50; corn, 8 bus. at 75c., 2½ bus. at 85c., 2½ bus. at 1.00; flax seed, 2 bus. at 1.25 .... 901 91

Tancock, J. A., horseshoeing, 91.13; Tennent & Barnes, veterinary services, 2.00 .... 93 13

Thomas, Geo. H., repairs to vehicles, 19.00; Thomson, A., cartage, 15.00. 34 00

Topping, A., travelling expenses, 5.89; Trafford, Wm., screens, 6 only at 2.65; pictures, 25 only at 1.00, 40.90 .... 46 79

Trustees. School Sec. No. 23, Twp. London, school rates for children of officials and attendants 200 00

Turner S. & Son, repairs to vehicles, 61.20; United States Express Co., cartage, 40c. 61 60

PUBLIC INSTITUTIONS MAINTENANCE.—*Continued.*

ASYLUM FOR INSANE, LONDON.—*Continued.*

EXPENSES.—*Continued.*

United Factories, Ltd., brushes, 1-3 doz. at 1.85, ½ doz. at 2.10, 2 doz. at 2.16, ½ doz. at 2.45, 1 doz. at 3.60, ½ doz. at 5.40, 1 doz. at 5.75, 1 doz. at 5.76, ½ doz. at 5.94, ¼ doz. at 5.96, ¼ doz. at 6.05, 1¾ doz. at 7.20, ¼ doz. at 8.46, 1½ doz. at 9.32, 1 doz. at 10.55, ½ doz. at 11.52, 7-12 doz. at 18.00, ½ doz. at 19.20, ½ doz. at 21.60, ¼ doz. at 22.50, ¼ doz. at 24.00, ½ doz. at 24.80, 1-6 doz. at 25.60, 1-12 doz. at 70.40; brooms, 1 doz. at 1.20, 35 doz. at 2.40, 15 doz. at 2.50; whisks, 1 doz. at 1.40, 2 doz. at 1.55; sundries, 7.85	269 93
Waide, D., lumber, 37.22; Walker & Logan, bricks, 25,000 at 7.75, 193.75	230 97
Watson, Wm., leather, 20 lbs. at 18c., 18¾ lbs. at 19c., 147 lbs. at 20c., 35¾ lbs. at 22c., 510½ lbs. at 29c., 13¾ lbs. at 30c., 4¾ lbs. at 70c.; linen thread, 4 doz. at 25c.; bristles, 1 doz. at 1.25; shoe making sundries, 18.77	232 74
Way, Wm., horseshoeing, 1.20; Webb, Jas., livery hire re religious services, 26.00	27 20
Westman, A., repairs to grain grinder, 3.35; keys, 1 doz. at 1.80; pulleys, 3 doz. at 1.25, 1 only at 1.10, 1 only at 2.00; paints, oils, etc., 26.63; diaphragms, 2 only at 3.00; flue brushes, 8 only at 1.10; gasoline torch, 1 only at 3.75; twine, 20 lbs. at 20c., 9 lbs. at 45c.; benzine, 45 gals. at 19c., horse clippers, 1 pr. at 2.75; glass, 10.50; stove cement, 20 lbs. at 8c.; bottle brushes, 1 only at 50c., 1 only at 1.50; brushes, 6 only at 65c.; air brick, 4 doz. at 5.40; rope, 16 lbs. at 18; castings, 76c.; axes, 1 only at 1.25; castors, 18 sets at 40c., 12 sets at 50c., carpet sweeper, 1 only at 3.50; barley forks, 3 only at 1.50; belting cement, 15 lbs. at 65c.; saw, 1 only at 1.25; harness weaving, 400 lbs. at 50c.; wheel barrows, 6 only at 3.50; hose, 50 ft. for 8.25; turpentine, 5 gals. at 23; paint scrapers, 2 only at 65c.; lawn mowers, 1 only at 16.85; knives, 6 only at 40c.; wrenches, 1 only at 1.00; rivets, 1 box at 1.00; packing, 25 lbs. at 28c.; books, 6 doz. at 50c.; sundries, 24.11	242 28
West Disinfecting Co., noisy burner, 1 only at 1.25; Western Oil Co., oils, etc., 102.00	103 25
Wheler, G., testing flour, 1.50; White, Geo. Sons & Co., repairs to boilers, 57.60; gear wheels, 4 only for 4.25; castings, 278 lbs. at 5c., 75.75	77 25
Wilcox, Thos., bull, 1 only at 45.00; Wilkins, J. D., expenses capturing eloper, 7.35	52 35
Wilkinson, Wm., threshing grain, 4½ days at 15.00, 67.50; Willis, W. D. & Co., lumber, 36.20	103 70
Wilson, W. J., veterinary services, 13.50; Winnette, R & Son, boiler plates, 126 lbs. at 3c.; repairs, 23.39, 27.17	40 67
Winnett, W. H., lumber, 412.28; coal, 813 1,790-2000 tons at 6.20, 2 tons at 7.00	5,472 42
Wood, R. J., turkey, 345 lbs. at 16c.; geese, 320 lbs. at 11c	90 40
Wortman & Ward Co., Ltd., repairs to boiler, 88c.; repairs to implements, 1.50; castings, 3,498 lbs. at 3½c.	122 36
Wright, James, & Co., paint, oils, etc., 416.26; glue, 50 lbs. at 20c.; babbit metal, 80½ lbs. at 15c.; rubber packing, 15¾ lbs. at 25c., 33 lbs. at 30c., 80 lbs. at 35c., 8¼ lbs. at 40c., 2 lbs. at 1.00; emery cloth, 4 quires at 90c., 2 quires at 95c., 1 quire at 1.10; gal'vd. iron, 47 lbs. at 5½c.; corundum wheel, 1 only at 3.50; oil cans, 1 set at 2.90; wright vise, 2 only, 194 lbs. at 13c.; plug taps, 1 only at 1.00; lightning stock, 1 only at 3.35; plow points, 24 only at 50c.; coal shutes, 2 only at 8.00; black pipe, 109 ft. at 2.30, 106 10-12 ft. at 3.00, 108 ft. at 3.85, 94½ ft. at 5.20, 115¾ ft. at 6.26, 162 7-8 ft. at 7.52, 119 ft. at 8.75, 57 ft. at 11.50 per 100 ft.; shafting, 180 lbs. at 3.75 cwt.; brushes, 1 doz. at 85c., 6 only at 90c., 6 only at 1.50; putty, 431 lbs. at 1.85 cwt., 460 lbs. at 2.50 cwt.; steel, 25 lbs. at 15c., 200 lbs. at 4.25 cwt.; wheels, cushion tired, 20.00; rod iron, 560 lbs. at 2.20 cwt., 559 lbs. at 2.25 cwt., 610 lbs. at 2.50 cwt., 151 lbs. at 2.55 cwt., 437 lbs. at 2.60 cwt., 48 lbs. at 2.70 cwt.; angle iron, 381 lbs. at 4c.; gaskets, 5¼ lbs. at 1.20; wrench, 1 only at 1.00, 1 only at 1.40; taper tap, 1 only at 1.00; lace leather, 5½ lbs. at 85c.; castings, etc., 44.36; leather belting, 20 ft. at 16c.; 30 ft. at 22c.; band iron, 745 lbs. at 2.75 cwt.; square	

PUBLIC INSTITUTIONS MAINTENANCE.—*Continued.*

ASYLUM FOR INSANE, LONDON.—*Continued.*

EXPENSES.—*Continued.*

iron, 864 lbs. at 2.50 cwt.; sundries, 41.54	890 08
Wright, Sons & Co.. hats, 12½ doz. at 2.00, 25.00; Wright Hat Store, hat, 1 only at 2.25	27 25
Wright, Jos., damages for injuries received by horse	50 00
York Mfg. Co.. mangle felt, 56 lbs. at 75c., 42.00; Young, R. J.. & Co., shirting 113¾ yds. at 12½c.; cotton, 64 yds. at 8½c., 60 yds. at 10c., 76¾ yds. at 11c.; table cover, 1 only at 2.00, 2 only at 4.00; sheeting, 32½ yds. at 27½c.; comforter, 1 only at 5.00; print, 236 yds. at 10c.; curtains, 2 pr. at 3.50, 1 pr. at 4.00; denim, 10 yds. at 20c.; muslin, 36 yds. at 15c.; scrim, 56 yds. at 12½c., 107.04	149 04

ASYLUM FOR INSANE, HAMILTON.

SALARIES ($39,871.79).

J. D. Russell, M.D. :	Twelve months' salary as	Medical Superintendent........	2,600 00
F. Beemer, M.D. :	do	Assistant do	1,400 00
Jno. Webster, M.D. :	do	First Assistant do	1,200 00
W. T. Wilson, M.D. :	do	Second do do	1,050 00
Annie Kelly :	do	Typewriter....................	400 00
L. E. Swazie :	do	Porter and Gatekeeper.........	375 00
Bidwell Way :	do	Bursar....................	1,600 00
A. Murray, Jr. :	do	Bursar's Clerk................	900 00
D. McCarthy :	do	Storekeeper................	1,000 00
L. McIntyre :	Five do	Assistant Storekeeper..........	250 00
Sidney Thompson :	Twelve do	Messenger and Stableman......	288 00
Joseph Ironside :	do	Engineer	650 00
Thos. Lawlor :	do	First Assistant Engineer.	700 00
Alex. Milne :	Nine do	Second do	225 00
Nathanial Reed :	Twelve do	Carpenter....................	550 00
Wm. Addison :	do	Assistant Carpenter............	500 00
Wm. Gatenby :	do	Tailor	549 00
Wm. McClure :	do	Baker	549 00
Robert Leslie :	do	Shoemaker....................	350 00
Wm. Scott :	do	Laundryman..................	450 00
Wm. Harper :	do	Butcher....................	400 00
Thos. McQueen :	do	Farmer :.....................	700 00
Nicholas Elliott :	do	Plowmam.....................	353 50
Farm Hands (2) :	do	....	671 50
W. S. Scott :	do	Gardener	600 00
Sara Shand :	Seven do	Matron.....................	291 67
H. E. Robertson :	Twelve do	First Assistant Matron.........	360 00
Minnie McKenty :	do	Second do	300 00
Cooks (8) :	do	....	1,412 87
Maids (4) :	do	....	572 00
Laundresses (4) :	do	....	838 71
Seamstresses (2) :	do	....	376 00
Maude Gill :	do	Trained Nurse......	220 00
Agnes Woodburn :	do	Chief Female Attendant.	240 00
Female Supervisors (10) :	do	....	2,271 50
Female Attendants (27) :	do	....	3,855 80
James Slater	do	Chief Attendant ....·........	450 00
Male Supervisors (9)	do	....	2,617 13
Male Attendants (30)	do	....	6,496 78
Stokers (5)	do	....	1,258 33

EXPENSES ($97,487.33).

Armstrong Cartage Co., cartage, 4.00; Almas, Geo. A., straw, 20.870 tons at 6.25, 127.72	131 72
Atteaux Dyestuff & Chem. Co., ammonia powder, 1,386 lbs. at 4¼c.; washing soda, 5,600 lbs. at 1¾c.	158 91
American Medico-Psycho. Asso'n, annual dues, 5.00; American Express Co., charges, 90c.	5 90

PUBLIC INSTITUTIONS MAINTENANCE.—*Continued.*

ASYLUM FOR INSANE, HAMILTON.—*Continued.*

EXPENSES.—*Continued.*

Bell Telephone, messages, 14.65; exchange services, 139.00; repairs, 2.65... | 156 30

Ben Hur Mfg. Co., laundry baskets, 3 only at 2.25, 6.75; truck castors, 1 doz. at 4.50; bed knobs, 200 at 3.00, 6.00; cartage, 50c. .... | 17 75

Bain, Jas. & Son, repairs to engines .... | 58 31

Bloomfield, Thos., cleaning chimneys, 16.25; Brit. *Canadian*, advertising *re* supplies, 4.80 .... | 21 05

Blachford & Son, interments .... | 60 00

Bennett Bros., chop corn, 58.150 tons at 22.00; flour, 1,000 lbs. at 1.95; beans, 20 bus. at 1.75; corn meal, 600 lbs. at 1.40 cwt., 4 sacks at 1.50, 2 bbls. at 3.20, 50 at 2.20, 2 bbls. at 3.45, 2 bbls. at 3.65; sundries, 40c.; ck. wheat, 1,600 lbs. at 1.75, 1,200 lbs. at 1.55, 1 ton at 31.00; split peas, 173 lbs. at 3.55; bran, 13.1330 tons at 16.50 .... | 1,681 62

Bruce, Jno. A., seeds, 390.99 plants, 36.00; pump sprayer, 1 at 23.00; sickles, 6 at 50c. ....: | 452 99

Bursar, sundries, 1.05; travelling expenses, 6.00 .... | 7 05

Bain & Adams, eggs, 100 doz. at 27c., 57 doz. at 18c.; lemons, 21 doz. at 30c., 7½ at 35c., 2 at 25c.; biscuits, 11½ lbs. at 8c.; berries, 1 crate at 2.50, 12 qts. at 18c., 2.16; cherries, 4 bas. at 1.00, 4.00, 2 bas. at 1.25, 2.50; cocoa, 3 tins at 35c.; flour, 1 bbl. at 4.50, 1 bbl. at 2.50, 2 bags at 63c.; tangle foot, 7 boxes at 50c.; sundries, 18.30; chickens, 3 prs. at 1.35, 2 prs. at 1.25; tomatoes, 8 lbs. at 10c.; capers, 6 bot.' at 20c.; seltzer, ½ doz. at 2.00; cream tartar, 10 lbs. at 35c.; fly traps, 4 at 20c.; tangle foot, 1 box at 3.00; stove polish, 6 tins at 10c.; peaches, 4 bas. at 1.00 | 113 08

Connell Anthracite Mining Co., coal, 247.910 tons at 5.75 .... | 1,422 86

Carpenter, John O., flour, 4 bbls. at 4.50; catsup flavor, 6 bot. at 25c.; berries, 1 bas. at 1.75; chickens, 1 at 1.10, 15 at 1.20, 4 at 1.25; peaches, 8 bas. at 1.00; melons, 3 at 20c., 2 at 30c., 2 at 25c.; puff rice, 6 lbs. at 30c.; cloves, 2 lbs. at 50c., ¼ lb. at 60c.; corks, 13 doz. at 10c., 10 doz. at 15c.; seltzer, ½ doz. at 1.50; biscuits, 9¾ lbs. at 8c., 6 lbs. at 10c.; pickle spice, 6 pkgs. at 25c.; lemons, 8 doz. at 50c., 2 doz. at 40c., 1 case at 10.50; mustard seed, 2 lbs. at 35c., ½ lb. at 40c.; putz cream, 3 tins at 80c.; plums, 8 bas. at 1.20; cucumbers, ½ bus. at 2.20; sundries, 49.70; jelly powders 2 doz. at 1.00; grapes, 2 bas. at 50c.; turkey, 13 lbs. at 23c. .... | 149 42

Clark, Adam, insertion tubing, 50 ft. at 12½c.; Jenkins' discs, 24 at 10.00; Jenkins' nuts, 24 at 5c., 48 at 10c.; soap holder, 1 at 1.25; boiler, 1 at 11.00; flange, 1 at 95c.; lead lined tank, 1 at 8.00; gaskets, 2 doz. at 1.80; closet bowl, 1 at 7.00; closet seat, 1 at 2.25; waste pipe, 1 length at 1.80; valves, 4 only at 2.50; sundries, 3.48 .... | 63 98

Cairns, Bernard, indelible ink, 1 qt. at 7.00; Case, H. Spencer, drugs, etc., 15.40 .... | 22 40

Canadian Pacific Ry., freight, 5.56; Canadian Rubber Co., garden hose, 150 ft. for 18.65; Gem nozzle, 35c. .... | 24 56

Canadian Time Recording Co., station watch clock dials, 4 boxes at 3.00... | 12 00

Crown Oil Refining Co., cylinder oil, 85 gals. at 60c., 43½ gals. at 65c.; scale powder, 200 lbs. at 10c.; sundries, 1.10 .... | 100 38

Croil, Jas., tweed, 48¼ yds. at 1.90, 91.68; Crawford Bros., gravel, 6 loads at 75c., 4.50 .... | 96 18

Common Sense Mfg. Co., roach exterminator, 24 tins at 1.00 .... | 24 00

Craig, Robt. L., V.S., professor's services, 20.50; Canadian Express Co., charges, 11.25 .... | 31 75

Commercial Oil Co., cylinder oil, 46 gals. at 60c.; engine oil, 47 gals. at 45c.; signal oil, 48 gals. at 1.25 .... | 108 75

Cambden, J. R., ham, 207 lbs. at 13½c., 160 lbs. at 14c., 65 lbs. at 14½c., 152 lbs. at 15c.; lard, 351 lbs. at 12½c. .... | 126 44

Central Prison Industries, flannel, 914 yds. at 25c.; 603 yds. at 50c., 600 yds. at 30c.; wrappers, 4.80; twine, 250 lbs. at 11½c.; yarn, 200 lbs. at 45c.; blankets, 426 lbs. at 45c.; buttons, 1 gro. at 7.50 .... | 1,032 75

Chadwick Bros., electric light wire, 330 ft. at 2c.; ceiling cleets, 50 prs. at 2½c.; sundries, 80c.; wire screens, 2 at 3.50; carbon holders, 6.00; arc lamp, 23.00; coal vase, 3.25; incandescent lamps, 500 at 19c.; electric

PUBLIC INSTITUTIONS MAINTENANCE.—*Continued.*

ASYLUM FOR INSANE, HAMILTON.—*Continued.*

EXPENSES.—*Continued.*

iron, 1 at 7.75; Edison sockets, 1 doz. at 2.40; installing electric wiring in outhouses, 96.85	249 90
Dean, M., music supplied and presents for patients' picnic, 35.00; Doyle, M. J., livery, 1.00	36 00
Dallyn, Jardine & Co., soda, 2,800 lbs. at 1¾c., 49.00; Donohue, D., tobacco stems, 252 lbs. for 2.00, 1,006 for 8.00; Dunlop Tire Co., rubber matting, 84½ lbs. at 39, 32.95	91 95
Dowswell Mfg. Co., rolls for wringer, 2 at 1.65; Dempster, Jas., oven grates, 4 at 2.50	13 30
Dunlop, The Jas. Co., bran, 23.923 tons at 15.50, 361.32; crk. wheat, 1,200 lbs. at 1.80, 3,500 lbs. at 1.60, 600 lbs. at 1.65, 9.90; beans, 6 bus. at 1.80, 36 bus. at 1.85; barley, 3,200 lbs. at 1.70; potatoes, 2,796 7-60 bus. at 66c.; split peas, 200 lbs. at 2.00, 800 lbs. at 2.15, 3,300 lbs. at 2.05; straw, 8.1900 tons at 6.00; linseed meal, 50 lbs. for 1.34; corn meal, 1,500 lbs. at 1.65 cwt.	2,630 71
Dominion Express Co., charges	6 27
Dalley, F. F. Co., Ltd., coffee, 2,700 lbs. at 25c.; pepper, 280 lbs at 19c.; cloves, 10 lbs. at 20c.; cinnamon, 85 lbs. at 25c.; cocoanut, 20 lbs. at 18c.; ginger, 75 lbs. at 23c.; flavoring extracts, 2 doz. at 12.00, 6 lbs. at 1.00; sundries, 35.24; allspice, 30 lbs. at 18c.; baking powder, 93 lbs. at 25c.; starch, 300 at 5¼c., 50 pkgs. at 7½c.; corn starch, 80 lbs. at 6c.; washing soda, 35 lbs. at 90 cwt.; vanilla, 6 bots. at 1.00; mustard, 4 doz. tins at 1.50; matches, 12 cases at 1.10; baking soda, 1 keg at 2.25; cream tartar, 40 lbs. at 25c.; blacking, 3 doz. at 75c.; blue, 10 lbs. at 14c.; nutmegs, 2 lbs. at 50c.	935 96
Eastwood, J. & Co., stationery, 9.95; amusements, 22.50; postage stamps, 31.00; sheet music, 2.00	65 45
Ellis, Norman, spectacles, 4 doz. at 3.60, ½ doz. at 7.20; repairing clocks, 38 70; mantel clock, 1 at 7.35, 1 at 4.88	68 93
Electric Supply Co., elec. stove, 1 at 7.50; Elliott, Nicholas, trav. exp., 3.50	11 00
Fearman, F. W. Co., Ltd., cheese, 2,595 lbs. at 14c., 451 lbs. at 13c., 1,368 lbs. at 13½c., 944 at 12c., 1,855 at 11¾c.; eggs, 167 doz. at 26c., 499 doz. at 19c., 175 doz. at 20c., 110 doz. at 21c., 117 doz. at 22c., 170 doz. at 23c., 226 doz. at 25c., 285 doz. at 16c., 228 doz. at 17c., 228 doz. at 18c., 58 doz. at 17½c., 57 doz. at 18½c., 59 doz. at 19½c., 38 doz. at 32c., 117 doz. at 27c.; ham, 195 lbs. at 12½c., 146 lbs. at 14c., 403½ lbs. at 15c., 322 at 16c.; bacon, 51 lbs. at 14c., 154 lbs. at 15½c., 685 lbs. at 16c.; honey, 1,394 lbs. at 9c., 1,490 lbs. at 8½c.; lard, 300 at 11¼c.; butter, 68 lbs. at 23c., 168 lbs. at 25c.	2,120 79
Fowler's Canadian Co., ham, 315½ lbs. at 15c.; lard, 600 lbs. at 11½c.; bacon, 301 lbs. at 16c.	164 49
Freed, Jno. B., boiler compound, 100 lbs. at 4½c.; wax, 12 lbs. at 8c.	5 21
Fleischmann & Co., 628 lbs. at 30c., 188.40; Foster Pottery Co., flower pots, 17.89; Finlay, Wallace, evergreens, 6 loads at 3.00, 18.00	224 29
Freeman, W. A. Co., Ltd., lime, 20 bus. at 25c.; manure, 28.50; fire clay, 1,110 lbs. for 11.10; bone meal, 1 ton at 28.50; cement, 3 sacks at 2.60, less sacks returned, 23.70	57 20
Farm Exchange, tallow, 2,550 2-3 lbs. at 4½c.; pork, 875 lbs. at 6½c.	171 68
Gripton, C., indelible ink, 1 bot. at 8.80; Gutta Percha Rubber Mfg. Co., aprons, 2 at 2.00, 4.00	12 80
Greening, B., Wire Co., screen, 1 at 6.00; repairing window guard, 1.25	7 25
Galloway, Wm., 2 loads sand at 50c., 1.00; *Globe* Printing Co., subs'n., 2 copies, 1 year, 8.00	9 00
Gunns, Ltd., butter, 37,399 lbs. at 23¾c., 8,882.26; Gurney, Tilden Co., Ltd., repairs *re* heating, 8.86	8,891 12
G. N. W. Telegraph Co., telegrams	2 61
G. T. Ry. Co., freight, 32.97; Gurney Foundry Co., repairs to boiler, 30.71	63 68
Good Roads Machinery Co., shears for drill plow, 2.50; castings, 285 lbs. at 4c.	13 90
Gilbert, H. J., rubber boots, 2 prs. at 4.50, 12 at 85c.; slippers, 1 pr. at 1.75, 6 at 1.50; shoes, 9 prs. at 2.50; overshoes, 2 prs. at 1.75	55 95

PUBLIC INSTITUTIONS MAINTENANCE.—*Continued.*

ASYLUM FOR INSANE, HAMILTON.—*Continued.*

EXPENSES.—*Continued.*

Gillard & Co., W. H., tea, 1,072 lbs. at 25c.; tapioca, 75 lbs. at 5½c.; starch, 380 lbs. at 7¼c., raisins, 224 lbs. at 6c.; salt, 3 bbls. at 1.30, 13 bbls. at 1.35; sugar, 1,516 lbs. at 3.89, 6,279 lbs. at 4.19, 3,222 at 4.29, 1,509 at 3.79; molasses, 48.9 gals. at 28; prunes, 3,600 lbs. at 6½c.; jam, 2,340 at 6¾c.; vinegar, 121.2 gals. at 25c.; dried apples, 1,145 lbs. at 6¾c.; mustard, 24 boxes at 44c.; rice, 2,645 at 3 7-8c.; currants, 691 lbs. at 6½c.; fish, 900 lbs. at 7½c., 8 doz. at 2.25, 100 boxes at 10c., 8 doz. at 1.70; canned vegetables, 6 doz. at 85c.; sundries, 22.01; soap, 67½ lbs. at 8c. 1,664 85

Gage & Berry, chickens, 3 prs. at 1.25, 23 prs. at 1.35; lemons, 13½ doz. at 20c.; celery, 5½ doz. at 50c., 6½ doz. at 1.00; oranges, 6 doz. at 20c., 7 doz. at 30c., 5 doz. at 50c.; baking powder, 22 lbs. at 30c.; eggs, 10 doz. at 30c.; sundries, 19.15; ham, 11½ lbs. at 15c.; fish, 2½ lbs. at 10c., 1 tin at 42c., 2½ lbs. at 8c., 1 bbl. at 7c.; biscuit, 17½ lbs. for 1.55, 1 tin at 25c.; bacon, 3½ lbs. at 18c. 93 35

Hamilton, F. Co., brushes, 3 at 35c.; bells, 2 sets at 2.50, 1 doz. at 2.50; sand screen, 5 yds. at 50c.; sundries, 47.35; meat cutters, 2 at 2.25; hair clippers, 2 prs. at 2.25; vegetable cutters, 2 at 1.75; nails, 1 keg at 2.40, 1 keg at 2.25, 75 lbs. at 2½c.; pulleys, 1 doz. at 1.20; putty, 200 lbs. at 2½c.; zinc, 149 lbs. at 10c.; brass screws, 2 gro. at 55c., 2 gro. at 66c.; rubber hose, 200 ft. at 15c.; wove wire, 5 yds. at 50c., 34 yds. at 35c.; spoons, 12 doz. at 1.85; razor bones, 3 at 45c.; razors, ½ doz. at 12.00, ⅓ doz. at 10.00; trays, ½ doz. at 3.75, 1 doz. at 4.00; base balls, 12 at 1.25; keys, 2 doz. at 1.50; screws, 2 gro. at 66c.; smooth planes, 1 at 2.00; wire, 273 ft. at 1.75; glue, 20 lbs. at 22c.; axe handles, ½ doz. at 3.75; wheelbarrow wheels, ½ doz. at 13.50; padlocks, ½ doz. at 7.25, 2 at 1.50; sash cord, 20 lbs. at 35c.; wood rasps, ½ doz. at 5.60; night latches, 3 at 2.25; chest locks, ½ doz. at 11.00; wood files, 3 at 40c; shears, 3 prs. at 80c.; mattress twine, 3 lbs. at 25c.; strap hinges, 50 lbs. at 5½c.; tar felt, 155 lbs. at 1.85; rim lock and knobs, 2 at 65c.; twine, 10 lbs. at 25c.; carvers, 1 set at 1.60; flat irons, 4 set at 1.00; hose, 50 ft. at 18c.; shellac, ½ gal. at 4.00; shutter hinges, ½ doz. sets at 2.00; hand saw, 1 at 1.75, 1 at 2.00; mirrors, 1 at 2.50, 4 at 12.00, 1 at 2.58; locks, 1 at 1.00; nails, 2 at 50; keyhole blades, ½ doz. at 3.00; hinges, 42½ lbs. at 6½c.; hammer handles, 1 doz. at 1.20; cupboard locks, 1 doz. at 1.75; meat grinder, 1 at 2.25; scales, 1 set at 4.25, 1 set at 5.75; twine, 25 lbs. at 25c., 18 lbs. at 55c., 12 lbs. at 40c.; chain, 65c.; copper floats, 3 only at 2.25; potato forks, 3 at 70c.; paint oils, etc., 188.74; mitts, 11 prs. for 5.00 ...... 638 37

Hazlett & Dawson, turkey, 1,360¾ lbs. at 18c., 244.95; fruit peel, 8 lbs. at 25c.; vanilla, 1 bot. at 1.25; borax, 10 lbs. at 10c.; cider, 4 gals. at 45c.; chickens, 6 prs. at 1.30, 20 prs. at 1.25; biscuits, 5 tins at 20c., 16 lbs. at 10c., 5 lbs. at 20c.; goose, 1 at 1.25, 799½ lbs. at 13c., 103.94; flour, 3 bbls. at 4.50, 50 lbs. at 2.20 cwt., 1,10; ducks, 5 prs. at 1.50; sundry groceries, 48.50 ...... 463 19

Hawkins, H. E., paris green, 70 lbs. at 20c.; wax, 100 lbs. at 11c.; dye, 2 doz. at 85c.; sundries, 1.55; insect powder, 2 lbs. at 25c. 28 75

Herald Printing Co., advertising, 3.33; subscription, 2 copies, 1 year, 6.00 ...... 9 33

Hoodless, J., Furniture Co., repairing piano stool, 1.00; chairs, 5 at 3.46, 1 at 3.45; repairing 2 lounges, 26.00 ...... 47 75

Hamilton and Toronto Sewer Pipe Co., 50 ft. pipe, 7.50; Hamilton and Barton Inc. Ry., use of railway 360.00 ...... 367 50

Hawkins, Ltd., drugs, chemicals, etc., 15.13; Hamilton water works, water, 4,090.57 ...... 4,105 70

Hamilton and Grimsby Elect. Ry., freight, 7.00; Hamilton Steamboat Co., freight, 7.47 ...... 14 47

Hamilton Engine Packing Co., packing, 29½ lbs. at 60c., 24 3-16 lbs. at 1.00; 26¾ lbs. at 80c.; covering heater with asbestos cement, 18.00; closet washers, 2 doz. at 25c. 81 32

Hamilton Brass Mfg. Co., water cocks, 2 at 2.00; repairing tap, 1.50; repairs, 2.75 ...... 8 25

PUBLIC INSTITUTIONS MAINTENANCE.—*Continued.*

ASYLUM FOR INSANE, HAMILTON.—*Continued.*

EXPENSES.—*Continued.*

Hamilton Stamp & Stencil Works, rubber stamps, 1 at 50c., 1 at 70c., 1 at 75c.	1 95
Halliday, Jas., milch cows, 5 at 60.00; purchase of meat, 13,447.93; Herald, I., tuning pianos, 13.50	13,761 43
Humphreys, F. F., berries, 12 crates at 2.25; candy, 190 lbs. at 15c.; cherries, 24 bas. at 1.25; apples, 18 bbls. at 3.00; raisins, 6¼ boxes at 3.00; figs, 95 lbs. at 13.00; cranberries, 2 bbls. at 11.00; oranges, 151 doz. at 25c.; oysters, 1½ gals. at 2.00; mixed nuts, 183 lbs. at 18.00; fish, 114 lbs. at 8c., 2,198 lbs. at 8½c., 3,133 lbs. at 9c., 145 lbs. at 9½c.	758 80
Hamilton Cemetery Board, interments, 24.00; Hislop, Jno., horseshoeing, 66.99	90 99
Howard, F. M., expenses *re* concert, 17.00; Hill, Geo., livery hire, 4.00; Hamilton Gas Light Co., gas, 632.70	653 70
Hedley-Shaw Milling Co., flour, 1,442 bbls. at 3.75	5,407 50
Hamilton C. P. & Light & Traction Co., elect. current, 3,086.73; repairs, 3.10	3,089 83
Imperial Chemical Co., paint, oils, etc., 112.77; Robert Junor, tea cups, 1 doz. at 8.00	120 77
Kenny, T. & Co., tea 600 lbs. at 22c., 132.00; Kirk, Jas., tobacco, 510 lbs. at 46c., 228 lbs. at 45c., 255 lbs. at 36c., 2 lbs. at 50c., 24 lbs. at 38c., 439.12	571 12
Lucas, Steele & Bristol, fish, 8 doz. at 1.70, 6 1-3 at 2.90, 100 at 15c.; tea, 1,023 lbs. at 25c.; starch, 192 lbs. at 7½c.; prunes, 3,600 lbs. at 7¼c.; bath brick, 4 doz. at 50c.; salt, 1 bbl. at 2.80, 13 bbls. at 1.35, 12 bags at 85c.; tapioca, 140 lbs. at 7c.; soap, 72½ lbs. at 8c.; sal soda, 375 lbs. at 90c. cwt., 1,125 lbs. at 95c. cwt.; pickles, 6 doz. at 2.25; corn starch, 40 lbs. at 6¾c.; molasses, 45 gals. at 32c.; sugar, 7,315 lbs. at 4.39, 3,463 lbs. at 3.99; sundries, 4.29; vinegar, 37 gals. at 25c.; syrup, 683 at 3 1-8c.; can vegetables, 16 doz. at 85c., 8 doz. at 1.25	1,194 99
Lewis, R. H., apples, 93 bbls. at 2.50, 232.50; Lafayette & Wilde, honey, 300 lbs. at 10c.	262 50
Lees, Wm. & Sons, bread, 14,630 lbs. at 2½c., less yeast, 2.55	363 20
Laidlaw, Jno. D., iron seat ends, 12 at 2.25; cartage, 75c.	27 75
Lumsden Bros., molasses, 43 gals. at 28c.; fish, 75 lbs. at 4¾c., 60 lbs. at 5½c., 106 lbs. at 6¾c., 2 cases at 6.25, 96 tins at 12c., 8 doz. at 2.00, 44 lbs. at 10c., 25 crates at 2.16; rice, 3,250 lbs. at 3¾c.; currants, 200 lbs. at 5¾c.; sundries, 43c.; corn starch, 40 lbs. at 7c.; laundry starch, 39 lbs. at 5c.; syrup, 145 gals. at 35c.; can vegetables, 8 doz. at 85c., 8 doz. at 67½c., 8 doz. at 1.30; bath brick, 2 cases at 75c.; molasses, 82 gals. at 28c.; currants, 565 lbs. at 5¾c.; raisins, 112 lbs. at 6½c.; prunes, 350 lbs. at 8c.; sugar, 8,186 lbs. at 4.29, 5,428 lbs. at 3.84; salt, 5 bbls. at 1.30, 6 bags at 75c., 1 bbl. at 2.90; tea, 414 lbs. at 25c.; tapioca, 146 lbs. at 6¾c., barrels 3 at 2.25; vinegar, 125 gals. at 25c.; cocoanut, 15 lbs. at 16c.; pipes, 2 boxes, at 90c.	1,157 70
Medcalf, D. M., trav. expenses *re* boiler inspection, 8.60; Matthews, Geo. Co., Ltd., lard, 600 lbs. at 13c., 78.00	86 60
MacKay, R. O. & A. B., coal, 25 130/2000 tons at 4.00, 100.26; Maxwell, D. Sons, rake teeth, 6 at 35c., 2.10	102 36
Melbourne, A. K. & Co., iron wheel, 1 at 1.25; manure forks, 1 doz. at 6.50; field hoes, 1 doz. at 4.00; shovels, 3 at 1.50; wheelbarrows, 3 at 3.50; wire nails, 1 keg at 2.50; staples, 20 lbs. at 5c.; horse brush, 1 at 1.25; paint, oils, etc., 7.25; axe handles, 1 doz. at 4.00; sundries, 75c.	43 50
Moore, The D. Co., dust pans, 1 doz. at 2.50; dish pans, 4 at 1.00; water carriers, 3 at 75c.; slop pails, 7 at 75c.; milk strainer, 1 at 1.75; milk can, 1 at 4.50; sprinkling cans, 3 at 50c.; pails, 3 at 35c.; boilers, 1 at 6.00; sauce pans, 1 at 2.50; galvanized iron, 5 sheets at 75c.; sundries, 7.55; pie plates, 1 doz. at 1.50; frying pans, 2 at 2.50; coffee boiler, 1 at 1.25; coffee strainers, 1 at 1.75; tin cullenders, 3 at 1.65, 3 at 1.20; gravy strainers, 2 at 1.50; coffee pots, 2 at 2.00; cake tins, 1 doz. at 1.20, 2 doz. at 1.00, 2 at 55c.	71 95
Ingles, Thos. & Sons, coal, 2,203 870/2000 tons at 5.99, 112 1860/2000 tons at 2.86, 112 640/2000 at 2.46, 8 tons at 6.25, 199 1060/2000 at 3.06, 897 230/2000 at 5.96, 39 tons at 6.23, 2 tons at 6.00	20,036 03

PUBLIC INSTITUTIONS MAINTENANCE.—*Continued.*

ASYLUM FOR INSANE, HAMILTON.—*Continued.*

EXPENSES.—*Continued.*

Marshall, Jas., lime, 40 bus. at 20c., 20 bus. at 18c., 11.60; Mail Ptg. Co.,
  subscription (2 copies), 1 yr., 8.00; 19 60
Murray, W. E., horse collar, 1 at 2.75; rubber rug, 1 at 2.75; harness
  repairs, 4.65 ....   10 15
Morris, J. & A., chickens, 2 prs. at 1.40, 2 prs. at 1.50, 1 at 75c.; celery,
  2¾ doz. at 1.00, 2 doz. at 1.10, 2½ doz. at 1.20, 1½ doz. at 1.50, 1½ doz.
  at 1.80; lettuce, 4⅜ doz. at 60c., 3¼ doz. at 80c., ½ doz. at 96c.; her-
  rings, 2 kegs at 1.00; pork, 27¼ lbs. at 15c.; biscuits, 8 boxes at 30c.,
  17¼ lbs. at 8.00; oranges, 5½ doz. at 30c., 1 doz. at 25c., 5 doz. at 40c.;
  oysters, 1 qt. at 50c.; baking powder, 19 lbs. at 30c.; coal oil, 5 gals.
  at 16c., 5 gals. at 17c.; lemons, 10½ doz. at 20c.; sundries, 11.46; veal,
  22 lbs. at 12½c., 53¼ lbs. at 15c.; apples, 2 bas. at 45c., 6 bas. at 50c.;
  ham, 5¾ lbs. at 16c.; spice beef, 8¼ lbs. at 12c.; syrup, 2 gals. at 1.15   78 83
Meakins & Sons, Ltd., brooms, 22 doz. at 3.00, 1 doz. at 7.00, 1 doz. at
  9.00, 3 at 12.80 per doz., 1-6 doz. at 7.04, 1-6 doz. at 7.36, 14 doz. for
  36.35, 10 doz. at 3.15; brushes, 13 doz. at 2.00, 12 doz. at 1.85, 1 doz.
  at 1.00, ½ doz. at 15.00, ¼ doz. at 4.20, ½ doz. lat 3.20, ¼ doz. at 5.44,
  ¼ doz. at 2.80, 1 doz. at 8.00; baskets, ½ doz. at 18.00; 2 doz. at 4.00,
  3 doz. at 3.25, 1½ doz. at 5.00; sundries, 2.09; cocoa mats, 1 doz. at
  13.50 ....t........   273 04
Moore, D. Co., repairs to cook stove, 1.35; swill can, 1 only at 5.75;
  repairs, 4.35; copper hot water tank, 1 at 14.00 ....   25 45
Mack, Jno., drugs, chemicals, etc., 815.98; Magee, Walton Co., filling
  ice houses, 1,643.00 ....   2,458 98
Morgan, Chas. E., trav. expenses, 5.95; Murton, D. & Sons, soap, 4,320 lbs.
  at 4c., 9,900 lbs. at 4½c., 2,078 lbs. at 5½c. 758 94
Massey-Harris Co., repairs to implements, 16.68; set of carriers for cutting
  box, 4.40; cutting box knives, 2 at 1.50; carrier slats, 8 at 15c.; sundries, 1.00 ....   26 28
Marshall, The E. R. Co., leather, 449½ lbs. at 30c., 218 lbs. at 22c., 521½
  at 28c., 150 at 50c., 285 at 29c., 84 at 52½c.; nails, 20 lbs. at 20c.; tan
  bark, 100 lbs. at 3½c.; shoe dressing, 1 gal. at 1.60; duck, 56½ yds. at
  16c.; ink, 1 gal. at 1.50; eyelets, 12 boxes at 35c.; heel taps, 24 doz. at
  85c.; bristles, 2 doz. at 1.20; shoe thread, 2 boxes at 78c.; white sill,
  2 lbs. at 5.50; bailey, jack, 1 at 4.50; sundries, 9.00; chrispin, jack,
  1 at 4.50; shoe buckles, 2 gro. at 1.50; shoe pegs, 3 bags at 35c.; iron
  nails, 20 lbs. at 7c.; sheep skins, 2 doz. at 6.00; webbing, 1 doz. rolls
  at 5.50; patches, 3 doz. at 1.00; top lifts, 12 doz. at 85c.; parisian
  paste, 10 lbs. at 25c. 646 57
McKay, S., stabling for horses, 1 yr., 25.00; McQueen, Thos., threshing
  wheat and oats, 3,307 bus., 66.14 ....   91 14
McLaughlin, M. & Co., bal. due on flour contract, 1905, 52.00; McIntosh,
  P. & Son, rolled oats, 85 bbls. at 5.25, 446.22 ....   498 22
McAllister, W. J., lumber 425 61
McDougall, W. T., soup tureen, 1 at 1.50, 1 at 1.75; vegetable dishes, 2
  doz. at 75c., 2 only at 60c., 3 doz. at 4.80; glassware, crockery, etc.,
  9.95; granite pot, 1 at 3.00; pepper shakers, 10 only at 12½c.; salt
  shakers, 10 only at 12½c.; mustard pots, 10 at 10c.; waste basins, 1
  doz. at 4.50; bowls, 20 doz. at 90c.; jardinieres, 4 at 1.25, 2 at 1.00,
  1 at 1.50, 1 at 1.40; pitchers, 1 doz. at 4.50, 1 doz. at 3.00; dinner
  plates, 1 doz. at 1.00; chamber sets, 1 at 5.50, 1 at 4.00; chambers,
  10 doz. at 3.60; water jugs, 2½ doz. at 3.00 ....   130 70
Nordheimer Piano and Music Co., violin strings, 2 doz. at 1.50; sheet
  music, 13.79; sundries, .72c.; repairs to clarionets, 2.50; clarionet
  reeds, 1 doz. at 1.50; clarionet, 1 at 15.00 ....   36 51
Ontario Rubber Mfg. Co., invalid cushions, 2 at 4.95, 2 at 5.85, 2 at 5.40;
  rub. bottles, 1 doz. at 16c.; hospital sheets, 24 only at 2.25 ....   86 20
Oak Hall, shirts, 23 at 1.00; handkerchiefs, 8 doz. at 1.20, 1 doz. at 1.50;
  ties, 7 1-6 doz. at 3.00; collars, 5 doz. at 1.20; sundries, 1.65 ....   63 25
Postmaster, rent of P. O. box, 8.00; Polson Iron Works, castings, 698
  lbs. at 5c.; Pendrith Machinery Co., bread pans, 10 doz. at 6.50 ......   107 90

PUBLIC INSTITUTIONS MAINTENANCE.—*Continued.*

ASYLUM FOR INSANE, HAMILTON.—*Continued.*

EXPENSES.—*Continued.*

Pratt, The T. H. Co., Ltd., dress goods, 254 yds. at 25c.; darning wool, 12 lbs. at 1.20; hoods, 2 doz. at 5.50; buttons, 2 gro. at 12.00, 4 gro. 2.50; table napkins, 2 doz. at 3.00, 1 doz. at 3.25, 1 doz. at 5.00; flags, 6 doz. at 90c., 17 doz. at 90c.; bed spreads, 76 at 1.50, 23 at 1.40, 1 at 2.75, 2 at 4.00; fringe, 12 yds. at 9c., 24 yds. at 10c.; frilling, 12 yds. at 18c., 84 yds. at 18c.; hessian, 150 yds. at 25c.; bunting, 60 yds. at 19c.; marking cotton, 5 doz. at 25c.; nett, 24 yds. at 50c., 26 yds. at 59c.; crochet cotton, 3 doz. at 80c.; ribbon, 96 yds. at 19c.; lace collars, 1 doz. at 3.00; shoes, 4 prs. at 1.75; hosiery, 5½ doz. at 4.00; aprons, ½ doz. at 6.00; shawls, 1 doz. at 6.00; lace, 3 doz. yds. at 1.00; pipes, 2.1-12 doz. at 2.70; belts, 1 doz. at 3.00; brooches, 3 doz. at 3.00; rubbers, 24 prs. at 60c.; tooth brush, 5 7-12 doz. at 1.20; ties, 2½ doz. at 3.00, 1 4-12 doz. at 2.28; cloth, 1 yd. at 3.00, 1 yd. at 3.75; quilts, 2 at 2.75, 1 at 6.50; ticking, 416 yds. at 25c., 300 yds. at 12½c.; sundries. 74.86; damask, 18 yds. at 50c.; madras, 88 yds. at 18c., 37½ yds. at 22½c., 29½ yds. at 50c., 72 yds. at 25c.; felt, 40 yds. at 69c., 33 yds. at 75c.; tapestry, 32 yds. at 72c.; butcher's linen, 12 yds. at 25c.; lace curtains, 9 prs. at 2.20, 12 prs. at 2.50; queen's cloth, 40 yds. at 13½c.; gingham, 349 yds. at 25c., 1,243½ yds. at 14c., 24 yds. at 15c., 117 yds. at 12½c.; sateen, 166½ yds. at 12c.; dress suitings, 219½ at 16c.; shoe laces, 3 gros. at 1.00; pillows, 1 pr. at 2.75; screen, 1 at 3.00; blinds, 2 at 4.50, 2 at 2.00, 5 at 1.85, 8 at 1.75, 5 at 1.65, 7 at 1.19, 7 at 1.25, 3 at 1.50; tabling, 455½ yds. at 1.25; galatea, 113¾ yds. at 18c., 434 yds. at 20c.; lining, 35 yds. at 25c.; thread, 29 gros. at 5.40, 6 lbs. at 1.25; sheeting, 15 yds. at 22½c., 100 yds. at 34c., 3,384 yds. at 22c., 419 yds. at 29c., 30 yds. at 33c., 32 yds. at 40c, 216½ at 28c.; cotton, 602½ yds. at 8c., 1,209½ yds. at 9c., 169½ yds. at 15c., 1,802¾ yds. at 9½c., 1,034 yds. at 7½c., 704½ yds. at 9c., 490 yds. at 10c., 100 yds. at 17½c., 69½ yds. at 12½c., 15 yds. at 20c.; towels, 4 1-3 doz. at 3.00, 6 doz. at 2.75, 3 doz. at 90c., 3 doz. at 83 1-3c., 2 doz. at 3.84, 2-3 doz. at 4.80; laces, 6 gro. at 1.00; duck, 83½ yds. at 10c., 107 yds. at 75c., 171½ yds. at 13c.; print, 2,362½ yds. at 11½c., 451 yds. at 10½c.; buttons, 45 gro. at 1.00, 24 gro. at 15c., 48 gro. at 10c., 1 at 1.10; scrim, 42 yds. at 12½c.; muslin, 6 yds. at 11c., 12 yds. at 22c., 78½ yds. at 22½c., 88½ yds. at 18c., 50½ yds. at 30c., 199½ yds. at 12c., 19 yds. at 16c., 30 yds. at 23c., 48 yds. at 17c., 50 yds. at 15c.; cretonne, 15 yds. at 16c., 56½ yds. at 22½c., 20 yds. at 18c., 40 yds. at 25c.; linen, 35½ yds. at 45c., 25½ yds. at 1.00, 351½ yds. at 1.25; hats, 12 at 25c., 9 doz. at 2.00, 5 doz. at 1.65, ½ doz. at 2.25, 12 at 99c., 11 4-12 doz. at 5.50, 12 at 49c.; yarn, 169½ lbs. at 45c., 165 lbs. at 43c.; towelling. 616½ yds. at 11½c., 600 yds. at 13c., 113 yds. at 12½c., 204½ yds. at 11c.; denim, 61½ yds. at 22c., 12 yds. at 18c., 20 yds. at 20c.; shirting, 278½ yds. at 13½c.; hair pins, 20 lbs. at 9c.; hat wire, 1 gro. at 1.20; needles, 4 M. at 1.50; oil cloth, 10 yds. at 2.70; tape, 30 pkgs. at 20c.; batting, 100 rolls at 9c.; cheese cloth, 317½ yds. at 5c.; pique, 20 yds. at 32c., 20 yds. at 23c.; table covers, 4 at 1.00. 1 at 2.45. 12 at 1.25, 1 at 5.00, 1 at 8.00, 2 at 7.50; bowls, 34 doz. at 84c.; ewers, 12 at 39c.; crockery sundries. 7.41; cups and saucers, 1 doz. at 1.80; 20 doz. at 75c., 1 doz. at 1.00, 1 doz. at 2.75; plates, 10 doz. at 78c., 10 doz. at 69c., 10 doz. at 59c., 1 doz. at 1.35, 2 only at 40c., 1 doz. at 85c., 1 doz. at 65c.. 1 doz. at 2.50, 1 doz. at 3.15; platters, 1 doz. at 6.60; chambers, 10 doz. at 4.00; jugs, 9 at 15c.. 15 at 25c., 9 at 35c., 2 at 60c.; pudding bowls. 8 at 19c.: tumblers, 16 doz. at 35c., 6 doz. at 45c.; vegetable dishes, 1 doz. at 5.28, 4 only at 50c.; trays, 6 only at 25c.; toilet paper, 1 case at 6.00, 1 case at 7.50 .... 5,796 90

Peebles. Hobson & Co., flour. 2 bags at 2.25, 3 bags at 60c., 3 bbls. at 4.50; veal, 66 lbs. at 15c., 10 lbs. at 18½c.; celery, 1 doz. at 60c.; onions, ¼ doz. at 2.00; lamb, ½ for 2.50; pineapples, 3 at 20c., 18 at 16 2-3c.; ham, 5 lbs. at 30c., 5½ lbs. at 16c.: silicon, 1 doz. at 1.50; can vegetables. ½ doz. at 1.00. ¼ doz. at 1.52; pineapples, 4 doz. at 2.00; roll oats. 25 lbs. at 3½c.; putz cream. 3 tins at 25c.; fly naper, 1 box at 60c.; sapolio, 6 pkgs. at 10c.; fish, 1,395 lbs. at 8c., 8.922 at 9c., 1,909

9 P.A.

PUBLIC INSTITUTIONS MAINTENANCE.—*Continued.*

ASYLUM FOR INSANE, HAMILTON.— *Continued.*

EXPENSES.—*Continued.*

at 10c., 4,647 at 8¼c., 1 doz. at 50c.; 4½ lbs. at 12c., 2½ lbs. at 15c.;
maple syrup, 30 gals. at 1.00; eggs, 144 doz. at 15c., 57 doz. at 23c.;
lemons, 10¼ doz. at 20c., 1½ doz. at 26c., 3 doz. at 25c.; sundries,
19.01; oranges, 4 doz. at 40c., 3 doz. at 50c.; lettuce, 7½ doz. at 90c.,
1¾ doz. at 1.00; apples, 7 bas. at 60c.; pork, 30¾ lbs. for 4.53; biscuits,
15 tins at 7c., 8 tins at 30c., 5 tins at 15c., 16½ lbs. at 8c.; baking pow-
der, 5 tins at 20c. 1,670 41
Patterson, J. D. & Co., repairs to vehicles, 73.25; Pease Foundry Co.,
repairs to range, 2.50 .... 75 75
Parke & Parke, wax, 120 lbs. at 11c.; chemicals, etc., 21.98; oriental dye,
  3 doz. at 1.00; sponges, 4 doz. at 75c.; chamois skins, 2 at 50c.; combs,
5 doz. at 4.00, 7 doz. at 3.25; lawn seed, 10 lbs. at 25c.; sundries, 65c.;
lineman's gloves, 2 prs. at 2.75; labels, 1,000 for 2.50; soap, 326½ lbs.
at 8c.; urinals, 1 doz. at 10.80 .... 133 00
Quinn, Richard, repairing boiler, 10.90; Russell, Jas., trav. expenses 3.50   14 40
Riddell, Jno. E., repairs to building, 289.83; smoke stack, 60.00; new venti-
lator, 37.50 .... 387 33
Rodger, R. S., horseshoeing, 99.90; repairs to implements, 27.45; repairs
to vehicles, 19.10 .... 146 45
Ramsay, Thos., toilet clippers, 2 prs. at 5.50; clipper springs, ½ doz. at
1.20; sundries, 13.84; rope, 48½ lbs. at 16c.; leather belting, 100 feet at
14½c.; copper measure, 1 at 2.00; force cups, 1 doz. at 9.90; lantern
globes, 1 5-6 doz. at 2.40; repairing thermometers, 3 at 5.65; fire brick,
500 at 38.00 M.; barrows, 6 at 4.00; paint, oils, etc., 6.75; cotton
waste, 123 lbs. at 12c.; iron pipe, 73 5-8 lbs. at 8c.; cast steel, 16½ lbs.
at 14c.; hoop iron, 72 lbs. at 5c., 69 lbs. at 6c.; cast iron elbows, 12
only at 10½c.; tripoli powder, 25 lbs. at 18c., bibbs, 1 doz. at 10.80;
monkey wrench, 1 at 3.00; scoops, ½ doz. at 16.20; copper wire, 5 lbs.
at 55c. 191 83
Sparrow, Geo. & Co., repairs to jacket kettles, 35.00; copper cover for
kettle, 9.00 .... 44 00
Soper, R., flag, 1 at 10.40; sundry newspapers, advertising supplies,
137.50; fuel, 22.75, 160.25 .... 170 65
Smith, W. D., automatic valves, 6 at 70c.; valve discs, 24 at 10c., 36 at
12c.; guage glasses, 48 at 11c.; sheet rubber, 22 lbs. at 1.35; key cock,
1 at 1.25; enamel bath, 1 at 30.00; sundries, 5.63 .... 82 83
Smith, E. D., jam, 4,500 lbs. at 8½c., 1,500 lbs. at 8½c., 750 lbs. at 7½c. 570 01
Singer Sewing Machine Co., needles, 12 doz at 20c.; oil, 10c.; sundries,
35c.; sewing machine, 1 at 30.40 .... 33 25
Stevenson, Thos., blankets, 2 prs. at 5.50, 1 pr. at 5.00; harness repairs,
31.25; whips, 2 at 1.00; metal polish, 10 tins at 25c.; harness dressing,
3 tins at 35c.; sundries, 2.00 .... 54 80
Sweeny, Hugh C., rice boiler, 3 at 1.10; dish pans, 12 at 1.50, 12 at 2.00;
dinner pans, 6 at 2.50; gravy strainers, 3 at 50c.; tea pots, 1 at 1.00;
steamers, 1 at 1.00; sundries, 6.84; scuttles, 3 at 1.25; pails, 6 at 1.00;
tea cans, 4 at 5.50; tea pail, 1 at 1.50; dippers, 1½ doz. at 2.40, 1 5-12
doz. at 6.00; milk pans, 3 at 2.25, 6 at 1.00; coffee pots, 3 at 1.50;
pie plates, 2 doz. at 1.70; pudding pans, 1 doz. at 3.00; milk cans, 3 at
6.25; granite pots, 1 at 1.10, 1 at 1.50, 1 at 1.75; saucepans, 3 at 75c.,
3 at 65c.; egg heaters, 6 at 75c.; repairs to tinware, 2.50 .... 159 94
Sanford, W. E. Mfg. Co., Ltd., cottonade, 1,235¾ yds. at 23c.; haircloth,
59 yds. at 27c.; italian 52½ yds. at 85c.; buttons, 3 gro. at 60c., 2
gro. at 1.50, 10 gro. at 1.50; holland, 44 yds. at 22c.; serge, 67 yds. at
2.50; sundries, 60c.; cloth, 1½ yds. at 3.25 .... 546 20
Stevens, The J. & Son Co., Ltd., drugs and chemicals, 48.40; medical appli-
ances, 10.80 .... 59 20
Shaw, Hugh, horseshoeing, 20.40; Spectator Ptg. Co., ptg., 251.11; adver-
tising, 2.91; subscription (2 copies), 1 yr., 6.00 .... 280 42
St. Mary's Cathedral, interments 27 00
Thompson, Jno. R., picture moulding, etc., 13.20;   Toronto Laundry
Machine Co., brass hinges, 2 at 1.50 .... 16 20

9a P.A.

PUBLIC INSTITUTIONS MAINTENANCE.—*Continued.*

ASYLUM FOR INSANE, HAMILTGN.— *Continued.*

EXPENSES.—*Continued.*

Taylor, Enoch, repairing lawn mowers, 36 for 33.05, 1 for 1.25; oil cans, 3 at 25c.; grinding shears, 25c.	85 30
Toronto *World*, subscription 1 yr., 3.00; Toronto *News*, subscription 1 yr., 3.00; Toronto *Saturday Night*, subscription 1 yr., 2.00	8 00
Times Printing Co., advertising, 2.91; subscription (2 copies), 1 yr., 6.00	8 91
Turner, Jas. & Co., can vegetables, 10 doz. at 95c., 10 doz. at 1.17½, 10 doz. at 90c.; sardines, 120 tins at 17½c.; salt, 16 bbls. at 1.35, 10 bags at 80c., 3 bbls. at 1.25; lobsters, 10 doz. at 4.00; can salmon, 10 doz. at 1.80; tea, 984 lbs. at 25c.; pickles, 5 doz. at 3.25; rice, 1,794 lbs. at 3 7-8c.; raisins, 280 lbs. at 9½c., 168 lbs. at 10c.; molasses, 41 gals. at 28c.; syrup. 1.317 lbs. at 2 7-8c.; tapioca. 278 lbs. at 7½c.; putz cream, 4 doz. at 2.25; sugar, 10.340 lbs. at 4.59; vinegar, 1,222½ gals. at 25c.; prunes. 200 lbs. at 8½c., 900 lbs. at 6½c., 1,800 lbs. at 6¾c.; dried apples, 1,138 lbs. at 5½c., 1,029 at 6¾c.; cod steak, 792 lbs. at 7½c.; sundries, 27.53; currants, 920½ lbs. at 7c.	1,769 87
Turnbull, A. C., stationery, 175.63; stamps, 122.10; subscription sundry periodicals, 56.25; post cards, 1.00; postal wrappers, 1.25	356 23
Toronto, Hamilton and Buffalo Ry., freight, 2.75; Troy Laundry Co., caustic potash, 720 lbs. at 8½c., 59.40	62 15
United Typewriter Co., Ltd., ribbons, ½ doz. coupons for 4.50; carbon paper, 1 box, 3.25	7 75
Vernon, H., city directory (1 copy) at	3 00
Warren Mfg. Co., cast iron fire pot, 1 at 4.50; Wilde, Lafayette, 480 lbs. at 10c., 48.00	52 50
Wright, Frank B., fire grate for stove, 1 only at 1.00; Wentworth Carriage Works, 1 waggon at 135.00	136 00
Wheler, G., testing flour, 1.50; Webster Floral Co., plants, 19.50; Wright, S., potatoes, 721½ bus. at 63c., 454.55; Wright, A. W., repairs to locks, 24.25	499 80
Wilkinson & Kompass. paints, oils, etc., 503.88; leather belting. 35 feet for 12.12; sundries, 1.09	516 34
Wallace, J. & Son, steam trap. 1 at 14.00; brass plugs, 2 at 1.25	16 50
Walker, Frank E. Co., Ltd., hair, 200 lbs. at 50c., 350 lbs. at 42c.; carpet. 36 yds. at 90c.; chairs, 12 at 2.05; rugs. 1 at 15.00. 1 at 18.00; gimp. 4 cards at 95c.; tow. 140 lbs. at 3½c.; sundries. 2.65; repairing chairs. 1.50; oil cloth mats. 12 at 50c.; felt paper, 54 yds. at 5c.; rubber mats, 12 at 1.00; carpet sweepers, 3 at 3.50	381 05
Woodman Bros., repairs to electric wires	71 00

ASYLUM FOR INSANE, KINGSTON.

SALARIES ($33,663.92).

E. Ryan, M.D.: Twelve months' salary as		Medical Superintendent	2,598 00
W. C. Barber, M.D.:	do	Assistant Physician	1,400 00
W. C. Herriman, M.D.:	do	Second do	1,100 00
W. R. Dick:	do	Bursar	1,500 00
A. Mackie: Seven	do	Clerk	495 83
John McManus: Five	do	Storekeeper	316 00
R. S. Graham: Six	do		450 00
W. Potter: Twelve	do	Engineer	740 00
Elizabeth Thompson: One	do	Stenographer	45 83
J. Dennison: Twelve	do	Carpenter	550 00
J. McMaster: Nine	do	Assistant do	247 90
Geo. Watson: Twelve	do	Tailor	500 00
Hugh Ross:	do	Farmer	550 00
T. W. McCammon	do	Baker	550 00
W. Carr	do	Gardener	501 00
J. Lawless: Six	do	do	165 00
J. Davidson: Twelve	do	Chief Attendant	400 00
J. Graham:	do	Assistant Engineer	500 00
T. C. Elliott: Eight	do	Painter	308 00

INSTITUTIONS MAINTENANCE.—*Continued.*

ASYLUM FOR INSANE, KINGSTON.—*Continued*

SALARIES.—*Continued.*

Geo. Ford:	Twelve months' salary as	Electrician........................	420 00
H. Derry: Six	do	Mason.....	300 00
J. Gillespie:	do	Assistant do......................	200 00
T. McGuire: Twelve	do	Butcher...............	350 00
A. McIver	do	Laundryman......................	450 00
Stokers (4):	do	....	1,174 17
W. Mullin:	do	Sewageman......................	300 00
L. McCrimmon:	do	Stableman.................	264 00
Roy Smith: Four	do	Messenger......................	80 00
Sara Webster: Twelve	do	Matron......................	500 00
Sara McNeil: Three	do	Assistant do......................	75 00
Minnie Gibson: Eight	do	....	200 00
Evelyn Dickson: Nine	do	Trained Nurse....................	300 00
Harriet L. Graydon:			
One and one-half	do	do	46 22
S. E. Winch: Twelve	do	Housekeeper......................	250 00
A. W. Arbuckle:	do	Musical Instructress	384 00
Annie C. Scott:	do	Musician......................	204 00
M. Dean:	do	Seamstress.....	180 00
Gertrude Burke:	do	Portress...........................	180 00
Male Supervisors (7): Twelve	do	....	1,927 90
Male Attendants (20):	do	....	6,316 71
Female Supervisors (6):	do	....	1,172 60
Female Attendants (16):	do	....	3,448 08
Cooks (2):	do	....	512 54
Laundresses (2):	do	....	396 00
Maids (4):	do	....	736 39
E. Mooney :	do	Temporary services................	378 75

EXPENSES ($67,645.23).

Abramson, Jas., felt hats, 6 doz. at 7.50; shoe laces, 2 gro. at 60; mitts, 2 loz. at 3.00; gloves, 1 doz. at 3.00; overalls, 1 doz. at 7.00; smocks, ½ doz. at 7.00; hosiery, 22 doz. at 1.20, 8 doz. at 2.00, 5 doz. at 3.00: mouth organs, 1 doz. at 2.25, 1¼ doz. at 3.00	129 10
Allan, F. A., tea, 335 lbs. at 25c.; baking soda, 20 lbs. at 3½c.; lard, 50 lbs. at 14c.; coffee, 370 lbs. at 25c.; vinegar, 31 gals. at 25c.; cocoa, 6 lbs. at 50c.; mustard, 20 lbs. at 25c.; corn starch, 40 lbs. at 7c.; laundry starch, 124 lbs. at 7c.; salt, 3 bbls. at 1.50	215 68
American Medico Psychological Ass'n., annual dues, 5.00; American Express Co., charges, 49.56 ....:	54 56
Anderson, Jno., meat, 970 lbs. at 5¼c., 53.35; Anglin, S. & Co., lumber, 539.34	592 69
Angrove Bros., phonograph records, 2 doz. at 7.80; phonograph needles, 3 boxes at 25c.; tennis balls, 1 doz. at 4.25, 1 doz. at 4.80; tennis net, 1 only at 6.50; jaws for chuck, 1 set at 2.00; bal. on band instruments, 10.00	43 90
Arbuckle, A. W., musical services, 13.50; Armstrong Bros., waggon, 1 only at 85.00	98 50
Bailey Broom Co., brooms, 68 doz. at 3.00, 204.00; Baker & Marshall, tobacco, 559 lbs. at 45c., 3 lbs. at 70c., 51 lbs. at 75c., 10 lbs. at 76c., 299.50 ....:	503 50
Bamford, Jas., carrots, 80 bags at 50c.; beets, 50 bags at 60c.; parsnips, 50 bags at 65c.; onions, 40 bags at 1.25; turnips, 80 bags at 30c.; cabbages, 12 bags at 2.00	200 50
Barber, Dr. W. C., travelling expenses, 65.90; Barber, W. C., musical services, 3.00	68 90
Barber, A. C., Mfg. Co., wicks, 2 doz. at 1.00, 2.00; Bassam, W. E., rent of cream freezers, 2.00	4 00
Bell Telephone Co., messages 56.40; rent of instruments, 115.50	171 90
Best. L. T.. drugs, chemicals, etc., 1.30; Bibby, F. A., livery hire, 18.00 ...	19 30
Bourk, S. C., cedar posts, 500 only at 13c., 65.00; *British Medical Journal*, subscription, 7.56	72 56

INSTITUTIONS MAINTENANCE.—*Continued.*

ASYLUM FOR INSANE KINGSTON.—*Continued.*

EXPENSES.—*Continued.*

Briscoe, C., services as laborer, 28½ days at 1.85, 52.72; Brown, Geo., lime, 320 bus. at 20c., 64.00	116 72
Burke, T. F., meat, 1,573 lbs. at 6¼c., 98.31; Burpee, W. A. & Co., seeds, 3.00	101 31
Bursar, to pay sundries, 30.38; Campbell, Mrs. P., milch cow, 1 only at 40.00	70 38
Canadian Practitioner and Review, subscription, 2.00; Canadian Express Co., charges, 19.05	21 05
C.P.R. Telegraph Co., messages, 2.09; Canadian Steam Boiler Equipment Co., grate bars, 514 lbs. at 5¼c., 26.98; cyclone grates, 1 doz. at 26.25, 53.23	55 32
Canadian Rubber Co., hose, 300 ft. for 38.48; sprinklers, 4 only at 1.50; sundries, 56c.	45 04
Canada Customs, custom duties, 10.21; Carnick, Wm., brick, 1,200 for 7.20	17 41
Carnovsky, W. H., cherries, 7 bas. at 1.35; apples, 10 bas. at 30c., 20 bas. at 35c., 1 bbl. at 2.00; muskmelons, 4 only at 25c.; plums, 8 bas. at 75c., 4 bas. at 85c., 22 bas. at 1.00; quinces, 2 bas. at 1.00; watermelons, 2 only at 75c.; berries, 200 boxes at 6¼c., 24 boxes at 8 1-3c., 6 boxes at 15c., 10 crates at 1.00; pears, 11 bas. at 75c.; peaches, 1 bas. at 85c.; sundries, 95c.	92 80
Carruthers, J. B., land adjoining asylum property, 1 year's rent	25 00
Castell, J., sausages, 250 lbs. at 8c.; meat, 1,078 lbs. at 7c., 2,017 lbs. at 7½c.	246 73
Cataraqui Cemetery Co., interments, 20.00; Central Prison Industries, flannel, 498 yds. at 25c., 1,029½ yds. at 30c.; braces, 24 doz. at 2.40; slippers, 30 prs. at 75c., 42 prs. at 90c.; tweed, 984½ yds. at 55c.; blankets, 2,494 lbs. at 45c.; croquet, 3 sets at 2.06 1-3; shoes, 25 prs. at 1.10, 1 pr. at 1.15, 1 pr. at 1.30, 50 prs. at 1.35, 49 prs. at 1.40, 26 prs. at 1.85; wrappers, 14.50, 2,449.87	2,469 87
Chandler, Ingram & Bell, drugs, chemicals, etc., 9.95; Chown, Edwin & Son, leather, 203 lbs. at 29c., 100 lbs. at 30c.; thread, 3 lbs. at 60c.; rasps, 4 only at 25c.; sundries, 3.16, 94.83	104 78
Chown, A. P., medical appliances, 103.02; drugs, chemicals, etc., 142.13	245 15
Cohen Bros., spectacles, 11-12 doz. at 16.00, 1¼ doz. at 1.50; cases, 1 doz. at 2.00; postage, 7c.	18 61
Common Sense Mfg. Co., roach exterminator, 5 lbs. at 1.00, 5.00; Couse, W., honey, 180 lbs. at 8c., 14.40	19 40
Crawford & Walsh, coats, 2 only at 8.00; suits, 5 only at 21.00	121 00
Crawford, James, split peas, 9 bbls. at 2.25; rolled oats, 40½ bbls. at 5.25; lemons, 5 doz. at 14c.	260 58
Crews, P. B., repairs to furniture, 4.45; Croft, Geo., rent of pasture and 20 tons of hay, 75.00	79 45
Croil, Jas., tweed, 43¾ yds. at 1.90, 83.13; Crothers, W. J. & Co., biscuits, 252 tins at 23c., 24 tins at 24c.; broken biscuits, 3,351 lbs. at 4c.; sundries, 1.36, 199.12	282 25
Crumley Bros., hats, 13 only at 50c., 6 only at 75c., 11.00; Corbett, Jno., transoms, 2 only at 50c.; cement, 2 bbls, at 3.00; sash tools, 1 doz. at 3.50, 10.50	21 50
Cullen, J., sugar, 605 lbs. at 4¼c.; soap, 5 boxes at 4.00; tea, 168 lbs. at 25c.; raisins, 58 lbs at 10½c.; turkey, 110¾ lbs. at 14½c.	109 58
Cummings, Geo., sheet music, 5.43; Cunningham, H., tuning pianos, 6.00	11 43
Dalton, W. B. & Sons, paints, oils, etc., 113.25; locks, 1 doz. at 1.20, 2 only at 1.45, 6 only at 1.50, 4 doz. at 2.00, 2 doz. at 4.00, 1 doz. at 4.55, 1 doz. at 6.00, 1 doz. at 7.00, 1 doz. at 7.83, 1 doz. at 13.25, ½ doz. at 20.00; spoons, 5 doz. at 75c., 1 doz. at 1.75, 1 doz. at 3.50, 2 doz. at 5.25; meat baskets, 1 doz. at 15.00; nails, 12 lbs. at 10c., 2 kegs at 2.25, 6 kegs at 2.30, 6 kegs at 2.35, 3 kegs at 2.40, 1 keg at 2.45, 1 keg at 2.50, 1 keg at 2.55, 3 kegs at 2.90, 1 keg at 3.25; drawer pulls, 6 doz. at 60c., 2 doz. at 75c.; latches, 1 doz. at 2.75, 1 doz. at 4.50; mattress twine, 10 lbs. at 40c.; wire hooks, 5¼ gro. for 7.73; cuspidors, 2 only at 2.50, 1 only at 3.00; hair clippers, 2 prs. at 2.50; tub, 1 only at 1.50; curled hair, 512 lbs. at 40c.; bronze numbers, 26 only at 15c.; sash cord, 6 lbs. at 35c.; mattress needles, 2 doz. at 1.20; glass, 16 boxes at	

PUBLIC INSTITUTIONS MAINTENANCE.—*Continued.*

ASYLUM FOR INSANE, KINGSTON.—*Continued.*

EXPENSES.—*Continued.*

2.25; paper, 4 rolls at 65c.; spoons, 3 doz. at 2.50, 3 doz. at 3.50; knives, 6½ doz. at 3.50, 1½ doz. at 3.75; castors, 24 sets at 10c.; brace, 1 only at 1.75, 1 only at 2.00; hockey sticks, 1 doz. at 4.00; rope, 407½ lbs. at 6c., 10 lbs. at 15c., 131 lbs. at 18c., 6½ lbs. at 30c.; hand bells, 3 only at 1.00, 1 only at 2.00; lanterns, 3 only at 85c.; gin block, 1 only at 6.25; forks, 1 doz. at 3.50; glue, 50 lbs. at 17c., 20 lbs. at 25c.; bronze letters, 8 only at 20c.; whiting, 336 lbs. at 1c.; planes, 1 only at 1.25, 1 only at 1.45; shears, 1 pr. at 10.00; rim knobs, 1 doz. at 1.00; pencils. 1 gro. at 4.00: sofa twine, 25 lbs. at 13c.; tacks, 12 doz. at 20c., 12 doz. at 24c., 6 doz. at 35c.; dualin, 116½ lbs. at 20c., 7½ lbs. at 25c.; hay fork handles. 1 doz. at 1.75; baskets, 5 only at 40c.; fire iron stands, 1 only at 6.75; moulding, 48 ft. at 4½c., 100 ft. at 5c., 48 ft. at 5½c., 100 ft. at 6c.; thermometers, 6 only at 50c., 1 only at 75c., 1 only at 1.00; saws, 1 only at 1.50; spirit level, 1 only at 1.00: toilet clippers, 2 only at 2.50; hinges, 1 doz. at 1.20, 1 doz. at 2.25; knobs, 2 gro. at 1.50; sofa springs, 4 gro. at 15.36; drawer locks, 1 doz. at 6.50; screws, 23.62; scales, 1 set at 7.00; leather belting, 50 ft. at 21.20, 40 ft. at 25.20, 80 ft. at 28.80 per 100 ft.; backing, 1,000 ft. for 9.00; weather strip, 108 ft. at 3c.; burnshine, 2 doz. pts. at 3.50; blistered steel, 64 lbs. at 9c.; cup books. 1 gro. at 1.25; dark lantern, 1 only at 75c.; iron hardware. etc., 74.33 .... 1,015 71

Darry, H., services as mason, 29½ days at 3.50, 103.25; Davies, Wm. Co., Ltd., sausages, 30 lbs. at 10c., 9 lbs. at 12c., 55 lbs. at 12½c., 7 lbs. at 13c., 11.95 .... 115 20

Davidson, J., expenses capturing eloper, 10.95; expenses taking patients to circus, 22.25 .... 33 20

Day, H. W., expenses capturing eloper, 2.00; straw, 3.470 tons at 5.00 ...... 18 14

Day, Harold, travelling expenses, 6.10; Dine, Dan., meat, 2,064 lbs. at 5.50 cwt., 113.52 .... 119 62

Dinnie, A., meat. 964 lbs. at 5½c., .53.24; Dinnie, E., veal, 200 lbs. at 6c., 12.00 .... 65 24

Dobbs. J. R. C., typewriter supplies, 14.50; Dolan, M., repairs to harness, 57.85; traces, 1 pr. at 4.00, 61.85 .... 76 35

Dominion Fish Co., fish, 21,876 lbs. at 5c., 300 lbs. at 6½c.; canned fish, 3 doz. at 1.10, 4 doz. at 1.20, 6½ doz. at 1.50, 8 doz. at 1.60, 1 doz. at 2.16, 1 doz. at 3.30; oysters, 1 1-8 gals. at 1.80, 1 pt. at 30c., 2 5-8 gals. at 2.00, 1 gals. at 2.20; chickens, 1 only at 48c.; 455 lbs. at 8c., 450 lbs. 8½c., 69 lbs. at 10c., 189 3-8 lbs. at 12½c.; geese, 2 only at 1.00. 106 lbs. at 11c., 20 lbs. at 12½c.; turkey, 423 lbs. at 15c.; venison, 95 lbs. at 8c.; sundries, 90c. 1,354 96

Dominion Express Co., charges, 6.10; Donohue, C., oats, 50 bus. at 38c., 234 bus. at 40c., 118 bus. at 42c.; cracked feed. 8.163 tons at 21.00, 2 tons at 24.00; wheat, 3.1747 tons at 16.00, 3.635 tons at 21.00; corn, 55¼ bus. at 62c.; bran. 1 ton at 19.00; bags, 80 only at 5c.; cartage. 8.30, 577.21 .... 583 31

Douglas & McIlquham, repairs to buildings, 53.80; Draper, Geo., turkey, 195 lbs. at 13c., 25.35 .... 79 15

Drury. Wm., lime. 107¾ bus. at 27c.; cartage, 2.00, 31.10; Eddy, E. B. Co., Ltd., paper. 5.82; paper bags, 4.34. 10.16 .... 41 26

Electric Boiler Compound Co., cup grease, 25 lbs. at 15c., 3.75; Elliott. T. C., apples, 1 bbl. at 2.00 .... 5 75

Fenwick. Wm. P., eggs. 17½ doz. at 15c., 16½ doz. at 17c., 67½ doz. at 17½c., 29½ doz. at 18c., 28½ doz. at 20c., 6½ doz. at 26c., 71½ doz. at 35c.; chickens, 17 only at 25c., 6 only at 42½c., 1 only at 45c. 62 20

Ferguson. T. H., lemons, 1 case at 4.00: Ferrel. The Co.. drugs, chemicals, etc., 9.90 .... 13 90

Fischer, Carl, sheet music, 13.47; Fisher Bros., grain, 59 loads at 3.00, 177.00 .... 190 47

Fletcher Mfg. Co.. almond paste, 10 lbs. at 38c., 3.80; Foden, J.. music provided. 60.25 .... 64 05

Foley, M., moving pianos, 6.00; Folger, Howard S., freight charges, 1.26 ... 7 26

PUBLIC INSTITUTIONS MAINTENANCE.—*Continued.*

ALYLUM FOR INSANE, KINGSTON.—*Continued.*

Expenses.—*Continued.*

Forster, A. S., strawberries, 486 qts. at 8½c.; cherries, 5 bas. at 1.20, 47.31; Frost, W. G., repairs to vehicles, 33.50	80 81
Gale, Geo. & Sons, nickelled springs, 4.20 lbs. at 7c., 29.40; Gallagher, T., inspecting scales, 6.50	35 90
Garlock Packing Co., repairs to boilers, 36.28; Gibson, W. W., drugs, chemicals, etc., 118.69; medical appliances, 6.95, 125.64	161 92
Gibson, Jno., meat, 31,117 lbs. at 4.15 cwt., 952 lbs. at 5c., 464 lbs. at 5¼c., 1,133 lbs. at 5½c., 1,000 lbs. at 6c., 2,071 lbs. at 6½c., 304 lbs. at 7c., 365 lbs. at 9c., 58 lbs. at 11c.	1,694 93
Gilbert, Jno., rolled oats, 35 bbls. at 5.40, 189.00; Gilmour, W., repairs to vehicles, 5.75	194 75
Gillett, E. W. Co., Ltd., perfumed lye, 3 cases at 3.50; baking powder, 6 doz. at 3.40, 6 doz. at 3.33 1-3; bi-carbonate soda, 1 case at 7.00	57 90
Glover, A., rice, 750 lbs. at 3¾c.; mustard, 52 lbs. at 20c.; sugar, 1,514 lbs. at 3.95 cwt., 609 lbs. at 4.50 cwt.; salt, 2 bags at 50c., 2 bbls. at 1.40; vinegar, 42 gals. at 25c.; flavoring extract, 4 doz. at 1.00; fruit peel, 14 lbs. at 15c., 7 lbs. at 20c.; tea, 570 lbs. at 25c.; chicory, 300 lbs. at 15c.; prunes, 100 lbs. at 5½c.; soap, 2 boxes at 4.00; allspice, 5 lbs. at 25c.; syrup, 1,005 lbs. at 3¼c.; finnan haddie, 30 lbs. at 9c.	385 16
Gowdey, Jas., meat, 480 lbs. at 5c., 2,280 lbs. at 6c., 9,859 lbs. at 7c.	850 93
Graham, Jas. G., expenses capturing eloper, 3.40; G.N.W. Telegraph Co., messages, 17.24	20 64
Grand Trunk Railway, freight charges, 148.43; Green, S., meat, 1,140 lbs. at 3.87½ cwt., 531 lbs. at 5c., 2,781 lbs. at 6c., 2,068 lbs. at 6½c.; milch cows, 6 only at 45.00, 1,041.13	1,189 56
Grimsby Co-Operative Fruit Growers' Ass'n., peaches, 56 bas. at 70c., 10 bas. at 75c.; pears, 1 bas. at 32c., 11 bas. at 42c.; grapes, 50 bas. at 18c., 50 bas. at 20c.	70 64
Guild & Hanson, city directory, 1 only at 2.00; Gunns, Ltd., butter, 5,252 lbs. at 21c., 14,456 lbs. at 23¾c., 4,545.04	4,547 04
Gutta Percha Rubber Mfg. Co., Ltd., hospital sheets, 24 only at 2.00	48 00
Haffner, P., matches, 5 gro. at 90c.; cocoa, 18 lbs. at 50c.; gelatine, 4 doz. at 1.50; coffee, 400 lbs. at 25c.; canned vegetables, 20 doz. at 1.00; chocolate, 18 lbs. at 50c.; sugar, 624 lbs. at 4.25 cwt.; syrup, 682 lbs. at 3¼c.	197 20
Halliday, Jas., difference in exchange of cows, 444.50; purchase of meat, 1,045.30	1,489 80
Hames. Jno., repairing and readjusting scales, 28.50; Hamer, J., repairing scales, 5.25	33 75
Hamilton, Peter, Co., repairs to implements, 6.90; Hanson, Geo., rubber stamps, 1 only at 1.00	7 90
Hand, F. W. Firework Co., fireworks, 27.40; Hartz, J. F. Co., Ltd., medical appliances, 68.46; drugs, 13.48, 81.94	109 34
Hawley, T. E., dyeing curtains, 2 prs. at 1.50, 3.00; Haywood, Howard, lecture, 6.00	9 00
Harrison, T. F. Co., fibre, 670 lbs. at 8c.; chairs, 12 only at 1.00; seats, 48 only at 17c., 24 only at 19c., 12 only at 2.75; rug, 1 only at 35.00; repairing chairs, etc., 60.85; invalid chairs, 1 only at 33.00; tassels, 2 doz. at 1.20; mirrors, 12 only at 60c., 1 only at 3.30; renovating mattress, 3.75; blinds, 2 only at 1.00, 4 only at 1.60; picture moulding, 20.28; rocker, 1 only at 15.00; furniture covering, 10 yds. at 1.25, 4 yds. at 2.00; silk gimp, 3 pcs. at 75c.; camp bed, 1 only at 1.50; bureau back, 1 only at 2.50; sundries, 9.05	336 30
Hay & Wilson, repairs to implements, etc., 18.55; Hedley Shaw Milling Co., flour, 1,000½ bbls. at 3.75, 3,751.89	3,770 44
Henderson, J. S., prunes, 600 lbs. at 6½c.; coffee, 379 lbs. at 25c.; starch, 40 lbs. at 6¾c.; onions, 1 bush. at 1.75; sugar, 1,864 lbs. at 4½c., 25 lbs. at 6½c., 1,800 lbs. at 3.95 cwt., 200 lbs. at 4.25 cwt., 1,161 lbs. at 4.30 cwt., 2,158 lbs. at 4.45 cwt.; syrup, 2,155 lbs. at 2 7-8c., 341 lbs. at 3c.; evaporated apples, 100 lbs. at 7½c.; olive oil, ½ gal. at 2.70; cocoanut, 5 lbs. at 22c.; currants, 147 lbs. at 6½c.; corn starch, 40 lbs. at 7c.; macaroni, 10 lbs. at 11½c.; ginger, 6 lbs. at 22c.; soap, 3	

INSTITUTIONS MAINTENANCE.—*Continued.*

ASYLUM FOR INSANE, KINGSTON.—*Continued.*

EXPENSES.—*Continued.*

boxes at 4.00; pepper, 5 lbs. at 35c.; melons, 1 doz. at 1.00; salt, 3 bbls. at 1.40; figs, 798½ lbs. at 5½c.; eggs, 30 doz. at 17c., 132 doz. at 19c., 30 doz. at 19½c., 25 doz. at 27½c.; biscuit, 12 tins at 12½c, 5 lbs. at 26c.; blacking, 6 doz. at 35c., 6 doz. at 45c.; L. & P. sauce, 1½ doz. at 3.50; pineapples, 4 only at 25c., 2 doz. at 1.70; bacon, 18 lbs. at 17c., 21½ lbs. at 18c.; tea, 180 lbs. at 25c., 5 lbs. at 40c.; raisins, 112 lbs. at 7½c.; lemons, ½ case at 5.00, 3 doz. at 25c., 3 doz. at 40c.; sapolio, 2 boxes at 2.85; vanilla, 4 doz. at 90c.; cream tartar, 10 lbs. at 30c.; matches, 1 case at 3.50; stove polish, 3 doz. at 45c.; vinegar, 31 gals. at 25c.; jelly powder, 2 doz. at 1.00; lard, 20 lbs. at 13c.; bovine cordial, 1 doz. at 11.00; mince meat, 110 lbs. at 9½c.; canned vegetables, 2 doz. at 92½c.; turkey, 220 lbs. at 14c.; mollasses, 4 gals. at 40c.; essence of almond, 2 doz. at 90c.; cranberries,, 12 qts. at 12c., 16 qts. at 12½c.. 849 57

Hendry, J. A., toilet paper, 3 cases at 6.40; paper bags, 2.45; wrapping paper, 7.95 .... 29 60

Hentig, Geo.; conductor pipe, 30 ft. at 10c.; diploma cases, 2 doz. at 2.50; kettle, 1 only at 2.50; tin dippers, 18 only at 20c., 6 only at 1.25; dust pans, 3 doz. at 6.00; dish pans, 1 doz. at 6.00; pot cover, 1 only at 1.50; roast pans, 2 doz. at 3.00; fish tins, 2 only at 2.00; tin dish, 1 only at 3.00; repairs to tinware, 32.90; centre dishes, 6 only at 3.00; gal'v. wash tubs, 2 only at 90c., 4 only at 1.00; boiler covers, 2 only at 75c., 2 only at 1.00; pails, 1 doz. at 3.25, 2 doz. at 3.50; tea jugs, 12 only at 1.10; sundries, 7.21 .... 150 96

Herriman, W. C., travelling expenses, 17.00; Hoag, F. J., drugs, chemicals, etc., 511.36; seeds, 26.84; soap, 100 lbs. at 8c., 37½ lbs. at 9c., 4 doz. at 40c.; medical appliances, 5.30; combs, 10 doz. at 60c.; sundries, 55c., 563.03 .... 580 03

Hogan, Wm., horseshoeing, 74.51; Hope, G. & Son., ferrets, 12.00 .... 86 51

Hopkins, Jno., Press, *American Journal of Insanity*, subscription 2 50

Horsey, S. J., double boiler, 1 only at 1.25; nails, 1 keg at 2.65, 1 keg at 2.75; paints, oils, etc., 172.63; stove door locks, 1 doz. at 9.00; tin, 1 box at 6.00; sad irons, 36 only for 21.00; brass polish, 1 doz. at 3.00; steel strap ends, 2 pr. at 1.00; clothes wringer, 1 only at 12.00; tea kettle, 1 only at 1.25; coffee pots. 1 only at 75c.; oil stoves, 2 only at 4.50; emery cloth, 1 only at 1.00; wrench, 1 only at 5.00; paint brushes, ½ doz. at 15.00; cap bath, 1 only at 4.50; clothes baskets, 4 only at 1.50; gasoline, 5 gals. at 30c.; pails, 3 doz. at 3.00, 2 only at 1.00, 1 only at 1.75; spoons, 3 doz. at 2.50, 3 doz. at 4.75; pans, 1 doz. at 1.50, ½ doz. at 3.00, ¼ doz. at 9.00; turpentine, 20 gals. at 1.25; mops, 1 doz. at 1.80; chambers, 10¼ doz. at 4.50; sundries, 16.45 .... 401 28

Imperial Steam Laundry Co., laundry, 947.47; marking tabs, 3.00......... 950 47

Imperial Chemical Co., soap, 1,034 lbs. at 5c., 51.70; Jackson, A.. music provided, 37.50 .... 89 20

Jackson, The, Press, printing, 78.75; Jennings, H., shoes, 19 prs. at 1.25, 14 prs. at 1.50; slippers, 3 prs. at 50c.; rubber boots, 2 prs. at 4.00; overshoes, 6 prs. at 1.75, 2 prs. at 2.25; rubbers, 12 prs. at 85c., 79.45 .... 158 20

Johnston, Mrs. T., laundrying, 14.10; Johnston, Jas., ribbon, 72 yds. at 3c.; silkoline, 10 yds. at 20c.; cambric, 50 yds. at 7c.; hairpins, 10 lbs. at 10c.; cotton, 579½ yds. at 10c., 123½ yds. at 10½c.; towels, 5 doz. at 2.50; thread, 24 doz. at 72c.; caps, 3 only at 38c.; laces, 2 gro. at 75c.; hosiery, 12 doz. at 3.00; print, 282½ yds. at 12½c.; yarn, 3 lbs. at 75c.; corsets, 1 pr. at 1.00; mittens, 6 doz. at 3.00; pins, 12 doz. at 20c.; shaker flannel, 143½ yds. at 10c.; shirting, 787½ yds. at 12½c., 130 yds. at 14c.; clothing, 2 suits at 6.50; butter cloth, 100 yds. at 5c.; needles, 40 papers at 5c.; muslin, 62 yds. at 25c; sheeting, 185½ yds. at 25c., 75 yds. at 30c.; wool hoods, 7 10-12 doz. at 9.00; sundries, 72c., 519.62 .... 533 72

Kay, Jno., Son & Co., brass placque, 1 only at 3.92; Kelly, W., dyeing curtains, 1.50 .... 5 42

PUBLIC INSTITUTIONS MAINTENANCE.—*Continued.*

ASYLUM FOR INSANE, KINGSTON.—*Continued*

EXPENSES.—*Continued.*

Kelly, Jas. & Co., bees wax, 57 lbs. at 33½c.; ham, 42½ lbs. at 16c.; sugar, 1,200 lbs. at 4.67 cwt., 700 lbs. at 4.75 cwt.; baking soda, 32 lbs. at 5c.; cream tartar, 5 lbs. at 40c.; eggs, 25 doz. at 35c.; salt, 8 bbls. at 1.45; prunes, 100 lbs. at 7½c.; coffee, 164 lbs. at 25c.; pipes, 1 box at 1.00 .... 188 64

Kenny, T. & Co., tea, 475 lbs. at 22c., 104.50; Kidd, Jno., repairs to vehicles, 13.05 .... 117 55

Kingston Milk Depot, milk, 5,926¼ qts. at 4c., 250.37; *Kingston News*, printing, 178.70 .... 429 07

Kingston Penitentiary, gravel, 75 bush. at 7c., 215 bush at 8c.; binder twine, 50 lbs. at 11½c.; toise macadam, 1.75 .... 29 95

K. P. & C. Electric Ry., car tickets, 120.00; cartage on posts, 9.75, 129.75; Kingston & Pembroke Ry., freight, 1.81 .... 131 56

Kingston Fire Brigade, services rendered at fire, 50.00; Kirkpatrick's Art Store, pictures, 6.60 .... 56 60

Lambert, Thos., canvas, 99¾ lbs. at 18c., 17.95; Laughern, Jas., paints, oils, etc., 114.00 .... 131 95

Leakey, F. J., soap, 131 lbs. at 6½c., 5 boxes at 4.00; syrup, 682 lbs. at 3½c., 1,349 lbs. at 3½c.; fish, 215 lbs. at 5½c.; coffee, 303¼ lbs. at 25c.; tobacco, 22 lbs. at 42c.; nutmegs, 4 lbs. at 75c.; tapioca, 160 lbs. at 7½c.; mustard, 20 lbs. at 25c.; cracked wheat, 12 lbs. at 20c.; starch, 100 lbs. at 8½c.; eggs, 65 doz. at 17c., 23 doz. at 20c., 25 doz. at 35c.; jam, 510 lbs. at 8½c.; matches, 1 case at 3.75; cocoa, 1 doz. at 3.00; sugar, 941 lbs. at 4½c., 25 lbs. at 8c.; tea, 184 lbs. at 25c.; cinnamon, 5 lbs. at 30c.; sundries, 3.20 .... 390 25

Lemmon & Sons, lanterns, 18 only at 65c.; coal oil, 91½ gals. at 20c.; lantern globes, 2 doz. at 1.00; locks, 6 only at 50c., 6 only at 65c.. 6 only at 85c., 6 only at 90c., 1 only at 1.50; poultry netting, 1 roll at 6.00; nails, 50 lbs. at 5c.; whisks, 1 doz. at 1.80; water cans, 6 only at 65c.; cement, 12 bbls. at 2.00; hose, 100 ft. at 12c., 100 ft. at 16½c.; forks, 3 only at 60c., 6 doz. at 2.25; garbage pails, 1 only at 2.00; snow shovels, 6 only at 50c., 6 only at 60c.; glue, 30 lbs. at 25c.; picture wire, 1 doz. pkgs. at 2.25; axe handles, 1 doz. at 3.00; whips, 3 only at 75c.; latches, 1 doz. at 1.20; washboards, 1 doz. at 3.00; sapolio, 1 case at 3.60; metal polish, 1 doz. at 3.00; brushes, 1 doz. at 3.00, 2 only at 75c.; lawn mowers, 1 only at 5.50; knives, 6 doz. at 3.00, 4 only at 1.25; butcher steel, 1 only at 1.00; towel rack, 1 only at 1.40; coal scoop, 1 only at 1.25; sundries, 21.07...... 225 02

Lewis, Rice & Son, coal scoop, 1 only at 5.72; fire set, 1 only at 8.00, 13.72; Lippincott, J. B. Co., medical books, 14.75 .... 28 47

Litton, C. S., tea, 280 lbs. at 25c.; prunes, 200 lbs. at 7c., 200 lbs. at 9½c.; sugar, 944 lbs. at 4.05, 637 lbs. at 4.35. 958 lbs. at 4.50 cwt.; soap, 5 boxes at 4.00; sapolio, 1 box at 3.25; tapioca, 180 lbs. at 9c.; cann. fish, 2 doz. at 1.10, 4 doz. at 1.65; cann. vegetables, 2 doz. at 1.30; sago, 100 lbs. at 6c.; jelly powders, 2 doz. at 1.10; rice, 100 lbs. at 3½c.; syrup, 2,032 lbs. at 3½c.; coffee, 220 lbs. at 25c.; currants, 166 lbs. at 9c.; honey, 216 lbs. at 8½c.; finnan haddie, 60 lbs. at 9c.; sundries, 2.40 .... 436 01

Macnee & Minnes, sheeting, 190 yds. at 19½c.. 1,551½ yds. at 20½c., 32¼ yds. at 22c., 30¼ yds. at 23c., 137 yds. at 26½c., 454½ yds. at 30c.; muslin, 60 yds. at 11c., 30 yds. at 16½c., 23 yds. at 18c., 32 yds. at 19½c.; tweed, 263½ yds. at 42½c., 191 yds. at 45c., 33½ yds. at 50c.; hospital cloth, 126½ yds. at 3½c.; buttons, 3 gro. at 1.00, 1 gro. at 1.20, 1 gro. at 1.50; duck, 60 yds. at 15c.; laces, 1 gro. at 2.50; chambray, 362½ yds. at 19c., 429 yds. at 21c.; hosiery, 25 doz. at 1.80, 12 doz. at 2.10, 4 doz. at 2.50; towels, 2 only at 50c., 2 only at 55c., 1 doz. at 1.45, 2 doz. at 3.25, ½ doz. at 3.75, ½ doz. at 4.00; overalls, 1 doz. at 7.20, 4 doz. at 9.00, 1 doz. at 9.25; white oilcloth, 6 pcs. at 3.25, 2 pcs. at 3.00; shirting, 449½ yds. at 12½c., 335 yds. at 13½c.; sateen, 42 yds. at 12½c., 50¾ yds. at 13½c., 25 yds. at 15c., 30 yds. at 19c.; cotton, 62 yds. at 7c., 501½ yds. at 8c., 172¾ yds. at 8½c., 368

PUBLIC INSTITUTIONS MAINTENANCE.—*Continued.*

ASYLUM FOR INSANE, KINGSTON.—*Continued.*

EXPENSES.—*Continued.*

yds. at 9c., 404¾ yds. at 9¾c., 722¾ yds. at 9 7-8c., 217¼ yds. at 10c., 244 yds. at 10¾c., 207¾ yds. at 13¾c.; thimbles, 3 gro. at 1.50; thread, 2½ gro. at 4.80, 5¾ gro. at 5.40; canvas, 50 yds. at 14c.; print, 41 yds. at 7½c., 502½ yds. at 9c., 169¼ yds. at 10c.; crash, 42½ yds. at 7¾c., 538½ yds. at 8c., 210½ yds. at 8½c., 438½ yds. at 9c., 12 yds. at 11c., 37 yds. at 12½c., 12 yds. at 24c.; ticking, 86½ yds. at 15c., 271½ yds. at 17½c., 326¾ yds. at 18½c.; cottonade, 62½ yds. at 22c.; quilts, 3 only at 1.75, 1 only at 3.00; butter cloth, 527½ yds. at 4½c.; batts, 150 lbs. at 13c.; combs, 6 doz. at 85c., 8 11-12 doz. at 1.70, 3 doz. at 1.75, 5 10-12 doz. at 2.25; handkerchiefs, 12 doz. at 95c.; curtain nett, 19¾ yds. at 52c.; needles, 3,000 at 1.25 m.; pillow cotton, 218¾ yds. at 13 7-8c., 87¾ yds. at 14¾c., 134¼ yds. at 14 7-8c., 88 yds. at 15c., 89 yds. at 15½c., 90½ yds. at 15¾c.; tray cloths, ¼ doz. at 4.00, 1 2-3 doz. at 7.00; doilies, 5 doz. at 50c.; carpet, 16 yds. at 40c.; lining, 93½ yds. at 25c.; bed spreads, 1 doz. at 13.50; flannelette, 1,470½ yds. at 8¼c., 239¼ yds. at 8½c.; denim, 54¾ yds. at 22c.; brushes, 6 doz. at 1.25, 3 doz. at 4.50; blankets, 1 pr. at 3.25; shawls, 4 only at 1.50, 4 only at 1.65, 4 only at 1.95; braces, 5 doz. at 2.50; mitts, 1 doz. at 2.25, 1 doz. at 2.50; linen, 46¾ yds. at 16½c., 31½ yds. at 25c., 107¾ yds. at 45c.; collars, 12 doz. at 75c., 10 doz. at 1.50; lawn, 62 yds. at 13c.; hessian, 57 yds. at 10½c., 56 yds. at 13½c., 56 yds. at 17c., 53 yds. at 20c.; ribbon, 144 yds. at 15c., 18 yds. at 17c.; curtains, 1 pr. at 5.50; hammocks, 2 only at 2.50, 1 only at 3.00; table covers, 3 only at 1.00; toilet covers, 2 only at 75c., 2 only at 3.50; tabling, 277½ yds. at 45c.; table napkins, 1 doz. at 8.50; scrim, 134 yds. at 10c., 84 yds. at 10½c., 31½ yds. at 12½c.; cretonne, 113½ yds. at 12½c.; satin duchess, 48 yds. at 25c.; mats, 2 only at 2.50, 2 only at 4.25; rugs, 1 only at 26.00; belts, 1 doz. at 2.50; caps, 1 doz. at 4.75; gloves, 1 doz. at 2.25, 1½ doz. at 2.65; handkerchiefs, 6 doz. at 1.20, 4 doz. at 1.50; ladies' coats, 27 only at 5.00; lawn, 96 yds. at 12c.; shirts, 1 doz. at 9.00; gingham, 118 yds. at 10c.; sundries, 41.47	3,049 61
Mackie, W. H., eggs, 51 doz. at 25c., 14.75; Mahood Bros., crepe paper, 30 rolls at 10c., 3.00	17 75
Manning, J. W., maple syrup, 20 gals. at 1.00, 20.00; Meakins Brush Co., white tampico, 300 lbs. for 39.69, 604 lbs. at 14c.; rice root, 112 lbs. for 24.15, 221 lbs. at 25c., less discount, 1.39, 202.26	222 26
Medcalf, D. M., travelling expenses *re* boiler inspection, 32.90; Mellville, P., meat, 1,050 lbs. for 30.00, 3,355 lbs. at 3c., 130.65	163 55
Metcalfe, Mrs. M. A., meat, 3,187 lbs. at 5c., 406 lbs. at 5½c., 1,547 lbs. at 7c., 2,266 lbs. at 7½c.; sausage, 308 lbs. at 8c.; lamb, 1 side at 2.25	486 81
Meyer Bros., washing soda, 4,200 lbs. at 1 7-8c.; analine blue, 4 lbs. at 3.50; hand seam dampers, 4 only at 75c.; sundries, 68c	96 43
Mills, Thos. C., hats, 5 doz. at 1.50, 5 doz. at 2.25; mitts, 6 doz. at 3.00, 4 doz. at 6.00, 1 doz. at 7.00	67 75
Monetary Times, subscription 2 years, 4.00; Montreal Transportation Co., lumber, 9.60	13 60
Morang & Co., books, 47.00; Morton & Sons, soap, 1 gro. at 2.40, 1 gro. at 3.60, 1 gro. at 5.40, 11.40	58 40
Morrison, Dr. C. A., professional services, 5.00; Morrison, Jas., Brass Mnfg. Co., hose nipples, 1-3 doz. at 5.01; lubricator, 1 only at 9.00, 10.67	15 67
Mott, J. L., Iron Works, brass gas jet, 1 only at 8.25; Murray, W. A. & Co., carpet, 34½ yds. at 1.50, 5½ yds. at 1.75, less discount, 3.05, 58.33	66 58
MacLean, H. N., straw, 5.1,540 tons at 4.00, 23.08; MacRow, D., evergreens, 2 loads at 1.50, 3.00	26 08
McAdoo, N., milch cows, 2 only at 35.00, 70.00; McAuley, Thos., subscriptions sundry magazines, 64.40; stationery, 318.53, 382.93	452 93
McCall, Jno., sheep, 59 only for 300.00; McCammon, services catering for annual ball, 5.00	305 00

PUBLIC INSTITUTIONS MAINTENANCE.—*Continued.*

ASYLUM FOR INSANE. KINGSTON.— *Continued.*

EXPENSES.—*Continued.*

McColl Bros. & Co., paints, oils, etc., 116.10; McClary Mnfg, Co., chambers, 12 doz. for 46.61 .... 162 71

McCrow, J., meat, 10,990 lbs. at 4¾c., 522.03; McDermott, J. F., repairs · to vehicles, 14.75 .... 536 78

McDermott Bros., sheet music, 8.30; McDermott, D. J., slippers, 27 prs. at 50c., 12 prs. at 60c., 6 prs. at 75c.; shoes, 33 prs. at 1.25, 16 prs. at 1.50, 1 pr. at 2.00, 1 pr. at 2.25, 2 prs. at 3.00; rubber boots, 3 prs. at 2.50, 5 prs. at 4.00; laces, 4 gro. at 25c.; long boots, 25 prs. at 3.25; gum rubbers, 1 pr. at 2.75; overshoes, 2 prs. at 1.75; knit ᵗox, 3 prs. at 1.00, 219.70 .... 228 00

McFadden, Ed., livery hire, 5.00; McGuire, T., travelling expenses, 8.00 13 00

McIntosh. P. & Son, oatmeal, 5 bbls. at 5.55, 27,75; McKelvey & Birch, ᵃnamelled bath, 1 only at 27.00; closet, 1 only at 2.75; bath cocks, ᴵ set at 2.50; enamelled sink, 1 only at 3.00; sundries, 2.09; time fitting bath, etc., 33.98, 71.32 .... 99 07

McLaughlin, J., oranges, 3 doz. at 30c., 3 cases at 3.00, 7½ cases at 3.50; raisins, 66 lbs. at 20c., 2 cases at 1.10, 1 case at 4.40; oakes, 20 doz. at 10c., 8 doz. at 20c., 5 only at 15c., 5 only at 25c., 8 only at 50c.; ᵖineapple cream, 5 gals. at 2.00; filberts, 50 lbs. at 15c.; lemons. 2 doz. at 25c., 4 doz. at 40c., 1 case at 3.25, 2 cases at 3.50, 1½ cases at 4.00, ½ case at 5.00, ½ case at 6.00; nuts, 15 lbs. at 18c.; candies, 50 lbs. at 10c., 20 lbs. at 25c.; pineapples. 2 doz. at 1.80; vanilla cream, 5 gals. at 1.50; almonds, 50 lbs. at 20c.; walnuts, 50 lbs. at 20c......... 150 70

McMahon, T. & Co., painting and paperhanging, 92.50; Napier, Jas., music supplied, 18.75 .... 111 25

Nanz & Neuner, plants, 15.00; *Napanee Beaver,* subscription, 1.00 ..... 16 00

Nesbitt, Wm. J., sausage, 250 lbs. at 8c ; prunes, 125 lbs. at 7¼c.; tea, 370 lbs. at 25c.; figs, 231 lbs. at 5¼c.; vinegar, 39 gals. at 25c.; cocoa, 24 lbs. at 50c.; syrup, 1,083 lbs. at 3c., 1,020 lbs. at 3½c.; coffee, 200 lbs. at 25c.; salt, 1 doz. bags at 1.20. 5 bbls. at 1.35; matches, 1 case · at 3.75; pepper, 75 lbs. at 25c.; cinnamon, 5 lbs. at 25c.............. 306 23

Newman & Shaw, napkins, 10 doz. at 1.25; towelling. 102 yds. at 8c., 199½ yds. at 10c.; lawn, 56 yds. at 12½c., 25 yds. at 15c., 23 yds. at 20c.; sheeting. 173 yds. at 30c., 36 yds. at 32c., 36 yds. at 35c.; print, 196¼ yds. at 10c., 580½ yds. at 12½c.; white suiting, 33 yds. at 30c.. 11 yds. at 37½c.; collars, 6 doz. at 1.40; flannelette. 244½ yds. at 10c., 187½ yds. at 12½c.. 11¼ yds. at 18c.; muslin, 50 yds. at 6c., 10 yds. at 10c., 37¼ yds. at 18c.; ribbon. 25 yds. at 3c., 40 yds. at 4c., 9¾ yds. at 10c., 36 yds. at 11c.. 14½ yds. at 12½c.; oilcloth, 12 yds. at 25c.: ticking, 160¾ yds. at 20c.. 166¼ yds. at 22c.; silesian, 51¼ yds. at 16c.; nett, 32 yds. at 25c.; lace. 23¾ yds. at 9c., 96 yds. at 10c., 24 yds. at 12½c.; thread, 93 doz. at 70c.. 24 doz. at 72.; linen damask. 126¾ yds. at 50c.; table linen, 154½ yds. at 7½c. 256¼ yds. at 8c., 266½ yds. at 9c., 169½ yds. at 10c.: felt, 4½ yds. at 80c.; shirting, 737½ yds. at 15c.; tweed. 82 yds. at 95c.: sateen, 10 yds. at 15c., 43¼ yds. at 20c.. 10 yds. at 25c., 60 yds. at 28c.; cambric, 38 yds. at 7c.; waisting. 15 yds. at 25c.; quilts. 50 only at 1.00. 10 only at 1.50; buttons, 40 doz. at 95c., 1 gro. at 1.50; crochet cotton, 2 doz. at 60c.; towels, 6 doz. at 1.50, 7 doz. at 1.75, 2 doz. at 2.85; insertion, 24 yds. at 5c.; hosiery. 5 doz. at 2.95, 5 doz. at 3.50, 5 doz. at 3.60; needles, 100 pkgs. at 3½c.; fringe, 36 yds. at 7c.: tongues. 2 2.3 doz. at 3.00; handkerchiefs, 41 doz. for 5.00; dress suitings. 390 5-8 yards at 19c.; lace curtains, 2 prs. at 2.25, 2 prs. at 2.50; thimbles, 1 gro. at 2.00; gingham, 30 yds. at 15c.; lustre, 8 yds. at 50c.; clouds, 6 only at 35c., 6 only at 50c.; fancy pins. 9 doz. at 50c.; shawls, ½ doz. at 3.00, 5-12 doz. at 6.00, ½ doz. at 12.00, ½ doz. at 15.00; sundries, 27.69 .... 1,266 53

Nicholls. Wm., veterinary services, 28.25; Nicholson's Cutlery Store, razor blades. 574 only at 5c., 28.70 .... 56 95

Nordheimer Piano & Music Co., sheet music, 32.90; sundries, 7.05......... 39 95

Nugent & Graham. paints, oils, etc., 79.44; lanterns, 1 doz. at 6.00; wire baskets, 3 only at 50c.; brushes, 2 only at 70c., 6 only at 90c.; hammers. ½ doz. at 7.20; hose, 50 ft. at 14½c.; cement, 7 bbls. at 2.20. 3

PUBLIC INSTITUTIONS MAINTENANCE.—*Continued.*

ASYLUM FOR INSANE, KINGSTON.—*Continued.*

EXPENSES.—*Continued.*

bbls. at 2.25; shovels, 6 only at 65c., 6 only at 75c.; glass. 66.07; spoons, 3 doz. at 2.00; turpentine, 42.50, gal. at 1.15; hose nozzles. ½ doz. at 6.00; picks. ½ doz. at 9.00; sash tools, 12 only at 40c.; manure forks, 6 only at 90c.; scissors, 6 pr. at 1.20; tea pot, 1 only at 1.75; whiting, 1 bbl. at 2.86; plaster paris, 1 bbl. at 2.25; sundries, 7.41	295 25
Ockley, V. & Sons, coffee, 200 lbs. at 25c.; jelly powder, 2 doz. at 1.20; soap, 15 lbs. at 15c., 5 cases at 4.00; tea. 100 lbs. at 25c.; baking powder, 4 lbs. at 60c.; barley, 4 bags at 2.75; tumblers, 6 doz. at 45c., 6 doz. at 70c., 24 doz. at 1.00; bowls, 6 doz. at 60c., 18 doz. at 1.25; toilet sets, 5 only at 4.25, 1 only at 4.50, 2 only at 5.00; jugs, 1 doz. at 2.10, 2 doz. at 3.00, 5¾ doz. at 4.00, 1 doz. at 5.40; ewers, 1 doz. at 4.50, 1 doz. at 4.80, 3 doz. at 6.00; basins, 1 doz. at 4.50, 2 doz. at 6.00; soap boxes, 1¾ doz. at 4.20; orange bowls, 1-6 doz. at 15.00; cups and saucers, 6 doz. at 75c., 61 doz. at 1.00, 1 doz. at 2.75, 2 doz. at 2.25, 1 doz. at 4.20, 1 doz. at 4.50; covered dishes, 3 doz. at 7.00, 1-6 doz. at 12.00; plates, 8 doz. at 75c., 9 doz. at 80c., 19 doz. at 1.00, 2 doz. at 1.50; dinner set, 1 only at 11.50, 1 only at 45.00; gem jars, 3 doz. at 65c., 3 doz. at 70c., 9 doz. at 95c.; flower pots, 1 doz. at 1.80, 1 doz. at 2.40; sundries, glassware, etc., 37.91	552 89
Ontario Rubber Co., hospital sheets, 24 only at 1.95, 46.80; Orwell, E., tobacco, 56 lbs. at 42c., 23.52	70 32
O'Connor, T. J., music provided, 15.75; O'Neil, C., music provided, 18.00	33 75
Pacific Surgical Mnfg. Co., medical appliances, 3.60; Parisian Steam Laundry Co., laundrying, 87.67	91 27
Parkhill, J. Y. & Co., potatoes, 1,672.54 bush. at 59½c.; eggs, 294 doz. at 14c., 392 doz. at 14½c., 294 doz. at 15c., 196 doz. at 15½c., 923 doz. at 16c., 755 doz. at 16½c., 588 doz. at 17c., 539 doz. at 17½c., 158 doz. at 18c., 109 doz. at 18½c., 98 doz. at 19c., 120 doz. at 21c., 188 doz. at 23c., 245 doz. at 23½c., 150 doz. at 24c., 326 doz. at 25c., 98 doz. at 27½c.; cheese, 82 lbs. at 12c., 85 lbs. at 12½c.. 90 lbs. at 13c., 149 lbs. at 13½c., 69 lbs. at 13¾c.; bacon, 60 lbs. at 13c., 11¼ lbs. at 14c., 10½ lbs. at 14½c., 42½ lbs. at 16½c., 25½ lbs. at 17c., 13¼ lbs. at 17½c., 39 lbs. at 18c.; fowl. 60 lbs. at 7½c., 38 lbs. at 8½c.; lard, 50 lbs. at 11c., 50 lbs. at 11½c., 50 lbs. at 11 3-8c., 50 lbs. at 12c., 50 lbs. at 12½c.; jam, 30 lbs. at 6¾c.; beans, 24 8-60 bush. at 1.65, 6 bush. at 1.75, 10 bush. at 1.77½; ham, 23½ lbs. at 12c.; eggs, 98 doz. at 27c., 188 doz. at 29c....	2,256 33
Partridge, F., making and putting up window guards, 25.00; covering 2 buckets with wire cloth, 2.00	27 00
Paul. Wm. J., tobacco, 100 lbs. at 41c.; pipes, 10 doz. at 1.50, 56.00; Peters, Wm. P. & Bro., oats, 1 ton at 24.00, 150 bush at 40c., 61 bush. at 65c., 10 bags at 80c., 500 lbs. at 1.30 cwt., 200 lbs. at 1.40 cwt.; flour, 2 bbls. at 4.80, 1 bbl. at 5.00, 25 lbs. for 70c.; oil cake, 100 lbs. at 2.00 cwt.; potatoes, 50 bags at 1.00, 125 bags at 1.20, 4 bags at 2.25; seed peas, 4 bush. at 1.30; corn, 17 bush. at 1.00; seed corn, ½ bush. at 6.00; peas, 200 lbs. at 1.50 cwt.; bran, 1 ton at 18.00, ½ ton at 19.50, 2¾ tons at 21.00; corn meal, 21 bbls. at 4.00; rock salt, 150 lbs. for 1.50; cracked feed. 1 ton at 21.00; mangle seed, 20 lbs. at 20c.; turnip seed, 2½ lbs. at 30c.; salt, 3 sacks at 70c., 634.30	690 30
Pickering, C. H., cann. vegetables, 4 doz. at 75c., 4 doz. at 1.00; breakfast food, 1 doz. at 1.50; starch, 126 lbs. at 7c.; tea. 100 lbs. at 25c.; salt, 3 bbls. at 1.50; bacon, 9 lbs. at 17c.; coffee, 404 lbs. at 25c.; soap, 10 boxes at 4.00; sugar, 594 lbs. at 4c.; sapolio, 1 case at 3.25; sundries, 2.35	218 71
Piper, N. L., Railway Supply Co., lanterns, 4 only at 85c.; signal oil, 10 gal. at 75c.; sundries, 2.78	13 68
Portsmouth, Village of, taxes, 14.00; Postmaster, postage stamps, 270.00	284 00
Price, H. F., candy, 140 lbs. at 10c., 15 lbs. at 12c., 7 lbs. at 15c., 38 lbs at 20c., 12 lbs. at 25c.; cornnicopias, 700 lbs. at 2½c.	44 95
Purdy, Chas., horseshoeing, 11.70; Purtell, M., tea, 600 lbs. at 25c.; chicory, 180 lbs. at 15c.; sugar, 624 lbs. at 4c.. 611 lbs. at 4½c.; mustard, 20 lbs. at 20c.; salt, 2 bbls. at 1.50; cornmeal, 2 bbls. at 4.00; prunes, 100 lbs. at 7c.; figs, 100 lbs. at 7c.; syrup, 1,335 lbs. at 3½c.; eggs,	

PUBLIC INSTITUTIONS MAINTENANCE.—*Continued.*

ASYLUM FOR INSANE, KINGSTON.—*Continued.*

EXPENSES.—*Continued.*

60 doz. at 30c.; rice, 100 lbs. at 3¼c.; coffee, 200 lbs. at 25c.; cheese, 79 lbs. at 14c.; sundries, 70c., 385.36 .... 397 06

Rankin, A. McGuin, crack feed, 3.1,205 tons at 21.00, 1 ton at 24.00, 99.65; Reddan, H. O., milk, 39 qts. at 5c., 1.95 .... 101 60

Reddan, Chas. oat straw, 4.1,760 tons at 4.00, 19.52; Rees, Henry, horse, 1 only at 150.00 .... 169 52

Reeves, Daniel, paints, oils, etc., 104.80; Reid, W. H., meat, 4,685 lbs. at 6c., 1,225 lbs. at 7c., 1,660 lbs. at 7¼c., 1,870 lbs. at 7½c., 636.28... 741 08

Reid, Robt. J., interments, 24.00; Reynolds, M. J., uniforms for nurses, 4 only at 2.00, 8.00 .... 32 00

Richelieu & Ontario Navigation Co., freight, 2.50; Richardson, Jas. & Son, kiln dried wheat, 82.20, bush. at 50c., 41.17 .... 43 67

Rigney, T. J., meat, 4,547 lbs. at 6c., 506 lbs. at 5c., 1,270 lbs. at 6½, 2,647 lbs. at 7½c.. 579 20

Rigney & Hickey, sugar, 1,878 lbs. at 3.82, 2.371 lbs. at 3.97, 1,225 lbs. at 4.37; soap, 5 boxes at 3.80, 5 boxes at 4.00; eggs, 5 doz. at 35c.; apples, 3 bush. at 75c., 2 bbls. at 1.75, 4 bbls. at 2.50; tobacco, 198 lbs. at 39c., 96 lbs. at 66c.; cann. vegetables, 12 doz. at 1.00; sago, 50 lbs. at 6¼c.; spice, 5 lbs. at 20c.; axle grease, 3 doz. at 50c.; mustard, 20 lbs. at 20c.; matches, 1 case at 9.00; currants, 165 lbs. at 7½c.; geese, 86½ lbs. at 10c.; syrup, 6,510 lbs. at 2 7-8c.; sapolio, ¼ gro. at 12.00; bacon, 15¼ lbs. at 16c.; spirits for hospital use, 11 gals. at 3.20; barley, 2 bbls. at 4.50; prunes, 200 lbs. at 6½c.; tea, 90 lbs. at 25c.; corn meal, 2 bbls. at 4.25; pepper, 20 lbs. at 20c.; raisins, 168 lbs. at 10c.; honey, 120 lbs. at 10c.; turkey, 353 lbs. at 14c.; sundries, 18.23 .... 850 55

Robertson, Nicolle & Co., beans, 11 bush. at 2.00; syrup, 3,735 lbs. at 2 7-8c., 1,336 lbs. at 3c.; salt, 4 bbls. at 1.30; soap, 976 lbs. at 5c., 1.758 lbs. at 5½c., 10 boxes at 3.85, 5 boxes at 4.00; sugar, 611 lbs. at 4.17 cwt.; sapolio, 3 doz. at 1.00; fish, 660 lbs. at 6½c.; pepper, 50 lbs. at 18c.; pickles, 1 pail at 4.00, 1 pail at 4.25; eggs, 60 doz. at 18c.; vinegar, 31 gals. at 20c.; cann. fruit. 10 doz. at 2.20 .... 506 22

Robertson Bros., ruby globe, 1 only at 2.25; sundries, 15c., 2.40; Rogers, J. H., sheet music, 1.50 .... 3 90

Rooney & Co., mitts, 6 doz. at 3.00, 6 doz. at 6.00; ties, 18 doz. at 1.50, 6 doz. at 2.25; hosiery, 8 doz. at 1.75, 16 doz. at 3.00; clothing, 25 suits at 6.50 .... 319 00

Ross, Dr. A. E., professional services, 5.00; Rouse, J. B. & Co., repairs to laundry, 9.75 .... 14 75

R. C. F. Artillery, manure, 57.50; Ryan, P., rent of pasture land, 67.50 125 00

Ryan, Dr., travelling expenses, 62.85; horse, 1 only at 130.00; buggy, 1 only at 60.00 .... 252 85

Saunders, Chas., sugar, 1,221 lbs. at 3.92 cwt.; 931 lbs. at 4.70, 603 lbs. at 4.77; tea, 300 lbs. at 25c.; prunes, 200 lbs. at 7½c.; raisins, 100 lbs. at 7c.; flavoring extract, 4 doz. at 85c.; rice, 500 lbs. at 3.65 cwt.; starch, 200 lbs. at 7c., 100 lbs. at 8½c.; blacking, 3 doz. at 85c.; coal oil, 44.20 gals. at 18½c.; vinegar, 54 gals. at 25c., barrel, 1 only at 2.00; figs, 198 lbs. at 6c., 100 lbs. at 6½c.; fish, 60 lbs. at 6½c., 300 lbs. at 7½c.; currants, 84 lbs. at 7c.; corn starch, 80 lbs. at 7½c.; tapioca, 100 lbs. at 7½c.; sundries, 1.15 .... 352 32

Sears, Geo., mirror plate. 1 light at 4.50; underlac, 1 gal. at 4.00; baskets, 2 only at 50c., 4 only at 1.00; floor wax, 4 lbs. at 60c.; hair broom, 1 only at 2.00; twine, 30 lbs. at 16c., 6 pkgs. at 1.00; paints, oils, etc., 224.75; wire cloth, 9 yds. at 20c., 2 yds. at 50c., sash tools, ½ doz. at 4.00, ½ doz. at 4.20; locks, 4 only at 85c.; mattress twine, 12 lbs. at 60c.; mop holders, 1 doz. at 1.50; hoes, 1 1-6 doz. at 6.00; pails, 4 only at 35c.; toilet clippers, 1 pr. at 4.00; mall elbows, 2 doz. at 1.20; hose, 100 ft. at 15c.; lawn sprinkler, 1 only at 6.00; pipe cutter, 1 only at 3.75; glue, 5 lbs. at 20c.; butter tryer, 1 only at 1.50; daulin, 40 lbs. at 20c.; nails, 2 kegs at 3.25; brushes, 2 only at 1.10. 2 only at 1.50, 1 only at 1.75, 2 only at 2.55; cement, 8 bags at 68¼c., 2 bbls. at 2.75; tile, 630 ft. at 7c.; rakes, 2 only at 75c.; shovels, 2 only at

PUBLIC INSTITUTIONS MAINTENANCE.—*Continued.*

ASYLUM FOR INSANE, KINGSTON.— *Continued.*

Expenses.—*Continued.*

75c.; vit. junctions, 6 only at 90c.; binder twine, 50 lbs. at 13.50 cwt.; cast elbows, 1 doz. at 1.80; pipe, 100 ft. at 5c., 100 ft. at 6c., 125 ft. at 10c.; bibs, 12 only at 1.00; whiting, 1 bbl. at 3.36; whips, 2 only at 70c.; detonator, 1 only at 1.20; fuse, 100 ft. for 75c.; beeswax, 50 lbs. at 45c.; sundries, 12.60 ....   490 41

Selby & Youlden, material and repairs to buildings, 120.22; Shales & Taugher, horseshoeing, 30.25 ....   150 47

Simmons Bros., lemon squeezers, 2 only at 60c.; glass, 70.80; fire clay, 1.572 lbs. at 1.00 cwt.; nails, 1 keg at 2.75; locks, 4 only at 65c.; paints, oils, etc., 139.79; saw blades, 1 doz. at 1.10; hammers, 2 only at 75c.; horse weight, 1 only at 1.75; zinc, 15 lbs. at 10c.; baskets, 10 only at 40c., 2 only at 60c., 2 only at 65c.; rubber hose, 100 ft. at 15c.; picture wire, 1 doz. at 1.50; harness polish, 6 tins at 30c.; nozzles, 6 only at 1.10, ½ doz. at 3.00; emery knife sharpeners, 1 doz. at 1.80; dishes, 2 only at 30c.; tin boxes, 6 only at 1.45; wood screw and die, 1 only at 1.30; fire brick, 31 lbs. for 2.48, 1,350 only at 4c.; bowls, 5 only at 50c.; rules, 6 only at 40c.; wrenches, 2 only at 1.15, 2 only at 2.00; metal polish, 2 qts. at 75c.; iron pipe, 118 ft. at 5½c., 111 ft. at 6½c.; Canada plate, 6 boxes at 3.25; wire netting, 40 yds. at 12c.; hedge shears, 1 pr. at 1.00; twine, 5 lbs. at 30c.; hose taps, 2 only at 75c.; asbestos cement, 10 lbs. at 10c.; cherry stoner, 1 only at 1.25; hose, 100 ft. at 15c.; hose nipples, 5 only at 25c.; mattress twine, 21 lbs. at 45c.; shovels, 6 only at 70c.; hose washers, 3 doz. at 1.50; valve spindles, 6 only at 40c.; trowel, 1 only at 1.60; brass hooks, 1 gro. at 3.25; gal'v. pipe, 30 lengths at 15c.; tubs, 3 only at 1.50; brushes, 1 only at 2.00, 1 only at 3.50; lids for range, 2 only at 65c.; cullendor, 1 only at 1.10; tile, 130 ft. at 13½c.; steam hose, 17½ ft. at 25c.; rakes, 2 only at 75c.; repairs, 57.96; hoes, 6 only at 45c.; valves, 2 only at 95c., 5 only at 1.25, 6 only at 1.50, 4 only at 2.40; candle wick, 2 doz. at 50c.; stoves, 1 only at 9.00, 1 only at 10.00; globe valves, 4 doz. at 2.45; sledge handles, 1 doz. at 1.75; blanket pins, 6 doz. at 50c.; plaster paris, 2 bbls. at 2.50; hatchet, 1 only at 1.25; castings, 15.24; pulleys, 1 only at 75c., 1 only at 1.25; hair, 1 bag at 2.50; brass letters, 30 only for 2.50; spice mill, 1 only at 10.00; sundries, 52.77 ....   692 65

Singer Sewing Machine Co., oil, 6 bottles at 10c.; repairing machines, 2.00; needles, 4 doz. at 20c.; sundries, 1.10 ....   4 50

Skinner, Henry & Co., wax, 115 lbs. at 11c.; playing cards, 2 doz. at 2.00, 1 doz. at 2.15; chloride of lime, 101 lbs. at 6c., 50 lbs. at 7c.; sundries, 1.91 ....   30 27

Sloan, S., turnips, 35 bags at 45c.; carrots, 30 bags at 50c.; apples, 4 bbls. at 2.00 ....   38 75

Smith, R., use of breeding horse, 8.00; Smith, N. L., cedar posts, 550 only at 1c., 5.50 ....   13 50

Sowards, Jno. F., horse, 1 only at 175.00; Sowards, Jas., cement, 3 bbls. at 2.20, 1 bbl. at 3.70; sand, 4 loads at 3.00; tar, 1 bbl. at 3.00; hair, 1 sack at 1.50; wood, 1½ cords at 8.00; coal, 476 tons at 2.17, 502.500 tons at 3.10, 1,653.760 tons at 5.10, 386.1,470 tons at 5.27; cartage, 50c., 13,049.28 ....   13,224 28

Spangenburg, F. W., graduation pins, 6 only at 2.75; repairs to watch, 2.00 ....   18 50

Spence, David M., hats, 2 doz. at 1.25, 2 doz. at 6.00; elastic, 3 doz. at 35c   15 55

Standard Silver Co., cruets, 1 only at 1.74, 1 only at 3.60, 5.34; Steele-Briggs Seed Co., seeds, etc., 125.06; air sprayer, 1 only at 5.50; flower pots, 11.80; shield hoes, 2 pr. at 1.20. 144.76 ....   150 10

Stevens, J. & Son Co., Ltd., medical appliances, 5.50; Stewart & Wood, paint, oils, etc., 3.70 ....   9 20

Suddard, E. S., soap, 5 boxes at 4.00, 5 boxes at 4.50; coffee, 100 lbs. at 25c.; sago, 200 lbs. at 8c.; tea, 180 lbs. at 25c.; clay pipes, 2 boxes at 1.00; sugar, 654 lbs. at 4¼c. 158 30

Sundry Newspapers, advertising *re* supplies, 118.00; advertising *re* fuel, 20.50 ....   138 50

PUBLIC INSTITUTIONS MAINTENANCE.—*Continued.*

ASYLUM FOR INSANE, KINGSTON.—*Continued.*

EXPENSES.—*Continued.*

Sutherland, J. H. & Bro., sole leather, 120½ lbs. at 30c.; leather, 143 lbs. at 31c., 50 lbs. at 45c., 50 lbs. at 75c.; ladies rubbers, 4 prs. at 60c.; shoes, 1 pr. at 2.00; sundries, 5.45	150 33
Swift, Jas. & Co., coal, 2 tons at 4.25, ¾ ton at 7.25; freight and cartage, 5.47	19 42
St. Elmo Cigar Store, tobacco, 162 lbs. at 45c., 60 lbs. at 65c., 111.90; St. Mary's Cemetery, interments, 12.00	123 90
Tait, Alex., threshing grain, 1,096 bus. at 2½c., 27.40; Taylor Publishing Co., subscription to *The Engineer*, 1.00	28 40
Taylor & Hamilton, tea pots, 4 only at 90c.; fire clay, 436. at 1.00 cwt.; cuspidors, 1 only at 3.00; registers, 6 only at 1.10; ash pit for No. 8 Oxford, 59.34; section of grate for No. 707 Oxford, 3.50; hot water section, 36.00; safety chain, 24 yds. at 10c.; tea kettle, 1 only at 1.75; lime, 10 bus. at 35c.; nickle plated hangers, ½ doz. at 6.50; tinsmith's shears, 1 pr. at 4.00; fire brick, 200 only at 4c.; valves, 2 only at 4.85; force cups, 4 only at 1.50; meat chopper, 1 only at 1.75; bath plugs, 14 only at 10c.; plyers, 3 prs. at 80c.; sundries, 18.07	178 62
Taylor, Jno. & Co., soap, 1,652 lbs. at 5c., 82.65; Thompson, F. C. & Co., thermometers, ½ gro. at 35.20, 17.60	100 25
Tomilson, Geo. R., electrical repairs, 117.10; electric lamps, 200 only at 20c.; trap valve, 1 only at 8.50; electric fixtures, 2 only at 7.50; electric shades, 1 doz. at 15.60; rubber covered wire, 1,800 ft. at 1c.; cleat rosettes, 24 only at 20c.; freight and customs charges, 2.45	221 45
Toronto Laundry Machine Co., making 1 pinion, 1.50; Toye, R. H., yeast, 253 lbs. at 30c., 75.90	77 40
Tracy, F., horseshoeing, 4.88; repairs to vehicles, 8.60	13 48
Van Winckel, N. P., interments, 40.50; Vicks, Jas. & Sons, seeds, 2.50	43 00
Waddington, H., sausages, 240 lbs. at 8c.; lamb, 1 side at 2.50; meat, 1,157 lbs. at 7c., 4,874 lbs. at 7½c.	468 24
Waldron, R., linoleum, 8 yds. at 65c.; water proof coats, 1 only at 11.50; ticking, 222 yds. at 21½c., 111¼ yds. at 23c., 414 yds. at 30c.; bed spreads, 84 only at 1.25; napkins, 1 doz. at 3.00, 1 doz. at 4.50; linen, 2 ends for 3.33, 30½ yds. at 25c., 94 yds. at 30c., 5 yds. at 50c., 5 yds. at 70c., 5½ yds. at 1.25; wrappers, 6 only at 1.00; shirting, 409 yds. at 11½c.; lustre, 25 yds. at 50c.; felt, 2 yds. at 75c.; cotton line, 9 3-8 yds. at 30c.; ribbon, 18 yds. at 18c.; curtain webb, 8 yds. at 40c.; gowns, 9 only at 75c.; shade cloth, 50 yds. at 20c., 80 yds. at 27c.; cashmere, 9 yds. at 50c.; shade rollers, 1 doz. at 2.00; duck, 54¾ yds. at 18c.; sheeting, 122½ yds. at 23c., 314½ yds. at 25c., 62 yds. at 35c., 177½ yds. at 29c.; tweed, 70 yds. at 50c.; hosiery, 10 doz. at 1.50, 7 doz. at 1.75, 12 doz. at 3.00; rug, 1 only at 25.00; lace, 3 doz. yds. at 60c., 3 doz. yds. at 1.50; tray cloths, 2 only at 1.60; bath mats, 1 only at 90c., 1 only at 1.25; flags, 5 only at 3.00, 2 only at 3.50; pillow cotton, 160 yds. at 17c.; linen thread, 1 lb. at 2.40; corsets, 3 prs. for 2.00; dress goods, 2 ends for 6.00; curtains, 3 prs. at 5.00; pillows, 6 only at 90c.; print, 542 yds. at 12½c.; gelly twine, 2 lbs. at 1.00; forfar, 63½ yds. at 24c., 402½ yds. at 30c.; sundries, 4.40	1,114 59
Walsh, P., lime, 20 bus. at 27c.; cartage, 50c., 5.90; Walsh, F. A., veterinary services, 60.00	65 90
Wartman, S., milk, 5 gals. at 20c., 1.00; Webster, Ed. S., tobacco, 144 lbs. at 45c., 153 lbs. at 75c.; sundries, 55c., 180.10	181 10
Whaley, Royce & Co., repairing musical instruments, 13.90; Wheler, G., testing flour, 1.00	14 90
Willard & Co., eggs, 60 doz. at 18c., 30 doz. at 25c.; express charges, 1.32, 19.62; Wilson, T. C. & Son, livery hire, 8.50	28 12
Wilmot, Peter G., shorts, 2 tons at 22.00, 4 tons at 23.00; bran, 2½ tons at 20.00; salt, 1 bbl. at 1.35; chop feed, 2 tons at 25.00; oats, 100 bus. at 40c., 200 bus. at 42½c.	362 35
Wingate, C. E., subscription to Medical Journal, 2.00; Wingate Chemical Co., medical appliances, 33.60	35 60
Wittbold, The Geo. Co., plants, 7.20; Wormouth & Co., repairing organ, 15.00	22 20

PUBLIC INSTITUTIONS MAINTENANCE.—*Continued.*

ASYLUM FOR INSANE, KINGSTON.—*Continued.*

EXPENSES.—*Continued.*

Wood, N. P., tea, 100 lbs. at 25c.; matches, 1 gro. at 80c.; cloves, 20 lbs. at 27c.; stove polish, 1 doz. at 1.10; chicory, 262 lbs. at 12½c.; starch, 152 lbs. at 6c., 100 lbs. at 10c.; mustard, 25 lbs. at 20c.; salt, 2 bbls. at 1.45; raisins, 56 lbs. at 10½c.; baking powder, 1 doz. tins at 5.25; ginger, 20 lbs. at 25c.; rice, 2 bags at 3.75, 400 lbs. at 4c.; sugar, 598 lbs. at 4.00 cwt., 683 lbs. at 4.25, 914 lbs. at 4.30, 926 lbs. at 4.65; soap, 2 boxes at 4.00; vinegar, 70 gals. at 25c.; barley, 250 lbs. at 4c.; sago, 100 lbs. at 9c. 311 51

York Mfg. Co., japan wax, 10 lbs. at 20c. 2 00

ASYLUM FOR INSANE, MIMICO.

SALARIES ($30,780.44).

N. H. Beemer, M. D.:	Twelve months' salary as	Medical Superintendent.......	2,600 00
Jas. M. Forster, M. D.:	do	Assistant "	1,400 00
Geo. M. Biggs, M. D.:	do	Assistant Physician...........	900 00
Josephine Wells: Six	do	Dentist	120 00
Mark Keilty: Twelve	do	Bursar.......................	1,500 00
W. P. Sturt:	do	Clerk........................	650 00
Robt. Elkin:	do	Steward	749 50
F. N. Wallis:	do	Storekeeper	800 00
John Gourley:	do	Engineer	700 00
James Ailles	do	do	526 00
Wm. Wilkinson:	do	Assistant Engineer	400 00
David Woodside: Two	do	do	60 00
Fireman (4)	do	....	825 81
Harry London: Nine	do	Electrician..................	186 00
A. Craib: Twelve	do	"	370 00
Robt. Maxwell	do	Carpenter....................	360 00
Jas. S. Doddridge: Eight and half	do	Assistant Carpenter...........	191 40
S. Matheson: Twelve	do	Gardener....................	575 00
George Dea:	do	Baker	500 00
B. Watson:	do	Mason.......................	500 00
Wm. Boulton:	do	Farmer ····················	550 00
Thomas Pattison:	do	Assistant Farmer.............	349 00
Ploughmen (3):	do	....	308 51
Jno. C. McMullen:	do	Laundryman.................	360 00
James Rice:	do	Sewageman.................	300 00
Wm. Patterson:	do	Stableman	300 00
F. W. Terry: Eight	do	Florist......................	80 00
George Stubbs: Twelve	do	Butcher	300 00
Wm. Bremner: Three	do	Shoemaker	60 00
Thos. Dunn: Ten	do	Messenger	300 00
Night Watch (2): Twelve	do	....	427 35
Marie H. Quinlan: Three	do	Matron	125 00
L. Gurd: Nine	do	do	375 00
B. Lukes: Twelve	do	Assistant Matron.............	300 00
Agnes Redick:	do	Tailoress....................	300 00
Seamstresses (2):	do	....	208 20
Cooks (3):	do	....	558 93
Maids (4):	do	....	461 87
Laundresses (4):	do	....	604 69
Female Supervisors (5):	do	....	820 50
Female Attendants (18):	do	....	2,570 27
Male Supervisors (6):	do	....	1,941 73
Male Attendants (20):	do	....	5,265 68

EXPENSES ($53,852.49).

Ash, H. J., pineapples, 1 case at 3.50; lemons, 1 case at 3.25, ½ case at 4.00, ½ case at 5.00, 1 case at 3.75. 1½ cases at 5.50, ½ case at 6.50; onions, 1 sack at 2.50; sundries, 4.72; melons, 2 at 35c., 1 at 65c.;

PUBLIC INSTITUTIONS MAINTENANCE.—*Continued.*

ASYLUM FOR INSANE, MIMICO.—*Continued.*

EXPENSES.—*Continued.*

peaches, 10 doz. at 30c., 10 doz. at 35c., 1 doz. at 40c., 10 bask. at 40c., 20 bask. at 50c., 7 bask. at 55c., 15 bask. at 65c., 2 bask. at 75c.; grapes, 1 bask. at 50c., 2 bask. at 60c.; berries, 4 cases at 2.25 .... 84 17

Ansley, A. & Co., hats, 3 doz. at 3.50, 7-12 doz. at 4.00, 6 doz. at 6.00; sundries, 1.18 .... 50 01

Adams Furniture Co., curled hair, 200 lbs. at 39c., 50 lbs. at 39c.; hair bags, 1 at 30c., 2 at 30c. 98 40

Alienist and Neurologist, 1 year's subscription, 5.00; Aikenhead Hardware Co., fitter tubes, 6 at 1.50, 9.00 .... 14 00

Brock, W. R. Co., Ltd., crash, 400 yds. at 10c.; towels, 25 doz. at 3.00; cardigan jackets, 1 doz. at 9.00; ties, 8 doz. at 2.25; hoods, 1 doz. at 4.50; table linen, 330 yds. at 37½c., 29 yds. at 45c.; batts, 6 doz. at 6.00, 5 doz. at 6.00; damask, 52¾ yds. at 55c.; denim, 555½ yds. at 18c.; lawn, 12 yds. at 20c.; curtain muslin, 120 yds. at 25c.; broadcloth, 1¼ yds. at 3.00; hessian, 539½ yds. at 12½c.; duck, 52 yds. at 17½c., 50½ at 18c.; crochet cotton, 3 gro. at 6.24; pillow cotton, 245½ yds. at 13½c.; towelling, 100 yds. at 8c., 210 yds. at 10c., 60 yds. at 15c., 100 yds. at 18½c.; velvet ribbon, 2 doz. yds. at 1.20; lace, 144 yds. at 2½c.; silkine, 5 doz. at 40c.; rifle laces, 10 gro. at 65c.; oufflin, 10 yds. at 20c.; sateen, 53 yds. at 15c.; suiting, 329 yds. at 12c.; interlining, 35 yds. at 30c.; rain coat, 1 at 4.27; italian, 54¾ yds. at 65c.; pocketing, 40 yds. at 18½c.; mitts, 8 doz. at 2.25; 10 doz. at 4.50; muslin, 251 yds. at 15c.; felt, 3 yds. at 55c.; hosiery, 10 doz. at 2.10, 10 doz. at 2.25; saxony, 7 lbs. at 1.00; gloves, 3 doz. at 2.25, ¼ doz. at 3.50, ½ doz. at 9.00, ½ doz. at 11.00; cotton, 1,525¾ at 9c., 359½ at 10c., 254½ at 11.00, 231½, 952½ at 12½c., 357 at 13½c., 331 at 14c.; gingham, 107¾ yds. at 10c., 97½ yds. at 19½c.; collars, 1 doz. at 1.25, 1 doz. at 1.80, 2 1-12 doz. at 2.25, 8 doz. at 95c.; ribbon, 36 yds. at 12½c., 36 yds. at 18½c.; combs, 12 doz. at 75c., 7 doz. at 90c., 1 gro. at 5.40; sweaters, 1 doz. at 6.50, 1 doz. at 9.00; thread, 4 doz. at 1.10, 6 doz. at 2.60, 18 gro. at 5.40, 1 doz at 1.00; frieze, 19½ yds. at 1.00, 5 yds. at 1.10; curtains, 3 prs. at 4.85; corsets, 6 doz. at 4.50; tweed, 36¾ yds. at 20c.; belts, 1 11-12 doz. at 2.25; linen, 100 yds. at 15½c., 46¾ yds. at 17½c., 94 yds. at 18½c.; silesia, 66 yds. at 17½c., 214½ at 18½c.; stoles, 6 at 1.25; canvas, 50 yds. at 13½c., 100 yds. at 16c.; serge, 19 yds. at 2.00; shawls, 1 doz. at 9c.; lining, 111 yds. at 18½c.; waists, 1½ doz. at 9.00, ½ doz. at 12.00; sundries, 54.76; sheeting, 200 yds. at 13½c., 1,271¼ yds. at 15c., 268¼ yds. at 17½c., 376¼ yds. at 19½c.; shirting, 3,186¼ yds. at 12½c.; handkerchiefs, 6 doz. at 80c., 12 doz. at 90c.; ticking, 1,045½ yds. at 17½c.; flannelette, 1,514 yds. at 10c., 522½ yds. at 11½c., 120¾ yds. at 12c.; muslin, 150½ yds. at 12½c., 80 yds. at 15c.; pins, 12 pkgs. at 12c., 12 pkgs. at 14c.; combs, 5 doz at 85c., 5 doz. at 90c.; corsets, 2 doz. at 4.50; sundries, 1.24; print, 1,843¼ yds. at 10c. 3,514 91

Bell Telephone Co., messages, 19.00; exchange service, 225.00 .... 244 00

Black, J. W., horses, 2 at 180.00 .... 360 00

Burns, P. & Co., coal, 1,286 570/2000 tons at 3.20, 34 1570/2000 tons at 3.60, 663 140/2000 tons at 5.52, 189 1740/2000 tons at 5.75 .... 8,993 23

Biggs, G. M., meals for patients and attendants at exhibition 15 00

Big Four Cap Co., caps, 8½ doz. at 3.00, 25.50; Bowden, F. A., lumber, 241.27 .... 266 77

Booth Copper Co., copper tube, 189 lbs. at 36c.; brass tube, 7½ lbs. at 33c. 70 43

Beal Bros., leather, 11 lbs. at 15c., 33½ lbs. at 28c.; sundries, 2.00 .... 13 03

British Medical Association, annual subscription 12 42

Bursar, to pay sundries, 20.62; commutation tickets, 28.00; street car tickets, 37.00 .... 85 62

Beemer, Dr., commutation ticket, 11.00; street car tickets, 12.00; travelling expenses, 67.50 .... 90 50

Bonners, Columbian, Insectitude, bug exterminator, 15 gals. at 2.50 .... 37 50

Canada Brokerage Co., rice, 2,240 lbs. at 3½c., cwt., 2,240 lbs. at 3.40; tobacco, 349¼ lbs. at 45c., 534 lbs. at 46c.; prunes, 1,000 lbs. at 6¾c., 1,500 lbs. at 6¾c.; rolled wheat, 10 bbls. at 2.65; currants, 158 lbs. at 5½c.; matches, 5 cases, 3.00; sugar, 1,107 lbs. at 3½c., 1,156 lbs. at 3 3-8c., 4,000 lbs.

PUBLIC INSTITUTIONS MAINTENANCE.—*Continued.*

ASYLUM FOR INSANE, MIMICO.—*Continued.*

EXPENSES.—*Continued.*

at 4.10; sundries, 8.94; pipes, 3 doz. at 75c.; tapioca, 169 lbs. at 6c., 184 lbs. at 6¾c.; camphor, 8 lbs. at 1.95; tea, 400 lbs. at 24c.; Dingman's blue, 10 doz. at 14c.; salmon, 4 doz. at 1.60; salt, 1 bag at 1.00 ..... 1,159 42

Canadian Fairbanks Co., globe valves, 6 for 3.92; brass locks, 2 for 1.88; bushings and castings, 9.41 .... 15 21

Canadian Practitioner and Review, subscription, 4.00; Campbell, E. P., car fares *re* concert for patients, 4.00 .... 8 00

Calham, J. E., gravel, 36 loads at 25c., 9.00; Canada Paint Co., paint, oils, etc., 85.29 .... 94 29

Canadian Horse Exchange, 1 horse at 180.00; Croil, Jas., tweed, 46¼ yds. at 1.90, 88.83 .... 268 83

Canadian Rubber Co., jar rings, 5 gro. for 3.64, 6 gro. for 4.37; tap washers, 100 for 58c.; army blankets, 12 at 2.00; rubber boots, 1 pr. at 3.50, 1 pr. at 3.57, 3 prs. at 4.20; sundries, 2.73 .... 54 99

Cockburn & Rea, assorted hats, 47 doz. at 50c., 23.50; Cowan, J. G., cleaning chimneys, 14.50 .... 38 00

Canadian Pacific Railway, freight, 2.62; Canadian Express Co., 72.30...... 74 92

Campbell Milling Co., choppings, 18.07; Carveth, J. A., books, 13.50...... 31 57

Cairns, Bernard, rubber stamp, 1 at 20c., 1 at 40c.; dater, 1 at 65c.; indelible ink, 3 qts. at 7.00, 3 bots. at 25c.; 1 pad at 25c................. 23 25

Chandler, Ingram & Bell, medical books, 5.00; medical appliances, 164.45... 169 45

Clappison Packing & Covering Co., gaskets, 11½ lbs. at 1.00, 5¾ lbs. at 1.25; mineral wool covering, 100 ft. for 20.80 .... 39 49

Central Prison Industries, tweed, 882 yds. at 55c.; packing, 1.45; shoes, 30 prs. at 1.40, 36 prs. at 1.80; yarn, 150 lbs. at 45c., 50 lbs. at 50c.; blankets, 108 lbs. at 45c.; binder twine, 50 lbs. at 11½c.; braces, 8 doz. at 2.40 .... 760 25

C. P. R. Telgraph Co., telegrams, 3.65; Craib, Jno., horseshoeing, 94.85... 98 50

Canadian General Electric Co., resistance wire, 2 5-8 lbs. at 85c.; lamps, 400 at 17c.; sundries, 1.10; reflectors, ¼ doz. at 2.40, 2 doz. at 3.86; globes, 3 doz. at 1.10; fuse plugs, 50 at 3.50 .... 85 30

Club Coffee Co., coffee, 500 lbs. at 17c., 100 at 22c., 100 at 25c.; chicory, 50 lbs. at 10c., 50 lbs. at 12c. 143 00

Canadian Oil Co., 529 gals. at 20c., 134 gals. at 20½c., 45.90 gals. for 6.18; cylinder oil, 40 gals. at 75c.; castor oil, 54 lbs. at 9½c.; benzine, 49 gals. at 20c. 173 33

Davidson & Hay, sugar, 8,140 lbs. at 4.23 cwt., 2,526 lbs. at 4.23, 1,151 lbs. at 3.50, 106 lbs. at 4.93; vinegar, 78.5 gals. at 25c.; tea, 663 lbs. at 24c., 1,050 lbs. at 25c.; nutmegs, 5 lbs. at 60c.; candles, 36 lbs. at 10½c.; tapioca, 178 lbs. at 5c.; biscuit, 65½ lbs. at 6½; salt, 10 bbls. at 1.40, 1 bbl. at 2.85; sundries, 9.36; prunes, 1,050 lbs. at 6½c., 1,375 lbs. at 6¼c.; sardines, 100 tins at 13c.; sal soda, 450 lbs. at 30c. cwt.; corn starch, 40 lbs. at 5½c.; currants, 68 lbs. at 5½c., 311 lbs. at 6c.; sapolio, 1 gro. at 11.30; rice, 2,398 lbs. at 3¼c.; can vegetables, 6 doz. at 1.25; brands sauce, 2 doz. at 2.00; raisins, 168 lbs. at 6c.; cornmeal, 10 bags at 1.75; tobacco, 450 lbs. at 40c.; matches, 5 boxes at 3.00; wrapping paper, 125 lbs. at 2½c.; sundries, 11.59; syrup, 1,912 lbs. at 2 7-8c.; tanglefoot, 2 cases at 3.75; essence of lemon, 2 doz. at 2.20½ 1,635 18

Dyson, W., expenses capturing eloper, 1.15; Dunn, Thos., expenses buying horses, 12.80; car tickets, 3.55 .... 17 50

Davis, F. A. Co., medical books, 7.00; Dallyn, Jardine & Co., wyandotte soda, 2,800 lbs. at 1 7-8c., 52.50 .... 59 50

Dunn, Wm., gravel, 53 loads at 20c., 10.60; Doyle, M. Fish Co., 15,350 lbs. at 8c., 1,228.00 .... 1,238 60

Devins, J. W., subscriptions to newspapers 1 yr., *Telegram* 3.00, *Star* 3.00, *Mail* 3.00, *Globe* 6.00, *News* 2.63, 10½ months............................ 17 63

Dalton Bros., pepper, 180 lbs. at 18c.; baking powder, 220 lbs. at 25c.; cinnamon, 60 lbs. at 25c.; nutmeg, 10 lbs. at 55c., 5 lbs. at 60c.; celery seed, 6 lbs. at 18c.; mace, 4 lbs. at 80c.; whole ginger, 6 lbs. at 20c.; ground ginger, 6 lbs. at 23c., 10 lbs. at 25c.; pickle spice, 6 lbs. at 20c.; sundries, 2.11; cloves, 10 lbs. at 24c., 10 lbs. at 25c. 128 47

10a P.A.

PUBLIC INSTITUTIONS MAINTENANCE.—*Continued.*

ASYLUM FOR INSANE, MIMICO.—*Continued.*

EXPENSES.—*Continued.*

Economical Mfg. & Supply Co., packing, 7 11-16 lbs. at 1.20, 8 9-16 lbs. for 10.07, 16½ at 1.15; valve twist, 2 spools at 1.00; sundries, 4.24......	44 82
Forster, Wm., sugar, 10 bags at 4.43; prunes, 250 lbs. at 7¾c.; sundries, 80c.	64 50
Farmers Advocate, subscription, 1.50; Foy, Geo. J., spirits for medicinal purposes, 20 gals. at 2.90, 5 at 3.00, 1 at 4.50	81 50
Fleischmann & Co., yeast, 234 lbs. at 30c.; Firstbrook Bros. Co., Ltd., shavings, 10.50	80 70
Forster, J. M., expenses *re* concert, 1.25; travelling expense, 3.26; Ferrier & Co., potatoes, 672.55 at 70c.	475 55
Gurney Foundry Co., repairs to range, 16.94; Grand & Toy, stationery, 40c.; printing, 20.00	37 34
Gordon, McKay & Co., cricket balls, 1 doz. at	11 52
Gutta Peroba Rubber Mfg. Co., water hose, 9½ ft. for 4.51; hospital sheets, 12 at 2.00; rubber shoes, 1 pr. 3.60	32 11
Gray, F. A., drugs, chemicals, etc., 5.05; Gurd, L., travelling expenses, 2.84	7 89
Grenadier Ice Co., ice, 372.41; Grand Trunk Railway, freight, 74.61	447 02
G. N. W. Telegraph Co., telegrams, 22.79; Gaby, Jos., horseshoeing, 75c.	23 54
Guinane, Jno., boots, 58 prs. at 1.25, 80 prs. at 2.50, 23 prs. at 3.50; laces, 10 gro. at 65c.; overshoes, 2 prs. at 2.00	384 50
Goldie, McCulloch & Co., 3 ft. diameter wheel, 1 at	14 00
Gowans, Kent & Co., jugs, 6 at 2.40, 2 at 1.20, 5 at 1.40, 1 at 4.80; bowls, 20 doz. at 30c.; sundries, 4.93; egg cups, ½ gro. at 5.40; cups and saucers, 10 doz. at 40c., 2 doz. at 75c.; butter dishes, 2 doz. at 2.25; tumblers, 2 gro. at 6.00, 1 1-3 gro. at 9.60; chambers, 1 doz. at 4.80; vase, 1-6 doz. at 6.00, 1-6 doz. at 9.00; covered dishes, 2 doz. at 5.40	113 45
Godden, C. P., sundry hardware, 5.70; axle grease, 15 lbs. at 10c.; scuttle, 2 at 65c.; putz cream, 1 doz. 2.75; oil cans, 1 doz. at 3.00; mouse traps, 2 doz. at 1.15; razors, 1 doz. at 13.00	29 55
Harcourt, E. H. Co., stationery, printing, etc., 56.05; Heather, H., repairs to buildings, 18.50	74 55
Harty, J. F. Co., medical supplies, 16.13; Hunter, Robert, market fees, 76c.	16 89
Hopkins, Jno. Press, subscription *American Journal Insanity*, 5.00; Hutchinson, M., lumber, 30.32	35 32
Harvey, Jno. G., phenyline disinfectant, 54 gals. at 1.25, 67.50; Hees, Geo. H., Son & Co., window shading, 35 yds., 5.49	72 99
Hope & Noden, screens, 25 yds. at 70c., 25 yds. at 85c.; dishes, 1 doz. at 15.00; boilers, 1 at 4.00, 1 at 3.00	60 75
Hamilton Dental Depot, dental apparatus, 37.50; Hortopp, Jas. A. & Co., bran, 2 tons at 20.00, 1 at 21.00, 1 at 22.00	120 50
Holdenby, G. W., milch cow, 1 at 50.00; Hedley, Shaw Milling Co., flour, 839 bbls. at 3.75, 20 bbls. at 3.76	3,271 25
Halliday, Jas. difference in exchange of cows, 166.29; purchase of meat, 6,390.18	6,556 47
Humphrey, F. W., sugar, 30 bags at 4.13, 3,000 lbs. at 4.33, 104 lbs. at 4.83; can vegetables, 8 doz. at 95c.; raisins, 420 lbs. at 4½c., 420 lbs. at 6¼c.; syrup, 3,392 lbs. at 2 7-8c., 1,686 lbs. at 3c.; sundries, 8.00; starch, 144 lbs. at 7¼c.; blacking, 3 gro. at 1.10; vinegar, 41 gals. at 25c.; borax, 50 lbs. at 6c.; salt, 20 bbls. at 1.35, 2 bbls. at 2.65; rice, 2,500 lbs. at 3½c.; corn starch, 80 lbs. at 5¼c.; sapolio, 2 gro. at 11.30	642 49
Inglis, Jno. Co., repairs, 30.00; Imperial Chemical Co., paint, oils, etc., 81.01; wax, 206 lbs. at 8½c.	128 01
Ivory, Jas., butter boxes, 5 at 1.62; pans, 1 at 2.50; ice cream can, 1 at 1.25; dippers, 2 at 35c.; repairs, 4.19	18 99
Jacobi, Philip, leather, 13 lbs. at 18c., 16¼ at 28c., 89¾ at 29c.; sundries, 2.77; bardash, 2.70	38 38
Jones Bros., repairing clippers . 1.00; Johnson, A., manure, 16.50	17 50
Keith & Fitzsimmons, ground balls, 12 at 50c.	6 00
Kemp, Mfg. Co., tinware, etc., 60.06; chambers, 10 doz. at 3.05; pitchers, 1 doz. at 4.50; bowls, 2 doz. at 1.02	103 10
Kinnear, T. & Co., starch, 372 lbs. at 7¼c.; prunes, 250 lbs. at 7c., 500 lbs. at 7¼c; soda biscuit, 410½ lbs. at 6½c.; mustard, 24 jars at 75c.; allspice,	

PUBLIC INSTITUTIONS MAINTENANCE.—*Continued.*

ASYLUM FOR INSANE, MIMICO.—*Continued.*

EXPENSES.—*Continued.*

10 lbs. at 18c.; sugar, 3,000 lbs. at 4.13, 3,000 lbs. at 4.23, 2,000 lbs. at 4.43; sapolio, 1 gro. at 11.30; currants, 144 lbs. at 6c.; sal soda, 225 lbs. at 90c.; syrup, 1,675 lbs. at 3c.; twine, 44 lbs. at 25c.; paper, 240 lbs. at 3c.	557 05
Kenny, T. & Co., tea, 1,500 lbs. at 22c., 330.00; Kay, Jno., difference in exchange of cow, 5.20	335 20
Kay, Jno., Son & Co., shade pulls, 70 at 3c., 2.10; Kelly, Lawrence, threshing 4½ days at 10.00; board, 1.00	48 10
Kirkpatrick, W. A. & Son, breeching straps, 3 at 1.00; hame straps, 4 at 20c.; tie straps, 2 at 80c.; repairs, 2.10	7 50
King's Printer, paper, 15.80; stationery, 15.05	30 85
Lyons, Geo. A., bran, 3¾ tons at 18.00, 6¾ tons at 20.00, 206.50; Lumbers, Jas. Co., soda biscuits, 259½ ibs. at 6½c., 16.87	223 37
Lawrence, W. J., plants	12 00
Lake, Wm. H., putty polish, 2 doz. at 90c.; scissors, 2 prs. at 75c.; carpet sweepers, 2 at 2.50; gasoline, 40 gals. at 25c.; sundries, 8.66; pails, 1 doz. 3.00; lanterns, 1 doz. 9.00; oil stoves, 6 at 1.10; chamois leather, 2 at 70c.; brooms, 2 at 75c.; paint, oil, etc., 1.15; axes, 2 at 1.00; stewers, 2,000 at 60c. M.; axe handles, ½ doz. at 1.50, ½ doz. at 2.25; creamers, 2 at 60c.; beeswax, 20 lbs. at 40c.; bowls, 10 doz. at 80c., 1 at 1.10; cups, 15 doz. at 45c., 5 doz. at 50c., 10 doz. at 75c; dishes, 1 at 5.40; plates, 10 doz. at 70c.; tumblers, 18 doz. at 63c.; chimneys, 2 doz. at 55c.; pick handles, ½ doz. at 1.80; keys, 6 doz. for 3.25; fork handles, ½ doz. at 2.00; spade handles, ½ doz. at 2.50; alabastine, 18 pckgs. at 30c.; putz cream, ½ doz. at 2.00; ewers, 1 doz. at 3.80; stone crocks, 6 at 55c.; lamp burners, 2 doz. at 1.00; plates, 10 doz. at 55c.; lantern globes, 2 doz. at 1.00; fruit dishes, 1 doz. at 1.60	151 48
Lemon, J. M., stabling horses and meals for messenger, December, 1905, 9.00; January, 1906, 9.10; February, 10.00; March, 9.75; April, 9.75; May, 8.00; June, 7.70; July, 10.50; August and September, 11.95; November, 18.15	103 90
Lynn, C., ferret at 3.00; Lane, Andrew, repairs to harness, etc., 64.35	67 35
Mail and Empire, wall charts, 12 at 25c.	3 00
Muldoon, J. & C., brick, 1,000 at 11.00; drain pipes, 4 at 50c.; fire clay, 685 lbs. for 4.11; tiles, 1,172 ft. 23.44, 600 ft. for 13.20; lime, 350 lbs. at 32½c.	54 89
Morton, David & Son, soap, 6,900 lbs. at 4c.	276 00
Murray, W. A. & Co., felt, 6 yds. at 1.00; linen, 10 yds. at 50c.; silk, 12 yds. at 25c., 12 yds. at 30c.; frilling, 9 doz. yds. at 60c.; cretonne, 59¼ yds. at 30c., 10 yds. at 35c.; muslin, 52 yds. at 15c.; silkoline, 38½ yds. at 15c.; oriental, 14 yds. at 15c.; floral, 35 yds. at 15c.; sateen, 40 yds. at 25c.; portiers, 6 prs. at 4.75; fringe, 71 yds. at 6c.; mattress covers, 2 at 3.50; denim, 15 yds. at 35c.	120 29
Mich, Chas. J., iron pot, 1 at 1.00; roasting pans, 2 at 10.00; repairs to strainer, 35c.; strainer, 1 at 90c.; fruit fillers, 3 at 30c.	5 15
Miller & Sons, plants, 27.40; Maddocks Bros., harness, 1 set at 40.00	67 40
Massey-Harris Co., Ltd., repairs, 1.51; binder twine, 50 lbs. at 5c., 2.50	4 01
Moore & Hortopp, 1 ton bran, 20.00; Muirhead, Andrew, turp., 5 gals. at 1.00	25 00
Massey, A. L. & Co., jaconet sheeting, 49 yds. at 1.00; drugs and chemicals, 6.15; absorbent cotton, 25 lbs. at 28c.	62 15
Medcalf, D. M., travelling expenses re boiler inspection	1 00
Matthews, F., sausages, 104 lbs. at 11c.; smoking bacon, 53 pieces at 7c.	15 78
Meredith, Thos. & Co., rope, 100 ft. for 5.04; sundries, 6.65; saws, 1 at 1.75, 1 at 2.50; nails, 1 keg at 2.20, 1 at 2.30, 1 at 2.35, 1 at 2.80, 1 at 3.00; discs, 24 at 7c.; gauge glasses, 2 doz. at 3.50; rod iron, 200 lbs. at 2.25, 205 lbs. at 2.30, 203 lbs. at 2.40, 200 lbs. at 2.70, 200 lbs. at 2.85	62 45
Metropolitan Soap Co., soap, 1,003 lbs. at 5c., 50.15; *Monetary Times*, subscription, 2.00	52 15
Maher, P., livery hire	28 00
May, Samuel & Co., repairs to billiard table, 4.15; repairs to cues, 3.20; cue cement, 20c.; cue tips, 3.00	10 55

PUBLIC INSTITUTIONS MAINTENANCE.—*Continued.*

ASYLUM FOR INSANE, MIMICO.—*Continued.*

EXPENSES.—*Continued.*

Musgrave, Chas. E., music for dances for patients, 146.50; Might Directory Co., Toronto city directory, 6.00	152 50
Musson, J. G., stationery	86 63
MacKay, Alex., work as baker, 12 days at 2.50	30 00
Macdonald, Jno. & Co., dress goods, 169½ yds. at 35c., 14¼ at 40c.; linen, 10 yds. at 32½c.; pongee, 63 yds. at 18½c.; art sateen, 48 yds. at 12½c.; butter cloth, 121 yds. at 4c.; print, 650½ yds. at 10½c.; thread, 5 gro. at 5.40; denims, 215 yds. at 19½c; costume cloth, 33 yds. at 50c.; sundries, 25.82; hessian, 532 yds. at 12¼c.	335 50
McNaughton, P., travelling expenses, 15.00; McLean Publishing Co., subscription to *Canadian Grocer*, 2.00	17 00
McKinnon, S. F. & Co., mantles, 14 at 2.00, 1 at 7.50; less discount, 1.78	33 72
McCann, Wm. Milling Co., oil cake, 500 lbs. at 1.75, 3,000 lbs. at 32.50; bran, 3,500 lbs. at 19.50	91 63
McDonald & Willson, sundry hardware, 1.90; McFarlane, Geo., extension ladder, 1 at 7.50	9 40
McPherson, J. A. L., services *re* drainage	5 00
McIntosh, P. & Son, 100 bbls. rolled oats at 5.25, 10 bbls. at 2.20; 10 bbls. at 2.50, 5 bbls. at 2.75	585 75
McLennan, Jno., recovering eloper, 4.00; McMurchy, Jno., hosiery, 32 doz. at 1.30, 13 doz. at 1.10; packing, 45c.; less discount, 1.69	58 66
Nerlich & Co., pipes, 2 doz. at 1.72, 2 doz. at 1.25, 2 doz. at 2.00, 1 doz. at 2.00; combs, 36 doz. at 85c., 1 doz. at 1.80; playing cards, 6 doz. at 90c.; sundries, 5.11; hair brush, 2 doz. at 3.75; mouth organs, 1 doz. at 2.25	64 60
Ontario Rubber Co., rubber boots, 1 pr. at 3.85; hospital sheets, 2 doz., 23.40; ladies' rubbers, 1 pr. at 62c.; rubber gloves, 6 prs. at 75c., 2 prs. at 1.25; syringes, 3 at 1.00; stomach tubes, 2 at 1.25; brushes, ½ doz. at 2.00, ½ doz. at 3.50; sundries, 20c.	66 72
Ontario Wind Engine & Pump Co., pump, 1 complete	17 00
O'Connor, Wm., berries, 300 qts. at 7c.; Ogilvie, Thos. & Son, 1 gro. at 1.50; silesia, 51 yds. at 17½c.; canvas, 75 yds. at 15½c.; sundries, 12c.	43 17
Ontario Lead & Wire Co., self-closing cocks, 4 at 2.42	9 68
Perkins, Ince & Co., vinegar, 88 gals. at 25c., 41.3 gals. at 25c.; biscuits, 344½ lbs. at 6½c.; boxes, 30 at 25c.; sundries, 12.21; syrup, 1,716 lbs. at 2 7-8c.; sago, 148 lbs. at 7c.; sugar, 5,000 lbs. at 4.43, 1,148 at 3½c.; tobacco, 546 lbs. at 36c.; coffee, 100 lbs. at 14c.; tea, 1,534 lbs. at 25c.; can vegetables, 4 doz. at 95c.	998 13
Piper, N. L. Railway Supply Co., lanterns, 1 doz., 8.10; Pease Foundry Co., castings for stoves, 183.53	191 63
Parsons, C. & Sons, Ltd., leather, 74 lbs. at 28c.; sundries, 1.94; Pilkington Bros., glass	124 29
Postmaster, stamps, 160.00; Plant, Geo., flower pots, 29.20	189 20
Perrin, F. J., coffee, 150 lbs. at 16c., 100 lbs. at 15c., 50 lbs. at 25c.; chickory, 20 lbs. at 14c., 2.80	46 30
Quinlan, W. H., commutation ticket, 30 trips for 1.10, 100 trips for 4.00	5 10
Queen City Oil Co., cylinder oil	32 93
Rice, T. G. Wire Mfg Co., wire screening, 30 sq. ft. at 25c.; wire cloth, 10 yds. at 27c.	10 20
Rowland, Hy. A., drugs and chemicals, 333.92; Reid & Co., lumber, 71.50	405 42
Rogers, Elias Co., Lt., coal, 238.790 tons grate at 5.77, 185.1052 tons grate at 5.77, 227.1540 slack at 3.50; wood, 16¼ cords at 4.50	3,316 44
Rooney, N., cotton, 245¾ yds. at 19½c.; pocketing, 53¾ yds. at 15c.; silesia, 215¼ yds. at 15c.; canvas, 52½ yds. at 12½c.; table linen, 246 yds. at 40c.; towels, 12 doz. at 1.60	193 44
Ruttan, J. W., expenses capturing eloper	75
Rice Lewis & Son, glass, 1 light at 94c.; sheet brass, 29½ lbs. at 23c., 17½ lbs. at 26c.; keys, 1 doz. at 4.00; locks, 1 doz. at 2.80, 1 doz. at 15.47, 1 7-12 at 3.45; rivets, 15¼ at 65c.; sundries, 59.35; knobs, ½ doz. at 3.90; shafting, 170 lbs. at 3c.; knives, 5 doz. at 1.25, 1 at 2.29; plate iron, 782 lbs. at 2¼c.; knives, 5 doz. at 1.25, 1 at 2.29; angle iron, 170 lbs. at 2½c.; mild steel, 100 lbs. at 3c., 80 lbs. at 2.20 cwt., 391 lbs. at 2.50;	

PUBLIC INSTITUTIONS MAINTENANCE.—*Continued.*

ASYLUM FOR INSaNE, MIMICO.—*Continued.*

Expenses.—*Continued.*

gin block, 1 at 3.84; curtain pole knobs, 36 sets at 32c.; band iron, 180 lbs. at 2.45 cwt.; valves, 2 at 1.10; shears, 1 pr. at 1.20, 3 prs. at 73c., ¼ at 6.40, 2 prs. at 1.05, 1 pr. at 5.66; manure forks, 1 doz. at 5.88, ½ doz. at 7c.; clippers, 1 pr. at 1.25, 1 pr. at 2.00, 1 pr. at 2.25, 1 pr. at 3.80; hoes, 1 doz. at 3.60, ½ doz. at 4.00; shovels, 1½ doz. at 10.45; lawn mowers, 12 at 3.97; spades, 1½ doz. at 10.18; cleaver, 1 at 5.00; butchers' steel, 1 at 1.92; packing, 20 lbs. at 25c.; graphite, 3 tins, at 4.65; horse clippers, 1 pr. at 13.00; carvers, 6 pr. at 1.11; spoons, 5 doz. at 79 4-5c.; solder, 50 lbs. at 25c.; frictionless metal, 50 lbs. at 20c.; auger bits, 1 set at 4.03; paris green, 100 lbs. at 17c.; Mrs. Pott's irons, 1 doz. sets at 8.82; pinions, 50 at 15c.; razor strops, 1 doz. at 5.50; molasses gaters, ½ doz. at 7.65; tin freezer, 1 at 4.30; galvd. griddles, ½ doz. at 7.90; sand paper, 1 ream at 6.25; horse weights, 2 at 1.00; sponges, 2 at 50c.; galvd. iron, 198 lbs. at 3.85; wall scrapers, 2 at 89½c.; kalsomine brush, 1 at 1.59; nails, 1 keg at 2.65; cricket gauntlets, 1 pr. at 3.90; bats, 6 at 6.30, 1 at 6.15, 2 at 4.50; barrow, 1 at 5.20; wire belt lacing, 4 pkgs. at 35c., 1.40; tarred fibre, 4 rolls at 40¼c.; boiler tubes, 144 ft. for 16.94; clay picks, 10-12 doz. at 4.30; sash locks, 2 doz. at 1.03; fire brick, 500 at 29.00 .... 557 31

Sundry newspapers, advertising supplies, 118.00; advertising *re* fuel, 20.50 138 50

Smith, J. C., inspecting scales, 3.20; Smith, E. S., jam, 300 lbs. at 7½c., 750 lbs. at 8½c., 300 at 8¾c., 300 at 10½c., less freight, 2.25 .... 144 95

Smith, A., veterinary services, 9.50; Storry, A. E., 5 days' wages at 12.00 per month, 1.93 .... 11 43

Stubbs, G., killing cattle, 5.00; Shuttleworth, E. B., Chemical Co., medical appliances, 8.75 .... 13 75

Sparrow, Wm. H., brass injection pump, 1 at 5 50

Sloan, Jno. & Co., corn meal, 4 at 1.75, 380 lbs. at 3c.; canned vegetables, 4 doz. at 72½c., 4 doz. at 95c., 4 doz. at 85c., 6 doz. at 1.25; sugar, 1,500 lbs. at 4 1-3c.; starch, 100 lbs. at 7c., 100 lbs. at 5½c.; soap, 37½ lbs. at 7½c.; prunes, 500 lbs. at 6½c.; jelly powder, 4 doz. at 90c.; gelatine, 3 doz. at 7.10, 3 doz. at 1.45; biscuits, 254 lbs. at 6½c.; currants, 147 lbs. at 8c., 254 lbs. at 7½c.; mustard, 12 doz. at 75c., 50 lbs. at 17c.; paper, 181 lbs. at 3½c.; rice, 2,500 lbs. at 3 5-8c.; sapolio, 3 gro. at 11.30; wash boards, 2 doz. at 2.00; sundries, 13.44; raisins, 72 lbs. at 10½c.; fruit peels, 21 lbs. at 12c., 28 lbs. at 22c., 28 lbs. at 11c.; cream tartar, 10 lbs. at 27c.; matches, 5 cases at 3.00; twine, 5 pkgs. at 75c.; blacking, 2 doz. at 90c.; Holbrook's sauce, 5-6 doz. at 3.00 .... 418 08

Steele, Briggs Seed Co., oil cake, 1½ tons at 33.50; seeds, 221.40; potash manure, ¾ ton at 36.00; linseed meal, 40 lbs. at 4c.; plants, 21.50 .... 312 75

Smith, T. H. & Co., cheese, 432 lbs. at 12c., 596 lbs. at 13½c., 434 lbs. at 11¾c., 340 lbs. at 14c., 349 lbs. at 14½c.; lard, 60 lbs. at 11½c.; beans, 24 lbs. at 1.65; geese, 529 lbs. at 17c. 444 18

Slater, Jno., repairs to vehicles, etc., 93.37; Slocum, Dr. T. A., cod liver oil, 1 bot. at 1.00 .... 94 37

Stanley, J., clocks, 2 at 4.50; clocks repaired, 4.75 .... 13 75

Stewart, Jas., recovering eloper, 2.00; Singer Sewing Machine Co., repairs to machines, 2.02; needles, 100 at 1.10; sewing machines, 1 at 27.20, 1 at 32.00 .... 64 32

Simpson, R. Co., Ltd., platters, 1 doz. at 1.80; plates, 15 doz. at 55c., 15 doz. at 75c.; wash basins, 1 doz. at 4.80; cups, 15 doz. at 50c.; tow, 200 lbs. at 3c.; sundries, 2.73; batts, 100 lbs. at 5c.; curtains, 5 prs. at 12.00; peaches, 25 lbs. at 15c., 30 lbs at 17c.; carpet, 37½ yds. at 1.10; Wilton rugs, 2 at 4.25; sewing and laying carpet, 37½ yds. at 7c.; prayer books, 1 at 50c., 6 at 25c. .... 165·56

Taylor, Jno. & Co., soap, 2,901 lbs. at 5c., 3,000 at 4½c., 1,059½ at 5½c., 6 doz. at 1.00, 9 gro. at 7.20 .... 536 34

Times and Guide, printing and stationery, 78.80; Toronto Laundry Machine Co., counter shaft, 1 at 15.00; repairs, 1.50 .... 95 30

Toronto St. Ry., car tickets, 16.00; Toronto *World*, sub'n., 1 yr., 3.00; *Saturday Night*, 2.00; Toronto Asylum, beeswax, 4.90 .... 25 90

PUBLIC INSTITUTIONS MAINTENANCE.—*Continued.*

ASYLUM FOR INSANE, MIMICO.—*Continued.*

EXPENSES.—*Continued.*

United Factories, Ltd., brooms, 20 doz. at 2.47½, 20 doz. at 2.61¼; brushes, 2 doz. at 2.25, 2 doz. at 2.07, 3 doz. at 2.25, 2 doz. at 2.68, 2 doz. at 3.82, 1 doz. at 9.00; mats, 1 1-12 doz. at 2.38, 1 at 6.48, 1 at 2.38, 1 doz. at 13.50, 2-3 doz. at 20.00; tubs, 1 doz. at 10.50; sundries, 4.64; whisks, 1 doz. at 1.30, 2 doz. at 2.00 .... 197 65
Vienna Pressed Yeast Co., yeast, 51 lbs. at 26c. 13 26
Vokes Hardware Co., milling tool, 1 at 2.50; iron handles, 5 doz. at 90c.; axe, 1 at 1.00; trowel, 1 at 1.25; hammer, 1 at 1.25; belt lacing, 2 pkgs. at 45c.; sundries, 11.38 .... 22 78
Willard & Co., butter, 27,697 lbs. at 22½c.; turkeys, 834 lbs. at 16c., 9½ lbs. at 15c.; goose, 10 lbs. at 9½c.; lard, 50 lbs. at 12c., 100 lbs. at 12¼c.; eggs, 480 doz. at 17c., 720 doz. at 18c., 1,320 doz. at 19c., 300 doz. at 20c., 360 doz. at 21c., 360 doz. at 22c., 600 at 23c., 120 doz. at 24c., 60 at 25c.; cheese, 573 lbs. at 13c., 1,286 lbs. at 13¼c.; syrup, 12 qts. at 28c., 2 gals. at 75c.; ham, 34 lbs. at 16½c., 11¾ at 16c., 21¾ at 17c.; ducks, 8 lbs. at 12c., 10 lbs. at 13c.; bacon, 20 lbs. at 16c., 8 lbs. at 18c., 14¼ at 17c.; chickens, 26¼ lbs. at 13c. 7,566 02
Wilson, T. A., bran, 1 ton at 20.00; Wheler, G., testing flour, 1.00 .... 21 00
Wells, Dr., Josephine, dental chair, 1 at 29 60
West, Taylor, Bickle & Co., brushes, 1 doz. at 2.00, 1 at 2.25, 1 at 2.75, 1 at 3.00, 1 at 3.80, 2¾ doz. at 4.95, 1 at 9.68, ½ doz. at 12.00; brooms, 10 doz. at 2.45, 10 doz. at 2.50 .... 83 93
Wilson, C. & Son, repairing scales, 6.80; Walsh, Rev. F., street car tickets, 6.30 .... 13 10
White & Co., figs, 10 lbs. at 11c.; oranges, 1 case at 3.00; walnuts, 100 lbs. at 14c.; lemons, 1 case at 3.25; filberts, 10 lbs. at 11c.; almonds, 10 lbs. at 13c.; raisins, 2 boxes at 3.50; chocolates, 30 at 15c.; candies, 210 lbs. at 9c. 54 15
Williamson, R. C., repairs to sewing machines 9 00
Wilson, Harold A. Co., subscriptions to magazines, 1906, *Architects and Builders'* mag., 2.00; *Burr McIntosh*, 3.00; *Black and White*, 6.00; *Harper's Weekly*, 4.00; *Harper's Mag.*, 4.00; London *News*, 6.00; *Ladies' Home Journal*, 1.25; *Strand*, 1.25; *Scientific American*, 3.00; *Munsey*, 1.00; *McClure's*, 1.00; *Outing*, 3.00 .... 35 50
Warwick Bros. & Rutter, printing 8 85
York Mfg. Co., duck, 16 yds. at 90c. 14 40

ASYLUM FOR INSANE, BROCKVILLE.

SALARIES ($27,821.38).

T. J. Moher, M. D.:	Twelve months' salary as Medical Superintendent			2,500 00
J. C. Mitchell. M. D.:		do	First Assistant Physician	1,400 00
H. Clare, M. D.:	Four	do	Second do	316 00
G. F. Weatherbead:	Six	do	do	415 66
Eric Sutherland:	Two	do	do	186 10
W. P. Dailey:	Twelve	do	Bursar	1,500 00
J. A. Laidlaw:		do	Storekeeper	950 00
R. A. Bush:		do	Engineer	650 00
D. McCrimmon:		do	Farmer	650 00
W. J. McKay:		do	Porter	475 00
James Weatherston		do	Carpenter	550 00
P. Crilly:		do	Tailor	500 00
P. Kilgour:		do	Baker	525 00
Jno. Richards:		do	Gardener	550 00
L. R. Tackaberry:	Seven	do	Farm hand	172 50
W. J. Fraser:	Twelve	do	Assistant Engineer	450 00
Wm. Ferguson:	do	do	Chief Attendant	400 00
Howard Wynn:	One	do	Messenger	18 76
R. C. Tennant:	Nine and half	do	do	186 90

PUBLIC INSTITUTIONS MAINTENANCE.—*Continued.*

ASYLUM FOR INSANE, BROCKVILLE.—*Continued.*

SALARIES.—*Continued.*

W. J. Connolly :	Eight months' salary as		Laundryman	229 00
Jno. A. Murphy :	Four	do	do ..	120 00
E. Rowson :	Five	do	Farmhand................	125 00
R. T. Stratton :	Twelve	do	Painter....................	360 00
James Bolger :		do	Butcher	300 00
Jennie R. Gibson :		do	Matron	500 00
M. A. Kitts :		do	Assistant Matron	300 00
Bertha Walsh :	Eight	do	Stenographer	165 00
Kate Melroy :	Four	do	do ..	89 30
N. Collins :	Twelve	do	Seamstress................	204 00
Maids (4) :		do	....	633 14
Laundresses (3)		do	....	571 20
Cooks (2)		do	....	592 83
Male Supervisors (6) :		do	....	2,076 00
Male Attendants (16) :		do	....	3,787 31
Female Supervisors (6) :		do	....	1,174 93
Female Attendants (14) :		do	....	3,203 76
Stokers (4) :		do	....	922 80
Sundry persons, temporary help :		do	....	71 69

EXPENSES ($62,828.24).

Abbott, A., hay, 6.500 tons at 7.50, 46.87 ; Abbott, Grant & Co., 47 lbs.
biscuits at 6½c., 3.79 .... 50 66

Adams, Mrs. A., clothes hamper, 1 only at 1.25 ; American Medico Psychological Ass'n., annual dues, 5.00 .... 6 25

Armour & Cunningham, sugar, 3,600 lbs. at 4.02 per cwt., 3,000 lbs. at 4.12,
1,000 lbs. at 4.42. 500 lbs. at 3.82, 50 lbs. at 5½c., 500 lbs. at 4.52 ;
prunes, 500 lbs. at 6½c., 700 lbs. at 7½c., 900 lbs. at 6c. ; pot barley, 200
lbs. at 2.50 ; evaporated apples, 400 lbs. at 14c., 200 lbs. at 9c. ; salt, 6
bags at 65c., 4 bags at 1.50 ; rice, 1,000 lbs. at 4c. ; brooms, 10 doz. at
2.10 ; twine, 5 lbs. at 30c. ; lard, 100 lbs. at 12½c., 200 lbs. at 13c., 100
lbs. at 14c. ; syrup, 665 lbs. at 3c. ; currants, 77 lbs. at 6½c., 82 lbs. at
8c. ; raisins, 28 lbs. at 6½c., 186 lbs. at 10c. ; cream of tartar, 10 lbs. at
28c. ; sundries, 1.56 ; cocoanut, 20 lbs. at 20c. ; mustard, 8 lbs. at 25c. ;
starch, 100 lbs. at 6½c., 100 lbs. at 7c. ; tobacco, 45 lbs. at 37c., 15 lbs.
at 39c., 15 lbs. at 48c., 48 lbs. at 50c. ; matches, 1 case at 4.00 ; jam, 42
lbs. at 8c. ; canned fruit, 3 doz. at 1.88, 3 doz. at 2.38, 2 doz. at 2.00 ;
potatoes, 40 bus. at 60c. ; sardines, 25 cans at 12½c. ; canned salmon, 4
doz. at 1.90 ; cranberries, 2 bbls. at 11.00 ; blue, 14 lbs. at 15c. ; figs, 324
lbs. at 5½c. 929 21

Ault & Reynolds, coal, 1.300 tons at 8.00, 2.081.510 tons at 6.08 .... 12,663 23

Atteaux Dye Stuff & Chemical Co., disinfectant, 43 gals. at 1.00 ; sal soda,
900 lbs. at 80c., bbl. 1.00 ; wyandott soda, 560 lbs. at 2c. 62 40

Baird Bros., sheeting, 1,085½ yds. at 12½c. ; ticking, 225 yds. at 20c. ; print,
501¼ yds. at 10c. ; flannelette, 497½ yds. at 12½c., 61¼ yds. at 15c. ;
hessian, 50 yds. at 20c. ; silkaline, 100½ yds. at 20c. ; towelling, 300 yds.
at 12½c. ; cotton, 142 yds. at 9c., 122¾ yds. at 10c. ; towels, 1 doz. at
2.40 ; print, 232¼ yds. at 10c. 420 63

Beddow, John, mutton, 36¼ lbs. at 12½c. ; veal, 34¼ lbs. at 10c. ; lamb, 52 lbs.
at 15c., 44½ lbs. at 20c. ; chickens, 39¾ lbs. at 15c. ; turkey, 7 lbs. at 16c. 31 80

Beggs, Robert, shoe repairing outfit, 20.05 ; sundries, 2.96 ; leather, 19¼ lbs.
at 28c., 18 lbs. at 29c., 21 lbs. at 30c., 2¾ lbs. at 80c. 42 19

Bell Telephone Co., repairs, 35.46 ; messages, 24.71 ; exchange service, 103.00 ;
bluestone, 53 lbs. at 7c. 166 88

Bickford, Mrs. W. H., dried apples, 125 lbs. at 5½c................................ 6 88

Booth, Vincent, dried apples, 160 lbs. at 5c. 8 00

Brock, Davis, milch cow, 1 only at 45.00 ; Brockville Light & Power Co.,
gas, 3,217.50 .... 3,262 50

Bradley, J. H., sugar, 5 bags at 4.00, 5 bags at 4.40 ; rice, 2 sacks at 3.30 ;
matches, 1 case at 4.00 ; prunes, 500 lbs. at 8½c. ; sago, 1 bag at 5.50 ;

PUBLIC INSTITUTIONS MAINTENANCE.—*Continued.*

ASYLUM FOR INSANE, BROCKVILLE.—*Continued.*

EXPENSES.—*Continued.*

tapioca, 171 lbs. at 7½c.; baking powder, 4 doz. at 1.83¾; pails, 1 doz. at 2.40; tobacco, 90 lbs. at 48c.	165 94
Brockville *Times*, printing, 150.75; stationery, 65.98; advertising, 8.55; subscription, 6.00	231 28
Brown & Semple, repairs to building, 12.51; lead pipe, 39 lbs. at 7c.; sundries, 1.69	16 93
Brock, W. R. & Co., Ltd., serge, 25 yds. at 2.61¼	65 31
Brockville Water Works Department, water supply	2,000 00
Brown, S. L., apples, 10 bus. at 50c.	5 00
Brockville & Prescott Joint Stock Road Co., commutations of tolls	10 00
Booth, N. F., 1 only, horse, 160.00; Bursar, to pay sundries, 29.70	189 70
Brown, H. & Son, bran, 2 tons at 18.00, 1 ton at 19.00, 1 ton at 20.00, ½ ton at 21.00, ½ ton at 18.00, 2 tons at 20.00; chop feed, 4 tons at 23.00, 1 ton at 24.00, 1 ton at 22.00, 1 ton at 22.50; oats, 200 bus. at 41c., 50 bus. at 45c, 150 bus. at 40c., 50 bus. at 42c.; straw, 1.59 ton for 7.20, 15.1977 tons at 6.60, 1.49 ton at 7.00, 2.358 tons at 7.50; seed corn, 12.32; seed peas, 5.75	634 81
Borthwick, John, carriage repairs, etc., 86.45; implements, 4.65; horse-shoeing, 62.35	153 45
Canadian Carriage Co., repairs to phaeton, 2.00; lamps, 1 pr. at 5.00	7 00
Canadian Express Co., charges	12 00
Canadian Pacific Telegraph Co., messages	2 05
Cairns, Bernard, indelible ink, 2 qts. at 7.00	14 00
Canada Customs, duties	2 55
Cadwell, B., lumber	3 00
Caldwell, H., apples, 49 bus. at 60c., 10 bus. at 70c.	36 40
Canadian Pacific Railway, freight	9 02
Canadian Steam Boiler Equipment Co., repairs to grate	3 83
Cameron, A. E., cartage, 90c.; bran, 1 ton at 18.00, 1 ton at 18.50, 4 tons at 19.00, 3 tons at 20.00; corn meal, 1 ton at 23.00; chop feed, 4 tons at 21.00, 1 ton at 20.00, 1 ton at 22.50, 1½ tons at 22.00, 1 ton at 23.00, 1 ton at 23.50; oats, 100 bus. at 41c., 100 bus. at 42c. ,100 bus. at 43c., 100 bus. at 44c., 200 bus. at 45c., 100 bus. at 40c.; herbagum, 8 lbs. for 1.00; rolled oats, 6 bbls. at 4.30; bran, 1 ton at 20.00, 1 ton at 21.00	781 70
Central Prison Industries, tweed, 1,034¾ yds. at 569.12; blankets, 1,106 lbs. at 45c.; packing, 7.10; shoes, 48 prs. at 1.15, 144 prs. at 1.40, 72 prs. at 1.80; yarn, 153 lbs. at 45c.	1,584 37
Chrysler, J. E. & Co., seed plates, 18 doz. at 60c.; jardiniere, 1 only at 3.75; fish knife and fork, 1 pr. at 4.00; table bell, 1 only at 2.75; knives, 1 doz. at 2.25, 1 doz. at 5.00; sundries, 6.80; fountain pen, 1 only at 3.50; portrait paper, 1 gro. at 1.50; spoons, 1 doz. at 2.50, 2 doz. at 1.87½; forks, ½ doz. at 7.00; lantern slides, 6 doz. at 50c.	53 10
Chandler, Ingram & Bell, drugs, medical appliances, etc.	42 35
Chisamore, James A., horses, 2 only at 166.75	333 50
Cottrill, J. F., services as veterinary	8 00
Craig, Robt. & Co., caps, 7 5-6 doz. at 4.50; hats, 26 doz. at 1.63, 4 only at 50c.	79 63
Croil, James, tweed, 46 yds. at 1.90; packing, 10c.	87 50
Copeland & McGrath, use of barn and shed, 6 mo., 50.00; livery hire, 2.00	52 00
Common Sense Mfg. Co., roach exterminator, 12 lbs. at 1.00	12 00
Cordingly Bros., violin strings, 13 only at 25c.; clarionet reeds, ½ doz. at 80c.	3 65
Culbert, J., yeast, 288 lbs. at 35c.; tea, 2,085 lbs. at 25c.; biscuits, 17 tins at 30c., 181¾ lbs. at 7½c.; grocery sundries, 37.39; jelly powder, 4 doz. at 1.00; syrup, 672 lbs. at 4c.; fish, 40 lbs. at 8c.; rice, 500 lbs. at 3½c.; sugar, 800 lbs. at 4.50, 2,100 lbs. at 4.25, 500 lbs. at 4.42, 500 lbs. at 4.00, 500 lbs. at 4.30, 500 lbs. at 4.45, 100 lbs. at 4.52; plates, 16 doz. at 1.00, 5 doz. at 70c., 13 doz. at 90c., 3 only at 35c., 6 only at 65c., 11 doz. at 80c.; cups and saucers, 15 doz. at 80c., 1 doz. at 1.25, 9 doz. at 60c., 6 doz. at 65c., 30 doz. at 55c., 20 doz. at 50c.; sago, 187 lbs. at 6½c.; glasses, 15 doz. at 50c., 6 doz. at 1.00, 10 doz. at 45c.; platters, 6 doz. at 80c.; brooms, 7 doz. at 2.10, 2 doz. at 2.00; fruit dishes, 15 only at 40c., 6 only at 65c.; figs, 25 matts. at 1.75, 2,112 lbs. at 6½c.; prunes,	

PUBLIC INSTITUTIONS MAINTENANCE.—*Continued.*

ASYLUM FOR INSANE, BROCKVILLE.—*Continued.*

EXPENSES.—*Continued.*

1,560 lbs. at 6¼c.; tobacco, 36 lbs. at 45c., 516 lbs. at 46c.; starch, 200 lbs. at 6c.; bowls, 5 doz. at 90c., 12 doz. at 1.00, 2 doz. at 1.20; chambers, 48 only at 40c., 4½ doz. at 4.50; basins, 18 only at 50c.; ewers, 18 only at 50c.; pitchers, 1 doz. at 3.00, 10 doz. at 4.80; syrup jugs, 6 only at 20c.; barley, 200 lbs. at 2½c.; canned fruit, 1 case at 6.50, 2 doz. at 2.87½; butter dishes, 12 only at 35c.; paper, 30 lbs. at 6c.; paper bags, 3,500 for 15.55; blue, 14 lbs. at 18c.; crock, 1 only at 1.00; borax, 50 lbs. at 10c.; clothes pins, 1 box at 1.00; lye, 1 case at 4.00; wash boards, ¼ doz. at 2.50; macaroni. 10 lbs. at 10c.; soap, 2 boxes at 4.00; salt, 2 bags at 1.50, 4 bags at 50c.; tapioca. 165 lbs. at 7c.; mustard, 1 jar at 1.00; breakfast food, 1 case at 5.75; vinegar jugs, 1 doz. at 3.00; vegetable dishes, 6 only at 65c.; slop jar, 1 only at 1.75; soap slabs, 1 doz. at 1.20; lard, 10 pails at 2.75; extract, vanilla. 3 doz. at 2.50; corn starch, 80 lbs. at 8c.; canned vegetables, 1 case at 2.00; matches, 1 case at 4.00; vinegar bottles, 1 doz. at 2.40; vegetable dishes, 5 doz. at 90c.; jugs, 2 doz. at 3.00; mustard pots, 8 only at 25c.; platters, 6 only at 75c. ... 2,002 29

Clutterbuck. James, bananas. 2 doz. at 25c., 3 doz. at 20c.; pineapples; 6 only at 30c.; oranges, 4 doz. at 40c., 6 doz. at 45c., 10 doz. at 50c.; lemons, 19 doz. at 25c., 1 doz. at 30c., 11 doz. at 40c.; peaches, 1 basket at 70c.; berries. 18 boxes at 12½c., 4 qts. at 15c.; grapes, 1 bas. at 35c.; melons. 3 only at 20c., 3 only at 30c 28 95

Davis, R., & Son. sheeting, 329 yds. at 20c., 415¾ yds. at 21c., 414¾ yds. at 21½c., 205¼ yds. at 22½c., 36½ yds. at 30c.; cotton, 1,121 yds. at 9c., 316 yds. at 11½c., 185 yds. at 12c., 129 yds. at 12½c., 506½ yds. at 13½c., 160 yds. at 7½c.; shaker flannel, 143¼ yds. at 10c., 202½ yds. at 12½c., 60 yds. at 14c.; braces, 6 doz. at 2.50; rubber sheets, 24 only at 2.75; shirting, 210½ yds. at 15c., 128 yds. at 19c.; crettone, 10 yds. at 15c., 10 yds. at 20c.; muslin, 50 yds. at 12c., 25 yds. at 12½c., 60 yds. at 17c., 10 yds. at 45c.; furniture covering, 15 yds. at 50c.; curtains, 12 prs. at 1.60; 12 prs. at 1.75, 17 prs. at 2.00; cloth. 523½ yds. at 18c.; duck, 52¾ yds. at 21c., 50 yds. at 25c.; ticking. 111 yds. at 22c., 105 yds. at 23c., 55 yds. at 2½c.; cocoa mats. 1 doz. at 13.00; lace curtains, 15 prs. at 1.00; felt, 7 yds. at 75c.; drapery. 91 yds. at 18c., 15 yds. at 50c.; print, 413¾ yds. at 10c. 74 yds. at 12½c.; sundries, 1.54; table linen, 5 yds. at 1.50; braces. 5 doz. at 2.50; cottonade, 60¼ yds. at 23½; denim, 38 yds. at 25c.; flannel. 61½ yds. at 25c., 36½ yds. at 30c.; flannellette, 152½ yds. at 13½c.; linen, 88½ yds. at 30c., canton flannel, 50¾ yds. at 18c.; sweaters, 2 only at 1.25 .... - 1,272 75

Dayman, W. H.. baskets, 2 doz. at 12.00 .... 24 00
Derosia, Paul, fish. 4,720 lbs. at 9c. 424 80
Dowsley, R., repairing shoes 1 45
Dominion Express Co., charges 7 55
Dunn, R. E., milch cow, 1 only at 47 00
Dudley, G. H.. apples, 4 bus. at 50c., 54½ bus. at 60c. 34 70

Donovan, D. D., wash tubs. 4 only at 1.15; salt, 6 bags at 65c.; sago. 164 lbs. at 6c.; ginger, 30 lbs. at 20c.; lard. 100 lbs. at 12½c.; mustard, 4 jars at 85c.; pepper. 10 lbs. at 22c.; prunes. 500 lbs. at 6c., 500 lbs. at 7½c., 300 lbs. at 7½c.; rice. 1,000 lbs. at 4½c.; vinegar. 61.7 gals. at 25c.; brooms, 14 doz. at 2.10; pipes. 2 boxes at 85c.; figs. 300 lbs. at 5c.; beans. 5 bus. at 2.00; sugar, 800 lbs. at 3.92. 400 lbs. at 3.82, 200 lbs. at 4.25, 700 lbs. at 4.32, 1,500 lbs. at 4.02. 1,000 lbs. at 4.12; sardines, 5.09; corn starch. 30 lbs. at 6½c.; French capers. 1 doz. at 1.35; scap. 1 box at 4.00; sal soda. 375 lbs. at 1c.; chocolate. 30 lbs. at 35c.; Gillett's lye. 2 cases at 3.95; apricots. 200 lbs. at 13½c.; biscuits. 12 tins at 28c.; barley. 8 bags at 3.00; blacking. 2 doz. at 90c.; shredded wheat. 3 cases at 5.75; baking powder. 4 doz. at 1.85; canned fruit. 2 doz. at 90c.. 6 doz. at 1.80, 2 doz. at 2.10, 4 doz. at 2.45, 4 doz. at 2.65; starch. 600 lbs. at 6c.; wax. 250 lbs. at 11c. powdered borax, 50 lbs. at 8c.; blueing. 28 lbs. at 15c.; washboards, ¼ doz. at 2.25 .... 704 92

Earl. James, straw, 1.630 lbs. at 6.00 .... 4 29
Eaton. Ross. apples. 10 bus. at 50c. 5 00
Edwards. Mrs. W. H., seeds. 8.41; Edwards, J., repairs to building, 54.25 .... 62 66

PUBLIC INSTITUTIONS MAINTENANCE.—*Continued.*

ASYLUM FOR INSANE, BROCKVILLE.—*Continued.*

EXPENSES.—*Continued.*

Ferguson, Wm., travelling expenses, 51.39; Foster Pottery Co., flower pots, 12.25	63 64
Foxton, A., sugar, 1,000 lbs. at 3.97, 500 lbs. at 4.37; pails, 1 doz. at 2.00; vinegar, 41¼ gals. at 25c.; canned vegetables, 4 doz. at 90c., 4 doz. at 1.20; sago, 200 lbs. at 5½c.; syrup, 657 lbs. at 3c., 341 lbs. at 3¼c.; salt, 2 bbls. at 3.00, 5 sacks at 1.35; rice, 250 lbs. at 3 3-5c.; soap, 1 case at 3.60; sapolio, 1 case at 3.00; Gillett's lye, 1 case at 3.80; matches, 1 case at 3.20; mustard, 5 jars at 85c.; bath brick, 1 case at 80c.. tobacco, 30 lbs. at 39c.; clay pipes, 3 boxes at 85c.; raisins, 36 lbs. at 10c.; jelly powder, 4 doz. at 95c.; gelatine, 2 doz. at 1.50; currants, 75 lbs. at 7c.; sundries, 5.10	200 37
Gardiner, O. L., apples, 12 bus. at 35c., 4 bus. at 60c., 5 bus. at 80c., 2 bus. at 1.00	12 60
Gananoque *Journal*, printing	8 50
Galbraith, John, repairs to implements, 6.75; repairs to vehicles, 2.25	9 00
Griffin, P., beef, 114 lbs. at 6c.; mutton, 415 lbs. at 8c., 183 lbs. at 9c., 407 lbs. at 10c.	97 21
Gilbert, N., portfolios, 6 only at 4.00	24 00
Gripton, C., dating stamp, 1 only at 3.75; postage, 25c.	4 00
Grey, R., oats, 90 bus. at 40c.	36 00
Gutta Percha Rubber Mfg. Co., hospital sheets, 96 at 2.00	192 00
Gillett, E. W. Co., Ltd., Gillett's lye, 1 case at 3.60; baking powder, 4 doz. at 1.65; sundries, 2.42	12 62
Gunns, Limited, butter, 19,933 lbs. at 23¾c., 4,734.09; less cartage, 6.07	4,728 02
Greening Wire Co., steel wire cloth, 24 sq. ft. for	9 40
Green, J. & Co., stationery, 132.78; sheet music, 12.68	145 46
Globe Clothing House, shirts, 2 only at 50c.; socks, 2 prs. at 25c.; sundries, 55c.	2 05
Grand Trunk Railway, freight, 59.83; Great North Western Telegraph Co., messages, 4.77	64 60
Gowan, S., dental services, 1.00; Gordon, J. F., yarn, 100 lbs. at 42c., 42.00	43 00
Halliday, James, purchase of meat	7,528 83
Hanton, R., eggs, 27 doz. at 15c., 36 doz. at 16c., 24 doz. at 20c., 18½ doz. at 25c., 15 1-6 doz. at 26c.	23 18
Harrison, W. H., repairs to tinware, etc., 26.45, cooking pans, 2 at 1.00, 2 only at 2.50, 3 only for 5.00; strainers, 2 only at 3.00; sprinkling cans, 3 only at 1.00; milk pails, 1 only at 1.15	48 60
Hayes, Eric, milch cow, 1 only at	37 50
Hewitt, Wm., eggs, 60 doz. at 25c.	15 00
Henderson, Ames Co., whistles, 1 doz. at 3.25; Henderson, J. J., hay (standing), 23 tons for 70.00	73 25
Henderson, J. J. & Son, sausage, 40 lbs. at 10c.; lamb, 58¼ lbs. at 12½c., 165 lbs. at 15c.; veal, 95½ at 10c.; turkey, 17¾ lbs. at 18c.; sundries, 20c.; chickens, 32½ lbs. at 15c., 16½ lbs. at 20c.; milch cow, 1 only for 39.00	96 22
Hogan, Wm., straw, 1.1100 tons at 6.00	9 30
Hunt Bros., flour, 910 bbls. at 3.85	3,503 50
Hutchinson, Geo., ticking, 208 yds. at 20c., 55 yds. at 22c.; shirting, 214 yds. at 11c., 334¼ yds. at 12½c., 386½ yds. at 13c.; print, 167¼ yds. at 11½c.; cheesecloth, 110 yds. at 5c.; corsets, 1 doz. at 9.00; thread, 25 gro. at 5.50; cotton, 106¾ yds. at 9c., 322¾ yds. at 10c., 226½ yds. at 11c.; flannelette, 425¼ yds. at 10c., 90 yds. at 11c., 173¾ yds. at 11½c.	479 66
Imperial Chemical Co., soap, 1,070 lbs. at 5c., 25 boxes at 2.10, 3 boxes at 3.00; paints, oils, etc., 58.86	173 86
Jackson, A. E., musical services, 15.00; Johnston, W. C., coffee, 50 lbs. at 23c., 11.50	26 50
Johnston, C. W., inspecting gas metres	26 00
Johnston's Cash Grocery, syrup, 333 lbs. at 3¼c.; jelly powder, 2 doz. at 1.00; sugar, 300 lbs. at 3.85, 600 lbs. at 3.92, 300 lbs. at 4.32, 500 lbs. at 4.02, 1,000 lbs. at 4.20, 500 lbs. at 4.25, 500 lbs. at 4.65; dried apples, 148 lbs. at 5½c., 150 lbs. at 8¼c., 200 lbs. at 11¼c.; mustard, 32	

PUBLIC INSTITUTIONS MAINTENANCE.—*Continued.*

ASYLUM FOR INSANE, BROCKVILLE.—*Continued.*

EXPENSES.—*Continued.*

lbs. at 20c.; pepper, 25 lbs. at 25c.; lard, 6 pails at 2.40, 3 pails at 2.50, 200 lbs. at 13c., 100 lbs. at 14c.; prunes, 300 lbs. at 6½c., 750 lbs. at 6¾c., 500 lbs. at 7½c., 200 lbs. at 8½c., 300 lbs. at 9½c.; brooms, 7 doz. at 2.10, 5 doz. at 2.35. figs, 200 lbs. at 5½c.; matches, 1 box at 4.00; chambers, 14 doz. at 4.00; coffee, 230½ lbs. at 23c.; rice, 1,300 lbs. at 4c.; cocoanut, 10 lbs. at 20c.; tobacco, 15 lbs. at 39c.; sundries, 4.25; bowls, 4 doz. at 90c.; currants, 74 lbs. at 8½c.; jams, 126 lbs. at 8c.; raisins, 36 pkgs. at 12½c.; twine, 5 lbs. at 28c.	677 33
Kemp, M., tuning piano, 2.00; Kenny, T. & Co., tea, 400 lbs. at 22c, 88.00, less freight, 12c.	89 88
Kincaid, V. F., drugs and chemicals	297 32
Kingston Asylum, brushes, 12 doz. at 2.00, 6 doz. at 2.50	39 00
Lee, Walter, apples, 5 bus. at 80c., 4.00; Lewis, Rice & Son, horse boots, 1 set at 11.76	15 76
Lorimer, Wm., apples, 7 bus. at 60c., 30 bus. at 80c., 20 bus. at 90c., 7 bus. at 95c.; sugar, 500 lbs. at 3.82, 500 lbs. at 3.92, 500 lbs. at 3.98, 500 lbs. at 4.00, 1,000 lbs. at 4.15, 500 lbs. at 4.42; corn starch, 40 lbs. at 7c.; starch, 100 lbs. at 6c., 300 lbs. at 6½c.; wash tubs, 3 only at 1.10; clay pipes, 2 boxes at 85c.; salt, 6 sacks at 1.50, 1 bbl. at 3.00; chocolate, 6 doz. at 40c., barrel, 1 only at 2.00; vinegar, 28 gals. at 25c.; prunes, 500 lbs. at 6c., 300 lbs. at 8½c., 400 lbs. at 9c., 650 lbs. at 9¾c.; lard, 200 lbs. at 13c., 40 lbs. at 13¾c., 2 pails at 2.75; matches, 1 case at 4.00; mustard, 6 jars at 90c.; nutmeg, 3 lbs. at 60c.; pepper, 25 lbs. at 20c., 10 lbs. at 22c., 10 lbs. at 30c; rice, 500 lbs. at 3.60; twine, 5 lbs. at 30c.; figs, 197 lbs. at 5½c.; brooms, 3 doz. at 2.10, 5 doz. at 3.00; sundries, 3.45; tobacco, 75 lbs. at 39c., 12 lbs. at 48c.; jam, 42 lbs. at 8c.; mops, 1 doz. at 1.25; honey, 15 lbs. at 18c.; apples, 4 bus. at 70c., 3 bus. at 80c., 25¾ bus. at 95c.; cider, 4 gals. at 25c.; canned fruit, 2 doz. at 1.65, 4 doz. at 2.25, 4 doz. at 2.65	636 85
Maley, W. L., shoes, 1 pr. at 55c., 45 prs. at 1.25, 60 prs. at 1.30, 1 pr. at 90c., 27 prs. at 1.32½, 4 prs. at 2.50, 4 prs. at 2.85, 10 prs. at 3.15, 18 prs. at 3.35; packing, 1.90	286 57
Maher, T. J., travelling expenses, 97.10; Mallock, Wm. & Co., 1 shaft pinion and keys, 9.00	106 10
Martin, Geo., potatoes, 2,147½ bus. at 60c., 1,288.20; Medcalf, D. M., travelling expenses *re* boiler inspection, 27.27	1,315 47
Miller, John, straw, 3.370 tons at 6.00	19 11
Miller, James, eggs, 7 doz. at 18c.; dried apples, 200 lbs. at 5c.	11 26
Mott, J. A., horseshoeing, 45.40; carriage repairs, etc., 34.25	79 65
Morton, David & Sons, Limited, soap, 2,520 lbs. at 4c.	100 80
Morrison, C. W., cigars, 200 for 8.00; pipes, 2 doz. at 2.25, 1 doz. at 3.00; billiard cues, ½ doz. at 12.00; cue tips, 100 for 1.00; cue cement, 3 bottles at 15c.; blackstone, 100 lbs. for 3.00; tobaccos, 1 doz. pkgs. at 1.20, 50 pkgs. at 4½c.	29 40
Moore & Mowat, worsted, 14 yds. at 1.00; serge, 50 yds. at 2.60; scarlet braid, 4 yds. at 4.00; canvas, 104 yds. at 15c., 50 yds. at 16c., 50 yds. at 16½c.; sundries, 14.62; sewing silk, 1 lb. at 12.00; machine silk, 11.50; buttons, 5 gro. at 1.50, 2 gro. at 1.25, 1 gro. at 1.60, 144 doz. at 6c.; tweed, 70 yds. at 60c.; linen spools, 18 doz. at 1.25; silesia, 57½ yds. at 17c.; buckles, 4 boxes at 50c.; thread, 7 lbs. at 1.25; wadding 24 doz. at 27c.; basting cotton, ½ gro. at 13.00	348 22
Murray, P. J., straw, 2.440 tons at 6.00, 13.32; Murphy, Anna, hay (standing), 15 tons at 3.00, 45.00	58 32
Mundle & Percival, print, 154½ yds. at 12c.; shirting, 90 yds. at 12c., 114 yds. at 15c.; flannelette, 243½ yds. at 12c.; cotton, 250 yds. at 10c.; starch, 40 lbs. at 7½c.; mustard, 2 jars at 85c.; coffee, 100 lbs. at 26c.	131 36
Mylhes, M., apples, 50 bus. at 60c.	30 00
McAlpine, D., veterinary services, 7.00; McCaw, J. F., lime, 4.55	11 55
McConkey, J. S., repairs to implements	3 40
McConkey, W. H., dried apples, 98 lbs. at 5½c.; vinegar, 18½ gals. at 20c.; coffee, 690 lbs. at 26c.	190 00
McEvoy, John, straw, 7.820 tons at 6.00, 2.1340 tons at 6.25	61 15

PUBLIC INSTITUTIONS MAINTENANCE.—*Continued.*

ASYLUM FOR INSANE, BROCKVILLE.—*Continued.*

Expenses.—*Continued.*

McEwen, J. W., matches, 1 case at 4.00; fruit peel, 14 lbs. at 20c.; raisins. 36 lbs. at 11c.; sapolio, 1 box at 3.00; brooms, 4 doz. at 2.10; syrup, 657 lbs. at 2 7-8c.; vinegar, 40.6 gals. at 21c.; salt, 6 sacks at 1.35, 3 sacks at 1.45; lard, 100 lbs. at 13½c., 100 lbs. at 14½c.; sugar, 1,500 lbs. at 4.02, 500 lbs. at 4.12, 500 lbs. at 4.22, 500 lbs. at 4.52; pepper, 10 lbs. at 25c.; sago, 476 lbs. at 5½c.; ground mace, 1 lb. at 1.15; sundries, 4.85; rice, 300 lbs. at 3.50; prunes, 50 lbs. at 7c., 50 lbs. at 8¼c.; tobacco, 45 lbs. at 39c., 30 lbs. at 40c.; chocolate, 6 lbs. at 35c.; jam, 84 lbs. at 8c.; ginger, 10 lbs. at 25c. 303 43
McColl Bros., signal oil, 28 gals. at 90c.; soap, 2,000 lbs. at 5c.; barrels, 3.25 .... 128 45
McDougall, H. D., lumber 9 00
MacGregor & Sanders, flannelette, 180¼ yds. at 9½c.; shirting, 119½ yds. at 10c.; cotton, 80 yds. at 10½c., ticking, 100¾ yds. at 20c.; chambers, 8 doz. at 4.00; bowls. 5 doz. at 90c.; plates, 6 doz. at 60c.; cups, 10 doz. at 50c.; tumblers, 8 doz. at 40c. 105 90
McIntosh, P. & Son, split peas. 6 bbls. at 4.90; rolled oats, 113 bbls. at 5.35 633 95
McHenrys, spirits for hospital use 37 30
McLane. Geo. A., milch cow, 1 only at 40.00; McLaren, Peter, lumber, 230.29 .... 270 29
Nerlich & Co., baseball bats, ¼ doz. at 10.20; mask, 1 only at 3.00; mitts, 1 only at 4.50; gloves, ¼ doz. at 27.00; baseballs, ¼ doz. at 12.00; sundries, 30c. 32 40
Neill, R., laces, 2 gro. at 25c., 2 gro. at 40c.; shoes, 1 pr. at 85c., 1 pr. at 1.05, 1 pr. at 1.20, 8 prs. at 90c., 3 prs. at 87c., 3 prs. at 1.10, 1 pr. at 1.60, 3 prs. at 1.18, 24 prs. at 1.35, 22 prs. at 1.80, 24 prs. at 3.08 ...... 163 57
Orme; J. L. & Son, tuning piano 2 00
Patterson, Thomas, rent of land and orchard as per lease 50 00
Postmaster, postage stamps, 190.00; post office, box rent, 5.40 .... 195 40
Quinsey, Wm., plough handle, 1 only at 1 00
Quirmbach, Geo. R., dressers, 2 at 7.75; wash stands, 2 at 2.25; interments, 80.00; hair, 200 lbs. at 33c.; tufts, 10 lbs. at 25c.; moss, 151 lbs. at 10c.; twine, 1 doz. balls for 3.00; tufting needles, 1 doz. at 1.70; bags, 4 only at 30c. 189 50
Recorder Printing Co., advertising, 33.70; Ritchie, F. J., subscription sundry dailies and magazines, 52.25 .... 85 95
Ross, D. W., milch cows, 2 at 37.50, 3 at 40.00, 1 at 45.00, 2 at 40.00 .... 320 00
Ross, G. & Co., bushing, 60c.; basin taps, 6 at 80c., 24 at 1.00, 1 pr. at 3.00; furnace grate, 1 only at 15.00; grate bar, 1 only at 3.75; basin, 1 only at 1.00; brass brackets, 1 pr. at 40c.; soil pipe, 1 length at 1.75; clean out, 1 only at 25c.; rubber. 15 lbs. at 30c.; sundries, 3.28 .... 59 33
Ross, H., milch cows, 3 only at 40.00, 120.00; Robinson, W. J., ice, 301.15 .... 421 15
Rudd Chas. R. & Co., team harness, 1 set at 45.00; blankets, 4 only at 2.50; whips, 2 only at 1.25; harness repairs, 77.40; robes, 2 only at 14.00 .... 162 90
Skinner, W. E., apples, 10 bbls. at 2.50 .... 25 00
Smart, James Mfg. Co., Limited, lawn mowers, 2 only at 4.25; lawn mowers sharpened, 13 only at 75c.; castings, 700 lbs. at 4c.; sundries, 2.52; brushes, 3 only at 45c. 50 12
Stayner, G. F., drugs, chemicals, etc., 147.83; Stephens, S. A., straw, 3.1930 tons at 6.50. 25.77 .... 173 60
Stewart, J. H., lamb. 70 lbs. at 15c.; chickens, 33½ lbs. at 15c.; turkey, 11 lbs. at 17c., 11 lbs. at 19c., 600 lbs. at 19½c.; geese 400 lbs. at 14½c.; sausage, 25 lbs. at 10c. 197 15
Steacy, D. R., locks. 1 10-12 doz. at 6.00. 1 doz. at 15.00; nails. 1 keg at 2.75, 2 kegs at 2.65; iron pipe. 52½ ft. at 3½c., 51¼ ft. at 4½c., 112 1-3 ft. at 5½c., 52¾ ft. at 7½c., 103 1-3 ft. at 9½c.; scoops. 6 doz. at 1.15; rubber hose, 50 ft. at 16c.; binding twine. 33 lbs. at 15c.; skates. 6 prs. at 50c.; belt laces, 3½ lbs. at 1.00; skate straps, 2 doz. at 1.00; reflector, 1 only at 2.25; furnace grates, 200 lbs. at 7½c.; coal oil heaters, 1 only at 5.00; metallic tape, 1 only at 2.75; scythe, 1 only at 1.00; poultry

PUBLIC INSTITUTIONS MAINTENANCE.—*Continued.*

ASYLUM FOR INSANE, BROCKVILLE.—*Continued.*

EXPENSES.—*Continued.*

netting, 25 yds. at 4c.; tile, 37½ ft. at 8c.; hose, 50 ft. at 10c.; hooked weeders, 3 only at 35c.; hoe beades, 2 only at 75c.; rollers for wringers, 2 only at 1.75; sash weights, 104 lbs. at 3c.; tailor's shears, 1 pr. at 13.00; oil cans, 4 only at 25c., 1 only at 1.75; Yale locks, 6 only at 75c.; whisks, 1 doz. at 1.50; lamp wick, 2 coils at 50c.; lanterns, 2 only at 50c.; dust pans, 2 doz. at 1.00; mantle globes, 6 only at 25c.; agate boiler, 1 only at 1.50; dish pan, 1 only at 1.25; gravy strainers, 2 only at 50c.; brushes, 1 only at 50c., 2 only at 75c., 4 doz. at 1.50; coach screws, 50 at 3.00 per 100; screws, 2 gro. at 77c., 2 gro. at 52c., 2 gro. at 1.75; batteries, 3 only at 35c.; tower bolts, 1 doz. at 1.75, 1 doz. at 2.25; drawer pulls, ½ gro. at 11.50, 6 doz. at 85c.; sheet steel, 4 pcs. at 90c., 3 pcs. at 70c.; basking couplings, etc., 25.64; auger, 1 only at 1.25; repairs to stove. etc., 12.00; plaster paris, 1 bbl. at 2.75; chest locks, 6 doz. at 85c., 6 doz. at 1.50; rope, 21 lbs. at 15c.; sash tools, 4 only at 22c., 8 only at 20c.; putty, 103 lbs. at 2¾c.; razors, 3 only at 1.00; shears, 3 prs. at 75c.; mantles, 1 doz. at 2.40; wheelbarrows, 2 only at 3.75, 1 only at 1.50; baskets, 9 only at 50c.; snow shovels, 2 doz. at 3.00; globe receivers, 4 doz. at 1.50; mirrors, 1 only at 25c., 1 only at 50c., 1 only 2.75; gas globes, 16 doz. at 2.25; shovels, 1½ doz. at 7.50; rakes, 2 only at 65c., 6 only at 70c.; hoes, ½ doz. at 4.75. 2 only at 1.00; wheelbarrow, 1 only at 3.50; axe handles, ½ doz. at 3.00; pick handles, 1 doz. at 3.00; axes, 2 only at 90c.; wringer, 1 only at 4.00; graining rollers, 1 set at 4.50; flue cleaners, 1 only at 2.75; valves, 1 only at 1.75, 2 only at 1.50, 6 only at 75c., 6 only at 90c., 2 only at 85c., 3 only at 1.00, 2 only at 1.10, 2 only at 70c.; sewer tile, 100 ft. at 8c.; pipe, 100 ft. at 3c., 100 ft. at 4c., 102 ft. at 3½c., 102½ ft. at 5½c., 6 ft. at 25c.; sheet rubber, 5 ft. at 35c.; glue, 8 qts. at 1.00; nails, 1 keg at 3.00, 1 keg at 2.75, 1 keg at 2.65, 25 lbs. at 5c., 1 keg at 3.25; expansion bits, 1 only at 1.50; picture books, 10 doz. at 10c.; picture wire, 2 doz. at 85c.; blacking, 1 doz. at 1.10; lantern burners, 1 doz. at 50c.; scissors, 2 prs. at 75c.; razors, 3 only at 1.00; rakes, 1 doz. at 7.50; hooks, 1 gro. at 1.25, 1 gro. at 1.50; pails, 2 only at 60c.; sad irons, 42 lbs. at 6c.; stable broom, 1 only at 1.25; barrow wheels, 2 only at 90c.; hose bilb, 6 only at 75c.; gas stove, 1 only at 2.00; coal tar, 1 bbl. at 6.00; rubber tubing, 30 ft. at 15c.; sash cord, 3 14-16 yds. at 45c.; paints, oils, etc., 19.41; putty, 116 lbs. at 3c.; arc globes, 2 only at 1.25, 10 doz. at 2.50, 1 only at 2.25; gas mantles, ½ doz. at 3.00, 10 only at 25c., 6 only at 20c.; sundries, 157.20; paints, oils, etc., 657.68; packing, 27½ lbs. at 50c., 33 lbs. at 50c., 5½ lbs. at 40c., 2½ lbs. 1.25; brushes, 1 doz. at 2.25, 29 only 26.85; polishing paste, 3 doz. at 3.00; glass, 1 case at 8.00, 1 case at 9.50, 1 case at 7.50, 1 light at 1.35. 40 lights at 15c., 1 case at 8.50, 1 case at 2.25, 1 case at 2.50, 400 lights at 3c., 2 cases at 10.50; brass plugs, 1 doz. at 3.00, 2 doz. at 1.30; brass cocks, 6 only at 70c.; thermometers, 1 doz. at 4.20, ½ doz. at 4.44; sheet iron, 70 lbs. at 6c., 98 lbs. at 6½c.; washer cutter, 1 only at 1.25; saw blades, 1 doz. at 1.20; hand lamp, 1 only at 1.10; galvanized pipe, 51½ ft. at 6c., 50 ft. at 8c.; galvanized elbows, 1 doz. at 1.25; ash doors, 1 only at 2.75; lindsay lights, 4 only at 1.50; metal ceiling, 10 sheets for 3.25, 3 doz. at 2.50; magnolia metal, 5½ lbs. at 25c.; files, 1 doz. at 1.75, 2 only at 25c., 6 only at 30c., 3 doz. at 50c., 1 only at 45c., ½ doz. at 2.25, ½ doz. at 2.75; belting, 50 ft. at 10c., 25 ft. at 13c., 50 ft. at 17c., 15 ft. at 28c.; gas pillars, ¼ doz. at 6.00; preserving kettle, 1 only at 1.15, 2 only at 2.00; chair nails, 2,000 at 65c.; night latch, 7 only at 1.50, 2 only at 2.00; steel brackets, 2 only at 1.50; cupboard locks, 1 doz. at 2.40; hay fork handles, 2 doz. at 2.00; shoe eyelets, 2,000 at 50c.; carvers and forks, 4 only at 1.25; dishes, 6 only at 25c.; dead locks, 1 doz. at 18.00; brushes, 3 only at 85c., 3 doz. at 1.75, 4 only at 80c., 4 only at 1.25, 4 only at 75c., 6 only at 20c., 2 doz. at 1.50 .... 1,679 97

Sanderson, J. A., cheese, 302 lbs. at 12½c. 37 75

Shaver, A. E., lard, 120 lbs. at 13c.; prunes, 490 lbs. at 6¾c.; sapolio, 1 case at 3.00, 2 bbls. at 2.90, 7 bags at 1.50, 4 bags at 65c.; starch, 100 lbs. at 5½c.; sugar, 500 lbs. at 3.82, 1,500 lbs. at 4.22, 1,500 lbs. at 4.02, 500

PUBLIC INSTITUTIONS MAINTENANCE.—*Continued.*

ASYLUM FOR INSANE, BROCKVILLE.—*Continued.*

EXPENSES.—*Continued.*

lbs. at 4.42; brooms, 7 doz. at 2.10; pipes, 2 boxes at 90c.; figs, 198 lbs. at 5½c.; dry apples, 267 lbs. at 6c., 250 lbs. at 9c.; salmon, 4 doz. at 1.80; rice, 1,000 lbs. at 4.00; sago, 500 lbs. at 6.00; apples, 1 bbl. at 3.00, 5 cases at 1.35; gelatine, 1 doz. at 1.25; matches, 1 case at 4.00; shoe polish, 1 doz. at 1.00; sundries, 3.95; sal soda, 375 lbs. at 1.00; vinegar, 40.7 gals. at 25c.; tobacco, 24 lbs. at 50c., 15 lbs. at 42c.; raisins, 28 lbs. at 10c.; pepper, 25 lbs. at 25c.; canned fruit, 4 doz. at 2.25, 2 doz. at 2.00, 2 doz. at 1.50, 2 doz. at 2.50; chloride of lime, 209 lbs. at 5c.; syrup, 342 lbs. at 3½c.	488 63
Shipman, J. A., apples, 6½ bus. at 80c.	5 20
Sheridan & Power, bread pans, 50 only at 24c.; coal oil, 219 gals. at 20c.	55 80
Shepard, Heman, denim, 117¾ yds. at 25c.; cottonade, 175½ yds. at 25c.	73 31
Simpson, Chas., medical services	16 00
Smart, James Mfg. Co., lawn mowers sharpened, 4 only at 75c.; repairs, 1.76; castings, 679 lbs. at 3¼c.; kegs, ½ doz. at 3.00	28 33
Smart, R. H., castings, 4.00; sundries, 1.55	5 55
Steacy, F. B., butter knives, 6 only at 85c.; repairing watch, 1.00	6 10
Stratton, R. & Son, repairs, carriage, etc., 70.15; horseshoeing, 20.60	90 75
Steel, Briggs Seed Co., seeds	24 79
Stagg, Fred. A., bacon, 579 lbs. at 16c.; ham, 653½ lbs. at 16c.; lamb, 12¼ lbs. at 13c.; sausage, 27 lbs. at 12½c.; fish, 6,200 lbs. at 7½c., 15¼ lbs. at 9½c., 30 lbs. at 10c., 60 lbs. at 9c.	677 54
Stewart, J. H., fowl, 13 lbs. at 15c., 137 10-16 lbs. at 20c.; lamb, 46 lbs. at 15c., 83 lbs. at 20c.; veal, 24 lbs. at 10c.	55 39
St. Lawrence Produce Co., butter, 100 lbs. at 23c.; eggs, 420 doz. at 26c., 1,140 doz. at 20c., 720 doz. at 25c., 780 at 18c., 180 doz. at 16c., 683 doz. at 17c., 180 doz. at 19c., 360 doz. at 21c., 240 doz. at 23c.	990 51
Sundry newspapers, advertising *re* supplies, 118.00; advertising *re* fuel, 20.50	138 50
Swartz, A. H., interments, 72.00; black hair, 300 lbs. at 33c.; tufts, 10 lbs. at 50c.; twine, 18 balls at 25c.; mirrors, 3 only at 75c., 1 only at 3.00	185 75
Taylor, John & Co., soap, 6,953 lbs. at 5c., 8 doz. at 40c., 1,500 lbs. at 4c., 8 gro. at 4.50, 2,143 lbs. at 6c.	561 93
Taber, W., syrup, 40 gals. at 85c., 34.00; Tompkins, Geo., hay (standing), 17 tons for 50.00	84 00
Troy Laundry Machinery Co., Ltd., repairs to stove	6 25
Vandusen, W., eggs, 14 doz. at 20c.	2 80
Watcheron & Co., tweed, 308½ yds. at 50c.; flannel, 57¾ yds. at 27c.; yarn, 102 lbs. at 45c.; packing, 1.05, less discount, 4.18	212 62
Warner, J., apples, 1¾ bus. at 70c., 6½ bus. at 50c.	4 30
Warren, John, apples, 5 bus. at 60c., 3.00; Weatherhead, G. F., travelling expenses for patients, 4.90	7 90
Wheler, G., testing flour, 1.00; Worden, A., sand, 150 bus. at 5½c., 8.25	9 25
West Chemical Co., disinfecting fluid, 74 gals. at 1.10	81 40
Webster, John, cheese, 388 lbs. at 12c., 624 lbs. at 12½c., 2,756 lbs. at 13c.	482 84
Williams, James, drugs, chemicals, etc., 396.80; wax, 474 lbs. at 14c.; hair brushes, ½ doz. at 6.60; cartage, 70c.; seeds, 13.60; Diamond dyes, 9 doz. at 1.00; tanglefoot, 1 case at 4.25; sundries, 1.00; Japan wax, 10 lbs. at 30c.	491 05
Wood, W. H., sawdust, 1,140 bus. at 1½c.	17 10
Wooding, Geo., rubbers, 1 pr. at 50c., 1 pr. at 1.40, 6 prs. at 2.75, 3 prs. at 85c., 1 pr. at 1.05, 4 prs. at 2.75, 18 prs. at 75c., 15 prs. at 1.35, 2 prs. at 1.00, 1 pr. at 1.10	69 85
Wright, H. B. & Co., oysters, 3 qts. at 40c., 6 gals. at 1.80; sundries, 7.20; oranges, 30 doz. at 25c., 2 doz. at 40c., 4 doz. at 50c., 2 doz. at 30., 2 doz at 35c., 1 doz. at 60c., 6 bbls. at 5.00; pineapples, 8 only at 20c., 8 only at 25c., 3 only at 30c.; cucumbers, 1 doz. at 1.00; bananas, 6 doz. at 25c.; cherries, 3 bas. at 1.25; gooseberries, 1 bas. at 1.10; lemons, 8 doz. at 20c., 3 doz. at 25c., 8 doz. at 30c., 6 doz. at 40c.; red currants, 1 bas. at 1.50; berries, 6 boxes at 10c., 24 boxes at 12c., 32 boxes at 12½c.; melons, 2 only at 75c.; peaches, 4 bas. at 1.00, 1 bas. at 1.25; plums, 2 bas. at 1.00; grapes, 1 keg at 6.50; candy, 250 lbs. at 9 9-10c.; nuts 200 lbs. at 15c.	162 38

PUBLIC INSTITUTIONS MAINTENANCE.—*Continued.*

ASYLUM FOR INSANE, BROCKVILLE.—*Continued*

EXPENSES.—*Continued.*

Wright, Robert & Co., butter dish, 1 only at 3.00; tea pot, 1 only at 1.10; tumblers, 1 doz. at 2.00; plates, 1 doz. at 1.30, 1 doz. at 1.93, 1 doz. at 2.90, 1 doz. at 2.75: boiler, 1 only at 1.10; saucepans, 3 only at 45c.; kettle. 1 only at 1.10; sheeting, 34 yds. at 50c.; platters, 1 doz. at 2.25; pillow cotton, 30 yds. at 25c.; cushion covers, 2 only at 69c.; linen, 5 yds. at 80c.; napkins, 1 doz. at 3.00, 2 doz. at 4.50; cloth, 6 pcs. at 2.70; art gimp, 98 yds. at 5c.; hoods, 3 doz. at 5.00; shawls, 2 doz. at 27.00; shirting, 197 yds. at 13c.; bureau covers, 2 only ab 2.00; chamber sets, 1 only at 4.50; quilts, 2 doz. at 14.40; soap, 2 boxes at 2.50; madras, 20 yds. at 30c.; vegetables, 4 doz. at 1.10; cups and saucers, 1 doz. at 2.75; shade cloth, 10 yds. at 19c.; tapestry, 14 yds. at 75c., 101¼ yds. at 85c., 10 yds. at 1.35, 1¼ yds. at 2.00; curtains, 3 prs. at 4.00, 3 prs. at 3.75, 20 prs. at 1.50; thimbles, 3 grs. at 3.00; bootees, 4 grs. at 1.00; ticking, 118¼ yds. at 25c.; towels, 1 doz. at 2.15, 10¼ doz. at 3.00; cards, 2 doz. at 1.50; needles, 3,000 at 1.25; corset laces, 2 grs. at 2.00; butcher linen, 69¼ yds. at 30c.; collars, 6 only at 25c., 1 doz. at 1.50, 2 doz. at 1.35; garters, 3 prs. at 39c.; mats. 8 only at 1.10, 2 only at 4.00; frilling, 7 doz. yds. at 1.00; curtain poles, 24 only at 30c.; jardiniers, 10 only at 50c., 3 only at 35c., 1 only at 75c.; vases, 14 only at 15c., 8 only at 25c.; art cord, 76¾ yds. at 10c.; gent's ties, 6 only at 20c., 4 doz. at 1.50; mosquito nets. 36 yds. at 5c., 48 yds. at 10c.; crochet needles, 2 doz. at 50c.; ribbons, 12 yds. at 20c., 9 yds. at 25c., 21 yds. at 15.; handkerchiefs, 2 doz. at 1.50, 2¼ doz. at 1.35; ladies' collars, 5 only at 30c.; pins, 7 doz. at 25c., 8 doz. at 17½c.; art muslin, 69 yds. at 20c., 5 yds. at 75c., 15¾ yds. at 30c., 5 yds. at 60c.; corsets, 3 doz. at 9.00; cretonne, 20 yds. at 20c.; canton flannel, 6 yds. at 20c.; combs, 10 doz. at 1.50; 8 yds. at 85c.; cotton, 62 yds. at 10c.; hair pins, 5 lbs. at 25c.; buttons, 2 grs. at 90c., 26 grs. at 65c.. 2 grs. at 75c., 1 grs. at 1.50, 1.grs. at 1.26; mending cotton, 10 doz. at 25c.; sundries, 52.18; braces, ½ doz. at 3.00; gloves, 2 prs. at 1.00; cuspidors, 2 only at 75c., 1 only at 50c.; combs, 40 doz. at 90c., 8 doz. at 85c.; laces, 22½ grs. at 1.00, 1 grs. at 2.00; print, 45 yds. at 13c., 298¾ yds. at 10c.; table linen, 202¾ yds. at 35c., 12 yds. at 1.15; dimity, 107½ yds. at 15c.; felt, 103¾ yds. at 12½c.; towelling 300 yds. at 11c., 12 yds. at 14c., 3 yds. at 25c.; batts, 100 yds. at 7½c., 100 yds. at 8c.; shades, 4 only at 1.15, 1 only at 75c., 9 only at 1.35, 2 only at 1.75, 2 only at 1.50, 7 for 27.75; pillow, 1 only at 2.10; sundries, 35.76; wrapperette, 15 yds. at 15c.; lawn, 48 yds. at 23c., 28 yds. at 15c.; buttons, 1 grs. at 1.80, 1 grs. at 1.35, 1 grs. at 1.75, 79 doz. at 5c.; oilcloth, 2 rolls at 2.65; hose, 3 doz. at 1.50; crochet cotton, 2 doz. at 50c.; pique, 8 yds. at 25c.; rugs, 1 only at 4.00; muslin, 57 yds. at 18c., 75 yds. at 25c., 80 yds. at 15c.; silk, 10 yds. at 75c.; scrim, 426¼ yds. at 18c.; gingham, 90 yds. at 13c.; toilet paper, 2 cases at 4.00; shades, 3 only at 95c., 3 only at 85c., 4 only at 90c., 2 only at 1.35, 5 only at 1.15, 2 only at 80c., 1 only at 1.10; cheese cloth, 711 yds. at 5c................................... 1,370 83

ASYLUM FOR INSANE, COBOURG.

SALARIES ($11,331.91).

Chas. M. Hickey, M.D :	Twelve months' salary as		Medical Superintendent....	2,100 00
H. M. Cockburn, M.D :	Ten	do	Assistant Superintendent...	540 00
Mary E. Snyder :	Three	do	Trained Nurse.............	100 00
M. J. Doyle :	Twelve	do	Bursar	1,250 00
D. Macpherson :		do	Clerk	468 00
P. Casserey :		do	Engineer.................	550 00
Jos. McDonough :		do	Baker.....................	550 00
W. K. Stewart :		do	Gardener and Messenger ...	600 00
Adam Watson :		do	Night Watchman..........	300 00

PUBLIC INSTITUTIONS MAINTENANCE.—*Continued.*

ASYLUM FOR INSANE, COBOURG.—*Continued.*

SALARIES.—*Continued.*

Agusta A. Nelles :	Twelve months' salary as Matron....................	500	00
Stokers (2) :	do	....	900	00
Cooks (2) :	do	....	408	00
Laundresses (2) :	do	... .	408	00
Seamstresses (2) :	do	....	167	00
Maids (2) :	do	....	312	00
Eliza J. Gunn :	do	Chief Attendant...........	240	00
Female Supervisors (3)	do	....	537	86
Female Attendants (7)	do	....	1,138	55
Sundry persons, temporary help			262	50

EXPENSES ($10,183.17).

Allen, W. L. & Co., brace. 1 at 2.50; sundries, 15.54; paint, oils, etc., 5.45; leather. belting, 14 ft. at 28c.; lace leather, 3 lbs. at 80c.; knives, 1 doz. at 2.50; carvers, 2 at 1.50; turpentine, 1 gal. at 1.20; baskets, 2 at 50c.; valves, 1 at 2.00	39	51
Atteaux, Dyestuff Chemical Co., ammonia powder, 1,257 lbs. at 4½c......	56	57
Atchison, Frank, turnips, 5 bags at 35c...............................	1	75
Brock, W. R. Co., Ltd., shirting, 119¾ yds. for 15.77, 119¾ yds. for 15.35	31	12
Burnet, W., crockery, glassware, etc., 3.30; rent for late J. W. Smith, 117.50	120	80
Baker, Ernest, tuning pianos	2	00
Bell Telephone Co., messages, 13.85; exchange service, 73.50	87	35
Bursar, to pay sundries	2	84
Brown, F. H., tea, 257 bs. at 25c.; sugar, 317 lbs. at 4.50, 309 lbs. at 4.00	90	87
Climo Bros.. 1 grate at 2.65; Canadian Express Co., charges, 25c.	2	90
Canadian Oil Co., wax, 4.66; paint, oils, etc., 66.28; soap, 7 cases at 3.75, 122 lbs. at 4½c., 7 cases at 3.75; white waste, 25 lbs. at 12c.; spiral packing, 59c.	132	52
Crossen Car Mnfg. Co., repairing engine, 9.32; Carveth, J. A. & Co., books, 10.00	19	32
Cobourg Water and Electric Co., water, 608.42; gas, 4.63; electric light, 571.76; repairs, 4.95	1,189	76
Chase Bros. & Co., shrubs, trees, etc., 27.90; Cann, Samuel, ice, 125.25	153	15
Cobourg's Book Store, subscriptions newspapers, 19.06; *Mail and Empire*, 4.00; *Globe*, 4.00; *Saturday Night*, 2.00; *Munsey*, 1.00; *Ladies' Home Journal*, 1.25; stationery, 9.45	21	70
Cobourg Cemetery Co., interments, 10.00; Cobourg taxes, 3.29	13	29
Dundas, A. R., saucepans, 2 at 75c.; sundries, 12.35; kettles, 2.50; valves, 1 at 2.40, 2 at 3.25, 2 at 3.00; basin plugs, 1 doz. at 3.00; valve washers, 1 doz. at 2.40; repairs, 16.28; 1 seat at 3.00; covers for vegetable cookers. 2 at 3.50; pipe, 1½, 18 ft. at 12c., 19 ft. at 7c.; closet bowl, 1 at 8.00; double boiler, 1 at 2.00; asbestos cement, 2 pckgs. at 50c.; food chopper, 1 at 2.50; taps, 2 at 1.50	82	92
Davies, Wm., Co., butter, 4,147 at 23c., 953.81; Delaney, W. J., teapot, 1 at 5.50; oil, 70c.; repairs, 1.10	961	11
Denton. D., seeds, 16.17; Dunlop Tire Co., hospital sheets, 6 at 2.50, 15.00	31	17
Dominion Gas Improvement Co., gas, 2.52; Davidson, J. H., admission of patients to fair, 1.00	3	52
Doyle. M. J., travelling expenses	18	00
Field & Bros.. blankets. 2 prs. at 1.50; rug, 1 at 2.50	5	50
Floyd. Wm. H.. repairs to shoes. 8.40; boots. 72 prs. at 1.25, 1 pr. at 1.50	99	90
Fleischmann & Co., yeast, 80½ lbs. at 30c.	24	15
Field Hardware Co., sundries, 8.06; waste, 20 lbs. at 12c.; screen doors, 2 at 1.50; putz cream. 6 tins at 25c.; screens. 2 at 50c., 2 at 25.	16	46

11 P.A.

PUBLIC INSTITUTIONS MAINTENANCE.—*Continued.*

ASYLUM FOR INSANE, COBOURG.—*Continued.*

EXPENSES.—*Continued.*

Guillett Bros., fish, 915¼ lbs. at 9c., 10 lbs. at 10c., 4 doz. at 1.65. 7 doz. at 35c., 92.53; sugar, 600 lbs. at 4.10, 300 lbs. at 4.00, 900 at 4.20, 200 at 4.60. 200 at 4.70. 400 at 4.50, 100 at 3.50, 200 at 4.80, 300 at 4.30. 200 at 4.80: sal soda, 900¾ lbs. at 3.75; canned vegetables, 6 doz. at 1.00, 4 doz. at 1.10; ham, 10 doz. at 14½c.; cream of wheat, 1 doz. at 2.25; fowl, 1 pr. at 60c.; salt, 5 bbls. at 1.50; currants, 60 lbs. at 7c., 46 at 7½c., 20 lbs. at 8c., 16 at 9c.; lemons, 13 doz. at 25c.; macaroni, 1 doz. at 1.20; gelatine, 2 doz. at 1.40; jelly powder, 2 doz. at 1.00; oysters, 9 qts. at 60c.; starch, 40 lbs. at 5¾c., 69 lbs. at 6c.; sundries, 60.43; oranges, 3 doz. at 30c., 15 doz. at 20c., 1 doz. at 60c.; pickles, 1 doz. at 2.75; tea, 200 lbs. at 25c.; eggs, 139 doz. at 15c., 34 doz. at 16c. 36 doz. at 17c., 72 doz. at 18c., 96 doz. at 19c., 24 doz. at 20c., 12 doz. at 21c.; 50 doz. at 25c., 40 doz. at 27c.; cabbage, 1 doz. at 1.20; corn starch, 2 doz. at 1.80; apricots, 25 lbs. at 16c.; apples, 1 bush. at 1.00, 6 bush. at 50c., 4 bush. at 60c., 2 bush. at 75c., 1 bbl. at 2.25; cheese, 11 lbs. at 17c., 10¼ lbs. at 14c., 12 lbs. at 12½c.; maple syrup, 1 gal at 1.25; flavoring extract, 1 qt. at 2.00, 2 qts. at 1.00; pine apples, 1 doz. at 1.75, ½ doz. at 1.20; syrup, 2 gals. at 90c., 2 gals. at 1.20; berries, 16 boxes at 10c.; bananas, 15 doz. at 25c.; blue, 1 box at 1.25; candy, 40 lbs. at 7½c., 50 lbs. at 7c.; bath brick, 1 doz. at 1.00; toilet paper, 1 case at 3.50; melons, 6 doz. at 15c.; gem jars, 4 doz. at 1.00; cocoanut, 5 lbs. at 25c.; beans, 1 bush. at 1.80; chickens, 3 prs. at 75c.; cream tartar, 10 lbs. at 30c.; brushes, ¼ doz. at 2.00; raisins, 10 lbs. at 12½c.; chocolate, 6 lbs. at 45c.; nuts, 10 lbs. at 15c............................ 605 25

Grafton Cheese & Butter Factory, cheese, 84 lbs. at 11½c.; Greer, Geo., livery hire, 3.50 .... 12 95

Gillett, E. W. Co., perfumed lye, 1 case at 3.29; cream tartar, 10 lbs. at 26¼c., 2.65 .... 5 94

Gillard, Jas., paints, oils, etc., 43.22; sundries, 7.75; shade cloth, 13¼ yds. at 20c.; blinds, 1 at 1.00, 1 at 65c., 2 at 40c., 12 at 90c.............. 66 92

Grosgean, Jno. L., cheese, 405 lbs. at 13¼c., 53.66; Gurney Foundry Co., repairs to range, 1.32 .... 54 98

G.N.W. Telegraph Co., messages, 8.27; George, R., seeds and plants, 6.16 .. 14 43

Hewson & Co., frilling, 7 doz. yds. at 1.00, 7.00; boot laces, 6 doz. at 30c.; whisks, 1 doz. at 1.60; cheese cloth, 379 yds. at 5c.; print, 511¼ yds. at 12½c.; oil cloth, 48 yds. at 25c.; galatea, 141 yds. at 16c.; sundries, 20.07; tea cloths, 1 at 3.50, 2 at 1.75, 1 at 1.50; gingham, 313¼ yds. at 14c., 166 yds. at 15c.; flannelette, 385¼ yds. at 10c.; ticking, 120¼ yds. at 18c., 61¾ at 15c.; chintz, 25 yds. at 25c.; sateen, 75 yds. at 25c.; muslin, 12 yds. at 10c., 45 yds. at 15c., 20 yds. at 20c., 35 yds. at 35c.; poles, 1 doz. at 3.00; combs, 2 doz. at 1.20; curtain stretchers, 1 at 2.00; buttons, 1 gt. gro. at 2.00, 1 gro. at 75c.; cotton, 251½ yds. at 8c., 101 yds. at 10c.; yarn, 42 lbs. at 55c.; thread, 9 doz. at 48c.; nett, 115 yds. at 13c.; linen, 5 yds. at 50c.; pillow cotton, 20 yds. at 22c.; sheeting, 48 yds. at 25c., 50¾ yds. at 35c.; lawn, 34 yds. at 15c.; curtain screens, 20 yds. at 10c.; safety pins, 12 doz. at 10c.; ribbon, 22½ yds. at 15c.; rugs, 2 at 2.00 507 40

Hoovey & Son, figs, 295 lbs. at 5½c., 345½ lbs. at 6c.; prunes, 1,000 lbs. at 7½c., 336 lbs. at 6¼c., 300 lbs. at 6¾c.; coffee, 350 lbs. at 25c.; sundries, 2.95 .... 243 65

Harcourt, E. H. Co., Ltd., printing and binding, 7.00; Honeywell, H., turkey, 70 lbs. at 13½c., 9.45 .... 16 45

Hickey, Dr. C. E., travelling expenses, 16.55; Hoskins, T., geese, 110 lbs. at 10c., 11.00; turkey, 77 lbs. at 14c.............................. 38 33

Haywood, H., entertainment for patients, 4.00; Huycke, J. P., carriage repairs, 3.85 .... 7 85

Hopkins, Jno., Press, subscription to *Journal of Insanity*, 5.00............... 5 00

Hunt Bros., 153 bbls. flour at 4.00 .... 612 00

Honor, J. F., tea, 250 lbs. at 25c.; sugar, 289 lbs. at 4.50, 309 lbs. at 4.10 88 17

Harvey, T. R. & Son, cups and saucers, 2 doz. at 65c............................ 1 30

Inglis, Jno. Co., castings, etc. 2 35

11a P.A.

PUBLIC INSTITUTIONS MAINTENANCE.—*Continued.*

ASYLUM FOR INSANE, COBOURG.—*Continued.*

Expenses.—*Continued.*

Johns, O. G., drugs and chemicals	130 22
Kewin, D., manure, 9.75; ploughing, 2 dys. at 3.50; removing old fence, 75c.	17 50
Leonard, E. & Sons, fencing, 26.12; apples, 1 bbl. at 2.75; scuffler, 1 at 8.00	36 87
Mitchell, T. & Son, beef, 15,577 lbs. at 7c.; mutton, 4,182 lbs. at 10c.; pork, 374½ lbs. at 12c., 300 lbs. at 12½c.; pluck, 19 at 10c., 1 at 5c.; tongues, 6 at 25c.; fowl, 1 pr. at 80c.; ham, 38 lbs. at 17c., 115¼ lbs. at 18c.; veal, 15½ lbs. at 10c., 356 lbs. at 9c.; bacon, 12 lbs. at 16c.; lard, 60 lbs. at 12c., 60 lbs. at 13c., 60 lbs. at 13½c.; lamb, 12¾ lbs. at 12½c., 1¼ for 1.25, 3 lbs. at 15c., 11¾ lbs. at 15c., 1.77; suet, 10 lbs. at 7c., 10 lbs. at 10c.; sausages, 4 lbs. at 12½c	1,688 67
Morton, David & Sons, Ltd., soap, 2,500 lbs. at 4½c., 110.00; Mulholland, R. A., paint, oils, etc., 10.00	120 00
Minaker & Co., carpet, 12 yds. at 45c., 5.40; Minaker & Staples, 10 yds. at 50c.	10 40
Minaker, D. H., interments, 11.00; May, W., 1 day's work in garden, 1.25	12 25
Morrison, Jas., Brass Mnfg. Co., repairing automatic injector	5 80
Mathewson's Sons, sugar, 5 bags for 18.73; tea, 89 lbs. at 16c., 14.24	32 97
Medcalf, D. M., travelling expenses *re* boiler inspection	10 15
McCallum, P. & Sons, muslin, 25 yds. at 25c.; silk, 1 end at 3.00; rugs, 1 at 3.00, 1 at 3.75	16 00
McBride, H. L., interments, 66.00; 22 bbls. rolled oats at 5.25; split peas, 2 bbls. at 4.90	66 00
McIntosh, Norman, rolling lawn, 3 dys. at 1.25, 3.76; McIntosh, P. & Son, 22 bbls. at 5.25; split peas, 2 bbls. at 4.90	129 06
McIntosh, J. D., cherries, 2 bus. at 1.40, 1 bus. at 1.00; berries, 14 boxes at 12½c., 30 boxes at 10c., 43 boxes. at 11c., 6 boxes at 11c.; sundries, 85c.; peaches, 1 bas. at 60c., 1 bas. at 50c.; melons, 1 bas. at 60c.; grapes, 1 bas. at 40c	16 89
Nichols, M. C., sausages, 92 lbs. at 11c.; lemons, 7 doz. at 25c., 3 doz. at 20c.; bacon, 8½ lbs. at 17c.; butter, 10 lbs. at 22c.; lard, 80 lbs. at 12½c.; apples 10 bus. at 60c., 1 bbl. at 2.00, 1 bbl. at 2.25, 9 bus. at 1.00, 5 bus. at 50c., 3 bbls. at 3.00; cheese 111 lbs. at 15c., 96 lbs. at 13c., 75 lbs. at 14½c.; sundries,, 24.40; eggs, 29 doz. at 15c., 11 doz. at 19c., 8 doz. at 20c.; chocolate, 3 doz. at 45c.; sausages, 14 lbs. at 11c.; 5 lbs. at 10c.; mustard, 10 lbs. at 25c.; canned vegetables, 2 doz. at 1.15; syrup, 326 lbs. at 3½c.; tobacco; 2 lbs. at 55c.; wash soda, 1,165 lbs. at 1½c.; maple syrup, 1 gal. at 1.20, ½ gal. at 1.10; soap, 72½ lbs. at 9c.; currants, 20 lbs. at 7½c., 20 lbs. at 7½c., 20 lbs. at 8½c.; cream tartar, 5 lbs. at 30c.; sapolio, 2 doz. at 1.08; berries, 50 boxes, at 8c.; 45 boxes. at 8 1-3c., 30 boxes at 10c., 12 boxes at 12c.; tomatoes, 1 case at 2.40; rhubarb, 6¾ doz. at 50c., 1 doz. at 50c.; baking powder, 1 doz. tins at 1.80; peanuts, 20 lbs. at 15c.; syrup, 30½ gals. at 41c.; vinegar, 5½ gals. at 35c.; matches, 16 boxes at 12½c.; pears, 2 bus. at 85c.; salmon, 4 doz. at 1.70; rice, 41 lbs. at 4½c.; bowls, 1 doz. at 1.15; starch, 50 lbs. at 6c.; coal oil, 5 gals. at 20c.; cups and saucers, 2 doz. at 85c.; sugar, 300 lbs. at 4.20, 200 lbs. at 4.60; fruit peel, 5 lbs. at 20c.; raisins, 12 lbs. at 11c	264 86
Nerlich & Co., croquet set	4 20
O'Neill, Jas. R., livery hire, 4.00; Otis Fensom Elevator Co., valve leathers, 3 at 70c.; postage, 4c.	6 14
Postmaster, stamps, 35.00; P. O. drawer rent, 3.00	38 00
Purser, Jno. G., tuning pianos, 2.00; Plunkett, Geo., coal, 80 255-2,000 tons at 3.71, 297.28	299 28
Rooney, D. & Son, fish, 813 lbs. at 8c., 385 3-8 lbs. at 7½c., 50 at 10c., 698½ at 10½c., 245½ at 11c., 14 doz. at 34c., 1 lot at 22.21	216 28
Routh, H., milk, 16,790 qts. at 4c	671 60
Roarabeck, Geo. A., currants, 20 lbs. at 7c., 20 lbs. at 8c.; tea, 330 lbs. at 25c.; brooms, 6 doz. at 2.45; lye, 2 doz. at 1.20; canned vegetables, 1 case at 2.40, 1 case at 1.90; sundries, 5.89; cream of wheat, 1 doz. at	

PUBLIC INSTITUTIONS MAINTENANCE.—*Continued*.

ASYLUM FOR INSANE, COBOURG.—*Continued*.

EXPENSES.—*Continued*.

2.40; eggs, 10 doz. at 17c.; pickles, 2 doz. at 1.00; cream tartar, 3.00; ginger, 5 lbs. at 30c.; roll oats, 1 bbl. at 2.50; candy, 50 lbs. at 6½c.; pepper, 4 lbs. at 25c	130 14
Stevens, J. & Son Co., felt, 2½ lbs. at 1.50; basins, 2 at 60c.	4 95
Sundry Newspapers, advertising *re* supplies, 72.00; advertising fuel, 10.50.	82 50
Service, Jas., repairing shoes, 6.45; Slattery, Thos. inspecting weights and measures, 2.50	8 95
Steid, J., sour krout, 1 bbl. at 5.00; Stone, Mrs. Geo., chickens, 2 pr. at 1.00, 22 pr. at 75c.; ducks, 2 pr. at 1.00	25 50
Smith, E. D., seeds, 9.00; jam, 240 lbs. at 8½ c., 90 lbs. at 8½c.; peaches, 6 bas. at 75c.; plums, 6 bas. at 55.; sundries, 1.95; grapes, 10 bas. at 22c.	49 23
Throop, J., painting, 21.73; Titford, C., freight and cartage, 32.28........	54 01
Taylor, Jno. & Co., soap, 600 lbs. at 4c., 3 doz. at 1.20, 1 doz. at 1.00, 1 doz. at 1.25, 530 lbs. at 4½c., 516 lbs. at 5c...............................	79 50
Thompson, Geo., potatoes, 658.90 bus. at 54c.; beans, 1 bus. at 1.60; salt, 1 bbl. at 1.50, 1 bbl. at 3.00; sundries, 90c...............................	363 32
Troop, Wm., rice, 300 lbs. at 4c., 300 lbs. at 4½c.; barley, 98 lbs. for 3.50, 200 lbs. at 3c., 100 lbs. at 3½; tapioca, 205 lbs. at 7c., 171 lbs. at 7½c.; sundries, 63c	65 98
Way, B., railway fares, exchanging patients, 5.95; Wilson, Isaac, stationery, 2.25	8 20
Wingate, C. E., medical books, 16.00; Williams, A. R., Machinery, Co., 9.60	25 60
Wheler, G., testing flour	1 00

ASYLUM FOR INSANE, PENETANGUISHENE.

SALARIES ($15,802.45).

P. H. Spohn, M.D.:	Twelve months' salary as		Medical Superintendent.....	2,400 00
Chas. E. Newton, M. D.:	Five and half	do	Assistant do	330 00
John Ronan:	Three	do	Bursar	194 11
Herman J. Spence:	Ten	do	do	880 89
R. H. Steadman:	Five	do	General Assistant	300 00
Jas. Lonergan:	Twelve	do	Storekeeper	750 00
P. Lanonette:		do	Engineer.....................	600 00
Geo. Bunt:		do	Assistant Engineer..........	450 00
A. E. McGinnis:		do	Carpenter	600 00
R. DeNure:		do	Farmer....	500 00
Thos. Harford:		do	Gardener.....................	500 00
A. Gendron:		do	Baker........................	500 00
Jos. Lemieux:		do	Messenger..........	400 00
Jas. Champion:		do	Laundryman	384 00
M. DeNure:		do	Stableman...................	384 00
Lillie Jones:	Four	do	Matron	167 00
Rose M. Smith:	Twelve	do	do	365 28
Eva M. Whiten:	Two	do	Stenographer	43 33
T. McLellan:	Three	do	do	52 00
E. McLachlan:	Seven	do	do	150 00
Delia Beaulieu:	Twelve	do	Seamstress..................	189 00
Female Supervisors (2):		do	....	344 00
Female Attendants (6):		do	....	1,168 50
Laundresses (2):		do	....	393 25
Cooks (3):		do	....	572 97
May Wilkie:	Four & half	do	Housemaid	58 50
Male Supervisors (2):	Twelve	do	....	660 00
Stokers (3):		do	....	372 67
Male Attendants (5):		do	....	1,914 25
Sundry persons temporary services...............................				178 70

PUBLIC INSTITUTIONS MAINTENANCE.—*Continued.*

ASYLUM FOR INSANE, PENETANGUISHENE.—*Continued.*

EXPENSES ($26.350.61).

Adams' Launch & Engine. Mfg. Co., dry cells, 14 at 30c.; spark plug, 1 at 2.00; repairs to engine, 2.95	9 15
Allen, Mrs. A. B., apples, 9 bags at 50c	4 50
Brock, W. R., Co., Ltd., serge, 45 yds. at 1.66¼; window shades, 10 at 1.47; furniture covering, 9 yds. at 1.50, 4 yds. at 1.42½; mats, 6 at 37½ pine flats, 108 ft. at 12.55; sundries, 44c.; lace curtains, 3 pr. at 6.25	142 70
Beck, C., Mfg. Co., electric lamps, 14 doz. at 2.85; 1 doz. at 4.00, 3 for 1.05	44 95
Beemer. Dr. F., trav. expenses. 14.70; Barlow. W., rep. clippers. 1.00	15 70
Burroughes, F. C. & Co., mattresses, 4 at 11.50; pillows, 3 at 1.65	50 95
Breithaupt Leather Co., 102 lbs. at 28c., 23 lbs. at 29c.; tanner's oil, 1 gal. at 75c	36 19
Bell Telephone Co., messages, 66.32; Exchage Service, 95.00	161 32
Bursar, sundries, 1.35; Beman, F. B., glazing, 9.58	10 93
Briggs. Wm., sheet music. 5.25; Blanchard, W., hair. 1 bag at 2.00	7 25
Cummings. J. M., rack irons. 2 sets at 6.50; bolts, 75c.	13 75
Cloutier. Jas., manure, 11.00; Coulson. Geo., threshing, 7.00	18 00
Canada Paint Co., paint. oils, etc., 120.90; Canada Foundry Co., hydrants, 4 at 34.50, 138.00	258 90
Central Prison Industries, shoes, 12 pr. at 1.10; blankets, 703 lbs. at 45c.; packing, 2.50	332 05
Charlebois. A. B. & Son. corn. ½ bus. at 2.00; cartage, 6.00	7 00
Charlwood, G. F., cow, 1 at 45.00; Croil, Jas., tweed, 47 5-8 yds. at 1.90, 90.49	135 49
Canadian Express Co., charges. 30.39; Can. Gen. Electric Co., electric light electric light supplies, 33.00	63 39
Campbell, E. D., plants, 11.00; Carr, Jos., veterinary services, 2.75	13 75
Canadian Oil Co., paint, oils, etc., 56.35	56 35
Copp Clark, Co., Ltd., almanacs, ¼ doz. at 3.30; postage, 28c.	1 11
Carter. W. S., stationery. 7.75; drugs and chemicals. 27.95	35 70
Copeland, G. & Sons. chop feed. 2 ton, 900 lbs. at 26.00; shorts, ½ ton at 22.00; chopping feed. 62 bags at 5c.; bran. ½ ton at 18.00; 3 600-2.000 ton at 22.00; oats, 662 22-34 bus. at 45c.; peas, 185.30 bus. at 80c., 25.47 bus. at 85c.; barley, 16 5-48 bus. at 60c	635 30
Dalley, F. F. Co., Ltd., coffee, 300 lbs. at 25c.; pepper, 50 lbs. at 17c.; mustard. 2 jars at 65c	84 80
Dusome. J. P., clothing, 16 suits at 8.50; Demure. D., 20 bus. oats at 45c.	145 00
Davies', Wm., Co., Ltd., butter, 7,773 lbs. at 23c., less cartage, 23.05	- 1,764 74
Day. G. E., Yorkshire, boar, 1 at 15.00; Dallyn Jardine & Co., 1,400 lbs. soda at 1 7-8c., 26.25	41 25
Devlin. Patrick. teaming coal	9 00
Enright & Labatt, livery hire, 1.50; Edwards, Geo., seedwheat, 12 bus. at 80c., 9.60	11 10
Elliott, Geo., milch cows, 2 at 45.00	90 00
Foster Pottery Co., flower pots. 25.86; *Farmers' Advocate.* sub'n., 1.50	27 36
Fleischmann & Co., yeast. 110 lbs. at 41c., 45.10; P. O. order, 3c.	45 13
Foster Pottery Co., flower pots. 25.86; Farmer's Advocate, subn. 1.50	27 36
Gignac. Louis. potatoes. 671 35.60 bus. at 65c., 436.53; G. N. W. Telegraph Co., messages, 5.85	442 38
Gidley & Co., H. E., lumber, 14.90; nails, 2.56; horseshoeing. 9.45; batteries, 7 at 35c.; dry cells. 6 at 35c.; gasoline, 5 gal. at 35c.	32 86
Georgian Bay Shook Mills, lumber. 6.90; Gropp Bros., lumber, 6.00	12 90
Gurney Foundry Co., set grates for oxford boiler, 10.00; repairs, 20.25	30 25
Grise. D., spirits for medical purposes, 15 gals. at 2.50. 37.50; Rev. F. W. Gilmour. burial services. 10.00	47 50
Gilbert, H. M., apples, 4 bus. at 50c.; berries, 178 qts. at 10c., 26 qts. at 11c., 35 qts. at 7c., 32 qts. at 9c., 22 qts. for 2.00	29 99
Grand Trunk Ry. freight	78 82
Gendron, S. A., sewing machine needles, 3 doz. for 1.00; smoke pipe, 1 at 1.65; chain. 64 ft. at 6½; sundries, 70c	7 35

PUBLIC INSTITUTIONS MAINTENANCE.—*Continued.*

ASYLUM FOR INSANE, PENETANGUISHENE.—*Continued.*

EXPENSES.—*Continued.*

Hartz, J. F. Co., Ltd., medical appliances, 66.58; drugs and chemicals, 20.09 .... 86 67

Humphrey, F. W., canned fruit, 2 doz. at 2.82½, 2 doz. at 1.67½, 2 doz. at 1.15; tobacco, 30 lbs. at 46c., 20 lbs. at 45c.; pickles, 2 doz. at 2.65... 39 40

Harvey, Jno. G., phenyline disinfectant, 58 gals. at 1.25; freight, 1.77... 74 27

Hartmann Bros., asbestos, 150 lbs. at 6c; axle grease, 3 doz. at 1.00; poultry netting, 50 yds. for 4.50; flue cleaner, 1 at 2.00; grass books, 1 doz. at 6.00; tape line, 1 at 3.00; wedge set, 1 at 2.00; wheel borrows, 6 at 3.00; boiler tubes, 28 ft. at 10c.; pitch fork handles, 6 at 20c.; tea kettle, 2.75; roast pans, 2 at 1.15; tubs, 6 at 1.00; feed bucket, 3 at 1.00; sal soda, 375 lbs. at 1.50; ladder, 1 at 5.50; wood screws, 10 gross at 25c., 5 gross at 27c.; drill, 1 at 5.00; boiler purge, 239 lbs. at 15c., 463 at 12½c.; plow, 1 at 12.50; mower knife, 1 at 3.85; hose, 250 ft. at 12c.; cement, 20 bbls. at 2.20; 12 sacks at 55c.; hardware sundries. 56.28; pans, 1 doz. at 1.80; 6 only at 75c., 1 doz. at 3.00; snaths, 2 at 75c.; scythes, 8 at 1.25; saws, 3 at 2.00, 1 at 75c., 1 at 6.50; axes, 2 at 1.25, 3 at 75c., 1 doz. at 11.00; paris green, 50 lbs. at 25c., 25 lbs. at 30c.; square, 1 at 1.25; shovels, 1½ doz. at 10.80, 1 doz. at 10.50, 2 doz. at 7.80, 18 only at 65c., 1 only at 1.25, 10 only at 2.25; meat chopper, 1 at 3.50; nails, 14 kegs at 2.40, 1 keg at 2.50, 12 lbs. at 12½c.; fork bar, 1 at 5.00; ice book, 1 at 1.34; sheet zinc, 4.56; ice plow, 1 at 35.00; paint, oils, etc. 144.30; glass 2 boxes at 5.00, 1 box at 5.50, 1 box at 4.00, 1 at 4.50; putty, 200 lbs. at 2½c., 100 lbs. at 2½c.; chest handles, 5 doz. at 75c.; chisels, 5 at 45c.; brushes, 1 doz. at 4.75. 3 only at 65c., 2 only at 1.00, 2 only at 22½c., 6 only at 1.75; liquid glue, 2 qts. at 75c.; plumb bab, 1 at 1.25; files. 3 doz. at 1.00; latches. 6 at 1.25; galv. wire 65 lbs. for 2.34, 136 at 3c.; sprinklers, 3 at 75c., 2 at 1.40; hammers, 1 at 2.00, 2 at 50c., 2 at 75c., 2 at 1.00; sash cord, 20 lbs. at 40c.; bitts, 1 set, 2.25; putz cream, 3 gals. at 2.00; lead, 50 lbs. at 6.25; 50 lbs. 5.50; axe handles, 3 doz. at 3.00, 2 doz. at 5.00; hoes, 17 at 45c.; rakes, 1 doz. at 7.20; sand plaster, 2 ton at 7.56; pitch forks, 6 at 55c.; rope, 54 lbs. at 18c.; tees, 6 at 70c.; key rings, 4 doz. at 50c.; elbows, 4 at 55c.; galv'd. pipe, 100 ft. for 6.00; 100 ft. for 7.00: castings, 21.85; coal oil, 10 gals. at 23c.; iron pipe, 105 lbs. at 3c.; forks, 1 doz. at 1.75; granite kettles, 1 at 1.25; brush books. 6 at 65c.; soal plates, 2 at 75c.; drain scoops, 2 at 1.00; fence staples, 1 keg. at 4.00; scuffler, 1 at 11.00; potato forks, 12 at 90, 2 at 1.40; steamer, 1 at 5.50; paint brushes, 1 at 1.75, 1 at 1.40, 1 at 90c., 1 at 75c.; belting, 16 lbs. at 15c., 24 ft. for 6.05; books and staples, 50 only at 3c., hinges, 6 pr. at 60c., 6 pr. at 20c.; white paper, 30 rolls at 50c.; barb wire, 100 lbs. at 3c.; halyard blocks, 12 only at 40c.; wardlocks, ½ doz. at 21.00; plyers, 1 pr. at 1.50; stone hammers, 84 lbs. at 12c.; hammer handles, 6 at 25c.; tar paper, 4 rolls at 1.00; bindertwine, 30 lbs. at 12½c., gasoline, 10 gls. at 30c.; knives, 1 doz. at 1.00; level, 1 at 1.25; hydrant fittings, 2 sets at 3.50; lace leather, 3 lbs. at 75c.; cow chains, ½ doz. at 2.00; ½ doz. at 2.50; stair fixtures, 1 doz. at 1.20; drawer locks, ½ doz. at 6.00; planes, 1 at 1.50, 1 at 2.25, 1 at 2.50, 1 at 3.00; root cutter, 1 at 18.00; stock food. 50 lbs. at 8c.; pails, 1 doz. at 3.00; scale powder, 62 lbs. at 12c.; valves, 6 at 75c., 6 at 65c., 6 at 60c. hose bibs, 6 at 75c., fire cleaner, 1 at 1.50; oil pumps, 2 at 3.00, 1 at 2.25; hose nipples, 3 at 75c.; rubber plugs, 4 doz. at 1.25; steel oilers, 1 set at 4.20, ½ doz. at 2.60; plow points, 6 at 30c.; screw plate taps, 1 set at 7.00; gasoline 10 gal. at 27c., 50 gals. at 28c., 20 gals. at 33c., 40 gals. at 30c.; sofa springs, 10 lbs. at 10c... 1,198 04

Hollisters, J. W., repairs, etc., to harness, 19.30; whips, 2 at 1.00; sweat pads, 3 pr. at 75c.; trace, 1 at 2.25; blankets, 1 pr. at 3.50............... 29 30

Hatley, J. J., beef, 41,243 lbs. at 6.95; pork, 5¾ lbs. at 14c., mutton, 59 lbs. at 6.95 .... - 2,871 04

Herald. Ptg. Co., ptg., 5.50; Heintzman & Co., music, 15.70.................. 21 20

Hunt Bros., flour, 445 bags at 2.00, 1.50 bags at 1.91½ .... - 1,177 25

Hood, D., V.S., professional services 17 00

PUBLIC INSTITUTIONS MAINTENANCE.—*Continued.*

ASYLUM FOR INSANE, PENETANGUISHENE.—*Continued.*

EXPENSES.—*Continued.*

Horrell, J. B. & Son, sugar, 300 lbs. at 4.60; cotton, 40 yds. at 8c.; beans, 8 bus. at 2.00; straw hats. 7 7-12 doz. at 1.50; print, 130 yds. at 18c., 136 yds. at 12c.; buttons, 3 gross, at 75c.; 1 gross at 1.25; jardinieres, 1 at 3.00, 5 at 50c.; thread, 3 gross. at 5.40; sateen 16 2-3 yds. at 12c.; comforter, 1 at 5.25; sundries, 6.20. .... 114 95

Johnson, M. J., rent corn cutter 5 00

Kemp Mfg. Co., tea pots, 2 11-12 doz. at 2.97; cups, 7 doz. at 1.13; bowls, 5 doz. at 1.13; pitchers, 2 doz. at 4.05, 2 doz. at 4.80; packing, 60c.; sundries, 4.33 .... 44 85

Kinnear, T. & Co., tea, 101 lbs. at 25c. 25 25

Kenny, T. & Co., coffee, 100 lbs. at 25c.; cloves, 5 lbs. at 23c.; cassia, 5 lbs. at 20c.; mixed spice, 5 lbs. at 22c.; borax, 1 pkg. at 3.25; cocoanut, 5 lbs. at 18c 32 40

Lahey & Co., D. A., tobacco, 365 lbs. at 50c., 182.50; sugar, 533 lbs. at 4.75, 887 lbs. at 4.60, 299 lbs. at 4.65, 603 lbs. at 4.50; cheese, 76 lbs. at 13c.; pipes, 2 boxes at 1.20; shirting, 26¼ yds. at 12c., 174 yds. at 14c.; duck, 32¼ yds. at 12c.; starch, 100 lbs. at 6c.; buttons, 1 gross at 20c., 8¼ doz. at 10½c.; bacon, 45 lbs. at 17c.; beans, 2 bus. at 2.00; eggs, 60 doz. at 18c., 30 doz. at 15c., 30 doz. at 17c., 115 doz. at 20c., 60 doz. at 25c.; figs, 701 lbs. at 5c., 336 lbs. at 6c.; jam, 750 lbs. at 7c.; sundries, 3.45; starch, 600 lbs. at 6c.; salt, 18 bbls. at 1.35; prunes, 500 lbs. at 7½c.; Rickett's blue, 24 lbs. at 7c.; corn starch, 40 lbs. at 7½ sapolio, 1 box at 3.15; currants, 84½ lbs. at 6½c., 50 lbs. at 7¼c., 130 lbs. at 8c.; fish 3 kegs at 7.00, 100 lbs. at 7c., 200 lbs. at 6c.; tea, 708½ lbs. at 25c.; wheatine, 500 lbs. at 3.75 cwt.; biscuit, 5 tins at 25c., barley. 50 lbs. at 4c.; brooms, 7 doz. at 3.25; soap, 1 box at 4.15; 1 box at 4.25, 1 doz. at 1.20, 1 box 4.25; cotton, 100 yds. at 5c., 686 yds. at 9c; corn meal, 4 bags at 2.20; cocoanut, 10 lbs. at 18c.; canned vegetables. 4 doz. at 1.17½; raisins, 23 lbs. at 6c., 28 lbs. at 6½c., 28 lbs. at 7¼. 9 boxes at 1.15; tanglefoot, 1½ boxes at 88c.; jelly powder, 1 doz. at 1.00; rice, 250 lbs. at 3½c.; towelling, 100 yds. at 15c., 50 yds. at 10c.; print, 510½ yds. at 12c.; flannelette, 300 yds. at 12½c.; laces, 1 gross at 75c.; apples, 21 bags at 75c., 14 bags at 1.00; hosiery, 20 1-3 doz. at 1.50; macaroni, 12 lbs. at 10c.; cheese cloth, 100 yds. at 5c.; underwear, 25 doz. at 6.00; tapioca, 200 lbs. at 7c.; smocks, 50 pr. at 75c.; corsets, 1 doz. at 9.00; handkerchiefs. 2 doz. at 2.00. 9 doz. at 1.00; shoes, 12 pr. at 1.25; ties, 2 doz. at 3.00, 7 doz. at 2.50; shirts, 1 doz. at 9.00; coal oil, 5 gals. at 23c.; collars. 7 doz. at 1.15; ginger, 5 lbs. at 30c.; sapolio, 1 doz. at 1.15; mitts, 80 prs. at 30c. 1,549 65

Little. Rev. H. M., burial services, 7.50; Lamb, W. T., recovering eloper, 5.00 .... 12 50

Lee, H. J., use of binder 4 00

Machin. Fannie, expenses recovering eloper, 5.00; Massey Harris Co., Ltd., 1 seed-drill, 75.66 .... 80 66

Midland Mercantile & Trading Co., ham, 52 lbs. at 17c.; macaroni, 12 lbs. at 10c.; salmon, 4 doz. at 1.75; tapioca, 100 lbs. at 8c.; sundries, 40c. 25 44

Milligan, S. A., bran, 4½ tons at 18.00, 1,500 lbs. at 18.00, ¼ ton at 8.66; shorts. 5.295 tons at 21.00, 520 lbs. at 20.00; chop wheat, 1,530 lbs. at 1.50, 2,000 lbs. at 1.25 .... 264 41

Midland Coal Dock Co., Pittsburgh slack, 1,293.1,900 tons at 2.80; egg and stove coal, 300.200 tons at 5.85 .... 5,378 64

Martin, Jas., honey, 180 lbs. at 8½c., 15.30; Medcalf, D. M., trav. expenses re boilers inspection, 20.00 .... 35 30

Morton, David & Sons, Ltd., soap, 1,980 lbs. at 4½c., 14 boxes at 2.40...... 121 80

Murdoch. Jas., inspecting scales 5 00

McIntosh, P. & Sons, rolled oats, 24 bbls. at 5.25; split peas, 3 bbls. at 4.90 .... 140 70

McIntaggart, Jno., use of engine, 6.00; McGliban, F. & Sons, lumber, 80.14 .... 86 14

McLellan, Tena, travelling expenses 8 50

PUBLIC INSTITUTIONS MAINTENANCE.—*Continued.*

ASYLUM FOR INSANE, PENETANGUISHENE.—*Continued.*

Expenses.—*Continued.*

McGuire, Jno., swing pole, 1 at 1.25; picture wire, 5 lbs. at 45c.; picture books, 1 gro. at 1.44; picture moulding, 400 ft. at 3c.; centre tables, 2 at 2.50; sundries, 3.26; tow, 81 lbs. at 3½c.; sofa springs, 10 lbs. at 10c. 29 03

McDonald, P. A., M.D., creolin, 40 gals. at 1.25; pot, 1.75; spectacles, 1 5-12 doz. at 3.00; drugs, chemicals, etc., 149.37; hair brushes, 1 doz. at 6.00, 2 doz. at 3.00; books, 2.55; stationery, 23.30; plants and seeds, 21.56; daily papers, 7.50; sundries, 10.75; soap, 5 lbs. at 20c.; razor strops, 4 at 50c.; whisks, 1 doz. at 2.50; lather brushes, 1 doz. at 2.50 .... 291 03

Nettleton, J. E., spectacles, 1 doz. prs. at 6.00; Nettleton, C. A., wall paper, 22.69 .... 28 69

Ontario Rubber Co., hospital sheets, 24 at 2.25; pneumatic mattress, 1 at 30.00 .... 84 00

Penetanguishene, Town of, water supply, 750.00; Postmaster, stamps, 62.30 .... 812 30

Penetanguishene & Midland Electric St. Ry., Light & Power Co., electric light 1 year 1,000 00

Payette, P. & Co., spiral packing, 3 1-8 lbs. at 80c.; flax packing, 1 lb. at 80c.; repairs, 52.37; flat iron, 43 lbs. at 3c., rod iron, 25 lbs. at 4½c.; asbestos, 27 lbs. at 6.62 cwt.; iron hardware casting, 10.75 .... 70 63

Picotte, H., cartage, 4.75; hire of cart horse, 12 wks. at 1.50 .... 22 75

Penetanguishene Liquor Store, spirits for medical use 25 00

Roderick, J. S., returning eloper, 5.00; Wm. Rennie, seeds, 10.42 .... 15 42

Rice, Lewis & Son, Ltd., grass catcher, 1 at 1.75; braided cord, ¼ doz. hanks at 2.00; sundries, 3.10 .... 5 85

Robitaille, A., manure 7 25

Simpson, R., Co., Ltd., pictures, 31 only for 33.05; 1 lot for 175.00........ 208 05

Sundry newspapers, advertising *re* supplies, 92.95; *re* fuel, 11.35 .... 104 30

Sanderson, Rev. A. R., burial services, 2.50; Spence, H. J., travelling expenses, 7.00 .... 9 50

Sinnott, M. A., apples, 12½ bags at 50c., 6.25; Steele, Briggs Seed Co., seeds and plants, 12.25 .... 18 50

Simmers, J. A., seeds, 48.85; implements, 4.22; tobacco stems, 100 at 3c... 56 07

Smith, Wm., peas, 101 bush. at 2.00; oats, 204.23 bush. at 45c............ 167 85

Smith, E. D., seeds, plants, etc, 29.81; jam, 600 lbs. at 7½c., 180 lbs. at 8½c., 60 lbs. at 10½c.; jelly, 3 pails at 75c., 3 pails at 58c.; preserves, 5 doz. qts. at 5.00, 3 doz. qts. at 6.00, less freight, 3.23 .... 140 62

Sinnott, Jas., grant for exemption from school rates of officials' children 150 00

Shanahan Carriage Co., repairs, 78.25; horseshoeing, 28.16; moss, 47 lbs. at 12c.; buttons, 90c... 112 95

St. Amant, S., horseshoeing, 31.15; carriage repairs, 51.85; iron, 28½ lbs. at 4c.; whiffletrees, 1 pr. at 2.00 .... 86 14

Thompson, Wm. M., hay, 3.1,160 tons at 6.94, 13.485 tons at 7.46, 3.1,035 tons at 14.75; straw, 10.35 tons at 5.44, 3.230 tons at 8.50; raisins, 10 lbs. at 12½c., 14 lbs. at 8c.; oats, 56 lbs. at 17c.; raisins, 56 lbs. at 9c.; sugar, 936 lbs. at 4.35, 909 at 4.85, 1,106 at 4.75; bacon, 36½ lbs. at 20c.; cranberries, 2 bush. at 3.00; corn starch, 40 pkgs. at 7c.; pickles, 2 doz. qts. at 2.50; oranges, 3 doz. at 60c., 4 boxes at 3.50; matches, 2 cases at 2.40; cinnamon, 5 lbs. at 35c.; cocoa, 1 doz. at 2.75; chocolate, 12 lbs. at 40c.; clay pipes, 1 box at 1.00; ham, 14 lbs. at 18c., 38½ lbs. at 20c.. 46 lbs. at 19c.; sapolio, 3 doz. at 1.05, 5 doz. at 1.15; tanglefoot, 8 boxes at 50c.; apricots, 50 lbs. at 18c., 25 lbs. at 20c.; currants, 229 lbs. at 8c.; figs, 300 lbs. at 8c.. 110 lbs. at 10c., 170 lbs. at 5c., 24 lbs. at 15c.; butter, 212 lbs. at 23c.; fish, 1,438 lbs. at 8c., 775 lbs. at 6½c.. 6 doz. at 20c., 3 gro. at 9.00, 4 doz. at 25c., 49½ lbs. at 12½c., 2,829 lbs. at 10c.; mustard, 2 jars at 85c., apples, 81 bags at 75c., 8 bags at 1.00, 11½ bbls. at 1.50; sugar, 2,659 lbs. at 4.60, 608 lbs. at 4.85, 318 lbs. at 4.90, 2.448 lbs. at 4.25, 606 lbs. at 4.50; soap, 2 boxes at 4.15, 2 boxes at 4.25, 1 box at 1.50, 30 lbs. at 15c.; salt, 7 bbls. at 1.35, 40 lbs. at 6½c.: malta vita, 1 doz. at 1.20; berries, 96 boxes at 10c.; tea, 315 lbs. at 25c.; sundries, 67.42: candies, 150 lbs. at 10c.; wheatine, 8 bags at 3.75; canned fruit, 2

PUBLIC INSTITUTIONS MAINTENANCE.—*Continued.*

ASYLUM FOR INSANE, PENETANGUISHENE.—*Continued.*

EXPENSES.—*Continued.*

doz. at 2.75; cornmeal, 7 bags at 2.20; biscuits, 5 tins at 30c.; macaroni, 12 lbs. at 9c.; nuts, 60 lbs. at 15c.; eggs, 30 doz. at 22c., 192 doz. at 20c., 90 doz. at 17c., 66 doz. at 15c., 102 doz. at 25c., 90 doz. at 23c.; coffee, 200 lbs. at 25c.; jam, 134 lbs. at 7c.; starch, 100 lbs. at 6c.; cocoanut, 5 lbs. at 20c.; borax, 2 doz. at 90c., 2 doz. at 1.00, 24 lbs. at 8 1-3c.; barley, 200 lbs. at 4c., 150 lbs. at 3½c.; lard, 90 lbs. at 14c., 28 lbs. at 13¾c., 50 lbs. at 13c., 50 lbs. at 12½c., 50 lbs. at 11½c.; sal soda, 355 lbs. at 1¼c.; cheese, 391 lbs. at 15c., 287 lbs. at 13c., 78 lbs. at 12½c., 71 lbs. at 13½c., 64 lbs. at 14c.; brooms, 7 doz. at 3.25; wash soda, 280 lbs. at 2¼c.; baking powder, 22 lbs. at 10c.; vinegar, 71½ gals. at 25c.; syrup, 2 gals. at 1.25, 678 lbs. at 3½c.; tobacco, 264 lbs. at 50c.; onions, 20 lbs. at 5c.; rice, 550 lbs. at 3½c.; dried apples, 123 lbs. at 9c.; prunes, 1,719 lbs. at 7½c.; lemons, 3 doz. at 25c., 5 doz. at 30c., 1 doz. at 35c., 6 doz. at 40c.; frilling, 1 doz. yds. at 2.25, 24 yds. at 20c., 24 yds. at 15c.; buttons, 2¾ gro. at 2.25, 6 doz. at 37½c., 6 doz. at 20c., 5 gro. at 1.00, 1 gro. at 1.50, 1 gro. at 75c., 1 10-12 gro. at 2.50; towelling, 203½ yds. at 12½c., 35½ yds. at 15c., 256 yds. at 10c., 8½ yds. at 20c.; print, 841½ yds. at 12c.; combs, 3 doz. at 1.25, 5 doz. at 1.00, 1 doz. at 3.00; cotton, 388¾ yds. at 10c., 266¾ yds. at 8c., 539½ yds. at 9c., 5 yds. at 12½c.; butter cloth, 70 yds. at 5c.; flannelette, 742 yds. at 12½c.; shirting, 1,097 yds. at 14c., 200 yds. at 20c., 200 yds. at 12c.; hessian, 10 yds. at 20c.; hosiery, 40½ doz. at 2.50, 5 doz. at 2.75, 8 pr. at 25c.; lounge cover, 1 at 2.75; cushion forms, 3 doz. at 6.00; linen, 8 yds. at 50c.; sateen, 20 yds. at 15c.; duck, 44 yds. at 15c., 28½ yds. at 22c.; wool mitts, 2 doz. at 3.00; cambric, 20 yds. at 12½c., 20 yds. at 15c.; suiting, 150 yds. at 18c.; smocks, 5 doz. at 9.00; overalls, 10 2-12 doz. at 9.00; door mats, 6 at 1.00; towels, 1 doz. at 9.00; boots, 25 prs. at 3.50, 13 prs. at 1.15, 16 prs. at 75c., 5 prs. at 65c.; table oil, 60 yds. at 25c.; carpet, 19 yds. at 50c.; thimbles, 1 gro. at 2.00; thread, 1 gro. at 5.40; 1 rug at 14.00; cloth, 15 yds. at 50c., 150 yds. at 14½c.; hair pins, 4 lbs. at 25c.; sateen, 7½ yds. at 20c.; plates, 3 doz. at 1.00; churn, 1 at 1.25; cups and saucers, 4 doz. at 1.00; snips, 1 pr. at 2.25; granite cups, 3 doz. at 1.32; shoe nails, 12 pkgs. at 15c.; silver polish, 1 gal. at 2.75; baskets, 2 at 1.25, 1 at 1.00, 6 at 50c.; braces, 100 prs. at 20c.; paint, oils, etc., 1.50; soup tureen, 1 at 1.50; vases, ½ dozen at 2.50; brushes, 3 doz. at 2.00; toilet paper, 1 case at 6.50; fly paper, 150 sheets for 3.00, 26 pkgs. at 8c., 4 boxes at 60c., 25 pkgs. at 10c.; jugs, 1 doz. at 3.00; gem jars, 15 doz. at 90c., 5 doz. at 1.15; paint cleaner, ½ gal. at 3.00; brass polish, 2 gals. at 2.00; vegetable dishes, 1 doz. at 4.80; tumblers, 1 doz. at 1.50; linoleum, 3½ yds. at 1.00; flannel, 200 yds. at 12½c.; mosquito netting, 12 yds. at 5c., 61 yds. at 6c.; sheeting, 497½ yds. at 22c.; quilts, 5 doz. at 9.00; awning cloth, 57½ yds. at 25c.; velour curtains, 1 at 10.00; velours, 8½ yds. at 1.75; buttons, 2 gro. at 2.40, 1 gro. at 1.00, 1 gro. at 1.25; mitts, 30 prs. at 30c.; caps, 12 doz. at 1.00, 12 doz. at 1.25; brooches, 6 at 50c.; ribbon, 25 yds. at 10c.; nett, 9 yds. at 25c. 4,058 90

Times, The and *Guide*, printing, 37.40; Taylor, Jno. & Co., soap, 7 boxes at 1.50, 1,736 lbs. at 5c., 97.30 .... 134 70

Toronto Laundry Co., mangle felt, 28 lbs. at 85c.; cotton duck, 12 yds. at 65c. 31 60

United Typewriter Co., Ltd., typewriter supplies 5 85

Williams, D., oats, 201 11-34 bush. at 40c., 39 19-34 bush. at 60c. 104 40

Wright, G. H., castings, 150 lbs. at 8c.; fitting castings, 5.25; fire brick, fitting, 1 at 3.00; varnish, 1 qt. at 50c... 20 75

Wheler, G., testing flour 1 00

Wright, C. E., fowl, 3 at 30c., 3 at 35c., 1 at 40c., 40 lbs. at 12½c., 9 lbs. at 10c., 17 lbs. at 12c., 9½ lbs. at 10½c., 7 prs. at 60c., 10 prs. at 75c., 1 pr. at 85c., 3 only at 38 1-3c., 1 pr. at 70c., 34 lbs. at 15c.; pork, 24 lbs. at 12½c.; veal, 106¾ lbs. at 12½c.; turkey, 255 lbs. at 16c.; tongue, 1 at 25c.; geese, 252 lbs. at 12½c.; shanks, 2 at 10c.; lamb, 3 qr. at 1.25, 1 qr. at 1.50, 8½ lbs. at 12½c., 69½ lbs. at 15c........................ 136 66

Western Foundry Co., covers for Huron range 6 60

PUBLIC INSTITUTIONS MAINTENANCE.—*Continued.*

ASYLUM FOR EPILEPTICS, WOODSTOCK.

SALARIES ($8,376.17).

J. J. Williams, M.D.:	Twelve months' salary as		Medical Superintendent	2,800 00
H. Clare, M.D.:	Eight	do	Assistant do	734 00
John Ronan:	Nine	do	Bursar	1,006 94
Ada Athoe:		do	Stenographer	108 00
M. Elliott:		do	Matron	375 00
Wm. C. Gimby:	Seven and half	do	Carpenter	375 00
Jno. E. Lang:	Eight	do	Assistant Carpenter	107 00
Cooks (3)	Twelve	do		315 62
M. Peach:	Four	do	Maid	56 00
Laundress (3)	Twelve:	do		143 19
M. German:	Nine	do	Seamstress	135 00
Walter Precious:		do	Engineer	375 00
S. McGurdy	Seven and half	do	Farmer	375 00
W. C. German:	Nine	do	Stoker	225 00
J. Grant:		do	Chief Male Supervisor	270 00
Susan Parker:		do	Chief Female Supervisor	162 00
Male Attendants (2)	Twelve	do		346 13
Female Attendants (2)		do		265 00
Sundry persons, temporary services				202 29

EXPENSES ($9,406.68).

Anderson, W. D., carpentering and material	199 37
Boles, Jno. E., flannelette, 63¾ yds. at 8c.; pins, ½ gro. at 11.50, ½ gro. at 6.00, ½ gro. at 10.00; shoe laces, 1 gro. at 1.75; chambray, 47¼ yds. at 14c.; cheese cloth, 54 yds. at 5c.; sundries, 45c.	30 37
Butler, R. E., Lumber Co., lumber, 81.98; Brown, H., grading grounds with team, 20.00	101 98
Brind, Dr. C., veterinary services, 5.00; Boles, Jas. P., clothing, 2 suits at 18.00, 36.00	41 00
Blake, Catharine, onions, 1 bag at 1.25, 1 bush. at 50c.; carrots, 2 bush. at 35c.; cauliflower, 8 head at 5c., 40c.	2 85
Baird, Wm., repairs, 3.99; Biggs, Geo. M., travelling expenses, 5.20	9 19
Bickle, J. R., meat, 24¾ lbs. for 2.41; Blackburn, J., meat, 32 lbs. for 3.39	5 80
Bursar, to pay sundries, 2.59; Bell Telephone Co., messages, 7.00; exchange service, 50.00	63 16
Bragg, H., freight and cartage, 8.95; Butler Bros., lumber, 9.43	18 38
Campbell Bros., towelling, 42½ yds. at 12½c.; drill, 45 yds. at 17½c.; cotton, 60 yds. at 9½c.; guernseys, 6 at 50c., 3.00; gingham, 53¼ yds. at 12½c.	28 58
Cullen, Jas., roll oats, 500 lbs. at 1.30; Connor & Co., flour cans, 1 at 50c., 1 at 75c., 1 at 1.00; toilet set, 1 at 2.25	11 00
Coppins, E. J., hose bibbs, 3 at 85c., 2.55; electric lamps, 1 at 3.00; sundries, 10c.; electric iron, 1 at 7.00	12 65
Chisnall, C., cartage	1 25
Coles, E. J., glasses, 1 doz. at 1.25, 1 doz. at 90c.; plates, 1 doz. at 72c., 8 doz. at 60c., 8 doz. at 54c.; paring knives, ½ doz. at 1.00; jug, 1 at 15c., 1 8-12 doz. at 1.00; dinner set, 1 at 20.00; toilet sets, 1 at 2.65, 2 at 1.00; slop jars, 2 at 2.00; cups and saucers, 8 doz. at 60c., 1 doz. at 1.00, 1 doz. at 70c.; bowls, 8 doz. at 1.00, 2 doz. at 60c., 2 doz. at 1.80; butter pats, 8 doz. at 25c.; fruit saucers, 8 doz. at 35c.; side dishes, 6 at 35c.; covered vegetable dishes, 24 at 45c., 2 at 1.10; bake boards, 2 at 75c.; tray, 1 at 2.70; sundries, 1.29	87 65
Cairns, Bernard, rubber stamp, 1 at 1.35, 4 at 35c., 1 at 25c., 2 at 85., 2 at 20c.; ink pack, 3 at 25c.; blue ink, 3 bots. at 25c., postage, 6c.	6 66
Clare, H., travelling expenses, 22.35; Cosford, T. H., bread, 181 loaves at 5c., 9.05	31 40
Canadian Express Co., charges	90
Davies, Wm., Co., Ltd., steak, 6 lbs. at 10c., 140 4-16 at 12c., 16 lbs. at 12½c., 33 lbs. at 15c., 29 4-10 at 15c.; beef, 424 7-16 at 9c., 1,425 at 9c., 11 7-8 at 10c., 565 at 8c.; ham, 40 lbs. at 16c., 11 lbs. at 18c.; pork, 140 at 15c., 88 lbs. at 14c., 10½ lbs. at 12½c.; mutton, 57 8-16 lbs. at 11c., 216 lbs. at 12c., 3 lbs. at 12½c., 16 11-16 lbs. at 14c.; veal, 7½ lbs.	

PUBLIC INSTITUTIONS MAINTENANCE.—*Continued.*

ASYLUM FOR EPILEPTICS.—*Continued.*

· EXPENSES.—*Continued.*

at 12½c.. 7¼ lbs. at 15c.; shank, 1 at 35c., 1 at 26c.; lamb, 48 at 15c., 7 6-16 at 15c., 30 lbs. at 14c.; chickens, 70 lbs. at 10c.; beef, 291 lbs. at 8c., 448 lbs. at 9c., 10 9-16 lbs. at 12c.; steak, 87 9-16 lbs. at 12c., 4 4-16 at 12½c., 41 4-16 at 15c.; mutton, 73 lbs. at 12c.; bacon, 39 15-16 lbs. at 17c.; suet, 10 lbs. at 10c....	534 79
Duval, Miss, travelling expenses, 3.50; Dominion Express Co., charges, 3.80	7 30
Dunn, Thos., grading grounds with team	17 00
Elliott, Miss M. C., travelling expenses	7 30
Fowell, Jno., 16 prs. shears at 30c.; neck yoke, 1 at 50c.; scraper, 1 at 10.00; wagon jack, 1 at 1.25	17 85
Frank, F., coal, 132.656 tons at 6.63	877 33
Fury & Thompson, fish, 30½ at 8c., 318 lbs. at 10c., 49¾ lbs. at 11c., 275 lbs. at 11c.; brooms, 2 doz. at 2.75, 2 doz. at 3.25; whisks, 1 doz. at 1.80	76 99
Frost & Wood, wagon, 1 at 72.00; whipple trees, 1 set at 3.00; stock rack, 1 at 18.00	93 00
Gingerich, A. H., paints, oils, etc., 1.77; seeds, 1 at 1.50; sweeper, 1 at 3.00; kettles. 2 at 65c., iron, hardware, etc., 5.30	12 87
Gardner & Co., lantern, 1 at 1.00; separator, 75c.; hat and cloak hooks, 10 at 10c.; door checks and springs, 4 at 7.50, 2 at 5.00; brackets, 5 at 80c.; putting up checks, 3.50; sundries, 85c.	51 10
Grafton & Co., mitts, 6 prs. at 50c.; G.N.W. Telegraph Co., messages, 80c.	3 80
Gustin, H. N., livery hire, 5.50; Grant, Jas., travelling expenses, 5.65	11 15
Grand Trunk Railway, storage and freight, 8.35; Goodeve, A., stationery, 3.60	11 95
Gray, J. S. & Son, tiles, 5 ft. at 1.25; German, W. C., use of horse and rig from Feby 5th to June 5th, 75.00; caretaking and heating of cottages, 9 weeks at 10.50. 94.50	175 75
Goodall, L., grading ground with team. 10 days at 4.00	40 00
Hollinrake & Co., sheeting, 30½ yds. at 25c.; pillow cotton, 36¼ yds. at 15c.; flannelette. 55 yds. at 10c.; towels, 5 doz. at 2.40, 1 doz. at 4.50, ½ doz. at 8.00; thread, 6 doz. at 45c.; sundries, 2.20	43 97
Hannan & Bull, horseshoeing, 14.05; Haight, Ed., settee, 1 at 7.00; laying carpet, 75c.	21 80
Harty, J. F., medical appliances. drugs, etc.	255 90
Hicks, W. R., livery hire. 1.00; Hammill. J. H. Co., 150.1264 tons at 6.67, 88.1176 at 6.67. 38.1800 at 6.98, 32.400 at 6.71	1.283 76
Hayward, Jas., milk, 13.058 lbs. at 1.35 cwt., 5,361 lbs. at 1.50 cwt.; Haywood, F., livery hire. 30.75	287 45
Hyde, F., drugs. chemicals, etc., 28.25; Hersee, Edwin, seeds, 14.65; sprayer, 1 at 90c.	43 80
Isbister, Jas., ice, 169.81; making cider, 5.30; Johnston, Rev. A. J., postal cards, 1.50	176 61
Karn, F. W., glass, 2 lights at 32½c., 2 at 65c., 3 at 1.75; tinner's snips, 1 at 1.75	8 95
King's Printer. stationery, 4.80; paper. 5.41	10 21
Karn, F. W., hardware sundries, 41.89; beeswax. 25 lbs. at 35c.; drawer locks, 2 at 50c., 6 at 45c.; wringer. 1 at 3.50; shellac, 1 qt. at 1.00; varnish, ¼ gal. at 2.00; wire cloth, 27 yds. at 15c.; lime, 3 bus. at 40c.; door pulls, 1 doz. at 1.20; paint, 1.13; wire, 600 ft. at 40c.; kettles, 2 at 1.25; cowbar, 1 at 1.50; brushes, 2 at 85c.; snow shovels. 3 at 35c., 3 at 30c.; brooms, 2 at 85c.; turpentine. 5 gals. at 1.20; roofing. 6 rolls at 3.25; tar paper. 3 rolls at 55c.; shovels, 3 at 1.15; door checks, 2 at at 6.00; chambers. 1 doz. at 4.20	125 97
Karn, W. A., drugs. chemicals, etc., 50.58; Kirk, Geo., hay, 231 lbs. at 60c.; rolled oats, 242 lbs. at 1.35, 500 lbs. at 1.30; bran, 500 lbs. at 1.00, 200 lbs. at 90c.; oats. 5 bus. at 45c.; seeds. 7.47; chop feed. 2.200 lbs. at 1.35. 4.000 lbs. at 1.20, 1,000 lbs. at 1.30, 500 lbs. at 1.40; bags, 4 doz. at 2.40	185 56
Lindsay, W. J.. 1 rocker at 2.50; dresser, 1 at 11.80; wardrobe. 1 at 10.50; rugs, 1 at 8.50, 1 at 3.00	36 30

PUBLIC INSTITUTIONS MAINTENANCE.—*Continued.*

ASYLUM FOR EPILEPTICS.—*Continued.*

EXPENSES.—*Continued.*

Millman, Fred., butter, 284 lbs. at 18c., 1,388 at 23c.; ammonia, 9 doz. at 86 2-3c.; tea, 155 lbs. at 25c.; coffee, 130 lbs. at 25c.; corn meal, 100 lbs. at 2.00, 100 lbs. at 1.80, 50 lbs. at 1.00; flour, 1,000 lbs. at 1.95, 25 lbs. at 2.80, 100 lbs. at 1.95; oat meal, 180 lbs. for 4.70, 360 lbs. for 9.40; lard, 50 lbs. at 11¼c., 10 lbs. at 13½c., 20 lbs. at 13c.; bacon, 35½ lbs. at 17c., 13 lbs. at 15c., 7 11-16 at 18c.; soap, 1½ doz. at 94c., 46 lbs. at 8c., 1 case at 2.10, 32½ lbs. at 7½c.; rice, 100 lbs. at 3¾c., 25 lbs. at 4c.; canned vegetables, 4 doz. at 1.10, 2 doz. at 90c., 4 doz. at 1.00, 2 doz. at 80c., 6 doz. at 80c., 10 doz. at 85c., 4 doz. at 90c., 18 doz. at 1.10; blue, 12 lbs. at 17c.; soda, 450 lbs. at 4.96; starch, 100 lbs. at 5.25, 1 doz. at 1.00; baking powder, 11 lbs. at 20c., 1 doz. at 4.00., 7 lbs. at 35c.; prunes, 150 lbs. at 7½c., 100 lbs. at 9¼c.; beans, 2 bus. at 1.75; peas, 1 bus. at 3.75; eggs, 102 doz. at 14c., 36 doz. at 15½c., 108 at 16c., 168 doz. at 17c., 132 doz. at 18c.; salt, 1 bbl. at 1.35; corn starch, 40 lbs. at 5¼c., 40 lbs. at 7c.; sauce, 1 doz. at 1.40; tapioca, 50 lbs. at 6c., 25 lbs. at 7c.; sugar, 346 lbs. at 4.35, 321 lbs. at 4.00, 321 lbs. at 4.10, 304 lbs. lbs. at 4.15, 303 lbs. at 4.20, 307 lbs. at 4.45, 309 lbs. at 4.50, 657 lbs. at 4.60; syrup, 366 lbs. at 2 7-8c.; vinegar, 30.4 gals. at 25c.; sago, 100 lbs. at 5c.; vinegar barrels, 1 at 2.00, 1 at 2.25, 3 at 2.00; barley, 50 lbs. at 3½c.; pickles, 1 doz. at 2.50, 1 doz. at 2.25, ½ doz. at 1.20; fish, 12 doz. at 10c., 6 doz. at 20c., 4 doz. at 1.55; canned fruit, 1 doz. at 2.75, 1½ doz. at 2.40, 2 doz. at 1.75, 2 doz. at 2.90, 11-12 at 3.00; bon ami, 3 doz. at 1.50; apples, 2 bags at 1.25; rolled wheat, 20 lbs. at 3½c., 100 lbs. at 8c., 100 lbs. at 2¾c.; sapolio, 4 doz. at 1.00; toilet paper, 2 cases at 6.00; jam, 112 lbs. at 7c.; cabbage, 1 doz. at 1.00, 1 doz. at 50c.; cheese, 40 lbs. at 14c.; figs, 28 lbs. at 4½c., 32 lbs. at 5½c.; currants, 25 lbs. at 6½c.; sundries, 67.65; silver polish, 1 doz. at 2.00; marmalade, 12 lbs. at 30c.; jars, 5 at 30c., 4 at 35c., 18 doz. at 75c.; baskets, 6 at 75c.; brushes, ½ doz. at 2.00, 4 at 40c., 4 at 50c.; potatoes, 130 bus. at 60c., 25 bags at 90c.; matches, 1 case at 4.25; pepper, 5 lbs. at 20c.; catsup, 1 doz. at 1.50; lye, 2 doz. at 1.00; berries, 24 boxes at 8c., 25 boxes at 8c.; lemons, 6 doz. at 25c., 1 doz. at 30c.; pork and beans. 2 doz. tins at 1.00; dried apples, 25 lbs. at 7c.; biscuits, 48 lbs. at 7c., 20 lbs. at 15c., 6 lbs. at 21c.; tumblers, 3 doz. at 1.00, 2 doz. at 50c.; basket, 1 at 25c.; metal polish, 1 doz. at 2.00; mustard, 4 lbs. at 42c.; peaches, 6 bas. at 80c.; brooms, 2 doz. at 3.00; canned vegetables, 2 doz. at 85c., 2 doz. at 80c., 2 doz. at 1.10; eggs, 36 doz. at 18c., 30 doz. at 20c., 30 doz. at 22c., 156 doz. at 23c., 60 at 24c.; brooms, 2 doz. at 3.00; chloride of lime, 10 lbs. at 11c.; butter crocks, 3 at 50c.; washing soda, 1 bbl. at 9.00; Kerr's polish, 1 doz. at 2.00; candy, 50 lbs. at 8½c.; oranges, 10 doz. at 25c.; turkey, 79 lbs. at 14c.; ducks, 19¾ lbs. at 11c.; nuts, 10 lbs. at 12c., 10 lbs. at 14c., 10 lbs. at 15c.; raisins, 1 box at 3.50; ham, 28¾ lbs. at 16c.; sapolio, 1 case at 2.88 .... 1,385 60

Milson, Jno., meat, 23 lbs. at 10c., 24¼ lbs. at 12½c., 16 2-3 at 15c.; sundries, 10.00 .... 17 85

Magee, J. V., bread, 6,302½ lbs. at 2c., 126.05; Martin, W. H., fitting locks, 75c. 126 80

Marshall, Miss E. J., services, cleaning building, 2.00; McKay, Alex., freight and cartage, 1.00 .... 3 00

McKay, Wm., 1 day's work with team, 8.00; McCurdy, Jas. S., travelling expenses, 3.00 .... 11 00

McIntyre, A., spirits for medicinal purposes, 28.75; McKiggon & Davidson, repairs to conductors, 6.90 .... 35 65

McDonald, Alex., 1 stove at 22.00; hardware sundries, 2.30 .... 24 30

Osborne, A. W., work with team, 48 hrs. at 40c. 19 20

Pott, F. & Son, raisins, 28 lbs. at 8c.,; sundries, 98c.; lye, 1 doz. tins at 1.00; eggs, 30 doz. at 12½c. 7 97

Poole & Co., vegetables, 1.23; figs, 32 lbs. at 4½c.; jam, 42 lbs. at 7c.; fibre pails, 1 doz. at 4.00; brushes, 2 at 1.25; eggs, 30 doz. at 15c.; raisins, 25 lbs. at 10c.; currants, 25 lbs. at 7½c.; sundries, 2.68 .... 23 66

PUBLIC INSTITUTIONS MAINTENANCE.—*Continued.*

ASYLUM FOR EPILEPTICS.—*Continued.*

EXPENSES.—*Continued.*

Pepper, J. T., indelible ink, 3.25; beeswax, 25 lbs. at 40c.; flavoring extract, 4 lbs. at 1.00; sundries, 5.60; razor strop, 1 at 1.00; drugs, chemicals, etc., .207.90; medical appliances, 32.60; soap, 34 lbs. at 8c., 1 doz. at 1.10, 34 lbs. at 8c.; sponges, 2 at 90c.; hair brushes, 2 at 90c.	274 49
Postmaster, stamps, 69.00; rent of P.O. box, 1.50	70 50
Parker, Miss S., travelling expenses	5 50
Richard Pure Soap Co., soap, 120 lbs. at 3c., 734 lbs. at 5c., 3 doz. at 41 2-3c., 1 gross at 3.00	59 55
Ronan, Jno., travelling expenses, 65.50; Rudd, S. C., services as veterinary, 11.00	76 50
Sutherland, J. & J., stationery, etc., 85.19; football, 1 at 1.75; toilet paper, 1 case at 4.00; subscriptions to Toronto *Globe* and *Mail and Empire*, 5 mos., 3.33	94 27
Sentinel Review, advertising, 1.02; subscription, 11.90	12 92
Spracklin, J. A., horse brush, 1 at 1.50; sundries, 35c.; horse blanket, 1 at 13.00; repairs to harness, 13.20; plush rug, 1 at 4.00	31 70
Sundry newspapers, advertising *re* supplies, 72.00; advertising *re* fuel, 10.50	82 50
Free, Wallace, seed wheat, 38 bus. at 80c.; grading grounds with team, 4 days at 4.00	46 40
United Typewriter Co., 1 typewriter	120 00
White, Jno. Co., Ltd., sheeting, 33 yds. at 25c.; linen, 12 yds. at 25c.; towels, 2 doz. at 1.50; handkerchiefs, 1 doz. at 4.20; collars, 1 doz. at 1.44; sundries, 2.06; towelling, 90 yds. at 12½c.; yarn, 2 lbs. at 75c.; thimbles, 2 doz. at 50c.	35 70
Woodstock Footwear Co., rubbers, 1 pr. at 1.00; Williams, Dr. J. J., travelling expenses, 10.20; rent of house, 100.00	111 20
Woodroofe & Son, clock, 1 at 1.25; Warwick Bros. & Rutter, printing, 24.85	26 10
Wheler, G., testing flour, 1.00; Williamett, J. P.. milk, 224 qts. at 5c., 11.20; Woodstock, Express Printing Co., printing, 53.86	66 06
Woodstock Electric Ligbt Co., electric current, 269.25; Woodstock Water Works, water rates, 1,250.00; Wallace, J. G., services, purchase Dunn's farm, 51.93	1,571 18

ASYLUM FOR FEEBLE MINDED, ORILLIA.

SALARIES ($24,360.65).

A. H. Beaton, M.D.:	Twelve months' salary as	Medical Superintendent.........		2,600 00
T. J. Norman, M.D.:	do	do	Assistant Physician.............	1,000 00
T. J. Muir:	do	do	Bursar.........................	1,350 00
P. McAulay:	do	do	Storekeeper....................	900 00
A. Jamieson:	do	do	Carpenter......................	450 00
A. Thompson:	do	do	Farmer.........................	503 00
H. Kilpatrick:	do	do	Baker	450 00
J. S. Gray:	do	do	Gardener	575 00
A. Maclean:	do	do	Tailor	400 00
A. Harvie:	do	do	Mason	450 00
J. H. Ross:	do	do	Engineer.......................	800 00
A. Allen:	do	do	Assistant Engineer..............	336 00
J. H. Ball:	One	do	Farmer.........................	45 83
R. Stewart:	Twelve	do	Laundryman	336 00
A. H. Sisson:	do	do	Chief Male Attendant	400 00
Male Night Attend'ts.(2)	do	do	....	405 00
Male Attendants (13):	do	do	....	4,202 10
C. Charpentier:	do	do	Stableman......................	276 00
J. Casey:	Four and half	do	Messenger.....................	108 00
R. Anderson:	Seven and half	do	do	195 16
J. Budd:	Twelve	do	Matron........................	500 00
L. McGillicuddy:	do	do	Assistant Matron...............	300 00
J. H. Hall:	Nine	do	Musician and Stenographer......	327 40
M. V. Nash:	Twelve	do	Teacher.......................	600 00

PUBLIC INSTITUTIONS MAINTENANCE.—*Continued.*

ASYLUM FOR FEEBLE MINDED, ORILLIA.—*Continued.*

SALARIES.—*Continued.*

A. E. Connor :	Twelve months' salary as	Teacher		300 00
M. Pinkham :	do	do	do	300 00
Female Attendants (12) do	do	do		2,498 04
Cooks (2) :	do	do		309 13
E. Calverly :	Nine	do	Dairymaid	126 00
Laundresses (3) :	Twelve	do		588 00
Seamstresses (3) :	do	do		639 00
Maids (8) :	do	do		1.063 07
Firemen (3) :	do	do		971 42
Sundry persons, temporary help				56 50

EXPENSES ($51,881.42).

Allan, Jno., pigs, 5 at 3.00; **Allan, Wm.**, milch cow, 1 at 40.00		55 00
Association of Institution Feeble Minded, yearly dues		10 00
Bailey, Dr. L., vet'y. prof'l. services, 58.75; Baye, Frank, turnips, 304.35 bus. at 10c.		89 21
Ball & Co., J. F., caps, 5 doz. at 6.75; ties, 2 doz. at 1.50; collars, 8 at 25c.		38 75
Brown, S., milch cow, 1 at 49.00: Bruce, Jno. A. & Co., seeds, 42.15		91 15
Burton, J., potatoes, 202.10 bus. at 40c.; apples, 4 bbls. at 1.50		86 87
Bethune, R., tea, 198½ lbs. at 23c.; coffee, 150 lbs. at 18c.		72 66
Ball, Jas., eggs, 60 doz. at 16c., 79 doz. at 13½c., 150 doz. at 14c., 98 doz. at 15c., 76 doz. at 15½c., 297 doz. at 17c., 184 doz. at 18c., 97 doz. at 19c.		169 79
Birney, Jno. J.. services as baker, 1 day, 1.50; Brown, Jas., pigs, 5 at 3.00		16 50
Black, W. O., scuffler, 9.00; Brammer, Jas., auto spray, 7.50		16 50
Bruce, Jno. A. & Co., punk, 2 doz. boxes at 9.00; Bursar to pay sundries, 2.97		20 97
Boyd. Moses, harness repairs, 53.30; rubber rugs, 3 at 2.00		59 30
Bell Telephone Co., messages, 9.30; exchange service, 70.00		79 30
Buckingdale, A., honey, 60 lbs. at 8c.; Boyle, W. J. O., straw, 8.763 tons at 5.50		50 90
Bell, F. A., oats, 57 2-34 bus. at 40c., 22.82		22 82
Brock. W. R. Co., Ltd.. tweed, 637½ yds. at 55c.; sheeting. 326½ yds. at 18½c.; homespun, 149½ yds. at 1.10; lace curtains, 8 'for 5.00; napkins, 2 doz. at 3.00; cotton, 413½ yds. at 7¾c.. 648 7-8 yds. at 10c., 204½ yds. at 6¾c., 31½ at 17c.; silesia. 66½ yds. at 15c., 73½ yds. at 16c., 27¼ yds. at 55c.; canvas, 50 yds. at 10c., 50 yds. at 15c.; serge, 51¼ yds. at 1.75; awning stripe, 108½ yds. at 19½c.; sundries, 10.18; hose, 8 doz. at 3.00; thread. 4 gro. at 5.40; handkerchiefs. 2 doz. at 55c., 2 doz. at 70c.; drill, 69¼ yds. at 12½c.; shirting. 2,685 yds. at 11½c.; machine twist, ¼ gro. at 11.00; elastic, 6 doz. at 75c.; hosiery, 10 doz. at 2.25, 10 doz. at 3.60; buttons, 1 gro. at 1.50: mitts. 2 doz. at 3.00; towels, 1 doz. at 6.00; braid. 1¼ gro. at 3.00: ticking. 655 yds. at 20c.; warp, 6 doz. at 1.15; towelling. 46 yds. at 18½c.; gingham, 266¼ yds. at 12½c.		1.535 80
Canadian Fairbanks Co., draper facing tools, 1 set at 15.90; Canadian Express Co., express freight. 2.25		18 15
Cuppage, Alex., potatoes, 81.30 bus. at 40c., 32.60; Jas. Croil, tweed, 43. yds. at 1.90, 81.70		114 30
Crockford, J.. potatoes, 312.40 bus. at 40c., 507.20 bus. at 10c.		175 80
Canadian Oil Co.. wax, 222 lbs. at 8c.; dynamo oil, 20 gals. at 65c.; cup grease, 100 lbs. at 10c.; sundries, 1.50; oils, etc., 73.90; candles, 144 sets at 10 1-3c.		130 98
Cairns, Bernard. indelible ink, 1 pt. at 3.50: linen marker, 1 at 50c.		4 00
Clark. D., interments, 93.00; Canadian Typewriter Co., letter books, 2 at 2.25		97 50
Central Prison Industries, slippers, 10 prs. at 90c., 10 prs. at 1.00., 50 prs. at 1.20, 109 prs. at 1.40; shoes, 20 prs. at 1.85, 50 prs. at 1.80, 104 prs. at 1.20. 68 prs. at 1.40. 20 prs. at 1.00; packing. 12.20; tweed, 3.015 yds. at 55c.; yarn. 66 lbs. at 45c.; flannel, 914 yds. at 25c.; blankets, 706 lbs. at 45c.		2.844 95
Church Bros.. horseshoeing. 66.20; carriage repairs, 131.49		197 69

PUBLIC INSTITUTIONS MAINTENANCE.—*Continued.*

ASYLUM FOR FEEBLE MINDED, ORILLIA.—*Continued.*

EXPENSES.—*Continued.*

Canadian General Electric Co., electrical repairs, etc., 59.23; heating oven, 1 at 7.50; stew pans, 3 at 2.00	72	73
Cooke, A. & Co., subs'n., sundry newspapers	16	50
Canada Wood Specialty Co., lumber, 93.46; Creelman Bros., repairs to plant, 2.58	96	04
Dalley, F. F. Co., pepper, 60 lbs. at 19c.; coffee, 250 lbs. at 25c.; vanilla, 1 qt. at 2.50; lemons, 1 qt. at 2.50; shoe polish, 3 doz. at 90c.; ginger, 30 lbs. at 23c.; corn starch, 200 lbs. at 6c.; chicory, 148 lbs. at 12c.; sundries, 1.19	119	45
Dwinell, Thos. A., filling ice house, 71.25; Duncan, Wm., hay, 4.440 tons at 8.00, 33.76	105	01
Davies, Wm. Co., Ltd., bacon, 100 lbs. at 14c.; ham, 53 lbs. at 13½c.	21	16
Dunn, W., milch cow, 1 at 38.00; Downs, J., hay, 1.525 tons at 9.50, 11.99	49	99
Dunlop, Jas., milch cows, 2 at 37.50, 75.00	75	00
Ellis, J. W., yeast, 280 lbs. at 30c., 84.00; express freight, 20.33; telegrams, 2.32	106	65
Failes, Jno., cutting meat, 25.00; Forrister, W., potatoes, 90 bus. at 40c., 36.27	61	27
Fletcher, D., oats, 56 16-34 bus. at 38c., 114 14-34 bus. at 40c.	67	22
Fletcher, W. J., repairs to shoes, 105.96; Frawley, N. J., spirits for hospital comforts, 5.00	110	96
Fletcher H., oats, 90 25-34 at 40c., 36.29	36	29
Gilpin Bros., brooms, 50 doz. at 2.75, 25 doz. at 2.70, 2 doz. at 1.50, 1 doz. at 1.25; brushes, 3 doz. at 2.00, 4 at 45c., 12 at 1.75, 8 doz. at 1.75, 2 doz. at 5.50, 1 at 3.15, 1 at 1.25; paint oils, etc., 105.20; putty, 175 lbs. at 3c., 25 lbs. at 4c.; bath brick, 9 doz. at 45c.; boot soles, 5 doz. for 16.26; boot heels, 5 doz. for 4.45; sundries, 66.38; dust pans, 1 doz. at 1.45; wash boards, 2 doz. at 4.00, ½ doz. at 2.50; knives, 1 doz. at 4.70, 1 doz. at 5.40; pails, 5 doz. at 2.20, 6 only at 35c., 3 doz. at 2.00, 3 doz. at 2.25; locks, 1 doz. at 18.00, 2 only at 70c., 5 only at 40c.; football, 1 only at 2.00; shovels, ½ doz. at 12.00, 2 only at 1.00, 1 doz. at 9.50; carvers, 3 prs. at 1.75; spoons, 1 doz. at 4.25; hair clippers, 3 prs. at 2.50; baskets, 2 doz. at 11.00, ⅓ doz. at 10.00; hampers, 2 at 2.25; sheet rubber, 21 lbs. at 35c.; whips, 3 only at 70c.; Paris green, 15 lbs. at 18c.; saws, 1 at 1.45; mops, 2 doz. at 1.50; garden shears, 1 pr. at 1.00; nails, 6 kegs at 2.20, 10 kegs at 2.60; fire bricks, 300 at 3.50; fire clay, 1 sack at 1.50; asbestos cement, 14 sacks at 2.75; alabastine, 140 lbs. at 7c.; glass, 3 cases at 4.25, 4 panes at 1.00; shears, 3 prs. at 75c.; preserving kettles, 2 at 1.50; hammers, 1 at 1.25, 3 only at 45c.; vise, 1 at 1.25; glue, 10 lbs. at 12c.; salt and pepper castors, 1 doz. at 1.10; wire, 32½ lbs. at 3½c.; Maple Leaf taps, 3 doz. at 3.25; lifts, 6 bags at 1.00; iron, 100 lbs. at 3c.; blue stone packing, 3 15-16 lbs. at 75c.; screw drivers, 3 at 40c.; asbestos sheet, 303 lbs. at 7c.; wire lath, 220 ft. at 16c.; bath bricks, 2 doz. at 55c.; razors, 2 at 1.50; rope, 29½ lbs. at 14c.; cake mixer, 1 at 2.75; milk pans, 1 doz. at 4.20; leather belting, 50 ft. at 17c.; packing, 9 1-8 lbs. at 95c.; grease cups, 6 only at 1.00, 2 only at 1.20; turpentine, 5 gals. at 95c.; skates, 2 doz. at 5.90; pipe cutter, 1 at 2.25, 1 at 3.25; cylinder lubricators, 3 only at 2.16 2-3; valves, 6 at 33 1-3c.; sleighs, 3 at 85c.; raisin seeder, 1 at 1.75; axes, 2 at 1.08	893	97
Grand Trunk Ry., freight, 122.01; electric wire, 1.00	123	01
Goss, Thos., hay, 11.139 tons at 7.50, 87.73; Gurney Foundry Co., repairs to range, 36.36	124	09
Geron, M., Delsarte entertainer, 1 at 2.10; sheet music, 1.32	3	42
Gammon, Owen, pigs, 6 only at 2.50, 15.00; Gallivan, Jno., straw, 1.130 tons at 5.50	20	86
Gellathy, A., oats, 64 19-34 bus. at 43c., 27.76; Gammon, Fred., straw, 2.490 tons at 5.50	40	11
Gale & Sons, Geo., assorted wires, 50 lbs. at 6.00 cwt.	3	00
Haywood, Thos., granite saucers, 6 doz. at 30 1-3c.; tea, 400 lbs. at 18c., 1,548 lbs. at 22½c.; figs, 1,661 lbs. at 4¾c.; prunes, 1,000 lbs. at 7½c.; syrup, 410 gals. at 37c.; apricots, 50 lbs. at 14c.; currants, 299 lbs. at 7 3-8c., 66⅓ lbs. at 7c.; starch, 190 lbs. at 5½c., 100 lbs. at 7c., 240 lbs.		

PUBLIC INSTITUTIONS MAINTENANCE.—*Continued.*

ASYLUM FOR FEEBLE MINDED, ORILLIA.—*Continued.*

EXPENSES.—*Continued.*

at 5¾c.; evap. apples, 100 lbs. at 11¾c.; sundries, 7.30; corn starch, 200 lbs. at 6c.; soap, 100 lbs. at 6½c., 8,516 lbs. at 5½c.; coffee, 1,000 lbs. at 24c.; ginger, 5 lbs. at 30c.; chicory, 483 lbs. at 10c.; molasses, 127 gals. at 35c.; jelly powder, 2 doz. at 2.00; raisins, 28 lbs. at 6c.; blue, 10 lbs. at 16c.; lemons, 3 cases at 5.00; cinnamon, 2 lbs. at 50c.; cherries, 4 bus. at 1.25; sapolio, 1 doz. at 1.10; biscuits, 17 lbs. at 8½c.; sal soda, 11,250 lbs. at 84c. cwt.; baking powder, 150 lbs. at 42c.	1,819 45
Hatley, Jas. J., fish, 74 lbs. at 9c., 790 lbs. at 10c.; ham, 32 lbs. at 15c., 13 lbs. at 16c., 12 lbs. at 16½c.; sausage, 121 lbs. at 10c., 152 lbs. at 11c.; meat, 1,041 lbs. at 7.20; pork, 1,336 lbs. at 7.20; mutton, 270 lbs. at 7.20; lard, 665 lbs. at 14c., 100 lbs. at 13c., 300 lbs. at 13½c., 400 lbs. at 12½c.; bacon, 80¾ lbs. at 16c., 68 lbs. at 17c., 34 lbs. at 18c., 43 lbs. at 20c.; tongue, 6 only at 40c.; chicken, 32½ lbs. at 11c., 8¼ lbs. at 15c.; sundries, 3.68; veal, 373 lbs. at 7.20; lamb, 327 lbs. at 23.56; turkey, 105 lbs. at 15c.; duck, 30½ lbs. at 12½c., 1 pr. at 1.30; milch cow, 1 only at 40.00	8,097 95
Hern, Jno., yarn, 54 lbs. at 45c., 24 lbs. at 50c., 97 lbs. at 47½c.	82 37
Hartt, J. I., potatoes, 202 15-60 bus. at 40c., 80.90; Horne, Wm., potatoes, 112 bus. at 40c., 44.80	125 70
Hazlett, Jno., pigs, 7 only for 18.00; turkeys, 224 lbs. at 14c.; ducks, 37 lbs. at 11c.; geese, 48 lbs. at 12c.	59 19
Harvie, Russell, recovering eloper, 2.00; Hewitt, J., turnips, 154 10-60 bus. at 10c.	17 42
Harvie, W., milch cow, 1 only at 39.00, 2 only at 40.00	119 00
Hedley, Shaw Milling Co., flour, 1,357¼ bbls. at 3.80	5,158 50
Harvie, D. M., apples, 6 bbls. at 1.50, 9 bbls. at 1.10; milch cow, 1 at 40.00	58 90
Hall Bros., printing, 50.25; Harvey, Jno. G., disinfectant, 40 gals. at 1.25, 50.00	100 25
Hazlett, Wm., milch cow, 1 only, at 35.00; exchange on cow, 12.00	47 00
Harvie, S. C., straw, 3.190 tons at 5.50	17 02
Imperial Chemical Co., cylinder oil, 47 gals. at 60c.; cup grease, 75 lbs. at 7c.	33 45
Johnston, Jas., straw, 2.1360 tons at 5.50; apples, 2 bbls. at 1.25; oats, 119 16-34 bus. at 38c.	62 30
Johnston, Robert, potatoes, 167.2 bus. at 40c., 66.82; Jones Underfeed Stoker Co., overhauling and repairing 2 stokers, 420.00	486 82
Jupp, R. H. & Co., clocks, 1 at 8.50, 1 at 6.50; repairing clocks, 1.25	16 25
Kenny, T. & Co., tea, 780 lbs. at 22c., 171.60; King's Printer, stationery, 40.50	212 10
Kingston Asylum, brushes, 5 doz. at 3.00	15 00
Kane & Kane, farmer's satin, 6 yds. at 75c.; lining, 6 yds. at 25c.; canvas, 12 yds. at 20c., 7 yds. at 15c.; silk twist, 1 box at 2.25; thread, 9 gro. at 5.40, 36 doz. at 45c., 1 lb. at 3.20, 1 lb. at 2.90; buttons, 3 gro. at 1.25, 12 gro. at 75c., 5¼ doz. at 75c., 12 gro. at 1.00, ½ gro. at 9.00, ½ gro. at 4.20, 1 gro. at 1.50; cotton, 848 yds. at 9c., 1,209 yds. at 10½c., 100 yds. at 14c., 159 yds. at 14½c.; ticking, 536½ yds. at 17c.; shirting, 1,137¾ yds. at 12.¾c.; denim, 34½ yds. at 17½c.; mole, 160 yds. at 20½c., 38 yds. at 16½c.; table oil, 12 pcs. at 2.50; dry good sundries, 14.33; moccasins, 24 prs. at 1.58, 2 prs. at 1.25; chicory, 134 lbs. at 11c.; coffee, 250 lbs. at 28c.; biscuits, 17½ lbs. at 7½c.; book and eye, 1 gro. at 3.00; tape, 6 doz. at 40c.; salt, 13 bbls. at 1.50; warp, 15 lbs. at 25c., 20 lbs. at 30c., 30 lbs. at 28c., 3 bunches at 1.40; sheeting, 532½ yds. at 19½c., 1,004½ yds. at 19½c.; yarn, 6 spools at 2.40; hosiery, 8 doz. at 2.70, 4 doz. at 5.10; laces, 1 gro. at 2.75; boots, 1 pr. at 1.75, 2 prs. at 2.00, 11 prs. at 1.50; gingham, 834 yds. at 12¾c.; linen, 136 yds. at 17½c., 112 yds. at 12½c.; towelling, 139 yds. at 20c., 50 yds. at 12½c.; cretonne, 32 yds. at 18¾c.; pocketting, 12 yds. at 12½c.; stay binding, 12 yds. at 15c.; table oil, 8 pcs. at 2.50; towels, 3 doz. at 2.75; eggs, 247 doz. at 18c., 49 doz. at 13½c., 98 doz. at 19c., 196 doz. at 17c.; corsets, 11 prs. at 50c.; sapolio, 1 doz. at 1.20; pins, 4 doz. at 25c.; grocery sundries, 1.33; sugar, 1,000 lbs. at 4.00, 200 lbs. at 4.40;	

PUBLIC INSTITUTIONS MAINTENANCE.—*Continued.*

ASYLUM FOR FEEBLE MINDED, ORILLIA.—*Continued.*

EXPENSES.—*Continued.*

bats, 5 doz. at 1.35; flannel, 89½ yds. at 25c.; table linen, 26 yds. at 1.10; napkins, 2 doz. at 3.25; handkerchiefs, 6 doz. at 85c.; mitts, 6 doz. at 3.25; muslin, 92¾ yds. at 10c.; hoods, 8 only at 50c.	1,774 68
Leigh, I., hay, 4.1413 tons at 8.00; straw, 4.420 tons at 5.00	62 80
Leigh, A., hay, 3.1005 tons at 7.00, 24.52; Langman, J. G., milch cow, 1 only at 40.00	64 52
Long, The E. Mfg. Co., repairs to tube expander, 4.00; Leskey, Wm., pigs, 17 at 2.50	46 50
Midland Coal Dock Co., coal, 138.1300 tons at 5.90, 2,396.889 tons at 3.25	8,606 48
Medcalf, D. M., travelling expenses, *re* boiler inspection	19 35
Martin, J., turnips, 221.40 bus. at 10c., 22.17; Moriarty, J., turnips, 40.40 bus. at 10c.	26 24
Mullett & Anthony, knife, 1 only at 1.00; twine, 3 balls at 60c., 2.80; Macnab Bros., grates, 1 set at 6.50	9 30
Murphy, Jno., turnips, 177¼ bus. at 10c., 461 bus. at 10c.; potatoes, 315 bus. at 40c.	189 83
Moore, Chris. Co., Ltd., butter, 780 lbs. at 21¾c., 169.65; Murdock, Jas., inspecting scales, 8.50	178 15
Matthews, Geo. Co., Ltd., lard, 20 lbs. at 11½c., 50 lbs. at 12½c., 100 lbs. at 12¾c.; ham, 41 lbs. at 16c.; sundries, 40c.; bacon, 102 lbs. at 18c.	46 62
Morton, David & Sons, Ltd., soap, 200 boxes at 2.40, 480.00; Murphy, Dennis, milch cow, 1 at 45.00; Murphy, John, milch cow, 1 at 40.00	565 00
McPherson, Chas., repairs to vehicles, 5.15; McGinn, Wm., boots and shoes, 24 prs. at 2.60, 10 prs. at 3.00, 8 prs. at 1.80; packing, 90c.	112 85
McGuire, I., travelling expenses, 6.70; McLeod, M., potatoes, 269.20 bus. at 40c., 107.73	114 43
McPhee, A., turkeys, 336 lbs. at 14c.; ducks, 66 lbs. at 11c.; 59 14-34 bus. at 38c. (oats)	76 88
McReynolds, T., music supplied, 15.00; admission of patients to circus, 22.00	37 00
McLean, D., milch cow, 1 only at 40.00; McKinley, D. M., stabling for horses, 1 yr., 36.00	76 00
McFadden, W. J., drugs and chemicals, 128.11; medical appliances, 1.00	129 11
Northway Co., Ltd., table linen, 43¼ yds. at 72c.; yarn, 96 lbs. at 45c., 3 lbs. at 75c.; thread, 2 gro. at 5.40, 25 doz. at 48c.; shoe laces, 1 gro. at 1.75; collars, 3 doz. at 1.35; linen, 261 yds. at 16c.; towelling, 83¾ yds. at 13½c., 999 at 13c.; corn starch, 200 lbs. at 6c.; laundry starch, 219 lbs. at 5½c.; sugar, 2,000 lbs. at 4.08, 20 bags at 3.88, 8 bags at 4.28, 2,000 lbs. at 3.98, 10 bags at 4.43, 20 bags at 4.03, 10 bags at 3.95, 2,000 lbs. at 4.13, 2,500 at 4.23; boots, 7 prs. at 1.75, 4 prs. at 2.00, 7 prs. at 1.50, 12 prs. at 1.60; moccasins, 3 prs. at 1.00, 1 pr. at 1.25, 6 prs. at 1.15; sundries, 24.83; corset steels, 1 doz. at 1.20; eggs, 256 doz. at 16c., 98 doz. at 15c., 98 doz. at 15½c., 49 doz. at 19c.; shirting, 184¾ yds. at 12¾c., 220¼ yds. at 12½c.; cotton, 25 yds. at 10c., 62¼ yds. at 13c., 25 yds. at 8c.; prunes, 300 lbs. at 6½c., 125 lbs. at 7½c.; figs, 64 lbs. at 4½c.; evap. apples, 100 lbs. at 10½c.; apricots, 50 lbs. at 14c.; hosiery, 5 doz. at 4.80, 2 prs. at 35c., 2 doz. at 3.00, 14 7-12 doz. at 96c., 5 doz. at 1.80; print, 10 yds. at 12c., 25¼ yds. at 8c.; corsets, 6 prs. at 50c.; window shade cloth, 200 yds. at 15½c.; crash, 293½ yds. at 13c.; pins, 4 doz. at 50c.; serge, 7 yds. at 50c.; honey, 60 lbs. at 11c., 25 lbs. at 14c.; lace, 6 doz. yds. at 60c., 10 yds. at 25c.; mufflers, 1 doz. at 2.75; ties, 2¼ doz. at 1.50; handkerchiefs, 20 doz. at 30c., 8 doz. at 60c., 8 doz. at 1.20; vests, 6 at 70c., 4 at 50c.; mitts, 3 doz. 10c., 101¾ yds. at 10½c.; rubbers, 12 prs. at 77c.	1,438 44
Northern Electric Supply Co., northern lamps, 250 at 15c.,	37 50
Nash, M. V., travelling expenses	5 25
Nerlich & Co., body protector, 4.50; baseball bats, 1-6 doz. at 8.40, ¼ doz. at 12.00	8 90
Ontario Reformatory for Females, shoes, 56 prs. at 1.00, 1 pr. at 1.25	57 25
Orillia, Town of, motor power, 1,323.59; Orillia Harness Co., repairs to harness, 1.30	1,324 89

PUBLIC INSTITUTIONS MAINTENANCE.—*Continued.*

ASYLUM FOR FEEBLE MINDED, ORILLIA.—*Continued.*

EXPENSES.—*Continued.*

O'Connor, P., turnips, 110.10 bus. at 10c., 11.02; O'Connor, C., turnips, 108 bus. at 10c., 10.80	21 82
Orillia Hardware Co., babbit metal, 10 lbs. at 15c.; asbestos, 18 lbs. at 10c., 3 sacks at 2.00; steam hose, 18 ft. at 35c.; packing, 5 ft. at 1.20, 3 lbs. at 55c., 10 lbs. at 50c.; glue, 5 lbs. at 22c.; brace, 1 at 2.50; cement, 5 bbls. at 2.00; octagon steel, 7 lbs. at 15c.; spirit level, 1 at 1.25; locks, 1 doz. at 4.25, 1 doz. at 1.20, 1½ doz. at 4.00; drawer pulls, 3 at 50c.; door checks, ½ doz. at 2.80, 5 only at 1.40; pig lead, 97 lbs. at 7c.; gate valve, 1 at 8.75; copper seal valves, 4 at 4.35; glass, 2 lights at 57½c., 12 lights for 1.92; razor strops, 3 only at 35c.; whiting, 50 lbs. at 2.00; sundries, 35.38; matches, 1 case at 3.60; refrigerator, 1 at 15.00; rope, 12 hank at 25c.; hay forks, 3 only at 50c.; hay rakes, 3 at 30c., 3 at 20c.; carvers, 4 prs. for 5.95; snips, 1 pr. at 1.50; screws, 2 gro. at 70c.; circular gaskets, 500 only for 18.00; lace leather, 6 lbs. at 85c.; castings, 24 lbs. at 9c.; carvers, 2 sets at 1.65; paint, oils, etc., 35.87; pail, 1 at 3.00; oat boiler, 1 at 2.25; mitts, 1 doz. at 4.50; cupboard turns, 2 doz. at 1.85; baskets, 4 only at 65c.; stove, 1 at 7.00; repairs, 27.80; auger, 1 at 1.25	294 92
Polson Iron Works, manhole gaskets, 1 doz. at 15.00; repairs to boilers, 157.91; tubes, 448 lbs. at 20c.	262 51
Pilkington Bros., glass, 22.85; Perryman, J., oats, 78 8-34 bus. at 40c., 31.30	54 15
Perryman, Wm., turkeys, 314 lbs. at 14c.; geese, 50 lbs. at 12c.	49 96
Postmaster, postage stamps, 136.00; rent of P. O. box, 2.00	138 00
Pomeroy, S., lavatory seats, 18 for 4.50; planing lumber, 3.75; lumber, 21.43; birch rollers, 3 at 1.90	31 58
Palmer & Co., fish, 292 lbs. at 9c., 641¼ at 10c., 4 doz. at 1.75, 12 doz. at 1.50	115 41
Phillips & Co., repairs to tinware, etc., 59.92; sundries, 17.27; wash basins, 6 at 28c.; teapots, 2 at 1.25; lanterns, 1 at 1.45, 3 at 40c.; bread pans, 1 doz. at 9.60, 1 doz. at 1.80; creamer cans, 2 at 75c.; making and fitting ventilation pipe, 11.00; tin pitchers, 6 at 75c.; pans, 3 at 1.50, 6 at 75c.; covers for kettles, 3 for 10.15; electric light shades, 8 at 1.00	139 57
Parsons, H., bowls, 2 doz. at 85c., 1 doz. at 60c., ½ doz. at 1.75, 3 doz. at 1.20; plates, 5 1-6 doz. for 3.62, 18 doz. at 60c., 2 doz. at 1.10, 2 doz. at 1.20, 2 doz. at 1.15, 1 doz. at 1.80; cups, 25 doz. at 47c., 2 doz. at 80c., 12 doz. at 1.10, 25 doz. at 65c., 2 doz. at 1.20; saucers, 25 doz. at 23c., 2 doz. at 40c., 25 doz. at 35c.; ewers, 12 at 45c.; tumblers, 12 at 50c.; sundries, 19.43; chambers, 5 doz. at 4.20; cuspidors, 6 only at 45c.; pans, 6 at 30c.; vegetable dishes, 2 at 98c., 6 at 45c.; jugs, 1 doz. at 1.65, 9 only at 58c., 9 only at 65c.; mouth organs, 6 only at 45c., 1 doz. at 1.10, 8 doz. at 55c.; milk pans, ½ doz. at 3.00, ¼ doz. at 3.35; dish pans, ¼ doz. at 10.80; dippers, 1 doz. at 1.70; tea set, 1 at 14.85; platters, 1 at 1.25, 1 at 49c.; books, 29.72; watches, 2 doz. at 1.00; dolls, 3 doz. at 50c., 3 doz. at 1.00; brooches, 2¾ doz. at 1.00, 1¾ doz. at 1.20	236 11
Palmer, G. E., raisins, 140 lbs. at 10½c.; starch, 42 lbs. at 6½c., 100 lbs. at 6¾c.; prunes, 500 lbs. at 7c.; sapolio, 1 doz. at 1.20; sundries, 1.80; fruit peel, 2 lbs. at 30c., 4 lbs. at 25c.; jelly powder, 1 doz. at 1.10; icing sugar, 20 lbs. at 8c.; shelled almonds, 3 lbs. at 40c.; candies, 200 lbs. at 7½c.; mixed nuts, 100 lbs. at 15c.; currants, 126 lbs. at 9c.; corn starch, 123 lbs. at 6¼c., 200 lbs. at 6¾c.	130 21
Rice, Lewis & Son, lawn mowers, 4 only at 4.65½, 2 only at 9.26½; boiler tubes, 530 ft. for 114.27	151 42
Robinson, R. A., cartage, 3.50; Regan, M. S., potatoes, 70 35-60 bus. at 40c.; turnips, 212 25 bus. at 10c.	52 98
Regan, P. potatoes, 48.30 bus. at 40c.; turnips, 172.40 bus. at 10c.	36 67
Regan, Jno. R., milch cows, 2 at 35.00; straw, 4.1005 tons at 5.50	94 76
Regan, Daniel, straw, 5.1590 tons at 5.00; turnips, 102 bus. at 10c.	39 18
Riordan, M., milch cow, 1 at 38.00; potatoes, 41.20 bus. at 40c.	54 53
Regan, Thos., hay, 1.1940 tons at 5.50, 2.890 tons at 7.00; potatoes, 212.25 bus. at 40c.; turnips, 261 10-60 bus. at 10c.	139 04

PUBLIC INSTITUTIONS MAINTENANCE.—*Continued.*

ASYLUM FOR FEEBLE MINDED, ORILLIA.—*Continued.*

EXPENSES.—*Continued.*

Rutherford, M., straw, 3.325 tons at 5.50	17 40
Sarjeant, The Co., fire brick, 300 at 2.80; plaster paris, 1 bbl. at 2.50; cement, 2 bbls. at 2.00; fire clay, 125 lbs. for 1.00; lime, 1,600 lbs. at 35c., 700 lbs. at 33c.; hair, 3 bus. at 25c.; tile, 200 at 3.60	31 76
Sundry newspapers, advertising *re* supplies, 118.00; *re* fuel. 20.50	138 50
Street, Geo., plants, 21.30; Smith, G., rent of pasture, 100.00	121 30
Smith, E. D., jam, 18 tins at 50c., 1 pail at 2.28	11 28
Shaw, R. S., tuning pianos, 6.00; subscriptions sundry magazines. 10.00	16 00
Slaven's Drug Store, stationery, 51.83; drugs and chemicals, 311.33; sundries, 22.69; toilet paper, 2 cases at 6.00. 12.00; sal soda. 8.250 at 85c.	468 03
Swinton, Wm. Music Hall, repairs to instruments, 3.45; machine needles, 6 doz. at 25c.; violin bow, 1 at 1.00; sheet music, 2.75; machine belts, 3 only at 15c., 45c.	9 15
Shaw, T., hay, 1.420 tons at 9.50; oats, 75 10-34 bus. at 40c.	41 62
Sinclair & Co., pickles, 12 bots. at 15c.; oranges, 15 doz. at 20c., 7 doz. at 30c.; lemons, 6 doz. at 20c., 3 doz. at 25c.; candy, 15 lbs. at 15c.; jelly powder, 2 doz. at 1.00; sugar, 16 lbs. at 8c., 600 lbs. at 4.53, 4,500 lbs. at 4.00, 1,500 lbs. at 4.73, 1,500 lbs. at 4.33; sundries, 32.28; beans, 2 bus. at 2.00; pepper, 30 lbs. at 18c., 34½ lbs. at 20c.; tobacco, 60 lbs. at 49c., 60 lbs. at 44c.; apricots, 25 lbs. at 15c., 25 lbs. at 17c.; sardines, 50 boxes at 9c.; biscuits, 104¾ lbs. at 7½c.; blue, 10 lbs. at 18c.; fish, 25 lbs. at 9c.; soap, 5 boxes at 4.25, 2 boxes at 4.50; prunes, 50 lbs. at 10c.; mustard, 6 jars at 90c.; sapolio, 1 doz. at 1.20, 1 doz. at 1.08; bath brick, 4 doz. at 50c.; sugar, 2,000 lbs. at 3.95, 600 lbs. at 4.33; ginger, 5 lbs. at 35c.; rice, 200 lbs. at 4c.; vanilla, 1 doz. at 2.00; peaches, 12 bas. at 80c., 1 bas. at 55c.; cherries, 2 bas. at 1.25; pears, 6 bas. at 65c., 6 bas. at 70c.; plums, 4 bas. at 80c.; peaches, 12 bas. at 65c.; gelatine, 1 doz. pkgs. at 1.50; matches, 2 cases at 4.00; corn starch, 80 pkgs. at 7c.	771 88
Tellier, Rothwell & Co., bark extract, 500 lbs. at 3½c., 17.50; Taylor Co., Jno., soap, 2 boxes at 3.25, 6.50	24 00
Telfer Bros., raisins, 28 lbs. at 6c.; split peas, 2 bags at 2.30; molasses, 26 gals. at 30c.; barley, 2 bags at 2.15; cheese, 148 lbs. at 12c.; Ideal blue, 10 lbs. at 14c.; corn meal, 2 bags at 1.75; currants, 149 lbs. at 6c.; sundries, 4.50; beans, 29 bus. at 1.60; biscuit, 35½ lbs. at 6½c.; rice, 1,000 lbs. at 3.90; vinegar, 79½ gals. at 22c.; tapioca, 179 lbs. at 6¾c.	171 75
Thompson. D. C., bran. 12 000 lbs. at 90c. 6,000 lbs. at 1.05, 1,200 lbs. at 1.00. 6,815 lbs. at 18.00, 1.300 at 19.00, 1.300 lbs. at 20.00; shorts. 3.500 lbs. at 1.00, 1,500 lbs. at 1.05. 5.100 lbs. at 1.10; rolled oats, 41 bbls. at 4.75; crushed oats, 1 ton at 25.00. 1¼ tons at 26.00	628 78
Thomson, A., milch cow. 1 only at 38.00; pigs. 13 only at 3.00. 77.00; Thomson, R.. oats, 112 2-34 bus. at 42c. 47.06	124 06
Thomson. Jas., apples. 10 bbls. at 80c., 2½ bbls. at 1.50, 11.75; Thomson, M. H., services as nurse. 37.00	48 75
Tudhope Carriage Co., repairs to vehicles	4 00
Vickers, Geo., table linen, 18 yds. at 48c.; toques, 2 only at 25c.; thread, 18 doz. at 45c.; ties, 5 doz. at 1.50; warp, 3 pkgs. at 1.35	28 79
Walker Bros., repairs to engine. 6.66; repairs to implements, 15.06	21 72
Warwick Bros. & Rutter, printing. 3.10; Wheler, G.. testing flour, 1.00	4 10
White, G. H., paints, oils, etc.. 65.73; steel, 8 lbs. at 15c.; dishes, 24 only at 5c., 24 only at 7c.; gaskets, 400 only at 4½c.; gauge glasses, 18 only at 10c.; galvanized pipe, 211 ft. at 9c.; spirit level. 1 only at 1.90; ratchet brace, 1 only at 1.25; drawer pulls. 3 doz. at 60c.; locks, 6 only at 75c.; graphite. 5 lbs. at 35c.; valves. 12 only at 50c.. 6 only at 90c.; canvas belting. 26 ft. at 15c.; saw vise, 1 only at 1.00; Stanley jointer, 1 only at 3.75; mitre box. 1 only at 14.50; sundries. 7.20	161 55
Wigg, H., straw. 2 1760 tons at 5.00; turnips. 229 bus. at 10c.	37 30
Willard & Co., butter, 27,120 lbs. at 20c.. 4.021 lbs. at 23½c.; lard, 50 lbs. at 11½c.	6,374 71
Wilson, Jno., seeds, 14.14; barley. 100 lbs. at 2½c.; cranberries, 12 qts. at 12½c.; linseed meal, 50 lbs. at 4c.; prunes, 150 lbs. at 7c., 50 lbs. at 7¼c.;	

PUBLIC INSTITUTIONS MAINTENANCE.—*Continued.*

ASYLUM FOR FEEBLE MINDED, ORILLIA.—*Continued.*

EXPENSES.—*Continued.*

salt, 24 bbls. at 1.50; rock salt, 100 lbs. for 1.50; sugar, 648 lbs. at 3.48 cwt.; rice, 2,600 lbs. at 4c.; lemons, 16 doz. at 20c., 7 doz. at 25c.; beans, 2 bus. at 2.15; oranges, 3 doz. at 25c., 21 doz. at 30c., 6 doz. at 40c.; fish, 15 lbs. at 8½c., 1 keg at 7.50; potatoes, 4 bags at 1.10; sundries, 3.64	239 79
Woods, S., turnips, 152.25 bus. at 10c., 15.24; Wood, W. Lloyd, drugs and chemicals, 1.55	16 79
World Furnishing Co., interments, 96.00; shade cloth, 6 yds. at 30c.; felt carpet, 5 yds. at 25c.; mirror plate, 1 only at 75c.; furniture covering, 2¼ yds. at 2.00; chairs, 4 only at 2.75; repairs to furniture, 29.06	144 86
Wright, Jno., pigs, 7 only at 2.50, 17.50; Wright, S., potatoes, 537 bus. at 85c.. 457.25	474 75
York, Peter, fish, 124¼ lbs. at 7c., 8.72; Young, S. J., board for 3 months, 15.00	23 72

MEDICAL RELIEVING OFFICER ($333.33).

St. Charles, W. P., Four months' salary as Relieving Officer	333 33

CENTRAL PRISON.

SALARIES ($30,379.46).

J. T. Gilmour, M.D.: Twelve months' salary as		Warden	2,750 00
M. Logan:	do	Deputy Warden	1,200 00
W. Sloan M.D.:	do	Physician	1,000 00
A. Jaffray:	do	Bursar	1,350 00
W. Arthur:	do	Storekeeper	800 00
G. W. Edgar:	do	Clerk	1,100 00
T. G. Crossen:	do	Stenographer	600 00
F. W. Lyons:	do	Sergeant	900 00
M. Clancy:	do	Foreman	599 00
A. Sangster:	do	Cook	700 00
W. Crackle:	do	Mason	700 00
W. R. Hardy:	do	Carpenter	600 00
Thos. Gill:	do	Janitor	420 00
E. A. Hammond:	do	Steamfitter	800 00
W. R. Hardy:	do	Guard foreman	75 00
Guards (27)	do		16,286 93
Sundry persons, temporary help			498 53

EXPENSES ($32,015.46).

Ashdown, Jno. baskets. 1 at 1.25, 2 at 1.00, 3.25	3 25
Atteaux Dyestuff & Chemical Co., soap clippings, 850 lbs. at 3½	29 75
Adams Furniture Co., oak diners, 48 at 1.25	60 00
Brock & Co., W. R., crash, 550 yds. at 8c., 250 yds. at 9½c., 427½ yds. at 10c.; shirts. 1 doz. at 6.41, 3 at 6.41 1-3. 19 at 6.75. 4 at 7.12¼. 2 at 6.41 1-6: cotton, 292½ yds. at 12c.; sundries, 14.38; handkerchiefs, 10 doz. at 50c.; mitts, 5 doz. at 2.85	403 43
Bruce, Jno. A. & Co., seeds, 27.45; Bramford, Jas., apples, 2 bbls. at 2.25, 4.50	31 95
Bursar, to pay sundries. 5.77; Bond, Robt., livery hire, 1.50	7 27
Burnham, Dr. G. H., professional services, 5.00; Bell telephone Co., exchange service. 95.25; messages, 10c.	100 35
Bingham's Pharmacy, drugs, chemicals, etc., 76.95; Bourdon, W. J., hats, 13 at 3.00, 39.00	115 85
Central Prison Industries, 7,867 lbs. soap at 1¼c., 1 box at 3.75, 750 lbs. at 1.00; beds, 1 at 5.12, 11 at 5.25; clothing repairs, 1,346.96; repairs to	

PUBLIC INSTITUTIONS MAINTENANCE.—*Continued.*

CENTRAL PRISON.—*Continued.*

EXPENSES.—*Continued.*

buildings, etc., 1,462.08; dish pans, 4 at 70c.; clothing, dry goods, shoes, etc., 3,688.63	6,692 59
Caulfield, Burns & Gibson, mitts, 8 1-3 doz. at 2.85; Consumers' Gas Co., gas, 396.76	420 51
Canadian General Electric Co., electrical repairs, 10.28; Canada Paper Co., toilet paper, 50 rms. for 36.36	46 64
C. P. R. Telegraph Co., messages, 3.41; Canada Paint Co., paint, oils, etc., 3.92	7 33
Canadian Express Co., express freight, 40c	40
Club Coffee Co., pepper, 80 lbs. at 18c.; baking soda, 5 lbs. at 3c., 20 lbs. at 5c.; cocoanut, 28 lbs. at 18c.; sundries, 30c.; corn starch, 40 lbs. at 6½c.; coffee, 625 lbs. at 16c., 350 lbs. at 26c.; tea, 300 lbs. at 25c.; flavoring extract, 6 lbs. at 60c., 1 pk. a 60c.; jam, 50 lbs. at 6½c.; jelly powders, 4 doz. at 85c	293 84
Consumers' Gas Co., gas, 107.76; City Water Works, dept., water, 155.03	263 39
Davidson & Hay, rice, 600 lbs. for 22.05, 900 lbs. at 3¾c.; sugar, 2,250 lbs, at 3.73, 1,200 at 3.83, 900 at 4.13, 600 at 4.23; syrup, 1,505 lbs. at 2 7-8c.; canned vegetables, 2 doz. at 85c., 2 doz. at 62½c., 4 doz. at 95c., 2 doz. at 1.30, 2 doz. at 1.35; currants, 63 lbs. at 6½c.; cheese, 37 lbs. at 14½c.; raisins, 28 lbs. at 9½c., 25 lbs. at 11c.; tobacco, 262 lbs. at 66c., 88 lbs. at 65 1-3c.; sundries, 18.10; evap. apples, 50 lbs. at 10¾c.; pails, 4 doz. at 1.85; brushes, 3 doz. at 1.00, 8 doz. at 1.25; baking powder, 6 doz. at 1.20; jelly powders, 3 doz. at 90c.; corn starch, 40 lbs. at 7c.; blacking, 3 doz. at 90c.; pepper, 70 lbs. at 19c.; brooms, 6 doz. at 2.50; cream tartar, 10 lbs. at 25c.; canned fruit, 2 doz. at 2.50; prunes, 110 lbs. at 6½c.; biscuit, 20 lbs. at 21c	653 42
Dominion Express Co., charges, 80c.; Doyle Fish Co., fish, 2,767 lbs. at 7½c., 207.53	208 33
Dominion Radiator Co., repairs to radiator, 1.80; Davies, Wm. Co., sausage, 425 lbs. at 11c., 50 lbs. at 8 1-3c., 50.91	52 71
Detective Pub. Co., subn. 1 year, 1.00; Detective Duncan, recapturing, escaped prisoners, 10.00	11 00
Fairles Milling Co., rolled wheat, 17 bbls. at 2.40, 42 bbls. at 2.50, 20 bbls. at 2.70; roll oats, 31½ bbls. at 5.20, 18 bags at 2.60; split peas, 44 bags at 2.25, 9½ bbls. at 4.50; pot barley, 5 bags at 2.20	574 40
Fleischmann & Co., yeast, 325 lbs. at 30c., 67.50; G. N. W. Telegraph Co., messages, 5.49	72 99
Grand & Toy, printing, stationery, &c., 36.00; Gray, F. A., drugs and chemicals, 59.30	95 30
Gurney Foundry Co., baker's oven grates, 4 at 2.50	10 00
Gilmour, Dr. J. T., travelling expenses, 116.10; Goodfellow, J., livery hire, 2.00	118 10
Grand Trunk Railway, freight, 19.00; repairs to siding, 824.92	843 92
Gunns, Ltd., beans, 26 bus. at 1.75c.; eggs, 60 doz. at 16c.; lard, 50 lbs. at 10¾c., 60 lbs. at 11½.; salt, 4 sacks, at 40c., 4 sacks at 50c., 80 sacks at 1.10; sausages, 400 lbs. at 11c., 25 lbs. at 7c., pork, 8 bbls. at 23.00	319 43
Globe Printing Co., subn.. 2 copies for 1 yr., 10.00; Golden's livery hire, 8.75	18 75
Gourlay, Winter & Leaming, organ rent, 24.00	24 00
Hunter & Smith, repairs to vehicles, 2.50	2 50
Hortop, Jas. A., chop feed, 1,000 lbs. at 1.40; oats, 105 bus. at 40c., 50 bus. at 42; bran, 1 ton at 20.00; 1 ton at 22.00; crushed oats, 1 ton at 26.00, 1,500 lbs. at 27.00	165 25
Harvey, Jno. G., disinfectant, 52 gals. at 1.25, 65.00; Harris, E. Co., marking ink, 1 qt. at 7.50	72 50
Humphrey, F. W., sugar, 1,000 lbs. at 3.83, 300 lbs. at 4.23; syrup, 336 lbs. at 2 7-8c.; currants, 79 lbs. at 6c.; canned vegetables, 2 doz. at 85c., 2 doz. at 62½c., 2 doz. at 1.20; figs, 64 lbs. at 4½, raisins, 28 lbs. at 5¼c.; sundries, 1.54; rice, 700 lbs. at 3¾	102 88
Hammill, J. H. Co., coal, 195 900-2000 tons at 3.06, 598.08; Hartz, J. F. Co., drugs and chemicals, 134.80	732 88
Harris Abattoir Co., pork, 521 lbs. for 50.10, 473 lbs. at 9¼c., 235 at 9½, 501 at 9¾c	165 03

PUBLIC INSTITUTIONS MAINTENANCE.—*Continued.*

CENTRAL PRISON.—*Continued.*

EXPENSES.—*Continued.*

Hall, F. & Sons, mitts, 1 doz. at 3.00; Howell & Co., drugs, chemicals, etc., 40.36 .... 43 36

Harcourt, E. H., stationery, 1.75; Hees, Geo. H., Son & Co., shades, 3 at 1.04, 3.12 .... 4 87

Halliday, Jas., difference on cows exchanged, 51.07; purchase of meat, 5,806.66 .... - 5,857 73

Hedley, Shaw Milling Co., flour, 805½ lbs. at 3.75, 3,020.63 .... - 3,020 63

Hunter, Moses, oats, 700 lbs. at 1.25, 61.26 bus. at 39½c.; bran, 500 lbs. for 4.75, 37.88 .... 37 88

Jeffrey & Eakins, photographic supplies, 61.27 .... 61 27

Junor, Wm., cups and saucers, 2 doz. at 2.00, 3 doz. at 3.50; salts and peppers, 12 doz. at 1.00; tumblers, 7 doz. at 45c.; plates, 2 doz. at 1.80. 33 25

Kent, Ambrose, & Sons, repairing clock, 2.75............................ 2 75

Kinnear, T. & Co., figs, 99 lbs. at 3½c.; tapioca, 25 lbs. at 6c., 40 lbs. at 7c.; biscuits, 69¾ lbs. at 6½c.; brooms, 6 doz. at 2.50; syrup, 1,705 lbs. at 2 7-8; canned vegetables, 4 doz. at 95c., 2 doz. at 62½c., 2 at 1.05, 2 at 1.35; raisins, 28 lbs. at 5c., 28 lbs. at 6½c.; sugar, 1,000 lbs. at 3.63, 1,200 lbs. at 3.73, 1,200 lbs. at 3.83, 200 lbs. at 4.03, 600 lbs. at 4.13, 300 lbs. at 4.23; rice, 1.700 lbs. at 3.75; sundries, 3.66; cream tartar, 5 lbs. at 25c., tobacco, 88 lbs. at 66c.; currants, .148 lbs. at 6½c.; prunes, 25 lbs. at 7c., 25 lbs. at 9¾; canned fruits, 2 doz. at 2.60; jelly powder, 8 doz. at 90c.; blacking, 3 doz. at 90c.; vanilla, 1 qt. at 2.50; jam, 40 lbs. at 7c.; cheese, 40¼ lbs. at 13½c 427 97

Kilgour Bros., rope tags, 1 m. at 66c., 1 m. at 1.18, 1.84; Kemp Mfg. Co., mugs, 12 doz. at 99c., 11.88 .... 13 72

Kincaid, G. & J. & Co., horseshoeing, 1.50; King's Printer, stationery 149.95; paper, 16.74, 166.19 .... 167 69

Lyons, Geo. A., bran, 1 ton at 18.50, 2 tons at 20.00, 1 ton at 20.50; ch. oats, 100 lbs. at 11.75, 1 ton at 24.00, 1 ton at 25.00, 100 bus. at 38c., 50 bus. at 30c.; straw, 1.05 .... 198 30

Leighton, R., apples, 3 bbls. ~' 3.00, 9.00; Livingston, E. J. & Co., tissue paper, 100 reams at 95c. 104 00

Lake Simcoe Ice Co., ice, 173½ tons at 85c., 147.26; Lake, Wm. H., cups and saucers, 4 doz. at 1.2 ., 4.80 .... 152 06

Myott Son & Co., tumblers, 2 doz. at 70c.; cups and saucers, 2 doz. at 90c.; plates, 2 doz. at 65c., jugs, ½ doz. at 1.80 .... 5 40

Mack, Chas. W., rubber stamp, 2 at 40c.; stamp pad, 1 at 30c.; Moore & Hortopp, cracked oats, 2,160 lbs. at 23.00 .... 25 94

Meakins & Sons, brooms, 5 doz. at 2.98, 5 doz. at 3.13 3-5, 30.58; Morton, David & Sons, soap, 1,200 lbs. at 4c., 48.00 .... 78 58

Muldoon, J. & Co., lime, 500 lbs. at 40c. cwt. 2.00; cement, 3 bbls. at 2.00, 6.00; gravel, 1 load at 2.00; cartage, 35c 10 35

Might Directories, Ltd., Toronto directory, 1 copy at 6.00.............. 6 00

Matthews, Geo. Co., Ltd., pork, 6 bbls. at 22.75, 5 bbls. at 24.50; bacon, 64 lbs. at 17c.; ham, 29 lbs. at 16c.; lard, 60 lbs. at 12¾......... 282 17

Mail Printing Co., subn., 1 yr. 4.00; Monetary Times, subn., 2.00 ...... 6 00

Macdonald & Co., Jno. & Co., cotton, 60 yds. at 6 5-8c., 3.98; McIntosh, P. & Son, rolled wheat, 2 bbls. at 2.40, 12.00 .... 15 98

National Prison Assn., membership dues for 1905 and 1906, 10.00........ 10 00

National Conference, Charities and Correction, membership dues for 1903, 1904, 1905 .... 7 50

Perkins, Ince & Co., sugar, 800 lbs. at 4.33, 2,500 lbs. at 3.93, 1,200 lbs. at 4.03; syrup, 671 lbs. at 3c., 306 lbs. at 3½c., 685 lbs. at 2 7-8c.; jelly powder, 7 doz. at 90c.; currants, 70 lbs. at 6½c., 72 lbs. at 7c., 169 lbs. at 8c.; raisins, 31 lbs. at 7c., 150 lbs. at 8½c.; prunes, 56 lbs. at 6½c.; jam, 28 lbs. at 7c.; rice, 500 lbs. at 3½c., 400 at 3¾c.; tea, 450 lbs. at 20c.; sundries, 33.88; blacking, 3 doz. at 90c.; tobacco, 176 lbs. 58.08; barley, 490 lbs. at 3½c.; canned vegetables, 8 doz. at 85c., 2 doz. at 1.15; brooms, 5 doz. 2.50; biscuit, 48 lbs. at 21c.; baking powder, 2 doz. at 1.20 .... 613 13

Perrin, F. J., tea, 160 lbs. at 20c.; coffee, 100 lbs. at 16c., 300 lbs. at 20c., 10 lbs. at 28c., 2 lbs. at 32c.; pepper, 70 lbs. at 15c.; baking powder,

PUBLIC INSTITUTIONS MAINTENANCE.—*Continued.*

CENTRAL PRISON.—*Continued.*

EXPENSES.—*Continued.*

36 lbs. at 10c.; spice, 5 lbs. at 20c.; nutmeg, 2 lbs. at 50c.; vanilla, 1 qt. at 1.20	128 74
Postmaster, stamps, 143.00; Prisoners' Aid Assocn, cab hire *re* religious services, 450.00	593 00
Potter, Chas. thermometer, 1 at 1.50	1 50
Rathbone, F. W., gloves, 1 pr. at 1.00; Rogers, Elias, Co., coal, 81.1400 tons at 3.38, 32.17 tons at 5.60	461 11
Roberts, E. H., keys, locks, etc., 5.80; Rennie, Wm., Co., seeds, 17.00	22 80
Robertson, Jas. Co., repairs, etc., 5.72; sundries, 40c	6 12
Rice Lewis & Son, sundry hardware, 10.77; columbia dry cells, 1 doz. at 11.25; key stations, 6 at 1.00; metal polish, 11-12 doz. at 3.00; lawn mowers, 2 for 22.05; wash bowls, 6 doz. at 1.22½; scythe stones, ½ doz. at 2.40; bell trap, 1 at 2.16; spades, 1 doz. at 9.98; padlocks, ½ doz. at 4.00; cleaver, 1 at 2.07	77 58
Sloan, Jno & Co., currants, 74 lbs. at 8c.; canned vegetables, 2 doz. at 85c., 2 doz. at 95c., 2 at 1.17½c.; jam, 50 lbs. at 7c.; nutmegs, 5 lbs. at 60c.; rice, 400 lbs. at 3¾c.; sugar, 1.200 lbs. at 4.03, 300 lbs. at 4.43; syrup, 340 lbs. at 4.43; tapioca, 40 lbs. at 7½c.; baking powder, 2 doz. at 1.20; pepper, 25 lbs. at 18c.; jelly powder, 4 lbs. at 90c.; tobacco, 88 lbs. at 66c.; sundries, 1.43	178 23
Simmers, J. A., disinfectant, 1 gal. at 30.00; seed, 200.36	230 36
Sparrow, Geo. & Co., knives, 4 at 1.00, 2 at 40c.; pie plates, 1 doz. at 1.25; double boilers, 1 at 4.00, 1 at 4.50	14 55
Standard Fuel Co., coal, 536.17 at 2.81, 94.01 tons at 5.28, 2,007.79; Stephenson, T. M., Canadian Almanac, 2 copies, 50c., 1.00	2,008 79
Shuttleworth, E. B. Co., drugs and chemicals, 15.05; Stanners, A. G., spectacles, 3 doz. at 2.50, 7.50	22 55
Simpson, R. Co., shades, 3 at 1.15; gloves, 1 pr. at 1.00; duck, 14½ yds. yds. at 35c.; sponge, 1 at 75c., 6 at 35c.; glasses, 1 doz. at 2.40, 1 doz. at 1.50; cups and saucers, 2 doz. at 2.65; plates, 1 doz. at 2.50; irons, 1 set at 1.00; rug, 1 at 76.38; sundries, 2.45	105 05
Smale, I. J., apples, 2 bbls. at 3.00; Shaw & Begg, insurance, 16.50	22 50
Stewart & Wood, ultra blue, 28 lbs. at 10c., 2.80; St. Michael's Cathedral, cab hire, *re* religious services, 187.50	190 30
Sundry Newspapers, advertising, supplies, 112.11; fuel, 16.00	128 11
Sundry persons, services and good conduct, 221.25	221 25
Taylor, Scott & Co., camp beds, ½ doz. at 15.00, 7.50; Toronto Water Works Depart., water, 49.41	56 91
Toronto Street Railway Co., car tickets, 80.00; Times and Guide, printing, 19.50	99 50
Taylor, Jno. & Co., soap, 1,377 lbs. at 3½c., 24 lbs. at 30c., 500 lbs. at 3¾c., 15 boxes at 6.00	164 15
Toronto Electric Light Co., electric current, 75.59; Toronto World, subn., 3.00	78 59
Toronto Weekly Railroad & Steamboat Guide, subn., 5.00	5 00
United Factories, brooms, 5 doz. for 14.72, 1-12 doz. at 13.80; paper, 100 lbs. at 4½c., 4.50	20 37
Vance & Co., potatoes, 1,456 bus. at 65c.; apples, 2 bbls. at 2.50, 5.00	951 49
Willard & Co., butter, 2,398 lbs. at 19c.; pork, 13 bbls. at 22.50, 19 bbls. at 21.25, 5 bbls. at 23.00, 4 bbls. at 24.00, 4 bbls. at 25.00; bacon, 43¼ lbs. at 15c., 100 at 16c., 38½ lbs. at 15½c., 57 lbs. at 17c., 42½ lbs. at 18c., 32½ lbs. at 18½c.; ham, 45¾ lbs. at 13½c., 48 lbs. at 14½c., 60½ lbs. at 16c., 38 lbs. at 17c.; eggs, 60 doz. at 16c., 60 doz. at 16½c., 60 doz. at 18c., 112½ at 19c., 100 at 20c., 45 at 22c., 87 at 23c.; lard, 50 lbs. at 11c., 100 lbs. at 11½c., 50 lbs. at 10¾c., 50 lbs. at 12c., 50 lbs. at 12¾c.; salt, 20 sacks at 40c., 4 sacks at 1.00, 12 sacks, at 1.10; beans, 72 bus. at 1.70, 12 bus. at 1.60; onions, 3 bags at 1.25; cheese, 86½ lbs. at 14c., 39¼ lbs. at 14½c.; apples, 4 bbls. at 2.50, 1 bbl. at 2.75, 1 bbl. at 3.25, 1 bbl. at 2.90; jam, 4 bbls. at 6.00; jam, 30 lbs. at 6¾c.; barley, 4 sacks at 2.00; corn meal, 1 sack at 1.60; turkey, 81 lbs. at 16c.; oysters, 1 pail at 3.15; carrots, 1 sack at 70c.	1,909 21
Warwick Bros. & Rutter, printing	63 85

PUBLIC INSTITUTIONS MAINTENANCE.—*Continued.*

CENTRAL PRISON.—*Continued.*

EXPENSES.—*Continued.*

Watson, Jno. T., hay, 2.1570 tons at 10.00, 1,750 tons at 11.00, 2.900 tons at 12.00, 1.520 tons at 13.00, 1.780 ton at 14.00, 1.540 ton at 15.00	148 13
White, E., sausages, 425 lbs. at 11c., 46.75	46 75
Wheler, G., testing flour, 1.00; Williams' Pharmacy, bug exterminator, 2 doz. tins at 2.50	6 00
Wilson, T. A., bran, 1 ton at 20.00; West Chemical Co., disinfectant, 83¾ gals. at 1.00	103 75
Webster, E. H., ice	42 75

CENTRAL PRISON, INDUSTRIES.

SALARIES ($13,714.15).

J. T. Gilmour :	Twelve months' salary as Warden...............................			500 00
J. O. Anderson :		do	Accoutant...............................	1,100 00
T. G. Crossen :		do	Shipping Clerk......................	100 00
W. W. Mason :		do	Engineer...........................	950 00
Jno. White :		do	Industrial Foreman.................	800 00
H. Able :		do	do	800 00
P. T. McKay :		do	do	1,000 00
S. Smith :		do	do	999 00
W. Houston		do	Gardener.................................	1,150 00
Geo. Moody :		do	Painter.................................	650 00
Geo. Ross :	One	do	Guard..................................	49 98
D. Robertson :	Six	do	do	275 00
John Harris :	Twelve	do	Machinist............................	700 00
A. J. Land :		do	do	700 00
W. W. Jackson :		do	Blacksmith............................	600 00
Wm. Hill :		do	Teamster..............................	450 00
F. Swallow :	Sixteen	do	Machinist (including arrears 1905)....	600 00
R. J. Linten :		do	Nightwatch............................	600 00
R. Borthwick :	Two	do	Gardener..............................	100 00
Jno. Ryan :	Ten	do	....	541 17
R. Gore :	Four	do	....	200 00
R. Lyon :	Eight	do	....	400 00
Guards (6) :	Twelve	do	....	449 00

EXPENSES ($45,190.87).

Atteaux Dye Stuff & Chemical Co., criterion blue, 10 gals. at 1.00; anthia aliz bordeau, 1 lh. at 97c.; dyes, 7.84	18 81
Allan, J. W., glass, 164.65; auger, 1 at 60c.; files, 1 doz. at 80c., 1 doz. at 90c., 1 doz. at 1.00; escutcheon pins, 2 lbs. at 45c.; screws, 5 gro. at 15c., 5 gro. at 22c.; chair backs, 2 doz. at 1.20; chair seats, 1 doz. at 1.50	174 60
Armstrong, Jno., coke. 25 bus. for 1.50; Ashcroft Mfg. Co., charts for Edison recording gauges, 10.00	11 50
Brock, W. R. Co., trousering, 2¾ yds. at 1.10, 2¾ yds. at 1.50, 1¼ yds. at 3.00; wadding, 40 doz. at 25c.; canvas, 50 yds. at 12½c., 50 yds. at 17¼c.; worsted, 37 yds. at 2.00; corticelli silk, 1 gro. at 12.50; hair cloth, 50 yds. at 35c.; melton, 9 yds. at 3.00, 2¼ yds. at 4.25; cheviot, 4 yds. at 2.50, 3¼ yds. at 2.60; canvas, 250 yds. at 8c., 10 yds. at 16½c., 50 yds. at 11c., 50 yds. at 16½c., 50 yds. at 18½c.; sundries, 43.74; cotton. 730 yds. at 8c., 367½ yds. at 9c.; tweed, 423½ yds. at 25c., 236 yds. at 75c.; serge, 32½ yds. at 1.50; italian, 1,325 at 25c., 51½ yds. at 30c., 109½ yds. at 65c.; suiting, 168¼ yds. at 85c., 2½ yds. at 1.50, 19 yds. at 2.25, 5¼ yds. at 2.50, 22¾ yds. at 3.00; padding, 40¼ yds. at 35c.; velvet, 1 yd. at 3.00, 1 yd. at 3.50, 2 yds. at 4.00; buttons, 2 gro. at 75c., 12 gro. at 45c., 2 gro. at 95c., 6 gro. at 1.25. 50 gro. at 7.12½.; denim, 3,357½ yds. at 23½c.; shirts and drawers, 4 doz. at 5.00. 4 doz. at 5.25, 4 doz. at 4.75, 2 doz. at 6.25, 4 doz. at 6.75; sewing silk, ½ gro. at 12.00; crash, 52 yds.	

PUBLIC INSTITUTIONS MAINTENANCE.—*Continued.*

CENTRAL PRISON INDUSTRIES.—*Continued.*

EXPENSES.—*Continued.*

at 8c.; silesia, 70 yds. at 10c., 49 yds. at 13½c., 55¾ yds. at 14½c., 66 yds. at 15c., 29 yds. at 18½c., 31 yds. at 25c.; pocketing, 54½ yds. at 16c.; braided twist, 1 gro. at 8.00; holland, 45 yds. at 12½c., 47½ at 13½c., 48 at 16½c.; cheese cloth, 112 yds. at 4c.; hessian, 308 yds. at 10c.; rubber tissue, 1 lb. at 1.25; stay binding, 2 boxes at 1.20; homespun, 18¾ yds. at 1.00; fancy lining, 141 yds. at 17½c., 26½ yds. at 1.00; beaver, 28¾ yds. at 3.00, 3 yds. at 5.50	3,029 79
Burns, P. & Co., coal, 1,027.400 tons at 2.85, 120.1500 at 3.43	3,341 71
Ballantyne, Jno. & Co., repairs to machinery, 4.45; Bourdon, W. J., hats, 17 at 3.00, 51.00	55 45
Burnett, Ormsby & Clark, premium on insurance	80 90
Beal Bros., uppers, 2 prs. at 2.15, 1 pr. at 1.85, 1 pr. at 2.05, 1 pr. at 2.25, 1 pr. at 2.50; heels, 3 doz. at 3.00; duck, 35 yds. at 16c.; sundries, 6.75; soft steel, 15 lbs. at 10c.; brass, 20 lbs. at 35c.; sponges, 1 doz. at 1.50	572 60
Brown Bros., Ltd., stationery, 46.54; Bywater, J., making caps, 2 at 1.75, 3.50	50 04
Bursar, to pay sundries, 14.84; Blaikie, Wm., bronze casting, 61 lbs. at 23c., 82 lbs. at 25c., 34.54	49 38
Bowden, Frank A., lumber, 108.45; Bell Telephone Co., messages, 30c.; exchange service, 116.00	224 75
Croil, Jas., tweed, 70½ yds. at 1.84¾, 91¼ yds. at 1.90	303 31
Canadian Heine Safety Boiler Co., heine boiler plugs and bridge, 24 at 60c., 14.40	14 40
Clarke & Clarke, skivers, 99¼ for 8.80; Canada Paper Co., paper, 300 lbs. at 3.50, 10.50	19 30
Clappison Packing & Covering Co., covering smoke box and pipes	67 53
Consumers' Gas Co., gas, 202.15; coke, 1.20; Crabb, Wm. & Co., b.c.s. pins, 2,000 at 25.00m., 50.00	253 35
Crickmore & Anderson, brokers' fees, 12.60	12 60
Canadian Rubber Co., rubber heels, 2 doz. at 2.62, 5.24; hose, 50 ft. for 6.37	11 61
Canadian Fairbanks Co., Ltd., packing, 31 lbs. at 1.00, 31.00; sundries, 6.74	37 74
Canadian Feather & Mattress Co., mattress, 1 at 2.25, 1 at 3.00, 1 at 3.10, 1 at 4.50, 25 at 2.85; packing, 3.75	87 85
Cotterill, Jno., plants	7 40
Colonial Cordage Co., rope, 142 lbs. for 25.56, 427 lbs. for 62.77; twine nipper, 1 at 6.50; twine, 150 lbs. at 9½c., 14½ lbs. for 4.48	113 56
Canadian Express Co., charges	5 75
Central Prison Maintenance, leather mitts, 2 2-12 doz. at 2.85	6 18
Canada Foundry Co., brass stuffing box, 1.80; pump fittings, 22.30	24 10
Canadian Pacific Rlwy., freight, 133.58; repairs to siding, 70.82	204 40
Canadian Oil Co., paint, oils, etc., 134.77; penoline, 46.20 gals. at 21c., 9.70; benzine, 41.66 gals. at 12c., 50 gals. at 18½c.	160 80
Canadian General Electric Co., Edison lamps, 90 at 17c., 10 at 23c.; inner flint globes, 2 doz. at 1.10; solid carbons, 500 for 11.18; batteries, 2 at 2.74; cod lines, 5 lbs. at 65c.; sundries, 41.56	93 49
Canadian Economic Lubricant, cylinder oil, 84 gals. at 60c.	50 40
Canada Paint Co., paint, oils, etc., 402.65; alabastine, 80 lbs. at 6c.; putty, 962 lbs. at 1.75 cwt.	424 29
Dominion Radiator Co., castings, etc., 161.78; repairs to valve, 4.50; ¾ black pipe,, 228.2 lbs. at 3.05; gauge glass washers, 1 lb. for 76c., 1 lb. for 69c.; valve, 1 at 8.82	191 41
Dominion Express Co., charges, 4.45; Dominion Suspender Co., 718¾ yds. for 47.80, 735 yds. for 55.86	108 11
Dineen, W. & D. Co., 1 cap at 1.50; Dunlop, Jno. H., plants, 60.50	62 00
Dominion Paper Box Co., boxes, 1,600 at 7c., 75 at 13c., 27.25; Douglas & Ratcliff, paper, 17.93	45 18
Davis, Jno. & Son, flower pots, 500 for 10.00, 500 for 20.00, 500 for 40.00, 500 for 50.00; fern pans, 100 for 50.00	170 00
Dodge Mfg. Co., wood pulleys, 1 at 7.00, 6 at 1.35, 18.90	25 90
Eaton, T. Co., Ltd., mantles, 12 at 20c.; chimneys, 12 at 10c.; logwood, 750 for 13.97, 1,600 lbs. at 1¾c., 28.00; potash, 236 lbs. at 7¾c.; wyan-	

PUBLIC INSTITUTIONS MAINTENANCE.—*Continued.*

CENTRAL PRISON INDUSTRIES.—*Continued.*

EXPENSES.—*Continued.*

dotte soda, 2,800 lbs. at 1¾c.; caustic soda, 1.150 lbs. for 42.27; essence of tan bark, 1 bbl. for 25.16	171 84
Empire Wall Paper Co., wall paper, 51.19; sponges, 4 for 1.75; glue, 6 lbs. at 30c.	54 74
Earle, Bourne & Co., tubing	150 30
Flett, Lowndes & Co., braid, ¼ gro. at 9.00; Frank & Bryce, thread, 72.47	74 72
Frederick, Jno. G., twine nippers, 50 at 6.50	325 00
Flagg, Stanley, G. & Co., castings, 937 lbs. at 9c.; pattern metal, 7 lbs. at 35c.; sundries, 90c.; making patterns, 8 hrs. time at 50c.; patterns, 140 lbs. at 9c.	104 28
Goldie & McCullock Co., repairs to valves	3 00
Gold Medal Furniture Mfg. Co., green drill, 4 yds. at 40c.	1 60
Gutta Percha Rubber Mfg. Co., gaskets, 42 lbs. at 75c.; balling machine rings, 13¼ lbs. at 1.65; kinkproof hose, 250 ft. for 39.55; shank couplings, 5 sets at 15c.; steam hose, 50 ft. for 21.77; packing, 15 lbs. at 30c.	121 36
Galloway, Taylor & Co., castings, 5,024¼ at 3c.; repairs, 35c.	151 08
Grand Trunk Railway, freight, 75.00; Grand & Toy, stationery, 23.00	98 00
..e & White, moccasins, 1 pr.	1 25
Hammill, J. H. & Co., coal, 257.535 tons at 2.72, 27.1200 tons at 3.02, 516.800 at 3.15, 472 tons at 4.00, 38.515 tons at 4.15	4,091 02
Harris, W. & Co., fertilizer, 200 lbs. for 2.75; Hamilton, W. Mfg. Co., fire bricks, 100 at 36c., 36.00	38 75
Harland, Wm. & Sons, enamel, 15 cans at 3.60 2-3	54 10
Harcourt, E. H. Co., stationery	22 45
770 yds. at 16½c., 770 for 102.70, 1,540 yds. for 205.40	846 25
Hamilton Cotton Co., beam warp, 1,540 yds. at 12¾c., 3,500 yds. at 5¾c.,	
Houston, Wm., travelling expenses	29 75
Hamilton Mfg. Co., flue cleaners, 1 at 3.75, 1 at 4.00; brushes, 2 at 50c.; tube tiles, 100 at 36c.; packing, ½ lb. at 80c., 58 lbs. at 1.20, 12 at 1.25; sundries, 1.16	131 71
Inglis, Jno. Co., valve, 1 at 25.00; indicator cock, 1 at 3.50; repairs, 100.23; cast iron boxes, 12 for 55.00; castings, 885 lbs. at 3½c.	214 71
Imperial Chemical Co., engine oil, 193 gals. at 35c., 42 for 14.26; engine grease, 350 lbs. at 8c.; spindle oil, 43 gals. at 35c., 91½ gals. at 40c.; paint, oils, etc., 287.27; lard oil, 46 gals. at 60c.	476 33
Imperial Varnish & Color Co., enamel, 206.12; paints, oils, etc., 180.30	386 42
Imperial Cap Co., cap peaks, 20 1-3 doz. at 75c.	15 25
Jessop, Wm. & Sons, Ltd., cast steel, 70 lbs. at 14c., 72 lbs. at 15c.	20 60
Jacques Electrical Co., repairing watchman's clock, 3.15; Jardine, A. B. & Co., dies, 4 at 1.50, 6.00	9 15
Joselin, J. S., patterns for bed, 8.70; Jones Underfeed Stoker Co., door liners, 8 at 1.75, 14.00	22 70
Kloepfer, C., repairs to vehicles, 16.04; cushion pads, 1 pr. at 95c.	16 99
Kennedy Hardware Co., castors, 50 set at 38c., 875 sets at 19¾c.	191 81
Kemp Mfg. Co., tin, 1 box at 10.90; galv. iron, 6.80; Karch, H. W., tongue plates, 2 at 2.50, 5 00	22 70
Leadlay, E. & Co., tallow, 839 lbs. at 5¼c., 1,691 lbs. at 5 7-8c., 1,184 at 6¾c.; pulled wool, 5,895 lbs. at 16c.; sacks, 80 at 25c.; fleece wool, 7,251 lbs. at 38½c.	3,978 17
Leckie, Jno., Ltd., brown duck, 20 yds. at 21c.; Lake, Wm. H., glass, 13.21	17 41
Meredith, Thos. & Co., iron, 44.70; horse rasps, ½ doz. at 9.00; copper, 4 lbs. at 50c.; sundries, 11.18; nuts, 10 at 10c.; drills, 1 doz. at 1.20; nails, 25 lbs. at 12c., 25 lbs. at 15c., 1 keg at 2.25, 1 keg at 2.35, 1 at 2.25, 1 at 2.50; screws, 25 at 3½c., 50 at 2.00, 5 gro. at 30c.; night latch, 1 at 2.00; 66 ft. tape line steel, 1 at 5.75; night latch, 1 at 2.00; perforated tins, 2 doz. at 3.00; rivets, 200 lbs. at 10c.	117 75
Muldoon, J. & Co., cement, 3 bbls. at 2.00, 5 bbls. at 2.15; gravel, 2 loads at 2.25; cartage, 1.05; lime, 2,200 lbs. for 10.20; bags, 30 at 10c.; sand, 3 loads at 2.00	41 50
Morrison, Jas., Brass Mfg. Co., basin cocks, 6 at 1.25; elbows, 2 doz. at 73c., 1 doz. at 1.68; sundries, 4.38; tees, 48 for 3.61; basin plugs, 2.10	20 73

PUBLIC INSTITUTIONS MAINTENANCE.—*Continued.*

CENTRAL PRISON INDUSTRIES.—*Continued.*

EXPENSES.—*Continued.*

Meakins & Sons. whitewash heads, 1 doz. at 29.12; Mason, W. W., travelling expenses, 3.95 .... 33 07

Mitchell, Jno. J. Co., *American Tailor and Cutter*, 1 yrs. sub'n. 7 60

McBain, Malcolm, sewing silk, ⅓ lbs. for 4.00; McBride, Sam'l., valuating lumber, 25.00 .... 29 00

MacGregor, Gourlay & Co., planer knives, 5 for 15.70, 7 for 19.66; cylinder bolts, 2 doz. at 3.00; pinion for moulder, 2.50; chuck, 1 at 6.00 .... 49 86

McMurchy, Jno., clothing fleece, 16,250 lbs. at 29½c.; sacks, 1 at 25c., 66 at 50c.; less freight, 2.04 .... 4,824 97

National Oil Co., spindle oil, 100 gals. at 35c. 35 00

Ontario Malleable Iron Co., malleable links, 389 lbs. at 4¼c.; bag, 1.40; patterns, 2 at 8.50; castings, 3,051 lbs. at 5c. 179 95

Ontario Reformatory for Females, making 1 doz. shirts, 2.00; shirting, 36 yds. at 12½c., 4.50 .... 6 50

Ontario Rubber Co., crutch tips, 8 1-3 doz. at 90c. 7 50

Ogilvie, Thos. & Son, hair cloth, 46½ yds. at 27½c.; col'd. mohair, 26½ yds. at 1.00; buttons, 1 gro. at 2.37, 18 10-12 at 50c., 1 gro. at 2.37; buckram, 8¼ yds. at 15c.; sundries, 12.07; French canvas, 759 yds. at 14½c.; canvas, 50 yds. at 8c.; holland. 47 yds. at 17½c.; machine silk, 2 lbs. at 12.50; grey drill, 410½ yds. at 9c.; silesia, 51 yds. at 17½c.; pocketing, 45¼ yds. at 17½c. 166 61

Postmaster, postage stamps, 80.00; post cards, 1.00; Pearson, Edwin B., insurance premium, 153.40 .... 234 40

Plant, George, flower pots, 5,000 for 36.00; Pilkington Bros., glass, 6.69 .. 42 69

Parsons. Chas. & Son, sole leather, 2,106¾ at 27c., 525 at 28c.; emery strop, 1 doz. at 3.00; iron, 40 lbs. at 6c.; silk, 1 lb. at 10.25; machine thread, 3 lbs. at 80c., 3 lbs. at 1.00; rivets, 20 lbs. at 30c., 5 lbs. at 75c.; books, 2 gro. at 1.25; color, 2 gals. at 55c.; buckles, 17 at 50c., 6 at 90c.; brace leather, 131¾ lbs. at 18c.; heels, 4 doz. at 3.00; sundries, 7.76; lace leather, 12¼ lbs. at 25c.; box calf, 120¼ lbs. at 25c.; duck, 216 yds. at 16c.; sewing awls, 1 gro. at 3.00; hammers, ½ doz. at 4.50; tacks, 20 lbs. at 25c.; knives, 1 doz. at 2.25; oak bands, 17 lbs. at 36c., 160 lbs. at 38c., 24 lbs. at 43c.; uppers, 1 pr. at 1.95, 1 pr. at 2.45, 2 prs. at 4.10; box sides, 188½ lbs. at 18c.; upper leather, 381 lbs. at 48c., 186 lbs. at 50c.; patent leather, 44 lbs. at 25c., 54 lbs. at 26c.; box leather, 867 at 20c.; sterling heels, 1 doz. at 3.00; shoe thread, 3 lbs. at 80c.; zinc, 20 lbs. at 15c.; rings, 12 gro. at 30c.; float tops, 4 at 50c.; rasps, 1 doz. at 2.50 .... 1,509 40

Queen City Oil Co., engine oil, 86 gals. at 35c., 58.62; cylinder oil, 40½ gals at 72c., 57.80 .... 116 42

Rennie, Wm., Co., seeds, 177.18; Robinson & Heath, broker's fees and freight, 17.95 .... 195 13

Rockers, Julius, seeds and plants, 456.00; Reid & Co., lumber, 213.72...... 669 72

Rice Lewis & Son, ratchet brace, 1 at 1.80; oil cans, ¼ doz. at 4.20; csk. rivets. 130 lbs. for 8.50; flat iron, 271 lbs. at 2.20, 279 lbs. at 2.35; gas pipe, 10.073½ ft. at 2.92 pr. 100 ft., 532½ at 2.09; socket scoops, ½ doz. at 18.00. 1-6 doz. at 20.00; rod iron, 500 lbs. at 2.70; weather proof wire. 25 lbs. at 30c.; shafting, 180 lbs. at 3.25 cwt.; ready roofing, 25 lbs. at 1.60; leather belting, 200 lbs. at 6 3-10c.; steel, 86 lbs. at 3.20 cwt.; saws, 6 at 3.04, ½ doz. at 16.58; drill gauge, 1 at 1.67; iron wire, 370 lbs. at 2.15, 423 lbs. at 2.20; sticker knives, 1 doz., 9.00; sticker blanks, 1 doz. at 4.20; screws, 2 at 1.90, 1 gro. at 59c., 1 at 90c., 1 at 98c.; tees and elbows, 52½ lbs. for 4.35; nails, 15 lbs. at 4-5c.; copper. 10¼ lbs. for 4.14: salamonica. 10 lbs. for 1.13; bolt books, 1 box for 1.00, 1 box for 1.57, 1 box for 1.50, 2 boxes at 2.50; blk. pipe, 5,039 lbs. for 116.04; night latch, 1 at 1.58; gem castors, 1,050 sets for 178.90; wrot. washers, 50 lbs. at 6.84 cwt., 35 lbs. at 7.00; wire cable, 33 lbs. at 11c.; pully block, 1 at 22.85; sheet brass, 9¾ lbs. at 22c.; cast steel. 55 lbs. at 8½c.; belt hook wire. 2.320 lbs. at 4.50; bead rivets. 20 lbs. for 1.27, 20 lbs. for 1.34, 10 lbs. for 2.05; jaw screws, 3 sets at 3.75; belt laces, 15 lbs. at 80c.; lace leather, 22½ at 75c.; files, 3 doz. at 3.64; rules, 1 doz. at 95c.; paper, 74½ lbs. at 4.15 cwt.;

PUBLIC INSTITUTIONS MAINTENANCE.—*Continued.*

CENTRAL PRISON INDUSTRIES.—*Continued.*

EXPENSES.—*Continued.*

nippers, 2 prs. at 2.50, ½ doz. at 14.40; nippers, 1 at 1.42; carriage bolts, 100 at 3.04; blank nuts, 10 lbs. at 10¾c.; galvd. iron, 585 lbs. at 3.50, 465 lbs. at 4.35, 317 lbs. at 4.23, 300 lbs. at 4.56; drill, 1 at 2.00; sprocket chain, 25 for 11c.; jaws for nippers, 1 doz. at 6.00; steel, 298 lbs. for 6.43, 137 lbs. at 3.25, 236 lbs. at 2.65 cwt., 1,180 at 2.35 cwt., 330 at 3.25, 648 at 3.00, 8,012 at 2.35, 462 at 3.00, 20,250 lbs. at 2.32 cwt.; machine bit, 1.04; sundries, 115.11; valves, etc., 48.25; twist drills, 1 doz. at 1.00, 7 doz. for 31.73, 4 at 1.60, 2 at 1.13; chuck jaws, 4 set at 1.50; packing, 5½ lbs. at 60c., 11½ lbs. at 1.20; jaw screws, 3 at 5.59; padlocks, ½ doz. at 18.00; angle iron, 8,010 lbs. at 2.20 cwt., 136 lbs. at 2.40, 93 lbs. at 2.60, 500 lbs. at 2.75; rod iron, 5,562 at 2.20, 968 at 2.35, 117 at 2.35, 391 at 2.45, 300 at 2.50, 500 at 2.75, 500 at 2.85, 721 for 15.60; zinc, 12 lbs. at 9c.; castings, etc., 15.41; sash lifts, 1 doz. at 1.95; wire cloth, 200 ft. for 5.68; band saw, 64 ft. for 25.73, 21 ft. for 7.89, 64 ft. for 21.83; corundum iron wheel, 2 at 2.65, 2 at 2.10; blue stone, 20 lbs. at 8c.; rubber cloth, 15½ lbs. at 16½c.; solder, 25 lbs. at 22c, 49¾ at 25c., 51¼ at 26¾c.; cotton waste, 595 lbs. at 9.20; shoe nails, 20 lbs. at 13c., 39 at 5 1-3c., 1 keg for 3.67; shoe rivets, 19 lbs. at 28c.	3,407 62
Robertson, James, Co., Ltd., brass pipe, 10 lbs. for 2.72; castings, 1.00; valve rubbers, 6 at 25c., 1.50	5 22
Rankin & Co., packing, 1.211 ton at 16.00	17 69
Reid, Geo. & Co., face geb. gear, 1 at 4.40; sundries, 90c.; small geb. gear, 1 at 1.55; latch needles, 1 box at 3.89; belts with steel teeth, 2 at 5.50; shuttles, 1 doz. prs. at 17.00; bow pickers, 1 doz. at 6.00, ½ at 6.83	48 15
Russell, J. S., gold sontache, 105 yds. at 18c.; gold cord, 50 yds. at 12 1-3c.	25 09
Remington Typewriter Co., carbon paper, 1 box at 4.00; Rathbun Co., lumber, 21.25	25 25
Rathbone, Geo., lumber, 618.58; Rogers, Elias & Co., 34.1700 tons coal at 3.38, 101.1200 at 3.38, 461.19	1,079 77
Smith, Baggs & Heaven, wax thread, 3 lbs. at 1.35; duck, 106¼ yds. at 16c.; rubber heels, 1 doz. at 3.25; linen thread, 1 lb. at 2.25; sundries, 1.85; leather, 202½ at 18c., 723½ at 19c., 157¾ at 20c., 884 lbs. at 26c., 602 lbs. at 26½c., 502 lbs. at 27c., 231 at 28c., 28½ at 35c., 147 lbs. at 48c., 76 lbs. at 48c.; nails, 10 lbs. at 6c., 10 lbs. at 14c.; eyelets, 10 gro. at 25c.; laces, 2 gro. at 70c., 2 gro. at 90c.; buckles, 1 gro. at 65c.; belt burrs, 10 at 35c., 13 at 60c.; belt rivets, 13 lbs. at 60c.; shoe packs, 20 lbs. at 15c.	1,085 02
Standard Fuel Co., slack coal, 1,380½ tons at 2.81, 3,879.61; Spence, B. & Co., files recut, 115 for 16.27	3,895 88
Smith, E. D., plants	97 00
Simpson, R., Co., wall paper, 8 rolls at 12½c., 25 yds. at 10c., 11 rolls at 25c.; tilters, 2 at 7.25; linoleum, 29 yds. at 1.00; laying linoleum, 1.45	51 20
Spooner, Alonzo W., wht. lace leather, 5 lbs. at 65c.; sundry newspapers, advertising, *re* fuel, 21.75	25 00
Smith's Falls Malleable Castings Co., castings, 20,202 lbs. at 4½c.; express on patterns, 40c	909 57
Smith, Jno. B. & Son, lumber, 143.34; Singer Sewing Machine Co., needles, 2.00	145 34
Simmers, J. A., seeds, plants, etc., 16.10; Standard Chemical Co., charcoal, 25 bush. at 13c., 3.25	19 35
Sadler & Haworth, talcott fasteners, 1 box, 1 inch, 2.00, 100 2 inch, 4.00, 100 2½ inch, 1.00, 4 inch, 18.00; apron belts, leather, 57½ ft. at 2.04, 37 ft. at 2.04; Stewart & Wood, glass, 9.93; alabastine, etc., 9.83	141 87
Spanish Cigar Factory, tobacco stems, 423 lbs. at 1c., 4.23; Simonds Canada Saw Co., saws, 3 for 3.97	8 20
Sundry persons for services and good conduct	716 30
Samuel, Benjamin, M. L. & Co., round steel, 68,679 lbs. at 2.02½ cwt.	1,390 75
Smith, Alf. W., insurance premium, 153.40; Steel, Briggs Seed Co., seeds, 16.41	169 81
Toronto St. Railway Co., car tickets	40 00
Taylor, Scott & Co., blocks, 5,000 at 4.50; sundries, 4.60; bobbin heads, 1,128 at 8½c.; croquet, 3 sets at 1.83⅓; washing boards, ½ doz. at 15.00; reel arms, 12 for 1.00; ladder, 2.18 ft. at 9½c.; repairs, 5.00	139 94

PUBLIC INSTITUTIONS MAINTENANCE.—*Continued.*

CENTRAL PRISON INDUSTRIES.—*Continued.*

EXPENSES.—*Continued.*

Turnbull Elevator Co., repairs, 1.00; elevator gates, 2 at 20.00; wire guard panels, 2 at 4.50	50 00
Turner, Jno. & Son, wire twisters, 6 at 1.25; boilers, 6 at 1.25; Toronto Water Works Dept., water, 638.61	653 61
United Factories, Limited, paper, 421 lbs. at 3½c., 480 at 3.00, 430 at 3½c.; brooms, 4 doz. at 3.10; varnish, ¼ doz. at 60c., ½ doz. at 1.20; brushes, 1 doz. at 5.40, 1 doz. at 4.05, 1 doz. at 6.00, ½ doz. at 12.60, 1 doz. at 27.20	118 41
Universal Specialty Co.. 1 dittograph	12 50
Vokes Hardware Co., locks, 1 at 1.25, ¼ doz. at 5.80, 2 doz. at 5.40, 2-3 doz. at 9.75; packing, 12¾ lbs. at 72c., 31¼ lbs. at 1.10; nails, 2 kegs at 2.65, 2 kegs at 2.35, 200 lbs. for 3.15, 2 kegs at 4.00; sundries, 67.90; shovels, 1 doz. at 10.80; horse shoes, 1 keg at 4.02; brass butts, 10-12 doz. at 3.50; cup locks, 11 sets at 95c.; sash cord, 10 lbs. at 33c.; auger bits, 28 for 6.52, 3 for 3.35; screws, 10 gro. at 46c., 5 gro. at 22c.; glue, 10 lbs. at 18c.; planes, 1 at 3.51; chisel handles, 3 doz. at 35c.; hollow auger, 1 at 5.00; wire cloth, 1 roll at 3.06; square, 1 at 2.50; files, 1 gro. at 12.64; door handles, 7 at 45c.; sand paper, 2 reams at 3.78; weather strips, 96 ft. at 2¾c.; brushes, 1 doz. at 6.00; drawer pulls, 2 doz. at 50c.; night latch, 1 at 12.00	266 74
West, Taylor, Bickle & Co., brooms, 10 doz. at 3.10, less discount, 25c.	30 75
discount, 25c.	30 75
Watson, Jno., hay, 1½ tons at 10.00, 15.00; Willard & Co., tallow, 1,639 lbs. at 5c., 2,086 at 5½c., 2,038 at 6c.	333 96
Williams, A. R., Machinery Co., gear for washers and pinion, 1 at 10.50; spring for drill, 1 at 1.00	11 50
Waterous Engine Works Co., stop valve, 1 at	27 95

ANDREW MERCER REFORMATORY FOR FEMALES.

SALARIES ($11,923.15).

Emma O'Sullivan:	Twelve	months' salary as	Superintendent	1,600 00
Lucy M. Coad:		do	Deputy Superintendent	650 00
M. Elliott:	Four	do	Principal Girls' Refuge	250 00
Bertha Borland:	Twelve	do	Secretary	350 00
Priscillia Bachus:		do	Chief Attendant	321 00
Female Attendants (8)		do		1,763 49
M. Madden:		do	Cook	240 00
Teachers: (4)	Four	do		400 00
John S. King, M.D.:	Twelve	do	Physician	800 00
Josephine Wells:	Four	do	Dentist	30 00
R. W. Laird:	Seven	do	Bursar	641 00
Thos. McKenzie:	Five	do	do	516 19
James Kelly:	Twelve	do	Engineer	650 00
James R. Laing:		do	Assistant Engineer	600 00
John Clark:	One and half	do	Nightwatchman	57 29
A. Francis:	Ten and half	do	do	493 03
Robt. Wheeler:	Twelve	do	Messenger	550 00
W. A. Hill:		do	Storekeeper	700 00
Frank Egan:		do	Caretaker	400 00
C. Machlin:		do	Gardener	550 00
Sunday persons, temperory help				361 15

EXPENSES ($11,929.01).

Allan, J. W., floor wax, 8 lbs. at 50c.; sundries, 10.83; paint, oils, etc., 23.35; chamber pails, 2 at 75c., 1.50	39 88
Austin, J. A., soap bark, 20 lbs. at 1.60; drug sundries, 1.05; drugs, chemicals, etc., 8.24	9 29
Atteaux Dyestuff & Chemical Co., sal soda, 1,350 lbs. at 5.40; chip soap, 620 lbs. at 5½c.; wyandotte soda, 560 lbs. at 2c., 1,400 lbs. at 1 7-8c.	80 81

PUBLIC INSTITUTIONS MAINTENANCE.—*Continued.*

ANDREW MERCER REFORMATORY FOR FEMALES.—*Continued.*

EXPENSES.—*Continued.*

Applegath, Jess., hats, 9 at 2.50	22 50
Brock, W. R. & Co., cotton, 100 yds. at 10c., 127½ at 13c., 86 at 8½c.; sheeting, 322¾ yds. at 15c.; linen, 258 yds. at 18½c.; duck, 10½ yds. at 1.00; dress goods, 129¼ yds. at 18½c., 38½ at 25c.; combs, 12 doz. at 85c.; sundries, 14.73; gingham, 212½ yds. at 11½c.; towels, 1 doz. at 2.25; towelling, 102 yds. at 8c.; print, 356¼ yds. at 10c.; warp, 6 bdls. at 1.25; Jap rugs, 1 at 4.50; handkerchiefs, 6 doz. at 60c.	332 79
Burns, P. & Co., stove coal, 91.1,920 tons at 5.45 and 6.150 tons at 5.45; slack coal, 389.1,695 tons at 2.90	1,664 86
Burns & Sheppard, horse at 167.50; Bursar, to pay sundries, 9.06	176 56
Belle Ewart Ice Co., ice	153 82
Blake, W. E., altar candles, 6 lbs. for 2.40; rosaries, 6 for 2.40; steni acid, 6 lbs. at 25c.; mission, 6 lbs. for 25c.; float oil, ½ gal. at 1.50	8 55
Bell Telephone Co., messages, 5.90; exchange service, 110.50	116 40
Beaver Soap Co., soap, 165 lbs. at 5½c., 9.08; Bethune, R., tea, 100 lbs. at 18½c., 18.50	27 58
Conger Coal Co., grate coal, ½ ton at 7.50, 3.75; wood ½ cord at 5.50, 2.75	6 50
Clark, David, repairs to furnace, 50.50; *Charities*, subscription, 2.00	52 50
Cross, Wm. G., livery hire, 6.00; Cahoon, A., repairs, paints, oils, etc., 510.63	516 63
Coulter Transfer Co., teaming, 119 hrs. at 50c., 59.50; loam, 3 loads at 3.00, 9.00	68 50
Catholic Register, subscription 1 yr. 1.50; Consumers' Gas Co., 1,104.25	1,105 75
Cox, S., manure, 50 loads at 50c., 25.00; Canada Pub. Co., printing, 2.25	27 25
Culham, T. G., hay, 1¼ tons at 12.50, 15.63; Cream, P., interments, 2.00	17 63
Cullen, Thos., helping gardener, 250 hrs. at 20c., 50.00, 240 hrs. at 20c., 48.00	98 00
Canada Paint Co., paints, oils, etc., 22.85; putty, 100 lbs. at 1¾c., 1.75	24 60
Central Prison Industries, repairs to shoes, 8.00; horseshoeing, 25.16; boiler compound, 4 lbs. at 2.50; repairs to implements, etc., 4.95; clothing, 1 suit at 17.00; 8 suits at 18.00; 8 prs. pants, 40.00; plants, 50.00, shoes, 36 prs. at 1.10, 1 pr. at 4.50, 6 prs. at 1.35; overcoats, 4 at 18.00	423 31
[illegible] Dairy Co., milk, 1,505 gals. at 18c., 278¼ gals. at 22c.	332 22
Davidson & Hay, Ltd., tea, 80 lbs. at 18½c., 251 lbs. at 3¾c.; cann. vegetables, 2 doz. at 85c., 2 doz. at 95c.; salt, 3 lbs. at 1.50; starch, 546 lbs. at 9c.; soda, 280 lbs. at 2c., 840 lbs. at 1.90; putz cream, 3 doz. at 2.00; sundries, 14.12; sago, 25 lbs. at 7c.; cocoa, 1 doz. tins at 9.00; wax tapers, 12 pckgs. at 10c.; prunes, 50 lbs. at 7c.; fish, 96 lbs. at 6½c.; syrup, 753 lbs. at 2 7-8c., 760 lbs. at 2 7-8c., 721 lbs. at 3c.; beans, 2 bush. at 1.70, 4 bush. at 1.75; sugar, 641 lbs. at 4.18, 312 lbs. at 3.88; malta vita, 1 case at 2.85; pepper, 5 lbs. at 18c., 5 lbs. at 28c., 5 lbs. at 30c.; corn starch, 40 lbs. at 7c.; barley, 98 lbs. at 2½c.; vanilla, ½ doz. at 2.25; gelatine, 4 doz. at 1.10; blue, 60 lbs. at 17c.; sapolio, ¼ gro. at 11.30	289 71
Dunn, Jas. R., hay, 1.1,220 ton at 10.50; commission, 50c.	27 90
Durie, D., sausage, 3 lbs. at 10c.; veal, 16½ lbs. at 14c.; potatoes, 16 bush. at 80c., 6 bush. at 90c., 4 bush. at 85c., 5 bags at 1.00, 4 bags at 1.05	41 61
Dominion Radiator Co., valve, 1 at 1.26, 1 at 1.65; radiator, 1 at 6.58; sundries, 27c.	9 76
Dunlop Tire Co., perforated mats, 2 at 3.15; cushion pads, 2 at 1.85	10 00
Down, M., relieving attendant from May 28th to July 18th	24 20
Elliott, M. C., coat, 1 at 3.98; boots, 1 pr. at 2.50; rubbers, 1 pr. at 50c.; umbrella, 1 at 1.00; stockings, 1 pr. at 1.00	8 98
Eaton, T. Co., Ltd., vases, 1 pr. at 35c., 4 prs. at 1.50; curtain stretchers, 2 prs. at 1.35	6 05
Evans, F. M., livery hire, 7.50; Fairles, G. H., rolled oats, 8 bbls. at 5.20, 41.60	49 10
Fleischmann & Co., yeast, 74¼ lbs. at 30c., 24.04; Fotheringham, D., inspection of refuge, 20.00	44 04
Fairles Milling Co., rolled wheat, 50 lbs. for	1 25
Gallagher & Co., fish, 11½ lbs. at 9c., 1,614½ lbs. at 10c., 5 lbs. at 11c., 3 doz. at 30c., 2 doz. at 25c., 2 doz. at 40c., 12 lbs. at 18c., 3 doz. at 50c.;	

PUBLIC INSTITUTIONS MAINTENANCE.—*Continued.*

ANDREW MERCER REFORMATORY FOR FEMALES.—*Continued.*

EXPENSES.—*Continued.*

oranges, 3 doz. at 25c., 5 doz. at 30c., 3½ doz. at 35c., 3 doz. at 40c., 1 case at 4.00; peaches, 1 bas. at 90c., 3 bas. at 85c.; cucumbers, 4 at 25c.; pears, 3 bas. at 60c., 1 bas. at 90c.; sundries, 12.67; berries, 6 boxes at 15c., 4 boxes at 25c., 4 boxes at 17½c.; currants, 1 bas. at 1.50, 2 bas. at 1.20; apples, 2 bas. at 40c.; cherries, 2 bas. at 1.40; lemons, 1 doz. at 20c., 1 doz. at 25c., 4 doz. at 40c., 2 doz. at 1.00; melons, 2 at 20c., 1 at 50c.	213 41
Gowans, Kent & Co., slop jars, 2 at 2.00, 4.00; Griffin, Peter, livery hire, 5.00	9 00
Goodfellow, J., livery hire, 11.00; Gutta Percha Rubber Mfg. Co., rubber boots, 3.19	14 19
Guinane, Jno., shoes, 8 prs. at 4.00, 32.00; Gillett, E. W., Ltd., baking powder, 4 doz. at 1.65, 6.60	38 60
Globe Printing Co., subscription 1 yr., 5.00; Golden's livery, livery hire, 18.00	23 00
Grand Trunk Railway, freight, 55c.; Gazey, Jas., Christmas gratuity for postman, 5.00	5 55
Halliday, Jas., purchase of meat	768 56
Hobbs, Samuel, zinc, 16 lbs. at 10c.; repairs, 4.05; paint, oils, etc., 4.65; ash pan, 1 at 1.25; sundries, 5.48; sundry dippers, 3 at 80c.; padlock, 1 at 1.50; cotton waste, 10 lbs. at 15c.	22 43
Heintzman & Co., loan of piano, 3.00; tuning piano, 2.00	5 00
Harris Abattoir Co., pork, 101 lbs. at 9½c., 213 lbs. at 9¾c., 209 lbs. at 9 5-8c., 202 lbs. at 10¼c., 71.17; Hendry, F., apples, 1 bbl. at 3.50	74 67
Hedley, Shaw Milling Co., flour, 102 lbs. at 3.80, 2 bbls. at 4.00, 1 bbl. at 3.80	399 40
Hichman Grocery Co., apples, 1 bbl. at 3.25; biscuits, 6 tins at 25c., 17 tins at 28c.; flour, 700 lbs. at 2.65; sundries, 6.69; cheese, 9½ lbs. at 17c.; corn meal, 25 lbs. for 75c.; rolled wheat 75 lbs. at 3 2-5	33 80
Hart & Co., drugs and chemicals, 56.25; medical appliances, 8.70; Harvey, Jno., ammonia, 43.43	108 38
Holloway, grocery sundries, 2.40; Hamilton, W. B. Shoe Co., 6 prs. at 70c., 4.20; shoe laces, 1 gro. at 2.20	8 80
Irwin, W. J., repairs to baker's oven, 19.10; Imperial Varnish & Color Co., soap, 440 lbs. for 21.34	40 44
Ivory, Jas., plumbing repairs, 82.12; Inglis, Jno. Co., Ltd., repairs to boiler, 13.04	95 16
Junor, Wm., teapot, 1 at 1.00; stand for soup tureen, 1 at 3.00	4 00
Jennings, C. A. B., repairs to furniture, 103.17; Johnson, D., repairing locks, 6.00	109 17
Jones & Moore Electric Co., Ltd., electrical repairs	70 62
Kinnear, T. & Co., tapioca, 25 lbs. at 5c.; malta vita, 1 case at 2.85; prunes, 50 lbs. at 7c.; cheese, 48 lbs. at 6c.; pepper, 10 lbs. at 18c.; canned vegetables, 4 doz. at 95c., 4 doz. at 85c., 2 doz. at 62½c., 4 doz. at 1.00; macaroni, 25 lbs. at 8½c.; gelatine, 4 doz. at 1.10; barley, 100 lbs. at 2½c.; salt, 1 bbl. at 1.50, 1 bbl. at 3.00; beans, 2 bus. at 1.80; figs, 33½ lbs. at 4c.; Riokett's blue, 60 lbs. at 17c.	53 40
Kemp Mfg. Co., mugs, 5 doz. at 90c.; nickel kettles, 1-12 doz. at 13.20, 1.10, ¼ doz. at 19.41; coffee pots, ¼ doz. at 4.50; sundry tinware, 12.03; pitchers, ¼ doz. at 5.40; saucepans, 2 at 60c.	26 16
Kenny, T. & Co., tea, 300 lbs. at 22c., 66.00; King's Printer, stationery, 75.00; paper, 13.04	154 04
Lake, Wm. H., plates, 3 doz. at 60c., 3 doz. at 70c., 3 doz. at 75c.; vegetable dishes, 3 at 40c.; surcingle, 1 at 1.00; sleigh bells, 1 string at 2.40; sundries, 3.50	14 25
Lyons, Geo. A., bran, 300 lbs. at 1.00, 400 lbs. at 2.00, 600 lbs. at 3.00, 200 lbs. at 2.20, 300 lbs. at 3.50; chop oats, 800 lbs. at 5c., 400 lbs. at 5.20, 400 at 4.80, 800 at 5.40, 800 at 10.00, 800 at 11.00; straw, 5.40; hay, 3.75	90 35
Luke, F. E., spectacles, 4 prs. at 1.50, 3 prs. at 2.00, 1 pr. at 2.75	14 75
Lammy, D. J., hay, 1.1005 tons at 12.00	18 03
Maddocks Bros., harness, 1 set, 35.00; sundries, 2.75; repairs, 1.50	39 25
Muldoon, J. & Co., lime, 2 bbls. at 80c.	1 60

PUBLIC INSTITUTIONS MAINTENANCE.—*Continued*.

ANDREW MERCER REFORMATORY FOR FEMALES.—*Continued*.

EXPENSES.—*Continued*.

Meredith, Thos. & Co., spoons, 3 doz. at 1.25; alabastine, 12 pkgs. at 40c., 4.80; glue, 20 lbs. at 9c.; floor wax, 6 lbs. at 3.60; sundries, 2.35.........	16 30
Meakins & Sons, brushes, 6 doz. at 1.80, 1 doz. at 1.40, 1-6 doz. at 15.60, 6 doz. at 1.80; sundries, 1.25	25 65
Meyer Bros., repairs to laundry, 32.75; Might Directory Co., city directory, 1 copy, 6.00	38 75
Maher, P., livery hire, 8.00; Macdonald, C. S., veterinary services, 3.00...	11 00
Morton, David & Sons, soap, 1,080 lbs. at 4c., 222 lbs. at 4½c.	53 19
Macklin, C. A., manure, 1.00; Moore, R. M., *Ladies' Home Journal*, subscription, 1.25	2 25
Mail Printing Co., subscription, 1 year (2 copies)	8 00
Macdonald, Jno. & Co., napkins, 2 doz. at 2.50, 2 doz. at 4.27½; curtain muslin, 50 yds. at 16½c., 36½ yds. at 22½c.; thread, 1½ gro. at 5.40; hose, 2 doz. at 3.00; galatea, 15½ yds. at .7½c., 152 yds. at 10c.; linen, 45 yds. at 15c., 49¼ yds. at 19½c.; cheese cloth, 108 yds. at 4c.; curtains, 1 pr. at 5.00; warp, 6 lbs. at 1.25; twine, 5 lbs. at 35c., 4 lbs. at 75c.; table cloth, 2 at 1.00; cotton, 243¼ yds. at 8c.; towelling, 200 yds. at 9½c.; sundries, 9.03	147 89
McCullough, W. A., fur caps, 4 at 5.00, 20.00; gloves, 8 prs. at 1.00, 8.00	28 00
McFadden, M., marking ink, 2 bots. at 1.50, 3.00; McMurchy, Jno., yarn, 25 lbs. at 39 1-5c., 9.80	12 80
McWilliam & Everist, cherries, 2 bas. at 1.25; berries, 27 boxes at 11c....	5 47
McKenzie & Co., picture frame and mat	3 50
National Prison Association, membership dues 1905-6	10 00
National Conference of Charities and Correction, membership dues for 1906	2 50
Nordheimer Musical Co., sheet music, 2.05; Neal, P. E., flowers, 8.00	10 05
Newell, Robert, livery hire	1 25
O'Sullivan, Mrs. E., travelling expenses, 65.50; Ontario Novelty Co., broom holders, 2 doz. at 75c., 1.50	67 00
Ontario Lead & Wire Co., closet bowl, 1 at	4 95
Perrin, F. J., coffee, 175 lbs. at 20c.; tea, 100 lbs. at 18½c.; chicory, 2 lbs. at 14c.	53 78
Perkins, Ince & Co., sugar, 313 lbs. at 3.98, 603 lbs. at 4.48; salmon, 4 doz. at 1.65; putz cream, 3 doz. at 2.00; matches, 1 case at 3.00; Perrin's sauce, ¼ doz. at 3.40; wax tapers, 1 case at 4.80; sundries, 12.04; prunes, 50 lbs. at 6¾c.; barley, 98 lbs. at 2½c.; codfish, 48 lbs. at 6½c.; figs, 58 lbs. at 5½c.; canned vegetables, 4 doz. at 92½c., 4 doz. at 95c., 4 doz. at 1.17½; raisins, 23 lbs. at 9½c., 23 lbs. at 18c.; currants, 80 lbs. at 9½c.; sauce, 1 doz. at 2.25; sapolio, ½ gro. at 11.30; gelatine, 2 doz. at 1.10	122 45
Postmaster, postal cards, 3.00; stamps, 40.00	43 00
Prisoners' Aid Association, cab hire for religious services	250 00
Rice Lewis & Son, carpet sweepers, 2 at 3.50; iron wheels, 2 at 1.25; hose, 100 ft. for 23.00, 25 ft. for 12.00; manure forks, 2 at 95c.; rakes, 2 at 60c.; sundries, 3.50; valves, 6 for 8.25; lard oil, 1 gal. at 1.25	51 60
Rogers, Elias Co., coal, 13.950 tons, 5.69, 1.1100 tons at 5.69	85 49
Roberts, G. R., postage stamps, 10.00; Riordon paper mills, paper, 3.82...	13 82
Rochester Lamp Co., lindsay mantles, 1 doz. at 1.92, 1 doz. at 2.40, 18 at 20c.; lindsay lamps, 6 at 90c.; gas cocks, 1 doz. at 2.40; silk gloves, 1 at 75c.; globes, ½ doz. at 1.80	17 32
Rathbone, G., lumber, 6.40; Ramesperger, A., tuning pianos, 2.00	8 40
Simmers, J. A., plants, 3.00; Savoy, The, candy, 6 lbs. at 40c., 2.40	5 40
Singer Sewing Machine Co., sewing machine, 1 at	27 20
Snows, R. B., oranges, 4 doz. at 30c.; lemons, 1 doz. at 20c.; berries, 5 boxes at 15c.	2 15
Simpson, R. Co., rain coats, 2 at 10.00; wallpaper, 10 rolls at 20c.; muslin, 8 yds. for 46c.	22 46
Stanners, A. C., alarm clock, 1 at 1.00; sundry newspapers, advertising *re* supplies 65.00, *re* fuel 10.50	76 50
Sullivan, E. O., telegrams, 1.03; patterns, 70c.; cab hire, 1.25............	2 98
Shaver, Sam., hot bed earth, 4 loads at 3.00............	12 00
Steele, Briggs Seed Co., seeds, 27.00; pruning knife, 1 at 35c.	27 35

PUBLIC INSTITUTIONS MAINTENANCE.—*Continued.*

ANDREW MERCER REFORMATORY FOR FEMALES.—*Continued.*

EXPENSES.—*Continued.*

St. Michael's Cathedral, cab hire for religious services	75 00
Smith Bros., tarpaulin and frame	10 00
Taylor, Scott & Co., step ladders, 21 ft. at 9½c.	2 00
Toronto Electric Light Co., electrical current, 597.20; repairing motor, 7.30	604 50
Taylor, Forbes & Co., float for steam trap, 1 at 3.60; repairs, 3.64; iron pipe, 10.07; castings, 16.16	29 83
Tyrrell, Wm. & Co., subscriptions *Wide World*, 1.20; *Ladies' Journal*, 1.25	2 45
Talbot & Talbot, scrub cloths, 2 doz. at 1.25, 2.50; Toronto, City of, water rates, 250.56	253 06
Toronto Street Ry., car tickets, 65.00; Taylor, Jno. & Co., soap, 955 lbs. at 5c., 1,254 at 5½c., 913 at 6c., 60 at 7½c., 60 at 8c., 184.79	249 79
Toronto Laundry Machine Co., mangle felt, 150 lbs. at 65c.; laundry nets 6 at 80c.; repairs, 1.50	103 80
Toronto Rug Works, 2 at 2.25, 4.50; United Factories, Limited, clothes baskets, 1 doz. at 2.75; 6 baskets at 2.00, 6 bas. at 2.50; scrub brushes, 5 doz. at 1.26; brooms, 4 doz. at 2.33½c, 45.40	49 90
Upper Canada Tract Society, sheet music	5 30
Vokes Hardware Co., locks, ½ doz. at 4.80; keg clasps, 1½ doz. at 1.75	5 03
Warwick Bros. & Rutter, printing, 82.42; Wheler, G., testing flour, 1.00	83 42
Walsh, F., prayer books, 4 doz. at 1.20	4 80
Willard & Co., eggs, 6 doz. at 21c., 48 doz. at 22c., 6 doz. at 23c., 16 doz. at 24c., 30 doz. at 25c., 32 doz. at 26c.; butter, 629 lbs. butter at 19c., 518 lbs. at 22½c.; turkey, 49 lbs. at 18c.; bacon, 35½ lbs. at 17c.; geese, 33 lbs. at 12c.; butter, 580 lbs. at 19c., 643 at 22½c.; eggs, 6 doz. at 16c., 8 doz. at 16½c., 19 doz. at 17c., 35 doz. at 18c., 30 doz. at 22c., 7 doz. at 21c., 36 doz. at 25c.; bacon, 94 lbs. at 15c., 12½ lbs. at 15½c., 130 lbs. at 16c., 19¾ lbs. at 17c., 11 lbs. at 16½c.; lard, 20 lbs. at 11c., 40 lbs. at 11¼c., 20 lbs. at 11¾c., 40 lbs. at 12c., 20 lbs. at 12½c.; ham, 15½ lbs. at 15c., 15½ at 16c., 14¾ at 16½c., 10 lbs. at 17c.; syrup, 2 gals. 90c.; cheese, 3¼ lbs. at 12¾c., 5 lbs. at 13c., 5 lbs. at 11¾c., 4¼ at 13¾c., 28¼ at 14½c.; pineapple, 1 case at 3.25; lemons, 1 doz. at 20c.; melons, 2 at 15c.; apples, 1 bbl. at 2.00, 1 bbl. at 2.50, 1 bbl. at 2.75, 1 bbl. at 3.00, 1 bbl. at 3.75	688 33
Wood, W. Lloyd, medical supplies, 60c.; Wright, S., potatoes, 83.45 bus. at 90c., 75.15	75 75
Wells, Josephine, D.D.S., dental services	13 25
Watkins, J. H. & Co., chopped oats, 400 lbs. at 1.25, 800 lbs. at 1.30; bran, 100 lbs. at 1.00, 300 lbs. at 1.00; linseed meal, 100 lbs. at 1.00; hay and straw, 8.49	28 99
Ward & Co., apples, 1 bbl. at 3.00, 1 bbl. at 3.50, 1 bbl. at 4.50; lemons, 4 doz. at 12½c.; potatoes, 6 bus. at 1.25	19 00
York Mfg. Co., duck, 10 yds. at 62c., 20 yds. at 63c.; wax, 10 lbs. at 15c.; starch, 10 lbs. at 7c., 627 lbs. at 8½c.; marking pens, 2 doz. at 25c.	74 79

TO PAY EXPENSE ACCOUNTS FROM DECEMBER 12TH TO DECEMBER 31ST, 1905.

ASYLUM FOR INSANE, TORONTO ($3,422.15).

Appleton, *Booklover's Magazine*, subscription	3 53
Brock, W. R. & Co., 1 doz. shirts and drawers	13 77
Bell Telephone Co., message	10
Coleman, C. W., repairing clock and cleaning	2 75
Consumers' Gas Co., gas	285 76
Common Sense Manufacturing Co., 12 tins rat exterminator	12 00
Canadian Oil Co., W. W. oil, 44 gals. at 17c.	7 48
Clark, Dr, soap and sundries	90
Corcoran, James (Bursar), 56 lbs. butter at 19¾c	11 07

PUBLIC INSTITUTIONS MAINTENANCE.—*Continued.*

ASYLUM FOR INSANE, TORONTO.—*Continued*

Doyle, M. Fish Co., fish, 860 lbs. at 8c.	68 80
Davidson & Hay, tapioca, 418 lbs. at 4¾c.; tea, 525 lbs. at 25c.; corn meal, 6 bbls. at 3.60; saltpetre, 10 lbs. at 8c.; candies, 192 lbs. at 12c.; granulated sugar, 3,066 lbs. at 4.23; syrup, 83 gals. at 34c.; citron peel, 7 lbs. at 13c.; oranges, 14 doz. at 11½c.; lemons, 21 doz. at 10½c.; evaporated apples, 500 lbs. at 7 7-8c; salt, 10 bbls. at 1.40	427 62
Elliott & Son, oak rail, 114 feet 1½ inches, at 4c.; frieze, 112 yds. at 15c.; picture rail, 500 feet 1½ inches, at 3½c.	38 86
Fleischmann & Co., yeast, 22½ lbs. at 30c.	6 75
Gray, Frank A., drugs and chemicals	59 30
Gowans, Kent & Co., butter dishes, 2 doz. at 2.25; box, 20c.	4 70
Godden, C. P., mops, 2 doz. at 6.50; rat traps, 1 doz. at 15.00; carpet felt, 6 rolls at 1.75; brass plug cocks, 2 at 4.50; pipe, 200 ft. ½ in. at 3c., 206 ft. ¾ in. at 4c., 312 ft. 3-8 in. at 3c.; asbestos sheeting, 696 yds. at 6c.; nipples, 24 3-8 in. at 3c., 24 ¾ at 4c.; elbows, 24 3-8 at 5c., 24 ¾ at 5½c., 12 ½ at 5c.	117 66
Howie, Josephine M., music	5 34
Hurd, H. E., V.S., professional services and medicine	4 50
Inglis, John Co., grate bars, 600 lbs. at 3½c.; repairing boiler, 7.63; repairing tank, 14.02; expanding tubes and new ones, 15.02; castings, 1.34; repairing laundry engiue and sundries, 4.00	66 16
Jacobi, Philip, sole leather, 185 lbs. at 28c.; sole leather roundings, 86 lbs. at 15c.; splits, 49¾ lbs. at 29c.; uppers, 52 lbs. at 50c.; russetts, 19¾ lbs. at 60c.; rivet's 15 lbs. at 10c.; hemp, 3 lbs. at 82c.; splitting machine, 10.50; awls, ink bristles, shoe knives, rasps, eyelets, 4.63	136 06
Knight, Mrs. H. T., wages, 28.00; Lawrence, J. W., stamps, 4.00	32 00
Miller & Sons, flowers	31 60
Mason & Risch Piano Co., tuning 2 pianos	10 00
Morang & Co., books	12 90
Matthews, F. W. Co., interments	16 00
Moore, Wm. & Son, apples, 3 bbls. at 4.00; nuts, 10 lbs. at 30c.; 10 lbs. at 15c.; candles, 1 lb. at 15c., 3 boxes at 40c.; paper, 3 rolls at 10c.; grapes, 10 lbs. at 20c.; candy, 5 lbs. at 25c.; oranges, 6 boxes at 3.50; cranberries, 1 bbl. at 14.00; biscuits, 7 lbs. at 13c., 11¼ lbs. at 19c.; oysters, 2 qts. at 50c.	60 95
McLaughlin & Co., flour, 10 bbls. at 4.55	45 50
McIntosh, P. & Son, rolled oats, 15 bbls. at 4.40	66 00
Nelson, H. W. & Co., ¾ gro. combs at 24.00	18 00
Ontario Rubber Co., jar rings, 10 gro. at 40c.; rubber boots, 1 pr. at 3.85; tubing, 5 3-16 lbs. at 80c.	12 00
Park, Blackwell & Co., butter, 1,680 lbs. at 19¾c.	243 32
Robertson, Jas. The, Co., sink and back with connections	19 50
Rogers' Hardware Store, 2 lanterns and oil	1 40
Ritchie, John, hay, 5,450 lbs. at 9.00 cwt.	24 50
Rathbone, G., lumber	60 68
Russell, E., wages	2 71
Ryan, Wm. & Co., butter, 275 lbs. at 15½c., 10 lbs. at 14c.; eggs, 360 doz. at 23c.	121 25
Simpson, The Robert, shoes, 1 pr. at 2.00; baskets, 2 at 25c., 1 at 30c.; hat, 1 at 2.25; gloves, 4 prs. at 25c.; collars, 4 stock at 50c.; brushes, 4 at 50c.; pins, 3 at 45c.; sundries, 2.00	13 40
Toronto Plate Glass Importing Co., glass	20 60
Toronto Electric Light Co., electric light	191 87
Timpson, G. J., music supplied	36 00
Toronto Laundry Machine Co., repairs, 1.50; rubber springs, 1.50	3 00
Turner & Porter, interment	8 00
Taylor, John & Co., soap, 3 gro. 1,620 lbs. at 7.20, 1,007 lbs. at 4½c.	61 52
Upper Canada Tract Society, The, 101 Presbyterian books	19 71
Wells, Josephine, medical comforts	13 25
Willard & Co., geese, 508 lbs. at 11c. chickens, 184 lbs. at 11c.; turkeys, 1,012 lbs. at 16c.	238 04
Water Works Department, water	765 34

PUBLIC INSTITUTIONS MAINTENANCE.—*Continued.*

ASYLUM FOR INSANE, MIMICO, ($2,034.16).

Ash, H. J., cranberries, 1 bbl. at 13.00; oranges, 2 boxes at 3.25; lemons, 1 box. at 3.25	22	75
Brock, W. R. Co., Limited, braces, 10 doz. at 1.80; towelling, 104 yds. at 7½c.; flannelette, 634¾ yds. at 10c.; white cotton, 405½ yds. at 12½c.; blue serge, 58½ yds. at 2.25; sundries, 1.80	273	40
Canadian Oil Co., oil, paints, etc	75	98
Canadian General Electric Co., lamps, 100 at 17c.; sundries, 2.26	19	26
Canada Brokerage Co., rolled wheat, 3 bbls. at 2.85; S. G. starch, 160 lbs. at 6c.; Prunes, 150 lbs. at 6¾c., 350 lbs. at 7c.; white pepper, 5 lbs. at 34c.; parafine candles, 36 lbs. at 10c.; paper, 1 ream, 4.88	66	43
Davidson & Hay, Limited, sugar, 1,145 lbs. at 4c., 2,000 lbs. at 4.33 cwt.; soda biscuits, 200½ lbs. at 6½c.; tobacco cutters, 2 only at 1.50; twine, 4 pkgs. at 85c.; canned vegetables, 6 doz. at 85c., 4 doz. at 62½c., 4 doz. at 95c.; salt, 5 bbls. at 1.40; rolled wheat, 5 bbls. at 3.00; corn meal, 3 bbls. at 3.50,; C. and B. capers, 1 doz. at 1.80; sundries, 40c	201	68
Dalton Bros., black pepper, 25 lbs. at 18c	4	50
Doyle, M., Fish Co., fish, 1,250 lbs. at 8c	100	00
Forster, Wm., sundry groceries	8	08
Godden, C. P., gauge glasses, 36 at 10c.; granite kettles, 2 at 1.25; sash fasteners, 1½ doz. at 50c., 2 doz. at 25c., 2 doz. at 1.20; cuspidors, 1 doz. at 4.50; castor oil, 1 gal. at 1.50; table spoons, 3 doz. at 2.50; brass screws, 3 gross at 60c.; locks, 1 doz. at 2.50; mouse traps, 1 doz. at 1.20; sundries, 4.93	33	68
Gurney Foundry Co., repairs to range	7	73
Hartz., The J. F. Co., Limited, ophthalmoscope, 1 only at 18.00; dry cell battery, 2 for 6.00	24	00
Hope, F. B., oak souvenir and feeder, 1 only at 21.00; rice boiler, 1 only at 1.35; baker's scraper, 2 only at 80c.; bells, 2 strings at 1.50c.; snow shovels, 2 doz. at 6.00; tube cleaner, 2 at 1.00, 6 at 1.25; saw blades, 1 doz. at 1.00; belting, 30 ft. at 41c.; special galvanized box, 1 only at 8.00; garbage cans, 3 only at 5.80; sundries, 3.32	90	47
Junor, Wm., plates, 3 doz. at 1.50, 3 doz. at 1.80; soup plates, 3 doz. at 1.50; tea plates, 3 doz. at 1.10	16	20
Lake, Wm., H., gasoline, 5 gals. at 25c., oil stoves, 6 at 1.10	7	85
Lane, Andrew, repairs to harness, etc	21	05
Lyons, Geo. A., bran, 4,000 lbs. at 18.00 per ton	36	00
Macdonald, John & Co., brooch, 2.25; tea, 5.00	7	25
McIntosh, P. & Son, rolled oats, 10 bbls. at 4.60	46	00
Maloney, Jno. & Co., lime, 750 lbs. for 2.44; plaster, 1 bbl. at 2.00	4	44
Matthews, F., sausage, 30 lbs. at 11c.; bacon, 25 lbs. at 7c	5	05
Murray, W. A. & Co., muslin, 12 yds. at 25c.; tarleton, 32¾ yds. at 15c., 32¾ yds. at 13½c.; embro, 20 yds. at 10c., 20 yds. at 15c	17	33
Ontario Rubber Co., rubber boots, 4 pairs at 3.85	15	40
Park, Blackwell & Co., Limited, butter, 1,120 lbs. at 19¾c	221	20
Rice, Lewis & Son, glass, 1 case at 4.00; 1 light, 1.25; apple parers, 1-6 doz. at 6.00; putty, 309 lbs. at 6.18; bolts, 2 doz. at 75c.; nails, 1 keg. at 2.35; shaving brushes, 3 doz. at 2.50; dessert forks, 3 doz. at 1.47; tea spoons, 5 doz. at 85c.; kettle stands and lamp, 1 only at 5.62; sundries, 7.42	45	48
Robertson, James, Co., Limited, thermometers for gegonstrom, 6 only at 4.75	28	50
Rowland, Henry A., drugs and chemicals	42	30
Roger's Hardware Store, steel hoes, 2 doz. at 6.00; sheep shears, 3 pair at 1.00; scythes, 6 at 1.00; milk cans, 10 only at 3.75; steamers, 6 only for 10.00; oval steamer, 1 only at 6.00; onyx cups, 5 doz. at 1.50; pie plates, 5 doz. at 1.50; kitchen bowls, 5 doz. at 1.55; rice boiler, 1 only at 1.25; skimmers, 1 doz. at 4.00; vegetable dishes, 20 doz. at 1.00; galvanized pipe, 116 ft. at 36c.; 101 ft. at 27¾c.; dishes, 1 doz. at 18.00; 1 doz. at 21.00; sundries, 5.10	243	02
Simpson, Robt. Co., Limited, wall paper, 79 rolls at 20c., 30 rolls at 15c.; border, 53 rolls at 6c.; oak moulding, 68 ft. at 2½c.; crepe paper, 24 rolls at 10c.; dolls, 1 doz. at 2.85	30	43

PUBLIC INSTITUTIONS MAINTENANCE.—*Continued.*

ASYLUM FOR INSANE, MIMICO.—*Continued.*

Smith, T. H., chickens, 34 lbs. at 12c.; turkey, 835 lbs. at 15c.; ducks, 13½ lbs. at 13c.; geese, 13½ lbs. at 12c.; cheese, 265 lbs. at 13c............... 167 15
Smith, Andrew, Dr. V. S., visits, attendance and medicines 25 00
Vienna, Pressed Yeast Co., yeast, 26 lbs. at 26c.................................. 6 76
Willard & Co., eggs, 240 doz. at 22c.; geese, 609 lbs. at 11c................. 119 79

ASYLUM FOR INSANE, LONDON ($6,535.13).

Adams & Tanton, wheat, 500 lbs. at 1.35 cwt.; corn 100 lbs. at 1.85c.; seed, 1 bus. at 80c.; prunes, 300 lbs. at 7½c.; canned tomatoes, 8 doz. at 95c. 39 50
Bell Telephone Co., messages, 60c.; repairs, 3.00; Bell, B. & Son, repairs to cutting box, 3.00 .... 6 60
Brick Manufacturing & Supply Co., tile, 1 6x6 glazed tile 50
Brock, W. A., repairs to syringe 25
Bott & Brown, 6 doz. perforated seats 11 50
Boyd, H. J., fish boiler, 2.25; 1 wash bowl, 25c.; tea kettle, 25c., 24 bake pans at 1.00; 1 cullender, 2.50; 1 doz. fish slicers, 3.00; enamelled chambers, 6 doz. at 6.60 .... 74 25
Canadian Express Co., charges 90
Canadian Packing Co., brawn, 570 lbs. at 8c.; lard, 200 lbs. at 11½c.; bacon, 22½ lbs. at 14c 71 72
Canada Brass Supply Co., 3 baths and supplies, 76.00; castings, bushings, etc., 22.99 .... 98 99
Childs, H. J., drugs and chemicals, 147.70; Creelman Bros., repairs to knitting machine, 8.92 .... 156 62
Citizens' Gas Control Co., gas 200 00
City Gas Co., gas 414 15
Canada Spice and Grocery Co., chicory, 20 lbs. at 12c.; nutmegs, 5 lbs. at 50c.; pepper, 20 lbs. at 19c.; ginger, 5 lbs. at 22c.; coffee, 158 lbs. at 27c., 138 lbs. at 18c.; rye, 40 lbs. at 3c 78 50
Canadian Oil Co., wax. 224 lbs. at 8c., 17.92, less 1 bbl., 1.00 .... 16 92
Cambridge, J. & Sons, fish, 230 lbs. at 10c 23 00
Chapman, Chas. writing paper, 100 pads at 25c.; typewriting paper, 4,000 sheets at 2.00 , m... 83 00
Clare, Robert, gravel, 11 cords at 3.50 .... 38 50
Chapman, John H., dolls, 5 at 1.25; caps. 7 doz. at 75c 6 50
Dennis Wire & Iron Works, 3 wire balloons 5 40
Darch & Hunter, 1 bbl. 3.50; lettuce, ½ doz. at 25c............................. 3 63
Dyer Bros., stabling horses, 32.00; manure, 31.05 .... 55 35
Dreaney Henry, manure, 27 loads at 50c 13 50
Everitt, George, brick, 2,500 at 7.50 per m.................................... 18 75
Fraser, D., horseshoeing 8 63
Fallon, P., milk, 138 gals. at 13½c 18 63
Gurd, Wm., & Co., 1 rubber stamp, 1.25; 1 rubber die, 75c.................... 2 00
Great N. W. Tel. Co., message, 25c.; Gurney Foundry Co., repairs to furnace, 20.00 .... 20 25
Grand Trunk Ry., freight charges 3 76
Howden, D. H. & Co., shovels, 1 doz. at 10.85; knives, 1 doz. at 4.25; carvers, 1 pr. at 1.40; twine, 16 lbs. at 30c................................... 21 30
Hueston, Robt., manure 50 00
Hookway, R. & Son, corn meal, 6 bbls. at 3.75................................. 22 50
Hunt Bros., coal contract. Pocahontas, 194 tons, 870 at 4.34; Briar Hill, 26 tons 1.300 lbs. at 5.00 .... 977 10
Hobb's Hardware Co., glass 8 30
Hoskens & Russell, horse shoeing 3 38
Howard, C. E., repairing wagon shafts 1 75
Higby, W. G., cab hire 8 00
Jenkins, Thos., pipes, 3 doz 5 40
Kingsmill, T. F., rugs. 18 only at 2.00; cloth, 51 yds. at 1.00. 200 yds. at 20c.; fringe, 24 yds. at 12c., 12 yds. at 12½c., 31 yds. at 5c.; denim,

PUBLIC INSTITUTIONS MAINTENANCE.—*Continued.*

ASYLUM FOR INSANE, LONDON.—*Continued.*

10 yds. at 22c.; carpet, 35 yds. at 1.50; silk, 4 yds. at 25c.; muslin 44 yds. at 28c., 16 yds. at 35c.; repp, 7½ yds. at 12½c.; table covers, 6 at 3.00, 3 at 50c.; 1 at 69c.; 2 at 1.00	229 80
Lawson & Jones, stationery and paper, 22.25; London Electric Co., electrical repairs, 6.60	28 85
London Crockery Co., chambers, 6 doz. at 4.80	28 80
Langford, A. A. Co., paper and stationery	25 40
London Engine and Supplies Co., gaskets, 6¾ lbs. at 1.20; valve, 1 angle and connections, 17.00	25 10
Ladell, A. E., tobacco, 204 lbs. at 45c., 210 lbs. at 46c	188 40
London Advertiser, subscriptions, Jan. 5th, to Dec. 31	11 99
Leonard, E. & Sons, repairs to boiler	2 50
Mann, John & Son, stove coal 144 tons, 4.80 at 6.20	894 29
May, Wm., horse shoeing	8 10
Mountjoy, R. & Son, apples, 1 bbl. at 3.00; cranberries, 2 qts. 25c.; lemons, 9 doz. at 3.30	6 55
Maker, Thos., cab hire, 15.00; Mallock, Wm. & Co., brass valve rods, 2 only at 2.15, 4.30	19 30
Malcolm, J. & Son, butter contract, 784 lbs. at 20 7-8c., 163.66; less cartage, 1.00	162 66
McMahon, Granger & Co., print, 341¾ yds. at 27½c.; corsets, 1 pr. at 1.25	95 23
McLaughlin, M. & Co., flour contract, 225 bbls. at 4.55	1,023 75
McInnis, A., farm labor	192 05
McCormick, C. J., chickens, 4 prs. 3.20; eggs, 220 doz. at 25c.; turkeys, 23¼ lbs. at 16c.; geese, 922 lbs. at 12c	172 92
McCormick, A. & Sons, tea, 285 lbs. at 22c	62 70
McCartney, Jas., manure, 5 loads at 50c.; horse hire, 18.50	21 00
McCallum, C. & Co., brushes, ½ doz. 30c.; soap, 1½ doz. at 1.20, 2 doz. at 1.20; baking powder, 6 doz. at 3.00; hops, 5 lbs. at 75c.	26 25
North, Ebenezer, cement pipe, 90c.; Onn, F. S., fish, 460 lbs. at 10c., 46.00	46 90
Perrin, D. S. & C., candy, 533½ lbs. at 12½c.; biscuits, 191¾ lbs. at 7c., 46¼ lbs. at 11c., 36½ lbs. at 12½c., 39½ lbs. at 13c	94 89
Parke, Davis & Co., kreso, 100 gals. at 85c	85 00
Peatt, J. Edward, borax, 10 lbs. at 9c.	90
Queen City Oil Co., oil, 44.80 gals. at 16c., 7.17; less 1 bbl., 1.00	6 17
Red Star News Co., organs, 7-12 doz. at 25c.; almanacs, ½ doz. at 75c.	6 25
Saunders, W. E. & Co., carbolic acid, 56 gals. at 21c.; absorbent cotton, 12 yds. at 29c	15 24
Scandrett Bros., yeast, 1 lb. at 36c.; almonds, 442 lbs. at 12½c.; raisins, 2 boxes at 2.25; corn starch, 40 lbs. at 6¾; sago, 158 lbs. at 5c., bags 500, 81c.; cider, 4 gals. at 30c.; brandy, ½ gal. at 2.00; syrup, 135 lbs. at 2¾; peels, 7 lbs. at 19c., 7 lbs. at 12c., 7 lbs. at 12c	114 91
Sutherland Bros., lamp burners, 1 doz. 2.00; cuspidors, 1 doz. at 55c.; thimbles, 1 doz. 1.00	9 60
Sifton & Co., 6½ M. mail bags	13 00
Southam Printing & Litho Co., printing and paper	24 50
Smith, Son & Clark, interments	18 00
Smith, Trethway & Co., boots, 2 pr. at 1.45, 18 pr. at 1.35; rubbers, 2 pr. at 60c	28 40
Tanton, John & Son, salt, 6 bbls. at 1.25; wheat, 10 bbls. at 3.03	37 80
Thomas, Geo. H., repairs to wagon	2 00
Tancock, J. A., horse shoeing	9 00
Westman, A., shade roller brakets and rings, 8½ doz. at 1.75; hardware, 15.06; lawn mower, 1 only at 16.75; netting, 50 yds. at 10c., 20 yds. at 20c., 8 yds. at 35c.; wire cloth, 100 ft. at 6c.; twine, 12 lbs. at 50c.	70 19
White, Geo. & Sons, repairs, 65.36; Western Oil Co., coal oil, 24.97	90 33
Wilson, W. J., medicine and veterinary services	27 25
Wood, H. G., tinware	15
Wortman & Ward, castings and repairs	28 46
Willis, W. D. & Co., flooring, 200 ft. at 35c.; shingles, 5 m. at 3.25; posts, 45 at 40c	41 25
Wright, Jas. & Co., cotton belting, 50 ft. at 25c.; rod iron, 7.77	20 27

PUBLIC INSTITUTIONS MAINTENANCE.—*Continued*.

ASYLUM FOR INSANE, HAMILTON ($5,900.98).

Anderson, Wm., evergreens, 9 loads at 2.50	22	50
Acton Tanning Co., ground bark, 2 bags for	1	82
Armstrong and Chapman, stabling for team, 2 years at 10.00	20	00
Bursar, to pay sundries	5	85
Bennett Bros., chop feed, 3 1,515-2,000 tons at 22.00; flour, 10 bags at 2.15, 10 bags at 1.90, 3 bags at 1.95	129	02
Bell Telephone Co., messages		25
Cambden, J. R., lard, 122 lbs. at 12½c	15	25
Canadian Express Co., express charges	1	15
Dominion Express Co., express charges		75
Dunlop, The James, Limited, potatoes, 384 50-60 bus. at 65c.; bran 3 1,680-2,000 tons at 15.50	309	66
Dundas Banner, subscription for 1906	1	00
Dalley, F. F. Co., Limited, pepper, 20 lbs. at 19c	3	80
Elliott, Nicholas, evergreens	5	00
Ellis, Norman, repairing clocks	2	25
Electric Supply Co., tinsel cord, 4 yds. at 30c.	1	20
Fleischmann & Co., yeast, 195 lbs. at 30c.	58	50
Fearman, F. W., Co., eggs, 126 doz. at 24c., 60 doz. at 25c., 60 doz. at 27c.; honey, 420 lbs. at 8¼	97	14
Farm Exchange, tallow, 320 lbs. at 4½c	14	40
G. N. W. Telegraph Co., messages	1	12
Gillard, W. H. & Co., starch, 123 lbs. at 4½c.; figs, 50¼ lbs. at 10c.; raisins. 4 boxes at 3.00, 1 box at 1.82; lobsters, 6 doz. at 2.10; salmon, 6 doz. at 1.70	47	22
Gurney Foundry Co., repairs to range	4	45
Globe Printing Co., subscription for 1906	8	00
G. T. Railway Co., freight	1	61
Hamilton Water Works, water	- 1,008	57
Humphreys, Frank F., fish, 393 lbs. at 8½c.. 1,091 lbs. at 9c., 117 lbs. at 9½c.; raisins, 6 lbs. at 20c.; nuts. 10 lbs. at 20c.. 160 lbs. at 12c.; oranges, 141 doz. at 13c.; cranberries, 2 bbls. at 13.25; figs, 11 lbs. at 15c.; sundries, 2.80	214	40
Hamilton, F. Co., Limited, twine, 5.25; hinges. 12 prs. at 40c.; locks, 1 only 1.00	11	05
Hamilton & Barton Incline Ry. Co., use of incline for December	30	00
Herald Printing Co., subscriptions for 1906	6	00
McLaughlin. M. & Co.. flour, 190 lbs. at 4.55, $864.50; less 80c., on 65 bbls. 52.00, (shipped December 30)	812	50
McIntosh, P. & Son, rolled oats. 14 bbls. at 4.60	46	00
Mack, Jno., drugs and chemicals	73	47
Myles. Thos., Sons. stove coal. 53.690 tons at 5.99; egg coal, 185.1670 tons at 5.99	- 1,432	69
Morgan, R. R., mine run coal, 22.850 tons at 3.90	87	45
Mail and Empire, subscriptions for 1906	8	00
Marshall, E. R. Co., leather, 267¼ ft. at 21c	56	12
Malcolm, J. & Son, butter, 1,264 lbs. at 20½c	259	12
Newport, W., candy. 100 lbs. at 20c, 75 lbs. at 15c	31	25
Nordheimer Piano Co., music stands, 3 at 85c.	2	55
Patterson, J. D. Co., repairs to waggons, sleighs, etc	75	40
Pratt. T. H., Co., Limited, ribbons, 107 yds. at 13.37; shawls, 9 only at 50c.; hose, 3 doz. at 3.00; tooth brushes, 6 doz. at 1.20; net, 48 yds. at 40c.; handkerchiefs, 16 doz. 15.60; ties, 5 doz. at 3.00; pipes, 4 doz. at 2.25; capes, 2 at 2.50; sundries, 15.33; belts. 1 doz. at 2.75	113	45
Ramsay, Thomas, hose, 50 feet 1½ inches, 3 ply at 25c.	12	50
Riddell, John E., repairs to buildings, etc.	34	89
Rodger, Robert S., horseshoeing	10	69
Russell, James, travelling expenses	4	00
Spectator Printing Co., printing, 9.50; subscriptions for 1906, 6.00	15	50
Smye. Wm.. Jr.. chickens, 15.15; turkey, 1,219 lbs.. 219.81; geese. 767 lbs at 12c., ducks, 5 pairs at 1.50; oranges, 7 doz. at 50c.; celery, 7½ doz. at 60c.; sweet potatoes, 12 lbs. at 6½c., 15 lbs. at 6½c.; jelly powder, 1 box at 1.00; capers, 6 bottles at 25c.; vanilla, 1 pint, 1.50; sapolio, 1 doz. at 1.20; coal oil, 5 gals. at 20c.; sundries, 20.53	370	98

PUBLIC INSTITUTIONS MAINTENANCE.—*Continued.*

ASYLUM FOR INSANE, HAMILTON.—*Continued.*

Sanford, W. E., Mfg. Co., serge, 112¾ yds. at 3.35	377 71
Sweeney, Hugh C., tinware	3 90
Shaw, Hugh, horseshoeing	8 10
Turnbull, A. C., stationery	5 25
Taylor, E., sharpening knives	· 1 75
Toronto World, subscription for 1906	3 00
Toronto News, do	3 00
Times Printing Co., do	6 00
Toronto Saturday Night, do	2 00
Warden, King & Son, Daisy fire pot complete with door, 18.00; washers, 1.00	19 00
Way, B., travelling expenses	2 75

ASYLUM FOR INSANE, KINGSTON ($2,828.59).

Anglin, S. & Co., lumber, 27.92; storm sash and vents, 59 at 1.10; doors, 2 at 3.75; cartage, 2.75	103 07
Abramson, Jos., hosiery, 12 doz. at 2.00	24 00
Brisco, C., services as helper to masons, 6 days at 1.85 per day	11 10
Bursar, to pay sundries	25
Carruthers, J. B., rent of land adjoining Asylum property	50 00
Croft, George, 21 tons hay and rent of pasture for 1905	125 00
Carnovsky, W. H., quinces, 3 baskets, 1.75; grapes, 6 baskets at 30c.; cranberries, 16 qts. at 15c.; oranges, 1 box, 2.50	8 45
Corbett, S. S., interments	13 00
Chown, A. P., drugs and chemicals	95
Derry, Hugh, services as mason, 6 days at 3.50 per day	21 00
Dominion Fish Co., oysters, 6 qts., 2.90; fish, 1,980 lbs., 103.50; fowl, 439½ lbs., 35.95	142 35
Dalton, W. B. & Sons, twine, 10 lbs. at 40c.; knives, ½ doz at 3.50; spoons, 3 doz. at 2.25, 3 doz. at 3.50; rope, 7¾ lbs. at 15c.; rope, 100 ft. at 15c.; books and eyes, 24 doz. at 10c.; sundries, 2.87	31 83
Dini, Evaristo, beef, 1,000 lbs. at 5.50 cwt.; mutton, 900 lbs. at 8c.	127 00
Engineer Publishing Co., 1 year's subscription	1 00
Fisher Bros., grains	171 00
Gravelle, O., cows, 5 at 45.00; use of binder for harvest, 1905, 10.00	235 00
Gibson, W. W., drugs and chemicals	1 20
Green, S., veal, 240 lbs. at 8c.; mutton, 1,420 lbs. at 8c.	132 80
Gibson, John, corned beef, 630 lbs. at 5c.; mutton, 580 lbs. at 8c.	77 90
Gowdey, James, beef, 560 lbs. at 5c.	28 00
Gilbert, John, contract butter, 293 lbs. at 17c.; rolled oats, 2 bbls. at 4.00	58 61
Grand Trunk Railway, freight	4 02
Herriman, Dr. W. C., travelling expenses	21 90
Hoag, Frank J., drugs and chemicals, 4.29; sundries, 35c.; soap, 37½ lbs. at 8c.	7 64
Hartz, The J. F. Co., Ltd., macintosh sheet, 1 only at 2.10; alcohol stove, 1 only at 4.00	6 10
Hogan, W., horseshoeing, 1.89; cart box and shafts, 15.00	16 89
Harrison, The F. F. Co., mattresses	6 50
Horsey, S. J., gasoline, 20 gals. at 25c.; souveneir range, 60.00; tinware, 1.75; oil stove, 7.50; repairs, 2.50	76 75
Henderson, J. S., spirits for medicinal purposes, 4.50; sundries, 3.05	7 55
Jackson Press, stationery and printing	18 00
Kingston Milk Depot, milk, 480 qts. at 4c.; whipped cream, 2 qts. at 40c.	20 00
Kelly, James & Co., sugar, 1,200 lbs. at 4.30 cwt.; salt, 12 bags at 10c., 4 bbls. at 1.35	58 20
Kingston News, printing	7 25
Lemmon & Sons, bath waste and overflow, 2.50; N. P. tap and flanges, 2 at 1.50; bath tap, 1 at 1.50; iron castings, etc., 3.25; lead bends, 2 at 75c.; horse blankets, 7, 14.50; repairs, 5 hours at 40c.; bells, 3 strings at 1.15; sursingles, 6 at 35c.; sundries, 2.90	36 70
La Fleur, Agnes G., services as dairy maid, 22 days at 12.00 per month	8 50
Macnee & Minnes, sateen, 24 yds. at 13c.; tabling, 54¾ yds. at 45c.; lawn,	

PUBLIC INSTITUTIONS MAINTENANCE.—*Continued.*

ASYLUM FOR INSANE, KINGSTON.—*Continued.*

30 yds. at 12½c., 24 yds. at 18½c.; muslin, 25 yds. at 15c.. 48 yds. at 18½c., 1 piece, 1.50; lace, 3 doz. yds. at 28c.; shawls, 1 doz., 18.00; cheese cloth, 108 yds. at 4¾c.; combs, 3 doz. at 1.50, 1 doz. at 1.35; handkerchiefs, 5 doz. at 1.00; tweed, 108 yds. at 40c., 98¾ yds. at 45c.; needles, 2½ m. at 1.00; pins, 6 pkgs. at 16c., 6 pkgs. at 18c.; bath towels, 2 doz. at 3.75, 2 doz. at 3.00	190	57
Mills, Thos., & Co., caps, 1 doz. at 9.00, ¼ doz. at 6.00	10	50
McGall, Jack, tobacco, 96 lbs. at 45c.	43	20
McColl Bros. & Co., cylinder oil, 1 bbl. 50 gals.	29	40
McAuley, Thos., stationery	32	01
McDermott, Jno. F., repairs to waggons, etc.	17	25
Nicholls, Dr., professional services	50	50
Newman & Shaw, oil cloth, 5 yds. at 25c.; pillow cotton, 82 yds. at 18c.; corsets, 4 pairs at 75c.; ties, 1 doz. at 1.75; waisting, 22½ yds. at 15c., 3½ yds. at 20c.; waists, 5 at 65c.	28	09
Peters, Wm. P. & Bro., bran, ½ ton at 18.00; cracked feed, 1 ton at 24.00; corn meal. 2 bbls. at 4.00	41	00
Pickering, C. H., cocoa, 6 lbs. at 50c.; coffee, 100 lbs. at 25c.; tea, 110 lbs. at 25c.	55	50
Purtell. M., chickory, 137 lbs. at 15c.; coffee, 100 lbs. at 25c.	45	55
Parkhill, J. Y. & Co., ham, 31½ lbs. at 13½c.; eggs, 147 doz. at 22½c., 49 doz. at 27½c.; lard, 50 lbs. at 11½c.	56	56
Postmaster, postage stamps	23	00
Rigney & Hickey, sugar, 667 lbs., 28.49; sundries, 1.50; syrup, 700 lbs. at 2 7-8c.; mustard, 5 jars at 1.00; turkey, 233 lbs., 34.08	89	20
Robertson, Nicolle & Co., soap, 8 boxes at 4.00, 2,000 lbs. at 5c.	132	00
Ryan, Dr. E., travelling expenses	58	50
Ross, H., expenses capturing escaped patient	1	05
Sowards, James, cement, 3 bbls., 7.70; wood, 1 cord, 7.50	15	20
Suddard, E. S., tea, 160 lbs. at 25c.	40	00
Tomlinson, Geo. R., electrical supplies, lamps, etc.	32	60
Uglow, R. & Co., stationery, 4.40; tennis balls, 2.00	6	40
Vincent, Ockley & Sons, cups and saucers, 6 doz. at 1.00; bowls, 6 doz. at 1.25; soup plates, 6 doz. at 1.00; candy dishes, ½ doz. at 7.00; plates, 1½ doz. at 1.75; sugar boxes, 6 only at 30c.; crockery sundries, 4.25	31	68
Waldron, R., saline, 46 yds. at 25c.	11	50
Wenger, Aaron, contract butter, 616 lbs. at 20¾c.	127	82

ASYLUM FOR INSANE, BROCKVILLE ($3,216.21).

Armour & Cunningham, prunes, 500 lbs at 6½c.; chocolate, 6 lbs. at 35c.; pot barley, 200 lbs. at 2½c.; evaporated apples, 500 lbs. at 9½	87	10
Armstrong, G. H., apples, 2½ bbls. at 2.25	5	63
Bursar, to pay sundries	1	60
Blair, Hiram, apples, 9½ bush at 50c.	4	75
Burns, James, apples, 15 bush. at 45c.	6	75
Brown, H. & Sons, oats, 100 bush. at 40c.	40	00
Bell Telephone Co., rent of instruments, 51.50; repairs, 4.02; messages, 60c.	56	12
Brockville Times, advertising, 1.75; printing, 14.50	16	25
Bedlow, Jno., lamb, 25½ lbs. at 12½c., 39½ lbs. at 15c.; sausage, 30 lbs, 3.10; turkey, 546¾ lbs. at 20c.; geese, 474 lbs. at 14c.	187	95
Cameron, A. E., teaming oats, bran, 2 tons at 17.00; corn meal, 1½ tons at 24.00; feed, 1 ton at 21.00	92	25
Canadian Express Co., express charges	1	25
Culbert, J., figs, 660 lbs. at 5c.; yeast, 28 lbs. at 35c.; soap, 1 box, 4.00; blue, 14 lbs. at 20c.; twine, 10 lbs. at 35c.; haddie, 15 lbs. at 10c.; tobacco, 33½ lbs. at 46	70	01
Central Prison, tweed, 110 yds. at 50c.; wrapper, 25c.	55	25
C. P. R. Telegraph Co., messages		25
Downey, D. W., men's rubbers, 5 prs. at 85c., 1 pr. at 65c.	4	90
Derosia, P.,, fish, 995 lbs. at 9c.	89	55
Dudley, Geo. H., apples, 13 bush. at 30c.	3	90
Farm Exchange, pork, 520 lbs. at 7½c.	39	00
Green, J. & Co., stationery	14	84

PUBLIC INSTITUTIONS MAINTENANCE.—*Continued.*

ASYLUM FOR INSANE, BROCKVILLE.—*Continued.*

Griffin, James, services as attendant, 5 days at 20.00 per month	3	22
Grey, Robert, meat blocks, 1 only at 1.50, 1 only at 1.00	2	50
G. T. Railway Co., freight charges		87
Harrison, W. H., repairs to tinware	5	25
Johnston's Cash Grocery, haddie, 30 lbs. at 7½c.; brooms, 2 doz., 5.45; currants, 76 lbs. at 6c.; raisins, 110 lbs. at 7½c.; raisins, 22 lbs. at 12½c.; sugar, 3 bags at 4.50; sundries, 2.10..	38	86
Jackson, E., recapturing eloper	5	00
Kincard, V. F., drugs and chemicals	53	17
McKinley, J. A., services as attendant, 14 days at 20.00 per month	9	03
McLaughlin, M. & Co., flour, 159 bbls. at 4.70	747	30
McLaren, Peter, lumber	32	50
McConkey, W. H., coffee, 100 lbs. at 26c...	26	00
McHenry's, spirits for medicinal purposes	3	00
Postmaster, postage stamps	10	00
Quirmbach, Geo., interments	8	00
Recorder Printing Co., subscription, 3.00; advertising, 2.15	5	15
Rudd, C. R. & Co., fur robes, 2 at 14.00; fur coat, 1 only at 17.00.........	45	00
Ritchie, F. J., cigars, 200 for 4.00; pipes, 1 doz. at 3.00......................	7	00
St. Lawrence Produce Co., eggs, 60 doz. at 25c., 300 doz. at 26.00.........	93	00
Stagg, Fred. A., bacon, 9 5-16 lbs. at 16c.; ham, 66¾ lbs. at 16c...........	12	17
Steacy, B. D., skates, 10 prs. at 50c.; straps, 1 doz. at 1.00, 1 doz. at 1.25, 1 doz at 1.50; padlocks, 6 only at 50c.; snow shovels, 1 doz. at 4.75, 2 doz. at 3.00; plaster paris, 1 bbl at 2.55; shackles, 11½ lbs. at 15c.; sundries, 3.40	32	93
Union Publishing Co., books	5	00
Water Works Dept., water	1,000	00
Wooding George, shoes, 17 pairs at 2.75, 52 pairs at 67½c., 5 pairs at 1.25, 1 pair at 1.60	89	70
Wright, Robert Co., curtains, 3 pairs at 1.75; boot laces, 5 gross at 1.00; stamping outfit, 6.00; sundries, 8.50	24	83
Wright, H. B. & Co., confectionery, 250 lbs. at 10c.; nuts, 200 lbs. at 15c.; grapes, 1 keg at 6.75; cranberries, 1 bbl at 13.00; oranges, 6 bbls at 4.50; oysters, 5 gals. at 1.60; sundries, 80c.............................	110	55
Williams, James, paraffin wax, 222 lbs. at 14c.; cartage, 50c...............	31	58
Webster, Jno., cheese, 298 lbs. at 12½c..	37	25

ASYLUM FOR FEMALE PATIENTS, COBOURG ($985.85).

Allen, W. L. & Co., screws, 2 doz. at 10c.; locks, 2 at 40c.	1	00
Bell Telephone Co., messages	1	05
Canadian Express Co., charges	3	35
Cobourg (Town), taxes on Lot 7, University Street	3	29
Clappison Packing & Covering Co., asbestos, 3 lbs. 9 oz. at 1.25	4	45
Cobourg Water & Electric Co., water, 104.76; light, 171.02	275	78
Canadian Oil Co., engine oil, 43.50 gals at 45c.	19	58
Canada Paint Co., white opalite, 45 lbs.	1	80
Dundas, A. R., iron and tinware	48	31
Duncan, John, Estate, potatoes, 60 bus. at 50c.; rolled oats, ½ bbl. at 4.50	35	85
DeLang, Wm., repairs	2	50
Dulmadge, Dr. J. D., professional services	3	50
Dempster, Jas., 1 grate	2	50
Ferguson, A. C., milk, 1,426 qts. at 4c.	57	04
Fleischmann Co., yeast, 6 lbs. at 30c.	1	80
Field Hardware Co., sundry hardware	5	52
Floyd, W. H., sundries	2	30
Gillard, James, sundries	6	19
Guillett Bros., squash, 3 at 10c.; grapes, 3 lbs. at 20c., 6 lbs. at 20c.; dates, 10 lbs. at 10c.; onions, ½ bus. at 1.00; haddies, 98¾ lbs. at 9c.; fish, 122 lbs. at 9c.; cranberries, 8 lbs. at 15c.; sapolio, 2 doz. at 1.10; celery, 12 pkgs. at 70c.; prunes, 10 lbs. at 10c.; raisins,, 98c.; peel, 4 lbs. at 13c.; pumpkins, 2 at 10c.; lemons, 1 doz. at 25c.; currants, 20 lbs. at		

PUBLIC INSTITUTIONS MAINTENANCE.—*Continued.*

ASYLUM FOR FEMALE PATIENTS, COBOURG.—*Continued.*

at 7c.; cider, 2 gals. at 20c.; oysters, 2 gals. at 2.27; nuts, 10 lbs. at 1.55; candy, 100 lbs. at 7c.; oranges, 15 1-6 doz. at 4.24; rice, 8 lbs. at 4c.; sausages, 4 lbs. at 12½c.	50 48
Hooey & Son, figs, 56 lbs. at 5c.; purnes, 149 lbs. at 7½c.; jam, 90 lbs. at 8c.	21 18
Hewson & Co., thread, 5¼ doz. at 48c.; frilling, 1 doz. at 2.00; muslin, 20 yds at 10c.; curtains, 13½ yds. at 1.00; rugs, 21.00	41 14
Harvey, T. R. & Son, dishes and glassware	12 51
Johns, O. G., drugs and chemicals	12 95
Kewin, D., 4 pair ducks at 1.00	4 00
Mitchell, T. & Sons, pork, 20 lbs. at 11c.; suet, 50c.; poultry, 33.57	36 27
Maher, W. J., beef, 1,519 lbs. at 7c.; suet, 10 lbs. at 12½c.	107 58
Macpherson, D., wages as temporary clerk	39 00
McBride, H. L., furniture	29 35
Newman, W. S., eggs, 90 doz.	18 60
Nichols, M. C., dishes, 7.65; sausages, 12 lbs. at 11c.; apples, 2.80; celery, 1 doz. at 55c.; biscuits, 55c.; oranges, 2 doz. at 50c.; soap, 1 box at 4.00; currants, 20 lbs. at 8c.; beans, 92 lbs. at 2 1-9c.	20 88
Ryan, Wm. Co., butter, 280 lbs. at 21¾c.	60 90
Steed, J., saurkrout, 1 bbl.	4 00
Troop, Wm., tapioca, 100 lbs. at 5c.; rice, 100 lbs. at 4c.; barley, 100 lbs. at 3c.	12 00
Throop, A. D., paint, 12 lbs. at 12½c.; time, 27 hours at 20c.; apples, 13 bus. at 70c.	16 00
Webster, J. T., mutton, 232 lbs. at 10c.	23 20

ASYLUM FOR INSANE, PENETANGUISHENE ($2,907.81).

Bell Telephone Co., messages	7 75
Breithaupt Leather Co., leather, 30 lbs. at 28c.	8 40
Campbell, S., beef and lamb, 2,960 lbs.	205 72
Chew Bros., horse hire	56 00
Copeland, G. & Sons, oat chop, 2,170 lbs. at 28.00 per ton; 100 bus. oats at 45c.; bran, 1 ton 18.00; shorts, 1 ton 23.00	116 38
Charlebois & Son, A. B., brick, 500, 4.00; cement, 20 bags 13.25	17 25
Cloutier, Joseph, manure, 47 loads at 25c.	11 75
Carter, W. S., drugs and chemicals	6 25
Corbeau, Mrs. N., wages as cook	2 00
Canadian Express Co., express charges	3 35
Dalley, F. F., The, coffee, 50 lbs. at 25c.	12 50
Darling, J. S., telegrams, 2.98; postage stamps, 7.00	9 98
Fleischmann & Co., yeast, 8 lbs.	3 31
Grise, D., spirits for medicinal purposes	12 50
Gignac, Louis, cups and saucers, 1 doz. at 1.00; butter, 584¼ lbs., 121.15	122 15
Gilmour, F. W., interments	5 00
Grand Trunk Railway, freight charges	82
Hartz, J. F. Co., The, surgical instruments and medical comforts	5 50
Hartman Bros., brushes, 3 at 30c., 3 at 50c.; knives, 6 at 35c., 2 at 30c.; butchers' steel, 1.00; glass, 12.00; tape line, 2.50; cork screw, 25c.	20 85
Herald, The, bill sheets	5 00
Hollister, J. W. & Co., 1 string bells, 2.75; saddlery, 90c.	3 65
Hunt Bros., 410 bags flour at 2.44	1,000 40
Little Henry M., interments	5 00
Labreau, F., interments	5 00
Lahey, D. A. & Co., raisins, 6 boxes at 75c.; peel, 1 lb. at 20c.; sugar, 29.07; figs, 123¾ lbs. at 4½c.; jam, 240 lbs. at 7¾c.; tobacco, 70 lbs. at 50c.; tea, 120 lbs. at 25c.; tapioca, 100 lbs. at 5c.; sago, 100 lbs. at 5c.; blue, 12 lbs. at 20c.; jardiniers, 3.20; shirts, 4 doz. at 5.50; drawers, 4 doz. at 5.50; cotton, 128 yds. at 10c.; socks, 2 doz. at 2.25; eggs, 30 doz. at 25c.	203 57
McDonald, P. A., drugs and chemicals	5 65
Ontario Rubber Co., rubber goods	30 24
Payette P. & Co., machinery and repairs	85 03
Pollard, Jno. R., postage stamps	5 00

PUBLIC INSTITUTIONS MAINTENANCE.—*Continued.*

ASYLUM FOR INSANE, PENETANGUISHENE.—*Continued.*

Robinson, George, horseshoeing	2 70
Shanahan Carriage Co., wagon and repairs	13 60
Steele, Briggs Seed Co., holly	1 00
Tudhope Carriage Co., The, repairs	19 00
Todd, S. E., 1,980 lbs. straw	5 45
Thompson, W. M., Tar paper, 7 rolls at 65c.; spray pump, 1.80; oakum, 10 lbs. at 10c.; sundry hardware, 3.03; pot barley, 148 lbs. at 4c.; peas, 98 lbs. at 4c.; washing soda, 360 lbs. at 1c.; bed pan, 50c.; fish, 500 lbs. 36.62; eggs, 120 doz. at 25c.; apples, 41 bags at 75c.; biscuits, 2 tins at 30c.; beans, 2 bus. at 2.00; ham, 44 lbs. at 15c.; brooms, 2 doz. at 2.50; corn meal, 3 bags at 2.20; cocoanut, 2 lbs. at 25c.; wheatine, 3 bags at 3.75; baking powder, 5 lbs. at 10c.; currants, 162 lbs. at 6½c.; raisins, 56 lbs. at 6c., 10 lbs. at 8c., 1 box layer, 3.75, 2 boxes layer, 2.20; rolled oats, 6 sacks, 15.45; prunes, 400 lbs. at 7½c., 100 lbs. at 9½c.; rice, 257 lbs. at 4c.; salmon, 4 doz. at 1.85; starch, 100 lbs. at 6c.; sugar, 293 lbs. at 4.90, 300 lbs. at 4.35; figs, 195 lbs. at 5c., 11¾ at 15c.; bacon, 18 lbs. at 17c.; baskets, 6 at 45c.; pipes, 1 doz. at 3.00; salt, 3 bbls. at 1.35; straw, 2,140 lbs. at 5.44 per ton; cotton, 175 yds. at 10c.; stockings, 1 doz. 2.50; corsets, 4 prs. at 75c.; gloves, 1 doz. at 2.50; handkerchiefs, 5.25; combs, 1 doz. at 2.25; ribbons, 18 yds. at 15c.; shawls, 7 at 49c.; ties, 6½ doz. at 2.25; laces, 18 yds. at 6c.; collars, 2 doz. at 1.20; shirts, 1 doz. at 7.00; oranges, 1 doz. at 50c., 1 box at 4.25, 2 crates at 3.75; candy, 30 lbs. at 18c.; molasses, 45.9 gals. at 33c.; nuts, 40 lbs. at 15c.; oysters, 2 qts. at 1.00; robes, 4 at 12.00; clothes, 50 suits at 6.00; bunting, 169½ yds. at 5c.; dishes, 1 doz. at 7.20; bowls, 6 doz. at 1.00; glass, 4 2-12 doz. at 40c.; napkins, 2 doz. at 3.50; cranberries, 5.30; hose, 3 doz. at 2.50; caps, 3 doz. at 1.00; shawls, 5 at 49c.; screw hooks, 1.25; screw eyes, 6 doz. at 5c.; twine, 1.10; polish, 1 tin 20c.; cord, 54c.	817 57
Wright, C. E., chickens, 8.05; turkeys, 200 lbs. at 16c.; geese and ducks, 226 lbs. at 14c.	71 69
Wright, G. H., traps, etc.	80

ASYLUM FOR FEEBLE MINDED, ORILLIA ($1,650.35).

Bell Telephone Co., messages	2 05
Boyd, Moses, blankets, 1 only at 1.90; robe, 1 only at 8.50; brushes, 1.25; combs, 60c.; repairs to harness, 1.25; sundries, 40c.	13 90
Brock, The W. R. Co., Ltd., flannel, 276¼ yds. at 32½c.; packing, 30c. (3 per cent. off), 87.38; tweed, 65¼ yds. at 95c.; packing, 30c. (5 per cent. off), 59.40	146 78
Central Prison, blankets, 715 lbs. at 50c.; wrappers, 5 at 50c.	360 00
Canadian General Electric Co., electrical supplies	4 84
Ellis, J. W., yeast, 14 lbs. at 30c.; express charges, 1.70	5 90
Failes, John, extra work cutting meat, 3 mos. at 5.00	15 00
Gilpin Bros., hardware sundries	3 58
Gattie, John, extra work as painter, 3 mos. at 5.00	15 00
Hazlett, John, turkey, 605 lbs. at 15c.	90 75
Hatley, J..J., contract, meat, 5,366 lbs. at 7.05 cwt.; fish, 125 lbs. at 9c.; sausages, 35 lbs. at 10c.; lard, 100 lbs. at 12½c.; suet, 40 lbs. at 10c.; bacon, 21 lbs. at 16c.	412 91
Haywood, Thos., granite cups	3 85
Hale Bros., advertising	3 50
Harvie, A., one month as mason	37 00
Harvie, D. W., apples, 15 bbls. at 1.50	22 50
Kane & Kane, salt, 6 bbls. at 1.50	9 00
Leigh, J., hay, 1.110 tons at 8.00	8 44
Moon, John, straw, 2.1165 tons at 5.00	12 91
Moore, The Chris. Co., Ltd., contract, butter, 1,101 lbs. at 18c.; turkey, 92 lbs. at 14c.	211 06
McFadden, W. J., drugs and chemicals	26 80
McCort, The Oil Co., candles, 144 set at 10c.; 68 lbs. cup grease at 10c.	21 20

PUBLIC INSTITUTIONS MAINTENANCE.—*Continued.*

ASYLUM FOR FEEBLE MINDED, ORILLIA.—*Continued.*

McPhee, A., fowl 55 05
Northway, The Co., Ltd., overshoes, 3 prs. at 1.65; rubbers, 1 pr. at 85c.; collars, 6 doz. 8.40; ties, 4 doz. at 1.50; corsets, 2 prs. at 50c.; spools, 1 gro. at 5.76; bath brick. 1 case at 1.00; eggs, 90 doz. at 25c.; sundries, 15c. 50 61
Phillips & Co., steamer, 1 at 7.00; dish pans, 4 only at 75c.; dippers, 2 at 20c.; repairs, 20c. 10 60
Portmaster, postage stamps 8 00
Slaven's Drug Store, books, 2.15; stationery, 2.30; sundries, 1.44 .... 5 89
Sinclair & Co., tobacco, 10.27; soap, 1 box 4.50; corn starch, 82 lbs. at 7¼c.; sago, 24 lbs. at 7c.; mustard, 4 jars at 90c.; blueing, 14 lbs. at 18c.; sundries, 2.98 .... 31 50
Thomson, D. C., contract, rolled oats, 6 sacks at 2.40; bran, 1,500 lbs. for 13.50; shorts, 500 lbs. for 5.00 .... 32 90
White, G. H., haliard, 5¼ lbs. 1.38; pocket knives, 3 at 90c.; sundries, 75c. 4 83
Watson, S., bricks, 3,000 at 8.00m. 24 00

CENTRAL PRISON, TORONTO ($2.366.82).

Bursar, to pay sundries 1 22
Bell Telephone Co., rent of instruments 70 75
Bourdon, N. J., fur caps. 7 only at 6.00 .... 42 00
Brock, W. R. Co., Ltd., shirts, 3 doz. at 6.75, 3 doz. at 7.50; cotton, 132¾ yds. at 7½c.; sundries, 4.23 .... 56 93
Canadian Oil Co., gasoline, 5 gals. for 1 50
Canadian General Electric Co., lamps, 200 at 17c.; solid carbons, 200 for 5.80; globes, 1 doz. at 1.25; sundries, 5.36 .... 46 41
Consumers' Gas Co., gas 128 96
Clubb Coffee Co., pepper, 25 lbs. at 18c.; vanilla extract, 2 pts. at 60c. ... 5 70
Central Prison Industries. clothing, etc. 42 74
Doyle, M., Fish Co., fish, 266 lbs. at 7½c. 19 95
Davidson & Hay. currants, 159 lbs. at 7c.; almonds, 5 lbs. at 26c.; sugar, 1,200 lbs. at 3.93. 300 lbs. at 4.33; rice, 500 lbs. at 3½c.; brooms, 10 doz. at 2.50; syrup, 698 lbs. at 2 7-8c.; biscuits, 81½ lbs. at 6½c.; canned vegetables, 2 doz. at 60c., 2 doz. at 82½c., 2 doz. at 92½c.; sundries, 1.27 .... 146 42
Fairles, G. H., rolled oats. 4 bbls. at 5.20; split peas, 7 bags at 2.25; rolled wheat, 5 bbls. at 2.70 .... 50 05
Fleischmann & Co., yeast, 51½ lbs. at 30c. 15 45
Gurney Foundry Co., repairs to furnace 2 50
Gazess, James, Christmas gratuity to letter carrier 5 00
Gunns, Ltd., pork, 2 bbls. at 21.50; pot barley, 5 bags at 2.15; salt, 3 bags at 50c.; eggs, 45 doz. at 22c. 65 15
Hunter, Moses, oats. 100.14 bus. at 40c., 828 lbs. at 1.20 cwt.; bran, 281 lbs. at 95c.; straw, 1,106 lbs. at 8.50 .... 62 61
Hamilton Mfg. Co., sheet packing. 32 lbs. for 12 80
Howland, H. S. Sons & Co., store door latches, 1-12 doz. at 15.00; inside lock sets. 1-6 doz. at 9.00 .... 2 75
Hartz, The J. F. Co., Ltd., hospital supplies 16 46
Harris, Dr., professional services 59 50
Halliday, James, cow 25 03
Hall, F. & Son, gloves. 11 prs. at 1.00 .... 11 00
Jeffrey & Eakins, photo supplies 14 75
Jones Bros. & Co., sharpening clippers, 3 prs. at 50c. 1 50
Johnston, Alex., repairing revolver 1 00
Kilgour Bros.; ¼ bbl (1,000). sacks 30 00
Monetary Times, subscription for 1906 .... 2 00
McLaughlin, M., & Co., flour, 75 bbls. at 3.75, 112 bbls. at 4.55 .... 790 85
McDonald & Willson, electric brackets, 2 at 2.25; shades, 3 at 40c., 3 at 3.50, 3 at 45c. 17 55
Postmaster, postage stamps 18 00
Queen City Oil Co. (Limited), cylinder oil, 42 gals. for 29 34
Rice Lewis & Son, iron, hardware, castings, etc. 30 58
Robertson, The Jas., Co., galvanized boiler, 1 only at 6.00; steam guage, 1 only at 2.00 .... 8 00

PUBLIC INSTITUTIONS MAINTENANCE.—*Continued.*

CENTRAL PRISON, TORONTO.—*Continued.*

Shuttleworth, E. B., Co., Limited, medical sundries	13 56
Smith, John B. & Sons, lumber, 35.80, covers, 129 at 15c.; waggon felloes 5 only at 50c.; butcher block, 1 only at 30.00; cedar posts, 60 at 30c.	155 65
Stewart & Wood, alabastine, 50 lbs. at 6c.; plaster, 1 bbl. at 2.10	5 10
Simpson, The R. Co., gloves, 25 pairs at 1.00; fur caps, 3 at 6.00; hats, 2 at 3.00	49 00
Sparrow, Geo. & Co., bread knife, 1 only at 1.00, 1 only at 1.50; raisin seeder, 1 only at 1.50; sundries, 60c.	5 60
Salvation Army, printing	12 50
Sharp, Charles, services as temporary guard	40 00
Sundry persons, extra work and good conduct	17 00
Toronto Electric Light Co., light	14 15
Toronto Water Works Dept., water for gate house	1 38
Toronto Street Ry. Co., car tickets	7 00
Vokes Hardware Co., latches, 1 only at 30c., 1 only at 1.75; B. D. hinges, 2 pairs at 85c.; scale beam, 4.05; sundries, 3.42	11 22
Vance & Co., potatoes, 45 bush. at 68c., 52 bush at 65c.; turkey, 74 lbs. at 17c., 82 lbs. at 17½c.; butter, 35 lbs. at 17c.; ham, 41 lbs. at 14c.; lard, 50 lbs. at 11½c.; pork, 2 bbls. at 21.50	151 36
Wicks, S., apples, 4 bbls. at 3.50, 4 bbls. at 3.00	26 00
White, E., sausages, 100 lbs. at 11c.	11 00
Watson, John, hay, 1.370 ton at 10.00	11 85

ANDREW MERCER REFORMATORY ($742.95).

Allan, J. W., glass, 1 light, 1.50; putty, 25 lbs. at 2½c.; pail, 1 at 50c.; paper, 1 quire, 25c.	2 88
Ashdown, John, repairing	4 00
Belle Ewart Ice Co., ice, 43½ cwt. at 13½c.	5 98
Brock, W. R. Co., shirting, 114 yds. at 12½c.; braize, 2 yds. at 3.20; thread, ¼ gross at 5.40; buttons, 1 gross, 1.19; hose, 1 doz., 2.85	26 57
Blake, W. E., pictures, 2.55; chapel supplies, 2.70; books, 5.25	10 50
City Dairy Co., milk	31 50
Cox, S., teaming	24 50
Central Prison Industries, boots, 24 pairs at 1.00; repairing, 1.00; boiler compound, 1 bbl., 2.50; horseshoes, 2.42	29 92
Consumers' Gas Co., gas	323 60
Davidson & Hay, figs, 7 lbs. at 4c.	28
Elliott, Miss M., subscriptions	4 00
Durie, D., eggs, 29½ doz. at 28c.; ham, 12 lbs. at 16c., 13 lbs. at 15½c.; bacon, 17¾ lbs. at 17c.; lard, 20 lbs. at 12½c.	17 75
Fleischmann & Co., yeast, 6½ lbs. at 30c.	1 95
Griffin, Peter, cab hire	4 00
Gallagher & Co., fish, 78 lbs. at 10c.; ciscoes, 1 doz. at 30c.	8 10
Johnson, D., repairs	1 10
Junor Wm., sauce tureen, 1.35; dishes, 25.50	26 85
Kennedy J. H., 4 pads	2 50
Monetary Times, subscription to October, 1906	2 00
Ryan, Wm., geese, 59 lbs. at 12½; turkey, 55 lbs. at 15½c.; cheese, 11 lbs. at 14c.; butter, 211 lbs. at 17c.	53 31
Robertson, James Co., repairs	10
Simpson, Robert, The, 1 hat	2 00
Shaver, S., ploughing	3 00
Snows, R. B., berries, 1.12; lemons, 3 doz. at 20c.; oranges, 2 doz. at 50c.; apples, 1 peck, 40c.	3 12
Simmers, J. A., moss, 50 yds. at 4c.; holly, 4 lbs. at 25c.; mistletoe, 25c.	3 25
Terry, F. G. Co., 1 load mortar and cartage	3 00
Toronto Electric Light Co., light	47 94
Upper Canada Tract Society, The, music, 6.32; instruments, 12 at 35c.	10 52
Watkins, J. H. & Co., oats, 400 lbs. at 13.00 ton; bran, 100 lbs. at 9.50 per ton; hay, 340 lbs. at 12.00 per ton	8 19
Water Works Department, water	80 54

Total Public Institutions Maintenance $1,016,252 37

AGRICULTURE.

FAIRS' BRANCH.

SALARIES ($1,720.00).

H. B. Cowan: Twelve months' salary as Superintendent	1,000 00
J. Lockie Wilson: One and two-thirds months' salary as Superintendent...	200 00
B. W. Elliott: Twelve months' salary as Stenographer .... •	520 00

·EXPENSES ($1,364.65).

Bell Telephone Co., messages, 23.45; rent of instruments, 38.76	62 21
Briggs, Wm., Co., 98 copies of *Guardian*, 2.94; C. P. R. Telegraph Co., telegrams, 15.57	18 51
Canadian Express Co., charges, 1.60; Cowan, H. B., travelling expenses, 250.00	251 60
Coo. W. C., reporting fair convention, 75.00; Dorman,. Jas., services as office boy at 10.00 per week, 181.99	256 99
Dominion Express Co., charges, 2.35; G. N. W. Telegraph Co., telegrams, 15.54	17 89
Galbraith Photo Co., lantern slides, 32.55; *Globe* Printing Co., 99 copies, 2.48	35 03
Hubertus, Mrs., postage stamps, 300.00; Hypson, M. L., services at 10.00 per week, 183.33	483 33
King's Printer, stationery, 60.84; paper, 2.25; Lee, Wm., to pay car fares, 60c.	63 69
McIlroy, Wm., preparing plan of fair grounds, Carleton County...........	3 00
News Publishing Co., 100 copies of paper, 3.00; Ottawa Valley *Journal*, copies of paper, 10.00	13 00
Pike. D., rent of tents, 40.00; Reading, A. J., operating lantern, 7.00...	47 00
Russill Hardware Co., hardware, 7.70; Smallfield & Son, 400 prize lists of Renfrew fair, 30.00	37 70
Toronto Star. 100 copies, 2.00; United Typewriter, supplies and repairs, 56.50	58 50
Warwick Bros. & Rutter, printing, 13.20; *Weekly Sun*, 100 copies, 3.00...	16 20

AGRICULTURAL AND HORTICULTURAL SOCIETIES ($76,378.00).

Grants to District Societies:

Addington District, 395.00; Camden E., 140.00; Hinchinbrook, 122.00; Kennebec, 87.00; Sheffield, 56.00	800 00
Algoma E. District, 380.00; Day, Wells and Bright, additional, 27.00; Gladstone and Bright, 90.00; Johnson and Aberdeen, 28.00; Laird, 58.00; Plummer additional, 86.00; St. Joseph Island, 47.00; Thessalon, 84.00	800 00
Algoma W. District, 436.00; Emo, Lavalle and Chapple, 112.00; McIrvine and Alberton, 140.00; Oliver, 112.00	800 00
Brant North District, 660.00; Onondaga, 140.00	800 00
Brant South District, 660.00; Brantford Horticultural, 140.00.........	800 00
Brockville District	800 00
Bruce Centre District, 380.00; Elderslie, 56.00; Greenock, 58.00; Huron, 66.00; Kincardine S., 65.00; Chesley Horticultural, 66.00; Kincardine Horticultural, 62.00; Paisley Horticultural, 47.00......	800 00
Bruce North District, 380.00; Amable and Albermarle, 77.00; Arran. 77.00; Bruce, 76.00; Eastnor, 38.00; Port Elgin Horticultural, 31.00; Saugeen, 27.00; Tara Horticultural, 32.00; Tiverton and North Kincardine, 62.00	800 00
Bruce South District, 380.00; Carrick, 117.00; Culross, 117.00; Kinloss, 110.00; Walkerton Horticultural, 76.00	800 00
Cardwell District, 450.00; Albion and Bolton Village, 140.00; Caledon, 140.00; Tecumseth, 70.00	800 00
Carleton District, 451.00; Fitzroy, 124.00; Huntley, 140.00; March. 85.00	800 00
Cornwall District	350 00
Dufferin District. 405.00; Luther East, 140.00; Melancthon, 128.00; Orangeville Horticultural, 127.00	800 00

AGRICULTURE.—*Continued.*

AGRICULTURAL AND HORTICULTURAL SOCIETIES.—*Continued.*

Dundas District, 380.00;   Matilda, 140.00;   Mountain, 140.00;
Winchester, 140.00 .... 800 00

Durham East District, 385.00;   Cavan, 126.00;   Hope, 140.00;
Millbrook Horticultural, 55.00;   Port Hope Horticultural, 94.00   800 00

Durham West District, 380.00;   Cartwright, 119.00;   Clarke, 109.00;
Darlington, 111.00; Bowmanville Horticultural, 81.00 .... 800 00

Elgin East District, 380.00;   Aylmer Horticultural, 64.00;
Bayham, 64.00;   Dorchester South, 64.00;   Malahide, 65.00;
Springfield Horticultural, 62.00; St. Thomas Horticultural, 37.00;
Yarmouth, 64.00 .... 800 00

Elgin West District, 520.00;   Aldborough, 140.00;
Southwold and Dunwich, 140.00 .... 800 00

Essex North District, 380.00;   Maidstone and Sandwich E., 105.00;
Rochester and Maidstone, 105.00; Tilbury W. and N., 105.00;
Windsor, Sandwich and Walkerville Horticultural, 105.00......... 800 00

Essex South District, 380.00;   Anderson and Malden, 105.00;
Colchester North, 105.00;   Colchester South, 105.00;
Mersea, 105.00 .... 800 00

Frontenac District, 380.00;   Kingston, 92.00;
Loughboro and Portland, 89.00;   Storrington, 103.00;
Wolfe Island, 136.00 .... 800 00

Grenville South District, 520.00;   Cardinal Horticultural, 140.00;
Edwardsburg, 140.00 .... 800 00

Glengarry District, 394.00; Charlottenburg, 140.00; Kenyon, 140.00;
Lancaster, 126.00 .... 800 00

Grey East District, 380.00; Artemesia, 51.00; Collingwood, 57.00;
Euphrasia, 74.00; Holland, 76.00; Osprey, 56.00; Proton, 76.00;
Thornbury Horticultural, 30.00 .... 800 00

Grey North District, 380.00;   Derby, 84.00;   Keppel, 61.00;
Owen Sound Horticultural, 49.00;   St. Vincent, 59.00;
Sullivan, 84.00; Sydenham, 83.00 .... 300 00

Grey South District, 380.00;   Bentinck, 97.00;
Durham Horticultural, 49.00; Egremont, 96.00; Glenelg, 82.00;
Normanby, 96.00 .... 800 00

Haldimand District, 380.00;   Cayuga Horticultural, 72.00;
Dunnville Horticultural, 68.00; Rainham and South Cayuga, 88.00;
Seneca and Oneida, 96.00; Walpole, 96.00 .... 800 00

Halton District, 380.00;   Esquesing, 100.00;   Nassagaweya, 82.00;
Nelson and Burlington, 100.00;   Oakville Horticultural, 70.00;
Trafalgar, 68.00 .... 800 00

Hamilton District 350 00

Hastings Centre District, 416.00;   Marmora, 140.00;
Stirling Horticultural, 104.00; Wollaston, 140.00 .... 800 00

Hastings East District, 455.00;   Hungerford, 140.00;
Tyendinaga, 123.00 .... 718 00

Hastings North District, 432.00;   Bangor, Wicklow, et al, 140.00;
Carlow, 88.00; Dungannon and Farraday, 140.00 .... 800 00

Hastings West District, 660.00; Belleville Horticultural, 140.00...... 800 00

Huron East District, 380.00;   Grey, 131.00;   Howick, 104.00;
Morris, 130.00; Turnberry, 55.00 .... 800 00

Huron South District, 380.00;   Hay, 90.00;   Stanley, 79.00;
Stephens and Usborne, 90.00;   Seaforth Horticultural, 72.00;
Tuckersmith, 89.00 .... 800 00

Huron West District, 408.00;   Ashfield and Wawanosh W., 140.00;
Clinton Horticultural, 100.00;   Goderich Horticultural, 85.00;
Turnberry, 67.00 .... 800 00

Kent East District, 380.00;   Cambden, 105.00;   Harwich, 105.00;
Howard, 105.00; Orford, 105.00 .... 800 00

Kent West District, 410.00; Chatham, Dover and Wallaceburg, 129.00;
Raleigh, 121.00; Romney, 140.00 .... 800 00

Kingston District, Kingston Horticultural, 140.00 .... 140 00

Lambton East District, 380.00;   Bosanquet, 96.00;
Brooke and Alvinston, 96.00;   Euphemia and Dawn, 87.00;
Plympton and Wyoming, 45.00; Warwick, 96.00 .... 800 00

AGRICULTURE.—*Continued.*

AGRICULTURAL AND HORTICULTURAL SOCIETIES.—*Continued.*

Lambton West District, 380.00;　　Enniskillen and Petrolia, 112.00;
　Moore, 112.00; Sarnia, 112.00; Sombra, 84.00 .... 800 00
Lanark, North, District, 380.00; Dalhousie, 125.00; Lanark Tp., 91.00;
　Lanark Horticultural, 100.00; Pakenham, 104.00 .... 800 00
Lanark South District, 380.00;　　Bathurst, 59.00;　　Drummond, 66.00;
　Sherbrooke South, 66.00;　　　　　　　Perth Horticultural, 111.00;
　Smith's Falls Horticultural, 118.00 .... 800 00
Leeds N. and Grenville, 434.00; Elmsley South, 120.00; Kitley, 140.00 694 00
Leeds South District, 411.00; Crosby North, 140.00; Lansdowne. 140.00;
　Rear of Leeds and Lansdowne, 109.00 .... 800 00
Lennox District, 384.00; Amherst Island, 137.00; Ernestown, 139.00;
　Napanee Horticultural, 140.00 .... 800 00
Lincoln District, 380.00;　　Clinton, 77.00;　　Grantham, 44.00;
　Grimsby South. 74.00; Grimsby Horticultural, 42.00; Louth, 77.00;
　St. Catharines Horticultural, 77.00 .... 771 00
London District. 210.00; London Horticultural. 140.00 .... 350 00
Manitoulin District, 380.00;　　Assignack. 99.00;　　Billings, 114.00;
　Campbell's and Providence Bay, 101.00; Howland, 106.00 .... 800.00
Middlesex East District, 380.00;　　　　　Dorchester North, 105.00;
　London Tp., 105.00; Nissouri West. 105.00; Westminster, 105.00... 800 00
Middlesex North District. 380.00;　Adelaide, 110.00;　Lobo, 110.00;
　McGillivray, 62.00; Williams East, 56.00; Williams West, 82.00... 800 00
Middlesex West District. 380.00;　　Caradoc, 84.00;　　Delaware. 84.00;
　Ekfrid and Mosa, 84.00;　　　　　　　　　　Metcalfe, 84.00;
　Strathroy Horticultural, 84.00 .... 800 00
Monck District. 380.00;　　Caistor, 95.00;　　Canboro, 38.00;
　Dunnville Horticultural. 44.00;　Moulton, 95.00;　Pelham, 95.00;
\　Wainfleet, 53.00 .... 800 00
Muskoka North District, 448.00;　　Humphrey and Cardwell, 72.00;
　Stephenson. 140.00; Stisted, 140.00 .... 800 00
Muskoka South District. 385.00;　　　　　　McLean, 58.00;
　Medora and Wood, 121.00;　　　　　　　Morrison, 96.00;
　Muskoka and Gravenhurst, 140.00 .... 800 00
Niagara, Town and Township 350 00
Nipissing East District. 520.00; Bonfield. 140.00; Ferris, 140.00 .... 800 00
Nipissing West District, 550.00; Widdifield, 250.00 .... 800 00
Norfolk North District, 380.00, arrears, 48.00;　　Middleton, 122.00,
　arrears, 22.00;　　　Simcoe Horticultural, 63.00, arrears, 26.00;
　Townsend, 113.00, arrears. 22.00; Windham, 122.00 .... 918 00
Norfolk South District, 380.00; Charlotteville, 122.00; Houghton, 123.00;
　Port Dover Horticultural, 52.00; Walsingham North, 123.00 ...... 800 00
Northumberland East District. 380.00; Brighton, 92.00; Cramahe, 85.00;
　Murray, 77.00; Percy, 73.00; Seymour, 93.00 .... 800 00
Northumberland West District, 520.00;　　　　Alnwick, 140.00;
　Cobourg Horticultural, 140.00 .... 800 00
Ontario South District 800 00
Ontario North District, 380.00;　　Brock, 86.00;　　Scott, 80.00;
　Scugog. 90.00; Thorah, 86.00 .... 722 00
Ottawa District 350 00
Oxford North District. 380.00;　Blandford, 35.00;　Blenheim, 86.00;
　Nissouri East. 77.00;　　　　Woodstock Horticultural. 65.00;
　Zorra East. 70.00; Zorra West and Embro, 87.00 .... 800 00
Oxford South District. 380.00; Dereham, 86.00; Norwich North, 86.00;
　Norwich South, 86.00;　　　　　　　　Oxford E. Tp., 37.00;
　Oxford N. and W. and Ingersoll, 86.00; Tilsonburg Hort., 39.00... 800 00
Parry Sound East District, 380.00; Chapman,.64.00; McMurrich, 67.00;
　Machar, 73.00; Perry, 131.00; Strong, 85.00 .... 800 00
Parry Sound North District 380 00
Parry Sound West District. 454.00;　Hagerman, Croft, et. al., 140.00;
　Humphrey and Cardwell, 66.00; McKellar, 140.00 .... 800 00
Peel District, 408.00;　　　　　　Brampton Horticultural, 112.00;
　Toronto Tp., 140.00 : Toronto Gore, 140.00 .... 800 00
Perth North District. 380.00;　Easthope North, 55.00;　Elma, 89.00;
　Listowel and S. Wallace, 96.00;　　　　　Mornington, 96.00;
　Stratford Horticultural. 84.00 .... 800 00

AGRICULTURE.—*Continued.*

AGRICULTURAL AND HORTICULTURAL SOCIETIES.—*Continued.*

Perth South District, 380.00; Blanshard, 117.00; Easthope S., 80.00; Fullarton and Logan, 118.00; Mitchell Horticultural, 105.00	800 00
Peterborough East District, 380.00; Douro and Dummer, 110.00; Galway, 122.00; Otonabee, 124.00; Peterborough and Ashburnham Horticulutral, 64.00	800 00
Peterborough West District, 395.00; Harvey, 75.00; Monaghan S., 114.00; Peterborough and Ashburnham Hort., 76.00; Smith. Ennismore, et. al., 140.00	800 00
Prescott District, 442.00; Alfred, 140.00; Plantagenet South, 140.00; Vankleek Hill Horticultural, 78.00	800 00
Prince Edward District. 410.00; Ameliasburg, 140.00; Picton Horticultural, 112.00; Sophiasburg, 138.00	800 00
Renfrew North District, 590.00; Grattan and Wilberforce, 70.00; Ross and Bromley, 140.00	800 00
Renfrew South District, 454.00; Grattan and Wilberforce. 70.00; Radcliffe and Raglan, 136.00; Renfrew Horticultural, 140.00	800 00
Russell District, 380.00; Cambridge, 108.00; Clarence, 112.00; Osgoode, 62.00; Russell, 138.00	800 00
Simcoe East District. 380.00; Matchedash, 104.00; Midland Horticultural, 51.00; Oro, 104.00; Orillia Horticultural. 57.00; Tiny and Tay, 104.00	800 00
Simcoe South District, 397.00; Essa, 54.00; Gwillimbury W. and Bradford, 140.00; Innisfil, 69.00; Tossorontio, 140.00	800 00
Simcoe West District. 380.00; Barrie Horticultural, 70.00; Collingwood Horticultural. 87.00; Flos, 87.00; Nottawasaga, 88.00; Vespra, 88.00	800 00
Stormont District. 407.00; Finch, 113.00; Osnabruck, 140.00; Roxborough. 140.00	800 00
Temiskaming District	380 00
Toronto District. 410.00; Toronto Horticultural. 140.00	550 00
Victoria North District, 380.00; Eldon. 138.00; Fenelon, 118.00; Somerville, 101.00	737 00
Victoria South District, 380.00; Emily, 83.00; Lindsay Horticultural, 84.00; Mariposa, 102.00; Ops, 64.00; Verulam, 87.00	800 00
Waterloo North District, 380.00; Elmira Horticultural, 59.00; Wellesley, 120.00; Woolwich, 121.00; Waterloo Horticultural, 120.00	800 00
Waterloo South District, 380.00; Galt Horticultural. 114.00; Hespeler Horticultural, 67.00; Preston Horticultural. 113.00; Wilmot, 126.00	800 00
Welland District, 380.00; Bertie, 107.00; Humberstone, 18.00; Niagara Falls Horticultural, 42.00; Stamford, 67.00; Thorold, 96.00	800 00
Wellington Centre District. 380.00; Elora Horticultural, 38.00; Erin, 91.00; Fergus Horticultural, 43.00; Garafraxa West, 77.00; Nichol, 81.00; Pilkington, 90.00	800 00
Wellington South District, 380.00; Eramosa, 105.00; Guelph Tp., 105.00; Guelph Horticultural, 105.00; Puslinch, 105.00	800 00
Wellington West District, 380.00; Arthur, 76.00; Clifford Horticultural, 73.00; Maryborough, 59.00; Minto, 60.00; Palmerston and N. Wallace. 76.00; Peel and Drayton, 76.00	800 00
Wentworth North District. 380.00; Beverley, 140.00; Flamboro East. 140.00; Flamboro West. 140.00	800 00
Wentworth South District. 380.00; Ancaster, 117.00; Binbrook, 81.00; Glanford. 106.00; Saltfleet. 116.00	800 00
York East District. 493.00; Markham, 97.00; Scarborough, 140.00; York and Weston. 70.00	800 00
York North District, 380.00; Georgina and N. Gwillimbury, 114.00; Gwillimbury East. 118.00; King, 117.00; Newmarket, Hort., 71.00	800 00
York West District. 456.00; Etobicoke, 134.00; Vaughan, 140.00; York Tp. and Weston. 70.00	800 00

14 P.A.

AGRICULTURE.—*Continued.*

AGRICULTURAL AND HORTICULTURAL SOCIETIES.—*Continued.*

Special Grants:

Brant South District: Tuscarora Indians	100 00
Haliburton District: Cardiff, 64.00; Dysart, et. al., 116.00; Glamorgan, 66.00; Minden, et. al., 112.00	358 00
Hastings Centre District: Madoc	380 00
Middlesex W. Dist.: Chippewa Indians, 75.00; Muncey Indians, 75.00; Oneida Indians, 50.00	200 00
Nipissing West District: Caldwell	140 00
Northumberland East District: Colborne Horticultural	140 00
Toronto District: Broadview Boys' Institute	50 00
Victoria North District: Dalton, Rama and Ryde	50 00

PORT ARTHUR AND FORT WILLIAM EXHIBITION ($1,800.00).

Burriss, R. A., Secretary-Treasurer, grant 1.800 00

EXPERT JUDGES ($9,425.43).

Name	Services	Expenses	Name	Services	Expenses
Alexander, J.,	$80 00	$67 50 ;	Brethour, J. E.,	$ 8 00	$ 2 65 ;
Ballantyne, W.W.,	10 00	11 55 ;	Boag, H. G.,	21 00	22 00 ;
Binstead, L.	6 00	3 60 ;	Bradley, T. W.,	9 00	12 10 ;
Bennett, J. E.,	12 00	15 10 ;	Beswetherick, W.,	132 00	41 55 ;
Boag, Jno. A.,	68 00	48 65 ;	Bradley, G. R.,	46 00	63 50 ;
Bollert, H.,	48 00	41 55 ;	Bishop, W.,	56 00	52 30 ;
Beattie, W. H.,	40 00	34 25 ;	Brooks, R. S.,	32 00	24 00 ;
Bell, W. J.,	36 00	27 70 ;	Conn, H. S.,	9 00	40 10 ;
Cockburn, J. A.,	44 00	28 75 ;	Cromarty, Jas.,	88 00	100 00 ;
Cardiff, G. B.,	9 00	20 20 ;	Cosh, N.,	52 00	29 65 ;
Clark, J. W.,	32 00	19 60 ;	Clark, J. G.,	14 00	14 80 ;
Donaldson, J.,	8 00	8 00 ;	Currie, C.,	15 00	15 10 ;
Davis, H. J.,	6 00	4 60 ;	Doherty, Alex.,	20 00	16 50 ;
Dundas, R. D.,	56 00		Douglas, A. B.	28 00	18 10 ;
Doherty,	72 00		Dale, W.,	64 00	1 50 ;
Elliott, Wm.,	24 00	13 05 ;	Darrock, H. J.,	6 00	6 95 ;
Field, R. H.,	22 00	15 70 ;	Elliott, W. R.,	92 00	164 65 ;
Gardhouse, W. J.	68 00	13 65 ;	Fuller, S. B.,	8 00	5 40 ;
Guy, Fred.,	3 00	19 80 ;	Gormley, A. G.,	51 00	75 00 ;
Green, Mary L.,	30 00	38 98 ;	Gray, Geo.,	62 00	51 95 ;
Graham, J. D.,	56 00	81 05 ;	Gibson, J. T.,	108 00	213 65 ;
Gray, Gertrude A.,	34 00	29 00 ;	Gilbert, Geo.,	68 00	46 40 ;
Gray, D. D.,	72 00		Gardhouse, Jno.,	44 00	13 45 ;
Hood, G. B.,	60 00	85 90 ;	Gardhouse, A. S.,	20 00	4 30;
Hall, R. J.,	80 00	70 45 ;	Harding, R. H.,	60 00	92 15 ;
Hillborn, J. D.,	12 00	7 80 ;	Henderson, Jas.,	56 00	38 80 ;
Holman, A. G.,	56 00		Hammer, D. G.,	28 00	12 50 ;
Irving, J. C.,	57 00	8 00 ;	Holes, Alfred,	27 00	24 30;
Jackson, Jno.,	72 00	114 75 ;	Honey, R.,	8 00	7 75 ;
Jarvis, O.,	40 00	35 80 ;	Jones, W.,	48 00	120 80;
Johnston, A.,	12 00	9 70 ;	Jeffs, E.,	72 00	......
Lawrason, P. S.,	33 00		Kydd, W. F.,	68 00	......
McClung, E.,	88 00	5 05 ;	Leigh, C.,	32 00	23 55 ;
McCallum, J. M.,	76 00	228 60 ;	McConnell, J.,	39 00	......
McCord, T. H.,	44 00	37 45 ;	McCallum, J. A.,	70 00	99 10 ;
McKay, D.,	81 00	7 05 ;	McMillan, T.,	8 00	5 40 ;
Maddock, R. Blanche	4 00		McTavish, A. D.,	16 00	15 50 ;
Milne, N. A.,	36 00	32 90 ;	Marshall, N.,	8 00	7 50 ;
Morrow, J. C.,	15 00	25 30 ;	Mortimer, R. E.,	62 00	49 10 ;
Mallory, B.,	28 00	21 85 ;	Mason, L. H.,	32 00	1 95 ;
Mallory, W. J.,	100 00	14 20 ;	Murphy, Annie,	9 00	11 45 ;
Oke, R.,	4 00	1 30 ;	Moscrip, W.,	15 00	6 50 ;
Parkinson, E.,	40 00	30 50 ;	Pollard, G.,	38 00	24 50 ;
Perry, A. D.,	36 00	32 50 ;	Pettit, A. G.,	52 00	50 75 ;
Reed, H. G., Dr.,	92 00	71 30.	Peer, W. E. A.,	24 00	21 50:

14a P.A.

AGRICULTURE.—Continued.

EXPERT JUDGES—Continued.

	Services	Expenses		Services	Expenses
Reid, T.R.,	44 00	45 35;	Reddick, G. W.,	18 00	47 70;
Reeves, F. F.,	6 00	7 50;	Richardson, M.,	6 00	2 60;
Russell, Jas.,	6 00	4 35:	Rettie, J.,	32 00	......
Snell, Jas.,	100 00	171 20;	Stonehouse, M.,	72 00	151 60:
Scott, T. H.,	20 00	14 25;	Stevenson, R. S.,	52 00	46 20;
Sangster, R. R.,	16 00	10 95:	Snider, F. D.,	......	40 00;
Smith, G. A.,	33 00	51 75;	Smith, Fred.,	24 00	11 15;
Scarf, Wm.,	18 00	22 20;	Smith, Agnes,	28 00	31 70;
Thompson, G.,	68 00	122 15;	Trew, D. C.,	50 00	49 60;
Thompson, E.V.,	54 00	......	Tolton, J.P.,	9 00	11 85;
Stewart, Mary M.,	7 50	......	Thorne, Wm.,	84 00	161 10;
Williams, G. H.,	68 00	48 45;	Whitelaw, Wm.,	136 00	......
Whitelaw, Geo.,	80 00	......	Wright, H.,	56 00	68 25;
Whitelaw, A.,	16 00	8 85;	Warren, C. Louise,	24 00	19 25;
Waters, B. J.,	24 00	21 90;	White, O. D.,	24 00	22 45;
			Yuill, J. A.,	3 00	10 25; 9,139 13

Brunnell, T. L., services at photographer 66 00
Campbell, Mrs. C., services, demonstrating, 24.00; travelling expenses, 18.45   42 45
Green, Annie W.,   do   63.00;   do   78.30   141 30
Simpkins, J. W., services as detective at 3.00 per day, 15.00; travelling
    expenses, 13.55 ....   28 55
Steele, S. H., services, demonstrating 8 00

LIVE STOCK BRANCH.

SALARIES ($3,120.00).

A. P. Westervelt, Twelve months' salary as Director.............................   1,500 00
D. T. Elderkin,   do   Clerk 1,100 00
M. Johnston,   do   Stenographer 520 00

EXPENSES ($647.82).

Bell Telephone Co., messages, 30.80; rent of instruments, 60.77 ....   91 57
Breeders' Gazette, subscription, 1.00; C. P. R., Telegraph, Co., telegrams,
    19.13 ....   20 13
Dorman, Jas., services as office boy, at 1.16 2-3 per day, 61.83; Doane Bros.,
    cab hire, 1.00 ....   62 83
Dominion Express Co., charges, 4.99; Donovan, H. B., book, 1.50 ....   6 49
Freyer, N., typewriting, 6.00; G. N. W. Telegraph Co., telegrams, 8.24...   14 24
Hubertus, Mrs., postage stamps, 125.00; International Railway Guide,
    subn., 2.00 ....   127 00
King's Printer, stationery, 135.66; Library Bureau of Canada, guide, 16.80.   152 46
Pettit, N. M., services as stenographer, at 10.00 per week 65 00
Shier, Beatrice, services as stenographer at 2.00 per day 30 00
United Typewriter Co., supplies, 56.40: services of stenographer, at 2.00
    per day, 7.00 ....   63 40
Warwick Bros. & Rutter, printing 14 70

GRANTS, ETC. ($24,126.43).

Eastern Live Stock and Poultry Show:
    Morgan, A. J., poultry coops, 227.00; Westervelt, A. P., Secy. Treas.,
       grant, 4,300.00 .... -   4,527 00
Horsebreeders' Association: H. Wade, Secy. Treas., grant .... -   1,000 00
Local Poultry Associations, grants:
    Brantford Poultry Association, 40.00; Brockville District Poultry and
      Pet Stock Association, 25.00; Forest Poultry and Pet Stock
      Association, 10.00; Guelph Poultry Association, 25.00; Hamilton,
      and Wentworth Poultry Association, 40.00; Huron Poultry Associ-

AGRICULTURE.—*Continued.*

GRANTS, ETC.—*Continued.*

ation, 40.00; London Poultry Association, 25.00; Meaford and Grey Counties Poultry Associations, 15.00; Midland Poultry, Pigeon and Pet Stock Association, 40.00; Napanee Poultry, Pigeon and Pet stock Association, 40.00; Northern Ontario Poultry Association, 40.00; Owen Sound Poultry and Pet Stock Association, 40.00; St. Thomas Poultry Association, 40.00; Toronto Poultry, Pigeon and Pet Stock Association, 40.00; Waterloo County Poultry and Pet Stock Association, 40.00 .... 500 00

Provincial Winter Fair, Guelph:
  Bond, Jno. M. & Co., wire railing for Main Building, 13.00; Cowan, W. A., tables, laying matting, etc., 81.50; Crowe's Iron Works. iron column, 16.05; Mahoney, R., lumber, locks, etc., 21.70; Richardson, G. A., cocoa matting, 127.38; Westervelt, A. P., Secy.-Treas., grant, 7,000.00; Prince of Wales' Prize, 50.00 .... 7,309 63

Pure Seed Fairs:
  Westervelt, A. P., Treasurer, grant, 230.00; Prizes Pure Seed Fair, Ottawa, 125.90; Guelph, 129.00 .... 484 00

Sales of Pure Bred Stock:
  Brown, J. A., Secretary, to assist in publication of catalogue, 18.00; Duff, J. M., Secretary, to assist in publication of catalogue, Guelph sale, 34.50; *Farmers' Advocate*, advertising 120.00; *Farming World*, advertising, 56.25; McMahon, E., Secretary to assist in publication of catalogue, Ottawa sale, 19.00; sundry persons, freight on animals purchased at sales, 159.45; *Weekly Sun*, advertising, 75.00 .... 482 20

Spring Stallion Shows and Investigations:
  Grants: Cannington Horse Show, 50.00; Carleton Place Horse Show, 50.00; Chatham Spring Stallion Show, 25.00; Clarksburg Spring Horse Show, 25.00; Drayton Entire Horse Show, 50.00; Elmira Spring Horse Show, 50.00; Elora Entire Horse Show, 50.00; Guelph Spring Stallion Show, 50.00; Huron County Spring Stock Exhibition, 50.00; Kennilworth Spring Horse Show, 50.00; Malton Spring Show, 50.00; Owen Sound Spring Horse Show, 50.00; Palmerston Spring Stallion Show, 50.00; Renfrew Spring Stallion Show, 25.00; Seaforth Spring Horse Show, 50.00; South Lanark Horse Show, 50.00; St. Thomas Horse Association, 50.00; Tara Spring Show, 50.00; Twp. of Erin Spring Horse Show, 50.00 .... 875 00

Horse industry, services as inspector at 6.00 per day and expenses:

	Services.	Expenses.		Services.	Expenses.
Arkell, H. S.,	......	63 00;	Boag, John A.,	114 00	47 65;
Bright, Jno.	198 00	78 35;	Cain, Wm.,	222 00	97 80;
Christie, Peter,	120 00	32 60;	Clarke, J. G.,	258 00	136 13;
Gardhouse, J.,	222 00	101 40;	Graham, J. D.,	258 00	145 61;
Gray, Geo.,	252 00	143 10;	Irving, James,	252 00	107 00;
Jones, Wm.,	198 00	90 15;	Kydd, W. F.,	222 00	130 49;
McMillan, T.,	198 00	86 28;	Mossip, W.,	228 00	108 53;
Reed, H. G.,	216 00	89 00;	Sinclair, J. A.,	180 00	89 80;
Smith, Wm.,	258 00	145 62;	Walsh, A. R.,	36 00	16 49;
Thom, Arthur,	66 00	26 20;			5,233 20

Services and expenses organizing Local Institute Districts :—

Amos, W. T.,	12 50	13 25;	Aylesworth, David,	12 50	9 40;
Aylesworth, J. B.,	10 00	3 00;	Bailie, Wm.,	11 88	9 15;
Bale, E. H.,	10 00	5 90;	Bass, W. M.,	11 25	15 40;
Binnie, Geo.,	11 25	3 50;	Bradshaw, J. W.,	10 00	7 25;
Brien, J. D.,	15 00	30 98;	Brown, Jno.,	11 25	16 50;
Campbell, D.,	10 00	4 25;	Carson, A.,	12 50	7 50;
Carson, G. W.,	10 00	4 00;	Channon, Wm.,	10 00	5 90;
Christie, W. A.,	12 50	6 00;	Clark, J. W.,	10 00	3 40;
Clemons, S. M.,	10 00	14 95;	Coatsworth, G. W.,	12 50	23 25;

AGRICULTURE.—*Continued.*

Services and expenses organizing Local Institute Districts.—*Continued.*

	Services.	Expenses.		Services.	Expenses.
Collins, Wm.,	12 50	3 50;	Comerford, F, A.,	15 00	30 50;
Craig, W. R.,	20 00	14 00;	Crawford, R, L.,	10 00	16 75;
Cullis, R.,	10 00	3 00;	Cumberland, T. J.,	12 50	10 00;
Culver, F. L.,	10 00	4 50;	Cummings, P.,	10 00	16 50;
Currah, A. L.,	10 00	22 50;	Donald, A. S.,	13 75	6 75;
Emerson, H. C.,	10 00	2 35;	Fallis, A. J.	12 50	7 55;
Field, R. H.,	5 00	3 42;	Forden, J. H.,	10 00	5 50;
Fox, J. P.,	12 50	6 50;	Gainer, W. H.,	10 00	4 50;
Goltz, Geo.,	12 50	6 50;	Graham, J. I.,	15 00	20 35;
Grant, R. H.,	20 00	10 50;	Haynes, W. G.,	10 00	5 85;
Heacock, F. W.,	11 25	4 75;	Hoar, H. C.,	12 50	6 00;
Hood, G. B.,	12 50	4 75;	King, R. E.,	12 50	5 75; .
Knight, Joshua,	10 50	5 05;	Lamb, Jas. A.,	12 50	7 50;
Leahman, R. A.,	11 25	5 61;	Lee, Erland,	10 00	2 50;
Leeson, F.,	10 20	5·60;	Lennox, W. J. W.,	10 00	4 50;
Longmoore, J. R.,	15 00	11 45;	McAlpine, W. J.,	15 00	11 05;
McArthur, P. A.,	10 00	4 50;	McKee, Jno.,	10 00	2 70;
McNaughton, J. P.,	15 00	27 50;	Macadam, Wm.,	20 00	10 50;
Maccoll, A.,	12 50	7 55;	Mackie, Chas. M.,	10 00	4 50;
Muirhead, D.,	10 00	7 65;	Nelson, R. J.,	10 00	4 50;
Nicholson, Chester,	12 50	7 00;	Nicholson, Geo.,	10 00	7 50;
Nixon, E. F.,	11 25	5 25;	Oliver, Geo.,	20 00	24 55;
O'Reilly, Chas.,	10 00	4 75;	Palmerston, N. S.,	10 00	4 90;
Pratt, Wm.,	15 00	9 40;	Purnell, Alf.,	10 00	11 00;
Reynolds, A. J.,	12 00	14 40;	Robins, Allan,	10 00	2 00;
Saunders, W. D.,	10 00	10 00;	Shantz, Allan,	10 00	12 15;
Shier, Wm.,	13 75	6 75;	Shields, Wm.,	12 50	8 35;
Slater, Wm.,	10 00	7 70;	Smith, J. L.,	12 50	8 40;
Swale, Cecil,	10 00	2 25;	Taylor, T. P.,	10 00	1 50;
Thurston,	10 00	2 75;	Ure, David,	13 75	23 00;
Wheaton, J. H.,	17 50	35 96;	Young, C. W.,	10 00	......
Young, Frank,	15 00	9 45;	Nodwell, R. D.,	10 00	9 38;	1,727 03

Livery hire *re* investigations:

Amos, J. E., 12.00; Annett, M., 12.00; Armstrong, Fred,13.00; Babe, Monat O., 15.00; Brooks, C., 18.00; Brownbridge, J. T., 15.00; Brunet. D., 24.00; Cameron. A. D., 20.00; Caldwell, Willard, 16.00; Caswell, G., 7.00; Carson, G. J., 7.50; Colby, Granville, 3.00; Copping, J., 16.00; Cooper, W. C., 4.00; Cromarty, J., 3.00; Field & Fawcett, 12.00; Finkle, C. H., 10.00; Frost, Thos., 12.00; Fry & Robertson, 12.50; Green, Geo., 31.50; Greer, Geo., 10.00; Guess, L., 8.00; Haas, C. D., 12.00; Hamilton, D. R. & Son, 7.00; Hart, John, 13.50; Hill, J. N., 10.00; Hollingsworth, J. 4.50; Hubbell, J. H., 4.50; Hunt & Coulter, 10.00; Hunt, Jos., 9.00; Jacks, J. L., 15.00; Jamieson, W., 7.00; Johnston & Soper, 6.00; Kennedy, A., 6.00; Killoran, L. E., 9.75; Lake, J. C., 10.00; Lomperd, Geo., 17.50; Larmer, A. J., 20.00; Leach, J., 3.00; Lush, Jno. 3.00; McCallum, Bros., 12.50; McCarter, Jno., 2.50; McCallum, T. G., 13.50; McFee, Chas., 22.00; McGregor, Colin. 3.00; McKee, Jno., 19.00; McLachlan, W. A., 12.00; McTavish, Peter, 16.00; Machell, B., 15.25; Marshall, J. W., 5.00; Owens, J., 15.00; Marlatt. D. A., 14.00; Millson & Hays, 2.00; Palmer Bros., 16.00; Pierce, Lewis and Son, 8.50; Pringle, A. & Co., 10.00; Purdy, F., 9.00; Readman, J. H., 12.00; Rennie, F., 12.00; Reynolds. F., 22.50; Robbins, A., 9.00; Robinson, Geo., 35.65; Robb, Geo., 11.00; Rowell, Thurlow. 10.50; Ryckman, C., 2.00; Schaus, J. W., 7.00; Sharp, Geo., 7.00; Spencer, F., 1.50; Suffel, E., 10.00; St. John, Robert, 1.50; Taylor, F., 12.00; Temple, J., 12.00; Tutle & Baker, 9.00; Walpole, T. N., 12.00; Wigg, E. J., 15.00; Wiggins, J., 6.75; Williams, G. H., 15.00; Willoughby, J. W., 9.00; York. H. L., 24.50; Young, R. M., 12.00 .... 913 40

Bell Telephone Co., messages, 1.30; Nunan, F., report books, 25.00 .... 26 30

Sundry Newspapers, advertising 27 42

Western Ontario Poultry Association, overdraft .... - 1,021 25

AGRICULTURE.—*Continued*

FARMERS' AND WOMEN'S INSTITUTES.

SALARIES ($3,192.00).

G. A. Putnam:	Twelve months' salary as Superintendent......................	1,800 00
do	arrears do 1905 do	200 00
A. Fox:	Twelve do . Stenographer	520 00
Ida McNicholl:	do do	468 00
M. M. Brough:	Four and quarter do do	204 00

EXPENSES ($3,192.01).

Ansley, E. R., copying charts, 7.50; Am. Fruit Pub. Co., subscription, 50c. ... 8 00

Bell Telephone Co., rent of instruments, 38.76; messages, 49.80 .... 88 56

Bennett, Chas., services at 75c. per day, 6.00; Brandon & Gilbert, cartage, 9.25 ... 15 25

Bengough, Thos. & Son, reporting convention 74 40

Briggs, Wm., labels for exhibition fruit, 4.00; Brough, M. M., services, 56.00 ... 60 00

Brough, E., mounting weeds, 12.00; Brodie, W., services at 10.00 per week, 365.00 ... 377 00

Brown, J. F. Co., rent of chairs, 7.00; *Breeder's Gazette*, subscription, 1.00 ... 8 00

Can. Express Co., charges, 50.44; Can. Typewriting Co., supplies, 1.50...... 51 94

C. P. R. Tel. Co., telegrams, 16.89; Creelman, G. C., annual dues Am. Association of Farmers' Institute Workers, 1905, 5.00; travelling expenses, 4.00 ... 25 89

Cummings, Mrs. E., 100 copies handbooks National Council of Women ... 27 00

Dom. Exp. Co., charges, 51.88; Duncan, R., services at 10.00 per week, 10.00 ... 61 88

Eaton, T. Co., valise for sets of weeds 14 00

Farmer's Advocate, 460 copies, 16.50; Globe Ptg. Co., advertising, 10.00... 26 50

G. N. W. Tel. Co., telegrams, 19.98; Gray, Gertrude A., preparing charts, 4.00 ... 23 98

Gripton, C., rubber stamps and pad, 3.50; Harcourt, E. H. & Co., programmes. 29.75 ... 33 25

Hypson, M. L., services at 10.00 per week, 67.34; Hubertus, Mrs., postage stamps, 475.00 ... 542 34

International Ry. Pub. Co., subscription, 2.00; Joy, Mrs. Jean, articles for report, 12.00 ... 14 00

King's Printer, stationery, 258.33; paper, 66.55; Kernahan, Josie, services at 1.25 per day, 11.25 ... 336 13

Lee, Wm., services as messenger at 4.00 per week, 85.34; car tickets, 2.60 ... 87 94

McIntosh, J. J., advertising 1 80

McLaren, Alex., services at 2.50 per day, 13.75; travelling expenses, 12.35 ... 26 10

Macpherson, M. C., article for report, 5.00; Miller, H. H., preparation of bulletin on weeds of Ontario, 32.65 ... 37 65

Musson Book Co., envelopes, 37.20; National Typewriting Co., supplies, 144.80 ... 182 00

National Drug and Chemical Co., chemicals, 23c.; Nunan, F., stationery, etc., 348.25 ... 343 48

Office Specialty Co., guides, folders, etc., 48.17; O'Burne, W. M., adv. meeting, 5.00 ... 53 17

Pike, D. & Co., rent of tent, etc., 36.25; Postmaster, unpaid postage, 5.64 ... 41 89

Putnam, Geo. A., travelling expenses, 179.49; Race, T. H., article for report, 5.00 ... 184 49

Reynolds & Son, banner for winter fair, 3.00; Riordon Paper Mills, paper, 1.70 ... 4 70

Russill Hardware Co., spirit stove for cooking kits, 1.50; Soules, Andrew, M., lecturing, 10.00 ... 11 50

Stanton, O. B., receipt books, 7.68; *Stratford Herald*, advertising meetings, 7.75 ... 15 43

Simpson, Robert Co., ribbons, etc., 19.40; Souch, W. J., services at 2.00 per day, 18.00 ... 37 40

Toronto Ry. Co., car tickets, 7.95; Toronto Engraving Co., charts for use of speakers, 16.50 ... 24 45

AGRICULTURE.—*Continued.*

FARMERS' AND WOMEN'S INSTITUTES.—*Continued.*

Thompson, Mrs. R., canning fruit for exhibition, 7.50; United Typewriter
     Co., supplies, inspection, etc., 74.25; exchange on typewriter, 70.00......   151 75
Walker, A. E. & Co., cotton for charts, 1.70; Warwick Bros. & Rutter,
     printing and binding, 128.64 ....   130 34
Weekly Sun, subscription, and copies of May issue, 40.30; Wells, Mrs. H.;
     article for report, 7.00 ....   47 30
White, G. G., services at 2.50 per day 17 50

GRANTS, LECTURES, ETC. ($19,239.64).

Treasurer, Farmers' Institutes :
   Addington, 25.00;   Algoma North, 25.00;   Algoma Centre, 25.00;
   Algoma East, 25.00;   Amherst Island, 25.00;   Brant North, 25.00;
   Brant South, 25.00;   Brockville, 25.00;   Bruce Centre, 25.00;
   Bruce North, 25.00;   Bruce 25.00;   Bruce West, 25.00;
   Carleton, 25.00;   Cornwall, 25.00;   Dufferin, 25.00;
   Dundas, 25.00;   Durham E., 25.00;   Durham W., 25.00;
   Elgin East, 25.00;   Elgin West, 25.00;   Essex, 25.00;
   Essex South, 25.00;   Frontenac, 25.00;   Frontenac, 25.00;
   Glengarry, 25.00;   Grenville South, 25.00;   Grey Centre, 25.00;
   Grey North, 25.00;   Grey South, 25.00; ·   Haldimand, 25.00;
   Halton, 25.00;   Hastings East, 25.00;   Hastings North, 25.00;
   Hastings West, 25.00;   Huron East, 25.00;   Huron South, 25.00;
   Huron West, 25.00;   Kent East, 25.00;   Kent West, 25.00;
   Lambton East, 25.00;   Lambton West, 25.00;   Lanark North, 25.00;
   Lanark South, 25.00;   Leeds North and Grenville North, 25.00;
   Leeds South, 25.00;   Lennox, 25.00;   Lincoln, 25.00;
   Manitoulin East, 25.00; Manitoulin West, 25.00; Middlesex East, 25.00;
   Middlesex North, 25.00;   Middlesex West, 25.00;   Monck, 25.00;
   Muskoka Centre, 25.00; Muskoka North, 25.00; Muskoka South, 25.00;
   Nipissing West, 25.00;   Norfolk North, 25.00;   Norfolk South, 25.00;
   Northumberland East, 25.00;   Northumberland West, 25.00;
   Ontario North, 25.00;   Ontario South. 25.00;   Oxford North, 25.00;
   Oxford South, 25.00;   Parry Sound East, 25.00;   Peel, 25.00;
   Perth North, 25.00;   Perth South, 25.00;   Peterboro East, 25.00;
   Peterboro West, 25.00;   Prescott. 25.00;   Prince Edward, 25.00;
   Rainy River South, 25.00; Renfrew North. 25.00; Renfrew South, 25.00;
   Russell, 25.00;   Simcoe Centre, 25.00;   Simcoe East, 25.00;
   Simcoe South, 25.00;   Simcoe West. 25.00;   St. Joseph Island, 25.00;
   Stormont, 25.00;   Temiskaming, 25.00;   Union, 25.00;
   Victoria East, 25.00;   Victoria West. 25.00;   Waterloo North, 25.00;
   Waterloo South. 25.00;   Welland, 25.00;   Wellington Centre, 25.00;
   Wellington East, 25.00;   Wellington South, 25.00;
   Welington West. 25.00;   Wentworth South, 25.00;
   Wentworth North. 25.00;   York East, 25.00;   York West, 25.00;
   York North, 25.00 ....   2,475 00
Treasurer Women's Institutes :
   Amherst Island, 10.00;   Brant North, 22.00;   Brant South, 22.00;
   Bruce Centre. 19.00;   Bruce, 13.00;   Bruce West, 19.00;
   Dufferin, 34.00;   Dundas, 10.00;   Durham East, 25.00;
   Durham West, 25.00;   Elgin East, 19.00;   Elgin West, 13.00;
   Essex North, 19.00;   Grey Centre, 34.00;   Grey North, 31.00;
   Grey South, 19.00;   Haldimand, 34.00; ·   Halton, 43.00;
   Hastings East, 19.00; Hastings North, 19.00; Hastings West, 19.00;
   Huron East, 19.00;   Huron South, 16.00;   Huron West, 22.00;
   Kent East, 10.00;   Kent West, 31.00;   Lambton East, 13.00;
   Lambton West. 13.00;   Lennox, 10.00;   Lincoln, 16.00;
   Middlesex North, 31.00;   Middlesex West, 16.00;   Monck, 22.00;
   Muskoka South, 28.00; Muskoka Centre, 10.00; Norfolk North, 19.00;
   Northumberland East, 19.00;   Northumberland West, 25.00;
   Ontario North, 10.00;   Ontario South. 22.00;   Oxford North, 25.00;
   Oxford South, 34.00;   Peel. 34.00;   Perth North, 16.00;
   Perth South, 16.00; Peterboro East. 10.00; Peterboro West, 10.00;
   Renfrew North, 19.00; Simcoe Centre. 34.00; Simcoe South, 10.00;

PUBLIC ACCOUNTS.

AGRICULTURE.—*Continued.*

FARMERS' AND WOMEN'S INSTITUTES.—*Continued.*

Simcoe West, 28.00;   Union, 16.00;   Victoria East, 16.00;
Victoria West, 19.00; Waterloo North, 22.00; Waterloo South, 28.00;
Welland, 25.00; Wellington Centre, 31.00; Wellington East, 25.00;
Wellington South, 28.00;   Wellington West, 22.00;
Wentworth North, 22.00;   Wentworth South, 34.00;
York North, 10.00;   York East, 25.00;   York West, 22.00.........   1,401 00

Treasurer, Branch Women's Institutes:

Brant North, 12.00;   Brant South, 12.00;   Bruce Centre, 9.00;
Bruce West, 9.00;   Dufferin, 24.00;   Durham East, 12.00;
Durham West, 12.00;   Elgin East, 9.00;   Essex North, 9.00;
Grey Centre, 33.00;   Grey North, 18.00;   Grey South, 9.00;
Haldimand, 33.00;   Halton, 33.00;   Hastings East, 9.00;
Hastings North, 9.00;   Hastings West, 9.00;   Huron East, 12.00;
Huron South, 6.00;   Huron West, 12.00;   Kent West, 12.00;
Lincoln, 6.00;   Middlesex North. 18.00;   Middlesex West, 6.00;
Monck, 12.00 Muskoka South, 12.00; Northumberland East, 9.00;
Northumberland West, 15.00; Ontario South, 12.00; Oxford North, 9.00;
Oxford South, 27.00;   Peel, 27.00;   Perth North, 6.00;
Perth South, 6.00;   Renfrew, 9.00;   Simcoe Centre, 21.00;
Simcoe West, 18.00;   Union, 6.00;   Victoria East, 9.00;
Victoria West. 12.00: Waterloo North, 12.00; Waterloo South, 6.00;
Welland, 15.00;   Wellington Centre, 21.00;
Wellington East, 15.00;   Wellington South, 12.00;
Wellington West, 15.00;   Wentworth North, 15.00;
Wentworth South, 30.00; York East. 15.00; York West, 12.00 ....   711 00

Treasurer, Women's Institutes in the Districts:

Algoma Centre, Goulais Bay, 3.00;   McLennan, 10.00;
    Tarentorus S. 3.00;
Manitoulin. East. Tehkummah 10.00;
    do   West, Gore Bay 10.00;
Nipissing, North Bay 3.00;
Parry Sound East, Golden Valley. 3.00; Loring, 3.00; Powassan, 3.00;
    Restoule 3.00;
Rainy River North, Dryden 10.00;
    do   South, Fort Frances 13.00;
St. Joseph's Island, Richard's Landing ....10.00;.
Temiskaming, Haileybury 10.00;
Thunder Bay. Dorion, 3.00;   Hymers, 3.00;   Murillo, 3.00;
    Ouimet. 3.00; Slate River Valley, 3.00 ....   109 00

Treasurer, Branch Women's Institutes in the Districts:

Algoma Centre, Des,arats. 3.00; Echo Bay, 3.00; Sault Ste. Marie, 3.00;
Manitoulin East. Green Bay 3.00;
    do   West, Poplar. 3.00;   Fernlee, 3.00;
Muskoka Centre. Allanville 3.00;
Rainy River North. Eagle River. 3.00;   Ox Drift, 3.00;
Rainy River South, Barwick, 3.00;   Emo, 3.00;   Sleeman, 3.00;
    Stratton 3.00;
St. Joseph's Island, Kentvale. 3.00; Markville, 3.00 ....   45 00

Services. lecturing at 5.00 per day:

Backus, Dr. A., 5.00; McMurchy, Dr. H., 5.00; Rose, Laura, 5.00...   15 00

Services, lecturing at 4.00 per day:

Anderson. D., 152.00; Campbell, Mrs. Colin, 16.00; Campbell, J., 180.00;
Caston, G. C., 92.00; Clark, J. W., 192.00; Cottrelle, G. R., 36.00;
Douglas, J., 4.00;   Drury, E. C., 184.00;   Elliott W., 36.00;
Elliott, A., 176.00;   Echlin. J. H.. 68.00;   Fraser, W. S.. 172.00;
Gardhouse, J., 40.00; Glendinning, H., 188.00; Hallman, A. C., 80.00;
Kydd, W. F., 364.00; Lavery, J. F., 28.00; Maddock. B. R., 16.00;
Mason. T. H., 220.00;   McMillan. T.. 196.00;   Nash, C. W., 276.00;
Orr, J. E., 8.00;   Paget. J. N.. 72.00;   Rose. Laura, 94.00;
Reed, H. G.. 388.00;   Rennie. S.. 112.00;   Shearer, W. C., 132.00;
Shepphard, T. A.. 68.00;   Shepphard, Jas.. 112.00;
Sherrington. A. E.. 164.00;   Smith, A. W., 36.00;
Stevenson. R. S., 176.00:   Stephen, W. F., 40.00;
Shuttleworth, L., 16.00; Zufelt. L. A., 32.00 ....   4,166 00

AGRICULTURE.—Continued.

FARMERS' AND WOMEN'S INSTITUTES.—Continued.

Services, lecturing at 3.00 per day:
Anderson, D., 63.00; Annis, L. E., 39.00; Backus, Dr. A., 187.50;
Bates, Mrs. J. W., 78.00; Beckett, H. L., 93.00; Clark, J. G., 48.00;
Campbell, Susie, 75.00; Campbell, Mrs. C., 129.00; Carlan, G., 69.00;
Carter, G., 114.00; Clarke, J. W., 36.00; Duncan, Bertha, 88.50;
Eager, W., 39.00; Echlin, J. H., 39.00; Foster, J. G., 45.00;
Glendinning, H., 63.00; Grey, G. A., 183.00; Gray, L. D., 236.50;
Grose, H., 117.00; Hilborn. W. W., 6.00; Johnson, D., 27.00;
Kinney, Mrs. E. M., 78.00; Kydd, W. F., 63.00; McIntosh, Janet, 102.00;
McLean, Alexr., 9.00; Maddock. B. R., 288.00; McMillan, T., 36.00;
McMurchy, Dr. H., 13.00; McTavish, Mrs. J. S., 117.00;
Millar, Bella, 168.00; Nash, C. W., 60.00; Paget, J. W., 69.00;
Pearce, J. S., 51.00; Rife, Isabel, 258.00; Rose, Laura, 147.00;
Ross, Annie, 6.00; Shearer. W. C., 147.00; Shepphard, J., 18.00;
Shuttleworth, L., 76.50; Smith, Agnes, 30.00; Stephen, W. T., 42.00;
Standish, J., 183.00; Warren, J. L., 93.00; Wells, Mrs. H,. 73.00;
Wilson, D. M., 54.00; Yuill, A. R., 15.00; Scott, J. H., 54.00 .... 4,031 00

Services, lecturing at 2.50 per day:
Barbour, G., 57.50; Campbell, Susie, 10.00; Duncan, Bertha, 42.50;
Govenlock, Mabel. 40.00; Grobie, A., 67.50; Lavery, J. F., 21.25;
Lavery, J. S., 30.00; McRae, A. D., 5.00; Mason, A. W., 22.50;
Morris, S. A., 15.00; Murray, Isabel, 95.00; Pease, I. J. C., 15.00;
Purvis. Mrs. W.. 37.50; Reynolds, Lulu, 47.50; Rivett, T. B., 5.00;
Sheffield, L. F., 60.00; Stewart, May, 52.50; Wagg, A. T., 17.50;
Watts. Mrs. P. W., 73.75 ...... 765 00
Backus. Annie. poultry charts, 1.50; Eaton. T. Co., cooking kits, 6.22..... 7 72
East & Co., fibre cases, 4.00; Hubertus, Mrs., postage stamps, 50.00...... 54 00
Warwick Bros. & Rutter, printing and binding 192 50

Travelling expenses:
Annis. L. E.. 10.35; Anderson. D.. 47.95; Arkell. H. S.. 30.80;
Backus, Dr. A., 115.42; Begg, Jas., 3.75; Barbour, G., 2.75;
Brodie, W.. 7.60; Cohoe, J. W.. 4.00; Campbell, Mrs. C., 90.80;
Campbell, J., 107.35; Campbell. Susie, 33.10; Caston, G. C., 51.45;
Carter, Gertrude, 12.35; Clark, J. W., 82.55; Cotterelle, G. R., 21.40;
Carlan, G., 19.20; Drummond, J., 55; Drury, E. C., 368.89;
Duncan, Bertha, 65.28; Dillon, T. J., 8.45; Day, G. E., 20.40;
Eager, W., 10.65; Elliott, A., 315.10; Elliott, W. (acctble), 100.00;
Echlin, J. H., 15.40; Field, R. H., 4.60; Farley, Mrs. W. W., 8.15;
Foster, J. G., 102.20; Fraser, W. S., 137.95; Gamble, W. P., 13.70;
Gardhouse, J., 6.40; Glendinning, H., 174.35; Graham, W. R., 12.25;
Graham, J. T., 1.15; Gray, Gertrude, 222.35; Gray, Lillian, 16.85;
Grose, H., 19.30; Groh, Anson, 4.80; Hallman, A. C., 6.15;
Harcourt, R., 8.05; Hatterman, R. F., 7.05; Hutt, H. L., 6.50;
James, D., 10.35; Johnson, W. J., 5.50; Johnson, D., 10.65;
Jones, H. (acctble) 125.00; Kenny, Mrs. E. M., 56.67;
Kydd, W. F., 394.63; Knowles, R. H., 1.45; Kerr, W. J., 20.40;
Lavery, J. F., 141.05; Lee, E., 6.70; Lemaire, L. R., 3.75;
McClure, Mrs. D., 2.85; McCallum, M., 5.25; McRae, A. D., 30.30;
McLean, A., 5.80; McMurchy, Dr. H., 5.15; McMillan, T., 36.10;
McTavish, Mrs. J., 95.00; Maddock, Blanche, 16.95; Mason, T. H., 51.36;
Miller, H. H., 3.05; Miller, Beila, 104.85; Murphy, R. G., 20.10;
Nash, C. W., 111.71; Oliver, Geo., 3.95; Orr, J. E., 1.70;
Price, L. G., 3.20; Philip, J. A., 5.95; Paget, J. W., 161.80;
Peer, W. E. A., 7.50; Pearce, J. S., 7.40; Putnam, Geo., 72.95;
Peart, H. S., 4.00; Quinn, J. F., 2.00; Reid, H. G., 438.70;
Rife, Isabel, 110.65; Rose, Laura. 108.15; Rayner, T. G., 50.00;
Reynolds, J. B., 9.50; Sanders, W. D., 1.95; Saule, A. M., 70.55;
Scott, J. H., 2.35; Shaw, Jno. C., 9.90; Sinclair, Jno., 75.00;
Shearer, W. C., 162.88; Standish, J., 106.80; Sheppard, F. A., 8.20;
Sheppard, Jas. 79.06; Sherrington, A. E., 27.75;
Shuttleworth, L., 70.15; Smith, W. L., 6.45; Smith, Agnes B., 64.32;
Stevenson, R. S., 72.45; Thompson, R., 10.15; Wagg, A. J., 9.00;
Warren, J. L., 29.20; Wilcox, O. J., 3.65; Wilson, D. M., 9.55;

AGRICULTURE.—*Continued.*
FARMERS' AND WOMEN'S INSTITUTES.—*Continued.*

Wismer, J. H., 1.15; Widdifield, J. W., 7.10; Zufelt, L. A., 41.50...	5,418 62
	19,390 84
Less Refunds on account of travelling expenses, 1905: Anderson, D., 38.85; Beckett, H. L., 65.25; Gray, G., 29.60; Maddock, B., 12.50; Yuill, A. R., 5.00	151 20
	19,239 64

BUREAU OF INDUSTRIES ($3,259.22).

Benning, A. J., tabulating agriculture and municipal statistics	440 00
Hewett, Alfred, 700 copies *Canadian Breeders' Tables*, 45.00; 600 copies *Can. Agriculture Annual*, 60.00	105 00
Hypson, M. L., services revising mail lists	30 00
King's Printer, paper, 50.55; stationery, 339.65	390 20
McIntyre, H., services, 28.00; Rightmeyer, F., services as stenographer at 12.00 per week, 492.00	520 00
Riordon Paper Mills, paper, 277.72; Souch, W. J., services, 276.00.........	553 72
Smith, H. G., services, 223.00; Stewart, H. A., meterological services, 50.00	273 00
Warwick Bros. & Rutter, printing and binding	947 30

DAIRY BRANCH, DAIRY INSTRUCTION.
SALARIES ($32,424.98).

Western District:

Geo. H. Barr: Nine months' salary as Chief Instructor.........			1,350 00
Jno. R. Burgess: Eight	do	Instructor............................•	800 00
F. Dean:	do	do	600 00
R. H. Green:	do	do	800 00
F. Herns:	do	do	800 00
E. N. Hart: Six	do	do	600 00
Alex. McKay: Eight	do	do	800 00
C. W. McDougall: Six	do	do	600 00
John H Scott: Eight	do	do	800 00
Geo. Travis:	do	do	800 00
W. W. Waddell:	do	do	800 00

Eastern District:

G. G. Publow, Eight and one-half months' salary as Chief Instructor............			1,275 00
C. A. Publow, One and one-third do		Instructor	133 33
W. J. Ragsdale, Eight	do	do	800 00
Geo. Robinson,	do	do	800 00
R. A. Rothwell,	do	do	800 00
J. F. Shingleton,	do	do	800 00
I. Villeneuve,	do	do	800 00
R. W. Ward,	do	do	800 00
A. H. Wilson,	do	do	800 00
D. M. Wilson,	do	do	800 00
E. Wilkinson,	do	do	800 00
L. A. Zufelt,	do	do	900 00
H. Brentnell: Six and one-half months' salary as Instructor....................			666 66
G. Bensley: Eight	do	do	800 00
J. Buro:	do	do	800 00
D. J. Cameron:	do	do	800 00
S. S. Cheetham :	do	do	800 00
Jos. Charbonneau: Six	do	do	600 00
W. Doole: Eight	do	do	800 00
J. H. Echlin: Two and one-third	do	do	233 33
R. E. Elliott: Eight	do	do	800 00
Claud Ferguson:	do	do	800 00
W. J. Gardiner: Six and two-thirds	do	do	666 66
R. J. Gray: Eight	do	do	800 00
Hugh Howie:	do	do	800 00
A. Herrity:	do	do	800 00
Jas. Irwin:	do	do	800 00
J. B. Lowery:	do	do	800 00
A. McDowell:	do	do	800 00
P. Nolan:	do	do	800 00
C. W. Norval,	do	do	800 00

AGRICULTURE.—*Continued.*

DAIRY BRANCH.—*Continued.*

EXPENSES ($1,679.80).

Barr, Geo. H., travelling expenses, 11.05; Burgess, J R., travelling expenses, 3.75	14 80
Canadian Express Co., charges, 12.45; Dean, Fred., travelling expenses, 214.75	227 20
Echlin, J. H., travelling expenses, 13.65; Green, R. H., travelling expenses, 2.35	16 00
Hubertus, Mrs., postage stamps, 50.00; Hart, E. W., travelling expenses, 245.35	295 35
King's Printer, stationery, 9.00; Kerns, Frank, travelling expenses, 1.25	10 25
McKay, Alex., travelling expenses, 2.95; McDougall, C. W., travelling expenses, 183.15	186 10
Musson Book Co., cheese factory reports, etc.	198 25
Publow, G. G., travelling expenses, 319.20; postage, 13.00	332 20
Prizes *re* Butter competition:	
Brown, F. E., 10.00; McKay, W. A., 20.00; McKenzie, D. E., 25.00	55 00
McQuaker, J., 15.00; Southworth, L. A., 30.00; Thompson, J. H., 5.00	50 00
Scott, J. H., travelling expenses	14 90
Travelling Expenses Eastern Instructors:	
Bensley, Geo., 10.85; Britnell, H., 11.75; Buro, J., 3.60; Cameron, D. J., 14.20	40 40
Charbonneau, Jos., 4.20; Cheetham, S. S., 8.85; Doal, W. W., 5.95; Elliott, R. E., 6.90	25 90
Ferguson, Claude, 3.25; Gardner, W. G., 7.80; Gray, R. T., 13.90; Herity, Anthony, 12.50	37 45
Howey, Hugh, 12.25; Irwin, J., 16.25; Lowery, J. B., 13.40; McDonnell, Allan, 3.20	45 10
Nolan, Peter, 9.05; Norval, C. W., 5.00; Ragsdale, W. J., 9.10; Robinson, Geo., 9.95	33 10
Rothwell, R., 3.85; Singleton, J. F., 7.50; Wilkinson, E., 2.85; Villeneuve, I., 3.85	18 05
Ward, R. W., 15.00; Wilson, A. H., 8.05; Wilson, D. M., 6.10; Zufelt, L. A., 4.85	34 00
Waddell, W.	3 70
Warwick Bros. & Rutter, printing and binding	42 05

EASTERN DAIRY SCHOOL ($9,194.82).

Mitchell, J. W.,	Twelve months' salary as Superintendant			1,500 00
do	Arrears, 1905			62 50
Connell, W. Y.,	Twelve months' salary as Bacteriologist			500 00
Publow, G. G.,	Three and one-half months' salary as Instructor in Cheese			525 00
Echlin, J. H.,	do	do	Assistant do	169 99
Stonehouse, Jas.,	do	do	Instructor in Butter	255 00
Buro, J.,	Three and two-third	do	do and Separator	172 50
do	Four one-half	do	Assistant Instructor Butter Dept.	25 00
Irwin, Jas.,	do	do	Assistant Instructor in Butter	161 33
Craig, J. A., services as Engineer				162 50
Singleton, J. F., services as Instructor Milk Testing				240 33
Gordon, Jessie, services as Office Assistant				190 00
Ross, Alex., do Caretaker				125 00
Ayer, A. A. & Co., cheese, 49.76; Anglin, S. & Co., paper files, 10.80; Am. Ex. Co., charges, 1.50				62 06
Annual Review Publishing Co., subscription, 3.50; Alexander, James. Ltd., loss on butter *re* experimental shipment, 55c				4 05
Bell Telephone Co., messages, 19.65; rent of instruments, 30.00				49 65
Bausch & Lomb Optical Co., hydrometers, 4.26; Bromley, F., pens and inkstand, 1.00				5 26
British Whig Publishing Co., advertising and subscription, 16.40; Burrell, D. H. & Co., dairy supplies, 10.19				26 59
Board of Education, rent of gymnasium, 60.00; Canadian Express Co., charges, 31.09				91 09

AGRICULTURE.—*Continued*.

EASTERN DAIRY SCHOOL.—*Continued*.

Chown, A. P., supplies, 6.10; stationery, 96c.; thermometers, 2.40	9 46
Canadian Dairy Supply Co., milk bottles, 3.45; C. P. R. Telegraph Co., telegrams, 25c.	3 70
Collector of Customs, duty charges, 2.29; *Creamery Journal*, subscription, 2.00	4 29
Carson, R., 1 bbl. salt, 1.60; Dominion Paper Co., paper, 24.00; Dobbs, J. R. C. & Co., stationery, 2.10	27 70
Dairyman Pubg. Co., advertising, 34.50; subscription, 1.00	35 50
Dean, F., cleaning and repairing school building and equipment	10 00
Derbyshire, D., supplies, 17.15; brushes, bottles, etc., 15.50; travelling expenses, 7.00	39 65
Dom. Ex. Co., charges, 1.30; Dobbs, J. R. C. & Co., typewriting supplies, 6.25	7 55
Eastern Ontario Dairymen's Association, advertising, 15.00; Eimer & Amend, hydrometers, chemicals, etc., 16.65......	31 65
Farming World, advertising, 10.00; *Farmer's Advocate*, advertising, 16.80	26 80
Firstbrook Box Co., boxes, 24.50; *Family Herald and Weekly Star*, subscription, 1.00	25 50
Farmer, Wallace's, subscription, 2.00; G. T. Railway Co., charges freight, 26.55	28 55
G. N. W. Telegraph Co., telegrams, 3.90; Gilbert, Jno., postage stamps, 45.25; groceries, 2.25	51 40
Guess, Leighton, livery hire, 6.00; Gibson, W. W., grass seed, 2.75........	8 75
Guild & Hanson, directory, 2.00; Graves Bros., 1 tape, 1.50	3 50
Hay & Wilson, wheelbarrow. 3.00; Hansen, C., laboratory supplies, 11.05	14 05
Hansen, Geo., advertising, 6.00; *Hoard's Dairyman*, subscription, 2.00...	8 00
Herns, F., cleaning and repairing school building and equipment..............	10 00
Hunter & Harold, erecting shelves, alterations, etc., 56.65; Jackson Press, printing, 35.25	91 90
Journal, The Ottawa, advertising, 12.50; *Kingston News*, subscription, 10.00	22 50
Kingston News, advertising, 11.85; printing, 105.75	117 60
Kelly, Jos., groceries, 1.50; Light Department, light, 33.25; fuel, 4.40...	39 15
Laidlaw, Jno. & Sons, dry goods, 9.60; Lyman, Sons & Co., supplies, 8.70	18 30
Lewis, M. J., shipping cream, 52.72; Lemmon, dairy supplies, etc., 80.71	133 43
McColl Bros. & Co., boiler compound, etc......	22 70
McKelvey & Birch, dairy supplies, hardware, 23.49; repairing leaks in cupola, 2.70	26 19
McAuley, Thos., stationery, 30.55; McFaul, R., blinds, 5.25	35 80
McKee, J. D., books	10 00
Mitchell, J. W., to pay broker duty charges, 40c.; travelling expenses and disbursements, 254.82	255 22
Mallen, James, 90.1750 tons soft slack coal at 3.75 per ton, 316.43; ½ cord slabs, 2.50	318 93
Mallen, James, manure	18 00
Montreal Star, advertising	18 00
Murphy, L. W., supplies, 7.10; Murphy, R. G., travelling expenses, 7.00	14 10
Montreal Star Publishing Co., supplies, 7.50; Mallory, A. W., shipping cream, 59.55	67 05
Mason, H., subscription to *Trade-Bulletin*, 2.00; Medcalf, D. M., travelling expenses *re* boiler inspection, 23.10	25 10
Newman, Wm., advertising, 6.00	6 00
Newlands, Wm., making plans, etc., *re* construction magazine cabinet...	4 00
Parkhill, J. Y., butter tub, 40c.; Powell, J., photos, 1.00......	1 40
Patton, L., travelling expenses	3 50
Queen City Oil Co., separators, cans, etc., 5.40; Robertson Bros., supplies, 13c	5 53
Robinson Bros., supplies, 23.88; Richardson, C. & Co., dairy apparatus, 80.00	103 88
Rees, S., harrowing lawn, manure, etc., 7.75; *Rural New Yorker*, subscription, 2.00	9 75
Roessler & Hasslocker Chemical Co., chemicals, 6.00; Reid, Robt., furniture, 13.50	19 50
Sears, Geo., hardware, etc., 17.00; Skinner, Henry & Co., supplies, 4.65	21 65
Sundry persons, milk supplied 2,515.11; hauling cream, 30.45.................	2,545 56

AGRICULTURE.—*Continued.*

EASTERN DAIRY SCHOOL.—*Continued.*

Summons Bros., hardware, dairy utensils	127 08
Silver Dust Mfg. Co., silver dust, 23.00; Stoddart, Arthur, rolling lawn, 1.50	24 50
Sears, Geo., hardware, 9.20; School of Mining and Agriculture, lecturing on Dairy Chemistry, 200.00	209 20
Sun Printing Co., subscription, 2.00; Tomilson, Geo. R., gas stove repairs, 8.85	10 85
Taylor & Hamilton, covering smokestack with asbestos	65 00
Uglow, R. & Co., stationery, 15.55; Water Works Dept., water, 100.00; *Weekly Sun*, advertising, 21.00	136 55
Wilson, T. H., lessons in soldering, 8.75; White & Gillespie, thermometer, 1.25	10 00
Weld, The Wm. Co., subscription to *Farmer's Advocate*	3 00

WESTERN DAIRY SCHOOL ($2,766.37).

Barr, Geo. H.,	Services as	Superintendant	450 00
Burgess, Jas. R.,	do	Instructor	225 00
Ballantyne, R. A.,	do	Engineer	140 00
Dean, Fred.,	do	Instructor	225 00
Hart, E. N.,	do	do	225 00
Herns, F.,	do	do	255 00
Walker, P.,	do	Milk Weigher	75 00

Brown, E. F., dairy supplies, 7.30; Ballantyne Dairy Supply Co., supplies, 21.50	28 80
Baird, W., express charges, 30c.; Bell Telephone Co., rent of instrument, 10.00	10 30
Bell Telephone Co., messages	1 55
Barr, Geo., butter for scoring instruction, 2.00; travelling expenses, 355.50	357 50
Burgess, J. R., travelling expenses, 2.60; Carr, T. E., painting, 18.25	20 85
Cunningham, Express, charges, 60c.; Can. Exp. Co., charges, 30c.	90
Carr & McNeil, painting butter room stairs	85 00
Depew Carbon Paint Co., paint, 2.50; *Dairyman* Publishing Co., advtg., 9.50	12 00
Dean, F., cleaning and repairing building, etc., 10.10; Dairymens' Ass'n. of Ontario, advertising, 10.00	20 10
Darch & Hunter, parchment, 38c.; Decorlis, E., travelling expenses, 12.60	12 98
Dyar, P. O., metal polish, 25c.; Electric Boiler Compound Co., boiler compound, 22.55	22 80
Evans Bros., subscription, 1.00; printing, 5.75; advertising, 19.21	25 96
Edwards, S. F., a pure culture, 25c.; East End Cheese Co., cheese, 2.80	3 05
Graham, D., soaps, lye, etc., 1.30; Grand Trunk Railway, freight charges, 2.52	3 82
Griffin, A., cartage, 7.07; Green, R. H., travelling expenses, 3.00	10 07
Harrison, F. L., rent of chairs, 2.00; Hare, A. E., plastering material and teaming, 8.40	10 40
Haney, Fred., pipe fittings, etc.	8 27
Hart, E. W., polish, 20c.; Hing Lee, laundrying, 5.54; Haldone, G. M., printing, 4.70	10 44
Herd, Jno., Board of Health charges, dairy school, 1.55; Herd, Geo. K., lime, 45c.	2 00
Herns, F., cleaning and repairing school buildings, 10.00; travelling expenses, 75c.; door mat and door keys, 50c.; postage stamps, 25c.	11 50
Johnston, Robt., lecturing, 2.50; Karn, W. A., chemicals, 5.00	7 50
Kilgour, D. L., toilet paper, 25c.; Kerry, Watson & Co., chemicals, 6.45	6 70
London Engine Supply Co., manhole gaskets, etc.	21 14
Lister, R. A. & Co., steel balls, 1.79; London Printing & Lithographing Co., stationery, 50c.	2 29
London Box Mfg. & Lumber Co., box lids, 1.00; London Advertiser Co., printing and stationery, 2.50	3 50
McKellar, Malcolm, iron work on boiler, 1.50; McColl. H., postage stamps, 2.00	3 50
McColl, D., postage stamps, 2.00; McKay, Alex., travelling expenses, 1.75	3 75
Mitchell, Gill & Co., cotton, 1.53; Meekison, J. D., subscription, 2.75; stationery, 75c.	5 03

AGRICULTURE.—*Continued.*

WESTERN DAIRY SCHOOL.—*Continued.*

Murray, W. H., duty on culture	19
Nicholl, Peter, repairing boiler arches, 2.50; Nicholson, R., 18.1530 tons steam coal at 4.50 per ton, 84.44	86 94
Noble, Jas., hardware, etc., 40c.; Pincombe & Donaldson, 1 load of kindling, 1.00	1 40
Richardson, C. & Co., cream scales and repairs, etc.	18 00
Robertson, J. & Son, galvanized iron tank and fixtures, hardware, etc.	40 09
Raymond. A. G., postage stamps, 14.00; Ray, E. W., photos, 2.75	16 75
Reed, J. H., travelling expenses	5 90
Strathroy *Despatch*, printing, 51.75; subscription, 1.00; advtg., 32.70; stationery, 75c.	86 20
Stevely, Wm. & Sons, cream pails	2 50
Scott & Gillies, 39.795 tons coal at 4.75 per ton, 127.70; 2 bbls. salt, 3.65	131 35
Strathroy, Town of, taxes, 90c.; sundry persons, milk, 30.18; butter and cheese, 11.02	42 10
Stepler, W. H., chemicals, 6.05; Statham, E. & Son, repairs to pump, 1.00	7 05
Scott, Jno. H., trav. expenses, 50c.; Taylor & McKenzie, card knife, 4.00	4 50
Travis, Geo., travelling expenses, 1.25; Vermont Farm Machine Co., freight on separator, 1.65	2 90
Whitelaw, R., liner plates, 1.00; Wright, Jas. & Sons, hardware, etc., 4.50	5 50
Welch, L. B., chemicals, 90c.; Whitehead, J. P., lecture on veterinary science, 5.00	5 90
Waddell, W., travelling expenses, 50c.; Wagner Glass Works, butter test bottles, 1.50	2 00
Westman, C., express charges	40

DAIRYMEN'S ASSOCIATIONS ($4,000.00).

Eastern Dairymen's Association, grant	2,000 00
Western Dairymen's Association, do	2,000 00

INSPECTION OF CHEESE FACTORIES AND CREAMERIES ($2,499.05).

Dillon. T. J., services as Inspector	668 27
do travelling expenses	532 38
Echlin. J. H., services as Inspector	750 00
do travelling expenses	548 40

OTTAWA CENTRAL FAIR ASSOCIATION ($4,000.00).

Ottawa Central Fair Association, grant	4,000 00

FRUIT, VEGETABLES, HONEY AND INSECTS. GRANTS, ETC. ($4,574.45).

Bee Keepers' Association, grant	500 00
Bee Keeper's Review list of bee keepers	2 40
Entomological Society, grant	1,000 00
Fruit Growers' Association, grant	1,800 00
Gemmill, F. A., travelling expenses	8 20
Grand Trunk Railway, freight charges	1 29
Hall, J. B., travelling expenses	6 95
Hershiser, Orel D., wax press for foul brood suppression	15 00
Harte & Lyne, duty, brokerage, charges, etc., on wax press	4 50
McEvoy, Wm., services as Inspector at 4.00 per day, 184.00; services as Inspector at 5.50 per day, 291.50; travelling expenses, 160.61	636 11
Vegetable Growers' Association, grant	600 00

EXPERIMENTAL FRUIT STATIONS, INSTITUTES AND HORTICULTURAL MEETINGS ($3,897.76).

Woolverton, L., salary as Secretary, Board of Control, and work on fruits of Ontario, 300.00; travelling expenses, 49.97	349 97

AGRICULTURE.—*Continued.*

EXPERIMENTAL FRUIT STATIONS, ETC.—*Continued.*

Allowances as Experimenter: Caston, G. C., 200.00; Dempsey, W. H., 200.00; Hilborn, W. W., 200.00; Jones, H., 200.00; Mitchell, John, 87.50; Pettit, M., 200.00; Peart, A. W., 175.00; Sherrington, A. E., 175.00; Stevenson, Rev. E. B., 75.00; — Woolverton, L., 175.00; Young, Chas., 100.00	1;787 50
Adams, E. E., assistance, Horticultural Show, at 3.00 per day, 65.00; travelling expenses, 16.60; vegetables, 5.00.	86 60
Briggs, Wm., printing, 20.50; Begg & Son, lettering banner, 1.00	21 50
Beattie, T., collection of fruit, Industrial Fair	1 50
Cutting, A. B., services, lecturing at 3.00 per day, 40.50; trav. exp., 40.00	80 50
Canadian Express Co., charges, 1.45; Caldwell, C., photos, 12.00	13 45
Creelman, G. C., travelling expenses, 16.55	16 55
Caston, G. C., assistance, Horticultural Show, at 3.00 per day, 6.00; trav. expenses, 1.60; fruit, 12.00	19 60
Dominion Express Co., charges, 25c.; Dempsey, W. H., services at 2.00 per day, 6.00; travelling expenses, 8.80	15 05
Flansburg & Potter Co., raspberry bushes, 3.50; Forbes, Wm., postage stamps, 5.00	8 50
Garrett, E., printing, 2.50; Gifford, A., services, lecturing at 3.00 per day, 27.00	29 50
Hutt, H. L., allowance for inspection, 100.00; travelling expenses, 146.24...	246 24
Hubertus, Mrs., postage stamps, 50.00; Haynes, A., collection of fruit, Industrial Fair, 6.05	56 05
Hodgetts, P. W., travelling expenses *re* fruit exhibit	65 00
Hunt, Wm., travelling expenses, 2.25; Hilborn, J. L., services as experimenter, 50.00	52 25
Johnson, D., services, lecturing, 69.00; travelling expenses, 128.45	197 45
Jones, H., services at 2.00 per day, 4.00; travelling expenses, 42.67	46 67
Lick, Elmer, services at 3.00 per day, 6.00; travelling expenses, 4.05	10 05
Macoun, W. T., services at 3.00 per day, 6.00; travelling expenses, 45.17; revising bulletin on Fruits of Ontario, 50.00	101 17
Mail Printing Co., advertising, 30.00; Mitchell, J. G., services at experimenter, 87.50	117 50
Niagara Peninsula United Fruit Growers' Association, grant	160 00
National Drug & Chemical Co., chemicals	1 21
Orr, W. M., services, revising Fruits of Ontario	4 00
Ottawa Nurseries, raspberry bushes	2 00
Ontario Horticultural Association, grant, 100.00; Pettit, M., collecting of fruit, 2.20	102 20
Peart, A. W., collecting fruit, 16.60; travelling expenses 8.40	25 00
Rivett, T. B., collecting fruit for exhibit at 2.50 per day	42 50
Smith, A. M., services at 3.00 per day, 24.00; travelling expenses, 14.35	38 35
Sherrington, A. E., services, lecturing at 4.00 per day, 64.00; travelling expenses, 90.45	154 45
St. Catharines Cold Storage Co., fruit	5 15
Smith, E. D., travelling expenses	32 30
Tufford, M. J., livery hire	8 00

EXPERIMENTAL FRUIT FARM ($2,172.25).

Arkell, H. S., travelling expenses, 7.45; Allen, A. A., postage stamps, 95c.	8 40
Baumgartner, F., wages as laborer at 33.00 per month	71 00
Black, J. K., bran, etc.	18 90
Culp, A. H., ha~ cats, manure, etc., 95.41; Carr, Fred., repairing implements, etc., 4.80	100 21
Canadian Stamp & Stencil Co., stamp, 25c.; Coy Bros. & Southcott, hardware, etc., 1.40	1 65
Canadian Express Co., charges, 25c.; Colgan, Robt., veterinary services, 1.00	1 25
Colégate, Geo., hardware, etc.	1 10
Day, Geo. E., travelling expenses, 9.85; Duncan, W. S., oats, 40.00	49 85
Elly, Wm., wages as laborer at 1.50 per day, 22.50; Eaton, T. Co., drugs, etc., 30c.	22 85
Ellis House, stabling horses	40

AGRICULTURE.—*Continued.*

EXPERIMENTAL FRUIT FARM.—*Continued.*

Fretz, F., barrels, 10.80; Lester, Jacob, ploughing at 40c. per hour, 23.60	34 40
Fry, D. W., hardware, etc., 55c.; Fairfield, C. A. D., drugs, etc., 1.35 ...	1 90
Griffin, J. P., team of horses, 500.00; Gummer, H., printing, 3.25	503 25
Greenwood, A. J. & Co., drugs, etc., 1.50; Hutt, H. L., travelling expenses re inspection Rittenhouse Farm, 4.90	6 40
Hunsburger, Wm., teaming at 3.75 per day	15 00
Hamilton, Grimsby & Beamsville Electric Railway Co., freight charges on tile	27 00
Jerome & Hammond, cultivator and barrow, 42.00; hill plow, 17.50	59 50
Jervis, John & Son, drain tile	102 00
McArthur, A. J., tools, etc., 14.20; McKenzie, Henry, ploughing, 7.00	21 20
Massey-Harris Co., implements, 88.00; Mills, Stanley & Co., 1 set harness, 28.00	116 00
Maxwell, David & Son, wagon, 70.00; Moyer, R. J., sleigh, plow, etc., 59.90	129 90
Merritt, Wm., horseshoeing, etc.	1 25
Peart, H. S., travelling expenses re inspection Rittenhouse Farm	3 15
Reynolds, J. B., travelling expenses, 11.80; Reid, John, hay, 27.00	38 80
Studler, A., wages as laborer at 33.00 per month, 71.00; Smure Co., hardware, oil, etc., 1.00	72 00
Shaefer, F., tile, 219.78; Tufford. L., wages as laborer at 1.50 per day, 36.37	256 15
Taylor, Chas., rolling coulter, 3.50; Van Norman & Robins, stationery, 25c.	3 75
Watts & Bates, hardware	52 46
Wood, John, wages as foreman at 45.00 per month, 270.00; travelling expenses, 4.50; freight on tile, 51.96	326 46
Wood Bros., harness, blankets, etc., 73.15; Woodand, W. R., oats, 40.60...	113 75
Wismer, A. K., Carriage Co., lumber, stone boat, etc.	12 32

COLD STORAGE EXPERIMENTS, GRANTS, ETC. ($151.28).

Canada Paper Co., wrapping paper, 5.40; Grigg, H. E., apples for storage, 48.00	53 40
Lyons & Marks, sample bottles and jars	22 25
National Drug & Chemical Co., chemicals	5 03
Rivett, T. B., collecting and packing fruit at 2.50 per day	67 50
Toronto Storage Co., storage on fruit	3 10

FRUIT, FLOWER AND HONEY SHOWS ($1,700.00).

Dunlop, J. H., grant to Ontario Horticultural Exhibition.....................	900 00
Niagara District Fruit, Flower and Honey Show, grant	500 00
Provincial Flower, Fruit and Honey Show account, grant	300 00

SAN JOSE SCALE, SPRAYING, ETC. ($3,026.88).

Arnott, Wilson, compensation for injury to orchard re spraying experiments	500 00
Bell Telephone Co., messages. 30c.; rent of instruments, 23.76	24 06
C.P.R. Telegraph Co., telegrams, 1.85; Carey, P. J., services, arbitrator Wilson-Arnott enquiry, 10.00	11 85
Cutting, A. B., services as Inspector, 31.00; travelling expenses, 60.80	91 80
Elliot & Co., copper sulphate	43 23
G.N.W. Telegraph Co., telegrams, 60c.; Gifford, A. B., services, self and team at 8.00 per day. 232.00	232 60
Hodgetts, P. W., services at director of spraying experiments, 100.00; travelling expenses, 58.29	158 29
Irwin, C. W., duty brokerage and cartage	3 44
Lymon Bros. & Co., freight charges on sulphur...................................	7 12
McCordick, W. F., lime	1 37
Niagara Sprayer Co., gas sprayer and repairing machine	103 05
National Drug and Chemical Co., chemicals	10 10
Poole, W. H., storage and cartage on machine	10 00
Peer, W. E. A., services in charge of spraying machine at 2.50 per day, 110.00; travelling expenses, 88.92	198 92

AGRICULTURE.—*Continued.*

SAN JOSE SCALE, ETC.—*Continued.*

Pettit, A. H., services inspecting, 20.00; travelling expenses, 30.00; services as arbitrator in Wilson-Arnott enquiry, 30.00	80 00
Rivett, T. B., services as inspector, 452.00; travelling expenses, 519.24...	971 24
Rittenhouse, D. B., expenses scale inspection	11 50
Smith, J. F., services as inspector at 3.00 per day, 171.00; travelling expenses, 142.73	313 73
Spramotor Co., hand spraying outfit	24 25
Toronto Liquid Carbonate Co., gas for operating	50 40
Treasurer Township Saltfleet, half expenses of inspection	179 93

MISCELLANEOUS.

ONTARIO EXPERIMENTAL UNION ($2,500.00).

Hutt, H. L., Treasurer, grant	2,500 00

PIONEER FARM ($943.21).

Annis, A. E., twelve months' salary as Superintendent, including house and supplies	140 00
Brignol, F. T., threshing, 20.50; Chase, W. S., 1. M. lath, 2.00	22 50
C. P. Railway Co., freight, 1.63; Cassidy & Son, groceries, 123.37	125 00
Daily Times-Journal, Fort William, advertising, 23.36; Dom. Express Co., 2.70	26 06
Gibson, J. E., groceries, 5.22; Godfrey, C. C., medical attendance on stock, 13.00	18 22
Hardy, H., wages, laborer (without board), 157.50; Hayes, J. G., rope, hardware, oils, etc., 26.55	184 05
Hutchinson, A. R., 3 sows, service, 4.50; Hatch, J. W., 9 sows, service, 9.00	13 50
Latimer, J., 1 sow, service, 1.50; McMillan, W., lumber, 4.95	6 45
Miner Publishing Co., advertising, 30.80; Orvis, A. L., supplies, 36.91	67 71
Pay lists, wages, farm laborers, 88.14; Rutter, L. V., bread, 44.00	132 14
Rhodes, Jno., binder twine, hardware, etc., 36.60; Reed, Jno., groceries, 118.76	155 36
Star Publishing Co., advertising, 30.80; Schellenberg, Max, harness repairs, etc., 8.45	39 25
Silver, Chas., services sale of effects, 10.00; Trist, R., groceries, 2.97	12 97

INCIDENTALS ($13,096.45).

Benning, J. E., services revising mailing lists at 10.00 per week	80 00
Can. Fairbanks Co., half cost of expenses of exhibit at Simcoe Fair	32 22
Grant, G., services at 2.50 per day	55 00
Hypson, M. L., services revising mailing lists at 10.00 per week	115 00
Harris, E., quail pamphlets and supplements for distribution	18 10
Johnston, G. T., supplies for Robert Reid	24 80
King's Printer, paper, 10.74; stationery, 295.63	306 37
Lynch, T., paste, 11.00; McIntyre, H., services mailing reports at 14.00 per week, 606.00	617 00
McMaster, M. H., postage stamps, 210.00; McCredie, A. L., special report on agriculture Co. Elgin, 35.00	245 00
Newell, O., services at 12.00 per week, 112.00; Potter, D., meal and supplies for Robert Reid, 6.00	118 00
Rightmeyer, F., services addressing envelopes, 2.00 per day, 120.00; Reynolds, J. B., travelling expenses, 137.24	257 24
Radcliffe. F. W., compensation for barberry hedge destroyed	10 00
Rivett, T. B., services investigating fruit crops at 2.50 per day	32 50
Riordon Paper Mills, paper for reports	7,409 68
Reid, Robert, services inspecting land for farm at 4.00 per day	88 00
Toronto Ry. Co., car tickets. 5.00; White. G. G., travelling expenses, 348.20	353 20
Warwick Bros. & Rutter. printing bulletins and pamphlets	8,334 34

AGRICULTURE.—*Continued.*

AGRICULTURAL COLLEGE, GUELPH.

SALARIES ($55,079.00).

Geo. C. Creelman: Twelve months' salary as	President.........................	2,000 00
H. H. Dean:	do　　Prof. of Dairy Husbandry.........	1,900 00
J. B. Reynolds:	do　　do　Physics and English.......	1,900 00
W. Lochhead: Four	do　　do　Biology....................	600 00
G. E. Day: Twelve	do　　do　Animal Husbandry........	2,000 00
C. A. Zavitz:	do　　do　Field Husbandry...........	2,000 00
H. L. Hutt:	do　　do　Horticultural..............	1,800 00
S. F. Edwards:	do　　do　Bacteriology..............	1,500 00
Robt. Harcourt:	do　　do　Chemistry.................	1,800 00
J. H. Reed:	do　　do　Veterinary Science(part time)	1,200 00
T. D. Jarvis،	do　　Lecturer in Biology..............	1,200 00
W. P. Gamble:	do　　do　Chemistry...............	1,400 00
H. S. Arkell:	do　　do　Animal Husbandry.......	1,200 00
Bronson Barlow:	do　　Demonstrator in Bacteriology.....	1,000 00
V. W. Jackson: Four and half	do　　　　do　　　Biology.........	266 00
J. E. Howitt: Four	do　　　　do　　　do　..........	234 00
E. G. de Coriolis: Nine	do　　　　do　　　Chemistry.......	750 00
H. L. Fulmer: Three	do　　　　do　　　do　..........	175 00
H. S. Peart: Twelve	do　　　　do　　　Horticultural....	1,000 00
M. R. Baker: Two	do　　Assistant Biological Laboratory....	70 00
W. H. Day: Twelve	do　　Lecturer in Physics..............	1,200 00
G. G. White: Three	do　　Fellow in Chemistry..............	112 50
J. Buchanan: Twelve	do　　Lecturer Field Husbandry........	1,200 00
Wm. Hunt· Nine	do　　Florist.........................	625 00
D. H. Jones: Twelve	do　　Dean of Residence...............	700 00
A. G. Rowsome:	do　　Teacher French and German and	
	Assistant Librarian............	800 00
E. Frew:	do　　Second Assistant in Library.......	450 00
H. L. Fulmer: Seven	do　　Fellow in Chemistry..............	262 50
W. R. Graham: Twelve	do　　Manager Poultry Department and	
	Lecturer.....................	1,400 00
W. Clark:	do　　Teacher in Drill and Gymnastics..	300 00
J. B. Fairbairn:	do　　President's Secretary and Assistant	
	in Residence..................	800 00
A. Hallett:	do　　Stenographer....................	500 00
S. Springer:	do　　Bursar and Superintendent...	1,600 00
A. A. Davidson:	do　　Bursar's Clerk....	750 00
W. B. Goldie: Five	do　　Clerk and Stenographer...........	208 00
E. Webb: Six	do　　do　　　do　　..........	250 00
S. E. Hardy: Twelve	do　　Matron.......................	500 00
W. O. Stewart:	do　　Physician (part time).............	600 00
R. W. Green:	do　　Engineer......................	950 00
A. Green:	do　　Assistant Engineer....	600 00
J. Boyle: Four	do　　Stoker.......................	172 50
J. Wilkie: Eleven	do　　do　.......................	450 00
J. Yates: Two	do　　do　.......................	90 00
S. A. Haggett: Seven	do　　do　.......................	270 00
F. G. Banfield One	do　　do　.......................	45 00
Geo. Barron: Nine	do　　Plumber and General man........	455 00
S. A. Hagget: Six	do　　Sewage Caretaker...............	240 00
John Squirrel: Twelve	do　　Night Watchman................	420 00
R. Masson:	do　　Messenger.....................	356 00
Geo. Agnew: One	do　　Sewage Caretaker...............	40 00
Geo. Barron: Three	do　　do　...............	120 00
R. Emmery: One	do　　do　...............	40 00
A. W. Bruce: Twelve	do　　Stenographer..................	300 00
E. Powell:	do　　do　....................	175 00
J. Teven:	do　　Janitor.......................	420 00
F. Sherman: Five	do　　Professor of Entomology..........	625 00
J. C. S. Bethune: Seven	do　　do　..........	875 00
E. J. Zavitz: Twelve	do　　Lecturer in Forestry..............	1,200 00
Wm. Holman:	do　　Painter.......................	700 00
L. Crowther:	do　　Baker........................	600 00
Mrs. Mathews:	do　　Janitress.....................	300 00
Mrs. F. A. White: Seven	do　　do　..................	160 00
R. Sunley: Five	do　　do　..................	125 00

15a P.A.

AGRICULTURE.—*Continued.*

AGRICULTURAL COLLEGE.—*Continued.*

SALARIES.—*Continued.*

Pay lists, wages, maids, cooks, laundresses, etc.	2,685 13
H. R. Rowsome, lectures on Apiculture	200 00
Geo. Agnew, services carrying mail, unloading coal, etc.	360 00
Prof. Harrison, three months prof. Bacteriology ......,........................	425 00
M. H. Smith, services switchboard	· 247 00
C. C. Thom, services in laboratory	230 00
Sundry persons, temporary services, etc.	300 13
Student labor	4,600 24

EXPENSES ($40,885.62).

Annual Review Pub. Co., subscription, 2.75; American Geographic Institute, atlas, 1.00	3 75
Arkell, T. R., first prize general proficiency, 10.00; American Educational Co., books, stationery, etc., 3.50	13 50
Anderson, C. & Co., note paper, envelopes, etc., 31.73; American Chemical Society, dues, 5.03	36 76
A. L. A. Publishing Board, Smithsonian Report, 1904, 84 titles at 4.00 per 100	3 36
Ambrose Kent & Sons, 9 fire drill badges, 10.00	10 00
Anderson, Peter, breakfast foods, 3 doz. at 1.80, 5.10; 2 doz. at 15c., 30c.; 4 doz. at 20c., 80c.; 4 doz. gem jars at 90c., 3.60	9 80
Adams Furniture Co., morris chair, 14.47; Arkell, H. S., travelling expenses *re* Chicago live stock show, 84.25	98 72
Buckingham, W. E., lectures, 78.00; examining papers, 22.00; Benson, Johnston & Co., stationery, 20.00	120 00
Buchanan, J., travelling expenses, 9.80; Bennett, L. H., photographs, 1.70	11 50
Burrow, Stewart & Milne, gas range 32.40, freight 95c.; Barker, R., cleaning and laying carpet, 8.25	41 60
Bethune, C. J., travelling expenses, 2.00; Bennett's newspaper and magazine sub agency, subscriptions *Saturday Evening Post* 1.50, *Ladies' Home Journal*, 1.25	4 75
Bowman, J. A., Aberdeen Angus bull, 300.00; lecture, 5.00; Barteldes, I. & Co., seeds, 1.06	306 06
Bausch & Lomb, laboratory supplies, 18.49; Burlington Canning Co., jam and canned fruits, 65.81	84 30
Broadfoot, J. B., laboratory supplies, 15.60; drug sundries, 4.55	20 15
Baker, M. R., travelling expenses, 14.50; Buskin, Geo., books, 1.25.........	15 40
Bond Hardware Co., galvanized pipe, 47.19; coal oil, 15.49: 1 bit, 2.00; 1 brace, 3.00; putty, 2.70; turpentine, 43 gals. at 97c., 41.81; repairs and furnishings, 79.48; sewage, 23.30; iron, hardware, etc., 201.75; 1 coal vase, 3.00; solder, 5.40; brushes, 5.00; jelly moulds, 1.50; wire, 9.42; saw, 1.50; packing, 8 lbs. at 1.00, 8.00; 2 prs. scissors, 1.60; paint, oils, etc., 60.77; 1 orange slicer, 3.00; cement, 6 bbls. at 2.50, 15.00, 12¼ at 2 25, 27.56; step ladders. 3 for 2.75; 1 gas plate, 4.50; nails, 17.10; belting, 18 ft. at 10c., 1.80; cartridges, 4 boxes at 60c., 2.40; 1 mop wringer, 1.75; Yale latches, 2 at 2.00, 4.00; screen 2.40; 2 sets hangers at 1.00, 2.00; track, 20 ft. at 8c., 1.60; door check, 1 at 6.00; 50 ft. hose at 12c., 6.00; 2 panes glass at 84c., 1.68, 1 box at 7.50; 2-3 doz. cup catchers at 1.80, 1.20	621 15
Bartholomew, E., books, 6.00; Brethour, J. E., travelling expenses *re* stock judging. 7.35	13 35
Beaver Flint Glass Co., platinum discs, 2.75; Bollert, E. R. & Co., furnishings, 2.23	4 98
Barlow, B., travelling expenses, 2.95; Buckbee, Wm., seeds, 2.32	5 27
Bolgiano. J. & Son, seeds, 2.55; Britnell, A., books, 10.00	12 55
Briggs, Wm., books, 709.68; advertising, 37.00; Burr & Ainsworth, bureau, 7.00; furnishings, 1.75	755 43
Borrowman, G. S., laboratory supplies, 2.55; Barclay, Jas., 9 bbls. apples, 12.90	15 45
Burpee, W. Atlee & Co., seeds, 6.40; Bruce, Jno. A. & Co., seeds, 28.58...	34 98
Barber, Chas. W., 1 blue heron mounted, 5.00; Beck Duplicator Co., 1 typewriter ribbon, 1.00	6 00

AGRICULTURE.—*Continued.*

AGRICULTURAL COLLEGE.—*Continued.*

Bell, W. J., travelling expenses *re* stock judging	11 85
Baldwin, L. H., travelling expenses, 3.00; lectures on poultry, 12.00; Bell Telephone Co., rent of instruments (1 year), 305.00; messages, 59.75	$79 75
Bursar, to pay sundries	6 26
Catto, Jno. & Son, sundry furnishings, 86.63; Copeland, Chatterson Co., Ltd., examination record blanks, 540 at 14.35 per 500, 15.50; current ledger binder, 1 at 12.00; 1 leaf index, 2.00	116 13
Canadian General Electric Co., pagoda shades, 7.79; repairs, 2.70; Canner Pub. Co., subscription, 3.00	13 49
Clemens, H. A. Co., lumber, etc., 529.00; Crowe's Iron Works, castings, 64 lbs. at 3½c., 2.24	531 24
Chicago Stock Judging Team, judging Fat Stock Show, Chicago	50 00
Coo, William, reporting poultry institute and supply copy of same	75 00
Chandler, Ingram & Bell, laboratory supplies, 3.38; Canadian Fairbanks Co., repairs, 12.12; wheelbarrows, 1 at 10.00, 1 at 12.50; steel tray for barrow, 1 at 4.59	42 59
Canadian Oil Co., cylinder oil, 45½ gals. at 80c., 36.40; *Canadian Breeders*, advertising, 30.00	66 40
Commercial Oil Co., engine oil, 42 gals. at 50c., 21.00; cotton waste, 13.23; floor oil, 44.38; can, 75c.	79 36
Castner, Curran & Bullitt. coal, 514.1200 tons at 3.55, 1,447.700 tons at 3.70, 10.1940 tons at 3.80	5,016 67
Cooper, Faber & Co., seeds, 1.19; Carter, Jas. & Co., seeds, 11.16	12 35
Canada Chemical Mfg. Co., laboratory supplies, 65.06; *Canadian Horticultural Annual*, advertising, 30.00	95 06
Canadian Typewriter Co., carbon paper, 1 box at 3.50	3 50
Catholic Publications Co., advertising, 10.00; Currie Bros., seeds, 49c.	10 49
Clark, W. A., repairing clock, 1.00; Corson, G. H., lectures, 15.00	16 00
Canada Customs, duties, 1,193.31; Chemists & Surgeons Supply Co., filter papers, 2 pkgs. for 1.12; laboratory supplies, 1.95	1,196 38
Cameron, W., groceries, 93.05; Canada Foundry Co., repairs, 27.95	121 00
Cash, Newton. lectures, 6.00; travelling expenses, 5.05; Canner Pub. Co., subscription, 3.00	14 05
Canada Newspaper Co., 6 mos. sub'n. to *Canada*, 3.00; Creelman, G. C., travelling expenses, 291.50	294 50
Canadian Pacific Railway, freight charges, 45.22; Canadian Pacific Railway Telegraph Co., telegrams, 2.25	47 47
Canadian Express Co., charges, 65.03; Central Electric & School Supply Co., laboratory supplies, 12.08	77 11
Dougall & Son, sub'ns. to magazines, 2.00; Doubleday, Page & Co., books, 21.60	23 60
Donovan, H. B., advertising, 12.60; Dowler Co., bedspreads, 8.95; napkins, 3.59; sundry furnishings, 17.82	42 96
Dooley, J. M., confectionery, 70.33; Day, T. J., subscription to *Daily Globe*, 1st May to 2nd December, 1904, 2.34	72 67
Dominion Bank, commission on drafts, 14.18; Day, W. H., trav. exp., 7.80	21 98
Day, G. E., travelling expenses, 9.55; re Live Stock Show, Chicago, 100.00	109 55
Dairy Department, butter, 277 lbs. at 15c., 41.55, 11 lbs. at 16c., 1.76, 2,020 at 21c., 432.60, 80 lbs. at 22c., 17.60, 115 lbs. at 23c., 26.45, 900 lbs. at 24c., 216.00, 4,695 lbs. at 25c., 900.00, 3,040 lbs. at 26c., 790.40, 200 lbs. at 27c., 54.00	2,480 36
Duckworth, Robt., repairs, 2.00; Dreer, Hy. A., seeds, 7.90	9 90
Duff. H. C., scholarship, 10.00: Davidson, John, kitchen table, 1 at 2.75; 11 knobs at 5c., 55c.; 6 handles at 10c., 60c.; gymnasium repairs, 1.25 ...	15 15
Davidson, Wm., shelter for horses and vehicles on Sundays, 26.00	26 00
Dominion Express Co., charges, 53.72; money orders, 4.59	58 31
Dominion School Supply Co., laboratory supplies. 7.59	7 59
Electric Boiler Compound Co., cotton waste, 123 lbs. at 12c., 14.76; separator oil, 5 gals. at 35c., 1.75; electric boiler compound, 480 lbs. at 6c., 28.80; oil, 27½ gals. at 80c., 22.00; supplies, 30.00; engine oil, 44 gals. at 50c., 22.00. 44 1-6 gals. at 50c., 22.08. 44 1-6 gals. at 50c., 22.08; 7 13-16 lbs. spiral packing at 1.20, 9.38; sundries, 70c.	173 55

AGRICULTURE.—*Continued.*

AGRICULTURAL COLLEGE.—*Continued.*

Elliott & Co., laboratory supplies, 28.90; Entomologist, N. C. Dept. of Agr., books, 30.00	58 90
Eureka Mineral Wool & Asbestos Co., covering boiler, 35.00; cup grease, 25 lbs. at 20c., 5.00; packing, 10 lbs. at 1.20. 12.00; sundries, 4.70; 30 lbs. wax at 25c.. 7.50; engine room supplies, 2 coils ½ hard hyd., 5½ lbs. at 85c., 4.68	68 88
Entomological Society of Ontario, 10,000 pins at 1.25 per m., 12.50; Ericsson, Elov., butter culture, 2 bottles at 50c., 1.00	13 50
Eimer & Amend, laboratory supplies, 363.99; Eaton, T. Co., Ltd., arm chairs, 12 at 4.50, 54.00; settees, 2 at 5.00, 10.00; tables, 2 at 4.50, 9.00; curtains, 4 prs. at 7.00, 28.00; fire fender, 5.75; wall paper, 13.60	484 34
Edwards, S. F., travelling expenses	4 65
Farmers' Advocate, book, 55c.; special advtg., Christmas No. 600.00; Fleischmann Co., yeast, 93.45	748 45
Foster, Thomas, repairs to boiler and furnace. 27.40	27 40
Farming World, advertising, 36.20	36 20
Fairbairn, J. B.. stationery, 2.08; Fairbairn, T. B., travelling expenses, 9.75	11 83
Frier, G. M., scholarship, 10.00: Ford Seed Co., seeds, 1.90	11 90
Ferry, D. M., seeds, 3.56; Farquhar, R. & J., seeds, 1.75	5 31
Funk & Wagnalls Co., sub'ns., 6.00; *Farmers' Advocate*, subs'n., 1.50	7 50
Fielding Chemical Co., laboratory supplies, 2.38	2 38
Fletcher. Dr.. travelling expenses, 5.00	5 00
Guelph Ice Co., ice, 22.75; Guelph Electrical Works, fittings, 58.73	81 48
Goldie. Jas. Co., flour, 733.63; bran, 4 tons, at 17.00, 68.00; ton middlings, 18.00	819 63
Guelph Paper Co., stationery, 13.90; Gosling, Jno., lectures, 76.00; trav. expenses, 74.00	163 90
G. N. W. Telegraph Co., 20.77; Gunns, Ltd., hams, 1,044.92; bacon, 48.25; sundries, 30c.	1,114 24
Green, R. W., travelling expenses, 11.25; Gordon, J. G., hardware sundries, 1.25	12 50
Geological Pub. Co., 26 vols. at 1.25, 32.50; Guelph Cartage Co., teaming coal, 36.08	68 58
Graham. W. R.. travelling expenses attending New York Poultry Show	51 95
Guelph Steam Laundry, 52c.; Grant & Armstrong, repairs to furniture. 93.50	94 02
Gemmell, T. H. & Co., cleaning lace curtains, 2.50; dyeing 2 chenille curtains, 3.00	5 50
Guelph Light & Power Co.. electric light, 441.19; Guelph Cigar Co., tobacco stems, 350 lbs. at 1.00, 3.50	444 69
Guelph Street Rlwy., car tickets, 28.40; delivering coal, 151.59	179 99
Globe Printing Co.. advertising, 40.75; Gummer, H., printing and advertising. 717.38; subscription to *Daily Herald*, 4.00	762 13
Grand Trunk Rlwy.. freight charges. 143.31; Grant, Thos. F., 2 pumps, 19.50	162 81
Gregory, Jas. H. & Son, seeds, 1.36; Gartons, Ltd., seeds, 7.99	9 35
Guelph Soap Co., soap. 50.69; Globe Wernicke Co., library supplies, 55.78	106 47
Gamble, W. P.. travelling expenses, 57.40; Guelph Stove Co., registers, 6 at 3.00, 18.00	75 40
Guelph Radial Rlwy. Co., cartage of coal	9 74
Guelph Paving Co.. laying cement floor in stable, 25.00; Grip, Ltd., half-tone engraving, 51.64	76 64
Guelph Spring & Axle Co., repairs, 1.25; Greenwood, A., peaches, 6 baskets, 3.50	4 75
Gordon, J. G.. repairs. 1.80; Ginn & Co.. books, 24.00	25 80
Guelph Waterproof Clothing, 1 piece rubber, 20c.; Green, R. W., travelling expenses, 9.00	9 20
Globe Printing Co., advertising, 20c.	20
Hammond Typewriter Co., 1 doz. shuttle shields, 1.50; Hales, Alfred, meat, 3.190.56	3,192 06
Hamilton, F. Co.. Ltd.. pruners, 2.75; pruning saw, 1.00	3 75
Hub Magazine Co., books, 14.25; Harper. H.. repairs. 2.40	16 65
Haugh, L., street car tickets, 3.00; Herod, Walter, laboratory supplies, 9.80	12 80

AGRICULTURE.—*Continued.*

AGRICULTURAL COLLEGE.—*Continued.*

Humphrey, Ralph W., groceries, 81.77; Hough, Robt., provisions, 3.85	85 42
Harcourt, E. H. Co., drawing cuts and printing land book, 421.88; Harvey, Jno. G., 833 lbs. ammonia at 6c., 49.98; 5 gals. disinfectant at 2.00, 10.00; Harvey's soap chips and freight, 21.16	503 02
Hunter, A. F., travelling expenses and lectures, 55.60; Hallman, A., expenses *re* stock judging, 5.20	60 80
Hacking, Robt., cigars, 46.50; Harkness, A. D., 6 boxes apples at 2.00, 12.00	58 50
Hutt, H. L., travelling expenses, 16.55; Hunt, Wm., trav. expenses, 2.75	19 30
Hanck, A., street car tickets, 3.00; Hansen, Chris., dairy supplies, 2.25...	5 25
Hewer, Jas. & Son, oil cake, 500 lbs. at 1¾c., 8.75; 16 lbs. linseed, 3 1-8c., 50c.; potatoes, 40 bags at 80c., 32.00; seeds, 35c.	41 60
Hibbard, G., travelling expenses, 3.75; Harcourt, R., trav. expenses, 71.65	75 40
Hewer, Jas. & Son, laboratory supplies, 1.50; Hood, G. B., school fees *re* employees' children, 90.60; 8 bbls. apples at 1.25, 10.00, 34 bbls. at 1.00, 34.00	134 60
Heffernan, J., ex. on express orders, 1.72; Hunter, Jas., seeds, 30.15	31 87
Henderson, Peter & Co., seeds, 1.99; Hammond, Jesse, seeds, 25c.	2 24
Huard, Victor A., subscription, 2.00; Historical Atlas Pub. Co., atlas of Wellington County, 15.00	17 00
Horticultural Pub. Co., subscription, 1.00	1 00
Iowa Seed Co., seeds, 2.52; Inland Revenue Dept., methylated spirits, 10 gals. at 1.08, 10.80; freight, 99c.	11 79
Imperial Varnish & Color Co., 5 gals. varnish at 3.50; 482 lbs. soap at 6c.; 43.11 gals. linseed oil at 57c.; 47.50 gals. turpentine at 90c.	113 79
James, D., seeds, 9.60; Johnston & Stokes, seeds, 7.71	17 31
Johnson, Benson E., stationery, 3.00; Jarvis, Jennie, trav. expenses, 5.70...	8 70
Jackson & Son, salt, 8.10; Jones & Moore, electric supplies, 27.00	35 10
Journal Printing Co., advertising, 16.80; Jarvis, T. D., trav. expenses, 58.30	75 10
Jarvis, Jennyson D., supplies, 11.95; Jones, Harold, 10 boxes apples, 10.00;	21 95
Journal Horticultural Soc'y., subscription, 2.00	2 00
Kay, Jno. Son & Co., 2 tables, 29.75; Kilgour Bros., paper, paper bags, etc., 26.43	56 18
Kloepfer & Co., coal, 516.58; freight, 92.37; Kenndy, R. B., photographs, 9.35	618 30
Kelly, Chas., tuning and repairs, 3.00; Krouse, F. W., honey, 441 lbs. at 8c., 35.28; 36 sections at 15c., 5.40; 372 lbs. at 9c., 33.48, 210 lb. cans, 2.00	76 16
King, W. S., electrical repairs, 2.25	2 25
Light & Power Dept., 95.39; Lawson & Jones, laboratory supplies, 51.55; Library Supply Co., books, 15.88	162 82
Lochead, W., travelling expenses, 48.95; Lee, J. W. & Son, 1 Yorkshire boar, 40.00	88 95
Library Bureau of Canada, books, 51.14; Lemen, C. A., 2 low water alarms, 4 at 35.00, 140.00; extra wire, 1,000 ft. for 10.00	201 14
Leitz, Ernst, laboratory supplies, 13.90; Library of American Museum of Natural History, books, 2.50	16 40
Library of Congress, sub'n. to catalogue cards, 12.46; Landreth, D., seeds, 2.65	15 11
Lovell, R. J. & Co., stationery, 16.89; Lyons & Marks, toilet paper, 4 cases at 16.75, 67.00; tumblers, ¼ gro. at 8.50, 12.75; mops, 3½ doz. at 1.85, 6.48	103 11
Love, Harry H. & Co., repairs to gymnasium, 6.30; flying rings, 7.00	13 30
Morris Harness & Stable Supply Co., blankets, 6.50; repairs, 5.00; robe, 12.00	23 50
Meacham, J. B., subscription, 2.00; Matthews, W. P., bridles, 3.50	5 50
Morris, E. B., livery, 23.00; Maule, Wm. H., seeds, 2.65	25 65
Miller, H. H., collection of weeds, 3.00; Moxley, Chas. E., electric magnets, 2.25	5 25
Market Scales, Guelph, 2.00; Morgan, A. T., score cards, 500, 1.75	3 75
Medcalf, D. M., travelling expenses, 17.60; Martin, Jno. S., lectures and travelling expenses, 11.35	28 95
Morlock Bros., repairs to furniture, 5.50; Milne, A., cutting fertilizer, 14 hours at 20c., 2.80	8 30

AGRICULTURE.—*Continued.*

AGRICULTURAL COLLEGE.—*Continued.*

Mills, Jno., books, 10.00; Morang & Co., books, 40.00	50	00
Michie & Co., preserved figs, 1 case, 8.50; Murray, W. A. & Co., quilts, 3 at 5.00, 15.00; stationery, 32.50; sundry furnishings, 17.95	73	95
Metal Shingle & Siding Co., feed box, 2.00; hay racks, 72.00; corner mangers, 13 at 2.00, 26.00	100	00
Morris, Geo. B., sundry hardware, 49.86; Morrison, Jas. Brass Mfg. Co., repairs, 73.18	123	04
Mahoney, J. J., repairs, 41.35; Mail Printing Co., sub., 2.84	44	19
McAinsh & Co., books, 39.80; McCormick & Robinson, furnishings and repairs, 147.88	·187	68
McLean & Dawson, mud rakes, 4 at 2.00; McKee, drugs and stationery, 10.75	18	75
McLaren, A. M., scholarship, 10.00; McDougall, Chas., 14 geese, 152 lbs. at 11c., 16.72	26	72
McCrea, J. A., groceries and provisions, etc., 3,684.73; meat, 357.96; furnishings, 744.90	4,787	59
McCready, S. B., travelling expenses, 12.00; McMillan Bros., sundry hardware, 124.27	136	27
Macdonald, D. E. & Bro., sundry furnishings, 74.38; McGibbon, D., repairs to stable, etc., 48.00	122	38
McHardy, J. & A., sausages, 190 lbs. at 12½c., 23.75, 470 lbs. at 14c., 65.80, 450 lbs. at 15c., 81.00	170	55
McLelland, R. B., 3 maps, 3.05; McKenzie, Duncan, horseshoeing, etc., 14.00	17	05
MacLaren, 82 lbs. cheese at 13c., 10.66; Macmillan Co., books, 2.71	13	37
McKee, J. D., laboratory supplies, 3.95; stationery, etc,. 1.75; repairs, 50c.; supplies, 2.00	10	20
McNaughton, apple butter, 73 lbs. at 6c., 4.38; McKay, Robt., seeds, 5.00	9	38
McIntosh, J. I., advertising	4	00
National Typewriter Co., supplies, 69.80; News Pub. Co., sub'n., 2.50; advertising, 75c.	73	05
Nordheimer Piano & Music Co., repairs, 10.00; North Am. Bent Chair Co., repairs, 8.40	18	40
Nelles, Chas. A., stationery, 141.58; Nixon, Chas. C., books, 2.50	144	08
Northrup, King & Co., seeds, 2.10; Nell, Philip, labels, 8.14	10	24
Nunan, F., printing and binding, 139.12	139	12
Occomore, H. & Co., sundries, 2.85; repairs, 139.22; Ohio Naturalist, books, 4.25	146	32
Orange, Judd Co., books, 1.13; Ottawa Field Naturalist Club, books, 1.00	2	13
Ontario Rubber Co., furnishings, 15.83; Office Specialty Mfg. Co., copying paper, 11.25; 3 card cabinets, 24.25; cards, 17.84; medium weight guides, 6.72; cupboard base, 19.00; special table and chair, 41.00	135	89
Olgenre, L. H., board for lecturers, short course, 23.50; Outlook Co., sub'n., 5.75	29	25
O.A.C. Review. 10,200 copies, 480.00; books, 16.10; Ontario Pub. Co., sub'n., 2.50; advertising, 25.00	523	60
Photo Engravers, advtg., 1.32; Pringle, G. D., stationery, etc., 24.15; repairs, 1.75; supplies, 19.45	46	67
Page, Hersey Iron & Tube Co., fire bricks, 400 at 2.00, 8.00; Peart, H. S., travelling expenses, 16.25	24	25
Petrie, A. B., drugs and chemicals, 182..24; Parisian Laundry Co., laundry, 5.76	188	00
Porter, E. L.,, .white wyandottes, 1 pr., 50.00; Palmer, Ed., livery hire, 1.00	51	00
Poultry Dept., 377 doz. eggs, 70.51; fowl, 1,049 lbs., 148.99; ducks, 17 prs., 25.60; chickens, 15 at 50c., 7.50; goslings, 3 at 1.50, 4.50	257	10
Painter, A. J., root maggot screens, 12 at 50c., 6.00; trav. expenses, 9.50	15	50
Postmaster, postage stamps, 514.40; State Incubator Co., universal brooders, 6 at 4.50, 27.00; thermometers, ½ doz. at 4.50, 2.25	543	65
Queen City Oil Co., compressor oil, 23.63 gals. at 60c., 14.18; Royal City Bottling Works, ginger ale, 5 cases at 75c., 3.75	41	56
Robertson, Jas. & Co., engine room supplies, 5.10; Rudd, T. E., repairs, 1.00	6	10
Ryrie Bros., stationery, 1.50; Richardson, C. & Co., butter prints, 2.50	4	00
Robertson, A. & Son, repairs, 79.51.; Ray Society, subscription, 5.11	84	62

AGRICULTURE.—Continued.

AGRICULTURAL COLLEGE.—Continued.

Russell, Wm., cement, 1 bbl. at 2.25; Richardson, G. A., furnishings, 126.34; hardware, etc., 195.31	323 90
Ryan, G. B. & Co., canton flannel, 12 yds. at 12½c., 1.50; Reading, Arthur J., printing photo, 4.45	5 95
Reed Bros., groceries, 2.25; Rennie, Wm. & Co., seeds, 178.95; Rittinger & Motz, advertising, 15.00	196 20
Reynolds, J. B., travelling expenses, 9.05	9 05
Reed, J. Hugo, care of horses during short course in stock judging, 6.00; Rose, D. M., scholarship, 20.00	26 00
Ramsey, J. G. & Co., laboratory supplies, 11.10; Robertson, James Co., Ltd., repairs, 116.08; sundries, 60.59	187 77
Reid & Ross, repairs to vehicle, 14.95	14 95
Sunley, Wm., repairs, 19.93; Shorthorn Society of Great Britain & Ireland, books, 51.14	71 07
Saunders, W. E., travelling expenses, 5.00; Simmers, J. A., seeds, etc., 19.15; budding knife, 1.25	25 40
Standard Fertilizer & Chemical Co., experimental manures, 15.70; Springer, S., travelling expenses, 10.45	26 15
Stevenson, Malcolm & Co., Welsbach light, 1.00; Steele, Jas., brass valve 36 lbs. at 5c., 1.80	2 80
Smith, Wm., travelling expenses, 8.35; Society of Chemical Industry, membership dues, 6.25	14 60
Smith, A. M., travelling expenses, stock judging, 9.15; Smale, F. J., expenses stock judging, 6.50	15 65
Sun Printing Co., advtg., 45.80; Sheppard Pub. Co., sub'n., 2.00	47 80
Steiger, Otto, seeds, 1.52; Stewart, Alex., dairy supplies, 5.81; laboratory supplies, 8.07	15 40
Steele Briggs Seed Co., seeds, 45.37; Sutton & Sons, seeds, 31.01	76 38
Sherman, F. J., trav. expenses, 10.75; Searle, H., 60 bus. turnips at 12c., 7.20	17 95
Southern Trust Co., books, 35.62; Stanton, O. B., stationery, 2.89	38 51
Snider, Jno. B., furniture, 4.50; sundry persons, conducting services in chapel, 97.50	102 00
Sheridan & O'Connor, contract, cement walks, 419.67; Smith, P., cutting fertilizer, 2.80	422 47
Serrit, H., scholarship, 10.00; Sanders, G. E., collection of weeds, 5.00; seeds, 35 bottles, 18.50	33 50
Sallows, H. D., horseshoeing, 3.13; Standard Vinegar Co., vinegar, 76½ gals. at 21c., 16.07; barrel, 4.02	23 22
Smith, Frederick, repairs, plumbing, etc., 29.61; Squair, Prof. J., travelling expenses, 5.00	34 61
Sentinel Pub. Co., advtg., 30.00; Shepherd, V., carpentering, 284.62	314 62
Salzer, Jno. A., seeds, 2.02; Sparrow & Co., sundry supplies, 47.70	49 72
Scott & Tierney, sub'n., 16.55; stationery, etc., 13.75; wall paper, 9.55	39 85
Spramotor Co., sprapaint, 100 lbs. at 11c., 11.00; sundries, 1.50	12 50
Sundry persons, temporary services, etc.	675 22
Sweeney, Jas., harness repairs, etc., 18.55; Sallows, H. D., repairs and horseshoeing, 13.38	31 93
Simplex Nett Co., laboratory supplies, 1.71; Stechert, G. E. & Co., books, 336.09	337 80
Siche Gas Co., rice carbide, 1 doz. 5 lb. tins at 70c., 3.50; Saunders, W. E. & Co., laboratory supplies, 9.95	13 45
Tilden, Josephine E., books, 2.25; Taylor, Forbes & Co., radiators, valves, etc., 301.58	303 83
Toronto Daily Star, advtg., 25c.; Toronto World, advtg., 93.00	93 25
Taylor & McKenzie, repairing, 2.60; Tolton Bros., 4.25	5 85
Thorp Co., 1 ton oil cake, 33.00.; 50 bush. barley at 50c., 25.00; 77.20 bags potatoes at 70c., 54.05	112 05
Thorburn, J. M. Co., seeds, 2.69; Tabard Inn Library, books, 1.03.........	3 72
Toronto Pottery Co., 24 water jars at 40c., 9.60; Thompstone, E., bed and mattress, 10.00; books, 2.00	21 60
United Typewriter Co., supplies, 25.95; stencil paper, 6 qrs. at 1.50	34 95
Vokes Hardware Co., 1 gross rubber chair tips, 3.00; Varsity, subsn., 1.00	4 00
Virtue & Co., books, 24.25	24 25

AGRICULTURE.—*Continued.*

AGRICULTURAL COLLEGE.—*Continued.*

Webster, H. B., scholarship, 10.00; Warden, King & Son, repairs, 30.00	40 00
Weld Co., Wm., advtg., 40.32; Waterous Engine Works Co., repairs, 33.50	73 82
Wallace, O. R., stationery, 25.10; Wolcott, Geo. R., repairs, castings, etc., 79.31	104 41
Wallace, O. R., stationery, 25.10; Wolcott, Geo. R., repairs, castings, etc., 59c.	25 49
Williams, Geo., confectionery, 42.06; Waters Bros., sundry furnishings, 35.73	77 79
Warren Manfg. Co., repairs, castings, etc., 24.15; Whitall, Tatum Co., laboratory supplies, 10.73	34 88
Westminster Co., subn., 2.50; Wealch, Jno., livery hire, 2.00	4 50
Weir, D., photographs, 5.00; Woods Fair, 25c.	5 25

MACDONALD INSTITUTE, GUELPH.

SALARIES ($16,088.00).

S. B. McCready:	Twelve	months' salary as	Professor of Nature Study	1,500 00
John Evans:		do	do Manual Training	1,400 00
M. U. Watson:		do	Director of Home Economics	1,300 00
E. W. Kendall:		do	Instructor of Manual Training	1,000 00
H. Givin:		do	do Domestic Science	900 00
G. Greenwood:		do	do Normal Methods	800 00
J. W. Eastham:	Five	do	do Domestic Arts	292 00
M. I. Speller:	Eight	do	do do	466 00
E. Thompstone:	Six	do	Demonstrator in Nature Study	400 00
E. Ferguson:	Six	do	Assistant Instructor Domestic Science	325 00
H. Holland:	Six	do	do	350 00
A. Ross:	Twelve	do	Instructor in Physiology and Home Nursing	600 00
A. Hoodless:	do	do	Superintendent Domestic Science	400 00
T. J. Moore:	One	do	Demonstrator Nature Study	60 00
J. Johnston:	Five and Three Quarters' salary as		Stenographer	145 50
M. Mills:	Seven	months' salary as	do	204 50
A. Clark:	Twelve	do	Engineer	650 00
R. Griest:	Four	do	Demonstrator Nature Study	267 00
P. Gauld:	Twelve	do	Stoker	540 00
J. T. Henderson:	do	do	Janitor	360 00
Mrs. Dodds:	do	do	Janitress	240 00
K. T. Fuller:	do	do	Lady Superintendent Macdonald Hall	700 00
E. Tennant:	do	do	Housekeeper Macdonald Hall	450 00
F. Hughes:	do	do	Janitor do	360 00
W. C. Walker:	do	do	Gardener and Supt. of Grounds	700 00
Pay Lists, Wages, Cooks, Maids, Etc.				1,678 00

EXPENSES ($16,685.86).

Anderson & Co., mucilage, 35c.; stationery, 1.92	2 27
Abbott, A. H., services teaching	5 00
Art Metropole, 12 scales from Philptecnic sets	3 24
Aikenhead Hardware Co., furnishings	6 00
Briggs, Wm., books, 143.09; Bach Specialty Co., washer, 14.00	157 09
Broadfoot, J. B., sundries, 4.77; Bond Hardware Co., sundry hardware, 86.93; sheet copper, 34½ lbs. at 37½c., 12.93	104 63
Barber, R. H., 1 gal. floor fluid, 3.00, ½ gal. do., 1.50	4 50
Borrowman, G. S., 1 1-3 doz. corks, 20c.; 10 oz. salts of lemon, 40c.; 4 oz. white pepper, 20c.; 3 lbs. glycerine at 35c., 1.05; sundries, 3.25	5 10
Bolas & Co., S. B., photos, 34 Cathedral prints, 29.34; Burrow, Stewart & Milne, gas range, 27.00	56 34
Bigelow, Miss Emma, teaching services	116 00
Brown Bros., Ltd., 2 skins blue morocco at 2.00; Bullock, S., furnishings, 22.75	26 75

AGRICULTURE.—*Continued.*

MACDONALD INSTITUTE—*Continued.*

EXPENSES.—*Continued.*

Buffalo Chemical Fire Extinguisher Co., 1 Cooker & Baker	6	00
Bausch & Lomb Optical Co., furnishings, 4.63; Beckett, Miss Janet, 1 loom complete, 25.00	29	63
Bell Telephone Co., messages, 9.35; ·Bigelow, Emma, 2 weeks board Xmas vacation, 7.00	16	35
Cranston & Son, florist supplies	4	87
Catto & Son, furnishings, 52.81; Cloke & Son, stationery, 50c...............	53	31
Can. Genl. Electric Co., 250 lamps at 19c., 47.50; repairs, 13.95; Cameron, W., groceries and provisions, 88.50 ...	149	95
Clemens, H. A. Co., lumber, etc., 144.38; Castner, Curran & Bullitt, run of mine coal 13,680 tons at 3.55, 485.65. 67,310 tons at 3.70, 1,791.17...	2,421	34
Collector of Customs, entry on 19 models, 30c.; duty on 2 rolls pictures, 1.50; duty on coal, 330.96; stone, 79c.; duty on baker and cooker, 1.80	335	35
Commercial Oil Co., floor oil, 75c., 40 gals. at 85c., 34.00, 3 cans at 75c., 2.25; ½ cans at 85c., 4.25	40	50
Can. Pacific Rlwy., telegraph, 27c.; Courian, Babyon & Co., 13 Japanese lanterns, 5.50	5	77
Can. Pacific Rlwy., freight, 181.83; Can. Express Co., charges, 27.55........	209	38
Dairy School, milk, 67,949 lbs at 1.60 cwt.; cream, 1,252½ qts. at 20c., 7 qts. at 30c., 63¼ qts. at 40c.; butter, 379 lbs. at 21c., 10 lbs. at 22c., 74 lbs. at 23c., 360 lbs. at 24c., 1,463 lbs. at 25c., 2,008 lbs. at 26c., 80¼ at 27c.	1,967	01
Doubleday, Page & Co., sub. *Garden Magazine*, 1.00; *Drawing and Manual Training Journal*, subn., 1.00	2	00
Dominion Publishing Co., a'dvtg., 33.33; Davidson, Wm., cab to and from Hospital, 1.25	34	58
Devlin & Galbraith, furnishings, 16.00; Diaz, Pelago, printing diplomas, 65 hrs. at 13c., 8.45	24	45
Davis & Son, Jno., sundries, 15.50; Dempsey, C. W., putting eyelets in carpets, 10c.	15	60
Day, T. J., subn. to newspapers for library, 8.76; Dooley, J. W., bread, 28 loaves at 10c., 2.80	11	56
Dowler Co., 5 doz. linen table napkins at 3.75, 18.75; Dom. Express Co., charges, 17.43	36	15
Educational Review, subn., 1.00; Electric Boiler Compound Co., 50 lbs. boiler compound at 7c., 3.50	4	50
Eaton Co., T., furniture, 69.85; Eddy, E. B. Co., 1 ream white tissue 20x30, 75c.; 3 reams manilla 20x30, 1.50	72	10
Fuller, Katherine T., travelling expenses, 3.75; Freshwater, F., 2½ dys. repairing at 1.00 per day, 2.50	6	25
Freke, Alfred, photo studies, 1.64; Foster, S., work on boiler, 45 hrs. at 40c., 18.00	19	64
Farmers' Advocate, subn., 1.50; advertising, 67.20; Fielding & McLaren, 200 lbs. tea at 18c., 36.00	104	70
Fleischmann Co., yeast, 2.70; Fidelity Trustee and Receiver Co., books for library, 61.00	63	70
Fletcher Manufacturing Co., sundry furnishings	9	93
Gutta Percha & Rubber Manftg. Co., hose, 232.75; Goldie, Jas., Co., flour and bread, 541.17	773	92
Gunns, Ltd., bacon and hams, 188.18; Globe Wernicke Co., furniture, 36.20	224	38
Gemmell & Co., T., furnishings, 1.50; Gordon, J. G., repairs, 1.75	3	25
Globe Printing Co., subn., 4.00; Gilchrist, Jas., plants, 21.30	25	30
Guelph Paper Co., paper and roll stand, 3.72; bags, 7.73, do., 2.25	13	70
Grant & Armstrong, chair cushion, 4.50; furnishings, 37.70; Gowans, Kent & Co., furnishings, 18.72	60	92
Guelph Electrical Works, 22.53; Gummer, H., printing and advtg., 69.00; stationery, 266.87	358	40
Guelph Cartage Co., coal, 156.18; furniture, 5.00; Guelph Light & Power Co., electric light, 152.65	313	78
Guelph Steam Laundry, laundry, 357.05; Guelph Ice Co., ice, 117.35	474	40
Guelph Rag & Metal Co., belting, 17.21; Guelph Soap Co., soap, 16.25 ...	33	46

AGRICULTURE.—*Continued.*

MACDONALD INSTITUTE.—*Continued.*

Expenses.—*Continued.*

Greenwood, Grace, travelling expenses	2	45
Guelph Radial Rwy. Co., cartage of coal, 25.32; Gowdy Bros., supplies, 11.10	36	42
Greist, Rosemina, travelling expenses, 16.95; Grand Trunk Rlwy. Co., freight charges, 34.13	51	08
Great North Western Tel. Co., telegrams, 1.41; Globe Wernick Co., office fittings, 23.99	25	40
Ginn & Co., 1 Wilson's laboratory astronomy, 1.00; Harcourt, E. H., envelopes and lithographing, 58.00	59	00
Hunter, D. M., laundrying. 221.00; Hewer & Son, Jas., 50 bags potatoes at 70c., 35.00; 45 lbs. clover seed at 25c., 11.25; seeds, 8.30	275	55
Herod, Walter, drugs and chemicals, 18.95; Hogg, W., 2 loads manure 50c. pr. load, 1.00	19	95
Hay, Rev. J., chapel service expenses, 15.00; Henderson, Peter & Co., seeds, 5.75; sun dial, 20.72	41	47
Hamilton Stamp & Stencil Works, rubber stamps, 2.89; Hannigan, Geo. D., 1 No. 101 stove, 3.15	6	04
Howell & Co., Jas., furnishings, 33c.; Hubbard, Leonidas, lecture on exploration work in Labrador, 25.00	25	33
Hales, Alfred, meat, 1,245.51; Hoodless, A., travelling expenses, 47.00...	1,292	51
Imperial Fine Art Corpn., furniture, 7.57; Imperial Varnish & Color Co., repairs, 32.06	39	63
Iwanami, J., repairs, 16.90; International Rlwy. Pub. Co., subn. to *Railway Guide*, 2.00	18	90
Junor, Wm., covered dishes and jugs, 12.30, ½ doz. do., 14.50; mustard, 1.50; 4 salts, 3.00; 1 dish, 75c.; 12 napkins, 2.00; 2 sugar, 1.00; 2 ice plates, 1.00; 1 dinner service, 50.00; saucers, plates, jugs, etc., 135.50; 4 doz. tea saucers, 8.60; 2 doz. plates, 9.44; 1 7-12 doz. round covered dishes, 38.95; ½ doz. oval fruit dishes, 10.80; 1-3 doz. bread plates, 4.20; 8 doz. butter crocks, 2.50 doz.; 4 doz. tea cups, 11.66	306	87
Jackson & Son, 32 gals. vinegar at 22c.; barrel, 2.00	9	04
Jarvis, T. D., 6 gals ice cream at 1.10	6	60
Kay, Jno., Son & Co., jardiniers, 25.55; furnishings, 41.18; Kennedy R. B., photos, 20.00	86	73
Kny, Scheerer Co., models, 60.65; Kelso, Jno. J., printing and stationery, 49.25	109	90
Kloepfer & Co., coal, 22.1808 tons at 5.30; freight on same, 20.61; 1,300 lbs. charcoal at 1c.	155	00
Krouse, F. W., services re Bees, 5.00; 2 cans honey, 124 lbs. at 9c.; Kaiser, Louis M., printing, 26.07	42	23
Kuchemann, Hy. K., furnishings, 1.05	1	05
Library Bureau of Canada, 15 binders, 18.12; Lyman, Knox & Clarkson, groceries, 6.23	24	35
Morton, K., 300 doz. eggs at 18c., 5.40; Morris, Geo. B., hardware, 80c. ...	6	20
Murphy, Dennis, manure, 2.50; Mahoney, J. J., repairs, 19.75	22	25
Macdonald, Jno. & Co., furnishings, 12.94	12	94
Macdonald Con. School, 33 bush. beets at 40c., 13.20; 10 bush. carrots at 40c., 4.00; 3 bush. onions at 60c., 1.80	19	00
Mitchell, R., postage stamps	100	00
Moore, Ray M., 2 copies *Ladies' Home Journal* at 1.25, 2.50; subscription *Pictorial Review*, 1.00; subscription 1 *Delineator*, 1.00	4	50
Mitchell, A. M., cab hire, 1.75; Max Grab Fashion Co., furnishings, 6.00...	7	75
Morris, E., livery hire, 1.75; Morgan, A. J., bulbs and plants, 13.05	14	80
Manual Arts Press, sub. to *Graining Magazine*, 1.00; Marriott & Co., uniforms, 42.00	43	00
McCready, S. B., travelling expenses, 18.30; McCormick & Robinson, repairing, 3.65	21	95
McCrea, J. A., groceries, provisions, etc., 2,531.64; McMillan, M., stamps, 2.50	2,534	00
McHardy, J. A., sausages, 13.15; McAinsh, D. T., books, 10.00	23	15
Macdonald, D. E. & Bro., sundry furnishings, 277.26; McKee, J. S., furniture and repairs, 9.18	286	44

AGRICULTURE.—*Continued.*

MACDONALD INSTITUTE.—*Continued.*

EXPENSES.—*Continued.*

Macmillan Co., books for library, 25.39; McMillan Bros., furnishings and repairs, 22.50	27 50
McKellard, R. B., map of Canada, 1.35	1 35
Nunan, Frank, stationery, 9.00; New England Pub. Co., subn. *Journal of Education*, 3.00	12 00
News, advertising, 100.00; National Educational Assocn., printing and publishing, 2.70	102 70
Nature Study Review, subn., 1.00; Napoli Macaroni Co., 18.20	19 20
Neill, J., rubber boots, 5.00; Nordheimer Piano Music Co., tuning pianos, pairs, 22.50	27 50
Nelles, Chas. L., stationery, paper, etc., 223.55; Nelson, A., travelling expenses, 7.25	230 80
North American Bent Chair Co., furniture, 89.00; National Typewriter Co., 35.90	124 90
Occomore & Co., repairs, 7.43; *O. A. C. Review*, advtg., 1.60	9 03
Ottawa Field Naturalist Club, reprints nature study, 10.00; Onto. Publishing Co., 5.00	15 00
Office Specialty Manuftg. Co., supplies, 100.51	100 51
Poultry Department, 2 doz. eggs, 50c., 3½ doz. eggs at 18c., 4 doz. at 18c., 27 doz. at 20c., 23 doz. at 20c.; 27 chickens, 114 lbs. at 15c.; 1 doz. eggs at 25c.	29 20
Pringle, G. D., rubber stamps and pad. 2.35; Potter, Chas., 3 oven thermometers at 1.25, 3.75, 9 do., 11.55	17 65
Petrie, A. B., drugs, 15.90; repairs, 5.35; Painter, A. J., plan for lantern slide, 1.00	22 25
Prang Educational Co., text books, 52c.; Phelps Pubg. Co., subn., 2.00	2 52
Preston & Rounds Co., Hellers catalogue of plants, 40c.; Polson Iron Works, repairs to boilers, 350.00	350 40
Postmaster, postage stamps, 93.50; Pringle, G. D., repairs, 7.75	101 25
Queen's Quarterly, subsn., 3.00	3 00
Reid & Ross, repairs, 1.65; Raymond Manftg. Co., furnishings, 93.86	95 51
Ryan & Co., G. B., sundries, 4.55; 6 iron beds at 11.50, 69.00; Rolph & Clark, stationery, 99 diplomas at 50c., 49.50	123 05
Reed Bros., 3 cases ginger ale at 75c., 2.25; 3 cases cream soda at 50c., 1.50; Robertson, Jas., Co., repairs, 4.08	7 83
Rice, Lewis & Son, 1 lb. copper rivets ¼x¼, 60c.; Russell, Harry, 60 doz. eggs at 20c., 12.00; express charges on crate, 15c.	12 75
Robertson & Son, repairs, 7.23; Richardson, G. A., iron, hardware, etc., 189.71	196 94
Richardson, A. S., furnishings, 13.00; Reid, N., postage stamps, 15.00	28 00
Robertson, Geo. A., 14 baskets cherries at 85c., 11.90	11 90
Standard Vinegar Co., W. W. vinegar, 11.01; Stewart, Alex., 1 lb. gum arabac, 75c.	11 76
Simplex Net Co., sundries, 8.50; Sparrow, Geo. & Co., sundry furnishings, 37.25	45 75
Sanderson, Harold C., refrigerators, 36.80, 32.40, 36.00; Steinberger, Hendry Co., stationery, 21.50	126 70
Simpson Co., Robt., 20 lbs. wax, 9.00; 1 gross needles, 7.20, 1 doz. do., 60c.; do., 60c.; 105 yds. carpet at 1.05, 110.25; 100 yds. carpet at 1.05, 105.00	232 05
Singer Sewing Machine Co., needles, 3.86; Sharpe, David, 2 doz. rhubarb roots at 1.50 per doz., 3.00	6 86
Sloan, Jno., dishes and platters, 7.05; Stanton & Co., O. B., stationery, 21.42	28 47
Strachan, Jno., duty on labels, 1.26; Stevenson & Malcolm, repairs, 4.25	5 51
Scott & Tierney, subscns., *Globe*, 2.75; *Mail and Empire*, 2.75; *Mercury* 2.75; *Herald*, 2.75	11 00
Strome, A. E., 4 loads manure at 50c., 2.00; Smith, E. D., sundries, 1.59	3 59
Standard White Lime Co., 425 lbs. lime at 1.40; Singer Sewing Machine Co., 4 machines at 23, 92.00	93 40

AGRICULTURE.—*Continued.*

MACDONALD INSTITUTE.—*Continued.*

EXPENSES.—*Continued.*

Sunbeam Incandescent Lamp Co., 1 lamp, 24c.; 24 lamps at 30c., 7.20; 9 at 50c., 4.50	11 94
Stechert, G. E. & Co., subsns. to periodicals, 32.10; Sunley, Wm., repairs, 2.25	34 35
Semple, J. P., travelling expenses	3 00
Thorp Co., 10 oz. rattan, 60c.; Tyrrell & Co., advtg., 2.90	3 50
Taylor, Forbes Co., 2 mowers, 21.60: Fowler & Co., furniture, 7.13	28 73
Taylor & McKenzie, repairs, 42.30; Teachers' College, Columbia University, 1 set meat photo, 1.50	43 80
Upper Canada Tract Socy., 6 knot cards at 25c., 150; 2 at 35c., 70; United Factories, Ltd., brushes, pails, etc., 8.59	10 79
United Typewriter Co., carbon paper, 7.00	7 00
Vokes Hardware Co., furnishings and repairs	55 61
Waters Bros., furnishings, 31.54; Watson Mfg. Co., 1 set of raising hammers, 6.00	37 54
Walker, W., slating blackboards in sewing and dressing room, 6 each, 12.00.	12 00
Wheadon & Co., R. L., 1 doz. ribbon at 45c.; furnishings, 1.40; 5 gingham, at 12½c., 63c	2 48
Williams. Geo., groceries, fruits. etc., 40.51; Watson, Mary Urie, travelling expenses, 7.45	47 96
Westminster Co., advertising in *Presbyterian*, 12.50; Whitham, S. F., 8 bush line at 25c., 2.00	14 50
Wills, H. J. B., 4 studies, 73c.; Watson, C. J., groceries, 75c	1 48
Wolcott, Geo. R., repairs, 17.55	17 55
Younger, W., 2 white willow chairs at 5.00, 10.00; 1 buff chair at 5.00, 5.00; 1 rush table at 5.00; 1 waste paper basket, 50c.; 2 waste paper baskets, 1.50, 3.00; 2 flower baskets at 1.75, 3.50	27 00

FORESTRY ($3,485.48).

Art Metropole, curve pen, 1.00; Abel, C. Co., trees, 457.13	458 13
Buckingham, W. E., legal work, *re* Holmwood farm	7 00
Bond, J. M. & Co., locks, 2.00; tape line, 200; iron hardware, etc., 23.46; garden line, 2 at 2.25; 1 vise, 2.50; 2 wheelbarrows at 3.50; 2 spades at 1.00; 3 spades at 1.25; 1 wrench, 1.75; line reels, 2 at 1.00; tiles, 737 ft. tile at 15c.; 2 bags cement, 1.70; leather gloves. 3 pr. at 25c	163 96
Canada Customs, custom duties, 11.80; Canadian Express Co., freight, 3.15; Clemens, H. A., lumber, 37.93	52 88
Cranston & Son, florist supplies, 9.80; Canadian Pacific Railway, freight charges, 72.38	82 12
Davidson, Jno., canvas, 12 pcs. for 1.50; Dominion Express Co., freight, 6.15	7 65
Davidson, J. F., 115 posts at 15c.; 130 rods fence at 57c., 1 gate, 6.50, 1 gate 6.75	104 60
Day, G. E., travelling expenses	3 20
Grand Trunk Ry., freight charges, 11.22; Guelph Electrical Works, 12¼ ft. flex at 3c.	11 60
Gummer, H., printing, 23.25; Guelph Cartage Co., cartage, 3.35	26 60
Guelph Street Railway Co., car tickets	12 00
Harcourt, R., travelling expenses, 3.25; Henderson, Peter, labels, 2 M at 4.00	11 25
Hill, D., seeds and plants, 105.20; Hewer, Jas. & Son, 8 lbs. grass seed at 17c.	106 56
Kilgour Bros., shipping tags, 1,000 for 1.40; Kelso, Jno. J., printing. 1.75	3 15
Morlock Bros., 104 yds. hessian at 6c.; Morris, G. B., 2 hammers, 2.00	8 24
McLelland, R. B., 1 map, 1.35; money order, 3c.; McMillan Bros., iron, hardware, etc., 203.82	205 20
McAllister, Geo., sawing lumber, 9.95; McKee. J. D., tubing, 4½ ft. for 1.00	10 95
Nelles, C. L., stationery, 6.06; National Typewriter Co., coupons, ¼ doz. at 9.00	10 56

AGRICULTURE.—*Continued.*

MACDONALD INSTITUTE.—*Continued.*

Office Specialty Co., book case, 15.30; cupboards, 52.42; cards, 1 M for 2.10; 3 sets guides, 2.10	71 92
Penfold, S. & G., 2 axe handles at 50c., 1.00; Postmaster, postage stamps, 12.00	13 00
Palmer, Ed., livery hire, 13.00; Painter, A. J., seeds, 13.90	26 90
Petrie, A. B., drugs, chemicals, etc.	147 15
Richardson, G. A., 1 saw, 2.00; 4 spades at 85c., 3.40; iron, hardware, etc., 12.19	17 59
Ramsey, J. G. & Co., photograph supplies, 28.60; 2 pkgs. tinted paper, 32c.	28 92
Sundry persons, temporary services	1,592 27
Siche Gas Co., rice carbide, 4 doz. tins at 1.00; Steele, Briggs Seed Co., spagum moss, 12 bales at 1.00; 2 hoes at 6.75	29 50
Stanton, O. B., stationery, 14.25; Sohne, J. H., trees, 122.40	136 65
Shepherd, V., carpentering, 4.50; Savage & Co., magnifying glass, 50c.	5 00
Thorp Co., seeds	63
Wolcott, Geo. R., repairs, castings, etc.	5 15
Zavitz, travelling expenses, 122.15; street car tickets, 3.00	125 15

ANIMAL HUSBANDRY, FARM AND EXPERIMENTAL FEEDING DEPARTMENT.

SALARIES ($5,043.70).

D. Douglas: Twelve months salary' as Forman			800 00
J. Masson:	do	Cattleman	504 00
J. Mutrie:	do	Assistant Cattleman	456 00
D. Luttrell:	do	do	456 00
J. Douglas:	do	do	456 00
E. Powell:	do	Stenographer	175 00
Pay Lists, wages, teamsters, laborers and etc.			2,196 70

EXPENSES ($12,048.69).

Arkell, H. S., travelling expenses	3 50
Barber, W. F., cow, 23.00; 47 hogs, 263.00; milch cow, 50.00	336 00
Barber, A., 30 steers, 1,473.20; Brethour, J. E., 6 hogs, 81.40	1,554 60
Bollert, E. R. & Co., 8 doz. bags at 2.40, 19.20; Bowman, Jas., 1 Angus bull, 300.00; 1 steer, 45.00	364 20
Bell Telephone Co., messages, 4.65; rent of instrument, 15.00; Barber, Robert, 19 hogs, 100.00	119 65
Bond Hardware Co., The, putty, 45c.; glass, 4.32; waste, 1.80; Japan, 38c.; coal oil, 7.40; gasoline, 1.50; car bolts, 2.22; 2 gates at 5.50, 11.00; screws and belt laces, 2.03; 5 gals. raw oil at 75c., 3.50; shoes and nails, 1.99; files, 40c.; cement, 1.70; brass cocks, 5.20; rod iron, 90c.; sundries, 6.72; iron, hardware, 104.39	155 90
Bisonette, A., wages	9 06
Clemens, H. A. Co., table, 75c.; lumber, 246.10; Clemens, G. W., 1 Holstein bull, 100.00	346 85
C. P. Ry., freight charges 51.09; Customs, charges, 30c.; C. P. Ry. Co.'s Telegraph, messages, 61c.	52 00
Canadian Express Co., express charges, 4.25; Coke, E. F., work on farm, 23.40	27 65
Cordova. A., labor on farm. 1.00; Chittick, J. T. Co., 2 tons oil cake at 33.00, 66.00	67 00
Day, G. E., travelling expenses	41 00
Duke. J. O., 7 bush. white cap. 8.75; Dominion Express Co., express charges, 25c.	9 00
Dawson, Robert, 2 days' running grader at 2.50, 5.00; Dominion Shorthorn Breeders' Association. subscription for 1906, 2.00	7 00

AGRICULTURE.—*Continued.*

FARM AND EXPERIMENTAL FEEDING.—*Continued.*

EXPENSES.—*Continued.*

Davis, H. J., 1 Shorthorn cow, 410.00; Davidson, J. F., 2 gates at 6.00, 12.00	422 00
Davies, Robert, 3 Clydesdale horses	2,600 00
Edwards, W. C. & Co., thoroughbred stock, 1,055.00; Elliott, W. R. & Sons, expenses *re* stock, 5.00	1,060 00
Ferry, D. M. & Co., 80 lbs. mangles, 8.00; Foster, T., work on farm, 7.60	15 60
Goldie, James Co., The, 27½ tons bran, 466.50; middlings, 428.50; 75 bush. oats at 38c., 28.50	923 50
Gummer, H., printing 1,500 score cards 12.50, 1,000 letter heads 5.50, 1,000 memo. heads, 4.50; envelopes, 15.00	37 50
Gowdy Bros., hair and cement, 6.68; 16 ft. sewer pipe, 10.40; G. N. W. Tel. Co., messages, 3.02	20 10
G. T. Ry., freight charges, 41.38; Grant, Thos. F., repairs to pump and piping, 34.50	75 88
Guelph Electrical Works, wire and sockets, 21.17; Guelph Paper Co., shipping tags, 35c.	21 52
Guelph Paving Co., cement floor	65 00
Hallman, A. C., 1 boar, 35.00; 1 sow, 30.00; Hamilton & Sons, repairs on mantel, 11.40	76 40
Hewer & Son, 7 lbs. turnip seed, 1.40; 10 lbs. rape seed, 50c.; 100 lbs. flax seed, 3.00; 591 bush. oats, 236.40; 2 tons chop, 50.00	291 30
Holstein Friesian Association, registration and transfer of stock	3 00
Hamilton, F. Co., Limited, 1 Niagara gas sprayer, 160.00; Hooper, John, 1 ton coal, 6.25	166 25
Hoyt, R. F., 1 grade milch cow, 48.00; Hosking, Benj., 1 low truck waggon, 45.00	93 00
Johnston, R. E., 3 Shorthorn heifers, 765.00; Jones Bros. Co., Limited, 1 cupboard, 40.00	805 00
Kloepfer, C., 6 spokes and rims	84
Lee, J. W. & Son, 1 Yorkshire boar, 40.00; Lynde, W. C., expenses and services, 8.15	43 15
Morris, Geo. B., pair plough lines, 90c.; Milne, F. E., work, 1.10	2 00
Massey-Harris Co., castings and repairs, 3.30; pulper, 13.00; mower, 35.00; binder, 135.00; blizzard and truck, 135.00; Milne, A., 10 pigs at 4.00, 40.00	361 30
Morris Harness and Stable Supply Co., repairing harness, 17.45; robe, 12.00	29 45
Metal Shingle and Siding Co., The, Morse feed box, 2.00; hay rack, 5.00; 13 cast iron corner mangers, 26.00; 13 cast iron corner mangers, 65.00; carrier track, 125.00; bar, 3 rod iron, 12.00; lumber, 26.66; clips, time. etc., 7.50; 45 lbs. material. 9.00	273 16
Monkhouse, J., 7¼ days' work at 2.00, 15.00; Matthews, W. P., bridle. 3.50	18 50
McKee, J. D., 50 lbs. sulphur at 4c., 2.00; McLelland, R. B., man. 1.35	3 35
McConnell's Carriage Works, waggon poles, 5.00; pole caps, 1.00; McMillan Bros., 400 lbs. Gold Medal twine. 56.25	62 25
McCrea, J. A., 2 bbls. salt, 2.70; molasses, 11.63	14 33
McGibbon, Duncan, 86 days' work at 2.00	172 00
Nelles, Chas. L., stationery. 4.50; Nunan. Frank, 2 doz. bulletin boxes, 4.32	8 82
National Live Stock Records, registration of stock. 15.42; Newhall, H. W., work on farm, 15.31	30 73
O'Neill, M. H., 1 Hereford heifer	150 00
Postmaster, postage stamps, 30.00; Petrie, A. B., drugs and chemicals, 14.60	44 60
Present, E. J., 143 bags chaff	8 58
Richardson, G. A., hardware, 36.46; horse blankets, 4.50; whitewash brush, 70c.; 700 lbs. nails, 14.20; sundries, 5.00; binder twine, 11.30; belt laces, 1.13; tin pail. 30c.; paper, 5c.; surcingle, 60c.	74 24
Robertson & Son, repairing machinery, 1.60; Robertson, Jas. W. Dr., Ayrshire bull, 250.00	251 60
Reid & Ross, repairing farm implements, 11.40; Reed, J. Hugo, V.S., attendance and medicines, 16.55	27 95
Rennie, Wm., Co., Limited, seeds 144.10, sacks 1.30; Rose, D. M., 14 days' work on farm, 21.75	167 15

AGRICULTURE.—*Continued.*

FARM AND EXPERIMENTAL FEEDING.—*Continued.*

EXPENSES.—*Continued.*

Sallows, Henry and David, horseshoeing and removing shoes, 19.24; Scott and Tierney, *Daily Journal*, 1.00 .... 20 24

Sweeney, James, harness and repairs, 32.25; Spramotor Co., ½ doz. nozzles, 4.70 .... 36 95

Sheridan & O'Connor, 2 bags cement, 1.50; Sheppard, V., carpentering, 83.70 .... 85 20

Taylor & McKenzie, repairs to boiler and engine, 99.05; 2 set screws, 2.10; Temple, A. J., registration of stock, 53c. 101 68

Thorpe Co., The, farm seed, 150.48; Thomas, C. R., registration of stock, 12.10 .... 162 58

Tolton Bros., harpoon fork, 4.00; 4 pulleys, 2.00; repairs, 24.55; shears, 2.40; sundries, 14.65 .... 47 60

Toronto and Hamilton Electric Co., cable 80 ft. at 35c. 28 00

Wolcott, Geo. R., stove pipes and elbow, 4.20; repairs to roof, 2.50; gasoline. 1.25; smoke stack 4.08; trough, 10.80; time on smoke stack. 4.85; chimney rims, 20c.; cartage, 35c. 28 23

Waterous Engine Works Co., governor valve 2 75

Zenner Disinfectant Co., The, 12 gals. zenoleum at 1.00 .... 12 00

FIELD EXPERIMENTS.

SALARIES ($6,128.20).

A. E. Whiteside: Twelve months' salary as Foreman.......................... 800 00
W. J. Squirrel: do   Specialist in Plant Breeding.......... 900 00
A. J. Bell: do   Asst.   do 700 00
M. Laughlin: Five and half do   Stenographer.................. 187 50
J. Coren: Seven   do   do 210 00
A. Cumming: do   Laborer.................... 456 00
Geo. Bard: do   do 456 00
Pay Lists, wages, teamsters, laborers.. 2,418 70

EXPENSES ($1,938.67).

American Abell Engine and Thresher Co., Limited, furnishings, 2.00; Anthony, Wm., 400 jute bags, 20.00 .... 22 00

Anderson, C. & Co., stationery, 55c.; Allen, R. J., 139 hours' work at 13½c., 18.77; Adams Furniture Co., furniture, 44.00 .... 63 32

Bond Hardware Co., The, Limited, hardware, 28.23; furnishings, 34.49; permanent improvements, 37.50 .... 100 22

Burpee, W. Attlee & Co., seeds, 7.68; postage, 1.16; Bruce, John A. & Co., seeds, 34.41; bags, 1.35 .... 44 60

Barteldes & Co., seeds, 1.06; Buckbee, H. W., seeds, 11.57; Briggs, Wm., stationery, 2.40 .... 15 03

Boddy, R. A., 172½ hours' work at 11c., 18.98; Baker, Wesley, 143 hours' work at 13½c., 19.31; Bell Tel. Co, rent of instrument, 15.00.......... 53 29

Can. Pac. Ry., freight charges, 4.32; Customs, duty, 7.81 .... 12 13

Canadian Express Co., express charges, 14.15; Clemens, The H. A. Co., lumber, 164.72 .... 178 87

Cooper, Taber & Co., rape seed, 1.19; Carter, James & Co., seeds, 11.16... 12 35

Currie Bros., seeds, 15c.; postage, 34c.; Clark. C. S., seeds. 4.12; bags, 50c. 5 11

Dominion Express Co., express charges, 18.76; Dibble, Edward F., seeds, 60c. 19 36

Duckworth, Robert, stoning cesspool, 2.00; Dreer, H. A., seeds, 85c.; postage, 13c. 2 98

Darch & Hunter Seed Co., Limited, seeds, 4.95; Duke. J. O., seeds, 1.00 ... 5 95

Davidson & Carter, farm implements 17 15

Ewing, Wm. & Co., seeds, 35c.; postage, 6c. 41

Ferry, D. M. & Co., seeds, 7.02; Ford Seed Co., seeds, 94c.; postage, 96c. 8 92

Guelph Paper Co., tags and twine, 3.94; stationery, 85.97; G. T. Ry. freight charges, 33.03 .... 122 94

AGRICULTURE.—*Continued.*

FIELD EXPERIMENTS.—*Continued.*

EXPENSES.—*Continued.*

Garton's Limited, assorted seeds, 7.99; Gregory, Jas. H., seeds, 84c.; postage, 52c.	9 35
Gunson, L. P. & Co., seeds, 7.60; Gerolamy, W. A., fanning mill, 25.00...	32 60
Guelph Sewage Department, 36 sticks dynamite, 7.20; Guelph Electrical Works, furnishings, 8.00	15 20
Guelph Rag and Metal Co., hardware	4 81
Hamilton, Mrs. A., 30 hours addressing envelopes, 3.03; Henderson, Peter & Co., seeds, 2.40; bags, 27c.	5 70
Hammond, Jesse, seeds, 25c.; Harris, Joseph Co., The, seeds, 50c.	75
Hunter, James, seeds, 30.15; Holmes Seed Co., seeds, 30c.; postage, 36c....	30 81
Hewer, James & Son, seeds, 37.20; furnishings, 10.60	47 80
Iowa Seed Co., seeds, 2.15; postage, 32c.	2 47
James, D., 8 bush. peas at 1.10, 8.80; bags, 80c.; Johnson & Stokes, seeds, 1.34	10 94
Kilgour Bros., 250 paper bags, 26.13; case, 30c.; Keith, George, ¼ lb. beet hybrid sugar, 10c.; postage, 2c.	26 55
Kitching, Perey, seeds, 8 25; Klinck, C. R., 17 days' work at 1.50 25.20...	33 75
Kelso, J. J., printing, 2,000 letter heads	7 50
Livingston Seed Co., The, seeds, 15c.; postage, 14c.; Landreth Seed Co., D., seeds, 2.65	2 94
Miller, A. H., refernce *re* noxious weeds, 2.50; Maule, Wm. Henry, 5 lbs. white turnip seed, 2.50; assorted seed, 2.65; postage, 50c.	8 15
Massey-Harris Co., Limited, gang plough, 33.00; drill plough, 18.00; thistle cutter, 4.00; sundries, 1.95	56 95
Macdonald, D. E. & Bro., dry goods, 1.30; Morris Harness and Stable Supply Co., The, repairs, etc., 9.75	11 05
May, L. L. & Co., seeds, 82 bags, 5c.; Morris, Geo. B., door bolt, 10c.	97
Milne, Alex., 5 days' work at 1.50, 7.50; Murnahan, John, 61 rods woven wire fence at 80c., 48.80; 4 wire gates at 4.80, 19.20; brace wire, 2.50	61 53
Metal Roofing Co. of Canada, Limited, 30 squares galvanized Eastlake at 5.05, 151.50; 77-132 squares galvanized Eastlake Startlers at 5.05, 2.94; 72 feet galvanized can and roll at 5c., 3.60; 7 rolls paper at 85c., 5.95; 30 lbs. galvanized nails at 8c., 2.40 166.39; less 5 per cent., 8.32	158 07
McLean & Dawson, testing pliers, 95c.; McKay, Robert, seed wheat, 5.00...	5 95
McAllister, Margaret, 4 weeks' work at 5.00, 20.00; McLelland, R. B., furnishings, 1.35	21 35
McGibbon, D., 29 days' work at 2.00, 58.00; McKenzie, Duncan, repairs and furnishings, 6.88	64 88
McMillan Bros., furnishings	2 65
Nelles, Chas. L., stationery, 27.68; Northrup, King & Co., seeds, 5.10; bags, 10c.; postage, 80c.	33 68
National Typewriter Co., copy holder, 3.50; ribbons, stationery, etc., 15.65; Norton Mfg Co., The, permanent improvements, 51.25	70 40
Occomore, H. & Co., waterfront, 7.00; furnishings, 2.75; Olds, L. L. Seed Co., seed corn, 30c.; postage, 21c.	10 26
Office Specialty Mfg. Co., furnishings	15 10
Pringle, G. D., 1 box type, 4 95; Petrie, A. B., furnishing, 4.28	9 23
Postmaster, postage stamps, 35.00; Penfield, S. & G., barrow teeth, 7.25...	42 25
Richardson, G. A., hardware, 15.92; Ryan, G. B. & Co., furnishings, 15.92; seeds, 18.00	49 84
Rennie, Wm. & Co., seeds, 38.93; bags, 20c.; Rimpau, W., seeds, 72c.	39 85
Roberts, W. B., 1½ bush. S, N. corn, 2.00; Reed, J. Hugo, V.S., medicine, 1.00	3 00
Sweeney, James, harness repairs 11.60, harness oil 1.25; Smith, Fred., plumbing, 12.10	24 95
Sexsmith, Geo. A., 1 bush. beans, 2.50; Salzer, John A. & Co., seeds, 2.02	4 52
Steiger, Otto, seeds, 1.52; Stevens, Fred. B. & Co., express on corn, 25c.	1 77
Standard Fertilizer & Chemical Co., chemicals 14.50, freight 1.20; Sutton & Sons, seeds, 12.93	28 63
Steele, Briggs Seed Co., seeds 22.20, bags, 18c.; Simmers, J. A., seeds, 2.55; postage, 12c.; labels, 1.20	26 25
Stewart, A., 2 doz. vials, 40c.; Smith, Mrs. E., making bags, 3.53	3 93

16 P.A.

AGRICULTURE.—*Continued.*

FIELD EXPERIMENTS.—*Continued.*

EXPENSES.—*Continued.*

Smith, Percy 4 days' work. 4.00; sundry persons. manure, 83.00............ 87 00
Shepherd, Victor, 15 days' work at 2.50, 33.75; Slater, A. E., work per-
formed, 115 hours at 13½c., 15.53 .... 49 28
Sanders, G. A., 30 hours' work at 13½c. 4 05
Thorburn, J. M. & Co., seeds, 3.23; postage, 36c.; Thorpe Co., The, seeds,
14.40; furnishings, 5.13; bags, 50c. 23 62
Teavens, J., 11¼ days' work at 50c., 5.75; Thom, C. C., 11 1-10 days' work,
16.65 .... 22 40
Twigg, C. R., 10 hours' work at 11c. 1 10
United Typewriter Co., Limited supplies 41 50
Vick, James, Sons, seeds 68
Wood, T. W. & Sons, seeds, 88c.; Whittaker, W., 14 3-10 days' work at
at 1.50, 21.45; Waters Bros., stationery, 30c. 22 63
Young, Wm., 65 posts at 19c. 12 35

EXPERIMENTAL DAIRY DEPARTMENT.

SALARIES ($2,498.50).

R. W. Stratton:	Nine months' salary as Foreman............................			585 00
C. H. Ralph:		do	Cheesemaker........................	444 00
G. R. Taylor:		do	Buttermaker........................	470 00
L. Hough:	Five	do	Engineer........................	175 00
J. Wright:	Three and One Half	do	do	122 50
Chas. Wood:	Twelve	do	Cattleman........................	540 00
L. Sparrow:	Nine	do	Stenographer........................	162 00

EXPENSES ($10,185.44).

Bissonette, G., work in stable, 3.42; Bell Telephone Co., messages, 1.35;
rent of instrument, 15.00 .... 19 77
Burrell, D. H. & Co., heifer mouthpieces, 3.03; milking machine, 150.00;
teat cups and mouthpieces, 6.00; vacuum pump and tank, 43.00;
vacuum safety valve, 3.50; stanchion cocks, 10.80; gauge, 1.65; sundries, 9.85 .... 227 83
Bond Hardware Co., hardware, 9.37; raw oil, 2.10; Bailey, Daniel, repairs
to harness, 3.35 .... 14 82
Ballantyne Dairy Supply Co., power belts, 2.00; cotton, 7.81; 2 bbls. salt at
1.65, 3.30; invoice books, 40c. 13 51
Benson Bros., groceries, 2.55; Burlington Blanket Co., cow covers, 1.40..... 3.95
Clemens, H. A. & Co., lumber, 39.79; Canadian Express Co., express
charges, 6.50 .... 46 29
Chickering, F. E., expenses, 1.75; Customs. duty on coal, 84.68................ 86 43
C. P. Ry., freight charges, 79c.; Coon. Wm., Jersey cow, 50.00 .... 50 79
Clark, W. A., paper knife, 35c.; Costello, John, balance on ice machine,
3.32 .... 3 67
Castner, Curran & Bullitt. 141.80 tons coal at 3.70 .... 524 66
Dominion Express Co., express charges, 4.00; Denniss. F. H., 19 days'
work, 22.50 .... 26 50
Dana. C. H., labels and punch, 2.75; Dean, H. H., travelling expenses,
43.96 .... 46 71
Douglas, J., board 8 00
Electric Boiler Compound Co., Limited, 443 lbs. electric boiler compound... 26 58
Eureka Mineral Wool and Asbestos Co., packing for pump 1 23
Firstbrook Box Co., The, Limited, shavings for bedding 81 45
Goldie, Jas. Co., The. Limited, 8 tons 500 lbs. bran, 166.50; G. T. Ry.,
freight charges, 9.88 .... 176 38
Gilmour, J. D., 132 hours' work at 12c.. 15.84; Gowdy Bros., repairs, 30c... 16 14
Guelph Paper Co., paper and twine, 1.35; Grant, Thos. F., repairs and
castings for pump, 7.75 .... 9 10
Guelph Soap Co., box Sterling soap, 3.75; soda ash, 4.45; Guelph Cartage
Co., teaming and shovelling coal, 58.44 .... 66 67

16a P.A.

AGRICULTURE.—*Continued.*

EXPERIMENTAL DAIRY DEPARTMENT.—*Continued.*

EXPENSES.—*Continued.*

Guelph Radial Ry. Co., Limited, hauling coal, 21.54; Guelph Electrical Works, rewinding armature, 18.00	39 54
G. N. W. Telegraph Co., messages, 53c.; Guelph Ice Co., ice, 5.00	5 53
Hewer, Jas. & Sons, oil cake, 13.00; gluten meal, 24.00; salt, 90c.; corn chop, 2.40	40 30
Hough, L., boarding machine expert, wages, 23.50; Holstein Friesian Association of Canada, registration of stock, 8.00	31 50
Kroeschell Bros. Ice Machine Co., repairs to ice machine	22 05
Leclair, J. M., work in stable, 6.48; Laing, W. J., load sand, 1.00	7 48
Latsch, F. P., 1 Jersey heifer	100 00
Morris Harness and Stable Supply Co., furnishing and repairs, 4.05; Moodie, Chas., 30 hours' work at 15c., 4.50	8 55
Mason, W., 7 bush. oats at 35c.	2 45
McAllister, Geo., feed, 8.50; McCartney, Robert, 98¼ bush. oats at 35c., 34.38	42 88
McKenzie, Duncan, horseshoeing, 2.75; McMullen Printing Co., The, 10,000 butter wrappers, 10.75	13 50
National Live Stock Record, registration of stock, 2.75; membership, 1.00	3 75
National Typewriter Co., Limited, furnishings	2 25
Owen Sound Creamery Co. Limited, butter paper, 75c.; preserver for butter, 1.50; 32 lbs. parchment, 2.20	4 45
Occomore, H. & Co., repairs to steam box, 1.70; repairs to boiler, 2.35	4 05
Presant, E. J., feed, 5.64; Penfold, S. & G., furnishings, 3.50	9 14
Petrie, A. B., chemicals	5 25
Richardson, G. A., hardware, 6.65; zenoleum and raw oil, 18.26; Rice, George, 2 Holstein cows, 700.00	724 91
Reid, J. Hugo, V.S., medicines, 3.80; Robertson, A. & Son, repairs to boiler, 6.81	10 61
Reid, N., postage stamps, 6.00; Rudd, T. E., repairs to oven, 2.15	8 15
Shepherd, V., 15 days' work at 2.18, 32.80; Stewart, Robert, bedding, 1.50	34 30
Smart Bag Co., Limited, 1 bale bags, 14.00; sundry persons, milk supplied, 7,564.33	7,578 33
Tolton Bros., repairs, 4.84; Thornton & Douglas, Limited, 4 prs. pants, 2.60	7 44
Taylor, Forbes Co., Limited, repairing machinery, 1.95; Taylor & McKenzie, repairs for ice machine, 40c.	2 35
Toronto Liquid Carbonate Co., Limited, 3 tubes liquid carbonic acid gas	9 00
Wolcott, Geo. R., repairs, 12.00; Weaver, J. B., 24 hours' work at 10c., 2.40	14 40
Weekly Sun, The, advertising	2 30

DAIRY SCHOOL.

SALARIES ($1,575.00).

W. Waddell: Three months' salary as Instructor in Buttermaking			240 00
C. H. Ralph:	do	do do	180 00
R. W. Stratton:	do	do do	240 00
C. W. McDougall:	do	do Separators	240 00
G. R. Taylor:	do	do do	180 00
L. Rose:	do	do Milk Farm Dairy	225 00
L. Sparrow:	do	Stenographer	75 00
L. Hough:	do	Engineer	105 00
J. H. McGillivray:	do	Assistant Engineer	90 00

EXPENSES ($5,888.89).

Bond, John M. & Co., hardware sundries, 22.86; Barr, Geo. H., travelling expenses, 1.00	23 86

AGRICULTURE.—*Continued.*

DAIRY SCHOOL.—*Continued.*

EXPENSES.—*Continued.*

Ballantyne Dairy Supply Co., Limited, 12 3-row floor brooms at 75c., 9.00; 144½ yds. cotton at 5c., 7.23; 2 gals. arnatto at 1.85, 3.70; 1,000 bleached circles at 70c. per c., 7.00; 4 gals. Hansen's rennet at 1.90, 7.60; sundries, 10.50 .... 45 03

Bollert, E. R. & Co., 20 yds. cotton at 12½c., 2.50; Benso Bros., 3 brooms, at 30c., 90c. 3 40

Canadian Dairyman, advertising 10.00; Commercial Oil Co., Limited, 5 gals. listerine at 85c., 4.25; can, 50c. 14 75

Canadian Express Co., charges 2.00; C. P. Ry., freight charges, 1.77...... 3 77

Canada Foundry Co., The, Limited, 2 water pistons and followers, tube liners, etc., 26.15; valve rod and stuffing, 1.80 .... 27 95

Clark, W. A., repairing clock, 1.00; Castner, Curran & Bullitt, 137.70 tons coal at 3.67, 503.30 .... 504 30

Canadian Oil Co., 1 doz. metal polish, 4.25; Customs, duty and entries, 73.90 .... 78 15

City Dairy Co., Limited, 100 butter cans. 30c.; postage. 15c.................. 45

Darch & Hunter Seed Co., Limited, 30,000 sheets parchment butter paper, 33.10; Dean, H. H., travelling expenses, 35.30 .... 68 40

Derbyshire, D., 1 set balls. 1.00; travelling expenses. 10.00; Davidson, Thos. Mfg. Co., Limited, appliance for school, 1.95 ....·····....... 12 95

Dairyman's Association of Western Ontario, advertising, 10.00; Dominion Express Co., charges, 50c. 10 50

Duncan, George, 6 days' whitewashing at 2.00 .... 12 00

Electric Boiler Compound Co., Limited, 20 gals. oil at 13.75; Ericsson, Elov, 2 bottles butter culture. 1.00 .... 14 75

Eureka Mineral Wool & Asbestos Co., 4 lbs. packing at 1.25 .... 5 00

Firstbrook Box Co., The , Limited, 500 butter boxes at 21c., 105.00; 213 butter boxes at 9¾c., 20.77 .... 125 77

Grand Trunk Ry., freight charges 23 69

Guelph Paper Co., The, 20 rolls manilla paper, 1.12; stationery, 1.30; Guelph Cartage Co., cartage on coal, 16.40 .... 18 82

Heffernan, A., duty on entry on milking machine, 1.20; Hansen's, Chr., Laboratory lactic ferment. 2.25 .... 3 45

Morris, G. B., painting, 4.35: Macdonald. D.E. & Bro., dry goods, 3.60... 7 95

Morris, E., back hire. 1.75; Muir, J. B., lecture to class, 6.00 .... 7 75

Morrison, The Jas. Manufacturing Co., Limited, valves, plugs and gauges 5 73

McCrea, J. A., groceries. 50c.; McIntosh. J. 1., advertising, 4.00 .... 4 50

McFeeters, J. A., 8 days' instructing dairy class 24 00

McMullen Printing Co., 20,000 butter wrappers at 1.00, 20.00; 10,000 plain parchment at 75c., 7.50: express charges, 1.15; case, 25c. 28 90

Nelles, Charles L., stationery 9 15

Postmaster, postage stamps, 32.00; Petrie, A. B., chemicals, 15.48 .... 47 48

Pringle, G. D., rubber stamp, .50c.; Quinn. E., postage stamps, 4.00 .... 4 50

Richardson. C. & Co.. 1 cooler. 52.00: 2 Eureko butter printers, 2.50; 1 can 500 lbs. and conductor, 14.00; skimming points. 80c. 69 30

Rudd. T. E., boiler, 3.00; repairing stack and oven. 3.90: 2 vats. 17.00: sundries. 2.15: Robertson. The Jas. Co.. repairs for basin. 3.00: Rogers, J. W.. advertising. 1.25 .... 30 30

Reid, N., postage stamps 5 00

Scott & Tierney, books and stationery, 12.65; Stewart, Alex., 190 lbs. sulphuric acid, at 2¾c., 5.21 .... 17 86

Sunley, Rachel, 16 days' cleaning dairy at 1.00; sundry persons. milk supplied, 4,494.54 .... 4,510 54

Taylor & McKenzie, repairs 13 35

United Factories, 2 doz. barrel brushes at 3.20, 6.40; United Typewriter Co., stationery, 3 50 .... 9 90

Wolcott. Geo. R., repairs on engine house. 6.54; Wagner Glass Works, butter test bottles and thermometer, 18.00 ....·.................. 24 54

Wood, Chas. S., travelling expenses and disbursements, 20.65; lime, 50c.... 21 15

Zimmerman Bros., 500 hoops at 4.00 per M, 20.00; 500 set heading at 5c., 25.00 .... 45 00

AGRICULTURE.—*Continued.*

POULTRY DEPARTMENT.

SALARIES ($714.65).

L. Sparrow: Twelve months' salary as Stenographer		120 00
J. R. Terry: do do Laborer		452 00
W. E. Todd: One do do		35 00
A. McKenny: Three do do		102 65
A. Twigg: do		5 00

EXPENSES ($3,133.64).

Allison, F. F., poultry, 35 lbs. at 9c., 3.15; Atkinson, George, poultry, 100 lbs. at 9c., 9.00	12 15
Brown, C. E., eggs, 200 at 5c., 10.00; Bailey, Dan'l., eggs, 35 at 5c., 1.75; 5 incubators, 55.00; harness furnishings, 4.90	71 65
Bell Telephone Co., messages, 1.60; rent of instrument, 15.00; Butterfield, T., poultry, 18.00	34 60
Bond, J. M. & Co., hardware, 15.72; Bell, W. J., 2 turkey pullets, 10.00...	25 72
Brown, W. A., wages, 21.75; Barclay, Jas., 95½ bus. wheat at 82¼c., 78.78, 54 bus. at 73c., 39.90, 53 bus. at 70c., 37.10	177 53
Broadfoot, J. B., drugs and chemicals, 7.10; Burton, Mrs. Thos., poultry, 8.00	15 10
Curtis, W. R. & Co., eggs, 100 pekin, 7.00; Canadian Express Co., express charges, 41.20	48 20
C. P. Ry. Freight, freight charges, 37.70; Clemens, H. A. Co., The, lumber, 55.67	93 37
Cyphers, Chas. A., Model Nursery food, 9.70; Customs, duty and entry, 21.85	31 55
Connecticut Agr'l. College, The, eggs, 15.00; Cockburn, John A., 27.49 bus. wheat at 70c., 19.47	34 47
Crow, J. W., poultry, 18.00; Colson, John, poultry, 20.00	38 00
Central Electric School Supply Co., electric supplies, 38.40; Chittick, J. T. Co., 20 bus. corn, 14.56	49 36
Cornell Incubator Mfg. Co., furnishings, 1.90; C. P. Ry. Telegraph, telegram, 33c.	2 23
Chemists & Surgeons Supply Co., Ltd., dispensing scales, 8.00; Canadian Shredded Wheat Co., 500 lbs. poultry food, 3.50	11 50
Daniels, C. J., 1 doz. burners, 4.00; 500 lbs. meal, 10.00; Dominion Express Co., express charges, 6.50	20 50
Davidson & Carter, 1 scuffler, 8.00; Dowler Co., The, 62 yds. cotton at 10c., 6.20	14 20
Dominion Poultry Station, poultry, 220 lbs. at 9c., 19.98; Davidson, J. F., building fence, 35.00	54 98
Foley, A. W., eggs, 200 at 5c.	10 00
Gummer, H., printing records, 14.50; stationery, 42.50; G. T. Ry., freight charges, 18.78	75 78
Goldie, James Co., The. Ltd., 50 bus. wheat at 70c., 35.00, 100 bus. at 80c., 80.00, 75 bus. at 75c., 56.25; 50 bus. oats at 38c., 19.00; 2,000 lbs. screenings, 20.00; 200 lbs. chopped wheat, 2.60	212 85
Gan, James, horse, 175.00; Green, Henry J., 4 thermometers, 80.54	255 54
Guelph Cartage Co., hauling coal, 4.10; Guelph Spring & Axle Co., Ltd., 1 axle box, 40c.	4 50
Guelph Electrical Works, rewinding motor, 3.40; 1 doz. batteries, 3.80	7 20
Guelph Radial Ry. Co., hauling coal, 1.02; Gowdy Bros., 7 bus. lime at 35c., 2.45	3 47
Gould, P., poultry, 6.00; Graham, W. R., scrubbing floors, 15.00	21 00
Hewer, Jas. & Son. 95 bus. barley at 50c., 47.50; 800 lbs. grit, 6.55; 500 lbs. oyster shells, 4.00; 20 bus. wheat at 80c., 16.00; seeds, 32.95; feed, 115.75; sundries, 22.40	245 15
Hohenadel, J., poultry, 75 lbs. at 9c., 6.75; Heffernan, A., 35 bags poultry feed, 13.90	20 65
Howitt, E., 16 loads gravel at 15c.	2 40
Johnston, J., poultry	6 08
Krouse. F. W., poultry, 47 at 50c., 23.50; eggs, 200 at 5.00, 10.00; Kloepfer & Co., 929 tons coal at 5.30, 49.15	82 65
Kloepfer, C., repairs to wagon	14 40

AGRICULTURE.—*Continued.*

POULTRY DEPARTMENT.—*Continued.*

EXPENSES.—*Continued.*

Lakewood Farm Co., poultry, 26.50; eggs, 40.60; Little, C. G., poultry, 10.28	77 38
Morgan, A. J., 5 gals. lice killer at 80c., 4.00; 40 trap nets at 90c., 36.00; 1 ton beef scraps, 56.50; 1 1-12 sanitary feeders, 5.40; 5 incubators at 10.00, 50.00; 1,000 sealed bands, 20.00; 5 thermometers, 3.13; 6 brooders, 2.00; 1 hydrometer, 2.50; 17 poultry bits, 1.07; 1 1-3 pigeon nests, 1.20, 1.60; 1,000 egg boxes for 8.50; 500 lbs. Puritan chicken feed at 3.75, 18.75; 500 lbs. Morgan chicken feed at 2.50, 12.50; 1 bone cutter, 17.25; 12½ doz. egg baskets at 1.25. 15.63. 4 1-6 do at 2.00, 8.34; sundries 90c.	264 07
Millard, I. K., purchase of stock, 30.00; Martin, John S., 350 eggs at 6c., 21.00; 20 Wyandotte pullets at 2.00, 40.00	91 00
Mason, Roy, 54½ lbs. poultry at 9c., 4.91, 34 lbs. at 7c., 2.38; Miller, Eliza, work, 17.00	24 29
Morris Harness Stable Supply Co., furnishings, 30c.; Morris, Geo. B., box shot sheds, 50c.	80
McColl Bros. & Co., 394.72 gals. oil at 23c., 90.78; McQuillan, A., 136½ lbs. poultry at 9c., 12.28	103 06
McCrea, J. A., furnishings, 4.45; McDougal, Chas., feed, 16.60	21 05
McNaughton, M., poultry, 8.03; McCrea, D., poultry, 13.12	21 15
McMillan Bros., 1 scale	19 00
Nelles, Chas. L., stationery, 8.66; Nottage, Dr. H. P., 500 eggs at 7c., 35.00	43 66
National Typewriter Co., furnishings, 2.75; Newhall, H. W., 19 hours' work, 2.20	4 95
Occomore, H. & Co., repairs to steam tank and box	3 57
Postmaster, postage, 50.50; Pickard, J. J., poultry, 18.00	68 50
Porter, E. L., poultry, 50.00; Prairie State Incubator Co., 6 incubators at 4.50, 27.00; 6 thermometers, 2.25	79 25
Petrie, A. B., chemical furnishings	10 88
Richardson, G. A., hardware sundries, 94.98; Robertson, G. A., poultry, 5.25; eggs, 3.00	103 23
Rice, W. E., 12 pairs squabs, 30.00; Reinhart, John, carriage supplies, 1.80	31 80
Redeker, A., poultry, 8.25; Robertson, M., poultry, 17.04	25 29
Ryde, Alice, poultry	7 68
Syracuse Rendering Co., 3,000 lbs. beef scraps at 40.00, 60.00; 200 lbs. cracked bone, 3.20; 300 lbs. bone meat meal, 4.50	67 70
Scaulan, J., 112 lbs. poultry at 9c., 10.08; Strachan, John, duty on eggs, 1.25	11 33
Sunley, Wm., furnishings and repairs, 19.93; Steele Briggs Seed Co., Ltd., 2 brooder stoves at 1.10, 2.20	22 13
Sheady, P., poultry, 35.00; Spratt's Patent, Ltd., 1 ton poultry feed, 23.50	58 50
Sheridan & O'Connor, 522 ft. concrete floor, 46.98; Scott, Wm., poultry, 7.35	54 33
Sutherland, John, 1,000 lbs. fine meal, 13.50; Sunley, T. J., poultry, 36.00	49 50
Thorpe Co., The, seeds, 19.25; 114 bus. corn at 58c., 60.32; 50 bus. barley at 50c., 25.00; 20 bus. oats at 45c., 9.00	113 57
Tavernor, James, 223 2-3 lbs. poultry at 9c., 20.19; Teale, W. J., poultry, 12.90	33 09
Tillson Co., The, Ltd., poultry feed, 8.75; Taylor, Forbes Co., Ltd., repairs, 1.25	10 00
Telfer, John B., 2 days' ploughing at 1.50, 3.00; Twiggs, C. B., 50 hours' work at 10c., 5.00	8 00
Webber, F. R., poultry, 6.00; Wolcott, Geo. R., furnishings, 1.80	7 80
Waters Bros., drawing paper	30

HORTICULTURAL DEPARTMENT.

SALARIES ($5,560.56).

W. Squirrel: Twelve months' salary as Head Gardener and Foreman				800 00
A. McMeans: Eight and half	do	do	do	566 50
W. Hunt: Three	do	Florist		175 00
W. Wells:	do	Assistant and Night Fireman		480 00
Geo. Collins: Nine	do	do	do	342 00
A. W. Bruce: Twelve	do	Stenographer		100 00
Pay Lists, Wages, teamsters, laborers				3,097 06

AGRICULTURE.—*Continued.*
HORTICULTURAL DEPARTMENT.—*Continued.*
EXPENSES ($3,328.05).

Anderson, C. & Co., stationery, 11.77	11 77
Bond, John M. & Co., 1 pump, 4.25; sundry hardware, 55.43; Bruce, John, A. & Co., seeds, 17.55 ....,	77 23
Bolgiano, J. & Son, seeds, 2.55; Burpee, W. Atlee & Co., seeds, 4.58	7 13
Becker, C., 10 loads manure at 50c., 5.00; Bailey, Daniel, repairing harness, 1.70	6 70
Bell Telephone Co., rent of instrument, 15.00: messages, 85c.; Blackie Bros., sulphur vaporiser, 6.00 ·....................................	21 85
Clemens, H. A. & Co., lumber, 167.88; Commercial Oil Co., 10 gals. lustreine at 85c., 8.50: 1 can, 75c.	177 13
Canadian Express Co., express charges, 8.15; C. P. Ry. Freight, freight charges, 5.70	13 85
Customs, duty and entries, 25.92; Cranston, John & Son, 2,000 flower pots, · 8.00; crate, 42c.	34 34
Carter, T., 4 loads manure at 50c., 2.00; Crossmore, Joseph, 7 loads manure at 50c., 3.50	5 50
Chemists & Surgeons Supply Co., furnishings, 7.40; Cordova, Ade, 25 hours' work at 11c., 2.75	10 15
Chadburn & Coldwell Mfg. Co., repairs to machinery, 4.90; Coke, E. F., 12 days, 15 hours' work, 17.25	22 15
Crow, J. W., 11 weeks' work at 12.50, 137.50; travelling expenses, 22.50 ...	160 00
Dominion Express Co., express charges, 4.20; Dreer, H. A., seeds, 10.37; . plants, 12.90	27 67
Dawson, C., 40 loads manure at 75c., 30.00; Duncan, G., whitewashing, 2.00	32 00
Davidson & Carter, 1 1-12 doz. cultivator points	4 25
Ewing, Wm. & Co., seeds	1 40
Ferry, D. M. & Co., seeds. 89c.; Farquhar & Co., seeds, 4.35	5 24
Flowers, Frank. 18 loads manure at 50c., 9.00; Foster, Thos., 21½ hours' work at 40c., 8.60	17 60
Freed, H., 1,000 cabbage plants	1 00
Guelph Cartage Co., hauling gravel. 5.40; Gadsby, James, 24 2-12 doz. lantern slides at 4.00, 96.65: boxes for same, 6.00	108 05
Guelph Light & Power Dept., fuel, 25.95; Gurney Foundry Co., boiler brushes, 6.00: repairs, 50c.	32 45
Gummer, H., stationery, etc., 20.17; Guelph Cigar Co., Ltd., 350 lbs. tobacco stems, 3.50	23 67
G. T. Ry. Freight, freight charges, 29.45; Guelph Paper Co., furnishings, 15.83	45 28
Guelph Ice Co., 2 loads manure at 50c., 1.00; Gammage, J. & Sons, plants, 4.80 ....,	5 80
Guelph Radial Ry. Co., Ltd., hauling coal	12 65
Henderson, Peter & Co., printing labels, 9.80; seeds, 1.39; 1 butter steel hand cart, 13.00	24 19
Hamilton, F. Co., Ltd., tools, 3.75; crop sprayer, 19.43; Hutt, H. L., travelling expenses, 13.40	36 58
Hunt, Wm., travelling expenses, 2.75; Hewer, Jas. & Son, seeds, 27.75; furnishings, 25c.	30 75
Hotson, J. W., building tool shed, 80.00; Howitt, Jas., 2 loads sand, 50c.; 60 loads gravel at 15c., 9.00	89 50
Iowa Seed Co., seeds	97
Johnson & Stokes, seeds, 6.37; Jackson, W. D., 25½ days' work at 1.30, 33.15	39 52
Kloepfer & Co., 28 tons coal at 5.60, 156.80, freight, 28.22: 4.1800 tons coal at 7.00, 34.30, freight. 18.15: 18 tons coal at 5.40, 97.20, freight, 18.65; 18.1260 tons coal at 5.30, 98.05, freight, 60.47; 600 tons coal at 5.40, 324.00; 19.80 tons of coal at 5.60, 107.24	943 08
Kandy Kitchen, The, 15 qts. ice cream	4 00
Lyman, A. B., trees	1 30
Macdonald, D. E. & Bro., 105½ yds. cotton at 10c., 10.58; 21 yds. muslin at 8c., 1.68; 25 yds. cotton at 8c., 2.00; 11½ yds. muslin at 15c., 1.73; 6 towels at 30c., 1.80	17 79
Morris, Geo. B., hardware, 4.62; Meehan, Thos. & Sons, seeds, 6.50; box and packing, 2.50: trees, 20.70	34 32
Morgan, A. J., bulbs, 97.16; transportation, 21.87	119 03

AGRICULTURE.—*Continued.*
HORTICULTURAL DEPARTMENT.—*Continued.*
EXPENSES.—*Continued.*

McAllister, Geo., 16 loads manure at 50c., 8.00; McMeans, A., travelling expenses and disbursements. 65.65	73	65
McLelland, R. B., 1 map of Dominion, 1.35; McGibbon, Duncan, 36 days' work at 2.00, 72.00	73	35
McMillan Bros., 6 pkgs. tacks, 30c.; butcher knife, 65c.; 8 balls cotton, 68c.; 2 horse blankets, 4.50; axle grease, 25c.	6	38
McLean & Dawson, repairs to lawn mower	11	00
Nelles, Chas. L., furnishings 1.50; Newhall, H. W., 5 hours' work at 11c., 55c.	2	05
National Typewriter Co., Ltd., supplies	5	00
Occomore, H. & Co., furnishings, 65c.; Office Specialty Mfg. Co., Ltd., furnishings, 8.20	8	85
Pringle, G. D., photographic supplies, 2.80; Postmaster, postage stamps, 36.00	38	80
Potter, Mrs. Stanley. 115 wax models at 2.25, 258.75, 14 do at 8.00, 112.00, 1 at 3.00, 4 at 4.00, 16.00, 1 at 7.00	396	75
Petrie, A. B., chemicals, 26.51; Peart, H. S., travelling expenses and disbursements. 37.10	63	61
Penfold, S. & G., 6 balls twine, 48c.; repairing mower, 1.37; sundries, 90c.	2	75
Painter. Mrs. F., making bags. 1.75; Palframan, Wm., 1 days' work, 1.50	3	25
Payn, Philip B., 28 hours' work at 15c.	4	20
Richardson, G. A., 200 ft. rubber hose at 16c., 32.00; hardware sundries, 50.35; wax fruit. 70c.; Robertson, A., 4 bus. lime, 1.00	84	05
Rennie, Wm. Co., Ltd., seeds. 5.20; Ryan, G. B. & Co., furnishings. 2.10	7	30
Robertson, A. & Son, furniture, 1.75; repairs to machine, 1.60; Reid & Ross, repairing wagon, 3.25	6	60
Sallows, H. & D., horseshoeing, 10.99; Scott & Tierney, stationery, 75c.	11	74
Smith, Fred. K., repairing gas meter, 5.05; Sunley, Wm., galv'd. iron pots, 7.50; brass sprayer, 1.95	14	50
Sutton & Sons. seeds. 18.08; Steele Briggs Seed Co., Ltd., seeds, 34.07; 6 hand weeders, 1.50	53	65
Simmers, J. A., 1 Iron Age double wheel hoe, 12.00 ;1 short handled budding knife, 1.25; seeds, 6.35	19	60
Shepherd, V., 2 days' work at 2.15, 4.30, 21½ days' work at 2.25, 48.38; Sloan, W., load manure, 50c.	53	18
Smith, E. D., plants. 30.55; Stevenson, E. B., plants, 4.05	34	60
Sundry persons, services picking berries. 80.76; Stokes, W. P., seeds. 18c.	80	94
Thorpe Co., The. 50 lbs. guano at 5c., 2.50; seeds. 35c.; Thornburn. J. M. & Co., seeds. 16.63	19	48
Thompstone. E., pair rubber boots, 2.00; Taylor & Forbes, repairs to greenhouse. 15.62	17	62
Twoltridge. T. H., 65 hours' work at 10c., 6.50; Toronto Liquid Carbonate Co.. Ltd., 125 lbs. gas. 7.50	14	00
Towell. John. 16 hours' work at 25c.	4	00
Vaughan Seed Store. seeds		13
Watson. C., 1 load manure. 50c.; Wolcott, Geo. R., work on tool house, 6.95; furnishings. 2.68	10	13
Zirngiebel, Augustus, seeds	1	00

MECHANICAL DEPARTMENT.
SALARIES ($800.00).

E. A. Crawford: Twelve months' salary as Mechanical Foreman	800	00

EXPENSES ($136.45).

Bond Hardware Co.. Ltd., tools and sundry hardware	80	93
Kloepfer, C., 1 fire traveller	2	00
Morris, Geo. B., tools	8	45
McKee. J. D., 3 sheets drawing paper, 25c.; McMillan Bros.. 13 wood screws, 52c.		77
Richardson. G., tools and sundry hardware	40	05
Wolcott. Geo. B., box stove. 2.50; granite pail, 1.00; granite cup, 10c.; 3 thimbles, 30c.; cartage, 35c.	4	25

Total Agriculture	$432,296	90

COLONIZATION AND IMMIGRATION.

PAMPHLETS AND ADVERTISING AND GENERAL COLONIZATION PURPOSES ($26,527.89).

Advertising:—
Annual Review Pubg. Co., 100.00; British American, 75.00;
Canadian Dairyman, 17.50; Canada First Pubg. Co., 41.74;
Catholic Register Pubg. Co., 46.80; Canadian Freeman, 65.00;
Canadian Baptist, 78.40; Commercial Handbook, 75.00;
Catholic Record, 83.20; Canada Churchman, 54.60;
Canada American, 150.00; Christian Guardian, 78.00;
Farmers' Advocate, 209.20; Farming World, 96.00;
Globe Printing Co., 320.00; Lord's Day Advocate, 52.00;
Mail Printing Co., 262.50; News Pubg. Co., 100.00;
O. A. C. Review, 48.00; Queen's Quarterly, 25.00;
Rittinger & Motz. 25.00; Toronto Daily Star, 13.50;
Toronto World, 48.00; Western British American, 75.00;
Weekly Sun, 104.00 .... 2,243 44
Baird, Jas., legal services re immigration investigation 164 00
Bell Telephone Co., messages, 19.63; Burling, R., interment, 30.00...... 49 63
Brownley, Rev. W. F., meals for immigrants, 4.50; railway fares for
immigrants, 9.90 .... 14 40
Brockville, Westport and Northwestern Railway Co., carriage of immi-
grants 29 00
Birmingham, R., services special officer Union Station at 3.00 per day,
564.00; accountable warrant, 15.75; travelling expenses, 22.40;
meals, 7.10; to purchase fruit for children, 4.75 .... 614 00
Brooks, Sandford, Hardware, Ltd., letter box plate 1 00
C. P .Railway, carriage of immigrants, 4,370.99; deporting immigrants,
9.60 .... 4,380 59
Crawford, Mrs. M. E., expenses returning immigrants to England 42 83
C.P.R. Telegraph Co., telegrams, 48.29; Cadieux, J., accountable, 100.00 148 29
Dominion Express Co., charges, 4.80; Duggan, Jno., cartage. 28.50;
Eplett, T. D., screens, pipe, etc, 2.08 .... 35 38
Flanagan, T. C., meals and lodgings, 670.15; Eaton, T. Co., supplies.
blankets, etc., 30.27; Evans, F. C., re deportation of immigrant, 12.55 712 97
G. T. Railway, carriage of immigrants, 6,434.95; Graves, D., meals and
lodgings, 27.50 .... 6,462 45
Galbraith Photo Co., developing plates, 32c.; Grace Hospital, 1 week's
fee for Eva Nott, 3.50 .... 3 82
G. T. Railway, baggage-master, storage, 2.25; G. N. W. Telegraph Co.,
telegrams, 47.28 .... 49 53
Irwin, C. W., brokerage charges, 5.37; Jones, R. A., services as clerk
Union Station at 2.50 per day, 645.00; expenses deporting immigrants.
1.50; accountable, 100.00; services as special representative interview-
ing immigrants placed on farms, 42.50 .... 794 37
King's Printer, paper, 3.48; stationery, 48.55 .... 52 03
Lundy, C. E., meals and lodging, 8.60; Leckie, Jno., Ltd., waterproof
blankets, 20.00 .... 28 60
Lord, Jas., storage of baggage, 1.60; Lee, F. G., travelling exp. re
transportation of insane immigrants, 5.00 .... 6 60
McColl, Dr. H. H., medical services for immigrants, 4.00; McTavish, J.,
cartage, 2.75 .... 6 75
McDonald, D. J., expenses deportation of immigrants, 22.35; May, A. J.,
photos, 7.00 .... 29 35
Mitchell, F., twelve months' salary as clerk at Union Station 767 50
Monthly Review, subscription, 5.00; Mail Printing Co.. subscription, 4.50 9 50
Murphy, R. G., meals and supplies, 22.83; Milnes, A. E., meals and lodg-
ings, 2.55 .... 25 38
Mitchell, F., services, clerk at Union Station at 2.50 per day 100 00
Morrison, P., travelling expenses of immigrant 5 20
Piper. Chas., expenses re deportation of insane immigrant 4 30
Pringle, A. W., photos, 4.00; Reading, A. J., lantern slides, 12.25 ...... 16 25
Ramsey, J. G. & Co., photo supplies. 6.05; Rice, T. G.. Wire Mfg. Co.,
letter box, 75c. 6 80
Riordon Paper Mills. paper, 2.55; Ruttan, J. H., expenses re deportation
of immigrant, 14.20 .... 16 75

COLONIZATION AND IMMIGRATION.—*Continued.*

PAMPHLETS AND ADVERTISING AND GENERAL COLONIZATION PURPOSES.—*Continued.*

Rankin, Wm., to pay express charges on immigrants effects to Ireland......	5 90
Riordon, Dr. Bruce, medical attendance, 5.00; Salvation Army, special grant, 7,000.00	7,005 00
Scobie, Jas., travelling expenses of immigrant, 5.20; Sharp, Rev. S. F., expenses forwarding immigrant, 2.00	7 20
Singular, Lot, board immigrants at Guelph, 6.00; Smith, S. G., expenses *re* deportation immigrant boy, 18.00	24 00
Sallows, R. R., photos for pamphlets, 26.75; Snider, B. D., expenses deportation of immigrant, 48.15	74 90
Theaker, F., photos, 3.50; Tutt, H. J., services as clerk Union Station, 749.00; accountable warrant, 54.03; advances to indigent immigrants, 14.00	820 53
Toronto Railway Co., car tickets, 14.00; Thompson, Jas., accountable, 500.00	514 00
Vick, Wm., moving into and cleaning new office, 6.15; Wawrick Bros. & Rutter, printing, 134.80	140 95
White, Henry, cartage, 95c.; Women's Welcome Hostel, grant, 1,000.00...	1,000 95
Wilson, Dr. R. J., medical attendance, 3.00; Women's Christian Temperance Union, salary of attendant at Union Station, 100.00	103 00
Wilkins, J. D., expenses *re* deportation of insane immigrant	10 75

LAND GUIDES FOR SETTLERS ($394.50).

Allan, W. J., 10.00;	Bond, H., 6.00;	Bertrand, P., 4.00;
Baxter, J. H., 8.00;	Bartlett, P. H., 12.50;	Cole, W., 6.00;
Connell, A., 4.00;	Carter, F. A., 5.00;	Curry, E., 4.00;
Dickenson, T., 20.00;	Davitson, G. E., 16.00;	Draper, A., 8.00;
Gurevity, A., 2.00;	Hughes, G., 4.00;	Hunt, R. D., 30.00;
Hough, J., 14.00;	Illingworth, H., 18.00;	Kiostad, O. J., 10.00;
Lowes, W., 16.00;	Levinson, D., 6.00;	McLean, J., 6.00;
Morrison, R., 4.00;	Mills, W., 2.00;	Moore, E., 8.00;
Martin, J., 4.00;	Maroney, S., 18.00;	Martin, Thos., 4.00;
Nicholl, E. A., 4.00;	Prouty, Chas., 66.00;	Pine, Jas., 4.00;
Robinson, W. J., 10.00;	Regan, D., 4.00;	Regan, J. T., 4.00;
Roach, Geo., 12.00;	Rogers, J., 4.00;	Smith, J. C., 6.00;
Serguff, G., 10.00;	Shortt, R. D., 4.00;	Stadelman, J., 4.00;
Storing, J., 3.00;	Stewart, H., 2.00;	Tardiff, H. F., 2.00;

Wilkins, H., 4.00; York, L., 2.00 ....   394 50

RENT AND MAINTENANCE OF OFFICE AT UNION STATION ($1,699.44).

Bell Telephone Co., messages, 8.85; rent of instruments, 52.75	61 60
C. P. R. Telegraph Co., telegrams, 48.47; Coyell, Alf., signs, 47.00	95 47
Canada Cabinet Co., desk cushion, etc., 33.94; Can. General Electric Co., desk lamps, etc., 4.41	38 35
Consumers' Gas Co., gas, 4.40; Eaton, T. Co., 87.61; G. N. W. Telegraph Co., telegrams, 37.71	129 72
G. T. Railway Co., rent of office, 675.00; *Globe* Printing Co., subscription, 5.00	680 00
Gripton, C., rubber stamps, etc., 7.30; Grand & Toy, toilet paper, etc., 25.00	32 30
King's Printer, stationery, 43.91; Lennox, Jno., office cleaning, 36.00	79 91
Mail Printing Co., subscription, 4.00; Might Directories, directory, 7.50	11 50
Meakins & Sons, map cloths, 1.96; Piper, N. L., Railway Supply Co., seats for immigration shed, 125.20	127 16
Rice, Lewis & Son, towel roller and hardware, 50c.; Russill Hardware Co., ladder, 5.00	5 50
Toronto Electric Light, wiring for lights, 40.30; light current, 3.75	44 05
Vick, Mrs. W., washing towels, 7.88; Vick, W., services as caretaker, 378.15	386 03
Warwick Bros. & Rutter, printing, 7.50; Williams, N. & Co., cartage, 35c.	7 85

COLONIZATION AND IMMIGRATION.—*Continued.*

WORK IN GREAT BRITAIN ($6,729.03).

Byrne, Peter: Twelve months' salary as Agent	2,366 43	
Byrne, E. A.: do do Clerk	700 80	
Byrne, Peter: To pay travelling expenses of self and staff...	235 30	
do advertising, 1,102.69; printing, 68.99...	1,171 68	
do office rent and caretaker, 317.79; fuel and light, 17.12	334 91	
do stationery, etc., 158.52; contingencies, etc., 431.80	590 32	
do office furniture, etc.	154 19	
Cash on hand Dec. 31st, 1906, to be accounted for	262 41	
Exchange on drafts	4 29	
	5,820 33	
Less cash on hand January 1st, 1906	141 99	
		5,678 34
G. N. W. Telegraph Co., telegrams	....	2 00
Thompson, James: Five months' salary as Special Agent......	500 00	
do travelling expenses and disbursements......	548 36	
Exchange on draft	33	
		1,048 69
Total Colonization and Immigration		$35,350 86

HOSPITALS, CHARITIES, SANITARY INVESTIGATIONS, ETC.

HOSPITALS AND CHARITIES ($209,362.59).

The Treasurer:

Barrie, Royal Victoria Hospital	1,181 04
Belleville, Belleville Hospital	952 88
Berlin, Berlin and Waterloo Hospital	697 97
Brantford, J. H. Stratford Hospital	1,414 07
Brockville, St. Vincent de Paul Hospital	1,892 09
do General Hospital	1,398 50
Chatham, St. Joseph's Hospital ...,...........................	1,242 46
do General Hospital	457 65
Cornwall, General Hospital	1,759 10
do Hotel Dieu Hospital	2,403 57
Collingwood, General and Marine Hospital	542 79
Fort William, Jno. McKellar Memorial Hospital	1,262 03
Gravenhurst, Muskoka Cottage	2,265 45
Galt, Galt Hospital	711 56
Guelph, General Hospital	2,445 34
do St. Joseph's Hospital	1,173 95
Hamilton, City Hospital	5,821 67
do do (arrears for 1905)	4,118 46
do St. Joseph's Hospital	1,427 24
Kenora, St. Joseph's Hospital	438 88
Kingston, General Hospital	3,045 90
do Hotel Dieu Hospital	5,611 55
Lindsay, Ross Memorial Hospital	491 01
London, General Hospital	4,059 70
do St. Joseph's Hospital	802 43
Mattawa, General Hospital	817 77
Midland, General Hospital	128 75
North Bay, Queen Victoria Memorial Hospital	587 37
Ottawa, General Protestant Hospital	2,714 92
do Misericorde Maternity Hospital	1,427 44
do do do do (arrears for 1905)..	1,389 02
do Maternity Hospital	384 67

HOSPITALS AND CHARITIES.—*Continued.*

HOSPITALS AND CHARITIES.—*Continued.*

The Treasurer—*Continued.*

Ottawa, Roman Catholic Hospital	4,374 54	
do St. Luke's General Hospital	3,245 51	
Owen Sound, General and Marine Hospital	910 23	
Pembroke, General Hospital	1,621 12	
do Cottage Hospital	786 57	
Peterborough, Nicholl's Hospital	1,037 93	
do St. Joseph's Hospital	1,364 59	
Port Arthur, St. Joseph's Hospital	1,284 08	
Renfrew, Victoria Hospital	375 30	
Sarnia General Hospital	1,117 33	
Sault Ste. Marie, General Hospital	2,037 14	
St. Catharines, General and Marine	1,329 89	
St. Thomas, Amasa Wood Hospital	335 94	
Smith's Falls, St. Francis Hospital	467 02	
Stratford, General Hospital	437 64	
Sudbury, St. Joseph's Hospital	996 17	
Thessalon, Victorian Hospital	380 95	
Toronto, General Hospital	12,147 42	
do Grace Hospital	3,255 05	
do Orthopedic Hospital	1,346 42	
do Sick Children's Hospital	7,131 00	
do St. Michael's Hospital	8,614 12	
do Western Hospital	4,710 01	
Walkerton, General Hospital	281 86	
Windsor, Hotel Dieu Hospital	977 29	
Woodstock, Woodstock Hospital	485 90	
		116,068 25

The Treasurer :

Belleville, Home for the Friendless	185 15	
Bowmanville Home for the Aged and Infirm	335 58	
Brantford, The Widows' Home	316 47	
Chatham, Home for the Friendless	454 65	
Cobourg, Home for the Aged and Infirm	242 13	
Cornwall, St. Paul's Home for the Aged	1,305 85	
Dundas, House of Providence	3,190 77	
Guelph, The Elliott Home	91 28	
do House of Providence	1,615 11	
Hamilton, Home for Aged Women	918 89	
do House of Refuge	2,596 09	
do St. Peter's Home	533 05	
Kingston, Home for Friendless Women	273 88	
do House of Industry	1,163 82	
do House of Providence	4,721 22	
Lindsay, Home for the Aged	596 82	
London, Convalescent Home	110 39	
do Home for Aged People	2,047 57	
do Home for Incurables	689 01	
do Roman Catholic House of Refuge	2,804 62	
Ottawa, Home for Aged	868 63	
do Home for Friendless Women	868 45	
do Home for Incurables	514 99	
do Refuge Branch Orphan's Home	538 93	
do Refuge of Our Lady of Charity	4,201 79	
do St. Charles' Hospice	4,980 71	
do St. Patrick's Refuge	2,582 02	
Peterborough, House of Providence	1,481 69	
do The Protestant Home	620 97	
St. Thomas, The Thomas Williams' Home	495 81	
Toronto, Aged Men's Home	663 60	
do Convalescent Home	590 35	
do Good Shepherd Female Refuge	2,477 61	
do Home for Incurables	5,373 90	
do House of Industry	4,060 14	

HOSPITALS AND CHARITIES.—*Continued.*

HOSPITALS AND CHARITIES.—*Continued.*

The Treasurer—*Continued.*

Toronto,	House of Providence	11,694 48	
do	Industrial Refuge	822 01	
do	Old Folks' Home	755 30	
do	St. John's Hospital	794 40	
do	The Haven	1,659 24	
Windsor,	Home for the Friendless	591 22	
			70,828 59

Treasurer:

Fort William, Orphans' Home		340 50	
Hamilton, Boys' Home		462 10	
do	Girls' Home	218 24	
do	Home for the Friendless	483 23	
do	Protestant Orphan Asylum	19 72	
do	Salvation Army Rescue Home	336 07	
do	St. Mary's Orphan Asylum	705 26	
Kingston, Hotel Dieu Orphanage		334 84	
do	House of Providence Orphanage	345 34	
do	Orphans' Home	446 94	
London, Protestant Orphans' Home		271 30	
do	Roman Catholic Orphans' Home	457 72	
do	Salvation Army Rescue Home for Women	529 65	
do	Womans' Refuge and Infants' Home	269 50	
Ottawa, Infants' home		268 10	
do	Orphans' Home	389 26	
do	Salvation Army Rescue Home & Children's Shelter	704 07	
do	St. Joseph's Orphan Asylum	1,373 22	
do	St. Patrick's Orphan Asylum	553 10	
Picton, Loyal True Blue Orphanage		255 88	
St. Agatha, St. Agatha Orphan Asylum		370 12	
St. Catharines. Protestant Home, Orphanage Branch		145 46	
Toronto, Boys' Home		739 50	
do	Girls' Home	704 02	
do	Infants' Home	918 84	
do	Protestant Orphans' Home	982 26	
do	Roman Catholic Orphan Asylum	2,466 46	
do	S. A. Home for Women	497 29	
do	St. Nichol's Home	428 08	
do	The Working Boys' Home	347 04	
			16,363 02

Infants' Home and Infirmary, Toronto:

Special grant for Infirmary work		500 00

Toronto General Hospital:

Special grant for Construction of a wing for treatment of Acute Neuresthenics		5,500 00
Riordon Paper Mills, paper for report		24 38
Warwick Bros. & Rutter, printing and binding report		78 35

COUNTY HOUSES OF REFUGE ($8,000.00).

Prince Edward Co., Treasurer, grant		4,000 00
Northumberland and Durham Co., Treasurer, grant		4,000 00

FREE HOSPITAL FOR CONSUMPTIVES. TWP. YORK (4,000.00).

Hammond, H. C., Treasurer, grant in aid of construction of building		4,000 00

HAMILTON HEALTH ASSOCIATION, HOSPITAL FOR CONSUMPTIVES ($4,000.00).

Hospital for Consumptives, grant		4,000 00

HOSPITALS AND CHARITIES.—*Continued.*

MAINTENANCE OF PATIENTS IN THE MUNICIPAL SANITORIA FOR CONSUMPTIVES ($10,253.39).

Treasurer, Muskoka Free Hospital, on account of maintenance	7,836	89
Treasurer, Toronto Free Hospital do	2,416	50

INDUSTRIAL SCHOOLS ($82,459.22).

Alexandra Industrial School, 1905..........................	812	25
1906	3,904	75
Grant, new cottage and alterations	20,000	00
St. John's Industrial School, 1905	2,073	43
1906	7,852	03
St. Mary's do do 1905	585	06
1906	2,205	73
Victoria do do 1905	4,715	17
1906	20,310	80
Grant, new cottage	20,000	00

SUNDRY GRANTS ($7,550.00).

Associated Charities	500	00
Prisoners' Aid Association	2,500	00
Royal Humane Society	250	00
Salvation Army	1,500	00
Society for Redemption of Inebriates	300	00
Victorian Order of Nurses	2,500	00

CHILDREN'S AID WORK ($6,957.89).

Allan, Mrs. A., board of children	43	46
Alexandra Industrial School, allowance towards cost, supervising girls' discharge from institution	200	00
Archer, Rev. W. H., travelling expenses *re* runaway girl	13	05
Bell Telephone Co., rent of instrument, 16.75; Belden, Dr. G. F., dentistry, 48.50	65	25
Blackstock, D., medicine and nursing child, 25.00; Bond, J. R., medicines, 16.15 ....*.	41	15
Boys' Home, board of children	76	00
Brown, H. A., services receiving and placing boys in foster homes. 25.00; travelling expenses, 3.25	28	25
Bray, Dr. R. V., services special Western agent, 100.00; travelling expenses, 33.15	133	15
Burns, P. & Co., 15.70 tons eggs coal at 5.45, 81.94; 5 tons nut coal at 5.45, 27.25	109	19
Central Prison Industries, beds and mattresses for Shelter	24	00
Campbell, Mrs. D., medical attendance and medicine, 3.85; board of children, 53.20; clothing for children, 8.25; travelling expenses, 3.65......	68	95
Canadian Conference of Charities, grant toward printing and distributing reports	250	00
C. P. Railway Co., fares of children, 100.63; Connor Bros., boots and shoes, 1.65	102	23
Consumers' Gas Co., gas, 12.40; Crawford, J. E., travelling expenses visiting children, 3.40	15	80
Children's Aid Society, London, grant *re* expenses of work outside district	400	00
Cunningham, Mrs. V. A., board of children, 1,388.70; allowance for sewing, 34.00; sundry disbursements, 28.75	1,380	45
Cunningham, D. C., expenses *re* children at Uxbridge	6	50
Dorland, Mrs. A., allowance for service placing girls	25	00
Eaton, T. & Co., clothing for children, 440.98; Fegan, D. L., rubbers, etc., 2.00	442	98
Fearnby, Geo., plastering, 5.00; G. T. Railway Co., fares of children, 193.10	198	10
Gurney Stove Co., repairs to hot water boiler, 107.39; Grand, Mrs. M. E., sewing, 5.50	112	89

HOSPITALS AND CHARITIES.—*Continued.*

CHILDREN'S AID WORK.—*Continued.*

Hospital for Sick Children, boots for Bertha Weston, 6.00; Howell, L., travelling expenses for child, 2.90	8 90
Hamilton, Grimsby and Beamsville Railway Co., fares of children	1 40
Herald, Mrs. B. F., services finding homes for children, 15.00; Haven, The, board of children, 20.00	35 00
Harris, Rev. P. C. D., services acting as agent at Guelph, 50.00; Harrington Bros., glass, 1.18	51 18
Hunter, W., expenses bringing boy from Hamilton, 3.50; Kettles, W. J., eye glasses, 2.75	6 25
Kearne, Jno., travelling expenses visiting children	67 85
Lediard, Rev. Jas., services organizing societies and visting children, 75.00; travelling expenses, 118.45	193 45
Lediard, Mrs. J., services of late Jas. Lediard, organizing and visiting children	150 00
McGill, Wm. & Co., ½ cord of pine, 3.25; McFaul, Dr. J. H., medical attendance, 6.00	9 25
McCallum, Rev. D., services visiting children, 61.60; Methodist Book Room, Christmas cards, 7.35	63 95
Miller, R. G., board of boy, 10.00; Mains, W. H., travelling expenses re May Miller, 5.90	15 90
Miller, Rev. C. R., expenses arranging for foster homes, etc.	25 00
Michall, T. C., services and expenses re child neglect case, 6.50; Nerlich & Co., toys, etc., 42.76	49 26
Menzies, Rev. A. D., board of child, 32.00; Park Bros., photos, 5.50	37 50
Richardson, W. K., salary at 600.00 per annum, 333.33; travelling expenses, 137.70	471 03
Rogers, Elias, wood, 3.25; Sacred Heart Orphanage, board of child, 29.47	32 72
Saunders, J., allowance for services	20 00
Sharpe, Mrs. E. E., board of boy, 7.50; travelling expenses, 12.90; visiting and supervising children, 15.00	35 40
Sedore, R. J., services assisting Rev. Jas. Lediard	5 00
Skinner, Dr. E. Lelia, medical service, 6.00; Stundon, A., services re V. Meyers, 23.40	29 40
Siche Gas Co., generator for Shelter, 15.75; St. Basil's Truth Secretary, 100 prayer books, 5.00	20 75
Thomson, S. M., services, 1,199.33; travelling expenses, 364.54; postage stamps, 4.00	1,567 87
Tolchard, D. F., dinners for Children's Aid officials re amending Act	2 00
Toronto Electric Light Co., light, 43.56; Toronto Orthopedic Hospital, boots, etc., for children, 34.40	77 96
Traill, A. J., services as agent, Brockville, 25.00; Trunk and Leather Goods Co., scopes, 21.20	46 20
Upper Canada Tract Society, books, 5.00; Western Hospital, board and nursing girl, 11.75	16 75
Webb, Rev. Jas., finding homes for girls, 45.00; Ward, A. R., photos of children, 13.97	58 97
Waterworks Department, water, 8.00; Wallis, F., plumbing, 1.50	9 50
Wilkinson, Jno., services special agent to foster homes	25 00
Young Women's Guild, board of children	12 00

SMALLPOX OUTBREAKS AND SANITARY INVESTIGATIONS (S1,586.47).

Bell, R. W., M.D., travelling expenses and disbursements	350 50
Birdil, D. M., travelling expenses re Vermillion River camps	10 00
Doane Bros., cab hire, 2.25; Dominion Express Co., charges, 6.20	8 45
Hamilton, Jno. A., M.D., medical attendance re smallpox outbreak French River	50 00
Irwin, C. W., brokerage	50
Lowe's Sanitarium, hospital model	17 25
McIlwain, S. C., services distributing posters of lakes in Muskoka, 10.00; travelling expenses, 9.75	19 75
Quibell, W. A., services re outbreak at Burton's Camp, 30.00; board, 6.00; telephone messages, 55c.	36 55
Sault *Star*, printing cards for quarantine purposes	3 00

HOSPITALS AND CHARITIES.—*Continued.*

SMALLPOX OUTBREAKS, ETC.—*Continued.*

Scott Samuel, salary as Sanitary Inspector Township Coleman, 600.00; travelling expenses, 251.57	851	57
Tucker Tent Co., tent model	15	00
Watts, Dr. F. S., services as Sanitary Inspector New Ontario, 125.00; travelling expenses, 98.90	223	90
Total Hospitals and Charities	$334,169	56

REPAIRS AND MAINTENANCE.

GOVERNMENT HOUSE ($14,228.88).

Armstrong, Fred. & Co., repairing electric wires, etc., 143.10; contract, hot water heating, greenhouse, 825.00	968	10
Banks, W. J., climbing and lining flagpole, 10.00; Beers, Wm., weather strips, 2.00	12	00
Bell Telephone Co., rent of instruments, 46.00; Brown, A. M., painting, etc., 90.06	136	06
Burroughes, F. C. & Co., rent of folding chairs, 17.50; Caine, T. H., painting, 53.00	70	50
Canadian Vacuum Cleaning Co., cleaning carpets	29	61
Catto, Jno. & Co., blankets, quilts, etc., 686.30; Chaney & Co., pillows, repairs to mattresses, etc., 19.15	705	45
Consumers' Gas Co., gas, 351.36; Cowan, J., cleaning chimneys, 11.00	362	36
Dinnis Richard & Son, lumber, etc.	450	35
Douglas Bros., repairing roofs, etc., 21.30; clearing snow off roof, 9.00	30	30
Durham Rubber Co., hose and couplings, 6.56; Eaton, T. & Co., curtains and rings, etc., 389.42	395	98
Fayle, V. P., expenses weighing coal	3	30
Gearing, T. V., contract building rose house, 2,523.75; repairing fence, 27.90	2,551	65
Godden, C. P., furnishings, 51.35; Gore, R., cleaning snow off walks, 50.00	101	35
Gowans, Kent & Co., glassware	44	96
Graham, Joseph, twelve months' salary as gardener and caretaker	550	00
Gurney Foundry Co., jackets, etc., 43.19; repairing boiler, 1.62	44	81
Guthrie, R., bulbs, evergreens for arch, etc., 199.30; Hutchinson, A. J., work on grounds, 21.00	220	30
Jennings, C. B., laying conservatory carpet, etc., 89.64; Junor, Wm., china and glassware, etc., 147.40	237	04
Kay, Jno., Son & Co., carpets, etc., 201.21; King Construction Co., iron framing for rose house, 333.57	534	78
Knickerbocker Ice Co., ice, 158.70; Littleford, W. O. & Son, repairing china, 2.20	160	90
McGill, Wm., 9 tons of nut coal at 6.00 per ton, 54.00; 23 tons of stove coal at 6.00 per ton, 138.00; 116.800 tons stove coal at 5.61 per ton, 653.00; 27 tons of nut coal at 5.61 per ton, 151.49	996	49
McLaughlin, Gourley, Ltd., repairing furniture, etc.	47	00
Miller & Sons, bulbs and plants, 73.73; Morrison, Jas. Brass Mfg. Co., gas brackets, etc., 25.47	99	20
Murray, J. G. & Co., oil, 1.25; Murray, W. A. & Co., linoleum, carpets, rugs, etc., 337.24	338	49
Newspapers, sundry advertising, 9.15; Ontario Lead and Wire Co., pipe, etc., 30.45	39	60
Ontario Lime Association, cement and mortar	4	58
Pay lists, wages of carpenters, plumbers, carter, etc.	2,645	75
Phillips Mfg. Co., Ltd., repairing mirror, 15.00; Pike, D. & Co., flags and repairs, etc., 229.25	244	25

REPAIRS AND MAINTENANCE.—*Continued.*

GOVERNMENT HOUSE.—*Continued.*

Queen City Concrete Paving Co., sand, gravel, etc., 14.50; Quinlon, Jas., clearing snow off walks, 3.00	17 50
Rice Lewis & Son, hardware, etc., 19.13; Robertson, Jas. Co., castings, etc., 3.37	22 50
Shipway Iron, Bell & Wire Mfg. Co., repairing electric bells, etc.	5 40
Smith's Toronto Dye Works, cleaning curtains, etc., 65.35; Stewart, Jno., painting fence, 267.00	332 35
Thomas, M., gravel, 78.00; Townley & London, painting, etc., 288.53	366 53
Toronto Electric Light Co., light current, 1,030.33; lamps, pipe, etc., 6.54; services man night of ball, 4.40; Prince Arthur's visit, 9.20; work of men repairing, 17.73	1,068 20
Wanless, Jno. & Co., table furnishings, etc., 259.51; Waterworks Department, water, 43.41	302 92
Urb'ach, C. A., cartage, 10.00; Vokes Hardware Co., hardware, etc., 34.64	44 64
Whitehead, F. W., clock, repairs, etc., 8.00; White, W. W., aigulettes for aides, 35.68	43 63

ATTORNEY-GENERAL'S DEPARMENT ($1,011.33).

Armstrong, Fred., desk lamps, etc.	27 45
Amsden, C., cleaning office, 6.86; Craik, Mrs., cleaning office, 18.29	25 15
Dunn, Wm. R. & Co., cupboard, etc., 73.50; Dennis, Richard & Son, lumber, 4.65	78 15
Geddes, J. W., picture frames, 6.00; Jennings, C. B., repairing furniture, etc., 7.25	13 25
Kent, B. & H. B., repairing clock, 1.50; Murray, W. A. & Co., cleaning, repairing, etc., 227.46	228 96
Monarch Typewriter Co., typewriter cabinet	32 50
O'Connor, Mrs., cleaning office	298 75
Pike, D. & Co., awnings	25 50
Rawlinson, L., furniture, etc.	92 95
Tangent Cycle Co., repairing messenger's wheel, 7.50; Townley & London, painting ceilings and walls, 179.16	186 66
Vokes Hardware Co., hardware, etc.	2 01

LANDS, FORESTS AND MINES ($3,557.33).

Armstrong, Fred. & Co., portable lamps, etc.	20 25
Baker, Mrs. L., office cleaning	319 75
Can. General Electric Co., supplies, 31.92; Craik, Mrs., office cleaning, 31.00	62 92
Canada Cabinet Manftg. Co., furniture, etc.	418 50
Dominion Portrait Co., frames and glass, 1.50; Dunn, Wm. R., desk and chairs, 46.00	47 50
Eaton, T. Co., chairs and cushions	27 00
Jennings, C. B., cleaning carpets, repg. furniture, etc.	26 52
Murray, W. A. & Co., linoleum, carpets, etc.	434 26
Office Specialty Manftg. Co., filing boxes, deal table, cases, etc.	1,924 85
Rawlinson, L., furniture, repairs, etc.	51 28
Taylor, J. J., adjusting door lock, 60c.; Townley & London, staining and varnishing, 1.25	1 85
United Typewriter Co., typewriter stand	7 50
Vokes Hardware Co., hardware, etc.	9 15
Wilson, Mrs., office cleaning, 204.00; Whitehead, F. W., repairing clocks, 2.00	206 00

PUBLIC WORKS DEPARMENT ($1,169.70).

Armstrong, Fred., portable lamps	7 00
Can. General Electric Co., desk lamps, 2.46; Craik, Mrs., office cleaning, 18.75	21 21
Dunn, Wm. R. & Co., furniture, 27.00; Dinnis, Richard & Son, lumber, 9.00	36 00
Fletcher Manftg. Co., carpet sweeper, etc.	12 30
Jennings, C. B., cleaning carpets, etc.	12 28

17 P.A.

REPAIRS AND MAINTENANCE.—*Continued.*

PUBLIC WORKS DEPARTMENT.—*Continued.*

Kay, Jno., Son & Co., wardrobe chair, etc., 7.75; King's Printer, document boxes, 21.00	28 75
Library Bureau of Canada, map cabinet, etc., 120.00; Lavery, Mrs. S., office cleaning, 330.00	450 00
Murray, W. A. & Co., linoleum, carpets, etc.	324 01
Rawlinson, L., repairing furniture	4 65
Reynolds, G. N. & Co., metallic pigeon hole case, 135.00; map case, etc., 60.70	195 70
Scheur, E., repairing clock	1 50
Townley & London, painting; etc.	73 06
Vokes Hardware Co., hat and coat hooks, etc.	1 74
Whitehead, L. W., repairing clock	1 50

TREASURY DEPARTMENT ($1,194.84).

Amsden, C., office cleaning, 230.26; Armstrong, Fred. & Co., lamp shade, 40c.	230 66
Coyell, Alf., telephone cabinet, 55.00; Craik, Mrs., office cleaning, 7.11...	62 11
Dunn, Wm. R. & Co., counter. 85.00; book case sections, etc., 17.00	102 00
Jennings, C. B., picture framing, 6.00; Library Bureau of Canada, document boxes, 42.65	48 65
Murray, W. A., carpets, 314.29; Office Specialty Mfg. Co., document boxes, 91.15	405 44
Ovens, T. A., varnishing, reglazing, etc., 12.00; Taylor, J. & J., on account time lock, 100.00	112 00
Townley & London, painting ceilings and walls	187 61
United Typewriter Co., typewriter, cabinet and chair	30 00
Vokes Hardware Co., pulleys, etc.	16 37

AUDIT OFFICE ($377.00).

Adams Furniture Co., couch, 55.00; Armstrong, Fred., portable lamps, buzzers, etc., 8.23	63 23
Dunn, W. R. & Co., desks and chairs, 110.00; Jennings, C. B., repairing chairs, furniture, etc., 14.75	124 75
McLaughlin, Gourley, Limited, re-covering table	11 75
Murray, W. A. & Co., carpets, linoleums, etc.	177 27

PROVINCIAL SECRETARY'S DEPARTMENT ($3,442.17).

Adams Furniture Co., wardrobes, 36.00; Amsden, C., office cleaning, 101.63	137 63
Armstrong, Fred. Co., shades, lamps, fixtures, etc	34 25
Barber, Mrs., office cleaning, 32.50; Canada Cabinet Co., cabinets, 79.36	111 86
Canada General Electric Co., desk lamps, etc., 16.37; motor fan, 13.95...	30 32
Clark, Mary, office cleaning, 269.60; Coyell, Alf., railing, 52.00	321 60
Craik, E., office cleaning, 16.25; Dinnis Rd. & Son, turned legs, 5.00	21 25
Dunn, Wm. R. & Co., furniture, etc., 647.50; Eaton, T. Co., awnings, 25.50	673 00
Jennings, C. B., repairing cushion, laying linoleum, etc	73 01
Kay, John, Son & Co., folding cabinet, 46.00; Lee, Mrs., office cleaning, 23.25	69 25
Library Bureau of Canada, cabinets, chairs, desks, etc	484 27
McLaughlin, Gourlay, Limited, repairing tables and chairs	12 75
Monarch Typewriter Co., cabinets and chairs, 100.50; Murray, W. A. & Co., carpets, rugs, etc., 645.78	746 28
National Typewriter Co., cabinets and chairs	31 75
Office Specialty Co., telephone brackets, special cabinets, etc.	321 50
Ovens, T. A., kalsomining, etc., 68.20; Queen City Carpet & Rug Renovating Co., laying carpets, repairing furniture, etc., 15.51	83 71
Rawlinson, L., repairing furniture, 11.05; Reynolds, G. N. & Co., chairs, desks, etc, 91.50	102 55
Ryan, M., office cleaning, 100.00; Ryrie Bros., clock, 3.50	103 50
Simpson, Robt., Co., chairs, 26.50; Taylor, J. J. & Co., changing safe combination, repairs, etc., 2.10	28 60
Townley & London, painting, varnishing, kalsomining, etc	38 79
Vokes Hardware Co., locks, door checks, etc.	16 3

17a P.A.

REPAIRS AND MAINTENANCE.—*Continued.*

DEPARTMENT OF AGRICULTURE ($1,321.41).

Armstrong, Fred., chandelier lamps, etc.	33 00
Carbonized Paper Co., typewriter chair, 7.00; Canada Cabinet Co., table, desk, etc., 68.40	75 40
Craik, Mrs., office cleaning	15 00
Dinnis, Richard & Son, lumber	3 71
Eaton, T. Co., awnings	8 50
Jennings, C. B., repairing furniture	3 25
Library Bureau of Canada. desk	21 50
Murray, W. A. & Co., carpets, linoleums, etc.	413 93
Office Specialty Co., document boxes, etc.	8 00
Patterson, Estate of A., framing photos	1 00
Rice, Lewis & Son, hooks, 2.70; Reynolds, G. N. & Co., table, 12.50	15 20
Rawlinson, L., furniture	133 00
Sangster, B., office cleaning at 7.50 per week	390 00
Townley & London, painting, kalsomining, etc.	174 92
United Typewriter Co., cabinet	25 00

PARLIAMENT BUILDINGS.

Salaries ($15,499.00).

B. O. Bryne :	Twelve months' salary as		General Clerk of Works.	1,200 00
J. P. Crotty :	do	do	Carpenter	800 00
M. J. Quinn :	Four and one quarter months' salary as		Mechanical Superintendent	479 00
J. J. Heydon :	Twelve months' salary as		Plumber	900 00
D. M. Medcalf :	do	do	Inspector of Boilers and Public Institutions	1,200 00
Thos. Burns :	do	do	Engineer	1,200 00
R. J. Griffiths :	do	do	Assistant Engineer and Steamfitter	720 00
John Bennett :	do	do	Fireman	650 00
S. Pears :	do	do	"	650 00
V. H. Annable :	do	do	"	650 00
Wm. Reddick :	do	do	Elevator Assistant	650 00
Richard Power :	do	do	"	650 00
Wm. Davidson .	do	do	Porter	650 00
Dan. Harrington:	do	do	"	650 00
G. W. Franks :	do	do	"	650 00
A. Currie :	do	do	"	700 00
S. Dunbar	do	do	Night Watchman	700 00
E. R. Lucas :	do	do	"	700 00
Robt. Armstrong:	do	do	"	700 00
J. W. Montgomery:	do	do	Porter	650 00
J. W. Houston :	do	do	Superintendent of Grounds and Gardens	350 00

Water, fuel and light ($8,756.33).

Consumers' Gas Co., gas 480.88; Fayle, V. P., expenses re weighing coal, 2.10	482 98
Grenadier Ice Co., ice	511 30
McGill, Wm. & Co., 696.1016 tons pea coal at 4.20 per ton, 2,940.46; 3 tons stove coal at 6.00 per ton, 18.00	2,958 46
Newspapers, advertising *re* fuel	9 15
Toronto Electric Light Co., power current, 358.54; light current, 3,846.50	4,228 64
Water Works Dept., water	565 80

Furnishings of Legislative Chambers and Speaker's Department ($1,803.93).

Armstrong, Fred., Lindsay lights, 1.80; Cairns. B., brass plate, 6.00	7 80
Canada Stationery Co., typewriter desk, 30.00; Dunn, Wm. R. & Co., furniture. etc., 31.28	61 28
Dorrien Plating Mfg. Co., repairing paper files, 18.35; Eaton, T. & Co., furniture. etc., 185.40	203 75
Geddes, J. W., framing pictures, etc., 3.75; Hobbs, Samuel, iron handles and stands, 1.20	4 95

REPAIRS AND MAINTENANCE.—*Continued.*

PARLIAMENT BUILDINGS.—*Continued.*

Harper, Wm., to pay gas burners for chamber, 10.00; duty, freight and brokerage on same, 4.45	14 45
Jennings, C. B., upholtsering, cleaning carpets, etc., 379.23; Kent, B. & H. B., repairing clock, and silverware, 5.25	384 48
Kent, Ambrose, repairing clock, 1.25; Kay, Jno., Son & Co., linoleum, etc., 168.62	169 87
Library Bureau of Canada, filing cases, etc., 26.50; Maas, W. T., picture glass, .28	26 78
Murray, W. A. and Co., linoleums, carpets, etc.	768 24
Ontario Compressed Air Dutsless House Cleaning Co., renovating carpets	12 50
Reynolds, G. N. & Co., furniture, etc., 78.00; Rawlinson, L., walnut chairs, etc., 62.40	140 40
Scheuer, E., repairing clock, 2.00; Vokes Hardware Co., night latch and hooks, etc., 4.93	6 93
Whitehead, F. W., repairing clocks	2 50

Supplies, tools, caretakers of grounds, and general repairs ($16,967.06).

Armstrong, Fred. & Co., electric supplies, 81.75; Beers, Wm., weather strips, 24.00	105 75
Bell Telephone Co., rent of instrument, 22.01; moving 'phone, 1.00..........	23 01
Brondon and Gilbert, saw-dust, 2.50; Clappison Packing and Covering Co., covering pipe, 6.75	9 25
Canadian General Electric Co., supplies, 95.24; Central Electric and School supply, etc., torch, 2.00	97 24
C. P. Railway Co., freight charges, 1.95; Crotty, P. J., travelling expenses, 7.50	9 45
Canadian Vacuum Cleaning Co., cleaning rooms, 25.00; Davidson and Hay, soap, sal soda, etc., 10.36	35 36
Dinnis, Richard & Son, lumber, closet seats, etc., 220.16; Douglas Bros., repairing roofs, 56.58	276 74
Dalton Bros., soap, 14.00; Dorrien Plating Co., branding irons, 9.00.......	23 00
Delmage, R. O., services temporary messenger, 34.00; Dominion Express Co., charges, 35c.	34 35
Elliott and Co., chemicals, 2.47; Elevator Specialty Co., repairing elevator, 24.50	26 97
Eaton, T. & Co., awnings, furniture, etc., 179.62; Godden, C. P., brooms, 8.20	187 82
Gilday, R., clearing snow from roof, 113.40; repairig roof gutters, etc., 248.62	362 02
Gurney, Tilden & Co., push plate, cylinders, etc., 55.93; Hobbs, Samuel, furnishing platform scales, 140.55	196 48
Imperial Varnish and Color Co., oil, soaps and turpentine, etc.	192 39
Inglis, John & Co., repairing boiler, 84.50; Jaynes Electrical Co., box station dials, 3.50	88 00
Jones, Jno., three months' salary as fireman, at 50.00 per month..........	150 00
King's Printer, toilet paper, 25.50; Lumbers, Jas. & Co., matches, sal soda, etc., 19.24	44 74
Littleford, W. O. and Son, repairing closet	2 75
Morrison, Jas., Brass Mfg. Co., castings, fixtures, etc..........	70 07
Moroney, J., felt boots for use of horse with roller, 11.00; Muirhead, A., chamois and sponge, 41.90	52 90
Mackenzie & Co., frame tablet, 23.55; Murray, W. A. & Co., feather dusters, 6.00	29 55
National Oil Co., oil soap, 29.10; National Drug and Chemical Co., chemicals, .40	29 50
Ontario Lead and Wire Co., sink, pipe, washes, etc.	151 61
Ovens, T. A., reglazing window reflectors, 24.00; Ontario Rubber Co., rubber cuspidors, etc., 7.50	31 50
Pay list, wages, carpenters, bricklayers, plumbers, laborers, etc.	9,358 66
Pay list, wages of dusters and cleaners, etc.	3,833 58
Power Bros., lowering flag pole, 5.00; Pike, D. & Co., splicing wire rope, 12.25	17 25
Polson Iron Works, repairing boilers, 23.39; Rice, Lewis & Son, hardware, etc, 51.22	74 61

REPAIRS AND MAINTENANCE.—*Continued.*

PARLIAMENT BUILDINGS.—*Continued*

Repairs Specialty Co., repairing elevators, 21.00; new cables for· elevators, 347.00 .... | 368 00

Robertson, Jas. Co., castings, etc., 11.34; Rochester Germicide Co., disinfecting appliances, 5.00 .... | 16 34

Seamen, Ken⁺ Co., tape for blinds. 56.48; Simonds Can. Saw Co., repairing saws, 1.50 .... | 57 98

Stewart, Jas., painting, 55.57; Townley & London, painting, glazing, etc., 506.90 .... | 562 47

Toronto Railway Co.. car tickets for workmen, 107.00; Thomas, M., gravel for walks, 224.25 .... | 331 25

Vokes Hardware Co., hardware, etc., 83.72; Williams, N., cartage, 1.75.. | 85 47

Whitehead, F. W., repairing clock, 1.00; Zenner, The Disinfecting Co., 30.00 | 31 00

Interior alterations ($1,780.90).

Armstrong, Fred and Co., contract electric fittings and wiring, 180.00; fitting railings, chandeliers, etc., 74.00; plumbing, 163.11 .... | 417 11

Browne, A. M., lettering cupboard, painting, etc. .... | 236 25

Coyell, Alf., storm windows. ash partitions, etc., 380.09; Dinnis, Richard and Son, lumber, 62.05 .... | 442 14

Gurney, Tilden & Co., altering and repairing cylinders, etc., 53.30; Haynes, W. J., plastering. 9.46 .... | 62 76

Jennings, C. B., cushions, 4.00; Morrison, Jas., Brass Mfg. Co., electric fixtures, air vents, etc., 59.47 .... | 63 47

Ovens. T. A.. painting walls. etc., 56.00; Office Specialty Mfg. Co., desks and chairs, 405.50 .... | 461 50

Rice Lewis & Son. coat hooks. 8.25; Vokes Hardware Co.. hardware. etc. 89.42 .... | 97 67

Trees. plants, shrubs, etc. ($468.28).

Dominion Transport Co., freight on trees, .76; Foster Pottery Co., flower pots, 11.87 .... | 12 63

King's Printer, sponges, etc., 3.50; Miller & Sons, plants, shrubs, etc., 329.98 .... | 333 48

Rice, Lewis & Son, hose, lawn mower, etc.. 71.17; Smith, E. D., trees, shrubs, etc., 51.00 .... | 122 17

Uniforms for messengers, attendants, etc. ($583.50).

Dineen, W. & D. Co., hats and police helmet .... | 43 50

Murray, W. A. & Co., uniforms for messengers .... | 540 00

Library fittings and shelving ($218.71).

Aikenhead Hardware Co., hinges, .40; Bawden, F. A., lumber, 109.16.. | 109 56

Hall, A., key for room, .15; Office Specialty Co., book racks, 109.00.:....... | 109 15

Archivist's office ($95.25).

Burroughes, F. C. & Co., linoleum .... | 80 01

Jennings, C. B., framing pictures .... | 15 24

Painting corridors and offices ($1,912.05).

Browne, A. M., on account of painting, plasterwork on walls and ceilings | 1,776 00

Townley and London, painting, oiling and kalsomining as per contract.... | 136 05

Outstanding accounts ($2,100.55).

Burroughes. F. C. & Co.. hire of chairs, 5.00; Coyell. Alf.. oak partition. etc., 60.60 .... | 65 60

Dominion Radiator Co., pipe, etc., 5.56; Eaton, T. & Co., dusters and mop cloths. 18.00 .... | 23 56

REPAIRS AND MAINTENANCE.—*Continued.*

PARLIAMENT BUILDINGS.—*Continued*

Imperial Varnish and Color Co., oil soap, 27.95; Jennings, C. B., upholstering, cleaning carpets, etc., 5.12	33 07
McGill, Wm. & Co., 391.1575 tons pea coal at 4.20 per ton, 1,645.95; Murray. W. A. & Co., denim, 10.85; cleaning and laying carpets, 54.66	1,711 46
Otis Fensom Elevator Co., cable, 47.60; work, 18.00	65 60
Pease Furnace Co., air vents, 5.10; Rawlinson, L., furniture repairs, 134.62	139 72
Smith, J. B. & Sons, lumber, 15.00; Vokes Hardware Co., hardware, 46.54	61 54
Total Repairs and Maintenance	$76,488 22

PUBLIC BUILDINGS.

ASYLUM FOR INSANE, TORONTO, ($11,060.17).

Engineers' supplies, repairs, etc., ($1,926.21).

Can. General Electric Co., supplies, 31.08; Canada Steam Boiler Equipment Co., grate, fire brick, etc., 133.22	164 30
Inglis, Jno. & Co., repairing boiler	28 48
Morrison, Jas., Bros. Manftg Co., water closets, etc., 291.60; Mott, J. L., iron works, shower baths, 890.00	1,181 60
Pickard, C. E. Co., motors	72 00
Robertson, Jas., Co., castings, baths, closets, sinks, etc.	160 44
Standard Ideal Sanitary Co., baths and fittings	281 26
Taylor, Forbes & Co., valves	38 13

Fittings for office, filing system, and surgical requirements ($922.70).

Canada Cabinet Co., cabinet desk, etc.	159 20
Hartz, J. F. Co., surgical appliances	558 75
Monarch Typewriter Co., typewriter, 110.26; cabinet, 22.50	132 75
Remington Typewriter Co., exchange on typewriter	72 00

Interior repairs and alterations to cold storage, furniture and furnishings ($4,468.11).

Adams Furniture Co., furniture	1,042 15
Brock, W. R. Co., carpets. etc.	174 03
Crown Furniture Co., furniture, 784.50; Cahoon, A., 43.70	828 20
C. P. Ry. Co., freight charges	16 96
C. P. Industries, hospital beds and blankets	1,398 95
G. T. Ry. Co., freight charges	6 77
Hibner, D., furniture	206 10
Jennings, C. B., upholstering, etc.	112 00
Phillips Manftg. Co., beds, moulding, etc., 68.95; Pike, D. & Co., hammocks, 18.00	86 95
Rice, T. G., Wire Manftg. Co., fire guards	120 00
Simpson, R. Co., beds, wall paper, linoleum, etc.	448 80
Singer Sewing Machine Co., sewing machine	27 20

Machinery and repairs for carpenter, shoe shop, laundry and kitchen, farm and garden ($2,647.55).

Gurney Foundry Co., steam carving table, platter, etc.	714 50
McClary Manftg. Co., heaters	56 05
Parmalee, W. H., jacket kettles, etc., 158.00; Phillips, Manftg. Co., mitering and vise machines for carpenter shop, 17.00	175 00
Reid & Co., lumber	170 00
Sparrow, Geo. & Co., rack clothes dryer, 800.00; Wilkinson Plough Co., pulper, straw cutter, 32.00	832 00
York Manftg. Co., 2 brass washers	700 00

PUBLIC BUILDINGS.—*Continued.*

ASYLUM FOR INSANE. TORONTO.—*Continued.*

Repairs to drains, roofs, etc. ($435.60).

Stewart, W. L. & Co.; repairs to roofs 435 60

Tents for tubercular patients ($160.00).

Turner, J. J. & Son, hospital tent 160 00

Fire protection and extinguishers ($500.00).

Alert Fire Appliance Co.. fire extinguishers 275 00
Gutta Percha & Rubber Manftg. Co., fire hose 225 00

ASYLUM FOR INSANE, MIMICO ($22,572.10).

Repairs to drains and subway ($980.00).

Ontario Sewer Pipe Co., pipe 980 00

Electrical Wiring and Improvements in Telephone system ($986.38).

Holmes Electric Protection Co., installation of switch boards and telephones 925 00
McDonald & Willson, lamp cord, shades, etc 61 38

Engineer's supplies and repairs, etc. ($1,178.23).

Canada Foundry Co., spiral stairs, etc., 502.37; Clarke, D., putting in galvanized iron pipe, 161.80 .... 664 17
Inglis, Jno. & Co., repairing boiler 89 48
Parmelee, W. H.. ventilators, 60.00; Power Specialty Co., blower; 50.00... 110 00
Standard Ideal Co., baths, etc. 314 58

Exterior repairs to buildings, etc. ($7,434.79).

Cathro & Co., overalls for diving suit 2 50
Dunn, T. H.; overalls 2 50
Fairbairn, R. P., travelling expenses 3 30
McFarlane, Geo., ladders and rods, 51.50; McQuillan & Co., time and material repairing intake pipe, 4,362.82 .... 4,414 32
Muldoon, J. & Co.. tile, 24.00; Musson, J. G., gravel. 24.00 .... 48 00
Ontario Paving Brick Co.. brick, 945.00; Ontario Rubber Co., sheet packing, etc., 14.05 .... 959 05
Owen Sound Portland Cement Co., cement 208 95
Pay lists, wages of men 465 50
Ross, Alex., services as foreman at 3.50 per diem, 217.00; services as diver, 16.00; travelling expenses self and man, 6.05 .... 239 05
Thomson, J., lumber 1,091 62

Fire protection, hose, escapes, ladders, etc. ($225.00).

Gutta Percha & Rubber Manftg. Co.. fire hose 225 00

Interior repairs and alterations, etc. ($2,512.07).

Burrows, Stewart & Milne Co., scales, 150.48; Burroughes, F. C. & Co., mattresses and pillows, 449.50 .... 599 98
C. P. Industries, asylum beds. etc. 1,038 20
Gurney Foundry Co.. range 150 00
Hees, Geo. H., Son & Co., poles, shades, etc., 40.61; Heintzman & Co., piano, 95.00 .... 135 61
Junor, Wm., furnishings 3 50
Murray, W. A. & Co.. furnishings 16 75
Rooney. N., furnishings 11 33
Singer Sewing Machine Co., sewing machines, 32.00; Simpson, Robt. & Co., furniture, 524.70 .... 556 70

Reconstruction of Cottage "A" ($5,055.19).

Butwell, H., brick, 144.00; Baillie, W., carpentering at 35c. pr. hour, 203.35 .... 347 35

PUBLIC BUILDINGS.—*Continued.*

ASYLUM FOR INSANE, MIMICO.—*Continued.*

Canada Foundry Co., columns, beams, bolts, etc., 150.00; Canada Paint Co., putty, turpentine, etc., 14.47	164	47
Canada General Electric Co., supplies	44	71
Doddridge, J. G., extra work as carpenter, 35.00; Douglas Bros., contract slate roofing. 856.00	891	00
Douglas Bros., galvanized iron work, 6.50; metal ceiling, 365.00	371	50
Gurney Foundry Co., screens and frames	17	70
Heakes, F. R., travelling expenses, 80c.; Hees, Geo. H., Son & Co., shades, 46.15	46	95
Lane, Andrew, felt	2	50
Moore, H. E., car tickets, 10c.; Muldoon, J. & Co., lime, 91.77	91	87
Meredith, Thos. & Co., wire nails, 26.20; Maxwell, R., extra work as carpenter, 90.00	116	20
McDonald & Willson, electrical fittings	50	88
Sundry newspapers, advertising for tenders	64	00
Ontario Lead & Wire Co., baths, castings, etc.	70	66
Pilkington Bros., glass, etc.	39	81
Rice Lewis & Son, bolts and steel bar, etc., 72.97; Roman Stone Co., stone, 58.00	130	97
Reid & Co., lumber, lath, etc., 216.56; Rice, T. G., Wire Manftg. Co., steel grill railing, 57.50	274	06
Scaife, W., doors and sash, 439.00; Simpson & Co., Robt., moulding, 12.75	451	75
Thompson, Jno., lumber, 1,799.00; Taylor, Forbes & Co., radiator valves, 29.81	1,828	81
Watson, B., carpentering	50	00

Machinery and repairs, kitchen, bakeshop, etc. ($1,350.44).

Can. Fairbanks Co., Pipe, etc., 150.58; Dodge Manftg. Co., belting, pulleys, shafts, etc., 142.00	292	58
Gurney Foundry Co., range, etc.. 104.20; Keys & Bull, waggon and implements, 339.00	443	20
Medcalf, D. M., travelling expenses, 1.00; Parmalee, W. W., jacket kettle, 98.00	99	00
Stanley, R. E., set of brass harness, 49.00; Toronto Jctn. Lumber Co., cedar posts, 100.00	149	00
Williams, A. R., Manftg. Co., iron straps	366	66

Underfeed stokers ($2,850.00).

Underfeed Stoker Co., installing stokers	2,850	00

ASYLUM FOR INSANE, LONDON ($9,074.06).

Repairs, drains, etc. ($430.65).

Horkie, Wm., lumber, 67.95; Walker & Logan, brick, 362.70	430	65

Engineer's supplies and repairs, etc. ($3,132.52).

Can. Steam Boiler Equipment Co., cyclone grate	212	50
Empire Manufacturing Co., drinking fountains, 90.00; Gurney Foundry Co., hot water heaters, 201.60; Howie, Wm., lumber, 916.33	1,207	93
Labatt Mfg. Co., pipes and bends. 227.45; Medcalf. D. M., travelling expense *re* renewal of boiler, 31.10	258	55
Parmelee, W. H., ventilating fan	42	00
Polson Iron Works, on account contract, 2 steam heating boilers	1,377	00
Wright, Jas., castings	34	54

Exterior repairs, improvements, etc. ($1,001.88).

Brick Manfg. & Supply Co., lime, 20.00; Heakes, F. R., travelling expenses, 10.75	30	75
Howie, Wm., lumber, 456.23; Kernahan, G. H., lumber, 114.41	570	64
Mann, Jno. & Sons, plaster paris, etc., 145.21; Winnett, W. H., lumber and posts, 255.28	400	49

PUBLIC BUILDINGS.—*Continued.*

ASYLUM FOR INSANE, LONDON.—*Continued*

Fire protection, hose, hydrants, etc. ($722.40).

Alert Fire Appliance Co., fire extinguishers	220	00
Dennis Wire & Iron Co., fire escapes, guards, screens, etc.	450	00
Wheeler, F. C., play pipe, hose, ladder, etc.	52	40

Interior repairs, alterations, etc. ($952.11).

Bott & rown, wardrobe and seats, 91.00; Burrow, Stewart & Milne. scales, 14.26	105	26
C. P. Industries, brass bed, 22.00; G. T. Ry. Co., freight charges, 10.37	32	37
Hibner, D. & Co., furniture, 276.30; Howden, D. H., scales, 19.50	295	80
Kingsmill, T. F.. carpet, etc., 151.45; McClary Manufacturing Co., brackets, etc., 88.83	240	28
Moore, H. E., travelling expenses, 8.40; Simpson, Robert, Co., pictures, 235.00	243	40
Singer Sewing Machine Co., sewing machine	35	00

Machinery and repairs to kitchen, etc. ($1,297.50).

Anderson, J. W., teaming, 21.00; Brand, W. H., power sprayer, etc., 125.00	146	00
Clare, Robt., gravel and teaming, 32.38; Crosbie, R., tile. 50.00	82	38
Dennis Wire & Iron Works Co., potato digger, 17.00; Glass, S. S., lathe, 270.00	287	00
Howie, Wm., lumber, 25.00; Joyce, Dane, trees, 20.00	45	00
Lamb, H. B. Fence Co., wire fencing, 243.88; Quinell, J., teaming, 8.75	252	63
Smith, E. D., trees, 99.19; Talbot, W. H. K., fanning mill, 7.00	106	19
Turner, Wm. & Son, waggon, 48.00; Toronto Laundry Machine Co., washer, 330.30	378	30

Railway switch into grounds ($1,537.00).

Can. Pacific Railway Co., track laying, ballasting, ties, etc.	1,537	00

ASYLUM FOR INSANE, HAMILTON ($9,751..75).

Repairs, drains, roofs, etc. ($575.07).

Corporation City of Hamilton, paving brick, 90.45; G. T. Ry. Co., freight charges, 49.00	139	45
Hendry & Co., cartage, 18.37; Hamilton & Toronto Sewer Pipe Co., pipe, 11.00	29	37
National Portland Cement Co., cement, 306.25; Riddell, Jno. E., felt and gravel roofing, 100.00	406	25

Paint shop ($245.52).

G. T. Railway Co., freight on cement, 32.20; Henry & Co., cartage on cement, 12.07	44	27
National Portland Cement Co., cement	201	25

Engineer's supplies, repairs, water supply, etc. ($680.62).

Clark, Adam, basin bowl, tap, etc.	11	03
Can. Steam Boiler Equipment Co., installing grates, etc.	70	16
Freeman, W. A. & Co., cement, 19.80; Gutta Percha & Rubber Mfg. Co., hose, coupling, etc., 106.45	126	25
Hamilton & Toronto Sewer Pipe Co., pipe	84	73
Morrison, Jas., Brass Mfg. Co., pipe whistle, 27.85; Rice, Lewis & Son, die stock, 39.10	66	95
Ramsay, L., iron pipe, 76.39; Smith, W. D., closet bowls, etc., 110.90	187	29
Woodman Bros., transformers	134	21

Enlarging steam mains ($1,759.03).

Clarke. Adam, pipe. valves, etc. 1,756.08; Heakes, F. R., travelling expenses, 2.95	1,759	03

PUBLIC BUILDINGS.—*Continued.*

ASYLUM FOR INSANE, HAMILTON.—*Continued.*

Renewal boilers ($3,255.95).

Buscombe, E. & J., brick, bricklaying, etc., 739.95; fire brick, clay, sand and lime, 116.10	856	05
Can. Steam Boiler Equipment Co., cyclone grates	212	50
Inglis, Jno. & Son, boiler, per tender, 555.00; Medcalf, D. M., travelling expenses, 24.40	579	40
Polson Iron Works, on account contract, 2 steam heating boilers	1,608	00

Exterior repairs and improvements, etc. ($835.36).

Crawford Bros., brick and gravel, 136.50; Freeman, W. A. & Co., cement for rink, 122.00	258	50
G. T. Railway Co., freight on cement, 35.00; Hendry & Co., cartage on cement, 13.12	48	12
McAllister, W. J., lumber and posts	297	44
National Portland Cement Co., cement	218	75
Wright, W. G., roller pounder, etc.	12	55

Main sewer iron pipe ($54.00).

Hamilton & Toronto Sewer Pipe Co., pipe	54	00

Interior repairs, alterations, etc. (825.79).

Fricker, D., moulding, etc., 48.12; Hamilton, F. & Co., picture wire, glass, etc., 18.76	66	88
Parmelee, W. H., jacket, kettles, etc., 103.00; Pickard, C. E., fan motors, 72.00	175	00
Riddell, Jno. E., canopy over range, 15.00; Singer Sewing Machine Co., machine, 30.40	45	40
Sparrow, Geo. & Co., jacket, kettles, etc., 55.00; Simpson, Robert & Co., pictures, 264.00	319	00
Walker, Frank E. & Co., furniture, carpets, laying of felt, etc.	219	51

Machinery and repairs for kitchen ($1,520.41).

Armstrong Bros., scavenger carts, 36.00; Alexander, A. G., roller splitting gauge, 9.00	45	00
Bain, James & Son, plumbing, castings, etc.	398	53
G. T. Railway Co., freight charges, 11.16; Massey, Harris Co., hoe drill, 68.25	79	41
Patterson, J. D. & Son, milk and meat wagon	37	00
Pendrith Machinery Co., dough mixer, 250.00; steel troughs and pyrometers, 115.00	365	00
Riddell, Jno. E., holders for scavenger carts, 10.00; Smith, E. D., trees, 152.28	162	28
Toronto Gas and Gasoline Engine Co., gas engine	302	00
Woodman Bros., transformer, etc.	131	19

ASYLUM FOR INSANE, KINGSTON ($27,369.80).

Repairs, drains, etc. ($289.72).

Heakes, F. R., travelling expenses, 10.55; Hentig. Geo., repairing conductor pipes, etc., 12.60	23	15
McFarlane, R. N. F., building drain, 127.00; Simmons Bros., repairing roof, 139.57	266	57

Engineer's supplies, repairs, etc. ($1,203.71).

Canadian Fairbanks Co., pump, 136.00; Conie, Wm., brick, 7.20	143	20
Douglas and McIlquham, masons' helper at 2.00 per day, 42.00; G. T. Railway Co., freight charges, 14.40	56	40

PUBLIC BUILDINGS.—*Continued.*

ASYLUM FOR INSANE, KINGSTON.—*Continued.*

Hydrotherapeutic Apparatus Co., baths, 464.00; Morrison, Jas. Brass Mfg. Co., pipe whistle, 27.85	491 85
Parmelee, W. H., ventilating fan. 42.00; Selby and Youlden, water work gauges, 14.00	56 00
Simmons and Son, sink and fittings, 28.50; Taylor and Hamilton, fitting up new closets, baths, etc., 427.76	456 26

Exterior repairs, cold storage, building root house, cow barns, etc., ($1,567.35).

Anglin, S. and Co., lumber, brick, etc., 789.29; Heakes, F. R., travelling expenses, 35.70	824 99
Hentig, Geo., ventilators, 24.00; Jamieson, A. and J., iron pipe steam trap, etc., 88.24	112 24
Knapp, A. C., skiffs. 121.00; Kingston Penitentiary, stone and gravel, 27.40	148 40
Mouldy, M., brick, 36.00; Partridge, F., wire guards, 260.06; Raney and Selby Co., Iron pot, 12.00	308 06
Storey, E. M., superintending work of repairs on laundry building	20 00
Sowards, J., cement, sand, etc., 74.50; Simmons Bros., cement, sand and building paper, 79.16	153 66

Fire protection, hose, hydrants, etc. ($176.50).

Canada Rubber Co., hose, coupling, etc.	58 00
Gutta Percha and Rubber Mfg. Co., hose, coupling, etc.	118 50

Instruments for band ($200.00).

Angrove Bros., brass instruments	200 00

Industrial Building material ($2,824.53).

Anglin, S. and Co., lumber, etc., 1,864.43; Brown, Geo., lime. 6.00	1,870 43
Dalton, W. B., hardware, etc., 204.81; Jamieson, A. and J., plumbing and castings. 82.51	287 32
Margent and Graham, paints and oils, 79.00; Grenville Asbestos Pipe Covering Co., covering, 64.62	143 62
Taylor and Hamilton, radiators, valves and plumbing	523 16

Interior repairs and alterations ($3,926.93).

Angrove, Henry, graphaphone and records, 105.00; Anglin, S. and Co., moulding, 1.60	106 60
Adams Furniture Co., furniture, 19.75; Bell Telephone Co., 2 phone sets and batteries, 10.50	30 25
Brock, W. R. and Co., 13.50; C. P. Industries, beds, 80.00; Chandler. Ingram & Bell, aseptic wash stand, 6.30	99 80
Dalton and Strange. Fairbank's scale, etc., 28.75; Dalton, W. B. and Sons, cutlery, 66.65	95 40
Gowans, Kent and Co., glassware, 23.75; G. T. Railway Co., freight charges, 4.48	28 23
Henderson, J. S., oil stove. 7.50; Horsey, S. J., range, etc., 71.07	78 57
Harrison, T. F. and Co., furniture, etc., 1,456.05; Hibner, D. and Co., desks and chairs. 112.50	1,568 55
Kav, Jno. Son & Co., rugs. 25.30; Kirkpatrick, M., picture moulding, 33.16	58 46
McFaul, R., comforter. 4.50; MacNee and Minnes, table furnishings, 510.46	514 96
Murray, W. A. and Co., curtains. etc., 35.45; Miller, A. H., cupboard, 14.50	49 95
Rooney, N., curtain. 22.50; Rice. Lewis and Son, grates, fenders, etc., 49.00	71 50
Sparrow, Geo., jacket, kettle, 55.00; Simpson, Robt. and Co., furniture. etc., 324.30	379 30
Simmons Bros., tinning dryer, etc., 68.23; Spangenberg, F. W., dessert set, 20.50	88 73
Smith Bros., clocks, 120.00; Taylor and Hamilton, iron pipe repairs, etc., 251.95	371 95
Tomilson, G. R., electrical supplies. 100.68; Oakley, Vincent and Sons, 34.00	134 68
Walkin, R. T., Estate, billiard table	250 00

PUBLIC BUILDINGS.—*Continued.*

ASYLUM FOR INSANE, KINGSTON.—*Continued.*

Machinery, repairs for kitchen, laundry, etc. ($1,632.69):

Dolan, M., harness, 98.00; Gallagher, L. L., mower and cultivator, 94.00 ...	192	00
Gurney Foundry Co., carving tables and hot water platters	406	08
G. T. Railway Co., freight charges, 2.42; Hermiston, C., plow, 13.00	15	42
Hentig, G., connecting pipe and castings, 50.40; Moore, H. E., travelling expenses, 14.10	64	50
MacGregor, Gourlay Co., rip table and saws, 103.85; Metcalf, D. M., trav. expenses, 15.05	118	90
Pay list, men employed, 68.50; Page Wire Fence Co., fence, 91.52	160	02
Raney, Selby and Co., castings, etc., 71.43; Spoor and Cosgrave, wagons, etc., 82.00	153	43
Steele Briggs Seed Co., hoe, 6.75; Smith, N. L., trees, 26.03	32	78
Spoor, R. J., barrow, horse lawn mower. 89.00; Smith, E. D., trees, 36.00	125	00
Simmons Bros., lawn mowers. plumbing, castings, etc.	328	86
Sparrow G. and Co., bread slicers, 13.50; Selby and Youlden, pulley, shafting, etc., 22.20	35	70

"New silo" ($430.00).

Simmons Bros., cement	430	00

Repairs to wharf and breakwater ($1,689.63).

Anglin, S. and Co., lumber, 553.15; Pay list, men employed, 456.01	1,009	16
Rathburn and Co., lumber, 132.11; Sears, Geo., hardware, 23.36	155	47
Sowards, Jas., lumber	525	00

Surgical appliances and library supplies ($532.77).

Chandler, Ingram and Bell. instrument cabinets	211	00
Chown, A. P., operating table, surgical appliance, 208.55; Down Bros., appliances, 17.52	226	07
Hartz, J. F. and Co., appliances, 25.60; Kny-Shearer Co., instrument tables, 22.00	47	60
Poole Publishing Co., books, 27.65; Stevens, J. & Son Co., appliances, 20.45	48	10

Furnishing attic in Nurses' Home ($607.25).

Anglin, S. and Co., lumber, 232.07; Horsey, H. S. and Co., rope and nails, 8.64	240	71
McFarlane, R. N. F.. carpentering work. 80.33; Sears. Geo., locks, bolts, etc., 39.40	119	73
Simmons Bros., wire weights, etc., 3.60; Taylor and Hamilton, radiators, soil pipe, bath pipe, etc., 188.00	191	60
Tomlinson, G. R., electric light supplies	55	21

Roof over boiler house, damaged by fire ($1,452.00).

McFarlane, R. N. F., contract for the whole work	1,452	00

Reconstruction of laundry and replacing machinery ($10,836.72).

Anglin, S. and Co., lumber, 69.80; Dalton, W. B. and Sons, belting, 38.64; Elevator Specialty Co., overhead elevators, sheaves, 12.50	120	94
Kingston and Pembroke Ry. Co.. freight charges	44	24
McFarlane, R. N. F., whole work, rebuilding contract, 7,593.00; additional work, plastering and sheeting, etc., 325.44	7,918	44
Selby and Youlden, castings and repairs, 366.67; Simmons Bros., castings and repairs, 234.43; water heating contract, 187.00	788	10
Standard Sanitary tubs	80	00
Toronto Laundry Machine Co., mangle and shirt machine, 1,805.00; repairing machinery, 25.00; services of man, 26.00; travelling expenses, 29.00	1,885	00

· PUBLIC BUILDINGS.—*Continued.*

ASYLUM FOR INSANE, BROCKVILLE ($11,684.70).

Covered way to women's cottages ($500.00)

Rice Lewis & Son, corrugated galvanized iron 500 00

Engineers' supplies and repairs, etc. ($618.92).

Black & Co., tank cover, steel plate, etc. 26 60
Brown & Semple, fittings for s$_p$ra$_y$ baths 103 50
Grenville Asbestos Co., covering 40 00
Mullen, R. J., carpentering 24 30
Parmelee, W. H., ventilating fan 50 00
Pay lists, wages, masons and carpenters 81 10
Ross, G. & Co., repairing baths, closets, radiators. etc. 292 17
Steacey, B. B., castings 1 25

Radiators main building and cottages, etc., ($889.75).

Canada Steam Boiler Equipment Co., cyclone grate 109 75
Canada Foundry Co., pump fo: hot water 150 00
Polson Iron Works, account contract steam heating boiler 630 00

Exterior repairs to brick work fence, etc. ($2,662.21).

Borthwick, J., blacksmithing 10 50
Davidson, Marcus, carpentering 189 00
Edwards, J., services as mason 264 25
Fitzsimmons, W. A.. carpentering 165 05
Horton, E., carpentering 25 00
McLaren, Peter, lumber 1,163 01
Mullen. R. J., carpentering 18 90
Olmsted, R. G., iron fence and gate 295 00
Patterson, S., carpentering 25 00
Pay lists. wages, carpenters 339 60
Steacy, B. D., cement, coal. tar. etc. 139 40
Worden, A., sand 27 50

Hot water boiler for cottages ($1.171.60).

Edwards, J., mason, work on foundations 45 50
Heakes, F. R.. travelling expenses 4 10
Ross, Geo. & Co.. new boiler 1,100 00
Steacy, B. D., cement 22 00

Fire escapes main building ($336.00).

Page Wire Fence Co.. fire escapes 336 00

Fire protection, hose, hydrants. etc. ($241.82).

Gutta Percha and Rubber Mfg. Co.. hose, etc. 132 79
Ross, G. & Co.. work on hose pipe, 46.00; pipe, valves, etc., 63.03............... 109 03

Interior repairs and alterations ($1,882.96).

Bell Piano & Organ Co., piano and stool 290 00
Canada Rubber Co., air beds 75 00
Chandler, Ingram & Bell, wheel chairs, etc. 71 00
Cordingly Bros., clarionet. 35.90; Curtin, J., tailoring machine, 47.50 ...... 83 40
Davis, R. & Son, curtains 194 70
Harrison, W. H., copper pairs 25 00
Northern Electric Mfg Co., supplies and installing telephones 142 25
Rice Lewis & Son, lawn bowls 31 61
Simpson. R. & Co., pictures. 245.00; Steacy. B. D.. picture glass, 29.50 ...... 274 50
Strathroy Furniture Co.. furniture 535.25; Swartz. A. H., furniture.
  etc., 23.75 .... 559 00
Wright, Robert & Co.. furniture, etc. 136 50

PUBLIC BUILDINGS.—*Continued.*

ASYLUM FOR INSANE, BROCKVILLE.—*Continued.*

Machinery and repairs for carpenter, laundry, etc. ($646.57).

Paris Plow Co., plow	14 00
Rice Lewis & Son, horse lawn mower	76 93
Stone & Wellington, trees	188 64
Toronto Laundry & Machine Co., extractor bowl, etc.	32 00
Wilkinson Plow Co., plow	45 00
York Manufacturing Co., washer	290 00

Repairs, drains, etc. ($400.44).

Deegan, J. E. & Co., balance extending eaves main building, 60.82; galvanized iron work, 42.10	102 92
Harrison, W. H., repairing	186 52
McLaren, Peter, lumber	111 00

Surgical appliances and library supplies ($465.55).

Carveth, J. A. & Co., medical books, 31.75; Chandler, Ingram & Bell, medical books, 4.00	35 75
Hartz, J. F. & Co., appliances	150 80
Lippincott, J. B. Co., medical books	4 00
Musson Book Co., medical books	275 00

Weigh scales ($469.37).

Gurney Scale Co., platform scale, 220.00; setting up scale, 58.10	278 10
Johnston, C. W., testing scale	5 50
McLaren, P., lumber	185 77

Root house ($1,399.51).

McLaren, P., lumber	228 12
Parlow, G. E. & E. A. Horton, contract whole work	1,067 00
Steacy, B. D., roofing	104 39

ASYLUM FOR FEMALE PATIENTS, COBOURG ($3,412.37).

Exterior repairs ($342.59).

Henderson Bros., window frame, sash, lumber, etc., 67.43; carpenter work, 19.25; building over weigh scales, 211.91	298 59
Leonard, E. & Sons, wire fencing	44 00

Interior repairs and alterations ($885.44).

Chandler, Ingram & Bell, wheel chairs	71 00
Dundas, A. R., furnishings, gas water heater. etc.	55 13
De Lancy, W., clock	5 75
Eaton, T. Co., chair	18 00
Gurney Foundry Co., cover for steam cooker	32 00
Henderson Bros., storm sash, lumber, hardware, etc.	237 82
Hibner, D. & Co., oak chairs, 81.00; Hewson & Co., furnishings, 28.00	109 00
McNicholl, E. C., furnishings, 135.00; McBride, H. L., furniture, etc., 35.75	170 75
Rice Lewis & Son, cutlery	36 29
Simpson, R. & Co., pictures	150 20

Fire protection. hose, hydrants, etc. ($170.00).

Alert Fire Appliance Co., fire extinguishers	110 00
Canada Rubber Co., fire hose	60 00

Underfeed stokers ($1,900.00).

Underfeed Stoker Co., underfeed stoker, per contract	1,900 00

REPAIRS AND MAINTENANCE.—*Continued.*

ASYLUM FOR FEMALE PATIENTS, COBOURG.—*Continued.*

Engineer's supplies and repairs, etc. ($114.34).

Dundas, A. R., copper covers, covering pipe and castings	114 34

ASYLUM FOR INSANE, PENETANGUISHENE ($10,664.86).

Addition to laundry ($1.013.24).

Blanchard, W., brick	398 75
Georgian Bay Snook Mills, lumber	382 26
McGibbon, F. & Son, lumber	232 23

Engineer's supplies and repairs ($441.71).

Clappison Packing and Covering Co., covering for pipe, boiler to greenhouse	24 00
Hartman Bros., valves, belt, packing, etc.	152 61
Morrison, Jas. Brass Manufacturing Co., whistle for pipe	27 85
Payette, P. & Co., iron pipes, valves, bolts, etc.	201 75
Shanahan Carriage Co., steel, 2.50; Street Railway Co., installing lights, 33.00	35 50

Exterior repairs to attendants' houses, wire fencing, etc. ($3,639.17).

Back, C. Mfg. Co., cedar shingles	55 60
Charlebois, A. B. & Son, cement, 28.47; Coulson, J. B., wire fencing, 144.00	172 47
Dewell, D., carpentering ....,	101 00
Firstbrook Box Co., flooring	109 33
Georgian Bay Snook Mills, lumber, 620.00; G. T. Railway Co., freight charges, 17.26	637 26
Hartman Bros., wire fencing, roofing, etc.	1,242 98
Ingram, W., mason work	57 16
King Construction Co., iron work	75 42
McGibbon, F. & Sons, lumber	595 89
Payette, P. & Co., iron pipe, roofing paper, etc., 141.38; pay list, wages men, 178.85	320 23
Tessier, A., cement, sash, lumber, etc.	247 83
West, Wm., brick	24 00

Fire protection, hose, hydrants, etc. ($237.50).

Alert Fire Appliance Co., fire extinguishers	220 00
Gutta Percha & Rubber Mfg. Co., hose hanger	17 50

Interior repairs and alterations ($1,955.63).

Burroughes, F. C. & Co., mattresses	230 00
C. P. Industries, hospital beds, blankets, etc., 250.45; Canada Oil Co., paints and filler, 5.10	255 55
Gendron, S. A., sewing machine, 30.00; plumbing contract dormitory, 390.00; castings, etc., 90.93	510 93
Heakes, F. R., travelling expenses, 16.85; Hartman Bros., locks. 10.50......	27 35
McGuire, Jno., furniture, wardrobe, etc., 125.50; McGibbon, F. & Sons, lumber, 249.92	375 42
Payette, N., moulding, etc., 11.40; Playfair, Preston Co., linoleum, etc., 105.70	117 10
Page Wire Fence Co., window guards	41 04
Steadman, R. H., electric light fixtures and curtains	32 00
Turner, J. J. & Sons, mattresses and pillows	126 00
Thompson, W. M., shellac, 3.50; Tuton, Geo. painting at 2.25 per day. 213.74	217 24
Tiropell, A., painting at 2.00 per day	23 00

REPAIRS AND MAINTENANCE.—*Continued.*

ASYLUM FOR INSANE, PENETANGUISHENE.—*Continued.*

Machinery and repairs for kitchen, laundry and farm ($677.95).

Charlebois, Frank, stone and stump machine	140 00
Georgian Bay Snook Mills, lumber, 405.42; G. T. Rlwy. Co., freight on tile, 18.90	424 32
Hollister, J. W., 2 sets double harness, 65.00; Hartman Bros., register, tar paper, steel wire, etc., 18.33	83 33
Wilkinson Plough Co., plough, etc..	30 30

Root house and silo ($1,992.88).

G. T. Ry. Co., freight on cement	96 26
Hartman Bros., sheet steel, iron, etc..	95 47
McGibbon, F. & Son, lumber	276 76
National Portland Cement Co., cement	437 50
Payette, P. & Co., iron collars, drills, etc., 5.89; pay list men employed, 267.86	273 75
Tessier, A., lime and lumber	88 14
West, Wm., brick	725 00

Repairs drains, etc. ($106.78).

Archer, Wm., services as carpenter	23 61
Dewell, D., services as carpenter	17 00
Hartman Bros., tile, 40.48; Scrigley, Ray, services as carpenter, 25.69...	66 17

Piano and pianola ($600.00).

Heintzman & Co., piano and pianola	600 00

ASYLUM FOR EPILEPTICS, WOODSTOCK ($68,405.48).

Balance of contracts ($3,472.83).

Austin, A. B., brushes and soap	40
Cole, Mrs. H., brushes and soap, 1.00; Coulter, J. E., galvanized iron work, etc., 21.57	22 57
Gurney, Tilden Co., castings	17 43
Keith & Fitzsimmons Co., electric and gas fixtures	430 00
Page Wire Fence Co., guards, 8.05; pay list, scrubbing and cleaning, 34.38	42 43
Purdy, Mansell Co., contract for spray bath and ventilation	2,960 00

Two cottages ($31,543.00).

Canadian Sportsman, advertising for tenders	9 00
Dominion Bridge Co., beams, girders, plates, etc.....................................	210 00
Fisher Co., account contract whole work	30,600 00
Heakes, F. R., travelling expenses, 31.35; Holmes, Jas., door handles, 1.25	32 60
Newspapers, sundry advertising for tenders	133 35
O'Byrne, B., travelling expenses	10 05
Tindall, J. D., services as Clerk of Works at 4.00 per day	548 00

Water supply ($4,161.33).

Bond, W. J., wages of bricklayer and laborer, 260.20; Baird, D., wrenches, etc., 7.25	267 45
Cherrett, E., brick, 209.00; C. P. Ry. Co.. services of inspector protecting company's track *re* watermain, 4.35	213 35
Fairbairn, R. P., travelling expenses	10 65
Gartshore-Thompson Pipe & Foundry Co., balance contract water pipe and valves	2,712 07
Hastings, A. & Son, cement, lime, etc..	83 90
McIntosh, A. J., balance of laying main, 302.40; Marshall, D. D., brick, 119.16	421 56

PUBLIC BUILDINGS.—*Continued.*

ASYLUM FOR EPILEPTICS, WOODSTOCK.—*Continued.*

Rapson, C. E., pipe, gravel, sand, etc.	185 60
Scott, J. J., levelling and filling in around cistern at 1.75 per day	14 88
Tindall, J. D., services as clerk of works at 4.00 per day	108 00
Whitelaw, R., maple frames, etc., 102.50; Whitney Bros., lead pipe and plumbing, 27.62	130 12
Waterworks system, repairing hydrants	13 75

Sewage ($3,570.90).

Birch, N. E., teaming, 8.00; Butler, R. E., Lumber Co., lumber, 32.10.	40 10
Fowell, Jno., barrows, 5.00; Francis, V. L., services inspecting sidewalk at 3.00 per day, 126.00	131 00
Fairbairn, R. P., travelling expenses, 24.10; Fisher & Co., cement, brick, etc., 153.67	177 77
G. T. Ry. Co., charges	81 44
Hannan & Bull, repairing tools, 9.50; Halford, A. J., travelling expenses, 25.85	35 35
Hasting, A. & Son, cement, etc.	76 28
Karn, Fred. D., shovels, picks, etc.	26 88
McIntosh Coal Co., lumber, pipe, cement, etc.	317 86
Odell, Wm. & Son, tile, 3.30; Owen Sound Portland Cement Co., 458.56	461 86
Pay lists men employed, 1,530.36; Purdy, Mansell & Co., putting in hydrant, 11.30	1,541 66
Rapson, C. E., excavating for septic tank and teaming	291 00
Tindall, J. D., services as clerk of works at 4.00 per day, 100.00; travelling expenses, 9.00	109 00
Whitney Bros., soil pipe	80 70

Roads and walks ($3,452.88).

Addison, A., work with team, grading	37 60
Brice, H., work with team, grading, 23.80; Birch, W. E., work with team at 4.00 per day, 188.00; oats and hay, 21.88	233 68
Coulter, J. E., lumber, labor, etc., sidewalk	91 15
Evans, H., work with team, grading	25 00
Fairbairn, R. P., travelling expenses	15 20
German, W. C., service as caretaker at 10.50 per week	42 00
Hayward, Jos., teaming	59 80
Maysey, R., work with team, 8.75; overseer at 2.00 per day, 28.00	36 75
Nagle & Mills, cement walks	922 75
Oxford, Treas. Co. of, sidewalk to bridge	305 00
Rapson, C. E., work with team, grading	25 60
Silica Bary Tie Stone Co., account contract cement sidewalks	1,500 00
Sparling, W. F., travelling expenses, 4.60; Scott, J. J., cleaning up lot and mowing at 1.75 per day, 8.75	13 35
Tindall, J. D., services as clerk of works at 4.00 per day	108 00
Ure, F. J., services surveying, etc.	37 00

Electric light and power ($924.35).

Coulter, J. E., material, labor, etc., 72.41; Coppins, E. S., electrical appliances and fuse plugs, 104.39	176 80
Heakes, F. R., travelling expenses, 5.85; Keith & Fitzsimmons Co., electrical fixtures, 50.95	56 80
McDonald & Willson, wiring	118 02
Woodstock Electric Light System, installing light and arc lamps	572 73

Fire protection, hose, etc. ($512.46).

Alert Fire Appliance Co., 20 extinguishers	220 00
Canada Rubber Co., hose couplings, etc.	39 21
Gutta Percha & Rubber Manftg. Co., hose couplings, etc.	253 25

18 P.A.

PUBLIC BUILDINGS.—*Continued.*

ASYLUM FOR EPILEPTICS, WOODSTOCK.—*Continued.*

Fencing ($420.61).

Canadian Fence Manuftg. Co., wire fence	413	65
Page Wire Fence Co., guards	6	96

Barns and stables ($1,780.25).

Butler, R. E,, Lumber Co., lumber, 60.10; Durkee, Wm., harness, 46.00	106	10
Frost & Wood, waggons and sleighs, 178.00; Fowell, Jno., farm implmts., 206.30; cutter robe, 68.25	452	55
German, W. C., horse, buggy and harness, 140.00; Heakes, F. R., travelling expenses, 9.95	149	95
Jenkins, W. H., harness, 25.00; Karn, Fred. W., farm implements, 11.60	36	60
Noxon Co., Ltd., implements, 102.75; Newspapers, sundry advertising for tenders, 54.60	157	35
Rick, E. F., team horses, 380.00; Sprocken, J. A., harness and repairs, 47.70	427	70
Sutherland, Angus, team of horses	450	00

Furniture and furnishings ($11,191.87).

Boles, Jno. E., sheeting, 87.01; Burrow, Stewart & Milne, scales, 18.85 ...	105	86
Bragg, H., freight and cartage, 33.96; Barr, Jos., clock, 1.25	35	21
Butler Bros., lumber, 252.81; Burroughes, F. C. & Co., packing and shipping goods, 19.95	272	76
Campbell Bros., oil cloth, sweepers, etc., 75.61; Connor & Co., Alf., groceries, cutlery, crockery, etc., 124.04	199	65
C. P. Industries, beds, blankets, 1,346.30; Coulter, J. E., lumber, carpentering, etc., 15.96	1,362	26
Carveth, J. A. & Co., books for library, 27.25; Coles, E. J. & Co., furniture and pictures, 205.20	232	45
Chamberlain Metal Weather Strips Co., weather strips, 52.95; Dymond, Sommerville Co., couches, etc., 249.30	302	25
Eureka Refrigerator Co., refrigerator, 388.00; Godard, G., window dips, 1.25	389	25
German, W. E., galvanized iron, 1.40; G. T. Rlwy. Co., freight charges on bed, 17.60	19	00
Gingerich, A. H., scale tools, etc., 182.83; Haight, Edw., furniture, etc., 5,232.72	5,415	55
Hollinrake & Co., quilts, towels, etc., 33.25; Karn, D. W. & Co., piano stool and drape, 275.00	308	25
Karn, Fred. W., granite ware, locks, etc., 289.34; King, Stephen & Co., furnishings, etc., 503.24	792	58
Lindsay, W. J., furniture, 626.24; Library Bureau of Canada, cabinet, cupboard, etc., 93.50	719	74
McDonald, Alex., copper kettles, boiler, etc., 17.45; Millman, Fred., meat boards, hamper, etc., 9.70	27	15
Maycock, J., papering, tinting, etc., 29.47; Montgomery, R. D., piano, violin and case, 310.00	339	47
Petit, A. H., moulding, painting, etc., 108.10; Poole & Co., crockery, glassware, etc., 19.55	127	65
Singer Sewing Machine Co., sewing machine, 28.00; Sparrow, Geo. & Co., laundry dryer, 380.00	408	00
Woodroofe & Son, clock, bell, etc., 19.55; White, Jno. & Co., screens, towels, etc., 93.71	113	26
Wyles, W. J., electric supplies, etc.	21	53

Purchase of land ($7,575.00).

Dunn, Catharine, purchase of land	7,575	00

18a P. 1.

PUBLIC BUILDINGS.—*Continued.*

ASYLUM FOR FEEBLE MINDED, ORILLIA ($3,159.78).

Engineer's supplies, repairs, etc. ($326.39).

Can. General Electric Co., supplies, 96.80; Canada Foundry Co., pipe, etc., 37.83	134 63
Gilpin Bros., water covering, etc., 54.11; Morrison, Jas. Brass Mfg. Co., pipe whistle, 27.85	81 96
Orillia Hardware Co., trough pipe, etc., 76.80; Parmelee, W. H., ventilating fan, 33.00	109 80

Exterior repairs to building ($754.48).

G. T. Railway Co., freight on cement	45 25
Hart, J. J., lumber, shingles, etc.	464 18
National Portland Cement Co., cement	218 75
Pomeroy, S., lumber, 1.70; Tait-Carss Lumber Co., lumber, 24.60	26 30

Fire protection, hose, escapes, etc. ($455.00).

Alert Fire Extinguisher Co., fire extinguishers	275 00
Gutta Percha & Rubber Mfg. Co., fire hose	180 00

Interior repairs, alterations, etc. ($609.03).

Burrow, Stewart & Milne, platform scale	28 03
Northern Electric Supply Co., lamps, sewing machine, motor	77 00
Orillia Mattress Factory, mattress and pillows	114 00
Simpson, Robert Co., pictures	150 00
Ward Furnishing Co., rug, linoleum, chairs, etc.	240 00

Machinery and repairs ($1,014.88).

Black, D. O., mower, buggy and wagon	181 00
Church Bros., 2 lumber wagons	89 00
Creelman Bros., knitting machine	56 25
Gerow, C. B., sewing machine, 45.00; G. T. Rlwy. Co., freight charges, 8.84	53 84
Hazlett, Wm., furnishing and building wire fence	30 55
Jones Underfeed Stoker Co., installing underfeed stokers	250 00
Medcalf, D. M., travelling expenses	5 00
Orillia Hardware Co., belting, pipe, etc.	40 47
Pendrith Machine Co., dough mixer	210 00
Phillips & Co., connecting tea and coffee urns, 36.00; copper, etc., 37.84	73 84
Walker Bros., pulleys, shafts, etc.	24 93

CENTRAL PRISON ($23,005.49).

Repairs, drains, etc. ($602.89).

American Blower Co., blower fittings	267 50
Creekmore & Anderson, duty and brokerage charges	80 80
Dominion Radiator Co., pipe	254 59

Boiler for north shop ($1,322.81).

Allison, H. J., steam separator for tubular boiler	180 00
C. P. Industries, lumber	50 30
Canada Foundry Co., boiler, 790.00; smoke connection and damper, 56.00; beams, 25.88	871 88
Muldoon, J. & Co., brick, cement, sand, etc.	100 63
Ontario Paving Brick Co., brick	120 00

Electric lighting, wiring, etc. ($914.42).

Can. General Electric, watchman's clock and supplies	727 59
Dominion Radiator Co., pipe, etc., 7.33; Rice Lewis & Son, pipe, 10.13	17 46

PUBLIC BUILDINGS.—*Continued.*

CENTRAL PRISON.—*Continued.*

Smith, Jno. B. & Son, lumber, 25.50; Taylor, Scott & Co., moulding, 10.00	35	50
Toronto Electric Light Co., wire connecting city light	133	87

Exterior repairs to buildings, etc. ($47.28).

Matthews, A., sky light frames, 28.64; Smith, J. B. & Sons, lumber, 18.64	47	28

Engineer's supplies and repairs, etc. ($1,479.53).

Canada Steam Boiler Equipment Co., cyclone grates	260	00
Lemen Low Water Alarm Co., water alarm	70	00
Matthews, A., concrete fan in workshop	632	00
Metal Roofing Co., galvanized sheet iron, nails, etc.	51	90
Petrie, H. W., drill, drill chuck. etc.	57	85
Polson Iron Works. grate bars, tiles. etc.	270	04
Sparrow, Geo. & Co., 40 gal pot	85	00
Taylor, Forbes & Co., pipe	52	74

Turn table, repairs and renewals for railway siding ($2,544.26).

Contractors' Supply Co., stove, 25.00; C. P. Industries, tiles, etc., 115.25; wages of carpenters, 11.80	152	05
Dominion Bridge Co., turn table, per tender	1,700	00
G. T. Railway Co., labor and material changing tracks	163	36
Muldoon, J., cement, sand, etc.	150	05
Ontario Paving & Brick Co., paving brick, 286.80; Rathbone, G., lumber, 92.00	378	80

Underfeed stokers ($3,800.00).

Underfeed Stoker Co., contract for stokers	3,800	00

Steam separators ($1,160.00).

Allison, H. J., 6 separators	1,160	00

Piano and two organs for religious services ($617.50).

Clegg, E. B., organ, 200.00; Gourlay, Winter & Leeming, organ, 47.50 ...	247	50
Mason & Risch, piano	370	00

Fencing ($686.14).

C. P. Industries, iron castings. paint. etc., 311.59; work of men. 205.10 ...	516	69
Muldoon, J., cement, gravel. sand, etc., 116.95; Ontario Brick Co., brick, 52.50	169	45

Machinery ($9,830.66).

Independent Cordage Co., balance on machinery installed	9,830	66

MERCER REFORMATORY ($2,608.86).

Engineer's supplies and repairs ($418.25).

Canada Steam Boiler Equipment Co., grate bars, fire brick, etc., 37.00; installing grates and relining fire box, 259.25	296	25
Parmelee, W. H., ventilating fan, 50.00; Pecaid, C. E., fan motors, 72.00	122	00

Exterior repairs to root house, fencing, etc. ($79.50).

Coyell, Alf., repairing and staying fences..	79	50

PUBLIC BUILDINGS.—*Continued.*

MERCER REFORMATORY.—*Continued.*

Interior repairs and alterations ($902.86).

Burroughes, F. C. & Co., mattresses, 32.40; Canada Feather and Mattress Co., mattresses, 26.25	58	65
Coyell, Alf., carpentering at work shop and other buildings	547	50
Musselman, Jacob, wages, laborer, 73.60; Smith, Wm., carpentering, 45.90	119	50
Stewart, John, paper, papering, painting, etc.	176	71

Machinery and repairs for kitchen, laundry, etc. ($238.10).

Massey, Harris Co., barrows, 9.50; Smith Bros., delivery wagon, 135.00 ...	144	50
Sparrow, Geo. & Co., cooking apparatus, 27.50; Toronto Laundry Machine Co., laundry machinery, 66.10	93	60

Changing Refuge to accommodate Asylum patients ($970.65).

Adams' Furniture Co.. chairs, 99.67; Brock, W. R. & Co., carpets, quilts and ticking, 370.11	469	78
Hutcheson, M., brick, flooring, 164.29; Rice Lewis & Son, hardware, cutlery, etc., 48.88	213	17
Rathbone. G., oak panels, doors, etc.	88	00
Sparrow, Geo. & Co., range and canopy, 115.00; kitchen furnishings, 84.70	199	70

NORMAL AND MODEL SCHOOLS, TORONTO ($5,207.59).

Repairs, drains, etc. ($151.19).

Armstrong, Fred., repairing electric wires, etc.	37	71
Gander, Thos. & Son, repairing walls and moulding	48	55
Lyon, J. D., repairing roofs	64	93

Metal ceilings in corridors ($326.74).

Dinnis, Richard & Son, lumber	152	31
Lyon, Jas., metal ceilings	172	00
Vokes Hardware Co., wire nails	2	43

Ventilation ($3,762.10).

Armstrong, Fred. Co., on account contract whole work, 3,500.00; altering and insulating wires, 46.62	3,546	62
Hamblin, Wm., brick and sand	12	00
Ontario Lime Association, cement and mortar	9	13
Toronto Electric Light Co., running underground power service for fans	194	35

Painting class rooms ($195.00).

Stewart, John, painting walls, ceilngs and glazing	195	00

Electric lighting class rooms ($277.00).

Armstrong, Fred., lamps and shades	32	00
Worrell & Keats, wiring rooms	245	00

Fire extinguishers ($143.00).

Alert Fire Appliance Co.. 13 fire extinguishers	143	00

Improvements and alterations Museum ($352.56).

Gearing, T. V. & Co.. building screen partitions, shelving, etc.	244	66
Stewart, John, painting, graining and varnishing	107	90

PUBLIC BUILDINGS.—*Continued.*

NORMAL AND MODEL SCHOOLS, OTTAWA ($3,809.31).

Repairs, drains, etc. ($87.59).

Canadian Steam Boiler Equipment Co., grates for boilers	40 50
McKinley & Northwood, plumbing, tinsmithing, etc.	47 09

Replanking play yards ($1,199.00).

Davis, S. J., contract flooring and planking	1,199 00

Renewals and improvements in plumbing ($1,922.85).

Edmonds, J. P. & F. D., tumbler holders	5 40
Heakes, F. R., travelling expenses	42 45
McKiney & Northwood, contract plumbing	1,875 00

Slate blackboards ($91.87).

Miller, A. K. & Son, setting blackboards	16 00
Steinberger, Hendry & Co., slate blackboards	75 87

Fitting rooms Normal and Model Schools ($272.00).

Howe, Wm., painting, graining, washing ceilings and walls	272 00

Radiators and storm sash ($236.00).

McKinley & Northcott, steam radiator	236 00

NORMAL SCHOOL, LONDON ($3,668.15).

Repairs, drains, etc. ($222.85).

Booth, Richard, building scaffold, painting, etc.	113 56
Heakes, F. R., travelling expenses	9 40
Johnson Temperature Regulating Co., repairing regulating apparatus	57 14
O'Byrne, B., travelling expenses	8 45
Winnett, Richard & Son, plumbing and castings	34 30

Painting walls of class rooms and corridors ($945.30).

Booth, Richard, contract painting	912 00
Heakes, F. R., travelling expenses	14 10
OByrne, B., travelling expenses	19 20

Purchase of additional land ($2,500.00).

Canada Trust Co., purchase of additional land	2,500 00

ADDITIONAL NORMAL SCHOOLS ($4,618.33).

Art Metropole, blue prints	3 78
Booker, A. H., purchase of land	592 50
Bartlett, F., taking levels and preparing plans of parks, streets and sewers, Peterborough	30 00
Drummond, F. S., survey and map of Government property, North Bay	10 00
Heakes, F. R., travelling expenses	27 00
Newspapers, sundry advertising for tenders	301 11
Parson, W. R. W., survey of grounds, Stratford	25 00
Russell, Peter, compensation *re* closing of lane, Hamilton	25 00
Tuckett, Geo., purchase of land	1,184 94
Trustees of C. P. Tuckett estate, purchase of land	2,394 00
Watkins, John, compensation *re* closing of lane, Hamilton	25 00

PUBLIC BUILDINGS.—*Continued.*

SCHOOL OF PRACTICAL SCIENCE ($70,080.00).

Repairs, drains, etc. ($500.00).

Morrison, Jas. Brass Mnfg. Co., packing, pipe, castings, etc.	14 36
University of Toronto, balance of appropriation	485 64

Grounds, roads, etc. ($1,500.00)

University of Toronto, balance of appropriation	1,500 00

Balance of contracts, chemistry and mining buildings ($31,500.00).

Brown, A. T., balance contract, carpenter and joiner work	6,200 00
Coyell, Alf., covering and screening frames in fan room, etc.	104 20
Douglas Bros., galvanized iron work in Observatory building	102 45
McGuire, D. J. & Co., amount contract electric wiring	1,220 00
Underfeed Stoker Co., balance of contract stoker to 2 boilers	175 00
University of Toronto, balance of appropriation	23,698 35

Electric light, Engineering building ($950.00).

W. J. McGuire & Co., electric shades contract	64 50
W. J. McGuire & Co., electric main contract, services to meter	27 50
University of Toronto, balance of appropriation	858 00

Wind break to ventilators ($225.00).

University of Toronto, balance of appropriation	225 00

Completing services, fittings, etc., Chemistry and Mining buildings ($7,175.00).

Armstrong, Fred., gas heater, lamps, etc.	88 70
Consumers' Gas Co., altering service pipe, labor, etc.	93 60
Coyell, Alf., book case, lumber, etc.	260 48
Dinnis, Richard & Son, lumber	68 77
Fiddes & Hogarth, castings, etc	52 65
Morrison, Jas. Bros. Mnfg. Co., brass plugs, etc.	53 62
Pease Foundry Co., door and frame castings	15 52
Pay lists, wages, carpenters, bricklayers, laborers, etc.	114 00
Polson Iron Works, painting engine	14 10
Reynolds, G. N. & Co., drawer locks, etc., for museum cases	37 00
Ross & Holgate, services and expenses of men testing motors	43 21
Stewart, John, painting, etc.	56 20
Vokes Hardware Co., brackets and hooks	47
University of Toronto, balance of appropriation	6,276 63

Furniture and equipment ($4,310.00).

Coyell, Alf., specimen cases	226 00
Ham. J. W., pressed brick	3 00
Morrison, Jas. Brass Mfg. Co., strainers	43 75
Reynolds, G. N. & Co., desk chairs, etc.	754 68
University of Toronto, balance of appropriation	3,282 57

Fire protection apparatus ($1,120.00).

Durham Rubber Co., hose, couplings, etc.	625 80
Diamond Dry Powder Fire Extinguisher Co., extinguisher	60 00
McCuaig, J. A. C., extinguishers	350 00
University of Toronto, balance of appropriation	84 20

Laboratory apparatus, instruments and supplies ($22,800.00).

Abbé Engineering Co., apparatus	25 00
Beardmore Belting Co., belting	50 27

PUBLIC BUILDINGS.—*Continued.*

SCHOOL OF PRACTICAL SCIENCE.—*Continued.*

Buckton, Joshua Co., lever testing machine	1,046 33
Can. Fairbank Co., cement testing machine	128 70
Cone, Wm., cherry boxes, binding posts, etc.	110 00
Can. General Electric Co., volt generator and rheostat	485 00
Cambridge Scientific Instrument Co., apparatus	411 02
Dodge Mnfg. Co., wood pulley	1 72
Electro Dynomic Co., motor and controller	210 00
Fielding & Platt, gas engines	456 59
Foster, James, compasses, chains, etc.	188 00
Gray, R. A. L., electrical apparatus	254 60
Hamilton, Wm. Mnfg. Co., mining machinery	4,400 00
Lufkin Rule Co., tape	51 24
Robinson & Heath, freight and brokerage charges	205 10
United Electric Co., switchboard, etc.	19 50
Volta Electric Repair Works, rheostats	40 00
Wanty, W., work of men installing exp. engine and brick work	50 90
Wanty, W., testing machine	35 53
Weston Electrical Instrument Co., apparatus	99 00
Westman & Baker, frame and slide for motor, etc.	23 25
Wetherell Separator Co., magnetic separator	1,000 00
Zeiss, Carl, night marine glass, etc.	63 28
University of Toronto, balance of appropriation	13,444 97

INSTITUTION FOR THE DEAF AND DUMB, BELLEVILLE ($3,700.86).

Repairs, drains, etc. ($381.37).

Alford, Walter, door frames, doors, sills, etc., 185.98; wages, carpenters. masons, laborers, etc., 185.54	371 52
Heakes, F. R., travelling expenses	9 85

Repairs to laundry machinery and boilers ($246.61).

Lewis, Jno. & Co., shafting and bricking in boilers, belting, etc	189 26
Manley, Thos., building extra walls re boilers, 40.00; Medcalf, D. M., travelling expenses, 17.35	57 35

Engine for laundry ($1,075.00).

Williams, A. R., Machinery Co., contract compound condensing engine...	1,075 00

Cement walks, crossings, etc. ($999.15).

Dolan and Sons, building cement walks and removing trees	999 15

Hedge fence in front of grounds, etc. ($221.00).

Herity, Fred., building wire fence	36 00
Reid, W. C., removing stone, hauling earth and trees	185 00

Extraordinary repairs outside ($177.73).

Alford, Walter, cement, stone, labor, etc., 146.48; Lewis, Jno. and Co., work on eaves, etc., 31.25	177 73

Hot water heater ($600.00).

Lewis, Jno. and Co., installing heater	600 00

INSTITUTION FOR BLIND, BRANTFORD ($4,112.20).

Repairs, drains, etc. ($230.67).

Howie & Feely, repairing down pipes, etc	189 62
Mann, Jno. and Sons, pipe, cement, etc., 36.60; O'Byrne, B., travelling expenses, 4.45	41 05

PUBLIC BUILDINGS.—*Continued.*

INSTITUTION FOR BLIND, BRANTFORD.—*Continued.*

New ice-house ($1,000.00)

Wright, Jas., on account contract	1,000 00

Shed for housing implements ($293.00).

Secord, P. H. and Son, contract	293 00

Cement walks and steps ($1,074.99).

Burrill, W. B., Co., crossing plates	60 77
Fisher Co., contract laying cement walks, 803.32; additional work hauling earth, etc., 75.80; cement crossings, steps and platform, 126.00	1,005 12
Heakes, F. R., travelling expenses, 4.60; O'Byrne, B., travelling expenses, 4.50	9 10

Outside repairs ($807.14).

Howie and Feely, painting roof and repairing slate, etc.	122 17
Secord, P. H. and Son, lumber, carpentering, etc.	222 97
Woolams, Geo., painting main building, work-shops, etc.	462 00

Renewing plank walks through Spruce Avenue ($106.40).

Secord, P. H. and Son, lumber	106 40

Verandah for Principal's residence ($600.00).

Secord, P. H. and Son, contract	600 00

ONTARIO AGRICULTURAL COLLEGE, GUELPH ($55,140.20).

Steel tank and tower, etc. ($1,107.84).

Amery, Richard. wages as laborer at 1.50 per day	30 00
Bond, J. M. & Co., pipes, etc.	38 90
Eureka Mineral Wool and Asbestos Co., packing	20 94
Fairbairn, R. P., travelling expenses	6 60
Medcalf, D. M., travelling expenses	3 35
McCann, Jas., contract foundation for water tower, 659.00; excavating and concrete work, 263.25	922 25
Robertson, A. & Son, castings, etc.	29 00
Taylor Bros, brick, labor, .etc	56 80

To complete work on compresser ($453.87).

Allen, E.,. splicing belt at engine house	6 45
Bond Hardware Co., belting, castings, etc.	137 16
Eureka Mineral Wool & Asbestos Co., packing	10 53
Guelph Cartage Co., cartage	25 00
Hughes, John, use of hog chains and jack screws	3 00
Pay lists, wages mason and helper	19 18
Robertson, Jas. & Co., castings	50 73
Robertson, A. & Son, castings	93 47
Taylor Bros., brick, cement, sand and labor	97 85
Toronto & Hamilton Electric Co., pulley	10 50

Additional apparatus for five laboratories ($3,984.15).

Allis, Chalmers & Co., experimental reduction machine	275 00
American Entomological Co., apparatus	23 85
Bausch & Lomb Optical Co., apparatus	518 74
Brooklyn Entomological Society, publication	4 00
Chemists' Surgeons Supply Co., water heater	12 50

PUBLIC BUILDINGS.—*Continued*.

ONTARIO AGRICULTURAL COLLEGE.—*Continued*.

Clemens, H. A. & Co., cupboard for apparatus	37 50
Carveth, J. A. & Co., apparatus, 12.65; Clark, J. A., thermometer shelter, 3.00	15 65
Canada Aluminum Works, aluminum microscope slides	3 15
Canadian Express Co., charges, 40c.; Canadian Pacific Railway, freight charges, 1.34	1 74
Collector of Customs, duty charges	1 00
Dominion Express Co., charges	7 46
Eimer & Amend, apparatus	638 18
Guelph Light & Power Co., apparatus	16 45
Greey, W. & J. G., separating shoe, 16.00;. Grant & Armstrong, tables, 12.25	28 25
Grand Trunk Railway Co., freight charges, 26.96; Green, Henry J., apparatus, 137.06	164 02
Greiner, Fredericks, apparatus	360 72
Hamilton Brass Mfg. Co., pump, tank, etc..	32 50
Heffernan. A., duty charges, 25.30; Holtzer Cabot Electric Co., apparatus, 2.00	27 30
Invincible Grain Cleaner Co., scourer	100 00
Jones & Moore Electric Co., motor	110 00
King, Scheerer Co., gas generators, 22.60; Kocbner, Jno., apparatus, 50.00	72 60
Leitz, Ernest, apparatus	197 30
Matheson, R., apparatus	35 10
Nelles. C. L., mimiograph, 10.00; Nambra, N., apparatus, 42.86............	52 86
Occomore H. & Co., trays, etc., 36.50; Office Specialty Mfg. Co., box drawer sections, 13.00	49 50
Petrie, A. B., microp slides, 2.00; Potter, Chas., apparatus, 66.50	68 50
Schaerer & Co., gaskets, 3.95; Scharmer & Leichmann, apparatus, 16.48	20 43
Spencer, Lewis & Co., apparatus, 110.25; Stevenson & Malcolm Co., plumbing and castings, 26.34	136 59
Taylor & McKenzie, apparatus, 193.00; Thomson Fred. & Co., electric bake ovens, 445.00	638 00
United Typewriter Co., typewriters and cabinets	275 00
Whitall, Tatum Co., apparatus, 57.26; Wagner Glass Works, test bottles, 3.00	60 26

Apparatus and furnishings for farm mechanics building ($919.59).

Canadian Fairbanks Co., gasoline engine, 146.00; Canadian Pacific Railway Co., freight charges, 2.07	148 07
Evans, John, travelling expenses, 4.10; Grand Trunk Railway Co., freight charges, 74c	4 84
Gesswein, T. W. Co., apparatus, 30.45; McMillan Bros., hanger frames. etc., 8.10	38 55
Taylor & McKenzie, apparatus	728 13

Cases and specimens for College Museum ($488.02).

Canadian Pacific Railway Co., freight charges	13 55
Grand Trunk Railway Co., freight charges	18 47
Jones Bros. & Co., cases	220 00
Moyer, M., on account of old relics	200 00
Morden, J. H., mounting specimens	8 00
Owen, R. E., stuffed lynx	20 00
Navitz, C. G., turkey buzzard	8 00

Additional Chemical Laboratories ($8,256.65).

Moore, H. E., travelling expenses	3 65
Whitham, S. F., account contract	8,253 00

Duck house, two experimental poultry houses and grain room ($599.99).

Barclay, James, posts, 7.50; Clemens, H. A. & Co., lumber, 443.96............	451 46
Davidson, J. F., gates, 17.85; Dowler Co.. cotton, 3.45	21 30

PUBLIC BUILDINGS.—*Continued.*

ONTARIO AGRICULTURAL COLLEGE.—*Continued.*

Pay list carpenters, 61.85; Richardson, G. A., cement, 40.83	102 68
Todd, W. E., labor	24 60

Laying cement walks, grading and planting Macdonald grounds ($1,997.75).

Cromwell, J., teaming, 93.76; Carter, T., manure, 1.00	94 76
Dooley, J. M., manure, 1.00; Guelph Cartage Co., cartage, 161.40	162 40
McCrea, J. A., manure, 1.00; McEllistrum, W., teaming, 506.60	507 60
McGinnis, R., manure, 18.00; Morris, J. A., teaming, 238.70	256 70
Morris, G. B., cement, 96.75; pay list men employed, 610.73	707 48
Sheridan, O. C., laying cement walks and steps	213 00
Weston, J. G., teaming, 55.31; Wagner, J., manure, 50c	55 81

Killman collection of insects ($1,000.00).

Killman, A. H., collection of insects	1,000 00

Rebuilding and repairing greenhouse ($4,999.04).

Canadian Sportsman, advertising for tenders	3 50
Crotty, P. J., travelling expenses	6 20
Bond Hardware Co., pipe	330 69
Eureka Mineral Wool & Asbestos Co., pipe covering, etc.	52 84
Guelph Cement Brick Block Paving Co., account contract cement foundations	180 00
King Construction Co., account cement superstructions	4,077 00
Moore, H. E., travelling expenses	6 55
Mahoney, Richard, services as clerk of works at 4.00 per day	208 00
Newspapers, sundry advertising for tenders	97 85
Robertson, James, Co., pipe	26 31
Sparling, W. F., travelling expenses	4 30
Taylor, Forbes Co., castings	2 10
Heakes, F. R., travelling expenses	3 70

Building for farm mechanics and instruments, demonstrations ($25,613.62).

Bond Hardware Co., iron pipe, castings, etc.	234 50
Canada General Electric Co., supplies, 242.97; Clemens, H. A. & Co., lumber, 44.44	287 41
Grand Trunk Railway, freight charges	5 28
Heakes, F. R., travelling expenses, 15.80; Hodgson, R., digging trenches at 2.00 per day, 40.00	55 80
McMillan Bros., shafting	94 25
Mahoney, R., services as clerk of works at 4.00 per day	865 00
Moore, H. E., travelling expenses	10 10
O'Hearn, Peter, excavating	43 29
Pringle, R. E. T. Co., electrical supplies	16 88
Richardson, G. A., hardware, etc.	10 50
Smith, Frederick, sheet lead, castings	24 45
Taylor & McKenzie, electric motor, lathe, drill, etc.	583 16
Toronto & Hamilton Electric Co., motor	280 00
Whitham, S. F., recount contract, whole work	23,103 00

Completion of the two cottages for Farm Foremen ($1,939.68).

Bond Hardware Co., pipes, elbows, etc.	34 62
Guelph Stove Co., erecting furnace, contract	210 00
Mahoney, R., services as clerk of works at 4.00 per day	75 00
Robertson, Jas. & Co., soil pipes, traps, etc.	145 06
Smith, Fred., baths, closets, boilers, etc.	145 00
Whitham, S. F., account contract	1,330 00

Glass for insects, physics and botany ($3,780.00).

King Construction Co., on account contract, superstruction	2,160 00
Witham, S. F., account contract, foundation	1,620 00

PUBLIC BUILDINGS.—*Continued.*

DISTRICT OF MUSKOKA ($92.99)

General repairs and furnishings ($93.99).

Ecclestone, Geo. W., plumbing, etc., gaol		87
Fenn, J. D., Sons & Co., furniture	21	40
Humphries, J. P., Dominion ensign	13	50
Phillips, F. A., storm sash, etc.	18	50
White, W. J. & Son, matting	39	72

DISTRICT OF PARRY SOUND ($4,165.53).

House for Gaoler, gaol kitchen and store-room ($2,328.85).

Canadian, The, advertising for tenders, 2.65; Clubb, W. H., account, contract, 1,962.00	1,964	65
Glassey, D., services as clerk of works at 4.00 per day	316	00
Macnabb & McKinley, installing soil and water pipe	16	20
Vokes Hardware Co., mantle, mirror, and grate	32	00

Alteration to Court House and general repairs ($1,086.68).

Clubb, W. H., account contract, brick, veneering and alterations to Court House	810	00
Fenn, A. N., scales, paint, etc.	33	50
Hillear, James, hose, reel, nozzle, etc.	13	70
Logan, Alex., office table	7	50
McKinney, S. L., carpentering	37	00
Moore, H. E., travelling expenses, 15.30; Macnabb & McKinney, metallic ceiling, 35.00	50	30
O'Byrne, B., travelling expenses	1	10
Riddell, J. D., carpentering	10	00
Walton, H. W., painting, tinting and papering	123	58

Lock-up, Powassan ($750.00).

Treasurer, Town of Powassan, grant to aid in building lock-up	750	00

DISTRICT OF ALGOMA ($320.31).

General repairs, gaol and lock-up, and fittings ($320.31).

Hesson, W. J. & Co., cedar and cedar posts	8	61
Hallam, W., wall paper, 11.00; contract papering, 71.00	82	00
McPhail, D. P., contract shingling roof, 86.00; locksmithing, 6.58	92	58
Moore & Browne, fire pots, stove pipes, etc., 7.70; field fence, wire gates, etc., 52.17	59	87
Sanderson, L., repairing walk and steps, 3.25; Simpson, T. E., chairs, 18.50	21	75
Woolrich, Geo., balance contract, painting	55	50

THUNDER BAY ($1,016.16).

Furniture and furnishings ($14.61).

Marshall, J. & Co., putting up partitions in attic	14	61

Exterior repairs, fencing, etc. ($12.30).

Moore, D. J., repairing wire door, window, etc.	12	30

Plumbing, Port Arthur gaol and Court House ($989.25).

Marshall, J. & Co., contract plumbing	965	00
Wells & Emmerson, weeping tile	24	25

PUBLIC BUILDINGS.—*Continued.*

RAINY RIVER DISTRICT ($517.20).

General repairs to Fort Frances lock-up ($78.50).

Wastell, W. G., repairs to gaol 78 50

Lock-up, Mine Centre ($421.70).

Gillon, J. D., services and expenses, 21.70; Gilbert, J. R., contract, whole work, 400.00 ....   421 70

Registry Office, Kenora, ($17.00).

Moon, Frank, teaming and levelling yard 17 00

DISTRICT OF NIPISSING ($9,627.50).

Completion of gaoler's house, North Bay ($2,299.80).

Marshall, J. H., services as clerk of works at 3.00 per day........................   234 00
North Bay Light, Heat & Power Co., wiring contract 62 50
Richardson & Co., contract hot water heating, 372.68; contract plumbing new lavatory, 255.57 ....   628 25
Richardson, J. W., window blinds, castings, etc. 15 05
Wallace, R. & Son, contract, whole work 1,360 00

Additions and alterations, North Bay Gaol and Court House ($2,049.50).

Canada Foundry Co., iron guards, per tender, 135.00; Central Prison Industries, cell gates 132.71 ....   267 71
Cole, Jas. & Co., door frames, 12.00; Connelly, J., reinforcing windows and repairing cell doors, 20.50 ....   32 50
Coyell, Alf., oak, iron-lined doors, per tender 89 00
Moore, H. E., travelling expenses, 27.25; Marshall, J. H., clerk of works at 3.00 per day, 57.00 ....   84 25
O'Byrne, B., travelling expenses 21 00
Purvis Bros., brushes, bolts, etc. 5 16
Richardson, J. W., radiator castings, plumbing, etc. 172 13
Small, John, flag pole for Court House, 5.00; repairing floor, 5.00 ....   10 00
Wallace, R. & Son, stone, cement, etc., 68.75; contract alterations, 1,100.00; alterations, on account, 199.00 ....   1,367 75

Repairs and alterations, Mattawa Lock-up ($91.15).

Gurney Foundry Co., grate bars, shaker, etc. 8 90
Simpson, W., papering and repairing ceiling and walls 82 25

Lock-up at Cobalt ($4,587.05).

Dreany Bros., stove furnishings, etc 53 90
Elliott, R. H., linoleum, window shades, etc. 37 27
Glassey, David, services as clerk of works at 4.00 per day, 292.00; travelling expenses, 50.00 ....   342 00
Galaska, A. S. & Co., chairs 9 30
Lavigne, D., board of D. Glassey at 2.00 per day, 18.00; board of D. Glassey at 1.50 per day, 57.00 ....   75 00
North Bay *Despatch*, advertising for tenders 3 00
New Liskeard *Herald*, advertising for tenders 2 08
Piper, N. L., Railway Supply Co., sanitary gaol pails 4 50
Pittam, E. D., contract, whole work, 3,805.00; building coal and wood house, 230.00; building chimney stacks, 25.00.......................................   4,060 00

Lock-up at Markstay ($600.00).

Treasurer, Township of Hogan, aid in building lock-up...........................   600 00

Total Public Buildings **$363,846 75**

PUBLIC WORKS.

MUSKOKA LAKES WORKS ($2,580.47).

Bartley, W. P., travelling expenses, 2.95; Batten & Son W. J., black-smithing, 6.96	9 91
Butterfield, B., lumber and sawing lumber	11 17
Child, Aaron & Son, hardware, 6.58; Chambers, F. C., travelling expenses, 1.85	8 43
Campbell, Peter, towing	25 00
Dolmage, C. R., travelling expenses and disbursements	18 55
Ecclestone. G. W., spikes, iron, etc.	46 46
Hanna, W. & Co., spikes, nails, etc., 18.35; Jenkins, A., travelling expenses, 4.05	22 40
McDermott, Isaac, towing, 12.00; McCutty, G., stove, 15.00	27 00
Mills, Ancil, travelling expenses, 46.76; Mickie, Dyment & Son, lumber, 351.10	397 86
Pay lists, men employed. 772.25; Palmer. Job, travelling expenses, 7.15	779 40
Rathbun Co., timber and lumber, 860.62; Ruddy & Cannell, board of men, 186.25	1.046 87
Thompson, Geo. A., lumber, 15.12; Wallis, J. S. & Co., lumber, 172.30....	187 42

Mary and Fairy Lakes works ($3,964.29).

Algoma Steel Bridge Co., account, contract, 2,160.00; Askin, J., timber, 94.94	2.254 94
Cullon Bros., drill and repairs, 80c.; Fairbairn, R. P., travelling expenses, 7.75	8 55
Huntsville, Lake of Bays & Lake Simcoe Nav. Co., scowing cement to locks and labor, 17.05; wood, 3.69	20 74
Hack, Mrs. S. J., board of men, 77.50; Jago & Martin, teaming, 3.70	81 20
Kennedy, D., trav. expenses. 7.90; Laidlaw, R., Lumber Co., lumber, 106.23	114 13
McEwen, J., Mrs., board of men. 132.74; McEwen, Jno., teaming, 15.00...	147 74
Muskoka Foundry Co., bolts, 24.88; Mills, A., travelling expenses, 31.24...	56 12
Mitchell. Jas., cartage, 1.15; Mosley, J. E., cement, etc., 86.62	87 77
Pay lists, men employed, 977.85; Ross. Alex., 26.85	1.004 70
Riverside Lumber Co., timber, 12.88; Robinson, W., board of men, 22.00	34 88
Smith, A. Sydney, lumber	31 20
Train, Fred, services, foreman at 3.00 per day, 63.00; trav. expenses, 12.15	75 15
Wright, Jas., blacksmithing, 6.75; White Bros., 40.42	47 17

Improvement to La Vase and Boon Creeks ($804.22).

Bell, J. H., dynamite, steel, etc., 25.58; Bernier, A. B., teaming, 9.00	34 58
Desourdy, A., sharpening drills. 8.25; Dennis, Stephen, dynamite, 2.50	10 75
Frederick, Ed., dynamite, 4.00; teaming. 1.75	5 75
Graft, David, team hire. 2.62; Graft, Mrs., team hire, 15.75	18 37
Garvin, O., drills, 75c.; Mick, Peter. blacksmithing, 1.40	2 15
Morrison Geo., tools, etc. 20.25; Miller, Adam, team hire. 3.50	23 75
Pay lists, wages of men. 689.74; Pilon, J. B., blacksmithing, 3.60	693 34
Porter & Co., tools, dynamite, 3.25; Richardson, J. W., steel, dynamite, etc., 12.28	15 53

Keewatin Bridge ($200.00).

Fraser, Jas., services inspecting, 25.00; Gilbert. Frederick, balance account, 175.00	200 00

Dredging entrance Neighick Lake ($898.15).

Brown, Jule, supplies. 7.27; Croft Co., slabs and cutting lumber, 25.11 ...	32 38
Hilliar, Jas., valves, supplies, water, etc., 11.55; McNight, Geo., supplies, 74.91	86 46
Mills. Ancil, travelling expenses, 17.50; Newell. W. R., supplies, 42.05	59 55
Pay lists, men employed, 651.28; Taylor, Fred., lumber, 27.69	678 97
Whalley. F. J., supplies	40 79

PUBLIC WORKS.—*Continued.*

MUSKOKA LAKES WORKS.—*Continued.*

Bridge at Rainy River ($1,990.52).

Bassett, Peter, piling, 70.00; Baldwin, W. C., supplies, 44.62	114 62
Brown, Alfred, painting and finishing building	14 00
Coates, J. O., travelling expenses, disbursements, 71.82; Can. Portland Cement Co., cement, 494.00	565 82
Dent, Jno., cartage, 2.00; Easton, G., supplies,.3.85	5 85
Gillon, D. J., services at 8.00 per day, 24.00; travelling expenses, 6.75 ...	30 75
Kennedy, Wm., travelling expenses, 45.00; McQuarrie and Grimshaw, supplies, 74.53	119 53
Pay lists, wages men employed, 1,034.25; Pearson, E. A., hardware, etc., 33.80	1,068 05
Piper, W. S., rule, 50c.; Rat Portage Lumber Co., lumber, etc., 57.70	58 20
Rasen and Coppleman, board of J. O. Coates, 12.00; Smith, R. O. and Co., stationery, 70c.	12 70
Service, Jas., taking out stone	1 00

Sleeman's Bridge and approaches ($1,044.80).

Armstrong, L., board of men, 31.03; Conroy, F. A., drift bolts, 36.33......	67 36
McIntyre and Son, timber, 200.29; Lee, Jno., tamarac stringers, 13.40 ...	213 69
Pay lists, men employed, 351.15; Pearson, E. A., hardware spikes, etc., 21.59	372 74
Rainy Lake and River Boom Co., pile driving hammer	96 00
Rat Portage Lumber Co., towing, teaming and loading, etc., 52.90; timber, 56.05	108 95
Reith, E., timber, 53.48; Sleeman, Geo., piling, 53.90; Weeks, Jno., ship auger, 45c.	107 83
Weir, David, accountable warrant	78 23

Goulais' River Bridge ($1,892.58).

C. P. Telegraph Co., telegrams, 1.50; C. P. Ry. Co., freight charges, 63.64	65 14
Dunn, Jas., tamarac piles, lumber, etc., 359.14; Loveland and Stone, lumber, 281.38	640 52
Lang, R., driving piles, per tender, 300.00; Moore and Browne, nails, bolts, etc., 40.32	340 32
Munro, W. H., services, superintendent at 5.00 per day	15 00
Plummer, W. H., and Co., timber, 213.60; Pay lists, men employed, 264.00	477 60
Robins, Louis, repairing tools, etc., 9.35; Tourongeau, Alex., services, superintendent at 5.00 per day, 170.00; trav. expenses, 174.65	354 00

Removing rock, North Bay ($986.07).

Fillon, C., services and expenses, 10.80; Jupp, R. H., services as overseer at 5.00 per day, 55.00	65 80
Orillia Construction Co., dynamite, etc., 183.00; Orillia Hardware Co., tools, oils, etc., 4.42	187 42
Pay lists, wages of men, 690.89; Perry, J. O., rubber boots, 27.00.........	717 89
Simmons, transportation tools and supplies, 6.50; Sargent & Co., 156 lbs. Smith's coal, 5.46	11 96
Thornton, S., use of stove and pipes	3 00

Sauble Bridge, Massey ($3,561.55). .

Armstrong Bros., lumber, 36.73; Art Metropole, blue prints, 1.05	37 78
Bowers, N. H., tools, etc., 80.56; Brown, Neil, board of J. O. Coates, 36.00	116 56
Coates, J. O., services as foreman at 3.00 per day, 36.00; trav. exps., 91.13	127 13
C. P. Railway Co., freight charges, 310.25; Chambers, E., lighting camp signals, 8.75	319 00
Fletcher, R. H., portable forge, 15.00; Halford, A. J., trav. exps., 10.90...	25 90
King, C., salt, 50c.; Latray, L., blacksmithing, 2.00	2 50
Lowe, J. S., lumber, 139.48; work of men and team, 15.75	155 23
Loveland and Stone, timber, 306.00; Merryer, Jas., cartage and uncovering gravel pit, 18.10 ....:...	324 10

PUBLIC WORKS.—*Continued.*

Sauble Bridge, Massey.—Continued.

Massey Station Mining Co., dynamite, fuse, etc.,. 47.20; Pay lists, men employed, 1,276.23	1,323 43
Raven Lake Portland Cement Co., cement	746 90
Spanish River Lumber Co., lumber, 377.62; coal, 1.35; Smith, R. O., stationery, 30c.	379 27
Tourongeau, Alex., travelling expenses	3 75

Spanish River Bridge ($5,560.37).

Barnes, Wm., travelling expenses, 39.60; Brown. F., timber, 6.00	45 60
C. P. Railway Co., freight charges, 497.32; Dominion Express Co., charges, 18.55	515 87
Dorey, Chas., spiles and logs, 68.25; Fairbairn, R. P., trav. exps., 34.20...	102 45
Gordon, Geo., red pine, 282.83; G. T. Railway Co., freight charges, 32.00...	314 83
Hews, C. P. & Co., hardware, 5.70; Halford. A. J., trav. exps., 10.30	16 00
Hinsperger Harness Co., tarpaulin, 13.80; Jelly, Wm., rent of timber for foundations of cement, 3.00	16 80
Kring, W. A., blacksmithing, 2.12; Loveland & Stone, lumber, 708.88	711 00
Lyde, D., wages, 4.80; McQuillan, A., timber and logs, 129.50; 23 cords wood at 1.75, 40.25	174 55
Morrison, Jas. Brass Mfg. Co., pressure gauge	1 75
Mickie, Dyment & Co,. freight on engine, 10.00; Owen Sound Portland Cement Co., cement, 711.76	721 76
Pay lists, wages of men .1 710.89; Paiement, A., acctble. warrant, 200.00	1,910 89
Purvis, C. A., dynamite, hose; etc., 234.13; Rodgers, W., towing, 2.00	236 13
Rollins. W. M., bolts, drills, etc., 40.00; Spanish River Lumber Co., timber, 21.35	61 35
Shakespeare Gold Mining Co., timber, 57.60; Sims Bros.. timber, 66.03 ...	123 63
Stinson, E., lumber and spiles	17 44
Tourongeau, Alex., services as superintendent at 5.00 per day, 400.00; trav. expenses, 190.32	590 32

Vermillion River Bridge, Twp. of Hanmer ($662.75).

Briscard, L., contract, erection of timber	600 00
Tourongeau, Alex., services, superintending at 5.00 per day, 30.00; trav. expenses, 32.75	62 75

Veuve River Bridge, Vernier ($4,487.17).

Allard, J. & Co.. storage of cement, 10.00; Beauchene, E., teaming, 7.00 ...	17 00
Bouffard, S., sand, 9.00; C. P. Railway, freight charges, 80.48	89 48
Cote, Paul, teaming. 29.09; Guenette, Jas., bolts, iron, etc., 4.25	33 34
Gordon, Geo. & Co., spiles, 74.00; International Portland Cement Co., cement, 294.00	368 00
Leblanc, C., sand and teaming, 9.75; Paiement, A., teaming, 1.50 ......:.....	11 25
Phillips, A., hauling spile driving outfit	9 00
Pay lists, men employed, 710.38; Paquettes. M., sand and teaming, 63.25...	773 63
Pilon, F., lumber, 104.02; Prieur, J. F., empty oil barrels, 25.00	129 02
Remillard, O., sand, 9.75; Ricard, Felix A., tools, nails, iron, etc., 56.74...	66 49
Sturgeon Falls Corporation. Town of, crushed stone	187 62
Tourongeau, Alex., services as superintendent at 5.00 per day, 270.00; trav. expenses, 132.34	402 34
Vance, James A., account contract, steel superstruction	2,400 00

Wrights' Creek Bridge, Temiskaming ($1,059.95).

Kerr, W. E., services as Inspector	15 00
Robertson, Geo. & Son. contract, erecting of timber bridge ...:.........	930 00
Tourongeau, Alex., services as superintendent at 5.00 per day, 55.00; trav. expenses, 59.95	114 95

North Road Bridge, Twp. of Dymond ($1,877.24).

Eplett, S. D., spikes, bolts, etc.	40 05
Irwin, D., contract, timber, 652.93; Jupp, R. H., acctble. warrant, 200.00	852 93

PUBLIC WORKS.—*Continued.*

North Road Bridge.—Continued.

Kerr, W. E., services as Inspector at 5.00 per day	65 00
Kerr, J. Harry, contract, erecting bridge, 549.94; Kennedy, A., spikes, 16.32	566 26
Pay lists, wages, men, 350.00; Tourongeau, Alex., travelling expenses, 3.00	353 00

Mattawa Bridge ($3,815.40).

Bell, J. H., rope, iron, etc., 56.13; C. P. R. Telegraph Co., telegrams, 1.75	57 88
Desormeau, F., timber, 1.53; Desourdy, A., hardware, 5.60; blacksmithing, 2.35	9 48
Doucette, F., timber and hardware, 3.74; Fink, J. A., timber, etc., 5.44	9 18
Fairbairn, R. P., travelling expenses, 7.25; Floorie, R., timber, 75c.........	8 00
Gauthier, Thos, repairing pump, 2.00; Halford, A. J., travelling expenses, 10.20	12 20
International Portland Cement Co., cement	82 12
Loughrin, J., nails, spikes, etc., 6.13; McMeekin, J., services *re* pay list and returns, 25.00	31 13
Mattawa Electric Light & Power Co., lighting temporary bridge	4 00
Mooney, Hugh, wages as foreman at 3.50 per day	185 75
Morrisette, G., loading concrete mixer, etc., 2.75; Morin, F., timber, 3.84	6 59
Pay lists, men employed, 3.243.01; Quimette, T., livery hire, 2.00...........	3,345 01
Sequin, L., loading concrete mixer	1 31
Tourongeau, Alex., services as superintendent at 5.00 per day, 35.00, travelling expenses, 27.25	62 25
Valois, A., cartage	50

Whitestone Bridge, McKenzie Township ($1,895.22).

Brunnell. Jno. & Sons, timber	313 67
Dixon, J. A., building stone approach, 100.00; spiles, etc., 41.50; board of men, 122.82	264 32
Holland & Graves, oats, hay, etc., 30.34; Leitch, Walter, hardware, hay, etc., 5.00	35 34
McIntosh, D. H., services as foreman at 3.00 per day, 12.00; travelling expenses, 85.54; livery and freight, 1.88	99 42
Pay lists, wages of men employed, 630.50; Simpson, Thos., timber, 23.64...	654 14
Strickland, A. D., spikes, blacksmith, etc.	28 33

Manitowaba Bridge, McKellar Township ($798.51).

Buchner, F., spikes, 2.90; Canning. W. L., bolts, etc., 19.91	22 81
Hilliar, Jas., hardware, rope, etc., 26.80; Leach, C. M., timber, 229.72...	256 52
McIntosh D. H., travelling expenses and disbursements, 84.38; Moyer, Geo., board of men, 61.50	145 88
Pay lists, wages of men employed, 283.45; Thompson. J., timber, etc., 89.85	373 30

Bala Bridge ($3,277.76).

Butterfield, B., lumber, 8.40; Burgess, J. W., hardware, 14.63..............	23 03
Burgess, Thos., teaming, 36.00; Cope, R.. teaming, 16.00 ..../...........	52 00
Currie. L.. board of men. 99.00: Curre. W. J.. teaming. 42.50	141 50
Campbell, P., towing cement mixer, 13.00; Dalmage, C. R., travelling expenses, 77.88	90 88
Edwards. J. G. & Co., steel tape line. 4.00; Hammill. R., board of men, 73.60; teaming, 5.75	83 35
Hussey. F., rent of cement mixer, 39.00; travelling expenses, 9.07...........	48 07
Jackson, A., unloading cement and teaming, 6.00; Knight, J. J., lumber, 6.00	12 00
Lakefield Portland Cement Co., cement, 340.00; McDevitt, W., board of men, 8.00	348 00
McDermott, I., towing, 124.25; Mickle, Oyment & Son, lumber, 246.56 ...	370 81
Mason, T., blacksmithing, 8.94; Ontario Bridge Co., account contract steel superstructure, 1,000.00	1,008 94
Pay lists, wages men employed. 843.86; Switzer, R. R., travelling expenses, 6.95	850 81

19 P.A.

PUBLIC WORKS.—*Continued.*

Bala Bridge.—Continued.

Thompson, Geo. A., lumber, 42.39; White, J., livery hire, 3.00; White, Mrs. J., board of men, 41.20	86	59
Whiting, W. O., gravel and teaming, 153.75; Wallace, Mrs. C. E., rent of boiler, 8.00	161	75

Canard River Bridge ($1,000.00).

Essex, Treas. County of, grant in aid of construction	1,000	00

Big East River Bridge ($800.00).

Chabbery, Treas. Township of, grant towards completion of bridge	800	00

La Mable Bridge, Dungannon Township ($1,271.43).

Davey Bros., cedar timber, 46.20; McConnell, T. C., grant in aid of construction, 700.00; services as foreman at 4.00 per day, 172.00; travelling expenses and disbursements, 84.51	1,002	71
Spurr, Jas., cedar timber and poles, 14.74; Tait, J. F., timber for piers, 253.98	268	72

Beaver Creek Bridge ($996.77).

Corrigan & Campbell, repairing scraper, 1.90; Ecclestone, G. W., cement, lime, etc., 14.20	16	10
Kaye, B. G., lumber, 14.00; Kaye, J. B., cedar posts, 2.40; repairing plow and scrapers, 2.50	18	90
Lake Rosseau Lumber Co., timber, 4.59; pay lists, wages of men employed, 936.93	941	52
Watson, Jno., sand, 1.65; Whitten, Jas., cement and lime, 18.60	20	25

Madawaska River Bridge ($5,000.00).

McNab, Treas. County of, grant in aid of construction	3,000	00

Sturgeon River Bridge ($267.75).

Hamilton Bridge Works Co., rods, spikes, bolts, etc.	267	75

South River and Eagle Lake Bridges ($673.13).

Claridge & Hillock, timber, 160.25; Campbell, W., drift bolts, 2.12	162	37
McIntosh, D. H., travelling expenses and disbursements, 47.77; pay list wages of men employed, 242.33	290	10
Robb, Chas., board of men, 13.50; Robb Lumber Co., lumber, 195.26	208	76
South River Mercantile Co., hardware, etc.	9	90
South River Lumber Co., sharpening drills	2	00

Black Duck and Indian River Bridges ($869.48).

Buckholy, A., cedar and oak, 33.88; Christink, R., use of plow, scraper, etc., 3.50	37	33
Dumouchel, H. L., tools, etc., 11.50; Dunlop & Co., hardware, 36.51	48	01
Hubert, R., cedar, 29.60; Kennedy, J. W., cedar, 92.88	122	48
Pembroke Lumber Co., lumber, 92.11; pay list, wages of men employed, 527.50	619	61
Synette, C., lumber	42	00

Wolsley River Bridge ($974.20).

Bertrand, Paul, tools, etc., 17.60; Croleon, Jno., spikes, etc., 38.50	56	10
Monette, C., dynamite, etc., 3.85; pay list, wages of men employed, 914.25	918	10

19a P.A.

PUBLIC WORKS.—*Continued.*

Axe Creek, Houseys, Outlet Creek and Kahskee Bridges ($1,221.57).

Brace, T. H., timber and spikes, 7.38; Brown, W. H., sawing trees, 6.60	13 98
Bernard, Jas., axe handle and nails, 49c.; Canning, Jno., wrench, bolts, etc., 1.08	1 57
Lowe, W. E., services as Inspector at 5.00 per day	40 00
McLean and Ridout, Treas. Townships of, timber, 62.94; Mickle Dyment & Son, timber, 137.89	200 83
Parker, Jno., spikes and nails, 3.05; pay lists, wages men, 726.41	729 46
Richardson Bros., nails. tools, etc., 10.30; Ruttan, C., planking, 99.45...	109 75
Rhodes, A. J., 44.95; Quinn, Wm., lumber, etc., 48.42; Steele, E., tamarac trees, 10.00	103 37
Thackaberry, W. J., bolts, plates, etc., 12.15; White Bros., cement, lime and nails, 10.46	22 61

Katrine Bridge, Armour Township ($1,257.23).

Appleby, R., board of men, 71.83; Clark, C. W., nails, iron, etc., 19.40...	91 23
Coulter, C. W., oak, 17.31; G. T. Railway Co., freight charges, 10.00	27 31
Hilliar, Jas., block and carpenter's pencils, 1.10; Knight Bros., tamarac piles, 92.80	93 90
McIntosh, D. H., travelling expenses, 32.18; Magnetewan River and Lake Steamboat Line, freight charges, 3.90	36 08
Pay lists, wages men, 803.29; Smith, H. J., bolts, books, etc., 6.95; Trussler Bros., lumber, 198.47	1,008 71

Burnt River Bridges ($2,017.11).

Barr, P. A., spikes, etc., 3.30; Brisbin, Jos., driving piles at 83¼c. each, 35.00	38 30
Baker & Bryan, cement, etc., 93.52; Craig & Auslin, timber, 37.49	131 01
Davis, Thos., gravel, 75c.; G. T. Railway Co., freight charges, 13.30	14 05
Horn Bros. Woollen Co., washing blankets, 2.65; Handcock, S. A., meals, 4.48	7 13
Hunter, Mrs. A., timber, 138.63; Kennedy, Wm., travelling expenses, 13.50	152 18
Lakefield Portland Cement Co., cement, 171.00; Mitchell, Jas., cartage, 1.70	172 70
Pay lists, wages men, 733.42; Robinson Bros., livery hire, 7.50; meals for P. R. Switzer, 2.60	743 52
Switzer, P. R., wages as foreman at 3.00 per day, 33.00; expenses and disbursements, 49.54	82 54
Switzer, Mrs. A. M., meals for men, 4.43; Vance, Jas. A., contract steel superstructure, 670.00	674 43
Wait, G., bolts, etc.	1 25

La Blanche River Bridge ($511.79).

Burlong, C. W., tamarac piles, 185.60; Fairbairn, R. P., travelling expenses, 32.60	218 20
Herald Publishing Co., advertising for tenders, 6.84; Houghton, J. W., tamarac piles, 195.20	202 04
Kerr, W. E., services measuring at 5.00 per day, 10.00; services inspecting at 5.00 per day 70.00	80 00
Kennedy, A., making auger, 3.50; New Liskeard, *Speaker*, printing and advertising, 8.05	11 55

SURVEYS, INSPECTIONS, ARBITRATIONS AND AWARDS ($663.82).

Armstrong, A. J., livery hire, 3.50; Burtch, B., assisting at surveys, 5.00...	8 50
Brown, A. N., assisting at survey, 8.25; Fairburn, R. P., travelling expenses, 150.42	158 67
Halford, A. J., travelling expenses, 220.30; Kennedy, Wm., travelling expenses, 45.65	265 95
LeBlanc, C., livery hire. 7.00; McIntosh, D. H., travelling expenses, 11.55	18 55
McLean, W. A. travelling expenses inspecting James Bay Railway	55 65
Moore A. J., V.S., livery hire, 8.00; Sylvester, O., services inspecting, 20.00; expenses, 1.50	29 50
Switzer, P. R., accountable warrant, 100.00; Stewart, Jas. D., services and expenses reporting township roads, 5.00	105 00
Thomas, R. A., hire of men and boat, 12.00; Whte, J., livery hire, 10.00	22 00

PUBLIC WORKS.—*Continued.*

LOCKMASTERS, BRIDGE TENDERS AND CARETAKERS' SALARIES ($4,299 17).

Wm. Kennedy :	Twelve months' salary as Superintendent....................			1,200 00
Wm. McIntosh :	Services as Lockmaster at Rosedale.........................			40 00
E. M. Davidson :	do	do	Port Carling	300 00
Jno. Makii s:	do	do	Lindsay........................	66 67
P. P. Young :	do	do	Young's Point....................	66 67
Wm. Robinson : .	do	do	Huntsville.........................,	300 00
Francis Stewart :	do	do	Magnetawan	300 00
David Galloway :	do	Caretaker	Elliott's Falls and Norland	10 00
Jno. Westlake :	do	do	Mississiqua and Bottle Lake	12 50
Jno. Westlake :	do	do	Eagle and Deer Lake..............	8 33
H. C. Austin :	do	do	Kinmount Dam	16 67
John C. Chesney :	do	do	Scott's Mills	8 33
Isaac White :	do	do	Bala	300 00
A. Sidney Smith :	do	do	Port Sydney.....................	100 00
Jacob Knoepffi:	do	do	Ahmic Lake	160 00
N. J. Harrison :	do	do	Keewatin........................	225 00
James Bayne :	do	do	Deer Lake Dam..................	360 00
Nils H. Hansen :	do	do	Keewatin........................	75 00
E. Cox :	do	Bridgetender	Port Sandfield	150 00
Colin Campbell :	do	do	Indian Point.....................	75 00
Geo. Selkirk :	do	do	Huntsville.......................	250 00
Andrew Miller :	do	do	Ryerson	250 00
Alfred McFayden :	Reading Gauge, Rainy River............................			25 00

MAINTENANCE LOCKS, DAMS AND BRIDGES ($10,426.82).

Ansley, A., lumber, 66.52; Andrews, Roger, board of men, 33.63	100 15
Appleby, R., board of men, 54.16; Arnberg, E., lumber for office of superintendent, 9.40	63 56
Arthur, Jas., supplies, 21.55; Batten, W. J. & Son., blacksmithing, 1.70...	23 25
Bailey, R. J., timber, 147.96; Bell Telephone Co., messages, 4.10	152 06
Bertrand, A. J., services in charge of timber slide, 84.00; Blake, J. C., livery hire, 4.75	88 75
Blair, J. T., cedar posts, etc., 3.15; Bottum, A. E., paint, hardware, etc., 3.75	6 90
Bobcaygeon *Independent*, advertising scow for sale, 2.00; Burgess, J. W., oil, 3.75	5 75
Bruce, R., lumber, 70.00; Broullard, A., towing, 11.00	81 00
Braithwaite, H., spikes, etc., 4.30; Braithwaite, F. Y. W., wire nails, etc., 15.57	19 87
Bridge Bros., tools and hardware, 21.20; Callow, A. & Sons, castings, etc., for dredging machine, 52.41	73 61
Callow, A. & Sons, work of men, 80.00; Carew, J., lumber, 26.75............	106 75
Calhane, T., lumber, 83.19; Carr, W., pine stringer, 5.00; Canadian Express, charges, 2.90	91 09
Cinnamon, D., hardware, etc., 28.27; Clark, C. W., paints, oils, etc., 41.55	69 82
Campbell, Peter, towing, 7.00; Cousineau, M., storage of tools and timber, 7.00	14 00
Cole, S., services as Inspector at 5.00 per day, 110.00; C. P. Railway Co., freight charges, 3.60	113 60
Coulter, J., Jr., meals for men, 2.40; man and team, 2.10	4 50
Cockburn, W., teaming, 1.75; Curtain, D., meals for men, 4.00; man and team, 2.55; timber, 1.63	9 93
Cullon Bros., blacksmithing, 2.00; Cox, Edward, teaming and board of men, 13.50	15 50
Coyne, Mrs., spiles, 6.00; Cockburn, S., work on bridge repairing break, 3.50	9 50
Dominion Express Co., charges, 2.80; Dolmage, C. R., work on stop logs, 7.50; travelling expenses, 26.80	37 10
Dunn. Jas., services protecting Goulais River bridge at 2.00 per day, 10.00; Deszrosseilliers, Jas., tools, etc., 8.37	18 37
Ecclestone. G. W., paint brush, etc., 11.35; Ferguson, J., chain, 2.00; Detman. F., meals, horse and man 40c..	13 75
Fairchild Co.. road scraper, 125.00; Foster, Jas., steel tape, 10.50.........	135 50

PUBLIC WORKS.—*Continued.*

MAINTENANCE LOCKS, ETC.—*Continued.*

Garlick, E. B., livery hire, 10.50; Gilbert, Fred., moving store house, 25.00; dressing lumber, 25.00	60 50
Goold Shepley Wire Co., gasoline engine and cement mixer, etc., 592.85; G. N. W. Telegraph Co., telegrams, 14.62	607 47
G. T. Railway Co., freight charges, 63.67; Grazelle, P., caretaker of dam at 2.25, 22.50; travelling expenses, 7.90	99 07
Griffith, J. W., jacking up bridge, 8.00; Georgian Bay Lumber Co., 46.20	54 20
Halford, A. J., travelling expenses, 43.80; Hamilton, W. H., stationery, 3.45	47 25
Haines, W., work repairing dam, 4.50; Harvie, W., repairing rods, augers, etc., 4.20	8 70
Hetherington, D., wood, 14.25; Hill, J. W., driving men and tools to Swamp Lake, etc., 10.00	24 25
Hill, S. J., carpentering, 7.00; Holcombe & Co., timber and plank, 58.46...	65 46
Hilliar, Jos., nails, oils. etc.. 6.95; Holden, H., caretaker of dam at 1.50 per day, 21.00; livery hire, 1.50	29 45
Hurley, P. J., rubber boots and socks, 8.50; Husband, R. J., water gauges, 6.50	15 00
Huntsville, Lake of Bays and Lake Simcoe Navigation Co., fares of men, towing, etc.	19 50
Jenkins, A., travelling expenses, 5.00; Jones Bros., towing bridge timber and timber, 12.02	17 02
Kennedy, W., travelling expenses and disbursements, 510.10; Keeling & Co., lumber, teaming, etc., 42.90	553 00
Kearny Timber & Mnfg. Co., timber	5 00
Knight Bros. Co., tamarac spiles, canning steel, etc., 104.15; King, W. A., draft bolts, 5.00	109 15
Kelly, C., sawing machine, 28.01; Knox, Jas., castings, 8.80	36 81
Lokay, D. J., painting. 92.40; Lebow. T., blacksmithing, 10.85	103 25
Langland, T. W., pine trees, 5.00; Ladell & Butchart, supplies, 10.64...	15 64
Liskeard Brick, Coal and Lumber Co.. cement, 6.80; Little Bros. & Co., lumber, 1.45	8 25
Lumb, Eli T.. rods, castings, etc., 66.31; Lucas, J. A., board and livery hire for Pickens, 2.75	69 06
Lynch, Jno. P.. board of men. 9.50; Lyttle. W. A.. bolts, spikes, etc., 8.25	17 75
McIntosh, D. H., services inspecting at 3.00 per day, 21.00; travelling expenses, 98.81	119 81
McLachlan, A. H., chain. hook, etc., 3.37; McKnight, G., rope, oil, etc., 8.15	11 52
McCrae, J., spikes, etc., 60c.: McIntyre, W. A., spikes. etc., 75c.	1 35
McKay, M., bolts, rods. etc.. 30.60; McKay. A.. timber, 41.61	72 21
McDermott, Isaac, towing. 10.00: McEachern, J, A.. board of men, 13.50...	23 50
McClure, J. H., board of men, 20.00; McGregor, W., travelling expenses, 3.65	23 65
McArthur, A., lumber. 17.00; McConnell, L. C., services as superintendent at 4.00 per day. 52.00; travelling expenses, 37.99	106 99
McKee. A., teaming, 20.00; Magnetawan River and Lake Steamboat Co., freight charges and fares of men. 16.76	36 76
Masin, Thos., blacksmithing, 4.00; Macnamara, Jno.. lumber, 28.25	32 25
Miller. A., painting swing bridge at 1.75 per day. 36.75; Mattawa Town Council, stone crusher. 600.00	636 75
Mitchell, Jas., cartage, 3.77; Mills, A., repairing dredging machine, 13.50; expenses and disbursements, 109.04	126 31
Mickle, Dyment & Son, stop log, etc., lumber. 375.55; Morrison, Jas. Brass Mnfg. Co., gauge, 14.00	389 55
Margach. Wm., travelling expenses, 16.70; Mowry & Sons, chain, wheels, etc., 20.75	37 45
Munro, W. H., repairs to bridge and services during freshet. 90.00; livery hire, 8.00	98 00
Muskoka Wood Mnfg. Co.. bridge pile, 6.50; Piper, N. L. Railway Supply Co., lamp, globe, etc., 1.75	8 25
Ontario Rubber Co.. diving dress and shoes. etc., 95.50; Owens, D., timber. plank, etc., 113.73	209 23
Pickens, J. M.. caretaker of dam at 2.25 per day, 29.25; travelling expenses, 3.50	32 75

PUBLIC WORKS.—*Continued.*

MAINTENANCE LOCKS, ETC.—*Continued.*

Pay lists, wages men, 2,600.68: Prieur. J. F., tools, bolts, etc., 37.15...	2,637 83
Roberts, J. D., board of men, 23.20; Roberts, D., board of men, 95.44......	118 64
Rice Lewis & Son, pulley block, 28.24; Robinson Bros., board and livery hire for Pickens, 8.00	36 24
Robinson, W., work on stop logs, etc., 8.25; postage, 2.00	10 25
Robertson, Robert, services protecting Goulais River bridge at 2.00 per day, 12.00	12 00
Ross, G. D., lock beams, pieces of oak, etc., 106.00; Reid, Robert, repairing railing steel bridge, 50c.	106 50
Ruddy & Connell, board of men, 71.80; Stinson, A., livery hire and teaming, 12.50	84 30
Stinson, Thos. & Sons, timber, 228.45; Smugge, H., painting, at 2.25 per day, 47.25	275 70
Smith, A. Sydney, lumber, 107.30; Scott, W. R., lumber, 15.00	122 30
Sutherland, W., hay, 1.50; Smith, H. J., bolts, etc., 5.45	6 95
Sheppard & Wallace. lumber. 355.35: Soward, H., spikes, 3.68	359 03
Shay, Ed., cartage, 2.25; Sylvester, O., services and expenses inspecting 20.00	22 25
Stringer, P., timber, 175.00; Stubbs, W., cartage, 5.00	180 00
Stewart, F., pumping out scow, 2.90; Tackett, A. A., taking up and re-placing stop logs, 75c.	3 65
Taylor, Eli, drift bolts, etc., 1.40; Thessalon Foundry and Machine Works, castings, etc., 33.75	35 15
Turnbull, Wm., service care of dam at Dryden	10 00
Tourongeau. A., services as superintendent at 5.00, 120.00; travelling expenses 55.30	175 30
Watchman,-Warder, The, printing posters, 1.75; Way, Jno.. plastering, 2.00	3 75
Walker. Geo., cartage, 4.00; Water, Light and Power Comm's., barrows and shovels, 7.00	11 00
Wallis, J. S., timber and sawing, 24.44; Welch, Jas., work, care of dams, 13.82	38 26
Windrum, W., taking up and replacing stop logs, 75c.; White, J., chains, 4.00	4 75
White Bros., hardware, spikes. etc., 24.72; Williams, A. R. Machinery Co., boiler fittings, etc.. 847.06	871 78
Westlake. J., iron for spiking timber, meals. etc., 9.30; Walton, Capt. A., loading, towing, etc., 36.25	45 55
White. Isaac. travelling expenses and disbursements, 13.77; teaming hay and lumber. 11.40; Wright. Jas.. spikes. blacksmithing, 2.00	27 17
Wannamaker, W. L., spikes. 80c.; Weddell. R.. iron bolts, 36.00	36 80
Young. E. J. F., paint	5 25

DRAINAGE ($14,010.00).

Treasurer Township—			
Bromley, grant towards completion of drainage works, Bromley Township ...			100 00
Drummond, grant towards construction of drainage works, McIntyre Creek			1,200 00
Medonte,	do	Medonte Township....	1,800 00
Mountain,	do	Baldwin	290 00
do	do	Silver Creek & Caistor	830 56
do	do	Miller...............	220 00
do	do	Caistor Extension and 8th Concession......	1,600 00
do	do	Allen Arcand........ .	2,200 00
Osgoode,	do	Silver Creek & Caistor	730 14
South Gower,	do	Silver Creek & Caistor	30 40
Tilbury East,	do	Dauphin	3,000 00
do	do	Big Creek............	1,000 00
Williamsburg,	do	Barkley Creek........	1,000 00
Winchester,	do	Silver Creek & Caistor	8 90

Total Public Works.....................................	$85,117 29

COLONIZATION ROADS, ($219,559.37).

Addington Road	York, M. P., overseer, 24 days at 2.25	54 00	
do	Pay lists, wages of men employed	231 75	
do	Fuller, W., powder, tools, etc	2 85	
do	Mallon, E., cedar	1 50	
do	Dawson, E., blacksmithing	· 1 40	
do	Jones, C., tools	1 30	
do	Sundry persons, cedar spikes, etc	1 45	
			294 25
Admaston Bridge	Butler, J. P., overseer, 39 days at 2.25	87 75	
do	Pay lists, wages of men employed	352 00	
do	Lester, B., spikes, washers, etc	33 24	
do	Butler, J., cedar, use of tools, etc	31 20	
do	Payne, J., stone for piers	10 00	
do	McVeigh, W., spikes	6 50	
do	Smith W. A., scantling	4 70	
do	Sundry persons, spikes, cedar, etc	05	
		530 44	
	Less advanced 1905 (Bonnechere bridge)	350 00	
			180 44
Airy Tp. Road	McConnell, T. C., paymaster		
do	Bloom, Herman, overseer, 27 days at 2.25	60 75	
do	Pay lists, wages of men employed	225 85	
do	Bradley, C., tools	7 60	
do	Holstein, H. L., repairs, etc	2 15	
do	Bloom. H., use of plow	1 90	
do	O'Neill, P., blacksmithing	1 75	
			300 00
Algona N.; 8 Con	Kavan, Adolph, overseer, 20 days at 2.25	45 00	
do	Pay lists, wages of men employed	229 00	
do	Thier, J. C., dynamite, etc	3 60	
do	Hock, G., blacksmithing	3 00	
do	Karron, W., timber	4 75	
do	McCann, M. J., repairs	1 10	
do	Switzer, J., repairs	50	
			286 95
Algona South Roads	Gallagher, Michael, overseer, 7 days at 2.25	15 75	
do	Pay lists, wages of men employed	96 25	
do	McGrath, W., overseer, 20 days at 2.25	45 00	
do	Pay lists, wages of men employed	229 50	
do	McGrath, W., cedar, 9.25; rent of tools, 12.40; postage, .50	22 15	
do	Rismer, Jno., overseer, 14 days at 2.25	31 50	
do	Pay lists, wages of men employed	160 50	
do	Rismer, J., use of plow	3 00	
do	Rismer, Aug., cedar	2 25	
do	Guthrie, J., tools	2 25	
do	McIntyre, J., tools	60	
do	Postage, stationery, etc	25	
do	Wilson, John, overseer, 14 days at 2.25	31 50	
do	Pay lists, wages of men employed	153 00	
do	Cameron, N., tools	8 25	
do	McMillan, S., timber and use of scraper	5 50	
do	Bremahan, rent of scraper	1 75	
			809 00
Alice Tp. Roads	Heisse, Ferdinand, overseer, 14 days at 2.25	31 50	
do	Pay lists. wages of men employed	154 81	
do	Dunlop & Co., scrapers, etc	15 30	
do	Heisse, Otto, plow points, etc	1 00	
do	Ziebell, Wm., overseer, 15½ days at 2.25	34 87	
do	Pay lists. wages of men employed	154 70	
do	Dunlop & Co., tools	6 75	
do	W. Bissenthal, lumber	2 25	
do	Sundry persons, tools, spikes, etc	1 43	
do	Born. Fred., overseer. 14 days at 2.25	31 50	
do	Pay lists, wages of men employed	100 50	

COLONIZATION ROADS.—*Continued.*

Alice Tp. Roads.—*Con.*	Laporte, J., cedar..................................	59 70	
do	Dunlop & Co., tools, dynamite, etc.........	5 80	
do	Schult, F., spikes.................................	2 50	
do	McCaughan, Wm., overseer 14 days at 2.25	31 50	
do	Pay lists, wages of men employed...........	73 50	
do	Honkie, Wm., overseer, 8 days at 2.25......	18 00	
do	Pay lists, wages of men employed...........	81 00	
do	Dunlop & Co., tools...............................	11 40	
			818 01
Anson, Minden and Lut-worth Tp. Rds.............	Mortimer, Jas., overseer, 35½ days at 2.25	79 88	
do	Pay lists, wages of men employed...........	401 50	
do	Stinson, T., plank.................................	25 00	
do	Mortimer, J., gravel..............................	13 00	
do	Sundry persons, blacksmithing, nails, etc.	1 92	
do	Mortimer, J. Sr., overseer, 7½ days at 2.25	16 87	
do	Pay lists, wages of men employed...........	83 25	
do	Taylor, R. J., overseer, 20 days at 2.25...	45 00	
do	Pay lists, wages of men employed...........	304 12	
do	Scott, Jno. J., overseer, 7½ days at 2.25...	16 87	
do	Pay lists, wages of men employed...........	83 00	
do	Postage, stationery, etc.........................	13	
do	Rogers, Geo., overseer, 8 days at 2.25......	18 00	
do	Pay lists, wages of men employed...........	81 37	
do	Leary, Thos., overseer, 12 days at 2.25...	27 00	
do	Pay lists, wages of men employed........	129 00	
do	Robertson, W. H., overseer, 5½ days at 2.25	12 37	
do	Pay lists, wages of men employed...........	87 37	
do	Anderson, B., powder.............................	42	
do	Peel, E., blacksmithing...........................	50	
do	Boldt, Adolphus, overseer, 13½ days at 2.25	30 37	
do	Pay lists, wages of men employed...........	275 62	
do	Hopkins Bros., tools...............................	1 75	
do	Walker, J., blacksmithing........................	75	
			1,735 06
Anstruther Road	Stephens, Thos., overseer, 14 days at 2.25	31 50	
do	Pay lists, wages of men employed...........	171 25	
			202 75
Ashdad Station and Mt. St. Patrick Rd...........	Windle, Patrick, overseer, 10 days at 2.25	22 50	
do	Pay list, wages of men employed...........	136 00	
do	Windle, P., board of men........................	35 00	
do	Devine & McGarry, tools, etc.................	32 75	
do	Quilty, Thos., overseer, 24 days at 2.25...	54 00	
do	Pay list, wages of men employed...........	553 50	
do	Quilty, T., cedar...................................	6 00	
			839 75
Aubrey Tp. Road	Robinson, W. J., overseer, 30 days at 2.50	75 00	
do	Pay lists, wages of men employed	557 01	
do	Beatty, A., provisions.............................	60 75	
do	Beddome, W. E., provisions......................	1 00	
do	Gardiner, A., provisions..........................	2 10	
do	French, Mrs. D., milk............................	3 20	
do	Postage, stationery, etc..........................	47	
			699 53
Aweres Tp. Road	Munro, W. H., paymaster......................		
do	Pay lists. wages of men employed........	200 12	
do	Stibbs, F. W., provisions........................	52 04	
do	Huston & Co., hay and oats..................	27 37	
do	Moore & Brown, dynamite......................	12 11	
do	Sims Lumber Co., lumber......................	4 80	
do	Algoma Iron Works, bolts....................	3 20	
			299 64
Badgerow, Cons. 2 & 5....	Labrosse, N. P., overseer, 19 days at 2.25	42 75	
do	Pay lists, wages of men employed...........	369 18	
			411 93

COLONIZATION ROADS.—*Continued.*

Badgerow, Cons. 4 & 5			
and Lots 8 and 9.........	Fillion, Frs., overseer, 24½ days at 2.25...	55 12	
do	Pay lists, wages of men employed.........	331 50	
do	Thivierge & Vissette, tools.....................	4 50	
			391 12
Bagot, 11 Con.................	Murphy, Thos., overseer, 27 days at 2.25	60 75	
do	Pay lists, wages of men employed...........	358 50	
do	Murphy, Thos., cedars, 36.00; use of tools, 7.00	43 00	
do	Windle, Patrick, overseer, 16 days at 2.25	36 00	
do	Pay lists, wages of men employed...........	126 50	
do	Windle, P., board of men, 42.25, cedar, 1.75..	44 00	
			668 75
Balkwell Road	Balkwell, W. J., overseer, 18¼ days at 2.00	36 50	
do	Pay lists, wages of men employed...........	367 50	
			404 00
Bancroft & Coe Hill Rd..	Nugent, W. H., overseer, 38 days at 2.25	85 50	
do	Pay lists, wages of men employed...........	336 75	
do	Muffett, C. E., provisions........................	26 97	
do	Gunter, W. B., do	29 37	
do	Nugent, W. H., do and material......	25 12	
do	Gilroy, N., do	24 58	
do	Vasson, J. E., do	5 20	
do	Henthorn, W. G., blacksmithing.............	2 95	
do	Postage, stationery, etc......................	27	
			536 71
Bancroft & Maynooth ...	Kirnighan, A., overseer, 26 days 3½ hours	59 28	
do	Pay lists, wages of men employed...........	188 68	
do	Gibson, W. G., repairing Selby Hill........	26 00	
do	King, John, right of way........................	20 00	
do	Sundry persons, dynamite, etc..................	7 16	
			301 12
Bar River Bridge and			
Road	Evoy, E. V., overseer, 14 days at 2.25...	31 50	
do	Pay lists, wages of men employed...........	84 66	
do	Evoy, W. H., timber........................	50 76	
do	Murray, R., plank..............................	22 00	
do	Wilson, R., plank..............................	3 07	
do	Collings, J. W., nails, etc.....................	4 95	
do	Moore & Brown, iron, etc.....................	3 00	
do	Postage, etc....................................	15	
			200 09
Barclay & Wabigoon Rd...	Bicknell, Wm. J., overseer, 25¼ days at 2.50......	63 75	
do	Pay lists, wages of men employed...........	431 09	
do	Sundry persons, tools, postage, express, etc.	5 16	
			500 00
Barrie Island & Mills Tp.	Griffith, Dan., overseer, 21 days at 2.25...	47 25	
do	Pay lists, wages of men employed...........	238 00	
do	Griffith, D. D., timber, hire of grader, tools, etc....................................	52 25	
do	Smith, Fred., spikes, etc......................	7 70	
do	McTaggart, F., stone boat....................	3 00	
do	Griffith, J. W., blacksmithing..................	1 80	
do	Griffith, Mrs., board of men....................	2 50	
		352 50	
	Less sale of tools...............................	2 50	
		350 00	
do	Shunkie, Chas., overseer, 16 days at 2.25	36 00	
do	Pay lists, wages of men employed.........	288 13	
do	Griffith, J. W., blacksmithing..................	9 86	

COLONIZATION ROADS.—*Continued.*

Barrie Island & Mills Tp	Loughead, T. R., tools	7 70	
do	Smith, F., powder, etc.	5 50	
do	Shunkie, Clayton, use of plow	4 00	
do	Baker, J. B., blacksmithing	1 60	
			702 79
Bass Lake Rd., Con. 4,			
Aberdeen	Torrence, Jos., overseer, 33 days at 2.25	74 25	
do	Pay lists, wages of men employed	207 50	
do	Somers, W. W., tools and dynamite	16 30	
do	Sundry persons, tools, dynamite, etc.	3 30	
			301 35
Bathurst & Althorpe Rd.	Dowdall, Thos., overseer, 14¼ days at 2.25	32 62	
do	Pay list, wages of men employed	195 60	
do	Reed, Jas., blacksmithing and repairs	6 58	
do	Conlon, Jno., gravel	5 00	
do	Dowdall. T., use of plows and scraper	5 25	
do	Sundry persons, tools, blacksmithing, etc.	3 70	
			248 75
Bear Lake and Nipissing			
Rd., Monteith Tp	Johnson, M., overseer, 22 days at 2.25	49 50	
do	do services, going over road with Inspector	1 83	
do	Pay lists, wages of men	241 67	
do	Nelson, O., fuse, etc.	4 25	
do	McCron, W., blacksmithing	1 40	
do	Sundry persons, tools, stationery, postage, etc.	1 35	
			300 00
Beaver Creek Rd., Kala-			
dar & Kennebec Tp	Patterson, Wm., overseer, 18 days at 2.25	40 50	
do	Pay lists, wages of men employed	157 12	
do	Loyst, G., blasting	2 00	
do	Postage, etc.	38	
			200 00
Bedford Tp. Road	Wilson, J., overseer, 21¾ days at 2.25	48 93	
do	Pay lists, wages of men employed	222 47	
do	Wilson, J. A., cedar, etc.	14 43	
do	Chown & Co., tools and expenses	10 02	
do	Wilson, D. J., blacksmithing	2 75	
do	Manley and Zimmerman, cedar	2 73	
do	Sundry persons, tools, postage, stationery, etc.	2 90	
			304 23
Bedford Road	Hamilton, G., overseer, 18 days at 2.25	40 50	
do	Pay lists, wages of men employed	144 75	
do	Hamilton, G., stoneboat and cedar	6 10	
do	Ming. W. J., tools	4 50	
do	Murphy. P., dynamite, etc.	2 00	
do	Affidavit, postage, etc.	1 15	
			199 00
Bellview Road	Legge, Joshua, overseer, 37 days at 2.50	92 50	
do	do do 13 do 2.00	26 00	
do	Pay lists, wages of men employed	302 30	
do	Carroll, R., tools	35 23	
do	Young, F. Rothwell, dynamite, fuse. etc.	10 80	
do	Algoma Central Ry., freight and fares of men	4 63	
do	Symons & Campbell, tools	3 85	
do	Ryan, T. S., repairs to tools	1 85	
do	Sundry persons, hardware, transport of tools, etc.	4 13	
			481 29

COLONIZATION ROADS.—*Continued.*

Belmont Tp. Roads	Sexsmith, Thos., overseer, 16 days at 2.25...	36 00	
do	Pay lists, wages of men employed	260 99	
do	Maloney, J.. wood for crusher	6 00	
do	Ryan, M., timber	5 05	
do	Sundry persons, wood, tools, dynamite, etc.	9 57	
do	Merriam, Robt., overseer, 9½ days at 2.25	21 38	
do	Pay lists, wages of men employed............	181 03	
do	Phillips Bros., tools	1 25	
do	McMaster, F. C., dynamite, etc.	1 30	
			522 57
Bethune Bridge. 5 S. L.			
Road	Lawson, T., overseer, 10 days at 2.25 ......·	22 50	
do	Pay lists, wages of men employed	105 00	
do	Griffin, M., plank	22 10	
do	Dunk, J., dynamite	2 85	
do	Woodruff, A. F., blacksmithing	2 35	
do	Sundry persons, tools, dynamite, timber, etc.	4 70	
			159 50
Bethune, 5 S. L. Road...	Dunk, John, overseer, 14 days at 2.25 ...	31 50	
do	Pay lists, wages of men employed	131 25	
do	Massey, Harris Co., plow	14 00	
do	Griffin, M., plank	9 60	
do	Brathwaite, H., tools	7 44	
do	White Bros., dynamite	4 35	
do	Sundry persons, blacksmithing and postage	1 85	
			199 99
Black Creek and Rankin			
·Road	Newman, August, overseer, 12 days at 2.25	27 00	
do	Pay lists, wages of men employed	114 40	
do	Dunlop & Co., dynamite	7 93	
do	Neuman, A., cedar	3 50	
do	Law, Z.. blacksmithing	2 30	
do	Pictine, Paul, overseer, 16 days at 2.25 ...	36 00	
do	Pay lists, wages of men employed	121 00	
do	Stewart, W. J., overseer, 14 days at 2.25	31 50	
do	Pay lists, wages of men employed	166 50	
do	Marion, T., tools	1 25	
do	Postage and freight	75	
do	Bromley, J. H., overseer, 11 days at 2.25	24 75	
do	Pay lists, wages of men employed	222 75	
do	Gordon, R. J., gravel............................	38 30	
do	Cecile, M., do	10 75	
do	Powder, fuse and postage	45	
			800 13
Blind River and Algona			
Road·	Martin. Robt., overseer, 26 days at 2.25...	58 50	
do	Pay lists, wages of men employed	321 87	
do	Brathwaite, F. W., tools and material ...	25 00	
			405 37
Blue Pratt and McCrossen			
Road	Buffy, Wm.. overseer, 48 days at 2.50	120 00	
do	Pay lists, wages of men employed	668 14	
do	Sleeman. G.. provisions	109 33	
do	McQuarrie & Grimshaw, provisions........	32 11	
do	Baldwin. W. C., do	12 99	
do	Sleeman, W. T., do	48 62	
do	Anderson, F., eggs	3 75	
do	Sundry persons. board and provisions, 5.52; freight, 3.30	8 82	
			1,003 76
Bonfield Tp. Roads	Pellerin. Alcide, overseer, 21 days at 2.25	47 25	
do	Pay lists. wages of men employed	250 13	
do	Cahill, J., tools	6 18	
do	Purvis Bros., dynamite	5 05	

COLONIZATION ROADS.—*Continued.*

Bonfield Tp. Roads	Sundry persons, blacksmithing, postage, affidavit, etc.	4 25	
do	Amyotte, Louis, overseer, 17 days at 2.25	38 25	
do	Pay lists, wages of men employed	216 00	
do	Purvis Bros., dynamite	14 00	
do	Larivere Bros., blacksmithing	6 15	
do	Farmer, Wm., overseer, 11½ days at 2.25	25 87	
do	Pay lists, wages of men employed	117 50	
do	Farmer, A., use of tools	3 00	
do	Lamarche, C., Jr., tools	3 60	
do	Postage	10	
do	Boisvert, Wm., overseer, 19 days at 2.25	42 75	
do	Pay lists, wages of men employed	223 12	
do	Sequin, J., tools, etc.	19 75	
do	Purvis Bros., dynamite, etc.	12 00	
do	Sundry persons, tools, blacksmithing, etc.	3 50	
do	Rose, Lena, overseer, 14 days at 2.25	31 50	
do	Pay lists, wages of men employed	144 75	
do	Rose, W., timber	11 08	
do	Brown, W., do	6 96	
do	Rose, A., dynamite, etc.	2 30	
do	Sundry persons, blacksmithing, etc., and postage	3 39	1,238 43
Bonfield and North Bay Road	Vaillancourt, P., overseer, 20 days at 2.25	45 00	
do	Pay lists, wages of men employed	219 62	
do	Purvis Bros., dynamite, etc.	26 87	
do	Sequin, Jno., tools and blacksmithing	10 25	
do	Vaillancourt, P., Jr., use of plow	2 50	
do	Gagnon, P., repairing drills	90	
do	Brigden, A. C., overseer, 7 days at 2.25	15 75	
do	Pay lists, wages of men employed	84 00	
do	Postage	25	405 14
Booth Road	Robinson, Jno., overseer, 37¼ days at 2.25	86 06	
do	Pay lists, wages of men employed	785 84	
do	Elliott, H., gravel, tile, etc.	22 80	
do	Dixon, R., cedar	0 34	900 04
Boulter Tp. Roads	Moltais, Prescol, overseer, 20 days at 2.25.	45 00	
do	Pay lists, wages of men employed	240 66	
do	Pacaud, L. J., plow	10 00	
do	Cahill, J., tools	2 20	
do	Sundry persons, tools and repairs	3 20	
do	Boissenault, Jos., Jr., overseer, 24 days at 2.25	54 00	
do	Pay lists, wages of men employed	289 08	
do	Lamarche, C., Jr., tools	6 00	
do	Postage, stationery, etc.	50	650 64
Brandy Creek and Port Carling Road	Cope, Stephen, Sr., overseer, 26½ days at 2.25	59 62	
do	Pay lists, wages of men employed	223 50	
do	Ecclestone, G. W., tools	7 46	
do	Hanna, Wm. & Co., tools, etc.	6 80	
do	Postage, affidavit, etc.	93	
do	Kaye, Jas., Jr., overseer, 36 days at 2.25	81 00	
do	Pay lists, wages of men employed	236 99	
do	Ecclestone, G. W., cement	19 50	
do	Butterfield, B., plank	26 40	
do	Glass, J., lumber	28 00	
do	Kaye, N., plow	7 00	
do	Sundry persons, blacksmithing, etc., and postage	1 11	

COLONIZATION ROADS.—*Continued.*

Brandy Creek and Port Carling Road	DeCaire, Francis, overseer, 13 days at 2.25	29 25	
do	Pay lists, wages of men employed	171 90	
			899 46
Bright Tp., Con. 4	Barker, A., overseer, 17¼ days at 2.25...	38 81	
do	Pay lists, wages of men employed	254 15	
do	Bridge Bros., tools	4 10	
do	Barker, A. cartage	2 75	
			299 81
Bright Tp., Rogers & Iron Bridge Road	Fowler, R., overseer, 29¼ days at 2.25	65 81	
do	Pay lists, wages of men employed	427 10	
do	Barker, R., use of plow, etc.	7 00	
do	Sundry persons, cartage, tools, etc.	4 15	
			504 06
Broder & Dill Road	Malette, Jos., overseer, 19 days at 2.25	42 75	
do	Pay lists, wages of men employed	254 00	
do	Evans, The Co., lumber	10 70	
do	Horne, R., tools	2 50	
do	Langlois, Alphonse, overseer, 24 days at 2.25	54 00	
do	Pay lists, wages of men employed	310 00	
do	Purvis Bros., tools	19 10	
do	Conway, J., plow	15 00	
do	Postage, affidavit, etc	75	
			708 80
Broder Tp., Kelly Lake Road	Wennerstrom, A., overseer, 14 days at 2.25	31 50	
do	Pay lists, wages of men employed	147 02	
do	Oliver, Thos., nails, etc	1 00	
do	Sundry persons, dynamite, postage etc	48	
			180 00
Broadbent and Edgington Road	Bartlett, Wm., overseer, 22 days at 2.25...	49 50	
do	Pay lists, wages of men employed	237 25	
do	Fenn, A. N., dynamite, etc	12 80	
do	Sundry persons, tools, dynamite, etc	2 57	
		302 12	
	Less sale of dynamite	2 12	
			300 00
Bromley Tp. Roads	Shinerman, Albert, overseer, 13 days at 2.25	29 25	
do	Pay lists, wages of men employed	107 43	
do	Berkart, E., plow	3 00	
do	Butt, Wm., cedar	7 50	
do	Sundry persons, dynamite and stone boat	3 00	
do	Gorman, M. P., overseer, 23 days at 2.25	51 75	
do	Pay lists, wages of men employed	241 50	
do	Sundry persons, use of waggon and tools	6 75	
			450 18
Bromley West T. L. and Cons. 3 and 16	Devine, Patrick, overseer, 12 1-5 days at 2.25	27 45	
do	Pay lists, wages of men employed	209 29	
do	Devine, P., cedar	43 20	
do	Leary, J., spikes, etc	8 66	
do	Dunlop & Co., tools, etc	8 66	
do	Wilson, T. R., blacksmithing, etc	1 65	
do	Miner, C. B., powder, etc	3 25	
do	McLaren, D., paymaster	....	
do	Pay lists, wages of men employed	100 50	
do	McIntyre, J. S., overseer, accountable...	250 00	
			652 66

COLONIZATION ROADS.—*Continued.*

Brougham and Admaston
Road ....Kennelly, Jos., overseer, 14 days at 2.25...   31 50
      do   Pay lists, wages of men employed......... 120 00
      do   Kennelly, Jos., board of men...................   39 00
      do   do   cedar 9 60
                                                                                        200 10

Brougham & Griffith Rd...Maloney, P. P., overseer, 15 days at 2.25   33 75
      do   Pay lists, wages of men employed......... 119 00
      do   Maloney, P. P., board of men...............   26 00
      do   do   cedar, 9.00; rent of plow
                    and scraper, 9.00...........................   18 00
                                                                            196 75

Bruce Mines & Sault Rd..Bryan, W., overseer, 27½ days at 2.25...   61 88
      do   Pay lists, wages of men employed........... 426 40
      do   Somers, W., dynamite, tools, etc............   14 04
      do   Horricks, Jno., plow repairs..................   4 00
      do   Chambers, J. H., plank........................   2 09
                                                                 508 41

Brudenell and South Al-
gona T. I ....Walsh, Michael, overseer, 16 days at 2.25   36 00
      do   Pay lists, wages of men employed........... 216 00
                                                                   252 00

Buckhorn Rd. North.......Simpson, Alex., overseer, 9 days at 2.25...   20 25
      do   Pay lists, wages of men employed........... 379 37
      do   Postage, hammer, etc...........................   95
                                                                 401 07

Burleigh & Apsley Rds...Coons, C. B., overseer, 27 days at 2.25   60 75
      do   Pay lists, wages of men employed........... 499 25
      do   Fitzgerald. H. G., tools, bolts, etc.......   11 50
      do   Dunford, J., wood for crusher...............   5 00
      do   Foster, J., stone and use of waggon.........   13 25
      do   Sundry persons, blacksmithing, hardware,
                    wood, etc......................................   7 05
                                                                 596 80

Burpee & Cockburn Isld..Goodmurphy, S. T.. overseer, 19 days at
                  2.25 ....   42 75
      do   Pay lists, wages of men employed........... 282 37
      do   McAlister Bros., tools and timber...........   13 95
      do   Bridge Bros., powder..........................   7 90
      do   Baillie, D., blacksmithing....................   2 25
      do   Bailey. W. T., overseer, 10 days at 2.25...   22 50
      do   Pay lists. wages of men employed........... 338 70
                                                                 710 42

Burris Tp., Lots 8 & 9...Martin, J., overseer, 9 days at 2.50.........   22 50
      do   Pay lists. wages men employed............... 757 00
      do   Holmes Bros., provisions....................... 159 93
      do   Martin, Mrs.,   do   23 50
      do   Shine, S.,   do   11 00
      do   Thompson, W. J., dynamite.................   14 25
      do   Sundry persons, provisions, blacksmith-
                    ing, etc. 15 34
                                                        1,003 52

Burton Rd., Field Tp.....Lecroix, Amedie, overseer, 18 days at 2.25   40 50
      do   Pay lists, wages of men employed......... 250 25
      do   Lillie, R.. dynamite.............................   4 20
      do   Prieur, J. F.. tools. etc........................   8 15
                                                               303 10

Balances, 1904. Stanley
and Fort William Rd....Ontario Bank, Port Arthur for N.
                  McDougall.
      do   Balance as per Pub. Accts. see page 198-1904... 1,208 16

COLONIZATION ROADS.—*Continued.*

Balances 1905, Balfour Tp. Roads	Cayen, A., overseer, 26 days at 2.25	58 50	
do	Pay lists, wages of men employed	321 60	
do	Cayen, A., tools, nails, etc.	18 22	
do	Belanger, E., timber	28 00	
do	Blonden, O., do	24 00	
do	Chenir, A., plank	50 00	
		500 32	
	Less advanced, 1905	450 00	
			50 32
Gillies, Con. 5 Road	McColl, D., overseer, 19 days at 2.25	42 75	
do	Pay lists, wages of men employed	443 75	
		486 50	
	Less advanced, 1905	480 00	
			6 50
Inspection	Munro, W. H., travelling expenses	52 75	
do	Houston & Co., storage of tools	4 75	
do	Soo Livery, cartage of tools	3 50	
do	Hodgings, R. S., services storing tools	5 00	
do	Pearl Laundry, washing blankets	3 00	
do	Graham, W. R., rent of barn for storage	10 00	
do	Postage, stationery, etc.	3 33	
			82 33
do	Moss, H. N., inspector, 6 days at 5.00	30 00	
do	C. A. Ry., freight on tools	7 60	
do	C. P. Ry. do	1 50	
			39 10
do	Pringle, W. W., Inspector, 11 days at 5.00	55 00	
Mattawa Tp. Road	Auger, Leon, overseer, 15 days at 2.00	30 00	
do	Pay list, wages of men employed	114 00	
do	Bell, J. H., dynamite	3 05	
			147 05
McIntyre and Neebing	Caldwell, A. B., overseer, 4 days at 2.25	9 00	
do	Pay lists, wages of men employed	190 00	
		199 00	
	Less advanced, 1905	195 00	
			4 00
Oliver Tp. Road	Caldwell, A. B., overseer, 23 days at 2.25	51 75	
do	Pay lists, wages of men employed	326 39	
do	Mark, Clavet, Dobie Co., dynamite	35 85	
		413 99	
	Less advanced, 1905	380 00	
			33 99
Road South Boundary Savard, Temiskaming	Barry & Foley, balance contract to chop, clear, stump and grub a road along S. boundary of Savard to Tp. Sharp at 400.00 per mile	300 00	
do	15 rods crossway at 1.25	18 75	
			318 75

COLONIZATION ROADS.—*Continued.*

Van Horne Road	Hayes, J. G., tents, tools, camp supplies omitted from 1905 accounts		153 00
Wright's Creek Bridge, Temiskaming	Armstrong, J. A., overseer, 23¼ days at 2.25	52 87	
do	Pay lists, wages of men employed	93 24	
do	Roberts, F., spikes	3 25	
do	Herron, W., spikes and rods	4 00	
		153 36	
	Less advanced, 1905	90 00	
			63 36
			953 40
Cache Creek Bridge	Renauld, Alex., contract 30 ft. bridge in Springer, Con. 2 and 3		500 00
Caldwell, Cons. 2 and 3 from Lot 9 west	Gingrass, P., overseer, 16 days at 2.25	36 00	
do	Pay lists, wages of men employed	245 50	
do	Guernette, E., blacksmithing, etc	21 50	
do	Ricard, F. A., dynamite, etc	2 79	
do	Lillie, R., do	4 60	
do	Postage	10	
			310 49
Caldwell and Badgerow T. L. Road	Dault, N., overseer, 12¼ days at 2.25	28 13	
do	Pay list, wages of men employed	163 80	
do	Ricard, F. A., scraper	8 00	
do	Postage	7	
			200 00
Caldwell, Kirkpatrick and McPherson T. L. Road.	Foisey, Ambrose, overseer, 19¼ days at 2.25	43 87	
do	Pay list, wages of men employed	236 58	
do	Guernette, J., tools	8 05	
do	Michael, N., blacksmithing	2 50	
do	Leveille, A., plank	14 00	
do	Riherd, M., dynamite	1 10	
			396 10
Calvin Tp. Road	Adams, Thos., overseer, 19 days at 2.25	42 75	
do	Pay list, wages of men employed	256 25	
do	Ryan, A., tools	1 20	
do	Postage	10	
			300 30
Calvin Tp., Patterson Creek Bridge	McCullough, Jas., overseer, 21 days at 2.25.	47 25	
do	Pay lists, wages of men employed	192 50	
do	Smith, Jas., spikes	14 60	
do	Hill, Jas., Jr., lumber	23 50	
do	Connelly, W., timber	17 40	
do	Ball, J. H., tools, etc	4 65	
			299 90
Campbell Tp	Reid, Duncan, overseer, 10 days at 2.25	22 50	
do	Pay lists, wages of men employed	217 30	
do	McKechnie, D., gravel and timber	6 00	
do	Colman, D., use of road machine	4 25	
do	Mimihen, O., overseer, 12¼ days at 2.25	28 12	
do	Pay lists, wages of men employed	197 25	
do	Slumkie, C., overseer, 9¼ days at 2.25	21 37	
do	Pay lists, wages of men employed	79 75	
do	Gamey, J. R., overseer, 5¼ days at 2.25	11 81	
do	Pay lists, wages of men employed	113 17	
			701 52
Capreol, Cons. 2 and 3	Forget, F., overseer, 29 days at 2.25	65 25	
do	Pay lists, wages of men employed	336 01	
			401 26

COLONIZATION ROADS.—*Continued.*

Carden Roads	Alton, Jno., overseer, 7 days at 2.25	15 75	
do	Pay lists, wages of men employed	184 17	
do	Ashley, J., overseer, 6 days at 2.25	13 50	
do	Pay lists. wages of men employed	86 50	
do	Irwin, J. J., overseer, 12¼ days át 2.25	28 12	
do	Pay lists, wages of men employed	170 75	
do	Thompson, F., hammer	1 29	
		500 08	
	Less sale of hammer	50	
			499 58
Carling Tp. North West Road	Madigan, Wm., overseer, 18½ days at 2.25.	41 62	
do	Pay lists, wages of men employed	261 90	
			303 52
Carpenter and Kingsford Road	McDermid, J. A., overseer, 39 days at 2.50.	97 50	
do	Pay lists, wages of men employed	663 75	
do	Langstaff, C. R., provisions	142 74	
do	Strachan, D., tools, etc	42 75	
do	Cameron. W. M.. provisions	16 65	
do	Quinn, A., provisions, butter, etc	17 60	
do	Reid, A., provisions	11 20	
do	Sundry persons, board, provisions, lumber, etc	14 40	
		1,006 59	
	Less amount of account unpaid	6 59	
			1,000 00
Cavendish Tp. Roads	White, Jno., overseer, 19½ days at 2.25	43 88	
do	Pay lists, wages of men employed	344 00	
do	Switzer, S., timber	10 00	
do	Sundry persons, tools, nails, stationery, etc	1 92	
			399 80
Centre Line Road, Bruce Mines to Cariboo	Steinburg, C., overseer, 23 days at 2.25	51 75	
do	Pay lists, wages of men employed	339 72	
do	Greigg Bros., tools	4 00	
do	McArthur, W. C., tools	2 70	
do	White, T. A., tools	3 45	
			401 62
Chalk River Bridge	Fields, W. S., overseer. 20 days at 2.25	45 00	
do	Pay lists, wages of men employed	223 00	
do	Fields, Jas.. lumber	180 20	
do	Dunlop & Co., spikes	10 00	
			458 20
Chaffey and Franklin	Morgan, F., overseer, 21 days at 2.25	47 25	
do	Pay lists, wages of men employed	143 37	
do	Morgan, F., cedar	7 50	
do	Sundry persons, tools, nails and postage	1 88	
do	White Abraham, overseer, 12¼ days at 2.25	28 12	
do	Pay lists, wages of men employed	171 74	
do	Irwin, W. E., overseer, 16¼ days at 2.25	37 12	
do	Pay lists, wages of men employed	246 46	
do	White Bros., dynamite	6 00	
do	Mosby, J. E., tools	3 20	
do	Wright, J., blacksmithing	3 10	
do	Postage, stationery, etc.	1 00	
			696 74
Chaffey Locks Road	Burtch, C. S., overseer, 18 days at 2.25	40 50	
do	Pay lists, wages of men employed	162 62	
do	Burtch, C. S., use of scraper and plow	2 30	
			205 42
Chandos Road	Hales, Jno., overseer, 15 days at 2.25	33 75	
do	Pay lists, wages of men employed	165 48	
do	McIlvina, J., tools	3 25	
			202 48

20 P.A.

COLONIZATION ROADS.—*Continued.*

Chapleau Tp.............	McAdams, J. D., overseer, 18 days at 2.25.	40 50	
do	Pay lists, wages of men employed	329 09	
do	Postage, affidavits, etc	1 46	
			371 05
Chisholm Tp. Roads	Kennedy, Donald, overseer, 20 days at 2.25	45 00	
do	Pay lists, wages of men employed	202 15	
do	Sundry persons, tools, livery, etc..............	3 50	
do	Anderson, T., overseer. 16 days at 2.25...	36 00	
do	Pay lists, wages of men employed	208 50	
do	Anderson, A. T., plank	5 00	
do	Brown, C. J., tools	2 25	
do	Lamb, Oliver, overseer, 14 days at 2.25......	31 50	
do	Pay lists, wages of men employed	149 37	
do	Porter & Co., tools.................................	12 70	
do	Brown, C. J., hardware ....:	3 50	
do	Sundry persons, powder, repairs etc.........	1 93	
do	Clement, Nap, overseer, 15 days at 2.25...	33 75	
do	Pay lists, wages of men employed	207 37	
do'	Porter & Co., tools	5 85	
do	Sundry persons, blacksmithing, etc., and postage	4 33	
do	McCharles, Jno., overseer, 16 days at 2.25.	36 00	
do	Pay lists, wages of men employed	183 43	
do	Knight, James, bolts and spikes	4 30	
do	Lewis, M. V., timber	17 50	
do	Porter & Co., tools	8 53	
do	Postage, etc	24	
do	Cherrier, J., overseer, 17 days at 2.25......	38 25	
do	Pay lists, wages of men employed	253 75	
do	Brown, C. J., tools	7 45	
do	Postage, affidavits, etc	80	
			1,502 95
Christie & McKellar Rd...	Orr, J., overseer, 18 days at 2.25.............	40 50	
do	Pay lists, wages of men employed	243 66	
do	Ross & Harris, dynamite	9 50	
do	Sundry persons, dynamite, blacksmithing, etc	6 67	
			300 33
Clarendon and Mississippi Road	Bushell, D., overseer, 17 days at 2.25......	38 25	
do	Pay lists, wages of men employed.............	211 37	
do	Allan, I., cedar, plank etc	49 68	
do	Riddell, D., dynamite	70	
			300 00
Clark's Bridge Road........	Elliott, Wm., overseer, 13 days at 2.25......	29 25	
do	Pay lists, wages of men employed.............	160 56	
do	Chambers, J. H., plank...........................	6 05	
do	White, T. A., tools	2 00	
do	Sundry persons, bolts, timber, etc	5 05	
			202 91
Coffin Tp. Road	Miller, Jas., overseer, 20 days at 2.25......	45 00	
do	Pay lists, wages of men employed.............	248 75	
do	White, T. A., tools	4 25	
do	Somers, W. W., tools	1 75	
do	Sundry persons, cartage, blacksmithing, etc	2 25	
			302 00
Combermere & Maynooth Road	Card, C. J., overseer, 15½ days at 2.25......	34 87	
do	Pay lists, wages of men employed	245 65	
do	Fair, R. C., tools	7 80	
do	Fallon, E., cedar	2 30	
do	Sundry persons, dynamite, tools, etc........	4 40	
			295 02

20a P.A.

COLONIZATION ROADS.—*Continued.*

Combermere and Palmer			
Rapids Road ....Johnson, J. F., overseer, 18 days at 2.25...	40 50		
do	Pay lists, wages of men employed............	130 00	
do	Johnson, J. F., tools, powder, etc...........	33 83	
do	Hudson, Mrs., board of men	51 00	
do	O'Brien, J. P., board of men	21 00	
do .	Devine & McGarry, tools	11 32	
do	Sundry persons, dynamite, blacksmithing, etc	4 79	
do	Litkie, B., overseer, 30 days at 2.25	67 50	
do	Pay lists, wages of men employed	367 12	
do	Litkie, B., tools, tent and cartage...........	25 37	
do	Schmelzie, S., tools	11 90	
do	Workman, A. & Co., tools	8 01	
do	Sundry persons, dynamite, camp outfit, etc	10 57	
		782 91	
	Less sale of tools, etc	14 00	
			768 91
Commanda Lake Road to			
Restoul Lake ....Porter, Geo., overseer, 16½ days at 2.25...	37 12		
do	Pay lists wages of men employed..............	160 32	
do	Brown, C. J., drills, powder, etc...........	3 85	
			201 29
Conmee Tp., Con. 1........Privat, Geo. A., overseer, accountable			780 00
Conmee Tp. between lots			
A. and 1 ....Privat, Geo. A., overseer, accountable			380 00
Constance Creek Bridge...Armitage, Jas., Reeve, paymaster			
do	Pay lists, wages of men employed	418 61	
do	Mayor, G., timber, cedar, etc.................	175 00	
do	Booth, J. R., timber, cedar, etc..............	20 00	
do	Sweeney, S., stone	19 00	
do	Andrews, A., iron rods, etc	42 80	
do	Baskins, G. H., cedar	5 00	
do	Armitage, J., cedar..............................	10 00	
do	Sundry persons, timber, paint, etc...........	8 39	
			698 80
Corkhill Road in Lobor-			
ough ....Corkhill, W. J., overseer, 10 days at 2.25.	22 50		
do	Pay lists, wages of men employed	159 39	
do	Darling, S. F., blasting supplies	12 59	
do	Dalton, W. B. & Sons, tools	3 25	
do	Austin, L. S., blacksmithing	2 20	
do	Roberts, J. S., tools	2 00	
			201 93
Corundum Mine Road ....Kernighan, A., overseer, 44 9-10 days at 2.25	101 02		
do	Pay lists of men employed	380 13	
do	Laundry, E., tools	2 40	
do	Bartlett, J., dynamite	2 30	
do	Kernighan, A., cartage and sharpening drills	3 40	
do	Sundry persons, dynamite, tools, black- smithing, etc	9 55	
			498 80
Crosby Rd. between Cons.			
3 and 4 ....Duval, C., overseer, 14 days at 2.25	31 50		
do	Pay lists, wages of men employed	167 25	
do	Desmarias. N., tools	3 50	
do	Quillier, W., blacksmithiing....................	2 00	
do	Postage, etc	55	
do	Taillon, A., overseer, 14 days at 2.25......	31 50	
do	Pay lists, wages of men employed	153 38	
do	Desmarias. N. tools	15 00	
do	Postage, etc	50	
			405 18

COLONIZATION ROADS.—*Continued.*

Cosby and Martland	......Lehais, H., overseer, 8 days at 2.25........	18 00	
do	Pay lists, wages of men employed............	82 25	
		100 25	
	Less amount of account unpaid........	25	
			100 00
Cosby & Martland Rd.	....Dione, F. X., overseer, 20¼ days at 2.25....	· 46 12	
do	Pay lists, wages of men employed	244 95	
do	Desmarias, N., tools	8 0ɔ	
do	Lafenier, D., rent of plow.......................	1 00	
do	Mulhern, W., blacksmithing	65	
			300 72
Creighton Road	............Brosseau, E., overseer, 23½ days at 2.25...	52 87	
do	Pay lists, wages of men employed	237 09	
do	Purvis Bros., tools	9 30	
do	Postage, stationery, etc	74	
			300 00
Croft Bridge, Lot 20, Con. 3	..............McIntosh, D. H., overseer, 5¼ days at 3.50	19 25'	
do	Pay lists, wages of men employed	61 48	
do	Knight Bros., lumber	267 52	
do	Crosswell, T., towing	6 00	
do	Hilliar, J., nails	2 65	
do	Bell, M., cartage	2 00	
do	Brown, J., nails	50	
			359 40
Croft Tp. Side Rd. between lots 30 and 31	...Farrelly, Thos., overseer, 19 days at 2.25	42 75	
do	Pay lists, wages of men employed	155 75	
do	Andrews, R., blacksmithing	1 00	
do	Newell, J. H., spikes	50	
			200 00
Dalton Road	................Montgomery, R., overseer, 7 days at 2.25	15 75	
do	Pay lists, wages of men employed	69 75	
do	Hunter, C., lumber and blacksmithing ...	4 50	
do	Montgomery, G., cartage	4 90	
do	Herring, E. H., tools, etc.	5 10	
do	Thompson, Chris., overseer. 11 days at 2.25	24 75	
do	Pay lists, wages of men employed	175 25	
do	Kitt, James, E., overseer, 8½ days at 2.25	19 12	
do	Pay lists, wages of men employed............	79 25	
do	Kitt, J. E., cedar	2 00	
do	Young, H., overseer, 6 days at 2.25	13 50	
do	Pay lists, wages of men employed	88 25	
dɔ	Postage, etc.	25	
			500 37
Dalton & Washago Rd.	....Boyd, Jno., overseer, 12½ days at 2.25 ...	28 12	
do	Pay lists, wages of men employed	252 02	
do	Bayley, J. T., gravel	22 00	
			302 14
Darling and Lanark Boundary Road	..........Barr, David, overseer, 14 days at 2.25	31 50	
do	Pay lists, wages of men employed	155 37	
do	Marshall, J., cedar	6 00	
do	Proctor, W. H., cedar and gravel	7 11	
			199 98
Darling, 8 Con. Line	......Barr, David, overseer, 15 days at 2.25 ...	33 75	
do .	Pay lists, wages of men employed	253 00	
do	McGee, H., gravel	6 44	
do	Moir, D., concrete pipe	5 00	
do	Hogan, M., blacksmithing	1 00	
do	Banning, O., powder and fuse	40	
			299 59

COLONIZATION ROADS.—*Continued.*

Day Tp., Con. 2	Grigg, Thos., overseer, 13½ days at 2.25 ...	30 38	
do	Pay lists, wages of men employed	155 94	
do	Taylor, A., blacksmithing and use of grader	7 75	
do	Cullis, J .R., dynamiting	4 00	
do	Bridge Bros., tools	2 50	
			200 57
Dean Lake and Blind			
River Road	Meeks, Jos., overseer, 21½ days at 2.25 ...	48 37	
do	Pay lists, wages of men employed	199 63	
do	Lizotte, E., blacksmithing	3 05	
do	Arnill, R., tools	2 00	
do	Forest, J., blacksmithing	65	
do	Thompson, L., tools	75	
			254 45
Dean Lake Mine Road....	Grant, Jas., overseer, 20 days at 2.25	45 00	
do	Pay lists, wages of men employed	333 50	
do	Braithwaite. F., tools	11 90	
do	Northern Ontario Copper Co., dynamite, etc.	9 25	
do	Postage, etc.	35	
			400 00
Desaulier Bridge & Field			
Road	Leduc, W., overseer, 21 days at 2.25	47 25	
do	Pay lists, wages of men employed	353 85	
do	Guernette, J., blacksmithing	10 00	
do	Lillie, R., dynamite	5 00	
do	Postage	10	
			416 20
Dilke Tp. Rd. North	McQuaker, Wm., overseer, 18 days at 2.50	45 00	
do	Pay lists, wages of men employed	314 47	
do	Proctor, H., provisions, etc......................	55 15	
do	Tilson Bros., do	28 52	
do	Longmore, F., butter	9 75	
do	Sheppard, W. G., provisions	5 00	
do	Gowdon, J., do	5 05	
do	Larogue, F., rent of camp	2 50	
do	Postage, etc.	16	
			465 60
Dinorwick & Sandy Lake			
Road	Smith, S., overseer, 26 days at 2.50	65 00	
do	Pay lists, wages of men employed	175 00	
do	Smith, S., use of tools, plows, etc.	10 00	
			250 00
Distress River Road	Milsop, Isaac T., overseer, 15 days 4½ hrs. at 2.25	34 76	
do	Pay lists, wages of men employed	151 82	
do	Hilliar, J., tools	9 10	
do	Sundry persons, blacksmithing, dynamite, etc.	4 31	
			199 99
Dobie Tp. Road	Luttrell, Alex., overseer, 18 days at 2.50...	45 00	
do	Pay lists. wages of men employed	395 45	
do	Gillies, M. Co., provisions	68 10	
do	Dixon, Geo., do	19 32	
do	Postage	50	
			528 37
	Less sale of lumber 12 00		
	Amount of account unpaid ... 16 37		
		28 37	
			500 00
Dorion Tp. Roads	Payton, Geo. C., overseer, 13 days at 2.25	29 25	
do	Pay lists, wages of men employed	164 25	
do	Marks, Clavet, Dobie Co., tools and freight	5 95	
do	Postage, affidavits, etc.	1 00	
			200 45

COLONIZATION ROADS.—*Continued.*

Dorion Tp. approaches to C.P.R. crossing	Payton, Geo. C., overseer, 5 days at 2.25	11 25	
do	Pay lists, wages of men employed	57 94	
do	Marks, Clavet Co, tools and freight	4 95	
do	Postage, affidavits, etc.	86	
			75 00
Dorion Tp. Road	Payton, Geo. C., overseer, 9 days at 2.25	20 25	
do	Pay lists, wages of men employed	108 44	
do	Postage	50	
			129 19
Dorion Tp. Bridge	Payton, Geo. C., overseer, 29 days at 2.25	65 25	
do	Pay lists, wages of men employed	245 48	
do	Mark, Clavet, Dobie Co., tools, etc.	32 32	
do	Woodside Bros., rods and bolts	7 26	
do	Roland, W., surveying	10 00	
do	Sundry persons, lumber, cartage, etc.	10 20	
			370 51
Donnegal and Fourth Chute Road	Turner, Robt., sr., overseer, 18 days at 2.25	45 50	
do	do do 7 do 1.50	10 50	
do	Pay lists, wages of men employed	132 00	
do	Turner, R., cedar and use of tools	8 91	
do	Sundry persons, tools, steel and powder	2 90	
			194 81
Drury, Denison and Graham	Ross, J. A., grant (expenditure, 1,182.33)	500 00	
Dryden Road North	Scott, W., overseer, accountable	200 00	
Dummer Tp. Road	Andrews, D., overseer, 9½ days at 2.25	21 38	
do	Pay lists, wages of men employed	169 60	
do	Patterson, E., gravel	4 00	
do	Sundry persons, tools, powder, blacksmithing, etc.	4 88	
			199 86
Dunchurch & James Bay Road	French, Ben., overseer, 61 days at 2.50	152 50	
do	Pay lists, wages of men employed	661 84	
do	Robertson Bros., provisions, etc.	150 74	
do	Taylor, M., do	35 51	
do	French, R., do	10 70	
do	Buchanan, A., do	4 10	
do	Postage, stationery, etc.	1 20	
			1,016 59
Douglas Station Road	Still, S. S., overseer, 16 days at 2.25	36 00	
do	Pay lists, wages of men employed	232 75	
do	Sutherland, A., tile	19 60	
do	Livingstone, H., tile	6 09	
do	Sundry persons, bolts, repairs, etc.	5 56	
			300 00
Dunnett & Cassimir Rd	Poisson, Chas., overseer, 25 days at 2.25	56 25	
do	Pay lists, wages of men employed	339 00	
do	Poisson, P., lumber	3 70	
do	Postage	04	
			398 99
Dunnett, between lots 8 and 9, Con. 5	Fournir, Nap., overseer, 17 days at 2.25	38 25	
do	Pay lists, wages of men employed	228 75	
do	Laporte, D., dynamite, etc.	30 50	
do	Lytle, W. A., blacksmithing	4 15	
do	Gagnon, A., overseer, 24 days at 2.25	54 00	
do	Pay lists, wages of men employed	209 61	
do	Gagnon, E., cedar	56 25	
do	Laporte, D. tools, etc.	32 65	
do	Lytle, W. A., spikes, etc.	17 84	
do	Keeling & Co., lumber	5 60	
do	Turgeon, F., overseer, accountable	80 00	
			782 60

COLONIZATION ROADS.—*Continued.*

Dysart & Sherburn Rds...	Roberts, Wm., overseer, 11 days at 2.25 ...	24 75	
do	Pay lists, wages of men employed	155 57	
do	Paul, Joseph, overseer, 8 days at 2.25	18 00	
do	Pay lists, wages of men employed	75 00	
do	Paul, J., cedar	6 00	
do	Sundry persons, blacksmithing, powder, etc.	4 25	
do	Cruikshanks, Robt., overseer, 10 days at 2.25	22 50	
do	Pay lists, wages of men employed	126 00	
do	Stevens, N., timber	2 00	
do	Loucks, J., overseer, 28 days at 2.25	63 00	
do	Pay lists, wages of men employed	200 17	
do	Louks, Mrs., board of men	71 64	768 88
Edgington and Humph- rey Road	Francour, Jno., overseer, 20 days at 2.25	45 00	
do	Pay lists, wages of men employed...........	246 43	
do	Bèlanger, J., tools................................	3 20	
do	Massey, G. R., blacksmithing..................	2 50	
do	Malkin, S. T., tools...............................	2 55	
do	Postage	12	299 80
Eganville & Perrault Rd..	Vendette, L., overseer, 22 days at 2.25...	49 50	
do	Pay lists, wages of men employed........	244 50	
do	McCann Bros., plow points.....................	1 05	
do	Vendette, L., use of plow.......................	4 20	
do	Sundry persons, blacksmithing, etc.........	1 20	300 45
Eganville & Scotch Bush Road	Wren, Thos., Sr., overseer, 21 days at 2.25	47 25	
do	Pay lists, wages of men employed........	253 50	
do	Black, W., blacksmithing.......................	1 20	
do	Postage	05	302 00
Eldon Three Quarter Line & Dalrymple Road	Steele, Jno., overseer, 6¼ days at 2.25...	14	
do	Pay lists, wages of men employed........	125	
do	Collins, T., gravel................................	10 62	
do	McFarlane, Jno., overseer, accountable...	120 66	269 87
Espanola Roads	Fisher, Alex., overseer, 28 days 9 hours at 2.25	65 03	
do	Pay lists, wages of men employed........	521 03	
do	Purvis, C. A., tools, etc........................	7 13	
do	Spanish River Pulp Co., dynamite..........	1 89	
do	Sheppard, H. E., affidavits	1 00	596 08
Eton Tp. Road	Robinson, W. J., overseer, 15 days at 2.50	37 50	
do	Pay lists, wages of men employed...........	371 91	
do	Hayes, J. G., tools....	1 50	
do	Begnall, F. T., plank.............................	53 90	
do	Latimer, J., spikes and tools..................	17 96	
do	Beatty, A., tools..................................	17 95	
do	Postage, etc.......................................	89	501 61
Faraday & Herschell	Mulcahey, Wm., overseer, 11 days at 2.25	24 75	
do	Pay lists, wages of men employed...........	66 00	
do	Rouse, M., rope, nails, etc.....................	9 50	100 25
Ferris Tp. Roads	Corbeilles, B., overseer, 19 days at 2.25...	42 75	
do	Pay lists. wages of men employed...........	259 13	
do	Purvis Bros., dynamite, chain, etc..........	13 83	
do	Corbeilles, B., plow..............................	9 00	
do	Pilon. J. B., blacksmithing.....................	6 30	
do	Morrison, G. E., tools............................	2 50	

COLONIZATION ROADS.—*Continued.*

Ferris Tp.	Roads	McDonald & Hay, dynamite	1 10	
	do	Dupuis, F., overseer, 14 days at 2.25	31 50	
	do	Pay lists, wages of men employed	150 75	
	do	Morrison, G. E., tools	11 75	
	do	Pilon, J. B., blacksmithing	1 30	
	do	Dupuis, F., use of plow, etc	4 70	
	do	Champagne, P., overseer, 10 days at 2.25	22 50	
	do	Pay lists, wages of men employed	119 00	
	do	Morrison, G. E., tools	6 75	
	do	Pilon, J. B., blacksmithing	1 50	
	do	Postage, etc.	25	
	do	Bouchard, R., overseer, 10 days at 2.25	22 50	
	do	Pay lists, wages of men employed	116 75	
	do	McDonald & Hay, dynamite, etc	7 15	
	do	Gauthier, V., blacksmithing	6 00	
	do	Postage	25	
	do	St. Jean, E., overseer, 14 days at 2.25	31 50	
	do	Pay lists, wages of men employed	164 11	
	do	Porter & Co., tools	4 50	
	do	St. Louis, A., repairing drills	60	
	do	Corbeilles, F., overseer, 20 days at 2.25	45 00	
	do	Pay lists, wages of men employed	215 75	
	do	Pelland, P., blacksmithing	2 00	
	do	Decari, B., plow	14 00	
	do	Morrison, G. E., tools	23 11	
	do	Postage	14	
	do	Rothwell, Thos., overseer, 14 days at 2.25	31 50	
	do	Pay lists, wages of men employed	154 75	
	do	McDonald & Hay, dynamite	4 75	
	do	Pilon, J. B., blacksmithing	5 00	
	do	Sundry persons, plow and tools	4 00	1,537 97
Ferry Road		Pringle, W. W., paymaster, accountable		200 00
Field and Badgerow Rd.				
from Sturgeon River		Aubin, Cyrus, overseer, 14 days at 2.25	31 50	
	do	Pay lists, wages of men employed	193 50	
	do	Guernette, J., tools	26 45	251 45
Field and Grant Smokey				
Falls Road		Lajeunesse, Chas., overseer, 33 days at 2.25	74 25	
	do	Pay lists, wages of men employed	335 88	
	do	Prieur, J. F., tools and dynamite	2 72	412 85
Field Rd. and Con. 6		Aubin, Eli, overseer, 19 days at 2.25	42 75	
	do	Pay lists, wages of men employed	242 25	
	do	Michaud & Levesque, scraper	11 00	
	do	Prieur, J. F., tools	6 50	
	do	Larocque, Max, overseer, 14½ days at 2.25	32 62	
	do	Pay lists, wages of men employed	168 75	
	do	Martin, Jos., overseer, 10½ days at 2.25	23 63	
	do	Pay lists, wages of men employed	165 25	
	do	Prieur, J. F., hardware, tools, etc	12 55	
	do	Aubin, O., scraper, etc	2 50	707 80
Fourth Lake Road		McLeod, Daniel, overseer, 14 days at 2.25	31 50	
	do	Pay lists, wages of men employed	167 17	
	do	Merrill, S. B., tools	3 15	
	do	McCullough, R., plowshare	25	202 07
Fossil Hill Road		Lewis, James, overseer, 13 days at 2.12	27 56	
	do	Pay lists, wages of men employed	370 02	
	do	Sundry persons, blacksmithing, hardware, etc.	2 42	400 00

COLONIZATION ROADS.—*Continued.*

French River Road ....Reekie, Albert, overseer, accountable..................		1,100 00	
Galbraith Tp. Road to			
McKenzie Bridge ....McPhee, M., overseer, 15¼ days at 2.25...	34 31		
do	Pay lists, wages of men employed.........	257 80	
do	McRae, A. J., tools............................	6 50	
do	Davidson, A., plow and repairs...........	60	
			299 21
Galway Roads ....Dutman, Wm., overseer, 11 days at 2.25	24 75		
do	Pay lists, wages of men employed...........	126 00	
do	Reid, Andrew, overseer, 9 days at 2.25...	20 25	
do	Pay lists, wages of men employed...........	129 75	
			300 75
Galway Tp. Roads ....Hunter, Wm., overseer, 16 days at 2.25...	36 00		
do	Pay lists, wages of men employed.........	210 25	
do	Hopkins Bros., tools.............................	3 75	
do	Dudman, Wm., overseer, 15 days at 2.25	33 75	
do	Pay lists, wages of men employed...........	216 75	
			500 50
Gamble's and Graham's			
Mill Road ....Graham, W. H., overseer, 15¼ days at 2.25	34 87		
do	Pay lists, wages of men employed...........	240 48	
do	Thornton, F., tools...............................	9 25	
do	Brais, D., repairs................................	3 00	
do	Bridge, J., use of grader and scraper......	4 50	
do	Sundry persons, dynamite, tools, etc.......	7 90	
			300 00
Gibbons, 3 and 4 Con..... Queeneville, A., overseer, 25 days at 2.25	56 26		
do	Pay lists, wages of men employed.........	343 50	
do	Postage	24	
			400 00
Gibbons, between Cons. 1			
and 2, lots 6 and 7 ......Couisseneau, M., overseer, 27¾ days at 2.25	62 43		
do	Pay lists, wages of men employed...........	373 75	
do	Prieur, J. F., block, chain and tools......	20 50	
do	Lillie, R., dynamite, etc........................	42 50	
			499 18
Gillies, Scobie and Pear-			
son Road ....Saunders, R., overseer, 30 days at 2.25...	67 50		
do	Pay lists, wages of men employed.........	427 28	
do	Hawker, E., blacksmithing....................	6 00	
do	Welsh, J. J., do	1 20	
do	Postage, etc.	28	
			502 26
Gilmour Station Bridge...McConnell, T. C., paymaster..................	....		
do	Pay lists, wages of men employed.........	262 00	
do	Sprockett, G., timber...........................	233 00	
do	Weddell, R., rods and bolts.....................	36 00	
do	Cox. J., spikes, etc...............................	10 74	
do	Walker, J. W., coal tar........................	3 00	
do	Sundry persons, spikes, tools, etc...........	7 52	
		552 26	
	Less amount account unpaid...........	52 26	
			500 00
Glamorgan and Cardiff			
Roads ....Shier, Jno., overseer, 6 days at 2.25........	13 50		
do	Pay lists, wages of men employed.........	76 50	
do	Kennedy, Jno., overseer, 6 days at 2.25...	13 50	
do	Pay lists, wages of men employed.........	80 00	
do	Walker, A., plow body...........................	3 25	
do	Sundry persons, powder, blacksmith-		
	ing, etc.	3 25	
do	Billings, Jas., overseer, 17 days at 2.25...	38 25	
do	Pay lists, wages of men employed........	133 50	

COLONIZATION ROADS.—*Continued.*

Glamorgan and Cardiff Roads	Sundry persons, blacksmithing, etc., and postage	3 25	
do	Curry, A., overseer, 19 days at 2.25	42 75	
do	Pay lists, wages of men employed	279 87	
do	Switzer, P. R., scraper	8 00	
do	Morrison, J., plank	4 70	
do	Wait, G., blacksmithing	1 50	
do	Postage	08	
do	Watson, T., overseer, 37½ days at 2.25	84 37	
do	Pay lists, wages of men employed	493 50	
do	Turner, J. J., tent	15 00	
do	Sundry persons, cedar, tools, blacksmithing, etc.	7 20	
			1,301 97
Golden Lake Road	Treas. County Renfrew, grant towards construction of bridge built in 1894		200 00
Golden Village Road	Murphy, Jno., overseer, 11 days at 2.25	24 75	
do	Pay lists, wages of men employed	174 35	
do	Stephens, M. J., blacksmithing	75	
do	Postage	15	
			200 00
Gordon and Allan	Treasurer Gorden and Allen, grant		500 00
Gordon, Allan & Billings	Shrigley, W. R., overseer, 30 days at 2.25	67 50	
do	Pay lists, wages of men employed	490 94	
do	Flannagan, S. C., road machine	12 00	
do	Shrigley. W. R., rent of plow, etc	6 90	
do	Loughead, T. R., tools, tar paper, etc	4 50	
do	Sundry persons, tools, blacksmithing, etc.	8 15	
do	McAusch, Wm., overseer, 9½ days at 2.25	21 37	
do	Pay lists, wages of men employed	168 50	
do	Allen. J. M., blacksmithing	4 25	
do	Munro, D., planks, spikes, etc	4 00	
do	Foster, G., cedar	1 87	
			789 99
Gordon Lake Road	McWhinney, Jno., overseer, 16½ days at 2.25	37 12	
do	Pay lists, wages of men employed	152 80	
do	McIeod, Jno., plank	4 65	
do	Clark, F., blacksmithing	4 62	
do	Postage, spikes, etc.	81	
			200 00
Gordon Lake & Sault Rd.	Ferguson, F., overseer, 20 days at 2.25	45 00	
do	Pay lists, wages of men employed	151 35	
do	Ferguson, R., tools	2 75	
do	Postage	06	
			199 16
Gornonville Rd., Widdifield Tp.	Larocque, O., overseer, 21½ days at 2.25	48 38	
do	Pay lists. wages of men employed	143 48	
do	Purvis Bros., dynamite, etc.	10 43	
do	Postage	11	
			202 40
Gore Bay and Providence Bay Road	Gamey. Jos., overseer, 31¼ days at 2.25	70 31	
do	Pay lists. wages of men employed	516 97	
do	Gamey. H.. plow	8 00	
do	Sundry persons, tools and postage	4 20	
			599 48
Gore Line Road, Indian River & Petewawa Rd.	Summers, Wm., overseer, 12 days at 2.25	27 00	
do	Pay lists. wages of men employed	123 50	
do	Mackie & Ryan, tools	1 00	
do	Postage	25	
do	Jackson. Jno., overseer, 11 days at 2.25	24 75	
do	Pay lists. wages of men employed	164 85	
do	Butt, Wm., cedar	4 80	

COLONIZATION ROADS.—*Continued.*

Gore Line Road, Indian River and Petewawa Rd..	McMunn, R., use of plow and repairs	4 60	
do	Jackson, W., cedar	1 00	
do	Drapeau, P., overseer, 16 days at 2.25	36 00	
do	Pay lists, wages of men employed	198 75	
do	Marett, P., gravel	14 90	
do	Prapeau, M., stone	35	
do	Hubert, R., overseer, 9 days at 2.25	20 25	
do	Pay lists, wages of men employed	71 62	
do	Kurth, F., cedar	7 21	
do	Dunlop & Co., tools	6 20	
do	Postage	25	
do	Hoffman, T., overseer, 10 days at 2.25	22 50	
do	Pay lists, wages of men employed	116 55	
do	Dunlop & Co., tools	16 97	
do	Hoffman, T., blacksmithing and postage	3 23	
		866 53	
	Less tools sold by R. Hubert... 3 50		
	do T. Hoffman.. 9 25		
		12 75	
			853 78
Goulais Bay Road	Munro, W. H., paymaster :		
do	Pay lists, wages of men employed	1,303 27	
do	Parker & Co., provisions	109 01	
do	Stibbs, F. W., do	202 69	
do	Huston & Co., hay, oats, etc.	177 45	
do	Moore & Brown, camp outfit	34 46	
do	Soo Livery, teaming	53 00	
do	Carroll, R., wagon and tools	67 45	
do	Ryan, T. S., blacksmithing	8 75	
do	Pratt, R. G., rubber boots	5 90	
do	Sundry persons, provisions	14 83	
do	do cartage, rent of camp, etc.	22 90	
			1,999 71
Grading Machinery	Good Roads Machinery Co., steel grader	237 50	
do	Sawyer, Massey Co., grader and extra blade bit	250 00	
do	do blade and bolt for grader	8 50	
			496 00
Gratton Tp. Road	Irving, Jno., overseer, 16 days at 2.25	36 00	
do	Pay lists, wages of men employed	176 00	
do	Irving, Jno., cedar, use of tools and postage	12 30	
			224 30
Gratton, 13 Con	Sutherland, P., overseer, 15 days at 2.25	33 75	
do	Pay lists, wages of men employed	165 00	
do	Sutherland, P., use of plow	2 00	
			200 75
Greenview Bridge over Papineau Creek	Anderson, Jas., overseer, 28 days at 2.25	63 00	
do	Pay lists, wages of men employed	127 50	
do	Cearins, A., cedar	62 20	
do	Grant, J., sawing timber	11 80	
do	Weddell, R., rods, nuts and washers	10 21	
do	Lumb, E. T., tar	7 00	
do	Sundry persons, sawing timber, cartage, etc.	6 55	
			288 26
Griffin Tp. Road	Chatson, O., overseer, 25 days at 2.25	56 25	
do	Pay lists, wages of men employed	437 06	
do	Chatson, W., dynamite, fuse, etc.	5 25	
do	Dual, Thos., ground rent	1 00	
do	Postage	48	
			500 04

COLONIZATION ROADS.—*Continued.*

Grimsthorpe Road	Byran, A. C., overseer, 14 days at 2.25	31 50	
do	Pay lists, wages of men employed	253 66	
do	Byran, A. C., timber	10 00	
do	Wagg, W. J., chain	4 54	
			299 70
Haggarty Tp. Roads	Stack, Patrick, overseer, 22 days at 2.25	49 50	
do	Pay lists, wages of men employed	330 00	
do	George & McGregor, tools	8 70	
do	Andrews, W. R., scraper	8 00	
do	Sundry persons, dynamite, blacksmithing, etc.	3 80	
do	Burant, Alex., overseer, 20 days at 2.25	45 00	
do	Pay lists, wages of men employed	226 50	
do	Prince, A., tools	28 98	
do	Longuskie, P., overseer, 7 days at 2.25	15 75	
do	Pay lists, wages of men employed	84 00	
do	Repairs, etc.	25	
			800 48
Hanmer Tp. Roads	Gatien, F., overseer, 26 days at 2.25	58 50	
do	Pay lists, wages of men employed	360 75	
do	Purvis Bros., dynamite	34 00	
do	Postage, stationery, etc.	50	
do	Lalonde. F., overseer, 13 days at 2.25	29 25	
do	Pay lists, wages of men employed	121 25	
			604 25
Harlowe and Myers Cave Road	Delyea, Alex., overseer, 13 days at 2.25	29 25	
do	do do 2 do 1.84	3 68	
do	Pay lists, wages of men employed	151 73	
do	Marble Lake Mfg. Co., cedar	9 00	
do	Brown, J. W., tools	4 75	
do	Sundry persons, caps, fuse and dynamite.	1 50	
			199 91
Harrowsmith and Sydenham Road	W. W. Proingle, paymaster, accountable		250 00
Harryett's Corners and Brudenell Road	Coyne, Sam'l., overseer, 18 days at 2.25	40 50	
do	Pay lists. wages of men employed	147 75	
do	Coyne, S., cedar and rent of plow	10 50	
do	Moran, J. P., cartage	60	
			199 35
Hartisbise Rd., Ferris Tp.	Rochefort, D.. overseer, 15 days at 2.25	33 75	
do	Pay lists, wages of men employed	247 00	
do	Gauthier, V., tools, blacksmithing, etc.	19 80	
do	Postage	25	
			300 80
Harvey Tp. Rd. North	Ingram, Jas., overseer, 35 days at 2.25	78 75	
do	Pay lists, wages of men employed	412 37	
do	Postage	50	
			491 62
Harvey Tp. Rd. South	Wier, J. O., overseer, 17 days at 2.25	38 25	
do	Pay lists, wages of men employed	260 63	
			298 88
Haveland & Fenwick Rds.	McLean, M., overseer, 21 days at 2.25	47 25	
do	Pay lists, wages of men employed	243 00	
do	Moore & Brown, dynamite	8 75	
			299 00
Hermina Mine Road	Houle, W., overseer, 24 days at 2.25	54 00	
do	Pay lists, wages of men employed	408 37	
do	Armstrong Bros., timber	14 00	
do	Bower, N. H., tools	6 55	
do	Sundry persons, blacksmithing, dynamite. etc.	6 57	
			489 49

COLONIZATION ROADS.—*Continued.*

Hermine & Bancroft Rd..	Bentley, Geo., overseer, 20 days at 2.25 ...	45 00	
do	Pay lists, wages of men employed	127 25	
do	Farnum, H. C., dynamite	15 00	
do	Bentley, G., use of wagon, etc.	8 00	
do	Ballard, Jno., tools, etc.	3 30	
do	Sundry persons, fuse and coal	1 40	
			199 95
Herschell, 3rd Con.........	Mulcahey, Wm., overseer, 25 days at 2.25	56 25	
do	Pay lists, wages of men employed	243 75	
			300·00
Hilton Road, Algoma	Brayley, Thos., overseer, 36 days at 2.25 ...	81 00	
do	Pay lists, wages of men employed	311 98	
do	Stienburg, T., tools	3 00	
do	Totten, W. J., tools	2 30	
do	Smith, W., gravel	2 10	
do	Sweedy, R. L., tools	50	
			400 88
Hilton Tp., "1 to K" Line	Burnside, James, overseer, 20 days at 2.25	45 00	
do	Pay lists, wages of men employed	259 03	
			304 03
Honora to Little Current..	Moore, Jno., overseer, 21½ days at 2.25 ...	48 37	
do	Pay lists, wages of men employed	439 63	
do	Kingsboro, J. G., tools, etc.	15 00	
do	Collins, Jno., lumber	1 50	
		504 50	
	Less sale of tools	3 75	
			500 75
Hollow Lake Road	Clayton, Jerry, overseer, 7 days at 2.25 ...	15 75	
do	Pay lists, wages of men employed	42 00	
do	Mackay & Co., spikes	2 57	
do	McKay, Angus, lumber	37 73	
			98 05
Howland and Bidwell	Hembruff, Jas., overseer, 9 days at 2.25 ...	20 25	
do	Pay lists, wages of men employed	173 70	
do	Hembruff, Jno., teaming	3 00	
do	Hembruff, Wm., do	3 00	
do	Postage	05	
do	Ferguson, L. W., overseer, 27 days at 2.25	60 75	
do	Pay lists, wages of men employed	418 47	
do	Trotter, W. L., tools, etc.	8 90	
do	Bradbury, F. G. R., tools	3 80	
do	Stringer, R., blacksmithing	3 45	
do	Gordon, W. H., plow points	4 00	
do	Postage	63	
			700 00
Hugel, between Cons. 2 and 3 and 4 and 5	Whelan, Jno., overseer, 14 days at 2.25 ...	31 50	
do	Pay lists, wages of men employed	168 75	
do	England, J., rent of plow	1 00	
do	Postage	10	
do	Akerland, J., overseer, 14 days at 2.25......	31 50	
do	Pay lists, wages of men employed............	156 00	
do	Guernette, J., tools, etc	12 45	
			401 30
Hugel & Badergow Rd...	Mayette, Leon, overseer, 27¼ days at 2.25	61 30	
do	Pay lists, wages of men employed	382 40	
do	Guernette, J., tools, blacksmithing, etc....	27 75	
do	Lillie, R., dynamite	15 00	
do	Portius, E., rent of plow	6 50	
do	Sundry persons, plank and rent of tools ...	6 45	
			499 40

COLONIZATION ROADS.—*Continued.*

Humphrey Tp. Road and
Bridge ....McCaus, Jno., overseer, 18 days at 2.25 ... 40 50
    do   Pay lists, wages of men employed 192 63
    do   Clubb, A. W., dynamite 12 00
    do   Lambert, W., blacksmithing 5 32
    do   Grant, W. M., do 2 50
    do   McCaus, R., use of wagon 1 00
    do   Postage 25
                                              254 20

Hungerford Tp. Road,
Tweed E.....................Dafoe, S. G., overseer, 11 days at 2.25 ...... 24 75
    do   Pay lists, wages of men employed 163 55
    do   Clark, G. V., timber 68 41
    do   Garrett, W. & Sons, iron rods 15 50
    do   Lonergan, A., cedar 10 00
    do   Cassidy, J., timber 9 00
    do   Rush, J., do 7 20
    do   Sundry persons, timber and nails 4 05
                                              302 46

Hydechute, Griffith Tp.... Fortin, Jos., overseer, 20 days at 2.25 ...... 45 00
    do   Pay lists, wages of men employed 318 50
    do   Fortin, J., cedar, teaming and use of plow 19 00
    do   King, J., cedar 11 00
    do   Devine & McGarry, tools 8 32
    do   Sundry persons, powder, spikes, etc. 4 71
    do   Doorly, Peter, overseer, 11 days at 2.25 ... 24 75
    do   Pay lists, wages of men employed 60 50
    do   Doorly, P., timber, board of men, etc. ... 13 70
    do   Sundry persons, powder, blacksmithing,
                 etc. 2 10
                                            507 58

Isbester Road .... McEvoy, R. W., overseer, 21 days at 2.25 47 25
    do   Pay lists, wages of men employed 251 00
    do   Collings, J. W., tools 1 50
    do   McEvoy, W. H., repairs 20
                                            299 95

Inspection .... Argue, D., services as Inspector,
                 99 days at 5.00 .... 495 00
  do   Postage 1 67
                                       496 67
  do   Bailey, Jno., services as Inspector,
                 81 days at 5.00 .... 405 00
  do   Cassidy, T., delivering telegrams,
                 etc. 2 50
  do   Mortimer, J., locating road 2 50
                                       410 00
  do   Bennett, G. W., services as Inspector, 78
                 days at 5.00 .... 390 00
• do   Besserer, L. W., services as In-
                 spector, 134 days at 5.00 670 00
  do   do   trav. expenses.. 18 00
                                     688 00
  do   Craig, Wm., services, Inspector, 77
                   days at 5.00 ...... 385 00
  do   do   postage, etc. 4 00
                                     389 00
  do   Cole, S., services, Inspector, 148 days at
                 5.00 .... 740 00
  do   Fraser, Jas., services, Inspector,
                 166 days at 5.00 ·830 00
  do   do   postage 5 00
                                     835 00
             Less amount of account unpaid 235 00
                                     600 00

COLONIZATION ROADS.—*Continued.*

Inspection...	Hunt, J. McK., services, Inspector, 115 days at 5.00		575 00
do	Jupp, R. H., services, Inspector, 26 days at 5.00		130 00
do	Kerr, W. E., services, Inspector, 220 days at 5.00 .... 1,100 00		
do	McKelvie, D., rent of storehouse...	4 16	
do	Pay list, wages of men, building storehouse	20 00	
do	Russell & Son, lumber for store-house	9 06	
do	Eplett, S., felt paper for store-house	2 00	1,135 22
do	Lowe, Wm., services, Inspector, 139 days at 5.00	695 00	
do	do postage	3 00	698 00
do	McConnell, T. C., services, Inspector, 67 days at 5.00		335 00
do	Moss, H. N., services, Inspector, 144 days at 5.00.	720 00	
do	do travelling expenses.	9 00	729 00
do	Munro, W. H., services, Inspector, 113 days at 5.00	565 00	
do	do postage	3 37	568 37
do	Pearson, Geo. M., services, Inspector, 76 days at 5.00...	380 00	
do	do postage	50	380 50
do	Pringle, W. W., services, Inspector, 128 days at 5.00	640 00	
do	do postage	8 56	648 56
do	Sylvester, O., services, Inspector, 129 days at 5.00	645 00	
do	do postage	4 70	649 70
do	Weir, D., services, Inspector, 99 days at 5.00	495 00	10,068 02
Jarlsburg Road	Nelson, Geo., overseer, 16 days at 2.25 ...	36 00	
do	Pay lists, wages of men employed	136 58	
do	Driscoll, R., plank	23 92	
do	Sundry persons, tools, plow point and postage	3 50	200 00
Jennings, 5 and 6 Con.....	Lignard, P., overseer, 29 days at 2.25......	65 25	
do	Pay lists, wages of men employed	369 75	
do	Dignard, A., lumber	42 75	
do	Coursol, F., do	16 00	
do	Sundry persons, nails, blacksmithing, etc.	9 75	503 50
Jennings and Appleby T. L. Road, lots 7 to 13...	Potvin, Jos., overseer, 21½ days at 2.25 ...	48 38	
do	Pay lists, wages of men employed	344 74	
do	Laporte, D... plow points	2 00	
do	Desgroosveilliers, crow bars	2 50	
do	Poulin, Geo., blacksmithing	50	398 12

COLONIZATION ROADS.—*Continued.*

Johnson and Plummer, Cariboo Lake to Port Lock Mill	Carter, Jno., overseer, 22½ days at 2.25 ...	50 62	
do	Pay lists, wages of men employed	334 10	
do	Carter, Jno. J., plank	10 20	
do	Sundry persons, tools	5 65	
			400 57
Johnson Tp. through Hincks' Location	McTavish, H., overseer, 21½ days at 2.25	48 37	
do	Pay lists, wages of men employed	342 95	
do	Prout, J. W., dynamite	9 00	
do	Sundry persons, dynamite, blacksmithing, etc	3 75	
		404 07	
	Less amount of account unpaid	4 07	
			400 00
Johnson Tp., Con. 3	Rutherford, Jno., overseer, 19¼ days at 2.25	43 31	
do	Pay lists, wages of men employed	253 30	
do	Somers, W. W., dynamite, blacksmithing, etc	11 83	
do	McLarty, R., plank	3 60	
do	Sundry persons, dynamite, tools, etc........	1 00	
			313 04
Jocelyn Tp., West Boundary	Burnside, Wm., overseer, 23 days at 2.25....	51 75	
do	Pay lists, wages of men employed	248 23	
			299 98
Jones Falls and Battersea Road	Burtch, C. S., overseer, 21 days at 2.25...	47 25	
	Pay lists, wages of men employed	262 87	
do	Burtch, L., gravel and plow paints	28 00	
do	Burtch, B., gravel	17 30	
do	Kenny, Thos., overseer, 10 days at 2.25 ...	22 50	
do	Pay lists, wages of men employed	126 00	
do	Harrison, F. S., dynamite, etc	2 71	
			506 63
Kagawong to Gore Bay...	Brown, Hugh, overseer, 24½ days at 2.25...	55 13	
do	Pay lists, wages of men employed	519 90	
do	Loughead, J. R., tools	7 60	
do	Brown, Robt., cedar	7 00	
do	Carter, J., plank	4 50	
do	Smith, Bros., tools	3 10	
do	Hilliar, J., repairs	2 00	
do	Sundry persons, tools, spikes, etc	5 40	
			604 63
Kill Bear Point Road in Carling Tp.................	Thompson, Andrew, overseer, 20 days at 2.25		45 00
do	Pay lists, wages of men employed	141 37	
do	Fenn, A. N., tools	4 95	
do	Thompson, Jno., rent of plow, tools, etc...	4 77	
do	Sundry persons, blacksmithing, etc	3 91	
			200 00
Killaloe & Brudenell Rd...	Hagarty, T., overseer, 28 days at 2.25	63 00	
do	Pay lists, wages of men employed	396 50	
do	Hagarty, Jerry, cedar	15 00	
do	Hagarty, Jas., dynamite	5 00	
do	Andrews, R., scraper	8 00	
do	George & McGregor, tools	7 20	
			494 70
Kirkpatrick, Cons. 4 & 5 & between lots 8 & 9...	Paquette, Felix, overseer, 10 days at 2.25...	22 50	
do	Pay lists, wages of men employed	173 26	
do	Guernette, J., blacksmithing	2 95	
do	Sundry persons, blacksmithing, etc	1 40	

COLONIZATION ROADS.—*Continued.*

Kirkpatrick, Cons. 4 and 5, and between lots 8 and 9..	Paquette, Alex., overseer, 13½ days at 2.25	30 38	
do	Pay lists wages of men employed	163 13	
do	Ricard, F. A., tools	6 30	
do	Postage	19	
			.400 11
Korah Roads	Everett, D., overseer, 28 days at 2.25......	63 00	
do	Pay lists, wages of men employed	427 42	
do	Moore & Brown, dynamite	8 75	
do	Plummer, Ferguson, Hardware. Co., tools.	1 30	
			500 47
Lake Clear Road	Gannon, M. J., overseer, 14 days at 2.25...	31 50	
do	Pay lists, wages of men employed	157 50	
do	Gannon, M. J., use of tools, etc	7 20	
			196 20
L'Amable & Bancroft Rd.	Moore, F., overseer, 40 1-5 days at 2.25...	90 45	
do	Pay lists, wages of men employed............	362 70	
do	Steel, E., wire fencing	145 50	
do	Sanderson, W. A., harness	29 35	
do	Lamb, Jno., cedar	15 00	
do	Mullett, C. D., blacksmithing	4 85	
do	Sundry persons, lumber, teaming, tools,		
do	etc	10 07	
		657 92	
	Less amount of account unpaid	257 92	
			400 00
L'Amable and Fort Stewart Road	Moore, F., overseer, 29½ days at 2.25......	66 37	
do	Pay lists, wages of men employed	438 32	
do	Sittl> & Culbertson, carts	45 00	
do	Fair, R. C., tools	11 97	
do	Mineral Range Iron Ffg. Co., dynamite...	4 19	
do	Lumbe, E., rent of tents. etc..................	6 00	
do	Stemars, W., cedar and stoneboat	4 00	
do	Hennessy, A., repairing carts	4 00	
do	Sundry persons, cartage, blacksmithing, etc	9 62	
			589 47
Laurier Tp., 9 & 10 Con.	Leighton, Fred, overseer, 17½ days at 2.25.	39 37	
do	Pay lists, wages of men employed........	160 07	
do	Postage	06	
			199 50
Lavalle and Burris Road between Secs. 26 & 27...	Weir. David, overseer, 31 days at 2.50......	77 50	
do	Pay lists, wages of men employed	673 65	
do	Saunders & Co., provisions and supplies ...	178 81	
do	Holmes Bros., provisions and tools	24 80	
do	McTavish, G., provisions	22 37	
do	Strachan, G., potatoes	11 00	
do	Martin, R. S., lumber	3 00	
do	Postage	12	
			991 25
Lefroy Second Line Rd...	Horricks, R., overseer. 21¼ days at 2.25 ...	48 37	
do	Pay lists, wages of men employed	209 50	
do	Fitzpatrick. timber	10 75	
do	Miller, F. A., timber	10 00	
do	Proud, V. W., timber	10 00	
do	McKay, M., blacksmithing	3 95	
do	Sundry persons, timber, nails, etc...........	2 57	
			295 14
Little Doe Lake Road ...	Stewart, Thomas, overseer, 14 days at 2.25	31 50	
do	Pay lists, wages of men employed	168 01	
do	King, T. L., use of plow	1 50	
do	Hilliar, J., dynamite	1 00	
			202 01

COLONIZATION ROADS.—*Continued*.

Little Pickerel River			
Bridge	Driver, Walter, overseer, 12 days at 2.25...	27 00	
do	Pay lists, wages of men employed.............	125 53	
do	Forsythe, E., spikes	2 25	
do	Driver, J., axe handles	75	
do	Postage	20	
			155 73
Long Lake Rd., Carlow			
Rd. & Musclow Hill Rd.	Stringer, P., overseer, 5 days at 2.00......	10 00	
do	Pay lists, wages of men employed	22 00	
do	Moore, F., overseer, 8¼ days at 2.25........	19 12	
do	Pay lists, wages of men employed	78 75	
do	Sagé, G. W., cartage	2 00	
do	Kernighan, A., overseer, 9 days at 2.25...	20 25	
do	Pay lists, wages of men employed	79 50	
			231 62
Lorimer Lake Road in			
Ferguson & Hagerman.	Steele, W. G., overseer, 22½ days at 2.25.	50 62	
do	Pay lists, wages of men employed	310 90	
do	Kangon, Emil, dynamite	10 80	
do	Beatty, Wm., Co., tools, etc..................	7 65	
do	Badger, W., dynamite	7 00	
do	Farley, R. J., use of forge	4 50	
do	Steele, G. R., teaming	5 25	
do	Sundry persons, tools, dynamite, etc	4 15	
			400 87
Lumsden Tp. Road	Masse, Leonard, overseer, 29 days at 2.25.	65 25	
do	Pay lists, wages of men employed	450 00	
			515 25
Leybster & Marks Post...	Faithful, Jas., overseer, 26 days at 2.25...	58 50	
do	Pay lists, wages of men employed	391 90	
do	Bishop, A. & Co., tools, etc....................	22 15	
do	Barden, G.. tent, tools and cartage	16 00	
do	Wells and Emmerson, tools, etc	10 20	
			498 75
Macaulay & Brunel	Rowe, Richard, overseer, 19¾ days at 2.25	44 43	
do	Pay lists, wages of men employed	153 99	
do	Mosley, J. E., tools	3 15	
do	Scott, R., spikes	60	
do	Postage	25	
do	Jackson, R., overseer, 37 days at 2.25 ...	83 25	
do	Pay lists, wages of men employed	307 23	
do	Ecclestone and Whitten, tools, etc	9 50	
do	Seeley, J. C., overseer, 19 days at 2.25......	42 75	
do	Pay lists, wages of men employed............	143 89	
do	White Bros., tools	9 18	
do	Sundry persons, tools, hardware, etc........	4 35	
			802 59
Machar & Lount Tp. Rds.	Smyth. G. C.. overseer, 16 days at 2.25......	36 00	
do	Pay lists, wages of men employed	148 88	
do	South River, Mercantile Co., tools, coal etc.	10 25	
do	Sundry persons, plow. tools, etc.............	4 87	
do	Quirt, Thos. H., overseer,, 14 days at 2.25.	31 50	
do	Pay lists, wages of men employed	160 35	
do	South River Mercantile Co., tools	5 50	
do	Vincent & Co., tools	2 65	
do	Leslie, Hy., overseer, 29 days at 2.25........	65 25	
do	Pay lists, wages of men employed	327 47	
do	Edgar, J., powder and use	3 61	
do	Sundry persons, steel blacksmithing, etc ...	3 67	
			800 00

21a P.A.

COLONIZATION ROADS.—*Continued.*

Maple Lake Station and Rosseau Road	Heaslip, James, overseer, 14 days at 2.25...	31 50	
do	Pay lists, wages of men employed	158 25	
do	Pearce. M.. powder and fuse	4 00	
do	Ross., D. M., rent of forge	2 00	
do	Sundry persons, coal, hire of plow, scraper, etc	4 25	
			200 00
Martland Rd. between 2 and 3	Dambremont, Frank, overseer, 14 days at 2.25	31 50	
do	Pay lists, wages of men employed	160 50	
do	Desmaris, Noel, tools	7 40	
do	Postage, affidavits, etc	1 00	
			200 40
Mason, Cosby and Delaware to C. P. Ry........	Lamarche, Peirre, overseer, 24½ days at 2.25	55 13	
do	Pay lists, wages of men employed	318 25	
do	Desmarsis, N., tools	19 80	
do	Bertrand, P., tools	5 05	
do	Postage, stationery, etc	1 07	
do	Ouilette, overseer, 22 days at 2.25...........	50 63	
do	Pay lists, wages of men employed	291 37	
do	Ouilette, F., tools, scraper, etc..............	48 50	
do	Desmarais, N., powder	5 25	
do	Monsen, C., dynamite	4 25	
			799 30
Massey Tp. from Salter and May	Cuthbertson, A., overseer, 27½ days at 2.25	61 87	
do	Pay lists, wages of men employed	412 37	
do	Massey Mining Co., rent of scraper	15 00	
do	Cuthbertson, A., plank	5 34	
do	Sundry persons, blacksmithing, 4.40; bank interest, 1.50	5 90	
			500 48
Matchedash Road	Barrow, Oliver, overseer, 17 days at 2.25...	38 25	
do	Pay lists, wages of men employed...........	510 75	
do	Balkewell, A., cedar and tile	23 33	
do	Gardiner, W., stone	14 80	
do	Hall, D., gravel	7 00	
			594 13
Mather and Dobie T. L. Road	Luthrell, Alex., overseer, 26 days at 2.50....	65 00	
do	Pay lists, wages of men employed	667 90	
do	Langstaff, C. R., provisions	147 59	
do	Hoover, B., provisions and lumber	43 90	
do	Strachan, D., tools	45 40	
do	Cameron, W., tools, provisions, etc	37 50	
do	Weston, T., storage and freight	4 00	
do	Postage, stationery, etc	75	
			1,012 04
Mattawan Tp. Roads	Dupuis. E.. overseer, 12½ days at 2.25......	28 13	
do	Pay lists, wages of men employed	122 25	
do	Belanger, W., overseer, 16 days at 2.25...	36 00	
do	Pay lists, wages of men employed	203 50	
do	Gilligan Bros., timber	5 00	
do	Levis Bros., tools	3 10	
do	Sunday persons, dynamite and tar paper ...	2 55	
do	Auger. Leon, overseer, 10 days at 2.25......	22 50	
do	Pay lists, wages of men employed	72 50	
do	Levis Bros., tools	2 70	
			498 23

COLONIZATION ROADS.—*Continued.*

Maynooth and Madawaska			
Road	Card, C. J., overseer, 37 days at 2.25...	83 25	
do	Pay lists, wages of men employed............	258 29	
do	Baragor, E. K., gravel and building culvert	41 00	
do	Wooton, E. A., tools...............................	4 62	
do	Weaver, G. E., axe handles, etc..............	85	
do	Postage, stationery, etc...........................	75	
			388 76
Medora, Wood & Baxter.	Wood, P. V., overseer, 20 days at 2.25...	45 00	
do	Wood, P. V., overseer, 4 days at 1.75...	7 00	
do	Pay lists, wages of men employed............	232 75	
do	Georgian Bay Lumber Co., tools...............	14 75	
do	Postage, stationery, etc...........................	50	
(Wood, Con. 16)...........	Armstrong, S., overseer, 19 days at 2.25	42 75	
do	Pay lists, wages of men employed............	154 26	
do	Young, J. F., tools.................................	5 00	
(Wood, Cons. 19-20).....	Armstrong, S., overseer, 8 days at 2.25...	18 00	
do	Pay lists, wages of men employed............	80 10	
do	Smith, J. G., plank...............................	6 00	
			606 11
Meldrum Bay and Silver-			
water Road	Falls, Thos., overseer, 23½ days at 2.25......	52 88	
do	Pay lists, wages of men employed............	522 85	
do	Baxter, J. L., scraper............................	7 50	
do	Sundry persons, repairs, blacksmithing, etc.	4 00	
			587 23
Mellick & Jaffrey Rd......	Talbot, D. C., overseer, 52 days at 2.50...	130 00	
do	Pay lists, wages of men employed.........	1,501 75	
do	Fife, A. T. & Co., camp outfit, tools, etc...	69 10	
do	Scott & Hudson Co., tools, hardware, etc.	29 15	
do	Hamilton Powder Co., dynamite.............	25 00	
do	Baker, F. J., building culverts..............	10.00	
do	Parrott, R., stove...............................:	10 50	
do	Griffith, D. M., blacksmithing.................	8 40	
do	Saunders, W., cartage..........................	6 00	
do ·	Sundry persons, dynamite, cartage, etc.	7 85	
			1,797 75
Methuen Tp. Roads	McCutcheon, R., overseer, 18 days at 2.25	40 50	
do	Pay lists, wages of men employed............	262 23	
do	Whitney, N., wood for crusher..............	4 00	
do	Sundry persons, plank, oil, postage, etc....	3 45	
			310 18
Michipicoten Road	Reid, G., overseer, 43 days at 2.50........	107 50	
do	Pay lists, wages of men employed............	792 77	
do	Speers & Burke, dynamite, etc..............	70 90	
do	Moore & Brown, tools............................	9 37	
do	Sundry persons, tools, spikes, etc...........	10 62	
			991 16
Mickle Steeps Rd., Cald-			
well Tp.	Graham, Alex., overseer, 14 days at 2.25	31 50	
do	Pay lists, wages of men employed............	162 38	
do	Sundry persons, tools, repairs, etc..........	2 37	
			196 25
Miscampbell Road	Lowe, Wilfred, overseer, 27 days at 2.25...	60 75	
do	Pay lists, wages of men employed............	254 00	
do	Gadd, T. J. P., board of men..................	150 07	
do	Wells Hardware Co., tools, dynamite, etc.	18 85	
do	McGuire & Penman, dynamite..............	20 50	
			504 17

COLONIZATION ROADS.—*Continued.*

Monk, between Rama Rd. and Rathbun	Mulvihall, Thos., overseer, 29 days at 2.25	65 25	
do	Pay lists, wages of men employed............	418 75	
do	Doolittle, S., dynamite...........................	9 00	
do	McNab Bros, do	3 80	
do	Cahill, M., blacksmithing.......................	2 80	
			499 60
Monmouth Roads	Summerville, W. J., overseer, 14½ days at 2.25	32 62	
do	Pay lists, wages of men employed............	264 60	
do	Cyle, J., repairing plow.........................	1 50	
do	Postage and blacksmithing.....................	57	
do	Graham, Thos., overseer, 29 days at 2.25	65 25	
do	Pay lists, wages of men employed............	418 85	
do	Cope, Jas., timber.................................	15 00	
do	Riley, Alex., nails.................................	1 00	
			799 39
Monteith Tp. 5th Side Road	Johnston, M., overseer, 20 days at 2.25...	45 00	
do	Pay lists, wages of men employed............	154 50	
do	Dixon, W. R., powder and fuse............	98	
do	Davis, T., blacksmithing.......................	50	
			200 98
Moores Bridge & Woolaston Road	Mulcahy, Wm., overseer, 33 days at 2.25...	74 25	
do	Pay lists, wages of men employed............	210 75	
do	Walker, Thos., blacksmithing..................	6 00	
do	I. B. & O. Ry., freight charges	5 00	
do	Sundry persons, bolts and lumber..........	4 10	
do	Nugent, Wm. H., overseer, 17 days at 2.25	38 25	
do	Pay lists, wages of men employed............	161 35	
do	Nugent, W. H., tools............................	6 40	
			506 10
Moose Creek Bridges	Littlejohn, D., repairing bridges.......................		6 98
Morley Rd. between Sec. 8 and 17 and west	Cameron, Wm., overseer, 35 days at 2.50	87 50	
do	Pay lists, wages of men employed.........	375 00	
do	Boucher, E. J., tent, provisions, etc.......	53 70	
do	McTague, J., provisions	57 63	
do	Cameron, Mrs., do	19 10	
do	Lockhart, E., tools	3 90	
do	Postage, stationery, etc.........................	50	
			597 33
Morley and Pattullo Town Line	Weir, D., overseer, 50 days at 2.50............	125 00	
do	Pay lists, wages of men employed.........	111 75	
do	Neilson, Mrs., board of men..................	13 20	
do	Hall, R., rent of camp...........................	5 00	
do	Anderson, A., lumber.............................	4 00	
do	Sundry persons, chain, express charges, etc.	10 85	
do	Neilson, M., 18 rods crossway (contract)	20 00	
do	Neilson, N., 110 rods ditching (contract)...	55 00	
do	McKenzie, A., 238 rods crossway and ditching (contract), 476.00, less deducted, 40.00	436 00	
do	Hampshire, F., 57½ rods, crossway (contract)	25 50	
do	Anderson, A., 35 rods crossway...	35 00	
do	Anderson, A., clearing out creek............	5 00	
do	Leatherdale, J. & J., 23 rods ditching...	28 75	
do	Spears & Draycott, 60½ rods crossway...	27 05	
do	Anderson, Reg., 244 rods crossway.........	75 00	
			977 10

COLONIZATION ROADS.—*Continued.*

Morrison Corner and Rose			
Tp. ....Inch, Thos., overseer, 11 days at 2.25......	24 75	
do	Pay lists, wages of men employed.............	163 40	
do	Chambers, J. H., plank.........................	5 25	
do	Somers, W. W., blacksmithing...............	3 65	
do	Sundry persons, use of plow, scraper etc.	3 13	
			200 18
Morrison & Rama T. L...Justin, H., overseer, 25 days at 2.25......	56 25	
do	Pay lists, wages of men employed.........	443 75	
			500 00
Muskoka Rd., Morrison			
and Muskoka ....Stephens, Thos., overseer, 29 days at 2.25	65 25	
do	Pay lists, wages of men employed.............	302 52	
do	Ecclestone, G. W., tools, dynamite, etc....	14 42	
do	Morris & Bartley, blacksmithing	4 05	
do	Stephens, J., cartage...........................	4 50	
do	Sundry persons, blacksmithing, use of		
do	tools, etc.	14 52	
do	Boyd, Wm., overseer, 18 days at 2.25......	40 50	
do	Pay lists, wages of men employed.........	335 63	
do	Mickle, Dyment Co., cedar, etc...............	13 08	
do	Sundry persons, spikes, tools, etc.........	2 40	
			801 87
Muskoka Road North of			
Ardtrea ....Gibson, Chris., overseer, 12½ days at 2.25	28 12	
do	Pay lists, wages of men employed.............	330 25	
do	Holmes, R. W., gravel...........................	31 30	
			389 67
McDonald Letherdale Rd.Orton, Jos., overseer, 24 days at 2.25......	54 00	
do	Pay lists, wages of men employed.............	232 27	
do	Macdonald, J., dynamite........................	9 00	
do	Walker, E., tile	7 88	
			303 15
McDonald, Meredith and			
Aberdeen Road ....Haldenby, S., overseer, 10 days at 2.25...	22 50	
do	Pay lists, wages of men employed.............	273 88	
do	Postage	12	
			296 50
McIntyre Tp. between			
lots W. and X..............Kallio, T. J., overseer, 28 days at 2.25...	70 00	
do	Pay lists, wages of men employed.........	779 85	
do	Marks, Clavet, Dobie Co., tools, etc.......	48 80	
do	Benson & Johnson, dynamite...................	1 50	
			900 15
McLean & California Rd.Von Volkenburgh, F., overseer, 17 days		
do	at 2.25	38 25	
do	Pay lists, wages of men employed.............	160 75	
do	Von Volkenburgh, F., tools.....................	1 00	
			200 00
McLean, Ridout and Sin-			
clair ....McKenzie, D. G., overseer, 15 days at 2.25	33 75	
do	Pay lists, wages of men employed.............	163 26	
do	Smith, J. D., hardware.........................	1 55	
do	Sundry persons, powder, etc...................	1 44	
do	Lowe, Jacob, overseer, 15 days at 2.25...	33 75	
do	Pay lists, wages of men employed.........	159 75	
do	Quinn, T., lumber..............................	3 00	
do	Sundry persons, tools...........................	4 10	
do	Bastedo, P. B., overseer, 10 days at 2.25	22 50	
do	Pay lists, wages of men employed.............	174 07	
do	Smith, J. D., tools...............................	2 75	
do	Sundry persons, drills, fuse, etc.............	1 37	
		601 29	
	Less amount Bastedo account unpaid...	69	
			600 60

COLONIZATION ROADS.—*Continued.*

McLennan and Bar River Road	Hollingsworth, E., overseer, 28 days at 2.25	63 00	
do	Pay lists, wages of men employed	301 25	
do	Young & Rothwell, dynamite	29 25	
do	Moore & Brown, tools	5 30	
do	Collins, J. W., hardware	80	399 60
McLennon Rd. in Laird.	Bradshaw, J., overseer, 20½ days at 2.25	46 13	
do	Pay lists, wages of men employed	245 12	
do	Murray, R., plank	8 04	
do	Robertson, D., spikes	40	299 69
McMurrich 25 S. L., 9th to 11th Con.	White, Robert, overseer, 23 days at 2.25	51 75	
do	Pay lists, wages of men employed	150 00	201 75
McPherson Tp., 5 and 6 Con.	Sylvester, Alfred, overseer, 19½ days at 2.25	43 88	
do	Pay lists. wages of men employed	251 64	
do	Ricard, F. A., tools	4 65	300 17
McPherson and Kirkpatrick T. L.	Garceau, A., overseer, 32½ days at 2.25	73 13	
do	Pay lists, wages of men employed	284 25	
do	Poisson, C. & Son, lumber	28 75	
do	Michel, N., blacksmithing	14 50	
do	Ricard, F. A., tools	3 13	403 76
Nairn & Lorne Tps	Fensom, Richard, overseer, 34 days at 2.25	76 50	
do	Pay lists, wages of men employed	694 60	
do	Purvis Bros., scraper, nails, etc	16 50	
do	Fensom. R. H., plank	11 35	
do	C. P. Ry., freight charges	1 05	800 00
Nelles between lots 4 and 5 and North	McQuaker, Wm., overseer, 26 days at 2.50	65 00	
do	Pay lists, wages of men employed	616 70	
do	Pearson, E. A., stove and camp outfit	99 60	
do	Proctor, H., provisions, tools, etc	99 70	
do	Baldwin, W. C., provisions	36 21	
do	Longmore, F., do	18 50	
do	Johnston, J., milk	19 04	
do	Tilson Bros., flour, etc	13 20	
do	Sundry persons, provisions and lumber	22 95	990 90
Neelon Road between 3 and 4 Cons	Dubruill. Alex., Jr., overseer. 16 days at 2.25	36 00	
do	Pay lists, wages of men employed	201 00	
do	Desaumi. T., contract (road work)	55 00	
do	Purvis Bros., dynamite	6 00	
do	Dubreuill, A., rent of tools	5 00	
		303 00	
	Less amount of account unpaid	53 00	250 00
Nipissing Road between Rye and Commanda	Haufschild, Wm., overseer, 12 days at 2.25	27 00	
do	Pay lists, wages of men employed	124 49	
do	Watt, D., plank	35 34	
do	Arthur, J. tools	5 40	
do	Sundry persons blacksmithing, and dynamite	4 15	196 38

COLONIZATION ROADS.—*Continued.*

Nipissing & Powassan Rd.	Rowlandson, R., overseer, 14½ days at 2.25.	32 62	
do	Pay lists, wages of men employed	156 48	
do	Eckensviller, S., plow and tools	9 20	
do	Richardson Bros., tools	2 50	
			200 80
North Grand Rd............	Badgar, Walter, overseer, 20 days at 2.25.	45 00	
do	Pay lists, wages of men employed	234 37	
do	Phillips, C. A., dynamite	18 00	
do	McKinley, W. S., dynamite	4 90	
do	Sundry persons, cedar and blacksmithing.	4 73	
		307 00	
	Less sale of dynamite	7 00	
			300 00
North Himsworth 5th Side Line	McQuoid, Jno., overseer, 19¾ days at 2.25...	44 43	
do	Pay lists, wages of men employed	243 84	
do	Brown, C. A., steel, tools, etc...............	4 10	
do	Porter & Co., tools, dynamite, etc...........	2 55	
do	Knight, Jas., drills	1 90	
do	Sundry persons, tools, blacksmithing, etc...	3 30	
			300 12
North Sherbrooke, 3rd Con.	Wilson, H., overseer, 20 days at 2.25......	45 00	
do	Pay lists, wages of men employed	199 50	
do	Wilson, Geo., timber	20 00	
do	McIntyre, D., timber	10 00	
do	McIntyre, M., blacksmithing	15 00	
do	Budd, W. H., dynamite	8 00	
do	Gordon, S., timber	2 50	
			300 00
Nosbonsing Station Road in Ferris Tp................	Racicot, Emery, overseer, 14 days at 2.25.	31 25	
do	Pay lists, wages of men employed...........	149 50	
do	Sequin, J. E., block, line and repairs......	14 50	
do	Richardson, W., dynamite, etc	4 75	
do	Postage, affidavits, etc	75	
			200 75
Oak Flats Road ....,......	Jeffray, Jas., overseer, 13 days at 2.25......	29 25	
do	Pay lists, wages of men employed	166 94	
do	Cragg, T. H., tools	4 25	
			200 44
Oakley, Draper & Ryde...	Merkeley, Hy., overseer, 11 days at 2.25...	24 75	
do	Pay lists, wages of men employed	266 88	
do	Davey, M., tools	4 50	
do	Brace, P. H., tools	3 75	
do	Postage, etc	25	
do	Johnson, Jas., overseer, 14 days at 2.25.	31 50	
do	Johnson, Jas., overseer, 7 3-5 days at 1.75	13 30	
do	Pay lists, wages of men employed	145 16	
do	Eccleston, G. W., tools	3 75	
do	Johnson, Jas., rent of plow, etc..............	5 50	
do	Postage	35	
do	Ketching, Wm., overseer, 23¼ days at 2.25	52 31	
do	Pay lists, wages of men employed...........	334 00	
do	Ecclestone, G. W., tools and powder........	8 73	
do	Pescal, T., blacksmithing	4 95	
			899 68
O'Connor Tp. Roads	Bull, W. H., overseer, 43½ days at 2.25...	108 75	
do	Pay lists, wages of men employed	343 40	
do	Sterrett, Jno., plank and spikes	12 50	
do	Wells, Emerson, tools	8 15	
do	Davidson, C. R., nails	50	
do	Bull, W. H., tools, travelling expenses, etc	19 20	
do	Irwin, D., contract to ditch, stump, build a culvert and cordurory	90 00	

COLONIZATION ROADS.—*Continued..*

O'Connor Tp. Road	Bryan & White, 79 rods crossway and 21 rods brushing and ditching as per tender	200 00	
			782 50
Olden Tp. Road	Crozier, Richard, overseer, 16 4-5 days at 2.25	37 80	
do	Pay lists, wages of men employed	157 84	
do	Crozier, R., cedar	3 00	
do	McDonald, J., tools	1 20	
do	Postage, etc	50	
			200 34
Oliver and McIntyre T. Line	Shanks, Allan, overseer, 19 days at 2.25	42 75	
do	Pay lists, wages of men employed	258 25	
do	Marks, Clavet, Dobie, Co., tools	75	
			301 75
Opinican Road, South Crosby	Teeples, Alex., overseer, 17 days at 2.25.	38 25	
do	Pay lists, wages of men employed	161 80	
do	McLean, J., cedar	5 00	
do	Sundry persons, tools and blacksmithing...	1 10	
			206 15
Papineau Tp. Roads	Viverais, Edwd., overseer, 12 days at 2.25.	27 00	
do	Pay lists, wages of men employed	165 00	
do	Viverais, Sam, timber	8 46	
do	Lalonde, A., overseer, 8 days at 2.25	18 00	
do	Pay lists, wages of men employed	173 50	
do	Bell, J. H., dynamite, etc	5 35	
do	Lalonde, N., use of plow	1 00	
do	Donville, Xavier, overseer, 14 days at 2.25.	31 50	
do	Pay lists, wages of men employed	146 25	
do	Bell, J. H., scraper	10 00	
do	Douville, Jos., cedars, tools etc	14 00	
do	Bantz, Herman, overseer, 11 days at 2.25.	24 75	
do	Pay lists, wages of men employed	168 70	
do	Lèvis Bros., tools	6 55	
do	Postage, etc	10	
			800 16
Parke Tp. Road	Munro, W. H., paymaster		
do	Pay lists, wages of men employed	273 62	
do	Moore & Brown, dynamite, etc	26 25	
			299 87
Parkinson Tp. Road	Acton, A., overseer, 26 days at 2.25	58 50	
do	Pay lists, wages of men employed	234 48	
do	Sargent, H., tools	4 80	
do	McKay, J. C., repairing tools	1 65	
			299 43
Patterson Hill Road	Wright, G. R., overseer, 14 days at 2.25	31 50	
do	Pay lists. wages of men employed	112 72	
do	Wright. G. R., use of tools	3 00	
do	Grigg Bros., use of scraper	1 75	
do	Stobie, J., dynamite, etc	1 59	
do	Sundry persons, blacksmithing, use of scraper, etc	1 70	
			152 26
Patton Tp., Lots 4 & 5	Rutledge, Wm., overseer, 27½ days at 2.25.	61 87	
do	Pay lists, wages of men employed	232 03	
do	Sargeant, H., tools, etc	6 35	
			300 25
Patullo Tp. Rd., S and E. of sec. 17	McQuaker, Wm., overseer, 38 days at 2.50	95 00	
do	Pay lists, wages of men employed	629 37	
do	Proctor, H., provisions	144 52	
do	Graham, J., provisions	19 87	
do	Tilson Bros., provisions	21 06	
do	Wier, F., provisions	12 50	

COLONIZATION ROADS.—*Continued.*

Patullo Tp. Rd., S. and E.
of sec. 17	Cameron, W., provisions	10 00	
do	Longmore, F., provisions	7 50	
do	Sundry persons, provisions, lumber, freight, etc.	22 39	
			962 21

Pembroke and Mattawa
Road and Bridge	Dunlop, Jas., overseer, 12 days at 2.25......	27 00	
do	Pay lists, wages of men employed............	121 00	
do	Dunlop, W. P., timber, tools, etc............	24 45	
do	Dunlop, J. H., timber	16 80	
do	Devlin, C. & Sons, scraper	9 35	
do	Ranger, Albert, overseer, 18 days at 2.25...	40 50	
do	Pay lists, wages of men employed	253 50	
do	Bell, J. H., tools	7 18	
do	Dunlop, W. P., overseer, 20 days at 2.25...	45 00	
do	Pay lists, wages of men employed............	218 50	
do	Dunlop, W. P., tools	4 50	
do	Curry and Thrasher, timber	38 17	
			805 95

Pembroke and Mattawa
Buchanan Road	Salafrane, Clement, overseer, 10 days at 2.25	22 50	
do	Pay lists, wages of men employed	112 50	
do	Salafrane, C., cedar and rent of plow	9 00	
do	Dumouchel, H. L., tools	6 00	
			150 00

Pennefather Tp. Road
...Munro, W. H., paymaster			
do	Pay lists, wages of men employed	388 74	
do	Moore & Brown, tools	12 24	
			400 98

Perry 15 and 16 Side Rd.,
Cons. 11 and 12	Gilpin, G., overseer, 19 days at 2.25.........	42 75	
do	Pay lists, wages of men employed	257 49	
			300 24

Perth Road to Loborough
Lake	Guthrie, Wm., overseer, 9 days at 2.25......	20 25	
do	Pay lists, wages of men employed	142 18	
do	Roberts, J. L., tools, dynamite, etc............	19 35	
do	Austin, L., blacksmithing	1 20	
do	Postage	25	
			183 23

Plevena, Ardoc & Claren-
don Roads	Pringle, W. W., paymaster, accountable............		750 00

Plummer and Aberdeen
Con. 2 Road	Robinson, Chas., overseer, 53 days at 2.25	132 50	
do	Pay lists, wages of men employed	1,298·70	
do	Somers, W. W., dynamite, tools, etc.........	64 67·	
do	McDonald, H., plow	18 00	
do	White, T. A., tools	4 50	
do	Gregg Bros., use of scraper	4 00	
do	Sundry persons, freight, telephones, etc...	4 00	
			1,526 37

Plummer, Aberdeen,
Johnson and Aberdeen
Additional	Williams, W. J., overseer, 22½ days at 2.25.	50 62	
do	Pay lists, wages of men employed............	239 25	
do	McRae, A. J., tools	12 85	
do	McQuarrie & McKay, dynamite	1 50	
do	Postage, etc	25	
		304 47	
	Less sale of tools	2 25	
			302 22

COLONIZATION ROADS.—*Continued.*

Pogue Lake Rd., Tp. of Sherwood	Romleskie, Peter, overseer, 14 days at 2.25.	31 50	
do	Pay lists, wages of men employed	159 00	
do	Dunnigan, M., plow	13 00	
do	Stafford & Co., tools, cedar, etc	6 90	
do	Sundry persons, use of tools, etc	4 85	
		215 25	
	Less sale of tools	7 55	
			207 70
Port Finlay and Echo Bay Road	Murray, T., overseer, accountable		250 00
Port Finlay and McLennan Road	Roswell, Chas., overseer 12 days at 2.25...	27 00	
do	Pay lists, wages of men employed	151 00	
do	Rosewell, D., gravel	17 04	
do	Junor, Jas., gravel	5 20	
do	McIntosh, P., blacksmithing	30	
			200 54
Port Severn Road	Lawson, Walter, Sr., overseer, 14 days at 2.25	31 50	
do	Pay lists, wages of men employed	248 75	
do	Oliver, W., stone	15 00	
do	Orland, H., tools	4 75	
			300 00
Prices' Hill Road	Eady, W. B., overseer, 16 days at 2.25 ...	36 00	
do	Pay lists, wages of men employed	241 75	
do	Devine & McGarry, dynamite	18 31	
do	Sundry persons, blacksmithing	2 25	
			298 31
Prince Tp. Roads	Munro, W. H., paymaster		
do	Pay lists, wages of men employed	490 75	
do	Moore & Brown, dynamite	5 79	
do	Soo livery, horse hire	3 00	
			499 54
Providence Bay towards Manitowaning	Kennedy, Wm., overseer, 37 days at 2.00.	74 00	
do	Pay lists, wages of men employed	516 39	
do	Gault, R., timber	8 00	
do	Wagg, W. J., tools	4 90	
do	Sundry persons, bolts, blacksmithing, etc ...	3 40	
			606 69
Purdy Mill Road	Segsworth, Geo., overseer, 25¾ days at 2.25	57 94	
do	Pay lists. wages of men employed	134 48	
do	Segsworth, G. cedar	4 50	
do	Trousdale, J. W., tools	3 40	
do	Sundry persons, tools, repairs, etc.	2 80	
		203 12	
	Less sale of tools	2 80	
			200 32
Quadville and Vambrough Road	Handke, Chas., overseer, 16 days at 2.25...	36 00	
do	Pay lists, wages of men employed	148 50	
do	Handke, C., teaming and use of plow	7 65	
do	Plant, X., dynamite	2 00	
do	George, W., axe and fuse	1 50	
			195 65
Railton Road, Loughboro Tp.	Joyce, Richard, overseer, 17 days at 2.25...	38 25	
do	Pay lists, wages of men employed	135 39	
do	Joyce, R., cedar, repairs, etc.	4 00	
do	Corbett, Jno., scraper and tools	10 65	
do	Sundry persons, tools	1 55	
			189 84

COLONIZATION ROADS.—*Continued.*

Rainy River Rd., Lots 10

and 11, Atwood	Buffy, Wm., overseer, 9 days at 2.50	22 50	
do	Pay lists, wages of men employed	240 07	
do	McQuarrie & Grimshaw, provisions	33 40	
do	Baldwin, W. C., do	20 59	
do	Easton, G., do	6 00	
do	Sundry persons, provisions, use of tools, etc.	9 27	
			331 83

Rama Con. L. Road ...... Cronk, Luther, overseer, 19 days at 2.25...   42 75
do   Pay lists, wages of men employed 215 59
do   Ecclestone, G., dynamite ....:. 36 25
do   Cronk, L., horse hire 5 00
do   Young, J. F., Estate, dynamite 1 40
do   Postage 25
                                                                   301 24

Ramsay Rd. between Lots

15 & 16, Cons. 4 & 8...	Stewart, Jno.. overseer, 22 days at 2.25 ...	49 50	
do	Pay lists, wages of men employed	622 61	
do	Torrance & Kaupnan, stove, camp supplies, etc	36 53	
do	Wylie, J., tent	16 50	
do	Dick, D. J.. provisions	27 24	
do	Williams. D., provisions	15 08	
do	Stevenson, N., provisions	41 10	
do	Donaldson, J., lumber	13 32	
do	Sundry persons, provisions	17 40	
do	do dynamite, freight, blacksmithing, etc.	11 51	
			85? 79

Rat Portage Rd. East..... Barr, Jno. D., overseer, 15 days at 2.25 ...   33 75
do   Pay lists, wages of men employed 202 00
do   Brett, J. T., provisions 38 89
do   Fife, A. T.. tools, etc. 12 40
do   Graham, R. T.. blacksmithing 4 30
do   Hudson's Bay Co.. rent of tent 4 00
do   Sundry persons, provisions, cartage, etc.. 7 40
                                                                   302 74
             Less deducted from pay list for board   54 50
                                                                   248 24

Ratter Tp. Rd................ Thebault, Alex., overseer, 10 days at 2.25   22 50
do   Pay lists, wages of men employed 160 81
do   Laporte, D., plow, etc. 17 50
do   Bartlett. R. A., overseer, 16 days at 2.25... 36 00
do   Pay lists. wages of men employed 222 92
do   Keating & Co., timber 17 50
do   Lytle, W. A., blacksmithing 12 86
do   Laporte, D., tools 10 30
                                                                   50? 39

Rayside Tp. Rds. .... Beaulieu, O., overseer, 25 days at 2.25 ... · 56 25
do   Pay lists, wages of men employed 269 15
do   Chenier, A., plank 96 75
do   Marcotte. M.. timber 52 00
do   Purvis Bros.. dynamite. etc. 10 25
do   Cayen, A., nails 9 60
do   Bonin, G., posts 60
                                                                   494 60

Rocher, Founder Road.... Paupore, Andrew, overseer, 15 days at 2.25   33 75
do   Pay lists, wages of men employed 188 36
do   Labine, Jos., cedar 34 77
do   Rennie. Robt.. lumber. spikes. etc. 5 36
do   Postage 50
                                                                   262 74

COLONIZATION ROADS.—*Continued.*

Rockingham and Palmer
Rapids Road	Moran, J. P., overseer, 16 days at 2.25 ...	36 00	
do	Pay lists, wages of men employed	330 00	
do	Devine & McGarry, tools	18 55	
do	Moran, J. P., dynamite, teaming, etc. ...	12 50	
do	Watson, J., chain	2 60	
do	G. T. Ry., freight charges	58	400 23

Rockville & Lehmans	Woods, A., overseer, 23¼ days at 2.25	52 87	
do	Pay lists, wages of men employed	333 75	
do	Trotter, W. L., tools	7 80	
do	Kingsboro, J., tools	6 20	
do	Sundry persons, powder, blacksmithing, etc.	4 32	404 94

Rolph, lots 18 & 19	Law, Jno., overseer, 15¼ days at 2.25	34 87	
do	Pay lists, wages of men employed	166 50	
do	Postage	13	201 50

Ryerson and Spence Road
to Burk's Falls	Stewart, Daniel, overseer, 17 days at 2.25	38 25	
do	Pay lists, wages of men employed	154 11	
do	Smith, H. J., blacksmithing	2 90	
do	Clarke, C. R., dynamite, etc.	5 15	200 41

Salter and Victoria Town
Line, Div. 5	Crothers, Geo., overseer, 25¾ days at 2.25...	57 93	
do	Pay lists, wages of men employed	297 81	
do	Thornton, F., tools	14 16	
do	Armstrong, J. W., plank	27 51	
do	Dacy Bros., blacksmithing	8 40	
do	Sundry persons, powder and use of road machine	5 49	411 30

Sanford Tp. Rds.	Robinson, W. J., overseer, 16 days at 2.50	40 00	
do	Pay lists, wages of men employed	362 81	
do	Beatty, Alex., provisions	90 62	
do	C. P. Ry., freight	4 30	
do	Hayes, J. G., dynamite	2 20	
do	Postage	07	500 00

Sanfield and Tehkummah
Road	Young, Myles, overseer, 15¼ days at 2.25 ...	34 87	
do	Pay lists, wages of men employed	258 72	
do	McGaulay, Jno., overseer, 24 days at 2.25	54 00	
do	Pay lists, wages of men employed	246 00	593 59

Sebastopol Tp. Road	Gallagher, E. H., overseer, 16 days at 2.25	36 00	
do	Pay lists, wages of men employed	168 00	
do	D'Lacy & Son, tools	3 00	
do	Gallagher, E. H., use of tools	1 00	
do	Postage, etc.	25	208 25

Sebastopol 7th Con	Plaunt, Xavier, overseer, 14 days at 2.25...	31 50	
do	Pay lists, wages of men employed	165 00	
do	Plaunt, X., cedar	8 40	
do	McCann, M. C., plow point and dynamite	6 20	
do	John, A., blacksmithing	4 00	
do	Postage, etc.	25	215 35

Shamrock & D'Acre	Keilly, Jno., overseer, 25 days at 2.25	56 25	
do	Pay lists, wages of men employed	226 50	
do	Keilly, Jno., cedar and use of plow	19 45	
do	Devine & McGarry, dynamite	3 57	
do	Hunt, Jno., blacksmithing	40	306 17

COLONIZATION ROADS.—*Continued.*

Sheffield and Hungerford
Road ....Gee, Robt., overseer, 7½ days at 2.25 ...... 16 87
  do   Pay lists, wages of men employed 82 48
  do   Powder, fuse and postage 65
                       100 00

Silver Mountain to 36
 Mile post, Lybster ......Faithful, T., overseer, 18 days at 2.25 ... 40 50
  do   Pay lists, wages of men employed 166 00
                       206 50

Silver Mountain Rd., Lybster Saunders, Robt., overseer, 16 days at 2.25 36 00
  do   Pay lists, wages of men employed 213 01
  do   Stirrett, Jno., timber 38 73
  do   Arthur, J., tools 13 25
  do   Welsh. J. J.. blacksmithing 3 15
  do   Postage, etc 24
                       304 38

Slate River Bridge ....Gillespie, A., overseer, 10 days at 2.25 ... 22 50
  do   Pay lists, wages of men employed 71 00
  do   Gammond, F., plank 36 25
  do   Judge, J., lumber 14 00
  do   McDonald, A., bolts 4 25
  do   Sundry persons, spikes, etc. 2 00
                       150 00

South and North Algona
Roads ....Gorman, Thos., overseer, 14 days at 2.25... 31 50
  do   Pay lists. wages of men employed 150 00
  do   George & McGregor, tools 13 15
  do   Gorman, T., cedar 6 85
  do   Beeckevald, Otto. overseer, 14 days at 2.25 31 50
  do   Pay lists, wages of men employed 157 20
  do   Cameron, N., tools 9 65
  do   Sundry persons, tools, blacksmithing. etc. 1 65
  do   Roesner, Julius, overseer, 14 days at 2.25 31 50
  do   Pay lists, wages of men employed 159 15
  do   Roesner, J., cedar, use of plow, etc. 11 30
  do   Groubeck. P., use of wagon 2 25
  do   Beyers. Chas., overseer, 14 days at 2.25... 31 50
  do   Pay lists. wages of men employed 168 00
  do   D'Lacy & Son, tools 5 80
  do   Postage 10
                       811 10

Spence Tp.. 21st Side
Line Road ....Fry, Arthur, overseer, 19 days at 2.25 ...... 42 75
  do   Pay lists. wages of men employed 236 93
  do   Vigras. P. J., tools, powder, etc. 2 60
  do   Fry. Richard. tools 6 85
  do   Blakeley, F., plank 5 60
  do   Doherty, S., timber 6 00
  do   McLachlan. A. H.. blacksmithing 60
  do   Stationery, postage, etc. 1 17
                       302 50

Springer Tp. Roads.........Duhane, A., overseer, 14 days at 2.25 ...... 31 50
  do   Pay lists, wages of men employed 161 50
  do   Li'lie. R.. dynamite 5 00
  do   Bellefennille. A., overseer, 13½ days at 2.25 30 38
  do   Pay lists, wages of men employed 157 13
  do   Lillie. R.. dynamite............................. 7 50
  do   Charles. F., blacksmithing 4 75
  do   Renaud. Alex.. overseer, 10½ days at 2.25 23 62
  do   Pay lists, wages of men employed 164 50
  do   Prieur, J. F., tools ....: 8 40
  do   Lillie. R.. dynamite 1 98
  do   Delome, Leon. contract to ditch between
        lots 8 and 9. Tp. Springer, from Con.
        B. to C., 250 rods 200 00
                       796 26

COLONIZATION ROADS.—*Continued.*

Stage Road	Pringle, W. W., paymaster, accountable		200 00
Stanhope & Snowden	Hewitt, W. G., overseer, 9 days at 2.25 ...	20 25	
do	Pay lists, wages of men employed	129 00	
do	Postage. etc.	30	
do	Long, Fred., overseer, 7 days at 2.25	15 75	
do	Pay lists, wages of men employed	84 25	
do	Sharples, B., overseer, 14 days at 2.25	31 50	
do	Pay lists. wages of men employed	168 50	
do	Newall, Michael, overseer. 8½ days at 2.25	19 13	
do	Pay lists, wages of men employed	126 84	
do	Newall, M., use of plow and postage	1 07	
do	Dawson, Richard, overseer, 18 days at 2.25	40 50	
do	Pay lists, wages of men employed	209 57	
do	Reynolds, Jas., overseer, 11 days at 2.25 ...	24 75	
do	Pay lists, wages of men employed	125 25	996 66
Stanley Bridge Road	Barrie, E., overseer, 34 days at 2.50	85 00	
do	Pay lists, wages of men employed	418 66	
do	Fraser Bros., provisions	186 27	
do	Fort William Hardware Co., tools, nails, etc.	8 15	
do	Sundry persons, blacksmithing, stationery, etc.	2 50	700 58
Stanley Bridge West	Barrie, E., overseer, 22 days at 2.50	55 00	
do	Pay lists, wages of men employed	155 00	
do	Routledge, J. E., provisions	78 78	
do	Judge, J., lumber	7 00	
do	Davidson, A. R., provisions	3 60	
do	Newsone, W. H., lumber	1 60	300 98
Stephenson and Watt	McKnight, Warren, overseer, 28¾ days at 2.25	64 69	
do	Pay lists, wages of men employed	311 32	
do	White Bros., dynamite	18 40	
do	Spragg, P., blacksmithing	3 34	
do	Sundry persons, do	2 71	
do	Suffern, W. A., overseer, 18 days at 2.25	40 50	
do	Pay lists, wages of men employed	240 36	
do	Ecclestone, G., dynamite	19 02	700 34
Stisted and Cardwell	Evans, Edward, overseer, 16½ days at 2.25	37 13	
do	Pay lists, wages of men employed	252 44	
do	Grant, D. M., tools	9 55	
do	Lambert, W. N., blacksmithing	1 30	
do	Postage	29	
do	Henderson, John, overseer, 24 days at 2.25	54 00	
do	Pay lists, wages of men employed	339 80	
do	White Bros., tools	11 93	
do	Sundry persons, tools and blacksmithing...	3 33	
do	West. Wm., overseer, 10 days at 2.25	22 50	
do	Pay lists, wages of men employed	69 25	
do	West Albert. cedar	8 00	
do	Grant, D. M., nails	25	809 77
Stoqua Road	Young, Samuel, overseer, 21 days at 2.25	47 25	
do	Pay lists, wages of men employed	343 25	
do	Dunlop & Co., dynamite, etc	5 89	
do	Nelson, R., blacksmithing	2 70	
do	Postage, etc.,	41	399 50
Stafford Proof Line	Ross, Wm., overseer, 9½ days at 2.25	21 38	
do	Pay lists, wages of men employed	352 50	
do	Hawkins, G., gravel	10 00	
do	Andrews, Samuel; cedar	5 00	

COLONIZATION ROADS.—*Continued.*

Stafford Proof Line	Butler, B., logs	4 00	
do	Sundry persons, spikes, use of waggons, etc.	7 10	
			399 98
Strathroy and Palmer Rapids Road	O'Brien, Jas., overseer, 16 days at 2.25...	36 00	
do	Pay lists, wages of men employed...........	150 00	
do	O'Brien, Jas., cedar and rent of tools...	14 00	
			200 00
Striker Tp. Road, Cons. 3 and 4	Trudeau, Jno., overseer, 32 days at 2.25.	72 00	
do	Pay lists, wages of men employed...........	420 85	
do	Braithwaite, F., dynamite, etc............	8 12	
			500 97
St. Joseph Tp. between lots 5 and 6	Burnside, Jas., overseer, 20 days at 2.25	45 00	
do	Pay lists, wages of men employed...........	250 88	
			295 88
St. Joseph Tp., U. to A. Concessions	Burnside, Jas., overseer, 17 days at 2.25	38 25	
do	Pay lists, wages of men employed...........	237 00	
do	Moore, Jas. A., dynamite.......................	14 65	
do	Foster & Co., tools................................	15 65	
			305 55
Sturgeon Creek Bridge, Shenstone Tp...............	Weir, D., paymaster...............................	....	
do	Pay lists, wages of men employed...........	118 00	
do	Turnbull, T., plank................................	32 25	
do	Ion, Arthur, tools, bolts, etc..................	16 62	
do	Can. Northern Ry., freight on pile driver	12 00	
do	McEachern, A., loading pile driver........	5 00	
			183 87
Sudbury and Blezard Valley Road	Pilon, Jas., overseer, 76¾ days at 2.50...	191 88	
do	Pay lists, wages of men employed.........	1,723 05	
do	Jacobs & Co., blankets	55 50	
do	Clairoux, J. M., tools	32 98	
do	Labelle, M., blacksmithing	16 63	
do	Purvis Bros., tools and dynamite...........	15 73	
do	Guy, R. J., chain, etc.	6 15	
			2,046 92
Summerville, Laxton and Bexley Roads	Peel, Arthur, overseer, 7½ days at 2.25...	28 12	
do	Pay lists, wages of men employed...........	166 60	
do	Peel. G., cedar	2 75	
do	Sundry persons, cedar, blacksmithing, etc.	3 15	
do	Armstrong, Wm., overseer, 8½ days at 2.25	19 12	
do	Pay lists, wages of men employed...........	82 38	
do	Davy, Thos., overseer, 11 days at 2.25...	24 75	
do	Pay lists, wages of men employed...........	174 39	
do	Repairs, powder, etc.	85	
do	Stewart, Wm., overseer, 13 days at 2.25...	29 25	
do	Pay lists, wages of men employed...........	167 25	
do	McDonald, Kenneth, overseer, 13¼ days at 2.25	30 37	
do	Pay lists, wages of men employed...........	168 12	
do	Hodges, F., powder	1 90	
do	Burgess, S., blacksmithing	55	
do	Henderson, Robt., overseer, 6 days at 2.25	13 50	
do	Pay lists. wages of men employed...........	82 50	
do	Hopkins Bros., tools	4 70	
do	Smith. Daniel, overseer, 5 days at 2.25	11 25	
do	Pay lists. wages of men employed...........	88 75	
do	Wilson. Jno., overseer, 15 days at 2.25...	33 75	
do	Pay lists, wages of men employed........	366 37	
			1.500 37

COLONIZATION ROADS.—*Continued.*

Sylvan Valley	Haldenby, S. R., overseer, 11½ days at 2.25	25 87	
do	Pay lists, wages of men employed	364 01	
do	Dukes, W., gravel, plow repairs, etc.	6 60	
do	Sundry persons, tools, postage, etc.	3 02	399 50
Tait Tp. Roads	Hughes, G. G., overseer, 39 days at 2.50	97 50	
do	Pay lists, wages of men employed	632 44	
do	Hughes, G. W., provisions	208 35	
do	Wier, B., potatoes	21 00	
do	McMillan, W., pork	10 66	
do	Hefferin, R., milk	12 50	
do	Todd, G. B., butter	15 20	
do	Postage, stationery, etc.	1 72	999 37
Tait and Mather T. L. to extend	Hughes, G. G., overseer, 53 days at 2.50	132 50	
do	Pay lists, wages of men employed	618 93	
do	Hughes, G. W., provisions and tools	166 77	
do	Hughes, M., provisions	18 00	
do	McMillan, D., do	17 40	
do	Ross, F., do	13 54	
do	McRae, A., do	13 00	
do	Sundry persons, provisions, board of men, etc.	14 86	995 00
Tarentorus Tp	McMullen, Benj., overseer, 30 days at 2.25	67 49	
do	Pay lists, wages of men employed	370 12	
do	McPherson, A., tools	4 00	
do	Lamon, H., use of plow	2 00	
do	Sims Lumber Co., plank	54 88	498 49
Tenby Bay Road	Hewitt, Geo., overseer, 19 days at 2.25	42 75	
do	Pay lists, wages of men employed	250 25	
do	Walker, Jas., gravel and timber	7 00	300 00
Thessalon River Bridge, Rock Lake	Wing, Chas., overseer, 30 days at 2.25	67 50	
do	Pay lists, wages of men employed	170 25	
do	Somers, W. W., bridge irons, bolts, etc.	17 20	254 95
Thessalon River Bridge between Rock and Gordon Lake	Ferguson, T., overseer, 25 days at 2.00	50 00	
do	Pay lists, wages of men employed	163 00	
do	McKay, G., plank	50 16	
do	Ferguson, T., timber, nails, etc.	26 30	
do	Somers, W., blacksmithing, bolts, etc.	10 40	
		299 86	
	Less amount of account unpaid	49 86	250 00
Trout Creek and Glen Roberts Road	McFadden, A., overseer, 10½ days at 2.25	23 63	
do	Pay lists, wages of men employed	176 62	200 25
Temiskaming Roads: Armstrong & Beauchamp Road	Hill, Harry, overseer, 94 days at 2.50	235 00	
do	Pay lists, wages of men employed	2,206 51	
do	Briscoe, T., provisions, camp supplies. etc.	258 54	
do	Smith, G. G., provisions, camp supplies, etc.	206 67	

22 P.A.

COLONIZATION ROADS.—*Continued.*

Armstrong and Beauchamp Road	Eplett, S. D., tools, etc.............	53 75	
do	Grills, N., blankets.....................	39 00	
do	Rumning, S., lumber	11 20	
do	Postage, stationery, etc.............	98	
		3,011 65	
	Less board of men Jean Baptiste, bridge repairs.........	11 55	
			3,000 10
Armstrong & Hilliard Rd.	Kerr, J. H., overseer, 36 days at 2.50	90 00	
do	Pay lists, wages of men employed	490 68	
do	Chrysler, Mrs., board and washing blankets	21 18	
do	Brown Bros., hay and oats......	23 21	
do	Eplett, S., dynamite, etc...........	15 90	
do	Taylor, G., chain.......................	14 10	
do	Briscoe, T., hay, tar paper, etc.	16 00	
do	Sundry persons, blacksmithing, washing blankets, etc.........	13 13	
do	Willard, Wm., overseer, 39 days at 2.50	222 50	
do	Pay lists, wages of men employed.	1,353 17	
do	Briscoe, T., provisions	279 83	
do	Eplett, S., tools, dynamite, etc..	83 45	
do	Smith, G., provisions and board...	41 45	
do	Welsh, H., provisions	41 41	
do	Running, S., lumber	33 60	
do	Grills, N., blankets	15 00	
do	Sundry persons, provisions, washing blankets, etc................	13 20	
do	Sherwood & Prest, contract to chop, clear, stump and grub a road between lots 2 and 3, Hilliard, 2 miles 150 rods at 500.00 per mile	1,234 37	
			4,002 18
Beauchamp between lots 4 and 5	Ireton, Samuel, overseer, 55 days at 2.50	137 50	
do	Pay lists, wages of men employed	651 87	
do	Briscoe, T., hay, provisions, etc.	164 90	
do	Smith. G. G.. hay, provisions, etc.	96 34	
do	Carruthers. W. H., blankets, etc.	35 85	
do	Ferguson & Cragg, camp material. etc.	25 08	
do	Running & Son, timber.............	10 60	
do	Sundry persons. provisions. cartage. blacksmithing, etc........	26 64	
do	Quittenton, Albert, contract to clear, stump and grub a road between lots 4 and 5. Beauchamp, thence west along 5th Con. to lot 3 Bryce 6 miles, at 500.00 per mile	3,000 00	
do	Crosswaying 400 rods at 1.50 per rod	600 00	
			4,748 78
Brethour Rd., lots 6 & 7.	Penman. Jos:, overseer, 113 days at 2.50	282 50	
do	Pay lists, wages of men employed.	3,162 69	
do	Ferguson & Cragg, tools	26 46	
do	Liddle, F., rubber boots	16 80	
do	McKnight, W. do	8 40	
do	Hendry. F. W., freight charges...	3 50	
do	Richards, W., cartage	50	
			3,500 85

22a P.A.

COLONIZATION ROADS.—*Continued.*

Casey, between lots 2 and 3, Con. 6	Robert E., overseer, 48 days at 2.50	120 00	
do	Pay lists, wages of men employed	664 29	
do	Malone, M. J., chain, cedar, etc.	7 50	
do	Sundry persons, rent of plows, etc.	5 50	797 29
Culverts T. L. Kearns & Hudson	Hammond, R., timber		4 25
Dack Tp. Bridges	Gardner, Thos., overseer, 28 days at 2.25	63 00	
do	Pay lists, wages of men employed	389 62	
do	Long Lake Co., dynamite and repairs	1 39	
do	Train, Fred., building bridge across south branch La Blanche River, lot 8, con. 5, Dack, as per contract	475 00	
do	Additional 8 feet on length of bridge	69 05	998 06
Evanturel, between lots 6 and 7	Houghton, J. W., overseer, 53 days at 2.50	132 50	
do	Pay lists, wages of men employed	1,259 59	
do	Clark, Jno., provisions, hay, blankets, etc.	329 24	
do	Eplett, S., scraper, etc.	32 50	
do	Brown Bros., feed	16 90	
do	Sword, T. J., potatoes	13 80	
do	Soutar, A., blacksmithing	3 95	1,788 48
Evanturel and Marter Boundary	Houghton, J. W., overseer, 18½ days at 2.50	46 25	
do	Pay lists, wages of men employed.	257 56	
do	Everett, W., provisions	30 97	
do	Clark, J., provisions	42 31	
do	Soper, L., timber and provisions.	12 81	
do	Woolings, W. C., meat	6 10	396 00
Firstbrook, Con. 5	Bray, Jno., overseer, 75 days at 2.50	187 50	
do	Pay lists, wages of men employed.	1,195 25	
do	Grills, N., provisions, etc.	260 44	
do	Eplett, S., dynamite, tools, etc.	243 98	
do	McCabe & Stinson, provisions, etc.	61 25	
do	Bray, J., board, plow, potatoes, etc.	30 00	
do	Slade, G., stove	15 00	
do	Sundry persons, provisions, repairs, etc	7 73	2,001 15
Grading Roads	Cragg, T., overseer, 89½ days at 2.50	223 75	
do	Pay lists, wages of men employed.	1,089 99	
do	Eplett, S. D., tent, oil, etc.	10 70	
do	Snider, J., lumber	12 42	
do	Kennedy, A. E., repairs	7 40	
do	T. & N. O. Ry., freight	3 26	
do	Sundry persons, repairs, nails, etc	2 48	
		1,350 00	
	Less amount of account unpaid	350 00	1,000 00

COLONIZATION ROADS.—*Continued.*

Haileybury to Firstbrook Road	Thompson, W. H., overseer, 28¼ days at 2.25	63 56	
do	Pay lists, wages of men employed.	432 59	
do	Norfolk, S., shovels	3 75	
do	Fleming, Jno. M., Jr., overseer, 16¼ days at 2.25	37 12	
do	Pay lists, wages of men employed.	398 75	
do	Norfolk, S., dynamite, tools, etc.	36 07	
do	Charlton and Wilson, dynamite, scraper, etc	15 65	
do	Fleming, G., plow, etc	13 00	1,000 49
Haileybury & Cobalt Rd.	Warner, F., overseer, 36 days at 2.50	90 00	
do	Pay lists, wages of men employed.	515 37	
do	Atkinson, E. & S., provisions.....	46 87	
do	McIntosh & Hamilton, provisions.	58 66	
do	Norfolk, S., camp outfit	62 86	
do	Murphy, A. J., rent of tent, etc.	18 80	
do	McMurdy, J. D., tools	4 00	796 56
Harley and Hilliard, Thornloe East	O'Hara, J., overseer, 51 days at 2.50	127 50	
do	Pay lists, wages of men employed.	634 84	
do	O'Hara, J., provisions	75 03	
do	Taylor Hardware Co., tools, dynamite, etc	57 66	
do	Doup, A., plow	12 00	
do	Latchford, J., plow	10 00	
do	Carruthers, W. H., provisions	49 93	
do	McMurray, W., provisions	8 84	
do	Eplett, S., scraper	10 00	
do	Sundry persons, tools, rent of camp, etc	10 30	996 10
Harris Rd., lots 2 & 3...	Huggins & Deleury, contract to chop, clear and grub a road along line between lots 2 and 3, from front of 3rd con. to front of 5 con., Tp. Harris, 3 miles at 165.00 per mile........	495 00	
do	Crosswaying 95 rods at 1.50 per rod	142 50	
do	Contract to. chop, clear and grub a road from the line between lots 2 and 3 along the front of con. 6, Twp. Harris to White River, 2¼ miles at 325.00 per mile	731 25	
do	Crosswaying 285 rods at 1.50 per rod	427 50	
do	Train, Fred, on account contract, road in Cassey Twp	157 50	
do	Ball. Geo. H., overseer, 66 days at 2.50	165 00	
do	Pay lists, wages of men employed.	1,089 63	
do	Grills, N., provisions	88 11	
do	Ball, H., butter and lumber........	57 05	
do	Carruthers, W. H., provisions ...	29 06	
do	Brown Bros., provisions	17 73	
do	Murray & Barlow	14 00	
do	A. Kennedy, blacksmithing and tools	12 95	

COLONIZATION ROADS.—*Continued.*

Harris Rd., lots 2 and 3	Sundry persons, hardware and provisions	9 20	
do	Ball, G. H., overseer, 49 days at 2.50	122 50	
do	Pay lists, wages of men employed.	806 04	
do	Murray & Barlow, provisions, etc.	114 99	
do	Eplett, S. D., camp outfit	82 90	
do	Young, A. J., blankets	24 00	
do	Marsland, J. T., plow, etc	15 00	
do	Sundry persons, provisions, etc....	31 40	
			4,633 31
Henwood, 4th & 5th Con..	Pacey, Geo., overseer, 81½ days at 2.50	203 75	
do	Pay lists, wages of men employed.	937 47	
do	Brown Bros., hay, oats, etc	117 65	
do	Welsh, H., provisions, supplies, etc	162 92	
do	Bennett, H., provisions	27 00	
do	Taylor, Geo., & Co., dynamite, etc.	36 95	
do	Grills, N., blankets	34 80	
do	Pacey, Mrs., provisions	21 97	
do	Pacey, S., cartage and board of men	14 00	
do	Bisber, S., rent of camp	10 00	
do	Sundry persons, provisions, tools, etc	35 45	
		1,601 96	
	Less sale of provisions and timber	16 86	
		1,585 10	
do	Bennett, H., contract to cut, stump and brush road along front of 5th con. of Henwood, from lot 6 to east boundary of Cane, 3 miles at 450.00 per mile	1,350 00	
do	Crosswaying 125 rods at 1.25 per rod	156 25	
			3,091 35
Hilliard Road between 4 and 5	Cook, J. E., overseer, 79 days at 2.50	197 50	
do	Pay lists, wages of men employed.	952 72	
do	Eplett, S., provisions, dynamite, etc	105 55	
do	Grills, N., provisions, oats, etc....	69 96	
do	Cook, J. E., hay, rent of house, etc	58 10	
do	Young, A. J., provisions	58 50	
do	Coutts, F., oats, provisions,. etc.	22 08	
do	Marsland, J. T., plow, repairs, etc	11 00	
do	Cook, W. A., board of men	28 56	
do	Sundry persons, tools, provisions, etc	12 38	
		1,516 35	
	Less sale of plow & tools	16 90	
			1,499 45
Hudson, Cons. 4 and 5...	Doughty, Robt., overseer, 45 days at 2.50	112 50	
do	Pay lists, wages of men employed.	499 28	
do	Eplett, S., stove, tools, dynamite, etc	164 62	
do	Grills, N., provisions	96 39	

COLONIZATION ROADS.—*Continued.*

Hudson, Cons. 4 and 5	Howie, R. G., dynamite etc	29 00	
do	Atchison, A. R., lumber	32 08	
do	Murray & Barbour, flour, blankets, etc	17 10	
do	Brown, T., provisions	12 00	
do	Sundry persons, provisions and blacksmithing	18 18	981 15
Hudson, 4 and 5 Cons	Jno. Bornstead, overseer, 10½ days at 2.50	26 25	
do	Pay lists, wages of men employed.	174 27	200 52
Hyslip and Charlton	Jack, Hugh, overseer, 75 days at 2.50	187 50	
do	Pay lists, wages of men employed	1,698 41	
do	Hovey, L. G., provisions, tools, etc	221 08	
do	Clark, J., provisions, lumber, etc...	283 29	
do	Woolings and Woolings, meat	24 45	
do	Ryan, W., hay, oats, etc	33 17	
do	Snowdon, W. B., board of men...	23 40	
do	Decou, J. E., rent of camp	10 00	
do	Soutar, A., bolts, blacksmithing, etc	14 60	
do	Sundry persons, hay, provisions, etc.	14 00	2,509 90
Interprovincial Line Rd	Aistrop, Jas., paymaster		
do	Pay lists, wages of men employed Less amount of account unpaid	50 37 37	50 00
Jean Baptiste Bridge	Kerr, J. H., overseer, 21 days at 3.50	73 50	
do	Pay lists, wages of men employed.	175 69	
do	Eplett, S., rope, tools etc	30 65	
do	Wicklem, E., moving pile driver...	19 75	
do	Taylor, Henderson & Co., rope ...	13 60	
do	Kennedy, A., blacksmithing	12 55	
do	Sundry persons, tools, freight, etc	15 10	340 34
Kearns and Armstrong T. L. Road	Welsh, Harry, overseer, 82 days at 2.50	205 00	
do	Pay lists, wages of men employed.	953 86	
do	Helsh, H., provisions, etc	296 09	
do	Harmer, W. H., teaming	5 00	
do	Mrs. Carr, washing blankets, etc.	3 60	1,463 55
Repairing Bridge, West Road	Kirker, E., repairing bridge		6 00
Repairing & grading Rds.	Cragg, T. E., overseer, 23½ days at 2.50	58 75	
do	Pay lists, wages of men employed.	201 00	
do	Ferguson & Cragg, wrench	1 40	
do	Eplett, S., oil, etc	50	261 65
Repairing Old roads and grading	Houghton, J. W., overseer, 38 days at 2.50	95 00	
do	Pay lists, wages of men employed.	492 71	
do	Brown Bros., hay, oats, etc	123 44	
do	Errett, W., provisions	65 70	
do	Woolings & Woolings, provisions...	42 44	
do	Smith, L., provisions	7 50	

COLONIZATION ROADS.—*Continued.*

Repairing old rds. & grading	Sword, T. J., provisions	5 75	
do	T. & N. O. Railway, freight	7 33	
do	Sundry persons, provisions, tools, etc	11 15	
		851 02	
	Less sale of provisions, etc....	12 00	
			839 02
Robilliard, Con. 4 Road	Chalmers, D., overseer, 96 days at 2.50	240 00	
do	Pay lists, wages of men employed.	1,022 59	
do	Hooey & Ryan, provisions, supplies, etc	237 04	
do	Hooey, L. G., provisions, blankets, etc	194 83	
do	Snowden, W. B., teaming	32 50	
do	Fraser, N. M., provisions	40 75	
do	Walton, W. C., provisions	37 45	
do	Clark, J., provisions, oats, etc	36 53	
do	Chambers, J., tent, stove and teaming	20 00	
do	Long Lake Co., provisions	23 62	
do	Sundry persons, teaming, freight, etc	30 00	
			1,915 31
Savard & Marquis Bdry	Hough, Jno. A., overseer, 34 days at 2.25	76 50	
do	Pay lists, wages of men employed.	497 07	
do	Hooey, L. G., tools	3 00	
do	Hough, Jno., Sr., tools	2 00	
do	Postage	8	
			578 65
Sheedy's, Taylor and Windigo Road	Peckover, Jno., overseer, 28 days at 2.25	63 00	
do	Pay lists, wages of men employed.	426 87	
do	Knox., J., plow repairs, blacksmithing, etc	4 35	
do	Eplett, S., plow point, tools, etc...	2 75	
do	Taylor Hardware Co., hardware....	2 95	
do	Scott, T., blacksmithing	40	
do	Judge, Wm., overseer, 15 days at 2.50	37 50	
do	Pay lists, wages of men employed.	685 61	
do	Gibbons, J. P., overseer, 15½ days at 2.25	34 87	
do	Pay lists, wages of men employed.	164 44	
do	Sundry persons, repairs, freight, etc.	2 00	
			1,424 74
	Total Temiskaming Roads		44,825 73
Venacker & Mallory Hill	Sallons, W. H., overseer, 20½ days at 2.25...	46 12	
do	Pay lists, wages of men employed	266 21	
do	Sallons, E., powder, etc	2 75	
			315 08
Van Horne Roads	Scott, Wm., overseer, 35 days at 2.25	78 75	
do	Pay lists, wages of men employed	351 60	
do	Reed, J., provisions	88 65	
do	Orvis, A. L., provisions	9 98	
do	McMillan, W., plank	28 32	
do	Silver, A., plank	13 50	
do	Newton, W., timber	7 45	
do	Mooney, E., provisions	11 75	
do	Sundry persons, spikes, livery, etc	9 10	
			599 10

COLONIZATION ROADS.—*Continued.*

Vermillion Bay Road ......Robertson, W. J., overseer, 19 days at 2.50	47 50	
do	Pay lists, wages of men employed	238 25	
do	Anderson, A., dynamite	13 00	
do	Postage, stationery and freight	1 41	
			300 16
Victoria Road ....McGaughey, Jos., overseer, 28½ days at 2.25	64 12	
do	Pay lists, wages of men employed	328 10	
do	McRae, J., cedar, powder, etc.	5 50	
do	Ryckman, D., blacksmithing	1 50	
do	Postage, affidavit, etc.	78	
do	Gilmour, Andrew, overseer, 25¼ days at 2.25	57 38	
do	Pay lists, wages of men employed	437 75	
do	McRae, J. A., tools..............................	4 17	
do	Postage, affidavits, etc.	70	
			900 00
Wabigoon Road North ...Alston, Hugh D., overseer, accountable		600 00
Wahnapitae and Sudbury			
Road ....Gauthier, M., overseer, 20½ days at 2.25	46 12	
do	Pay lists, wages of men employed	335 89	
do	Purvis Bros., tools, supplies, etc.	42 95	
do	Gauthier, E., cedar	30 00	
do	Gauthier, M., hay, oats, etc.	11 05	
do	Labelle, G., cedar	6 00	
do	Robillard, S., cedar	5 00	
do	Postage	41	
			477 42
Waito Station Rd., Wylie,			
Con. 12 and Rolph ......Berndt, Aug., overseer, 10 days at 2.25 ...	22 50	
do	Pay list, wages of men employed	111 25	
do	Berndt, A., cedar, use of tools, etc.	17 50	
do	Sundry persons, tools, blacksmithing, etc. ·	2 40	
do	McAnulty, Thos., overseer, 15¾ days at 2.25	35 43	
do	Pay list, wages of men employed	146 61	
do	Dunlop & Co., tools	12 25	
do	McAnulty, D., timber	5 44	
do	Postage, cartage, etc.	1 10	
do	Kannegiesser, Herman, overseer, 17 days at 2.25	38 25	
do	Pay lists, wages of men employed	154 50	
do	Dunlop & Co., tools	6 00	
do	Sundry persons, axe handles, postage, etc.	1 25	
do	Oalkie, Chas., overseer, 12½ days at 2.25 ...	28 13	
do	Pay lists, wages of men employed	121 50	
do	Oalkie, Chas., overseer, 12½ days at 2.25...	28 13	
do	Clarke & Andrews, blacksmithing	35	
do	Hoffman, Paul, overseer, 15 days at 2.25...	33 75	
do	Pay lists, wages of men employed	166 25	
do	Hoffman, P., use of tools	1 25	
			908 21
Wainwright Tp. Roads....Richardson, Wm., overseer, 33 days at 2.50	82 50	
do	Pay lists, wages of men employed	349 71	
do	Cassidy & Son, provisions	26 65	
do	Tuck, M., do	4 75	
do	Orvis, A. L., do	21 35	
do	Hayes, J. G., tools, etc.	9 60	
do	Sundry persons, provisions, repairs, etc....	5 42	
			499 98
Warren & Markstay Rd...Belanger, N., overseer, 14 days at 2.25 ...	31 50	
do	Pay lists, wages of men employed	158 05	
do	Laporte, D., tools	7 35	
do	Langlois, A., do	3 10	
do	Blanchette, Thos., overseer, 32 days at 2.25	72 00	
do	Pay lists, wages of men employed	491 80	
do	Laporte, D., tools, etc.	29 00	

COLONIZATION ROADS.—*Continued.*

Warren and Markstay Rd	Lytel, W. A., blacksmithing	5 95	
do	Barette, J., grindstone	1 00	
do	Postage, etc.	25	
			800 00
Warren and Monnettville Road	Therin, Theo., overseer, 25 days at 2.25	56 25	
do	Pay lists, wages of men employed	341 25	
do	Dupuis, A., repairing plow	3 50	
do	Ritcher, Arthur, overseer, 14 days at 2.25	31 50	
do	Pay lists, wages of men employed	171 25	
do	Boufford, Nap., overseer, 15¼ days at 2.25	34 88	
do	Pay lists, wages of men employed	250 50	
do	Bertrand, P., tools	9 00	
do	Lillie, R., dynamite	2 61	
do	Stationery, postage, repairs, etc.	2 00	
			902 74
Washago Rd., east into Rama	Cronke, Luther, overseer, 19 days at 2.25	42 75	
do	Pay lists, wages of men employed	238 75	
do	Cronke, A., dynamite	10 00	
do	Carrick, J. T., do	4 00	
do	Cronk, L. A., blacksmithing	3 96	
do	Sundry persons, blacksmithing, etc.	2 86	
			302 32
Waters Tp. towards White-fish	Robinson, D., overseer, 27 days at 2.25	60 75	
do	Pay lists, wages of men employed	485 87	
do	Moxam, J. B., timber, lumber, etc.	23 85	
do	Robinson, D., cedar	9 60	
do	Gagnon, W., do	6 00	
do	Oliver, Thos., tools	6 45	
do	Sundry persons, dynamite, blacksmithing, etc.	2 92	
			595 44
West Bay and Slash Rds.	Leason, Wm., overseer, 15 days at 2.25	33 75	
do	Pay lists, wages of men employed	255 05	
do	Hinds, O., tools, etc.	11 10	
do	Postage	10	
		300 00	
	Less paid by Township Council	50 00	
		250 00	
do	Cormier, Jno., overseer, 16 days at 2.25	36 00	
do	Pay lists, wages of men employed	202 49	
do	Baxter, A., tools	2 55	
do	Hawke, G., crowbar and blacksmithing	3 50	
do	Hay, D., tools	3 73	
do	Marshall, W., use of plow, etc.	4 00	
			502 27
Westphalia Road	Brown, Wm., overseer, 10 days at 2.25	22 50	
do	Pay lists, wages of men employed	162 36	
do	Ladel & Butcher, tools	4 18	
do	Drinkwater, J., blacksmithing	4 55	
do	Brown, W., tools	6 40	
			199 99
Westphalia Road, Trout Creek to Commanda	Osborne, Thos., overseer, 23¼ days at 2.25	52 31	
do	Pay lists, wages of men employed	243 97	
do	Ladell & Butcher, powder, fuse, etc.	2 40	
do	Trussler Bros., blacksmithing	1 40	
			300 08
Westport Bridges, Maberly and Perth Roads	Treasurer Westport, contribution towards construction of bridge		900 00

COLONIZATION ROADS.—*Continued.*

Whitefish Bridge, O'Con-			
nor Road	Hunt, J. McKay, overseer, 9 days at 5.00	45 00	
do	Pay lists, wages of men employed	218 25	
do	Fort William Hardware Co., dynamite, etc.	13 35	
do	Wadson, A. & Co., tools	80	
do	Postage, stationery, etc.	50	277 90
Whitefish Lake Road and			
West Mountain Road	Kennelly, Jos., overseer, 20 days at 2.25	45 00	
do	Pay lists, wages of men employed	258 00	
do	Maloney, Jas., J. overseer, 21 days at 2.25	47 25	
do	Pay lists, wages of men employed	243 00	
do	Devine & McGarry, dynamite, etc.	5 00	
do	Cotter, J. J., cedar	2 00	
do	Sundry persons, blacksmithing, etc.	2 70	
do	Dodge, Francis, accountable	280 00	882 95
White Lake Rd., Paken-			
ham Tp	Morphy, Jno. A., overseer, 16 days at 2.25	36 00	
do	Pay lists, wages of men employed	159 00	
do	Morphy, Wm., cedar	5 00	200 00
Widdifield Tp. Roads	Stockdale, Jno., overseer, 13 days at 2.25	29 25	
do	Pay lists, wages of men employed	200 00	
do	Richardson & Co., dynamite	18 30	
do	Garvin, O., blacksmithing	2 45	
do	Newbury, Wm., overseer. 14 days at 2.25	31 50	
do	Pay lists, wages of men employed	158 26	
do	Thebualt, Major, overseer, 9½ days at 2.25	21 37	
do	Pay lists, wages of men employed	112 87	
do	Richardson, J. W., tools	11 11	
do	McDonald & Hay, tools, etc.	2 35	
do	Sundry persons, plank and use of scraper	4 00	
do	Besserer, Louis, overseer, 39½ days at 2.25	88 87	
do	Pay lists, wages of men employed	494 25	
do	Purvis Bros., tools and dynamite	18 60	1,193 18
Wilberforce Roads	Hutchke, Hy., overseer, 30 days at 2.25	67 50	
do	Pay lists, wages of men employed	402 80	
do	Dunlop & Co., dynamite	9 64	
do	Lipke, L., blacksmithing	3 30	
do	Hutchke, Hy., use of tools, etc.	20 00	
do	Bissenthal, Otto, overseer, 14 days at 2.25	31 50	
do	Pay lists, wages of men employed	164 00	
do	Bissenthal, O., use of plow and scraper	3 65	
do	Hingle, F., plank	85	
do	Rickzen, Chas., overseer, 12 days at 2.25	27 00	
do	Pay lists, wages of men employed	100 37	
do	Switzer, J., tools	8 88	
do	Rickzen, C., cedar and rent of tools	9 80	
do	Proukie, Albert, rent of scraper	3 00	
do	Sundry persons, dynamite, blacksmithing, etc.	1 80	
do	Hubert, Aug., overseer, 4 days at 2.25	9 00	
do	Pay lists, wages of men employed	36 50	
do	Dunlop & Co., dynamite	4 00	
do	Schutt, F., blacksmithing	50	904 09
Wilberforce, Con. 12 and			
5th Line	Maloney, Jno., overseer, 20 days at 2.25	45 00	
do	Pay lists, wages of men employed	324 00	
do	Beiderman, Wm., overseer, 7 days at 2.25	15 75	
do	Pay lists, wages of men employed	70 50	
do	Dunlop & Co., dynamite, etc.	4 84	
do	Beiderman, Wm., cedar, use of tools, etc.	8 50	

COLONIZATION ROADS.—*Continued.*

Wilberforce, Con. 12 and 5th

Line	Postage, etc.	41
do	Sack, Frank, overseer, 14 days at 2.25 ...	31 50
do	Pay lists, wages of men employed	155 75
do	Sack, Aug., cedar, use of plow, etc.	9 26
do	Acton, J. A., tools, etc.	4 13
do	Sack, Ferdinand, use of scraper	2 50
do	Bimm, E., blacksmithing	40
		672 54
Wylie Tp. Roads	Schoenfeldt, Wm., overseer, 14 days at 2.25	31 50
do	Pay lists, wages of men employed	140 85
do	Thur, J. C., tools	8 00
do	Dunlop & Co., dynamite, etc.	3 35
do	Schoenfeldt, H., rent of scraper	3 50
do	Schoenfeldt, W., cedar and rent of plow, etc.	12 10
do	Hock, G., blacksmithing	70
		200 00

Commission on post office orders 1 80

	219,596 44
Less refund, Cardiff and Dysart Rd., 1905......	37 07
Total Colonization Roads ....$	219,559 37

CHARGES ON CROWN LANDS.

BOARD OF SURVEYORS ($200.00).

Secretary-Treasurer Association of Ontario Land Surveyors 200 00

AGENTS' SALARIES AND DISBURSEMENTS ($42,351.94).

Jno. H. Anderson:	Twelve months' salary as Crown Timber Agent, Tory Hill...			300 00
A. E. Annis:	Four and one half months' salary	do	Dryden.....	72 50
Jas. B. Brown:	Twelve months' salary as Crown	do	Bracebridge.	900 00
Thos. Buchanan:	do		do	Thessalon...	300 00
Robert J. Byers:	do		do	Massey......	500 00
Chas. Booth:	do		do	Denbigh·....	100 00
C. W. Burns:	do		do	Sundridge...	900 00
Jas. Barr:	One	do	do	Fort Frances.	100 00
W. P. Christie:	Twelve	do	do	Parry Sound	1,600 00
Thos. Chester:	Six and one half months' salary	do	NewLiskeard	678 90
Wm. Campbell:	Twelve months' salary		do	Stratton St'n.	300 00
Jno. M. Deacon:	do		do	Mattawa	300 00
James Ellis:	do		do	Parry Sound	500 00
T. G. Eastland:	do		do	Apsley......	300 00
J. S. Freeborn:	do		do	Magnetawan.	500 00
R. J. Groulx:	Eight	do	do	Chelmsford .	400 00
Jno. J. Grills:	Twelve months' salary		do	NewLiskeard	500 00
Chas. Henderson:	do		do	Sndbury.....	1,400 00
Robt. G. Howie:	do		do	NewLiskeard	1,200 00
S. J. Hawkins:	do		do	Webbwood..	1,400 00
J. McK. Hunt:	Four	do	do	Fort William	200 00
E. Handy:	Twelve months' salary		do	Emsdale	500 00
Wm. Hartle:	do		do	Winden.....	350 00
C. J. Hollands:	do		do	Fort Frances.	300 00
W. H. Hesson:	do		do	PortArthur..	500 00
Williams, Hugh:	do		do	Heaslip	500 00
Jno. Kennedy:	do		do	Pembroke...	1,600 00

CHARGES ON CROWN LANDS.—*Continued.*

AGENTS' SALARIES AND DISBURSEMENTS.—*Continued.*

Jos. A. Levis:	Twelve months' salary as Crown Timber Agent, SturgeonFalls				500 00
Wm. Margach:	do		do	Kenora......	1,600 00
J. Maughan:	do		do	Sault Ste. Marie.....	1,400 00
Hector McDonald:	do		do	Thessalon....	1,400 00
J. K. McLellan:	do		do	Sudbury.....	500 00
Alex. McFadden:	do		do	Emo.........	300 00
Jno. A. Oliver:	do		do	Port Arthur..	1,200 00
R. H. Pronger:	Seven and one half months' salary		do	Dryden	191 42
Adam Prince:	Twelve do		do	Wilno	500 00
Isidore Queeneville:	Seven and one half months' salary		do	Sturgeon Falls	386 15
Arthur Stevenson:	Twelve months' salary		do	Peterboro	1,400 00
M. Seegmiller:	do		do	Kenora	800 00
W. F. Scott:	Five do		do	New Liskeard	500 00
J. S. Scarlett:	Twelve do		do	Powassan.....	500 00
J. R. Tait:	do		do	L'Amable	500 00
Jas. Wilson:	do		do	Kinmout	150 00
D. B. Warren:	do		do	Pembroke....	300 00
Earnest Wright:	do		do	Warren.......	250 00
W. B. Whybourne:	do		do	Marksville....	150 00
Jas. York.	Eleven do		do	Fort Francis..	1,100 00
H. N. Young:	Twelve do		do	Sault Ste. Marie.......	300 00
J. P. Watson:	do		do	New Liskeard	912 50

Bracebridge Agency:
    Brown, Jas. B., travelling expenses and disbursements, 249.08; postage, 10.45; to pay Bastedo, D. E., stationery, 5.25; Jones, O. R., postage stamps, 6.80 .... 271 58

Dryden Agency:
    Annis, A. E., postage and rent of box, 37.70; to pay Miner Publishing Co., envelopes, 4.50; Pronger, R. H., postage, 7.62 .... 49 82

Emo Agency:
    McFayden, A., postage and stationery, 44.20; Postmaster, money orders, 1.40; Stewart, C. B., stationery, 3.25 .... 48 85

Elmsdale Agency:
    Handy, E., postage 17 64

Fort Frances Agency:
    York, James, travelling expenses and disbursements, 302.65; to pay Scott, J. C., rent of office, 118.00 .... 420 65

Heaslip Agency:
    Williams, Hugh, postage, 24.77; to pay *Haileyburian*, printing, letter paper, 2.00; Newsome & Gilbert, stationery, 8.50; Zahalan, K. G., letter press, 7.00 .... 42 27

Kenora Agency:
    Art Metropole, builders' level, 17.00; Gardener & Co., 16.50 .... 33 50
    McMurphy, Flora, services as stenographer at 1.50 per day 195 00
    Margach, Wm., travelling expenses and disbursements, 213.50; board of men, 85.20; to pay, Bret, J. P., horse feed, 15.95; Blue Bud, Jno., services, examining territory at Big Grassey River, 1.50; Cox, Anna, washing camp blankets, etc., 4.50; Campbell, Jno., examining territory at Big Grassey River at 3.00 per day, 9.00; C. P. Railway Co., freight charges, 61.97; C. P. R. Tel. Co., telegrams, 7.95; Dominion Express Co., charges, 2.50; David, Sam., 3 days' services canoeing Margach, Wm., 5.25; Griffith, D. M., blacksmithing, 16.00; Great West Saddlery Co., harness, horse blankets, etc., 44.90; Hudson's Bay Co., supplies, 18.45; use of horse 1 day, 4.00; Henderson, Jas., services assisting Margach, Wm., at Big Grassey River at 6.00 per day, 9.00; Johnson's Pharmacy, medicine for horses, 2.45; Kendall, E. F., meals and fares, 15.00; King, Wm., harness, etc., 3.25; McDonald, Thos., services, inspecting on Dore Lake, 28.00; board, 2.75; McLean, E. W. & Co., team of horses, 280.00; Margach, Wm., office rent, 80.00; Ogenagene, Wm., services as guide, 10.00; board, 6.00; Pither, R. J. N., rent of stables, 25.00; Parsons, A. J., postage stamps, 42.00; rent of post office box, 4.00; Preston, A. M., drawing

CHARGES ON CROWN LANDS.—*Continued.*

AGENTS' SALARIES AND DISBURSEMENTS.—*Continued.*

maps of timber berth, 2.00; Railway fares of men, 17.60; Robinson, W. J., 1 day's service examining lots, 3.50; Revell, L. O., board for driver and stabling for team, 11.60; Riley, Mrs., meals for driver, 34.80; Riley, E., wages as driver at 1.50 per day, 175.50; disbursements for self and horse, 59.25; Rice, Lewis & Son, 2 log rules, 2.50; Sargent, Fred., 2 days' inspecting Blumb timber lot, 5.00; Scott & Hudson Building Co., repairing sleigh, etc., 4.50; Smith, G. W., stationery, 2.90; Miner Pubg. Co., stationery and postage, 18.50; Scovil, Dr. S. S., rent of office, 360.00; Seegmiller, M., postage, 10.00; Sterling, C. N., canoe paddle, etc., 69.25; United Typewriter Co., shipping machine, 1.00; wages men, 226.75 .... | 2,002 77

Massey Agency:
Byers, R. J., postage, 8.83; to pay, Mervyn, Jas., hire of horse, 1.00; Payton, A., care of office, 1.00 .... | 10 83

Marksville Agency:
Whybourne, R. E., postage .... | 2 00

Mattawa Agency:
Deacon, J. N., postage .... | 5 08

New Liskeard Agency:
Chester, Thos., travelling expenses .... | 76 14
Grills, J. J., postage, 21.18; to pay, Stephenson, E. F., stationery, 14.50 .... | 35 68
Howie, R. J., travelling expenses and disbursements, 96.98; to pay, Brown Bros., horse feed, 29.39; Eplett, S. D., supplies, 4.10; Herron's, livery hire, 109.00; Hill, Fred., wages as guide and axeman, 60.00; Hill, Harry, board, 10.50; McGrath, R. H., wages as cook and packer, 34.00; King's Printer, stationery, 10.00; McKnight, Wesley, 2 tourist bags, 1.00; McCosh, D., rent of office, 45.00; Morrison, Wm., groceries, 26.98; Postmaster, postage stamps, 5.00; Scott, Walter F., travelling expenses and disbursements, 157.85; Watson, L. P., travelling expenses and disbursements, 277.60 .... | 867 40

Port Arthur Agency:
Munro, Hugh, Estate of, rent of office .... | 77 00
Oliver, J. A., travelling expenses and disbursements, 154.75; accountable, 300.00; to pay, Brown, Johnson, wages, 122.50; Bruce, D. R., rent of typewriter, 18.00; Central Book Store, stationery, 4.90; Cresswell, Dawson, wages, 172.50; Cooper, W. E., tents, 22.75; C. P. Railway Co., freight charges, 5.00; C. P. Tel. Co., telegrams, 2.40; Davidson, Jas., livery hire, 13.00; Dominion Express Co., 10.65; Fisher & Hart, groceries, 5.75; Murray, Jas., wages, 10.00; Postmaster, postage stamps, 30.94; Port Arthur Bazaar, Ltd., stationery and typewriter ribbon, 18.00; Parker, Ed., wages, 27.50; Rapsey, M., postage stamps, 14.00; *Superior* Ptg. Co., stationery, 18.00; Smith Premier Typewriter Co., typewriter, 50.00; Walsh, Louis, Coal Co., coal, 32.50; Wells & Emmerson, canoes, hardware, etc., 101.25; Williams, Ann., scrubbing, 2.00 .... | 1,136 39
Chronicle Ptg. Co., postage and stationery, 8.75; Foster, Jas., compass and chain, 16.75 .... | 25 50
Hesson, W. H., postage .... | 18 50

Powassan Agency:
Scarlett, J. S., postage .... | 2 50

Parry Sound Agency:
Christie, W. P., travelling expenses and disbursements .... | 361 54
Ellis, Jas., postage .... | 25 57
Moore, Geo., rent of office, 48.00; Pirie & Stone, rent of office, 21.00...... | 69 00

Pembroke Agency:
Kennedy, J. C., travelling expenses and disbursements, 1905, 280.15;
    do   do   do   do   1906, 272 17;
to pay, Dom. Express Co., charges, 2.92; Hogarth, Wm., blankets, 8.20; Moffat, Alex., postage stamps, 5.00; Mitchell, T. E., stationery, 1.25; Munro, Mrs. J. W., rent of office, 40.00 .... | 609 69

Peterborough Agency:
Bell Telephone Co., rent of instrument .... | 15 00

CHARGES ON CROWN LANDS.—*Continued.*

AGENTS' SALARIES AND DISBURSEMENTS.—*Continued.*

Peterboro Review, stationery and postage 13 80
Stevenson, Arthur, travelling expenses and disbursements, 176.25;
postage and telegrams, 5.51; to pay Bell Tel. Co., rent of instrument, 15.00; Gibbs, R., livery hire, 35.00; *Peterboro Review,* postage,
and stationery, 16.55; Toronto Savings & Loan Co., rent of office,
175.00 .... 423 31
Sudbury Agency:
Henderson, C., travelling expenses and disbursements, 46.42; to pay,
Conway, Jno., livery hire, 8.00; Dominion Express Co., charges,
7.60; *Journal* Ptg. Co., postage and stationery, 4.00; Lennan, Geo.
H., supplies, 15.55; Lough, R. J., rent of office, 48.00; McLennan,
J. K., postage, 15.33; stationery, 2.25; Post Office box rent, 2.00;
Sudbury Mining News, stationery, 5.50 .... 154 65
Sault Ste. Marie Agency:
McLean, Dr. Jas., medical services, disinfecting papers, 20.00; Mc-
Fadden & McFadden, rent of offices, 91.00 .... 111 00
Maughan, Jas., travelling expenses and disbursements, 243.88; post-
age, 6.25; to pay Adams, C. T. & Co., postage stamps, 6.00; rent of
post office box, 4.25; Bell Telephone Co., messages, 5.45; rent of
instrument, 12.50; C. P. R. Tel. Co., telegrams, 3.96; Colt, Mrs.,
scrubbing office, 1.00; Dom. Express Co., charges, 1.57; Foster, J.
G. & Co., directory, 2.00; Ganley, Jas., rent of office, 39.00; Hutton
Bros., livery hire, 13.00; *Sault Star,* ptg., 6.75; Templeton, A. &
Sons, livery hire, 7.00; Young, H. N., 5.25 .... 357 86
Stratton Station Agency:
Campbell, Wm., postage and stationery 36 65
Sundridge Agency:
Burns, C. W., travelling expenses and disbursements 591 74
Thessalon Agency:
Algoma Advocate, printing and stationery 8 55
Dyment, N. & A., rent of office, 98.35; Bridge Bros., wood for office, 15.00 113 35
Macdonald, Hector, travelling expenses and disbursements, 228.52;
to pay, McDougall, G., wood, 7.20; Needles, J. W., use of tug, 30.00;
Preston, Frank, livery hire, 85.50; Simon, A. D., rent of office, 60.00 411 22
Webbwood Agency:
Hawkins, S. J., travelling expenses and disbursements, 179.15; to pay
Dom. Express Co., charges, 60c.; Hawkins, S. J., rent of office,
49.00; Hargraves, Geo., assisting in scaling sample measurement
berth 108, 3.50; McMillan, J. C. & Co., stationery, 2.10; Pidgeon,
E., assisting scaling and measuring at 1.75 per day, 5.25; Purvis,
C. A., log rule, 2.25; Postmaster, postage stamps, 12.00; *Sault Star,*
printing and stationery, 6.00 .... 259 85
Ames, D. H., services as caretaker Day and Loboro Lakes, 1905 .... 20 00
Armstrong, J. E., services assisting Jas. Murray at 2.50 per day 82 50
Best, S. G., postage, 1905 .... 9 14
Bilton, Geo., services as caretaker Mud and Loon Lake Islands......... 25 00
Byers, R. J., services inspecting N. & S. ¼ lots 3 & 6, Shedden, 8.00;
lots 10 & 4 in Merrit, 16.00; Boyd, Jas., services inspecting lots in
Houghton, 10.00 .... 34 00
Beckett, J. R., services inspecting Cameron & Lauder at 3.00 per day,
30.00; to pay Burritt, E. A., services assisting, 8.00; Smiley, W.
H., services assisting, 7.00 .... 45 00
Christie, Malcolm, services inspecting at 2.00 per day 180 00
Christie, Jno., services assisting H. May inspecting Twp. of Burpee
at 2.00 per day 74 00
Cruise, W. W., valuation fee, block 16 and 19, Windsor. 10 00
Davis, S., caretaker Leonard Islands 20 00
Deacon, E., services inspecting and valuating lots 7 & w. ½ 8 & 9,
South Sherbrooke 10 00
Groulx, R. J., travelling expenses, 70.90; Gibbs, R., livery hire, 4.00 74 90
Hunt, J. McKay, services, inspection of lots, 45.00; expenses, 6.00;
to pay Letterman, Mark, services as guide at 4.00 per day, 14.00;
Johnson, Jas., stationery, 2.40 .... 67 40

CHARGES ON CROWN LANDS.—*Continued.*

AGENTS' SALARIES AND DISBURSEMENTS.—*Continued.*

Jervis, Henry, travelling expenses, 10.00; to pay Heroy, J. S., wages cooking and packing at 5.00 per day, 35.00	45 00
Kelly, Thos., services inspecting Twps. McClure, Herschell and Mayo at 5.00 per day, 395.00; travelling expenses, 14.60; to pay Kelly, Jno., wages assisting Inspector at 2.00 per day, 28.00; expenses, 15.80	453 40
McLennan, J. K., inspecting E. ½ lot 7, con. 2 Broder, 5.00; lot 8 in 1, Garcon, 10.00	15 00
McKelvie, D., services as Inspector Twps. Crawford and Carnegie at 3.00 per day, 114.00; expenses and disbursements, 107.55	221 55
McConnell, T. C., services inspecting mill site reserve	20 00
McGowan, W., services inspecting lots Conger and Burpee	40 00
May, H., balance services inspecting Twp. Burpee at 5.00 per day, 85.00; Burton & Brown at 5.00 per day, 450.00	535 00
Murray, Jas., services special inspection Twps. Murphy and Hoyle at 3.50 per day, 120.00; expenses and disbursements, 98.60	218 60
Moir, G. A., services Asst. Inspector Twps. of Crawford and Carnegie at 2.50 per day	85 00
Potts, H. F., services and expenses inspecting land	10 00
Quenneville, Isidore, travelling expenses, 105.10; to pay Cockburn, D. C., stationery and postage, 1.00; Leslie, R., steel tape and compass, 7.00	113 10

OTTAWA AGENCY ($3,779.60)

E. J. Darby, Twelve months' salary as Agent	1,500 00
S. C. Larose, do Clerk	1,000 00
Darby, E. J., disbursements 1905, 7.31; Fotheringham and Popham, printing and stationery, 10.75	18 06
Hope, Jas. and Son, stationery, 27.15; Kyle, S. J., platform of plan cabinet, 3.10	30 25
McNeil, E. R., duplicator composition, 5.00; Might Directories, Ottawa Directory, 4.00	9 00
Ottawa Electric Light Co., light, 1.29; post office, postage, 9.00; rent of box, 4.00	14 29
Rainboth, E. J., retaining fees as surveyor	700 00
Sun Life Assurance Co., rent of office, 500.00; Starr, J., repairing gold lettering, 8.00	508 00

QUEBEC AGENCY ($2,010.70)

Byron, Nicholson, Twelve months' salary as Agent	1,500 00
Department of Trade and Commerce, rent of office one year	125 00
Harney, T., salary as mesenger and caretaker, 150.00	150 00
Nicholson, B., balance disbursements (1905), 2.20; travelling expenses and disbursements, 112.80; accountable warrant, 50.00	165 00
To pay:—American Lumberman, book, 4.00; Clement & Clement, repairing typewriter and sundries, 12.40; Commercial Printing Co., stationery, 10.00; Chronicle Printing Co., subscription, 3.00; Deegan, M., office cleaning, 8.00; Heyden, A. J., clerical services, 15.00; Mulroney, W. J. and G., postage stamps and stationery, 14.30; Postmaster, rent of box, 4.00	235 70

FOREST RANGING ($45.165.61)

Services and expenses as Ranger at 7.00 per day:

McCreight, J., services, 455.00; travelling expenses and disbursements, 39.60; expenses accountable, 850.00; to pay Algoma Commercial Co., supplies, 23.40; Algoma Central and Hudson Bay Railway Co., freight charges, 1.48; Bassineau, P., cook and packer, at 2.50 per day, 170.00; MacKay Bros. & Co., cotton bags, .75; Plummer, W. H. & Co., supplies, 13.50; Sayers, E., packer and chopper, at 2.00 per day, 94.00; Stibbs, F. D., supplies, freight and tally boards, etc., 77.88	1,725 61

CHARGES ON CROWN LANDS.—*Continued.*

FOREST RANGING.—*Continued.*

Services and expenses as Ranger at 5.00 per day:

Ansley, J. J., services, 740.00; expenses accountable, 275.00	1,015 00
Allen, R. A., services, 1,080.00; expenses, 20.00; expenses accountable, 250.00	1,350 00
Archer, A. E., services, 465.00; travelling expenses, 120.20; to pay board of men, 7.50; Blain, Sinclair & Smith, counsel, 30.00; Cragg, W. V., one trunk line, 1.00; Dominion Express Co., charges, 3.93; Draper, R., services at 2.50 per day, 70.00; Eplett, S. D., camp stove, etc., 9.00; Grills, W., supplies. 49.46; Herron's Livery, livery hire, 3.00; Jack Hugh, services at 2.50 per day, 70.00; MacKnight, W., one pack bag, 2.50; Salter, W. H., groceries, 3.46; Turner, J. J. & Son, tent, 9.35; Taylor, Geo. Hardware Co., one canoe paddle, 1.40; Thompson, J. L., water bottle, 1.00; T. & N. O. Railway Co., freight charges, 6.00......	852 80
Baulke, G. R., services, 235.00; travelling expenses, 2.50; to pay Burley, Roy, services as assistant at 2.50 per day, 20.00	257 50
Bliss, L. E., services, 1,295.00; expenses accountable, 75.00....................	1,370 00
Barrett, Thos., services, 800.00; expenses accountable, 200.00	1,000 00
Brody, Jno., services, 545.00; travelling expenses, 28.50	573 50
Cameron, W. B., services	230 00
Gorman, Pat., services, 605.00; expenses accountable, 275.00	880 00
Hill, Joshua, services, 1,080.00; expenses accountable, 100.00	1,180 00
Huckson, A. H., services, 995.00; expenses accountable, 275.00	1,270 00
Halliday, James, services, 1,210.00; expenses accountable, 75.00	1,285 00
Hickerson, M. L., services, 225.00; services estimating timber on Deer River at 10.00 per day, 50.00...	275 00
Hutton, J., services, 900.00; travelling expenses, 20.90; expenses accountable, 175.00	1,095 90
Hurdman, W. H., services, 570.00; expenses, 4.50; expenses accountable, 325.00	899 50
Jervis, H., services, 1,090.00,; travelling expenses, 5.70; expenses accountable, 100.00	1,195 70
Johns, Alex., services, 670.00; expenses accountable, 150.00	820 00
Johnson, S. M., services, 1,535.00; travelling expenses, 88.82; expenses accountable, 150.00; to pay Halliday, Jas., services inspecting at 3.00 per day, 65.00; Wait, J. T., rent of office, 50.00	1,888 82
Lozo, Jno., services	835 00
Lee, Jas. B., services, 895.00; expenses accountable, 75.00	970 00
Lucas, R. G., services, 545.00; travelling expenses, 30.70; expenses accountable, 175.00	750 70
McNamara, J., services, 815.00; expenses accountable, 200.00	1,015 00
McDougall, J. T., services, 585.00; expenses accountable, 175.00	760 00
Menzies, A., services, 1,225.00; expenses accountable, 300.00	1,525 00
Manico, Wm., services, 1,350.00; expenses accountable, 75.00	1,425 00
Murray, Wm., services, 1,255.00; expenses accountable, 75.00	1,330 00
Macdonald, S. C., services	815 00
Margach, J. A., services, 300.00; travelling expenses, 13.50; expenses accountable, 100.00; to pay Ripple, Jno., services as assistant at 1.50 per day, 31.50; board, 14.40	459 40
Newburn, D., services	475 00
Revell, L. O., services, 810.00; expenses accountable, 200.00	1,010 00
Robinson, Wm., services, 900.00; to pay Oulette, S., services as guide, 3.00; Quirt, Henry, services as guide, 1.00; Verslegers, Casple, services as guide, 2.00	906 00
Shaw, Geo., services, 720.00; expenses accountable, 275.00	995 00
Taylor, L. G., services, 950.00; travelling expenses, 51.55	1,001 55
Vincent, H. T., services, 1,035.00; expenses accountable, 200.00	1,235 00
Whelan, J. P., services, 810.00; expenses accountable, 100.00..................	910 00
Watts, Geo., services, 1,485.00; travelling expenses and disbursements, 80.30; to pay Bell, A., work and board at 3.00 per day, 81.00; Creighton, L., work and board at 3.00 per day, 93.00; Fort Francis Times, printing and stationery, 34.00; Knox, E. F., rent of office, 28.00; Martin, R. H., wood, 5½ cords for 9.25; Rat Portage Lumber Co., wood, 2½ cords for 9.63; Watson & Floyd, tent, oil, etc., 10.45; Williams, H. rent of office, 60.00	1,890 63

CHARGES ON CROWN LANDS.—*Continued.*

FOREST RANGING.—*Continued.*

Yuill, Thos., services, 665.00; expenses accountable, 200.00	865 00
Services at 4.00 per day:	
Whyte, J. L., services, 484.00; travelling expneses, 73.20	557 20
Services at 3.50 per day:	
Chalmers, Geo. J., services, 399.00; travelling expenses, 33.70; expenses accountable, 175.00	607 70
Rawson, C. E., services, 126.00; travelling expenses, 19.55	145 55
Ritchie, J. A., services, 329.00; travelling expenses, 8.85; expenses accountable, 140.00	477 85
Whyte, J. T. G., services, 318.50; travelling expenses, 34.90	353 40
Services at 3.00 per day:	
Brinkman, A. B., services, 240.00; expenses accountable, 225.00.........	465 00
Huckson, A. H., services	48 00
McPherson, J. S., services, 329.00; travelling expenses, 16.50; expenses accountable, 300.00	645 50
McCallum, Thos., services	171 00
McCow, J. G., services, 216.00; expenses accountable, 175.00	391 00
Welch, Harold, services, 423.00; expenses accountable, 100.00	523 00
Services at 2.50 per day:	
Riley, Ed., services, 262.50; travelling expenses, 3.90	266 40
Ansley, W. E., expenses accountable, 150.00; Arnill, Wm., expenses accountable, 100.00...	250 00
Coburn, Jno., expenses accountable, 175.00; Corrigan, R. L., expenses accountable, 100.00	275 00
Chemer, E. A., expenses accountable, 100.00; Durrell, Wm., expenses accountable, 75.00	175 00
French, L., expenses accountable, 100.00; Foster, E. G., expenses accountable, 150.00	250 00
Fairbairn, W. H., expenses accountable, 100.00; Hartley, C., expenses accountable, 225.00	325 00
Herring, E. C., expenses accountable, 100.00; Lalonde, E., expenses accountable. 300.00	400 00
Loudry, W. E., expenses accountable, 200.00; Playfair, A., expenses accountable, 100.00	3〔.〕 00
Ross, Geo., expenses accountable, 875.00; Shaw, Alfred, expenses accountable, 150.00	1,025 00
	45,989 21
Less refund by D. L. Mather for expenses of J. T. White and Ed. Riley re measuring	823 60
	45,165 61

FOREST RESERVES ($27,913.19)

Tapping, Thos., salary as Superintendent of Western Forest Reserve.........	339 14

Services and expenses as Ranger:

Adams, Morris:	services at 2 50 per day,	332 50 ;	travelling expenses,	60 23	392 73
Angus, Robert:	do	325 00 ;	do	5 90	330 90
Black, Davidson:	do	357 50 ;	do	29 90	387 40
Bonneycastle, R. H.:	do	210 00 ;	do	60 30	270 30
Bassineault, Sam:	do	192 50 ;	do	6 80	199 30
Bay, John:	2 00				8 00
Clendenning, C. S.:	2 50	345 00 ;	do	30 90	375 90
Clark, W. A.:	do	310 00 ;	do	62 10	372 10
Crawford, Jas. P.:	do	287 50 ;	do	58 10	345 60
Carruthers, R. A.:	do	357 50 ;	do	18 30	375 80
Coleman, R. M.:	do	325 00 ;	do	24 60	349 60
Cox, G. B.:	do	292 50 ;	do	32 40	324 90
Cruise, G. A.:	do	370 00 ;	do	30 80	400 80
Campbell, J. L.:	do	382 50 ;	do	9 00	391 50
Chemones, John:	do	134 00 ;	do	2 40	136 40
Chenapess, Sandy:	2 00				133 00

23 PA.

CHARGES ON CROWN LANDS.—*Continued.*

FOREST RESERVES.—*Continued.*

Dann, E. M.: services at 2 50 per day 362 50; travelling expenses, 34 70 — 397 20
Deacon, Edgar: do 50 00; do 8 40 — 58 40
Dorsey, C. F.: do 340 00; do 19 50 — 359 50
Dreany, Alex: do 332 50; do 7 00 — 339 50
Donnell, M. O.: do 350 00; do 9 65 }
for R. O. Donnell, funeral expenses 130 28 } 489 93
Duke, William: do 120 00; travelling expenses 67 30 — 187 30
Ellis, Jno.: do 462 50; do 5 90 — 468 40
Eilber, Geo.: do 365 00; do 29 25 — 394 25
Foster, Jas.: compass and pins 6 25
Fawcett, J. R.: services at 2 50 per day, 30 00; travelling expenses, 30 00 — 60 00
Ferguson, W.: do 67 50; do 4 30 — 71 80
Graham, Jno.: do 337 50; do 21 95 — 359 45
Godkins, J.: 2 00 .... 262 00
Hunter, Frank: 2 50 357 50; do 23 90 — 381 40
Harnidge, R. L.: do 232 50; do 34 85 — 267 35
Hamilton, C. D., expenses acountable 200 00
Jefferson, L., services at 2.50 per day 247 50
Klotz, H. W.: do 362 50; do 21 60 — 384 10
Knowles, F. B. do 175 00; do 13 60 — 188 60
Kinney, William: 4 00 588 00; do 12 10
To pay: Brock, W. R. Co., Ltd., blankets. 30.60; C. P. Railway Co., freight charges, 11.84; Hudson Bay Co., tools, etc., 27.88; Peterboro Canoe Co., canoes, 84.15; Turner, J. J. & Sons, tents, 26.75 .... 781 32
Kennedy, G. K.: services at 2 50 per day, 312 50; travelling expenses, 21 60 — 334 10
Kent, H.: do 362 50; do 23 90 — 386 40
Lewis, R. G.: do 285 50; do 24 70 — 309 70
Lamarche, A.: do 455 00; do 8 40 — 463 40
Leitch, P. A., travelling expenses. 296.28; to pay W. R. Brock Co., Ltd., blankets, 46.80; C. P. Railway Co., freight charges on canoes, 13.62; Dominion Express Co., charges on tents, 3.50; English, Wm. Canoe Co., 3 canoes and crating, 107.00; Hudson Bay Co., tools, etc, 1.90; Revillon Bros., camp furnishings, 109.66; Turner, J. J. & Sons, tents, 44.63 .... 623 39
Lambert, N. P.: services at 2 50 per day, 270 00; travelling expenses, 23 70 — 293 70
Langerine, A.: 2 00 .... do — 10 00
McCullogh, D.: 2 50 302 50; do 19 70 — 322 20
McGregor, C.: 2 00 — 270 00
McGregor, Peter: 2 50 507 50; do 13 10 — 520 60
McGuire, T. C.: 3 00 85 00; do 8 80 — 93 80
McDonald, S. C.: 4 00 952 00; do 3 60 ....
To pay: W. R. Brock Co., Ltd., blankets. 31.45; English, Wm. Canoe Co., canoes and crating, 120.00; Hudson Bay Co., supplies, 53.17; Peterboro Canoe Co., canoes, 73.95; Turner, J. J. & Sons. tents, 9.25; wages men extinguishing fire, 124.40 .... 1,367 82
McKay, D. L.: services at 2 50 per day, 340 00; travelling expenses, 28 50 — 368 50
McLeod, B.: do 255 00; do 6 00 — 261 00
Markell, F.: expenses accountable 25 00
Manes, Jno.: services at 2 50 per day, 360 00; travelling expenses, 10 40 — 370 40
Montgomery, Alex.: do 447 50; do 14 90 — 462 40
Metcalf, M. E.: do 280 00; do 20 10 — 300 10
Neelon, J. A.: do 297 50; do 28 20 — 325 70
Oliver, J. A.: salary as Supervisor Sibley Reserve 100 00
Prudhomme, A.: services at 2 50 per day, 442 50; travelling expenses, 35 55 — 478 05
Patterson, Frank K. do 350 00; do 27 90 — 377 90
Powell, Jno. J.: do 260 00; do 15 80 — 275 80
Petront, Wm.: do — 307 50
Presley, W. H.: do 330 00; travelling expenses, 19 50 — 349 50
Ross, K. G.: 4 00 588 00; do 29 40 ....
To pay: C. P. Railway Co., freight charges, 8.82; Chenapess, Sandy, assisting putting out fire, 6.00; Dominion Express Co., charges, 2.40; Hudson Bay Co., cod lines, etc., 43.36; Horne, R., nails, 4.00; Novire, Jas., assisting putting out fire, 2.00; Peterboro Canoe Co., 3 canoes and paddles, 73.95; Shawinigabo, assisting putting out fire, 4.00; Turner, J. J. & Sons, 3 tarpaulins, 27.68; 789 61

CHARGES ON CROWN LANDS.—*Continued.*

FOREST RESERVES.—*Continued.*

Rochon, Jas., services at 2.50 per day, 455.00 travelling expenses, 8.40;		463 40
Robillard, A. E.: do 285 00; do 59 60		344 60
Robertson, L. B.: do 100 00; do 16 00		.116 00
Scrimgeour, W. G.: do 310 00; do 61 85		371 85
Shields, Wm., expenses accountable		100 00
Stata, Sam., services at 2.50 per day, 335.00; travelling expenses, 3.20......		338 20
Smith, W. J., to pay Bell Telephone Co., messages...........................		80
Scott, C. M., services at 2.50 per day, 302.50; travelling expenses, 29.80;		332 30
Smyth, W. J., services and inspection re instructions to Jno. Laycock		5 00
Saville, Thos., balance re services for 1905 at 2.50 per day		140 00
Spaniel, Alex., services at 2.50 per day, 360; travelling expenses,)2.20;		362 20
Tapping, Thos., services assisting in extinguishing fire....................		1 50
Teasdale, J. D.: services at 2 50 per day, 382 50; travelling expenses, 9 00		391 50
Thompson, M.: do 300 00; do 9 10		309 10
Tyrrell, A. J.: do 370 00; do 16 50		386 50
Thomson, Harry: do		337 50
Turner, Jno.: do		407 50
Taylor, A.: do 380 00; travelling expenses, 9 00		389 00
Taylor, Wm.: do 382 50; do 9 00		391 50
Tookey, W. E.: do 277 50; do 23 90		301 40
Thomson, F.: do 405 00; do 19 65		424 65
Viverois, D.: do 440 00; do 8 40		448 40
Webb, C. E.: do 360 00; do 29 90		389 90
Washburn, C. F.: do 305 00; do 31 20		336 20

FIRE RANGING ($57,611.65).

Services at 5.00 per diem:

Gagne, F., services, 795.00; trav. expenses, 22.40; to pay: Bell & Co., J. H., tools, etc., 60.93; Brock, W. R. & Co., blankets, 30.52; freight and cartage, 2.35; Turner, J. J. & Sons, tents and express, 18.00	929 20
Robinson, Wm., services, 390.00; travelling expenses, 25.65; Thomas, M., services, 30.00	445 65

Services at 4.00 per diem:

Barrett, T., services	104 00
Duval, C. A., services, 574.40; travelling expenses and disbursements, 120.30	
To pay, Prieur, J. F., supplies, 429.91; wages of men, 324.60......	1,449 21
Marchant, J., services, 560.00; travelling expenses, 10.00................	570 00

Services at 3.00 per diem:

Brinkman, A. B., services, 345.00; travelling expenses, 48.50	393 50
Fairbairn, N. H., do 354.00...	354 00
Gemmill, J., do	396 00
McCaw, J. G., do	291 00
Newborn, W., on account of services	350 00
Scott, Robt., services, 359.00; travelling expenses, 50.60	409 60
Urquhart, J., do 294.00; do 170.25	464 25
Wilkins, G. N., do 279.00; do 68.70	347 70

Services at 2.50 per diem:

Allison, M. B.: services, 357 50; travelling expenses, 18 10	375 60
Armstrong, W. H.: do 335 00; do 22 25	357 25
Ames, Romney: do 170 00; do 14 20	184 20
Bone, A.: do	307 50
Biggs, A.: do 352 50; do 19 80	372 30
Biggs, Jos.: do 350 00; do 14 80	364 80
Buchanan, A.: do 352 50; do 19 30	371 80
Bradburn, O. E.: do 345 00; do 17 30	362 30
Burger, W.: do 335 00; do 26 35	361 35
Bertrand, P.: do 355 00; do 5 50	360 50
Brown, J. B.: do 220 00; do 29 25	249 25
Carson, J. G.: do 270 00, do 29 25	299 25
Coulter, C.: do 340 00; do 23 30	363 30
Cousineau, A.: do	327 50

CHARGES ON CROWN LANDS.—*Continued.*

FIRE RANGING.—*Continued.*

Corrigan, I. O.:	services,	257 50;	travelling expenses,	25 50		283 00
Carey, D. V.:	do	192 50;	do	26 00		218 50
Cox, Stewart :	do	340 00;	do	14 85		354 85
Davidson, G. L.:	do	320 00;	do	18 10		338 10
Delmage, R. D.:	do	300 00;	do	34 80		334 80
Dever, W.:	do	357 50;	do	11 90		369 40
Enright, Owen:	do	152 50;	do	16 70		169 20
Enright, Thos.:	do	337 50;	do	19 65		357 15
Elliott, Jackson:	do	357 50;	do	15 10		372 60
Faries, R.:	do					352 50
Flanigan, P.:	do	340 00;	do	20 20		360 20
Ferguson, Wm.:	do	292 50;	do	1 40		293 90
Gauthier, A.:	do	302 50;	do	5 65		308 15
Glazier, M. B.:	do	355 00;	do	22 20		377 20
Guertin, Godfrey:	do	117 50;	do	12 65		130 15
Gorselin, J.:	do	90 00;	do	5 50		95 50
Guthrie, Wm.:	do	352 50;	do	6 20		358 70
Hawley, D. J.:	do	307 50;	do	26 60		334 10
Hodgins, Thos.:	do	360 00;	do	13 70		373 70
Helliwell, Paul:	do	265 00;	do	19 15		284 15
Hall. M. E.:	do	305 00;	do	22 00		327 00
Irwin, Oscar :	do	317 50;	do	21 40		338 90
Jackson, Jno.:	do	292 50;	do	14 55		307 05
Kelly, J. J.:	do	325 00;	do	17 40		342 40
Keyes, Thos. R., deceased:	do	267 50;	do	11 20		278 70
			funeral expenses,			127 10
King, F. G.:	do					307 50
Lamarche, A.:	do	257 50;	travelling expenses,	11 00		268 50
Lambert, N. P.:	do	45 00;	do	11 00		56 00
Lees, J.:	do	307 50;	do	10 65		318 15
McCurdy, J. L.:	do	207 50;	do	20 20		227 70
McCullough, C.:	do	342 50;	do	27 00		369 50
McClure, A.:	do	67 50;	allowance for board, self and assistant, 1905,	11 00		68 50

McDougall, J. T.: services, 725 00; travelling expenses, 28 07; to pay assistance and supplies for men.........................465 74   1,218 81

McIntosh, A. A: rent of room, 77 00; Storage of camp outfit, 21 00; Walbourn, W. H., papering room.............................2 00   100 00

McDonald, F.:	services,	350 00;	travelling expenses,	1 40		351 40
McKay, Hugh:	do	337 50;	do	34 75		372 25
McIver, Hugh:	do	355 00;	do	33 20		388 20
McDougall, E. H.:	do	202 50;	do	20 65		223 15
Maguire, L. C.:	do	240 00;	do	8 80		248 80
Morrow, R.: acc't	do					50 00
Moore, L. E.:	do	25 00;	do	22 00		47 00
Matte, Jno.:	do	237 50;	do	3 40		240 90
Macalpine, C. D. H.:	do	310 00;	do	28 00		338 00
Macdonell, N.:	do	285 00;	do	2 95		287 95
Merchant, A.:	do					350 00
Morand, L.:	do	340 00;	do	6 50		346 50
Mustard, W. H.:	do	325 00;	do	16 10		341 10
Mitchell, Grant:	do	152 50;	do	18 50		171 00
Nadon, F.:	do	357 50;	do	4 60		362 10
O'Connor, Jas.:	do	355 00;	do	7 40		362 40
Pennell, G.:	do	330 00;	do	10 65		340 65
Prestley, J.: acc't	do					50 00
Pew, Murray:	do	307 50;	do	23 50		331 00
Quigley, Wm.: acc't	do					100 00
Quilty, J.:	do	365 00;	do	14 90		379 90
Readman, R. E.:	do					202 50
Russell, J. F.	do					152 50
Savard, A.:	do	160 00;	do	2 80		162 80
Smith, A. L.:	do	335 00;	do	22 00		357 00
Stellan, F.:	do	317 50;	do	2 75		320 25
Sterrett, J. T.:	do	292 50;	do	29 65		322 15

CHARGES ON CROWN LANDS.—*Continued.*

FIRE RANGING.—*Continued.*

Stubbs, Jno.:	services,	287 50;	travelling expenses,	28 95	316 45
Stetham, H. A.:	do				105 00
Taylor, A. E.:	do	142 50;	do	27 35	169 85
Trembley, Jno.:	do	330 00;	do	3 20	333 20
Taggart, Ralph:	do	322 50;	do	33 65	356 15
Thompson, M.:	do	27 50;	do	4 75	32 25
Whitmore, Wm.:					307 50
Wickett, E.:	do	117 50;	do	14 40	131 90
Wickett, J. A.:	do	317 50;	do	28 35	345 85
Yocum, J.:	do	360 00;	do	20 50	380 50

Services at 2.00 per diem:
Burns. G. F., 6.00;   Campbell, R., 9.00;   Carville, H., 8.00;
Greenshields, E.. 10.00;   Levesque, E.. 4.00;   McDermott, R., 7.00;
McDonald. A.. 5.00;   Monaghan. J. R., 10.00;   O'Brien, M.; 9.00;
Smith, Jas., 1905;   travelling expenses, 11.50;   Turner, R., 5.00;
Turner, G., 15.00 ....   99 50

Services at 1.50 per diem:
McDonald. Thos., 94.50; Stellar, Fred, 190.50 ....   285 00

Services at 1.25 per day:
Crowe, Wm.. 106.00; Cartwright. Thos.. 131.00; Cousineau, T.. 131.00;
Cullen. M. T.. 91.00;   Christie, J.. 113.00;   Conboy. T.. 131.00;
Cottenham. W.. 131.00; Cousins. Jas.. 131.00; Carlin, Thos., 131.00;
Conture. N.. 78.00;   Calwag. S. H., 66.00;   Cannon, J. V., 151.00;
Christlow. H.. 131.00;   Collins. C.. 131.00;   Campbell. R.. 63.00;
Cutham, D.. 142.00; Corrigan, M. B.. 131.00;   Peeler. Chas.. 98.25;
Russell, Jno., 115.00 ....   2,202 25

Services at 1.00 per diem:
Ambrose. A. W.. 131.00;   Allison, Jno.. 42.00;   Allen. Geo.. 55.00;
Arnoth, W., 130.00; Armstrong, J. C., 130.00; Atkinson, Thos., 140.00;
Archer, J.. 131.00;   Allison. Jas., 42.00;   Beaton. W., 125.00;
Bertrand, F., 82.00;   Bellyeville, O.. 132.00;   Barb, Ben., 131.00;
Bethune, D., 54.00;   Baur, A., 131.00;   Brown. A., 120.00;
Burgess, W. H., 1905. 131.00;   Burgess, W. H., 1906, 131.00;
Bissett, J. C., 131.00;   Beggs, D., 93.00;   Boisbert, J., 106.00;
Brewer. C. E.. 131.00; Bowland, Mrs. J.. 131.00; Bowie, L., 119.00;
Burton. R.. 83.00;   Bruno, Paul. 131.00;   Brooks, T. H., 132.00;
Buchanan. R.. 89.00;   Burns, Wm.. 131.00;   Brown, Jno., 131.00;
Conolly. J.. 100.00;   Cartier, F.. 132.00;   Cox, Jos.. 98.00;
Cooney. J. C., 118.00; Conway, R., 143.00; Cuthbertson, W., 124.00;
Campbell. H., 128.00;   Crombie, J. (deceased), 132.00;
Caron. Vital. 131.00;   Cole, Geo., 132.00;
Coghlan,. T.. 131.00;   Cameron, A.. 126.00;   Connorette, Wm., 66.00;
Cardiff. G. F.. 131.00;   Curtain, D.. 131.00;   Chartrand, L.. 99.00;
Dube, Jno.. 125.00;   Dawson, D., 132.00;   Delgarm, J., 131.00;
Dennison, Harry. 131.00; Didieu,. L. P., 130.00; Dawkins. J.. 131.00;
Doyle, T. J., 129.00;   Davis, W. J., 75.00;   Datour. A., 89.00;
Duff, A. S., 12.00;   Draycott. E. A., 115.00;   Driver, Jos., 130.00;
Dunn, Thos.. 131.00;   Dilworth, W., 74.00;   Duplesis, Alex., 82.00;
Dunne, J. F., 118.00;   Dufond, Ignace, 125.00;   Elliott, W., 119.00;
Edwards, E. D.. 131.00;   Erwin. T.. 131.00;   Feeley, P.. 106.00;
Fortier, Jos.. 111.00; Fairbairn, W. H.. 31.00; Fidler, S. J.. 89.00;
Filiater. Jas.. 125.00;   Finley, B., 131.00;   Flynn. Jno., 127.00;
Foley, P.. 106.00;   Groney. C.. 131.00;   Gavnon, J., 129.00;
Gervais, L. X.. 131.00;   Gould. F.. Sr.. 134.00;   Gault. Jas.. 90.00;
Gauthier. A.. 19.00;   Gill. J. W.. 74.00;   Gallagher, J.. 131.00;
Gibson, Thos.. 44.00; Greenshields. E.. 151.00; Gongeon, A.. 119.00;
Growberger. L.. 132.00;   Godin. Wm.. 48.00;   Graham, J.. 41.00;
Gillies. J. P.. 72.00; Gervais, W., 132.00; Grozelle. W. D.. 115.00;
Grant, B. A.. 76.00;   Groulx, A.. 131.00;   Groulx, F., 56.00;
Gorman, M.. 131.00;   Grant, J. D.. 131.00;   Harper, T.. 105.00;
Haskin. D.. 131.00;   Hennesy. R. E.. 85.00;   Haley. E.. 131.00;
Helmer, J., 113.50;   Harper, Thos., 131.00;   Hones, J. L., 45.00;
Hance, A., 113.00;   Haldsworth, J., 126.00;   Hurd, E., 121.00;

CHARGES ON CROWN LANDS.—*Continued.*

FIRE RANGING.—*Continued.*

Hatton, A., 79.00; Hunt, J. W., 81.00; Hogarth, H., 134.00;
James, F., 131.00; Jackson, R. Sr., 42.00; Kirk, W. J., 79.00;
King, Alex., 69.00; Kennedy, M., 130.00; Kirby, H., 131.00;
King, Jas., 30.00; Koch, Jno., 116.00; King, Chas., 131.00;
Kennedy, J. J. 154.00; Larivere, J., 131.00; Law, W. J., 131.00;
Lamothe, M., 1905, 132.00; Lamothe, M., '06, 131.00; Larivie, J., 114.00;
Lamothe, H., 105.00; Lorenz, C., 133.00; Lafrance, T., 130.00;
Lablanc, O., 131.00; Lamarche, J., 131.00; Lemyre, M., 60.00;
Leahy, Jno., 132.00; Lindsay, J. A., 121.00; Ludgate, A., 77.00;
Lynch, M. D., 106.00; Lavois, B., 131.00; Loring, F., 115.00;
Long, H. E., 120.00; Lowe, W. D., 131.00; Massey, Geo., 131.00;
Mulvaney, W., 131.00; Marion, Isidore, 84.00; Munro, J. H., 131.00;
Morre, D., 130.00; Milne, A., 131.00; Murphy, Peter, 104.00;
Morris Hoff, J. S., 108.00; May, Wm., 131.00; Matte, Jos., 25.00;
Moriarty, M., 131.60; Montroy, J. J., 131.00; Megean, J., 131.00;
Magar, H., 131.00; McDonald, M., 69.00; McCaffrey, J., 133.00;
McCreary, W., 133.00; McAulay, D., 124.00; McKinney, J., 131.00;
McIrny, D., 33.00; McDougall, D., 64.00; McMullen, Alex., 130.00;
McGarrey, R., 131.00; McKenzie, W., 131.00; McColl, A., 132.00;
McAmmond, J., 113.00; McGuire, Hugh, 132.00; McAdam, Wm., 131.00;
McFarlane, Jas., 130.00; McBain, J., 48.00; McGuey, O., 134.00;
McKay, Angus, 131.00; McInnes, D. C., 95.00;
McDonald, A. J., 1905 4.00, 1906 83.00, McCaw, B. E., 90.00;
McFarlane, B. L., 131.00; McIntyre, W., 131.00; McGahie, C., 132.00;
McGregor, J., 129.00; McLaughlin, J., 131.00; McPhee, L. V., 132.00;
McNabb, Alex., 98.00; Montray, T., 124.00; McRae, Alex., 131.00;
Manseau, L., 81.00; Macdonald, H. C., 131.00; Mercer, W., 104.00;
Macdonald, A., 82.00; May, Albert, 120.00; Mitchell, W., 90.00;
Murphy, W., 37.00; Newton, T., 131.00; Nolan, Peter, 90.00;
O'Brien, Martin, 153.00; O'Brien, P., 74.00; Oulette, J., 108.00;
Owens, R., 131.00; Ouimette, C., 131.00; Page, W., 127.00;
Patterson, T., 72.00; Plourde, C., 132.00; Pane, Wesley, 131.00;
Playfair, A., 84.00; Powell, S., 131.00; Paquette, Jos., 47.00;
Rawson, C. E., 120.00; Raymond, C., 134.00; Rogers, Fred., 4.00;
Rivers, Jno., 79.00; Richardson, J., 100.00; Ryan, D. J., 68.00;
Ross, A. C., 81.00; Reynolds, J., 104.00; St. Pierre, W., 128.00;
Stanley, L., 103.00; Saucier, Ovid., 131.00; Stewart, D. R., 136.00;
Shipman, C., 106.00; Sheahan, D., 133.00; Sauve, A., 131.00;
Stevenson, W., 72.00; Sicord, F., 132.00; St. Armour, J., 131.00;
Snowden, T., 113.00; Smith, Jos., 131.00; Shields, Thos., 110.00;
Shields, Geo., 135.00; Shields, F., 131.00; Spreadborough, W., 132.00;
Stevenson, W., 93.00; Smith, Wm., 178.00; Sharbot, J., 131.00;
Sheahan, D., 1.00; Thongie, Xavier, 131.00; Thomas, G. J., 131.00;
Thomas, Peter, 132.00; Thomas, Wm., 132.00; Tremblay, E., 125.00;
Thomas, Jas., 103.00; Traynor, D., 36.00; Took, S., 50.00;
Tullock, W. A., 95.00; Towers, O., 131.00; Troppier, A., 131.00;
Tyson, T., 130.00; Turner, Geo., 158.00; Turner, Robt. Sr., 151.00;
Vincent, Jas., 41.00; Vermette, J., 132.00; Voker, P. D., 131.00;
Wilson, J., 122.00; Wallace, Geo., 131.00; Walters, T., 88.00;
Walker, Jas., 131.00; Welsh, W., 1905 72.00, 1906 114.00;
Weigold, J., 131.00; Williams, Allen, 52.00; Williams, W., 131.00;
Wright, Jno., 1905, 33.00, 1906, 41.00; Yandou, J., 131.00;
Youill, J. A., 131.00 .... 28,647 50

Assistance extinguishing fires:

Aikens, G., 132.00; Algoma Commercial Co. 123.29 .... 255 29
Booth, J. R., 340.71; Carpenter, T. G., 2.50 .... 343 21
Can. Copper Co., 7.00; Colonial Lumber Co., 60.00 .... 67 00
Charlton, J. & A. A., 281.38; Cook Bros., 10.95 .... 292 33
Conger bark limit, 3.00; Dyment, N. & A., 3.00 .... 6 00
Grant, D. Inglis, 2.63; Gillies Bros., 1,164.60 .... 1,167 23
Georgian Bay Lumber Co., 92.88; Gordon Geo. & Co., 26.00 .... 118 88
Henderson, C., 158.75; Hawkesbury Lumber Co., 53.50 .... 212 25
Kennedy, J. C., 10.00; Loveland & Stone 20.63 .... 30 63
McDougall, J. T., 17.50; McGregor, Peter 12.00 .... 29 50

CHARGES ON CROWN LANDS.—*Continued.*

FIRE RANGING —*Continued.*

McLachlin Bros., 395.53; Northern Construction Co., 96.00............	491 53
Northern Lumber Co.. 48.75; Parry Sound Lumber Co., 7.00............	55 75
Rathbun & Co.	25 88
Smith, J. B. & Son. 7.63; Spanish River Pulp & Paper Co., 28.00.........	35 63
Tapping, T., 3.00; Thessalon, lumber, 3.75.........:.........................	6 75
Victoria Harbor Lumber Co..	76 00
Bertrand, Isaac, services at 26.00 per month, 109.50; Brock, W. R. & Co., blankets, 45.40	154 90
Blanchet & Fitzpatrick, tents, blankets, etc., for C. T. McDougall............	26 43
Conway, J., livery hire, 28.00; Carter, J. & Son, tent and blankets, 28.00.	56 00
English. Wm. Canoe Co., canoes and crating for J. C. Kennedy..............	60 00
Henderson, E., 2 cedar canoes, 72.00; Jalbert, O., rubber sheet, 1.80; 2 cords wood, 10.10	83 90
Kennedy, J. C., to pay for ranger's outfit, 31.25, C. P. Ry., freight charges., 5.46; Dom. Express, charges, 1.40	38 11
Lennox, G. H., supplies for Henderson, 110.65; Maxwell, J., services at 75c. per day, 16.50	127 15
Moore, D., bal. travelling expenses, 3.75; Peterboro Canoe Co., canoe paddles for J. C. Kennedy, 73.95	77 07
Playfair, A. M., services at 70.00 per mo., 80.77; Purvis Bros., camp supplies, 30.30	111 07
Richardson, J. W., tents, blankets, etc., for C. T. McDougall	34 50
Turner, J. J. & Sons, tents for J. C. Kennedy, 26.70; T. & N. O. Ry., repairing 4 velocipedes for C. T. McDougall, 67.62	94 32
Wells Hardware Co., canoe, paddles etc	22 85
	66,905 86

Less refunded b- T. N. O. Railway, half cost of fire ranging	9,286 71	
Thos. Saville. balance accountable warrant, 1905.....................	7 50	
		9,294 21
		57,611 65

CULLERS' ACT ($180.35).

Currie, D. H., services at 4.00 per day, 28.00; travelling expenses, 39.05	67 05
Cooke, A. M.. rent of hall for examiners, 2.00; Fisher, George, services at 4.00 per day, 20.00	22 00
Gardner, Jno., services, 4.00; Jordan, S., services moving logs, 6.00...............	10 00
Kennedy, J. C., travelling expenses and disbursements. 29.00; McNabb, A. D., services at 4.00 per day. 8.00; Miner Pub. Co., advertising and printing, 6.00	43 00
Margach, Wm.. travelling expenses. 24.00; Oliver. J. A., travelling expenses, 6.50	30 50
Port Arthur Bazaar, ink. 30c.; Sims Lumber Co., sawing logs, 7.50........:	7 80

SURVEYS ($125,003.39).

American Tent and Awning Co., tent. pack sacks, etc		26 40
Beatty, H. J., survey Township Gamey, 1 840.65: allowance for running boundaries. 300.00; Township Borden, 1,338.48; allowance for running boundaries. 150.00; Township Lackner. 2,144.24; Township McNaught, 1,992.08; less advance, 3.500.00 (1905)...		4,765 45
Beatty, Walter, survey Township Cochrane, 2,293.04; less advance. 1,500.00 (1905)		793 04
Township D'Arcy, 2,209.64; less advance, 1,500.00 (1905)............		709 64
Township McGee, 2 124.64: less advance 1,500.00 (1905)............		624 64
Township Chapleau. 2,157.00: advance, Gallagher and Streathem, 3,000.00; accountable warrant, 1,000.00		6,157 04
Byrne, Thos., survey Township Scollard		2,675 20
Bollon. E. D., survey Township Nesbit 2,296.30: Township Aubin. 2,313.50		4,609 80
Cavana & Watson. survey Townships Duff and Lucas, 3,538.30: Township Calder. 5,403.84		8,942 14
Code, A. S., survey Township Ottawa, 2,426.76; Township Fournier, 2,442.60		4,869 36
Copp. Clark Co.. maps of districts and townships...................................		1,100 00

CHARGES ON CROWN LANDS.—*Continued.*

SURVEYS.—*Continued.*

DeMorest R. W., survey timber berths Algoma at 7.00 per day, 371.00; wages, assistance, 479.00; travelling expenses, 199.03; supplies, etc., 202.55; rent of canoe and camp outfit, 20.00; less advance, 400.00 (1905) ... 871 58

Dickson, Jas., services inspection of surveys at 8.00 per day 1,848.00; services at Toronto at 3.00 per day, 24.00; to pay wages men, 2,358.25; transportation and supplies, 1,304.65; less advance, 1,900.00 (1905)... 3,634 90

Francis, J. J., services at 8.00 per day, 24.00; travelling expenses, 12.50... 36 50

Filton, C. E., survey Townships Reid and Carnegie, 4,537.80; less advance, 1,000.00 (1905) 3,587 80

Fitzgerald, J. W., survey Township Bradburn, 5.627.59; Township Beck, 2,392.10 .... 8,019 69

Galbraith, W., advance, survey Township Clute, 4,000.00; accountable warrant, 1,000.00 .... 5,000 00

Gillon, D. J., survey timber berths Rainy River at 7.00 per day, 427.00; rations, 5.00; travelling expenses. 24.30; supplies, outfits, etc.. 296.56; transportation, 125.08; wages of assistants, 575.75......................... 1,453 69

Halford, A. J., survey Townships Moody and Leslie, 4,845.80; less advance, 3,500.00 (1905) 1,345 80

Harcourt, E. F. Co., 2,000 maps Coleman Township 65.00; 10,000 maps Coleman, Loraine and Bucke. 260.00; 500 maps Ontario, 500.00; maps of pulpwood timber berths, 270.00; 5,000 maps Abitibi, 465.00; 1,000 maps Huron and Ottawa, 1,180.00; 3.000 plans timber berths. 286.00; 5 maps Loraine and Bucke, 155.00; 1,000 maps Barr, 42.00; 5,000 maps Coleman, 105.00 .... 3,328 00

Hutcheson, J., survey Township Dargavel, 2.451.40; survey Township Lennox, 2,448.60 .... 4,900 00

King's Printer, maps 592 30

McMillan, W. stakes, 1.25 advance, survey Townships Temple and Langton, 1,000.00; accountable warrant, 500.00 .... 1,501 25

Newman, J. J., surveys Township Sherring. 2,309.70; Township Marathon, 2,823.82 .... 5,133 52

Niven, Alex., surveys base and meridian lines Algoma 9,405 00

Patton, T. J., re Inter-Provincial boundary, services, 3,048.00; assistants' wages, 4,450.62; travelling expenses, 612.29; stationery, 6.00; less one-half paid by Province of Quebec, 4,058.46; less advance, 3,000.00 (1905) 1,058 46

Patton, T. J., accountable warrant, 500.00; advance re Inter-Provincial boundary line, 2,000.00; advance, surveying Township Bowyer, 1,000.00 3,500 00

Rorke, L. V., services at 7.00 per day, 504.00; services at 8.00 per day, 120.00; travelling expenses, 27.30; surveys. Townships Paul and Pattinson, 4,401.07; survey Township Collins, 2,269.00; less advance, 1,750.00; (1905), 519.00; to pay supplies, etc 440.30; transportation, 264.99; wages of assistants, 900.35.. 7,177 01

Rice Lewis & Son, iron picks 430 00

Seager, E., services at 9.00 per day 245.00; work on maps at 8.00 per day, 48.00; wages of assistants. 500.75; travelling expenses 111.65; supplies, 136.35; survey Township Pellatt, 2,759.00; less advance. 1,500.00 (1905), 1,259.00; advance re survey Township Redditt. 1.800.00...................... 4,100 75

Smith. Jas. H., survey Township Sweatman, 2,593.20; Township Stinson, 2.283.30 .... 4,876 50

Speight. T. B., survey of marsh lands adjoining Mud Creek Reservation at 8.00 per day, 48.00, services inspecting bridge Haileybury and New Liskeard at 12.00 per day. 144.00; assistants' wages. 50.00; travelling expenses, 122.35 .... 364 35

Speight & Van Nostrand. survey re base and meridian lines, Algoma....... 9,885 70

Stull, D., survey Township Allan. 2,121.94; Township Ringwood. 2.043.04... 4,164 98

Tarling, C. & Co., mounting maps 140 10

Tyrrell & McKay, survey Township Sydere 5,185 40

Whitson. J. F., travelling expenses 37 40

CLEARING ALONG TEMISKAMING RAILWAY ($89,412.95).

Begg Bros., boots, rubbers, blankets, etc., 600.28; Bell, J. H., chain blocks, shovels, hardware, etc.. 469.06 .... 1,069 34

Borden's Condensed Milk Co.. milk. 37.00; C. P. Railway Co., freight charges. 13.08 .... 50 08

CHARGES ON CROWN LANDS.—*Continued.*

CLEARING ALONG TEMISKAMING RAILWAY.—*Continued.*

Cameron, W., groceries, etc., 208.56; Chaput, L. Fils Cie, tea, 108.00...	316 56
Davies, Wm. & Co., meat, etc., 4,352.79; Dunlop & Co., tools, 176.13.........	4,528 92
Floyd, J. A., boots. stationery, optical supplies, etc.	446 62
Howland, H. S. & Sons, hardware, etc., 685.00; Hudson's Bay Co., boots, etc., 30.50	715 50
Lamarche, C., Jr., hay, etc., 354.25; Lumbermen's Supply Co., shoes overalls, shirts, etc., 450.78	805 03
Levis Bros., groceries, 1,752.93; McDonald & Hay ranges, kettles, etc., 594.80	2,347 73
Matthews, Geo. Co., meats, 70.33; Morel & Co.. meats. 1,125.18...........	1,195 51
Ogilvie Flour Mills Co., flour, 891.75;* Pay list, wages of men, 70,143.56...	71,035 31
Pink, Thos., bill hooks, bolts, etc.	67 00
Richards. D., soap, etc. 107.25; Richardson, J. D., tools, bolts, iron, etc.. 842.31	949 56
T. & N. O. Railway freight charges. 1.47; Torrance, Parks Co., groceries, 107.23	108 70
Young, A. J., groceries, etc.	5,777 09

[*NOTE. A small portion of the above amount is made up of freight charges and travelling expenses not separated from the accounts.]

COMPENSATION FOR LOSS OF TIMBER ON BERTHS TOWNSHIPS MARTLAND AND COSBY ($10.000.00).

Carswell & Anderson, compensation	10,000 00

MINING DEVELOPMENT, INSPECTIONS, EXPLORATIONS, ETC. ($30,678.03).

W. G. Miller,	Twelve months' salary as	Provincial Geologist	3,600 00
A. P. Coleman,	do	do	Geologist and Mineralogist........	500 00
E. T. Corkill,	do	do	Provincial Inspector of Mines.....	1,600 00
S. Price,	Seven and one quarter	do	Mining Commissioner.	1,799 32
E. R. Mickle,	Three and one half	do	Assistant do	1,056 86
George T. Smith,	Twelve months'	do	Mining Recorder.................	1,800 00
A. G. Burrows,	do	do	Provincial Assayer...............	1,000 00
M. H. Smith,	do	do	Stenographer and Clerk..........	480 00
do	arrears, 1905,		do	100 00
Sidney Bowker,	Seven months'	do	Mining Inspector................	291 66
H. J. McAuley,	Eight and one half	do	do	763 15
A. H. Robinson,	Seven and one half	do	do	1,065 18
R. A. Ferguson,	Four	do	do	232 50
F. F. Lemieux,	Six	do	do	250 00
H. F. McGuire,	Three	do	do	125 00
C. H. Shera,	Five	do	do	207 00
T. A. McArthur,	Five	do	do	333 00
C. W. Belyea,	One	do	do	82 00

Belleville Office:

Allan, N., coal, 8 tons, 56.00; Belleville Gas Co., gas, 68.98	124 98
Brown, Mrs., scrubbing and cleaning, 1.00; Canadian Express Co., charges, 2.75	3 75
Chown, W. W., nails, etc., 1.85; Clarke, F. C., gasolene, lye, etc., 94.12	95 97
C. P. Ry. Telegraph Co., telegrams, 50c.; Corporation City of Belleville, water, 45.00	45 50
Dominion Express Co., charges, 5.30; Embury, W. J., services as assistant assayer at 5.50 per diem, 330.22	335 52
Greenleaf & Son, work on engine, 26.60; G. T. Railway Co., freight charges, 11.44	38 04
Gunyon, Mrs. E., washing towels, 25c.; Hart, Mrs., cleaning, 10.00 ...	10 25
Hoskins & Co., fire brick, 25.00; *Intelligencer*, printing and stationery, 10.00	35 00
Lewis, Jno. & Co.; repairing stove, gas fixtures, etc...............	5 83
Lyman Bros. & Co., chemicals, 342.61; London, J. W., carbon paper, 55c	343 16
McCrodan, A. J., matches, soap, etc., 2.30; McCurdy, J. O. R., repairing cylinder, 15c.	2 45

CHARGES ON CROWN LANDS.—*Continued.*

MINING DEVELOPMENT, ETC.—*Continued.*

McGill, Wm., repairing water meter, etc., 13.55; Martin, G., cartage 25c.	13 80
Newspapers and Periodicals, subscriptions, 45.40; Postmaster, stamps, 35.00; rent of P. O. box, 4.00	84 40
Soal, T., cartage, 6.00; Scantlebury, C. B., stationery, twine, etc., 1.75	7 75
Slater, T., rebuilding assay furnace	3 35

Haileybury Office:

Cobbold, P. A., postage stamps, 21.00; Dominion Express Co., charges, 10.86	31 86
Farr, Mrs. C. C., rent of office, 343.00; Ferguson, R. L., services mining recorder's office, 130.00	473 00
Galoska & Co., broom, 40c.; *Herald* Printing Co., 3.33	3 73
King's Printer, stationery, 496.89; McCool, C. A., fireproof safe, 175.00	671 89
Mitchell, A. W., wood, 10 cords, 20.00; Office Specialty Mnfg. Co., desk and chair, 41.00	61 00
Alton & James, table, 3.50; Ardley, E., preparing micro-rock sections, 9.87	13 37
American Express Co., charges, 1.10; Armstrong & Comisky, desk, 20.00; office rent, 50.00	71 10
Art Metropole, cross section paper, 13.67; Armsbrust, D. K., services with mickle, 159.30	172 97
Bowker, Sidney, travelling expenses, 20.18; Bouchard, Antoine, wages, 44.00	64 18
Brown, E. W., services at 2.00 per day, 50.00; Baker, M. B., services, 734.29; travelling expenses, 242.10	1,026 39
Breck, T. H., typewriting, 5.30; Byers, R. J., services as inspector, 5.00	10 30
Brown, T., services at 60.00 per month, 60.00; Burrows, W. A., office rent, 40.00	100 00
Brewer, Geo. L., moving safe, 12.00; Coleman, A. P., travelling expenses, 172.43	184 43
Campbell, W. C., services as surveyor at 100.00 per month, 200.00; travelling expenses, 27.30	227 30
Clay, D. C., services guarding mining claims, 556.50; travelling expenses, 15.60	572 10
C. P. R. Telegraph Co., telegrams, 3.46; Corkill, E. T., travelling expenses and disbursements, 665.38	668 84
Caretaker, Orange Hall, services, 6.00; Dube, Arthur, wages at 40.00 per month, 40.00	46 00
Desjardins, Alf., repairing chair, 1.50; Duff, R. A., wages at 60.00 per month, 120.00	121 50
Denny, Jas., 46 rock sections at 40c., 18.40; Dominion Express Co., charges, 64.23	82 63
Dominion Business College, carbon paper, stationery, etc.	14 75
Dreany Bros., gold pan, coal, hardware, etc.	21 20
Dinel, Gerry, wages at 40.00 per month, 77.60; Elliott, R. H., office chair and table, 21.35	98 95
Enright, E., 41 rock sections at 10c., 4.10; Evans, J. W., assaying ore for nickle, 7.75	11 85
Fraleck, A. L., services, 400.00; travelling expenses, 363.95	763 95
Fenn, A. N., stove pipe, etc., 17.65; Ganley, Jas., rent of office, 52.00...	69 65
Galt, Gerald, assistant surveyor, 156.00; travelling expenses, 26.90	182 90
Goldie, J. D., drawing map of Michipicoton District	39 00
Goldie & McCullogh Co., safe, 322.75; Harper, A. E., photo supplies, 14.20	336 95
Haileybury Orange Hall, rent for use of commission	43 00
Hore, R. E., services as Geologist, 225.00; travelling expenses and disbursements, 112.08	337 08
Hardy, Jno., wages as guide, 178.25; Harris, J., cartage, 75c.	179 00
Hudson Bay Co., blankets, etc., 4.15; Hill, Jas., wages at 2.00 per day, 34.00	38 15
Hay, H., services at 40.00 per month, 40.00; *Haileyburian, The,* advertising, 15.45	55 45
Hearst, W. H., legal services Attorney General-General *v.* Brown	150 00
Kerns, M. C., services as guardian of mining locations at 2.50 per diem	260 00
Kenny, R. T., services guarding mining locations, 49.50; travelling expenses, 3.85	53 35

CHARGES ON CROWN LANDS.—*Continued.*

MINING DEVELOPMENT, ETC.—*Continued.*

Knight, C. W., services as Geologist, 500.00; travelling expenses, 34.80; 26 rock sections, 11.60	546 40
King's Printer, stationery, 390.71; Kilburn, Geo. H., services at 50.00 per month, 58.33	449 04
Logan, Alex., desks, chairs, etc., 42.55; Laing, A. T., preparing map of Coleman and vicinity, 4.00	46 55
Leslie, J., express charges, 25c.; Lemieux, F. F., services, 41.00; postage, 8.90	50 15
Lyman Bros. & Co., bottles for cuttings from gas wells	2 91
McKay, M., services, laborer at 2.00 per day	74 00
McArthur, T. A., trav. expenses, 15.00; postage stamps, 2.00; to pay office cleaning, 3.00	20 00
McQuire, H. F., rent of office Parry Sound, 18.75; McKinley-Darragh-Savage Mines, 1 canoe, 20.00	38 75
Marsh, A. H., counsel fee preparing charges Attorne-General v. O'Brien	250 00
Mitchell, Geo., salary as stenographer re mining commission, 376.20; travelling expenses, 381.53	757 73
Mickle, G. R., trav. expenses, 295.38; Micklethwaite, photo supplies, 32.61	327 99
Miller, W. G., trav. expenses, 343.71; expenses accountable, 200.00	543 71
Moore, S. E., services at 100.00 per month, 150.00; trav. expenses and board, 94.72	244 72
Menzies, Jas., services at 50.00 per month, 78.00; Newton, services as asst. surveyor, 79.50	157 50
Newspapers and periodicals, subscriptions and advertising	62 00
Orton, Edward, cone, 4.00; Peppard, H., services as surveyor, 90.00; trav. expenses and disbursements, 1.60	95 60
Patterson, Nan. C., typewriting, 6.00; Peterboro Canoe Co., 2 canoes and paddles, 77.53	83 53
Pike, D., 2 prospector's bags, 12.00; Plaskett, T. S., electroscope, 15.00	27 00
Postmaster Cobalt, stamps, 8.50; Postmaster Haileybury, stamps, 1.70	10 20
Price, Samuel, trav. expenses and disbursements re mining commission	583 14
Ramsey, J. G. & Co., photo supplies, 5.40; Remington Typewriter Co., rent of machine and supplies, 22.90	28 30
Revillon Bros., supplies, 200.69; Reading, A. J., lantern slides, etc., 20.28	220 97
Ritchie, C. H., accountable warrant on account of disbursements of witness fees re Attorney-General v. Hargrave title to mining property	1,000 00
Robinson, A. H. A., trav. expenses and disbursements, 440.76; Ralph, Michael, wages as guide, 75.00	515 76
Ray, Ferdinand, wages at 1.60 per diem, 19.20; Simpson, T. E., office furniture, 135.25	154 45
Scott, H. J., wages, 34.00; Simms, Jas., team hire for Mickle, 3.00	37 00
Stewart, Wm., 44 rock slides at 25c., 11.00; Sullivan, F. A., typewriting report of commission, 6.00	17 00
Sutherland, W. A., services as guardian mining locations at 3.00 per diem	99 00
Taylor, Geo., Hardware Co., 1 paddle, 1.25; Trail, J., wages at 50.00 per month, 58.33	59 58
Tomlinson, W. Harold, rock sections and slide box to order	24 50
T. & N. O. Railway, freight charges	29 16
Vendome Hotel, rent of hall for sitting of commission	3 00
Wilson, Isaac, livery hire, 7.00; United Typewriter Co., typewriter, 60.00	67 00
White, Jos. W., services assisting Prof. Miller, 10 00; trav. expenses, 22.14	32 14
Mining Conventions (1905):	
Armstrong, May, typewriting, 2.50; Bain & Calicott, pamphlets, 25.00	27 50
Copp & Co., 50 copies of U. S. Codes for general expenses	18 60
Goodwin, E. C., typewriting, 2.34; Jackson Press, printing, 4.00	6 34
Moffatt, A., services reporting mining conventions	117 00
St. Ann's Rectory, rent of hall, 12.00; Sault Star, printing, 4.00	16 00
Sundry Newspapers, advertising, 136.32; Wilson, P. R., post cards and printing, 4.25	140 57

EXPERT TREATMENT OF ORES AND COLLECTION OF MINERALS ($61.03).

McLeod & Glendinning, balance on silver nugget	61 03

CHARGES ON CROWN LANDS.—*Continued.*

DIAMOND DRILLS ($5,243.95).

Alabastine Co., supplies, 55.18; Bell, J. H. & Co., tar paper, nails, etc., 22.72	77 90
Bandler, Bernard & Son, carbons, 911.37; Brewer, G. L., teaming, 7.00	918 37
Canada Foundry Co., duplex pump, 33.50; Couturier, D., wood, 25¾ cords at 1.25, 31.98	65 48
Canadian Fairbanks Co., rent of gasolene engine	15 00
Dreany Bros., gasolene pipe, etc., 60.92; Dominion Express Co., charges, 11.60	72 52
Eadie, J., hauling drill, 11.00; Ferguson, R. A., storage of drill, tools, etc., 9.00	20 00
Irwin, R. D., lumber, 32.45; Kelly, Jas., travelling expenses and disbursements, 4.45	36 90
Little Bros. & Co., lumber, 1.88; Lonsdale, C., hauling drill, 10.00	11 88
Martin, O., hauling drill and pipe, 6.00; O'Connor, D. & Co., teaming, 7.50	13 50

Pay lists:

Bagley, Wm., helper, at 2.65 per diem	12.54
Dyer, Fred. C., runner, at 2.30 per diem	161.82
Kelly, Jas., manager, at 3.75 per diem	119.05
Killeen, Jas., helper, at 2.65 per diem	143.10
McGregor, Jno., helper, at 2.00 per diem	65.00
Mason, Wm., runner, at 2.25 per diem	71.43
Morris, Allan, assistant runner, at 2.00 per diem	63.50
Murphy, M. J., helper, at 2.00 per diem	155.12
Murdoch, M. P., helper, at 2.00 per diem	23.00
Plunkett, Jno., helper, at 2.65 per diem	214.65
Roche, E. K., manager, at 100.00 per month	753.79
Rouleau, Joe, helper, at 2.65 per diem	273.87
Woodhouse, Geo., helper, at 2.65 per diem	251.75

2,308 62

Poppleton, G., repairing machinery, 24.84; blank bits, oil, etc., 18.90; storage of boiler, 6.00; travelling expenses, 2.60	52 34
Pipe & Presley, tar paper, 2.91; Petrie, H. W., plunger pump, 90.00; hose, belt, etc., 13.71	106 62
Roche, E. K., travelling expenses and disbursements, 38.95; Rond, Jenckes Co., belting, batteries, etc., 42.50	81 45
Reichmau, C., boxes	6 40
Stewart, R. M., hauling drill and removing machinery	45 00
Sullivan Machinery Co., feed screws, etc., 166.21; Stanicrond, D., hauling wood, 15.37	181 58
Stanicrond, Jos., cutting wood, 19.37; Taylor, Geo., Hardware Co., pipe, etc., 86.04	105 41
Turnor, G. F., lumber, etc., 30.20; T. & N. O. Railway, freight charges, 24.05	54 25
Temiskaming-Cobalt Mine, wood, 43 cords at 2.25, 96.75; 51 cords at 2.00, 102.00, coal oil, etc., 2.25; work of men, 9.38	210 38
Triefus, S. & E., carbons, 857.35; Wright, E. C., cement, 3.00	860 35

SUMMER MINING SCHOOLS ($1,196.14).

Bain, J. W., services at 5.00 per diem, 340.00; Goodwin, P., services at 5.00 per diem, 395.00; travelling expenses and disbursements, 333.31	1,068 31
Jackson Press, printing mineral tickets, 20.50; Lindsay, R. J., box for lantern, 1.92	22 42
Ottawa Carbide Co., carbide, 3.50; Pike, D. & Co., tent screen door, etc., 20.00	23 50
Pratt & McIvor, printing posters, etc., 4.50; Richardson, W. L., slides, 21.50	26 00
Thompson, A. T. & Co., slides and box, 43.56; Van Winkle, H., bags for minerals, 2.50	46 06
Ward's Natural Science Establishment, samples of minerals	9 85

CHARGES ON CROWN LANDS.—*Continued.*

CANCELLATION OF MINING LEASES, ETC. ($1,889.70).

Registering cancellation of leases:

Lamarche, C., 73.00; Lount, J. E., 2.05; McCurry, P., 50.10	125 15
McNamara, V., 125.00; Morrow, B., 2.32; Munro, J. M., 229.20 ...	356 52
Preston, R. E., 901.50; Sissons, H. J. F., 489.00; Thompson, J. D., 17.53	1,408 03

GILLIES' TIMBER LIMIT ($19,159.48).

W. G. Miller and E. L. Corkhill, to pay:

Apala, Henry, services as laborer, 120.00; Alane, Juha, wages at 2.00 per day, 83.00; Art Metropole, drawing paper, etc., 12.67; Aikenhead Hardware Co., prospecting picks, 90c.; Allandorf, H., wages as laborer, 18.00; American Tent & Awning Co., tents, blankets, etc., 7.45; Anterson, J., wages at 2.00 per day, 142.00; Antia, A., wages at 2.00 per day, 140.00; Benoit, E., wages as laborer, 10.00; Blas, Joe., services at 2.75 per day, 38.50; Belrose, F., groceries, 82c.; De Bruque, D., dynamite, 4.80; Baggage Transfer, Toronto, cartage, 50c.; Bigars, E., services as inspector, 17.50; Baker, F. Godfrey, services as assistant, 180.00; travelling·expenses and disbursements, 45.60; Brown, E. W., services as laborer, 8.00; Brown, Thos., services as prospector, 180.00; Brageon, O., services as prospector, 3.75; Campbell, D. C., services as assistant, 225.00; travelling expenses, 50c.; Culbert, E. A., shoulder straps, 90c.; Cooper, Jas., wages at 2.00 per day, 183.20; Cooper, M., wages at 2.00 per day, 209.20; Craig, Adam N., services as cook, 427.00; Can. Express Co., charges, 55c.; Chawnce, Frank, services as prospector, 3.75; Chawnce, Jack, services as prospector, 3.75; Dehuey, J. S., services as geologist, 225.00; travelling expenses and disbursements, 43.61; Dominion Express Co., charges, 6.90; Dreany Bros., stove, cooking utensils, etc., 204.28; Desjardines, Alf., repg. awning. steel chain, 1.50; Duff, R. A., services as assistant, 308.00; Dummett, A., services at 2.00 per day, 6.00; Deeneree, Frank, cutting wood. 73.75; Dufour, N., wages as laborer, 7.42; Eaton, T. Co., spoons, desks, etc., 8.79; Evans, Robt., 4 cots and mattresses, 10.00; Evans, J. W., services assaying, 7.50; Fox, E., services as prospector, 22.50; Gauthier, A., services at 2.75 per day, 38.50; Gauthier, L., services at 2.75 per day, 38.50; Ginty, T., services at 2.00 per day, 8.00; Galt, Gerald, services as assistant, 120.00; Goodwin, W. M., services as assistant. 252.00; travelling expenses and disbursements, 84.42; Golaska, A. S., groceries, etc., 21.70; Graeel, P., services as prospector, 17.50; Hore, R. E., services as assistant geologist, 300.00; Hoskinen, Emile, wages at 2.00 per day, 226.00; Hilli, E., wages at 2.00 per day, 150.00; Hill, Matti, services as laborer, 109.00; Hope, Jas., wages at 2.00 per day, 60.00; Hill, Jas., wages as laborer, 51.00; Hudson's Bay Co., cotton, 9.80; Hardy, Thos., hauling lumber, 27.00; Huronen, Kalli, services as laborer, 115.50; Isakeson, Matti, services as prospector, 121.70; Isakson, Yack, services as laborer at 2.00 per day, 151.00; Johnson, Hy., wages as laborer, 22.00; Jack, L., carpenters' helper at 2.75 per day, 11.00; Korpela, D., services as laborer, 164.50; Knight. C. W., services as geologist, 250.50; Lindscock, Jno., services as laborer, 158.20; Lindsay, Geo., services as prospector, 48.75; Lottenan, T., services as laborer, 168.00; McKinnon, & Walker, lumber and timber, 374.32; McLaren, G. R., services as prospector, 150.00; McGoldrick. Jno., services as prospector, 22.50; McNeil, Hugh A., canoe, 55.00; McKinnon, A., services as carpenter at 3.50 per day, 42.00; McKie, Geo., services as assistant cook, 80.50; McLellard, Argus, services as prospector, 48.75; Maki, Jan, services as laborer at 2.00 per day, 121.20; Maki, H., wages at 2.00 per day, 155.00; Maki, Matti, services as laborer, 115.50; Muller, W. G., travelling expenses and disbursements 31.55; Murphy, Geo., services as prospector, 11.25; Menzies, Jas., tent, 8.50; Neome, Jno., services as laborer, 156.50; Parizeane, C., services as prospector, 11.25; Petaniene, Yani, services as laborer at 2.00 per day, 20.00; Pietitainen, David, contracts sinking shafts, 988.40; Peppard, Hugh, services with survey party, 120.00; Pipe & Preasley, groceries, 66.13; Prospect House, Cobalt, board of men, 12.50; Postmaster, rent of box, 2.00; postage stamps, 9.00; Reamsbottom, Edwards & Co., groceries, provisions, etc., 2,283.74; Rice Lewis & Son, cor-

CHARGES ON CROWN LANDS.—*Continued.*

GILLIES' TIMBER LIMIT.—*Continued.*

undum and emery, 86c.; Ran, Tencke, mining tools and apparatus, 554.61; Rista, Emile, services as laborer, 165.50; Rash, Paul, wages as laborer, 18.00; Smith, H. R., carpenters' help, 18.00; Scott, H., services as carpenter, 22.50; Sharpe, Geo., wages at 2.00 per day, 72.00; Smith, A. V., services as laborer at 2.50 per day, 8.75; Sink, Y., services as laborer, 43.00; Stewart, H. J., contracts sinking shafts, 2,400.00; Teasdale, C. M., services as surveyor, 375.00; travelling expenses, 48.00; Trotter, R., wages at 2.00 per day, 108.00; T. & N. O. Railway, freight charges, 7.85; Turner & Henderson, lumber, etc., 68.98; Tourner, H., services as laborer, 122.00; Taylor, Geo., Hardware Co., 50 ore sacks, 4.25; Tang, Jno., cutting wood at 1.15 per cord, 8.48; Vandett, Joe, services as cook, 130.00; Westman, Peter, services, trenching at 2.00 per day, 4.00; Wes, Tentor, services as laborer, 121.00; Whitson, J. F., charges on dog, etc., 2.40	14,905 96
Art Metropole, steel tape, etc., 23.67; Abbe Engineering Co., apparatus, 110.00	133 67
Brown, T., reward for discovery of valuable veins	525 00
Canadian Aluminum Works, aluminum bronze, 9.00; Connell, J., iron work, etc., 10.75	19 75
Dominion Express Co., charges, 5.05; Duff, R. A., travelling expenses, 21.70	26 75
Dreany Bros., tents, blankets, etc.	96 61
Eaton, T. Co., hats, white cover, etc., 84.15; Eimer & Amend, chemicals, 15.95	100 10
Galoska, A. S., blankets, etc., 13.75; Hand, Thos., services patrolling, 417.00	430 75
Jessop, C. W., services guarding minerals at 3.00 per diem	258 00
Kirkpatrick, S. F., services making tests of reduction prices on silver cobalt ore	240 00
Lindsay, Robt. L., carpentering, 35.94; lumber, 6.37; Lyman, Sons & Co., chemicals, 26.03	68 34
McKelvey & Birch, aluminum stop cock, etc., 9.16; McKinnon & Walker, stove pipe, nails, etc., lumber sockets, 143.47	152 63
McLaren, G. R., reward for discovery of valuable veins, 525.00; Potter, Chas., compasses, level, etc., 130.64	655 64
Reamsbottom, Edwards & Co., groceries, blankets, etc.	379 85
Simmers Bros., hose, belting, etc.	48 53
School of Mining, Kingston, work and expenses *re* experimental treatment of silver cobalt ore	600 00
Smart Bag Co., sacks and twine, 62.50; Tang, Jno., services, 417.00	479 50
Whitson, J. F., travelling expenses	38 40

ALGONQUIN NATIONAL PARK ($11,501.70).

Bartlett, G. W.:	Twelve months'	salary as	Superintendent	847 55
Bell, J. H.:	do	do	Chief Ranger	647 57
Armstrong, J. A.:	do	do	Ranger	547 55
Balfour, R.:	do	do	do	547 55
Becker, R.:	One and one-half	do	do	75 00
Bell, W. D. M.:	Twelve	do	do	547 55
Bell, W.:	One and one-half	do	do	75 00
Bonfield, J.:	Seven and one-half	do	do	330 89
Bowke, W.:	Nine months'	do	do	412 84
Colson, E.:	Eleven and one-half	do	do	522 55
Godda, Geo.:	Twelve	do	do	547 55
Gorm n, J. O.:	do	do	do	547 55
Hunta W.:	Three	do	do	150 00
Lett, R. C. W.:	Seven	do	do	297 55
Ross, D. A.:	Twelve	do	do	547 55
Sawyers, J.:	do	do	do	547 55
Waters, S.:	do	do	do	547 55
McCoy, E.:	One	do	Teamster	30 00
Nevin, J.:	Four	do	do	120 00
Smith, A.:	Six	do	do	180 00
Cox, M. B.:	Twelve	do	Housekeeper	399 96

Bell, J. H., travelling expenses self and ranger, 2.10; Bell, Wm., travelling expenses, 7.30	9 40

CHARGES ON CROWN LANDS.—*Continued.*

ALGONQUIN NATIONAL PARK.—*Continued*

Becker, A. J., travelling expenses, 2.45; Birkett, Thos. Son & Co., tarred felt and nails, 36.90	39 35
Bartlett, G. W., travelling expenses, 1.60; postage, 19.69; account of addition to Rangers' house, 500.00; to pay Booth, J. R., pitch cotton bags, etc., 26.50; board of men at hotel, South River, 12.50; transportation, 15.04; Canadian Express Co., charges, 54.37; Canadian Atlantic Railway Co., freight charges, 111.80; telegrams, 3.83; Cook, Ed., cartage, 2.00; Vincent, The Co., stove pipes etc., 1.90; Holstein, H. L., hardware, 1.00; Hilliar & Clark, hardware, etc., .45; Leacock, Geo., teaming, 2.00; McKinley & Northwood, 3.60; less advanced (1905), 30.00...	726 28
Barnet, A. & Co., hardware, etc., 12.30; hay, etc., 72.71	85 01
Booth, J. R., nail saw, etc., 10.94; Bate, H. N. & Son., candles, 2.88	13 82
Bryson, Graham & Co., supplies, 2.85; Bush, W., travelling expenses, 12.15; ammunition .60, 12.75	15 60
Canadian Express Co., charges, 2.40; Devine & McGarrry, hay 41.03, tools, pipe, etc., 39.20	82 63
Dodds, J. W., straps and loops for snowshoes, 6.00 Dunlop & Co., cement, 29.40	35 40
Doligan, W., house on lot 20, concession 14, Township Peck	100 00
English, Wm. Canoe Co., canoes, 105.00; Esmonde, J. P. & F. W., tar paper, pans, etc., 22.72	127 72
Fetterly, D., carting rangers and supplies, 5.00; Graham Bros, seeds, 24.96	29 96
Goodrean, Geo., squatter's claim to a 100-acre lot, 50.00; Greaves Bros., tin pails, 1.60	51 60
Jamieson Lime Co., lime, 10.00; King's Printer, paper; 17.60; stationery, 17.95, 35.55	45 55
Leacock, Geo., livery hire and teaming, 12.00; McCleary Mfg. Co., ranges, etc., 66.17	78 17
McLean, Jas., travelling expenses, 15.20; McKinley & Northwood, tools, etc., 41.82	57 02
Montgomery, R. S., harness supplies, 4.05; Nelson, J., carting stove to shelter house, 1.00	5 05
Peterboro Canoe Co., canoe, 23.80; Queen City Oil Co., oil, 26.28	50 08
Renfrew Milling Co., flour, bran and oats, 148.90; Rice, Lewis & Co., Canadian ensign, 12.65	161 55
Ritchie, W. D., on account contract, for Rangers, house,	1,048 00
Standard Drug Co., drugs, 25.48; St. Anthony Lumber Co., lumber, 15.00	40 48
Turner, J. J. & Sons, sleeping bags, 114.00; Taylor, H. C., roofing materials, 67.50	181 50
Waters, S., travelling expenses, 9.60; Warren Sporting Goods Co., revolver cartridges, etc., 10.40	20 00
Woods, J. W., sleeping bag, 12.75; Warwick Bros. & Rutter, printing, 15.47	28 22

RONDEAU PROVINCIAL PARK ($3.301.40).

Gardiner, Isaac, Twelve months' salary as Superintendent, 450.00; postage, 4.00	454 00
Gardiner, H., do Assistant Superintendent	353 00
American Express Co., charges, 3.25; Bawden, P., medicine, 3.80	7 05
Bates, W. T., teaming, 3.00; Bates, F. D., gasoline, 2.40	5 40
Bell Telephone Co., rent of instruments, 10.00; messages, .90	10 90
Buller, T. L., cedar posts. 18.00; contract erection of refrectory, 1,500.00...	1,518 00
Canadian Carbon Light Co., gas mantles, 7.00; Canadian Flour Mills Co., wheat, oats, etc., 105.76	112 76
Clark, J. F., travelling expenses, 12.20; Conway, W. P., bounty on four skunks, 2.00	14 20
Craig & Co., window shades, 4.50; Cattle, Sam'l, whips, brush, and repairing blankets, 2.45	6 95
Davis, Mark, gravel and scraping road, 6.60; Dominion Express Co., charges, .45	7 05
Elliott & Co., chicken feed, 2.25; Gardiner, Oscar, hay, 4.00	6 25
Gardiner, W. T., cutting thistles at 1.50 per day, 15.00; services during absence of H. Gardiner, 21.00	36 00

CHARGES ON CROWN LANDS.—*Continued.*

RONDEAU PROVINCIAL PARK.—*Continued.*

Gillings, G., hauling gravel and general teaming, 123.80; Green, W., V.S., exchange on horse, 25.00	149 80
Halford, A. J., travelling expenses, 11.75; Handy, F., clover hay, 8.00	19 75
Handy, G. W., mowing grass, 6.00; Harrison, H. B., meat, meal and flax seed, 10.05	16 05
Johnston, E., hauling and spreading gravel, 86.25; Locke, J. C., chairs for pavilion, 4.00	90 25
McDonald, W., teaming, etc., 7.00; McDougall, N., hauling and spreading gravel, 68.30	75 30
McLean, Jas., hay, 35.95; McKinlay, Robt., seats, 50.00	85 95
McMaster, W. F., paint, oils, etc., 26.82; Michigan Central R'y., freight charges, .76	27 58
O'Bryne, B., travelling expenses, 12.40; Pere Marquette R'Y., freight charges, .47	12 87
Ridgetown Milling Co., buckwheat and oats, 44.49; Reynolds, Mrs. W., hay, 5.40	49 89
Ritchie, A., blacksmithing, 13.50; Rose, W., wire fencing and gate, 21.00; hay and wheat, 12.40, 33.40	46 90
Smith, Jas. R., lawn mower, 5.50; Westman, A., netting, 60.50	66 00
Waterloo Mutual Fire Insurance Co., premium on policy on buildings for 3 years	31 15
Wigle, W. D., crating and cartage of wild fowl	2 60
Weir, F. D., services repairing dock, 4.00; West, C., corn and oats, 38.05	42 05
Whitson, J. F., travelling expenses, 34.80; Wilson, D., gravel, 19.20	54 00
Total Charges Crown Lands	$476,660 81

REFUNDS.

EDUCATION ($1 932.87).

Examination fees:—

Adams, T.. 2.00; Allison, D., 1.00; Atkinson, Ernest E., 1.00; Avery, Edna, 3.00; Baird, E., 2.00; Banden, A., 2.00; Bell, C., 1.00; Bell, Margaret P.. 3.00; Boyle, M. E., 2.00; Boquelle, Maggie, 3.00; Brady, Bernard, 3.00; Brown, W. C., 1.00; Brown, K., 2.00; Brownfitt, G. N. 2.00; Bowen, Lulu, 3.00; Burgess, W. M., 2.00; Burt, Edith M., 1.00; Bunt, H., 2.00; Campbell, Roscoe, 2.00; Cartier, H., 2.00; Carruthers, Lillian, 2.00; Casselman, W., 2.00; Caverley, Evelyn, 2.00; Cameron, E., 2.00; Christie, B. R.. 2.00; Clarke, B., 2.00; Coleman, J. H., 2.00; Collins, Dollie E.. 3.00; Conneny, Jennie. 3.00; Cross, M., 2.00; Cotter, Cecily, 3.00; Cotter, Gladys, 3.00; Craig, Annie M., 2.00; Coyne, G., 2.00; Dafoe, G., 2.00; Donnelly, Marcella, 3.00; Dormer, Sadie, 3.00; Dryburgh, J. D., 2.00; Edmison M., 2.00; Fawcett, W. J.. 2.00; Fetterly, D. K.. 3.00; Ford, H. L., 2.00; Ford, C. E., 3.00; Forsyth. O., 2.00; Fox, Nettie, 3.00; Fox, E. M., 2.00; Fraser. Agnes R.. 3.00; Free, H., 2.00; Gates, R. J., 2.00; Garthan, B., 2.00; Gaulin, M., 2.00; Gilbert, C. S., 3.00; Glashan. J. C., 9.00; Gordon, Ernest, 2.00; Gordon, James L.. 2.00; Gordon. J., 2.00; Grassie, Annie, 2.00; Green, C. E., 2.00; Gregg, C., 3.00; Griffith, Reba, 1.00; Hacking, Mary. 3.00; Henry. A. P.. 3.00; Headrick. L., 2.00; Hewitt, O., 2.00; Hoag, J. P., 4.00; Howell, C., 2.00; Howie. J. V.. 3.00; Howill Frank F.. 2.00; Hewer. Winton. 1.00; Hunter. Jessie, 3.00; Hunt, Mabel, 1.00; Irwin, H., 1.00; Innis, C., 2.00; Johnston, Jno., 3.00; Jones, R. S., 2.00; Kearnes. E.. 2.00; Kennedy. S. A., 2.00; Keyes, Rita, 3.00; Killen, J. J.. 3.00; Kirkwood, Jas.. 2.00; Knight. A. E., 2.00; Labelle C., 2.00; Laur, M., 2.00; Lear, Amelia. 3.00;

REFUNDS.—*Continued.*

EDUCATION.—*Continued.*

Lees, Margaret A., 3.00;   Lewis, F., 2.00;   Leonard, Agatha 3.00;
Little, M. M., 2.00;   Little E., 2.00;   Lukes, K., 3.00;
McAskile, James E., 2.00;   McBride. C., 1.00;   McCallum, Janet, 3.00;
McCaig, J. B., 2.00;   McCormack. Bernie, 3.00;   McCoy, Kate, 3.00;
McCullough, Jennie, 3.00;   McDonald, F., 2.00;   McGregor. M., 2.00;
McLachlan, C., 2.00;   McLean, Bertha, 3.00;   McLean, Amelia, J., 3.00;
Maclean, R., 2.00;   Maley, Harry, 2.00;   Marchall, G., 2.00;
Martin, B., 2.00;   Martin, Mary. 2.00;   Mason, Ruth, 3.00;
McMurche, J., 1.00; Meach, F., 2.00; Morgan, F., 2.00; Moore, H., 2.00;
Murton, G. F., 1.00;   Neale, W. J., 2.00;   Neale, J. P., 3.00;
Norman. W., 2.00;   Norrish V. E., 2.00;   Orr, T. S., 1.00;
O'Sullivan, Anastasia, 2.00;   Popplewell, Amy B., 3.00;
Parker, M., 3.00;   Peacock. Gertie, M., 3.00;   Pollock, Rose, 3.00;
Phillips, C., 2.00;   Quinlan, J., 2.00;   Ripley, Alberta, 2.00;
Rixen, E., 2.00;   Robideau. F., 2.00;   Robinson, I. H., 2.00;
Rowe, Ida I., 2.00; Rogers. Mabel F., 2.00; Robertson Catharine S., 2.00;
Rutherford, R., 2.00;   Russell, P. B., 2.00;   Salmons, Eliza, 3.00;
Shanks, G. B., 3.00;   Shaw, Lena M., 3.00;   Shaw, F. C., 2.00;
Sheppard, F. W., 2.00;   Sellers Roberta. 2.00;   Sinclair, R., 2.00;
Scott, R. S. 2.00;   Smith, D. G., 3.00;   Smith, E., 3.00;
Stewart, A., 2.00;   Strothers. L., 2.00;   Sugden, Carrie M., 2.00;
Tackaberry. R., 2.00;   Taylor, L., 2.00;   Tapping, W., 2.00;
Theobald, H., 2.00;   Tinchborn, K., 3.00;   Trick, H., 2.00;
Trott, Ina, 2.00;   Trusdale Lillian, 3.00;   Waddell Jessie, 3.00;
Whitmarsh, G., 2.00;   Wilkins, C., 2.00;   Wilson, R. E., 3.00;
Witton, J. G., 2.00;   Winali, Mary 3.00;   Wood, Boyd, 1.00;
Wright, Muryl, 3.00 .... 374 00

Normal School fees:
Acton, A. A., 10.00; Alga, E. J., 3.00; Aylesworth, R. W. P., 3.00;
Baker, J., 10.00;   Baskin, K. C., 10.00;   Bassett, G. N., 10.00;
Bartlett, F., 10.00;   Bartlett, E. M., 10.00;   Bier, V. L. A., 10.00;;
Binkley, L. N., 10.00;   Briggs, M. E., 10.00;   Brown. J., 10.00;
Brown, M., 10.00;   Burroughs, E., 10.00;   Caldwell, M., 3.00;
Campbell, J., 10.00;   Carr, A. F., 10.00;   Chester, M., 10.00;
Colson, M., 10.00;   Dawson, F. H., 10.00;   Dawson, J., 10.00;
Delavunt, L. M., 10.00; Dewart, E. M. 10.00; Dean. E. D., 10.00;
Decker, H. G., 10.00;   Dohn, L. A., 5.00;   Ellis. V., 10.00;
Farrell, P. L., 10.00;   Ferguson, D. M., 10.00;   Fletcher. M., 3.00;
Foster, M., 10.00;   Fox. M. J., 5.00;   Frederick. O., 10.00;
Gibbons, J. M., 10.00; Godbolt, E. A., 10.00; Gordon, J. T., 10.00;
Gracey, E. M., 10.00; Hazelton, S. B., 10.00; Hamilton. A. E., 10.00;
Hayes, J., 10.00;   Herron, E., 10.00;   Hodson, A. M., 10.00;
Houlden. F. D., 10.00;   Hughes. L. G., 10.00;   Hunt, Stella, 10.00;
Jamieson, M. K., 10.00;   Johnston, M., 10.00;   Jones, M. M., 10.00;
Lake, F., 10.00;   Longan, M. A., 10.00;   McCutcheon. E. B., 10.00;
McDonald, J., 5.00;   McGill. G. W., 10.00;   McGill, E. N., 10.00;
McGill, E. C., 10.00;   McGill. G. W., 15.00;   McGee, M. E., 10.00;
McGinnigh, E., 10.00; McEachren, J. G., 15.00; McKerroll, B. A., 10.00;
McLaughlin. E. E., 10.00;   McLuman, D. J., 10.00;
McMaster, J. S., 10.00;   McNaughton, J., 10.00;
McRitchie. J., 10.00;   McTavish, J., 10.00;
Marshall, L. G., 10.00; Might, M. J., 10.00; Mickle, G. R., 10.00;
Millin M. L., 10.00;   Mosey, Annie. 15.00;   Morgan, A., 10.00;
Moyer, H. E., 3.00;   Neely. M. C., 10.00;   Neilson. M., 10.00;
Parker, Marv M., 10.00;   Pigott, D., 10.00;   Rielly, L., 10.00;
Ritson, N. F., 10.00;   Ross. M. L., 10.00;   Richard, O. S., 15.00;
Russell. B. A., 15.00;   Sarles. L. 10.00;   Sawle. J. E., 10.00;
Scidmore. I., 10.00;   Scrimgeour, J. V., 10.00;   Shannon, Bella, 10.00;
Shaver, C. A., 15.00;   Sheppard, C. R., 10.00;   Siblew, H., 10.00;
Simpson, L. A., 10.00;   Slater, K. C., 10.00;   Sutcliffe, E. V., 10.00;
Thompson C., 10.00;   Thorpe, E. H., 10.00;   Vandulin. D., 10.00;
Warner, M., 10.00;   Warwick, I. M., 10.00;   Whicker, Edna. 10.00;
Winter, M., 10.00 .... 980 00

24 P.A.

REFUNDS.—*Continued.*

EDUCATION.—*Continued.*

School of Practical Science fees:
Kyle, A. J. 33 00
Superannuated Teachers' fees:
Collart, estate of late Jno., 59.13; Gillman, estate of late Jas., 374.08;
Learn, Jas. N., .27; Mills, L., 39.00; Sinclair, estate of A. H., 36.66;
Thomson, J. W., 7.00; Musson Book Co., returned registers, 3.00......... 545 87

CROWN LANDS ($32,844.62).

Refunds of lands and mining locations:
Armstrong, J., on agricultural location 10.00..............................
Attridge, Jno., S½ 1-3 Armstrong, 5.00...............................
Angus, R. B., W½ of S½ Mather, 20.00...............................
Ash, T. J., N¼ 6 in 1 Brethour, 5.00......................................
Armstrong, W. H., 1 and 2 in 12 Patterson, 20.00..............
Armstrong, Wm., Island Y. 6, 10.00...................................
Armstrong, G., Island Y. 7, Georgian Bay, 10.00.................
Allen, B., 2 in 3 Dowling. 5.16...
Blaney, W., 14 in 5 Matchedash. 40.00..............................
Bragdon, C. A., north part lots 4 and 5 in con. 21 Patterson, 5.00...
Bowman, J., R. 586, 10.00...
Bergeron, G., E½ 4 in 1 Dunnedon, 20.00.........................
Beninger, R., E½ of S½ 6 in 1 Mather, 20.00.....................
Beath, E. H, P. T., 14 in 2 Davis...
Bronson, C., 10 in 4 Cobden, 10.00..................................
Byers, O., pt. of town plot reserved Grafton, 8.50..............
Beamolt, Bernard, NE 40 acres S½ 4 in 3 James, 70.00.......
Bradley, Mrs. C., SE¼ of S½ in Dymond, 125.00..................
Brewster, Muirhead & Heyd, S½ 23 in 2 Bayham, 531.25.......
Bavery, Jas., 295 E. Island Winnipeg River, 60.00................
Bragdon, Clara D., N 10 acres 7 in 2 Hardy, 10.00..............
Black, David, NW¼ section 2 Shenston, 75.00.....................
Booth, J. R., S½ lot 11 4 con. Harley, 565.95.....................
Christie, L., lots 1 in 3, Farrington, 200.00.........................
Cooper, W., E½ of S½ 1 in 1 Kingsford, 50.00....................
Carley, A., land rear of Keewatin, 5.00...............................
Clarke, J. M., part of Cobalt Lake. 70.00............................
Crawford, T., 3 in 4 Coleman, 29.35....................................
Clark, Bowes & Swabey NE¼ N¼ 6 in 6 Coleman, 10.00.......
Coffey, Mrs., S½ 12 in 2 Strange, .75.................................
Chilloot, T. E., Duck Island, 99.00....................................
Cameron. W. G., H. P. 409 district R. R.. 40.00..................
Clarke, W. J., S½ 14 and 15 in 2 Bucke, 10.50....................
Crumley, D.. 16 in 13 Sherbourne, 50.50.............................
Cassels. Brock, Kelly & Falconbridge, water lot in front of lot 12 in
3 Toronto, 10.00...
Connor, Jno., NW¼ sec. 13 Salter, 20.00............................
Crowley. J., N¼ 4 in 5 Bucke. 40.00.................................
Craig, H. J., berths 142 and 143 ground rent, 144.00...........
Causley, B., N¼ 11 in 1 Striker. 9.75.................................
Chapin, W.. N part 5 and 9 McClintock. 4.00......................
Caulfield. W., S½ 2 in 5 Bucke. 85.00................................
Colter. E. C., 32 in 15 Faraday. 200.00..............................
Cody & Burritt. S½ of N½ 14 in 6 Carlow. 12.50.................
Denton, Dunn & Boultbee, W. D. 528 and 510, 77.00...........
Dingman. W.. 5½, 1 in 6 Calvert. 2.00...............................
Durst. Chas., township 29 range 22 north of Sault. 5.00.......
Dinnick, C. R. S., Island 7T0 Temagami, 32.00...................
Dawson, Jno., Iron, Thorne and Gaffney Islands, 25.00.......
De Long. B. F.. NE¼ sec. 10 Blake. 14.00...........................
Elstone, E., 31 and 32 in 12 Minden, 7.00...........................
Ellis, J. A. part of Island H. B. 2, 14.20.............................

24a P.A.

REFUNDS.—*Continued.*

CROWN LANDS.—*Continued.*

Empire Limestone Co., water lot in front lot 6 in 1 Humberstone, 25.00

Edmison, A. H., S. 189 and 201, 265.00

Elder, T., N½ 11 in 5 Evanturel, 30.00

Folger, A. L., W. 2 14 and W. 2 18, 152.00

Frappier, O., W½ 8 in 3 Hanmer, 50.00

Ferguson, J., lot A, Lake Temagami, 100.00

Farr, Miss L. G., 11 in 3 Bucke, 6.00

Foster, T., N¼ of 9 and 4, Fairbank, 8.50

Fowler, J., SW¼ 6 in 4 Waters, 20.05

Fallis, Geo., 10 and 11 in 17 Patterson, 20.00

Ferguson, D., 17 and 18 in 1 Patterson, 20.00

Foulis, J. C., N. T. 27, 5.00

Fagan & McKillop, township 23, range 10. District Algoma, 40.00

Fagan, Geo. F., township 23 range 10, 80.00

Graham, H. D., 5½ 8 in 1 Cook, 20.00; L. O. 56 and 7 District Nipissing, 90.00

Gillman, J. C., W. D. 502 District of Thunder Bay, 120.00

Gerard, Oscar, land on Montreal River, 10.00

Graham, J. A., Island K. C., Georgian Bay, 46.12

Gelinas Bros. Co., berth 5 Caldwell Township, 25.00

Gauthier, F. X., E. S½ 3 in 3 Bucke, 9.75

Gilliland, Mrs. T. B., part reserve 4 Euginia, 45.00

Goetz, A., mining claim, 20.00

Gallagher, Z., S. W. part 3 in 5 Coleman, 25.00

Grieve & Grieve, S½ 3 in 2 Savard, 4.50

Gregory & Gooderham, 10 in 5 Bucke, 10.50

Grant, F. D., water lot front 18, Prince Arthur Landing, 5.00

Gordon & Fowler, 11 and 12 concession 11 Monmouth, 200.00

Hanes, C. S., SW¼ 7 in 6, Coleman, 40.00

Hetherington, G., 7 and 8 con. 18 Hardy, 20.00

Harwood, T. J., W. D. 529, 40.00

Hodge, A., N½ 6 in 6 Pellatt, 10.00

Harvie, J. T., 8 and 9 in 4 Joly, 100.00

Holland & Groves, lot S¾ 3 in 2 Garcon, 80.25

Harris, J. I., N½ 11 in 4 Bright, 15.00; 5½ 3 in 5 Day, 15.00

Heyworth, A. T., Island 72 in Burnham, 10.00

Hausman, M. G., S½ 4 in 2 Armstrong, 22.46

Hearst, W. H., S½ 11 in 1 Baldwin, 240.00

Hopkins, G. H., limits n Glenmorgan, 108.00

Howard, Mrs. A., S½ 12 in 1 Evanturel, 40.00

Hills, Jas., 16 and 17 in 5 Hardy, 20.00

Harris, Elizabeth, N¼ 8 in 3 Patton, 10.00

Hamilton, G. D., 18 and 19 in 10 Barrie, 20.00

Hoskin, Alfred, lots 7, 8 and 15 Patterson, 20.00

Hodgins, B. J., N¼ S½ 8 in 6 Aubrey, 7.50

Hewson, W. H., G. B. 2 and 3, 76.50

Inglis, Jno. Jr., Island in Hollow Lake, 25.00

Imperial Lumber Co., J. S. 25, 26 and 27 Bay Lake, 190.00

Johnston, J. H., Thorn Island, Georgian Bay, 150.00; Island B. 9 in 26 Bear Lake, 25.00

Johnston, H., 30 in 8 Wood, 5.00

Johnston, W. J., N½ of NW¼ in 4 Tarentorus, 40.00

Johnston, McKay, Dodds & Grant, N. S. 4, 5.00

Kelsey, E. H., 26 in 3 Wilson, 27.00

Keenan, Mrs. F. H. E. S. A. Chapleau, 5.00

Kobbo, S., Temagami permit, 10.50

Keown, A. L., 13 and 14 A. Franklin, 45.00

Keating, W. J., Island 732, 5.00

Kennedy, D., 8 in 5 Chisholm, 50.00

Levi, E., H. W. 652 and 654, 26.00

Love, Jno. S., SW¼ section 32 Tennyson, 40.00

La Plante, Frank H., W. 738 on Coulture Lake, 1.46

REFUNDS.—*Continued.*

CROWN LANDS—*Continued.*

Longworthy, W. F., H. W. 738 on Coulture, .71
La France, J., W½ 11 in 3 Martland, 40.00
Leduc, D., E½ of E½ 5 in 6 Blezard, 3.12
Lafave. A., lot 3 con. 1, Hagar, 81.00
McConachie, Roy, 4 and 5 in 12 Franklin, 10.00
McBride, H., 5½ 3 in 6 Henwood, 5.25
McDonald & Bowland, M. C. A., 285 and 286, 139.00
McBride, E., SE¼ N½ 1 in 12 Lorraine 10.00
McKenzie, J. D., D. 248, 40.00
McFadden, J. Sr., 29 in 7 Digby, 20.00
McNamara, J., E½ 19 in 3 Widdifield, 40.00
McEvoy, F., Island A. Long Lake, 80.00
McCallum, A., 27 in 4 McKenzie, 44.00
McBryan, H., 1 in 3 Lybster, 15.00
McNamara, J. M., J. S. 59, 58.50
McPherson, W. D., J. S. 54, 15.33
McGibbon, Chas., 49 in 5 Gibson, 90.00
McCoughey & McCurry, J. S., 63, 22.00
McCall, Alex., Dudley, 1.03
McDougall, Mrs. M., No. 944, 140.00
McArthur, T. A., 5 in 4 Coleman, 10.00
McCallum, Geo. P., Whiskey Lake, 100.00
Marriott, A. J., N½ 2 in 1 Harley, 40.00
Murphy & Fisher, K. 222, S. 294, J. O. 113 and J. O. 133, 11.60
Matheson, W. A., 4 in 5 concession 3 Marks, 50.00
Morton, Jno., 754 and 757 District of R. R., 103.50
Mann, Thomas M. C., parts of lots 11 and 12 in 6 and 7 Butt, 10.00
Milligan & Meldrum, L. O. 3 Nipissing, 60.00
May, H. H., N½ 8 in 3 Miscampbell, 20.00
Matheson, W. A., lot 3 concession 5 Connell, 40.00
Morrison, E., N½ 4 in 4 Widdifield, 40.00
Macdonald, C. G., H. W., 738 Coulture Lake, 20.00
Morrah, Frank, H. W. 738 on Coulture Lake, 2.08
Morrison, Geo., J. S. 28 town plot Latchford, 25.00
Mattice, Jno., S½ lot 11 4 con. Harley, 361.16
Millward, Wm., overplus 40 acres 35 and 36 in 15 Patterson, 20.00
Moffatt, T., 22 in 9 Patterson, 11.00
Meyer, F. J., 8 in 6 Laurier, 99.00
Murray, J. A., 11 and 12 in 6 Patterson, 11.50
Moffatt, W. A., 13 and 14 Alexander Street, Petawawa, 12.00
Mackenzie, P. E., W. 305, 160.00
Morrah, Frank, B. G. 165 and 166, 15.00
Nelles, J. H., 8 in 6 Laurier, 99.00
Nickson, W., 374, 375 and 376 H. P., 24.00
O'Brien, W. B. 259, 260, etc. 522.75
Ontario Gold Mining Co., 38 P. to 69 P., 1,700.00
O'Byrne, P., 16 in 11 Seymour, 670.00
Peever, T. H., 24 in 9 Ross, 89.60
Paine, W. E., Island H. B. 2 Georgian Bay, 5.00
Primrose, H., NE¼ 6 in 8 Jaffray, 60.50
Pratt, E. S., 11 and 12 in A. McDougall, 111.00
Perry, Frank, ground rent Township of Ancres, 57.00
Paine, H. M., parcel No. 5 Island H. B. 2, 13.60
Perry, Fred., A. P. 219, 40.00
Palen, B., 27 in 9 and 10 Wilson, 3.00
Payton, Geo. O., W½ 7 in 3 Dorion, 5.00
Ritter, J. K., N½ 8 in 2 Duck, 40.00
Reilly, J., NW¼ N½ 1 in 12 Loraine, 10.00
Rogers, Fred., 2 in 3 Chesley, 320.00
Rosamond, A., N½ in 3 Richards, 26.00
Raney, Jno., S½ 1 in 1 Dymond, 40.00
Ryan, Bernard, 11 in 6 McMahon, 94.75
Rates, A., 6 in 3 McMahon, 20.00

REFUNDS.—*Continued*

CROWN LANDS.—*Continued.*

Richards, W. J., 4 in 4 in 12 and 1 Stisted, 100.00.............. ....
Russell, R. K., NW part 3 in 5 Coleman 14.50.......'......................
Swartz, C., 35 in 10 Pringle, 25.00...
Shiell, R. T., 31 in 1 S. Canonto, 10.00 ....
Smith, A. H., M. C. A. 297 and 298, 7.30................................
Swartymeier O. B., S. part 1 in 1 Van Horne, 14.75.......... ....
Sawyers, H. R., Island 5 Y., 10.00.......................................
Shain, T. A., parts 11 and 12 Bridgeland, 15.00........................ ....
Stiles, Rev. W. H., Island 71 Lower Rideau Lake, 40.00.................
Shaw, J. H., Marshall's Island, Lake Nipissing, 20.00....................
Slattery, R. J., 16 in 12 McNabb, 40.00....................................
Thorloe, W. E., 2 in 10 Wood, 10.00; Right of way, 5 in 4 Medora, 5.00
Tollison, J., 1 in 3 Dorrien, 16.50; 1 in 3 Doran. 3.50......................
Teeter, L. V., Indian Reserve, 10.00..
Telgman, Otto E., land near Flying Post, blocks 1 and 7, 90.00; Ground
     Hog River, 584.00...
Tharle, H. J., H. W. 246, 40.20..
Toronto General Trusts Co N½ 4 in 1 Spence, 13.50...................
Varey, W. A., 17 and 18 in con. 3 Stisted, 3.14........................
Vandusen, G. E., 6 and 7 in 8 Patterson, 2.00.........................
Watson, Joseph, overplus 13 in 13 Bangor, 6.00......................
Wickson, W., P. 101, 25.00.'..
Watson, Smoke & Smith, 350 in 137 N. S. Lake Huron, 37.60; B. G.
     32 to 35 District R. R., 100.00...
Walsh, Mrs. C., 14 and 16 W½ 5 in 13 Sheffield. 48.00....................
Warde, O. S., R. 588 19.00; R. 574 and 575, 50.50......................:
Williams, J. H., Island 140 Bertram, 50.00...............................
Whitmore, R.. H. P. 368, 5.00...
Williams, T. E., SW¼ sec. 3 Lefroy, 80.00...............................
Wagnusson, C. lot 1 in 1 Pellatt, 61.00.......................................
Young, A. J., J. S. 35 and 41, 325.70; S. W. part of town plot Cobalt,
     37.25 ....
Young, J. M.. Islands Y. 2, 3 and 4. Georgian Bay, 50.00..............
Zabalon, R. G.. S½ 12 in 4 Martin, 40.00.................................... 13,734 42
Timber Dues to Settlers:
     Beatty, Blackstock & Co., 94.30; Central Ontario Railway Co., 13.20;
     Fortune, W. F., 378.60; Fremli . W. D.. 2,269.29; Garside, B.. 3.30;
     Greer, G. & Co., 1.00;   Hogan, E. W. & Son. 496.95;
     Kennedy, H. W., 14.48;   Klock. R. H. & Co, 106.20;
     McDonald, D., 21.45;   Pellon, E., 16.25;
     Saginaw Lumber & Salt Co., 263.47;   Stewart & Smiley, 9.79;
     West, H. A., 3.75; Whalen, J. & G. 12.50; York, L., 6.35.............. 3,710 88
Miners' Licenses and Permits:
     Adams, C., 21.50;   Abitibi Mining Co.. 10.00;   Brush, T. H., 5.00;
     Bonegard, A., 5.00;   Belanger. Pierie, 5.00;   Browning, A. G., 5.00;
     Campbell. A. M., 5.00; Cockerline, G. P.. 5.00; Charpentier, Jas., 5.00;
     Dreány, H., 5.00;   Donaldson. D. G.. 5.00;   Evans, J. W., 20.00;
     Enright, J. S.. 5.00;   Friar, G.. 5.00;   Faskin. D., 10.00;
     Green, J. F., 5.00;   Goetz, Alois. 7.50;   '   Gray, Jno., 45.00;
     Hassett, M., 5.00;   Hille F.. 10.00;   Harris, R., 5.00;
     Hunt, Jas., 5.00;   Irwin. R. T., 10.00;   Jackson, Jno. J., 10.00;
     Kehoe. J. J., 5.00;   Kent Bros., 10.00;   Legault, T., 5.00;
     Ledut, W. M., 5.00;   Leroy. G. E., 10.00;   Logan, Thos., 40.00;
     Lindsay, Jas. J.. 5.00; McClure. A.. 30.00; McKeown. D. J., 5.00;
     McNamara. J. M.. 79.00; McGarry. P. W., 5.00; McGillis. Geo. 5.00;
     Marsh, F. H.. 10.00;   Mole, Wm., 10.00;   Macmillan, D. A., 5.00;
     Petermann. J. M.. 5.00;   Pipin, F. D. & Co., 5.00;
     Robertson & Coughlin, 60.00; Reynolds, M., 10.00; Roadhouse. J., 20.00;
     Rowell,' Reid. Wilkie & Wood. 24.00;   Selby, H. W., 21.00;
     Sands, J., 5.00;   Stewart, E. J.. 10.00;   Sissons & Tibbetts, 5.00;
     Seegmiller, M.. 5.00;   Swenson, O. W.. 20.00;   Specht. E., 10.00;
     Usher, F. M. C., 10.00; Williams, H., 10.00; Watling, C. A., 5.00;
     Zanus, G., 5.00; Yates, J., 5.00....................................... 683 00

REFUNDS.—*Continued.*

CROWN LANDS.—*Continued.*

On account road allowance, Treasurer Township of:
Anglesea, 125.53; Anstruther, 236.01; Burleigh N., 25.11; Brougham, 2.99; Burns, 21.66; Cardwell, 74.53; Cavandish, 66.65; Cashel, 2.94; Canato S., 5.42; Cardiff, 8.44; Chapman, 12.68; Carlow, 7.15; Christie, 62.41; Carling, 22.84; Cobalt Lake, 20.00; Denbrigh, 1.84; Darling, 3.91; Dalton, 1.31; Digby, .97; Ferris, 8.70; Faraday, 6.30; Fraser, 15.82; Galway, 2.67; Glenmorgan, .86; Grimsthorp, 69.05; Griffith, 1.89; Hagerman, 131.47; Harvey, 15.53; Herschell, 19.76; Humphrey, 1.32; Himsworth S., 6.03; Himsworth, W., 12.19; Jones, .92; Joly, 46.84; Kennebeck, 1.37; Lavant, 2.55; Lawrence, 66.83; Lutterworth, .94; Lake, 16.10; Livingstone, 13.12; McClintock, 94.13; McLean, 4.08; McDougal, 6.95; McKellar, 135.30; Medora, 3.96; Matawachan, 9.62; Methune, 1.14; Miller, 1.92; Monmouth, 3.18; Oakley. 63.58; Radcliffe, 1.02; Richards, 13.32; Raglan, 11.30; Ridout, 25.59; Sherwood, 1.30; Snowden, .85; Wollaston, 1.30; Wood, 114.74 .... 1,635 93

Chappell, H. S., culler's fee, 4.00; Hall & Lewis, cost of survey, 20.00... 24 00

Heith, C. K., charges *re* diamond drill, 11.72; McPherson, W. D., cost of survey, 7.67 .... 19 39

McMurchy, A., overpayment on ballast pit, 3.00; Mackenzie, P. E., cost of surveys, 80.00 .... 83 00

Pratt, D. S., overpayment of transfer fees 4 00

Samuels, F., amount paid for documents to be used in court 2 00

Shelvin, T. H., bonus paid bv Mr. Shelvin at 1903 sale *re* berth 33 R. R. District, berth having been bid on in error.................... 12,705 00

MUNICIPALITIES FUND ($243.32).

Mrs. Martha Cronyn, widow's pension *re* clergy reserve 243 32

LAND IMPROVEMENT FUND ($1,911.31).

On account of Crown Lands sales, Treasurer Township of:
Arthur, 92.22; Bagot, 8.89; Darling, 13.40; Digby, 28.01; Greenock, 42.52; Howey, 7.24; Kinloss, 15.04; Melancthon, 12.84; Osprey, 32.42 .... 252 58

On account of School Land sales:
Ashfield, 43.24; Arthur, 29.61; Admaston, 27.19; Arron, 94.00; Bentinck, 141.01; Bruce, 152.04; Egremont, 24.73; Elderslie, 130.95; Glenelg, 256.29; Holland, 43.00; Huron, 92.20; Kincardine, 170.24; Matchedash, 9.40; Normanby, 120.74; Sullivan, 178.40; Saugeen, 83.40; Wallace, 62.29 .... 1,658 73

MISCELLANEOUS ($11,309.36).

Fishery Licenses:
Adamson, T., 10.00; Bishop, A., 100.00; Brickenden, F. G., 5.00; Bowman, A., 15.00; Brayley, Jno., 10.00; Bernier, F., 10.00; Benjamin, F. E., 2.00; Brum, A., 1.00; Clark, B., 10.00; Colton, S., 9.00; Cryderman. J. F., 5.00; Dean, W., 1.00; Detler, P. A., 1.00; Forget, Rev. J. W., 3.00; Frink, R., 1.00; Flick, A. F., 1.00; Gerhard, Geo., 1.00; Gegue, L., 10.00; Graham, J. J., 1.00; James, M., 10.00; Kidd, Jno., 15.00; Knight, W., 10.00; McLeod, J., 1.00; McEwen, J. W., 5.00; McDonald, Mary, 5.00; Moore, H. J., 5.00; Marsh, W. J., 10.00; Miller, Hildreth. 10.00; Macdonald, L., 5.00; Moses, Alex., 5.00; O'Neil, J. R., 200.00; Pixley, G., 1.00; Proulx, C. B., 10.00; Raney, Bros., 100.00; Schell, C., 1.00; Spence, Wm., 2.00; Sells, Albert, 1.00; Strong, E. E., 1.00; Sweeney, Z. T., 2.00; Simpkins, W., 1.00; Sallows, W. H., 1.00; Taafe, Jno., 5.00; Urquhart, W., 10.00; Vancott, J. A., 35.00; Warren, E., 1.00; Wood, Jas., 5.00; Wheeler, J. E., 20.00; Wager, Jas., 5.00; Wilford, R., 1.00; Whealan, C., 1.00; Young, J., 10.00.................. 690 00

REFUNDS.—*Continued.*

MISCELLANEOUS.—*Continued.*

Marriage Licenses:
Armstrong, W. J., Estate of, 2.80; Akins, Jas., 2.40; Ashley, H., 4.20; Ames, Mrs. G. P., 4.80; Briscoe, H., 4.80; Bouck, R. E., 2.60; Beacock, Mrs. W. J., 5.00; Bellinger, B., 1.40; Bundy, D. H., 60c., Bonck, R. E., 2.60; Baker, J., 4.80; Bucke, S. M., 1.00; Birkley, M., 4.80; Box, R. S., 2.20; Castner, J. N., 2.00; Calvert, D. S., 1.20; Coleman, J. A., 4.20; Clegg, J., 4.20; Dwyer, W. D., 2.20; Dickson, J. H., 4.80; Disher, Estate of S. M., 3.80; Davies, E. F., 4.60; Gillian, T., 3.60; Goring, F., 5.00; Heaslip, R. S., 5.00; Holmes, R., 5.60; Haney, A., 4.20; Hycke, H. C., 1.20; Huber, Isaac, 6.40; Johnson, J. H., 3.00; Kellerman, J., 5.40; Lowes, W. H., 80c.; Lamarche. A., 1.80; McKay, J. G., 3.20; McLeod, J., 4.00; McLachlan, J. F., 4.20; McMurchid, J., 3.40; McPherson, E. A., 4.40; McVeigh, A. H., 2.60; McDougal, Alex., 4.60; Mossip, S. S., 8.00; Miller, P. E. R., 60c.; Miller, J., 4.40; Minto, A., 5.00; Melville, T. R., 6.00; Morrish, Jas., 5.00; Moore, W. C., 2.60; Minto, A., 5.00; Newman, R. S., 3.60; Norman, J., 3.80; O'Neil, G., 4.60; Ortwein, J. W., 2.60; Oliver, Jas., 20.00; Palmer, E. J., 4.40; Phillips, Rev. J. R., 2.80; Ross, Jas., 4.00; Robinson, C. A., 4.20; Read, S. J., 60c.; Stewart, W. H., 4.40; Somers, F., 2.00; Shields, A., 2.40; Smith, J. R., 2.80; Stewart, A. J., 1.00; Scott, J. R., 1.00; Stewart, W., 1.80; Sweeney, W. O., 5.00; Smith, F. W., 2.60; Tait, A. H., 5.00; Tucker, W. J., 4.00; Weston, W. H., 2.80; Welch, C. D., 2.20; Westland, H. W., 3.80; Willoughby, J., 5.00; Wegg, F., 5.60 .... 278 00

Algoma Taxes:
Cassels, Hamilton, 156.74; Cowan, Wm., 2.30; Doyle, B., 1.52; Gooderham, G., 3.89; Hodgins & McMurrich, 8.50; McLennan, Allan, 1.40; MacKenzie, Mann & Co., 8.91; Nelson, A. F., 60c.; Pim, Jos., 246.53; Ripley, M. T., 3.01; Scott, J. C., 61c.; Wilkie, D. R., 1.77; Wright, A. V., 4.25; Whitaker, Wm., 23c. 440 26

Incorporation Fees:
Blake, Lash & Cassels, 403.50; Bruce, B. C. & Counsel, 100.00; Burton & Bro:, 12.00; Beatty, Blackstock, Hasken & Riddell, 135.00; Chisholm, A. G., 3.00; Colonial Cordage Co., 194.38; Gurney Oxford Stove & Furnace Co., 2.00 .... Gormully, Orde & Powell, 385.00.. Gigson, Osborne, O'Reilly & Levi, 185.00; Kerr, Ball & Shaw, 75.00; Keefer, F. H., 75c.; Lewis & Richards, 32.50; Lees, Hobson & Stevens, 75.00; Little, H. A., 100.00; McDonald & Macintosh, 122.50; Miller & Sims, 160.00; Mosten, Star & Spence, 2.00; Miller, Ferguson & Hunter, 100.00; Royce & Henderson, 94.35; Rodd & Wigle, 50.00; Robb Engineering Co., 10.00; Shaw, A. D., 2.00; Spotton, W. H. B., 100.00; Scotland Tobacco Co., 3.00; Summit Lake Gold Mining Co., 5.00.. Sleeman's Brewing & Malting Co., 50.00; Tudhope, M. B., 75.00; Toronto General Trusts Co., 82.65; Williams, H. J. C., 5.00; White, Peter, Sr., 110.00 .... 2,674 63

Auto Fees:
Brien, G. R., 1.00; Cargill, W. D., 1.00; Corby, H., 4.00; Clench, Johnson, 1.00; Goudy, J. O., 1.00; Harvey, W. C., 3.00; Hall, Dr. G. W., 1.00; Hog & Lytle, 1.00; Irish, Mark, 4.00; Jackson Bros., 7.00; Mackie, R., Bugg & Co., 2.00; Potts, Jno. M., M.D., 2.00; Spragge, W. E., 1.00; Woodman Bros., 1.00; Willis, J. F., 1.00 .... 31 00

Liquor Licenses:
Brooks, O. S., Estate of, 142.50; Clarke, Mrs. M. A., 33.33; Coughlin, J. J., 9.53; Girard, Noe., 16.66; Hunt, John, 8.33; Hansen, P., 1.00; Reaume, Frank, 22.23; Tumyson, P., 30.00; Wilson, Pike & Gundy, 100.00 .... 462 58

REFUNDS.—*Continued.*

MISCELLANEOUS.—*Continued.*

General :

Buggs & Fost, overpayment of mining license, 200.00.........................
Code & Burrett, license fee Crown Lumber Co., 25.00.........................
Botsford, J. H., Notary fee, 3.00...
Carradoc, Treas. Twp. of, interest on Drainage Debentures, 159.04...
Davis, A. H., coroner's fee, 13.00...
Easthorpe S., Treas. Twp. of, interest on Drainage Debentures, 145.53;
Elgin, Treas. Co. of, surplus fees, 130.93; Grey, G. H., notary fee, 3.00;
Gardner, R. J., M.D., one paymt. commissioner as coroner, 6.50.....
International Railway Co., supplementary tax, 58.00....................
Inspector of Prisons & Public Charities, maintenance of Wm. Harrison,
   80.12 ....:.............
McLeister, E., lost book since found, 50c. ....
Rosenthal, M., printing exercise, 25.00.......................................
Sunnidale, Treas. Twp. of, interest on Drainage Debentures, 17.63...
Shopper, Jas., part fine imposed, 192.00.....................................
St. Thomas, City of, surplus fees, 21.12......................................
Supreme Council of Royal Arcanum, registry fee, 25.00.................
Toronto, Treas. of, surplus fees, 1,746.04....................................
York, Treas. of, surplus fees, 2,210.28... 5,0(1 69

Private Bills :

Allison, R., 84.10;   Bicknell & Bain, 94.00;
Blake, Lash & Cassels, 76.85;   Cassels, Hamilton, 82.35;
Cassels, Brock, Kelly & Falconbridge, 94.10; Cronyn & Betts, 70.40;
Copeland, W. A., 89.40;   Gray, F. R., 94.35;
Kingsmill & Hellmuth, 80.10;   Loscombe, T. H., 70.75;
McCarrow, M. J., 85.35;   McIntyre, D., 94.15;   Mickle, W. C., 93.35;
Preston, T. H., 81.10;   Robertson & Coughlin, 88.40;
Rowell & Reed, 96.70;   Staunton & O'Hearn, 70.90;
Thornton, Rt. Rev. Bishop, 82.00;   Trinity Church, 42.85;
Wilson, Pike & Gundy, 100.00... 1,671 20

Total Refunds $48,241 48

MISCELLANEOUS.

LAW STAMPS ($2,361 50).

McMahon, Jas., Twelve months' salary as Law Stamp Distributor......... 2,200 00
British American Bank Note Co., printing law stamps........................... 159 00
Dominion Express Co., charges 2 50

LICENSES ($161.74).

Canadian Express Co., charges ....:...... 40
Canadian Printing Co., 12,000 forms License Inspectors reports on appli-
   cations 85 00
Hubertus. Mrs., postage stamps. 460.00; King's Printer, stationery, 251.19 711 19
Riordon Paper Mills, paper, 24.77; Warwick Bros. & Rutter, printing and
   binding, 798.30 .... 823 15

                                                                 1,619 74
Less refund on account, printing, stationery, paper, postage stamps, etc. 1,458 00

                                                                 161 74

RAILWAY SUBSIDY FUND.—*Continued.*

SUCCESSION DUTY, LEGAL EXPENSES, VALUATIONS, ETC. ($7,664.19).

Legal Services:
Crothers & Price, 10.00;   Fraser & Moore, 17.83;
Henderson, Gordon, 32.12;   Hollimake, C. E., 13.41;
Holland, H. F., 82.93; Hagar, A. E., 137.72; Hancock, J. H., 47.00;
Ingersoll & Kingstone, 83.41;   Ingersoll, J. H., 200.00;
Logan, J. R., 28.87;   McCarthy, Boyes & Murchison, 3.52;
Macdonald & Drew, 19.99;   Nelles, Matheson & Thompson, 161.95;
O'Brien & O'Brien, 61.45;   O'Brien & Hall, 2.60;
Pousette, A. P., 25.00; Ruttan, G. F., 55.99; Rogers & Stewart, 31.06;
Reade, Wm., 64.38; Smith & Steele, 245.99; Stewart, H. A., 26.48;
Scott & Robertson, 25.16; Smith, J. F., 55.00; Trip, A. E., 13.02;
Wallace, J. G., 60.07;............... Wilson, Pike & Gundy, 86.36;
Wilson, A. W., 107.63; Williams, Jno., 3.15.........................   1,702 09

Services as Valuator:
Anderson & Williams, 5.00.;   Butler, E. W. D., 50.00;
Brown, C. A. B., 724.00; Bolton, Milford, 132.50; Cross, W. H., 130.50;
Case, G. A., 100.00;   Devlin, J. T., 26.60;   Defoe, D. M., 800.00;
Evans, R. W., 105.08; Ego, Donald, 10.00; Fraser & Moore, 12.25;
Goldman, C. E. A., 54.00; Gwyer, H. C., 14.04; Garrioch, W. S., 10.00;
Henderson, Elms, 417.50;   Hollingrake, W. A., 40.00;
Hope, Geo. F., 20.00;   Hewlett, James, 5.00;   Horsie, Jno., 46.33;
Hutton, F. R., 15.00;   Jones, Wm., 25.00;   Knell, Henry, 5.00;
Keefer, Frank, H., 20.00; Leetham, E. S., 35.00; Logan, J. R., 21.69;
Mothersill, G. B., 83.61;   Moore, C. H., 28.50;   Mulligan, H., 9.65;
Mackay, R., 25.00; Mendenball, M. F., 20.00; Neman, J. P., 6.00;
Pousette, A. P., 300.00; Pearson Bros., 300.00; Proctor, J. O., 29.10;
Puser, S., 26.65;   Robertson, H. H., 14.12;   Ross, L. W., 15.40;
Radenhurst, G. A., 10.00;   Stewart, F. J., 630.00;   Scully, J., 7.00;
Small, Sidney, 32.00;   Shore, F. H., 10.00;   Sletter, H., 5.00;
Thompson. S. A., 6.25; Thompson, Jas., 50.00; Vigeon Harry, 30.50;
Wade, Osler, 44.00; Whitney, J. W. G., 800.00; Wallace, J. G., 500.00;
Wallace, Edward, 100.00 ....   5,907 27

Bowlby, Clement & Fennell, cost *re* appeal 46 98
McLeod, J. B., to pay registration fees, 1.60; Rowland, J. S., travelling
   expenses and disbursements, 6.25 ....   7 85

FIDELITY BONDS ($2,285.44).

Premium on bonds:
Dominion of Canada Guarantee Accident & Insurance Co., 463.25.........
Employers' Liability Assurance Co., 1,994.73 ....
Empire Accident and Surety Co., 35.00..
London Guarantee and Accident Co., 1,222.19 ....
Medland & Jones, 849.24 ....   4,564 41
Less refunds 2,278 97

                                                  2,285 44

AUTOMOBILE TAGS AND ENFORCEMENT OF LAW ($5,595.69).

Canadian Express Co., charges, 1.35; Dorrien Plating & Mfg. Co., designs,
   patterns and tags, 4.350.08 ....   4,351 43
Dominion Express Co., charges, 7.30; Frisby, E., services as Provincial
   Auto Constable at 2.50 per diem, 227.50, travelling expenses and disbursements, 55.46, 282.96 ....   290 26
Kavanagh, W. H., services as special constable at 2.50 per diem, 230.00,
   travelling expenses, 101.15 ....   331 15
King's Printer, stationery, 6.00; McLachlan, J. B., travelling expenses,
   6.50 ....   12 50

MISCELLANEOUS.—*Continued.*

AUTOMOBILE TAGS AND ENFORCEMENT OF LAW.—*Continued.*

Mack, C. W., shield, badges for constable	2 50
Mulkins, Frank, services as special constable at 2.50 per diem	177 85
Riordon Paper Mills, paper	17 00
Stanley, Jno., services as special constable at 2.50 per diem, 152.50, travelling expenses and disbursements, 27.50, rent of stop watch, 3.00.	183 00
Van Nierop, E. T., services as special constable at 2.50 per diem	230 00

ALGOMA TAXES ($244.25).

G. N. W., Telegraph Co., telegrams, .50; Gripton, C., rubber stamps, 1.25.	1 75
Hubertson, Mrs., postal cards, 10.00; Newspapers, Sundry, advertising tax sale, 179.95	189 95
Taylor, Percy S., services at 8.00 per week	52 55

ENFORCEMENT OF LIQUOR LICENSE ACT ($10,859.64).

Jno. A. Ayearst, Seven months' salary as special officer	875 00
Geo. E., Morrison, Twelve months' salary as special officer	1,025 00
Henry Totten, Two months' salary as special officer	200 00
Ayearst, J. A., travelling expenses and disbursements	462 90
Beamish. T. A., legal services defending detectives at Ottawa	10 00
Bell Telephone Co., messages	2 10
Bicknell, Morine, Bain & Strathy, law costs, 15.00, value of liquor destroyed Rex. V. Hansen, 15.00	30 00
Browning, A. G., legal services *re* O'Neill	38 00
Gordon, J. W., travelling expenses, 619.17; King's Printer, stationery, 21.90	641. 07
McCrae, Chas., legal services	25 00
Morrison, Geo. E., travelling expenses and disbursements	1,290 42
Salaries and expenses of detectives of liquor license service	6,096 03
Slaght, T. R., legal services	75 00
Tisdale, Tisdale & Reid, legal services enforcing act	79 10
White, H., legal services and expenses *re* London assault case	10 02

FISHERIES ($25,510.21).

Services and travelling expenses of overseer:

Addington County	Irish, John	salary,	25 00;	expenses,	80;
do	Purcell, H. R.	do	25 00;	do	77 48;
Algoma District	VanNorman. R.	do	250 00;	do	337 00;
Brant County	Johnston, Hy.	do	150 00;	do	17 20;
do	Kern, Jacob	do	40 00;	do	19 20;
Bruce	Jermyn, John W.	do	150 00;	do	40 40;
do	Kehoe, Daniel	do	100 00;	do	16 10;
do	Robertson. David	do	150 00;	do	55 36;
Carleton	Green, Adam	do	25 00;	do	12 15;
do	do (arrears 1905)	do	6 25;		
do	Loveday, E. T.	do	75 00;	do	17 40;
do	Major, Wm.	do	50 00;	do	8 25;
do	Younghusband, Dan'l.	do	25 00;	do	2 20;
Carleton and Lanark	Knox, Archibald, jr.	do	50 00;	do	22 30;
Dufferin	Moffatt, Geo.	do	18 33;	do	1 50;
do	Small, John	do	20 00;		
Dundas	McNairn, James	do	50 00;	do	11 30;
Durham	Twamley, Chris	do	25 00;		
do	do (arrears 1905)	do	6 25;		
do	Watson, John	do	75 00;	do	138 80;
do	Worden, Frank	do	25 00;		
Durham and Northumberland.	Covell, John	do	75 00;	do	10 35;
Elgin.	McClennan, K.	do	100 00;	do	66 65;
do	McEwan, Arch.	do	100 00;	do	40 60;
do	do (arrears 1905)	do	25 00;		

MISCELLANEOUS.—*Continued.*

FISHERIES.—*Continued.*

Essex	Drouillard, Arzase....	do	100 00;	do	11 75;
do	Laframboise, R.......	do	100 00;	do	7 55;
do	Wigle, Lewis	do	150 00;	do	34 95;
do	do (arrears 1905)	do	37 50;		
Frontenac	Barstow, J. D........	do	4 99;		
do	Brickwood, J. H.....	do	100 00;	do	111 28;
do	Davis, J. W..........	do	50 00;	do	1 45;
do	Donaldson, W. J.....	do	25 00;	do	33;
do	Drew, Henry	do	50 00;	do	93 35;
do	Esford, Henry.......	do	75 00;		
do	Irish, Samuel........	do	18 75;	do	1 25;
do	Knight, U. R........	do	50 00;	do	13 85;
do	Shellington, N.......	do	35 00;	do	23 75;
Grenville	Boyd, J. H..........	do	75 00;	do	34 50;
do	Fraser, J.A. and launch	do	200 00;	do	59 85;
Grey	Gillespie, Jas........	do	60 00;	do	55;
do	Kennedy, John	do	100 00;	do	25 55;
do	Meyers, Jas..........	do	40 00;	do	9 15;
do	Robinson, T.W.......	do	150 00;	do	80;
Haldimand	Farrell, John	do	21 33;	do	2 00;
do	Fredenburg, Daniel...	do	38 60;	do	18 10;
do	Lee, Edward	do	150 00;	do	60 88;
do	Vokes, James........	do	59 54;	do	87 63;
Haliburton	Gainsforth, Wm	do	35 00;	do	2 60;
do	do (arrears 1905)	do	8 75;		
do	Switzer, H.W........	do	35 00;	do	13 55;
Halton	Sargent, Wm	do	100 00;		
Hastings	Cunningham, Jas. A..	do	14 08;		
do	Gault, Thos. G.......	do	75 00;	do	62 45;
do	Glass, Irving.........	do	100 00;	do	71 30;
do	do (arrears 1905)	do	25 00;		
do	Green, John	do	50 00;	do	5 00;
do	do (arrears 1905)	do	12 50;		
do	Morton, John........	do	25 00;		
do	Parsons, John ...,...	do	10 25;		
do	St. Charles, Charles ..	do	25 00;	do	1 58;
do	Sweet, B.H..........	do	25 00;		
Howe Island	Cox, Matthew	do	75 00;	do	60;
Huron	McMurray, Robt.....	do	150 00;	do	21 85;
Kent	Crotty, John.........	do	75 00;	do	3 81;
do	Fitzpatrick, Jerome ..	do	150 00;	do	16 58;
do	Forbes, Hy..........	do	50 00:		
do	do (arrears 1905)	do	12 50;		
do	Osborne, Hy........	do	75 00;	do	2 20;
do	Peltier, Theo	do	100 00;	do	17 75;
Lambton	Blunden, H.A........	do	150 00;	do	32 33;
do	do (arrears 1905)	do	37 50;		
do	Little, Richard.......	do	150 00;	do	275 40;
Lanark	Deacon, E	do	40 00;	do	5 00;
do	Stewart, Jas.........	do	40 00;		
do	Wilson, H...........	do	25 00;		
do	do (arrears 1905)	do	6 25;		
Leeds	Acton, Nassau	do	75 00;	do	25;
do	Birch, Wm. J.	do	25 00;	do	32 55;
do	Covell, H. N.........	do	25 00;	do	4 01;
do	Hull, Chas	do	50 00;	do	86 95;
do	McGuire, John	do	50 00;	do	84 15;
do	Slate, Geo	do	50 00;	do	15 20;
do	Spence, Wm.........	do	75 00;	do	20 00;
do	Taylor, H. C	do	125 00;		
do	Townsend, Jas.......	do	25 00;	do	10 68;
Frontenac	Phillips, J· H........	do	433 33,	do	36 60;
Lennox and Addington	Huffman, E. M.......	do	100 00;	do	17 40;
do	Murdock, John.......	do	100 00;	do	10 10;
Lincoln	May, Jas. C.........	do	100 00;	do	48 76;

MISCELLANEOUS.—*Continued.*

FISHERIES.—*Continued.*

Manitoulin Isl'd	Hembruff, Jos	do	35 00;	do	2 85;
do	Hunter, Wm	do	50 00;		
do	Oliver, Richard	do	300 00;	do	63 19;
Middlesex	Boler, Wm	do	20 00;		
do	Campbell, John	do	25 00;	do	38 70;
do	Corsant, A	do	50 00;	do	4 20;
do	Gibson, J. W	do	25 00;	do	35;
do	Hunter, Frank	do	25 00;		
Maganetewan R. and Georgian Bay	Free, John	do	50 00;		
Michipicoten Isl'd	Daveneau, H	do	25 00;		
Muskoka	Bettes, Almon	do	16 06;	do	8 41;
do	Doolittle, Herbert	do	25 00;	do	31 00;
do	do (arrears 1905)	do	6 25;		
do	Hewitt, James	do	29 17;		
do	Langford, N	do	50 00;	do	12 30;
do	do (arrears 1905)	do	12 50;		
do	Silverwood, H	do	50 00;		
do	Wilmott, J. H	do	50 00;	do	11 82;
Muskoka and Simcoe	Dusang, B. A	do	33 94;	do	73 80;
Muskoka and Parry Sound	Smith, Wm	do	100 00;	do	2 80;
Nipissing District	Baechler, F	do	25 00;		
do	Carter, Alfred	do	50 00;	do	50;
do	Huntington, S. A	do	100 00;	do	31 95;
do	McKelvie, D	do	50 00;		
Norfolk	McColl, Geo. D	do	51 94;	do	5 45;
do	Pierce, J. P	do	158 77;	do	98 75;
Northumberland	Cassen, C. H	do	60 00;	do	88 20;
do	Cryderman, Jerome	do	60 00;	do	41 61;
do	Fleming, Edw	do	25 00;		
do	Hayes, Hy	do	60 00;	do	15 41;
do	Hess, James	do	60 00;	do	12 50;
do	Johnston, Wm. Hy	do	100 00;	do	19 97;
do	McAllister, John	do	100 00;	do	27 54;
do	Merriam, Enoch	do	100 00;	do	31 88;
do	Stuart, D	do	60 00;	do	87 55;
do	do (arrears 1905)	do	15 00;		
Ontario	Bowerman, J	do	40 79;	do	112 05;
do	McPhee, Donald	do	50 00;	do	70 80;
do	Macdonald, Hector	do	50 00;	do	48 65;
do	Mansfield. Thos	do	9 26;		
do	Mayne, Wm	do	25 00;	do	3 50;
do	do	do	6 22;		
do	Swift, Thomas	do	9 26:		
do	Thompson, Hy	do	50 00;		
do	do	do	12 50;		
do	Timlin, Michael	do	50 00;	do	132 10;
do	Willis, Jas. M	do	40 79;	do	50;
Parry Sound	Johnston, Thos. H	do	75 00;	do	18 95;
do	Laughington, Hy	do	200 00;	do	54 69;
do	Olton, W. P	do	none;	do	90;
do	Paul J	do	56 25;		
do	Wood, John	do	75 00;	do	7 20;
Parry Sound and Nipissing	Bailey, Geo. L	do	25 00;		
Peel	Clunis, A. A	do	50 00;	do	11 35;
do	Walker, R. J	do	50 00;	do	1 59;
Peterboro	Brown, John	do	36 62;	do	3 40;
do	Caskey, Thos. C	do	63 54;		
do	Clarkson, Wm	do	100 00;	do	39 90;
do	Dickson, John	do	10 42;	do	5 50;
do	Johnston, David	do	100 00;	do	110 85;
do	Lean, W	do	17 15;	do	17 95;
do	MacIntyre, A	do	50 00;	do	44 45;

MISCELLANEOUS.—*Continued.*

FISHERIES.—*Continued.*

Peterboro	Moore, F. J	do	100 00;	do	24 60;
do	Shewen, P. W. C.	do	4 44;		
do	Watt, John	do	100 00;	do	49 00;
Pelee Island	Henderson, H. A.	do	100 00;		
Prescott and Russell	Bourgeon, J. B	do	100 00;	do	62 31;
Prince Edward	Clark, M	do	200 00;	do	259 95;
Rainy River	Nash, John	do	300 00;	do	5 50;
do	Perry, John	do	37 50;		
Renfrew	Christink, Irwin	do	200 00;	do	129 90;
do	Taylor, Chas	do	50 00;		
Renfrew and Nipissing	Dunlop, James	do	27 19;	do	9 05;
Simcoe	Coulter, Samuel	do	60 00;		
do	do (arrears 1905)	do	15 00;		
do	Dodds, Wm	do	60 00;	do	20 50;
do	McGinn, Wm	do	75 00;	do	23 55;
do	Mayor, Harry	do	60 00;	do	30 60;
do	Robinson, Geo.	do	60 00;		
do	do (arrears 1905)	do	15 00;		
do	Williams, John T.	do	50 00;		
Stormont, Dundas and					
Glengarry	Blondin Isaac	do	50 00;	do	10 00;
Thunder Bay	Ashworth, J. C.	do	100 00;		
do	Leitch, P. A.	do	177 74;	do	8 90;
Victoria	Bradshaw, Arch	do	75 00;	do	10 45;
do	Burtcheall, Chris.	do	12 77;	do	20 15;
do	Merriam, David	do	40 00;	do	7 05;
do	Nicholls, Garner	do	25 00;	do	45 90;
do	Sinclair, Neil	do	25 00;		
do	Toole, Ira	do	21 22;	do	10 95;
Welland	Cook, H. G. A.	do	14 36;		
do	Kraft, Samuel	do	75 00;	do	81 90;
do	Shelley, Geo.	do	none	do	185 05;
Wellington	Robertson, Colin	do	25 00;	do	1 50;
Wentworth	Kerr, Chas. J	do	100 00;	do	100 41;
Wolfe Island	Holliday, Hy	do	100 00;	do	22 98;
do	do (arrears 1905)	do	25 00;		
York	Godfrey, Jas.	do	25 00;	do	60;
do	do (arrears 1905)	do	6 25;		
do	Tillett, Robt	do	100 00;	do	38 35;
do	Wood, W. R.	do	150 00;	do	55 65;	$17,309 76

Services as Special Guardians:
Cosgrove, R., 25.00; Guerin, L., 7.50; Goldie,. E. J., 20.00;
Holyome, Fred., 10.50 .... 63 00
Jole, Ernest. 35.00; Kyle. James. 20.00; Perdue, S. (1905), 25.00;
West, Chas., 60.00; West, G. D., 60.00 .... 200 00

Steamer Gilphie:
Allen, W. T., services and expenses *re* delivery of steamer 5 40
Collingwood *Enterprise Messenger*, advertising *re* sale of Gilphie 6 25
Hill, T., caretaker of Gilphie, Dec. 8th to April 1st 35 00
Mail printing Co., advertising *re* tenders sale of Gilphie 22 05
Owen Sound *Times*, advertising sale of boat 8 50
Scottish Union Insurance Co., insurance on boat 62 50
Sims, T. C. & Co.. 3 tons coal at 4.50 .... 13 50
White Star Laundry, laundrying 10 20

Steamer Eva Belle:
Wing, P. L.. services as engineer 303 00
British American Assurance, premium on policy 15 60
Crane, John, painting and lettering sign 3 00
Clark & Lewis, oil stive, rope, etc., 38.01; Deman, J. M., carpenter
work on steamer, 37.00 .... 75 01
Foster & Co., coal 155 07

MISCELLANEOUS.—*Continued.*

FISHERIES.—*Continued.*

Steamer I'll See:

Ache, Jos., use of tow line, 10.00; Automobile Equipment Co., celluloid, 1.00	11 0u
Burnett, Jas. W. & Son, gasoline, rope, oil, etc.	37 32
Bulmer, W. B.. refrigerator, etc., 56.80; work of men, 65.00	121 80
Bartlett, McDonald & Gow, comforters	3 00
Carroll, W. B., legal services *re* purchase of launch	45 00
Caulkins, H. J. & Co. platinum, 4.53; Dodge, G. B., supplies, 8.99	13 52
Dinean, C., salary as engineer, 70.00; allowance for board, 2.00	72 00
Drake, J. W., Furniture Co., blankets, clothes, etc.	36 95
Ebere, W., repairing launch. 3.00; Green, H. R., wheel blades, 5.50...	8 50
Grand Trunk Railway Co., freight charges on boat	60 00
Gidley, W. C., services as captain, 140.00; board of men, 34.30; to pay assistance, 4.25; travelling expenses. 5.25	183 80
Haynes, Nelson & Co., gasoline, etc., 146:66; Halliday, J., cells and spark plugs, 4.10	150 76
Housey, E., repairs and supplies. 249.64; Hadley Lumber Co., lumber, 1.20	250 84
Hogan, F., services as engineer, 140.00; allowance for board, 12.40; travelling expenses and disbursements, 26.66	179 06
Jackson, J. A., *re* purchase of launch, 2.00; Johnston, G. L., broom and soap, 60c.	2 60
Leckie, Jno., Ltd., electric bells, 2.00; Little, A., loading boat on cars, 80.19	82 19
McClung, W. J., gasoline. 6.25; McCormack, Jas, repairing fender, 50c.	6 75
Major, R., repairs to yacht. 1.50; Melach, J. D, putting boat on ways. 12.75	14 25
Marrentette, E. J., services as captain at 2.00 per diem, 292.00; travelling expenses and disbursements, 84.50; wages of mate, 16.00	392 50
Menard. M. L., blacksmithing. 14.23; Montreand, C., board of Captain Gidley, 4.75	18 98
Nelson Hardware Co., gasoline, etc., 102.86; Oulette, A., repairing patrol boat, 61.91	164 77
Pratt, Thos., services, assisting C. F. Pratt	34 00
Pratt. Chas. F.. taking patrol I'll See from Gananoque to Windsor, 34.00; travelling expenses and disbursements, 98.37	132 37
Potter, Chas., compass, etc.	22 00
Predhomme. A., services, assisting Pratt, 20.00; trav. expenses, 6.15	26 15
Reynolds. R. A. & Son. agents Commercial Union. premium on policy	58 50
Schug, Elec. Mfg., spark coil, 5.00; Selby & Youlden, gasoline, 5.40...	10 40
Sweeney, P. J., trav. expenses, 55c.; assistance keeping boat afloat. 6.00	6 55
Shaw, A., services, measuring yacht. 2.00; expenses. 2.70	4 70
Swift, Jas., wharfage, 25c.; Smith, W. H.. towing boat to Windsor, 25.00	25 25
Smith, Thorn, wages as cook. 15.48; Tucker, W., services. 2.00	17 48
Windsor Awning & Tent Works, repairing canvas. 4.00; Wessel, C. B.. spark coil and plug, 13.75	17 75
Wigle. W. D.. supplies. etc., 19.52; allowance for board. 6.00	25 52
Yeomans. J. W., putting out and setting launch in water	3 00
Sailboat for Overseer McGuire, Landen, C. F. boat	50 00
Sailboat for Overseer Purcell, Tisdale. Alex., boat	32 00

Commissions on sales of Angling Permits:

Bradshaw A., 75c.; Beacher, F., 25c.; Blais, D., 50c.; Buckley, G. E.. 181.75; Birch. W. J., 1.50	184 75
Brickwood, J. H., 48.75; Briggs, T. J., 3.00; Cassan, C. H., 8.50; Clarkson, W.. 9.50; Corel. H. W., 50c.	70 25
Clark, Marshall, 26.50; Dean. W., 3.00; Doolittle, H., 29.50; Drew, H , 1.25; Dodd. W. T., 1.25	61 50
Dusang, B. A., 26.50; Francis. Wm.. Sr., 15.25; Free, Jno., 50c.; Green. Jno.. 4.25; Gault, Thos., 50c.	47 00
Hunter. Wm.. 50c.; Hull. Chas., 20.25; Huffman. E. M., 1.25; Hewitt. J., 1.25; Hess, Jas.. 50c.	23 75
Henderson. H. A., 13.25; Henbruff, J., 2.75; Huntington. S. A.. 28.75; Halliday, H.. 8.00	52 75

MISCELLANEOUS.—*Continued.*

FISHERIES.—*Continued.*

Johnston, Thos., 1.25; Johnston, D., 1.25; Johnson, W. H., 25c.; Knight, N. K., 21.75; Kraft, S., 4.25	28 75
Laughington, H., 48.75; Little, R., 29.75; Lee, E., 2.25; Langford, Newton, 50c.; McGinn, W., 1.50	82 75
McFee, Donald, 25c.; McGuire, G., 34.50; McAllister, J. R., 8.25; Macdonald, S. C., 119.00	162 00
Merriam, D., 2.00; Murdoch, J., 12.00; Merriam, E., 9.00; Macdonald. Hector, 50c.; Moore, F. J., 33.75	57 25
Nichols, G., 52.25; Nash, Jno., 75c.; Oliver, R. C., 19.00; Pierce, J. P., 13.25; Phillips, J. H., 24.50	109 75
Purcell, H. R., 3.75; Shellington, N., 1.50; Spence, W., 22.75; Smith, Wm., 1.25; Tillitt, Robt., 50c	29 75
Townsend, J., 2.00; Watt, Jno., 25c.; Wood, W. R., 25c.; Willmott, J. H., 18.00; Williams, J. T., 17.25	37 75
Van Norman, R. M.	22 25
Bowerman, C., boat hire, transporting live bass	10 00
Brandon, C., services on fish car at 2.00 per diem, 16.00; trav. exp., 8.75	24 75
Bennett, Norman E., services and expenses transportation of bass	11 00
Brandon & Gilbert, cartage, 5.50; Bell Telephone Co., messages (for Taylor), 3.05	8 55
Bush, Wm. T., canoe and paddles for Overseer Dusang	40 00
Beatty, J., travelling expenses, assisting Dusang, 10.25; Canadian Express Co., charges, 1.50	11 75
Canadian Pacific Railway Co., freight charges, 70c.; Coons, Jno., 1 canoe (Clarkson), 15.00	15 70
Chauvin, Victor, services at 2.00 per diem, 428.00; travelling expenses and disbursements, 199.35	627 35
Cook & Perkins, use of tug for. Overseer Oliver	72 00
Cook, Wm., use of launch for season 1906, 100.00; Dusang, B. A., to pay assistance, 12.25	112 25
Dominion Express Co., charges, 2.50; Dedrick, Adam, services and expenses re transporting bass, 11.00	13 50
Ferris, Jas., 5,714 parent bass at 7c., 399.88; 200 dead bass at 4c., 8.00	407 88
Findlay, C., services assisting Overseer Shelley	4 50
France, W. Jr., services patrolling Georgian Bay at 5.00 per diem, 595.00; expenses and disbursements, 95.77	690 77
Gidley, W. C., services capturing trap nets in Georgian Bay	20 00
Gammon, J. H., services assisting Overseer Shelley, 7.50; Grand Trunk Railway Co., freight charges, 2.68	10 18
Hutchinson, J., services assisting Dusang, 5.00; House, E., services assisting Overseer Shelley, 3.00	8 00
Hat, D., services assisting Overseer Shelley	9 00
King's Printer, stationery, paper and printing, 310.14; Keefer, F. H., legal services, collecting outstanding revenue, 75.00	385 14
Lake, H., services assisting Overseer Shelley, 23.40; Leatherdale, R., rent of tent, 3.00	26 40
Leckie, Jno., Ltd., lanterns, etc., 12.10; Midgley, Geo. B., printing, 1.50	13 60
Matthews, R. E., services, 55.00; expenses, 18.40; Martin, A. T., ice for Shelley, 3.75	77 15
Murray, G., cartage on fish, 50c.; Mill Lake Navigation Co., services of yacht Peace, patrolling Georgian Bay, 800.00	800 50
O'Hara, J., services assisting Overseer Dusang, 40.00; Piper, Wilfred, services assisting Dusang, 4.50	44 50
Prue, C. B., fish boxes, 6.20; Shelley, Geo., one-half of proceeds from sale of confiscated fish, 350.00	356 20
Street, Jos., pair of oars (Phillips), 3.00; Sweet, W. H., services assisting J. F. Cryderman, 2.25	5 25
Temagami Transportation Co., half cost, rent of steamer for 43 days	118 94
Times Printing Co., Hamilton, advertising, 1.50; Walker, L. A., services assisting Overseer Shelley, 4.50	6 00

MISCELLANEOUS.—*Continued.*

GAME PROTECTION ($10,966.65).

Burt, Wm.:	Six months' salary as Warden		175 00
Fitzgerald, G. W.:	Twelve	do	600 00
Gill, Jno. A.:	Six	do	175 00
Hand, T. A.:	do	do	300 00
Hearst, Jno.:	Six and one quarter	do	263 67
Pardiac, W. D.:	Twelve	do	563 67
Watson, Henry:	Four	do	167 00
Wigle, W. D.:	Twelve	do	563 67
Willmott, Jno.H.:	do	do	450 00

Expenses and disbursements as Warden:

Burt, W., 13.26; Fitzgerald, G. W., 59.10; Hand, T. A., 145.10; Hearst, Jno., 52.70 .... 270 16

Pardiac, W. D., 252.63; Wigle, W. D., 458.96; Willmott, J. H., 167.09 878 68

Services and expenses as Deputy Warden:

Chauvin, Victor, services. 56.00; travelling expenses, 21.35 .... 77 35

Hines, Jno.. services, 180.50: travelling expenses, 229.75 .... 410 25

Loveday, E. T., services, 300.00; trav. expenses and disbursements, 10.45 .... 310 45

Miller, B. B., services, 242.40; travelling expenses, 13.15 .... 255 55

Enforcement of Act:

Armstrong, J., services, 45.00; Askew, Geo., services, 11.40; Brickwood, J. H., services, 45.00 .... 101 40

Barnes, M., services, 47.50; Boate, J. R., services, 15.00; Baultbee, M. M., legal services, 5.00 .... 67 50

Blea, D., services, 500.00; Clarkson, Wm., services, 40.00; Calbeck, A., services. 8.00; expenses, 90.50 .... 638 50

Cornwall, F., services, 40.00; Code & Burritt, legal services, 30.00; Conway, W. P., services, 50.00 .... 120 00

Christink, E., expenses and disbursements, 29.85; Dixon, J., court costs, 9.80 .... 39 65

Diamond, T., services, 62.50; Draycock, F. W., services, 40.00; Driver, Jos., services 50.00 .... 152 50

Evans, W. E., services, 40.00; Ford, E., services, 92.00; Goldie, E. J., services, 47.50 .... 179 50

Goring, F.. services, 12.00; travelling expenses, 3.05; Graydon, H. M., services. 58.85 .... 73 90

Gunn, Jno., services, 3.00; Hughes, David, services, 42.50; Hewitt, Jas.. legal services, 67.50 .... 113 00

Hammond, J..H., 5.00; Hazel, Jno., services, 30.00; Haight, W. O., legal services and expenses, 12.50 .... 47 50

Hore. Wm., services, 50.00; Jenkins, W. T., services and expenses, 2.50; Jarmain, G. D., legal services, 26.15 .... 78 65

Johnston, J. P.. services, 37.50; Jackson, A. R., services, 47.50; Kerr, E. J., services, 50.00 .... 135 00

Kime, Geo., services, 50.00; Killen, Wm., services, 57.50; Lalor, W. J., services, 37.50 .... 145 00

McDiarmid. F. A., services and travelling expenses, 10.00; McDougall, N., travelling expenses, 24.70 .... 34 70

McAmmond, W., services, 37.50; Mitchell, Geo., services, 55.00; Norval, G. F.. services. 51.00 .... 143 50

Pierce, J. P., services, 73.10; travelling expenses, 7.00.; Raphail, J. C.; services. 86.00 .... 166 10

Rogers, J. E., special services, 45.00; Russell, Jno. F., services, 37.50; . Rowntree. J. H., services, 37.50 .... 120 00

Stewart, Alex., services. 45.00; Stromberg, Nils, services. 42.50; Smith, Walter, services, 14.00 .... 101 50

Smith. Jno., services, 14.00; Simmons, Matt., services, 24.00; Simmons, W. H., services, 6.00 .... 44 00

Simpson, J., services, 37.50; Senical. Jno., services, 38.00; Swift, Thos.. services. 38 00; expenses. 6.00 .... 119 50

Steeper, Jno., services, 50.00; Todd, T. R., legal services, 25.00; Loulouse, Jas., services, 40.00 .... 115 00

MISCELLANEOUS.—*Continued.*

GAME PROTECTION.—*Continued.*

Taylor, Wm., services, 11.00; Taylor, H., legal services, 5.35; Todd, T. R., services, 25.00	41	35
Travis, Jno., services, 60.00; Taylor, Fred., services, 50.00; Urwin, Walker, services. 52.50	162	50
Walker, F., services, 90.00; Watson, H., legal services, 366.00; Williams, T., legal services and expenses, 5.00	461	00
Welsh, Jno., services, 26.00; Wood, Jno., services, 72.50; White, Harry, sevices, 72.50; Wilson, J., services, 50.00	221	00
Angus, Geo., services. propagating game; 91.67	91	67
Allison, M. B., travelling expenses and disbursements	18	65
Askin, Geo., use of gasoline launch, 6.00; Bell Telephone Co., rent of instruments, ·27.00; messages, 85c.	33	85
Buchanan, S., travelling expenses as commissioner	63	20
Canadian Pacific Railway Co., freight charges, 2.32; Canadian Express Co., charges, 3.50	5	82
Casement, W. H., travelling expenses as commissioner	51	25
Dominion Express Co., charges	42	64
Purchase of Quail:		
Graydon, H. M., to pay care of birds, 10.00; Canadian Express Co., charges, 59.80; cartage, etc., 2.45; Payne, C., 90 doz. quail, 901.00	973	25
Grand Trunk Railway Co., freight charges		80
King's Printer, stationery, 83.60; McLean, R. G., advertising, 75.00	158	60
McVannel, Jno., livery hire	ɪ2	50
Maisonville, H. C., accountable warrant *re* expenses acting Secretary of the meeting of Ontario Game Commissioners at Ottawa, 35.00; travelling expenses, 25.30	60	30
Ottawa Transfer Co.. cartage, 1.50; Pierce, J. B., hire of boat and board of self and man. 38.50	40	00
Pratt, C. F., use of launch and crew, 15.00; Rice Lewis & Son, 4 pairs of handcuffs, 18.00	33	00
Schwaufer, F., dressing furs, 11.65; Toronto Cold Storage Co., storage, 23.62	35	27
Thompson, J. E., travelling expenses *re* commission	144	20
Temagami Transportation Co., rent of steamer Marie and fuel	118	95

DESTRUCTION OF WOLVES ($8,367.00).

Bounty:

Andrew, J., 30.00;	Appleton, E.. 210.00;	Alexander, E., 15.00;
Austin, F. P., 15.00;	Anakeezik, 30.00;	Archimusquee, 45.00;
Andrews, Wm., 15.00;	Aitkins, B.. 15.00;	Ahtisqua, 15.00;
Austin, W. J., 15.00;	Akewise, J., 15.00;	Beaver, Geo., 30.00;
Bowen, J. W., ·30.00;	Boyden, J., 60.00;	Blair, B. L., 15.00;
Bodtka, E. W.. 15.00;	Bellomy, E., 15.00;	Burns, D., 15.00;
Ball, A. E., 30.00;	Bell, J. H.. 15.00;	Boulard,. A., 30.00;
Belanger, B., 15.00;	Bowen, H., 15.00;	Both, S., 15.00;
Bell, W. D. M., 15.00;	Brough, D. D., 15.00;	Burgess, W. H., 15.00;
Bowes, E. W., 15.00;	Black, J. R., 15.00;	Busch, W. F., 15.00;
Bishabo,, Wm., 15.00;	Batis, M., 30.00;	Bowes, R., 6.00;
Brown, T. E., 15.00;	Burrnell, H., 15.00;	Balfour, R., 30.00;
Bourne, R. A., 15.00;	Bannon, A., 120.00;	Bay, Jno., 6.00;
Balfour, R., 15.00;	Big Bear, 15.00;	Brunsell, G., 15.00;
Babcock, E. G., 15.00;	Bothwell, J., 24.00;	Bouhomme, L., 30.00;
Bonfield, J., 30.00;	Courchene, F., 15.00;	Contine, J., 15.00;
Cronk, M., 12.00;	Clark, D., 15.00;	Chearey, M., 15.00;
Commanda, Moses, 15.00;	Cronce, P., 15.00;	Chambers, T., 15.00;
Chouron, J., 30.00;	Chi chis, Canoe. 30.00;	Cain, P., 15.00;
Cheminesi, J., 15.00;	Cunningham, J. T., 15.00;	Crate, E., 15.00;
Chena, Jas., 15.00;	Commanda, Alex.. 15.00;	Chaney, M., 15.00;
Couch, T. H., 15.00;	Chemegut, Joe., 15.00;	Cathro. Wm. H., 15.00;
Clement, H., 15.00;	Donivan, J., 30.00;	Day, Geo., 30.00;
Dobie, W., Sr., 15.00;	Desosiers, J., 60.00;	Deveque, A·., 15.00;
Duhamel. Chas. 15.00;	Detweiler, J. A., 15.00;	Dumond, A. E., 15.00;
Dakis, M., 15.00;	Dickson, Saml., 15.00;	Dawkins, Jno., 15.00;
Dickson, B. W., 45.00;	Dick, A. E., 30.00;	Deschamps, F., 15.00;
Dick, Jno. 45.00;	Evans, G., 15.00;	Elliott, W. E.. 6.00;
Friday, Jas., 30.00;	Finlayson, A., 6.00;	Foley, P., 150.00;

MISCELLANEOUS.—*Continued.*

DESTRUCTION OF WOLVES.—*Continued.*

Forsyth, W., 45.00; Ferguson, E., 18.00; Francois, Jno., 12.00;
Fairfield, W., 15.00; Froncour, D., 12.00; Furlong, F., 6.00;
Falley, Tony, 15.00; Faille, M., 15.00; Frichette, O., 15.00;
Geandes, A., 60.00; Gadbois, J., 60.00; Geroux, J., 480.00;
Gauthier, J. V., 15.00; Gostmier, D., 15.00; Gostmier, D., 15.00;
Goldt, F. Jr., 6.00; Gregory, G., 75.00; Godda, G., 60.00;
Gregory, W., 15.00; Gutcher, J., 15.00; Groulx, A., 15.00;
Golightly, R., 15.00; Gardner, Jas., 15.00; Gill, Wm., 18.00;
Geroux, A., 75.00; Harrison, T., 75.00; Holmes, J., 12.00;
Houson, H., 60.00; Hawk, Chas., 15.00; Hughes, G. W., 15.00;
Haskin, W., 15.00; Hood, Thos., 30.00; Haskin, Jno., 30.00;
Hoath, A., 15.00; Hill, W., 15.00; Howse, Geo., 15.00;
Hoskin, W., 135.00; Hughes, Geo. W., 15.00; Heppelle, E., 15.00;
Helman, M., 15.00; Jourdine, P., 15.00; Jacobs, H., 15.00;
Jones, Paul, 15.00; Jackson, J. H., 54.00; Johnson, G., 15.00;
Kootangay, 30.00; Kring, J. W., 6.00; Kellar, G. H., 6.00;
Ke Ka, 15.00; Kee-ua-quash-King, 15.00; Kipling, E., 165.00;
Knox, J., 6.00; Kearns, P. E., 15.00; Kagass, 15.00;
Kahkaykusik, 30.00; Ralk. a-nis. nobby, 45.00; Ka Ka, Eabs, 30.00;
Kath, A., 15.00; Kewaise, W. A., 15.00; Keeley, M., 15.00;
Kelly, Chas., 15.00; King, S. A., 30.00; Kayhewaweuse, 15.00;
Lalonde, D., 15.00; Leveille, F., 30.00; Laundry, Alex., 150.00;
Lyons, A., 15.00; Lawson, E., 15.00; Lauzon, J., 30.00;
Lloyd, E., 6.00; Lamb, Moses, 60.00; Languwai, J., 15.00;
Lamb, Thos., 15.00; LaBrash, F., 15.00; Lonsdale, W., 15.00;
Legris, C., 15.00; Lapelle, J., 15.00; Lindberg, G., 15.00;
Lindsay, A., 15.00; McRae, Angus, 150.00; McLaughlin, J., 15.00;
McGarvey, G., 18.00; McCrackon, F., 30.00; McAdam, Arch., 6.00;
McArthy, F., 6.00; McArthy, Patrick, 6.00; McGraw, R. J., 15.00;
McOuat, J., 15.00; McGuire, H., 105.00; McIntyre, Wm., 15.00;
Miller, A., 6.00; Mec-big-gesek, 15.00; Matthews, J. J., 30.00;
Matheson, Roy., 15.00; Martin, F., 15.00; Maungosse, 30.00;
Morgan, M., 15.00; Murray, Patrick, 36.00; Mones, Albert, 18.00;
Moore, Jos., 15.00; Moriarty, M., 30.00; Morand, Louis, 30.00;
Martin, H. G., 15.00; Marcoux, Peter, 30.00; Martin, D., 30.00;
Mangoose, J., 60.00; Nicholson, A., 6.00; Newton, J. S., 75.00;
Nichols, G., 12.00; Necauegaboo, 15.00; Netuhmajezhie, 15.00;
Neweqwetwith, E. E., 15.00; Ogemausignob, 45.00; O'Donnell, D., 45.00;
Otto, W. H., 330.00; Ok-a-pia-kesek, 15.00; Pellerin, E., 15.00;
Pringle, A., 18.00; Pillon, Davies, 15.00; Phillips, H., 60.00;
Price, T., 15.00; Paquette, A., 6.00; Pet-as-o-meek, 15.00;
Pastway, J., 75.00; Petwaweash, 15.00; Pierce, P. H., 15.00;
Peshabo, Wm., 15.00; Pieere, 15.00; Pense, M., 15.00;
Pete-kogo-neb, 15.00; Phillips, H. S., 15.00; Quick, Jno., 30.00;
Quick, W., 15.00; Redekie, Peter, 15.00; Robinson, D., 15.00;
Ronger, A., 15.00; Robinson, J., 45.00; Ryan, Mike, 15.00;
Russell, A., 15.00; Red-ski, Peter, 30.00; Robertson, J., 150.00;
Regan, D., 30.00; Rectoul, Frank, 15.00; Roy, N., 15.00;
Red Fox, Jacob, 15.00; Shortreed, J., 60.00; Stevens, J., 15.00;
Single, Geo., 15.00; Springsteed, A., 15.00; Sandison, Isaac, 75.00;
Swartz, A., 15.00; Stepeguay, Mark, 30.00; Spence, T., 15.00;
Sundberg, N., 30.00; Sawyer, C., 15.00; Stevenson, G., 15.00;
Sammons, P. B., 75.00; Stevens, Wm., 60.00; Sarazin, L., 12.00;
Shebisquash, Peter, 45.00; Sawyer, A., 15.00; Schutt, C., 15.00;
Spence, G., 6.00; Smith, Melvin, 15.00; Stewart, D., 15.00;
Sell, H., 30.00; Ste. Marie Jos., 15.00; Shortend, G. E., 15.00;
Sawyer, Jas., 45.00; Smyth, W., 30.00; Stone, W. E., 15.00;
Schwieg, F., 15.00; Simpson, W. A., 15.00; Scott, Alex., 105.00;
Thompson, W., 15.00; Thompson, J., 6.00; Turcotte, Jno., 6.00;
Story, Thomas, 6.00; Tait, J. O., 30.00; Terrill, L. J., 30.00;
Turner, G., 15.00; Torrance, J., 15.00; Toland, Geo., 15.00;
Tossie, G., 15.00; Villnebb, E., 18.00; White Crow's second son, 15.00;
Whitmore, T., 30.00; Waddlington, E., 6.00; Wilson, Jno., 30.00;
Wager, W. A., 6.00; Wa-Wa-the-be-tunk, 15.00; Wissiau, M., 15.00;

25a P.A.

MISCELLANEOUS.—*Continued.*

DESTRUCTION OF WOLVES.—*Continued.*

Wabie, Angus, 15.00; Windsor, B., 6.00; Wah-ka-be-ness, 15.00;
Wilson, A., 15.00; Washburn, Chas., 15.00; Walters, S., 135.00;
Wabi, 15.00; Williams, W., 30.00; White, F., 15.00;
Wa Wa Giesie, 15.00; Yournam, J., 15.00; York, J., 30.00;
Zeekik, 45.00; Zayman, F., 30.00 .... 8,367 00

EXPENSES OF ELECTIONS ($2,991.19).

Can. Express Co., charges, 2.95; Dawson, Thos., Returning Officer, costs of
  of bye-election, Kingston, 412.97 .... 415 92
Dom. Express Co., charges, 7.93; Elliott, Alex., court crier at Port Arthur
  election trial, 4.00 .... 11 93
Guerard, H. D., livery hire, 2.00; Grant, C. S., travelling expenses *re* Port
  Arthur election, 150.36; Prince Edward, 33.35................................. 135 71
Horton, E. E., travelling expenses, 85.15; Holden, G. C., cost of bye-elec-
  tion, Hamilton, 669.69 .... 754 84
King's Printer, paper, 29.62; stationery, 78.90 .... 108 52
McDermott, Wm., cost of bye-election, Cardwell, 57.58; Mowat, Fred., R.
  O., costs of bye-election, N. Toronto, 1,281.77· 1,339 35
Mowat, Fred., *re* attendance at court, Kingston election trial, 5.00; attend-
  ance at court *re* Norfolk election trial, 5.00; attendance at court *re*
  Port Arthur election trial, 5.00 .... 15 00
Teetzel, Justice, allowance *re* Port Arthur election trial, 30.00; travelling
  expenses, 65.00 .... 95 00
Thompson, A. W., attending court *re* Port Arthur election trial 15 00
Warwick Bros. & Rutter, printing and binding, 48.67; Williams, N. Co.,
  cartage, 1.25 .... 49 92

MANHOOD SUFFRAGE REGISTRATION ($15.00).

Price, Judge, services as chairman, 10.00; MacWatt, Judge, services as
  chairman, 5·00 .... 15 00

VOTERS' LISTS ($3,745.96).

Algoma, Judge Johnston, 109.10; Bruce, Judge Barrett, 117.53 .... 226 63
Carleton. Judge O'meara, 8.60; Dufferin, Judge McArthur, 47.50.............. 56 10
Elgin, Judge Ermatinger, 117.67; Judge Coulter, 125.55 .... 243 22
Essex, Judge McHugh, 32.90; Judge Howe, 44.90 .... 77 80
Frontenac, Judge Price 23 70
Grey, Judge Widdifield, 45.70; Judge Hatton, 19.00 .... 64 70
Haldimand, Judge Douglas, 25.64; Hastings, Judge Fralick, 104.65 .... 130 29
Huron, Judge Doyle, 77.90; Halton, Judge Gorham, 91.93..................... 169 83
Kent, Judge Dowlin, 11.15; Judge Bell, 99.20 .... 110 35
Lennox & Addington, Judge Madden, 85.30; Lincoln, Judge Carman, 92.80 78 10
Leeds and Grenville, Judge Reynolds, 44.20; Lanark, Judge Sinclair, 40.28 84 48
Lambton, Judge MacWatt, 85.25; Judge Hardy, 68.20 .... 153 45
Muskoka, Judge Mahaffy, 175.15; Manitoulin, Judge McCollum, 49.00...... 206 15
Middlesex, Judge Macbeth, 41.50; Judge Elliott, 71.57 .... 113 07
Northumberland and Durham, Judge Benson, 105.50; Judge Ketchum, 68.20 173 70
Norfolk, Judge Robb 31 75
Ontario, Judge McCrimmon, 59.00; Judge McIntyre, 90.80 .... 149 80
Oxford, Judge Finkle, 112.40; Perth, Judge Barron, 164.37 .... 276 77
Parry Sound. Judge McCurry, 78.70; Peterboro, Judge Weller, 12.50 ...... 91 20
Peel, Judge McGibbon, 100.30; Prescott and Russell, Judge Constantineau,
  15.75 .... 116 05
Prince Edward, Judge Morrison, 107.40; Renfrew Judge Donahue, 27.70... 135 10
Rainy River, Judge Chapple, 86.15; Nipissing, Judge Valin, 94.32........... 180 47
Simcoe, Judge Ardagh 104 50
Stormont, Dundas and Glengarry, Judge Liddell, 115.00; Judge Jamieson,
  101.80 .... 216 80
Thunder Bay, Judge O'Leary, 18.80; Victoria, Judge Harding, 14.30; Judge
  McMullan, 25.65 .... 58 75
Wentworth. Judge Snider. 121.75; Waterloo, Judge Chisholm, 123.00; Wel-
  land, Judge Wells, 128.45 .... 373 20

MISCELLANEOUS.—*Continued.*

ARMY AND NAVY MONUMENT ($1,000.00).

P. H. Drayton, Legislative grant 1,000 00

ONTARIO RIFLE ASSOCIATION ($1,000.00).

Capt. Colin Harbottle, Legislative grant 1,000 00

ONTARIO ARTILLERY ASSOCIATION ($500.00).

R. Myles, Legislative grant 500 00

CANADIAN MILITARY INSTITUTE ($300.00).

O. Heron, Legislative grant 300 00

UNITED EMPIRE LOYALISTS ($200.00).

United Empire Loyalists, Legislative grant 200 00

R. M. C. RIFLE ASSOCIATION ($100.00).

R. M. C. Rifle Association, Legislative grant 100 00

CANADIAN MINING INSTITUTE ($300.00).

Can. Mining Institute, Legislative grant 300 00

FORESTRY ASSOCIATION ($300.00).

Can. Forestry Association, Legislative grant 300 00

INSURANCE ($397 09).

Can. Assurance Co., premium on policy, Dairy School Kingston.................. 45 00
Commercial Union Assurance Co., premium on policy Dairy School, Kingston 45 00
Commercial Union Assurance Co., premium on policies three years, pictures,
    Normal School, Toronto 75 00
Norwich Union Fire Insurance Co., premium on policy, Dairy and Poultry
    Buildings, Guelph· 56 75
Queen's Insurance Co., premium on policy three years, School of Science
    Observatory 58 04
Royal Insurance Co., premium on policy, Dairy and Poultry Buildings,
    Guelph ...:.. 56 75
Waterloo Mutual Fire Insurance Co., premium on policy, brick dwelling,
    college heights, Guelph 3 30
Western Insurance Co., premium on policy, Dairy and Poultry Buildings,
    Guelph 56 75

ARBITRATION, CANADA AND QUEBEC ($7,034.75).

Butcher, N. R., typewriting 9 78
Collison, B. F., services re statement Common School lands 282 00
Ewart, Osler & Co., security for costs, Ontario vs. Canada, 136.72, legal
    service and disbursements, Northwest angle treaty No. 3, 60.04; trust
    funds, 27.39; Dominion vs. Ontario, 21.33 .... 245 48
Irving, Æ., legal services, Northwest angle treaty, 1,345.00; re trust funds,
    650.00 .... 1,995 00
Margach, Wm., expenses giving evidence re Treaty, No. 3.................... 65 90
Macdonald, Shepley, Middleton & Donald, legal services re trust funds,
    1,250.14; Northwest angle treaty No. 3, 1.501.14........................... 2,751 28
Registrar of Exchequer Court of Canada, stenographers' fee, etc., Dominion
    vs. Ontario 117 15
Smith, W., Asherton, legal services re appeal to Supreme Court re trust
    funds 593 29
Warwick Bros. & Rutter, printing and binding 638 45
White. H. S., legal services assisting Æ. Irving................................. 336 42

MISCELLANEOUS.—*Continued.*

ANNUITIES AND BONUSES TO INDIANS UNDER TREATY NO. 9 ($16,124.00).

Receiver General, Dominion of Canada, repayment of amount paid as gratuity to Indians 16,124 00

COMMITTEE OF HOUSE FOR ART PURPOSES ($950.00).

Forster, J. W., portrait of Hon. J. P. Whitney 500 00
Forster, J. W., portrait. of Rt. Hon. Sir Jno. A. Macdonald.................. 250 00
Robinson, Kathleen, bust of Christopher Robinson, K. C........................ 200 00

HYDRO ELECTRIC POWER COMMISSION.

SALARIES ($12,925.98).

C. B. Smith:	Thirteen months' salary as Chief Engineer..................			3,791 68
P. W. Sothmann:	Four	do	do do	1,166 68
H. G. Acres:	Thirteen	do	Assistant do	1,625 00
W. G. Chace:	Five	do	do	750 00
S. B. Clement:	Seven	do	do	875 00
C. P. Fowler:	Six and one-half	do	do	845 00
A. D. Griffin:	Three	do	do	329 25
G. T. Jennings:	One	do	do	108 87
A. H. McBride:	Two	do	do	204 00
E. Richards:	Thirteen	do	do	1,650 00
J. S. Richmond:	Two	do	do	250 00
W. Todd	One	do	do	100 00
F. W. Wilkins:	Three	do	do	290 00
A. V. Bax:	Four	do	Secretary	181 00
E. C. Settell:	One and one-half	do	do	120 50
G. Sproule:	Eight and half	do	do	639 00

EXPENSES ($13,074.02).

Acres, H. G., travelling expenses and disbursements, 2.075.40, accountable, 50.00 .... 2,125 40
Ayers, John, reading of Moira gauge, 44.00; Anderson, Jas., reading of Fort William gauge, 40.00 .... 84 00
Art Metropole, printing, 1.48; pencils. 1.25; mdse. 6.50; blue prints, 13.31; steel tape, 3.57; 1 only rule at 50c.; 20 yds. transparent profile paper, 7.20; 1 only rose tracing cloth. 5.50; 100 sheets tracing paper, 6.75; ½ doz. 2B.K. pencils, 50c.; box rubber bands, 20c.; tracing linen. 1.08; 1 only French curve, No. 1 for 25c.; 1 only French curve No. 5 for 25c.; 1 only French curve, No. 13 for 20c.; ½ doz. circular ink erasers, 21c.; ½ doz. Robin erasers, 30c.; 2 bottles green ink, 50c.; 1 roll cross section paper. 10.00; ¼ doz. pen holders. 30c.; sundries. 4.48...................... 64 33
Arcade Printing Co., The, 300 industrial reports, 2.75; 750 forms, 4.50; 500 forms, 3.50; 300 cards 3.00; forms, 3.00 .... 16 75
Andrews, W. S., services and expenses, 381.65; Armour & Mickle,. legal services. 1.610.98 .... 1,992 63
Beldam, E., 12 days work and travelling expenses, 124.90; Bell Telephone Co., 6 months' rent of instrument, 31.00; messages, 12.90.................. 168 80
Beck. Hon. Adam. accountable. 200.00; expenses. 200.00; Bax, Archd. V., petty office expenses, 32.28 .... 432 28
Chace, W. G., expenses and disbursements, 362.03; Chattle, R. H., reading Nipegon. gauge, 100.00 .... 462 03
Campbell. Florence. services as stenographer, 90.00; W. Coo, reporting and expenses, 53.25 .... 143 25
Chase. W. S., reading Wabigoon gauge to Jan. 6th, 5.62; C. P. Ry.. Telegraph, telegrams, 36.91 .... 42 53
Clement. S. R.. 6 months' expenses, 299.43; Canadian Engineer, advertising. 13.50 .... 312 93
Canadian Electrical News, advertising 10 00
Eaton, The T. Co., curtains, etc., 17.37; Electrical Review, advertising, 12.00 .... 29 37

MISCELLANEOUS.—*Continued.*

HYDRO ELECTRIC POWER COMMISSION.—*Continued.*

EXPENSES.—*Continued.*

Electrical World, (New York), advertising, 10.68; Ellis, P. W., honorarium as Commissioner, 600.00	610 68
Foster, James, 3 hand levels at 8.00, 24.00; Ford, James, 7 months' reading Port Frances gauge, 49.50	73 50
Fowler, C. P., expenses and disbursements	164 98
Grand and Toy, stationery. 60.60; Galbraith, W., plan of South Falls, 5.00	65 60
Griffin, A. D., expenses and disbursements	664 29
Hart and Riddell, stationery, 3.00; Hure, W. C., reading Port Severn gauge, 40.00	43 00
Harrison & Co., 1 only calculating instrument, 35.00; Hicks, T. L., wiring office, 5.20	40 20
Jennings, G. T., accountable	250 00
King's Printer, 1 m. headings, 2.70; 1 m. envelopes, 2.50; embossing 2 m. sheets 2.50; 1 only die. 5.00	12 70
Lockhart Photo Supply Co., blue prints	12 60
Mail Job Printing Co., printing reports, etc	327 00
Mackay, John & Co., advice and services, 600.00; Mowat, Fred, services as Sheriff, 22.20	622 20
McMurdie, C. E., reading of Winnipeg river, gauge	24 00
McBride, A. H., 12 days' work at 4.00	48 00
Neil, J. W., 19 days' horse hire at 2.50, 47.50; board of horse and expenses, 16.25	63 75
Office Specialty Manfacturing Co., book case, 6.00; flat top, desk, 18.00; 1 base, 5.00; 1 only box, drawer section. 13.00; legal blank section, 9.00; glass door sections, 12.00; top, 4.00	67 00
Passmore, H. N., services and expenses, 51.15; copy Detroit City charter, 2.25	53 40
Richards, E., 13 months' expenses and disbursements, 626.76; accountable, 50.00	676 76
Richmond, J. Stanley, expenses and disbursements	58 56
Saturday Night. Limited, printing, 41.25; reports at 10c., 412.50; printing reports, 1,675.00	2,087 50
Settell. E. C., expenses of commission, 47.55; petty office expenses, 47.72; accountable. 46.77	142 04
Staunton & O'Heir, legal expenses at Hamilton, 18.57; Smith, C. B., expenses and disbursements, 91.22	109 79
Sproule, Gordon, expenses and disbursements	123 78
Sothmann, P. W., 3 months travelling expenses and disbursements	98 05
Steinberger, Hendry Co., map of Quebec, 3.50; Stevens, Horace J., 1 only copy Copper handwork, 5.00	8 50
Simpson, T. T., travelling expenses	22 70
T. & N. O. Ry. Co., to pay laundrying, 8.76; rent. light and telephone. 589.72	598 48
Toronto Electric Light Co., lamps and fixtures	6 50
United Typewriter Co., inspections of typewriter	6 00
Wilkins, F. W., travelling expenses and disbursements	48 16
Weddell, R. G., reading Trent river, gauge	8 32

Balance in bank 31st Dec., 1906	237 18	
Less balance in bank 1st January, 1906	190 50	
		46 68

UNIVERSITY OF TORONTO COMMISSION ($6,625.37).

Honorariums as Commissioners:

Bruce, Rev. Dr. D., 800.00;	Cody, Rev. H. J. 800.00;	
Colquhoun, A. H. U., 800;	Flavelle, Jas., W., 800.00;	
Meredith, Sir W. R., 800.00;	Smith, Goldwin, 800.00;	
Walker, Byron E., 800.00		5,600 00
Colquhoun. A. H. U., services as secretary for preparation of report		1,000 00
King's Printer, stationery		13 37
United Typewriter Co., rent of machine		12 00

MISCELLANEOUS.—*Continued.*

COMMISSIONS *RE* SUNDRY INVESTIGATIONS ($12,370.44).

Andrews, W. S., on account of service and expenses as counsel *re* commission on insurance	1,000 00
Briggs, A. W., services as Assistant Counsel	100 00
Butcher, N. R., copy of proceedings Insurance Commission	378 18
Casselman, A. S., accountable warrant *re* Text Book Commission	2,700 00
Cross, H. C., services as special examiner, York County Loan and Savings Co	1,000 00
Cross, H. C., stenographer's fees, 157.50; registrar's fees, *re* titles, 37.40...	194 90
Clarkson, G. F., services on account	375 00
Hellmuth, J. F., on account of services and expenses as counsel *re* Commission on Insurance	3,000 00
Gerry, G. R., on account of services and expenses as counsel, *re* Commission on Insurance	2,000 00
Jarrett, Minnie M., special services as stenographer, Bastedo investigation	128 00
Judd, Joseph C., services as Commissioner do	500 00
Judd, Joseph C., travelling expenses do	65 00
Masten, C. A., services and disbursements as Counsel	725 63
Mickle, M. C., payment on account, procuring evidence	75 00
Morphy, H. B., legal services and disbursements *re* investigation, C. E. Whitshaw and Registrar of Deeds S. Perth	128 73

GRATUITIES ($17,410.00).

Bush, R. A., engineer Brockville Asylum	275 00
Barron, Robt., gardener Mercer Reformatory	500 00
Boyd, Mrs. W. B. and Miss Mary Murray, daughters of the late J. W. Murray	1,900 00
Clarke, Chas., allowance on retiring position clerk Legislative Assambly	2,500 00
Cummings, Miss L., teacher Ottawa Normal School	150 00
Daughters of Kivas Tully, consulting engineer Public Worke Department	1,000 00
Elliott, Miss M. E., matron Woodstock Hospital	250 00
Ferris, M. J., clerk Crown Lands Department	575 00
Guthrie, Donald, further allowance to the Misse's Smith, grand-daughters of Mrs. Laura Secord	300 00
Gaffney, Patrick, engineer Toronto Normal School	400 00
Kerr, Hugh, attendant Kingston Asylum	360 00
Laird, R. W., bursar Mercer Reformatory	500 00
McManus, Jno., storekeeper Kingston Asylum	600 00
McCutcheon, Thos., gratuity	300 00
McNichol, E. C., M.D., allowance on retiring Superintendent Cobourg Asylum	1,000 00
McBrearty, M., engineer School of Practical Science	600 00
Moore, Jno., allowance on retiring position as gardener Deaf & Dumb Institute	225 00
Miller, Mrs. Cathrine, widow of Jno. Miller, M.A., late Deputy-Minister of Education	2,700 00
Pope, Miss M. A., matron London Asylum	250 00
Quinlan, Miss M. H., matron Mimico Asylum	200 00
Sisters of Hugh D. Sinclair, chief clerk Land Titles	1,100 00
Sharkey, Miss Sarah, head laundress Hamilton Asylum	125 00
Sippi, C. A., unmarried daughters of, late bursar London Asylum	1,000 00
Thompson, A., farmer Orillia Asylum	200 00
Wood, Miss Jane, attendant Brockville Asylum	150 00
Watson, Miss Jessie, matron Hamilton Asylum	250 00

REMOVAL OF PATIENTS TO ASYLUMS ($5,396.11).

Simpser, P., Twelve months' salary as Bailiff	1,100 00
Johnson, Mrs. J. J., do do do	704 00
Applegath, Jess., hats, 6.00; Angus, Geo., travelling expenses, 5.40	11 40
Canadian Transfer Co., bus for patients, 3.50; Central Prison Industries, Bailiff's clothing, 30.00	33 50
Dick, W. R., to pay cab hire, 4.50; Enright & Labatt, livery hire, 18.00	22 50
Grand Trunk Ry. Co., railway fares, 579.90; Guinane, Jno., shoes, 8.00	587 90

MISCELLANEOUS.—*Continued.*

REMOVAL OF PATIENTS TO ASYLUMS ($5,396.11).

Gorman, J., expenses removal of patients, 11.00; Hodgson, S. D., travelling expenses, 6.85	17 85
Hawley, F. M., trav. expenses, 6.10; Johnson, Mrs. J. J., travelling expenses, 986.10	992 20
Kilty, Wm., trav. expenses, 1.40; Macdonald, Jno. & Co., clothes and gloves, 22.16	23 56
Middleton, R. J., cab hire, 2.00; Ogilvie, Thos. & Sons, suiting, 10.45...	12 45
Simser, P., trav. expenses, 1,712.05; Smith, S. G., trav. expenses, 21.40	1,733 45
Spence, S. J., expenses of discharged patient, 22.00; Thompson, A. W., Sheriff, trav. expenses, 135.00	157 00
Toronto Railway Co., street car tickets	30

INVESTIGATIONS AS TO FEEBLE MINDED ($551.80).

Lancashire & Cheshire, pamphlets	1 30
McMurchy Dr. Helen, services *re* census of the feeble minded in Ontario, 525.00; travelling expenses, 25.50	550 50

EXPENSES ENTERTAINMENT OF PRINCE ARTHUR ($1,035.19).

Macdonald, Jas. Fraser, expenses incurred *re* visit	1,035 19

WILLIAM SHERRING, VICTOR OF MARATHON RACE ($500.00).

Sherring, William, grant	500 00

EXPERIMENTAL SEWAGE FARM, BERLIN ($4,000.00).

Treasurer, Town of Berlin, grant towards expenses	4,000 00

BRITISH MEDICAL ASSOCIATION ($5,000.00).

Ross, J. F. W., M.D., Honoray Treasurer, grant	5,000 00

IRISH AND SCOTCH BOWLING ASSOCIATION ($400.00).

Postlethwaite, C. R. W., Secretary Ontario Bowling Association, grant ...	400 00

ONTARIO RAILWAY AND MUNICIPAL BOARD.

SALARIES ($10,120.01).

James Leitch:	Seven months' salary as Chairman of Board			3,500 00
A. B. Ingram:	Six and one-half	do	Commissioner	2,177 77
H. N. Kittson:	Six and two-thirds	do	do	2,266 66
H. C. Small:	do	do	Secretary	1,133 33
Wm. C. Coo:	Five and one-quarter	do	Stenographer	657 25
Dora Ault:	Seven	do	do	250 00
Grace Dunkin:	Four	do	do	135 00

EXPENSES ($2,793.59).

Bell Telephone Co., messages, 17.80; Cairns, B., seal and stamps, 15.70...	33 50
Can. Express Co., charges, 75c.; Coo, Wm. C., travelling expenses and disbursements, 58.80; copy of evidence Grand Trunk Pacific, 150 folios at 5c., 7.50; 3 copies of evidence *re* Ottawa City *v.* Ottawa Electric, 293 folios, 20.51	87 56
C. P. Tel. Co., telegrams, 1.16; Domn. Express Co., charges, 1.10	2 26
Emsley, R. S., services as Civil Engineer. *re* Metropolitan Railway, 13.33; overlooking plans of G. T. P. Rlwy. 173.33; travelling expenses, 81.00	267 66
G. N. W. Tel. Co., telegrams, 96c.; Heaton's Agency, commercial handbook, 1.00	1 96
Hubertus, Mrs., postage stamps, 90.00; House postmaster, unpaid postage, 12c.	90 12
Ingram, A. B., travelling expenses, 443.43; King's Printer, stationery, 342.09	785 52

MISCELLANEOUS.—*Continued.*

ONTARIO RAILWAY AND MUNICIPAL BOARD.—*Continued.*

Kitson, H. N., travelling expenses, 209.88; Leitch, travelling expense, 476.88	686 76
Mail Job Printing Co., printing rules and regulations, 132.00; Martin, Lily, services as office assistant, 66.00	198 00
Newspapers and Periodicals, sundry subscriptions, 17.50; Pringle & Cameron, services as stenographer, 10.00	27 50
Pringle, R. A., services *re* investigation collision G. T. Rlwy. & Hamilton Co	50 00
Remington Typewriter Co., typewriter, 108.00; clerk, etc., 16.50	124 50
Small, H. C., travelling expenses, 311.10; to pay hotel expenses of self and commissioners at Hamilton, 24.65; postage stamps, 10.00	345 75
Toronto Rlwy. & Steamboat Guide, subn., 2.60; Warwick Bros. & Rutter, printing and binding, 12.40	15 00
Wise & Middlemost, stop watch, camera, etc	77 50

COMMUTATION VOLUNTEER VETERAN'S LAND GRANTS ($71,800.00).

Veteran's surrender of military certificate at 50.00 each:

Acton, J. A.; Aitkin, W. J.; Algie, J.; Allan, W. R.; Allen, M.; Amer, T. A.; Amess, C.; Anderson, Chas. Elliott; Anderson, A. H.; Anderson, D.; Anderson, J.; Anderson, J. W.; Anderson, R.; Andison, Jas.; Aneman, J.; Anning, C.; Anthony, J.; Ardell, A. E.; Armour, J.; Armstrong, Geo. W.; Armstrong, John; Armstrong, Thos.; Armstrong, W. H.; Arnold, Jas.; Arnold, Joshua; Arnold, Margaret (late F. G. Arnold); Arnold, W. G.; Arthur, C.; Arthur, W.; Atchison, T.; Atkinson, G. K.; Atkinson, W. H.; Augustus, F. G.; Abbott, C. C., for D. Thompson; Abbott, C. C., for Geo. Watt; Auger, M., for W. J. Butterfield; Auger, M., for Dan. Cox; Auger, M., for R. N. Castle; Auger, M., for J. A. Payne; Armstrong, S. A., for J. Stephen; Armstrong, S. A., for C. Noble; Armstrong, S. A., for R. Patterson ...... Aylesworth, B. & Co., for R. Halsburg...... Anderson, Isabella, for J. Anderson; Allan, S., for Jas. Moore; Allen, Frdk.; Adams, E.; Alexander, Robt.; Bailey, J. T.; Baker, J. B.; Balch, Thos.; Baldwin, E.; Baldwin, G. S.; Baldwin, John; Ball, E. W.; Ballantyne, J.; Ballard, Ben. Geo.; Ballard, Sarah Jane (late H. E. Ballard); Banner, John; Bauslaugh, L. P.; Banting, John G.; Barber, D. W.; Barnard, W. H.; Barnet, Aaron; Baron, G.; Barton, E. J. W.; Barton, Thos.; Battams, S.; Battye, J.; Beard, J. Markham; Baxter, J. B.; Bearinger, Wm.; Beattie, J.; Beatty, Jas.; Beaven, N.; Beckett, Joseph; Bedley, J.; Begin, J.; Begin, J. L.; Begley, J.; Belderson, J. M.; Belford, W.; Benjamin, F. P.; Bell, Annie (late John Bell); Bell, C. McC.; Bell, T.; Benness, W.; Bennett, J.; Bennett, Sam.; Berry, G. P.; Berryman, S. J.; Berube, Geo. Bernard; Best, George; Bickerstaff, R. E.; Bidwell, W. E.; Bingham, George; Bingham, J.; Bird, B.; Bird, B. M.; Bird, M.; Bishop, A.; Black, A.; Blackeby, A. E.; Blackstock, John; Blackwell, F.; Blain, E. B.; Blair, Alex.; Blair, Wm.; Blake, Elias Darch; Bleakley, R.; Blight, J.; Boae, J.; Boland, T.; Bond, G.; Bond, W. A.; Book, Adam; Book, George; Book, Jas. Hamilton; Book, Mary Ellen (for late M. E. Book); Borthwick, C.; Boswell, T. E.; Bott, J.; Bovay, R. H.; Bowles, W.; Box, Albert Jno.; Boyd, James; Boyd, L.; Boyd, M.; Boyd, Robt.; Boyd, Sam'l Irvine; Boyd, Wm. Sam'l; Boyle, C.; Boyle, J. B.; Boyle, J. N.; Braden, Wm. Oliver; Bradley, S.; Bradley, W. H.; Bray, C.; Brington, J. Sanderson; Brinkman, J.; Brinkman, W.; Britton, James; Broadfoott, Isaac D.; Brock. Wm.; Brockingshire, J.; Brophy, M.; Brothers, T.; Brown, Alex.; Brown, C. A.;

MISCELLANEOUS.—*Continued.*

LAND GRANTS.—*Continued.*

Brown, David H.;   Brown, John;   Brown, R.;   Brown, S.;
Brown, Thos.;   Brown, Wm. John;   Bruce, H.;
Bryden, Stephen F.;   Buderick, J. H.;   Burgess, W.;   Burk, M.;
Burniston, J.;   Burns, R.;   Burrows, Jas.;   Bushfield, F.;
Buskard, A;   Busteed, John;   Butter, R.;   Byrne, T.;
Bye, Geo.;   Barber, H. L., for L. Brooks;
Barber, H. L., for D. Gillies;   Barber, H. L., for John Innes;
Boyle, A. (Executor);   Brown, Martha A., for S. Brown;
Brodie, Geo., for Wm. Spry ....
Book, Mary Ellen, widow of assignee late M. E. Book;   Bright, H.;
Bishop, Washington (1089);   Burt, Thos.;   Buchanan, R.;
Brown, O. P.;   Beaven, L. E.;   Brown, Geo.;   Briggs, G. H.;
Brown, Jno.;   Blackburn, R. C.;   Bredin, J. W.;   Bissett, J.;
Bissett, W. G.;   Blackmore, Jas.;   Barker, Jas. R.;   Braden, S.;
Brais, E.;   Burr, Rd.;   Bell, Neil;   Brockenshire, G.;
Bywater, J.;   Brenan, J.;   Boughner, A. P.;   Bushy, Jas.;
Burch, J. N.;   Brown, Alex.;   Caldwell, W. T.;   Caldwell, Hugh;
Cameron, Albert;   Cameron, Colin S.;   Cameron, Dan'l;
Cameron, D.;   Campbell, A.;   Campbell, Angus;   Campbell, C.;
Campbell, John;   Campbell, Wm.;   Carmichael, J.;   Carpenter, John;
Caron, C. E.;   Carr, Daniel;   Carr, S. T.;   Carre, Henry;
Carrick, Henry;   Carrier, Antoine;   Carrier, Augustus;
Carson, J.;   Carson, R. J.;   Carson, W. J.;   Cartier, T.;
Case, Henry;   Cathcart, J.;   Cathroe, John;   Catt, Henry;
Cavanagh, J.;   Cavanagh, W.;   Caxius, Thos.;   Cedar, A.;
Chadwick, F. A. P.;   Chalmers, G.;   Chapman, C.;   Charters, J.;
Chasse, Phillipe;   Chester, A.;   Christie, A.;   Christie, E.;
Ching, Richd.;   Chrysler, Wm.;   Clark, Jas.;   Clark, S. A.;
Clark, W. T. C.; Clark, Margt. J., for J. G. Morris; Clarke. W. D.;
Clarkson, R.;   Clearihue, Gordon;   Cleverdon, Thos. E.;
Cobbold, Jas. R.; Cole, Aaron; Cole, A. G.; Coleman, A.; Coleman, R.;
Collinge, S.;   Colter, M.;   Cook, Angus;   Cook, E. H.;
Connor, T. A.;   Cooper, J. A.;   Cooper, Jas. G.;   Cooper, R.;
Cope, G.;   Copt, Joseph;   Connell, G.;   Connell, N. S.;
Costello, S.;   Cottingham, D.;   Coulter, F.;   Coulter, S. A.;
Coursey, John;   Courtney, R.;   Couse, Aylmer;   Cousins, R.;
Covell, Robt.;   Cox, Wm.;   Coyne, Isaac;   Craig, W. M.;
Cresswell, J.;   Crewe, H. S.;   Crichton, Peter;   Croom, Joseph;
Crouch, W. T.;   Crowe, Edward;   Cruggan, G.;   Cummings, R.;
Current, W. N.;   Curry, Jno.;   Cutler, J.;
Cunningham, W. B., for G. W. Reid...........................:........
Coleman, V. B., for S. G. Grimeson ....
Chadwick, C. A., for Jno. Jollife ....
Campbell, C. V., adm'r estate of P. C. Campbell ....
Cox, E., for Robert Cox;   Creech. Wm.;
Cockrell, T., for A. Millerarty;   Conroy, D., for J. R. Dundas;
Conroy, D., for C. Shanahan;   Conroy, D., for Robt. Thompson;
Cameron, Susan ....
Clarke, Adele, Louise & Marian Trickey, for late W. T. C. Clarke...
Campbell, W. E.;   Corrigan, J. L.;   Cline, I. H.;   Cherry. Jno.;
Cotterill, I. S. L.;   Cox, Wm.;   Christie, A.;
Craig, Wm.;   Cansley, Rd.;   Coulter, J. W.;   Christie, V.;
Cook, Wm.;   Clifford, Jno.;   Cudmore, A.;   Cudmore, J.;
Campbell, D.;   Chapman, C.;   Crickington, J.;
Dack. W. B.;   Dale, H. S.;   Dalton, W.;   Daly, Timothy;
Darnbough, R.;   Darwin, J.;   Dasavra, L.;   Davey, N. H.;
David, Henry A.;   Davidson, J.;   Davidson, P.;   Davies. R.;
Davis J.; Day. Sarah (late Joseph Day); Daziel, A. H.; Deacon. W. S.;
Dean, Purvis E.;   Deans, Alex.;   Deans, James;   Decker, J. E.;
Deleree, Jno.;   Delf. James P.;   Dennison, S. J. A.;   Denmark, E.;
Denis, A.;   Dent, Wm.;   Derick, T. H.;   Dickie, A. M.;
Dickinson, S. W.;   Distin, J.;   Doan, J. B.;   Dodd, Joseph;
Donnelly, J. R.;   Donnelly, R.;   Donner, C.;   Dowling, J. E.;
Doyle, John;   Draper, C. E.;   Drewrey, R.;   Duggan, Gilbert C.,

MISCELLANEOUS.—*Continued.*

LAND GRANTS.—*Continued.*

Dulmadge, F.; Dunbar, Wm. A.; Dunlop. J. B.; Drags, L. for J. Drags; DeLury, J. S. for Jas. Hallam; DeLury, J. S. for J. J. Keleher; Dowling, J. F. for W. T. Walby; Dunn, Robt.; Dunn, Thomas; Dunning, Gregory; Durfy, I.; Durham, R. S.; Durval, A.; Dyer, A. G.; Douglas, Wm. and Ada; Dumphy, Jas.; Dempsey, M.; Draper, Wm.; Dick, D. E.; Daniel,, Jas.; Dubois, Chas.; Davis, Wm.; Davidson, J.; Ecker, Wm. H. Y.; Edge, Elias; Egerton. W. T. for N. T. Bowman; Egerton. W. S. for T. Hutchinson; Edmonston, J.; Eitle, J. V.; Elford, J. H.; Elliott, G.; Embrey, Jas.; Erskine, D. M.; Erwin, W. J.; Elliott, C. L.; Elliott. A. M.; Emery, Henry; Embury, Angus; Evans, T.; Emerson, I.; Eamon, Jas.; Easton, C.; Esson, Wm.; Fanning, V.; Farrell, D.; Ferguson, D.; Ferguson, J.; Finch, S. E.; Fisher, Charles; Fissitte. Isaiah; Fitzgerald, M.; Fitzgerald, T.; Fitzsimmons, W. A.; Fleet. S. M.; Fleming, W.; Follis, G.; Forbes, Wm.; Ford, S. M. A.; Ford, Wm.; Foster, Eliza (late Jno. Foster); Fox. W. C.; Fox, E. T. for J. Campbell; Fraser, Thos. H.; Fraunch, F.; Freed, Wm. Judson; Freeman, A. P.; Fuller, Jacob; Furnival, Wm.; Fife, J. A. for J. W. Eastland; Eurler, C. for J. Clendennen; Fuller, J. for Jas. Chester; Forde, J. C.; Fryes, W. H.; Fernholm; A. G.; Freeborn, W. B.; Freeborn, H.; Fuller, E. L. for L. Brock; Frame, Jno.; Fulton, A. G.; Field, N.; Faulkner, Ann E. M. (8206); Fernholm, A. G.; Gahan, E. H. Gahan, W. F.; Gallarno, Alex.; Gamble, F. C.; Garbutt, S.; Garrett, J.; Gault, W.; Gauthier, John; Gee, Fred.; Gelley, Marie .T. for C. Gelley; Gentleman, C.; German, J. L.; Gerou. D.; Gerou, W.; Gibson, Goodwin; Gibson, T.; Gill, Wm.; Gillis, Thos.; Gilmore, Isaac; Gilmore, Smith; Gilmour. Walter G.; Gimblett, W. H.; Glenn. George; Glenn, J. E.; Glenn, S.; Glover, W. J.; Gohm, Wm.; Gonyon, J.; Good, Thos.; Good, W. H.; Goodwin, A.; Gordon, W.; Gorrel, D.; Gorrie, Geo. T., Gough, J.; Gould, Wm.; Gow, J. F.; Gowanlock, A. T.; Gowans, Wm. W.; Grady, J. H.; Graham, Donald; Grant, A. G.; Grant, John Peter; Grant, W. S.; Gray, John; Gray, R. T.; Green, Alex.; Green, James; Green Rachael (late Thos. Green); Green, Thos.; Greenwood, A.; Gregory, R. W.; Griffin, Wesley; Griffith, Wm.; Guay, L.; Gindsay. H.; Guman, J. L.; Gelley, Marie T. for C. Gelley; Green, Rachael for R. Mooney; Gribble, F. J. for A. J. Heaslip; Gogo, G. J. for J. River; Gibson, Francis for V. A. Hall; Gauthier. F. X. for Mada Malette; Gleeson, Wm. for Thos. Joyce; Gleeson, Wm. for A. J. Monteith; Gleeson, Wm. for W. Foster; Gleeson, Wm. for H. Ware; Gauthier. F. A. for L. Gauthier; Gesnell, G. for S..J. Press; Garner, Eliza Anne; Green, Erasmus; Graham, Jas.; Gray, Alex. C.; Giles, Cyrus; Gilroy. Alfred; Greenway, W. R.; Graham, D.; Gledhill, H.; Goodall, A.; Gerrie, Geo.; Gamble, Jno.; Grisdale, R.; Gates, Joseph; Greenway, J.; Graham, T.; Graham, J.; Gilkinson, W.; Graham, Wm.; Gordon. P. J.; Gunn. D.; Green. Rachael (late R. Mooney); Haggart, John; Hall, John; Hall, J.; Hall. John; Hall, W. H.; Hallett, Geo. A.; Hamilton, A.; Hampden. Edward; Hanna, W.; Hanson, T.; Harbour, R.; Harden. A.; Harkness. F. J. for J. W. Sill; Harmer, H.; Harper, C. L.; Harrison, E.; Harrison, J. J.; Harrison, Robt.; Hartford, D. P.; Hartwick, P.; Hatt, James; Hawkins. W. H.; Hawley, J. W.; Hay, L.; Hayes. E.; Heakes, Sam'l. Rich.; Hedden, B.; Henderson. R.; Henderson, Thos.; Henry, D.; Henry, J.; Hepburn, W.; Hewitt, James; Hewitt. Jno.; Hewson, T. J.; Hickman, D. A.; Higgins, H. N.; Higgins. Rich'd.; Higinbotham, Nath'l.; Hill, C.; Hill, Geo. A.; Hill. John; Hills. Chas.; Hills. James; Hinde W.; Hinton, Jno.; Hoard, Isaac; Holihan, H.; Holland, Wm.; Holt. P.; Holthy. A. V.; Hope. J.; Hopwood, T.; Horne. Thos.; Hornoe, F. B.; Hostrawser, W.; Hotson, J. A.;

MISCELLANEOUS.—*Continued.*

LAND GRANTS.—*Continued.*

Howard, A. W.;   Howard, Wm.;   Hawes, Wm.;   Hubbs, F. S.;
Hukstep, T.;   Hughes, John;   Hull, Thos.;   Hume, Walter;
Hunt, Thos.; Hunter, Chas.; Hunter, John Geo.; Huntley, Edward;
Hurcomb, Deborah;   Hurdman, Alex.;   Hurkett, Caleb;
Hutchinson, Mrs. Annie (late R. A. Hutchinson); ....
Horton, Robt. Wm. T., and Edith, A., executors estate of H. Horton;
Hay, W. D. and A. D., executors of A. D. Hay ....
Hartford, Lucy, executors estate of A. J. Hartford ....
Harkness, F. J., for Jno. Alexander;   Humphrey, Clara A. (1152);
Holmes, S.;   Hall. R. R.;   Hindem, J. N.;   Hood, F. C.;
Humber, G., for T. Harkness;   Harkness, T. J., for J. W. Sill;
Hubbard, Mary, for J. W. Fingland;   Hall. John;   Harris. Jas.;
Henderson, Jno.;   Hardie, H.;   Hemphill, C.;   Hemphill, I.;
Hamilton, U. C.;   Florence Peers, and Eliz. Thompson (1697);
Harris, Jas.;   Harrison, R. S.;   Hoover. S. B.;   Hack, Chas.;
Hilliner, E.;   Healey, Jno. H.;   Ironside, G.;   Irving, Robt.;
Irwin, John;   Illiff, Thos., ex. est. W. J. Illiff;   Invice, A. (4337);
Jack, James;   Jackman, A.;   Jackson, J.;   Jackson, John;
Jacques, Jno.;   Jamieson, R.;   Jarvis, Wm.;   Jeffers, J.;
Jefferson, Martha (late Wm. Jefferson); Jennings, G. L.; Johns, Geo.;
Johnston, E. A.;   Johnston, G.;   Johnston, H. H.;   Johnston, J. E.;
Johnston, K. G.;   Jones, A.;   Jones, Fred. A.;
Jordan, C. E., for Wm. Jordan; Jose, Rich.; Joseph, H.; Joynt, R. L.;
Johnston, E.;   Johnston, D.;   Johnston, I. N.;   Johnston, Jno.;
Johnston, Jas.;   Johnston, W. A.;   Jamieson, Edward;   Kane, W.;
Keefer, H. F.;   Keeler, G. H.;   Kelly, D. B.;   Kelly, W.;
Kennedy, D.;   Kennedy, J.;   Kennedy, J. W.;   Kent, C. C.;
Ketchum, J.;   Kettell, E. J.;   Kigman, R.;   King, Geo.;
King, R.;   King, W, J. A.;   Kirk, J. Y. S.;   Kirk, R. J.;
Kirkpatrick, E.;   Kennedy, W. L., for J. Blackburn, Jr.;
Kennedy, J. E., for Wm. Meade; Kearns, M. S.; Kilmer, Irving (16.67);
Kemp, V.; Kenard, I. N.; Kelso, H.; Karl, Sarah Ann (late L. Rowe);
Kilmer and Irving (16.67);   Kincard. J. B.;   Kyle. Thomas;
Lafferty, John;   Laflamme. H.;   La Fountaine, H.;   Laird, A.;
Lamont, R.;   Lang, M. R.;   Langstaff, G.;   Lapointe, L. A.;
Larkin, P.;   Lattimer, R. E.;   Lawerence, O.;   Lawrie. J. W.;
Lauzon, Alex.;   Leach, James;   Lebo, Chas.;   Lebo, Geo.;
Leech, Caroline (late H. Leech); Leek, W.; Leggitt. J. E.; Leitch, R.;
Leroy. L. J.;   Lewis, W. H.;   Lewis, W. J.;   Lighthall, A.;
Lile, Enam;   Lillie, Robt.;   Lincoln. J.;   Lindsay, A. P.;
Litchfield. S.;   Lloyd, J. H.;   Lockhart, Robt. G.;   Logan, Wm.;
Logan, T.;   Long, A. R.;   Long, D.;   Lough. W. R.;
Lougheed, Jno.;   Luck, C. A.;   Luther. A.;   Lapassie, J. B.;
Loucks, N.;   Lowry, Jno.;   Lobie, W. C.;   Lusk. Isaac;
Loyst, P.;   Laeon, W. T.;   Lapp, Samuel (4550);   Lescilles, D.;
Lang, J. W.;   McAvony, Thos.;   McBryan, H.;   McBryen, J.;
McBurney, Wm.; McCallum, Arch.; McCarney, Jno. W.; McCarthy, W.;
McCarthy, Wm., for C. Mason;   McIllroy. W., for G. E. McIllroy;
McNee, G., for G. L. Tripp;   McLennan, for E. Mirault;
McLennan, for F. C. Askwith;   McCarthy, W. H.;   McCauley, J.;
McClelland, J.; McClint, Leonard, McConnell, Jas.; McCoombs, T.;
McCosh, A. P. S.;   McCoy, Henry;   McCoy, Wm.;   McCrea, J.;
McCollock, Geo.;   McCumber, W.;   McDonald, Frank C.;
McDonald, Thos. S.;   McDonald, W. C.;   McDougall, Arch.;
McDowell, Alex.; McFadden, J.; McGeein, Bernard; McGill, R. S.;
McGill, Sydenham C.;   McGillivray, J.;   McGregor, A.;
McGregor W.;   McGregor, W.;   McInain. J. A.;   McIntosh, G. H.;
McIntosh. Lorre;   McIntyre, A.;   McIntyre, J.;   McJames, S.;
McKay, A. F.; McKay, J. B.; McKay, John Randolph; McKay, Robt.;
McKellar. Peter P.; McKenzie. Daniel; McLaid, W.; McLean. A. N.;
McLean, J. A., for U. W. Root;   McLean, J. A., for M. Ryan;
McLean, N.;   McLean, W.;   McLeod, G. A. K.;   McLeod, Hugh;
McMann, Alex.;   McMann, J.;   McNeill, N.;
McLennan, A. R., for A. Povrier;   McMann, R.;   McMaster, R.;

MISCELLANEOU'S.—*Continued.*

LAND GRANTS.—*Continued.*

McMaster, M.; McMaster, Wm.; McMaster, W. F.;
McMillar, Mrs. James (late Jas. Mc.); McMillar, J.;
McMillan, R. H. T.; McMurchy, R.; McNabb, R.; McNally, H. Y. W.;
McNee, Geo.; McPhadden, Arch'd. D.; McPhee, A.; McPherson, W. W.;
McQuade, J.; McRorie, W.; McWhinnie, N.; McCann, J. G.;
McCleary, T.; McCall, W. O.; McDonald, Geo.; McKenzie, M.;
McKee, D. J.; McPherson, Jas.; McKay, Hector; McRoskie, W. A.;
McKaskill, Mary (6203); McMaster, Thos.; McDonald, Jno.;
McDonald, Jno. A.; McDonald, Jas.; McCallum, A. H.;
McGregor, Donald; McIvan, I. A.; McNab, A.; McNab, James;
MacDiarmide, W.; MacDonald, for W. H. Manson; MacDonald, W. J.;
Mackie, J.; MacLennan, D. B.; MacLeod, H. A. F.; MacPherson, E.;
Magee, James; Magill, A.; Magill, W. E.; Mann, H.;
Manley, Ed.; Markland, Wm. Hy.; Marr, J. M.; Marsh, A. A.;
Martin, Rich.; Martyn, G. H.; Mason, Chas.; Mason, J.;
Matchett. E. L.; Matchett, J.; Mathieson, C. A.; Maulson, F. H.;
May, G. H.; Mayne, Jas.; Meek, W.; Melach, J.;
Meloche, F. X.; Maven, I. D., for J. Whalen;
Meates, Emily, ex. of J. W. Selles; Marshall, Israil B. (786);
Murch, Thos. (11456); Mulligan, the widow & A. ex. of Wm. Mulligan;
Murch, Thos. (11843); Mackenzie, Isabella (9306); Meloche, J. M.;
Menzies, Chas.; Merrett, T.; Merrick, A. C.; Messenger, G. E.;
Might, W.; Miller, A.; Miller, G.; Miller, James;
Millgate, Robt.; Mills, Wm.; Millward, W.; Milner, Wm. A.;
Mimms, Geo.; Murden. H. McM.; Mitchell, Fred.; Mitchell, Geo.;
Mitchell, Joseph; Mitchell, Thos.; Moffatt, J. N.; Moffatt. T.;
Moore, Geo.; Moore, Geo.; Moore, J. C.; Moore, T. D. S.;
Moore, Wm. Hy.; Morison, D. N.; Morran, J.;
Morris, Fanny (late J. Morris); Morris, Harvey; Morrison, Marshall B.;
Morrow, Chas.; Morrow, Thos.; Morrow, Wm.; Mowatt, D.;
Mullett, G. R.; Morison, D. W.; Might, J. M.; Might, G. W.;
Mulligan, Eliza Jane (late Wm. Mulligan); Murray, Dan'l.; Murray, J.;
Murray, J. A.; Mustill, J.; Morrison, M. B., for Geo. Clarke;
Murphy, A. G.. for W. F. Page; Murphy, R. G., for R. E. Bellamy;
MacDonald. J. W.; MacDonald, D.; Mallock, P.; Moore, Wm.;
Mitchell, Wm.; Menzies, A. B.; Mitchell, N.; Murray, Christopher;
Monteith, W.; Milmine, Alex.; Mills, Thos.; Miller, Wm. (468);
Midveney, R. L. (12351); Marshall, Thos.; Mathews, R.; Malcolm, F.;
Mosier, A. H.; Morrow, Robt. J.; Morrison, W.; Munro, A.;
MacDiarmid, D.; Morgan, Cosbie; Mills, Wm. Walter; Marns, Robt. G.;
Mills, W. H.; Nagle, John, for John, Wilson; Naylor, Jas.;
Nicholson, W.; Newman, Jno.; Nasmyth, W. W.; Needham, S.;
Negg, R.; Neill, J. A.; Nelles, Jos.; Nelles, J. T.;
Nelmes, D. T.; Nelson, Theo. H.; Nettleton, C.; Newcombe, J.;
Nevill, M. P.; Nichol, R. H.; Nisbet, Wm.; Noller, J.;
Northwood, J. M.; Norton, W.; Nott. Fred.; Noverre, F. A.;
Noiton, W.; Oakley, G. F.; Oelschlager, A.; O'Connell, W. H.;
O'Neil, James: O'Neil. J. F.: Orange. Geo. H., for J. Mayberry (33.33);
Orange, Geo. H., for Z. R. Rowe (33.33); Orde, F. W.; Orr, Jos. E.;
Orr. Wm.; Ough, Chas. Rd.; Page, Henry; Palmer, J. M.;
Paris, Geo. R.; Parker, R.; Parnell, Isaac, Patos, Fred.;
Patten, R.; Patterson, C.; Patterson, W.; Patterson, Wm.;
Pattie. Wm.; Paul, Robt.; Pawson, B.; Payne, Jas.;
Peat, James; Pierce, J. W.; Perkins, Jno.; Perry, Jas.;
Phillip. Wm. H.. for T Pavette; Phillips. R.. for T. Weston;
Peat, Oswald, for J. Weston; Perry, I., next of kin C. Perry;
Perry, J. B.; Perry, W. B.; Petes, W. D.; Peters, W. L.;
Peterson, Nicholas A.: Pettet. Geo.; Pettigrew, N.; Pettigrew, R.;
Phillips, G. A. C.; Phillips. R. R.; Phipps, F. T.; Pickering, J.;
Pickering, J. M.; Pickrell, C. E.; Pidd, L.; Pittard, W. W.;
Plank, L.; Plummer, F.; Pollock, W.; Pouliot. J.;
Powell, A. B.; Powell, G. E., Sr.; Powell, R.; Power. E. A.;
Pratt, Jas. Isaac; Prebble, Kathleen M. (late A. H. Prebble;

MISCELLANEOUS.—*Continued.*

LAND GRANTS.—*Continued.*

Price, S. R.;   Prime, A.;   Prime, Arthur;   Prout, Wm.;
Pugh, J.;   Pauher, E. F.;   Patterson, John;   Parliament, Henry, J.;
Parnell, E. J.;   Phillips, Ranton;   Pike, W. S. C.;   Post, C. W.;
Powell, Jno. J.;   Payn, W. L.;   Patterson, Tucker (10200);   Peer, I.;
Pearson, A. D.;   Phillips, J. H.;   Pepper, I. P.;   Pritchards, W.;
Phillips, R. R.;   Pearce, J.;   Pitsworth, Jos.;
Radford, Rd.;   Rae, Cecil R.;   Ramsay, W. J.;   Rance, J. E.;
Randle, Jas.;   Rapleje, C. C.;   Rath, S.;   Rayner, J. A.;
Read, Hector;   Real, D.;   Redfern, J. W.;   Reid, Henry;
Ross, Margt., for Thos. W. Ross;   Ross, Sarah, for J. McCowell;
Riddell, A., for J. H. Bessey;   Russell, W.;   Reeves, Henrietta (2889);
Rannie, Alex.;   Reden, Corey H. (12988);   Reeves, Capt.;
Rennie, Geo.; Richardson, Marcella P.; Richmond, Jas.; Riddle, Geo.;
Ridley, J. A.;   Rimellard, J.;   Rions, Eliza, for Wm. Rions;
Ritchie, C.;   Robb, G. T.;   Roberts, Peter;   Robertson, Jno. H.;
Robertson, J. P.;   Robertson, Jas. W.;   Robinson, F.;
Robinson, G. H.;   Robinson, John;   Robinson, W.;   Robitaille, C.;
Robson, A.;   Robson, W. B.;   Rochon, D.;   Rochon, D. Jr.;
Roe, Jason;   Rose, S.;   Ross, H. H.;   Ross, Jas. M.;
Ross, W.;   Roy, Prosper;   Runchey, Cyrus;   Russell, Gavin;
Russell, G. F. B.;   Russell, N. W.;   Rutherford, G.;   Ryan, J. C.;
Robertson, D. M., for Hugh Caldwell ....

do	J. W. Patterson ....
do	Late James Hughes ....
do	Thomas Roach ....
do	Levi Buck ....
do	Wm. J. King ....
do	A. Winegarden ....
do	J. B. Hatton ....
do	Robt. Irwin, Sr. ....
do	Thos. S. Hooper ....
do	Stan Huet ....
do	Jas. F. Rooney ....
do	Wm. M. Allyn ....
do	J. Curry ....
do	Jos. Mann ....
do	W. H. Stevenson ....
do	A. Kennedy ....
do	S. Tobin ....
do	John Hannafur ....
do	Geo. Colling ....
do	J. A. Benn ....
do	Andrew Boa ....
do	J. D. McPherson ....
do	W. T. Tucker ....
do	Ed. Rooney ....
do	Orlando Gammond ....
do	Ulvie DeLisile ....
do	A. Crooks ....
do	R. Warren ....
do	J. E. Harrison ....
do	Albert Brown ....
do	G. H. May ....
do	C. Quackenbush ....
do	W. Pollock ....
do	J. W. Brown ....
do	A. J. McClinkie ....
do	C. H. Walker ....
do	J. W. Soper ....
do	John Milne ....
do	R. Greenlan ....
do	R. J. Barrett ....
do	A. Watson ....
do	R. Pollock ....

MISCELLANEOUS.—*Continued.*

LAND GRANTS.—*Continued.*

Rorke, Hugh E., for Jno. Brown;   Russell, W.;   Rankin, H. C.;
Ryan, Chas.;   Ryan, W.;   Ryan, C. W.;   Robertson, D.;
Ross, Chas. H.;   Ryan, W.;   Sabine, H. G.;   Sainschney, A.;
Sanders, T. W.;   Sanders, W.;   Sanderson, Geo.;   Sanderson, R.;
Savage, P. G.;   Sawyer, A.;   Schroeder, J.;   Schroeder, Martin;
Scott, Saml.;   Scriver, J. F.;   Simpson, Phoebe;
May Gunner and Annie Simpson for Late R. Simpson ....
Stinson, J., for W. Hammon;   Stinson, J., for J. Redden;
Stevenson, J., for R. Stevenson;   Scratch, A. J.;   Scurrah, G.;
Selby, J.W. ;   Senn, Phillip M.;   Servos, Alex.;   Shaver, L. J.;
Shaw, J. F.;   Shepherd, J. L.;   Sherwood, T.;   Shier, Luke;
Shouldice, W.;   Sidney, Adam;   Silcox, E. D.;   Simmons, G.;
Simmons, J.;   Simmons, R.;   Simpson, C.;   Simpson, Geo.;
Simpson, J.;   Simpson, J.;   Simpson, W. C.;   Sisson, Jno.;
Skelton, James;   Skinner, L. D.;   Sloan, J.;   Sloan, James;
Smail, John;   Small, Robt.;   Smeeth, F.;   Smith, Alex.;
Smith, Andrew;   Smith, C. J.;   Smith, H.;   Smith, John James;
Smith, R. T.;   Smith, T. L.;   Smyth, W. A.;   Snell, Thos.;
Snetsinger, R;   Snook, J. A.;   Sparkman, J.;   Sparling, W.;
Spencer, W. E., for J. Kefler;   Sargent, Jos., for D. Albright;
Spanton, Mary (130 35);   Spink, W. B.;   Springford, Chas. M.;
Stabback, J. B.;   Stafford, A.;   Stanley, B.;   Staples, R. F.;
Steele, A. E.;   Steinbach, D.;   Stenton, Geo.;   Stephens, E. Code;
Stephens, Jas;   Stephens, L. A.;   Stephens, S.;   Stevenson, G. F.;
Stewart, John;   Stephenson, John;   Stevenson, W. J.;   Still, J.;
St. John, Geo.;   Stoneham, J.;   Storey, John H.;   Storms, J.;
Storrs, Archd.;   St. Pier, Anthony;   Straley, W.;   Street, L. J.;
Strong, C. S.;   Sturgis, G. T.;   Sullivan, J.;   Sutherland, A. B.;
Sutton, Ernest;   Swain, Jos.;   Swan, Henry;   Swarts, E.;
Swayze, M. W.;   Sweet, C.;   Sweet, J.;   Sweet, Wm.;
Syme, Jas.;   Sypher, Peter;   Sampson, Jas.;   Scurray, Arthur E.;
Shaw, D. W.;   Shelrick, Mark;   Shearer, W. R.;   Strong, Geo.;
Sernor, Peter G.;   Stephens, W. B.;   Snell, Jas.;
Smith, Eliza E., Ex. Estate of Late John Smith; Snetsinger, Geo. H.;
Snell, Jas.;   Smith, D.; Smith, Jas.; Sootheran, I. H.. for Jas. Wilson;
Sweetman, C.;   Steedmark, M.;   Steele, A. F.;   Sterling, W. H.;
Stevenson, Jno.;   Stevenson, Thos.;   Taylor, Marg't., for John Taylor;
Taylor, Alex.;   Taylor, H. C.;   Taylor, Isaac;   Taylor, Joseph;
Telford, W. P.;   Tisdale, S., for F. Ladd;   Thomas, John D.;
Toronto General Trust, for W. S. Fraligh; Terence, J.; Thomas, D. H.;
Thomas, W.;   Thompson, Arch'd.;   Thompson, A. F.;
Thompson, Chas.; Thompson, Geo.; Thompson, John; Thompson, J.H.;
Thompson, W. C.;   Thompson, Robt.;   Thompson, W. J.;
Thomson, E. W.;   Thomson, F. L.;   Thorburn, T.;   Thornton, W. H.;
Tice. G. W.;   Ticknor, J.;   Timmis, J. A. (4658);   Tierney, John;
Tinkiss, R. N.;   Tobin, R. A.;   Tomilson, F. B.;   Tovell, J. E.;
Towers, T. A. P.;   Trail, D. (488);   Tranter, J.;   Trew, D. C.;
Trudell. E.;   Trott, Vincent Jas.;   Tufford. Leonard;   Turcott, J.;
Turnbull, D.;   Turnbull, I. I.;   Turnbull, J.;   Twillie. R.;
Turchell, G. A.;   Thomas, F. H.; VanDusen, E. D.; VanDusen, G. E.;
Van Tyle, L. G.;   Vanness, P.;   Veitch, Wm. M.;   Verral, C.;
Verral, J. H.;   Verral, Wm. H.;   Vicary, Sidney;   Vint, John;
Vertice, R. H.;   Vivian. J. H.;   Vohl. L. P.;
Wagar, A.;   Wagoner, S.;   Wakeley. T.;   Walker, John J.;
Walker. Wm. Thomas;   Wallis, T.;   Wallis. T.;   Wallis, Wm.;
Wand, A.;   Ward, Geo.;   Ward, W. W.;   Warren, B.;
Watson, T. E.. for Jno., Walsh; Wager, Marg,t. B. for W. Latimer;
Walsh, G. L.. for John Walsh;   Wallis, Irene. for A. McLean;
Ward, Elinor, (10,248); Walsh, E. J., for J. J. Walsh; Warren, Chas;
Wass, John; Watson, Saml., Waters. J.; Waters. W.; Wattin, W.;
Watt. W.; Watts. T.; Waugh, J. C.; Webster. T.; Weidmark, J.;
Welsh, W.; Welsh, Roht.; Wells. G.; Welsh. S. H.; Welshead, Benjm;
Weston. N.; Westway, J.; Wheeler, C.; White, J.; Whiteworth, S.;

MISCELLANEOUS.—*Continued.*

LAND GRANTS.—*Continued.*

Whitmarsh, Fred Morris; Wholey, Thos.; Wickem, E. A.; Wiley, John; Wilcox, J. J.; Weidman, T. C.; Wiley, G.; Wilford, J. T.; Wilkins, Ed.; Wilkinson, John R.; Williams, Jno., for J. Valois; Williams, Thos.; Williams, W.; Wills, H.; Wilson, Herbert, E.; Wilson, J.; Wilson, Jas.; Wilson, John; Wilson, John; Wilson, John W.; Wilson, N. W.; Wilson, J. S.; Wilson, R. H.; Wimbs, P.; Wingrove, John; Winstanley, Chas. J. H.; Winter, John; Wise, Alex.; Wishop, Jas. A.; Witty, H. S.; Wright, John J.; Woodley, Jas.; Woodard, Marshall; Yearsley, S.; Yeigh, Grace, Late E. H. Yeigh; York, Ephm. B.; Young, Alex.; Young, C. W.; Young, H. Y.; Young, James; Young, Wm.; Young, P. E., for Wm. Fraser; Young,. P. E., for H. L. Palmer; Young, P. E., for F. W. Bradfield; Young, P. E., for T. A. Sheldon; Young, Margt. V., (late R. Young); Young, Sarah J., for Jacob Young ... $71,830 00

INCIDENTAL EXPENDITURES ($12,995.72).

American Bank Note Co., debenture certificates, 40.00; stock certificates, 25.00; engraving and printing bonds and coupons, 26.00	2,665 00
Bank of Commerce, charges *re* certain drainage coupons	183 63
Baldwin, Mrs. E. C. & A. M. & Mrs. L. M. Baldwin Cooke, allowance as daughters of the late C. J. Baldwin	350 00
Case, Geo. A., services as valuator, 140.00; Draper, A. W., services as valuator, 125.00	265 00
Dewar, D. R., expenses *re* entertaining British bowlers	235 95
Ford, The Florist, floral cross for late Hon. Mr. Prefontaine, 100.00; wreath for late Alex. Muir, 20.00	120 00
Grant, S. P., special services auditing fire accounts	100 00
Hodgins, Frank E., legal services *re* Ontario Bank, 40.00; Lloyd, R. J., luncheon entertainment, medical Assn., 343.50	383 50
Imperial Bank, commission retiring annuity certificates	17 50
Mail Printing Co., 200 proofs of advertisement	2 00
Meredith, Judd & Meredith, legal services *re* escheated estate of late James Craigie	33 32
Miller & Sons, flowers, etc., supplied to Countess Grey	48 00
Newspapers, sundry, advertising *re* Government loan	4,768 26
Pearson Bros., services as valuators	10 00
Price S., legal services and expenses *re* Investigation of charges against Registrar of Deeds, South Perth	24 72
Pittaway, A. G., 20 copies of group of Premiers	100 00
Reburn, Henry, services *re* circus, 42.00; allowance for incidentals, 21.00; trav. expenses, 58.65	121 65
Ritchie Ludwig & Ballantyne, accountable warrant actions *re* mining claims	1,000 00
Rogers, J. E., and expenses *re* circuses	148 96
Street, G., & Co., sundry newspapers, England advertising Government loan	19 44
Stewart, A. M., services *re* supplementary revenue, 75.00; services *re* act to amend lunatic asylums, act, 75.00	150 00
Sundry persons *re* commission on distribution of law stamps	2,204 79
Watt, Jas., services preparing index to Registry act and amendments	30 00
Walker, E., design for funeral of the late Mr. Carscallen	14 00

Total Miscellaneous ... $285,972 53

RAILWAY SUBSIDY FUND ($130.860.68).

(Authority for payment, 52 Vict., chap.
35, and 53 Vict., chap. 46.)

Port Arthur, Duluth
and Western Railway...On account of grants in aid of line
from Port Arthur to Western Pro-
vincial boundary, 85.54 miles.

payment due 1st January, 1906	5,596 80		
do 1st July, 1906 ...	5,596 80		11,193 60

(Authority for payment, 53 Vict. chap.
46, 56 Vict. chap. 34, 57 Vict. chap.
49, 58 Vict. chap. 36, 52 Vict.
chap. 35, 59 Vict. chap. 48, and
60 Vict. chap. 40.)

Ottawa, Arnprior and
Parry Sound Railway.....On account of grants in aid of line
from Eganville to Scotia, 146.1
miles, and 3.33 miles at Depot Bay.

Payment due 1st January ,1906	10,221 15		
do 1st July, 1906 ...	10,221 15		20,442 30

(Authority for payment, 52 Vict. chap.
35, and 53 Vict. chap. 46.)

Parry Sound Coloniza-
tion Railway ....On account of grants in aid of line
from Scotia to Depot Bay, 47.75
miles. .

Payment due 1st January, 1906	3.340 59		
do 1st July, 1906 ...	3,340 59		6,681 18

(Authority for payment, 52 Vict. chap.
35, and 56 Vict. chap. 34.)

Irondale, Bancroft and
Ottawa Railway...........On account of grants in aid of line
from Irondale easterly, 35 miles.

Payment due 1st January, 1906	3,132 12		
do 1st July, 1906 ...	3,132 12		6,264 24

(Authority for payment, 58 Vict. chap.
36, and 56 Vict. chap. 34.)

Tilsonburg, Lake Erie
and Pacific Railway.....On account of grants in aid of line
from Tillsonburg to Port Burwell,
15.846 miles, and connecting Grand
Trunk and Michigan Central Railways at Tillsonburg, 3.262 miles—
19.108 miles.

Payment due 1st January, 1906	891 19		
do 1st July, 1906 ...	891 19		1,782 38

(Authority for payment, 59 Vict. chap. 48.)

Ontario, Belmont and
Northern Railway.........On account of grant in aid of line
extending from Junction with
Central Ontario Railway, 9.57
miles.

Payment due 1st January, 1906	446 57		
do 1st July, 1906 ...	446 57		893 14

26 P.A.

RAILWAY SUBSIDY FUND.—*Continued.*

(Authority for payment, 60 Vict. chap. 40.)

Montreal and Ottawa
Railway...................On account of grant in aid of line from
Boundary line between the Prov-
inces of Ontario and Quebec, extending westerly 50 miles.

Payment due 1st January, 1906	2,332 00	
do 1st July, 1906 ...	2,332 00	
		4,664 00

(Authority for payment, 50 Vict. chap.
48, and 61 Vict. chap. 22.)

Pembroke Southern
Railway...................On account of grants in aid of line
from Golden Lake, northerly, 18½
miles.

Payment due 1st January, 1906	1,294 26	
do 1st July, 1906 ...	1,294 26	
		2,588 52

(Authority for payment, 57 Vict. chap.
49, 58 Vict. chap. 36, 62 Vict. chap. 23.)

Ontario and Rainy
River Railway ....On account of grants in aid of line extending westerly from the junction
with the Port Arthur, Duluth and
Western Railway, 40.32 miles.

Payment due 1st January, 1906	25,017 70	
do 1st July, 1906 ...	25,017 70	
		50,035 40

(Authority for payment, 62 Vict. chap. 23.)

Central Ontario Railway.. On account of grant in aid of line from
Village of Ormsby, 21 miles.

Payment due 1st January, 1906	1,469 18	
do 1st July, 1906...	1,469 18	
		2,938 36

(Authority for payment, 61 Vict. chap. 22.)

Ottawa & New York
Railway Co...............International Railway Bridge.

Payment due 1st January. 1906	816 22	
do 1st July, 1906 ...	816 22	
		1,632 44

(Authority for payment, 63 Vict. chap. 29.)

Dominion Bridge Co........Interprovincial Bridge.

Payment due 1st January, 1906	1,166 05	
do 1st July, 1906 ...	1,166 05	
		2,332 10

(Authority for payment, 1 and 2 Edw.
VII. c. 22 and 25.)

Bruce Mines and
Algoma Railway ....

Payment due 1st January. 1906	1,144 57	
do 1st July. 1906 ..	1,144 57	
		2,289 14

RAILWAY SUBSIDY FUND.—*Continued.*

(Authority for payment, 2 Edw. VII.
c. 25.)

James Bay Railway.........	Payment due January, 1906	345 15	
do	do July 1st, 1906	345 15	
			690 30

(Authority for payment, 2 Edw. VII.
c. 25.)

Bay of Quinte Railway....	Payment due January, 1906	1,990 36	
do	July, 1906	1,990 36	
			3,980 72

(Authority for payment, 2 Edw. VII.
chap. 25.)

Lindsay, Bobcaygeon & Pontypool Railway........	Payments due January 1st, 1906.........	1,226 43	
do	July 1st, 1906	1,226 43	
			2,452 86

(Authority for payment, IV. Edw. VII.
cap. 18 and 6 Edw. VII. cap. 19.)

Huntsville & Lake of Bays Railway	Cash payment	....	10,000 00

ANNUITIES ($102,900.00).

Treasurer, Ontario...........	To pay annuity certificates due June 30th, 1906	51,450 00	
do	...........To Pay annuity certificates due December 31st, 1906	51,450 00	
			102,900 00

COMMON SCHOOL FUND ($6,038.73).

Dominion Government. amount accountable bv Ontario *re* Common School lands during year ended December. 1905	6,038 73

DRAINAGE DEBENTURES MUNICIPAL ($37,307.18).

Debentures issued by the municipality for the construction of drainage works : Treasurer Township of Amaranth, 507.41; Ekfrid, 5.137.20; Stephen, 6.118.45; Sunnidale, 1,150.01; South Easthope. 8,426.48; West Flambcro, 2,209.30; West Zorra, 6 712.33; Zorra East, 7,046.00...	37,307 18

DRAINAGE DEBENTURES (TILE) ($1,800.00).

Debentures issued by municipality for construction of Tile Drainage works : Treasurer Townshin of Brooks. 300.00: Dawn, 200.00; Ekfrid.. 100.00; Harwich, 200.00; Orford, 300.00: Raleigh, 600.00; .Sarnia, 100.00	1,800 00

GOOD ROADS ($95,141.89).

(1 Edward VII., Cap. 32.)

Treasurer, County of Hastings, account grant				16,834 40
do	Lanark,	do		8,023 23
do	Lincoln,	do		3,441 50
do	Simcoe,	do		35,962 31
do	Wellington,	do		10,659 02
do	Wentworth,	do		20,221 42

SUGAR BEET INDUSTRY ($75,000.00).

(1 Edward VII., Cap. 44.)

Wallaceburg Sugar Co., Ltd., bounty on 11,276,066 lbs	40,684 68
Ontario Sugar Co., Ltd., bounty on 9,510,753 lbs.	34,315 32

UNIVERSITY OF TORONTO ($30,000.00).

(5 Edward VII., Cap. 37.)

Trustees, University of Toronto, to meet certificates due June 30th, 1906	30,000 00

UNIVERSITY OF TORONTO (SUCCESSION DUTY) ($86,629.00).

(6 Edward VII., Cap. 55.)

Bursar, University of Toronto, grant from succession duty receipts	86,629 00

FORFEITURE IN THE GAMEY CASE ($2,000.00).

(6 Edward VII., Cap. 5.)

Treasurer, Sick Children's Hospital, special grant	2,000 00

INTER-PROVINCIAL CONFERENCE, OTTAWA ($435.50).

Horace Wallis, to pay expenses of Ministers and Secretaries *re* Inter-Provincial Conference at Ottawa	435 50

PROVINCIAL BOUNDARIES CONFERENCE, OTTAWA ($73.65).

Horace Wallis, to pay expenses of Ministers and Secretaries *re* Provincial Boundaries Conference at Ottawa	73 65

PURCHASE OF PROPERTY FOR IMMIGRATION PURPOSES ($12,000.00).

Jas. W. Alexander and Agnes M. Alexander, purchase of property, corner Wellington and Peter Streets	12,000 00

PURCHASE OF HEMP ($12,596.71.)

Independent Cordage Co., purchase of hemp 12,596 71
    Harwich, 200.00; Oxford. 300.00; Raleigh, 600.00; Sarnia, 100.00   1,800 00

DISTRIBUTION TO MUNICIPALITIES UNDER SUPPLEMENTARY REVENUE ACT ($81,060.99).

(6 Edward VII., Cap. 9.)

Treasurer Ontario, to pay municipalities 81,060 99

INTEREST, CHARGES AND SINKING FUND ON ONTARIO GOVERNMENT INSCRIBED STOCK ($158,154.47).

(5 Edward VII., Cap. 2 and 3.)

Bank of Montreal............Interest on loan, £1,200,000 May 15th to December 31st, 1906 .... 128,005 82
    do   ....Sinking Fund, ¼ of 1 per cent. (half yearly)... 29,129 14
    do   ....Charges for services, £210 .... 1,019 51

        Total Expenditure $6,720,179 07

No. 21.

STATEMENT OF EXPENDITURE by the Treasurer of Ontario, shewing the amount expended, unexpended and over-expended for the twelve months ended December 31st, 1906.

Service.	SUB-SERVICE.	Appropriation.	Expended.	Unexpended.	Over-expended.
Civil Government	Lieutenant-Governor's Office............salaries	2,600 00	2,600 00		
	do ....ex pces	1,700 00	1,700 00		
	Œce of Premier and President of the Council..salaries	11,200 00	11,200 00		
	do expenses	3,000 00	2,127 23	872 77	
	ral's Department.............salaries	15,800 00	15,800 00		
	do expenses	2,310 00	2,055 32	254 68	
	Eion do at............. aes	22,382 00	22,016 65	365 35	
	do expenses	2,550 00	2,763 45		213 45
	Department of Lands, Forests and Mines.....salaries	55,100 00	54,024 56	1,075 44	
	do expenses	17,000 00	25,852 82		8,852 82
	Bureau of Mines.........salaries	6,150 00	4,473 99	1,676 01	
	do expenses	6,000 00	9,101 55		3,101 55
	Public Wks Department....... rées	21,200 00	20,130 16	1,069 84	
	do ; epes	5,000 00	5,385 16		385 16
	Highways Branch. ....salaries	1,950 00	1,950 00		
	do expenses	1,500 00	1,455 64	44 36	
	Colonization Roads Branch.......sal ries	4,050 00	4,050 00		
	do expenses	1,000 00	417 21	582 79	
	Fisheries Branch......... ines	6,150 00	5,150 50	999 50	
	do ; pes	1,500 00	2,069 14		569 14
	Game Ban Branch.........salaries	2,400 00	2,400 00		
	do expenses	600 00	563 86	36 14	
	Labor Bureau. ....salaries	2,100 00	2,100 00		
	do expenses	1,050 00	929 48	120 52	
	Treasury Department ....salaries	17,400 00	17,004 16	395 84	
	do expenses	4,575 00	4,572 25	2 75	
	Succession Duty Office.........salaries	5,500 00	5,329 43	170 57	
	do expenses	1,500 00	1,696 28		196 28
	Provincial Auditor's Office..........salaries	12,200 00	11,427 68	772 32	
	do expenses	1,600 00	1,515 44	84 56	
	Provincial Secretary's Department.......sal ries	21,225 00	21,108 32	116 68	
	do ? ées	5,650 00	7,290 94		1,640 94
	Inspection Public Institutions.......... es	21,430 00	18,275 00	3,155 00	
	do ? pes	10,500 00	16,852 73		6,352 73
	License Branch.............salaries	9,450 00	9,000 00	450 00	
	do expenses	700 00	1,367 23		667 23

Registrar General's Branch............salaries	12,200 00	12,200 00		
do ....expenses	3,980 00	3,576 34	403 66	
Provincial Board of ....salaries	8,650 00	8,050 66	599 34	
do ....expenses	14,600 00	6,804 77	7,795 23	
Children's Branch............sal	5,700 00	5,700 00		
do ....expenses	2,600 00	3,007 81		407 81
it of Justice Accounts Branch............salaries	2,300 00	2,300 00		
do	200 00	161 84	38 16	
Insurance Branch ....salaries	7,000 00	7,000 00		
do ....expenses	3,600 00	2,330 93	269 07	
Department of Agriculture............	23,128 00	23,128 00		
do ....expenses	2,000 00	1,682 78	317 22	
n d Forestry............sal	7,700 00	6,679 88	1,020 12	
do ....expenses	3,000 00	3,881 85		881 85
Factory Inspection Branch............	6,400 00	6,400 00		
do	4,500 00	4,040 16	459 84	
Miscellaneous:—				
King's Printer ....salaries	4,600 00	4,600 00		
do ....expenses	200 00	171 87	28 13	
tial tle	6,000 00	5,843 67	156 33	
Inspection Registry Offices	2,250 00	2,250 00		
Municipal Auditor............	2,700 00	2,713 72		13 72
Total Civil Government............	428,330 00	428,280 46	23,332 22	23,282 68
Salaries............	25,050 00	25,050 00		
Clerks of Committees............	5,500 00	3,279 00	2,221 00	
Sessional Writers, Messengers and Pages............	17,000 00	15,890 00	1,110 00	
Postage and Cost of House Post Office............	2,300 00	1,842 03	457 97	
Stationery, Printing and Binding............	53,000 00	52,339 93	660 07	
Library............	4,000 00	4,055 00		55 00
Indemnity to Members............	101,000 00	100,901 40	98 60	
Expenses............	7,000 00	11,838 00		4,838 00
Total Legislation............	214,850 00	215,195 38	4,547 64	4,893 00
Supreme Court of Judicature............salaries	37,150 00	36,874 65	275 35	
Expenses:—				
Registrar Supreme Court and Court of Appeal............	75 00	10 50	64 50	
Master-in-Chambers............	400 00	314 67	85 33	
Master-in-Ordinary............	200 00	177 04	22 96	
Taxing Officers............		46 80		46 80
Judge's Library, etc............	944 80	944 80		

Legislation......

Administration of Justice......

No. 21.—Statement of Expenditure by the Treasurer of Ontario, etc.—Continued.

SERVICE	SUB-SERVICE	Appropriation	Expended	Unexpended	Over-expended
		$ c.	$ c.	$ c.	$ c.
Administration of Justice—Cont'd	Court of Appeal ... salaries	3,200 00	3,200 00		
	do ... expenses	1,050 00	1,011 06	38 94	
	High Court ... salaries	2,800 00	2,800 00		
	do ... expenses	400 00	132 55	267 45	
	...al Office ... salaries	14,094 00	14,094 00		
	do ... expenses	1,550 00	736 53	813 47	
	Registrar's Office ... salaries	10,400 00	10,400 00		
	do ... expenses	800 00	82 66		82 66
	Wk'ly Court ...	1,650 00	1,637 05	12 95	
	Exchequer Division ...	750 00	750 00		
	Surrogate ... salaries	3,025 00	3,025 00		
	do ... expenses	250 00	122 24	127 76	
	Surrogate Judges and Local Masters	28,603 00	28,428 57	174 43	
	...an Legal Offices	3,500 00	3,500 00		
	Inspection of Division ...	700 00	718 30		18 30
	do	5,000 00	5,000 00		
	Land ...s Office	1,400 00	1,744 30		344 30
	do	6,650 00	650 00		
	...rs of Titl e ...	68 00	68 99	1 01	
	Drainage Trials Act ... sal	947 03	5,366 62	580 41	
	do ... ex	5,050 00	5,954 23		304 23
	Deputy Clerks of the Crown	60 00	65 84		65 84
	Local Registrars	17,550 00	16,438 03	1,111 97	
	...	7,300 00	6,793 00	507 00	
	...al Administration of ... Jus.	11,000 00	11,023 00	577 00	
	...ers of Criminal ...	180,305 00	191,951 45		11,351 45
	...cal Services	2,000 00	4,180 00	925 00	
	Sheriff's Fees	2,000 00		2,000 00	
	Seals and other Contingencies	11,000 00	12,255 30		1,255 30
	Litigation of Constitutional ...	300 00	179 88	120 12	
	...s Act	600 00	5,377 91	622 09	
	...	1,200 00	44 70	755 30	
	Shorthand Reporters ... salaries	500 00		500 00	
	do ... expenses	14,800 00	1,500 00	1,200 00	
	County Law Library, London and Ottawa	1,200 00	1,372 85		172 85
	Expenses ...ly Court, London and Ottawa	1,200 00	1,200 00		
		100 00	100 00	100 00	

Osgoode Hall, Maintenance —				
Fuel, Light and ⬛ Wer. ⬛ ⬛	7,500 00	3,489 08	4,010 92	
Salaries of Engineer, ⬛ and	1,880 00	1,810 06	70 00	
Furniture and ⬛ ⬛	1,500 00	1,372 06	127 94	
Fittings for ⬛alts and ⬛	2,500 00		2,500 00	
Fire Protection, ⬛, etc.	1,300 00	1,252 90	47 10	
General Repairs, Drains, ⬛	1,600 00	2,294 86		694 86
Repairs to Main Entrance and Stone Work	700 00			
New ⬛	90 00	172 00	700 00	
Painting Walls, etc., ⬛ Room	1,100 00	820 03	228 00	
To Renew Roof of Boiler House	800 00		279 97	
Telephone and Telegraph Service	175 00	175 00	800 00	
District of Algoma	19,701 00	18,422 55	1,278 45	
do ⬛er Bay	12,650 00	16,090 14		3,440 14
do Rainy River	15,900 00	16,211 29		311 29
do Nipissing	22,950 00	26,502 87		3,552 87
do ⬛a	8,650 00	9,307 43		657 43
do Parry Sound	13,150 00	13,671 72		521 72
do Manitoulin	9,955 10	10,583 13		578 03
Provisional ⬛ity of Haliburton	1,650 00	1,426 35	223 65	
⬛de to District Judges		2,840 00		2,840 00
Provincial Police, Niagara and Detroit Rivers	13,890 00	13,756 13	133 87	
Revision of ⬛	30,000 00	5,026 54	24,973 46	
Total Administration of Justice	564,844 93	544,826 60	46,256 40	26,238 07
Public and Separate Schools	241,610 59	241,472 25	138 34	
Poor and District Schools	77,000 00	76,997 63	3 37	
Special Grant, Public, Separate and Rural Schools	60000 00	59,982 72	17 28	
⬛ry ⬛nn, P. S. ⬛et ⬛	300 00	300 00		
Kindergarten Schools	3,500 00	3,463 20	36 80	
Night Schools	250 00	249 35	65	
Instruction in Agriculture and Horticulture in Rural Schools	2,000 00	124 50	1,875 50	
Continuation ⬛ls	32,000 00	31,785 33	214 67	
Mel ⬛ols	11,000 00	10,168 31	831 69	
French-English ⬛ng Schools	2,00 00	405 09	1,594 91	
Teachers' Associations	3,000 00	3,068 25		68 25
Inspection of ⬛chools	83,667 00	80,86 28	3,210 72	
Departmental Examinations	6,850 00	6,850 00	-	
do salaries	24,050 00	28,688 69		4,638 69
Toronto Normal and Model Schools salaries	29,350 00	29,350 00		
do do expenses	3,245 00	3,055 43	224 57	
Ottawa do salaries	24,010 00	23,552 33	457 67	
do do expenses	2,935 00	1,457 10	1,477 90	

No. 21—Statement of Expenditure by the Treasurer of Ontario, etc.—Continued.

SERVICE	SUB-SERVICE	Appropriation.	Expended.	Unexpended.	Over-expended.
		$ c.	$ c.	$ c.	$ c.
Education.—Continued....	Ottawa Normal and Model Schools......maintenance	5,600 00	3,210 08	2,389 92	
	London do ....salaries	9,200 00	9,156 00	44 00	
	do do ....expenses	3,600 00	2,688 71	911 29	
	do do ....maintenance	4,000 00	2,257 78	1,742 22	
	High Schools and Coll ... Institutes......salaries	5,700 00	4,773 86	926 14	
	do do ....expenses	116,800 00	116,180 32	619 68	
	... H. S. Cadet Corps.........salaries	12,500 00	12,500 00		
	... H. S. Cadet Corps ...	2,500 00	1,600 00	900 00	
	Ontario Normal Coll ....expenses	6,700 00	6,450 00	250 00	
	do ....salaries	7,975 00	8,282 49		307 49
	Library and Museum.........salaries	8,500 00	8,307 33	192 67	
	do ....expenses	7,050 00	7,029 59	20 41	
	School of Practical Science ....salaries	58,747 00	58,747 00		
	do ....expenses	10,075 00	10,075 00		
	do ....maintenance	18,525 00	18,525 00		
	Public Li... ....salaries	2,650 00	2,650 00		
	do ....Grants	47,200 00	28,301 12	18,898 88	
	Art Schools and ... Museums	4,800 00	4,260 85	539 15	
	Library and ... etc.	4,200 00	4,200 00		
	...	2,200 00	1,900 00	300 00	
	... Education	31,620 00	26,798 50	4,821 50	
	Superannuated ...	63,300 00	63,190 00	110 00	
	Provincial University..........	134,352 23	123,837 91	10,514 32	
	School of Mining, Kingston........	37,000 00	37,000 00		
	... Faculty of ... College for promotion of	50,000 00	50,000 00		
	... Educational Buildings........	13,240 00	10,818 87	2,421 13	
	...	11,646 72	10,458 71	1,188 01	
	... Advisory Council.........	400 00	1,240 09		840 09
	... for ... Deaf and Dumb........salaries	26,783 00	25,788 01	994 99	
	do ....expenses	26,350 00	23,197 09	3,152 91	
	do ....Repairs to Buildings	3,785 00	3,700 13	84 87	
	Institution for the Blind.........salaries	19,121 00	17,989 64	1,131 36	
	do ....expenses	16,760 00	14,242 92	2,517 08	
	do ....Repairs to Buildings	1,809 10	138 25	1,670 85	
	Total Education........	1,381,491 64	1,320,921 71	66,424 45	5,854 52

Public Institutions Maintenance

Item				
Asylum for Insane, Toronto	41,296 00	39,624 81	1,671 19	
do	74,200 00	86,803 63		12,603 63
do London	51,759 00	46,060 34	5,098 66	
do	96,400 00	93,443 28	1,956 72	
do Hamilton	45,311 00	39,871 70	5,439 21	
do	90,200 00	97,487 33		7,287 33
do Kingston	36,272 00	33,663 92	2,608 08	
do	57,850 00	67,645 23		9,795 23
do	32,194 00	30,780 44	1,413 56	
do Brockville	51,050 00	53,852 49		2,802 49
do	30,362 00	27,821 38	2,540 62	
do	63,200 00	62,828 24	371 76	
do	12,590 00	11,331 91	1,258 09	
do Penetang	13,000 00	10,183 17	3,416 83	
do	17,106 00	15,802 45	1,303 55	
do Woodstock	23,900 00	26,350 61		2,450 61
Asylum for Epileptics	12,823 33	8,376 17	4,447 16	
do	15,250 00	9,406 68	5,843 32	
Asylum for Feeble Minded, Orillia	25,458 00	24,360 65	1,097 35	
do expenses	50,150 00	51,881 42		1,731 42
	333 33	833 33		
Relieving Officer	30,420 00	30,379 46	40 54	
do	41,150 00	32,015 46	9,134 54	
Central Prison	14,185 00	13,714 15	470 85	
do	53,500 00	45,190 87	8,309 13	
Mercer Reformatory for Females	12,450 00	11,923 15	526 85	
do	17,600 00	11,929 01	5,670 99	
To pay pensions December 12 to 31, 1905.				
Asylum for Insane, Mimico	3,422 15	3,422 15		
do	2,073 01	2,034 16	38 85	
do Hamilton	6,535 13	6,535 13		
do	5,952 98	5,900 98	52 00	
do Brockville	2,854 97	2,828 59	26 38	
do	3,216 21	3,216 21		
do Penetang	1,051 10	985 85	65 25	
do	2,976 25	2,907 81	68 44	
Asylum for Feeble-Minded, Orillia	1,650 35	1,650 35		
Central	2,366 82	2,366 82		
Mercer	742 95	742 95		
Total Public Institutions Maintenance	1,042,451 58	1,016,252 37	62,869 92	36,670 71

Agriculture

Item				
Agricultural and Horticultural Societies … salaries	1,720 00	1,720 00		
do … expenses	1,500 00	1,364 65	135 35	
do … grants	79,000 00	76,378 00	2,622 00	

No. 21.—STATEMENT OF EXPENDITURE by the Treasurer of Ontario, etc.—*Continued*

SERVICE.	SUB-SERVICE.	Appropriation. $ c.	Expended. $ c.	Unexpended. $ c.	Over-expended. $ c.
Agriculture.—*Continued*	Agricultural and Horticultural Societies, Port Arthur & Fort William Exhibition	1,800 00	1,800 00		
	Agricultural & Horticultural Societies..E[rpt] Judges	11,000 00	9,425 43	1,574 57	
	[...] S[ub] Branch	3,120 00	3,120 00		
	do [...]	1,000 00	647 82	352 18	
	do [...] nts	22,291 95	24,126 43		1,834 48
	Farmers' and W[...] Institutes	3,612 00	3,192 01	420 00	
	do grants	3,200 00	3,192 00	7 99	
	do grants, lectures, &	20,000 00	19,239 64	760 36	
	Bureau of I [...]	5,500 00	3,259 22	2,240 78	
	Dairy Branch—				
	Dairy Instruction ......salaries	32,700 00	32,424 98	275 02	
	do ......expenses	2,000 00	1,679 80	320 20	
	Eastern [Dry] School	11,000 00	9,194 82	1,805 18	
	W[m] do [...]	3,500 00	2,766 37	733 63	
	Dairymen's [...]	4,000 00	4,000 00		
	Ge[...] [Cal] Fair [...] Factories and Creameries	2,500 00	2,499 05	95	
	[...] [...] [...] Vegetables and Insects......grants	4,000 00	4,000 00		
	Experimental Fruit Sta[...], &c	4,500 00	4,574 45		74 45
	Experimental Fruit Farm	5,000 00	3,897 76	1,102 24	
	Cold Storage, Experiments......grants	2,000 00	2,172 25		172 25
	[Fit] [...] [...] and Honey Sale	2,500 00	151 28	2,348 72	
	San Jose Scale	1,700 00	1,700 00		
	[do] Experimental Union	4,100 00	3,026 88	1,073 12	
	[Br] Farm	2,500 00	2,500 00		
	[Idl] s...	2,000 00	943 21	1,056 79	
	[Go] [...] [College] ......salaries	22,000 00	18,095 45	3,903 55	
	do [...] [late] [...] ......expenses	57,180 00	55,079 00	2,101 00	
	[Md] [...] [ad] Hall ......salaries	41,128 00	40,885 62	242 38	
	do ......expenses	16,400 00	16,088 00	312 00	
	Forestry	17,200 00	16,685 86	514 14	
	[...] [al] Farm and Feeding	3,500 00	3,485 48	14 52	
	Field Experiments	17,100 00	17,092 39	7 61	
	[...] Dairy	8,290 00	8,086 87	223 13	
	[al] Dairy School	16,392 00	12,683 94	3,708 06	
	Poultry Department	9,640 00	7,463 89	2,176 11	
		4,135 00	3,848 2[9]	286 71	

Horticultural Department	8,898 00	8,888 61	9 39	
Mechanical Department	960 00	936 45	13 55	
Total Agriculture	460,550 95	432,296 90	30,341 23	2,081 18
Pamphlets, Advertising and General Colonization purposes	28,000 00	26,527 89	1,472 11	
Land Guides for Settlers	2,000 00	394 50	1,605 50	
Rent and Maintenance of Office, Union Station	1,500 00	1,699 44		199 44
Work in Great Britain	7,065 00	6,729 03	335 97	
Total Colonization and Immigration	38,565 00	35,350 86	3,413 58	199 44
Grants	327,799 40	325,625 20	2,174 20	
Children's Aid Societies	8,000 00	6,957 89	1,042 11	
Sanitary Investigations	5,000 00	1,586 47	3,413 53	
Total Hospitals and Charities	340,799 40	334,169 56	6,629 84	
G t ne e Department	18,000 00	14,228 88	3,771 12	
... s Department	1,050 00	1,011 33	38 67	
Dep t nt Lands, Forests and Mines	5,400 00	3,557 33	1,842 67	
Public Wks Department	1,600 00	1,169 70	430 30	
... ry Department	1,200 00	1,194 84	5 16	
Provincial Auditor's Office	500 00	377 00	123 00	
Provincial Secretary's Department	3,300 00	3,442 17		142 17
Department of Agriculture	1,150 00	1,321 41		171 41
Parliament Buildings ... salaries	16,170 00	15,499 00	671 00	
do ... maintenance	41,340 00	34,686 56	6,653 44	
Total Repairs and Maintenance	89,710 00	76,488 22	13,535 36	313 58
Asylum for I ne, To	9,385 00	11,060 17		1,675 17
do ... I Mo	23,225 00	22,572 10	652 90	
do London	10,300 00	9,074 06	1,225 94	
do Hamilton	16,375 00	9,751 75	6,623 25	
do Kingston Fde	27,343 00	27,369 80		26 80
do Grg	12,800 00	11,684 70	1,115 30	
do Penetang	6,050 00	3,412 37	1,637 63	
do	13,300 00	10,664 86	2,635 14	
Asylum for Epil... is, Woodstock	89,500 00	68,405 48	21,094 52	
Asylum for Idle... Mid, Orillia	6,450 00	3,159 78	3,290 22	
Mercer Reformatory for Females, Toronto	15,110 00	23,005 49		7,895 49
...	6,445 00	2,608 86	2,836 14	
Osgoode Hall, To	35,000 00		35,000 00	

Colonization and Immigration

Hospitals and Charities

Repairs and Maintenance

Public Buildings

No. 21.—STATEMENT OF EXPENDITURE by the Treasurer of Ontario, etc.—Continued.

SERVICE	SUB-SERVICE	Appropriation.	Expended.	Unexpended.	Over-expended.
		$ c.	$ c.	$ c.	$ c.
Public Buildings.—*Continued.*	Normal [and] [Model] Schools, Toronto	6,150 00	5,207 59	942 41	....
	do do Ottawa	5,150 00	3,809 31	1,340 69	....
	Normal School, London	4,000 00	3,668 15	331 85	....
	[Additional] N[ormal] [and] [Model] Sch[ool]s	100,000 00	4,618 33	95,381 67	....
	School Practical [Science]	70,080 00	70,080 00	....	....
	Blind [Institution], Belleville	5,800 00	3, 00 86	089 14	....
	[Deaf and] [Dumb] [Institution]	7,640 00	4, 12 20	3,627 80	....
	Agricultural College, [Guelph]	70,345 00	55, 40 20	15,204 80	....
	Dist[r]ict of [Muskoka]	100 00	93 99	6 01	....
	do Parry Sound	4,300 00	4, 65 53	34 47	20 31
	do [Muskoka]	300 00	30 31	... 53	....
	do Thunder Bay	1,600 00	06 16	583 84	....
	do Rainy River	1,600 00	57 20	1,082 80	....
	do Nipissing	10,400 00	9,627 50	72 50	....
	Total Public Buildings	556,748 00	368, 86 75	197,519 02	9,617 77
Public Works....	[Muskoka] Lakes Works	2,800 00	2,580 47	219 53	....
	M[a]ry [and] [Fairy] [Lakes] [Works]	5,250 00	3,964 27	1,285 71	....
	Dredging Entrance Neighick Lake	900 00	898 15	1 85	....
	[outlet] to La Vase [and] Boon Creeks	950 00	804 22	145 78	....
	[...] Bridge	200 00	200 00	....	....
	Bridge at [...] [Bridge]	2,000 00	1,990 52	9 48	....
	Goulais River [...]	1,200 00	1,044 80	155 20	....
	Removing [rock] N[orth] [of] River	4,500 00	1,892 58	3,607 42	....
	Sauble Bridge [...]	950 00	956 07	....	36 07
	Spanish River Bridge	3,700 00	3,561 55	138 45	....
	[...] River Bridge	7,500 00	5, 60 37	1,939 63	....
	Venve River Bridge	800 00	5, 662 75	137 25	....
	[...] [Creek] [...]	4,500 00	4,487 17	12 83	....
	[North] [...] [Road]	1,400 00	1, 69 95	340 05	....
	[...] Bridge	2,000 00	1,877 24	122 76	....
	[...] Bridge	9,800 00	3,815 40	5,984 60	....
	[...] Bridge	1,500 00	1,395 22	104 78	....
	[...]	800 00	798 51	1 49	....
	[...] River Bridge	3,000 00	3,277 76	....	277 76
	[...] River Bridge	1,000 00	1, 00 00	....	....
	Big East River Bridge	800 00	800 00	....	....

		Appropriation	Expended	Unexpended	Over-expended
	L'Amable Bridge	700 00	1,271 43		571 43
	Beaver Creek Bridge	1,000 00	996 77	3 23	
	Draper Bridge	500 00		500 00	
	Madawaska River Bridge	3,000 00	3,000 00		
	Sturgeon River Bridge	275 00	267 75	7 25	
	South River and Eagle Lake Bridges	700 00	673 13	26 87	
	Black Duck and Indian River Bridges	900 00	869 48	30 52	
	Wolsley River Bridge	975 00	974 20	80	
	Axe Creek, Housey's outlet Creek & Kahshee Bridges	1,400 00	1,221 57	178 43	
	Katrine Bridge	1,500 00	1,257 23	242 77	
	Burnt River Bridge	1,800 00	2,017 11		217 11
	La ... River Bridge	4,000 00	511 79	3,488 21	
	Surveys, Inspections, etc.	2,000 00	663 82	1,336 18	
	Lockmasters' and Bridgetenders' Salaries	4,700 00	4,299 17	400 83	
	Maintenance, ...ks, Dams and Swing Bridges	10,800 00	10,426 82	373 18	
	Drainage	27,210 00	14,010 00	13,200 00	
	Total Public Works	117,010 00	85,117 29	32,995 08	1,102 37
Colonization Roads.........	Colonization Roads	235,010 00	219,559 37	15,450 63	
Charges on Crown Lands	Board of Surveyors	200 00	200 00		
	Agents' Salaries	40,000 00	42,351 94		2,351 94
	...wa Agency	3,850 00	3,779 60	70 40	
	... Agency	2,075 00	2,010 70	64 30	
	Forest Ranging	46,000 00	45,165 61	834 39	
	Forest Reserves	25,000 00	27,913 19		2,913 19
	Fire Ranging	70,000 00	57,611 65	12,388 35	
	Cullers' Act	200 00	180 35	19 65	
	Surveys	150,500 00	125,003 39	25,496 61	
	Clearing along Temiskaming Railway	50,000 00	89,412 95		39,412 95
	Compensation for loss of ...ber on berths, Townships Martland and Cosby	10,000 00	10,000 00		
	Mining Development, Inspections etc.	37,000 00	30,678 03	6,321 97	
	Experimental treatment of ores, collection of minerals and cases, etc.	1,100 00	61 03	1,038 97	
	Diamond Drills	8,000 00	5,243 95	2,756 05	
	Summer Mining Schools	1,200 00	1,196 14	3 86	
	Cancellation of Mining Leases	2,500 00	1,889 70	610 30	
	Gillies Timber Limit	25,000 00	19,159 48	5,840 52	
	Algonquin National Park	13,100 00	11,501 70	1,598 30	
	Rondeau Provincial Park	6,500 00	3,301 40	3,198 60	
	Total Charges Crown Lands	492,225 00	476,660 81	60,242 27	44,678 08

No. 21.—STATEMENT OF EXPENDITURE by the Treasurer of Ontario, etc.—*Continued.*

SERVICE.	SUB-SERVICE.	Appropriation.	Expended.	Unexpended.	Over-expended.
		$ c.	$ c.	$ c.	$ c.
Refunds......	Education..........	2,000 00	1,932 87	67 13	
	Crown Lands........	33,474 29	32,844 62	629 67	
	Municipalities Fund......	243 32	243 32		
	Land Improvement Fund....	1,911 31	1,911 31		
	Miscellaneous.........	10,000 00	11,309 36		1,309 36
	Total Refunds........	47,628 92	48,241 48	696 80	1,309 36
Miscellaneous....	Law Stamps	4,200 00	2,361 50	1,838 50	
	Licensees...........	2,000 00	161 74	1,838 26	
	Succession Duty, legal expenses......	8,000 00	7,664 19	335 21	
	Fidelity Bonds	2,500 00	2,285 44		285 44
	Enforcement Mobile Law........	4,500 00	5,595 69		1,095 69
	Algoma Taxes.........	500 00	244 25	255 75	
	Enforcement Liquor Li... Act.	7,500 00	10,859 61		3,359 64
	Fisheries	28,000 00	25,510 21	2,489 79	
	Game Protection and Importation of Game Birds...	17,000 00	10,966 65	6,033 35	
	Wolf Bounty.........	8,372 00	8,367 00	5 00	
	Expenses of Elections.........	10,000 00	2,991 19	7,008 81	
	Manhood Suffrage and Registration.....	500 00	15 00	485 00	
	Revision of Voters' Lists........	3,500 00	3,745 96		245 96
	Insurance...........	7,000 00	397 09	6,602 91	
	Arbitration Canada and Quebec......	5,000 00	7,034 75		2,034 75
	Annuities and Bonus to Indians, Treaty No. 9....	10,000 00	16,124 00		8,124 00
	Legislative Committee for Art Purposes....	2,500 00	950 00	1,550 00	
	Ontario Rifle Association.........	1,000 00	1,000 00		
	Monument Army and Navy ...	1,000 00	1,000 00		
	Ontario Artillery Association.....	500 00	500 00		
	Canadian Military Institute......	300 00	300 00		
	United Empire ...	200 00	200 00		
	R.M.C. Rifle Association.....	100 00	100 00		
	Canadian Mining Institute.......	300 00	300 00		
	Canadian Forestry Association.......	300 00	300 00		
	York Pioneers........	200 00		200 00	
	Hydro- ...ic Power Commission...	18,000 00	26,000 00		8,000 00
	University of Toronto Commission....	7,200 00	6,625 37	574 63	
	Commission re Sundry Investigations...	5,000 00	12,370 44		7,370 44
	Gratuities...........	20,000 00	17,410 00	2,590 00	

Rem...al of Patients	7,000 00	5,396 11	1,603 89	
Investigations as to Feeble-minded	600 00	551 80	48 20	
Expenses entertainment of Prince Arthur	1,035 19	1,035 19		
William Sherring, victor Marathon race	500 00	500 00		
Experimental ...ge Farm, Berlin	4,000 00	4,000 00		
British Medical Association	5,000 00	5,000 00		
Visit of English Bowling Associations	400 00	400 00		
Ontario Railway and Municipal Board	8,000 00	12,913 60		4,913 60
Commutation Volunteer ...ans' Grants	50,000 00	71,800 00		21,800 00
Incidentals	10,000 00	12,995 72		2,995 72
Total Miscellaneous	261,207 19	285,972 53	33,459 90	58,225 24
That Supply Bill	6,271,333 61	5,888,180 27		
Railway Subsidy Fund		0,860 68		
Annuities		102,900 00		
Drainage ...bentures, Municipal		37,307 18		
do Tile		1,800 00		
Common School Fund		6,038 73		
G ...Roads (1 Edw. VII. Cap. 32)		95,141 89		
Sugar Beet Industry (1 Edw. VII. Cap. 44)		75,000 00		
University of Toronto		30,000 00		
do do (Succession ...ty)		86,629 00		
Forfeiture of money in the ...ody of the Supreme Court in the Gamey ...se (6 Edwl. VII, Cap. 5)		2,000 0		
Inter-provincial Conference, Ottawa		435 50		
Provincial Boundari ...Conference, Ottawa		73 65		
Purchase of Property for Immigration purposes		12,000 00		
Purchase of Hemp from Independent Cordage Co		12,596 71		
Distribution to Municipalities from Railway Tax		81,060 99		
...est Charges and Sinking Fund, etc. (5 Edw. VII. Cap. 2 and 3		158,154 47		
Grand Total Expenditure		6,720,179 07		

27 P.A.

No. 22

Comparative Statement of Expenditure during the years 1905 and 1906.

SERVICE	SUB-SERVICE	Expenditure 1905. $ c.	Expenditure 1906. $ c.
Civil Government......	Lieutenant-Governor's Office..........salaries	2,140 00	2,600 00
	do ....expenses	1,700 00	1,700 00
	Premier and President Executive Council Department..salaries	8,710 00	11,200 00
	do ..expenses	1,533 16	2,127 23
	they ☐ral's Department ....salaries	15,409 33	15,800 00
	do ....expenses	2,445 94	2,055 32
	Audit of Justice Account's Branch..........salaries	2,150 00	2,300 00
	do ....expenses	190 34	161 84
	Insurance Branch ....salaries	6,800 00	7,000 00
	do ....expenses	2,579 54	2,330 93
	Education Department..........salaries	16,579 00	22,016 65
	do ....expenses	2,425 62	23 45
	Department of Lands, Forests and Mines......sal ries	49,046 29	54,024 56
	do ....expenses	17,679 05	25,852 82
	Bureau of Mines..........salaries	4,491 00	4,473 99
	do ....☐s	4,258 34	9,101 55
	Public Works Department..........salaries	23,869 50	2030 16
	do ....expenses	8,874 24	5,385 16
	High ☐ss Branch ....salaries	....	1,950 00
	do ....expenses	....	1,455 64
	Colonization Roads Branch..........salaries	....	4,050 00
	do ....expenses	....	417 21
	Fisheries Branch ....salaries	5,654 00	5,150 50
	do ....expenses	1,419 38	2,069 14
	Game Branch..........☐es	2,250 00	2,400 00
	do ....☐s	507 84	63 86
	Labour Bureau ....salaries	2,100 00	2,100 00
	do ....expenses	1,126 80	99 48
	Treasury Department..........salaries	20, 00 86	17,004 16
	do ....expenses	5,052 67	4,572 25
	Suc ☐ion Duty Branch ....salaries	....	5,329 43
	do ....expenses	....	1,696 28
	Provincial Audit Office ....salaries	9,450 00	11,427 68
	do ....expenses	1,018 82	1,515 44
	Provincial Secretary's Department..........salaries	19,738 75	2108 32

	Provincial Secretary's Department	expenses	7,563 30	7,290 94
	Inspection Public Institutions	salaries	16,331 82	18,275 00
	do	expenses	6,565 69	16,852 73
	License Branch	salaries	8,400 0	9,000 00
	do	expenses	982 96	1,367 23
	Registrar General's Branch	salaries	11,415 48	12,200 00
	do	expenses	2,415 47	3,576 34
	Provincial Board of Health	salaries	8,803 95	8,050 66
	do	expenses	7,659 54	6,804 77
	Neglected Children's Branch	salaries	4,750 0	5,700 00
	do	expenses	2,543 56	3,007 81
	Department of	salaries	20,788 28	23,128 00
	do	expenses	1,946 85	1,682 78
	Colonization and Forestry	salaries	8,000 00	6,679 88
	do	expenses	4,022 65	3,881 85
	Factory Inspection	salaries	5,950 00	6,400 00
	do	expenses	4,207 60	4,040 16
	King's Printer	salaries	4,400 00	4,600 00
	do	expenses	174 88	171 87
	Official Gazette	expenses	6,007 80	5,843 67
	Inspection of Registry Offices		2,250 00	2,250 00
	Municipal Auditor		2,594 70	2,713 72
	Total Civil Government		374,975 69	428,280 46
Legislation	Salaries		23,057 41	25,050 00
	Clerks of Committees, etc.		15,504 39	3,279 00
	Sessional Writers, Messengers and Pages			15,890 00
	Postage and Cost of House Post Office		2,089 96	1,842 03
	Stationery, Printing and Binding		55,853 69	52,359 83
	Library		3,566 67	4,055 00
	Indemnity to Members		101,003 60	100,901 40
	Expenses		10,031 37	11,838 00
	Total Legislation		211,107 09	215,195 36
Administration of Justice	Supreme Court of Judicature	salaries	37,161 89	38,368 46
	Court of Appeal	salaries	4,144 46	3,200 00
	do	expenses		1,011 06
	High Court	salaries	2,855 96	2,800 00
	do	expenses		132 55
	Central Office	salaries	13,899 04	14,094 00
	do	expenses		736 53
	Registrar's Office	salaries	11,585 20	10,400 00
	do	expenses		882 66

No. 22—COMPARATIVE STATEMENT of Expenditure during the years 1905 and 1906.—*Continued.*

SERVICE.	SUB-SERVICE.	Expenditure 1905. $ c.	Expenditure 1906. $ c.
Administration of Justice.—*Cont'd.*	Weekly Court	1,799 20	1,637 05
	Exchequer Division ....salaries		750 00
	Surrogate	3,182 60	3,025 00
	do ....expenses		122 24
	Surrogate Judges and Local Masters	273 01	28,428 57
	Inspection of Legal Offices	3,941 83	3,500 00
	Inspection of Division Courts ....expenses		718 30
	do ....salaries	6,056 96	5,000 0
	do		1,744 30
	Land Titles Office	5,971 69	6,650 00
	do ....expenses		648 99
	Local Masters of Titles	4,518 99	5,366 62
	Drainage Trials Act	590 38	5,954 23
	do ....expenses		665 84
	Deputy Clerks of the Crown	16,745 67	16,438 03
	Deputy Clerks of the Crown as Local Registrars	69 33	6,793 00
	Crown Prosecutions	7,986 14	10,423 0
	General Administration of Justice in Counties	178,756 51	191,551 45
	Inspectors of Criminal Actions	645 00	4,180 00
	Sheriffs' Fees, etc	11,824 92	12,255 30
	Seals and other Contingencies	104 05	179 88
	on of Constitutional Questions	24 24	5,377 91
	Grouped Counties	782 30	444 70
	Shorthand Reporters ....salaries	12,169 10	13,600 00
	do ....expenses		1,372 85
	ty Law Libraries	1,200 00	1,200 00
	Osgoode Hall Maintenance	14,722 64	11,385 93
	District of Algoma	293 27	18,422 55
	do Thunder Bay	16,353 18	16,090 14
	do Rainy River	15,860 88	16,211 29
	do Nipissing	21,331 12	26,502 87
	do Muskoka	684 06	9,307 43
	do Parry Sound	12,332 58	13,671 72
	do Manitoulin	8,770 44	10,533 13
	Provisional County of Haliburton	1,662 20	1,426 35
	Allowance to District Judges		2,840 00
	Provincial Police Niagara and Detroit River	12,060 94	13,756 13

Revision of Statutes		200 00	
Special Services			5,026 54
	Total Administration of Justice	501,524 78	544,826 60
	Public and Separate Schools	242,289 96	241,472 25
	Poor and ﬕﬗ Kdis	64,672 87	76,997 63
	Special Grants, Public, Separate and Rural Schools		59,982 72
	Military Istruction—P.S. ﬕt Corps		300 00
	Nﬔt Schools	3,213 33	3,463 20
	Kindergarten Schools	235 20	249 35
	Instruction in Agriculture in grouped rural schools	85 86	124 50
	Continuation ﬕﬔs	21,265 67	31,785 33
	Model Schools	10,078 97	10,168 31
	French-English Training Schools	800 00	405 09
	ﬕﬕs Associations	2,541 63	3,068 25
	Inspection of Schools	71,235 67	80,456 28
	ﬕﬔl Examinations ..... salaries	31,749 91	6,850 00
	do ..... expenses		28,688 69
	Toronto N ﬔﬕal and Model Schools ..... ﬕﬕs	26,863 00	29,350 00
	do do ..... expenses	3,216 74	3,055 43
	ﬕﬕwa do ..... salaries	22,661 66	23,552 33
	do do , ... eﬕﬔ	2,197 41	1,457 10
	do do ..... ﬕﬔce	4,105 56	3,210 08
	London ﬕﬕﬔal Sﬕol ..... ﬕﬕs	8,550 00	9,156 00
	do do ..... expenses	3,602 82	2,688 71
	do do ..... ﬕﬔce	2,788 00	2,257 78
	High Schools and Collegiate Insti ﬔﬕs ..... ﬕﬕﬔs	118,560 78	4,773 86
	do do ..... expenses		116,180 32
	Military Instruction, H. S. Cadet Corps		1,600 00
	S b ﬕ ﬕﬕﬔts for ﬕﬔt ﬕﬕs		12,500 00
	Ontario Normal College ..... ﬕﬕs	11,805 06	6,450 00
	do ..... expenses		8,282 49
	Departmental Library and Museum ..... salaries	6,663 00	8,307 33
	do ..... expenses	6,584 82	7,029 59
	School ﬕ ﬕal Science ..... salaries	43,301 90	58,747 00
	do do ..... expenses	8,287 68	10,075 00
	do do ..... maintenance	17,464 26	18,525 00
	Public Libraries	31,662 41	30,951 12
	Art ﬕﬕls and Art Museum	2,031 30	4,260 85
	Literary and Scientific	4,100 00	4,200 00
	Historical Sﬕﬔs	1,400 00	1,900 00
	Technical Education ﬕﬔs	21,563 89	26,798 50
	Superannuated	62,663 65	63,190 00
	Provincial University	130,789 51	123,837 91

Education

No. 22.—COMPARATIVE STATEMENT of Expenditure during the years 1905 and 1906.—Continued.

SERVICE.	SUB-SERVICE.	Expenditure, 1905.		Expenditure, 1906.	
		$	c.	$	c.
Education—Continued.	School of Mining, Kingston.	37,000	00	37,000	00
	Medical Faculty of Queen's College for promotion of Medical Education			50,000	00
	Maintenance Educational Buildings.	11,127	74	10,818	87
	Miscellaneous	2,366	78	10,468	71
	Election expenses, Advisory Council			1,240	09
	Istitution for Deaf and Dumb, Belleville ...... salaries	24,558	25	25,788	01
	do expenses	25,825	44	23,197	09
	do repairs to buildings			3,700	13
	Institution for the Blind, Brantford ...... salaries	17,745	82	17,989	64
	do expenses	15,142	72	14,242	92
	do repairs to buildings			138	25
	Total Education	1,131,799	17	1,320,921	71
Public Institutions Maintenance...	Asylum for Insane Toronto...... salaries	35,718	59	39,624	81
	do expenses	79,135	85	86,803	63
	do London...... salaries	43,327	45	46,660	34
	do expenses	101,489	57	93,443	28
	do Hamilton...... sal ars	38,034	82	39,871	79
	do expenses	95,932	63	97,487	33
	do Kingston...... salaries	29,199	48	33,663	92
	do expenses	67,306	40	67,645	23
	do Mimico...... salaries	27,994	94	30,780	44
	do expenses	53,728	94	53,852	49
	do Brockville...... salaries	24,966	37	27,821	38
	do expenses	65,956	47	62,828	24
	do Cobourg...... salaries	10,021	81	11,331	91
	do Penetang...	14,777	72	10,183	17
	do	15,164	80	15,802	45
	do expenses	24,774	68	26,350	61
	Asylum for Epileptics Woodstock...... al as			8,376	17
	do expenses	902	06	9,406	68
	Asm for Fble Med, Orillia...... salaries	22,215	52	24,360	65
	do do expenses	49,840	52	51,881	42
	Mdl Relieving Officer...	000	00	333	33
	Central Prison Toronto......salaries	25,698	61	30,379	46

Central Prison do .... expenses	48,076 93	32,015 46	
do salaries		13,714 15	
do fin .... expenses		45,190 87	
Mercer Reformatory for Females ...... salaries	12,511 18	11,923 15	
do .... expenses	19,442 30	11,929 01	
To pay expenses Dec. 12-31, 1905:			
Asylum to date, Toronto		3,422 15	
do Mimico		2,034 16	
do London		6,535 13	
do Hamilton		5,900 98	
do Kingston		2,828 59	
do Brockville		3,216 21	
do Cobourg		985 85	
do Penetang		2,907 81	
do Orillia		1,650 35	
do Central Prison		2,360 82	
do Mer Reformatory ..		742 95	
Total Public Institutions Maintenance		907,307 19	1,016,252 37
Agricultural aid tal Societies	90,136 40		90,688 08
Live Stock Branch	18,378 12		27,894 25
Farmers' and Women's Institutes	25,033 75		25,623 65
Bureau of hs	1,876 53		3,259 22
Dairy Instruction	36,841 47		34,104 78
Eastern Dairy School	10,345 53		9,194 82
Mrn do	3,208 59		2,766 37
Dairymen's Associations			4,000 00
Inspection Cheese Factories and Creameries			2,499 05
Ca al Fair Association			4,000 00
Fruit, Honey, Vegetables and Insects ..... Grants	6,06 70		4,574 45
Experimental Fruit ons, etc	4,497 62		3,897 76
Experimental Fruit Farm			2,172 25
Cold Storage	637 22		151 28
Fruit, her and Honey Shows			1 00
Onio Experimental Union	5,889 97		3,06 88
San José Scale	2,000 00		2,60 00
br Farm	59 93		93 21
Incidentals	22,919 32		18,96 45
Agricultural College .... salaries	45,010 98		55,079 00
do expenses	44,839 87		40,85 62
Macdonald Institute and Hall .... salaries	13,659 15		16,68 00
do expenses	17,022 26		16,65 86
Forestry			3,485 48
Experimental Farm and Feeding	13,668 78		17,092 39

Agriculture ...

No. 22—Comparative Statement of Expenditure during the years 1905 and 1906.—*Continued.*

SERVICE.	SUB-SERVICE.	Expenditure, 1905.	Expenditure, 1906.
Agriculture.—*Continued.*	Field Experiments	7,476 40	8,066 87
	Experimental Dairy	14,892 15	12,683 94
	Dairy School	7,722 34	7,463 89
	Poultry Department	2,931 79	3,848 29
	Horticultural Department	7,950 81	8,888 61
	Mechanical Department	949 08	936 45
	Total Agriculture	405,534 76	432,296 90
Colonization and Immigration	Pamphlets, Advertizing and General Colonization Purposes	13,026 59	26,527 89
	Land Guides for Settlers		394 50
	Rent and Maintenance of Office, Union Station		1,699 44
	Work in Great Britain	19,198 83	6,729 03
	Total Colonization and Immigration	32,225 42	35,350 86
Hospitals and Charities	Grants	262,280 96	325,625 20
	Children's Aid Societies	4,204 57	6,957 89
	Sanitary Investigations	1,697 15	1,586 47
	Total Hospitals and Charities	288,182 68	334,169 56
Repairs and Maintenance	Government House	11,889 87	14,228 88
	Attorney-General's Department	672 55	1,011 33
	Department Lands, Forests and Mines	3,280 56	3,557 33
	Public Works Department	1,493 51	1,169 70
	Treasury Department	871 32	1,194 84
	Provincial Audit Office		377 00
	Provincial Secretary's Department	2,158 45	3,442 17
	Department of Agriculture	885 19	1,321 41
	Parliament Buildings	52,082 23	50,185 56
	Total Repairs and Maintenance	73,333 88	76,488 22
Public Buildings		234,977 40	368,846 75
Public Works		69,853 29	85,117 29
Colonization Roads		178,313 02	219,559 37

Charges Crown Lands			
...al of Surveyors	200 00		
Agents' ...	42,351 34	27,564 46	
... Agr ...	3,779 60	2,722 57	
... do	2,010 70	1,903 91	
... Agr	45, 65 61	35,421 70	
Forest Reserves	27,913 19	18,773 20	
Fire Ranging	57,611 65	54,295 24	
...	180 35	49 35	
Surveys	125,003 39	107,102 49	
Clearing along ...ng Railway	89,412 95	33,808 61	
... for ...ds of ... b..., Townships			
Martland and Cosby	10, 00 00		
Mining ...ul, in ..., etc.	30,678 03	16,409 54	
Experimental ...ment of ..., collection of minerals,			
etc. ...ai drills	61 03	500 00	
	5,243 95	1,508 09	
Summer mining ...de	1,196 14	1,198 84	
...on of mining l...ases	1,889 70		
Gillies' ...tir ...l Park	19,159 48	8,226 89	
	11,501 70	2,046 35	
Rondeau Provincial Park	3,301 40		
Total Charges on Crown Lands		321,731 28	476,660 81
Refunds			
Education	1,932 87	1,058 15	
Crown Lands	32,844 62	32,621 16	
Municipalities Fund	243 32	364 98	
Land Improvement Fund	1,911 31	1,763 72	
Miscellaneous	11,309 36	122 51	
Total Refunds		35,030 52	48,241 48
Miscellaneous			
...w S...e	2,361 50	2,385 70	
...s	161 74	83 48	
Succession ...ty, legal ...	7,064 19	5,514 14	
Fidelity Bonds	2,285 44	1 ...6 28	
...at Auto ...de ...t... al ...to Tags	5,595 69	...3...2 50	
Algoma Taxes	244 25		
...l...ent Liquor License Act	10,859 64	4,185 99	
	25,510 21	24,063 98	
...e ...ta	10,966 65	8,727 46	
...Mf ...ity	8,367 00	5, ...6 00	
...s of Elections	2,991 19	84, ...0 37	
...al Suffrage ...gation	15 00	...26 95	
...vision of ...y lists	3,745 96	3, ...0 36	

No. 22.—COMPARATIVE STATEMENT of Expenditure during the years 1905 and 1906.—*Continued.*

SERVICE.	SUB-SERVICE.	Expenditure 1905.	Expenditure 1906.
Miscellaneous.—*Continued.*	ce	4,785 75	97 09
	A, d Qc	2,393 07	7,64 75
	s d s to s By No. 9.		16,24 00
	Committee of e or At s..		900
	o e t y d y e.	750 00	1,000 00
	o t e.	1,000 00	1,00 00
	o A e.		60 00
	t e e s o .	500 00	80 00
	R. M. C. e e.	300 00	80 00
	Mining ti n.		80 00
	y of t.	100 00	80 00
	Statue e Sir Gr t.		
	c r .	300 00	26,000 00
	o o Investigations ...	6,500 00	5 37
	re .	6,639 95	12,370 44
	l of s as to eble- Med .	2,000 25	17,410 00
	Expenses dt of ce Ar ..		5,396 11
	Sherring, r M ne ..	32,210 00	51 80
	Experimental Sewage .	5,312 44	1,035 19
	Visit of l g s..		60 00
	o d M 3 d		90 00
	n Volunteer s Land s.		6,000 00
			90 00
	Telephone Service ...	5,954 81	12,913 60
	Eastern l s	200 00	71,800 00
	Memorial South s.	300 00	
	e e i ..	1,891 88	
	i t s...	10,382 68	
		13,655 43	12,995 72
	Total Miscellaneous ...	**238,699 47**	**285,972 53**

Rail w Subsi y Fund		130,860 68
As	120,860 68	102,900 00
Drainage ds, Municipal	102,900 00	37,307 18
do Te	14,107 88	1,800 00
6a School Fd	1,500 00	8,038 73
Good Roads (1 Edwd. VI. cap 32)	7,692 67	95, 11 89
Sugar t y (1 Edwd. VI. cap. 44)	46,081 59	25,000 00
do o	74,191 55	30,000 00
e of ey i e ly the Supreme		86, 00
t in e ay e (6 Edw. VI, cap 5)		
r- o oll s e, e, a		2,000 00
t, nt s al Sinking Fund on Ontario		435 50
al 3. i Stock, (5 Edwd. VI. cap 2		73 65
e of y of s		
e of Hemp from t Cordage Co.		158,154 47
n to s m Supple ry		12,000 00
Revenue (6 d. VI. cap. 9)	15,236 19	12,596 71
n Mining Fund, R.S.O. 97, cap. 36.		
School of Mining, t (1 Edwd. VII. cap. 44,	22,500 00	81,060 99
s. 1)	5,450 54	
Stati y d over Distribution		
Total Expenditure	5,396,016 74	6,720,179 07

I'NDEX.

Estimates

of the

Province of Ontario

For the Year Ending 31st December,

1907

PRINTED BY ORDER OF
THE LEGISLATIVE ASSEMBLY OF ONTARIO

TORONTO:
Printed and Published by L. K. CAMERON, Printer to the King's Most Excellent Majesty.
1907.

WARWICK BRO'S & RUTTER, Limited, Printers,
TORONTO.

SUMMARY

Of the Estimated Expenditure of the Province of Ontario for the Financial Year
ending 31st December, 1907.

No.	SERVICES.	To be voted.		
		For current expenditure.	On capital account.	For other purposes.
		$ c.	$ c.	$ c.
I	Civil Government................	530,982 00		
II	Legislation	224,500 00		
III	Administration of Justice	612,394 29		
IV	Education	1.396,266 27		
V	Public Institutions Maintenance ...	1,040,058 50		
VI	Agriculture.....................	485.453 00		
VII	Colonization and Immigration.....	46.065 00		
VIII	Hospitals and Charities..........	303,663 53		
IX	Maintenance and Repairs of Government and Departmental Buildings	89,795 00		
X	Public Buildings—			
	(1) Repairs	45,760 00		
	(2) Capital Account	....	493,935 00	
XI	Public Works—			
	(1) Repairs	21,200 00		
	(2) Capital Account	....	140,400 00	
XII	Colonization and Mining Roads ..	....	....	298,311 00
XIII	Charges on Crown Lands	525,800 00		
XIV	Refunds Account...............	33,172 39		
XV	Miscellaneous Expenditure	231,375 30		
		5,586,485 28	634,335 00	298,311 00

1.   Current Expenditure for 1907 .... 5,586,485 28

2.   On Capital Account..................... 634,335 00

3.   Other purposes 298,311 00

     Amount of Estimates................ $6,519,131 28

ESTIMATES OF EXPENDITURE

OF THE

PROVINCE OF ONTARIO

FOR THE YEAR

1907.

1. CIVIL GOVERNMENT.

AMOUNT TO BE VOTED, $530,982.00.

No. of Vote.	Salaries and Contingencies.	1906	1907
		$ c.	$ c.
1	Lieutenant-Governor's Office..............	4,300 00	4,300 00
2	Office of the Prime Minister and President of the Council............................	14,200 00	14,550 00
3	Attorney-General's Department.............	30,210 00	64,462 00
4	Education Department.....................	24,932 00	29,899 00
5	Lands, Forests and Mines Department.......	84,250 00	110,600 00
6	Public Works Department..................	48,500 00	50,150 00
7	Treasury Department	28,975 00	31,125 00
8	Provincial Auditor's Office	13,800 00	14,550 00
9	Provincial Secretary's Department...........	116,685 00	145,670 00
10	Department of Agriculture.................	46,728 00	49,726 00
11	Miscellaneous	15,750 00	15,950 00
		428,330 00	530,982 00

I. CIVIL GOVERNMENT.—*Continued.*

No. of Vote.	SERVICE.	Salaries and Expenses.	
		1906	**1907**
1	**Lieutenant-Governor's Office.**		
	Official Secretary	1,400 00	1,400 00
	Assistant Secretary	600 00	600 00
	Messenger...............................	600 00	600 00
	Contingencies	1,700 00	1,700 00
		4,300 00	4,300 00
2	**Office of the Prime Minister and President of the Council.**		
	Prime Minister and President of the Council...	7,000 00	7,000 00
	Chief Clerk and Prime Minister's Secretary....	2,000 00	2,250 00
	Clerk...................................	700 00	800 00
	do	500 00	500 00
	Messenger for Executive Council and Caretaker	1,000 00	1,000 00
	Contingencies...........................	3,000 00	3,000 00
		14,200 00	14,550 00
3	**Attorney General's Department.**		
	Attorney-General	4,000 00	4,000 00
	Deputy Attorney-General	3,500 00	3,500 00
	Clerk of Executive Council.................	1,950 00	2,200 00
	Solicitor................................	....	3,000 00
	Assistant Clerk of Executive Council and Attorney-General's Secretary............	1,650 00	1,750 00
	Stenographer and Assistant................	500 00	550 00
	Law Secretary...........................	800 00	800 00
	First-Class Clerk	1,300 00	1,400 00
	Second-Class Clerk	1,100 00	1,150 00
	do do	1,000 00	1,050 00
	Messenger...............................	....	312 00
	Contingencies...........................	2,310 00	2,000 00
	Audit of Justice Accounts—		
	Auditor of Criminal Justice Accounts......	1,800 00	1,900 00
	Stenographer............................	500 00	550 00
	Contingencies............................	200 00	200 00
	Insurance Inspection—		
	Inspector of Insurance, and Registrar of Friendly Societies and Loan Companies.	3,000 00	3,000 00
	Assistant Registrar of Friendly Societies...	1,400 00	1,450 00
	Clerk...................................	1,000 00	1,100 00
	do	950 00	950 00
	Stenographer............................	650 00	650 00
	Printing, blank returns and forms.........	1,300 00	1,300 00
	Travelling expenses, books, postage, stationery, etc.........................	1,300 00	1,300 00
	Actuarial Calculating Machine	....	350 00

I. CIVIL GOVERNMENT.—*Continued.*

No. of Vote.	SERVICE.	Salaries and Expenses.	
		1906	**1907**
3	**Attorney General's Department.**—*Con.*		
	Ontario Railway and Municipal Board—		
	Chairman		6,000 00
	Vice-Chairman		4,000 00
	Member of Board		4,000 00
	Secretary		2,000 00
	Court Reporter		1,500 00
	Messenger and Entry Clerk (transferred from Mtce., and Repairs of Public Buildings)		750 00
	Stenographer		550 00
	do		550 00
	Travelling Expenses		3,000 00
	Experts and Counsel		4,000 00
	Supplies, Stationery, etc.		500 00
	Telegrams and Long Distance Telephones		500 00
	Postage		400 00
	Books for Library		500 00
	Technical Periodicals, etc.		50 00
	Copies of Evidence at Hearings		500 00
	Printing and contingencies		1,200 00
		30,210 00	64,462 00
4	**Education Department.**		
	Minister of Education	4,000 00	4,000 00
	Deputy Minister	3,000 00	3,000 00
	Superintendent of Education (half-year, 1906)	1,750 00	4,000 00
	Minister's Secretary and Departmental Secretary	1,300 00	1,800 00
	Chief Clerk and Accountant	1,650 00	1,800 00
	Clerk of Records	1,500 00	1,800 00
	do of Correspondence	1,350 00	1,400 00
	Assistant Clerk of Correspondence	900 00	900 00
	Assistant Clerk of Records	1,000 00	1,000 00
	Clerk of Statistics	1,000 00	1,050 00
	do · and Assistant Accountant	900 00	950 00
	do and Stenographer	900 00	900 00
	Junior Clerk	600 00	800 00
	Messenger	312 00	400 00
	Stenographers (3)	1,620 00	1,774 00
	Caretaker, including offices, museum, etc	600 00	600 00
	Postage	450 00	450 00
	Printing and binding, paper for circulars and blanks, etc.	800 00	800 00
	Office stationery, account books and sundries.	500 00	500 00
	Books, periodicals and contingencies	600 00	600 00
	Travelling and other expenses	200 00	400 00
	Purchase of Burroughs' Adding Machine		375 00
	Advertising in Educational Journals		600 00
		24,932 00	29,899 00

I. CIVIL GOVERNMENT.—*Continued.*

No. of Vote.	SERVICE.	Salaries and Expenses.	
		1906	**1907**
5	**Lands, Forests and Mines Department.**		
	Minister..........	4,000 00	4,000 00
	Deputy Minister of Lands and Forests.......	3,500 00	3,500 00
	Minister's Secretary......................	1,600 00	1,700 00
	Law Clerk................................	2,400 00	2,400 00
	Secretary to Department	1,500 00	1,550 00
	Stenographer	600 00	600 00
	do		550 00
	Land Sales and Free Grants—		
	Chief Clerk	2,000 00	2,000 00
	Clerk of Free Grants.................	1,000 00	1,400 00
	do	1,000 00	1,050 00
	do	1,050 00	1,050 00
	do	1,000 00	800 00
	do		750 00
	do		800 00
	Stenographer	600 00	600 00
	do	500 00	500 00
	Military Grants—		
	Chief Clerk.......................	1,500 00	1,550 00
	Clerk	700 00	750 00
	Stenographer	500 00	550 00
	Surveys and Patents—		
	Director	2,300 00	2,400 00
	Surveyor and Draughtsman.............	1,750 00	1,900 00
	Clerk	1,100 00	1,100 00
	Draughtsman	1,250 00	1,250 00
	Clerk	900 00	950 00
	do	900 00	950 00
	do		750 00
	do		750 00
	Draughtsman	900 00	950 00
	Stenographer	500 00	550 00
	Clerk of Patents	1,750 00	1,800 00
	Clerk	900 00	1,000 00
	do	1,050 00	1,100 00
	do	950 00	1,000 00
	do		800 00
	Woods and Forests—		
	Chief Clerk.......................	2,000 00	2,000 00
	Clerk	1,150 00	1,200 00
	do	1,300 00	1,350 00
	do	1,000 00	1,100 00
	do	900 00	950 00
	do	850 00	900 00

I. CIVIL GOVERNMENT.—*Continued.*

No. of Vote.	SERVICE.	Salaries and Expenses.	
		1906	**1907**
5	**Lands, Forests and Mines Department.**		
	Woods and Forests—		
	do	800 00	850 00
	do		750 00
	do		750 00
	do		750 00
	Stenographer		500 00
	Accounts Branch—		
	Accountant	2,000 00	2,100 00
	Clerk	1,200 00	1,200 00
	do	1,150 00	1,150 00
	do	800 00	
	do	1,000 00	950 00
	do		750 00
	do		750 00
	Registrar.............................	1,500 00	1,500 00
	Clerk................................	1,100 00	1,100 00
	Messenger, etc.......................	650 00	700 00
	Contingencies, plans, maps, etc...........	17,000 00	25,000 00
	Advertising		2,000 00
	Bureau of Mines—		
	Deputy Minister......................	3,000 00	3,000 00
	Secretary............................	1,200 00	950 00
	Clerk		750 00
	Clerk		750 00
	Clerk	700 00	750 00
	Clerk and Stenographer	550 00	750 00
	Clerk	700 00	
	Contingencies, plans, maps, etc..........	6,000 00	10,000 00
	Advertising...........................		2,000 00
		84,250 00	110,600 00
6	**Public Works Department.**		
	Minister..............................	4,000 00	4,000 00
	Deputy Minister......................	3,000 00	3,000 00
	Clerk and Minister's Secretary	1,500 00	1,600 00
	Engineer.............................	2,000 00	2,000 00
	Assistant Engineer	1,200 00	1,300 00
	Architect.............................	2,000 00	2,000 00
	Assistant Architect	1,300 00	
	Draughtsmen (2)		2,000 00
	Secretary Public Works..................	1,250 00	1,250 00
	Accountant	1,450 00	1,500 00
	Clerk................................	1,200 00	1,200 00
	Clerk and Stenographer.................	600 00	600 00

I. CIVIL GOVERNMENT.—*Continued.*

No. of Vote.	SERVICE.	Salaries and Expenses.	
		1906	**1907**
6	**Public Works Department.**		
	Clear and Stenographer..........................	....	600 00
	do do	450 00	500 00
	Clerk of Files.............................	600 00	600 00
	Messenger and Caretaker	650 00	700 00
	Contingencies.............................	5,000 00	5,000 00
	Highways Branch—		
	Clerk	1,000 00	1,100 00
	Stenographer........	500 00	550 00
	do	450 00	500 00
	Stationery and printing	500 00	500 00
	Travelling expenses and contingencies:....	1,000 00	1,000 00
	Colonization Roads—		
	Superintendent........................	1,900 00	1,900 00
	Accountant	1,200 00	1,200 00
	Clerk	950 00	950 00
	Contingencies.........................	1,000 00	1,000 00
	Fisheries—		
	Deputy Commissioner..................	2,200 00	
	Chief Clerk	1,400 00	
	Clerk	950 00	
	do and Stenographer.................	600 00	
	do	550 00	
	do	450 00	
	Contingencies	1,500 00	
	Game Protection—		
	Chief Warden	1,500 00	
	Clerk................................	900 00	
	Contingencies.......	600 00	
	Fisheries and Game—		
	Superintendent........................	....	1,800 00
	Fish and Game Inspector	....	1,400 00
	Chief Clerk...........................	....	1,500 00
	Clerk	....	1,000 00
	do	....	600 00
	do and Stenographer................	....	600 00
	do do	....	500 00
	Clerk................................	....	950 00
	Contingencies.........................	....	2,100 00
	Labor Bureau—		
	Secretary............................	1,500 00	1,500 00
	Clerk and Stenographer	600 00	600 00
	Contingencies	1,050 00	1,050 00
		48,500 00	50,150 00

I. CIVIL GOVERNMENT.—*Continued.*

No. of Vote.	SERVICE.	Salaries and Expenses. 1906	1907
7	**Treasury Department.**		
	Treasurer	4,000 00	4,000 00
	Assistant Treasurer	3,000 00	3,000 00
	Clerk and Minister's Secretary	1,000 00	1,200 00
	Clerk of Bonds and Algoma Taxes	1,800 00	1,800 00
	Chief Clerk and Accountant	1,600 00	1,700 00
	Cashier	1,300 00	1,300 00
	Second Class Clerk	1,000 00	1,200 00
	do	850 00	900 00
	do	850 00	950 00
	Junior Second Class Clerk	700 00	750 00
	do		550 00
	Clerk and Bank Messenger	800 00	800 00
	Messenger and Clerk	500 00	500 00
	Contingencies	4,575 00	4,575 00
	Succession Duties Branch—		
	Solicitor under Succession Duties Act	2,400 00	2,600 00
	Assistant Solicitor	1,100 00	1,200 00
	Second Class Clerk	1,000 00	1,100 00
	Accountant		1,000 00
	Stenographer	550 00	550 00
	Junior Stenographer	450 00	450 00
	Contingencies and extra assistance	1,500 00	1,000 00
		28,975 00	31,125 00
8	**Provincial Auditor's Office.**		
	Provincial Auditor	3,000 00	3,000 00
	Assistant Auditor	1,800 00	1,800 00
	Chief Clerk and Accountant	1,700 00	1,700 00
	First Class Clerk	1,450 00	1,400 00
	Second Class Clerk	1,200 00	1,150 00
	Clerk	1,050 00	800 00
	do	700 00	800 00
	do	700 00	800 00
	do	600 00	750 00
	do		750 00
	Extra Clerks *re* Public Accounts	1,000 00	1,000 00
	Contingencies	600 00	600 00
		13,800 00	14,550 00
9	**Provincial Secretary's Department.**		
	Secretary and Registrar	4,000 00	4,000 00
	Assistant Secretary	3,000 00	3,000 00
	Deputy Registrar	1,550 00	1,600 00
	Assistant do	1,350 00	1,400 00
	First Class Clerk and Minister's Secretary	1,600 00	1,650 00

I. CIVIL GOVERNMENT.—*Continued.*

No. of Vote.	SERVICE.	Salaries and Expenses.	
9	**Provincial Secretary's Department.**—*Con.*	1906	**1907**
	First Class Clerk	1,500 00	1,550 00
	do	1,450 00	1,200 00
	Second Class Clerk	1,200 00	1,250 00
	Junior Second Class Clerk	900 00	950 00
	do	900 00	950 00
	Clerk	700 00	750 00
	Stenographer	600 00	650 00
	do	600 00	650 00
	Junior Clerk .... }	1,050 00	650 00
	do .... }		450 00
	do	....	550 00
	Messenger and Caretaker..................	650 00	700 00
	Junior Messenger.......................	175 00	400 00
	Printing and binding, including Marriage Licenses, Joint Stock Company forms, etc.	2,250 00	3,000 00
	Stationery, postage and contingencies........	3,400 00	3,400 00
	Installing new filing system (including temporary services).......................	....	2,000 00
	Automobile tags and law enforcement (transferred from Miscellaneous)..............	....	3,500 00
	Inspection Public Institutions—		
	Inspector of Asylums	2,500 00	2,600 00
	do Hospitals and Charities......	2,600 00	2,600 00
	do Asylums and Prisons........	2,500 00	2,600 00
	First Class Clerk	1,450 00	1,500 00
	do	1,350 00	1,400 00
	do	1,350 00	1,400 00
	do	1,350 00	1,400 00
	do	1,300 00	1,350 00
	Second Class Clerk....................	1,100 00	1,100 00
	do	....	1,200 00
	do	....	1,200 00
	Junior Second Class Clerk..............	850 00	900 00
	do	900 00	600 00
	do	....	550 00
	Junior Second Class Clerks (2)	930 00	....
	Stenographer	500 00	550 00
	do	450 00	550 00
	do	450 00	500 00
	do	450 00	500 00
	Clerk and Stenographer................	500 00	....
	Clerk	900 00	900 00
	Travelling expenses for Inspectors	1,000 00	1,500 00
	Printing, stationery, postage and contingencies	2,300 00	4,200 00
	Changes *re* book-keeping. including new books........................	4,200 00	....

I. CIVIL GOVERNMENT.—*Continued.*

No. of Vote.	SERVICE,	Salaries and Expenses.	
9	**Provincial Secretary's Department.**—*Con.*	1906	**1907**
	Inspection Public Institutions—		
	Special investigations...................	3,000 00	3,500 00
	Temporary Assistance....................	....	9,500 00
	License Branch		
	Chief Officer....	2,200 00	2,300 00
	Provincial Inspector....................	2,000 00	2,000 00
	First Class Clerk	1,800 00	1,850 00
	Second Class Clerk....................	1,100 00	1,150 00
	Junior Second Class Clerk.............	800 00	1,000 00
	do do	800 00	850 00
	Stenographer.........................	450 00	500 00
	Clerk and Messenger..................	300 00	400 00
	Stationery, postage and contingencies....	700 00	1,000 00
	Registrar-General's Branch		
	Deputy Registrar-General and Secretary Board of Health...................	2,750 00	2,800 00
	Chief Clerk...........................	1,200 00	1,250 00
	Second Class Clerk....................	1,150 00	1,200 00
	do	1,050 00	1,100 00
	do	1,050 00	1,100 00
	do	1,050 00	1,100 00
	do	950 00	1,000 00
	do	900 00	1,000 00
	do	900 00	1,000 00
	Stenographer	600 00	600 00
	Messenger............................	600 00	650 00
	Printing and stationery................	2,000 00	2,500 00
	Postage and contingencies...:.........	600 00	600 00
	Travelling expenses...................	300 00	200 00
	Temporary services...................	300 00	300 00
	District Registrar's fees...............	400 00	400 00
	Typewriters...........................	380 00	....
	Addressograph	....	320 00
	Provincial Board of Health—		
	Chairman	400 00	400 00
	Medical Inspector......................	2,050 00	2,200 00
	Provincial Analyst in charge of Laboratory	1,600 00	1,900 00
	Provincial Chemist..........	1,100 00	1,400 00
	Assistant Bacteriologist (Kingston)......	500 00	500 00
	Chief Clerk...........................	1,100 00	1,150 00
	Clerk.................................	700 00	750 00
	Stenographer	550 00	600 00
	Laboratory Clerk (messenger last year)...	650 00	700 00
	Printing, binding, stationery and sanitary literature	1,000 00	1,500 00

I. CIVIL GOVERNMENT.—*Continued.*

No. of Vote.	SERVICE.	Salaries and Expenses.	
		1906	**1907**
9	**Provincial Secretary's Department.**—*Con.*		
	Provincial Board of Health—(Con.)		
	Per diem allowance and travelling expenses of Members of Board and Secretary..	2,000 00	2,000 00
	Rent of Laboratory	500 00	500 00
	Laboratory investigations, including maintenance and equipment.............	3,000 00	3,000 00
	For the analysis of sewage.............	1,000 00	....
	Sewage and Water Investigations, including equipment and analysis of sewage.	6,000 00	7,000 00
	Contingencies........................	500 00	700 00
	Temporary services....................	600 00	....
	Assistant Bacteriologist	....	600 00
	" Chemist	....	600 00
	Messenger for Laboratory	....	300 00
	Tuberculosis Exhibit..................	....	1,000 00
	Outbreaks of communicable diseases and sanitary investigations	....	5,000 00
	Neglected Children's Branch—		
	Superintendent and Inspector	2,100 00	2,200 00
	Inspector............................	1,200 00	1,200 00
	Clerk and Stenographer...............	600 00	....
	Stenographer.........................	....	600 00
	Clerk................................	450 00	500 00
	Children's Caretaker (from Children's Aid Work)	600 00	600 00
	Special literature.....................	200 00	500 00
	Children's Visitor.....................	750 00	750 00
	Travelling expenses and contingencies....	2,400 00	2,600 00
	Temporary Assistance	....	400 00
		116,685 00	145,670 00
10	**Department of Agriculture.**		
	Minister..............................	4,000 00	4,000 00
	Deputy Minister and Secretary of Bureau of Industries..........................	3,000 00	3,000 00
	Assistant Secretary	1,800 00	....
	Chief Clerk and Statistician.............	1,750 00	1,800 00
	First Class Clerk and Minister's Secretary....	1,600 00	1,600 00
	Second Class Clerk.......................	1,200 00	1,250 00
	do	1,200 00	1,250 00
	do Municipal Statistics.......	1,200 00	1,250 00
	do	1,200 00	1,250 00
	do	1,200 00	1,250 00
	do	1,050 00	1,100 00
	do	....	950 00
	do Accountant transferred from Agriculture.............	1,200 00	....

I. CIVIL GOVERNMENT.—*Concluded.*

No. of Vote.	SERVICE.	Salaries and Expenses.	
		1906	**1907**
10	**Department of Agriculture.**—*Con.*		
	Accountant and Secretary of Fruit Growers' and Beekeepers' Associations	....	1,600 00
	Junior Second Class Clerk..................	700 00	750 00
	do do	700 00	750 00
	do do	....	624 00
	do do	....	520 00
	Messenger	600 00	600 00
	Junior Messenger..........................	260 00	312 00
	Stenographer	468 00	520 00
	Contingencies............................	2,000 00	1,500 00
	Colonization and Forestry—		
	Director...............................	2,000 00	2,100 00
	Forester...	1,700 00	....
	Clerk.................................	1,000 00	1,000 00
	do	800 00	850 00
	do (9 months in 1906)	600 00	850 00
	do at Station......................	1,000 00	1,100 00
	Clerk and Stenographer................	600 00	600 00
	Contingencies	3,000 00	5,000 00
	Factory Inspection Branch—		
	Inspector	1,150 00	1,200 00
	do	1,150 00	1,200 00
	do	1,100 00	1,200 00
	do	1,100 00	1,200 00
	Female Inspector......................	700 00	750 00
	do do	650 00	700 00
	Clerk and Stenographer................	550 00	600 00
	Contingencies	4,500 00	5,500 00
		46,728 00	49,726 00
11	**Miscellaneous.**		
	King's Printer's Office :		
	King's Printer.......................	1,600 00	1,600 00
	Assistant King's Printer...............	1,100 00	1,150 00
	Chief Clerk	1,000 00	1,050 00
	Clerk	900 00	950 00
	Contingencies, including stationery, postage, etc............................	200 00	250 00
	Cost of Official Gazette....................	6,000 00	6,000 00
	Inspector of Registry Offices...............	1,750 00	1,750 00
	do do Travelling and other expenses........	500 00	500 00
	Municipal Auditor.........................	2,100 00	2,100 00
	do · Travelling and other expenses	600 00	600 00
		15,750 00	15,950 00
	Total Civil Government.........	428,330 00	530,982 00

II. LEGISLATION.

Amount to be voted, $224,500 00.

No. of Vote.	SERVICE	Salaries and Expenses.	
12	**II. Legislation.**	1906.	**1907**
	Mr. Speaker's salary......................	2,500 00	2,500 00
	Clerk of the House.......................	2,000 00	2,000 00
	Clerk Assistant and Clerk of Routine	1,800 00	1,800 00
	Sergeant-at-arms	1,400 00	1,500 00
	Law Clerk...............................	1,500 00	1,500 00
	do Assistant.......................	1,500 00	1,500 00
	Stenographer	600 00	600 00
	Postmaster	. 1,500 00	1,500 00
	Assistant Postmaster.....................	950 00	1,000 00
	Clerk	....	800 00
	Librarian	2.000 00	2,00υ 00
	Assistant Librarian	1,100 00	1,100 00
	do for annex...............	650 00	700 00
	Messenger—Assistant in Library (transferred from Mtce. and Repairs of Public Buildings)	....	700 00
	Archivist	1,500 00	1,700 00
	Clerk to Archivist........................	800 00	850 00
	Archives—Stenographer	550 00	550 00
	Accountant of the House (also King's Printer).	400 00	400 00
	Housekeeper and Chief Messenger...........	1,000 00	1,100 00
	Assistant Housekeeper	900 00	900 00
	House Messengers (4).....................	2,400 00	2,400 00
	Clerks of Committees, Secretaries of the Speaker and Leader of the Opposition	5,500 00	5,500 00
	Sessional Writers, Messengers, Elevator Men and Pages............................	17,000 00	17,000 00
	Postage and Cost of House Post Office.......	1,800 00	1,900 00
	Carriage of Mail..........................	500 00	.500 00
	Stationery, including printing paper, printing and binding	50,000 00	55,000 00
	Printing Bills and distributing Statutes.......	3,000 00	4,000 00
	Library, for books and binding, etc..........	4,000 00	4,000 00
	Indemnity, to members including mileage.....	101,000 00	102,000 00
	Subscription to newspapers and periodicals....	1,000 00	1,000 00
	Contingencies	4,500 00	4,500 00
	Documents, Binding and contingencies, Bureau of Archives...........................	1,500 00	2,000 00
		214,850 00	224,500 00

III. ADMINISTRATION OF JUSTICE.

Amount to be voted, $612,394 29.

No. of Vote.	SERVICE.	Salaries and Expenses	
	III. Administration of Justice.	1906.	**1907**
13	Salaries and Expenses.............	162,288 83	176,742 46
14	Miscellaneous...........................	283,860 00	304,958 50
15	Administration of Justice in Districts.........	118,696 10	130,693 33
		564,844 93	612,394 29
13	**Salaries and Expenses.**		
	Supreme Court of Judicature—		
	Allowance to Judges under R.S.O. cap. 52.	17,000 00	17,000 00
	Registrar Supreme Court and Court of Appeal..............................	2,000 00	2,100 00
	Contingencies, printing, etc.............	75 00	75 00
	Master-in-Chambers	3,200 00	3,300 00
	Clerk...............................	1,850 00	1,950 00
	Assistant Clerk........................	1,100 00	1,200 00
	Entering Clerk........................	700 00	700 00
	Contingencies........................	400 00	500 00
	Master-in-Ordinary	4,000 00	4,000 00
	Chief Clerk and Accountant.............	2,000 00	2,000 00
	Clerk and Stenographer...............	1,300 00	1,400 00
	Contingencies........................	200 00	200 00
	Senior Taxing Officer..................	2,200 00	2,300 00
	Junior do.	1,800 00	1,850 00
	Contingencees	....	50 00
	Judges' Library	700 00	700 00
	Copies Holmstead & Langton's Judicature Act for Judges...............	244 80	14 40
	Court of Appeal—		
	Assistant Registrar and Clerk of Election Court......................	1,500 00	1,500 00
	Usher and Messenger...............	800 00	850 00
	Contingencies........................	1,050 00	1,050 00
	Secretary to Judges...................	900 00	950 00
	High Court—		
	Clerk of the Process..................	1,400 00	1,400 00
	Printing Writs, Forms, etc.............	300 00	300 00
	Contingencies........................	50 00	50 00
	Clerk of Assize.......................	1,400 00	1,500 00
	Contingencies	50 00	50 00
	Central Office—		
	Clerk of the Crown...................	2,500 00	2,500 00
	Clerk of Records and Writs.............	1,550 00	1,700 00
	Judgment Clerk.................	1,150 00	1,250 00

2 E.

III. ADMINISTRATION OF JUSTICE.—*Continued.*

No. of Vote.	SERVICE.	Salaries and Expenses.	
		1906	**1907**
13	**Salaries and Expenses**—*Con.*		
	Central Office—Con.		
	Clerk..............................	1,100 00	1,100 00
	do	1,100 00	1,200 00
	do	900 00	1,000 00
	do	750 00	850 00
	do	900 00	1,000 00
	do	850 00	900 00
	Messenger........................	400 00	500 00
	Housekeeper and Messenger...........	700 00	800 00
	Two assistants....................	744 00	....
	Assistant Housekeeper		650 00
	Assistance		264 00
	Messenger.........................	650 00	650 00
	Housekeeper.......................	400 00	400 00
	Assistant Housekeeper.............	400 00	400 00
	do allowance for artificial feet	150 00	....
	Contingencies.....................	1,400 00	1,400 00
	Registrar's Office—		
	Senior Registrar and Referee of Titles....	3,000 00	3,000 00
	Junior Registrar.....................	2,200 00	2,200 00
	Clerk..............................	1,200 00	1,300 00
	do of Non Jury Sittings...............	1,500 00	1,600 00
	Usher and Stenographer to Judges.......	900 00	900 00
	do and Stenographer...............	900 00	900 00
	do and Stenographer...............	700 00	700 00
	Contingencies	800 00	1,100 00
	Weekly Court—		
	Registrar and Clerk of Weekly Court (exclusive of $400 paid from surplus interest lund)	1,600 00	1,600 00
	Contingencies.......................	50 00	50 00
	Exchequer Division—		
	Usher and Stenographer................	750 00	800 00
	Surrogate Court, Surrogate Judges, Local Masters, etc.		
	Surrogate Clerk......................	2,000 00	2,000 00
	Clerk	800 00	900 00
	Stenographer, part time................	225 00	250 00
	Contingencies..	250 00	250 00
	Commutations of Fees—		
	Judges of Surrogate..................	15,351 00	17,913 66
	Local Masters.......................	9,752 00	9,752 00

III. ADMINISTRATION OF JUSTICE.—*Continued.*

No. of Vote.	SERVICE.	Salaries and Expenses.	

13	**Salaries and Expenses**—*Con.*	1906	**1907**
	Commutations of Fees—Con.		
	Allowance to Crown Attorney, Toronto, (63 Vic., chap. 17).................	3,500 00	3,500 00
	Allowance to District Judges under 6 Edward VII., Cap. 19, Sec. 16.....	....	4,500 00
	Inspection of Legal Offices—		
	Inspector...........................	2,200 00	2,350 00
	Clerk and Stenographer...............	1,300 00	1,350 00
	Travelling and other expenses..........	700 00	700 00
	Inspection of Division Courts—		
	Inspector...........................	1,800 00	1,800 00
	Assistant Inspector	1,400 00	1,500 00
	Clerk	1,050 00	1,150 00
	do	750 00	900 00
	Travelling expenses and contingencies....	1,400 00	1,800 00
	Land Titles Office—		
	Master of Titles, Toronto..............	3,000 00	3,000 00
	do (Inspector other L.T. Offices)	500 00	500 00
	Chief Clerk..........................	1,100 00	1,200 00
	Clerk...............................	900 00	950 00
	do	800 00	850 00
	do	350 00	650 00
	Registration and Index Books...........	150 00	150 00
	Stationery, contingencies and occasional assistance	100 00	700 00
	Shelves and fittings	200 00	400 00
	Travelling expenses (Inspector)..........	200 00	200 00
	Master at Sault Ste. Marie..............	546 60	606 00
	do Parry Sound..................	649 50	731 40
	do Bracebridge..................	427 10	360 40
	do Port Arthur...	160 50	309 00
	do North Bay	1,118 30	1,687 00
	do Kenora......................	306 05	361 80
	do Gore Bay....................	100 00	100 00
	do Fort Frances.................	448 98	427 80
	Registry and Index books..............	400 00	400 00
	Forms and other contingencies..........	600 00	800 00
	Rent of office at Sault Ste. Marie for Local Master (with heating)..............	250 00	250 00
	Fittings for safe of Local Master at Parry Sound...........................	540 00	540 00
	Fittings for safe of Local Master at Sault Ste. Marie............	400 00	....
	Light and Attendance..................	....	300 00

III. ADMINISTRATION OF JUSTICE.—*Continued.*

No. of Vote.	SERVICE.	Salaries and Expenses.	
		1906	**1907**
13	**Salaries and Expenses.**—*Concluded.*		
	Drainage Trials Act—		
	Salary of Referee......................	3,500 00	3,500 00
	Additional Drainage Referee (6 months in 1906)	1,250 00	2,500 00
	Stenographer	900 00	900 00
	do.		600 00
	Contingencies....	600 00	600 00
	Deputy Clerks of the Crown................	17,550 00	17,550 00
	do do as Local Registrars....	7,300 00	7,300 00
		162,288 83	176,742 46
14	**Miscellaneous.**		
	Crown Counsel prosecutions..............	11,000 00	12,000 00
	General Administration of Criminal Justice in Counties.......................	180,000 00	195,000 00
	Inspectors of Criminal Investigation, salaries	5,000 00	5,000 00
	" Accident Insurance policies....	105 00	105 00
	Special Services.......................	2,000 00	2,000 00
	To pay Sheriffs, Criers and Constables in attending Courts of Assize, County Courts, Deputy Clerks of the Crown and Pleas attending Assizes, and their postages, etc.....................	11,000 00	13,000 00
	Seals and other contingencies	300 00	300 00
	Litigation of constitutional and other questions......................	6,000 00	6,000 00
	For Revision of Statutes, including payment of Officers of Civil Service and others in connection therewith (notwithstanding anything to the contrary in the Public Service Act)................	30,000 00	30,000 00
	Expenses of County Judges in grouped counties..........................	1,200 00	1,200 00
	Judges' travelling expenses *re* Ditches and Water Courses Act.................	500 00	500 00
	Shorthand Reporters at the Assizes and Election Courts....................	14,800 00	14,800 00
	Shorthand Reporters at the Assizes and Election Courts, Contingencies.......	1,200 00	1,200 00
	Typewriter for Court Reporter............	....	98 50
	County Law Libraries (Circuit and County Judges)...........................	1,200 00	1,200 00
	Expenses incident to weekly court at London and Ottawa................	100 00	100 00

III. ADMINISTRATION OF JUSTICE.—*Continued.*

No. of Vote.	SERVICE.	Salaries and Expenses.	
14	**Miscellaneous.**—*Concluded.*		
	Osgoode Hall Maintenance—		
	Fuel and light..........................	5,000 00	5,000 00
	Salaries of Engineer, Fireman and Care-taker.............................	1,880 00	1,880 00
	Water	2,500 00	2,500 00
	Furniture and incidentals..............	1,500 00	1,500 00
	Fittings for vaults and offices (part revote)	2,500 00	2,800 00
	Appliances for fire protection, hose, etc....	1,300 00	500 00
	General repairs, drains, etc..............	1,600 00	1,600 00
	Painting walls, etc., ...	1,100 00	1,000 00
	Repairs to Main Entrances and Stone work	700 00	....
	Exterior Repairs, (including repairs to stone-work, outside painting, plaster work and roof at gables...................	....	2,500 00
	Telephones............................	400 00	400 00
	Grant towards expenses of Telephone and Telegraph Service	175 00	175 00
	To renew roof of Boiler House...........	800 00	....
	Two Steam Heating Boilers and Connections	....	2,600 00
		283,860 00	304,958 50
15	**Administration of Justice in Districts.**		
	District of Algoma—		
	Sheriff's salary.........................	1,400 00	1,400 00
	Clerk of the Peace and District Attorney...	400 00	400 00
	Clerk of the District Court..............	600 00	600 00
	Magistrate at Sudbury..................	1,000 00	1,000 00
	Arrears of salary, late Police Magistrate, Sault Ste. Marie....................	266 00	....
	Magistrate at Thessalon.................	1,000 00	1,000 00
	Travelling expenses of Police Magistrate..	300 00	300 00
	Administration of Justice, etc............	9,260 00	9,260 00
	Salaries of Lock-up Keepers, Matrons, Turnkeys, Surgeons	2,300 00	2,350 00
	Fuel for Gaol and Lock-ups	525 00	625 00
	Lighting and Water....................	250 00	150 00
	General maintenance, gaol clothing, gro-ceries, etc.	2,400 00	1,500 00
		19,701 00	18,585 00
	District of Thunder Bay—		
	Sheriff's Salary	1,000 00	1,000 00
	House, fuel and light	250 00	250 00
	Clerk of the District Court..............	450 00	450 00
	Chief Constable.......................	400 00	400 00
	Police Magistrate at Fort William and West, including expenses	1,000 00	1,000 00

III. ADMINISTRATION OF JUSTICE.—*Continued.*

No. of Vote.	SERVICE.	Salaries and Expenses.	
		1906	**1907**
15	**Administration of Justice**—*Continued.*		
	District of Thunder Bay—Concluded.		
	Police Magistrate at Port Arthur and East including expenses	1,000 00	1,000 00
	Police Magistrate for certain portions of Districts of Thunder Bay and Rainy River (salary and expenses)	....	1,300 00
	do arrears of salary 1906.	....	433 33
	Clerk of the Peace and District Attorney ..	250 00	250 00
	Administration of Justice, etc.	4,600 00	8,000 00
	Salaries of Lock-up Keepers, Matrons, Turnkeys, Surgeons................	2,000 00	2,200 00
	Fuel for gaol and lock-ups	600 00	600 00
	Lighting and water....................	100 00	100 00
	General maintenance, gaol clothing, groceries, etc.........................	1,000 00	1,500 00
		12,650 00	18,483 33
	District of Rainy River—		
	Sheriff's Salary	1,000 00	1,000 00
	Registrar and Clerk of District Court.....	700 00	700 00
	Clerk of the Peace and District Attorney...	250 00	250 00
	Police Magistrate	750 00	750 00
	Police Magistrate, Town of Rainy River ..	600 00	600 00
	Arrears of Salary, late Police Magistrate, Town of Rainy River..............	900 00	....
	Police Magistrate at Fort Frances (formerly paid out of Administration of Justice)..	400 00	400 00
	Police Magistrate for Mining Districts	1,000 00	1,000 00
	Travelling Expenses..................	300 00	300 00
	Administration of Justice...............	5,700 00	6,000 00
	Salaries for Lock-up Keepers, Matrons, Turnkeys and Surgeons.............	2,800 00	2,650 00
	Fuel for gaol and lock-ups	550 00	575 00
	Lighting and Water...................	150 00	150 00
	General maintenance, gaol clothing, groceries, etc.........................	800 00	800 00
		15,900 00	15,175 00
	District of Nipissing—		
	Sheriff's Salary	750 00	750 00
	Clerk of the Peace and District Attorney..	250 00	250 00
	Clerk of the District Court	450 00	450 00
	Administration of Justice, etc.	6,400 00	10,000 00
	Salaries of Lock-up Keepers, Matrons, Turnkeys and Surgeons.............	3,350 00	3,350 00
	Fuel for gaols and lock-ups	1,200 00	1,500 00
	Lighting and water....................	250 00	300 00

III. ADMINISTRATION OF JUSTICE.—*Continued.*

No. of Vote.	SERVICE.	Salaries and Expenses.	
15	**Administration of Justice**—*Continued.*	1906	**1907**
	District of Nipissing—Concluded.		
	General maintenance, gaol clothing, groceries, etc............................	2,800 00	3,500 00
	Salary and expenses of Special Constable..	1,200 00	1,200 00
	Additional Constables...................	5,200 00	5,200 00
	Police Magistrate, Temiskaming Railway and settlements	750 00	750 00
	do to cover travelling expenses	350 00	350 00
		22,950 00	27,600 00
	District of Muskoka—		
	Sheriff's salary	500 00	500 00
	Clerk of the Peace and District Attorney..	250 00	250 00
	Clerk of the District Court..............	450 00	450 00
	Police Magistrate's salary and travelling expenses........	500 00	500 00
	Administration of Justice	5,675 00	6,675 00
	Salaries of Lock-up Keepers, Matrons, Turnkeys and Surgeons.............	750 00	750 00
	Fuel for gaol and lock-ups	150 00	200 00
	Lighting and water....................	75 00	75 00
	General maintenance, gaol clothing, groceries, etc....	300 00	500 00
		8,650 00	9,900 00
	District of Parry Sound—		
	Sheriff's Salary	500 00	500 00
	Police Magistrate	600 00	600 00
	Police Magistrate	250 00	250 00
	Clerk of the Peace and District Attorney ..	250 00	250 00
	Clerk of the District Court	450 00	450 00
	Constable at Depot Harbor ($200 formerly paid out of vote for Administration of Justice...........................	400 00	400 00
	Administration of Justice	8,000 00	8,500 00
	Salaries of Lock-up Keepers, Matrons, Turnkeys and Surgeons.............	1,500 00	2,000 00
	Fuel for gaols and lock-ups..............	500 00	600 00
	Lighting and water	100 00	150 00
	General maintenance, gaol clothing, groceries, etc..........................	600 00	1,000 00
		13,150 00	14,700 00
	District of Manitoulin—		
	Sheriff............................	500 00	500 00
	Clerk of the Peace and District Attorney ..	250 00	250 00
	Salary of Registrar of Deeds and Master of Titles..............................	600 00	600 00

III. ADMINISTRATION OF JUSTICE.—*Concluded.*

No. of Vote.	SERVICE.	Salaries and Expenses.	
		1906	**1907**
15	**Administration of Justice.**—*Concluded.*		
	District of Manitoulin.—Con.		
	Salary of Clerk of District Court and Surrogate Court	450 00	550 00
		30 10	....
	do Arrears of Salary, 1905	1,000 00	1,000 00
	Stipendiary Magistrate..................	5,400 00	6,000 00
	Administration of Justice		
	Salaries of Lock-up Keepers, Matrons, Turnkeys and Surgeons............	700 00	750 00
		400 00	400 00
	Constable	150 00	150 00
	Constable, Nairn Centre	200 00	200 00
	Fuel for gaol and lock-ups	25 00	25 00
	Lighting and water....................		
	General maintenance, gaol clothing, groceries, etc..........................	250 00	300 00
		9,955 10	10,725 00
	Provisional County of Haliburton—		
	Police Magistrate for Haliburton and points north, including expenses	800 00	800 00
	Junior Judge, in lieu of travelling expenses holding Courts	400 00	400 00
	Registrar of Deeds....................	200 00	200 00
	Administration of Justice	250 00	250 00
		1,650 00	1,650 00
	Provincial Police on Niagara and Detroit Rivers, etc.		
	Police Magistrate, Bridgeburg and Fort Erie	500 00	500 00
	Arrears of Salary, late Police Magistrate, Bridgeburg.....................	475 00	....
	Administration of Justice...............	9,415 00	9,475 00
	Administration of Justice—Detroit River ..	3,500 00	3,500 00
	Provincial Constable at Goderich (six months in 1906)..................	200 00	400 00
		14,090 00	13,875 00
	Total Administration of Justice..........	564,844 93	612,394 29

IV. EDUCATION.

Amount to be voted, $1,396,266 27.

16	Public and Separate School Education........	629,167 59	896,667 45
17	High School and Collegiate Institutes........	152,175 00	155,593 75
18	Departmental Library and Museum	15,550 00	18,518 95
19	School of Practical Science	87,347 00	....

IV. EDUCATION.—Continued.

No. of Vote.	SERVICE.	Salaries and Expenses.	
		1906.	**1907**
	Education—Continued.		
20	Public Libraries, Art Schools, Literary and Scientific	61,050 00	60,500 00
21	Technical Education	31,620 00	31,620 00
22	Superannuated Public and High School Teachers	63,300 00	63,650 00
23	Provincial University and Mining Schools.....	221,352 23	50,707 40
24	Maintenance Education Department and Miscellaneous	25,286 72	24,736 72
25	Institution for the Deaf and Dumb, Belleville..	56,918 00	56,056 00
26	Blind Institute, Brantford..................	37,690 10	38,216 00
		1,381,456 64	1,396,266 27
16	**Public and Separate School Education (Details).**		
	Aid from Municipalities Fund, to be added to Public and Separate School grant (50 Vic. c. 5).....	1,610 59	2,932 45
	Public and Separate Schools, old districts.....	240,000 00	....
	Rural Public and Separate Schools (Counties), grants and equipment..................	....	380,000 00
	Urban Public and Separate Schools (Counties and Districts).....................	....	120,000 00
	Public and Separate Schools, new districts (including Poor Schools)...............	77,000 00	....
	Special Grant Public and Separate Rural Schools, Counties	60,000 00	....
	Public and Separate Schools, new Districts ...	....	50,000 00
	Assisted Public and Separate Schools, new Districts	....	35,000 00
	Assisted Public and Separate Schools, Counties	....	25,000 00
	Military Instruction Public School Cadet Corps	300 00	750 00
	Kindergarten Schools	3,500 00	5,000 00
	Night Schools............................	250 00	300 00
	Instruction in Agriculture and Horticulture in grouped rural schools, and aid to grouped rural schools........................	2,000 00	2,000 00
	Continuation Classes......................	22,000 00	....
	do do (for libraries and scientific equipment)	10,000 00	....
	Continuation Classes, ordinary grants and equipment......................	....	40,000 00
	Model Schools (including reference books and special grants)	11,000 00	11,000 00
	French-English Training Schools	2,000 00	2,000 00
	Teachers' Associations, including grant to Ontario Provincial Association, $1,000.00....	3,000 00	3,250 00

IV. EDUCATION.—*Continued.*

No. of Vote.	SERVICE.	Salaries and Expenses.	
16	Public and Separate School Education—*Con.*	1906	**1907**
	Paper, postage, printing, stationery and incidentals for above services...............	....	1,500 00
	Inspection of Public and District Schools.....	65,000 00	67,500 00
	Inspection of Continuation Classes (4 mos., 1906)	667 00	2,000 00
	Inspection of Separate Schools..............	5,700 00	5,700 00
	Inspection of Bilingual Schools..............	2,900 00	3,400 00
	Inspection of Normal and Model Schools	2,000 00	2,000 00
	Inspection of Technical Schools (from Technical Education)	1,900 00	1,900 00
	Travelling expenses, Inspectors	4,000 00	4,000 00
	Stationery, postage, printing, binding and incidentals	1,500 00	2,000 00
	Examiners for Departmental Examinations, including travelling expenses...........	21,000 00	25,500 00
	Paper, postage and supplies for Examiners and Assistants	3,050 00	3,050 00
	Assistants in connection with Departmental Examinations.........................	....	2,000 00
	Registrar Education Department	2,000 00	2,000 00
	Clerk and Secretary Board of Examiners	1,750 00	1,750 00
	Clerk of Examinations	1,100 00	1,100 00
	Assistant Clerk of Examinations............	1,000 00	1,000 00
	Printer.................................	1,000 00	1,000 00
	Electric Motor for Printing Office...........	....	125 00
	Expenses Advisory Council, including travelling expenses, allowances to members, printing, postage, papers, books, stationery and incidentals	....	5,000 00
	Lectures on special subjects at Normal Schools, including arrears and car fare of students to attend Nature Study classes	....	450 00
	Normal and Model Schools, Toronto. Details (a)..................................	32,595 00	35,835 00
	Normal and Model Schools, Ottawa. Details(b)	32,545 00	34,475 00
	Normal and Model Schools, London. Details (c)	16,800 00	16,150 00
		629,167 59	896,667 45
	(a) Normal and Model Schools, Toronto.		
	The Principal	2,600 00	2,700 00
	The Vice-Principal.......................	2,100 00	2,200 00
	Drawing Master.........................	1,200 00	1,280 00
	French Master	300 00	300 00
	Music Master	1,050 00	1,150 00
	Head Master of Model School..............	1,800 00	1,880 00
	Assistants, Boys' Model School (4)..........	4,675 00	5,030 00
	Head Mistress of Girls' Model School	1,100 00	1,200 00

IV. EDUCATION.—*Continued.*

No. of Vote.	SERVICE.	Salaries and Expenses.	
		1906	**1907**
16	**Public and Separate School Education**—*Con.*		
	Four Assistants of Girls' Model School	3,500 00	3,670 00
	Pianist....................................	150 00	170 00
	Drill Master	250 00	270 00
	Instructor in Calisthenics for Girls' Model School	550 00	550 00
	Instructor in Sewing......................	550 00	550 00
	Instructor in Reading	500 00	500 00
	Director of Kindergarten	1,100 00	1,200 00
	Assistant Director of Kindergarten..........	650 00	750 00
	Instructor of Manual Training..............	1,200 00	1,300 00
	Clerk and Stenographer	500 00	550 00
	Instructor of Household Science............	750 00	840 00
	Head Gardener...........................	650 00	700 00
	Assistant Gardener.......................	500 00	550 00
	Engineer (part year 1906).................	250 00	....
	Engineer	550 00	....
	Fireman and Watchman....................	....	700 00
	Fireman..................................	....	550 00
	Laborers on grounds......................	1,000 00	1,500 00
	Janitors of Normal School (including cleaning,(2)	950 00	950 00
	Janitor of Boys' Model School (including cleaning).................................	525 00	600 00
	Janitor of Girls' Model School (including cleaning).................................	400 00	400 00
	Reference books and pictures...............	200 00	200 00
	Stationery, apparatus, chemicals and contingencies.............................	1,350 00	1,350 00
	Text and blank Books, etc., for Model School pupils..............................	500 00	500 00
	Supplies for Kindergarten.................	150 00	150 00
	Domestic and Sanitary Science and Manual Training supplies......................	1,000 00	800 00
	Annual Grant in aid of Boys' and Girls' Model School Games......................	45 00	45 00
	Apparatus and supplies, chemical and physical, for new laboratory	....	750 00
		32,595 00	35,835 00
	(b) Normal and Model Schools, Ottawa.		
	The Principal	2,500 00	2,600 00
	Vice-Principal............................	2,100 00	2,200 00
	Drawing Master	1,100 00	1,200 00
	French Master	650 00	650 00
	Music Master............................	1,050 00	1,150 00
	Drill Instructor..........................	200 00	220 00
	Head Master of Boys' Model School	1,700 00	1,800 00
	Three Assistants of Boys' Model School.......	3,150 00	3,450 00
	Head Mistress of Girls' Model School........	1,100 00	1,200 00

IV. EDUCATION.—*Continued.*

No. of Vote.	SERVICE.	Salaries and Expenses.	
16	**Public and Separate School Education**—*Con.*	1906.	**1907**
	(b) Normal and Model Schools, Ottawa.—*Con.*		
	Three Assistants of Girls' Model School	2,250 00	2,520 00
	Instructor of Calisthenics for Girls' Model School	800 00	800 00
	Director of Kindergarten....................	1,100 00	1,200 00
	Assistant Director of Kindergarten	550 00	750 00
	Instructor of Manual Training..............	1,100 00	1,200 00
	Instructor of Household Science	800 00	840 00
	Secretary and Librarian	450 00	450 00
	First Engineer and Gardener...............	700 00	700 00
	Second Engineer and Gardener.............	550 00	550 00
	Laborer on Grounds	400 00	400 00
	Janitor Normal School (including cleaning)....	500 00	500 00
	Caretaker	760 00	760 00
	Nightwatchman and fireman...............	500 00	500 00
	Reference Books and pictures	400 00	400 00
	Stationery, apparatus, chemicals and supplies.	900 00	1,200 00
	Text books for Model School pupils.........	500 00	500 00
	Library and Supplementary reading books....	150 00	150 00
	Supplies for Kindergarten	150 00	150 00
	Domestic and Sanitary Science supplies......	200 00	200 00
	Manual training..........................	200 00	200 00
	School decorations	150 00	150 00
	Lantern slides...........	100 00	100 00
	Equipment science teaching................	150 00	150 00
	Annual Grant in aid of Boys' and Girls' Model School Games	35 00	35 00
	Maintenance.		
	Expenses of grounds......................	400 00	400 00
	Fuel and light...........................	2,800 00	2,800 00
	Water	600 00	600 00
	Furniture, incidentals, snow-cleaning, etc.....	1,800 00	1,800 00
		32,545 00	34,475 00
	(c) Normal and Model Schools, London.		
	The Principal	2,600 00	2,700 00
	The Vice-Principal........................	2,100 00	2,200 00
	Drawing and Writing Master..............	275 00	275 00
	Music Master............................	275 00	275 00
	Kindergarten Teacher.....................	125 00	125 00
	Drill, Gymnastics and Calisthenics	175 00	175 00
	Instructor Manual Training................	1,100 00	1,200 00
	Instructor Household Science	400 00	400 00
	Stenographer and Clerk	500 00	550 00

IV. EDUCATION.—*Continued.*

No. of Vote.	SERVICE.	Salaries and Expenses.	
		1906	**1907**
16	**Public and Separate School Education**—*Con.*		
	(c) Normal and Model Schools, London—*Con.*		
	Engineer	650 00	650 00
	Caretaker	450 00	450 00
	Gardener	550 00	550 00
	Stationery, apparatus, chemicals, incidentals and supplies..........................	1,200 00	1,200 00
	Reference books and pictures	400 00	400 00
	Payment to London School Board	1,500 00	1,500 00
	Supplies for Manual Training, Sanitary and Domestic Science	500 00	500 00
	Maintenance.		
	Fuel, light, etc.	2,000 00	1,000 00
	Water	500 00	500 00
	Furniture, incidentals, etc.	500 00	500 00
	Expenses of grounds, trees, etc.............	500 00	500 00
	Scrubbing, cleaning, cartage, etc...........	500 00	500 00
		16,800 00	16,150 00
17	**High Schools and Collegiate Institutes.**		
	High Schools and Collegiate Institutes, including districts	115,000 00	128,500 00
	Military instruction, High School Cadet corps and expenses re sub-target guns and arrears	2,500 00	2,500 00
	Purchase of sub-targets for Cadet Corps under contract of 1904 (re-vote)...............	12,500 00	....
	Two Inspectors of High Schools............	5,700 00	6,000 00
	Travelling Expenses	1,000 00	1,000 00
	Stationery, postage and incidentals	800 00	800 00
	Principal Ontario Normal College...........	3,000 00	....
	Vice-Principal, including $500.00 arrears 1905 and $500.00 January to June 1906, as Acting Principal	1,500 00	....
	Vice-Principal Normal College, 9 months $375, as Acting Principal for school year 1906-7, $1,000.00	....	1,375 00
	Instructor Manual Training (9 months).......	1,100 00	825 00
	Instructor Household Science (9 months)......	650 00	281 25
	Clerical Services (9 months)................	450 00	337 50
	Printing and examinations..................	300 00	....
	Printing, stationery, postage and incidentals ..	....	300 00
	Manual Training, Sanitary and Domestic Science supplies...............................	800 00	500 00
	Grant to Normal College (Hamilton Board of Education (9 months)...................	4,500 00	3,375 00

IV. EDUCATION.—*Continued.*

of Vote.	SERVICE.	Salaries and Expenses.	
17	**High Schools and Collegiate Institutes.**—*Con.*	1906	**1907**
	Contingencies and Library, including grants to Students' Societies	350 00	300 00
	For special services of Hamilton Collegiate Institute, masters as lecturers in Normal College 1905 and 1906, partly arrears	2,000 00	....
	For special services of Hamilton Collegiate Institute masters as lecturers in Normal College 1906 and 1907, partly arrears, and special service of University Professors, Sanitary Science Lecturers, including travelling expenses......................	....	3,500 00
	Grant to Literary Society of the Ontario Normal College.........................	25 00	....
	Agricultural training in High Schools.........	....	6,000 00
		152,175 00	155,593 75
18	**Departmental Library and Museum.**		
	Historiographer	2,200 00	2,200 00
	Librarian	1,600 00	1,600 00
	" arrears, 1905.......................	300 00	....
	Superintendent of Museum	1,600 00	1,600 00
	Clerk	900 00	900 00
	Clerk in Museum...........................	1,000 00	1,000 00
	Stenographer	500 00	500 00
	Postage and stationery	100 00	200 00
	Incidentals and purchases..................	600 00	600 00
	Binding and repairing books, pamphlets and periodicals............................	200 00	300 00
	Educational and technical books for reference..	800 00	800 00
	Binding pamphlets, Library	100 00	....
	Subscriptions to newspapers...............	....	400 00
	Expenses of Archæological researches, purchase of collections, pictures, busts, cases, paintings, extra services, manuscripts, furnishings, travelling expenses, etc...........	2,500 00	3,000 00
	Natural History collection, and supplies, incidentals and Inspection	500 00	1,500 00
	Services Dr. Brodie arranging collection......	1,000 00	1,000 00
	Assistant to Dr. Brodie	450 00	450 00
	Catalogue for Museum	500 00	500 00
	Guard in Museum..........................	700 00	700 00
	Paper, printing, labels and sundries..........	....	500 00
	Unpaid accounts 1906....	....	768 95
		15,550 00	18,518 95

IV. EDUCATION.---Continued.

No. of Vote.	SERVICE.	Salaries and Expenses.	
		1006	**1907**
19	**School of Practical Science.**		
	Salaries and Maintenance (transferred to University of Toronto)	87,347 00	....
20	**Public Libraries, Art Schools, Historical, Literary and Scientific Societies.**		
	Superintendent Public Libraries..............	1,700 00	2,000 00
	Clerk do	950 00	1,000 00
	Public Libraries Grants.....................	40,000 00	37,000 00
	Paper, postage, printing, stationery and incidentals................................	....	1,000 00
	Travelling Libraries, cost of books, services and expenses	....	3,000 00
	Ontario Library Association.................	200 00	300 00
	Grant in Aid Reading Camps...............	1,000 00	1,000 00
	Rural school libraries......................	6,000 00	5,000 00
	Art Schools and Art Museum expenses	2,000 00	2,000 00
	Art School, Hamilton	2,000 00	2,000 00
	Ontario Society of Artists.	800 00	800 00
	Canadian Institute, Toronto.................	1,500 00	1,500 00
	Institute Canadien, Ottawa	400 00	400 00
	Ottawa Literary and Scientific Society........	400 00	200 00
	Ottawa Field Naturalist Society	300 00	300 00
	St. Patrick Literary Association	200 00	100 00
	Hamilton Scientific Association.............	400 00	400 00
	Association of Chemical Industry	200 00	200 00
	Astronomical Society, Toronto	600 00	600 00
	Wellington Field Naturalists' Society.........	100 00	100 00
	Ontario Historical Society	600 00	600 00
	Essex Historical Society....................	100 00	100 00
	Women's Wentworth Historical Society (land)	100 00	300 00
	Lundy's Lane Historical Society......	200 00	200 00
	Niagara Historical Society..................	100 00	100 00
	Women's Canadian Historical Society........	100 00	100 00
	Middlesex and London Historical Society	100 00	100 00
	Simcoe Historical Society...................	....	100 00
	Miscellaneous Grants 1906, omitted in 1907...	1,000 00	....
		61,050 00	60,500 00
21	**Technical Education.**		
	Technical Education, including grants, Summer schools, scholarships, equipment, books, stationery, printing and other expenses....	30,000 00	30,000 00
	Toronto Technical High School, arrears 1905..	1,620 00	1,620 00
		31,620 00	31,620 00

IV. EDUCATION.—*Continued.*

No. of Vote.	SERVICE.	Salaries and Expenses.	
		1906	**1907**
22	**Superannuated Teachers.**		
	Annual retiring allowance to Teachers and Inspectors.........................	63,000 00	63,500 00
	Medical examination fees, printing, paper and incidentals.....	300 00	150 00
		63,300 00	63,650 00
23	**Provincial University and Mining Schools.**		
	Agricultural Examination—University Degree B.S.A..............................	425 00	425 00
	Statutory Grant to University (60 Vic., cap. 59)	7,000 00	7,000 00
	Grant from the sale of lands (60 Vic. cap. 59, 5 Edw. VII, cap. 36, 5 Edw. VII, cap. 37...	1,186 06	1,082 40
	University of Toronto (Sec. 16, cap. 41, I Edw. VII.)................................	53,460 67	....
	University of Toronto, estimated deficit.......	70,830 50	....
	do (unpaid deficit 1903-4, re-vote)	600 00	....
	University of Toronto, Collection and Historical Papers..............	150 00	....
	Purchase of Historical Papers for Educational Department	....	200 00
	University of Toronto Domestic Science Dept. Supplementary	700 00	....
	School of Mining, Kingston (Maintenance)....	29,500 00	34,500 00
	do for Equipment	7,500 00	7,500 00
	Medical Faculty of Queen's College for promotion of Medical Education	50,000 00	....
		221,352 23	50,707 40
24	**Maintenance Education Department and Miscellaneous.**		
	Maintenance.		
	Furniture and furnishings..................	700 00	1,000 00
	Scrubbing, cleaning and supplies (Education Dept., and Toronto N. School)..........	600 00	700 00
	Expenses of grounds, including wages of extra laborers and supplies..................	1,200 00	1,500 00
	Painting fences (re-vote $300.00)	400 00	....
	Fuel and light.............................	5,700 00	5,700 00
	Water.....................................	1,000 00	1,000 00
	Repairs, carpentry work (including material, incidentals, etc.)	2,300 00	2,300 00
	Fire appliances............................	150 00	150 00
	Carpenter..................................	650 00	700 00
	Wages of Night Fireman and Watchman	540 00	540 00

IV. EDUCATION.—*Continued.*

24	**Maintenance Education Department and Miscellaneous.**—*Concluded.*	1906	**1907**
	Miscellaneous.		
	For proportion of cost of Minister's Report ...	1,500 00	1,500 00
	High and Public School Registers............	1,500 00	1,500 00
	Purchase of text books by schools...........	1,000 00	1,000 00
	Printing Documentary History of Education ..	2,646 72	2,646 72
	Printing and supplying School Act to Trustees, and contingencies (part re-vote)..........	3,000 00	3,000 00
	Cost of Investigations (special law costs, etc.)..	500 00	500 00
	Legal Services *re* Revision and Consolidation of School Act..........................	1,500 00	1,000 00
	Election Expenses, Advisory Council...........	400 00	....
25		25,286 72	24,736 72
	Institution for the Deaf and Dumb, Belleville, Ontario.		
	◄(226 pupils.)		
	Salaries.		
	Superintendent and Principal (including allowances)...............................	2,500 00	2,000 00
	Physician...............................	600 00	600 00
	Bursar.................................	1,000 00	1,000 00
	Matron and Housekeeper...................	500 00	500 00
	Teachers—Literary Department (14).........	10,450 00	10,450 00
	Instructor Manual Training and Teacher	650 00	450 00
	Teacher Domestic Science	400 00	400 00
	Storekeeper, Clerk and Assistant Supervisor ..	600 00	600 00
	Engineer	650 00	650 00
	Stoker	384 00	384 00
	Farmer and Gardener	450 00	450 00
	Teamster	288 00	300 00
	Baker and Meat Cook.....................	450 00	450 00
	Night Watchman and Stoker...............	384 00	384 00
	Foreman Carpenter and Assistant (2)	800 00	800 00
	Foreman Shoemaker	500 00	500 00
	Printing Instructor	550 00	550 00
	Messenger..............................	264 00	300 00
	Cook	240 00	240 00
	Small Boys' and Girls' Nurses (2)...........	360 00	360 00
	Laundresses, Assistant Cooks, Housemaids, etc. (15)............................	2,448 00	2,448 00
	Supervisor of Boys	500 00	500 00
	Instructress in Sewing and Supervisor of Girls.	350 00	350 00
	Stenographer and Clerk	400 00	400 00
	Trained Nurse	400 00	400 00
	Temporary Assistance.....................	300 00	400 00
	Man on sewage works.....................	365 00	365 C0
		26,783 00	26,231 00

3 E.

IV. EDUCATION.—*Continued.*

25	**Institution for the Deaf and Dumb.**—*Con.*	1906.	**1907**
	Expenses.		
	Medicine and medical comforts	350 00	350 00
	Butchers' meat, fish and fowl................	3,350 00	....
	Flour, bread, etc.............................	1,600 00	....
	Butter and Milk............................	2,600 00	....
	Groceries...................................	2,600 00	....
	Fruit and Vegetables.......................	700 00	....
	Fruit and vegetables, groceries and provisions (including fruit, butter, milk, bread, flour, vegetables, meat, fish, fowl, etc.)	....	11,000 00
	Bedding, clothing and shoes	750 00	750 00
	Lighting............................	1,050 00	1,050 00
	Fuel....,...................................	6,950 00	6,400 00
	Laundry, soap and cleaning	700 00	750 00
	Furniture and furnishings	650 00	700 00
	Farm, feed and fodder.....................	700 00	700 00
	Repairs and alterations, ordinary	900 00	900 00
	Advertising, Stationery, Printing, Postage....	800 00	800 00
	Books, apparatus and appliances	650 00	650 00
	Unenumerated and Miscellaneous...........	1,000 00	1,000 00
	Sewage works, Chemicals, etc	100 00	100 00
	Water supply, under contract.	900 00	900 00
	Repairs to Buildings, Furniture, etc.		
	Adjustable desks...........................	250 00	....
	Cement floor, metal ceiling, fitting up room in basement for boys' play-room, floor in Engineers' workshop, etc...........	300 00	....
	Furniture and furnishings, carpeting in officers' quarters, hot water heater, etc..........	400 00	....
	Furniture and furnishings, extra...............	....	1,050 00
	Bedding, sheeting and towelling.............	....	300 00
	Metal sheeting for eleven school-rooms sitting-rooms, etc..........................	960 00	400 00
	.Maple floor in girls' sitting-room and hallways.	350 00	....
	Lumber for boys to make tables, seats, etc....	325 00	325 00
	Chapel repairs, metal sheeting, painting, decorating and regraining seats..............	450 00	450 00
	Lumber, hardware, plaster, oil, etc., for buildings generally.......................	350 00	350 00
	Wages of extra carpenter, painter, plasterers, etc.................................	400 00	500 00
	Piano for officers' parlor....................	....	400 00
		56,918 00	56,056 00

IV. EDUCATION—*Continued.*

No. of Vote.	SERVICE.	Salaries and Expenses.	
		1906	**1907**
26	**Blind Institution, Brantford.**		
	(111 pupils.)		
	Salaries.		
	Principal (including allowances).............	2,400 00	2,400 00
	Assistant Principal.......................	1,200 00	1,200 00
	Physician	500 00	500 00
	Bursar and Storekeeper (including allowances).	1,100 00	1,200 00
	Matron................................	450 00	450 00
	Teachers (11)............................	4,850 00	5,150 00
	Musical Director	100 00	100 00
	Trades Instructors	900 00	500 00
	Supervisor of Boys	400 00	400 00
	Visitors' Attendant	180 00	180 00
	Carpenter	550 00	550 00
	Engineer................................	600 00	650 00
	Assistant Engineer.......................	475 00	• 475 00
	Fireman in Winter, farm hand in Summer	375 00	400 00
	Farmer and Gardener.....................	500 00	500 00
	Teamster...............................	350 00	350 00
	Porter and Messenger....................	260 00	260 00
	Baker..................................	425 00	450 00
	Cooks (2)..............................	348 00	348 00
	Maids (10)..............................	1,300 00	1,300 00
	Laundresses (3)	508 00	508 00
	Nurses (2)..............................	550 00	550 00
	Night Watchman.........................	375 00	375 00
	Temporary Assistance....................	425 00	400 00
		19,121 00	19,196 00
	Expenses.		
	Medicine and medical comforts.............	200 00	200 00
	Butchers' meat, fish and fowl..............	1,600 00	
	Flour, bread and biscuits..................	600 00	
	Butter and lard..........................	1,100 00	
	General groceries........................	1,400 00	
	Fruits and vegetables.....................	300 00	
	Groceries and provisions, including flour, butter, fruits, vegetables, meat, fish and fowl, etc		5,300 00
	Bedding, clothing and shoes	500 00	500 00
	Fuel	3,800 00	3,800 00
	Electric light and gas.....................	1,200 00	1,200 00
	Laundry, soap and cleaning........	350 00	350 00
	Furniture and Furnishings.................	700 00	700 00
	Farm, feed and fodder	700 00	800 00
	Repairs and alterations...................	1,000 00	1,000 00

IV. EDUCATION.—*Continued.*

No. of Vote.	SERVICE.	Salaries and Expenses.	
26	**Blind Institution, Brantford.**—*Con.*	1906	**1907**
	Advertising, printing, stationery, postage.....	700 00	700 00
	Books, apparatus and appliances............	800 00	1,300 00
	Unenumerated	1,100 00	1,000 00
	Pupils' sittings at the churches.............	200 00	200 00
	Rent and hydrants.......................	160 00	160 00
	Water supply...........................	350 00	350 00
	Repairs to Buildings, Furniture, etc.		
	School desks..:..........................	50 00	....
	Piano and reed organ	500 00	....
	Repairs to pianos and organs..............	500 00	250 00
	Hardwood floors	130 00	165 00
	New Lavatory for Hospital.................	100 00	....
	Hardware...............................	200 00	260 00
	Alteration in heating Principal's residence.....	50 00	....
	Carpets and Furniture, Officers and teachers..	200 00	....
	Sewer...................................	79 10	....
	Library, shelving and metal ceiling..........	....	75 00
	Renewing and painting line fence	....	12b 00
	Workshop...............................	....	250 00
	Laundry, repairs and renewals.............	....	125 00
	Kitchen, steam cooking kettles.............	....	75 00
	Covering for steam pipes	....	50 00
	Relining tanks	....	35 00
	Tools for engineer	....	50 00
		37,690 10	38,216 00
	Total Education.....................	1,381,456 64	1,396,266 27

V. PUBLIC INSTITUTIONS MAINTENANCE.

Amount to be Voted, $1,040,058.50.

27	Asylum for Insane, Brockville	$93,562 00	$98,023 00
28	" Cobourg	26,190 00	25,252 00
29	" Hamilton................	135,511 00	139,530 00
30	Kingston................	94,122 00	100,434 00
31	London	147,159 00	148,100 00
32	Mimico	83,244 00	88,230 00
33	Orillia	75,608 00	76,988 00
34	" Penetanguishene	41,006 00	43,916 00
35	Toronto.................	115,496 00	134,319 50
36	Woodstock..............	28,073 33	28,176 00

V. PUBLIC INSTITUTIONS MAINTENANCE.—*Continued.*

No. of Vote.	SERVICE.	Salaries and Expenses.	
		1906	**1907**
37	Central Prison, Toronto	$71,570 00	$67,420 00
38	" Industries	67,685 00	66,220 00
39	Mercer Reformatory, Toronto	30,050 00	23,450 00
40	Medical Relieving Officer..................	333 33	
		1,009,609 66	1,040,058 50
41	To pay balance 1905 accounts..............	32,841 92	....
27	**Asylum for Insane, Brockville.**		
	(661 patients.)		
	Salaries.		
	Medical Superintendent	2,500 00	2,500 00
	Assistant Superintendent..................	1,400 00	1,400 00
	Assistant Physician	1,000 00	1,000 00
	Bursar	1,500 00	1,500 00
	Storekeeper..............................	950 00	950 00
	Clerk	600 00	600 00
	Stenographer	250 00	250 00
	Matron...................................	500 00	500 00
	Assistant Matron.........................	500 00	300 00
	Cooks (3)................................	648 00	
	Housemaids (4)..........................	516 00	
	Dairymaid...............................	168 00	2,424 00
	Laundresses (3).........................	648 00	
	Seamstress	204 00	
	Tailor....................................	500 00	500 00
	Laundryman	360 00	360 00
	Baker....................................	525 00	525 00
	Butcher	300 00	300 00
	Engineer	650 00	650 00
	Assistant Engineer.......................	450 00	450 00
	Stokers (5)..............................	1,200 00	1,500 00
	Carpenter	550 00	550 00
	Mason and Bricklayer....................	....	600 00
	Painter..................................	....	420 00
	Farmer..................................	675 00	650 00
	Farm Hand..............................	300 00	
	Cowman..................................	240 00	900 00
	Messenger...............................	252 00	
	Gardener	550 00	600 00
	Chief Attendant..........................	400 00	
	Supervisors (6) Male.....................	2,088 00	7,768 00
	Ordinary Male Attendants (16)	4,272 00	
	Night watch (2) Male	576 00	

V. PUBLIC INSTITUTIONS MAINTENANCE.—*Continued.*

No. of Vote.	SERVICE.	Salaries and Expenses.	
27	**Asylum for Insane, Brockville.**—*Continued.*	1906	**1907**
	Salaries—Concluded.		
	Chief Attendant, Female.....................	$ 250 00	
	Supervisors (6) "	1,368 00	
	Ordinary Attendants (1f) Female	2,700 00	$5,326 00
	Night " (2) "	372 00	
	Temporary Assistance.....................	400 00	400 00
		30,362 00	32,923 00
	Expenses.		
	Medicines and Medical Comforts............	900 00	900 00
	Groceries and Provisions (including Flour, Butter, Fruit & Vegetables, Meat, Fish and Fowl)...............................	29,200 00	29,000 00
	Heating and Lighting......	16,000 00	16,000 00
	Clothing.................................	4,500 00	5,000 00
	Laundry, Soap and Cleaning........	1,500 00	1,500 00
	Repairs and Replacements (including Furniture and Furnishings and Bedding)..........	5,000 00	5,000 00
	Office Expenses...........................	800 00	700 00
	Farm Expenses...........................	2,000 00	4,000 00
	Miscellaneous (including Water)......... ..	3,300 00	3,000 00
		93,562 00	98,023 00
28	**Asylum for Female Patients, Cobourg.**		
	(146 patients.)		
	Salaries.		
	Medical Superintendent.....................	$2,100 00	$2,100 00
	Assistant Superintendent....................	720 00	
	Trained Nurse	....	400 00
	Bursar and Storekeeper.....................	1,250 00	1,250 00
	Clerk and Stenographer	600 00	600 00
	Portress.................................	180 00	180 00
	Matron	500 00	500 00
	Cooks (2)..............................	456 00	
	Housemaids (2)...........................	336 00	
	Laundresses (2)...........................	408 00	1,464 00
	Seamstress...............................	216 00	
	Baker...................................	550 00	550 00
	Night watch (1) Male	300 00	300 00
	Engineer.................................	550 00	550 00
	Stokers (2)..............................	900 00	900 00
	Gardener.................................	600 00	600 00

V. PUBLIC INSTITUTIONS MAINTENANCE.—*Continued.*

No. of Vote.	SERVICE.	Salaries and Expenses.	
28	**Asylum for Female Patients, Cobourg.**—*Con.*		
	Salaries—Concluded.		
	Carpenter...............................	$ 600 00	$ 600 00
	Chief Female Attendant.................	216 00	
	Supervisors (3) Female.................	696 00	
	Female Attendants (6)..................	1,044 00	2,158 00
	Night Watch (female)..................	168 00	
	Temporary Assistance..................	200 00	200 00
	Expenses.	12,590 00	12,352 00
	Medicines and Medical Comforts...........	200 00	200 00
	Groceries and Provisions (including Flour, Butter, Fruit, Vegetables, Meat, Fish and Fowl)	6,200 00	6,300 00
	Heating and Lighting....................	3,500 00	3,000 00
	Clothing...............................	600 00	800 00
	Laundry, Soap and Cleaning.............	500 00	450 00
	Repairs and replacements (including Furniture, Furnishings and Bedding)	900 00	600 00
	Office Expenses........................	300 00	250 00
	Farm Expenses.........................	300 00	300 00
	Miscellaneous (including water)...........	1,100 00	1,000 00
		26,190 00	25,252 00
29	**Asylum for the Insane, Hamilton.**		
	(1,083 patients).		
	Salaries.		
	Medical Superintendent	2,600 00	2,600 00
	Assistant Superintendent...............	1,400 00	1,400 00
	Second Assistant Physician.............	1,200 00	1,200 00
	Third " "	1,050 00	1,050 00
	Bursar................................	1,600 00	1,600 00
	Clerk and Stenographer.................	900 00	1,000 00
	Stenographer..........................	400 00	450 00
	Storekeeper...........................	1,000 00	1,000 00
	Assistant Storekeeper	700 00	....
	Matron...............................	500 00	500 00
	Assistant Matron (O.H.)................	360 00	360 00
	Second Assistant Matron................	300 00	300 00
	Cooks (8).............................	1,704 00	
	Housemaids (4)........................	700 00	3,640 00
	Laundresses (4)........................	804 00	
	Seamstresses (2)......................	432 00	
	Tailor.................................	550 00	550 00
	Shoemaker	350 00	450 00

V. PUBLIC INSTITUTIONS MAINTENANCE.—*Continued.*

No. of Vote.	SERVICE.	Salaries and Expenses.	
		1906	1907
29	**Asylum for the Insane, Hamilton.**—*Con.*		
	Salaries—Concluded.		
	Laundryman	$ 450 00	$ 500 00
	Baker	550 00	550 00
	Assistant Baker........................	350 00	350 00
	Butcher................................	400 00	420 00
	Engineer...............................	650 00	700 00
	Engineer at pump house................	700 00	600 00
	Assistant Engineer.....................	300 00	300 00
	Stokers (6)............................	1,500 00	1,800 00
	Carpenters (2).........................	1,100 00	1,150 00
	Painter	....	420 00
	Farmer.................................	700 00	700 00
	Assistant Farmer	475 00	475 00
	Gardener	600 00	600 00
	Assistant Gardener.....................	450 00	500 00
	Messenger and Stableman (2)............	600 00	
	Farm hand.............................	300 00	} 1,500 00
	Cowman	300 00	
	Chief Attendants, Male (2)....	850 00	
	Supervisors, Male (9)..................	3,072 00	} 11,521 00
	Male Attendants (27)..................	6,720 00	
	Porter and Gatekeeper.................	450 00	
	Trained Nurse.........................	400 00	400 00
	Chief Attendant (1), Female.............	240 00	
	Supervisors (10) Female	2,388 00	} 7,444 00
	Ordinary Female Attendants (27)	4,716 00	
	Temporary assistance...................	500 00	500 00
		45,311 00	46,530 00
	Expenses.		
	Medicines and Medical Comforts............	1,000 00	1,000 00
	Groceries and Provisions (including Flour, Butter, Fruit and Vegetables, Meat, Fish and Fowl)........................	41,000 00	43,000 00
	Heating and Lighting....................	26,000 00	24,000 00
	Clothing..............................	5,000 00	6,000 00
	Laundry, Soap and Cleaning	1,700 00	2,000 00
	Repairs and replacements (including Furniture and Furnishings and Bedding)...........	6,800 00	6,000 00
	Office Expenses.........................	1,200 00	1,000 00
	Farm Expenses.........................	3,000 00	4,000 00
	Miscellaneous (including Water)............	4,500 00	6,000 00
		135,511 00	139,530 00

V. PUBLIC INSTITUTIONS MAINTENANCE.—*Continued.*

No. of Vote.	SERVICE.	Salaries and Expenses.	
		1906	1907
30	**Asylum for the Insane, Kingston.**		
	(602 Patients.)		
	Salaries.		
	Medical Superintendent	$ 2,600 00	$ 2,600 00
	Assistant Physician.........................	1,400 00	1,400 0₀
	Second Assistant. Physician..................	1,100 00	1,100 00
	Bursar	1,500 00	1,500 00
	Clerk and Stenographer	600 00	600 00
	Storekeeper...............................	900 00	900 00
	Portress...................	180 00	180 00
	Matron	500 00	500 00
	Assistant Matron..........................	300 00	300 00
	Cooks (4).................................	840 00	
	Servants, Dairymaid, etc. (6)	1,008 00	
	Laundresses (3)	576 00	2,884 00
	Seamstress	180 00	
	Tailoress	240 00	
	Tailor....................	500 00	500 00
	Laundryman...............................	450 00	480 00
	Baker	550 00	550 00
	Butcher	350 00	350 00
	Engineer...................................	740 00	740 00
	Assistant Engineer.........................	500 00	500 00
	Electrical "	420 00	450 00
	Stokers (4)	1,440 00	1,440 00
	Carpenter	550 00	550 00
	Asst. Carpenter...........................	360 00	360 00
	Painter................................,.....	420 00	480 00
	Bricklayer and Mason.....................	600 00	650 00
	Farmer....................................	550 00	550 00
	Gardener	500 00	500 00
	Asst. Gardener............................	360 00	360 00
	Stableman and Messenger (2)...............	264 00	900 00
	Night Sewage man	264 00	
	Chief Attendant...........................	400 00	
	Supervisors (7) Male	2,160 00	
	Attendants (20) Male.......................	5,932 00	10,340 00
	Night Watchers (4)	1,200 00	
	Trained Nurse for Infirmary	400 00	400 00
	Supervisor Leahurst	250 00	250 00
	Supervisors (6) Female.........	1,332 00	
	Attendants (17) "	2,892 00	5,116 00
	Night Watchers (4) "	360 00	
	Musical Instructress	204 00	204 00
	Temporary Assistance.....................	400 00	400 00
		36,272 00	38,034 00

V. PUBLIC INSTITUTIONS MAINTENANCE.—*Continued.*

No. of Vote.	SERVICE.	Salaries and Expenses.	
30	**Asylum for the Insane, Kingston.**—*Continued.*	1906	**1907**
	Expenses.		
	Medicines and Medical Comforts	1,000 00	1,000 00
	Groceries and Provisions (including flour, butter, fruit, vegetables, meat, fish and fowl)	27,500 00	27,500 00
	Heating and Lighting.....................	12,000 00	13,000 00
	Clothing	4,000 00	5,000 00
	Laundry, Soap and Cleaning................	1,300 00	1,300 00
	Repairs and replacements (including Furniture, and Furnishings and Bedding)...........	5,250 00	7,000 00
	Office Expenses..........................	1,100 00	1,100 00
	Farm Expenses	2,700 00	4,500 00
	Miscellaneous (including water).............	2,000 00	2,000 00
	Brush Industry	1,000 00	
		94,122 00	100,434 00
31	**Asylum for the Insane, London.**		
	(1,061 patients).		
	Salaries.		
	Medical Superintendent	2,600 00	2,600 00
	First Assistant Physician..................	1,400 00	1,400 00
	Second Assistant Physician................	1,100 00	1,050 00
	Third Assistant Physician..................	1,000 00	1,000 00
	Bursar	1,600 00	1,600 00
	Clerk and Stenographer	800 00	800 00
	Storekeeper.........................:.....	1,000 00	1,000 00
	Typewriter and Fortress (2)...............	450 00	450 00
	Matron..................................	500 00	500 00
	Assistant Matron.........................	....	300 00
	Cooks and Assistant Cooks (7).............	1,584 00	
	Housemaids (6)	1,080 00	
	Dairymaid...............................	180 00	4,248 00
	Laundresses (4)	924 00	
	Tailoress and Seamstress (2)	480 00	
	Tailor...................................	560 00	560 00
	Shoemaker...............................	350 00	400 00
	Laundryman..............................	360 00	400 00
	Baker...................................	450 00	450 00
	Assistant Baker...........................	240 00	240 00
	Butcher	425 00	450 00
	Engineer.................................	800 00	800 00
	Assistant Engineer	450 00	450 00
	Second Assistant Engineer.................	420 00	420 00
	Engineer (Infirmary) and Blacksmith........	360 00	360 00

V. PUBLIC INSTITUTIONS MAINTENANCE.—*Continued.*

No. of Vote.	SERVICE	Salaries and Expenses.	
		1906	1907
31	**Asylum for the Insane, London.**—*Continued.*		
	Salaries—Concluded.		
	Stokers (7)	$ 2,300 00	$ 2,300 00
	Bricklayer and Plasterer....................	600 00	1,140 00
	Assistant Bricklayer	500 00	
	Carpenter and Asst. do....................	1,150 00	1,150 00
	Tinsmith	400 00	450 00
	Painter...................................	450 00	550 00
	Farmer....................................	800 00	800 00
	Assistant Farmer.......................	450 00	500 00
	Gardener	650 00	650 00
	Assistant Gardeners (2)....................	600 00	660 00
	Sewage-man...............................	500 00	500 00
	Porter and Messenger.....................	240 00	
	Yardman..................................	300 00	
	Ploughman................................	300 00	1,500 00
	Farm Night Watchman....................	300 00	
	Cowman and Dairyman	300 00	
	Chief Attendants (3) Male.................	1,200 00	
	Supervisors (7) Male......................	2,484 00	13,124 00
	Bandmaster and Supervisor................	360 00	
	Ordinary Male Attendants (32).............	8,664 00	
	Trained Nurse	420 00	420 00
	Chief Attendant (Female).................	250 00	
	Supervisors (8) (Female)..................	1,848 00	9,178 00
	Ordinary Female Attendants (38)...........	6,468 00	
	Night Attendants (3) (Female).............	612 00	
	Temporary Assistance.....................	500 00	500 00
		51,759 00	52,900 00
	Expenses.		
	Medicine and Medical Comforts............	1,000 00	1,000 00
	Groceries and Provisions (including Flour, Butter, Fruit and Vegetables, Meat, Fish and Fowl)...................................	42,500 00	42,500 00
	Heating and Lighting.....................	25,500 00	25,000 00
	Clothing..................................	9,000 00	9,000 00
	Laundry, Soap and Cleaning...............	2,500 00	2,500 00
	Repairs and Replacements (including Furniture and Furnishings and Bedding)..........	9,500 00	9,500 00
	Office Expenses	1,400 00	1,000 00
	Farm Expenses............................	3,000 00	3,500 00
	Miscellaneous (including Water)	1,000 00	1,200 00
		147,159 00	148,100 00

V. PUBLIC INSTITUTIONS MAINTENANCE.—*Continued.*

No. of Vote.	SERVICE.	Salaries and Expenses.	
		1906.	**1907**
32	**Asylum for Insane, Mimico.**		
	(580 patients).		
	Salaries.		
	Medical Superintendent	$2,600 00	$2,600 00
	Assistant Superintendent...................	1,400 00	1,400 00
	2nd Physician............................	900 00	1,050 00
	Bursar	1,500 00	1,500 00
	Clerk and Stenographer	650 00	650 00
	Porter and Typewriter	180 00	300 00
	Storekeeper	900 00	900 00
	Matron..................................	500 00	500 00
	Assistant Matron.........................	300 00	300 00
	Steward.................................	750 00	750 00
	Cooks (4)...............................	852 00	
	Housemaids (2)	584 00	
	Laundresses (5)	720 00	2,720 00
	Seamstress	204 00	
	Tailoress	360 00	
	Shoemaker	350 00	350 00
	Laundryman	360 00	400 00
	Baker...................................	500 00	540 00
	Butcher and Dairyman	300 00	300 00
	Engineer at main building	700 00	750 00
	Engineer at the pump house	525 00	525 00
	Assistant Engineer	400 00	450 00
	Electrician...............................	400 00	420 00
	Stokers (4)	1,296 00	1,396 00
	Carpenter	360 00	500 00
	Assistant Carpenter......................	240 00	300 00
	Bricklayer and Mason.....................	500 00	500 00
	Farmer	550 00	600 00
	Assistant Farmer.........................	350 00	400 00
	Gardener................................	575 00	575 00
	Attendant at sewage works................	300 00	360 00
	Messenger...............................	300 00	
	Plowman................................	288 00	1,050 00
	Stableman	300 00	
	Male Supervisors (6).....................	2,040 00	
	Male Attendants (16)	4,152 00	8,140 00
	Night Watches (2) Male..................	576 00	
	Supervisors (5) Female...................	1,068 00	
	Attendants (18)	2,616 00	4,304 00
	Night Watches (2) Female	348 00	
	Temporary assistance	400 00	400 00
		32,194 00	34,930 00

V. PUBLIC INSTITUTIONS MAINTENANCE.—*Continued.*

No. of Vote.	SERVICE.	Salaries and Expenses.	
		1906	**1907**
32	**Asylum for Insane, Mimico.**—*Continued.*		
	Expenses.		
	Medicine and Medical Comforts.............	$1,000 00	$ 900 00
	Groceries and provisions (including flour, butter, fruit and vegetables, meat, fish and fowl)..	25,500 00	26,000 00
	Heating and lighting......................	12,350 00	12,500 00
	Clothing.................................	4,200 00	5,000 00
	Laundry, soap and cleaning................	1,500 00	1,500 00
	Repairs and replacements (including furniture and furnishings and bedding)............	3,400 00	3,000 00
	Office expenses..........................	1,000 00	900 00
	Farm expenses...........................	1,200 00	2,500 00
	Miscellaneous (including water)	900 00	1,000 00
		83,244 00	88,230 00
33	**Asylum for Feeble Minded, Orillia.**		
	' · (761 patients.)		
	Salaries.		
	Medical Superintendent...................	2,600 00	2,600 00
	Assistant Physician	1,000 00	1,100 00
	Bursar	1,350 00	1,350 00
	Storekeeper	900 00	900 00
	Stenographer and Teacher.................	400 00	400 00
	Matron	500 00	500 00
	Assistant Matron	300 00	300 00
	Cooks (3)...............................	540 00 ⎤	
	Housemaids (8)..........................	1,152 00 ⎟	
	Dairymaid	168 00 ⎬ 3,156 00	
	Laundresses (3).........................	540 00 ⎟	
	Seamstress (3)	756 00 ⎦	
	Tailor	400 00	400 00
	Laundryman	336 00	336 00
	Baker	450 00	450 00
	Engineer	750 00	800 00
	Assistant Engineer.......................	375 00	360 00
	Stokers (3).....	1,000 00	1,080 00
	Carpenter	450 00	450 00
	Painter.................................	....	420 00
	Mason and Bricklayer....................	450 00	450 00
	Farmer	550 00	550 00
	Gardener	575 00	550 00
	Messenger, Porter and Stable-keeper (2)......	600 00	660 00
	Chief Attendant	400 00 ⎤	
	Supervisors (2) male	720 00 ⎟ 5,576 00	
	Ordinary Male Attendants (13)	3,516 00 ⎬	
	Nightwatches (2) male	600 00 ⎦	

V. PUBLIC INSTITUTIONS MAINTENANCE.—*Continued.*

No. of Vote.	SERVICE.	Salaries and Expenses.	
33	**Asylum for Feeble Minded, Orillia.**—*Con.*	1906	**1907**
	Salaries.—Concluded.		
	Ordinary Female Attendants (12) ˩	$ 2,208 00 ⎱	$2,700 00
	Night Attendants (2)	372 00 ⎰	
	Teachers and Industrial Instructors (3)........	1,200 00	1,200 00
	Temporary assistance	300 00	300 00
	Expenses.	25,458 00	26,588 00
	Medicines and Medical Comforts	500 00	500 00
	Groceries and Provisions (including flour, butter, fruit and vegetables, meat, fish and fowl)	23,850 00	24,000 00
	Heating and Lighting	10,200 00	10,000 00
	Clothing...............................	6,000 00	6,500 00
	Laundry, Soap and Cleaning	1,800 00	1,800 00
	Repairs and replacements (including Furniture and Furnishings and Bedding)	4,000 00	3,000 00
	Office Expenses...........................	500 00	500 00
	Farm Expenses............................	1,800 00	2,600 00
	Miscellaneous (including water).............	1,500 00	1,500 00
		75,608 00	76,988 00
34	**Asylum for the Insane, Penetanguishene.**		
	(242 patients.)		
	Salaries.		
	Medical Superintendent	2,400 00	2,400 00
	Assistant to the Superintendent........	900 00	720 00
	Bursar	1,100 00	1,100 00
	Storekeeper.............................	750 00	750 00
	Stenographer.............................	260 00	260 00
	Matron..................................:....	500 00	500 00
	Cooks (3)...............................	648 00 ⎫	
	Housemaid	168 00 ⎬ 1,528 00	
	Laundresses (2)	408 00	
	Seamstress...............................	204 00 ⎭	
	Laundryman.............................	360 00	360 00
	Baker and Butcher........................	500 00	500 00
	Engineer	600 00	600 00
	Assistant Engineer and Night Watch	450 00	450 00
	Stoker (2)...............................	360 00	720 00
	Carpenter	600 00	600 00
	Painter	....	420 00
	Farmer..................................	500 00	500 00
	Gardener......	500 00	500 00

V. PUBLIC INSTITUTIONS MAINTENANCE.—*Continued.*

No. of Vote.	SERVICE.	Salaries and Expenses.	
		1906	1907
34	**Asylum for Insane, Penetanguishene.**—*Con.*		
	Salaries.—Concluded.		
	Stableman and Assistant Farmer	$ 340 00	
	Messenger and Dairyman....................	400 00	$ 1,200 00
	Plowman.................................	....	
	Male Supervisors (2).......................	360 00	
	Male Attendants (8)....	1,992 00	2,852 00
	Chief Female Attendant....................	250 00	
	Female Supervisors (2)....................	456 00	2,506 00
	Female Attendants (11)...................	1,800 00	
	Temporary assistance.....................	300 00	300 00
	Expenses.	17,106 00	18,766 00
	Medicine and Medical Comforts	500 00	500 00
	Groceries (including Flour, Butter, Fruit, Vegetables, Meat, Fish and Fowl)	10,500 00	10,000 00
	Heating and Lighting.....................	4,500 00	5,000 00
	Clothing.................................	1,500 00	1,750 00
	Laundry, Soap and Cleaning...............	700 00	700 00
	Repairs and replacements (including Furniture and Furnishings and Bedding)	2,000 00	2,500 00
	Office Expenses..........................	500 00	400 00
	Farm Expenses..........................	1,700 00	2,500 00
	Miscellaneous (including water).............	2,000 00	1,800 00
		41,006 00	43,916 00
35	**Asylum for Insane, Toronto.**		
	(832 Patients.)		
	Salaries.		
	Medical Superintendent................. ..	2,600 00	2,600 00
	do do allowance	....	450 00
	do do 15 mos. arrears to Dec. 31, 1906	....	562 50
	Assistant Superintendent	1,400 00	1,400 00
	Second Assistant	1,050 00	1,050 00
	Clinical Assistant	....	1,200 00
	Bursar	1,700 00	1,700 00
	Storekeeper..............................	900 00	950 00
	do Arrears for 1906................	....	50 00
	Clerk and Stenographer	600 00	600 00
	Stenographer	250 00	250 00
	Matron..................................	500 00	500 00
	Assistant Matron.........................	300 00	300 00
	Steward	850 00	850 00

V. PUBLIC INSTITUTIONS MAINTENANCE.—*Continued.*

No. of Vote.	SERVICE.	Salaries and Expenses.	
35	**Asylum for Insane, Toronto.**—*Concluded.*	1906	**1907**
	Salaries.—Concluded.		
	Cooks (9)...............................	$ 1,296 00	
	Housemaids (3)	540 00	
	Dairymaid	180 00	$ 4,396 00
	Laundresses (7)	1,488 00	
	Seamstress	216 00	
	Tailor.................................	600 00	600 00
	Baker.................................	525 00	800 00
	Assistant Baker	275 00	
	Butcher	324 00	324 00
	Engineer	850 00	850 00
	Assistant Engineers (2)..................	850 00	900 00
	Stokers (4)	1,104 00	1,440 00
	Bricklayer and Mason...	625 00	625 00
	Carpenters (2)..........................	1,150 00	1,200 00
	Painter................................	600 00	600 00
	Attendant Tradesman	600 00	600 00
	Farmer	600 00	600 00
	Gardener..............................	525 00	550 00
	Teamster and Messenger	300 00	300 00
	Chief Attendant, Male	850 00	
	Male Supervisors (8).....................	2,968 00	
	Ordinary Male Attendants (26)	5,376 00	12,032 00
	Male Night Watchers (4)	1,224 00	
	Porter	300 00	
	Trained Nurse	400 00	400 00
	Female Supervisors (10)..................	1,968 00	
	Female Ordinary Attendants (23)...........	3,804 00	8,800 00
	Female Night Attendants (4).............	768 00	
	Musical Instructress	240 00	240 00
	Temporary Assistance...................	600 00	600 00
	Expenses.	41,296 00	48,319 50
	Medicines and Medical Comforts............	900 00	1,000 00
	Groceries and Provisions (including Flour, Butter, Fruit and Vegetables, Meat, Fish and Fowl).............................	39,900 00	45,000 00
	Heating and Lighting.....................	15,500 00	18,000 00
	Clothing	3,500 00	4,500 00
	Laundry, Soap and Cleaning...............	1,600 00	2,200 00
	Repairs and Replacements (including Furniture and Furnishings and Bedding)	5,000 00	6,000 00
	Office Expenses	800 00	800 00
	Farm Expenses	4,000 00	4,500 00
	Miscellaneous (including Water)............	3,000 00	4,000 00
		115,496 00	134,319 50

V. PUBLIC INSTITUTIONS MAINTENANCE.—*Continued.*

No. of Vote.	SERVICE.	Salaries and Expenses.	
		1906	1907
36	**Asylum for Epileptics, Woodstock.**		
	(80 patients.		
	Salaries.		
	Medical Superintendent (4 months arrears, 1905)	$2,833 33	$2,100 00
	Asst. Physician...........................	1,050 00	1,000 00
	Bursar and Storekeeper	1,000 00	1,300 00
	do rent allowance.......	250 00	....
	Typewriter and Portress	144 00	180 00
	Matron................................	500 00	500 00
	Cooks (3)...............................	600 00	
	Laundresses (2)	410 00	
	Seamstress.............................	180 00	1,900 00
	Housemaids (1)..........................	156 00	
	Baker, Butcher and Dairyman (1)...........	400 00	400 00
	Engineer...............................	500 00	500 00
	Stokers (2)..............................	600 00	600 00
	Carpenter	600 00	600 00
	Farmer	600 00	600 00
	Farm hands (2)..........................	....	600 00
	Gardener	600 00	600 00
	Messenger and stableman..................	240 00	240 00
	Supervisor (male),.......................	360 00	
	Male Attendants (3)......................	804 00	1,500 00
	Nightwatch (male)	240 00	
	Supervisor (female).......................	216 00	
	Female attendants (3)	540 00	756 00
	Temporary keep assistance.................	....	200 00
		12,823 33	13,576 00
	Expenses.		
	Medicines and Medical Comforts	300 00	500 00
	Groceries and Provisions (including Flour, Butter, Fruit and Vegetables, Meat, Fish and Fowl)	5,500 00	5,000 00
	Heating and Lighting	3,000 00	3,000 00
	Clothing...............................	800 00	500 00
	Laundry, Soap and Cleaning	750 00	500 00
	Repairs and replacements (including Furniture and Furnishings and Bedding)...........	1,000 00	500 00
	Office Expenses..........................	600 00	600 00
	Farm Expenses..........................	800 00	1,500 00
	Miscellaneous (including water).............	2,500 00	2,500 00
		28,073 33	28,176 00

V. PUBLIC INSTITUTIONS MAINTENANCE.—*Continued.*

No. of Vote.	SERVICE.	Salaries and Expenses.	
		1906	**1907**
37	**Central Prison, Toronto.**		
	(400 Prisoners.)		
	Salaries.		
	Warden	$ 2,750 00	$ 2,750 00
	Deputy Warden	1,200 00	1,250 00
	Sergeant Guard	900 00	950 00
	Guards (30)............................	17,000 00	17,500 00
	Bursar	1,350 00	1,350 00
	Clerk (Chief)	1,100 00	....
	Storekeeper............................	800 00	1,000 00
	Clerk and Stenographer	600 00	600 00
	Physician..............................	1,000 00	1,000 00
	Carpenter	600 00	600 00
	Plumber and Steamfitter.................	800 00	800 00
	Mason and Bricklayer...................	700 00	700 00
	Cook and Baker........................	700 00	700 00
	Janitor................................	420 00	420 00
	Temporary assistance	500 00	500 00
		30,420 00	30,120 00
	Expenses.		
	Medicines and Medical Comforts	500 00	500 00
	Groceries and Provisions (including Flour, Butter, Fruit and Vegetables, Meat, Fish and Fowl)	19,000 00	17,000 00
	Heating and Lighting.....................	5,000 00	4,000 00
	Clothing................................	7,000 00	6,000 00
	Laundry, Soap and Cleaning	2,000 00	1,800 00
	Repairs and replacements (including Furniture and Furnishings and Bedding).......	3,000 00	3,500 00
	Office Expenses	500 00	700 00
	Farm Expenses	1,400 00	1,300 00
	Miscellaneous (including water)	2,750 00	2,500 00
		71,570 00	67,420 00
38	**Central Prison Industries.**		
	Salaries.		
	Warden.................................	500 00	500 00
	Accountant	1,100 00	1,200 00
	Shipping Clerk.........................	100 00	100 00
	Teamster..............................	450 00	500 00
	Night Watch	600 00	600 00
	Engineer	950 00	950 00

V. PUBLIC INSTITUTIONS MAINTENANCE.—*Continued.*

No. of Vote.	SERVICE.	Salaries and Expenses.	
38	Central Prison Industries.—*Concluded.*	1906	1907
	Salaries—Concluded.		
	Consulting Engineer (3 mos.)	$ 75 00	
	Foremen Cordage Shop (2)...................	....	$1,600 00
	Machinists, Cordage Shop (2)..............	1,400 00	1,500 00
	Industrial Guard, Cordage Shop......... ...	150 00	150 00
	" " " "	....	50 00
	Machinist, Woodworking Shop (including 4 months arrears 1905)...................	600 00	450 00
	Industrial Guard, Woodworking Shop	100 00	100 00
	" " " "	50 00	50 00
	Gardener...............................	1,500 00	1,500 00
	Assistant Gardeners (2) .....'..	1,260 00	1,320 00
	Foreman Machine Shop	1,000 00	1,000 00
	Foreman Painter, Machine Shop	650 00	650 00
	" Blacksmith, Machine Shop	600 00	600 00
	Industrial Guard, " .:.................	50 00	50 00
	Foreman Shoe Shop	800 00	800 00
	" Tailor "	800 00	800 00
	" Woolen Shop....................	1,000 00	1,000 00
	Industrial Guard, Woolen Shop	50 00	50 00
	Temporary assistance	400 00	400 00
		14,185 00	15,920 00
	Expenses.		
	Shoe Shop.......:....................	4,000 00	4,000 00
	Tailor "	6,000 00	4,500 00
	Woodworking Shop	5,000 00	1,500 00
	Woolen "	12,000 00	12,000 00
	Machine "	10,000 00	9,000 00
	Cordage	4,000 00	2,000 00
	Greenhouse...........................	500 00	1,500 00
	Fuel and General Expenses	12,000 00	15,000 00
	Carpenter shop...................	....	800 00
		67,685 00	66,220 00
39	Andrew Mercer Reformatory for Females.		
	(60 inmates.)		
	Salaries.		
	Superintendent..........................	1,600 00	1,600 00
	Deputy Superintendent	650 00	650 00
	Physician............................	800 00	800 00

V. PUBLIC INSTITUTIONS MAINTENANCE.—*Continued.*

No. of Vote.	SERVICE.	Salaries and Expenses.	
39	**Andrew Mercer Reformatory.**—*Concluded.*	1906	**1907**
	Salaries—Concl ded.		
	Principal of Refuge (4 months)..............	$ 250 00	....
	Teachers (4) (4 months)	400 00	....
	Bursar	1,100 00	$ 1,200 00
	Storekeeper and Carpenter..................	700 00	700 00
	Stenographer	350 00	350 00
	Messenger.................................	550 00	550 00
	Cook..	240 00	240 00
	Gardener....................................	550 00	550 00
	Stableman..................................	400 00	400 00
	Carpenter's and Gardener's Assistants........	850 00	850 00
	Engineer	650 00 }	1,300 00
	Assistant Engineer.........................	600 00 }	
	Night Watch	550 00	550 00
	Chief Attendant	350 00 }	2,310 00
	Attendants (8).............................	1,760 00 }	
	Temporary assistance	100 00	100 00
		12,450 00	12,150 00
	Expenses.		
	Medicines and Medical Comforts............	200 00	200 00
	Groceries and Provisions (including Flour, Butter, Fruit and Vegetables, Meat, Fish and Fowl).................................	4,800 00	3,200 00
	Heating and Lighting.................. ..	3,250 00	2,000 00
	Clothing...................................	1,000 00	800 00
	Laundry, Soap and Cleaning...............	850 00	900 00
	Repairs and replacements (including Furniture and Furnishings and Bedding)..........	2,000 00	1,000 00
	Office Expenses	450 00	450 00
	Farm Expenses.............................	1,050 00	750 00
	Miscellaneous (including water, manufacturing operations, library, schools, etc.)........	4,000 00	2,000 00
		30,050 00	23,450 00
40	Medical Relieving Officer (4 mos.)	333 33	....

V. PUBLIC INSTITUTIONS MAINTENANCE.—*Concluded.*

No. of Vote.	SERVICE.	Salaries and Expenses.	
41	**To Pay Expense Accounts from December 12th to December 31st, 1905.**	1906.	1907
	Toronto Asylum............................	$3,422 15	....
	Mimico "	2,073 01	....
	London "	6,535 13	....
	Hamilton "	5,952 98	....
	Kingston "	2,854 97	....
	Brockville "	3,216 21	....
	Cobourg "	1,051 10	....
	Penetang "	2,976 25	....
	Orillia "	1,650 35	....
	Central Prison	2,366 82	....
	Mercer Reformatory	742 95	....
		32,841 92	....
	Total Public Institutions Maintenance....	1,042,451 58	1,040,058 50

VI. AGRICULTURE.

Amount to be Voted, $485,453.00.

42	Agricultural Societies, etc..................	$95,020 00	$100,292 00
43	Live Stock................................	26,411 95	23,482 00
44	Farmers' Institutes	26,812 00	26,816 00
45	Bureau of Industries.......................	5,500 00	5,500 00
46	Dairies	59,700 00	56,150 00
47	Fruit, Vegetables, Honey and Insects	19,800 00	29,022 00
48	Miscellaneous	26,500 00	30,500 00
49	Agricultural College :—		
	Salaries and Expenses	98,308 00	108,375 00
	Macdonald Institute	33,600 00	33,250 00
	Forestry	3,500 00	4,000 00
	Animal Husbandry, Farm and Experimental Feeding...........................	17,100 00	20,610 00
	Field Experiments......................	8,290 00	8,990 00
	Experimental Dairy.....................	16,392 00	14,495 00
	Dairy School	9,640 00	9,560 00
	Poultry	4,135 00	3,835 00
	Horticulture..........................	8,898 00	9,626 00
	Mechanical Department.................	950 00	950 00
		$460,556 95	$485,453 00
42	*Agricultural and Horticultural Societies :*		
	Grants to Agricultural and Hort'l Societies.	$79,000 00	$79,000 00
	Special grants under Agricultural Societies Act, Sec. 37.......................	....	5,000 00

VI.   AGRICULTURE.—*Continued.*

No. of Vote.	SERVICE.	Services and Expenses.	
		1906	1907
42	*Agricultural and Horticultural Societies.*—Con.		
	Port Arthur and Fort William Exhibition..	$ 1,800 00	....
	Expert Judges, services and expenses.....	11,000 00	$11,000 00
	Superintendent.........................	1,200 00	2,200 00
	Stenographer	520 00	572 00
	Clerk..................................	....	520 00
	Contingencies.........................	1,500 00	2,000 00
		$95,020 00	$100,292 00
43	*Live Stock Branch :*		
	Provincial Winter Fair (Guelph).........	$7,000 00	$6,300 00
	Winter Fair, alterations to building	225 00	....
	Winter Fair Building (Guelph) re vote	34 70	....
	Poultry Coops, Winter Fair	227 00	400 00
	Overdraft, W. Poultry Association........	1,021 25	....
	Pure Seed Fairs, 1905 and 1906..........	484 00	360 00
	Eastern Live Stock and Poultry Show.....	4,300 00	4,100 00
	Local Poultry Associations	500 00	1,000 00
	Sales of Pure Bred Stock	1,000 00	1,000 00
	Ontario Horse Breeders' Association	1,000 00	2,000 00
	Spring Stallion Shows and investigations (under regulations of Department)....	6,000 00	2,000 00
	Director of Live Stock Branch...........	1,500 00	2,300 00
	Live Stock Advisory Board	500 00	500 00
	Clerk..................................	1,100 00	1,400 00
	Stenographer	520 00	572 00
	Prince of Wales Prize..................	....	50 00
	Contingencies.........................	1,000 00	1,500 00
		$26,411 95	$23,482 00
44	*Institutes :*		
	Farmers' Institutes, grants, lectures, etc...	$13,000 00	$12,000 00
	Women's " " " " ..	7,000 00	7,000 00
	Superintendent........................	1,800 00	1,900 00
	Superintendent Women's Institutes, arrears 1905.................................	200 00	....
	Clerk	624 00	624 00
	Stenographer.........................	520 00	572 00
	Stenographer	468 00	520 00
	Contingencies.........................	3,200 00	4,200 00
		$26,812 00	$26,816 00
45	*Bureau of Industries :*		
	Printing forms, extra services in compiling statistics, printing and distributing bulletins, reports, etc.	$5,500 00	$5,500 00

VI. AGRICULTURE.—*Continued.*

No. of Vo	SERVICE.	Salaries and Expenses.	
		1906	1907
46	*Dairy Branch :*		
	Dairymen's Association, Eastern Ontario..	$2,000 00	$2,000 00
	Dairymen's Association, Western Ontario .	2,000 00	2,000 00
	Dairy Instruction...............	30,000 00	....
	Dairy Instruction and Inspection	....	35,000 00
	Eastern Dairy School...................	11,000 00	10,500 00
	Western Dairy School	3,500 00	1,750 00
	Chief Instructor, Eastern Ontario (9 months)	1,350 00	1,450 00
	do do Western Ontario do	1,350 00	1,450 00
	Inspection of Cheese Factories and Creameries.............................	2,500 00	....
	Ottawa Central Fair Association, for Dairy Purposes, (under direction of Dept. of Agriculture)	4,000 00	....
	Contingencies.......................	2,000 00	2,000 00
		$59,700 00	$56,150 00
47	*Fruit, Vegetables, Honey and Insects :*		
	Fruit Growers' Association	$1,800 00	$1,700 00
	Experimental Fruit Stations	4,000 00	4,000 00
	Experimental Fruit Farm	2,000 00	10 ,000 00
	Fruit, Flower, Vegetable and Honey Shows	1,700 00	2,000 00
	Fruit Institutes and Horticultural Meetings	1,000 00	1,000 00
	Bee-Keepers' Association................	500 00	450 00
	Inspection of Apiaries..................	600 00	1,200 00
	Entomological Society	1,000 00	1,000 00
	San Jose Scale, spraying, etc.	4,000 00	4,000 00
	Director of Spraying Experiments, 1905...	100 00	....
	Vegetable Growers' Association..........	600 00	600 00
	Stenographer.........................	....	572 00
	Cold storage, experiments, grants, and contingencies	2,500 00	2,500 00
	(Note.—Salary of Secretary of Fruitgrowers and Beekeepers Associations transferred to Vote No. 10.)	$19,800 00	$29,022 00
48	*Miscellaneous :*		
	Ontario Experimental Union............	$2,500 00	$2,500 00
	Pioneer Farm (Northern Ontario)........	2,000 00	3,000 00
	Incidentals :		
	Sundry services in connection with agricultural work ; printing and distributing reports and bulletins, special investigations in agricultural conditions, growing of crops, outbreaks of diseases, etc., agricultural instruction, travelling expenses and contingencies not otherwise provided for.................	22,000 00	25,000 00
		26,500 00	30,500 00

VI. AGRICULTURE.—*Continued.*

No. of Vote.	SERVICE.	Salaries and Expenses.	
		1906	**1907**
49	**Ontario Agricultural College.**		
	Salaries.		
	President......................................	$ 2,000 00	$ 2,100 00
	Professor of Dairy Husbandry...............	1,900 00	2,000 00
	" Physics and English.............	1,900 00	....
	" English	....	2,000 00
	" Biology........................	1,800 00	....
	" Botany and Nature Study........ :...		1,800 00
	" Animal Husbandry..............	2,000 00	2,000 00
	" Field Husbandry.	2,000 00	2,000 00
	" Horticulture	1,800 00	1,900 00
	" Bacteriology	1,500 00	1,600 00
	" Chemistry	1,800 00	1,900 00
	" Veterinary Science (part time)....	1,200 00	1,200 00
	" Entomology	1,500 00	1,500 00
	" Harrison's salary, 3 mos., 1905...	425 00	....
	Lecturer in Chemistry....................	1,400 00	1,500 00
	" Animal Husbandry..............	1,200 00	1,300 00
	" Biology......................	1,200 00	....
	" Entomology.....................	....	1,300 00
	" Physics	1,200 00	1,300 00
	" Field Husbandry............	1,200 00	1,300 00
	" Forestry......................	1,200 00	1,300 00
	Demonstrator in Biology....................	800 00	....
	" Botany and Entomology..		800 00
	Demonstrator in Botany (transferred from Macdonald Institute)	....	800 00
	" Chemistry..................	1,000 00	700 00
	Demonstrator in Chemistry (9 months)		525 00
	" Bacteriology	1,000 00	1,100 00
	" Horticulture	1,000 00	1,100 00
	" Physics............................		700 00
	Fellow in Chemistry............	450 00	450 00 ·
	Florist ....:........	800 00	900 00
	Manager of Poultry Department and Lecturer.	1,400 00	1,500 00
	Dean of Residence........................	700 00	700 00
	Teacher in French and German, Assistant Librarian..............................	800 00	800 00
	Second Assistant in Library..................	450 00	450 00
	Teacher in Drill and Gymnastics.............	300 00	300 00
	President's Secretary, Assistant in Residence..	800 00	800 00
	Lecturer in Apiculture.....................	200 00	200 00
	Stenographer.............................	500 00	550 00
	Stenographic Assistance, 3 Depts.. Biol., Phys., Chem., 100 each; Entomological, Bacteriological, Library, ½ time, 155...........	475 00	....
	Stenographers (2) for 6 Departments........	....	810 00
	Bursar and Superintendent.................	1,600 00	1,800 00

VI. AGRICULTURE.—*Continued.*

No. of Vote.	SERVICE.	Salaries and Expenses.	
49	**Ontario Agricultural College.**—*Continued.*	1906	**1907**
	Salaries—Concluded.		
	Bursar's Clerk..........................	750 00	800 00
	Clerk and Stenographer	500 00	500 00
	Matron	500 00	500 00
	Physician (part time)...................	600 00	600 00
	Engineer	950 00	950 00
	Assistant Engineer	600 00	600 00
	Painter...............................	700 00	700 00
	Plumber and General man...............	600 00	600 00
	Baker................................	600 00	600 00
	2 Stokers	1,080 00	1,080 00
	Night Watchman.......................	420 00	420 00
	Janitor...............................	420 00	420 00
	Messenger............................	360 00	360 00
	Operator for Telephone Switchboard........	....	260 00
	Temporary Assistance...................	1,000 00	....
	2 Janitors, looking after 6 laboratories and Massey Hall.......................	600 00	600 00
	Student Labor	5,000 00	....
	Servants' pay list (including laundryman).....	3,000 00	3,900 00
		57,180 00	55,875 00
	Expenses and Maintenance.		
	Meat, bread, groceries, laundry, engine room supplies and fuel	25,600 00	28,000 00
	Advertising, Printing, Postage and Stationery.	3,000 00	4,000 00
	Maintenance, 5 laboratories...............	3,000 00	3,000 00
	Expenses, Short Courses.................	600 00	1,000 00
	Advisory Board of College...............	200 00	200 00
	Temporary Assistance (transferred from salaries)	....	1,000 00
	Student Labor (transferred from salaries).....	....	5,000 00
	Travelling Expenses and Extra Lectures......	1,100 00	1,100 00
	Library	2,000 00	2,750 00
	Scholarships	100 00	100 00
	Telephone Service, rent, etc...............	403 00	400 00
	Furnishings and repairs	3,500 00	4,000 00
	Sewage...............................	500 00	500 00
	School assessment......................	125 00	100 00
	Contingencies	1,000 00	1,350 00
		98,308 00	108,375 00

VI. AGRICULTURE.—*Continued.*

No. of Vote.	SERVICE.	Salaries and Expenses.	
		1906	**1907**
49	**Macdonald Institute and Hall.**		
	Salaries.		
	Professor of Nature Study (transferred to College)...............................	1,500 00	....
	Professor of Manual Training...............	1,400 00	1,500 00
	Director in Home Economics...............	1,300 00	1,400 00
	Instructor in Manual Training.............	1,000 00	1,000 00
	" " Domestic Science.............	900 00	1,000 00
	" " Normal Methods..............	800 00	900 00
	" " Domestic Art...............	700 00	800 00
	Demonstrator in Nature Study (transferred to College).....	800 00	....
	Assistant Instructor in Domestic Science......	700 00	700 00
	" " Domestic Art (9 months)	....	450 00
	Lecturer in Physiology and Home Nursing....	600 00	600 00
	Instructor in Laundry and Household Administration......................	....	600 00
	Supt. of Domestic Science.................	400 00	400 00
	Teacher in Drill Gymnastics...............	....	300 00
	Stenographer...........................	350 00	360 00
	Engineer.	650 00	650 00
	Stoker	540 00	540 00
	Janitor................................	360 00	360 00
	Janitress..............................	240 00	240 00
	Lady Superintendent, Macdonald Hall........	700 00	700 00
	Housekeeper " "	450 00	500 00
	Janitor " "	360 00	400 00
	Gardener and Supt. of Grounds.............	700 00	700 00
	Servants' Pay List......................	1,950 00	1,950 00
		16,400 00	16,050 00
	Expenses.		
	Bread, meat, groceries, furnishings, repairs, engine room supplies and fuel, and labor on Grounds............................	13,000 00	13,000 00
	Maintenance of Laboratories in Institute......	3,000 00	3,000 00
	Library and Stationery...................	1,200 00	1,200 00
		33,600 00	33,250 00
49	**Forestry.**		
	Expenses in Forestry.	3,500 00	4,000 00
49	**Animal Husbandry, Farm and Experimental Feeding Department.**		
	Permanent Improvements.................	500 00	500 00
	Wages of Men and Foreman and Stenographer	4,750 00	5,500 00

VI. AGRICULTURE.—*Continued.*

No. of Vote.	SERVICE.	Salaries and Expenses.	
		1906	1907
49	**Animal Husbandry, Farm and Experimental Feeding Department.**—*Continued.*		
	Purchase of Live Stock...................	8,000 00	6,000 00
	Maintenance of Stock	1,500 00	1,500 00
	Farm Maintenance (including repairs, blacksmithing, binder twine, seed, furnishings, fuel, light, advertising, printing, stationery, tools, implements, etc.).................	2,000 00	2,800 00
	Contingencies.............................	350 00	350 00
	Experimental Dairy Herd (transferrred from Experimental Dairy Department) :—		
	Herdsman...........................	....	540 00
	Assistant Herdsman	....	420 00
	Purchase of Cows	....	2,000 00
	Feed and Fodder...................	....	1,000 00
		17,100 00	20,610 00
49	**Field Experiments.**		
	Permanent Improvements..................	500 00	650 00
	Assistant, Specialist in Plant Breeding, Stenographer, Foreman, Teamsters and Laborers	6,350 00	6,860 00
	Seeds, Manure and Special Fertilizers........	590 00	575 00
	Furnishings, implements, repairs (blacksmithing, etc.).............................	525 00	580 00
	Printing, postage, stationery, contingencies,etc.	325 00	325 00
		8,290 00	8,990 00
49	**Experimental Dairy Department.**		
	Permanent Improvements..................	500 00	500 00
	Wages, including Foreman, Cheesemaker, Buttermaker, Engineer, Stenographer and Book-keeper	2,742 00	2,295 00
	Milk for Experimental cheese and buttermaking	10,000 00	10,000 00
	Purchase of Cows.........................	800 00	....
	Feed and Fodder	650 00	....
	Furniture, furnishings, repairs, etc., laboratory expenses, gas, chemicals, etc., and contingencies.............................	1,000 00	1,000 00
	Fuel and light............................	700 00	700 00
		16,392 00	14,495 00
49	**Dairy School.**		
	Permanent improvements, cement floors, walks, etc...................................	300 00	200 00
	Wages of instructors, engineer, janitor, stenographer and book-keeper...............	1,590 00	1,710 00
	Cleaning, painting, repairs and contingencies..	300 00	300 00

VI. AGRICULTURE.—*Concluded.*

No. of Vote.	SERVICE.	Salaries and Expenses.	
		1906	**1907**
49	**Dairy School**—*Continued.*		
	Dairy appliances, separators, vats, expenses cheese and butter judges, inspecting factories, etc.............................	$600 00	$500 00
	Advertising, printing, stationery, postage, books, papers, etc......................	250 00	250 00
	Fuel and light..............................	600 00	600 00
	Purchase of milk for use in school.......	6,000 00	6,000 00
		9,640 00	9,560 00
49	**Poultry Department.**		
	Wages of assistant, stenographer, and temporary assistance......................	830 00	805 00
	Poultry Institute, Short Courses (Transferred to College)......	300 00	....
	Furnishings and repairs.....................	500 00	500 00
	Permanent improvements....................	100 00	100 00
	Purchase of stock.........................	200 00	200 00
	Purchase of horse.........................	175 00	....
	Fuel, light and contingencies...............	330 00	330 00
	Experiments with incubator, fattening and feed	1,700 00	1,900 00
		4,135 00	3,835 00
49	**Horticultural Department.**		
	Permanent improvements...................	200 00	400 00
	Head gardener and foreman, assistant in plant breeding, assistant and night firemen, teamsters, assistant gardener, stenographer and laborers	5,898 00	6,101 00
	Manure, trees, plants, bulbs, seeds, cold storage experiments, implements, tools, furnishings, repairs and contingencies................	1,400 00	1,500 00
	Fuel and light..............................	1,000 00	1,000 00
	Wax fruit models...........................	400 00	400 00
	Purchase of Horse.........	....	225 00
		8,898 00	9,626 00
49	**Mechanical Department.**		
	Salary of foreman..........................	800 00	800 00
	Tools, fuel and light.......................	150 00	150 00
		950 00	950 00
	Total Agriculture....................	460,556 95	485,453 00

VII. COLONIZATION AND IMMIGRATION.

Amount to be voted, $46,065.00.

No. of Vote.	SERVICE.	Salaries and Expenses.	
		1906.	**1907**
50	Pamphlets, advertising and general colonization purposes, including extra help........	$20,000 00	$25,000 00
	Land Guides for settlers and veterans.........	2,000 00	2,000 00
	Rent and maintenance of office at station	1,500 00	2,000 00
	Women's Welcome Hostel	1,000 00	1,000 00
	Salvation Army	7,000 00	7,000 00
	Work in Great Britain.		
	Agent in Liverpool	2,365 00	2,365 00
	Clerk " "	700 00	700 00
	Contingencies............................	4,000 00	6,000 00
		38,565 00	46,065 00

VIII. HOSPITALS AND CHARITIES.

Amount to be voted, $303,663.53.

No. of Vote.	SERVICE.	Salaries and Expenses.	
		1906	**1907**
51	For Institutions, mentioned in Schedule "A" of Statutes (including arrears)	116,071 88	130,000 00
	For Institutions in Schedule "B"...........	70,828 59	76,243 31
	For Institutions in Schedule "C"...........	16,363 02	15,954 81
	For printing, stationery and other contingencies	300 00	300 00
	Industrial Schools.....................	32,000 00	35,000 00
	do arrears from 1904......	7,468 27	....
	do arrears from 1905......	717 64	....
	Prisoners' Aid Association	2,500 00	2,500 00
	Children's Aid Work	8,000 00	8,000 00
	Canadian Humane Society	250 00	250 00
	Victorian Order of Nurses in new districts.	2,500 00	2,500 00
	Salvation Army Prison Gate Work	1,500 00	1,500 00
	Associated Charities....................	500 00	500 00
	Society for Reclamation of Inebriates	300 00	300 00
	Infants Home and Infirmary	500 00	500 00
	Smallpox outbreaks and Sanitary Investigations (transferred to Vote 9)	5,000 00	....
	For Children's Shelter, Toronto	....	10,000 00
	Changes in Toronto General Hospital *re* treatment of acute neuresthenics	5,500 00	....

VIII. HOSPITALS AND CHARITIES.—*Concluded.*

No. of Vote.	SERVICE.	Salaries and Expenses.	
51		1906	**1907**
	Grant new Industrial School Building, Mimico (Revote)l..............................	5,000 00	....
	Grant new Industrial School Building.........	15,000 00	....
	For Alexandra School, new cottage and alterations to old buildings	20,000 00	....
	Maintenance of patients in Municipal Sanitoria for Consumptives, including arrears for 1905	10,500 00	8,115 41
	Free Hospital for Consumptives, Township of York	4,000 00	....
	Hamilton Health Association, Hospital for Consumptives	4,000 00	....
	County House of Refuge, Prince Edward	4,000 00	....
	do do Northumberland and Durham	4,000 00	....
	do do Hastings (revote)...	4,000 00	4,000 00
	do do Prescott and Russell	....	4,000 00
	do do Peterborough......	....	4,000 00
		340,799 40	303,663 53

IX. MAINTENANCE AND REPAIRS OF GOVERNMENT BUILDINGS

Amount to be voted, $89,795 00

No. of Vote.	SERVICE.	Salaries and Expenses.	
52	Government House	18,000 00	18,000 00
53	Parliament and Departmental Buildings.......	71,710 00	71,795 00
		89,710 00	89,795 00
52	**Government House.**		
	Gardener and Caretaker		
	Fireman and assistant gardener.............		
	Assistant gardener........................		
	Extra gardener...........................		
	Water...................................		
	Gas.....................................	18,000 00	18,000 00
	Fuel		
	Repairs..................................		
	Furnishings..............................		
	Contingencies............................		
	Paving on Simcoe St., proportion of cost		

MAINTENANCE AND REPAIRS OF GOVERNMENT BUILDINGS.—*Con.*

No. of Vote.	SERVICE.	Services and Expenses.	
53	**Parliament and Departmental Buildings.**	1906	**1907**
	Attorney - General's Department, furniture, cleaning, etc..........................	900 00	....
	Lands and Mines Department, furniture, cleaning, etc...............................	900 00	....
	do fittings for vaults.............. :.....	4,500 00	....
	Public Works Department, furniture, cleaning, etc.......... '................	1,100 00	....
	do vault fittings....................	500 00	....
	Treasury Department, furniture, cleaning, etc..	1,200 00	....
	Provincial Audit Office, furniture, cleaning, etc.	500 00	....
	Provincial Secretary's Department, furniture, cleaning, etc..........................	2,100 00	....
	do shelving Criminal Justice accounts branch.....................	150 00	....
	do vault fittings, Registrar's Branch..	200 00	....
	do filing cabinets, Public Institutions office......................	600 00	....
	do vault fittings, License Branch.....	400 00	....
	Department of Agriculture, furniture, cleaning, etc............................	1,150 00	....
	Archivist's Office...........................	800 00	....
	Water and Fuel...........................	9,000 00	9,000 00
	Electric power and light current and gas......	5,500 00	5,000 00
	Furnishings of Legislative Chamber and Speaker's apartments..................	2,000 00	....
	Supplies, tools, etc., for engine room and general repairs......................	2,000 00	2,000 00
	Caretakers of grounds, repairs and cleaning of buildings, etc...................	9,500 00	....
	Caretakers of grounds and maintenance of drives and walks	....	4,500 00
	Repairs and cleaning of buildings, etc........	....	13,500 00
	Vault fittings and shelving	....	5,000 00
	Furniture and furnishings for buildings	....	8,000 00
	Interior alterations........................	2,000 00	2,000 00
	General Clerk of Works	1,200 00	1,200 00
	Carpenter...............................	800 00	800 00
	Plumber................................	900 00	900 00
	Mechanical Superintendent.................	1,150 00	....
	Engineer	1,200 00	1,200 00
	Assistant engineer and steam fitter..........	720 00	720 00
	Firemen in boiler room (3).................	1,950 00	2,100 00
	Passenger elevator attendants (2)...........	1,300 00	1,300 00
	Porters in charge of entrances and corridors (4 in 1907)...........................	3,300 00	2,800 00
	Nightwatchmen (3) (2 last year)	2,100 00	2,175 00
	Superintendent of grounds and gardens......	350 00	....
	Garden shrubs, etc., for grounds............	500 00	500 00

MAINTENANCE AND REPAIRS OF GOVERNMENT BUILDINGS.—*Con.*

No. of Vote	SERVICE.	Salaries and Expenses.	
		1906	**1907**
53	**Parliament and Departmental Buildings,** *Con.*		
	Uniforms for messengers, attendants, etc	600 00	600 00
	Library fittings and shelving	500 00	. . . .
	Painting corridors and offices.	5,000 00	2,000 00
	Painting outside work.	1,200 00	1,200 00
	Inspector of Boilers, Public Institutions.	1,200 00	1,300 00
	Telephone service.	. . . .	4,000 00
	To pay outstanding accounts of 1905.	2,740 00	. . . .
		71,710 00	71,795 00

X. PUBLIC BUILDINGS.

Amount to be voted, $539,695 00

No. of Vote.	SERVICE.	To be voted for 1907	
54	Public Institutions (revote $32,730 00.)	193,825 00	
55	Educational (revote $115,162 00).	318,725 00	
56	Districts	27,145 00	
			539,695 00
	Capital account $493,935 00		
	Repairs 45,760 00		
		$539,695 00	

Public Institutions.

54	*Brockville Asylum :*		
	Green House addition	1,850 00	
	Interior repairs and alterations	5,000 00	
	Exterior repairs.	3,500 00	
	Balance due on boilers and setting up same	500 00	
	Alteration to boiler house	1,500 00	
			12,350 00
54	*Cobourg Asylum :*		
	Interior repairs and alterations	2,000 00	
	Exterior repairs and alterations	1,600 00	
			3,600 00

X. PUBLIC BUILDINGS.—*Continued.*

No. of Vote.	SERVICE.	1906	
	Public Institutions—*Continued.*		
54	*Hamilton Asylum :*		
	Improvement to heating plant............	3,000 00	
	Paint Shop (part revote)	2,000 00	
	Entrances, main building, male and female side	1,000 00	
	Interior repairs and alterations	6,500 00	
	Exterior repairs and alterations	3,000 00	
	Repairs to sewers (revote)	700 00	
			16,200 00
54	*Kingston Asylum :*		
	Local Telephone System	1,500 00	
	Industrial Building·	6,500 00	
	Extension to water pipe and repairs to breakwater and wharf	6,000 00	
	Interior repairs and alterations	3,000 00	
	Exterior repairs and alterations	2,000 00	
			19,000 00
54	*London Asylum :*		
	Balconies at east and west ends of main building	2,500 00	
	Barn on the North Farm...	3,500 00	
	Green House in the Sewage Farm........	1,750 00	
	Hot Water Heating Boilers for North Bldg.	600 00	
	Balance to pay on boilers and setting up same	750 00	
	Interior repairs and alterations...........	3,500 00	
	Exterior repairs and alterations	3,000 00	
			15,600 00
54	*Mimico Asylum :*		
	Repairs and extension to wharf	3,000 00	
	Renewals of boilers and steam separators..	3,300 00	
	Etobicoke Township for closing road	250 00	
	Railroad switch......................	500 00	
	Extension of water supply pipe (part revote)	4,000 00	
	Interior repairs and alterations	2,500 00	
	Exterior repairs and alterations	2,000 00	
	Barn on McNeil Farm	2,500 00	
			18,050 00
54	*Orillia Asylum ;*		
	Additional farm lands	4,000 00	
	Interior repairs and alterations	1,600 00	
	Exterior repairs and alterations	1,700 00	
			7,300 00
54	*Penetanguishene Asylum :*		
	Renewals of boilers and extension of boiler house	5,000 00	
	Alterations to kitchen and bakery (part revote)	2,000 00	

5 E.

X. PUBLIC BUILDINGS.—*Continued.*

No. of Vote.	SERVICE.	1907	
	Public Institutions—*Concluded.*		
54	*Penetanguishene Asylum*—Concluded.		
	To complete addition to laundry (part revote)	3,500 00	
	Reconstruction of building to accommodate additional patients....	9,000 00	
	Interior repairs and alterations..........	1,500 00	
	Exterior repairs and alterations	2,000 00	
			23,000 00
54	*Toronto Asylum :*		
	Interior repairs and alterations	5,500 00	
	Exterior repairs and alterations	2,000 00	
			7,500 00
54	*Woodstock Asylum :*		
	Completion of cottages, including contracts, refrigerators, wire guards, electric fixtures, hardware, etc., etc (part revote)	21,125 00	
	Sewage (revote)......................	4,700 00	
	Roads, walks and grounds (revote)	2,000 00	
	House for Farmer..................	2,500 00	
	Electric light and power plant...........	600 00	
	Barns, stables and silo (part revote)	6,500 00	
	Driving shed	400 00	
	Stable and coach house	2,500 00	
	Furniture and furnishings	12,500 00	
	Farm and garden, ice house, piggery, reservoir, farm implements, live stock, exterior repairs and painting	7,000 00	
			59,825 00
54	*Central Prison :*		
	Interior repairs and alterations..........	2,500 00	
	Exterior repairs and alterations	3,500 00	
			6,000 00
54	*Mercer Reformatory :*		
	Steam engine to run laundry............	500 00	
	Fencing..............................	500 00	
	Interior repairs and alterations..........	2,500 00	
	Exterior repairs and alterations	1,900 00	
			5,400 00
	Total Public Institutions		193,825 00

Educational.

No. of Vote.	SERVICE.	1907	
55	*Normal and Model Schools, Toronto*—		
	Repairs and Drains	500 00	
	Painting Class Rooms.................	350 00	
	Electric Lighting, renewing wiring Education Department Building Normal School and Model School and wiring and fixtures for three class rooms, Normal School....................	1,100 00	

X. PUBLIC BUILDINGS.—*Continued.*

No. of Vote.	SERVICE.	1906	
	Educational.—*Continued.*		
	Ventilating Model School similar to Normal School	4,000 00	
	Metal Ceilings in centre corridors	400 00	
	Improvements and alterations in Normal School, including fitting up Chemical Laboratory, additional plumbing, electric clock and bells	1,500 00	
			7,850 00
55	*Normal and Model Schools, Ottawa*—		
	Repairs, Drains	400 00	
	Ventilation af Normal School	4,500 00	
	Alterations and improvements to Normal School - including re-arrangement of Class rooms, painting, plumbing constructing lavatory in basement, fitting up Chemical Laboratory, metal ceilings furnishing and fittings	6,650 00	
	Equipment for Science Teaching	800 00	
	Electric Light Normal and Model School ..	1,000 00	
	Programme Clock	200 00	
	Cement Walks to Normal School	600 00	
	Telephone System for School	250 00	
	Slate Blackboards	150 00	
	Fitting up two rooms in Model School	400 00	
	Improvements in lighting windows (re-vote)	200 00	
	Improvements in Plumbing (part re-vote) Normal School	200 00	
	Furnishings, renewals and additional for re-arrangement of class rooms, including 100 desks and chairs, tables for art room, lockers for students, desks and tables for private rooms, carpets and furnishings for library	1,800 00	
			17,150 00
55	*Normal School, London*—		
	Repairs, Drains, etc	300 00	
	Painting Exterior of Building	400 00	
	Improvements and Alterations, re-arrangement of Class Rooms, fitting up of Chemical Laboratory	5,000 00	
	Ventilation	6,000 00	
			11,700 00
55	*Additional Normal Schools ($100,000 re-vote)* ..	....	200,000 00
55	*Deaf and Dumb Institution, Belleville*—		
	Repairs and Drains	400 00	
	Implement Shed and Poultry House (part re-vote)	800 00	

. X. PUBLIC BUILDINGS.—*Continued.*

No. of Vote.	SERVICE.	1906	
	Educational.—*Continued.*		
	Greenhouses (part re-vote).............	2,500 00	
	Exterior Repairs.......................	500 00	
	Improvements in Plumbing.............	1,000 00	
	Ventilation System	3,500 00	
	Interior Repairs........:...........	400 00	
			9,100 00
55	*Institute for the Blind, Brantford—*		
	Repairs and Drains....................	300 00	
	Cement Walks........................	800 00	
	Plank Walks and Roadways.............	450 00	
	Outside Repairs, including pointing brickwork, wood and galvanized iron work, painting...........................	800 00	
	Completing Icehouse..................	50 00	
			2,400 00
55	**Ontario Agricultural College.**		
	To complete contracts for rebuilding Greenhouses...............................	1,450 00	
	To complete contract for two cottages.......	475 00	
	To complete glasshouse for Insects, Physics and Botany..........................	2,100 00	
	To complete Farm Mechanics Building, and Heating, Plumbing and Hoist (part re-vote)	13,000 00	
	To complete addition to Chemical Laboratory (part re-vote).........................	3,000 00	
	Steel Tank and Tower for 5,000 gallons of water to supply College, Macdonald Institute and Hall (part re-vote)............	6,200 00	
	Addition to Main Building (to accommodate 40 Students)........................	18,000 00	
	Machinery and Furnishings for new Machinery Hall................................	4,000 00	
	Coal Bin to hold 3,000 tons of Coal.........	5,000 00	
	Additional apparatus for five Laboratories and Gymnasium..........................	3,000 00	
	Cases and Specimens for College Museum.....	500 00	
	Laying Cement Walks....................	1,000 00	
	Motor for Pumping Machinery, Steam Separators and Grate Bars..................	4,000 00	
	Building for storage of Fruit and Vegetables..	3,000 00	
	Heating, Lighting and Furnishing new Chemical Laboratory	3,800 00	
	New Roof for Main Building..............	2,000 00	
			70,525 00
	Total Educational................		$318,725 00

X. PUBLIC BUILDINGS.—*Continued.*

No. of Vote.	SERVICE.	1907	
56	**Districts.**		
	Muskoka :		
	General Repairs, Furnishings, including drain construction......................	....	300 00
	Parry Sound:		
	Addition to Gaol yards and enlargement of Gaol.............................	3,000 00	
	Cement Floor in basement of old part of Court House and new W.C.'s........	200 00	
	General Repairs and alterations...........	460 00	
	Furniture and furnishings for Court House	300 00	
	Completion of Contracts for Gaoler's House and Veneering and alterations to Court House...............................	560 00	
	Addition to Registry Office for Land Titles Office, including heating and plumbing	3,500 00	8,020 00
	Manitoulin :		
	Addition to Gore Bay Gaol...............	1,200 00	
	Alterations and Repairs to Manitowaning Lock-up..................	100 00	
	Furnishings for District.................	100 00	1,400 00
	Rainy River District:		
	Repairs and alterations including painting at Kenora Gaol, Court House and Gaoler's House.......................	350 00	
	Repairs and alterations to Lock-ups.......	100 00	
	Grant to assist in erection of a new Lock-up at Fort Frances.....(conditional..,...	1,000 00	
	Fittings and Furnishings for Land Titles and Registry Office, Kenora (part re-vote).............................	800 00	
	Furnishings for District.................	100 00	
	Cement floor and storm sash, Registry Office, Fort Frances	125 00	2,475 00
	Algoma :		
	Repairs and alterations at Sault St. Marie Gaol and at Lock-ups, including painting, new sidewalks, new eave-troughing, new roof for Gaolers' House and general repairs....................	900 00	
	Furnishings for the District.............	100 00	
	New Lock-up at Massey (grant to municipality)	600 00	
	Improvements to Registry Office, Sault Ste. Marie, including heating and plumbing	1,800 00	3,400 00

X. PUBLIC BUILDINGS.—*Continued.*

No. of Vote.	SERVICE.	1907	
	Districts—*Concluded.*		
	Nipissing:		
	Repairs to North Bay Gaol and Court House including new fence around Gaol......	2,000 00	
	To Complete alterations to North Bay Gaol	200 00	
	Alterations to provide increased cell accommodation at Sudbury Lock-up, a new furnace, closets, baths, new plumbing, repairs to Gaol fence, painting.	3,000 00	
	Repairs and alterations to Sturgeon Falls Lock-up............	100 00	
	Repairs and alterations to Cobalt Lock-up, including new fence...............	250 00	
	Furnishings for the District.............	100 00	
	Repairs and alterations at Mattawa Lock-up	300 00	
	Lock-up at Haileybury... (grant revote)...	1,000 00	
	" " New Liskeard....(grant).......	1,000 00	7,950 00
	Thunder Bay:		
	Buildings separate house for Gaoler and present quarters occupied by Gaoler to afford additional cell accommodation for prisoners......................	2,500 00	
	Alterations and general repairs at Gaol, Court House and District Lock-ups.........	1,000 00	
	Furnishings for the District.............	100 00	3,600 00
	Total Districts	....	$27,145 00
	Total Public Buildings	....	$539,695 00

XI. PUBLIC WORKS.

Amount to be voted, $161,600.00

		Re-Vote.	New Vote.
57	High Bridge, Marys and Fairys Lake Locks...	$1,200 00	$500 00
	Embankment along river in Dover Township..	....	500 00
	Pier and Boom, Huntsville Bridge............	....	600 00
	White River Bridge, Pacaud Boundary.......	....	900 00
	North and Black Rivers Improvement........	....	900 00
	Hills Bridge	....	700 00
	Oxtongue Bridge............................	....	1,200 00
	Veuve River Bridge, Verner	....	1,300 00
	Still River Bridge, Byng Inlet..............	....	1,000 00

PUBLIC WORKS.—*Concluded.*

No. of Vote.	Service.	Revote.	New Vote.
57	**Public Works.**—*Concluded.*		
	La Blanche River Bridge and Approaches	$3,500 00	$1,500 00
	Port Severn, Axe Lake and Cooper Bridges.....	....	1,500 00
	Bala Bridge (to complete)	....	2,000 00
	Extension to Wharf at Port Carling..........	....	2,000 00
	Sauble River Bridge	800 00	4,300 00
	Mississippi, Grant, McKenzie and Egan Bridges	....	2 400 00
	Bridges on Round Lake Road...............	....	2,400 00
	Goulais River Bridge	2,500 00	2,800 00
	White River Bridge and Approaches, Marter Township.......................	....	2,800 00
	Thessalon and Larchwood Bridges..........	....	3,000 00
	Gooderham and Kinmount Bridges	....	3,500 00
	Minden Bridge............................	....	3,500 00
	Mattawa Bridge..........................	6,000 00	4,800 00
	Bridge at Eau Claire......................	....	3,800 00
	Houseys Rapids Bridge	....	3,800 00
	New Liskeard Bridge, Grant...............	....	4,000 00
	Mississauga River Bridge, Thompson Township	....	4,600 00
	Kearney, Bridge	....	4,800 00
	Improving Kemps Channel	....	5,000 00
	West Arm Lake Nipissing Bridge	....	3,000 00
	Wabigoon Bridge	....	7,600 00
	Spanish River Bridge and Approaches........	1,900 00	9,500 00
	Espinola Bridge..........................	....	8,800 00
	Massey Bridge, Spanish River..............	....	14,000 00
	Surveys, Inspections, Awards, etc..........	....	1,000 00
	Superintendent of Public Works............	....	1,200 00
	Lock Masters, Bridges Tenders, Caretakers, etc., Salaries........................	....	3,500 00
	Maintenance Locks, Dams, Bridges, Dredging, etc...........................	....	12,000 00
	Maintenance, Equipment, Instruments, Machinery, etc............................	....	3,500 00
	Drainage :		
	Whitebread Drainage Works, Kent	4,000 00	....
	Ruscombe Drainage Works, Essex.......	2,500 00	1,000 00
	Cavan Township Drainage Works........	4,000 00	....
		26,400 00	135,200 00
	Capital Account..........................	140,400 00	
	Repairs, etc.............................	21,200 00	
	Total Public Works, 1907	....	161,600 00
	Total vote for 1906	....	117,010 00

XII. COLONIZATION ROADS, 1907.

Amount to be voted, $298,311.00.

No. of Vote.	SERVICE.	To be voted for 1907	
58	North Division............................	$89,236 00	
59	West Division	27,800 00	
60	East Division	93,425 00	
61	Temiskaming Division	62,350 00	
62	General "	25,500 00	
			$298,311 00

58

Northern Division.

Aberdeen, Concession 1 and 2..............	$300 00	
Aberdeen, 3rd Concession Bridge	200 00	
Allan and Gordon (Conditional)	500 00	
Ansonia Bridge....................	200 00	
Aubrey Township Roads (Conditional)	400 00	
Aweres to connect with Bellevue Road	600 00	
Assiginac (Conditional)....................	500 00	
Billings (Conditional)	500 00	
Beaver Creek Bridge.......................	300 00	
Bellingham and Montgomery Road (In Montgomery Township)	500 00	
Balfour Road.	500 00	
Bridgeland Road	500 00	
Bruce Mines and Mill Town Road	300 00	
Bright Additional, Lots 1 to 12, 4th Concession	400 00	
Bruce Mines and Macbeth Bay Road	500 00	
Blue, Pratt and McCrossan Road............	4,000 00	
Burpee and Cockburn Island	700 00	
Bidwell School to Manitowaning............	500 00	
Bridge, Campbell Township, 10th Concession..	300 00	
Burpee, Concessions 5 and 6	200 00	
Burris and Carpenter Town Line............	500 00	
Bellingham and Grassett...................	750 00	
Cariboo and Port Lock Road...............	500 00	
Cartier and Chelmsford Road........	500 00	
Cobden and Striker Road..................	400 00	
Collins Bridge, McLeod's Creek	250 00	
Carpenter Road, between Lots 6 and 7......	1,000 00	
Carnarvon and Sandfield Road	900 00	
Carnarvon (Conditional).....	500 00	
Creighton Township and Killarney..........	600 00	
Campbell Township and Gore Bay Road......	900 00	
Conmee Road between A and 1, and Blind Line	800 00	
Carnarvon, 25th Side Line.................	300 00	
Day and Goldenburg Road	500 00	
Darlington Bay Road	800 00	
Dunvalley and Houghton Road	500 00	

XII. COLONIZATION ROADS.—*Continued.*

No. of Vote.	SERVICE.	To be voted for 1907
58	**Northern Division.**—*Continued.*	
	Dean Lake and Iron Bridge Road	300 00
	Dean Lake and Dayton Road	500 00
	Desbarats Location Road..................	250 00
	Devlin and Burris Road	1,000 00
	Dilke, between 33 and 34 and Northerly......	1,000 00
	Dryden Road North. (To pay balance for work done in 1905)	286 00
	Dobie Township Road	500 00
	Dorion Township Roads...................	900 00
	Eton Township Roads	600 00
	Espanola, Menit and Baldwin Road..........	600 00
	Foster's Road in Gould...................	250 00
	Fort Frances and Emo Road................	4,000 00
	Goulais Bay Road	2,000 00
	Galbraith, 3rd and 4th Concession Road	250 00
	Gordon and Rock Lake Road and Bridge	900 00
	Gore Bay and Meldrum Bay Road	1,500 00
	Gorham and Dawson......................	600 00
	Gordon, Allan and Billings................	750 00
	Gillies, Scoble Town Line and Pearson Road ..	500 00
	Gillies, 4th Concession, between Lots 4 and 5	200 00
	Hilton Township Road....................	800 00
	Howland, Shequiandah and Bidwell..........	800 00
	Howland, Shequiandah and Bidwell (Conditional).............................	500 00
	Haviland and Vankoughnet Town Line.......	200 00
	Isbester Station Road....................	500 00
	Jocelyn Road	700 00
	Johnston, Tarbutt and Tarbutt Additional	750 00
	K Line between side roads 5 and 10, St. Joseph Township	250 00
	Kirkwood Township Road.................	500 00
	Kingsford and Mather Town Line	1,000 00
	Kingsford, 2nd and 3rd Concession	500 00
	Keewatin and Darlington Bay..............	600 00
	Kagawong and Providence Bay	800 00
	Korah, between Sections 22 and 27	600 00
	Lumsden Road..........................	500 00
	Lee Valley Road, May Township	500 00
	Lake Shore Road........................	500 00
	Laird and McDonald Town Line............	200 00
	Laird Township Roads....................	600 00
	Lonely Lake Road.......................	250 00
	Lavallee and Burris Road	1,000 00
	Little Current to Manitowaning	900 00

XII. COLONIZATION ROADS.—*Continued.*

No. of Vote.	SERVICE.	To be voted for 1907
58	**Northern Division**—*Continued.*	
	Lybster, 36 Mile Post to Marks Township	300 00
	Miscampbell Township Road................	500 00
	Moran and McMahon Town Line	500 00
	Massey Road, Salter Township.............	500 00
	May Township, 2nd Concession	500 00
	Mather and Potts Town Line...............	1,000 00
	Mather West Town Line	500 00
	Morley Bridge, Lot 25, River Range	700 00
	Morley and Shenston North Town Line	1,000 00
	Mellick and Jaffray Road	800 00
	Mills and Barrie Island....................	700 00
	McKinnon Tote Road.....................	300 00
	McDonald, Meredith and Aberdeen Additional	600 00
	McDonald and McPhee Valley Road	500 00
	McIntyre and Oliver Town Line (Conditional)	300 00
	Nelles and Patullo Town Line	1,000 00
	Nairn and Worthington	600 00
	Northern Road through Plummer and Aberdeen	2,000 00
	O'Connor Township Road.................	800 00
	Patton Road, between Lots 10 and 11, Con. 4	400 00
	Prince Road	500 00
	Pickerel Creek Bridge.....................	200 00
	Paipoonge Township Roads................	950 00
	Parkinson and Gould Town Line	400 00
	Parkinson and Bellingham Road............	400 00
	Pattullo, between Sections 3 and 4, North	1,000 00
	Patton, Marsh River Bridge and Road, Con. 3	500 00
	Rainy River Road	3,000 00
	Robinson and Dawson ....'............	500 00
	Rayside Road............................	500 00
	Rydal Bank and Rose Township Road	500 00
	Road between Sections 19 and 20, Tarentorus	300 00
	Schreiber Bridge	500 00
	St. Joseph Township, between Lots 10 and 11, Concession 0.........................	250 00
	St. Joseph A line, between Lots 33 and 37	250 00
	Shenston and Ball	500 00
	Stanley Road (Conditional)	900 00
	Shakespeare Road........................	500 00
	Spanish River Road in Shedden	500 00
	Salter Road, Section 23, and between 22 and 15	500 00
	Sanfield Township Bridge..................	150 00
	Sand Bay Road	200 00
	Tait and Richardson Road.................	1,000 00
	Tait and Pattullo Town Line	1,000 00
	Tehkumah and Assiginac	700 00
	Tehkumah (Conditional)	500 00
	Thessalon Road..........................	800 00

XII. COLONIZATION ROADS.—*Continued.*

No. of Vote.	SERVICE.	To be voted for. 1907	
58	**Northern Division**—*Concluded.*		
	Thompson, Marsh River Road and Bridge	500 00	
	Thessalon River Bridge, Lots 19 and 20......	800 00	
	Tarentorus Township (Conditional grant)	500 00	
	Van Horne Road	700 00	
	Victoria and Shedden Town Line	500 00	
	Wainwright Road	600 00	
	West Bay Road............................	500 00	
	Whitefish and Waters Road	600 00	
	Wells Township Road	600 00	
	Webbwood Bridge Road....................	1,000 00	
	Walford Road, Victoria Township	500 00	
	Wells Road, Concession 3	300 00	
	Zealand Road.............................	200 00	
			$89,236 00
59	**Western Division.**		
	Amhic Lake road and bridge	300 00	
	Armour and Ryerson town line.............	300 00	
	Axe Lake and Banbury road, 7th to 2nd Con. Monteith...............................	300 00	
	Artray and Washago road..................	400 00	
	Booth Line road	300 00	
	Balkwell road	400 00	
	Brunel and Chaffey township roads...........	700 00	
	Bethune road between 12 and 13	200 00	
	Bethune and Novar road	300 00	
	Christie and McKellar road................	300 00	
	Croft and Hagerman town line across cons. 6 and 7...........................	200 00	
	Croft between cons. 13 and 14 North road to lot 31	200 00	
	Chisholm and Himsworth town line, 2nd to 4th concession	300 00	
	Centre road, McKellar, cons. 4 to 9.........	500 00	
	Dunchurch and James Bay road	700 00	
	Dillings Port road in Shawanaga.........	300 00	
	Draper, McCauley town line and Jackson Hill.	600 00	
	Dalton and Washago road.................	300 00	
	Franklin and Sinclair road................	600 00	
	Foley Township, 11th concession line........	300 00	
	Foley Township between lots 120 and 121 to Conger	400 00	
	Fifth Side road, South Himsworth 10 to 12th con	200 00	
	Great North road, 7th to 12th con. Ferry	300 00	
	Gibson and Baxter road...................	600 00	
	Heeley Settlement and Orange Valley road, in Christie...............................	300 00	

XII.　COLONIZATION ROADS.—*Continued.*

No. of Vote.	SERVICE.	To be voted for **1907.**
59	**Western Division**—*Continued.*	
	Himsworth, con. 4 and 5	450 00
	Humphrey, Pt. Colborne to Black's Crossing..	250 00
	Joly, 10th side road, cons. 10 to 12	200 00
	Kill Bear Point road in Carling..............	300 00
	Lindsay and St. Edmunds road..............	500 00
	Mill road, McKenzie Township..............	300 00
	Matchedash roads	800 00
	Morrison and Muskoka road...............	800 00
	Medora and Wood road....................	800 00
	Machar Township, 20th side road and bridge..	450 00
	Monteith road between cons. 9 and 10, lots 12 to 22	200 00
	Machar and Strong town line and cons. 9 and 10	300 00
	McMurrich 15th and 20th side road..........	400 00
	McMurrich and Ryerson town line..........	200 00
	McConkey and Wilson town line, to extend ...	500 00
	McLean and Ridout roads.................	700 00
	McDonald Line...........................	400 00
	Macaulay, to lower Duck Lake and improve Baysville and Draper road	400 00
	North West road, McDougall and Carling....	600 00
	Nipissing road from lot 5 to 23 Monteith......	300 00
	Nipissing Township, 10th side road from Rosseau	200 00
	North Himsworth, 5th side road 20th to 24th concession............................	500 00
	Otter Lake road, in Foley..................	200 00
	Perry and Monteith road, Sprucedale west....	200 00
	Parry Sound and Beveridge Creek road	500 00
	Powassan and Callendar road..............	350 00
	Pringle road between cons. 10 and 11........	250 00
	Powassan to Chisholm, 12th con	300 00
	Port Severn road........................	400 00
	Road leading to Rondeau Park (grant).......	500 00
	Rainy Lake road in Ryerson..............	200 00
	Ryerson between lots 5 and 6, cons. 5 and 6..	300 00
	Road along lot 11, con. A, Croft...........	300 00
	South Himsworth, 6th con., boundary to 5th side road............................	200 00
	Strong, 5th side road, 5th to 8th concessions..	400 00
	Strong and Joly town line	300 00
	South River to the 10th side line in Laurier ...	250 00
	Spence Tp. road between cons. 4 and 5	200 00
	South Himsworth road between 24th and 25th concessions	300 00
	South River bridge in Machar	300 00
	Scotia Junction South road	400 00
	Stephenson road deviation.................	800 00
	Stisted and Oakley roads............. ...	600 00

XII. COLONIZATION ROADS.—*Continued.*

No. of Vote.	SERVICE.	To be voted for 1907.	
59	**Western Division.**—*Continued.*		
	Sandfield and Carling road	300 00	
	Watt and Cardwell roads...:...............	700 00	
	Whitestone Valley road, Burton and McKenzie	500 00	
	Whitehall Station road.....................	200 00	
			27,800 00
60	**Eastern Division.**		
	Appleby and Jennings town line road and bridge	500 00	
	Alice and Fraser road	1,000 00	
	Airy Township road........................	300 00	
	Anson, Hindon and Dysart.................	700 00	
	Addington road from Cloyne to Massanaga ...	400 00	
	Addington road from Kaladar to Cloyne	400 00	
	Arden and Oso road	200 00	
	Arden and Harlow road	300 00	
	Bark Lake and Barrys Bay road....	500 00	
	Brougham, Griffith and Matawatchan.........	1,000 00	
	Brudenell and Lyndoch road	600 00	
	Bagot, Blythfield and Admaston	800 00	
	Battersea and Sunbury road in Storrington, (conditional)	300 00	
	Burridge road in Bedford Township.........	200 00	
	Battersea and Keelerville road	200 00	
	Burley and Apsley road	700 00	
	Belmont Township roads	600 00	
	Booth road, South	200 00	
	Buckhorn road	300 00	
	Burgess Mine road	600 00	
	Bancroft and Maynouth road	300 00	
	Bancroft and Hermine road	400 00	
	Bancroft and Coe Hill road	600 00	
	Bessmer Mine and Long Lake road	600 00	
	Bronson Bridge, (Grant conditional)	600 00	
	Boulter and Bonfield town line and bridge	400 00	
	Bonfield Township roads	1,600 00	
	Boulter roads	200 00	
	Blezard road, between 5 and 6 concession	500 00	
	Blezard, 1st con. and between lots 10 and 11..	400 00	
	Blezard road, 5th concession...............	400 00	
	Bedall road in Springer....................	200 00	
	Button road in Field and Springer	500 00	
	Badgerow, 1st concession, LaBrosse road	600 00	
	Bastedo South, town line, lots 10 to 13	300 00	
	Bromley Township, 5th line................	150 00	
	Bromley Township, 6th concession	400 00	
	Bulmer's Creek Bridge	500 00	
	Constance Creek road.....................	300 00	

XII. COLONIZATION ROADS.—*Continued.*

No. of Vote.	SERVICE.	To be voted for 1907
60	**Eastern Division**—*Continued.*	
	Cosby, South Boundary....................	500 00
	Cosby, first and second concessions..........	700 00
	Cassimer road, between concessions 2 and 3 ..	300 00
	Cassimer road, between concessions 3 and 4 ..	200 00
	Capreol road, between lots 10 and 11, 1st concession :.........................	200 00
	Capreol, 1st and 2nd concessions............	800 00
	Caldwell and Badgerow, town line..........	400 00
	Crerer East, town line road	500 00
	Caldwell and McPherson town line	500 00
	Calvin Township roads	1,000 00
	Cameron Township roads	400 00
	Chisholm Township roads	900 00
	Chisholm right of way, concession 6, lot 11 ...	25 00
	Carden roads............................	500 00
	Corundum Mine road	600 00
	Carlow Township roads	200 00
	Clarendon and Ardoch road...............	300 00
	Chandos Township roads....	500 00
	Cavendish roads	400 00
	Carden and Mara town line, opposite concessions 3, 4, 5 and 6......................	200 00
	Chaffey's Locks and Opinicon	300 00
	Collins' Lake road in Kingston Township.....	300 00
	Donegal road............................	500 00
	Dacre and Coldwell Station road	500 00
	Darling, 8th concession road...............	200 00
	Dalton road	500 00
	Dunnett Township, 1st and 3rd concessions...	500 00
	Dunnett and Cassimer town line............	500 00
	Dunnett, between lots 8 and 9, concession 5...	200 00
	Dunnett, between lots 4 and 5 in the 6th, 5th and 4th concessions....................	200 00
	Dill Township road	400 00
	Desarmeau road in Grant..................	200 00
	Douglas Station road	300 00
	District Line............	400 00
	Frawley and Timmerman road in Bedford.....	200 00
	Fourth Concession, Lavant	300 00
	Faraday and Herschell road................	200 00
	Ferris Township roads	1,600 00
	Gore Line	500 00
	Garson and Capreol town line	500 00
	Gibbons and Bastedo road.................	500 00
	Gibbons Township road...................	300 00
	Greenview road	250 00
	Gilmour road, approaches.................	200 00
	Glamorgan and Cardiff	1,400 00

XII. COLONIZATION ROADS.—*Continued.*

No. of Vote.	SERVICE.	To be voted for 1907
60	**Eastern Division**—*Continued.*	
	Gull Creek and Horse-shoe Lake road........	200 00
	Galway Township roads....................	900 00
	Hills-Bridge, Dalton Township.............	600 00
	Hartington and Conway's Creek road, Portland Township	200 00
	Harvey Township roads, North..............	800 00
	Harvey roads, South......................	500 00
	Harlow and Northbrook road	200 00
	Herschell road	300 00
	Hanmer and Capreol town line	600 00
	Hugel, 2nd and 3rd concessions	200 00
	Hugel, 4th concession road	400 00
	Hawley, concessions 1 and 2...............	300 00
	Jones Falls and Battersea road.............	500 00
	Jennings road, between 3rd and 4th concession	200 00
	Jones Falls and Morton	200 00
	Kingston and Perth road, Bedford Townships.	300 00
	Kirkpatrick, between 2nd and 3rd concessions.	200 00
	Kirkpatrick, 4th concession, lots 1 to 7.......	200 00
	Leduc road, 5th concession, Gibbons........	500 00
	Long Lake road in Broder.................	300 00
	Lerock road in 6th concession Field.........	300 00
	Leduc Bridge	400 00
	Lyell road to Madawaska Station...........	200 00
	Lanark and Darling town line..............	200 00
	Longford Mills and Orillia road	300 00
	Loboro, 8th and 9th concessions............	200 00
	L'Amable and Bancroft....................	500 00
	L'Amable and Fort Stewart road	800 00
	Murray Lake and Markstay road	400 00
	Mount St. Patrick bridge and road..........	300 00
	Monck road, west of Seabright.	500 00
	Mountain Grove and Long Lake road in Olden.	200 00
	Monmouth and Sherbourne	1,400 00
	Montague, West Boundary, conditional.	750 00
	Minden and Lutterworth	1,000 00
	Mattawan Township roads.................	800 00
	Mattawa and Pembroke road, Head, Clara and Maria	600 00
	Mason and Scollard town line..............	500 00
	Mason North, town line	2,000 00
	Martland South, Boundary.................	500 00
	Martland, first concession.................	500 00
	Markstay and Appleby	800 00
	McPherson, 5th concession	500 00
	McPherson North, town line...............	600 00
	McKenzie Lake road......................	500 00
	North Algona	500 00

XII. COLONIZATION ROADS.—*Continued.*

No. of Vote.	SERVICE.	To be voted for 1907
60	**Eastern Division.**—*Continued.*	
	Neelon, concession 3, road..................	400 00
	North Bay and Bonfield road................	500 00
	North Sherbrooke, 4th concession	100 00
	North Smith..............................	200 00
	North Shore road in Loboro...............	200 00
	North Elmsley, East Boundary, conditional...	750 00
	Oak Lake road............................	300 00
	Oak Flats road in Hinchenbrook...........	200 00
	Opinicon to Perth road....................	200 00
	Pembroke and Eganville road..............	1,200 00
	Paquett's Rapids road.....................	200 00
	Pembroke and Mattawa road...............	1,000 00
	Paradis road.............................	500 00
	Papineau Township roads.............	1,600 00
	Parnham Village to Parnham Station	200 00
	Parnham and Arden road in Hinchenbrook, Olden and Kenebec	200 00
	Plevna and Levant	500 00
	Proving line, between 11th and 12th concessions of Hagarty............................	500 00
	Ross town line...........................	300 00
	Ross, 4th concession......................	300 00
	Road South of Sturgeon River in Field......	400 00
	Road North of Sturgeon River in Field......	400 00
	Road between lots 7 and 8 Kirkpatrick......	300 00
	Robilliard Hill	400 00
	Richmond Township road..................	500 00
	Road between lots 6 and 7 concession 3, Cosby	200 00
	Road between lots 10 and 11 from town line to concession L., Rama	300 00
	Rama concession L., Washaga to lot 5.......	300 00
	Raglan and Radcliffe roads	800 00
	Road between Killaloe and Brudenell........	1,000 00
	Roads between Wilno and Barrys Bay and Wilnos and Killaloe in Hagarty..........	600 00
	Sebastapol roads	600 00
	Stoney Lake and Norwood.................	200 00
	Somerville, Bexley and Laxton	1,800 00
	Stanhope and Snowden....................	1,000 00
	Smokey Falls road in Field	500 00
	Sudbury and Blezard Valley road	2,000 00
	South Algona road...........	1,400 00
	Stafford road	600 00
	St. Charles and Appleby road	500 00
	Tryon road in Olden	200 00
	Victoria Road	600 00
	Wolfe Grove town line, Ramsay Township....	900 00
	White Lake road, Pakenham...............	300 00

XII. COLONIZATION ROADS.—*Continued.*

No. of Vote.	SERVICE.	To be voted for 1907	
60	**Eastern Division.**—*Continued.*		
	Widdifield Township roads	1,000 00	
	Westport and Sherbrooke road.............	300 00	
	Wollaston Township road	300 00	
	Wilberforce	500 00	
	Westmeath, 8th concession	500 00	
	Westmeath, 1st concession	400 00	
	Wylie road	500 00	
	Warren and Cosby road..............	800 00	
	Warren and Markstay road.................	1,500 00	
	Warsaw to Young's Point road.............	200 00	
	Wilson road in Bedford Township	300 00	
	Whitefish and Black Donald road and Bridge..	300 00	
			93,425 00
61	**Temiskaming.**		
	Armstrong, concession 4	350 00	
	Otter Creek road........................	400 00	
	Casey, between lots 6 and 7 con. 4 north, conditional	500 00	
	Dymond, concession 2	500 00	
	Kearns, concession 5, lots 10, 11 and 12......	500 00	
	Evanturel, lots 4 and 5, Tomstown road north.	500 00	
	Taylor road	500 00	
	Bucke, between lots 6 and 7...............	500 00	
	Renewing Peterson's bridge over Mill Creek, Bucke	700 00	
	Moose Creek bridges	900 00	
	Harley, front of concession 5...............	1,000 00	
	Armstrong and Beauchamp town line, concessions 2 and 3	1,000 00	
	Hudson, 3rd concession	1,000 00	
	Evanturel, lots 10 and 11, concession 6 to Englehart	1,000 00	
	Brethour road between lots 6 and 7..........	1,000 00	
	Savard, South boundary...................	1,200 00	
	Ingram, South boundary..................	1,500 00	
	Grading old roads	1,500 00	
	Kearns and Hudson, town line to Uno Park...	1,500 00	
	Kearns and Armstrong town line...........	1,500 00	
	Harley and Hilliard town line, to complete....	1,500 00	
	Dack and Robilliard, front of 3rd concession ..	1,500 00	
	Cane Township road......................	1,500 00	
	Henwood east, boundary	1,500 00	
	Cobalt and Haileybury road	1,500 00	
	Kearns and Harley town line...............	2,000 00	
	Hudson Township grant, conditional........	2,000 00	

6 E.

XII. COLONIZATION ROADS.—*Concluded.*

No. of Vote.	SERVICE.	To be voted for 1907	
61	**Temiskaming**—*Concluded.*		
	Haileybury and Firstbrook road............	2,000 00	
	Charlton and Hyslop road.............·...	2,000 00	
	Tomstown and Wendigo road ....··	2,000 00	
	Marter Township road	2,000 00	
	Henwood road and bridge	2,300 00	
	Hilliard, lots 4 and 5, front of concession 4....	2,500 00	
	Harris, from centre of con. 6 north to con. 2 Casey, then east to Keys road	2,500 00	
	Harley and Casey, front of con. 4, north road, to White River	3,000 00	
	Armstrong and Hilliard road............. ·	3,000 00	
	Beauchamp road	3,000 00	
	Chamberlain road..................	4,000 00	
	Charlton and Mud Lake road ....·	5,000 00	
			62,350 00
62	**General.**		
	New short roads, bridges and repairs	10,000 00	
	Inspections, incidental expenses in connection therewith, storage of tools, supplies, etc ..	12,000 00	
	To pay balances Road Accounts and inspection, 1906 and 1905	2,500 00	
	Road Making Machinery ....·........	1,000 00	
			25,500 00

XIII. CHARGES ON CROWN LANDS.

Amount to be voted, $525,800 00

No. of Vote.		1906.	**1907**
63	Expenditure on account of outside service, and surveys	397,825 00	363,900 00
64	Expenditure on account of Mining Development	74,800 00	142,300 00
65	Expenditure on account of Parks............	19,600 00	19,600 00
		492,225 00	525,800 00

XIII. CHARGES ON CROWN LANDS.—*Continued.*

No. of Vote.	SERVICE.	Salaries and Expenses.	
63	**Outside Service and Surveys.**	1906.	**1907**
	Board of Surveyors	200 00	200 00
	Agents' salaries and disbursements	40,000 00	45,000 00
	" Ottawa Agency	3,150 00	3,900 00
	" Quebec "	2,075 00	2,100 00
	Forest ranging.............................	40,000 00	45,000 00
	Forest reserves...........................	25,000 00	30,000 00
	Fire ranging..............................	60,000 00	60,000 00
	Cullers' Act..............................	200 00	200 00
	Surveys :		
	Surveys of Townships in new districts	113,000 00	100,000 00
	Maps, preparation of, engraving and printing same....................	6,000 00	7,000 00
	Base and meridian lines	20,000 00	20,000 00
	Survey of outlines of blocks to be granted Grand Trunk Pacific Railway, Thunder Bay District	....	24,000 00
	Surveys of limits chargeable to limit holders	5,000 00	2,500 00
	Special surveys in Mining Districts, Vote 64	2,500 00	....
	Survey of Timber berths in new districts .	....	5,000 00
	Inspection of surveys	4,000 00	4,000 00
	Clearing along Temiskaming Railway....	50,000 00	....
	Retaining fee of E. J Rainboth for three years and a half at $200.00 per annum as Surveyor to the Ottawa Agency	700 00	....
	Fire Ranging along Railway Lines, etc.......	10,000 00	10,000 00
	Exploration and Estimation of Timber Berths	6,000 00	5,000 00
	Caswell & Company, compensation for loss of timber on Berths in Townships of Martland and Cosby	10,000 00	....
		397,825 00	363,900 00
64	**Mining Development.**		
	Provincial Geologist	3,600 00	4,000 00
	Assistant Geologist.......................	....	3,300 00
	Provincial Inspector of Mines..............	1,600 00	1,800 00
	Geologist and Mineralogist	500 00	500 00
	Expenses assay office and assayer, Belleville ..	2,300 00	2,300 00
	Experimental treatment of ores and collection of minerals, Parliament Buildings, and cases	1,100 00	1,100 00
	Diamond drills, working expenses (percentage refunded by persons employing same)	8,000 00	8,000 00

XIII. CHARGES ON CROWN LANDS.—*Continued.*

No. of Vote.	SERVICE.	1906.	1907
64	**Mining Development.** *Continued.*		
	To cover special services and unforeseen expenses......	3,000 00	3,000 00
	Summer Mining Schools...............	1,200 00	1,200 00
	Mining Recorder, Haileybury	1,800 00	2,000 00
	Geological explorations :		
	To pay salaries, wages, subsistence, travelling and other expenses to parties exploring in Northern Ontario ; also travelling and other expenses of Provincial Geologist, Inspector of Mines and other field officers ..	10,700 00	10,700 00
	Special Surveys in Mining Districts (transferred from Vote 63)................	....	3,000 00
	Cancellation of Mining Leases to pay registration fees, Local Masters of Titles	2,500 00	....
	Expenses Mining Conventions.............	500 00	200 00
	Mining Commissioner ; salary and expenses...	4,000 00	4,200 00
	Clerk ; salary and expenses	....	3,000 00
	Mining Recorders ; salaries (other than at Haileybury) and expenses	5,000 00	5,000 00
	Inspection of Mining Claims, Guarding locations, etc.	4,000 00	4,000 00
	Gillies Timber Limit ; expenses preliminary operations, including surveying, purchase of machinery, mining, treatment of ores, etc.........................	25,000 00	60,000 00
	Sampling Plant...........................	....	25,000 00
		74,800 00	142,300 00
65	**Parks.**		
	Algonquin National Park—		
	To cover erection of shelter lodges, salaries of Superintendent and Rangers, game animals and birds, administration of Justice and other expenses........... } Addition to headquarters building. ...... }	13,100 00	12,100 00
	Rondeau Provincial Park—		
	To cover salaries, Ranger and Assistant, extra ranger during shooting season, making buildings, roads and dock, game animals and birds, and other expenses..	6,500 00	7,500 00
		19,600 00	19,600 00
	Total Charges on Crown Lands	492,225 00	525,800 00

XIV. REFUND ACCOUNT.

Amount to be voted, $33,172 39

		1906.	**1907**
66	Education	2,000 00	2,000 00
67	Crown Lands	33,474 29	18,500 00
68	Municipalities Fund	243 32	243 32
69	Land Improvement Fund	1,911 31	2,429 07
	Miscellaneous	10,000 00	10,000 00
		47,628 92	33,172 39

To be voted for
1907

66   Education.

To pay withdrawals from Superanuation Fund 2,000 00

67   Crown Lands.

For payments made to the credit of the Department on account of uncompleted purchases, and afterwards returned to proposed purchasers on purchases not being carried out 7,500 00

For two per cent. of timber dues payable to Municipalities for timber cut on road allowances ... 6,000 00

Refund to settlers under the settlement of Free Grants Act of 1880 ... 5,000 00

     18,500 00

68   Municipalities' Fund.

Amount collected in 1906 .... 3,969 71
Less 20 per cent. for commission 793 94
Vide Stat. Can. 18 Vic. C. 2 and 19 Vic. C. 16 .... 3,175 77

To be added to grant to Public and Separate School (50 Vic. C. 5) 2,932 45

To pay Widows' Pensions, 1907 ....   243 32

69   Land Improvement Fund.

Moneys collected from sales of Crown Lands subject to the Land Improvement Fund for the year ending 31st December, 1906 .... 2,438 74
Less 6 per cent. for cost of collection and management 146 32

     2,292 42

XIV. REFUND ACCOUNT.—*Concluded.*

No. of Vote.	SERVICE.		To be voted for 1907
69	**Land Improvement Fund.**—*Concluded.*		
	One-fifth to the Land Improvement Fund.............. Vide Stat. Can. 16 Vic. C. 157 and Con. Stat. Can. C. 26..		458 48
	Moneys collected from the sale of Common School Lands subject to the Land Improvement Fund for the year ending 31st December, 1906	8,385 51	
	Less 6 per cent. for collection and management	503 13	
	To be distributed as follows.....	7,882 38	
	One-quarter to the Land Improvement Fund	1,970 59	
			2,429 07

XV. MISCELLANEOUS.

Amount to be voted, $231,375 30

No.	SERVICE			
70	Collection of Revenue :			
	Law Stamps........................		4,200 00	2,500 00
	Licenses............................		2,000 00	2,000 00
	Succession Duty—Legal Expenses, valuations, arbitrations.................		• 8,000 00	8,000 00
	Fidelity Bonds		2,000 00	2,000 00
	Automobile Tags		1,500 00	....
	Algoma Taxes.......................		500 00	500 00
	Enforcing Liquor License Act..............		7,500 00	7,500 00
	Fisheries............................		28,000 00	28,000 00
	Game Protection.....................		16,000 00	16,000 00
	Importation of Game Birds................		1,000 00	1,000 00
	Wolf Bounty..........................		8,000 00	8,000 00
	do Claims disallowed by Provincial Auditor on account of irregular certificates..................		372 00	....
	Expenses of Elections...		10,000 00	10,000 00
	do (Manhood Suffrage Registration)		500 00	500 00
	do (Revision of Voters' Lists)		3,500 00	3,500 00
	Insurance........................		7,000 00	7,000 00
	Arbitration, Canada and Quebec.....		5,000 00	5,000 00
	Annuities and bonuses to Indians under Treaty No. 9.............................		10,000 00	9,000 00

MISCELLANEOUS.—*Concluded.*

No. of Vote.	SERVICE.	1906.	1907
70	**Miscellaneous.**—*Continued.*		
	Legislative Committee for Art Purposes	2,500 00	2,500 00
	Grant to Ontario Rifle Association	1,000 00	1,000 00
	do do Artillery Association........	500 00	500 00
	do Canadian Military Institute..........	300 00	300 00
	do Royal Military College Rifle Association............................	100 00	100 00
	do Army and Navy Veterans for Monument (part re-vote)..............	1,000 00	140 00
	do York Pioneers....................	200 00	200 00
	do United Empire Loyalists...........	200 00	200 00
	do Canadian Mining Institute	300 00	200 00
	do Forestry Association ....'...........	300 00	300 00
	Commission *re* Hydro-Electric Power........	18,000 00	18,000 00
	do University of Toronto	7,200 00	....
	Commissions *re* Sundry Investigations........	5,000 00	5,000 00
	Gratuities................................	20,000 00	10,000 00
	Removal of Patients to Asylums............	7,000 00	7,000 00
	Investigation as to Feeble Minded...........	600 00	600 00
	Incidentals..............................	10,000 00	10,000 00
	Automobile Law enforcement...............	3,000 00	
	Railway and Municipal Board Expenses......	8,000 00	....
	Towards payment commutation Volunteer Veterans land grants......................	50,000 00	50,000 00
	Statute of Hon. John Sandfield Macdonald....	....	10,000 00
	Grant toward Tablet, Batoche Column	....	200 00
	South African Monument	....	2,500 00
	Expenses of Members to funeral late G. N. Kidd, M.P.P...............................	....	135 30
	Bell Telephone Memorial, Brantford	....	2,000 00
	Miscellaneous Grants, omitted in 1907........	10,935 19	....
	Total Miscellaneous...................	261,207 19	231,375 30
71	To defray the Expenses of Legislation and Maintenance and Salaries of the Officers of the Government and Civil Service, and other Services for the month of January, 1908................................	250,000 00	250,000 00

SUPPLEMENTARY ESTIMATES, 1907.

CIVIL GOVERNMENT.

Attorney General's Department.

Insurance Inspection—Stenographer................... $ 50 00

Lands, Forests and Mines Department.

Law Clerk	100 00
Stenographer......................................	50 00

Land Sales and Free Grants.

Clerk	50 00

Surveys and Patents.

Draughtsman.....................................	50 00
Clerk.....:	50 00

Woods and Forests.

Clerk..........	50 00
Stenographer	50 00
Clerk (Registrar's, Accounts Branch)	100 00

Bureau of Mines.

Clerk and Stenographer (omitted from Main Estimates)..	600 00
do do ..	550 00
Advertising (additional)...........................	2,000 00

Public Works Department.

Chief Architect...................................	200 00
Fisheries and Game—Game Reports, etc	500 00
Labor Bureau Agencies............................	1,200 00

Treasury Department.

Junior Second-class Clerk	750 00
Adding Machine (re-vote)...........................	375 00

Succession Duties Branch.

Stenographer.....................................	50 00
Stenographer....	50 00
Inspector of Insurance, actuarial work *re* Succession Duties................................	250 00

Provincial Auditor's Office.

Chief Clerk and Accountant......................... $ 50 00

Provincial Secretary's Department.

Engrossing Clerk..................................   520 00
First Class Clerk..................................   240 00
Refunds...   5,000 00

Inspection of Public Institutions.

Clerk...   50 00
Second Class Clerk................................   50 00
Deportation of undesirable immigrants..............   1,000 00

Registrar-General's Branch.

Stenographer 50 00

Provincial Board of Health.

Allowance for salary and expenses of Chairman and
    Members of Board.............................   2,400 00
Temporary Services 500 00
Smallpox Claims—Townships of Belmont and Methuen..   350 00
        do   Township of Chandos,............   600 00
        do   do   do Burleigh.............   150 00

Department of Agriculture.

Minister's Secretary and Secretary to the Department...   100 00
Factory Inspectors (3) 3,600 00
                                                         ————————   21,735 00

71   LEGISLATION.

Mr. Speaker Crawford. 500 00
Bureau of Archives—Printing, paper, binding, last re-
    port, (re-vote)...............................   400 00
                                                         ————————   900 00

72   ADMINSTRATION OF JUSTICE.

Supreme Court of Judicature.

Entering Clerk....................................   50 00
Chief Clerk and Accountant........................   250 00

Land Titles Office.

Clerk...   50 00
Clerk...   50 00
Transfer of Titles to Registers of District of Sudbury... 1,000 00
Registers and other books, District of Sudbury 200 00
Transferring entries of ownership into new registers and
    other work in connection with transfers, District of
    Sudbury.......................................   1,000 00

Miscellaneous.

Porter at Osgoode Hall (transferred from Parliament Buildings)	$ 650	00
Typewriter for Shorthand Reporter	58	00
Refund of expenses in connection with Baskin Extradition	125	00
Refund to Michael Flaherty in the case of Flaherty *vs.* Lamont, Farquhar and Dixon, assault	75	00
Insurance, Osgoode Hall	1,200	00

District of Thunder Bay.

Constable on line of Grand Trunk Pacific	600	00

District of Rainy River.

Constable at Fort Frances	400	00
Constable at Emo	400	00
Constable at Rainy River	400	00

District of Nipissing.

Constable at Blizzard Valley	150	00
Constable at Warren	150	00

District of Parry Sound.

Constable on line of C. P. R.	600	00
Arrears for 1906	300	00

District of Sudbury.

Sheriff's Salary	750	00
Clerk of the Peace and District Attorney	250	00
Clerk of the District Court	450	00
Administration of Justice	5,000	00

14,158 00

73　　　EDUCATION.

Public and Separate School Education.

Teachers' Associations (Grant to Dominion Educational Association	500	00
Inspection of Continuation Classes	500	00
Text Book Commission	8,200	00
Purchase of flags for Rural School Houses	5,000	00
Stenographer (Departmental Examinations)	550	00
Inspector of Technical Schools	100	00
Janitors of Toronto Normal and Model Schools	100	00
Re-organized Normal School Staffs and Expenses	5,000	00
To Queen's University, Kingston, first annual payment for three years, in aid of "Education of Teachers". (Payments to be made on certificate of Minister of Education that regulations of Education Department have been) complied with.)	5,000	00

Professional Training of First-Class Teachers and High
  School Assistants (for part of year) $6,000 00
Model Plans, with specifications, for Rural Public Schools   750 00
To provide temporary teachers, Normal Schools, in cases
  of illness.................................... 500 00
Gratuities 8,000 00
Costs *re* S. S. 16, Township of Peel Trustees.......... 502 00

Departmental Library and Museum.

Superintendent of Museum......................... 200 00
Additional amount of purchases.................... 500 00

Public Libraries, Art Schools, Historical, Literary and Scientific Societies.

Ottawa Literary and Scientific Society 200 00
St. Patrick Literary Association................ 100 00
Huron Institute, Collingwood....................... 100 00
Grant to Markham Library for the Blind 200 00

Repairs and Maintenance, Education Department and Toronto Normal and Model School Buildings.

Alterations to Buildings............................ 1,200 00
Cleaning, etc., Education Department Offices, Museum
  and Normal Schools 500 00
                         43,702 00

PUBLIC INSTITUTIONS, MAINTENANCE.

Hospital for Epileptics, Woodstock.

Miscellaneous, including water...................... 500 00
Consulting Surgeon................................. 600 00
Engineer 100 00
Supervisor (male)
Male attendants (3) } 1,500 00
Night watchman (male)
Supervisor (female)
Female attendants (3) } 950 00
Night watch, (female 1)
Cooks (2)... 450 00
Stoker (1).. 300 00

Asylum for the Insane, Hamilton.

Mason and bricklayer................................ 600 00

Asylum for the Insane, Mimico.

Engineer at pump house, allowance for 1906.......... 50 00
  do   do   allowance for 1907 .... 50 00

Asylum for the Insane, Toronto.

Butcher 156 00
Engineer 50 00
Stenographer 50 00

Central Prison, Toronto.

Investigation and cost of preliminary steps for removal.. $3,000 00

London Asylum.

Interior repairs and alterations...................... 1,000 00

Kingston Asylum.

Pathological Expert................................ 300 00
                                                        ————   9,656 0

15!   AGRICULTURE.

Agricultural and Horticultural Societies.

Port Arthur and Fort William Exhibition 1,800 00

Live Stock Branch.

Director of Live Stock Branch 100 00
Clerk 100 00
Investigation into horse industry, grants for improving
    same, and Contingencies in connection with horse
    breeding 2,000 00
Transportation, International Horse Show............. 2,000 00
Sales of Pure Bred Stock (additional) including expenses
    of meetings and advertising..................... 500 00
Contingencies (additional) 500 00

Institutes.

Contingencies (additional) 1,000 00

Dairy Branch.

Western Dairy School 1,500 00

Fruit, Vegetables, Honey and Insects.

Grants to assist co-operative associations of fruit growers
    in purchase of power sprayers and in expenses of
    spraying, organization, instruction and inspection in
    connection with same.......................... 6,000 00
Experimental Fruit Farm, Fruit Building and Residence. 5,000 00
Contingencies...................................... 500 00

Ontario Agricultural College.

Plant Breeding Investigations, services and expenses.... 1,000 00
                                                        ————   22,000 0

76   COLONIZATION AND IMMIGRATION.

Salvation Army (additional)................................$	3,000 00	
Rent and maintenance of office at Union Station (additional)....................................	600 00	
Work in Great Britain, contingencies (additional)......	6,000 00	
		9,600 00

77   HOSPITALS AND CHARITIES.

New Liskeard : New hospital for the Northern Nipissing District..$	2,000 00	
Salvation Army : Prison Gate Work	500 00	
Boys' Industrial School, Mimico : Remodelling and repairing......................................	15,000 00	
Girls' Industrial School, East Toronto : Remodelling and repairing	10,000 00	
Hamilton Mountain Sanitarium	4,000 00	
Toronto Free Hospital for Consumptives..............	4,000 00	
Society for Reclamation of Inebriates	200 00	
London Hygienic Institute..........................	50,000 00	
		85,700 00

78 MAINTENANCE AND REPAIRS OF GOVERNMENT BUILDINGS.

Parliament Buildings.

Renewal of Elevators...............................$	6 500 00	
Blue Printing Machine..............................	400 00	
Insurance (3 years)................................	7,500 00	
Elevator Attendants (2)............................	100 00	
Filing Cabinet, office furniture, including ledger desk and safe (Inspection of Public Institutions)	600 00	
Office Fittings (Provincial Board of Health)...........	400 00	
		15,500 00

79   PUBLIC BUILDINGS.

London Asylum.

Receiving Tank and Pump...........................$	250 00

Orillia Asylum.

Boiler Feed Pump..................................	175 00

Toronto Asylum.

Changes..	100,000 00

Colonization and Immigration.

Immigration Lodging House........................	5,000 00

Agriculture.

Heating, Lighting and Furnishing addition to Main Bldg.	2,000 00
Coal Bin (additional)...............................	4,700 00

Institute for Deaf and Dumb.

Renewing, Painting and Re-setting Windows, Main
  Building.. $ 500 00

Provincial Board of Health.

Fittings and Equipment for Laboratory...............   275 00

Muskoka District.

Repairs and alterations to District Court House, including new sidewalk...............................   300 00

Parry Sound District.

Lock-up at Callander 300 00
  do   at Court House at Powassan..... ....   500 00
Furnishing for Registry Office......... ....   600 00

Algoma District.

Lock-up at Echo Bay..............................   500 00
Registry Office, Sault Ste. Marie................... 6,000 00
Furniture and Fittings.............................   700 00
Land Titles Office, Sault Ste. Marie................. 2,000 00

Manitoulin District.

To complete alterations at Gore Bay Gaol............. 1,800 00

Nipissing District.

Repairs and Furniture for Registry Office, North Bay...   500 00
Repairs and alterations to Cobalt Lock-up, including new
  fence (additional)........................... .   100 00

Thunder Bay District.

Heating and plumbing Gaol and Gaoler's house........   600 00
New Registry Office at Port Arthur... .... 6,000 00
Furniture and Metallic Fittings.....................·   700 00

Sudbury District.

Court House and Gaol, Sudbury..................... 25,000 00
Furnishings... 1,000 00
Registry Office, Sudbury........................... 6,000 00
Furniture and Metallic Fittings 700 00
                                                   ———————   166,200 00

80   PUBLIC WORKS.

Draper Bridge, Revote............................. $ 500 00
North River Improvement to complete...............   600 00
Otter Creek Bridge at Copp's Falls.... ....   500 00
Dysart Township Bridge, Haliburton 600 00

Himsworth Bridges......	$ 900	00
Concrete Mixing Machine...'......................	950	00
Bells Rapids Bridge, grant........................	1,000	00
Larchwood and Thessalon Bridges to complete in steel..	2,800	00
Repairs Dredge Nation.River (grant conditional).......	3,500	00
City of St. Thomas *re* Toll Road taken over...........	3,000	00
Township of London towards purchase Proof Line Toll Road...	3,300	00

Drainage Grants.

Aux Sable River Drainage Works, Bosanquet,.........	5,000	00
Pelee Drainage Works, Mersea.;.....................	3,000	00
Nottawasaga River.....................................	5,000	00
Hardy Creek Drainage Works, Adelaide & Metcalf.....	2,500	00

33,150 0

81   COLONIZATION ROADS.

North Division.

Bellevue Road ....,........	$ 800	00
Dowling concession, 4 from Balfour town line to lot 5...	500	00
Drury, Dennison and Graham (conditional)...........	500	00
Fort Frances and Emo road	900	00
Kashabowia to Tip Top Mine.......................	3,000	00
Mine Centre road....................................	500	00
Tarentorus Township, between sections 19 and 30......	600	00
Survey of Colonization road from Sudbury to Sault Ste. Marie...	5,000	00

West Division.

Alsace road and West Phalia road..............	900	00
Cockburn and Maple Lake road.....................	400	00
North road from Pickerel River to Ferry Township.....	400	00
McKellar, 2nd concession road......................	300	00
Rose Point and Parry Sound road...................	400	00
Seguin Falls and Orrville road......................	500	00

East Division.

Alice, 14th road and bridge.........................	450	00
Antoine Creek bridge and Snow road.................	500	00
Astorville and Wisawasa road......................	400	00
Arden and Kaladar.................................	300	00
Boulter, concessions 9 and 10......................	500	00
Capreol, 3rd concession............................	500	00
Ferry roads..	400	00
Forester's Falls road and bridge, (conditional)	500	00
Hanmer Township, between lots 6 and 7..............	500	00
Marlbank road.....................................	250	00
Morton and Jones Falls road.......................	200	00
Monmouth Township road...........................	900	00
Pembroke and Eganville road....	300	00

Sharbot Lake to Titchbourne and Crow Lake .... $	500 00	
Trout Lake to North Bay............................	500 00	
Wahnapitae Lake Road.............................	1,500 00	
Cross Lake and Madawaska.........................	500 00	
Oso and 'Maberly Road............................	300 00	

Temiskaming.

Ingram, South Boundary and Cane (to complete contracts)	300 00	
Wendigo Lake Bridges.............................	900 00	

General.

New Roads in Abitibi District.......................	10,000 00	
		34,900 00

82   CHARGES ON CROWN LANDS.

Outside Service and Surveys.

Ottawa Crown Timber Agent, Special Services.......	200 00	
Estimating Temagami Reserve	5,000 00	
Fire Ranging, Additional along Railways	10,000 00	
Balance of Clearing on T. & N. O. Railway, to close up small accounts................................	2,000 00	
Exploration Survey Branch of T. & N. O. Ry., Cobalt to Sudbury	12,000 00	

Mining Development.

Mine Assessor and other Expenses under Supplementary Revenue Act, 1906..........................	7,000 00	
Mining Recorders (new Divisions, etc.) additional......	2,500 00	
Inspection of Mining Claims (additional)..............	5,000 00	
Inspector of Mines (additional)......................	200 00	
Expenses visit of Mining Institute, Engineers..........	1,000 00	
		44,900 00

83   MISCELLANEOUS.

Enforcing Liquor License Act	7,500 00	
Fish and Game....................................	6,000 00	
Law Society fees for various officers	200 00	
Misses Elizabeth and Mary Ann O'Carroll, losses 1837..	400 00	
		14,100 00

Total	$516,201 00

2 E.

FURTHER
SUPPLEMENTARY ESTIMATES, 1907

MISCELLANEOUS.

Grant towards completion of scheme of drainage in Townships of
   Osnabrook, Cornwall and Roxborough, known as the River Raisin
   drainage scheme $4,000 00
To Mrs. Helen St. John, widow of Mr. Speaker St. John........... 4,000 00
To Miss Winnie St. John, daughter of Mr. Speaker St. John......... 1,000 00
Caretaker, Osgoode Hall..... .... 50 00

               Total... $9,050 00

REPORT

OF THE

Minister of Lands, Forests and Mines

OF THE

PROVINCE OF ONTARIO

For the Year

1906.

PRINTED BY ORDER OF
THE LEGISLATIVE ASSEMBLY OF ONTARIO

TORONTO
Printed and Published by L. K. CAMERON, Printer to the King's Most Excellent Majesty
1907.

Printed by WARWICK BRO'S & RUTTER, Limited, Printers,
TORONTO.

1a L.M.

CONTENTS.

iii.

CONTENTS—*Continued.*

REPORT OF THE

Minister of Lands, Forests and Mines

Of the Province of Ontario, for the year 1906.

To His Honour the Honourable WILLIAM MORTIMER CLARK,
Lieutenant-Governor of the Province of Ontario.

MAY IT PLEASE YOUR HONOUR:

As required by law, I submit for the information of your Honour and the Legislative Assembly, a report for the year ending on the 31st December, 1906, of the management of the Crown lands of the Province.

CLERGY LANDS.

The area of Clergy lands sold during the year was 785 acres, aggregating in value $1,367.20. The collection on account of these and former sales amounted to $3,969.71. (See Appendix No. 3, page 6.)

COMMON SCHOOL LANDS.

The area of Common School lands sold during the year was 30½ acres for $70. The collection on account of these and sales of former years was $9,218.61. (See Appendix No. 3, page 6.)

GRAMMAR SCHOOL LANDS.

The area of these lands sold during the year was 76 acres, for $133.00. The collection on account of these and sales in former years was $2,669.52 (See Appendix No. 3, page 6.)

UNIVERSITY LANDS.

The area of these lands sold during the year was 1,411½ acres, for $705.75. The collection on account of these and sales of former years was $1,082.40. (See Appendix No. 3, page 6.)

CROWN LANDS.

There have been sold for agricultural purposes during the year 69,860½ acres for $72,204.31. The collection on account of these and former sales was $83,851.64. There were sold for mining purposes 4,877 acres for $11,988.05, and collected on account of mining sales $118,243.62.

[v.]

There were leased for mining purposes 13,384 acres for $13,177.00. There was collected on account of mining leases $46,620.69. There were 942½ acres of Crown lands leased for other than mining purposes. The collection on account of these and former leases was $3,372.83. The total area of land disposed of during the year was 91,367 acres. The total collections on account of lands sold and leased during the year was $100,399.81. (See Appendix No. 3, page 6.)

The Temiscamingue region has continued to attract the largest number of settlers, and this is not to be wondered at in view of the prosperity and future prospects of that great district. The existence of immense areas of fertile land, the discoveries of silver in different sections, the abundance of employment afforded by railway construction, mining and lumbering, the ready market for all varieties of farm and garden produce, the easy access afforded by the T. & N. O. Ry., are all factors which make that northern region a splendid field for those desiring to secure homes for themselves and their families. When the illimitable areas of good land lying north of the present settled area, and extending beyond the Transcontinental Railway line and east and west along that line for long distances, are opened up by the construction of that railway, an enormous population will certainly flow in, and the construction itself will give employment to an army of laborers who will require to be fed, thus affording a market for all farm and garden products.

An appropriation has been taken by the Public Works Department to construct trunk lines of road in that region, thus making it accessible from the Railway.

The Department has continued to insist upon a strict compliance with the regulations as to the performance of settlement duties in those townships which are open for sale. Two Homestead Inspectors have been actively engaged during the year in the work of inspecting lots sold, and where they have reported neglect to occupy and reside, the delinquents have been notified that unless they went into occupation by a certain date their claims would be cancelled. The Salvation Army has been meditating placing a colony in this region and should they carry out their plans, an object lesson would be afforded in systematic settlement and co-operative farming. The foreign population in this district is small in numbers, but 't is interesting to know that there is a Russian Jewish colony in the Townships of Chamberlain and Pacaud, who are reported to be industrious and energetic, earning good wages and putting the money back into their farms. The agent reports them to be a very law-abiding sober people, anxious to become British subjects and learn the English language.

In the old Free Grant districts there has not been any great influx of population. The areas suitable for settlement have been pretty well taken up, and the lots remaining unlocated are largely broken lots, not well suited for agriculture. In certain localities small areas suitable for settlement are still to be found, but these are the exception. The Department has instituted a system of homestead inspections in order to enforce compliance with the conditions of settlement, and has not hesitated to cancel locations where improvements are not diligently prosecuted. Owing to the increased value of woods other than pine, there has grown up a desire to take up lots not suitable for agricultural purposes in order to be in a position to dispose of the timber. To prevent such abuses the Department has provided for a system of inspecting lots applied for, with a view of ascertaining if there is a sufficient proportion of good land in them to warrant the expectation that a living could be made by farming. If there is, the lands are located, but where it is palpable that the lands are not capable of affording a living by agriculture, and are being applied for in order to get the timber, location is refused. The Free Grant districts of Muskoka and Parry Sound, about which there were many shakings of the head when they were opened for settlement, now contain a population of nearly 50,000 with 8 or 10 important towns.

The Rainy River and Thunder Bay districts have received their share of attention, although their proximity to the great prairie region tells against them, but the fact remains that the valley of the Rainy River is one of the most fertile and beautiful areas in the Province.

In the Sudbury region, the following townships have been opened under the Free Grants Act, and are being rapidly located:—Blezard, Broder, Garson, Hanmer, Neelon, Balfour, Rayside, West part of Capreol.

In every section of the Province prosperity prevails, and the settlers are as a rule contented and comfortable. The Department is everywhere requiring settlers to proceed with taking up residence and the perform-ance of settlement conditions, as it is only by so doing that population can become dense and the burden of taxation, etc., be equitably distributed.

MILITARY GRANTS.

There were 400 certificates issued during the year, authorizing veter-ans to select their lands, under I Edward VII. Cap. 6. This brings the total number issued under this legislation up to 13,000. Location certi-ficates, confirming veterans in the lands selected upon prescribed condi-tions, were issued to 500, making a total of 2,902. Eight hundred and twenty locations were made during the year, nearly all in the Abitibi region, bringing the number of locations up to 5,220. As already stated 13,000 certificates have been issued and there are in the Department new applications for certificates to the number of 250. The Legislation of last Session, authorizing the redemption by the Treasurer of the Province of unlocated military certificates at $50.00 each, has resulted in the surrender of 1,400 certificates. This will materially lessen the outstanding number but it still leaves about 6,000 to be provided for. Patents under the amended Act have issued to 301 veterans for their locations.

MINING INDUSTRY.

In the year 1906 the mining industry of the Province reached high-water mark in the quantity and value of the output of mines and metal-lurgical works. The production of nickel from the deposits of the Sudbury region reached the large aggregate of 10,932 tons, valued in the matte at $3,836,419, while of copper the output was 5,940 tons worth $998,548. The steady growth of this branch of the industry has placed Ontario indisput-ably at the head of the nickel-producing countries of the world. The devel-opment of the silver-cobalt area discovered on the line of the Temiskaming and Northern Ontario Railway in 1903 has gone on with great rapidity, The yield of silver which in 1904 was 206,875 ounces. increased in 1905 to 2,451,356 ounces, and in 1906 to about 5,400,000 ounces. The total value of the silver produced from the Cobalt mines up to the end of 1906, was upwards of $5,000,000. Late in the season new discoveries of silver-cobalt ore were reported from points on t'e Montreal River, 30 or 40 miles northwest of Cobalt, and if, as seems probab'e, these reports should be verified, the silver-bearing area will be materially enlarged. The chief source of iron ore continues to be the Helen mine in the Michipicoten region, but at Bessemer, in the County of Hastings, and at Radnor mine, in the County of Renfrew, important deposits of magnetite are being opened up. Shipments from the former are being made to blast furnaces at Midland and Sault Ste. Marie. The magnetic ore bodies at Moose Mountain, in the township of Hutton, are also under development, the branch line of the Canadian Northern to the mines being nearly finished. The other substances, both metallic and non-metallic, in the long and varied list of mineral products of Ontario, have been produced in about the usual quantities, except petroleum which has decreased, and natural gas which has largely increased.

The natural result of the great activity in mining has been an increased demand for mining lands, the property of the Crown. This is reflected by the growth in the revenue from mining sources. Under the new law, very considerable sums are received from the sale of miner's licenses and other fees, particularly in times of mining excitement like the present. The beds of Cobalt and Kerr Lakes, in the township of Coleman (except portions already granted), were offered for sale by public tender towards the close of the year. The former containing 51 acres, sold for $1,085,000, ten per cent. of which was paid in before 31st December. The tenders for Kerr Lake not being considered satisfactory, fresh bids were advertised for, and in January, 1907, the parcel was sold for $178,500, and a royalty of ten per cent. on the gross value of the minerals extracted.

COLLECTIONS.

The total collection from all services was $2,266,387.94. Of this, $269,029.06 was from lands sold and leased; $1,900,914.62 was from woods and forests; $85,256.06 from mining licenses and fees, and royalty on mines. (See Appendix No. 4, page 7.)

DISBURSEMENTS.

The gross expenditure of the Department for the past year was $616,259.80. The principal services were: agents' salaries and disbursements, $42,351.94; forest ranging, $45,165.61; fire ranging, $57,611.65; mining development. $28,195.02: forest reserves, $27,913.19; surveys, $125,003.39: refunds, $32.844.62; Algonquin Park, $11,501.70; Temagami timber cutting, $89,412.95; Veterans' commutation, $71,800.00. (See Appendices Nos. 6 and 7, pages 9 to 33.)

WOODS AND FORESTS.

(The total revenue from this branch was $1,900,914.62.) Of this, $535,970.57 was from bonuses, $1,295,378.53 from timber dues; $66,118.47 from ground rent, and $3,447.05 from transfer fees. (See Appendix No. 4, page 7.)

(The lumber trade has continued in a prosperous condition, and there has been a marked increase in the value of stumpage. The outlook for the present season is that the output of logs will exceed that of last season. A number of berths suitable for tie purposes were sold during the year at satisfactory prices. The Montreal Pulp Concession which had been forfeited for non-performance of conditions, was also put up for sale and a bonus of $300,000 received for the right to cut the pulpwood thereon. The output of pulpwood for the year was 84,961 cords, being 12,285 cords in excess of last year. The pulp mills at Sault Ste. Marie, Spanish River and Sturgeon Falls have been running to their full capacity during the year.)

FIRE RANGING.

There were 509 fire rangers on duty during the past summer, including those in the forest reserves. Of this number 345 were employed on territory under timber license, half of their wages and expenses being paid by the licensees, and the other half by the Crown. Along the line of construction of the T. & N. O. Ry. the Canadian Northern, and the Grand Trunk Pacific, west of Port Arthur, fire rangers were put on duty. The total cost to the Department of this service was $57,611.65. No serious fires occurred, the supervision, especially along the railway lines, being very close.

CULLERS' EXAMINATIONS.

Cullers' Examinations were held at North Bay, Port Arthur, Sault Ste. Marie, Fort Frances and Kenora, during the year. Sixty candidates were successful, and were granted certificates giving them authority to act as Cullers. (For list of Licensed Cullers see Appendix No. 60 page 145.)

ALGONQUIN AND RONDEAU PARKS.

The reports of the Superintendents of these parks will be found in appendices Nos. 58 and 59, pages 142 to 144.

CROWN SURVEYS.

The following Crown Surveys have been carried out this year:—
Three hundred and fifty one miles of base and meridian lines have been run in the District of Algoma, these lines forming the outlines of nine mile townships. The Inter-provincial boundary between the Provinces of Ontario and Quebec has been completed from the eighty-eighth mile to the one hundred and fortieth mile north of the head of Lake Temiskaming, by the Commissioners appointed, respectively, by the Provinces of Ontario and Quebec. Mr. T. J. Patten, O.L.S.. being the Commissioner for Ontario. and Mr. J. H. Sullivan, P. L. S., the Commissioner for Quebec. By the courtesy of the Chief Astronomer, Dr. W. F. King, of the Dominion Astronomical Observatory, Ottawa, the Department has been furnished with the geographical position of monument A on the Inter-Provincial Boundary between Ontario and Quebec, at the north end of Lake Temiskaming as computed by Dr. Klotz, Dominion Astronomer. This monument was set by the Commissioners appointed by the respective Provinces in the year 1874, on the north side of the channel called Chenail du Diable, as the initial point for commencing the Inter-Provincial boundary at the head of Lake Temiskaming. This point has been found to be situate in latitude 47 degrees, 33 minutes, 43.14 seconds north, and longitude 79 degrees, 30 minutes, 56.32 seconds west. Twenty-seven townships have been subdivided into lots and concessions, four of these being surveyed on the new nine mile square system, the follow-

ing being a list of the names and districts in which they occur: In the District of Nipissing, the townships of Sweatman, Stimson, Allen, Bigwood, Scollard, Sherring and Marathon, seven in all   In the District of Algoma, the townships of Bradburn, Sydere, Calder, Clute, Beck, Dargavel, Lennox, Ottaway, Fournier, Gallagher, Chapleau, Aubin, Nesbitt, Strathearn, Mc-Naught, Lackner, Pattinson and Paul, eighteen in all.   In the District of Rainy River, the townships of Langton and Redditt. The surveyors of the base and meridian lines, forming the outlines of sixteen townships nine miles square, report the land covered by their survey to be almost all good farming land.   The other townships in Northern Ontario situate in what is called the Clay Belt are reported to be almost all good clay and clay loam land, the most of the land being already well suited for agricultural purposes and nearly all the other with a moderate amount of drainage can be utilized for agricultural purposes.

Reviewing the surveys of the last few years in this part of the country it is safe to say that at least eighty-five per cent. of the land is first class agricultural soil. Some of the townships sub-divided have been reported to be absolutely all good land, not one acre unfit for settlement, a thing unparalled in the history of townships in this Province.

About seventy-two townships of thirty-six square miles each have been sub-divided in this northern part of the Province and four townships of nine miles square, each containing about fifty-two thousand acres, and about fourteen hundred miles of base and meridian lines have been run altogether, these lines forming the outlines of townships.

The townships of Allen, Bigwood and Scollard, situate on the north side of French River, in the district of Nipissing, have a number of settlers already squatted in the townships. Portions of these townships are very good agricultural land. The townships near Chapleau have not turned out as valuable for agricultural purpose as was anticipated, although there is a large quantity of timber of various sorts on these townships.

A number of timber berths in the Districts of Rainy River, Algoma, Thunder Bay and Nipissing were also surveyed during the year.

Several other minor surveys have been performed also.

The summer, similar to that of the season before, was a very favorable one, so that the surveyors were able to finish their contracts.

The surveyors' reports so far as received and examined will be found in appendices 18 to 57 inclusive, pages 46 to 142 inclusive.

MUNICIPAL SURVEYS.

The only municipal surveys for which instructions issued during this year was that of a survey in the township of East Oxford, in the county of Oxford, for which instructions were issued to O. L. S. F. J. Ure, on the petition of the municipal council of East Oxford, to survey the road allowance between the third and fourth concessions from the original monument between lots twelve and thirteen across lots fourteen to twenty inclusive.

The municipal survey of the line between concessions eight and nine from lot twenty southerly to lot number fourteen, both inclusive, in the township of Hinchinbrooke, in the county of Frontenac, has been performed by O. L..S. E. T. Wilkie, and has been confirmed under the provisions of the Revised Statutes of Ontario, 1897, chapter 181, sections 14 and 15, such survey so confirmed being final and conclusive.

The particulars relating to these surveys will be found in appendix No. 14, page 42.

MINING AND OTHER SURVEYS.

The Mines Act requires that applicants to purchase or lease mining lands in unsurveyed territory shall file in the Department surveyor's plans (in triplicate) of their proposed mining locations and mining claims, with field notes and descriptions by metes and bounds, before any sale or lease can be carried out, and under Orders-in-Council dated 23rd January, 1892; 3rd December, 1892; 29th April, 1886; 22nd September, 1893; 26th February, 1906, applicants to purchase islands, or locations for agricultural purposes, in unsurveyed territory, are required to file surveyor's plans (in triplicate) of their locations or islands as the case may be, with field notes and descriptions by metes and bounds; the locations to be of the form and size, wherever practicable, prescribed by the Mines Act, together with the necessary affidavits as to their being no adverse claim by occupation or improvement, etc.

Under the above Act, Orders-in-Council and regulations, in the Districts of Parry Sound, Nipissing, Algoma, Thunder Bay, Rainy River, an area of 14,065 221-300 acres has been sold and patented during the year, for which the sum of $18,813.70 has been received; and an area of 7,096 98-100 acres has been leased at $1,00 per acre for the first year's rental.

F. COCHRANE,
Minister.

Department of Lands, Forests and Mines,
Toronto, December 31st, 1906.

APPENDICES.

Appendix No. 1.

Returns of Officers and Clerks of the Department of Lands, Forests and Mines for the year 1906.

Branch.	Name.	Designation.	When appointed.	Salary per annum.	Remarks.
				$　　c.	
	Hon. F. Cochrane	Minister	06, May 13	4,000 00	
	Aubrey White	Deputy Minister	1882, Jan. 1	3,500 00	
	George Kennedy	Law Clerk	1872, Feb. 1	2,400 00	
	Geo. W. Yates	Minister's Secretary	1899, Feb. 26	1,600 00	
	E. S. Williamson	Secretary to Department	1889, May 1	1,500 00	
	Janet Garvie	Stenographer	06, Jan. 1	600 00	
Sales and Free Grants	J. J. Mphy	Chief Clerk	1872, May 1	2,000 00	
	W. R. Leer	Clerk	1894, Feb. 5	1,000 00	
	Selby Draper	do	1903, Jan. 1	1,050 00	
	Wler Cain	do	1903, Mar. 6	1,000 00	
	May Bengough	Stenographer	1896, Oct. 23	600 00	
	W. A. Collins	Clerk	1906, July 1	800 00	
	M. C. Jaffray	Stenographer	1904, Nov. 9	450 00	Resigned October, 1906.
Military Grants	R. H. Browne	Chief Clerk	06, Mar. 2	1,500 00	
	R. T. Wir	Clerk	09, Jan. 13	700 00	
	E. F. O'Neil	Stenographer	09, Dv. 9	500 00	
Surveys and Patents	Geo. B. Kirkpatrick	Director of Surveys	1886, Jn.30	2,300 00	
	J. F. Won	Surveyor and Draughts man	1892, Sept. 1	1,750 00	
	W. F. Lewis	Clerk	1872, Feb. 5	1,100 00	
	D. G. Boyd	Draughtsman	1897, Sept. 27	1,250 00	
	E. M. Jarvis	Clerk	1904, Oct. 19	900 00	
	J. B. Proctor	Stenographer	1897, Jan. 15	900 00	
	H. Fy	Draughtsman	1904, Jan. 13	900 00	
	M. H. W. Kirkland	Stenographer	1904, Nov. 23	900 00	
	C. S. See	Kief Clerk Patents	1880, May 22	560 00	
	C. E. Burns	Clerk	1900, April 9	1,750 00	
	W. S. Sutherland	do	1902, Jan. 13	900 00	
	W. Carrell	do	1904, Jan. 15	1,050 00	
				960 00	

	Name	Position	Date	Salary	Remarks
Woods and Forests	J. A. G. Crozier	Chief Clerk	1867, Dec. 1	2,000 00	
	Kenneth Miller	Clerk	1891, Nov. 1	1,150 00	
	J. B. Ok	do	1898, Aug. 1	1,300 00	
	H. Gillard	do	1900, April 9	1,000 00	
	F. J. Niven	do	1903, Jan. 1	900 00	
	W. F. Trivett	do	1904, Jan. 13	850 00	
	R. H. Hodgson	do	1904, Nov. 23	800 00	
Accounts	D. George Ross	Accountant	1861, April 15	2,000 00	
	E. Leigh	Clerk	1873, Dec. 20	1,200 00	
	M. J. Ferris	do	1892, April 1	1,150 00	Resigned December 31, 1903.
	A. E. Robillard	do	1894, May 4	800 00	
	H. M. Lount	do	1904, Jan. 13	1,000 00	
	F. Yeigh	Registrar	1886, March 1	1,500 00	
	H.		1893, Oct. 1	1,100 00	
	H. Brophy	Messenger	1893, Oct. 1	650 00	
Bureau of Mines	T. W. Gibson	Deputy Minister	1891, June 19	3,000 00	
	Anne Moffat	Stenographer	1901, March 1	700 00	
	W. H. Morris	do	1906, Jan. 1	700 00	
	Ethel Craig	do	1906, Jan. 1	550 00	

D. GEO. ROSS,
Accountant.

AUBREY WHITE,
Deputy Minister.

Appendix No. 2.

List of Land Agents for the year 1906.

Name.	Post Office Address.	District or County.	Date of Appointment.	Salary per annum.	Remarks.
				$ c.	
Anderson, Jno. H	Hill	Part of Hastings and Peterboro	1905, May 31	300 00	Agent for sale of land ; resigned 7th Mch, 1906.
Annis, A. E.	Dryden	do District of Rainy River	1895, Nov. 28	200 00	
Barr, James	Fort Frances	Homestead Inspector	1906, Nov. 23	1,200 00	Agent for sale of land.
Boa, Chas.	Plevna	Part of Frontenac and Addington	1905, Oct. 20	100 00	Agent for sale of land.
Brown, James B	Bracebridge	Homestead Inspector	1905, July 28	900 00	Agent for sale of land.
Byers, R. J		Part of Algoma District	1905, July 3	500 00	Agent for sale of land without salary
Bishop, H. E.		Town Plot of Hilton	1896, Mch 23		Agent for sale of land.
Buchanan, Thos	Thessalon	Part of Algoma District	1901, Nov. 30	300 00	
Burns, C. M.	Parry Sound	Head Inspector	1905, Nov. 15	900 00	
Caldwell, Wm.	Stratton Station	Part of Rainy River District	1897, Aug. 12	300 00	
Deacon, Jno. M.	New Liskeard	Head Inspector	1906, June 8	1,200 00	
Eastland, T. G.	Mattawa	Part of Nipissing District	1905, July 8	300 00	
Ellis, James	Apsley	City of Peterboro	1896, July 10	300 00	
Freeborn, Dr. J. S.	Parry Sound	Parry Sound District	1898, Dec.	500 00	
Grills, Jno. J.	Maganetawan	do	1905, Oct. 10	500 00	Agent for sale of land.
Groulx, R. J.	New Liskeard	Lake Temiskaming, District of Nipissing	1905, July 3	500 00	
Handy, E.	Ernsdale	Homestead Inspector	1906, My 7	600 00	
Hartle, Wm.		Part of Parry Sound	1879, July 3	500 00	
Hollands, C. J.	Fort Frances	do Victoria	1895, Nov. 28	350 00	Mining and land agent.
Hunt, J. H. McK.	Fort William	Town Plot of and Rainy River	1892, 12	300 00	Agent for sale of and.
Hugh, Williams	Heaslip	Homestead Inspector	1906, May 12	600 00	
Ellis, Jos. A.	Port Arthur	Part of District of Nipissing	1905, July 14	500 00	Agent for sale of land.
MacLennan, J. K.	Sturgeon Falls	District of Thunder Bay	1903, July 8	500 00	Mining and land agent.
McFayden, Alex	Sudbury	District of Nipissing	1905, July 3	500 00	
Prince, Adam	Emo	District of Algoma	1905, July 3	300 00	
Patton, W. H.	Wilno	District of Rainy River	1905, Sept. 8	500 60	
Pronger, R. H.	Killarney	Renfrew	1905, July 12	Commission	Agent for sale of land.
Quenneville, Isadore	Dryden	Town Plot Killarney	1895, March 2	300 00	do
Scott, W. F.	Sturgeon Falls	Part of District of Rainy River	1906, My 7	600 00	
Seegmiller, M.	Rat Portage	Homestead Inspector	1906, May 7	1,200 00	Resigned May 15, 1906.
		District of Rainy River	1903, Nov. 21	800 00	Mining and land agent ; removed Dec. 31, 1906.

Appendix No. 2.—Concluded.

List of Land Agents for the year 1906.

Name.	Post Office Address.	District or County.	Date of Appointment.	Salary per annum.	Remarks.
				$ c.	
Scarlett, J. S.	Powassan	Part of District of Parry Sound	1880, June 17	500 00	
Tait, J. R.	L'Amable	do	1869, May 28	500 00	
...n, Jaes	Kinmount	do	1905, May 31	150 00	
Warren, D. B.	Pembroke	do	1905, July 3	300 00	
Wright, E. A.	Warren	do	1905, July 14	250 00	
Whybourne, W. E.	Marksville	St. Joseph Island	1905, April 7	150 00	Agent for sale of land.
...n, T. P.	Ridgetown	Assistant Homestead Inspector	1905, May 10	912 50	do
...g, H. N.	Sault Ste. Marie	Part of Algoma District	1901, Nov. 23	300 00	Free grant and sale agent.
..., James	Fort Frances	Homestead Inspector	1905, July 6	1,200 00	Resigned 30th Nov., 1906.

D. GEO. ROSS,
Accountant.

AUBREY WHITE,
Deputy Minister.

2 L.M.

Appendix No. 3.

STATEMENT of Lands Sold and Leased, amount of Sales and Leases, and amount of Collections
for the year 1906.

Service.	Acres sold and leased.	Amount of sales and leases.	Collections on sales and leases.
		$ c.	$ c.
Crown Lands—			
Agricultural	69,860½	72,204 31	83,851 64
Mining	4,877	11,988 05	118,243 62
Clergy Lands	785	1,367 20	3,969 71
Common School Lands..........................	30½	70 00	9,218 61
Grammar School Lands	76	133 00	2,669 52
University Lands	1,411½	705 75	1,082 40
Leases—			
Mining..	13,384	13,177 00	46,620 69
Crown	942½	754 50	3,372 83
	91,367	$100,399 81	$269,029 02

D. GEO. ROSS,   AUBREY WHITE,
    Accountant.   Deputy Minister.

Appendix No. 4.

STATEMENT of the Revenue of the Department of Lands, Forests and Mines for the year 1906.

Service.	$ c.	$ c.	$ c.
LAND COLLECTIONS.			
Crown Lands—			
Agricultural	83,851 64		
Mining	118,243 62		
		202,095 26	
Clergy Lands	....	3,969 71	
Common School Lands	....	9,218 61	
Grammar School Lands.......................	....	2,669 52	
University Lands.............................	....	1,082 40	
Railway Lands...............................	....	22 25	
Rent—			
Mining Leases	46,620 69		
Crown Leases................................	3,372 83		
		49,993 52	
Mining Licenses and Fees.....................	70,256 06		
Royalty on Mines............................	15,000 00		
		85,256 06	
			354,307 33
WOODS AND FORESTS.			
Bonus..	....	535,970 57	
Timber dues..................................	....	1,295,378 53	
Ground rent..................................	....	66,118 47	
Transfer fees.................................	....	3,447 05	
			1,900,914 62
Casual fees...................................	645 83		
Cullers' fees	348 00		
Assay fees	1,655 20		
		2,649 03	
Rondeau Park	189 00		
Algonquin Park..............................	296 50		
Forest Reserves...............................	1,353 50		
		1,839 00	
			4,488 03
REFUNDS.			
Temagami timber cutting......................	....	3,531 54	
Diamond Drill................................	....	2,855 37	
Fire Ranging	....	83 90	
Mining Inspection	....	21 75	
Bureau of Mines	....	53	
Inspection...................................	....	12 00	
Agents' salaries..............................	....	172 87	
			6.677 96
			2,266,387 94

D. GEO. ROSS,   AUBREY WHITE
    Accountant.   Deputy Minister.

Appendix No. 5.

STATEMENT of the Receipts of the Department of Lands, Forests and Mines for the year 1906, which are considered as Special Funds.

Service.	$ c.	$ c.
Clergy Lands.		
Principal..	2,748 90	
Interest...	1,220 81	
		3,969 71
Common School Lands.		
Principal..	3,202 43	
Interest...	6,016 18	
		9,218 61
Grammar School Lands.		
Principal..	1,241 20	
Interest...	1,428 32	
		2,669 52
University Lands.		
Principal..	838 98	
Interest...	243 42	
		1,082 40
Railway Lands.		
Principal..	12 50	
Interest...	9 75	
		22 25
		$16,962 49

D. GEO. ROSS,   AUBREY WHITE.
    Accountant.   *Deputy Minister.*

Appendix No 6.

STATEMENT of Disbursements of the Departments of Lands and Mines for the year 1906.

Name.	$ c.	$ c.	$ c.
AGENTS' SALARIES.			
Land.			
Annis. A. E..	72 50		
Anderson, J. H....................................	300 00		
Buchanan, Thos....................................	300 00		
Brown, Jas. B.....................................	900 00		
Byers, R. J....................................	500 00		
Both. Chas.......................................	100 00		
Campbell, Wm....................................	300 00		
Deacon, J. M.....................................	300 00		
Ellis, James	500 00		
Eastland, T. G....................................	300 00		
Freeborn, Dr. J. S................................	500 00		
Grills, John J....................................	500 00		
Handy, E..	500 00		
Hartle, Wm.......................................	350 00		
Hollands, C. J....................................	300 00		
Hesson, W. H.....................................	500 00		
Hugh, Williams....................................	500 00		
Levis, J. A.......................................	500 00		
MacLennan, J. K...................................	500 00		
McFayden, Alex....................................	300 00		
Prince, Adam......................................	500 00		
Pronger, R. H.	191 42		
Seegmiller, M.....................................	800 00		
Scarlett, J. S....................................	500 00		
Tait, J. R..	500 00		
Warren, D. B......................................	300 00		
Wilson. James.....................................	150 00		
Wright, E. A......................................	250 00		
Whybourne, Wm. E..................................	150 00		
Young, H. N.......................................	300 00		
Timber.		11,663 92	
Christie, W. P....................................	1,600 00		
Hawkins, S. J.....................................	1,400 00		
Henderson, Chas...................................	1,400 00		
Howie, R. G.	1,200 00		
Kennedy, John.....................................	1,600 00		
McDonald, Hector	1,400 00		
Margach, Wm.......................................	1,600 00		
Maughan, Jos......................................	1,400 00		
Oliver, J. A......................................	1,200 00		
Stevenson, A......................................	1,400 00		
Homestead Inspectors.		14,200 00	
Barr, James	100 00		
Burnes, C. W......................................	900 00		
Chester, Thos.....................................	678 90		
Carried forward	1,678 90	25,863 92	

Appendix No. 6.—Continued.

Name.	$ c.	$ c.	$ c.
Brought forward..........................	1,678 90	25,863 92	
HOMESTEAD INSPECTORS.--*Concluded.*			
Groulx, R. J..................................	400 00		
Hunt, J. McK.................................	200 00		
Quenneville, Isadore	386 15		
Scott, W. F..................................	500 00		
Watson. T. P	912 50		
York, James.................................	1,100 00	5,177 55	
AGENTS' DISBURSEMENTS.			
Land.			
Annis, A. E	42 20		
Brown, Jas. B..	271 58		
Byers, R. J. :................................	34 83		
Campbell, Wm................................	36 65		
Deacon, J. M.................................	5 08		
Ellis, James	25 57		
Grills, Jno. J.................................	35 68		
Handy, E.	17 64		
Hesson, W. H................................	27 25		
Hugh, Williams..............................	42 27		
MacLennan, J. K.............................	27 08		
McFayden, Alex..............................	48 85		
Pronger, R. H	7 62		
Seegmiller, M................................	372 40		
Scarlett, J. S.................................	2 50		
Whybourne, Wm. E	2 00		
Young, H. N	11 50	1,010 70	
Timber.			
Christie, W. P................................	430 54		
Hawkins, S. J	259 85		
Henderson, Chas.............................	142 57		
Howie, R. G	431 95		
Kennedy, John...............................	609 69		
McDonald, Hector	533 12		
Margach, Wm	1,861 27		
Maughan, Jos................................	457 36		
Oliver, J. A	1,230 14		
Stevenson, A.................................	381 11	6,337 60	
Homestead Inspectors.			
Burnes, C. W	591 74		
Chester, Thos................................	76 14		
Groulx, R. J.................................	70 90		
Quenneville, Isadore	113 10		
Scott, W. F......	157 85		
Watson, T. P	277 60		
York, Jas	420 65	1,707 98	
Carried forward	....	40,097 75	

Appendix No. 6.—Continued.

Name.	$ c.	$ c.	$ c.
Brought forward	....	40,097 75	
Miscellaneous.			
Ames. D., Caretaker Dog Lake.......................	20 00		
Armstrong, J. E., *re* inspection Hoyle & Murphy......	82 50		
Best, S. G., postage 1905	9 14		
Britton, Geo., Caretaker Mud and Loon Lakes........	25 00		
Beckett, J. R., *re* inspection Cameron and Papineau, etc.	45 00		
Boyd, Jas. " Houghton.....	10 00		
Christie, M. " Burton and Brown	180 00		
Christie, John . " Burpee	74 00		
Cruise, W. W " 16 and 19 plan 146, Windsor	10 00		
Deacon, E. " lots in Oso..............	10 00		
Danis, Samuel, Caretaker Leonard Island.............	20 00		
Hunt, John McK., *re* inspection Conmee.............	65 00		
Jervis, Henry " Phelps..............	45 00		
Kelly, Thos. " Hershel and McClure.	453 40		
Moir, G. A. " Crawford & Carnegie..	85 00		
May, Henry " Burpee, etc..........	535 00		
Murray, James " Hoyle and Murphy...	218 60		
McGowan, Wm. " lots in Conger........	40 00		
McConnell, T. C. " mill site 67 E. H. R., Tudor	20 00		
McKelvie, Daniel, *re* inspection Crawford & Carnegie..	221 55		
Potts, H. T. " lots in Southampton ...	10 00		
Toronto Savings and Loan Co., rent of Peterborough office	75 00		
		2,254 19	
Ottawa.			42,351 94
Darby, E. J., Agent................................	1,500 00		
Larose, S. C., Clerk	1,000 00		
		2,500 00	
Rent	416 67		
Disbursements	862 93		
		1,279 60	
Quebec.			3,779 60
Nicholson, B., Agent...............................	1,500 00		
Harney, Thomas, Clerk.............................	150 00		
		1,650 00	
Rent	125 00		
Disbursements.....................................	235 70		
		360 70	
Wood Ranging.			2,010 70
Allan, R. A.......................................	1,330 00		
Disbursements	20 00		
		1,350 00	
Ansley, J. J	....	1,015 00	
Ansley, W. E	....	150 00	
Arnell, Wm	....	100 00	
Archer, A. E......................................	465 00		
Disbursements	387 80		
		852 80	
Carried forward.................................	....	3,467 80	48,142 24

Appendix No. 6.—Continued.

Name.	$ c.	$ c.	$ c.
Brought forward..........................	....	3,467 80	48,142 24
WOOD RANGING—*Continued.*			
Baulke, George R................................	235 00		
Disbursements................................	22 50		
		257 50	
Barrett, Thos..................................	....	1,000 00	
Bliss, L. E....................................	....	1,370 00	
Brady, John....................................	545 00		
Disbursements................................	28 50		
		573 50	
Brinkman, A. B	....	465 00	
Bell, Angus....................................	....	81 00	
Cameron, W. B.................................	....	230 00	
Chalmers, Geo. J	574 00		
Disbursements................................	33 70		
		607 70	
Chenier, D. A	....	100 00	
Coburn, John..................................	....	175 00	
Corrigan, R. T.................................	....	100 00	
Creighton, Thos	....	93 00	
Durrell, Wm...................................	....	75 00	
Fairbairn, N. H................................	....	100 00	
Foster, E. G...................................	....	150 00	
French, L	....	100 00	
Gorman, Pat...................................	....	880 00	
Halliday, James	....	1,350 00	
Hartley, Chas	....	225 00	
Herring, E. C	....	100 00	
Hickerson, M. T...............................	....	275 00	
Hill, Joshua	....	1,180 00	
Huckson, A. H.................................	....	1,318 00	
Hurdman, W. H................................	895 00		
Disbursements................................	4 50		
		899 50	
Hutton, John..................................	1,075 00		
Disbursements................................	20 90		
		1,095 90	
Jervis, H......................................	1,190 00		
Disbursements................................	5 70		
		1,195 70	
John, Alex.....................................	....	820 00	
Johnson, S. M..................................	1,685 00		
Disbursements................................	138 82		
		1,823 82	
Lalonde, E	....	300 00	
Lee, James B..................................	....	970 00	
Londry, W. E	....	200 00	
Lozo, John	....	835 00	
Lucas, R. G	720 00		
Disbursements................................	30 70		
		750 70	
McCallum, Thos	....	171 00	
McCaw, John..................................	....	391 00	
McCreight, John...............................	1,305 00		
Disbursements................................	420 61		
		1.725 61	
Carried forward	....	25,451 73	48,142 24

Appendix No. 6.—Continued.

Name.	$ c.	$ c.	$ c.
Brought forward		25,451 73	48,142 24
WOOD RANGING.—*Continued.*			
McDonald, S. C.		815 00	
McDougall, J. T.		760 00	
McNamara, John		1,015 00	
McPherson, J. S	629 00		
Disbursements	16 50		
		645 50	
Manice, Wm		1,425 00	
Margach, J. A.	400 00		
Disbursements	59 40		
		459 40	
Menzies, A.		1,525 00	
Murray, Wm		1,330 00	
Newburn, Wm		475 00	
Playfair, Andrew		100 00	
Rawson, Chas. E.	126 00		
Disbursements	19 55		
		145 55	
Revell, L. O		1,010 00	
Ritchie, Jas. A	469 00		
Disbursements	8 85		
		477 85	
Robinson, Wm	900 00		
Disbursements	6 00		
		906 00	
Ross, George		875 00	
Riley, E.	262 50		
Disbursements	3 90		
		266 40	
Shaw, Alfred		150 00	
Shaw, George		995 00	
Taylor, T. G.	950 00		
Disbursements	51 55		
		1,001 55	
Vincent, H. T.		1,235 00	
Watts, George	1,485 00		
Disbursements	231 63		
		1,716 63	
Welch, Harold		523 00	
Whalen, P. J.		910 00	
White, Jno. T. G.	802 50		
Disbursements	108 10		
		910 60	
Yuill, Thos		865 00	
		45,989 21	
Mather, D. L., refund		823 60	
			45,165 61
FIRE RANGING.			
Allison, Jno.		42 00	
Allison, Jos.		42 00	
Allison, M. B.	357 50		
Disbursements	18 10		
		375 60	
Carried forward		459 60	93,307 85

Appendix No. 6.—Continued.

Name.	$ c.	$ c.	$ c
Brought forward	....	459 60	93,307 85
FIRE RANGING.—*Continued.*			
Allen, Geo.............................	....	55 00	
Algoma Commercial Cc.......................	....	87 75	
Ames, Romney	170 00		
Disbursements...........	14 20		
		184 20	
Archer, Geo......	....	131 00	
Ambrose, A. W.......................	131 00		
Disbursements.............................	3 94		
		134 94	
Armstrong, J. C...........................	....	130 00	
Armstrong, W. H......................	335 00		
Disbursements......................	.22 25		
		357 25	
Arnott, Wm.	....	130 00	
Aikins, Geo...........................	....	132 00	
Atkinson, T. S......................	140 00		
Disbursements.........................	35 54		
		175 54	
Barb, Ben.............................	....	131 00	
Barrett, Thos.........................	....	104 00	
Barr, Archie...........................	....	131 00	
Beaton, Wm............................	....	125 00	
Beggs A...............................	352 50		
Disbursements	19 80		
		372 30	
Beggs, Wm............................	....	93 00	
Bellefenille, Oliver....................	....	132 00	
Bertrand, Paul.......................	355 00		
Disbursements........................	5 50		
		360 50	
Bertrand, Felix.......................	....	82 00	
Bertrand, Isaac	....	109 50	
Bethune, Donald.....................	....	54 00	
Beggs, Jos............................	350 00		
Disbursements........................	14 80		
		364 80	
Bissett, J. C..........................	....	131 00	
Bone, A..............................	....	307 50	
Bowland, Jno.........................	....	131 00	
Bowie, Louis	....	119 00	
Booth, J. R...........................	....	340 71	
Boisvert, Jno.........................	....	106 00	
Bradburn, E. O.......................	345 00		
Disbursements.........................	17 30		
		362 30	
Brewer. Chas. E.	....	131 00	
Brinkman, A. B.......................	345 00		
Disbursements.........................	48 50		
		393 50	
Carried forward	....	6,058 39	93,307 85

Appendix No. C.—Continued.

Name:	$ c.	$ c.	$ c.
Brought forward....................		6,058 39	93,307 85
FIRE RANGING.—*Continued.*			
Brooks, T. H........................		132 00	
Brown, J. B........................	220 00		
Disbursements...................	29 25		
		249 25	
Brown, Jno........................		131 00	
Bruno, Paul.......................		131 00	
Buchanan, A.......................	352 50		
Disbursements...................	19 30		
		371 80	
Burns, Wm........................		131 00	
Buchanan, Robt....................		89 00	
Burns, Alex.......................		120 00	
Burgess, W. H.....................		262 00	
Burger, Wm.......................	335 00		
Disburssments...................	26 35		
		361 35	
Burton, R.........................		83 00	
Canadian Copper Co................		7 00	
Cannon, J. V.......................		151 00	
Cardiff, G. F.......................		131 00	
Carpenter, T. G....................		2 50	
Campbell Henderson................		128 00	
Campbell, Rory....................		63 00	
Cameron, Albert...................		126 00	
Caron, Vital.......................		131 00	
Carson, Jas. G.....................	270 00		
Disbursements...................	29 25		
		299 25	
Cartier, Felix.....................		132 00	
Carlin, Jas. Thomas................		131 00	
Charlton, J. and W. A..............		281 38	
Chartrand Theophile...............		99 00	
Christie, Jno......................		113 00	
Christilan, Henry..................		131 00	
Coghlan, Thos.....................		131 00	
Cartwright, Thos..................		131 00	
Colonial Lumber Co................		60 00	
Cook Bros. Lumber Co..............		10 95	
Cole, Geo		132 00	
Cottenham, Wm...................		131 00	
Collins, Chas......................		131 00	
Colway, G. H......................		66 00	
Conboy, Timothy..................		131 00	
Connolly, Jno......................		100 00	
Conorette, Wm....................		66 00	
Conway, Richard		143 00	
Cooney, J. C.......................		118 00	
Couture, Nelson		78 00	
Conger Bark, Limited..............		3 00	
Corrigan, M. B.....................		131 00	
Corrigan, S. O.....................	257 50		
Disbursements	25 50		
		283 00	
Carried forward..................		11,891 87	93,307 85

Appendix No. 6.—Continued.

Name.	$ c.	$ c.	$ c.
Brought forward............................	....	11,891 87	93,307 85
FIRE RANGING.—*Continued.*			
Coulter, Chas..................................	340 00		
Disbursements...........................	23 30		
		363 30	
Cousins, Jas...............................	....	131 00	
Cosineau, Arthur	....	327 50	
Cox, Stewart	340 00		
Disbursements............................	14 85		
		354 85	
Cox, Jos..................................	....	98 00	
Crombie, Jno..............................	....	132 00	
Culhane, Daniel	....	142 00	
Curtin, D................................	....	131 00	
Crowe, W.................................	....	106 00	
Cosineau, Thos...........................	....	131 00	
Cullen, M. T.............................	....	91 00	
Curry, D. V..............................	192 50		
Disbursements...........................	26 00		
		218 50	
Cuthburtson, Wm..........................	....	124 00	
Davidson, G, T	320 00		
Disbursements	18 10		
		338 10	
Davis, M. J..............................	....	75 00	
Dawkins, Jno.............................	....	131 00	
Delgarno, Jas............................	....	131 00	
Delamage, R. D..........................	300 00		
Disbursements............................	34 80		
		334 80	
Dennison, Hugh...........................	....	131 00	
Dever, Wm...............................	357 50		
Disbursements............................	11 90		
		369 40	
Didier, L. P.............................	....	130 00	
Dillworth, Wm...........................	....	74 00	
Dowe, Wm................................	....	131 00	
Doyle, T. J..............................	....	129 00	
Draycott, E. A...........................	....	115 00	
Duval, C. A..............................	576 00		
Disbursements............................	873 21		
		1,449 21	
Dunn, J. F...............................	....	118 00	
Duff, A. S...............................	....	12 00	
Dunn, Thos...............................	....	131 00	
Dufond, Ignace...........................	....	125 00	
Dube, Jno	....	125 00	
Driver, Jos..............................	....	130 00	
Duplisis, Alex	....	82 00	
Dyment, N. and A.........................	....	3 00	
Erwin, Thos..............................	....	131 00	
Enright, Thos	337 50		
Disbursements........................	19 65		
		357 15	
Carried forward		18,994 68	93,307 85

Appendix No 6.—Continued.

Name.	$ c.	$ c.	$ c.
Brought forward	....	18,994 68	93,307 85
FIRE RANGING.—*Continued.*			
Enright, Owen.................................	152 50		
Disbursements	16 70		
		169 20	
Elliott, Jackson...............................	357 50		
Disbursements	15 10		
		372 60	
Elliott, Wm	....	119 00	
Edwards, E. D................................	....	131 00	
Fairburn, N. H	....	385 00	
Faries, Richard..............................	....	352 50	
Ferguson Wm..	292 50		
Disbursements..............................	1 40		
		293 90	
Fiddler, S. J.................................	....	89 00	
Filiater, James...............................	....	125 00	
Finley, Barney	....	131 00	
Flynn, Jno...................................	....	127 00	
Flanagan, Peter..............................	340 00		
Disbursements	20 20		
		360 20	
Foley, Pat...................................	....	106 00	
Fortier, Jos..................................	....	111 00	
Frappier, August	....	131 00	
Feeley. Pat..................................	....	106 00	
Gagne, F.....................................	795 00		
Disbursements	134 20		
		929 20	
Gagnon, Jas	....	129 00	
Gault, Jas	....	90 00	
Gauthier, Arthur	302 50		
Disbursements	5 65		
		308 15	
Gauthier, Alfred	....	19 00	
Gemmell, Jno	....	396 00	
Gervais, N....................................	....	132 00	
Gervais, F. X.................................	....	131 00	
Gibson, Thos.................................	....	44 00	
Gill, Jno. W.................................	....	74 00	
Gillies, J. P..................................	....	72 00	
Glazier, M. B................................	355 00		
Disbursements	22 20		
		377 20	
Godkin, Jacob................................	....	3 00	
Goden, Wm..................................	....	48 00	
Gongeon, Arsene	....	119 00	
Gorman, M..........e........................	....	131 00	
Gosselin, Jos	90 00		
Disbursements	5 50		
		95 50	
Gould, Ferdinand............................	....	134 00	
Grant, B. A..................................	....	76 00	
Grant, J. D..................................	....	131 00	
Brought forward............................	....	25,543 13	93,307 85

Appendix No. 6.—Continued.

Name.	$ c,	$ c.	$ c.
Brought forward...............................		25,543 13	93,307 85
Fire Ranging.—*Continued.*			
Graham, Jno...............................		41 00	
Graney, Christopher		131 00	
Grawberger. Thos.....................		132 00	
Greenshields, E..........................		151 00	
Groulx, F. K...........................		56 00	
Groulx, Arthur..........................		131 00	
Grozelle, A. D..........................		115 00	
Guertin, Godfrey	117 50		
Disbursements..........................	12 65		
		130 15	
Guthier, Wm...........................	352 50		
Disbursements..........................	6 20		
		358 70	
Gallagher, Jas..........................		131 00	
Gillies, Bros		1,252 60	
Georgian Bay Lumber Co		88 94	
Gordon, Geo. & Co.		26 00	
Hawkesbury Lumber Co.		53 50	
Haggart, Ralph.........................	322 50		
Disbursements..........................	33 65		
		356 15	
Hanes, J. L.............................		45 00	
Hall, M. E..............................	305 00		
Disbursements..........................	22 00		
		327 00	
Haley, Edward..........................		131 00	
Harper, Thos............................		105 00	
Harvie, Andrew		113 00	
Haskin, William.........................		131 00	
Hawley, D. J............................	307 50		
Disbursements..........................	26 60		
		334 10	
Helliwell, Paul	265 00		
Disbursements..........................	19 15		
		284 15	
Helmer, Jno.............................		113 50	
Henderson, Chas........................		399 70	
Hennesy, B. E...........................		85 00	
Hodgins, Thos...........................	360 00		
Disbursements..........................	13 70		
		373 70	
Hogarth, Henry		134 00	
Hoff, J. T. M...........................		108 00	
Holdsworth, Jno.........................		126 00	
Holton, Arthur		79 00	
Hurd, Edward...........................		121 00	
Hunt, J. W..............................		81 00	
Irwin, Oscar M.	317 50		
Disbursements..........................	21 40		
		338 90	
James. Thos.............................		131 00	
Jackson, Robert.		42 00	
Carried forward......................		32,300 22	93,307 85

Appendix No. 6.—Continued.

Name.	$ c.	$ c.	$ c.
Brought forward		32,300 22	93,307 85
FIRE RANGING.—*Continued.*			
Jackson, Jno.	292 50		
Disbursements	14 55		
		307 05	
Kennedy, J. C.		254 16	
Kennedy, Michael		130 00	
Kennedy, Jno. J.		154 00	
Kelly. Jno. J.	320 00		
Disbursements	22 40		
		342 40	
Keys, Thos. R.	267 50		
Disbursements	11 20		
Funeral expenses	127 10		
		405 80	
King, Chas.		131 00	
King. Frank G.		307 50	
King, James		30 00	
King, Alex.		69 00	
Kirby, H.		131 00	
Kirk, J. W.		79 00	
Koch, Jno.		116 00	
Lamarch, A.	257 50		
Disbursements	11 00		
		268 50	
Lamarch, Jno.		131 00	
Lamothe, H.		105 00	
Lambert, N. P.	45 00		
Disbursements.	11 00		
		56 00	
Lamothe, Michael 1905	132 00		
do ... 1906	131 00		
		263 00	
Lafrance, Thos.		130 00	
Latour, Alfred		89 00	
Lauviere, Jos.		131 00	
Lavois, Benj.		131 00	
Law, W. J.		131 00	
Lawson, David		132 00	
Lees, Jno.	307 50		
Disbursements	10 65		
		318 15	
Leblanc, Oliver.		131 00	
Leahey, Jno		132 00	
Larrivee, Jos.		114 00	
Lemyre, Middy		60 00	
Lindsay, J. A.		121 00	
Lorenz, Chas.		133 00	
Lorenz, Fred.		115 00	
Long, Henry E.		120 00	
Ludgate, Anthony		77 00	
Lynch, M. D.		106 00	
Loveland, & Stone.		151 63	
McAdam, Wm.		131 00	
McAmmord, Jos.		113 00	
Carried forward		38,147 41	93,307 85

Appendix *No. 6.—Continued.*

Name.	$ c.	$ c.	$ c.
Brought forward.................	....	38,147 41	93,307 85
FIRE RANGING.—*Continued.*			
McAulay, D...		126 63	
McBain, R.		48 00	
McCaw, Jno. G....		291 00	
McCaffery, Jas...		133 00	
McColl, Archibald ...		132 00	
McCaw, James...		90 00	
McCreary, Wm ...		133 00	
McClure, A....		78 50	
McCullough, Christopher....	342 50		
Disbursements ...	27 00		
		369 50	
McDonald, F ...	350 00		
Disbursements ...	1 40		
		351 40	
McDonald. M...		69 00	
McDonald, A. J...		87 00	
McDonald, Wm...		94 50	
McDonald, A...		82 00	
McDougall, E. G...	202 50		
Disbursements...	20 65		
		223 15	
McDougall, D...		64 00	
McDougall, Jas. T...	725 00		
Disbursements ...	739 86		
		1464 86	
McFarlane, Jas...		130 00	
McFarlane, R. L...		131 00	
McGregor, Jas...		129 00	
McGregor, Peter ...		12 00	
McGuey, Denis...		134 00	
McGuire, Hugh...		132 00	
McGarvey, Robt ...		131 00	
McGhie, Chas...		132 00	
McIlroy, Daniel...		33 00	
McInnis, D. C...		95 00	
McIntyre, Wm...		131 00	
McIver, Hugh...	355 00		
Disbursements......	33 20		
		388 20	
McKay, Angus...		131 00	
McKenzie, Wilbert...		131 00	
McKinsey, Jos...		131 00	
McLaughlin John...		131 00	
McMullen, Alex...		130 00	
McNabb, Alex...		98 00	
McLaughlin Bros...		395 53	
McPhee, Hugh...		132 00	
McRae, Alex...		131 00	
MacAlphine, C. D. H...	310 00		
Disbursements...	28 00		
		338 00	
Carried forward...	....	45,311 68	93,307 85

Appendix No. 6.—Continued.

Name.	$ c.	$ c.	$ c.
Brought forward		45,311 68	93,307 85
FIRE RANGING.—*Continued.*			
MacCurdy, J. T.	207 50		
Disbursements	20 20		
		227 70	
MacDonald, H. C.		• 101 00	
MacDonald, Norman	285 00		
Disbursements	2 95		
		287 95	
MacKay, Hugh	337 50		
Disbursements	34 75		
		372 25	
Maguire, T. C.	240 00		
Disbursements	8 80		
		248 80	
Major, H.		131 00	
Marion, Isadore		84 00	
Massey, Geo.		131 00	
Matte, Jos.	262 50		
Disbursements	3 40		
		265 90	
Manseau, Louis		81 00	
Maxwell, Jno.		16 50	
May, Wm		131 00	
May, Albert		120 00	
Megean, Jos.		131 00	
Mercer, Whitefield		104 00	
Merchant, Ambrose		350 00	
Merchant, Jno.	560 00		
Disbursements	10 00		
		570 00	
Mitchell, Walter		90 00	
Mitchell, Grant	152 50		
Disbursements	18 50		
		171 00	
Milne, Albert		131 00	
Moore, David 1905		3 75	
Moore, S. E.	25 00		
Disbursements	22 00		
		47 00	
Moore, Donald		130 00	
Montroy, J. J.		131 00	
Moriaty, M.		131 00	
Morrow, R.		50 00	
Morand, Louis	340 00		
Disbursements	6 50		
		346 50	
Montroy, Tuffield		124 00	
Mulvaney, Neil		131 00	
Munro, J. H.		131 00	
Murphy, Wm		37 00	
Murphy, P.		104 00	
Mustard, W. H.	325 00		
Disbursements	16 10		
		341 10	
Carried forward		50,764 13	93,307 85

3 L.M.

Appendix No. 6—Continued.

Name.	$ c.	$ c.	$ c.
Brought forward..................................	....	50,764 13	93,307 85
FIRE RANGING.—*Continued.*			
Nadon, Xavier.....................................	357 50		
Disbursements................................	4 60		
		362 10	
Newburn, Wm......................................	....	350 00	
Newton, Thos.....................................	....	131 00	
Noland, Peter.....................................	....	90 00	
Northern Construction Co..........................	....	96 00	
Northern Timber Co...............................	....	48 75	
O'Brien, Martin...................................	....	153 00	
O'Brien, Phil......................................	....	74 00	
O'Connor, Jas.....................................	355 00		
Disbursements	7 40		
		362 40	
Oulette, Jos.......................................	....	108 00	
Ouimette, Chas.............................1905	....	131 00	
Owens, R..	....	131 00	
Page, Noe...	....	127 00	
Paquette, Jos.....................................	....	47 00	
Patterson, Thos...................................	....	72 00	
Paul, Wesley......................................	....	131 00	
Pennell, Geo......................................	330 00		
Disbursements................................	10 65		
		340 65	
Peeler, Chas......................................	....	98 25	
Playfair, Andrew..................................	....	164 77	
Pew, Murray......................................	307 50		
Disbursements................................	23 50		
		331 00	
Plourde, Chas.....................................	....	132 00	
Powell, Samuel....................................	....	131 00	
Prestley, Jas......................................	....	50 00	
Parry Sound Lumber Co............................	....	7 00	
Quilty, Jno..	320 00		
Disbursements................................	14 90		
		334 90	
Quilty, Jos..	....	45 00	
Quigley, Wm......................................	....	100 00	
Rawson, Chas. E...................................	....	120 00	
Rathburn Company................................	....	25 88	
Raymond, Chas....................................	....	134 00	
Readman, R. E....................................	....	202 50	
Reynolds, Jas.....................................	....	104 00	
Richardson, Josh..................................	....	100 00	
Rivers, Jno.......................................	....	79 00	
Rogers, Fred......................................	....	4 00	
Ross, A. C..	....	81 00	
Robinson, Wm.....................................	390 00		
Disbursements................................	25 65		
		415 65	
Russell, Jno......................................	....	267 50	
Ryan, Daniel J....................................	....	68 00	
St. Amour, Jno....................................	....	131 00	
St. Pierre, Wm....................................	....	128 00	
Carried forward..................................	....	56,773 48	93,307 85

3a L.M.

Appendix No. 6—Continued.

Name.	$ c.	$ o.	$ c.
Brought forward............................	....	56,773 48	93,307 85
FIRE RANGING.—*Continued.*			
Savard, August................................	160 00		
Disbursements.................................	2 80		
		162 80	
Sauve, Antoine.................................	....	131 00	
Saucier, Ovid...................................	....	131 00	
Scott, Robt.....................................	359 00		
Disbursements.................................	50 60		
		409 60	
Sharbott, Jos...................................	....	131 00	
Sheahan, Daniel................................	....	134 00	
Shipman, Chas..................................	....	106 00	
Shields, Foster.................................	....	131 00	
Shields, Thos	....	110 00	
Shields, Geo....................................	....	135 00	
Sicard, F. K....................................	....	132 00	
Smith, Jos......................................	....	131 00	
Smith, Jas......................................	....	11 50	
Smith, A. L.....................................	335 00		
Disbursements.................................	22 00		
		357 00	
Smith, Wm......................................	....	131 00	
Smith, Wm......................................	....	47 00	
Snowdon, Thos..................................	....	113 00	
Spanish River Pulp and Paper Co...............	....	28 00	
Spreadborough, Newell.........................	....	132 00	
Stanley, Leonard................................	....	103 00	
Stellar, Fred....................................	508 00		
Disbursements	2 75		
		510 75	
Stephenson, Wm...........................1905	72 00		
Stephenson, Wm...........................1906	93 00		
		165 00	
Stewart, D. R...................................	....	136 00	
Stethen, H. A...................................	....	105 00	
Stirrett, J. T...................................	292 50		
Disbursements.................................	29 65		
		322 15	
Stubbs, Jno.....................................	287 50		
Disbursements.................................	28 95		
		316 45	
Smith, J. B. and Son...........................	....	7 63	
Taylor, A. E....................................	142 50		
Disbursements.................................	27 35		
		169 85	
Thomas, G. T...................................	....	131 00	
Thomas, Peter..................................	....	132 00	
Thomas, Jas....................................	....	103 00	
Thomas, Wm....................................	....	132 00	
Thomas, Wm....................................	....	30 00	
Thompson, Milton..............................	27 50		
Disbursements.................................	4 75		
		32 25	
Thorgie, Xavier................................	....	131 00	
Carried forward.............................	....	61,964 46	93,307 85

Appendix No. 6—Continued.

Name.	$ c.	$ c.	$ c.
Brought Forward..........................	....	61,964 46	93,307 85
Fire Ranging—*Continued.*			
Thessalon Lumber Co.........................	....	3 75	
Tooke, Samuel...............................	....	50 00	
Tower, Orastus..............................	....	131 00	
Trainer, Wm................................	....	36 00	
Tremblay, Jas...............................	330 00		
Disbursements	3 20		
		333 20	
Tremblay, Emerie	....	125 00	
Turner, Robert..............................	....	151 00	
Turner, Geo.................................	....	158 00	
Tullock, W. A...............................	....	95 00	
Tyson, Thos.................................	....	130 00	
Urquhart, A.................................	294 00		
Disbursements...............................	170 25		
		464 25	
Victoria Harbor Lumber Co....................	....	76 00	
Vermette, Jno...............................	....	132 00	
Vincent, Jas................................	....	41 00	
Volker, P. D................................	....	131 00	
Wallace, Geo................................	....	131 00	
Walker, James...............................	....	131 00	
Watts, Geo	....	62 75	
Watters, Thos...............................	....	88 00	
Weigold, Jno................................	....	131 00	
Welch, Wm.......................1905	72 00		
Welch, Wm.......................1906	114 00		
		186 00	
Whitmore, Wm...............................	....	307 50	
Williams, Alex..............................	....	52 00	
Wickett, Jno. A.............................	317 50		
Disbursements.......................	28 35		
		345 85	
Wickett, Emerson............................	117 50		
Disbursements..............................	14 40		
		131 90	
Wilkins, G. W...............................	279 00		
Disbursements..............................	68 70		
		347 70	
Williams, Wm...............................	....	131 00	
Wilson, Jas.................................	....	122 00	
Wright, Jno.................................	....	74 00	
Yandon, Jos.................................	....	131 00	
Yocom, Jno.................................	360 00		
Disbursements	20 50		
		380 50	
Yuill, J. A.................................	....	131 00	
		66 905 86	
Refunded.................................	....	9 294 21	
			57,611 65
Carried forward	....	....	150,919 50

Appendix No. 6.—Continued.

Name.	$ c.	$ c.	$ c.
Brought forward.............................	....	....	150,919 50
BELLEVILLE ASSAY OFFICE.			
Burrows, A. G., salary......	1,000 00		
Embury, W. J., clerk	318 22		
		1,318 22	
Disbursements...............................	295 90		
Supplies..	539 53		
Repairs...	3 35		
		838 78	
MINING DEVELOPMENT.			2,157 00
Exploration.			
Baker, M.B., services.............................	734 29		
Disbursements...............................	261 06		
		995 35	
Byers, R. J., services.............................	....	5 00	
Coleman, A. P., services.........................	500 00		
Disbursements...............................	1,167 80		
		1,667 80	
Fraelick, E. L...................................	400 00		
Disbursements	363 95		
		763 95	
Ferguson, R. A., services........	....	102 50	
Kerr, H. L., services	11 00		
Disbursements...............................	19 60		
		30 60	
Mitchell, George................................	616 60		
Disbursements	329 43		
		946 03	
Silver, L. P., services........................	9 87		
Disbursements...............................	24 40		
		34 27	
White, Jos. W., services..........................	10 00		
Disbursements...............................	22 14		
		32 14	
Ritchie, C. H., Attorney General vs. Hargrave........	1,000 00		
Hearst, W. H., Attorney General vs. O'Brien.........	150 00		
Marsh, A. H., do.	250 00		
		1,400 00	
Lyman Bros., Supplies	2 91		
Advertising.....................................	70 20		
		73 11	
Guarding Mines.			
Clay, D. C., services.............................	556 50		
Disbursements...............................	15 60		
		572 10	
Kenny, R. T., services...........................	....	53 35	
Kearns, M. C., do	....	260 00	
Sutherland, W. A., services	....	99 00	
Mining Inspectors.			
Smith, Geo. T., services..........................	1,800 00		
Carried forward	1,800 00	7,035 20	153,076 50

Appendix No. 6.—Continued.

Name.	$ c.	$ c.	$ c.
Brought forward	1,800 00	7,035 20	153,076 50
Mining Inspectors.—Concluded.			
McAulay, N. J., clerk	763 15		
Smith, M. H., stenographer	580 00		
Disbursements	738 48		
		3,881 63	
McArthur, T. A., assistant.............	417 00		
Disbursements..............................	557 46		
		974 46	
Corkill, E. T..............................	1,600 00		
Disbursements....................	2,636 76		
		4,236 76	
Mickle, G. R., services	1,056 86		
Disbursements	515 98		
		1,572 84	
Robinson, A. H. A., services......................	1,065 18		
Disbursements..............................	440 76		
		1,505 94	
Mining Recorders.			
Bowker, S., services............................	291 66		
Disbursements..	207 43		
		499 09	
Belyea, C. W., services	....	125 00	
Lemieux, F. F., do	250 00		
Disbursements	8 90		
		258 90	
McQuire, services	125 00		
Disbursements	78 95		
		203 95	
Shera, C. H., services	207 00		
Shera, W. L. do	43 00		
Disbursements..............................	40 00		
		290 00	
Price, Samuel, Mining Commissioner.................	1,799 32		
Disbursements..............................	498 15		
		2,297 47	
Miller, G. W., Provincial Geologist..................	3,600 00		
Disbursements............................	773 64		
		4,373 64	
King's Printer..............................	887 60		
Express..............................	49 08		
Telegrams	3 46		
		940 14	
			28,195 02
CULLERS' ACT.			
Currie, D. H., services............................	28 00		
Disbursements	39 05		
		67 05	
Fisher, G. W., services..........................	....	20 00	
Gardiner, John, do	....	4 00	
Kennedy, J. C., disbursements	....	29 00	
McNabb, A. D., services	... .	8 00	
Margach, Wm., disbursements	....	36 00	
Carried forward.............................	....	164 05	181,271 52

Appendix No. 6.—Continued.

Name.	$ c.	$ c.	$ c.
Brought forward................................	....	164 05	181,271 52
CULEERS' ACT.—*Concluded.*			
Maughan, Jos., disbursements.......................	....	7 50	
Oliver, J. A. do	....	8 80	
			180 35
· FOREST RESERVE.			
Temagami Reserve.			
Angus, Robt.......................................	325 00		
Disbursements.............................	5 90		
		330 90	
Boissonnault, Samuel	192 50		
Disbursements.............................	6 80		
		199 30	
Carruthers, R. A....	357 50		
Disbursements.............................	18 30		
		375 80	
Coleman, R. M....................	325 00		
Disbursements.............................	24 60		
		349 60	
Deacon, Edgar....................................	50 00		
Disbursements.............................	8 40		
		58 40	
Dreany, Alex.....................................	332 50		
Disbursements.............................	7 00		
		339 50	
Dorsey, C. F.....................................	340 00		
Disbursements.............................	19 50		
		359 50	
Eilber, Geo.......................................	365 00		
Disbursements...	29 25		
		394 25	
Ellis, John	462 50		
Disbursements.............................	5 90		
		468 40	
Ferguson, Wm....................................	67 50		
Disbursements.............................	4 30		
		71 80	
Graham, Geo.....................................	337 50		
Disbursements............	21 95		
		359 45	
Hamilton, C. D.,................................	....	200 00	
Jefferson, Leonard	....	247 50	
Kennedy, G. N...................................	312 50		
Disbursements.............................	21 60		
		334 10	
Klotz, H. N......................................	362 50		
Disbursements.............................	21 60		
		384 10	
Knowles, F. B...................................	175 00		
Disbursements.............................	13 60		
		188 60	
Carried forward	....	4,661 20	181,451 87

Appendix No. 6.—Continued.

Name.	$ c.	$ c.	$ c.
Brought forward...................	....	4,661 20	181,451 87
Forest Reserves.—*Continued.*			
Temagami Reserve.—Continued.			
Lamarche, Alphonse	455 00		
Disbursements	8 40		
		463 40	
Lambert, N. P.................................	270 00		
Disbursements	23 70		
		293 70	
Lewis, R. G...................................	285 00		
Disbursements...............................	24 70		
		309 70	
Maguire, T. C................................	85 00		
Disbursements...............................	8 80		
		93 80	
Manes, Jno	360 00		
Disbursements	10 40		
		370 40	
Macdonald, S. C.............................	955 60		
Disbursements	412 22		
		1,367 82	
Montgomery, Alex............................	447 50		
Disbursements	14 90		
		462 40	
McGregor, P..................................	507 50		
Disbursements..............................	13 10		
		520 60	
McKay, D. L.................................	340 00		
Disbursements...............................	28 50		
		368 50	
Petrant, Wm.................................	....	307 50	
Powell, John	260 00		
Disbursements.............................	15 80		
		275 80	
Presley, W. H	330 00		
Disbursements	19 50		
		349 50	
Prudhomme, Adolphe...........................	442 50		
Disbursements...............................	35 55		
		478 05	
Robertson, Bruce	100 00		
Disbursements	16 00		
		116 00	
Rochon, Joseph...............................	455 00		
Disbursements...............................	8 40		
		463 40	
Shields, Wm.................................	....	100 00	
Stata, Sam..................................	335 00		
Disbursements	3 20		
		338 20	
Saville, Thomas.............................		140 00	
Carried forward	....	11,479 97	181,451 87

Appendix No. 6.—Continued.

Name.	$ c.	$ c.	$ c.
Brought forward....................		11,479 97	181,451 87
FOREST RESERVES.—*Continued.*			
Temagami Reserve.—Concluded.			
Thompson, Milton	300 00		
Disbursements	9 10		
		309 10	
Tookey, W. E.......................	277 50		
Disbursements	23 90		
		301 40	
Turner, John	....	407 50	
Tyrell, A. J........................	370 00		
Disbursements	16 50		
		386 50	
Viverais, Dave.....................	440 00		
Disbursements	8 40		
		448 40	
Metagami Reserve.			
Black, Davidson	357 50		
Disbursements	29 90		
		387 40	
Clendenning, C. S..................	345 00		
Disbursements	30 90		
		375 90	
Cox, G. B..........................	292 50		
Disbursements	32 40		
		324 90	
Dann, E. M.........................	362 50		
Disbursements	34 70		
		397 20	
Hornidge, R. L.....................	232 50		
Disbursements	34 85		
		267 35	
Hunter, F. K.......................	357 50		
Disbursements	23 90		
		381 40	
Kent, Hubert.......................	362 50		
Disbursements	23 90		
		386 40	
Markell, F. K......................	....	25 00	
McLeod, Barnard	255 00		
Disbursements	6 00		
		261 00	
Patterson, F. H....................	350 00		
Disbursements	27 90		
		377 90	
Ross, K. G.........................	489 01		
Disbursements	588 00		
		1,077 01	
Spaniel, Alex......................	360 00		
Disbursements	2 20		
		362 20	
Carried forward		17,956 53	181,451 87

Appendix No. 6.—Continued.

Name.	$ c.	$ c.	$ c.
Brought forward......................		17,956 53	181,451 87
FOREST RESERVE.—*Continued.*			
Temagami Reserve.—Concluded.			
Webb, C. E.........................	360 00		
Disbursements	29 90		
		389 90	
Mississaga Reserve.			
Campbell, J. L.....................	382 50		
Disbursements.....................	9 00		
		391 50	
Cruise, Geo. A.....................	370 00		
Disbursements.....................	30 80		
		400 80	
Fawcett, Jas. R....................	30 00		
Disbursements.......	30 00		
		60 00	
Kinney, Wm........................	588 00		
Disbursements.....................	193 32		
		781 32	
Metcalf, N. E......................	280 00		
Disbursements..:..................	20 10		
		300 10	
McCullough, D.....................	302 50		
Disbursements............	19 70		
		322 20	
Neelon, G. M.......................	297 50		
Disbursements.....................	28 20		
		325 70	
O'Donnell, Roy....................	350 00		
Disbursements....................	9 65		
Funeral expenses.................	130 28		
		489 93	
Scott, Clarence M..................	302 50		
Disbursements.....................	29 80		
		332 30	
Smyth, W. J.......................	3 00		
Disbursements.............	2 80		
		5 80	
Taylor, Angus.....................	380 00		
Disbursements.......	9 00		
		389 00	
Taylor, Wm........................	382 50		
Disbursements.....................	9 00		
		391 50	
Teasdale, Jno. D.:.................	382 50		
Disbursements.....................	9 00		
		391 50	
Thompson, Fred....................	405 00		
Disbursements.....................	19 65		
		424 65	
Thomson, Harry....................		337 50	
Washburn, Chas. F.................	305 00		
Disbursements....................	31 20		
		336 20	
Carried forward		24,026 43	181,451 87

Appendix No. 6,—Continued.

Name.	$ c.	$ c.	$ c.
Brought forward...............................		24,026 43	181,451 87
FOREST RESERVE.—*Continued.*			
Nepigon Reserve.			
Adams, Morris.................................	332 00		
Disbursements..:............................	60 73		
		392 73	
Bonnycastle, R. H.............................	210 00		
Disbursements..............................	60 30		
		270 30	
Clarke, W. A..................................	310 00		
Disbursements..............................	62 10		
		372 10	
Crawford, Jas. P..............................	287 50		
Disbursements....	58 10		
		345 60	
Duke, Wm...................................	120 00		
Disbursements.............................	67 30		
		187 30	
Leitch, P. A..................................	....	623 39	
Robillard, A. E...............................	285 00		
Disbursements	59 60		
		344 60	
Scrimgeour, W. G.............................	310 00		
Disbursements	61 85		
		371 85	
Eastern Reserve.			
Foster, Jas..................................	....	6 25	
Godkin, Jacob...............................	....	262 00	
McGregor, Chas..............................	270 00		
Disbursements'..............................	1 50		
		271 50	
Tapping, Thomas.............................	....	339 14	
Sibley Reserve.			
Oliver, J. A..................................	....	100 00	
			27,913 19
SURVEYS.....................................	....	....	125,003 39
BOARD OF SURVEYORS.........................	....	....	200 00
GILLIES LIMITS...............................	....	....	19,159 48
CANCELLATION OF LEASES.....................	....	....	1,889 70
MINERAL COLLECTIONS.........................	....	....	61 03
Carswell and Co., compensation for loss of timber on berths in Townships of Martland and Cosby.......	....	....	10,000 00
REFUNDS......................................	....	....	32,844 62
Carried forward	....	....	398,523 28

Appendix No. 6.—Continued.

Name.	$ c.	$ c.	$ c.
Brought forward.......			398,523 28 '
CONTINGENCIES.			
Bureau of Mines.			
Printing and Binding........	1,629 32		
Stationery and Paper.............................	2,436 18		
		4,065 50	
Postage....:...............................	367 60		
Telegraphing...............................	152 19		
Express and cartage	95 01		
		614 80	
Advertising................................	262 80		
Subscriptions........, ..	200 18		
Books....................................	63 80		
Maps.....................................	353 47		
		880 25	
Gibson, Thos. W., travelling expenses.........	45 50		
Thompson, P., services..	32 00		
		77 50	
Typewriter, repair, etc........................	132 25		
Bell Telephone Co., rent......................	23 76		
		156 01	
Extra clerks	3,245 32		
Sundries......................................	62 17		
		3,307 49	
Departmental.			9,101 55
Printing and binding	2,620 92		
Stationery	3,745 92		
		6,366 84	
Postage...	1,858 68		
Express	279 08		
		2,137 76	
Telegraphing......................................	469 83		
Telephone messages	12 05		
Telephones rent	309 89		
Cab hire	20 75		
Car fare.	60 00		
		872 52	
Subscriptions	191 00		
Advertising.......................................	4,071 03		
		4,262 03	
Typewriter, rents and repairs.	....	419 75	
Kirkpatrick, G. B., travelling expenses. ,..............	86 20		
White, A. " "	386 50		
Yates, G. W. " "	62 95		
		535 65	
Extra Clerks..,...............................		11,001 14	
Arnoldi, F., legal expenses.	200 00		
Sundries.......................................	57 13		
		257 13	
			25,852 82
			433,477 65

D. G. ROSS,   AUBREY WHITE,
  Accountant.   Deputy Minister.

Appendix No. 7.

STATEMENT of Expenses on account of various services, under the direction of the Department of Lands and Mines, for the year 1905.

Name.	$ c.	$ c.	$ c.
DIAMOND DRILL.			
Roche, E. K., salary	753 79		
Disbursements	39 15		
		792 94	
Kelly, Jas., salary	119 05		
Disbursements	6 15		
		125 20	
Labor	1,446 06		
Freight, express and cartage	131 42		
		1,577 48	
Supplies	600 91		
Drill Furnishings	2,147 42		
		2,748 33	
			5,243 95
MINING SCHOOLS			1,196 14
ALGONQUIN PARK			11,501 70
RONDEAU PARK			3,301 40
TEMAGAMI TIMBER CUTTING			89,412 95
ONTARIO MINING CONVENTION			326 01
VETERANS' COMMUTATION			71,800 00
			$182,782 15

D. GEO. ROSS,   AUBREY WHITE,
Accountant.   Deputy Minister.

Appendix

WOODS AND

Statement of Timber and Amounts accrued from Timber Dues,

Agencies.	Area covered by timber licenses	Saw Logs.				Boom and Dimen	
		Pine.		Other.		Pine.	
	Sq. miles.	Pieces.	Feet B. M.	Pieces.	Feet B.M.	Pieces.	Feet B. M.
Western Timber District.......	12,523	9,692,617	496,783,253	1,105,864	45,998,680	184,260	23,035,162
Belleville Timber District.......	1,402	372,445	25,958,868	316,333	14,235,110	7,826	1,777,495
Ottawa Timber District.	6,138	2,202,701	152,058,344	185,459	6,712,197	37,616	4,704,825
	20,063	12,267,763	674,800,465	1,607,656	66,945,987	229,702	29,517,482

QUANTITY AND

GENERAL STATEMENT

Agencies.	Cord Wood.		Tan Bark.	Railway Ties.	Posts.	Telegraph Poles.	Shingle Bolts.	Head Bolts.	Car Stakes.
	Hard.	Soft.							
	Cords	Cords	Cords	Pieces	Cords	Pieces	Cords	Cords	Pieces
Western Timber District.	5,437	8,227	10,964	1,709,091	74	4,519	......	4,352	591
Belleville Timber District.	21	311	1,306	18,944	712	718	......	......	......
Ottawa Timber District.......	....	5,547	....	12,407	1,019	2,857	9	......	......
	5,458	14,085	12,270	1,740,442	1,805	8,094	9	4,352	591

J. A. G. CROZIER,
    Chief Clerk in Charge.

No. 8.

FORESTS.

Ground Rent and Bonus during the year ending 31st December, 1906.

DESCRIPTION OF TIMBER.

sion Timber.		Square Timber.				Pile Timber.		Pile Timber.		Cedar.	
Other.		Pine.		Ash, Birch, Elm & Hml'k							
Pieces.	Feet B. M.	Pieces.	Feet Cubic.	Pieces	Feet Cubic.	Pieces	Feet lineal	Pieces	Feet B. M.	Pieces	Feet lineal.
33,332	5,307,240	11,851	638,228	a 236 b 23 e 8	9,493 691 209	887	48,415	6,930	648,609	3,817	125,111
6,502	1,268,612	....	....	......	......	......	......	....	....	......	....
34,761	1,931,635	......	....	......	h 8,224	......	......	....	....	......	1,061
74,595	8,507,487	11,851	638,228	a 236 b 23 e 8 h 8	9,493 691 209 8,224	887	48,415	6,930	648,609	3,817	126,172

OF TIMBER, ETC.—*Continued.*

Pulp Wood. Cords.	Amounts Accrued.						
	Transfer Bonus.	Interest.	Trespass.	Timber Dues	Bonus.	Ground Rent.	Total
	$ c.	$ c.	$ c.	$ c.	$ c.	$ c.	$ c.
71,660	3,251 65	6,333 90	14,091 51	942,366 37	540,458 98	42,389 00	1,548,891 41
7	....	555 69	94 94	37,171 45	....	4,134 00	41,956 08
13,294	195 40	969 26	909 81	177,860 40	....	19,288 00	199,222 87
84,961	3,447 05	7,858 85	15,096 26	1,157,398 22	540,458 98	65,811 00	1,790,070 36

AUBREY WHITE,
Deputy Minister.

Appendix No. 9.

WOODS AND FORESTS.

Statement of Revenue collected during the year ending December 31st, 1906.

	$	
Amount of Western collections at Department.............................	1,591,993	82
do do Quebec....................................	33,428	53
Amount of Belleville collections...	43,758	24
Amount of Ottawa collections	231,600	24
do do at Quebec	133	79
	$1,900,914	62

J. A. G. CROZIER,   AUBREY WHITE,
  Chief Clerk in Charge.   Deputy Minister.

Appendix No. 10.

PATENTS BRANCH.

Statement of Patents, etc., issued by the Patents Branch during the year 1906.

	Number.
Crown Lands......	675
School do	54
Mining do	129
Public do (late Clergy Reserves)	13
Free Grant Lands (A.A.)	74
do (under Act of 1880)	296
Rainy River Lands (Mining and Crown)...................................	47
Mining Leases...	112
Licensee of Occupation...	15
Rondeau Harbor Leases..	3
Crown Leases	8
Crown Lands (University) Patents	8
Under Act of 1901 (Veterans)...	301
Temagami Leases...	34
Total..	1,769

CHARLES S. JONES,   AUBREY WHITE,
  Chief Clerk.   Deputy Minister.

Appendix No. 11.

Statement showing the number of Locatees and of acres located, of purchasers and of acres sold; of lots resumed for non-performance of the settlement duties ; and of patents issued under "The Free Grants and Homesteads Act," during the year 1906.

Township.	District or County.	Agent.	No. of persons located.	No. of acres located.	No. of purchasers.	No. of acres sold.	No. of lots resumed.	No. of patents issued.
Baxter	Muskoka	J. B. Brown, Bracebridge	8	1,226	4	114	6	1
Brunel	"	"	2	200				3
Chaffey	"	"	1	98			1	
Draper	"	"						
Franklin	"	"	6	806	2	113	5	3
Macauley	"	"	2	300	2	101	3	3
Medora	"	"	2	253	3	112	3	4
Monck	"	"						
Morrison	"	"			1	6		4
Muskoka	"	"	1	100	4	685	2	4
McLean	"	"	8	1,020	3	138	10	
Oakley	"	"	10	1,174	1	100	9	3
Ridout	"	"	3	394			2	2
Ryde	"	"			1	4		1
Sherbourne	Haliburton	"	1	190	2	132		1
Sinclair	Muskoka	"	12	1,892	5	139	11	8
Stephenson	"	"	1	100	1	1	1	2
Stisted	"	"	2	257			2	6
Watt	"	"	2	299	1	1	3	4
Wood	"	"	10	1,633	6	350	14	4
Cardwell	"	Jas. Ellis, Parry Harbor	7	846			5	3
Carling	Parry Sound	"	5	841	9	231	7	
Christie	"	"	3	478			2	5
Conger	"	"	5	1,009	8	142	2	2
Ferguson	"	"	2	263	2	17	4	
Foley	"	"	1	200			2	3
Hagerman	"	"	4	559	1	3	1	4
Humphrey	"	"	1	187			5	
Harrison	"	"	1	189	35	139		
McConkey	"	"	5	884	3	169	9	1
McDougall	"	"	1	111	2	40	2	7
McKeller	"	"	2	301			2	1
McKenzie	"	"	8	1,152	3	131	5	
Monteith	"	"	3	399	2	3		6
Shawanaga	"	"	6	1,157			5	
Wilson	"	"	4	432	1	62	4	1
Cowper	"	"			1	26		
Chapman	"	Dr. J. S. Freeborn, Maganetawan	10	1,344			2	1
Croft	"	"	13	1,984	4	163	13	5
Ferrie	"	"						
Gurd	"	"	15	2,249	6	389	9	9
Lount	"	"	3	400	1	4	1	1
Machar	"	"	7	906	1	2	7	3
Mills	"		5	800	2	44	3	14
Pringle	"		5	823				4
Ryerson	"		7	755	1	20	9	14
Spence	"		10	1,174	3	81	14	1
Strong	"		3	500			2	4

4 L M.

Appendix No. 11.—Continued.

Township.	District or County.	Agent.	No. of persons located.	No. of acres located.	No. of purchasers.	No. of acres sold.	No. of lots resumed.	No. of patents issued.
Armour......	Parry Sound..	E. Handy, Emsdale....	5	519	5	108	2	4
Bethune......	"	" "	5	784	2	119	3	2
Joly........	"	" "	4	600	....	....	6	1
McMurrich...	"	" "	5	496	1	100	4	1
Perry........	"	" "	7	1,072	1	2	10	5
Proudfoot.....	"	" "	7	1,166	5	313	21	4
Chisholm.....	Nipissing	J. S. Scarlett, Powassan	16	2,104	2	104	10	16
Gibson.......	Parry Sound..	" "			1	90		
Hardy........	"	" "	4	589	2	17	1	2
Himsworth...	"	" "	17	2,587	1	66	26	12
Laurier.......	"	" "	13	2,180	2	25	21	9
Nipissing.....	"	" "	11	1,569	9	93	15	11
Patterson.....	"	" "	5	859	6	173	4	....
Anson........	Haliburton....	Wm. Hartle, Minden...						
Glamorgan....	"	" "	5	610	....	....	2	1
Hindon.......	"	" "						
Lutterworth ..	"	" "	6	666	....	....	2	5
Minden.......	"	" "	2	223	....	....	1	1
Snowdon.....	"	" "	3	400	....	....	4	3
Stanhope.....	"	" "	4	390	....	....	3	1
Anstruther ...	Peterboro.....	T. G. Eastland, Apsley..	8	1,133	1	35	5	1
Burleigh.....	"	" "						3
Chandos.....	"	" "	2	276	....	....	2	1
Methuen.....	"	" "	1	100	1	7		1
Cavendish.....	"	Jas. Wilson, Kinmount	2	204	3	124	2	....
Galway......	"	" "	4	384	....	....	2	1
Cardiff.......	Haliburton....	J.H.Anderson, Tory Hill	5	693	....	....	2	3
Monmouth....	"	" "	14	1,632	3	140	13	13
Bangor........	Hastings......	" "	6	515	2	86	....	1
McClure......	"	" "						
Wicklow......	"	" "						
Carlow	"	J. R. Tait, L'Amable....						1
Cashel.......	"	" "	3	376	....	....	3	...
Dungannon...	"	" "	1	78	1	28	1	....
Faraday......	"	" "	11	1,360	4	97	12	5
Herchel......	"	" "	5	374	....	....	6	2
Limerick.....	"	" "			1	5		
Mayo........	"	" "						
Monteagle	"	" "	13	1,419	1	15	10	10
Wollaston	"	" "	4	531	....	....	9	6
Algona S......	Renfrew......	Adam Prince, Wilno....	1	100	....	....	....	5
do N......	"	" "	6	445	1	60	....	7
Brougham....	"	" "						
Brudenell....	"	" "	4	415	....	....	1	....
Grattan.......	"	" "	5	767	....	....	1	....
Griffith	"	" "						
Hagarty......	"	" "	7	647	....	....	2	12
Jones.........	"	" "	1	90				
Lyell.........	Nipissing	" "	1	100	3	95	1	1
Lyndock......	Renfrew......	" "	3	302	1	2	....	1
Matawatchan..	"	" "	1	56	....			
Richards......	"	" "	5	669	1	20	1	2

4a L.M.

Appendix No. 11.—Continued.

Township.	District or County.	Agent.	No. of persons located.	No. of acres located.	No. of purchasers.	No. of acres sold.	No. of lots resumed.	No. of patents issued.
Radcliffe	Renfrew	Adam Prince, Wilno	14	1,713			5	1
Raglan	"	" "	6	836	2	42	4	13
Sebastopol	"	" "						
Sherwood	"	" "	10	1,107	1	2	2	7
Wilberforce	"	" "	1	100			1	4
Alice		D. B. Warren, Pembroke	1	98			2	1
Buchanan	"	" "	4	384	1	5	2	4
Cameron	"	" "						
Fraser	"	" "			1	22		4
Head	"	" "						
Maria	"	" "						
McKay	"	" "						
Petewawa	"	" "			9	23		5
Rolph	"	" "	2	257			2	2
Wylie	"	" "						1
Bonfield	Nipissing	J. M. Deacon, Mattawa	4	600			2	10
Calvin	"	" "	1	200				
Ferris	"	" "	15	1,688	2	3	20	15
Mattawan	"	" "			1	2		3
Papineau	"	" "	2	200				
Korah	Algoma	H. N. Young, S.Ste.Marie					3	1
Park	"	" "						
Prince	"	" "	3	320			3	2
Plummer	"	Thos. Buchanan, Thessalon	4	277			1	
do add	"	. "	1	199				1
St. Joseph Isl'd	"	W. E. Whybourne, Marksville	15	1,587	6	19	15	12
Blake	Thunder Bay.	W.H.Hesson,Port Arthur	4	640			4	3
Conmee	"	" "	14	2,410			13	
Crooks	"	" "			1	40		1
Dawson Rd	"	" "						
Dorion	"	" "	16	2,591	3	306	12	1
Gillies	"	" "	4	552	1	3	4	10
Gorham	"	" "	11	1,728	3	70	7	
Lybster	"	" "	11	1,790	6	97	18	6
Marks	"	" "	4	642			10	
McIntyre	"	" "	5	801			6	
McGregor	"	" "	14	2,264	4	14	3	
O'Connor	"	" "	16	2,453	3	245	14	11
Oliver	"	" "	5	809	3	50	4	7
PaipoongeN.R.	"	" "	6	652	1	100	4	2
do S.R.	"	" "	15	1,662	1	12	19	3
Pearson	"	" "	16	2,491	3	39	1	
Pardee	"	" "						
Scoble	"	" "						
Strange	"	" "	15	2,383	3	403	6	2
Atwood	Rainy River	Wm. Campbell, Stratton	1	81			1	
Blue	"	" "	12	1,764	8	189	10	1
Curran	"	" "	6	970			3	

Appendix No. 11.—Concluded.

Township.	District or County.	Agent.	No. of persons located.	No. of acres located.	No. of purchasers.	No. of acres sold.	No. of lots resumed.	No. of patents issued.
Dewart	Rainy River	Wm. Campbell, Stratton						
Dilk	"	"	5	568	1	2	3	3
Morley	"	"	5	813	2	38	4	5
McCrosson	"	"	14	2,194	2	6	8	
Nellee	"	"	9	1,289			12	1
Pattullo	"	"	10	1,367	7	260	12	2
Roseberry	"	"						
Shenstone	"	"	4	630	1	84	4	2
Spohn	"	"	10	1,561	2	77		
Sutherland	"	"	9	1,437			8	
Sifton	"	"					1	
Tait	"	"	10	1,444	4	102	9	
Tovell	"	"	6	991	5	310	3	
Worthington	"	"	2	327			2	
Aylsworth	"	Alex. McFayden, Emo	1	164	2	310	1	1
Barwick	"	"						
Burriss	"	"	10	1,717	4	220	12	3
Carpenter	"	"	7	1,136	8	239	6	7
Crozier	"	"	12	1,757	6	170	11	6
Dance	"	"	7	1,197	1	80	4	
Devlin	"	"	6	976	2	6	4	7
Dobie	"	"	9	1,362	3	96	5	5
Kingsford	"	"	13	2,130			9	2
Lash	"	"	5	769	3	43	8	2
Mather	"	"	15	2,349	7	375	11	1
Miscampbell	"	"	10	1,598	1	19	9	
Potts	"	"	2	324	1	2	1	
Pratt	"	"	4	641	1	21	5	
Roderick	"	"			2	123		1
Richardson	"	"					1	
Woodyatt	"	"	2	308	3	468	1	3
Blezard	Nipissing	J.K.McLennon, Sudbury						
Broder	"	"						
Balfour	Algoma	"						
Capreol, W]	Nipissing	"						
Garson	"	"						
Neelon	"	"				3	496	
Rayside	Algoma	"						
Abinger	Lennox and Addington	Chas. Both, Denbigh						
Clarendon	Frontenac	"	2	183			1	4
Denbigh	Lennox and Addington	"	7	1,299	2	12	2	6
Canonto S	Frontenac	"						
do N	"	"						
Miller	"	"			1	2		2
Palmerston	"	"						
Totals			893	126,085	316	10,833	755	492

W. C. CAIN,
 Clerk in Charge.

AUBREY WHITE,
 Deputy Minister.

Appendix No. 12.

Statement of work done in the Military Branch of the Department of Lands, Forests
and Mines during the year 1906.

```
Letters received.....................................................................   10,000
   "    written ....................................................................    9,000
Certificates issued...................................................................      400
Documents issued in connection with certificates ....................................    2,000
Maps       "        .................................................................    3,000
Forms      "        .................................................................      500
Location Certificates issued .........................................................      500
Locations made  .....................................................................      820
Surrenders............................................................................    1,400
References for Patents issued ........................................................      301
```

R. H. BROWNE,   AUBREY WHITE,
   Clerk in charge.   Deputy Minister.

Appendix No. 13.

Statement of the number of Letters received and mailed by the Department
in 1904, 1905 and 1906.

| Year | Letters received | | | | | Names indexed. | Orders-in-Council. | Returned Letters. | Letters, circulars and reports mailed from Department. |
	Sales and Free Grants.	Surveys.	Woods and Forests.	Mines.	Totals.				
1904....	17,960	6,735	5,786	3,250	41,970	48,230	79	47	52,110
1905....	19,932	8,018	7,126	4,000	46,220	53,100	220	60	55,400
1906....	21,525	11,490	9,620	7,702	50,337	59,250	262	80	60,000

FRANK YEIGH,   AUBREY WHITE,
   Registrar.   Deputy Minister.

Appendix No. 14.

Statement of Municipal Surveys for which Instructions Issued during the year 1906.

No.	Name of Surveyor.	No.	Date of Instructions.	Description of Survey.	Date when confirmed under R.S.O. 1897, cap. 181, Sects. 10 to 15 inclusive.
1	F. J. Ure..	658	April 18th, 1906	To survey the road allowance between the 3rd and 4th concessions of the township of East Oxford, in the County of Oxford from the original monument between lots 12 and 13 across lots Nos. 14 to 20 inclusive or as much further as may may be necessary to find an original monument and to mark the road allowance across lots Nos. 14 to 20 with permanent monuments on each side of said road allowance.	

GEORGE B. KIRKPATRICK,
　　　　　Director of Surveys.

AUBREY WHITE
Deputy Minister Lands and Forests.

Appendix No. 15.

Statement of municipal surveys confirmed during the year 1906.

No.	Name of Surveyor.	No.	Date of Instructions.	Description of Survey.	Date when confirmed under R. S.O., 1897, cap 181, secs. 10 to 15 inclusive.
1	E. T. Wilkie..	657	October 16, 1906	To survey the line between concessions Nos. 8 and 9 from lot No. 20 southerly to lot No. 14, both inclusive, in the township of Hinchinbrooke, in the county of Frontenac, and to plant permanent monuments on each side of the said concession road allowance.	November 26, 1906.

GEORGE B. KIRKPATRICK,   AUBREY WHITE,
      Director of Surveys.   Deputy Minister Lands and Forests.

Appendix No. 16.

Statement of Crown surveys in progress during the year 1906.

No.	Date of Instructions.	Name of Surveyor.	Description of Survey.	Amount Paid.
1	May 15, 1906.	W. Galbraith	Survey of Township of Clute, District of Algoma.	$5,000 00
2	May 15, 1906.	W. Beatty	Survey of Townships Gallagher and Strathearn, District of Algoma.	4,000 00
3	May 31, 1906.	J. J. Francis	Survey of Townships Langton and Temple, District of Rainy River.	1,500 00
4	June 14, 1906.	T. J. Patten......	Survey of portion of Boundary between Ontario and Quebec.	2,000 00
5	June 11, 1906.	T. J. Patten......	Survey of Township of Boyer, District of Nipissing.	1,500 00
6	July 6, 1906.	E. Seager	Survey of Township of Redditt, District of Rainy River.	1,800 00
				$15,800 00

GEORGE B. KIRKPATRICK,   AUBREY WHITE,
      Director of Surveys.   Deputy Minister Lands and Forests.

Appendix No. 17.

Statement of Crown lands surveyed, completed and closed during the year 1906.

No.	Date of Instructions.	Name of Surveyor.	Description of Survey.	Amount paid.	No. of acres.
				$ c.	
1	May 31st, 1905	Walter Beatty	Survey of townships of Cochrane, D'Arcy and McGee, District of Algoma	2,127 32	68,930
2	May 31st, 1905	H. J. Beatty......	Survey of townships of Borden and Gamey, District of Algoma.......	629 13	46,069
3	May 31st, 1905	C. E. Fitton......	Survey of townships of Carnegie and Reid, District of Algoma..	3,587 80	45,878
4	May 31st, 1905	Cavana and Watson	Survey of townships of Duff and Lucas, District of Algoma	3,538 30	45,383
5	May 31st, 1905	L. V. Rorke	Survey of township of Collins, District of Algoma	519 00	22,980
6	June 16th. 1905	James Dickson....	Inspection of Surveys	803 89	
7	May 31st, 1905	A. J. Halford.....	Survey of townships of Moody and Wesley, District of Nipissing.....	1,345 80	48,458
8	July 27th, 1905	T. J. Patten	Survey of Interprovincial Boundary, Ontario and Quebec.............	1,058 46	
9	Aug. 2nd, 1905	Edmund Seager...	Survey of township of Pellatt, District of Rainy River..........	1,259 00	31,050
10	Sept. 19th,1905	R. W. DeMorest ..	Survey of timber berths Nos. 182 and 176, District of Nipissing	871 58	
11	Jan. 20th, 1906	D. J. Gillon	Survey of timber berths, District of Rainy River....................	1,453 69	
12	Jan. 26th, 1906	Edmund Seager...	Survey of timber berths, District of Rainy River................o..	1,041 75	
13	Nov. 15th, 1905	T. B. Speight.....	Survey of certain marsh land, Mud Creek Reservation	80 20	
14	May 15th, 1906	Alex. Niven	Survey certain base and meridian lines, District of Algoma........	9,405 00	
15	May 15th, 1906	T. B. Speight.....	Survey certain base and meridian lines, District of Algoma........	9,885 70	
16	May 15th, 1906	E. D. Bolton	Survey of townships of Nesbitt and Aubin, District of Algoma	4,609 80	46,098
17	May 15th, 1906	James Hutcheon..	Survey of townships of Lennox and Dargavel, District of Algoma.....	4,900 00	46,000
18	May 15th, 1906	Tyrrell & MacKay	Survey of township of Sydere, District of Algoma.................	5,185 40	51,854
19	May 15th, 1906	H. J. Beatty......	Survey of Townships of Lackner and McNaught, District of Algoma	4,136 32	46,079
20	May 15th, 1906	A. S. Code........	Survey of townships of Ottaway and Fournier, District of Algoma	4,869 36	45,705
21	May 15th, 1906	J. W. Fitzgerald ..	Survey of township of Bradburn, District of Algoma	5,627 59	51,773
22	May 15th, 1906	L. V. Rorke	Survey of townships of Paul and Pattinson. District of Algoma....	4,401 07	45,662
23	May 25th, 1906	J. H. Smith	Survey of townships of Sweatman and Stimson, district of Nipissing.	4,876 50	45,765
24	May 15th, 1906	Cavana and Watson	Survey of township of Calder, District of Algoma.................	5,403 84	51,783
25	May 29th, 1906	W. W Stull.......	Survey of townships of Allen and Bigwood, District of Nipissing...	4,164 98	48,906
26	Feb. 26th, 1906	T. B. Speight.....	Survey re connecting point for longitude of boundary between Ontario and Quebec................	284 15	
27	May 23rd, 1906 June 25th, 1906 }	James Dickson..	Inspection of surveys (1906).......	2,831 01	

Appendix 17.—Concluded.

No.	Date of Instruction.	Name of Surveyor.	Description of Survey.	Amount paid.	No. of acres.
28	Jan. 26th, 1906	L. V. Rorke	Survey of timber berth WR9......	119 05	
29	June 27th, 1906	J. W. Fitzgerald ..	Survey of township of Beck, District of Algoma................	2,392 10	23,171
30	Aug. 24th, 1906	J. J. Francis......	Survey of certain lots Dryden town plot	37 75	
31	May 15th, 1906	J. J. Newman	Survey of townships of Sherring and Marathon	5,133 52	48,196
32	July 26th, 1906	L. V. Rorke	Survey of timber berths, District of Rainy River....................	2,137 89	
33	July 19th, 1906	Thomas Byrne....	Survey of township of Scollard, District of Nipissing................	2,675 20	33,440
34	Nov. 23rd, 1906	J. F. Whitson ...	Survey of Kerr and Cobalt Lakes, District of Nipissing............	37 40	
35	May 15th, 1906	W. Beatty........	Survey of township of Chapleau, District of Algoma.............	2,157 04	23,213
			The Copp, Clark Co., lithographing maps...........................	1,100 00	
			C. Tarling & Son, mounting maps..	140 10	
			E. H. Harcourt & Co., lithographing maps	3,659 00	
			Rice Lewis & Son, iron posts......	430 00	
			American Tent and Awning Co., tent and tarpaulin..............	26 40	
			King's Printer, mounting maps	261 30	
				109,203 39	916,373

GEORGE B. KIRKPATRICK,   AUBREY WHITE,
Director of Surveys.   Deputy Minister of Lands and Forests.

(*Appendix No. 18*).

BASE AND MERIDIAN LINES, DISTRICT OF ALGOMA.

HALIBURTON, ONT., December 13th, 1906.

SIR,—I have the honor to submit the following report on the survey of certain base and meridian lines forming the outline of the townships nine miles square, between the Missanabie and Mattagami Rivers, in the District of Algoma, under instructions from your Department, dated fifteenth of May, one thousand nine hundred and six.

I left Toronto on the sixth of June last, and proceeded to Missanabie on the Canadian Pacific Railway, thence by canoes to Dog Lake, Missanabie Lake, and down Missanabie River to where my base line of nineteen hundred crosses said river, arriving there in the afternoon of the eighteenth of June.

I obtained on the same evening an observation of Polaris for azimuth, and the following morning commenced my survey by running south astronomically from the ninty-ninth mile iron post on said base line, the boundary between the townships of Staunton and Barker. At the ninth mile on this line I turned and ran west astronomically on a nine mile chord to the line run by Ontario Land Surveyors Speight and Van Nostrand, as the west boundary of the township of Staunton. This line I intersected at nine miles one chain and eighteen links, and eighty-three links north of their nine mile post.

After removing their post to my line I returned to the line between the townships of Staunton and Barker, and ran east astronomically on nine mile chords, a base line of sixty-three miles, forty-six chains, and six links to a meridian line, run by Ontario Land Surveyor Speight, in nineteen hundred and five, intersecting this line three chains and seventy-one links south of his fifteen mile iron post.

These nine mile chords formed the southern boundaries of the townships of Barker, McCrae, Idington, Williamson, Teetzel, Gurney and Beardmore. the boundaries between which were also run north astronomically as I went along from the nine mile points to my base line of nineteen hundred.

From the intersection of the boundaries between McCrae and Idington, Idington and Williamson, and Teetzel and Gurney, with the seventy-two mile base line, nine mile lines were run south astronomically for boundaries of townships not yet named. A line was also run seven miles due south from corners of Williamson and Teetzel, and one and a half miles of due south line was also run from corners of Barker and McCrae, making a total mileage of one hundred and seventy-one miles.

As I had already drawn some supplies from the Transcontinental Railway Caches, and was afraid of being short on the way home, the survey was discontinued at the end of the seventh mile on line south from corners of Williamson and Teetzel, just after crossing the Kapuskasing River, which was on our way to the Canadian Pacific Railway. I reached Missanabie with my party on the twenty-eighth of September and Toronto on the evening of the twenty-ninth.

The details of the survey will be found in the field notes. The lines were well opened out and well blazed. Iron posts one and seven-eighth inches in diameter were planted alongside of wooden posts at the corners of each township (excepting where an iron post had already been planted near by) and marked with cold chisel with the name of the township on side next the township. Wooden posts were similarly marked, bearing trees taken, and course and distance noted from the posts. Observations for azimuth were frequently taken. The magnetic variation of the needle was comparatively steady at six degrees west.

General Description.

The tract of country surveyed is generally level, but with a little fall to the north. In some places it is a little rolling. The soil is almost all clay, a little sandy occasionally on slight elevations. Very rarely gravel or stone, with very few outcrops of rock. In fact rock or stone is scarcely ever seen excepting at the rivers, there it is mostly granite or gneiss, sometimes Huronian. Owing to the nature of the soil, and the level country, the water cannot get away, and much of what might be called swamp is really clay flat, and will become the best of farming land by the ordinary drainage incidental to settlement. Much of the ground is covered with a heavy growth of moss, but this rests upon clay, and will be burnt off with the clearing of the land.

Timber.

The timber is nearly all spruce generally red or black from four to fourteen inches in diameter. White spruce and poplar grows along the banks of river and creeks, and on the more elevated portions of the country much of it of large size running up to twenty and thirty inches in diameter. Balm of Gilead of large size is found in many places, and is always an indication of good land, clay covered with black muck. White birch is found on some of the higher portions of the country of good size, and a few black birch trees were met with. Balsam is freely intermixed with the other kinds of timber. There has been a large amount of tamarac in the country, but it is now nearly all dead. Very few living trees are left. The small trees however are mostly green. There is no white or red pine in the country, and I only saw one growth of banksian pine.

There is not much cedar in the country, only along river banks. Much of the timber has been blown down, making it very difficult to get through. The country is very brushy with young balsam, spruce and alder.

Water.

The rivers running through the survey are the Missanabie, Opaszatika (meaning poplar) Kapuskasing and Ground Hog, besides a number of smaller runs and streams.

The Missanabie is the largest of these, and varies in width from three hundred to one thousand feet with many rapids and falls. The Opaszatika is from two to four chains wide, with muddy water tributary to the Missanabie. The Kapuskasing is from three to five chains wide, with many beautiful falls, and the Ground Hog will average four to five chains in width, the last two being tributary to the Mattagami River. There are falls on all of these rivers capable of producing a large amount of power.

The southern boundary of the township of Gurney runs through Lake Remi, a beautiful sheet of clear water three miles wide on the line, and extending south and southwest from five to seven miles.

The National Transcontinental Railway will skirt Lake Remi on the south, and run through seven or eight of the townships outlined, and settlement will no doubt speedily take place on the completion of this undertaking. About ninety per cent. of these townships may be put down as good farming land. A fire ran over a considerable area about five years ago, and some fire got out during the past summer along the location of the railway line.

Game.

The country abounds with moose; bears were frequently seen, partridge were scarce, wild ducks plentiful. The usual kinds of fish were found in the waters, pike, pickerel and salmon trout.

No minerals were met with. There were a few frosts during the summer, but I have no reason to suppose the country would compare unfavorably with more southern parts of Ontario when they were in the same condition.

Herewith will be found the field notes, and plan of survey, and account in triplicate.

I have the honor to be,
Sir,
Your Obedient Servant,
(Signed) ALEX. NIVEN,
Ontario Land Surveyor.

The Honorable,
　The Minister of Lands, Forests and Mines,
　　Toronto.

(Appendix No. 19).

BASE AND MERIDIAN LINES, DISTRICT OF ALGOMA.

TORONTO, Dec. 12th, 1906.

SIR,—We have the honor to submit the following report on the survey of certain base and meridian lines, forming outlines of townships nine miles square, in the District of Algoma, made by us during the past summer under instructions from your Department, dated 15th May, 1906.

At the earliest possible date, we made arrangements with the Hudson's Bay Company to transport the bulk of the season's supplies from Missanabie to Brunswick House Post at the east end of Missanabie Lake, and later, to the point where the Opazatika River is crossed by "Niven's base line of 1900."

With O. L. S., E. R. Bingham as first assistant, and seven men from older Ontario, we left Toronto in two detachments on 23rd and 24th May, respectively, and on arriving at Missanabie were joined by thirteen Indians, whose services had been previously arranged for.

The journey from Missanabie to the point where the Missanabie River is crossed by Niven's base line, a distance of 125 miles, including twenty-eight portages, occupied eight days. Of these portages, the majority were short and generally good, it being found necessary in only five or six instances to carry the canoes overland. The rapids at nearly all these portages are very swift and dangerous for any but experienced hands to attempt to run them, even with empty canoes.

The initial point of the survey, namely, the end of the 102nd mile on the base line run in 1900 by Ontario Land Surveyor Alex. Niven, from the 198th mile post on the district boundary, having been reached, the work was proceeded with, and the following lines were run, viz., the north and west boundaries of the townships of Staunton, Devitt, Eilber, McCowan, Neely, Nixon, Pearce and Torrance, with the exception of the east three miles of the south boundary of the township of Staunton.

Following verbal permission from your Department to extend, under favorable circumstances, the scope of the survey, we prolonged the west boundaries of the townships of Eilber, Nixon, Pearce and Torrance, each for a distance of nine miles north, and continued due west three and a half miles from the north-west corner of the township of Staunton. The prevalence of forest fires in the vicinity of the Kapuskasing River rendered unsafe the continuation of the work to the east of the township of Torrance, and the latter part of the survey covered by the instructions was left unfinished.

All lines were well opened out and blazed, and iron posts one and seven-eighth inches in diameter were planted at the north-west corners of the following townships, viz., Staunton, Devitt, Eilber, McCowan, Neely, Nixon, Pearce and Torrance, the name of each adjacent township being clearly marked by cold chisel upon the sides of the iron posts. At all other mile points on east and west lines, and one and one-half miles on meridians, the posts planted were of wood, each bearing the distance in miles from the initial point of the line upon which it stood. The north and south lines were run as true meridians, and the east and west lines were nine mile chords of parallels of latitude.

Numerous astronomical observations were taken during the progress of the work.

General Features.

In general, the surface of the country in this region may be termed flat and gently undulating and lying at an elevation of from ten to twenty-five feet above the numerous streams which traverse it. Not less than thirty-five per cent. of the area is high and undulating, the numerous creeks which traverse it affording excellent drainage facilities. The remainder of the region traversed is flat, and with one or two exceptions there were no muskegs of any extent.

Soil.

The soil is chiefly clay and clay loam, only a small outcropping of rock being seen, except in the river beds and rapids, and the shores of some of the lakes. The usual peat moss of the clay belt prevails, but this, as is now well known, is a condition easily removed when the land is required for cultivation. The presence of this moss preserves the winter's ice until late in the summer. Facilities for artificial drainage are good, but there will not be much necessity for expensive drainage work when once the moss has been cleared away by fire. Near the Kapuskasing River, on the north boundary of the township of Torrance, a marked example of this was seen, a tract of several miles in extent which had recently been burned over, having been changed from apparently flat moss grown area to level clay land, needing only slight labor to fit it for immediate cultivation.

In passing Brunswick House Post in the latter part of May, we noticed that preparations were being made, with the primitive means available for planting potatoes, and on our return, we were, by the kindness of the Hudson's Bay Company's officers, presented with a substantial sample of the fruits of their labors. A member of our party who is thoroughly acquainted with farming in older Ontario was delegated to dig the potatoes, and he assured us he had never seen better specimens, nor a more abundant yield.

Climate.

The northern part of the territory crossed by the survey is slightly south of the latitude of Winnipeg, and our previous experience of the clay belt region had led us to expect a climate quite as temperate as that of Manitoba. The summer of 1906 bears out this estimate, as the only severe frosts noted were in the latter part of May, and one slight frost occurred in August. When the necessary drainage and removal of peat moss and its products have been brought about by the settlement of the country, it may be confidently expected that the summer frost will almost, if not entirely, disappear.

Timber.

The timber met with is chiefly spruce, poplar, tamarac, balm of Gilead, and white birch, (and a few scattered "scrubby" cedar) of sufficient quality and quantity for the ordinary needs of settlers, besides furnishing a considerable amount of pulpwood for industrial purposes. As is usual in these northern latitudes, the larger timber is found in the immediate vicinity of the rivers and attains a maximum diameter of 30 inches, that more remote being dwarfed by the shortness of the season for growing. Poplar, which usually occupies the ridges and banks of rivers, reaches a maximum of from 10 to 15 inches, and is of excellent quality.

Water Power.

The Missanabie is a fine stream 400 to 500 feet wide, with a depth of 4 to 10 feet, the Opazatika being similar but less than one-third its volume, while the Kapuskasing equals the Missanabie in size and volume, but with no fall of consequence. In addition to the above streams, the country is well watered by springs and spring creeks or rivulets.

There are no water powers of any considerable magnitude within the limits of the survey. There is a chute of about 10 feet on the Missanabie River, nearly opposite the third mile in the north boundary of the township of Eilber. North of this township, and on the Missanabie River there are numerous rapids in the first six miles, and these will some day serve a good purpose.

Another chute of about 10 feet occurs on the Opazatika River, near the north boundary of the township of Nixon, and it will some day be drawn upon for a limited supply of power.

Minerals.

Nearly all the territory embraced by this survey lies within the Huronian formation with an occasional small outcrop of granite and gneiss. So far as our observation goes, no evidence of the presence of economic minerals was met with.

Game.

Moose tracks were frequently seen, but are not so numerous as to indicate the presence of the animal in large numbers. Occasional marten and mink were seen. Fish were not found in abundance.

General Remarks.

Briefly, the country and conditions met with are very similar to those covered by our report on a part of the clay belt surveyed in 1905, the superiority if anything, being in favor of that of 1906.

We feel confident that when the National Transcontinental Railway is completed, and this will be under construction through this region in 1907, fully seventy-five per cent. of this land will be converted into excellent farms, and will compare well with any agricultural section of the older part of the Province.

Accompanying this report are a general plan, field notes and triplicate accounts.

We have the honor to be,
Sir,
Your Obedient Servants,
(Signed) SPEIGHT & VANNOSTRAND,
Ontario Land Surveyors.

The Honorable,
The Minister of Lands, Forests and Mines,
Toronto.

_____

(*Appendix No. 20.*)

Township of Clute, District of Algoma.

BRACEBRIDGE, ONT., Dec. 29th, 1906.

SIR,—I have the honor to submit the following report of the survey of the township of Clute, in the district of Algoma, performed under instructions from your Department, dated May 15th, 1906.

I commenced the survey at the south-east angle of the township, by chaining O. L. S. Patten's base line. which forms the south boundary, and running the different side roads due north from this base line. At one hundred and twenty chains north from the south-east angle, the line between the second and third concessions was run west from the district boundary, and the survey of the several concession lines and side road allowances proceeded with, making the regular lots 25 chains 25 links in width, and 59 chains, 50 links in depth.

An iron post one and seven-eighths inches in diameter was planted at the south-east angle of the township, marked "R" on four sides, "Clute", on the north-west side and "Fournier" on the south-west side.

Iron posts one and one-quarter inches in diameter were planted between lots 12 and 13 on the south boundary, between lots 12 and 13 on the line between the 6th and 7th concessions, and between 12 and 13 on the north boundary, and also on the east and west boundaries at the line between the 6th and 7th concessions; these iron posts were marked "R" on four sides and also marked with the number of the concession on the north and south sides.

The iron posts previously planted at the north-east and south-west angles of the township were marked "R" on four sides, and "Clute" on the side facing the township; an iron post one and one-quarter inches in diameter similarly marked was planted on the north boundary at the edge of the lake in the north-west corner of the township.

The west boundary was run by O. L. Surveyors, Cavana & Watson.

General Features.

The township is situated in the great northern clay belt and the soil is a rich clay loam throughout the greater part, with a considerable area of a lighter sandy loam, with clay sub-soil extending over the western portion of the township, and is well adapted for agriculture.

About fifteen per cent. consists of swamp or muskeg, and the remaining eighty-five per cent. of the land may be classed as good agricultural land, with no stones or boulders to interfere with cultivation.

The greater part of the township is undulating or rolling, affording good natural drainage, while to the east of the Frederick House River, there are extensive level tracts of land, and as nearly all of these level portions are traversed by creeks with good current, they will be comparatively easily drained.

The timber is black spruce, balsam, poplar, white birch and a few cedars, with some white spruce of larger size near the rivers. There is also in many places a thick growth of underbrush and alders.

In the westerly part of the township a fire took place, evidently in 1905, and extended from concession four to the north boundary; the area of this burnt timber is shown on the timber map.

Outcroppings of rock occur in the bed of the Frederick House River, in concessions 11 and 12, and in the Bush-ke-gow River at lot 13, which rock is apparently gneiss of Laurentian formation.

No other rock in place was observed, but numerous boulders are scattered along the beds of the rivers.

Water.

The Frederick House River is from three to six chains in width with many rapids, where the river-bed is thickly covered with stones and large boulders. The water is colored with clay in solution, and on account of the rapid current it is a difficult river to ascend in canoes.

The Bush-ke-gow River, from one and one-half to two chains wide, is a fine stream of comparatively clear water, with banks about 20 feet high, but is not navigable for canoes on account of the rapid current. The lower portion of this stream is a succession of rapids caused by layers of boulders and stones which have been deposited in the bed of the river.

A number of small lakes are found in the westerly portion of the township, draining into a stream about one chain wide which flows northerly, crossing the north boundary in lot 25.

These lakes are shallow with clay and gravel beds, and generally marshy shores, they are supplied by numerous springs, making the water clear and good.

A small amount of water power could be developed on the Bush-ke-gow River, at lot 13, concession 6; this is more of a rapids than a falls, and the number of horse power that would be available without great expense would be sixty or seventy: the volume of water flowing in this stream is not large during the summer.

The line of the National Transcontinental Railway as now surveyed, crosses this township, and the construction of this railway will afford an easy means of access to extensive tracts of good land.

The magnetic variation ranges from eight to eleven degrees west, the average variation was found to be eight degrees forty-five minutes west.

There are no settlers or improvements on any of the lots.

Accompanying this report are a plan of the township, timber map and field notes made out in the usual form.

I have the honor to be,

Sir,

Your Obedient Servant,

(Signed) W. GALBRAITH,

Ontario Land Surveyor.

The Honorable,
The Minister of Lands, Forests and Mines,
Toronto.

(Appendix No. 21.)

TOWNSHIP OF BORDEN, DISTRICT OF ALGOMA.

EGANVILLE, ONT., February 26th, 1906.

SIR,—I have the honor to submit the following report of the survey of the Township of Borden, in the District of Algoma, made under instructions from your department dated May 31st, 1905.

This township is bounded on the west by the Township of Cochrane, on the north by the Township of McGee, both of which were surveyed by Ontario Land Surveyor Walter Beatty, and on the east by the Township of Gamey, and on the south by unsurveyed lands of the Crown.

There is a good canoe route from the Village of Chapleau on the main line of the Canadian Pacific Railway to Moose Factory, which passes through this township in a north-easterly course and is used for putting in supplies for the Transcontinental Railway.

The north and west boundaries of this township were surveyed by O. L. S. Walter Beatty and the east boundary by Ontario Land Surveyor, L. V. Rorke.

I commenced my survey as instructed, at the south-east corner of the Township of Cochrane, where I found iron and wooden posts marked, "Con. I." on the north, "Cochrane" on the north-west, and "I" on the west sides, and which I further marked "Borden" on the north-east and "XII" on the east sides. I then ran a chord of latitude east astronomically to intersection with the meridian run by Ontario Land Surveyor, L. V. Rorke, where I planted an iron post one and seven-eighths inches in diameter, marked "I" on the west side, "Borden" on the north-west and "Con. I" on the north sides, this being forty-three links north of his "XII" mile post; thus making

5 L. M.

each lot forty chains wide excepting lot No. "I" which is only thirty-eight chains wide. I planted an iron post one and one-quarter inches in diameter between lots six and seven, marked "VI" on east, "Con. I" on north and "VII" on west sides..

From this line as a base, I made my sub-division survey in accordance with instructions, by projecting meridians north astronomically from posts established on south boundary. The concession lines were made to agree with concession lines in the Township of Cochrane and posts established by Ontario Land Surveyor Walter Beatty were used for commencing the different concession lines in the Township of Borden, the additional marking of lot No. "XII" being added to his posts. To the one and one-quarter inch iron post planted by him at the intersection of the line between concessions three and four with his west boundary I added "XII." I found the one and seven-eighths inch iron post at north-west corner of Borden marked "Con. VI" on south, "Borden" on south-east, "I" on east, "McGee" on north-east, "Con. I" on north, "D'Arcy" on north-west, "XII" on west and "Cochrane" on south-west sides, this being the corner of the four townships. I planted an iron post one and one-quarter inches in diameter at the intersection of the line between concessions three and four with line between lots six and seven marked "Con. IV" on north, "VI" on east, "Con. III" on south and "VII" on west sides, and as the line between concessions three and four intersected the east boundary at the fifteenth mile post established by Ontario Land Surveyor Rorke, this iron post is marked "XV M" and "Con. III" on south, "XII" on west, "Con. IV" on north and "I" on east sides, it being also the commencing point of the line between concessions three and four in the Township of Gamey. The north-east corner of the township was established by O. L. S. Walter Beatty. I planted an iron post one and one-quarter inches in diameter at the intersection of the line between lots six and seven, concession 6 with the south boundary of the Township of McGee, marked "VI" on east side, "VI" on west side, and "Con. VI" on south side. This post is three chains and fifty links east of the post established by O. L. S. Walter Beatty, for line between lots six and seven, concession I, Township of McGee.

Frequent observations were taken throughout the survey. On each island a prominent tree was blazed and numbered. The only islands of any size are number "I" in Loon Lake and number "I" in West's Lake, both of which are well timbered, the former being rough and broken while the latter is level and suitable for camping purposes.

The magnetic variation is fairly constant at four degrees west, but I found considerable variation in the vicinity of intersection of lines between lots ten and eleven with line between concessions four and five. The surface is fairly level, but slightly hilly in the vicinity of the chain of lakes running through the township in a north-easterly direction. The soil is mostly sandy and generally stony and I do not consider that more than fifteen per cent. is suitable for agricultural purposes.

The south boundary is nearly all in brule which extends from ten to sixty chains north into the township. The remainder of the township is covered by a heavy growth of jack pine, spruce, birch, balsam and poplar from 4 inches to 12 inches in diameter, excepting in swamps where the timber is spruce and dry tamarac, the spruce being of fair quality from 4 inches to 12 inches in diameter. There is some pine of fair quality on lots ten and eleven, concession two, and some scattered pine on lots 8 and 9, concessions 2 and 3; lots 6 and 7, concession 5, and lots 4 and 5, concessions 5 and 6.

5a L. M.

The township is well supplied with water which occupies about one-eight of the total area. Pike abound in all the lakes and some trout of about 4 lbs. weight were caught in Emerald Lake, which is a beautiful sheet of water, very clear and deep. Small speckled trout were caught in creek flowing out of Emerald Lake, and there is good trout fishing in Nemegisenda River, at foot of falls, on lot one, concession two; we caught them up to eighteen inches in length. Loon River, which enters the township in lot 12, Con. 5, and runs north-easterly, and leaving township on north boundary of lot 3, Con. 6, is a small stream varying in width from twenty to seventy-five links. It is shallow and rapid in places and is not navigable by canoes excepting on lots 3 and 4, where it is from one and one-half to two chains wide and from one to three feet deep. The River Némegisenda enters township on lot I, concession 2, on the east boundary and flows northerly, crossing the east boundary of the township near the south-east corner of lot I, concession 5. It has a good strong current, is navigable by canoes and is from seventy to one hundred links in width, with low marshy banks. There is one fall on lot I, concession 2, of about twenty feet, but the supply of water is not constant enough nor of sufficient volume to make it a valuable water power in my opinion.

No indication of economic mineral was seen.

Taken as a whole, I consider this township unsuitable for agricultural purposes and its principal asset to be pulpwood.

Accompanying this report are a general plan, timber plan and field notes.

> I have the honor to be,
> Sir,
> Your obedient servant,
> (Signed) HERBERT J. BEATTY,
> Ontario Land Surveyor.

The Honorable,
The Minister of Lands, Forests and Mines.
Toronto.

(*Appendix No. 22.*)

TOWNSHIP OF COLLINS, DISTRICT OF ALGOMA.

TORONTO, October 17th, 1906.

SIR,—I have the honor to submit the following report on the survey of the Township of Collins, in the District of Algoma, performed by me under instructions from your Department, dated the Thirty-first of May, nineteen hundred and five.

This township lies to the north and adjoining the Township of Chewett, also surveyed by me under instructions of the same date.

Having completed the survey of the Township of Chewett, I proceeded with the survey of the Township of Collins by continuing the east boundary of the Township of Chewett due north for six miles and running the concession lines for the Township of Collins due west therefrom.

On the twentieth of October I found it necessary, owing to the possibility of the small lakes on the canoe route freezing over, to abandon the survey

for the season, leaving twenty-three miles of line, including the north boundary unfinished. I returned to the work on the tenth of June, nineteen hundred and six, and completed the survey in the usual way.

Wooden posts were planted at the front angles of all the lots and marked for the several lots and concessions for which they were placed. Iron posts one and one-quarter inches in diameter were planted at the following points: At the intersection of the front of concession four with the east and west boundaries of the township, and also at the intersection of the line between lots six and seven with the north and south boundaries of the township, and with the front of concession four, and these were marked according to the lots and concessions they were placed to define. Iron posts one and seven-eighths inches in diameter were planted at the north-east and north-west angles of the township and at the intersection of the west boundary of the northerly shore of Trout Lake, and the name of the township was marked on these in addition to the number of the lot and concession. The iron posts of the same dimensions formerly planted at the north-east angle of the Township of Chewett and at the intersection of the north boundary of that township with the easterly shore of Trout Lake were also properly marked for the Township of Collins, that is to say:—

The iron post at the north-west corner of the township is marked "Collins" on the south-east side, "Con· VI" on the south side, and "XII" on the east side.

The iron post at the north-east corner of the township is marked "Collins" on the south-west side, "Con. VI" on the south side, "I" on the west side.

The iron post at the south-east corner of the township is marked "Collins" on the northwest side, "Chewett" on the southwest side, "Con. I" on the north side, "Con. VI" on the south side, "I" on the west side.

The iron post at the intersection of the south boundary with the easterly shore of Trout Lake is marked "Collins, Con. I" on the north side, "Chewett, Con. VI" on the south side, "X" on the east side.

The iron post at the intersection of the west boundary with the northerly shore of Trout Lake is marked "Collins" on the north-east side, "Con. I" on the north side, "XII" on the east side.

Trout River, the outlet of Trout Lake, runs diagonally from south-west to north-east through the township. The land is rough· and hilly for some distance back from the shore, the remaining part being high and rolling, interspersed with swamps.

Timber.

A fire during the spring of 1905 swept over that part of the township east and south of Trout River destroying the timber, which is principally Banksian Pine and Spruce, excepting in some swamps along the east boundary, where spruce, cedar and dead tamarac ·from four to ten and twelve inches still remains green.

The north-easterly part of the township is also brule of some fifteen years and is grown up with second growth scrub.

The western part of the township is fairly well timbered wnth Banksian pine, birch, balsam, spruce, poplar and dead tamarac, accompanied by a thick growth of underbrush. Where not thickly wooded this timber averages from ten to twenty inches in diameter, but the greater portion runs from four inches to ten in diameter. Some Red and White pine is still standing on lots nine and ten, concession two and three, and on lots five and six, concessions five and six, in size from eight to twenty-four inches in diameter.

Soil.

The soil throughout the township varies from a light sand to a rich sandy loam, the latter being more particularly found in the western one-third of the township, but is too stony to be classed as desirable for agricultural purposes, though several separate areas may be termed suitable, perhaps in all about twenty-five or thirty per cent. of the area, for agricultural or grazing purposes when the seasons will permit.

Minerals.

The rock formation is Laurentian, consisting principally of granite. Few exposures were seen excepting along the shores of Trout Lake. Numerous large and small boulders, both angular and rounded, are found throughout the township. No indications of economic minerals were seen.

Game and Fish.

A scarcity of the larger game which might be expected to inhabit that country was notable. The waters of Trout Lake and River abound with trout, white fish, pike and pickerel.

Accompanying this report are a general plan, timber map and field notes of the survey.

I have the honor to be,
　　Sir,
　　　　Your obedient servant,
　　　　　　(Signed) L. V. RORKE,
　　　　　　　　Ontario Land Surveyor.

The Honorable,
　　The Minister of Lands, Forests and Mines.
　　Toronto.

————

(Appendix No. 23.)

TOWNSHIP OF CHAPLEAU, DISTRICT OF ALGOMA.

DELTA, ONT., Dec. 19th, 1906.

SIR,—I have the honor to submit the following report on the survey of the Township of Chapleau, in the District of Algoma, pursuant to your instructions dated the fifteenth day of May, 1906.

This township is bounded on the east by the Township of Gallagher, surveyed by me this season, and on the south, west and north sides by unsurveyed lands of the Crown. Having completed the survey of the Township of Gallagher, I commenced my survey by running a chord of latitude due west astronomically from the south-west corner of said township, planting durable wooden posts every forty chains marking the corners of the respective lots excepting the south-west corner of lot twelve which is broken by a lake at the shore of which I planted an iron bar one and seven-eighths inches in diameter alongside a spruce post, both of which were marked "XII" on east side, "Con. I" on north side and "Chapleau" on north-east side. The west boundary was established by off-setting around the lake the required distance to make lot twelve forty chains wide. From this as a base, meridians were projected north astronomically and the subdivision was performed in accordance with instructions, durable wooden posts being planted at the corners of all lots excepting where such corners came in water in which case posts were planted at the shore in manner called for in instructions. On the line between lots six and seven iron bars one and one-quarter inches in diameter was planted alongside wooden posts at the following corners : at its intersection with the south boundary, marked "VI" on east, "Con. I" on north, and "VII" on west sides; at its intersection with line between concessions three and four marked "Con. IV" on north, "Con. III" on south, "VI" on east and "VII" on west sides, and at its intersection with north boundary marked "Con. VI" on south, "VI" on east and "VII" on west sides. I planted an iron bar one and one-quarter inches in diameter marked "Con. III" on south, "XII" on east and "Con. IV" on north sides at intersection of line between concessions three and four with shore of lake which west boundary crosses. At the north-west corner of the township I planted an iron bar one and seven-eighths inches in diameter marked "Con. VI" on south. "XII" on east, and "Chapleau" on south-east sides, this post being two chains and forty-five links east of O.L.S. McAree's post, which is now the south-east corner of the Township of Strathearn. I also planted a one and one-quarter inch iron bar at the intersection of line between concessions three and four with the east boundary marked "Con. IV" on north, "I" on west and "Con. III" on south sides, and the one and seven-eighths inch iron bar at the north-east corner of the township was marked "XII" on east, "Gallagher" on south-east, "Con. VI" on south, "Chapleau" on south-west and "I" on west sides, while the one and seven-eighth iron bar at the south-east corner was marked "XII" on east, "Gallagher" on north-east, "Con. I" on north, "Chapleau" on north-west and "I" on west sides, these posts being also the north-west and south-west corners of the Township of Gallagher.

Frequent observations for azimuth were taken.

The whole of the township is rolling and broken, the soil being sandy and stony with frequent outcroppings of rock and with many large boulders scattered over the surface. Small areas of light sandy soil are scattered throughout the township, on one of which the Village of Chapleau is built. None of it would make good farming land, the soil being too light for growing crops, though some very good potatoes are grown in the gardens in the village.

Excepting a narrow strip along the south boundary and the greater portion of lots eight, nine, ten, eleven and twelve, concessions three, four, five and six, the township is all brûle, the above excepted areas being covered by banksian pine, white birch, poplar, spruce and balsam from three to twelve inches in diameter and from which all timber of any value except for fuel has been removed.

As will be seen by reference to the general plan, the township is well watered, there being a good water route through the same navigable by canoes excepting a few short portages. The only water power of any value is in Block A, and belongs to a company operating a saw-mill and electric light plant which supplies the Village of Chapleau.

The fishing in the lakes is fairly good and quite a few red deer were seen in the southerly part of the township.

The magnetic variation of the needle is from three and one-half to four degrees west and is fairly constant in the northerly portion of the township, but is not to be relied upon in the southerly portion.

Taken as a whole, this township is not of great value either for timber or agricultural purposes.

Accompanying this report is a general plan, timber plan, traverse sheet and field notes of the entire survey.

I have the honor to be,

Sir,

Your obedient servant,

(Signed) WALTER BEATTY,

Ontario Land Surveyor.

The Honorable,

    The Minister of Lands, Forests and Mines.

    Toronto.

(Appendix No. 24).

TOWNSHIP OF LACKNER, DISTRICT OF ALGOMA.

EGANVILLE, ONTARIO, October 6th, 1906.

SIR,—I have the honor to submit the following report of the survey of the Township of Lackner, in the District of Algoma, performed under instructions from your Department dated May fifteenth, 1906.

This township is bounded on the west by the Township of McNaught, on the north by the Township of Gamey and on the east and south sides by unsurveyed lands of the Crown, and can best be reached by Nemegos Station on the main line of the Canadian Pacific Railway, via Nemegosenda River to lot three, concession two, of the Township of McNaught, from which there is a fairly good portage to lake on lot twelve, concession two, of this township.

I commenced my survey by running a chord of latitude east astronomically a distance of six miles from an iron bar one and seven-eighth inches in diameter marked "VI. M" on south side, planted by Ontario Land Surveyor L. V. Rorke, planting posts for the respective lots as instructed. From the easterly end of this chord, I ran the east boundary of the township north astronomically to intersection with the south boundary of the Township of Gamey, produced thirty-nine links easterly, and subdivided the township in the usual manner, planting substantial wooden posts duly marked at the corners of the respective lots. Frequent observations for azimuth were taken.

I marked the iron bar at the south-west corner of the township "XII." on east, "Lackner" on north-east, and "Con. I." on north sides, and planted a one and seven-eighth inch iron bar marked "I." on west, "Lackner" on northwest, and "Con. I." on north sides at the southeast corner of the township. Also an iron bar, same diameter, marked "Con. VI." on south, "Lackner" on southwest, and "I." on west sides, at the northeast corner of the township, and to the iron bar planted at the southwest corner of the Township of Gamey I added "Con. V." on south, and "Lackner" on southeast sides.

To the one and one-quarter inch iron bar planted by Ontario Land Surveyor L. V. Rorke and marked "IX. M" on south side, I added "Con. III." on south, "XII." on east, and "Con. IV." on north sides.

I planted one and one-quarter inch iron bars alongside of wooden posts at the following corners:—At the intersection of line between lots six and seven with the south boundary, marked "VI." on east, "Con. I." on north, and "VII." on west sides. At intersection of same line with line between concessions three and four, marked "Con. IV." on north, "VI." on east, "Con. III." on south, and "VII" on west sides. At its intersection with the north boundary, marked "Con. VI." on south, "VI." on east, and "VII." on west sides; and at intersection of line between concessions three and four with east boundary, marked "Con. IV." on north, "I" on west and "Con. III." on south sides.

The surface of lots eight, nine, ten, eleven and twelve, concessions two, three, four and five, is rough and rocky with large boulders and broken with hills rising from sixty to three hundred feet, and in this area the magnetic variation is very erratic, due doubtless to magnetic iron.

The remainder of the township is rolling, sandy land, stony with boulders scattered throughout, and broken by lakes and rocky ridges.

About eighty per cent. of the township has been burned over about twelve or fifteen years ago, and is now covered with a thick growth of banksian pine, white birch, poplar, and alders from one to three inches in diameter. The southeasterly portion prior to the fire was covered with a splendid growth of banksian pine.

The township is well watered with numerous small streams: the Nemegosenda River passes through its northwest corner on lot twelve, concession six, and the only other stream of importance enters the township on lot ten, concession one, flows in a northeasterly direction and is joined by another small stream on lot five, concession three, and leaves the township near the southeast corner of lot one, concession five, where it empties into a chain of lakes extending to the northeast. It is very crooked, varying in width from twenty-five to fifty links, and in depth from six inches to four or five feet. It is navigable with small canoes through concessions three and four, but is obstructed in many cases by fallen trees.

Moose were very plentiful throughout this township, and pickerel were easily caught in the lake on lot eight, concession four; and in stream on lot one, concession four, fresh beaver dams were seen in three places.

With the exception of a few lots, this township is unsuitable for agricultural purposes, the soil being either too light and sandy or too rocky, and there is little timber of any commercial value.

Accompanying this report are a general plan, timber plan and field notes.

I have the honor to be,
          Sir,
          Your obedient servant,
          (Signed) HERBERT J. BEATTY,
               Ontario Land Surveyor.

The Honorable
     The Minister of Lands, Forests and Mines,
          Toronto.

(Appendix No. 25.)

TOWNSHIP OF McNAUGHT, DISTRICT OF ALGOMA.

EGANVILLE, ONTARIO, October 26th, 1906

SIR,—I have the honor to submit the following report on the survey of the Township of McNaught, in the District of Algoma, performed under instructions from your Department, dated the fifteenth of May, 1906.

This township is bounded on the east by the Township of Lackner, on the north by the Township of Borden, on the west by the Township of Gallagher and on the south by unsurveyed lands of the Crown.

I commenced my survey at the south-west corner of the township at an iron bar planted by Ontario Land Surveyor John McAree alongside a cedar post marked "XXXVII" on south-east side and "XXXVIII" on south-west side and "XXX" on north-west side, and from this I ran a chord of latitude for south boundary east astronomically to intersection with meridian run by Ontario Land Surveyor L. V. Rorke last summer, where I planted an iron bar one and seven-eighths inches in diameter alongside a wooden post, both of which were marked "Con. I." on north, "McNaught" on northwest, and "I" on west sides. These posts are seventy links north of Ontario Land Surveyor Rorke's six mile post. I chained easterly on this boundary planting wooden posts at every forty chains for the corners of the respective lots excepting lot one which is thirty-nine chains and eighty-nine links wide.

I planted a new iron bar one and seven eighths inches in diameter and a spruce post, marked "XII" on east, "McNaught" on north-east, and "Con. I" on north sides alongside Ontario Land Surveyor John McAree's posts at the south-west corner, and an iron bar one and one-quarter inches in diameter alongside a spruce post marked "Con. I" on north, "VI" on east and "VII" on west sides between lots six and seven, and performed my survey by projecting meridians north astronomically from the post at the south-west corner of the township, and posts between lots. ten and eleven, eight and nine, six and seven, four and five, and two and three, making the respective concessions eighty chains in depth as nearly as practicable.

I planted iron bars one and one-quarter inches in diameter on the line between concessions three and four at its intersection with the west boundary with the line between lots six and seven, and also at its intersection with the east boundary of the township, also at the intersection of line between lots six and seven with the south boundary of the Township of Borden. The west boundary intersected the south boundary of the Township of Cochrane eighty-eight links west of the south-west corner of said township, where I planted an iron bar one and seven-eighths inches in diameter alongside a dry banksian pine post, both of which were marked "Con. VI" on south, "McNaught" on south-east, and "XII" on east side. To the one and seven-eighths inch iron bar planted alongside a wooden post at the south-east corner of the Township of Borden, which is also the north-east corner of the Township of McNaught, I added "Con. VI" on south, and "McNaught" on south-west sides.

Wooden posts of as durable material as could be procured were planted at the corners of lots except where corners came in water, and in the latter case posts were planted at the shores in accordance with instructions .

Frequent observations for azimuth were taken. Magnetic variation is fairly constant at from three and one-half to four degrees west of the astronomic north.

The Canadian Pacific Railway passes a little less than a mile south of the south-west corner of the township and runs in a south-easterly direction so that it is five miles south of the south-east corner. The River Nemegosenda crosses the Canadian Pacific Railway at Nemegos Station, about two miles south of the south boundary and flows in a north-westerly direction entering the township near the south-east corner of lot six and leaves the township near the south-east corner of lot one, concession six. This stream averages about forty feet in width and flows through a marshy valley, has low banks which it overflows for a considerable time in the spring and after any heavy rains during the summer. It has a good strong current, is very crooked and is navigable by canoes, there being two short portages in the township and three portages between the south boundary and the railway. In high water this forms a fairly good route through the easterly portion of the township. There is also a chain of lakes from the west boundary in concession five to lot five, concession three, draining into Nemegosenda River on lot three, concession three. The outlet of these lakes is navigable only in high water for about thirty chains from its entrance to the river and there is a good portage from this point to the lake on lot five.

The surface is fairly level except that portion lying east of the Nemegosenda River, which is rough and broken with rocky sandy soil. That part lying west of the river and south of the chain of lakes is nearly all brule, the soil being light and sandy, quite barren in places, while the portion north of the chain of lakes and west of the river is also fairly level and broken with many small lakes and is about half brule, the soil being light and sandy and rather stony for a mile or two north-west of the river.

Red deer were seen in the south-westerly portion of the township and moose are quite plentiful in the westerly portions. There are plenty of fish in the lakes.

Magnetic iron occurs on lots one and two, concessions two, three, four and five.

The only timber of commercial value is banksian pine, and this is restricted to lots three to twelve, concessions four and five, the remainder of the timber having been destroyed by fire about fifteen years ago.

Taken as a whole, I do not consider this township suitable for agricultural purposes, the soil being too light for profitable farming.

Accompanying this report are a general plan, a timber plan, traverse sheet and field notes of the entire survey.

> I have the honor to be,
> Sir,
> Your obedient servant,
> (Signed) HERBERT J. BEATTY,
> Ontario Land Surveyor.

The Honorable
The Minister of Lands, Forests and Mines,
Toronto.

(*Appendix No. 26.*)

TOWNSHIP OF McGEE, DISTRICT OF ALGOMA.

DELTA, March 6th, 1906.

SIR,—I have the honor to submit the following report of the survey of the Township of McGee, in the District of Algoma, made under instructions dated May 31st, 1905.

This township is bounded on the south by the Township of Borden, on the east by the Township of Chewett, on the north by the unsurveyed lands of the Crown, and on the west by the Township of D'Arcy, and can easily be reached by a good canoe route from the Village of Chapleau, on the main line of the Canadian Pacific Railway, to Moose Factory, which passes through the south-east corner of the township via Loon River.

I commenced my survey at the eighteenth mile post planted by Ontario Land Surveyor L. V. Rorke, this post being the corner of the Townships of Borden, Gamey, Chewett and McGee, and is marked "XVIII" miles and "Con. VI" on south, "Gamey" on the south-east, "I" on east, "Chewett" on north-east, "Con. I" on north, "McGee" on north-west, "XII" on west, and "Borden" on south-west sides. I then surveyed the south boundary by running a chord of latitude west astronomically, planting wooden posts properly marked every forty chains excepting where the lot corners came in lakes; in these cases I established posts in manner shown in field notes. I planted an iron bar one and one-quarter inches in diameter alongside wooden post between lots six and seven, concession I, marked "VI" on east, "Con. I" on north, and "VII" on west sides, and at the intersection of this chord with the east boundary of the Township of Cochrane I planted one and seven-eighth inch iron bar marked "Con. VI" on south, "Borden" on south-east, "XII" on east, "McGee" on north-east, "Con. I" on north, "D'Arcy" on north-west, "I" on west, and "Cochrane" on south-west sides, this being the corner of the four townships and thus making lot twelve thirty-eight chains and seventy-eight links in width. From this corner I ran the west boundary north astronomically and, from the south boundary as a base, I made my sub-division survey in accordance with instructions by running side lines north astronomically between lots two and three, four and five, etc., and I used nineteenth and twentieth mile posts planted by Mr. Rorke for the starting points of lines between concessions one and two and two and three. Owing to the north-east corner of the township coming in Neme-gisenda Lake, I established the north boundary by running a chord of lati-tude east and west from the line between lots four and five at a point six miles north of the south boundary of township, planting an iron bar one and seven eighths inches in diameter at the intersection of north boundary with west shore of Nemegosenda Lake marked "Con. VI" on south, "McGee" on south-west and "I" on west side. I also planted an iron bar one and one-quarter inches in diameter at the intersection of line between lots six and seven with the north boundary, marked "VI" on the east, "Con. VI" on north, and "VII" on west side, and also planted an iron bar one and seven-eighths inches in diameter at the intersection of north boundary with west boundary of township, marked "XII" on east, "McGee" on south-east, and "Con. VI" on south side. I also planted an iron bar one and one-quarter inches in diameter at intersection of line between lots six and seven with line between concessions three and four marked "VI" on east, "Con. IV" on north, "VII" on west, "Con. III" on south side, and an iron bar one and one-quarter inches in diameter at the intersection of line between concessions three and four with west boundary marked "Con. III" on south, "XII" on east, and "Con. IV" on north.

The surface generally is fairly level, but somewhat broken and hilly along the east boundary.

The soil is sandy and mostly stony, being too light to make first-class farming land.

The township is heavily timbered with jack pine, spruce, poplar, balsam and white birch from 4 inches to 12 inches in diameter, excepting a strip of brule from ten to forty chains wide on lots eleven and twelve, concessions four, five and six.

There are considerable areas of spruce swamps in which the timber is suitable for pulpwood.

The township is well watered throughout with numerous lakes and streams, none of the latter being navigable by canoes, excepting Loon River, which runs through lots one, two and three, concession one, and is from one and a half to two chains wide, and from ten inches to three feet deep, with sandy bottom and a fair current.

The fishing is fairly good, pickerel, pike, white fish and trout being taken in Nemegosenda Lake.

There are no islands of any importance, no water powers and no indications of economic minerals. The magnetic variation is fairly constant at four degrees west.

Observations for Azimuth were taken in southerly portion of township, but owing to dull, cloudy and rainy weather I could not get any observations in northern portion of township.

I do not consider that there is a sufficient amount of arable land to warrant this township being opened for settlement.

Accompanying this report are a general plan, timber plan and field notes.

I have the honor to be,

Sir,

Your obedient servant,

(Signed) WALTER BEATTY,

Ontario Land Surveyor.

The Honorable
    The Minister of Lands, Forests and Mines,
                    Toronto.

(*Appendix No. 27.*)

TOWNSHIP OF D'ARCY, DISTRICT OF ALGOMA.

DELTA, March 31st, 1906.

SIR,—I have the honor to submit the following report of the survey of the Township of D'Arcy, in the District of Algoma, made under instructions dated May 31st, 1905.

This township is bounded on the west and north by the unsurveyed lands of the Crown, on the east by the Township of McGee, and on the south by the Township of Cochrane, both of which I have surveyed and already reported on.

The township is easily reached by water from the Village of Chapleau on the main line of the Canadian Pacific Railway, by a route navigable for boats not drawing more than five feet of water, via Chapleau River through Township of Cochrane, entering D'Arcy on lot seven, concession one, and this route is navigable as far as the rapids on lot four, concession three.

I commenced my survey at the south-east corner of the township, this corner having been established when surveying the Township of McGee where there is an iron bar one and seven-eighths inches in diameter marked "D'Arcy" on the north-west side, "Con. I" on the north side, "McGee" on the north-east side, "12" on east side, "Borden" on south-east side, "Con. VI" on south side, "Cochrane" on south-west side and "I" on west side. From this post I ran a chord of latitude west astronomically to intersection with the west boundary of the Township of Cochrane, thereby establishing the south-west corner of the township, this being also the north-west corner of Cochrane. I planted an iron bar one and seven-eighths inches in diameter which is marked "Con. I" on north, "D'Arcy" on north-east, "12" on east, "Cochrane" on south-east and "Con. VI" on south side. From this post I chained east, planting posts as shown on the field notes every forty chains, leaving lot "I" thirty-seven chains and forty-eight links. I planted an iron post one and one-quarter inches in diameter on this line between lots six and seven, marked "VI" on east, "Con. I" on north and "VII" on west side. I ran the west boundary north astronomically from post planted at the south-west corner, a distance of six miles, planting an iron post one and one-quarter inches in diameter at the line between concessions three and four, marked "Con. III" on south, "12" on east, and "Con. IV" on north side; also an iron post one and seven-eighths inches in diameter at the north-west corner marked "Con. VI" on south, "D'Arcy" on south-east, and "12" on east sides, and from this post the north boundary was run east astronomically to intersection with production of the west boundary of the Township of McGee, where I planted an iron post one and seven-eighths inches in diameter marked "I" on west, "D'Arcy" on south-west, and "Con. VI" on south sides. I also planted an iron post one and one-quarter inches in diameter at the intersection of the line between lots six and seven with the north boundary marked "VII" on west, "Con. IV" on south, and "VI" on east sides, and on an iron post of same size at the intersection of line between lots six and seven with line between concessions three and four marked "VI" on east, "Con. IV" on north, "VII" on west, and "Con. III" on south sides.

The sub-division was performed in accordance with instructions by projecting meridians from the proper posts on the south boundary, making the different concessions eighty chains more or less in depth, suitable posts of the most durable wood were planted where required.

Observations were taken as frequently as was necessary, and I found the variation of the magnetic needle to be fairly constant at four degrees west of the astronomic north.

The percentage of brule is not large, the township generally being covered with a thick growth of spruce, balsam, jack pine, poplar and white birch, varying from four to twelve inches in diameter. There is a considerable quantity of spruce pulpwood in swamps scattered throughout the township. The bulk of the jack pine adjacent to Henderson Lake has been taken off.

No indications of economic minerals were seen.

About twelve per cent. of the total area of the township is water. There are a few islands in Henderson Lake from which most of the merchantable timber has been removed; some of these are suitable for camping purposes. Red deer were fairly plentiful and a few bear were seen. Partridge were scarce.

The surface is fairly level, rolling and broken in places, with hills from forty to fifty feet high.

The soil is generally sandy and stony.

The northerly part of the township is in what is said to be the beginning of a clay belt extending down the Chapleau River.

I have the honor to be,

Sir,

Your obedient servant,

(Signed) WALTER BEATTY,

Ontario Land Surveyor.

The Honorable
    The Minister of Lands, Forests and Mines,
        Toronto.

(*Appendix No. 28.*)

TOWNSHIP OF COCHRANE, DISTRICT OF ALGOMA.

DELTA, ONT., March 25th, 1906.

SIR,—I have the honor to submit the following report of the survey of the Township of Cochrane, in the District of Algoma, made under instructions from your department dated May 31st, 1905.

The township is bounded on the east by the Township of Borden, on the north by the Township of D'Arcy, and on the west and south by Townships "33" and "30," both of which are unsurveyed.

The south-west corner of the township is about one and one-half miles distant from the Village of Chapleau, on the main line of the Canadian Pacific Railway, and there is a good canoe route from Chapleau through the southerly part of the township which is used for transportation of supplies by the Transcontinental Railway.

I commenced my survey as instructed at an iron post planted by Ontario Land Surveyor John McAree, marked "XXXI" on south and "XXX" on south-east sides, and from this post I ran the west boundary north astronomically and also a chord of latitude east astronomically for the south boundary, and made my subdivision survey in accordance with instructions.

I planted an iron bar one and seven-eighths inches in diameter marked "Con. I" on north side, "Cochrane" on north-east side, and "XII" on east side alongside O. L. S. McAree's post. I planted an iron bar one and one-quarter inches in diameter, marked "Con. I" on north, "XII" on east, and "Con. III" on south sides at the intersection of line between concessions three and four with west boundary; and an iron bar one and seven-eighths inches in diameter, marked "Con. I" on north, "D'Arcy" on north-east,

"XII" on east, "Cochrane" on south-east, and "Con. VI" on south sides at the north-west corner of the township, being the south-west corner of D'Arcy. On the south boundary I planted an iron bar one and one-quarter inches in diameter three miles east of the south-west corner, marked "VII" on west, "Con. I" on north, and "VI" on east sides; also an iron bar one and seven-eighths inches in diameter, six miles east of the south-west corner, south-west, "I" on west, "D'Arcy" on north-west, "Con. I" on north, sides, this being the south-east corner of the township, and from this I ran the east boundary of the township north astronomically, planting an iron bar one and one-quarter inches in diameter at its intersection with line between concessions three and four, marked "Con. III" on south, "I" on west, and "Con. IV" on north sides, and an iron bar one and seven-eighths inches in diameter at intersection with south boundary of Township of McGee, making this post the corner of the four Townships of Cochrane, D'Arcy, McGee and Borden. It is marked "Con. VI" on south, "Cochrane" on south-west, "I" on west, "D'Arcy" on north-west, "Con. I" on north, "McGee" on north-east, "XII" on east, and "Borden" on south-east sides. From this post the north boundary of Cochrane was run west astronomically to intersection with east boundary and an iron bar one and one-quarter inches in diameter, marked "VI" on east, "Con. VI" on south, and "VII" on west sides being planted at the intersection of line between lots six and seven with the north boundary. I also planted. an iron bar one and one-quarter inches in diameter, marked "VI" on east, "Con. IV" on north, "VII" on west, and "Con. III" on south sides at intersection of line between concessions three and four with line between lots six and seven.

The south boundary crosses a large island on Loon Lake, in which no posts were planted.

A sufficient number of observations for azimuth were taken to ascertain the bearing of lines, and the variation of the magnetic needle was fairly constant at four degrees west of the astronomic north.

The surface is rolling, with very few hills of a greater elevation than forty feet, with spruce and tamarac swamps and small lakes scattered through the township, and in addition to these small lakes there are three or four large lakes, viz., Chapleau, Sinclair's, Henderson's and Loon, making the water area about seventeen per cent. of the whole township.

There are a number of islands in Loon Lake, a few of which are suitable for camping purposes, but otherwise of no apparent value; the large island on the south boundary is rocky and stony and nearly all brule. Of the other islands, Nos. 1 and 2 in Chapleau Lake, being within easy reach of Chapleau Village, are suitable for camping purposes.

The fishing is fairly good in all the waters and specially so in Loon Lake where large pike are plentiful, and I understand large grey trout are also taken, although I did not get any myself.

Most of the timber of commercial value has been removed from the east half of the township. This consisted of jack pine and spruce with a few scattered red and white pine. Spruce suitable for pulpwood is found in the swamps throughout the township, and jack pine up to 15 inches in diameter is found scattered through the east half, the timber generally benig poplar, spruce, balsam, jack pine and white birch.

Chapleau and Henderson Lake are connected by a sluggish stream from one to eight chains wide, navigable for small boats drawing less than four feet, this being the only navigable stream in the township. Loon River, the outlet of Loon Lake, is a small shallow stream from thirty to seventy-five links wide, with a strong current, rapid in places.

No water powers or indications of economic minerals were seen. The soil
is generally light and stony and not suitable for agricultural purposes, though
limited areas of fairly good soil are scattered throughout the township.

Where obtainable, prominent trees were blazed and marked on each island.

I have the honor to be,

Sir,

Your obedient servant,

(Signed) WALTER BEATTY,

Ontario Land Surveyor.

The Honorable
    The Minister of Lands, Forests and Mines,
       Toronto.

(Appendix No. 29).

TOWNSHIP OF PATTINSON, DISTRICT OF ALGOMA.

TORONTO, December 3rd, 1906.

SIR,—I have the honour to submit the following report on the Township
of Pattinson, in the District of Algoma, performed under instructions from
your Department dated the fifteenth day of May, nineteen hundred and six.

This township is bounded on the east by the Township of Collins,
surveyed by me under instructions from your Department in nineteen hundred
and five, and on the south by the Township of McGee, surveyed by Ontario
Land Surveyor Walter Beatty.

The north boundary of the township was run due west from the north-
west corner of the Township of Collins, and the east boundary due north
from the north-east corner of the Township of D'Arcy.

The depth of concession one is consequently short. The width of the lots
on the front of concession two, with the exception of lot twelve, were all
made the exact forty chains and the lines between lots were run south to
intersect the south boundary.

Posts of the most durable wood available were planted at the front
angles of all lots and properly marked according to instructions, and iron
posts were planted in addition thereto at the following points —:

An iron post one and seven-eighths inches in diameter was planted at
the north-west corner of the township and marked "Pattinson" on the south-
east side. "Con. VI" on the south, "XII" on the east.

The iron post one and seven-eighths inches in diameter planted at the
north-east corner of the township is marked "Pattinson" on the south-west,
"Collins" on the south-east, "Con· VI" on the south, "XII" on the east,
"I" on the west.

The iron post one and seven-eighths inches in diameter planted at the
intersection of the east boundary of the township with the north shore of
Trout Lake is marked "Pattinson" on the west, "Collins" on the north-east,
"Con. I" on the north, "XII" on the east. "I" on the west.

The iron post one and seven-eighths inches in diameter planted by
Ontario Land Surveyor Walter Beatty at the intersection of the north boundary of the Township of McGee with the westerly shore of Trout Lake was
also marked "Pattinson" on the north-west, "Con. I" on the north.

The iron post one and seven-eighths inches in diameter planted by Ontario Land Surveyor Walter Beatty at the north-west corner of the Township of McGee was also marked "Pattinson" on the north-east, "Con. I" on the north, "XII" on the east.

An iron post one and one-quarter inches in diameter was planted at the intersection of the line between lots six and seven with the south boundary of the township and marked "Con. I" on the north, "VI" on east, "VII" on west side.

An iron post one and one-quarter inches in diameter was planted at the intersection of the front of concession four with the west boundary of the township and marked "Con. III" on the south, "Con. IV" on north, "XII" on east side.

An iron post one and one-quarter inches in diameter was planted at the intersection of the front of concession four with the east boundary of the township and marked "Con. III" on south, "Con· IV" on north, "I" on west side.

An iron post one and one-quarter inches in diameter was planted at the intersection of the line between lots six and seven with the north boundary of the township and marked "Con. VI" on the south, "VI" on the east, "VII" on the west side.

The iron post intended for the centre of the township was lost somewhere in transportation and consequently there was none planted at this point.

General Features.

The land in this township is high, broken with hills and ravines with numerous swamp areas and on the whole stony. About twenty-five per cent. of the whole area might be termed suitable for cultivation. This area is principally comprised in the eastern one-quarter of the township. The western half of the township is rough and more broken, especially that part through which the Chapleau River runs.

The soil varies from a light sand to a good sandy loam, in the north-eastern portion of the township.

Timber.

The township is well timbered throughout with the exception of a small area of brule at the south-west corner. Where the timber has attained a good merchantable size it is sparse and open, with a heavy growth of underbrush. There is some good spruce scattered along the river shores and in the swamp areas, also cedar in a few smaller areas in the south-eastern part of the township. The tamarac varies in diameter up to twelve inches, but is dry and beginning to rot. On the higher ground Banksian pine, birch and balsam is the principal timber, running in size from six to eighteen inches in diameter.

Rocks and Minerals.

Only a few exposures are noticeable, but where seen the rock was granite. No mineral was found in the township. There was a strong magnetic attraction in the easterly half of concessions three and four. The surface of the whole township was more or less covered with boulders, both round and angular.

6 L.M.

Water Powers.

The rapids on the Chapleau River are flat and the banks not suitable for developing the different falls, which may be noted as follows.—
On lot twelve concession one, rapids five feet fall.
On lot twelve concession two, rapids four feet fall.
On lot eleven concession two, rapids fifteen feet fall.
On lot eleven concession three, rapids five feet fall.
On lot ten concession three, rapids six feet fall.
On lot seven concession six, rapids nine feet fall.

Fish and Game.

Pike and pickerel were caught in the Chapleau River. Only a few indications of large game were seen.
Accompanying this report are plans and field notes of the survey.

I have the honour to be,
Sir,
Your obedient servant,
(Signed) L. V. RORKE,
Ontario Land Surveyor.

The Honourable,
The Minister of Lands, Forests and Mines,
Toronto.

———

(Appendix No. 30).

TOWNSHIP OF BECK, DISTRICT OF ALGOMA.

PETERBOROUGH, ONTARIO, December 5th, 1906.

SIR,—I have the honour to submit with this report the field notes and plan of the survey of the Township of Beck, in the District of Algoma, performed under instructions from your Department, dated June 27th, nineteen hundred and six.
I commenced the survey, as instructed, at the south-west angle of the township; from this point I chained northerly along Ontario Land Surveyor Patten's meridian, which forms the west boundary, giving the first three concessions a uniform depth of eighty chains, my chaining along the meridian agreeing with that of Mr. Patten's. I adopted the first, second and third mile posts, and from them ran the line for the front of concessions two, three and four east astronomically to the east boundary of the township. The lines in front of concessions five and six I ran west astronomically from the east boundary of the township.
From the south-west angle of the township I chained easterly along Ontario Land Surveyor Patten's base line until I reached the iron post planted by him to mark the sixth mile. I gave all the lots along this line a uniform frontage of forty chains with the exception of lot one, which is forty-one chains and thirty-two links. From the iron post planted by Ontario Land Surveyor Patten to mark the sixth mile on his base line, I ran the east boundary north astronomically to its intersection with the south

6a L. M.

boundary of the Township of Fournier, which it strikes one chain and forty-four links east of the south-west angle of the said township.

All the side lines I ran north astronomically from the proper points on Ontario Land Surveyor Patten's base line.

On the iron and wooden posts planted by Ontario Land Surveyor Patten at the south-west angle of the township, I marked "Beck" on the north-east side, "Con. I" on the north side, and "Lot XII" on the east side.

On the iron and wooden posts planted by Ontario Land Surveyor Patten at the south-east angle of the township I marked "Beck" on the north-west side, "Reaume" on the north-east side, "Con. I" on the north side, "Lot XII" on the east side, "Lot I" on the west side.

On Ontario Land Surveyor Patten's base line at its intersection with side line between lots six and seven, I planted an iron post one and one-quarter inches in diameter marked "Con. I" on the north side, "Lot VI" on the east side, and "Lot VII" on the west side.

An iron post one and one-quarter inches in diameter was planted on the east boundary line at its intersection with the line in front of concession four, marked "Con. IV" on the north side, "Con. III" on the south side, and "Lot I" on the west side.

An iron post one and one-quarter inches in diameter was planted at the intersection of the line in front of concession four with the line between lots six and seven marked "Con. IV" on the north side, "Con. III" on the south side, "Lot VI" on the east side, "Lot VII" on the west side.

On the iron post one and one-quarter inches in diameter at the intersection of the line in front of concession four with the west boundary, "concession four" was marked on the north side, "Con. III" on the south side, and lot "twelve" on the east side.

An iron post one and seven-eighth inches in diameter was planted at the north-east angle of the township marked "Beck" on the south-west side, "Reaume" on the south-east side, "Con. VI" on the south side, "Lot I" on the west side, "Lot XII" on the east side.

An iron post one and one-quarter inches in diameter was planted on the north boundary line at its intersection with the line between lots six, and seven, marked "Con. VI" on the south side, "Lot VI" on the east side, and "Lot VII" on the west side.

On the iron post one and seven-eighth inches in diameter planted by Ontario Land Surveyor Code at the north-west angle of the township "Beck" was marked on the south-east side, "Con. VI" on the south side, "Lot XII" on the east side.

The Township of Beck, which lies about midway between the Mattagami and Frederick House Rivers, may be described as a generally level or gently undulating country timbered with spruce up to twelve inches in diameter, dead and decaying tamarac up to ten inches in diameter, scattering white birch, poplar and balsam of average size and quality, a few balm of gilead and some scrub cedar; the whole country interspersed with spruce and tamarac swamps, alder and willow underbrush and considerable windfall, especially along the creeks. There are a few white pine running from twelve to fourteen inches in diameter on lots four and five, concession three.

The soil on the uplands is a rich black loam from ten to twelve inches in depth, free from stone with clay sub-soil. On the lowlands and in the swamps the soil is a black mucky clay free from stone. Only a few small outcroppings of rock (Huronian) were noticed, one especially along the line in front of concession four on lots three and four.

The township is traversed by a large stream and two creeks of fair size, but there are no lakes or ponds.

The average magnetic variation I found to be about eight degrees and thirty minutes west. All the survey, however, was made independent of the magnetic needle.

No indications of mineral were noticed.

The usual kinds of game and fur were seen.

On the whole I consider about fifty per cent. of the township suitable for settlement, and with a proper system of drainage I am of the opinion that at least thirty-five of the remaining fifty per cent. can be utilized.

Hoping this report and the accompanying returns will be found satisfactory,

I have the honour to be,

Sir,

Your obedient servant,

(Signed)   J. W. FITZGERALD,

Ontario Land Surveyor.

To the Honourable,
    The Minister of Lands, Forests and Mines,
        Toronto.

————

(Appendix No. 31).

TOWNSHIP OF PAUL, DISTRICT OF ALGOMA.

TORONTO, ONTARIO, November 21st, 1906.

SIR,—I have the honour to submit the following report on the Township of Paul, in the District of Algoma, performed by me under instructions from your Department, dated the fifteenth day of May, nineteen hundred and six.

This township lies to the north-east of the Township of Collins, surveyed by me under your instructions dated the thirty-first day of May, nineteen hundred and five, the north-east angle of that township being my starting point for the survey of the Township of Paul.

Having reached my starting point on the tenth day of June, and after taking an astronomical observation, I proceeded to run the south boundary of the Township of Paul due east for six miles and to run the east boundary due north from this point and to sub-divide the township lots in the usual way.

Wooden posts were planted at the front angles of all lots and marked for the several lots and concessions for which they were placed.

Iron posts were planted at the side of the wooden posts and marked as follows:—

The iron post one and seven-eighth inches in diameter previously planted at the north-east angle of the Township of Collins and marked "Collins" on the south-west, "Con. VI" on the south, "I" on the west, was also marked "Paul" on the north-east, "Con. I" on the north, and "XII" on the east.

An iron post one and seven-eighth inches in diameter was planted at the intersection of the south boundary of the township with the water's edge of the lake on lot one and marked "Paul" on the north-west, "Con. I" on the north, "I" on the west.

An iron post one and one-quarter inches in diameter was planted at the north-east corner of the township and marked "Paul" on the south-west, "Con. VI" on the south, "I" on the west.

An iron post one and seven-eighth inches in diameter was planted at the north-west corner of the township and marked "Paul" on the south-east, "Con. VI" on the south, "XII" on the east.

An iron post one and one-quarter inches in diameter was planted at the intersection of the south boundary of the township with the line between lots six and seven and marked "Con. I" on north, "VII" on west, "VI" on east.

An iron post one and one-quarter inches in diameter was planted at the south-east corner of lot one concession four and marked "Con. IV" on north, "Con. III" on south, "I" on west.

An iron post one and one-quarter inches in diameter was planted at the intersection of the north boundary of the township with the line between lots six and seven and marked "Con. IV" on south, "VII" on west, "VI" on east.

An iron post one and one-quarter inches in diameter was planted at the intersection of the west boundary of the township with the front of concession four marked "Con. IV" on the north, "Con. III" on the south, "XII" on the east.

An iron post one and one-quarter inches in diameter was planted at the intersection of the front of concession four with the line between lots six and seven and marked "Con. IV" on north, "Con. III" on south, "VII" on west, "VI" on east.

Physical Features.

The township, as a whole, is hilly and rocky and not suitable for agricultural purposes, the western part especially being broken with high, rocky hills while the easterly part is high and rolling land consisting of sandy hills and swamps covered with boulders where not rocky.

Trout River, the outlet of Trout Lake, enters the township in concession three and runs northerly through the north-westerly part, crossing the north boundary on lot eleven.

Timber.

With the exception of about four thousand acres the whole area of this township is a brule grown up with small second growth. At the south-east part of the township the country is timbered with spruce, birch and banksian pine from four to eighteen inches in diameter. A few scattering white pine is to be seen on south halves of lots three, four, five, six and seven, in the first concession, which average from eight to twenty-four inches in diameter. A large swamp area of green spruce and dry tamarac from four to twelve inches in diameter adjoins Trout River in concessions three, four and five. On lots three and four, concession five, there is another smaller area similarly timbered. Throughout the large area of brule several small swamps are met with containing green cedar, spruce and dry tamarac from four to fifteen inches in diameter.

Rocks and Minerals.

The rock formation is the Laurentian granite throughout the township. No economic minerals were found.

Water Powers.

There is no.single fall or rapid on Trout River within this township of sufficient magnitude to develop to advantage, but the several rapids on the river in east half of lot eleven and west half of lot ten, concession six, might be combined to produce about one thousand horse-power.

Fish and Game.

Several indications of bear, moose and caribou were seen. White fish, pike, pickerel are plentiful in Trout River and speckled brook trout in the smaller streams.

Accompanying this report are a general plan, timber plan and field notes of the survey.

I have the honor to be,
Sir,
Your obedient servant,
(Signed) L. V. RORKE,
Ontario Land Surveyor.

The Honourable,
The Minister of Lands, Forests and Mines,
Toronto.

(Appendix No. 32).

TOWNSHIP OF OTTAWAY, DISTRICT OF ALGOMA.

ALVINSTON, Dec. 28th, 1906.

SIR,—I have the honor to submit the following report of the survey of the Township of Ottaway immediately west of Fournier made under instructions dated May 15th, 1906.

After finishing the survey of Fournier I proceeded, after observation for Azimuth (Polaris) to run the south boundary west astronomically for a distance of three miles, planting posts at intervals of 40 chains, then after starting concession lines I and II, and II, III west from the east boundary, I ran north three miles, thence east to the east boundary, and as the survey checked at the east boundary with 12 links I produced the line between concessions III and IV west and the line between lots 6 and 7 north, laying out the township in the usual way. I then produced the south boundary west to the west boundary, which it strikes at an angle of 898 and 55' from east to north as does also the line between concessions III and IV. The lines have been well opened out and blazed and care has been taken in the planting and marking of posts.

The following iron posts were planted in Ottaway:—

At the south-east angle the one and seven-eighths inch iron post marking the south-west angle of Fournier is marked on the north-west "Ottaway," on the north "Con. I," and on the west "I" for the number of the lot.

On the south boundary of lot line between lots 6 and 7, one and one-quarter inch iron post, marked on the east "VI," and on the west "VII" for the number of the lot and on the north "Con. I."

At the south-west angle one and seven-eighths inch iron post was planted, marked on the north-east "Ottaway," on the east "XII" for the number of the lot and on the north "Con. I."

At the east boundary at the intersection of concession line III and IV, one and one-quarter inch iron post was planted marked on the north "Con. IV," on the south "Con. III," and on the west "I" for the number of the lot.

At the intersection of lot line 6 and 7 and concession line III and IV, one and one-quarter inch iron post was planted marked on the north "Con. IV," on the south "Con· III," on the west "II," and on the east "VI," for the numbers of the lots.

At the west boundary at the intersection of concession line "III and IV" one and one-quarter inch iron post was planted marked on the north "Con. IV," on the south "Con. III," and on the east "XII" for the number of the lot.

At the north-east angle the one and seven-eighths inch iron post planted to mark the north-west angle of Fournier was marked on the south-west "Ottaway," on the south "Con. VI" and on the west "I" for the number of the lot.

At the north-west angle the one and seven-eighths inch iron post marking the 30th mile of the meridian run by O. L. S. Patten was marked on the south-east "Ottaway," on the south "Con. VI," and on the east "XII" for the number of the lot.

One and one-quarter inch iron post was lost on the way and I was unable to plant an iron post at the intersection of lot line 6 and 7 at the north boundary. The wooden post is however 2.88 chains west from O. L. S. Patten's one and, one-quarter inch iron post marked III M.

General Features.

The township is generally level except some portions at the north boundary to the east. The greater portion will require drainage which will be easily accomplished owing to a fair general fall. The heavy moss now covering the country retards the flow of water and when this is removed there will be a good natural drainage not apparent at present. The greater portion is flat and creeks are not numerous. At the south-west angle there is considerable dry muskeg, but about 75 or 80 per cent. will be good agricultural land.

Soil.

The soil is a sandy clay slightly browner than the usual clay soil. It is covered with a coating of rich loam and a heavy moss. This soil will be much easier worked than clay owing to its small percentage of sand and I would consider this township will be a good tract of farming land.

Timber.

The township is covered by a growth of spruce, dead tamarac, poplar, balsam, birch, with a few cedar and Balm of Gilead. The timber is generally mixed with the exception of some belts of birch and poplar. The tamarac is still sound. The sizes run from five to ten inches and in places to fifteen and eighteen inches.

Minerals.

The few exposures of rock are along the river in the 6th concession. These are a gray slaty rock of Huronian origin. No economical minerals were seen.

Waters.

In the centre of the east half of the township Muskego Creek or River, a stream from three to eight feet deep and nearly two chains wide, flows north. There are a few small rapids in the 6th concession but the water falls so low in the creek that they cannot be of much value as water powers. This stream enters the Frederick House River in the Township of Clute to the north.

Two lakes occur in the north-west quarter of the township, having clear water. The larger has deposits of a marly clay to the south side which may perhaps be used for the manufacture of cement.

Fish and Game.

In the Muskego River a very small species of shad may be caught with the hook, but the lakes do not appear to be very well stocked. Game was at one time plentiful in the township from the appearance about old Indian camps, but not much is seen at present.

The magnetic variation runs from $7\frac{1}{2}$ to 10 degrees west. I herewith submit a general plan, a timber map, field notes and traverse of the lakes and river.

All of which is respectfully submitted.·

I have the honor to be,
.   Sir,
Your obedient servant,
(Signed) A. S. CODE.
Ontario Land Surveyor.

The Honorable,
The Minister of Lands, Forests and Mines,
Toronto.

_____

(Appendix No. 33).

TOWNSHIP OF FOURNIER, DISTRICT OF ALGOMA.

ALVINSTON, ONT., Dec. 28th, 1906.

SIR,—I have the honor to submit the following report of the survey of the Township of Fournier, in the District of Algoma, made under instructions dated May 15th, 1906.

After arranging for men and supplies, I left Alvinston June 6th and proceeded to New Liskeard where I was met by my party, and after some delay owing to non-arrival of canoes, we left for the end of the Steel T. & N. O. Railway on 21st June. This train was however wrecked and we again re-. turned to New Liskeard. On the 22nd June we were able however to reach the end of the Steel—then at the third crossing of the Blanche River.

We paddled then up Blanche River, down White Clay River, Black River, and down Abitibi River to the mouth of the Frederick House River, then up the latter until we arrived at the boundary line between Algoma and Nipissing. The trip was made without accident though we found the rapids on Frederick House River very difficult to ascend, and the party were obliged to wade some four and a half days to ascend seven miles of the river.

Commencing at the 156th mile post on the district boundary I ran west astronomically along the south boundary, planting posts at intervals of forty chains and checking the bearing by Azimuth observation (Polaris) at 2 miles and 70 chains, similarly with concession lines two and three. Unfortunately after finishing the south-easterly part of the township a tree, rotten at the centre, fell upon one of the transits and put it entirely out of commission and I was forced to proceed with one transit and one picket line party. This was somewhat difficult in Fournier owing to the gently rolling nature of the country in the eastern part. Owing to fluctuating variation it is impossible to use a magnetic compass. The survey was then laid out in the usual way, and after this the west boundary was run with Transit. Observation for Azimuth was made at one mile north of the south boundary also at the intersection of concession line IV and V and lot line 6 and 7. The lines have been well opened out and blazed and care has been taken in planting and marking posts.

The following iron posts have been planted in Fournier:—

One and one-quarter inch iron where the line between concessions III and IV intersects the east boundary. This is marked on the west "I" for the number of the lot, on the north "Con. IV," on the south "Con. III."

One and one-quarter inch iron where the line between concessions III and IV intersects lot line 6 and 7. This marked on the west "VII" for the number of the lot, on the east "VI" for the number of the lot, on the north "Con. IV," and on the south "Con. III."

One and one-quarter inch iron where the line between concessions III ond IV intersects the west boundary. This is marked on the east "XII" for the number of the lot, on the north "Con. IV," on the south "Con. III."

One and one-quarter inch iron where the line between lots 6 and 7 intersects the south boundary. This is marked on the east "VI" for the number of the lot, on the west "VII" for the number of the lot, and on the north "Con. I."

One and one-quarter inch iron where the line between lots 6 and 7 intersects the north boundary. This is marked on the east "VI," on the west "VII" for the numbers of the lots, and on the south "Con. VI."

One and seven-eighths inch iron at the south-west angle marked on the north-east "Fournier," on the north-west "Ottaway," on the north "Con. I" and on the east "XII" for the number of the lot.

One and seven-eighths inch iron at the north-west angle marked on the south-east "Fournier," on the south-west "Ottaway," on the south "Con. VI," on the east "XII" for the number of the lot.

At the south-east angle the present one and seven-eighths inch iron was marked with a cold chisel on the north "Con. I," on the west "I" for the number of the lot, and on the north-west "Fournier." At the north-east angle the present one and seven-eighths inch iron was marked on the south-west "Fournier," on the south "Con. VI," and on the west "I" for the number of the lot.

General Features.

The township is generally level or gently undulating and fairly dry, with portions at the south-west and north-east angles somewhat lower and more level than the central portion. Numerous small lakes occur but none are large. A ravine of muskeg commencing on lot 7, concession I and running parallel with the Frederick House River apparently gives an under-drainage and connects the tier of small spring lakes. The land will be easily drained in the creeks and gullies present. The heavy moss now covering the country retards somewhat the flow of water. Bush covers the whole area. About 70 per cent. will, when cleared and drained, become agricultural land. When opened up this township will be pretty in its scenery.

Soil.

The soil in general is a sandy clay or clay with a slight mixture of sand which will render it easily workable. Pockets of gravel appear to exist. A belt of rather sandy land lies just east of the chain of lakes parallel with the Frederick House River.

Timber.

The township is covered with a growth of spruce, dead tamarac, poplar, birch, balsam, with a few Balm of Gilead and cedar. It is generally mixed, and belts with the exception of birch and poplar are uncommon. The sizes generally run from 5 inches to 10 inches and in places to 15 inches. The tamarac is practically all killed by the insect pest which passed over this country some years ago. It is still sound however. The general use of timber would be for building purposes, railway ties, poles, etc.

Minerals.

There are a few exposures of Huronian origin and of a gray slaty nature at the rapids in the 5th concession, but no economic minerals were found.

Waters.

The Frederick House River, a stream about 3 chain 75 links wide flows through the township. This stream has a slow current through the southerly four concessions and the 6th concession, but is quite swift in the 5th concession in places. Just north of the line between the 4th and 5th concessions a rapid occurs with an available fall of about seven feet, having an available power of about 320 h.p. at average low water stage. The water in the Frederick House is rather dark but wholesome. The small lakes occurring are generally spring lakes and seem to be connected underground by runs of muskeg in a north-west and south-east direction.

Fish and Game.

The Indians have depleted this country of game, which from appearances about numerous old camps, was very plentiful. In the river, maskinonge are to be had with the aid of the net and a species of small shad with the hook and line.

In the lakes that have not muskeg shores large pike are very plentiful and can be easily caught with the troll.

The magnetic variation is very variable, running from 7½ to 10½ degrees west.

I submit with this report, field notes and traverse notes a general plan and a timber map.

All of which is respectfully submitted.

I have the honor to be,
Sir,
Your obedient servant,
(Signed) A. S. CODE.
Ontario Land Surveyor.

The Honorable,
The Minister of Lands, Forests and Mines,
Toronto.

(Appendix No. 34).

TOWNSHIP OF BRADBURN, DISTRICT OF ALGOMA.

PETERBOROUGH, ONTARIO, December 5th, 1906.

SIR,—I have the honor to submit the following report on the survey of the Township of Bradburn, in the District of Algoma, performed under instructions from your Department dated May fifteenth, nineteen hundred and six.

This township is surveyed on the new method of survey approved by Order-in-Council of date April twenty-fourth, nineteen hundred and six.

As instructed I commenced the survey at the north-east angle of the Township of Mabee, being at the intersection of Ontario Land Surveyor Speight's base and meridian lines surveyed last season; from this point I chained northerly along the meridian a distance of nine miles, giving the concessions thereon a uniform depth of forty-nine chains and fifty links. allowing fifty links for half road allowance on the north side of the base line, one chain for road allowance between each alternate concession, and fifty links for half road allowance on the south side of the north boundary line. My measurements along the meridian practically agreeing with that of Mr. Speight's, I adopted the iron posts planted by him at the third, sixth and ninth mile as the starting points for the lines in the centre of the road allowances between concessions four and five, eight and nine, and the north boundary respectively.

The west boundary I ran north astronomically from the iron post planted by Ontario Land Surveyor Speight to mark the third mile on his base line. The east boundary I ran north astronomically from the iron post planted by Ontario Land Surveyor Patten to mark the sixth mile on his base line.

All the concession lines, including the north boundary, were run due east and west astronomically from the proper points on Ontario Land Surveyor Speight's meridian to their intersections with the east and west boundaries of the township.

The side line in the centre of the road allowance between lots twenty-four and twenty-five I ran north astronomically from Ontario Land Surveyor Speight's base line

The side lines in the centres of the road allowances between lots six and seven, and twelve and thirteen, were run north and south astronomically from the proper points on the line in the centre of the road allowance between concessions two and three.

As will be seen by the plan, I did not run the side line in the centre of the road allowance between lots eighteen and nineteen through concessions one, two, three and four. I thought it better to leave lots eighteen and nineteen through these four concessions extend to the road allowance along the Mattagami River on either side, that part of the above side line through concessions five to twelve inclusive was run north and south astronomically from the proper point on the line in the centre of the road allowance between concessions six and seven.

To all the regular lots I gave a uniform width of twenty-five chains and twenty-five links, allowing a side road allowance of one chain between lots six and seven, twelve and thirteen, eighteen and nineteen, twenty-four and twenty-five, also a half road allowance of fifty links along the west side of the east boundary and along the east side of the west boundary.

Good durable wooden posts properly made marked and planted were placed along the concession lines between the lots one on the line itself as a guide post with the numbers of the lots on the east and west sides and R on the north and south sides, one fifty links north of the guide post and one fifty links south of the guide post with the numbers of the lots on the east and west sides and the number of the concession or R on the north and south sides as the case might be.

At the intersection of the centre line of the different concession road allowances with the centre line of the different side road allowances, good durable wooden posts were planted marked "R" on the north, south, east and west sides.

Good durable wooden posts were also planted at the angle of each of the four adjoining lots marked with the number of the concession on the north or south sides as the case might be, and the number of the lot on the east and west side, as the case might be, with R on the two sides facing the concession and side road allowances; these posts were planted at a distance of fifty links from the centre of the concession road allowance and fifty links from the centre of the side road allowance.

Where the front angle or angles of a lot came in a lake or in the Mattagami River, the posts were projected to the proper points on the north or south or on the north and south shores therof, and planted at a perpendicular distance of one chain from high water mark; these posts were marked with the numbers of the lots on the east and west sides and the number of the concession or R facing the north or south sides, as the case may be, in order that these projected posts may be easily located; guide posts were planted on the shore north or south of the lot posts with the numbers only of the lots marked on the east and west sides and where trees were found near these guide posts they were blazed in a conspicuous manner.

A road allowance of one chain in perpendicular width is allowed for along each side of the Mattagami River through the township, also around all large lakes, and around all lakes cut by the concession and side road allowances; all these road allowances are delimited by durable wooden posts planted on the lines of survey at a perpendicular distance of one chain from high water mark, with the letter R marked on the side facing the road allowance.

To all the posts, with the exception of the guide posts and those defining a road allowance along lakes or rivers suitable bearing trees were taken properly marked and recorded.

To make the survey permanent in case of fire, iron posts of the following dimensions were planted at the following points:—

An iron post one and seven-eighths inches in diameter at the north-east angle of the township marked "Bradburn" on the south-west side and the letter "R" on the south-east and west sides.

An iron post one and seven-eighths inches in diameter at the north-west angle of the township, marked "Bradburn" on the south-east side and the letter "R" on the north, south, east and west sides.

An iron post one and one-quarter inches in diameter at the intersection of the north boundary line with the line in the centre of the road allowance between lots twelve and thirteen, marked "Con. XII" on the south side and the letter "R" on the south, east and west sides.

An iron post one and one-quarter inches in diameter on the east boundary line at its intersection with the line in the centre of the road allowance between concessions six and seven, marked "Con. VII" on the north side, "Con. VI" on the south side, and the letter ' R" on the north, south, east and west sides.

The intersections of the centre lines of the road allowance between lots twelve and thirteen with concessions six and seven falling in Shallow Lake, an iron post one and one-quarter inches in diameter was planted at the intersection of the centre line of the road allowance between lots twelve and thirteen with the north limit of the road allowance on the north shore of said lake, marked "Con. VII" on the north side and the letter "R" on the north, south, east and west sides.

An iron post one and one-quarter inches in diameter was planted on the west boundary line at its intersection with the line in the centre of the road allowance between concessions six and seven, marked "Con. VII" on the north side, "Con. VI" on the south side, and the letter "R" on the north, south, east and west sides.

On the iron post one and seven-eighths inches in diameter planted by Ontario Land Surveyor Patten, which post marks the south-east angle of the township "Bradburn" was marked on the north-west side and the letter "R" on the north, south, east and west sides.

An iron post one and seven-eighths inches in diameter was planted at the south-west angle of the township marked "Bradburn" on the north-east side, and the letter "R" on the north, south, east and west sides.

An iron post one and one-quarter inches in diameter was planted on the south boundary line at its intersection with the line in the centre of the road allowance between lots twelve and thirteen, marked "Con. I" on the north side and the letter "R" on the north, south, east and west sides.

The chief feature of the Township of Bradburn is the Mattagami River which enters the township from the south on lot eighteen and flowing west of north leaves it at lot twenty-seven, concession twelve. It is a fine stream, being from five to ten chains in width with good current and a depth of from five to fifteen feet, with vegetation as a general rule almost to the water's edge. Numerous rapids and falls occur on the river in its course through the township, the most notable of which are Loon Rapids on lot eighteen, concession three; Yellow Falls on lot twenty-one, concession six;

Island Falls on lots twenty-three and twenty-four, concessions six and seven.
I made a careful survey and estimate of the power available at each of the
above points, full particulars of which will be found in the notes.   There
are a few small islands in the river in the township which are of little value
either for agriculture or as summer resorts.

The east branch of the Muskego River flows north-westerly through the
south-westerly part of the township; it is a stream having an average width
of about one chain and a depth of from three to five feet, with a rather
sluggish current.   I do not consider it of a sufficiently navigable nature to
allow any reservation for a road along its shores.

Several lakes, some of which have considerable area, occur in the various
parts of the township; as a rule these lakes are shallow with low shores, and
are connected by small creeks.

That portion of the township lying west of the Mattagami River is of
a more or less rolling character timbered with spruce up to sixteen inches
in diameter, Balm of Gilead up to twenty inches in diameter, poplar, white
birch and balsam of average size and quality, dead and decaying tamarac
with alder and willow underbrush and considerable windfall throughout.
The soil of the uplands is of a rich black loam from ten to twelve inches
in depth, free from stone, with clay sub-soil in the lowlands and swamps,
which, owing to the nature of the country here, can be readily drained.   The
soil is black muck with clay sub-soil, free from stone.

That portion of the township lying east of the Mattagami River may
be described as a generally level or gently undulating country, timbered
with spruce up to fourteen inches in diameter, with birch, poplar, balsam
and balm of gilead of average size and quality.   In this portion of the township there is a considerable area covered with spruce and tamarac swamps;
all these swamps, however, admit of easy drainage.

On the uplands the soil is a rich black loam from ten to twelve inches
in depth, with clay sub-soil free from stone.

A few small outcroppings or rock (Huronian) are to be met with along
the Mattagami River at the various falls and rapids.

No traces of minerals were discovered.   The average magnetic variation
I found to be eight degrees and thirty minutes west.   All the lines of survey were, however, run north and south and east and west astronomically
entirely independent of the magnetic needle, the total area of the township
being within one and one-half acres of the theoretic area of a nine mile township surveyed under this system in that latitude.

Taking the township as a whole, I would consider fully sixty per cent.
suitable for immediate settlement, and I have no doubt that with proper
drainage, which can be easily effected, nearly all the remaining of the forty
per cent. can be made suitable for farming purposes.

Two trial lines of the proposed Transcontinental Railway crosses the
township in a north-westerly direction.   I think, however, as the location
of the road in that locality has not yet been decided upon, that it would
only confuse the returns to show these lines in the field notes or on the plan.

Fish, game and fur of the usual kind common to this section of the
province are to be found in abundance.

Wild fruit such as strawberries, raspberries, etc., were fairly plentiful.

Frequent observations for azimuth were taken on Polaris at elongation, also solar observations for latitude, records of which will be found in the notes.

Trusting that this report, with the accompanying plans, field notes, etc., of the survey will be found complete and satisfactory to your Department,

I have the honor to be,

Sir,

Your obedient servant,

(Signed) J. W. FitzGerald,

Ontario Land Surveyor.

To the Honorable
    The Minister of Lands, Forests and Mines,
        Toronto.

(*Appendix No. 35.*)

Township of Sydere, District of Algoma.

Hamilton, Ont., Dec. 11th, 1906.

Sir,—In compliance with your instructions dated the 15th of May, 1906, to survey the Township of Sydere, west of the Mattagami River, in the District of Algoma, I have the honor to report as follows:—With as little delay as possible I secured the services of two experienced field assistants, Messrs. W. M. Stewart and F. W. Paulin, together with fifteen other men, and provided with five large Peterborough canoes, we assembled at Metagama Station, on the Canadian Pacific Railway, on the 6th of June. Thence we proceeded by way of Lakes Muskegogoma and Minnisinagua to Fort Mattagami, and from there followed the Mattagami River route to the mouth of the Muskego Creek.

In passing it may be mentioned that the Mattagami River affords an excellent canoe route thus far.

Though containing numerous rapids and falls, the portages are not long as a rule, and between the portages the water in the river is good for canoes or small boats.

Several of the falls on the Mattagami afford very excellent water powers which should prove of great value in the future development of the country. The Muskego Creek is of but little consequence, as it is too small to afford either a practical boat route above the forks or permanent power for development purposes.

We managed to work our canoes up the Muskego as far as the forks without much difficulty. The forks occur upon lot four or five in the ninth concession of Sydere, and here on the 18th of June, upon a point on the east bank of the stream, we made a secure cache of our supplies. We had thus occupied twelve days in covering the distance and transporting our supplies from Metagama Station to the Township of Sydere, and no time was lost in the undertaking.

With light canoes we now worked our way up the east branch of the Mushego until we reached the road allowance between concessions four and five in the Township of Bradburn recently run by O. L. S. Fitzgerald.

Here canoes were cached and our necessary outfit portaged westerly and south-westerly and camp made on the south end of lot I in the fourth concession of Sydere.

Our east boundary was found to have been already run by Mr. Fitzgerald, so the commencement of our survey was made in rechaining and posting our south boundary and in running the concession line between II and III, which was turned off from the east boundary on an assumed course four minutes north of west so as to make a straight chord to the west boundary.

By astronomical observation the true course of this line was afterwards found to be north 89 degrees 58 min. west, and the line was deflected two minutes to the south at the side road between lots 12 and 13 and carried through to the west boundary where it struck nine links south of Speight's one and one-half mile tally. In running this concession line westerly, as with others throughout the township, the fronts of all lots on both sides of the road as well as on the centre lines were made and posted in uniform widths of 25.25 chains, excepting adjoining the east and west boundaries where some broken distances were made.

From these posts so planted at uniform distance upon the concession roads, the side roads were run and opened out from south to north and the adjacent concessions made of equal depth between the several concession roads, but no posts were planted at the blind lines on the side roads.

At the intersection of all concession and side roads wooden posts marked to indicate their respective lots and concessions were planted at the several lot corners as well as at the intersection of centre lines.

In order to make the survey more permanent in case of fire, nine iron posts were planted as follows: At the centre of road intersections at each of the four corners of the township posts, one and seven-eighths inches in diameter and three feet long, marked with the names of adjoining townships and "R" on each of the four sides.

At the centre of road intersections between lots twelve and thirteen and the north and south boundaries, as well as road between concessions six and seven, iron posts one and one-quarter inches in diameter and three feet long and marked as follows: That on the north boundary, "Con. XII" on the south side, and "R" on the four sides; that on the road allowance between conlessions six and seven, "Con. VII" on the north and "R" on the four sides; that on the south boundary, "Con. I" on the north and "R" on the four sides; and in the centres of the road intersections on the east and west boundaries between concessions six and seven iron posts one and one-quarter inches in diameter and three feet long and marked "Con. VII" on the north and "R" on the four sides.

Astronomical observations were taken from time to time in order to determine true courses of lines.

The general character of the country may be described as rolling rather than hilly, the higher lands being chiefly wooded by white poplar and some white spruce and birch, whereas the lower lying portions are more or less swampy and wooded with black spruce and occasional clumps of cedar.

Few rock exposures occur upon the township, those noted being in the north and north-western parts where several exposures of granite were noted. Granite also makes its appearance at several points along the banks of the Muskego Creek.

With these few exceptions the surface of the township is composed of alluvial clay, sandy clay and muskeg with clay subsoil.

Some choice sections occur in various parts of the township, but as a whole, for agricultural purposes I would class Sydere as only medium. The

Township of Sydere is heavily wooded with the following varieties of timber named in the order of their abundance: Black spruce, white poplar, white spruce, white birch, tamarac, Balm of Gilead and cedar. A few large white spruce occur in various localities suitable for milling purposes, but they are not found in sufficiently large numbers to warrant the setting aside of the township as a timber reserve, but there is sufficient white spruce timber to supply the demand for local building purposes, and the township as a whole is well covered with pulpwood and fuel.

Several preliminary lines of the Grand Trunk Pacific Railway pass through or close to the Township of Sydere, and when this road is constructed it will furnish a convenient means of access and shipping facilities for local products. Sydere is fairly well watered by the Muskego and a few other small creeks and little lakes, all of which contain good water.

In regard to climate, I have to report that two nights during the first week in July heavy frosts were experienced.

Some varieties of game, particularly moose, were observed to be abundant.

Throughout the survey particular care was exercised at all times to prevent the occurrence of forest fires, and I am glad to be able to say that none were started by us.

I have now had prepared under my direction a copy of field notes, including astronomical observations, affidavit re settlers and oaths of chainmen, a plan of township on mounted paper and a timber plan on tracing linen, all of which, together with account in triplicate, are submitted herewith.

I have the honor to be,

Sir,

Your obedient servant,

(Signed) J. W. Tyrrell.

Ontario Land Surveyor.

The Honorable
    The Minister of Lands, Forests and Mines,
        Toronto.

(Appendix No. 36).

Township of Calder, District of Algoma.

Orillia, December 31st, 1906.

Sir,—In compliance with instructions received from you bearing date of May 15th, 1906, for the survey of the Township of Calder, in the District of Algoma, our party left Metagama in canoes on the nineteenth day of June following, having experienced some delay in outfitting, and procuring proper men to carry out the work. The route followed was the same as that of previous years via the Hudson Bay Post, at Mattagami, and thence following the waters of the Mattagami River to Loon Portage, in the Township of Bradburn. At this point we cached our canoes and proceeded to pack the supplies over the portage trail to the Driftwood River or Creek which passes from south to north through the above township of Calder. The water in all the streams traversed en route was found to be exceptionally high for this season of the year, but was rapidly

7 L.M.

falling as we travelled north. As we found that O. L. S. Fitzgerald had already commenced the boundary line between the Townships of Calder and Bradburn, we at once began operations. On the first of August we had the misfortune to have our camps totally destroyed by fire, and were forced to return to civilized limits to procure clothing and a new camp outfit. This incident with its attendant evils consumed much valuable time, and it was the beginning of September before we were again in the field. The origin of the fire we were unable to ascertain, as the cook who was absent from the camp for a short time, states that all fires were extinguished before his leaving, and the chainmen who visited the camp in the interval, say that no sign of fire was visible. The fire scorched an area of perhaps four acres, the damage to timber being infinitesimal, its only serious effect being the destruction of the camp as above stated. The weather throughout the season was exceptionally warm and dry, the woods resembling a huge tinder-box, requiring the utmost care and vigilance to prevent a conflagration. This has been the only season we have experienced in that part of the country where any difficulty was found in obtaining an abundant supply of water when working on the lines. By the end of the first week in October, the weather, which had continued up to that time exceptionally mild and summerlike, took a decidedly colder turn, with snow storms and freezing temperature, and although we were almost finished, we deemed it advisable to send out the main body of the party with the canoes by the route traversed in coming in, four of us remaining to finish and travel over the Transcontinental Railway trail to Abitibi River, and thence up that stream. and the Black River to MacDougal's Falls, to which point the T. & N. O. Railway had been graded.

In accordance with the instructions above referred to, the lots in this township were laid out with a frontage of 25.25 chains, a road allowance of one chain in perpendicular width being laid out between lots 6 and 7, 12 and 13, 18 and 19, 24 and 25, and on the several boundaries, and a similar road allowance between concessions II-III, IV-V, etc., at intervals of two concessions. The concession lines were run due east and west, and the side lines due north and south astronomically in the centre of the road allowances. On the lines in the centre of the concession road allowances, and the north and south boundaries posts were planted at the intersections of the several lot lines, and marked with the proper lot numbers from number one at the east to number twenty-eight at the westerly boundary; and at the intersections of the various side lines with four R's. At a distance of fifty links north and south of these lines where such point fell within the township, posts were also planted at the several lot corners, and marked with the lot and concession numbers to which each referred and R. fronting the road allowance in accordance with the system of double fronts. No posts were planted on the side lines to mark the blind concessions. Road allowance posts were also planted where necessary to mark the road allowances around lakes. In addition to the wooden posts above referred to, iron posts were planted or marked at the intersections of the road allowances (centre lines), at the following points:—At the four angles of the township, iron posts one and seven-eighths inches in diameter marked with the name "Calder" facing diagonally into the township, and four R's.; on the side line between lots 12-13 on the south boundary, on the line between concessions VI-VII, and at the north boundary, posts one and one-quarter inches in diameter, markd with concession numbers and four R's.; and on the line between concessions VI-VII, at the east and west boundaries. The lines in the centre of the road allowances on the north.

7a L.M.

and east boundaries intersect directly at the water's edge of the small lake at that place, a steep hill rising from the water, but as this was a firm sandy soil, and we concluded that the post at this point could be planted securely enough to be safe from ice, it was planted directly at the intersection; this course being considered preferable to marking it as a witness post. Two bearing trees were marked for this post.

This township throughout its area has a gently undulating character just sufficient to produce effectual natural drainage, the only rough land being at the north-easterly corner where steep ridges and ravines cover but a small area. This latter part is occupied by an old brule. The fire appears to have swept from the east, and extends but a very short distance west of the boundary.

The soil is uniformly of excellent quality, being clay and clay loam with generally a light deposit of black mould, and in the lower lands a considerable peaty deposit overlying it. In only one or two instances was sandy soil encountered and then only locally and of shallow depth, and in only one or two cases was the clay found to bake on exposure to fire heat. This township is by far the most readily adaptable to agricultural purposes that we have yet been called upon to survey, owing to its uniformly rolling and well drained surface.

The main drainage channel is formed by the Driftwood River or Creek flowing in an almost due north course, and following closely the side line between lots twenty-four and twenty-five. This stream expands to a width of about two chains through the northerly half of the township, a width out of all proportion to the volume of water passing through, as in August last the flow might easily have been passed through a pipe of twenty inches in diameter. It is held up at intervals by natural dams of boulders forming small rapids, and which, if removed, would greatly reduce its size and increase its carrying capacity. The banks along this stream are uniformly good, poplar and birch growing quite up to the edge. which would not occur if much overflowing occurred. The balance of township is also well drained by smaller streams flowing mostly towards the North. Only a few lakes, mostly of small size and shallow, were met with; the only one deserving special mention, owing to the crystal purity of its water, being that at the extreme north-east. The water in all the streams and small lakes met with was of good quality, but an extremely dry season rendered some of the former somewhat muddy, and of scarcely perceptible current.

Spruce forms the chief timber, and is usually of small size, seldom exceeding twelve inches in diameter. Poplar, white birch and tamarac of small size are also plentiful, and occasionally balsam. In only a few places was any quantity of timber of a merchantable size met with, notably through concession VII, along the easterly boundary where large birch, poplar and spruce occur in diameter up to twenty inches. As a whole the township cannot be considered as a valuable timber prospect, but will furnish abundance for domestic supply. The bush is generally thick, and crowded with undergrowth of alder, small cedar, balsam and moosewood. A thick growth of elderberry was noticed for the first time in the northeast corner, near the lakes on the burnt ground.

No rock outcrops were met with in the township.

Numerous signs of beaver in large numbers were evident in the large number of dams on all suitable streams. Some of these dams were of large size, but although some fresh work was met with, by far the greater number of beaver appear to have been killed out. Large meadows and the numerous dams attest the former activity of the animal, and from the abundant supply of

easily accessible food still available, it would not appear that starvation had
driven them out.   Bears were found to be exceptionally plentiful as we
discovered to our cost, these animals taking away a large cache of provisions, carrying the full bags of flour, &c., bodily off into the woods, and
no doubt discussing their contents at leisure.   Mink seemed plentiful along
the Driftwood, as also the other fur-bearing animals native to the country.
Nearly all the small lakes and streams appear to be inhabited by fish,
chiefly pike.

A party of Transcontinental engineers were at work in the township,
and a large number of lines have been run in various parts.   Only those
lines were noted which we understand to be practically on the final location.   In the southerly part of the township a considerable fluctuation was
noticed in the magnetic meridian, the variation reading from two to fifteen degrees west, but north of the line between concessions two and three,
the compass needle appeared remarkably steady, and from a large number
of readings the normal variation appears to be about nine and one-half
degrees west.

We have the honor to be,

Sir,

Your Obedient Servants,

(Signed) CAVANA & WATSON,

Ontario Land Surveyors.

The Honorable,
    The Minister of Lands, Forests and Mines,
        Toronto.

(Appendix No. 37).

TOWNSHIP OF DUFF. DISTRICT OF ALGOMA.

ORILLIA, April 21st, 1906.

SIR,—In keeping with instructions received from you for the survey of
the Townships of Duff and Lucas, in the District of Algoma, we proceeded
to carry out the same with all possible celerity.   The route followed to reach
the Township of Lucas has been described in our report on the survey of
that township, the present township being approached through it from the
west.   For reasons also stated in the above report, it was necessary to prose-
cute the work in the winter, but as the ground was not frozen even when we
had finished the work, no difficulty was experienced in properly planting
the posts on the survey lines.

The several concession lines were run due east and west and the side
lines due North and South astronomically, the South boundary was rechained and posts planted at the angles of the several lots, the mile posts
planted by Ontario Land Surveyor T. J. Patten being taken as starting points
for the several side lines.   In this work and throughout the survey a steel
band chain eight chains in length was used and was found to be well adapted
for the level character of the country, giving uniform and satisfactory re-
sults.   In some cases a few links difference has been made from the chaining previously done on the outline, and in such cases our own measurements
have been shown.   The north boundary was not rechained, the distances
shown on the plan on this line being deduced from the connections with the
mile posts planted thereon by O. L. S. Patten.   Wooden posts were planted
on the lines at the front of the several concessions to mark the boundaries
between lots, and were marked in the manner prescribed for single-fronted

concessions, the lot numbers being placed on east and west sides, and the concession numbers on north and south sides at side line intersections, and on the north side only on posts marking the boundary between the lots in each block. In addition to the wooden posts iron posts one and one-quarter inches in diameter, marked in a similar manner to the wooden posts, were planted at the following points: on the line between Concessions III. and IV., at its intersection with the easterly boundary of the township; at its intersection with the line between lots six and seven; at its intersection with the westerly boundary of the township. As the line between lots six and seven intersects the north boundary in a lake, an iron post was planted near the southerly shore and marked on the south side "W. P. 54," 65, on the east "VI," and on the west "VII." The iron post planted by O. L. S. Patten at the end of his ninth mile on the base line forming the southerly boundary of this township, was marked on the east side "VI," on the west "VII," and on the north "Con. I." The iron post planted by O. L. S. Patten on the line between the Districts of Nipissing and Algoma to mark the north-east angle of the Township of Tully and the south-east angle of the Township of Duff, was marked on the north-west "Duff," and on the north "Con. I." The iron post planted by O. L. S. Niven at the 150th mile on the above district line, being at the north-east angle of the Township of Duff, was marked on the south-west side "Duff," on the south side "Con. VI," and on the west "I." The iron post planted by O. L. S. Patten at the end of his sixth mile, being the south-west angle of the Township of Duff, was marked on the north-east "Duff," on the north-west "Lucas," on the north "Con. I." on the east "I." and on the west "XII." An iron post one and seven-eighths inches in diameter was planted where the line between the Townships of Duff and Lucas intersects the northerly boundary of the same, and was marked on the south-east "Duff," on the south-west "Lucas," on the south "Con. VI." on the east "XII," and on the west "I."

For purposes of description, a line drawn from the intersection of the side line between lots two and three with the southerly boundary to the intersection of the line between lots seven and eight with the northerly boundary of the township divides the township into two distinct areas. West of this line is found a generally level or gently rolling country timbered chiefly with spruce of comparatively small diameter; while east of it the rolling character is more pronounced with the occurrence of ravines, larger timber and the occasional predominance of poplar and white birch as a factor in the forest growth. A string of small lakes marks this division and are peculiarly interesting owing to their nearly exact alignment, marking as it were a cleavage plane in the natural character of the country. In the immediate neighborhood of these lakes, notably that crossed by the line between Concessions II and III. the country to the east of Crawfish Lake (so named on account of its peculiar shape), and the small lakes crossed by the line between Concessions V and VI west of lot four, the country is high and somewhat rough and broken by ravines. This rough character, however, does not extend far on either side of the lakes and the area rendered unfit for cultivation on this account is insignificant. The drainage of the westerly area above referred to appears to move regularly toward the north-west through small creeks, the largest of which crosses the south boundary at the line between lots eight and nine and passes into the neighboring Township of Lucas, in the southerly part of the fourth concession. This latter creek has an average width of from fifty to sixty links and banks from six to ten feet high, with a moderate current. The area to the east appears to drain more directly into the Frederick House Lake. The water in both lakes

and small streams is clear and good. The soil throughout is clay and clay
loam with, in a few places in the rolling country about the lakes, a slight
sandy admixture, and has usually a considerable deposit of black vegetable
mould overlying it and in common with the rest of the country is moss covered. There are some small areas of flat land forming the characteristic,
semi-open swamps, with small scrubby clumps of spruce, which would require
to be drained before they could be brought into a state of cultivation, but,
as far as could be observed, no exceptional obstacles are offered to thorough
drainage. The land is free from stone and offers good prospects to the agriculturist.

No rock outcrops nor indications of valuable minerals were observed.
The entire land area is covered with forest, which is chiefly composed
of spruce, and, excepting on the rolling lands and creek banks, seldom exceeding twelve or fourteen inches in diameter. Dead tamarac is scattered through
it and a minor proportion of balsam, white birch and poplar, the last two
rather rare and always small, excepting in the rolling country near the
lakes. The north-eastern portion of the township, especially about Crawfish
Lake and the small lakes to the north and north-west, contains some large
and fine timber, spruce, tamarac and poplar of twenty inches in diameter
being common, and also large white birch. A few specimens of the jack
pine were also met with in the latter locality and about half a dozen trees
of white pine, the latter punky and valueless. This township appears to
have escaped fire in recent years, although in a few places the lines passed
through a very thick and lusty growth of young spruce and tamarac, apparently an aftergrowth following a fire of distant date. The usual game of
the country is to be found, although the moose (the staff of life for the Indian
population) was absent, probably yarding in a more favorable locality. Few
grouse were seen, although plentiful in the autumn. A single large covey
of prairie chicken were met with. In fur-bearing animals marten appeared
to be most plentiful.

The weather during the progress of this work was all that could be de-
sired, "Buckskin weather" being the rule, and only on one or two occasions
did the thermometer dip to 22 degrees. It was not till about Christmas time
that we were forced to take to snowshoes, but after this the depth of snow
increased rapidly and in the first week in January measured nearly four
feet. The long tramp from this township to Biscotasing was extremely ardu-
ous, especially on the river stretches, where the snow lay deep, with an
accumulation of slush from six inches to a foot in depth underneath, rendering the use of hand-drawn toboggans and sleighs so difficult that most
of the party abandoned these and took to the pack strap in preference. It
was a surprise to hear, when travelling along these river stretches with the
mercury ranging well below zero, song birds pouring out notes closely resembling those of our canary with all the vim we are accustomed to hear
from this June bird. The party, with the exception of one man, whom it
was necessary to leave at Joe Moore's on account of frozen feet, arrived at
Biscotasing on January the 19th of the present year.

We have the honor to be,
Sir,
Your obedient servants,
(Signed) CAVANA & WATSON,
Ontario Land Surveyors.

The Honorable,
The Minister of Lands, Forests and Mines,
Toronto.

(Appendix No. 38).

TOWNSHIP OF LUCAS, DISTRICT OF ALGOMA.

ORILLIA, April 21st, 1906.

SIR,—Following your instructions for the survey of the Townships of
Duff and Lucas, in the District of Algoma, bearing date of May 31st, 1905,
we proceeded at once to make preparation to carry out the same. Considerable difficulty was experienced in obtaining men capable of carrying out
the work, and it was not until the 8th day of July that our party was in
readiness to leave the railway. On the above date we left Metagama on the
main line of the Canadian Pacific Railway and followed the canoe route
usually taken by parties entering the above district, over the waters tributary to the Spanish River south of the height of land, and to the Mattagami
River north of it, passing on our way north the Hudson's Bay post of Mato-
gami. In order to escape the long and difficult portages and shallow, snag-
infested creeks leading from the Mattagami River to the Frederick House
River by way of Porcupine Lake, we proceeded further down the river and approached the Township of Lucas from the west, packing in to the westerly
boundary over the line between concessions two and three of the Township of
Crawford. Work was commenced from the above boundary from the posts
planted thereon by Ontario Land Surveyor T. J. Patten and developed in the
usual manner, having regard to the special details set forth in the above
mentioned instructions.

Owing to disaffection among the Indians employed, we could not finish
the work during the season of open navigation and were compelled to return
to the railway and organize a new party, and at the same time make preparation for a winter trip. All this consumed time, and it was not until the
third day of January of the present year that the surveys outlined in 'the
instructions above referred to were fully completed, and we were ready to
face the long snowshoe trip that lay before us on the return journey.

Although a portion of the Township of Lucas was surveyed during the
early winter, the season was exceptionally favorable, the early snowfall
having prevented the frost from entering the ground, and posts were driven
as readily as in summer. The concession lines were run due east and west
and the side lines due north and south astronomically. Along the lines at
the front of each concession wooden posts were planted to mark the angles
of the several lots and were marked in the manner prescribed for single-
fronted concessions. The south boundary was rechained and posts planted
at intervals of forty chains to mark the lot corner, the mile posts previously
planted by O. L. S. Patten being taken as starting points for the several side
lines. The north boundary was not rechained, with the exception of that
part crossing lots nine and ten, where there has apparently been an error
in the original chaining. This part was rechained and the corrected distance placed on the plan of the township. Other distances along the above
line have been deduced from the connections with the mile posts planted
thereon. In addition to the wooden posts iron posts one and one-quarter
inches in diameter, marked with the concession numbers and lot numbers corresponding to their several positions, were planted at the following points:
On the line between Concessions III and IV, at its intersection with the
line between lots six and seven; and on the line between lots six and seven
at its intersection with the northerly boundary of the township. The iron

post planted by O. L. S. Patten at the end of his 15th mile on the meridian forming the westerly boundary of the Township of Lucas, was marked "Con. IV" on the north side, "Con. III" on the south side, and "XII" on the east; and the iron post planted on the south boundary at the end of his third mile was marked "Con. I" on the north side, "VI" on the east, and "VII" on the west. An iron post one and seven-eighths inches in diameter was planted at the intersection of the boundary between the Townships of Lucas and Duff with their northerly boundary and marked on the east side "XII." on the west "I," on the south "Con. VI," on the south-east "Duff," and on the south-west "Lucas." The iron post planted by O. L. S. Patten at the end of his sixth mile and marking the south-east angle of the Township of Lucas and the south-west angle of the Township of Duff, was marked on the east side "XII." on the west "I," on the north "Con. I." on the north-east "Duff," and on the north-west "Lucas." The iron post marking the south-west angle of Lucas was marked on the north-east side "Lucas," on the north side "Con. I," and on the east side "XII." The iron post at the north-west angle of the township was marked on the south-east side "Lucas," on the south "Con. VI," and on the east "XII."

This township embraces a section of country of generally even or nearly level surface dipping toward the north, and, with the exception of a burnt area in the south-westerly part, and a few patches of partially open swamp, is thickly covered with forest. The main drainage appears to pass through two creeks, the principal one entering across the south boundary on lot eight and passing out across the north boundary on lot ten, thus having a general course a little west of north, and the other flowing north-westerly from the east boundary in concession three and crossing the north boundary on lot four. Both these creeks contain good water and ample banks and could be readily improved so as to furnish a means of transport for the timber of the country. We were informed by the native Indians that these creeks drain into the Frederick House River. No lakes were met with but the water supply is excellent and abundant, being contained in small creeks. On either side of the creek first above mentioned, through concessions I, II and III, the forest has been destroyed by fire of recent date. This burnt area probably includes thirteen or fourteen hundred acres.

The soil throughout is clay and clay loam, covered by a deposit of black vegetable mould of varying depth and having a growth of moss on the surface. It is free from stone, has good drainage facilities and is well adapted for agriculture. When ordinary improvements in the way of drainage are carried out, there will be no waste land in this township.

From an economical standpoint the forest is chiefly valuable as a producer of tie and pulp timber. although on the banks of creeks and rolling land larger trees are met with.

The spruce appropriates most of the available root space and generally ranges from six to twelve inches in diameter. Tamarac is next in importance, scattered among the spruce, in size from eight to sixteen inches and nearly all dead. Balsam is usually of small size and often replaces alder as a thick undergrowth. Poplar and white birch are sparsely scattered and unimportant, likewise cedar.

No rock outcrops were met with nor indication of valuable minerals.

The usual game and fur-bearing animals of the district are found here. Grouse were very plentiful in the autumn but were rarely seen after the snowfall. Signs of moose were observed, but this does not appear to be a favorite ground for these animals. Beaver occupy the creeks, but not, as far as observed, in considerable numbers, and the Indians report that large numbers of these animals died throughout the country in the preceding spring from some unknown cause. Of the other fur-bearers, mink and marten are probably most numerous.

We have the honor to be,
Sir,
Your obedient servants,
(Signed)   CAVANA & WATSON,
Ontario Land Surveyors.

The Honorable,
The Minister of Lands, Forests and Mines,
Toronto.

(Appendix No. 39).

TOWNSHIP OF CARNEGIE, DISTRICT OF ALGOMA.

· ORILLIA, March 26th, 1906.

SIR,—In compliance with instructions received from you dated the thirty-first day of May, 1905, for the survey of the Townships of Carnegie and Reid, in the District of Algoma, the party organized for that purpose left Metagama on the eighth day of July following; some difficulty having been experienced in obtaining suitable men to carry out the work. The canoe route traversed was that usually taken by surveyors entering the above district, via the Hudson's Bay Post at Mattagami, and thence down the several lakes and streams forming the Mattagami River to the locality of the survey. Actual survey work was commenced on July 24th.

As it was found that the south boundary of the above township had not been run, but that the north boundary had been run by O. L. S. Fitzgerald, the survey was commenced from the latter, running the concession lines due east and west, and the side lines due south astronomically. A single row of posts was planted on the lines in front of the several concessions and were marked in the manner set forth in the above mentioned instructions for single fronted concessions, the numbers of the concessions to the south of the lines being marked on the posts only at the intersections of the side lines or boundaries. In addition to the wooden posts, iron posts one and one-quarter inches in diameter were planted at the following points:—On concession line "III" and "IV" at its intersection with the boundary between Carnegie and Reid, marked on the north side "Con. IV," on the south side "Con. III." on the east "XII." and on the west "I"; at its intersection with side line "6' 'and "7," marked on the north side "Con. IV," on the south side "Con. III," on the east "VI," and on the west "VII," at its intersection with the boundary between Carnegie and Prosser, marked on the north side "Con. IV," on the south side "Con. III," and on the west "I." Iron posts similar to the above were planted on the line between lots "6" and "7," at its intersection with the south boundary of the township, marked on the east side "VI," on the west side "VII." and on the north side "Con. I." The line between lots "6" and "7" intersecting the north boundary of the township at the iron post planted by O. L. S. Fitzgerald, this post was marked "Con. VI" on the south side. An iron post one and seven-eighths inches in diameter was planted on the boundary between Carnegie and Reid at its intersection with the south boundary, and marked on the north-east side "Carnegie," on the north-west side "Reid," on the north "Con. I," on the east "XII," and on the west "I." The boundary between Carnegie and Reid intersects the north boundary at the iron post planted by O. L. S. Fitzgerald to mark the line between the Townships of Crawford and Mahaffy, and this post was marked on the south-east side "Carnegie," on the south-west side "Reid," on the south "Con. VI," on the east "XII," and on the west "I." The iron post at the north-east angle of the township was marked on the south-west side, "Carnegie."

The surface of the township is of a generally level character, dipping gently toward the north-west, and draining into the Mattagami River. It is traversed by two main streams, the first of these entering across the south boundary on lot eight, taking a north-westerly course to lot twelve, and thence northerly, joining the other principal stream on lot twelve, concession four. This second stream above referred to flows from lot one in the second concession in a north-westerly direction to its junction with the former, and thence across the westerly boundary of the township in the southerly part of concession five. Both the above streams have ample banks to accommodate a large volume of water, the valleys generally occupying a level of twenty-five to thirty-five feet below the adjacent land surface. Excellent drainage facilities are thus provided for all but the extreme north-east corner of the township. The water in these and all smaller streams is of excellent quality for drinking purposes. No lakes of any considerable extent were met with, the few small ponds encountered being shown on the plans returned herewith.

The soil over nearly the whole of the area embraced within the boundaries of this township is clay overlaid with a deposit of black vegetable mould, varying from a few inches to more than a foot in depth, and this in turn covered with moss. Some small areas of sandy loam were met with, and in places a shallow deposit of sand overlies the clay subsoil. The whole is well adapted for agricultural purposes.

No rock outcrops were met with nor any indication of valuable minerals. The entire area is occupied by forest with the exception of about sixteen hundred acres in the south-westerly part of the township which has been burnt over, leaving only small patches of green bush. Spruce forms by far the greater part of the timber, and does not usually exceed twelve inches in diameter on the level bush lands, but on slopes and creek banks where the drainage is ample, numerous trees are met with of a diameter of twenty inches. Tamarac also forms a considerable proportion of the forest, and although all but very young trees are dead, they are still sound in most cases, and for a few years to come would be available for tie timber, for which their size is in general suitable. Poplar is conspicuous only on the higher well drained lands, where it attains a diameter of about two feet. White birch occurs to some extent but generally of such small size as to be of little importance, the largest trees being observed on the rising ground on lots four and five in concession five. Balsam forms an important part of the forest growth, being generally ranked as an undergrowth, but, like the rest, attains larger dimensions on well drained land. Wherever this latter tree occurs in any size and quantity, windfall is the sure result, and the openings so made are quickly taken possession of by moosewood, alder and hazel. On lot five in concessions five and six, there is a clump of white pine containing probably one hundred trees in diameter from fifteen to eighteen inches. This is the only place where this tree was observed.

In common with the surrounding country, numerous signs of moose were observed, and to a lesser extent of red deer. Grouse were very plentiful, and in some localities hares. Few signs of beaver were seen, probably on account of the lack of desirable food growth. Mink, marten and otter complete the list of valuable fur-bearing animals. A remarkable phenomenon not noticed in former years was the large numbers of wood mice. These little animals, of a size between the ordinary domestic mouse and the house rat, were everywhere in evidence, the moss being burrowed in every direction by their runways.. One had only to stand a moment or two anywhere in the woods to see large numbers of these rodents moving about. Owls, hawks, ravens, whiskey-jacks, wood-peckers, crossbills, and many of the birds commonly seen in more southern latitudes, take up their summer homes in this locality.

I have the honor to be,

Sir,

Your obedient servant,

(Signed) CHAS E. FITTON,

Ontario Land Surveyor.

The Honorable,

The Minister of Lands, Forests and Mines,

Toronto.

(Appendix No. 40).

TOWNSHIP OF REID, DISTRICT OF ALGOMA.

ORILLIA, March 26th, 1906.

· SIR,—In compliance with instructions received from you bearing date of May 31st, 1905, for the survey of the Townships of Carnegie and Reid, in the District of Algoma, I beg to submit herewith returns for the survey of the Township of Reid. The route of travel to reach this township has been described in the report on the survey of the Township of Carnegie. For similar reasons to those given in the latter report, the survey was begun from the northerly boundary run by O. L. S. Fitzgerald, and the concession lines run due west, and the side lines due south astronomically. A single row of posts was planted on the line at the front of each concession marked in the manner prescribed in the above instructions to govern single fronted concessions. In addition to the above wooden posts, iron posts one and one-quarter inches in diameter were planted at the following points:—On concession line III and IV at its intersection with the easterly boundary of the township, marked on the north side "Con. IV," on the south side "Con. III," on the east side "XII," and on the west side "I," at its intersection with the side line between lots six and seven marked on the north side "Con. IV," on the south side "Con. III," on the east "VI," and on the west "VII," and at its intersection with the westerly boundary marked on the north side "Con. IV," on the south side "Con. III." and on the east "XII," on the side line between lots lots six and seven, at its intersection with the south boundary marked on the north "Con. I," on the east "VI," and on the west "VII." As this side line intersects the north boundary of the township at the iron .

post planted by O. L. S. Fitzgerald, this post was marked "Con. VI," on the south side, the proper lot numbers being already marked thereon. The iron post at the north-east angle of the township being the same planted by O. L. S. Fitzgerald to mark the line between the Townships of Crawford and Mahaffy, was marked on the south-west side "Reid," on the south side "Con. VI," and on the south-east side "Carnegie." The iron post planted by O. L. S. Fitzgerald at the south-west angle of Mahaffy was marked on the south-east side "Reid," and on the south side "Con. VI." An iron post one and one-quarter inches in diameter was planted on the south boundary, at the line between Reid and Carnegie, marked on the north-east side "Carnegie," on the north-west side "Reid," on the north "Con. I," on the east "XII," and on the west "I." The iron post planted at the south-west angle of Reid by O. L. S. Niven, was marked on the north-east side "Reid," on the north "Con. I," and on the east "XII."

In running down side line between lots 4 and 5, it was found that through concessions III, II and I it would run close to the Mattagami River, leaving a narrow irregular strip of land to the east or west between the line and the river, the balance of the lot being on the other side of the river. As this strip would be practically useless to an owner across the river, it was deemed inadvisable to run this line across the above concessions, and it was accordingly discontinued at the line between concessions III and IV, the river being made the boundary between lots 4 and 5 through those concessions.

The Mattagami River flows through this township in nearly a due north course, its point of crossing the north boundary on lot two being only about one and a quarter miles farther east than where it enters across the south boundary, and between these points the channel is remarkably straight. It occupies a valley of from thirty to forty feet below the level of the surrounding country, and from fifteen to twenty chains across. The banks extend usually ten or twelve feet above the average water level, and in most places a bench of a few chains extends back to the sides of the valley. The river has an average width of about five chains, and a generally even current of about two miles per hour. There are no rapids or falls in its course through this township, but in places large numbers of boulders occupy the channel, and where these occur a swifter current runs, rendering careful navigation necessary. The banks are of clay, with an occasional outcrop of schist rock at the waters edge. A ledge of the latter extends nearly across the channel from the westerly bank a short distance above the line between concessions II and III. The rock outcrops do not rise high enough to form the banks, being deeply covered by the overlying clay, and are unimportant in extent. Pike and pickerel abound in some parts of the river, and although none were taken within the limits of this township, speckled trout (the genuine S. Fontinalis) were caught at points farther up and down the stream, at the foot of falls and rapids, and of a size and possessing fighting qualities that might well entice the enthusiastic angler over many miles of country to catch. A creek about one chain in width enters across the easterly boundary in the southerly part of concession five, and flows in a nearly due north direction across the north boundary, entering the main river about a mile lower down. This creek has a valley about twenty-five feet in depth, and a good current. Another creek, having a width of thirty to fifty links, traverses the westerly part of the township, taking an easterly course from lot twelve in concession one, till it reaches lot eight concession two, and thence northerly and westerly crossing the north boundary on lot twelve. This creek has a good current, the banks running from four to ten feet in height above average water level, and affords a good drainage outlet for the surrounding lands. The Indians who hunt in this neighborhood say that this creek abounds in speckled trout, a statement that opportunity did not permit of verifying. The township as a whole is well watered, and the water of excellent quality.

The land surface in the vicinity of the Mattagami River, and especially on its easterly side, is broken by ravines running into the river, the balance being of a level or gently rolling character. The soil is clay and clay loam overlaid by a deposit of black vegetable mould varying from a few inches on the high land to more than a foot in the swamp areas. It is uniformly covered with moss. Nearly all of this township is available and well suited for agricultural purposes, the flat lands offering no exceptional difficulties to drainage.

Aside from the unimportant rock exposures already mentioned as occurring at the water level of the Mattagami River, the only rock outcrop noticed was on side line six and seven a short distance north of its intersection with the line between concessions three and four. Here the line passes over a rise some twenty feet above the surrounding land level, and covering but a small area. This rise is composed of schists resting at a steep angle with splashes of quartz. No indications of minerals of economic value were observed.

Of one character or another the whole area is covered with forest, and for the greater part thickly timbered. Spruce forms the chief, and in many parts the only forest tree, especially in that part lying west of the above named river. This tree ranges from three inches in the undrained flats to nearly two feet in diameter on high rolling ground. There is a good deal of tamarac dead, but mostly sound, and well suited for railway ties. Poplar, white birch and balsam grow on the higher lands. East of the river where the country is cut by ravines and rolling, giving ample drainage, the timber is in general larger than on the west side, and contains a larger proportion of poplar, white birch and balsam, but also a great deal of windfall and thick undergrowth of alder, moosewood and hazel. Along the river bank there are some scattered large spruce and cedar, the latter having a diameter up to twenty-four inches, but generally short and very limby.

Abundant signs of the usual game of the country were seen, including moose and red deer. Grouse were numerous, and in fur-bearing animals mink and marten are especially plentiful.

As the notes of the north boundary of this township would be merely a repetition of those already furnished by O. L. S. Fitzgerald for the south boundary of Mahaffy, it has not been deemed necessary to repeat them. It will also be noticed that the magnetic declination has not been shown on plans. This was found to be exceedingly variable, and in notes of a careful transit traverse of the Mattagami River, the declination has been entered at each change station.

> I have the honor to be,
> Sir,
> Your obedient servant,
> (Signed) CHAS. E. FITTON,
> Ontario Land Surveyor.

The Honorable,
The Minister of Lands, Forests and Mines,
Toronto.

(Appendix No. 41).

TOWNSHIP OF DARGAVEL, DISTRICT OF ALGOMA.

GUELPH, ONT., Nov. 12th, 1906.

SIR,—I have the honor to submit the following report of the survey of the Township of Dargavel, in the District of Algoma, made in accordance with instructions from your Department dated the 15th day of May, 1906. I proceeded to work by way of Biscotasing Station, on the Canadian Pacific Railway and the Mattagami River canoe route, leaving the railway on June 8th and arriving at the township on June 26th.

As instructed, I commenced the survey of the south boundary of the township at the six-mile post planted by Ontario Land Surveyor Speight on the meridian line which forms the west boundary of this township and ran east astronomically, planting posts at regular intervals of forty chains apart.

The township was laid out into lots of 320 acres each, or thereabouts, in the usual way, the concession lines being run due east and west one mile apart and the side lines due north and south also one mile apart, that is, between alternate lots.

Wooden posts six inches square were planted on the concession lines every half mile. The mile posts, that is, those planted at the intersections of the lines, were marked with the numbers of the concessions on the north and south sides, and with the numbers of the lots on the east and west sides.

The half-mile posts were marked with the numbers of the lots on the east and west sides and the number of the concession to which they referred on the north side.

On the north boundary posts were planted only at the intersections of the side lines one mile apart, and were marked with the lot numbers on the east and west sides and the concession number on the south side.

An iron post one and seven-eighths inches in diameter was found along-side of the wooden post at the south-west angle of the township and was marked "Dargavel" on the north-east side, "Con. I" on the north side, and "Lot XII" on the east side. A similar iron post was found beside the wooden post at the north-west angle of the township and was marked with the name of the township on the south-east side, "Con. VI" on the south side and "Lot XII" on the east side. Iron posts one and seven-eighths inches in diameter were also planted beside the wooden posts at the south-east and north-east angles of the township. The former being marked "Dargavel" on the north-west side, "Con. I" on the north side, and "Lot I" on the west side, and the latter marked "Dargavel" on the south-west side, "Con. VI" on the south side, and "Lot I" on the west side.

An iron post one and one-quarter inches in diameter was placed beside the wooden post at each of the following points: (1) On the south boundary at the line between lots six and seven and marked "Lot VI" on the east side, "Lot VII" on the west side, "Con. I" on the north side. (2) On the east boundary at the line between concessions three and four marked "Con. III" on the south side, "Con. IV" on the north side, "Lot I" on the west side. (3) At the intersection of the line between the third and fourth concessions with the line between lots six and seven, marked "Con. III" on the south side, "Con. IV" on the north side, "Lot VI" on the east side, "Lot VII" on the west side. (4) On the west boundary at the line between concessions three and four, marked "Con. III" on the south side, "Con. IV" on the north side, "Lot XII" on the east side. (5) On the north boundary at the line between lots six and seven marked "Con. VI" on the south side, "Lot VI" on the east side, "Lot VII" on the west side.

The lines of the survey were well opened out and well blazed.

The land in the western part of the Township along the Mattagami River is rolling and is covered with mixed timber, a large percentage of which is tamarac, now dead and falling to the ground. Eastward from the river the land becomes level with an occasional low ridge of drier land.

The principal timber on the level land is spruce, which is mostly of fair size and good quality. This land is covered with a thick growth of moss, which holds the water and ice and thereby gives the country a swampy appearance. In general there is a gentle slope to this land, so that when the timber is removed and the moss burned off it will be found to be fairly dry and easily drained.

In the north-east corner of the township, part of the land is swampy and the timber small, and considerable drainage will be needed to fit the land for pasturage.

The Mattagami River enters the township in lot eleven of the first concession, flows north through lot eleven of the second concession, then turns to the west and leaves the township near the middle of the third concession. It re-enters the township in lot twelve of concession four, but leaves it again in the same lot. It again enters the township at the south-west corner of lot twelve of the sixth concession and flows north through that lot to the north boundary of the township. This river is here a large stream, averaging over five chains in width and is of considerable depth and flows with a good current. The other streams in the township are small.

There are no rock exposures except a very small one on the right bank of the river in Lot "XII," "Con. IV."

The township, on the whole, is a fairly good one and with a moderate amount of drainage practically the whole of it can be utilized for agricultural purposes.

Game is not plentiful; some moose were seen and traces of caribou, but no red deer. There are a few beavers on the small streams but no large colonies.

The variation of the magnetic needle ranged from seven to about eight degrees west of north.

Accompanying this report are the field notes of the survey and a plan of the township with a timber plan.

I have the honor to be,

Sir,

Your obedient servant,

(Signed)   James Hutcheon,

Ontario Land Surveyor.

The Honorable,
    The Minister of Lands, Forests and Mines,
        Toronto.

(Appendix No. 42).

TOWNSHIP OF LENNOX, DISTRICT OF ALGOMA.

GUELPH, ONT., Dec. 18th, 1906.

SIR,—I have the honor to submit the following report of the survey of the Township of Lennox, in the District of Algoma, made in accordance with instructions from your Department dated the 15th day of May, 1906.

Immediately after completing the survey of Dargavel, I proceeded with the survey of this township by producing the south boundary east astronomically to intersect the meridian line run by O. L. S. Patten in 1904.

Posts were planted on this south boundary at regular intervals of 40 chains apart, the excess in distance, amounting to 38 links, being added to lot number two. The side lines were run due north from alternate posts on this boundary, that is, one mile apart. The concession lines were run due east also one mile apart.

Wooden posts six inches square were planted on the concession lines every half mile, dividing the township into lots of 320 acres or thereabouts. The mile posts were marked with the concession numbers on the north and south sides and the lot numbers on the east and west sides. The half-mile posts were marked with the number of the concession on the north side and the numbers of the lots on the east and west sides.

An iron post one and seven-eighths inches in diameter was placed beside the wooden post at each of the four corners of the township and were marked in the following manner, so far as they referred to this township: That at the south-west corner was marked "Lennox" on the north-east side. "Con. I" on the north side, "Lot XII" on the east side. That at the south-east corner was marked "Lennox" on the north-west side, "Con. I" on the north side, "Lot I" on the west side, and also "Nesbitt" on the south-west side. "Con. VI" on the south side, according to instructions.

That at the north-east corner was marked "Lennox" on the south-west side, "Con. VI" on the south side, "Lot I" on the west side. That at the north-west corner was marked "Lennox" on the south-east side, "Con. VI" on the south side, "Lot XII" on the east side, and "Dargavel" on the south-west side.

An iron post one and one-quarter inches in diameter was placed beside the wooden post at each of the following points: (1) On the south boundary at the line between lots six and seven and marked "Lot VI" on the east side, "Lot VII" on the west side, "Con. I" on the north side. (2) At the intersection of the line between concessions III and IV with the line between lots six and seven marked "Con. III" on the south side, "Con. IV" on the north side, "Lot VI" on the east side, "Lot VII" on the west side. (3) On the west boundary at the line between concessions III and IV marked "Con. III" on the south side, "Con. IV" on the north side, "Lot XII" on the east side. (4) On the north boundary at the line between lots six and seven marked "Con. VI" on the south, "Lot VI" on the east side. "Lot VII" on the west side. The survey lines were well opened out and well blazed.

The south-western part of the township is well drained by two streams of about equal size, which unite to form Driftwood Creek. The east branch enters the township in lot six, concession one, and the west branch enters in lot eleven, concession one. These streams converge as they flow northward and unite in lot nine, concession four, forming a good stream which flows nearly due north and leaves the township at the line between lots nine and ten. The land in the western part of the township is moderately level and the most of it is covered with a thick growth of moss. In the eastern part of the township the land is a little more rolling and is drained by a small stream which enters in lot one, concession two, and flows north-westerly, crossing the north boundary at lot six. The soil is a clay loam and on the rolling land it is first class. Where the land is level the thick growth of moss retains the water and gives the country a swampy appearance, which will disappear to a very large extent when the land is cleared. The largest area of wet land is on the south boundary of lots three, four and five, which are mostly swamp. The timber on this land is small and thin. The soil is a black muck of considerable depth and the ground water stands within a few inches of the surface.

This land can probably be drained without much difficulty into the east branch of Driftwood Creek. A few other similar swamps are found in different parts of the township, but they are not extensive in area.

With a moderate amount of drainage, practically the whole of this township will be available for agricultural or pasturage purpose.s

There is no rock and the only boulders observed were in the bed of the east branch of Driftwood Creek.

The timber in the eastern and western parts of the township is principally spruce of good quality and fair size. On the dry land there is also some good white birch, balsam and poplar.

In the central part of the township, extending from the south boundary to the north and comprising nearly one-third of its area, the land had been burned over a number of years ago and is now grown up with a thick growth of small spruce and tamarac, the latter of which is now mostly dead.

Accompanying this report are the field notes of the survey, a plan of the township and a timber plan.

I have the honor to be,

Sir,

Your obedient servant,

(Signed)   JAMES HUTCHEON,

Ontario Land Surveyor.

The Honorable,
The Minister of Lands, Forests and Mines,
Toronto.

(Appendix No. 43).

TOWNSHIP OF AUBIN, DISTRICT OF ALGOMA.

LISTOWEL, Dec. 10th. 1906.

SIR,—In pursuance with instructions dated May 15th, 1906. from the Honorable the Minister of Lands, Forests and Mines, I beg leave to submit the following report. I proceeded with as little delay as possible to survey the Township of Aubin in the District of Algoma. I encountered some difficulty at the outset in getting good canoe men for my journey in. I also found that canoes of the proper size were hard to get, Peterboroughs 19 feet in length and having a capacity of from 1,500 to 2,000 pounds, are the best

8 L.M.

for a surveyor's use in that part of the Province. I obtained most of my supplies from the Hudson's Bay Company at Biscotasing, and found them reliable to deal with. On June 6th I left Toronto by C. P. Railway and arrived at Biscotasing on June 7th. On June 9th I left Biscotasing with 6,000 pounds of provisions and outfit, with six canoes and fourteen men, and on July 3rd arrived at O. L. S. Nivens' base line on the Mattagami River, a distance of about 200 miles. In travelling this distance there are about seventeen portages to cross, varying in length from about three chains to one and three-quarter miles; eleven of these portages are south of the height of land and six are north. After surveying the Township of Nesbitt, on August 15th, I commenced the Township of Aubin by running north from the south boundary between lots two and three and then running west from the east boundary between concessions one and two, and finished the township on September 21st. During the time of this township the weather was hot and dry, rain fell on five days, a heavy thunder storm occurring on the 16th. While in this township we camped on the west bank of the Mattagami River and occupied two cabins built by the Grand Trunk Pacific people and used as a cache. They afterwards built other caches about twenty miles farther down the river. Behind one of these caches one day my men discovered some green peas almost ripe, full grown and of a good sample; evidently the seed had been thrown out by the previous occupants of the cabin. This is one proof that the country is productive. On our trip out in the fall we stopped at Joe Moore's cabin on the river. This cabin is about forty miles south of O. L. S. Niven's base line and is about on the edge of the clay belt. Mr. Moore is one of the oldest settlers in this part of the country. He has a good garden surrounding his cabin and every year grows a lot of vegetables. This year he had about sixty bags of potatoes, which were of good quality and a splendid crop. The iron post one and seven-eighths inches in diameter and three feet long planted alongside a wooden post at the south-east angle of the Township of Aubin is marked "Aubin" on the north-west side, "Nesbitt" on the north-east side, "Con. I" on the north side, "XII" on the east side, and "I" on the west side. The wooden post is similarly marked.

The iron post one and seven-eighths inches in diameter and three feet long, planted alongside a wooden post at the north-east angle of the Township of Aubin, is marked "Aubin" on the south-west side, "Nesbitt" on the south-east side, "Con. VI" on the south side, "XII" on the east side, and "I" on the west side. The wooden post is similarly marked.

The wooden post planted at the south-west angle of the Township of Aubin is marked "Aubin" on the north-east side, "XII" on the east side, and "Con. I" on the north side.

The iron post one and seven-eighths inches in diameter and three feet long planted alongside a wooden post at the north-west angle of the Township of Aubin is marked "Aubin" on the south-east side, "Dargavel" on the north-east side, "XII" on the east side, and "Con. VI" on the south side. The wooden post is similarly marked.

The iron post one and one-quarter inches in diameter planted alongside a wooden post on the east boundary of the township, on the line between concessions three and four, is marked "Con. III" on the south side, "Con. IV" on the north side, and "I" on the west side. The wooden post is similarly marked. The iron post one and one-quarter inches in diameter planted alongside a wooden post on the south boundary of the township, on the side line between lots six and seven, is marked "Con. I" on the north side, "VI" on the east side, and "VII" on the west side. The wooden post is similarly

8a L.M.

marked. The iron post one and one-quarter inches in diameter planted alongside a wooden post on the west boundary of the township, where the line between concessions three and four intersects it, is marked "Con. III" on the south side, "Con. IV" on the north side, and "XII" on the east side. The wooden post is similarly marked.

The iron post one and one-quarter inches in diameter planted alongside a wooden post on the north boundary of the township, where the side line between lots six and seven intersects it, is marked "Con. VI" on the south side, "VI" on the east side, and "VII" on the west side. The wooden post is similarly marked.

The iron post one and one-quarter inches in diameter planted alongside a wooden post, at the centre of the township where the side line between lots six and seven intersects the concession line between concessions three and four, is marked "Con. III" on the south side, "Con. IV" on the north side, "VI" on the east side, and "VII" on the west side. The wooden post is similarly marked.

Under the head of timber I beg to report the following:— The kinds of timber found in this township are, in order of their relative abundance, black spruce, poplar, tamarac, balsam, white birch, balm of gilead, white spruce and cedar. The black spruce is much harder in its nature than the white, and the limbs grow downward and are always thicker on one side of the tree; the bark of the black is much rougher than that of the white, and the wood is much darker in color. The limbs of the white spruce are more evenly distributed around the tree and have not the same tendency to grow downward as that of the black. The bulk of the timber in this township is black spruce, but the best of it is scattered all over, and not any great quantity in any one place. Small black spruce is the only kind of timber I found growing in the muskegs. There is also a great quantity of poplar in this township and is found on slightly higher ground, the best of it also being scattered over the township, but all of it is of sufficient size for pulpwood and the best of it is suitable for lumber. There is quite a quantity of it along the banks of the Mattagami River. With regard to tamarac, I found that nearly all of this kind of timber is half dead, and there seemed to be very little green foliage on the trees. I cannot explain this unless it might be caused by a succession of either dry or wet seasons. The balsam I found was mostly of small dimensions and only suitable for pulpwood. The white birch, which grows on higher land, is mostly of smaller dimensions, but is good sound timber. Some patches of white birch I found growing along the banks of the Mattagami River. With regard to cedar and white spruce, I would say that the best of it is found along the river, but there is very little of it in the township. The largest and best timber in this township is found along the banks of the river, and I would suggest that one mile back on each side of the river for the whole length of the township be reserved for lumbering. There are no rapids or waterfalls on the river in this township, but there is one place you will see marked in the field notes where there are a few rocks in the channel. There are no bad places in the river. The average current would be about two miles an hour. In July when we arrived at O. L. S. Nivens' base line the river was high, and within about three feet of the top of the bank. In September when we returned to civilization the water was from three to four feet lower. In coming out we had in many places to get out of our canoes and pull them up over the rocks on account of the water being so low. In both the Townships of Aubin and Nesbitt we saw considerable big game, moose, caribou and red deer, also plenty of rabbits and partridge. Just below the Wawaitan portage, at the lower end of Lake Mattagami, where a small stream enters the river, there is a spot where brook trout are very plentiful; some were caught this summer weighing three pounds.

Under the head of soil, I beg to report that I found it to be clay and clay loam. In the swamps there is a heavy growth of moss, then from 6 to 18 inches of black muck before you reach the clay. This muck holds the water like a sponge, and often to get water we required to dig down into the clay and the water would run down out of the muck into the hole. The water in this township is good. Clay loam I found on the higher land, where the coating of moss was very thin. In the muskegs, where nothing but black spruce grows, I found a thin layer of moss, then the muck about six inches in depth and then the clay. These muskegs are not very wet and they all have solid clay bottoms, and can hardly be called true muskegs. The land can easily be cleared as the roots of the trees do not penetrate the clay, but seem to run along between the clay and the muck, and once the land is burnt over and drained, the stumps can be easily moved. The country, although flat and level, can easily be drained into the Mattagami River. The banks of the river in the fall, when the water is low, will average seven feet in height. There is a strip of land along each side of the river which is rolling; this strip is about ten chains back from the river in extent. Under the head of minerals, I beg to report that I found no outcropping of rock, nor any stony land or boulders, and consequently found no trace of minerals.

With regard to observations, I beg to say that I took three in the township. The first was taken on the east boundary, at the N. E. angle of lot I, concession II. The date of this observation was August 20th. I found my line at this point to be of the right bearing. The second observation was taken at about chainage 18.00 on the south boundary of lot six, concession four, on August 31st.

The third observation was taken on the west bank of the Mattagami River at chainage 4.72 on the south boundary of lot II, concession III, the date being September 12th. I found the line at this point to be of the right bearing.

The method used in observing was the greatest elongation of Polaris, the Azimuth at elongation being 1 degree 50 minutes for latitude 48 degrees 50 minutes (approx.). I cannot give the full details of these observations as the small note book in which I took them has been misplaced and cannot now be found.

With regard to the opening up and development of the country, I would say that I learned from the Hudson's Bay Company that the Grand Trunk Pacific survey line crosses the Mattagami River about forty miles to the north of this township, and when this line of railway is built the land should become quickly settled, as it will be easy of access and should soon contain a prosperous community.

I have the honor to be,

Sir,

Your obedient servant,

(Signed)   E. D. Bolton,
Ontario Land Surveyor.

The Honorable,
    The Minister of Lands, Forests and Mines,
        Toronto.

(Appendix No. 44.)

TOWNSHIP OF NESBITT, DISTRICT OF ALGOMA.

LISTOWEL, Dec. 10th, 1906.

SIR,—In pursuance with instructions dated May 15th, 1906, from the Hon. the Minister of Lands, Forests and Mines,. I beg leave to report the following:—I proceeded with as little delay as possible to survey the Township of Nesbitt, in the District of Algoma. I encountered some difficulty at the outset in getting good canoe men for my journey in. I also found that canoes of the proper size were hard to get, Peterboroughs 19 feet in length, and having a capacity of from 1,500 to 2,000 lbs., are the best for a surveyor's use in that part of the Province. I obtained most of my supplies with the exception of meats from the Hudson's Bay Co., at Biscotasing, and found them reliable to deal with. On June 6th, I left Toronto by the Canadian Pacific Railway, and arrived at Biscotasing on June 7th. On June 9th, I left Biscotasing with 6,000 lbs. of provisions and outfit, with 6 canoes and 14 men. On July 3rd, I arrived at O. L. S. Niven's base line on the Mattagami River, a distance from Biscotasing of about 200 miles. This base line forms the south boundary of the Townships of Aubin and Nesbitt. In travelling this distance, there are 17 portages to cross, varying in length from about three chains to one and three-quarter miles, eleven of these portages being south of the height of land, and six being north of the height of land. From the river, with two weeks' provisions and outfit, I proceeded easterly along O. L. S. Niven's base line, a distance of ten miles to the south-east angle of the Township of Nesbitt, and commenced the survey of said township on the 7th day of July. I commenced the survey by running from O. L. S. Patten's meridian line between concessions I and II, and running north from O. L. S. Niven's base line, between lots II and III, Con. I. I finished the survey of the township on August 18th. During the survey the weather was hot and comfortably dry, rain having fallen on four days, with one thunder storm, not very heavy.

The iron post one and seven-eighths inches in diameter, and three feet long, planted at the south-west angle of the Township of Nesbitt alongside a wooden post is marked "Nesbitt" on the north side, "Aubin" on the north-west side, "Con. I" on the north side, "XII" on the east side, and "I" on the west side. The wooden post is marked similarly.

The iron post one and seven-eighths inches in diameter and three feet long, planted at the north-west angle of the Township of Nesbitt, alongside a wooden post is marked "Nesbitt" on the south-east side, "Aubin" on the south-west side, "Con· VI" on the south side, "XII" on the east side, and "I" on the west side. The wooden post is similarly marked.

The wooden post planted at the south-east angle of the Township of Nesbitt is marked "Nesbitt" on the north-west side, and is marked "Crawford" on the south-west side, "Con. I" on the north side and "I" on the west side.

The iron post one and seven-eighths inches in diameter and three feet long, planted at the north-east angle of the Township of Nesbitt alongside a wooden post, is marked "Nesbitt" on the south-west side, "Con. VI" on the south side, and "I" on the west side.

The iron post one and one-quarter inches in diameter, planted alongside a wooden post, on the east boundary of the township between concessions

III and IV is marked "Con. III" on the south side, "Con. IV" on the north side, and "I" on the west side. The wooden post is similarly marked.

The iron post one and one-quarter inches in diameter planted alongside a wooden post, on the south boundary of the township, on the side line between lots six and seven, is marked "Con. I" on the north side, "VI" on east side, and "VII" on the west side. The wooden post is similarly marked.

The iron post one and one-quarter inches in diameter planted alongside a wooden post, on the north boundary, where the side line between lots six and seven intersects it, is marked "Con. VI" on the south side, "VI" on on the east side, and "VII" on the west side. The wooden post is similarly marked.

The iron post one and one-quarter inches in diameter planted alongside a wooden post, at the centre of the township, where the side line between lots six and seven intersects the line between concessions three and four is marked "Con. III" on the south side, "Con. IV" on the north side, "VI" on the east side, and "VII" on the west side. The wooden post is similarly marked.

Under the head of timber, I beg leave to report the following: The kinds of timber found in this township are, in order to their relative abundance, black spruce, poplar, tamarac, balsam, white birch, balm of gilead, white spruce and cedar. The only place where I found white spruce and cedar was in the swamps and along the banks of Driftwood Creek and other smaller creeks. The underbrush consists of moose maple, alder, hardhack, and ground cedar. The black spruce is much harder in its nature than the white, and the limbs grow downward, and are always thicker on one side of the tree. The bark of the black spruce is rougher than that of the white, and the wood is much darker in color. The limbs of the white spruce are more evenly distributed around the tree, and have not the same tendency to grow downward as the black. The bulk of the timber in this township is black spruce, but the best of it is scattered all over the township, and not any great quantity in any one place. Small black spruce is the only kind of timber I found growing in the muskegs. There is also a large quantity of poplar in this township, which is found on slightly higher land, and the best of it is also scattered over the township, but all of it is of a sufficient size for pulpwood, and the largest of it is suitable for lumber. With regard to tamarac, I found that nearly all of this kind of timber is half dead, and there seemed to be very little green foliage on the trees. I cannot explain this, unless it might be a succession of either wet or dry seasons. The balsam I found was mostly of small dimensions, and only suitable for pulpwood. The white birch is mostly of small dimensions, but is good sound lumber. With regard to cedar and white spruce, I would say that there is very little of it in this township.

Under the head of soil, I beg leave to report that I found it to be of clay and clay loam. In the swamps there is a heavy growth of moss, then from 6 inches to 18 inches of black muck before you reach the clay. This black muck holds the water like a sponge, and often to get water, we required to dig down into the clay and the water would run out of the muck into the hole. The water found in this township is good. I found clay loam on the higher land where the moss was very thin. In the muskegs, where nothing but black spruce grows, I found a thin layer of moss, then about 6 inches of muck, and then clay. These muskegs are not very wet, and they all have solid clay bottoms, and can hardly be called true muskegs. The land can be easily cleared, as the roots of the trees do not penetrate far into the clay, but seem to run along between the clay and the muck, and once the land is burnt over and drained, the stumps can easily be moved. The country although flat and level can easily be drained, as the bottom of Driftwood Creek and other smaller creeks is quite a bit lower than the level of the swamps and muskegs. The bank of Driftwood Creek, on an average, has a height of about four feet.

Under the head of minerals, I beg leave to report that I found no outcropping of rock in the township, nor any stony land or boulders, and consequently found no trace of minerals.

In regard to observations, I beg to state that I took two in the township and one on the boundary between Aubin and Nesbitt. The first I took was at the north-west angle of lot 4, concession 2, on July 14th. I used the method of greatest elongation of Polaris, the azimuth at elongation being 1 degree 50 minutes for north latitude 48 degrees 50 minutes (approx.). My line was correct at this point.

The next point of observation was at the north-west angle of lot 8, concession 4, and was taken on July 31st, my line running about two minutes too far to the east; from this point I corrected tne line running north.

The next point of observation being on the boundary of the two townships and at the north-east angle of lot I concession II, Township of Aubin; the date of this observation was August 20th. I found my line at this point to be running correctly. I cannot give all the details of these observations for the reason that the small note book in which I took them has been misplaced and cannot be found. I always used the method of greatest elongation.

With regard to the opening up and development of this land, I may say that I learned from the Hudson's Bay people, at Fort Mattagami, that the Grand Trunk Pacific survey line crosses the Mattagami River about 40 miles north of this township, and when this line of railway is built, the land will be easy of access, and should become settled very fast, and within the next few years should contain a prosperous community.

I have the honor to be,

Sir,

Your obedient servant,

(Sgd.) E. D. Bolton,

Ontario Land Surveyor.

The Honorable,
    The Minister of Lands, Forests and Mines.
    Toronto.

————

(Appendix No. 45).

Portion of the Boundary Line Between Provinces of Ontario and Quebec, District of Nipissing.

Toronto, Ont., Dec. 29, 1906.

To the Hon. Frank Cochrane, Minister of Lands, Forests and Mines for the Province of Ontario, and the Hon. Adelard Turgeon, Minister of Lands, and Forests for the Province of Quebec.

Sirs,—In accordance with your instructions dated June 14, 1906, to define the portion of the boundary line between the Provinces of Ontario and

Quebec from the intersection of the Okikodosek River in the 88th mile, to O. L. S. Speight's base line, we proceeded on the 13th of July by way of New Liskeard, Ontario. After arranging for our supplies and a full complement of men, a number of the men having been by mutual agreement engaged on the Manitoulin Island, Lake Huron, and the transport of supplies to Klock's farm on Quinze Lake, we started from Klock's on the 23rd, and arrived at Abitibi, Hudson Bay Co.'s. post, Saturday, 28th July, at noon. We remained at the post until Tuesday morning, 31st, having been windbound on Monday.

On account of an epidemic of measles among the Indians at Abitibi, we were unable to procure a guide for the country north of Abitibi Lake. However, after proceeding with the work sometime we engaged for that purpose an Indian named Joe, who lives on Joe Lake, west of the 106th mile.

On the evening of the 31st July, we arrived at the first intersection of the Okikodosek River, our starting point, and after observing the eastern elongation of Polaris, on the same night in order to find the meridian, we proceeded next morning to continue the boundary due north astronomically from the post planted by the Commissioners in 1905, at 87 miles, and 60 chains on the south bank of the said river to the end of the 140th mile, which is 46 chains and 52 links north of the intersection of the said O. L. S. Speight's base line, and which base line we intersected at a point one chain and ninety-three and one-half links east of the 70 mile post, planted by him in 1900 to mark approximately the position of the Inter-provincial boundary.

Having completed the boundary to the end of the 140th mile on the 27th of September, we, after a day spent in repairs to our canoes, commenced our return by way of the Woman River, which stream our canoemen on the way north had found to be a fairly good route, and while travelling we made a track survey of it, also of the Okikodosek River. A portage of about six miles connects the headwaters of the two streams.

On Saturday, the 6th of October, we reached Abitibi post, having been delayed nearly a day by a heavy rain storm. On account of being short of provisions, we did not complete the stadia survey of the lower portion of Okikodosek River. We remained at Abitibi over Sunday, and were obliged to remain in camp there during a severe blizzard which lasted nearly two days. On Wednesday, 10th October, we left Abitibi and reached Klock's farm on Sunday 14th, at noon, a heavy head wind on the previous day, having delayed us considerably. On the evening of the 15th we reached North Temiskamingue village, and on the evening of the 16th arrived at New Liskeard, where we remained until the 20th in paying our men. We might say that through a delay in receiving our cheques when we arrived at New Liskeard, we were obliged to remain over there on Thanksgiving Day, the 18th of October. On the 20th we left New Liskeard, and arrived at our homes a day or two later.

On level ground the bush was cut out three feet on each side of the line, making a total width of six feet. In the rolling and hilly portions a somewhat greater width was cut, in order to gain a clear sight of about 40 to 50 chains. The trees nearest the line were blazed on the north and south sides, also on the side facing the line.

At the end of every mile a post of iron tubing one and seven-eighths inches in diameter, and three feet long, was driven about two feet in the ground, and close to the north side a wooden post 6 inches square, of the most durable timber convenient, was also planted and whenever stones were convenient, a large cairn was built around them. These cairns are shown in the accompanying field notes. On each post was cut on the south side the number of miles in Roman numerals, counting from the head of Lake Temiskaming. On the east side was cut "Que.,", and on the west side "Ont."

With the exception of one or two places where no timber was near, at each mile post two bearing trees were marked "B. T." The course and distance to said trees from the post is shown in the field notes.

At each intersection of the Hannah Bay River a wooden post was planted on the south bank, and marked similarly to the mile posts. Also at the intersection of Speight's base line, an iron post of the above dimensions, also a wooden post, were planted and similarly marked.

The line was produced by alternate sights, with reversals of two Troughton & Simms transits, on a 6 inch limb, the other a 5 inch, to a steel pointed picket on a hub. A tack was then driven in the hub at the mean of the two sights.

All observations for azimuth were taken from an elongation of Polaris by both instruments, and a mean taken.

Observations for latitude by meridian altitudes of the sun were also made.

Each mile was carefully measured with a 66 feet steel tape of standard length. It was then remeasured with a 100 feet steel tape as a check.

All base lines for determining the widths of lakes and rivers were carefully measured twice.

The magnetic variation averaged about ten degrees west of north, and was very steady.

The survey lines of the Transcontinental Railroad were intersected in the 90th, 91st, 92nd and 94th miles.

The line crosses the Okikodosek River frequently to the 98th mile post.

The rock is principally red granite and greenstone. No economic minerals were found. The soil is all good clay, mostly rolling, and suitable for agriculture from the beginning of the season's work to the middle of the 101st mile. Here the hills forming the divide between the Okikodosek and Woman Rivers begin, and continue until the lake on the latter river in the 107th mile is reached. This divide is mostly rolling country with sand and boulders on the hills, and occasional rock exposures with clay and occasional muskegs in the lower levels. The hills are from 20 to 60 feet high. In the 101st mile a ridge running nearly east and west, and about 250 feet high was crossed.

From the lake mentioned in the 107th mile the country is mostly clay, and rises to the 110th mile, where the divide between the Woman and Hannah Bay Rivers is reached. This divide is similar to the one just described, and extends to about the end of the 118th mile, where the line descends to the valley of the Hannah Bay River.

From the 118th to the middle of the 131st mile the country is all good clay land, mostly level, with an occasional elevation from 20 to 40 feet high. A large percentage of this portion is wet, the water being prevented by the moss from draining off. From the 131st mile to the end, the country is nearly level. The elevations are generally not more than six feet. A large percentage of this is also wet land covered with moss. From about the end of the 137th mile to the end, and as far north as could be seen, the country is mostly marshes covered deep with moss, and in places with timber varying from scattered, scrubby spruce to small thickets of the same to about 10 inches in diameter.

The Hannah Bay River was crossed in the 130th and 134th miles, and below its confluence with the Woman and Burnt Bush Rivers, opposite the 132nd mile, is about 8 to 10 chains wide.

The creek on the Ontario side emptying into the Woman River opposite the 124th mile is used by the Indians as a canoe route. The mouth of it appeared to be blocked some with logs when we returned.

In the 136th mile a deep stream, about a chain wide, was crossed. This stream the Indians say is a canoe route to the west.

The Woman River is about 2 chains wide at its mouth up to the falls opposite the 126th mile. Canoeing on it in low water with loads is tedious on account of numerous boulders, otherwise it makes a good canoe route. The portages are mostly short. On account of the shorter portage at the divide it might be preferred to the Hannah Bay River route. The land along it is mostly clay and well timbered. The timber throughout the line consists of black spruce, jack pine, poplar balm of gilead, white birch, and dry tamarac, varying mostly from 6 to 18 inches. In some localities it attained a greater diameter. The poplar would make beautiful wood for cabinet makers, and for floors, as it is white, straight and sound. In a few places along the larger streams large white spruce occurs. The spruce is of the best quality for pulpwood and building timber. The jack pine is mostly fine tall timber, and free of limbs to near the top. With the exception of along the Hannah Bay River very little balsam was seen. From near the end of the 137th mile as mentioned above, the timber, on account of the muskeg and moss, dwindles to scrubby spruce with an occasional small thicket of large spruce. This appears to be the southern limit of the great muskeg.

From about the middle of the 103rd mile to near the lake in the 107th mile, shown in the notes as Lake Billy, also east of this lake and north of it some distance parallel to the line, the country has recently been burned. Along the Woman River in places an older brule is found.

Lots of pickerel and pike were procured by the party, and in the small brooks speckled trout. Along the Hannah Bay River the Indians brought in a few of the large speckled trout.

Very few partridges or rabbits were seen. The Indians who hunt there say that on account of the rain storms last winter the above game when under the snow at night perished under the resulting heavy crust.

There are evidences of moose and deer. We were told a great number of them have been killed in the country recently.

From the falls on the Woman River a considerable amount of power could be developed.

The climate we found to be similar to that of similar latitudes in Ontario and Quebec. On the nights of the 13th and 14th of August, the water froze in our water vessels, but no effect of the frost was seen on the lakes or rivers. We had beautiful ripening weather all the time, with sufficient rain. On the night of the 16th of September we had a considerable frost. On the 6th of October, when we arrived at the Hudson's Bay Company's post at Lake Abitibi, the potatoes and garden flowers were quite green.

Mr. Moberly, one of the engineers in charge on the Transcontinental Railroad survey, gave us some samples of wheat, oats and barley, which he grew at the Whitefish River, a river flowing into the Abitibi Lake, at the north-east corner.

There is no doubt that the country when sufficiently cleared up will be quite free from summer frosts.

We have the honor to be,

Sir,

Your obedient servants,

(Sgd.)　T. J. PATTEN, O.L.S.,
Commissioner for Province of Ontario.

(Sgd.)　J. H. SULLIVAN, P.L.S.,
Commissioner for Province of Quebec.

(Appendix No. 46).

BOUNDARY BETWEEN THE PROVINCES OF ONTARIO AND QUEBEC.

MONTREAL, Feb. 1st, 1906.

SIRS,—The undersigned, Thaddeus J. Patten, Ontario Land Surveyor, for the Province of Ontario, and Francois Charles Laberge, Provincial Land Surveyor for the Province of Quebec, joint commissioners acting under instructions from the Governments of the Provinces of Ontario and Quebec, respectively, have the honor to report as follows:—

That the appointment of T. J. Patten, as commissioner for Ontario, is dated in the month of July, 1905, and that the appointment of F. C. Laberge, as commissioner for Quebec, is also dated in the month of July, 1905, and that the instructions received from Ontario and Quebec are dated the 27th day of July, 1905.

These instructions were for the special object of determining and tracing a part of the boundary line between the two Provinces, from a point known as the 42nd mile, northward from the initial point of that part of the boundary line running from the head of Lake Temiscaming, due north astronomically to James Bay.

The said 42 miles of said line had been determined and traced in 1874, by W. W. O'Dwyer, P.L.S., representing the Province of Quebec, and J. L. P. O'Hanly, O.L.S., representing the Province of Ontario.

According to the Act passed the 12th of August, 1889, by the Parliament of the United Kingdom of Great Britain and Ireland, to define the boundaries of the Province of Ontario, 52 and 53 Victoria, Chap. 28, a line running due north from the head of Lake Temiscaming to James Bay, is one of the boundaries, and it was this said boundary line, 42 miles of which were determined in 1874, as aforesaid, and from the said 42nd mile northward, that was to be determined according to the instructions received by each commissioner.

The documents that were furnished were the following:—

A plan of the boundary line between the Provinces of Ontario and Quebec, prepared by W. W. O'Dwyer, and J. L. P. O'Hanly, boundary commissioners, dated Ottawa, December, 1874.

A plan of a portion of a route from the river Ottawa to Hudson's Bay, signed by Lindsay Russell, dated Ottawa the 16th of March, 1868.

A copy of part of a plan of base line by T. B. Speight, O. L. S., in 1900.

Traverse of part of Upper Lake Abitibi, by T. B. Speight, O. L. S.,
dated Toronto, November 17th, 1900.

After having received the instructions from their respective departments, the two commissioners met in Toronto, on the first day of August,
1905, to examine their respective documents, and to decide all the particulars of the expedition. The expedition assembled at New Liskeard,
Ontario, on the 6th day of August following, and then crossed on the 7th,
to North Temiscaming, where the hiring of men and the final arrangements for the survey were completed.

On the 11th of August, the party left North Temiscaming by canoes
up the Quinze River, but the supplies were carted 15 miles over the road
to Klock's farm, situated on Quinze Lake. From Klock's everything was
transported by the party in canoes, by the Abitibi route to Island Lake,
and from thence up a river into Labyrinth Lake, arriving on Thursday, the
17th day of August, at the southern end of said Labyrinth Lake, near the
prolongation of the boundary line as traced and noted by the two commissioners in 1874, and on the same day proceeded to the monuments at the
Height of Land.

The boundary line, as prolonged by O'Dwyer and O'Hanly to Labyrinth Lake, was easily detected. The opening made in the forest in 1874
being plainly visible, was followed easily to the Height of Land, where the
two stone monuments, shown on the maps provided, were found, and to the
42nd mile boundary stone planted in 1874, where the work was to begin.

On the night of the 17th of August several independent successful astronomical observations were made to determine the direction of the true
meridian, and on Friday, the 18th of August, a start was made from the
said 42nd mile stone monument north astronomically to determine the
boundary line according to instructions.

For plainly marking and permanently designating the said boundary
line, it was determined on the ground by an opening through the forest of
at least 6 feet in width, and the standing trees nearest to the line were
blazed on the north and south sides, and also on the side facing the line.
At every mile an iron post, made of tubing, 3 feet long and one and seven-
eighths inches in diameter, outside measurement, was, where possible, well
driven, and close to the north side of it was also driven a wooden post not
less than six inches in diameter and of the best timber available.

On these posts were well marked the number of miles in Roman numerals,
on the south side, reckoned from the initial point of the line at the
head of Lake Temiscaming. On the east side was marked "Que." and on
the west side "Ont."

At the intersection of the lakes and principal streams a wooden post
was planted marked with the miles in Roman numerals on the south side.
The plus chainage was marked in Arabic and "Ont." and "Que." on the
respective sides.

Where a mile came in a lake or bay, at the intersection of the nearest
shore an iron post was also planted and similarly marked.

In several places, where the clay was very hard, holes were dug about
2 feet and the posts well planted.

Whenever loose rocks were convenient, substantial cairns were built
around the posts; these cairns are indicated in the field notes.

Two bearing trees were marked and noted at every post where it was
possible.

The measurement of the line was carefully made with a 66 ft. steel tape of standard length; a plumb-bob was used by each chainman. The measurement of each mile was carefully checked with a 100 ft. steel tape of standard length, and whenever the measurements differed materially it was remeasured.

All base lines of triangles were carefully measured twice and a mean taken.

The true meridian was determined from astronomical observations on Polaris at its eastern elongation. The azimuth of the star was calculated by different methods and a mean taken.

The bearing of the rear picket on the boundary already determined was read at each observation, and the error was seldom more than 20 seconds, and in several instances, only a few seconds. This is noted in the records of astronomical observations.

An observation for latitude by a meridian altitude of the sun was made at $54\frac{1}{2}$ miles. The result corresponded very closely with that deduced from the latitude given for the Height of Land monuments.

The production of the line was done with a sight and a reversal sight from a transit to a steel picket on a hub. A tack was driven in the hub midway between the two sights. In mountainous country, sights were taken from hill to hill and at times exceeded a mile in length. In such cases the line was accurately defined in the intervening valleys with a transit.

The boundary line was continued across Lake Abitibi, a total distance of nearly 46 miles, to the south bank of the Okikodosek River in the 88th mile. This river empties into the large bay on the north side of Abitibi Lake.

Fearing that the cold weather prevailing at the time might freeze this bay, which is very shallow, operations were discontinued on the 13th day of October, and on the following day the return journey, by way of Abitibi, Hudson's Bay Company's post, was begun, following the Abitibi route to Klock's farm on Quinze Lake, and from there to North Temiscaming and New Liskeard, which latter place was reached on the 23rd of October.

The party, while returning, was delayed by wind and bad weather for more than a day. On the 23rd of October, the party was paid off and they left for their respective homes the following day.

During the course of the survey sketches of lakes were made, and in some instances canoe surveys with magnetic directions, or micrometer surveys, also with magnetic directions, were made of the islands or shores of rivers and lakes situated in the immediate vicinity of the boundary line.

The line as traced on the ground is very plainly visible, and in some places a sky line was cut through the woods to allow of longer sights to be taken.

At station 75 miles plus 47.50 chains, one of the prominent points in Lake Abitibi was merely touched by the line, and for that reason it was named boundary point on the plan.

The timber from the height of land to Labyrinth Lake is principally jack pine up to 12 inches in diameter, and tall and clean, and would make good lumber for some purposes. With it there is some white birch and balsam of good size.

Around Labyrinth Lake there is some large white pine scattered. There is also large white spruce, balsam, cedar and white birch.

From Labyrinth Lake to Abitibi Lake the timber is the same, but includes large poplar and balm of gilead, and in the swamps large black spruce and dry tamarac. Cedar is found around the lakes and streams, and much of it is unsound at the butt. Jack pine is found to 24 inches in diameter and is also clean tall timber. Some large white pines, about 24 inches in diameter, scattered, were found on the 53rd, 55th, 56th and 63rd miles. Near the south shore of Abitibi Lake there are also a few white and red pines.

In some low spots black ash is found. To the east of the 52nd mile there is a fine tract of black and white spruce.

On the large island called Kenosha Obyowa, in the Abitibi Lake, the timber is much smaller. The reason of this, the Indians say, is that about 35 years ago a severe rain storm in the winter deposited so much ice on the trees that the boughs were all destroyed.

None of the country traversed has been burned for a great many years.

The most important character of the soil is that it is constituted for the greater part of clay which is well drained, and therefore after the forest has been cut good farming land will be developed in the valleys.

From the 42nd mile to the 58th mile the country is hilly, and the rock crops out at every hill top in the form of ridges and bluffs of a very broken character.

From the 58th to the 68th mile, although rocky on the hills, the country is less broken and the hills have more gentle slopes. From the 68th mile to Abitibi Lake the line descends into a valley, principally good clay land.

From the north shore of Abitibi Lake to the end of the line the country is principally low land covered with black spruce, with higher land adjoining the streams.

The general direction of the hills is east and west, and they are separated by valleys of from one half mile to one mile in width, and these valleys are connected at intervals by hollows, gulleys or creeks, thus rendering them easily accessible from one to the other.

The waters flowing in the streams and accumulated in the lakes are colored by sediments, the more as Lake Abitibi was approached.

In Lake Labyrinth the water is colored slightly whitish, and only in Trout Lake clear water was found.

The other waters are colored by the clay held in suspension.

The bottom of Lake Abitibi is all clay, and on account of its shallowness the water is always muddy.

The rock that constitutes the hills is mostly a fine grained greenish rock, sometimes passing into diorite.

These rocks belong to the Huronian formation and are very broken.

In a few places quartz veins were visible but no mineral of importance was noticed in them.

The Acipimocasi River, which was crossed in the 61st mile, is a fine stream. It forms a portion of the canoe route from Blanche River to Abitibi Lake, by way of Metawagogig or Upper Lake, into which it empties. The valley of this river contains fine farming land.

Nothing was crossed or seen which might form the Abitibi River which is dotted on the maps.

Labyrinth Lake, Trout Lake and the smaller lakes abound with fish, principally pike, pickerel and bass. In Lake Abitibi the same fish are found, also lake trout and white fish.

Moose and red deer were seen, also bear tracks. There is also an abundance of smaller game.

Accompanying this report are forwarded plan, field notes and account, which bear the same date, Feb. 1st, 1906.

We have the honor to be, .

Sir,

Your obedient servants,

(Sgd.) T. J. PATTEN,

Ontario Land Surveyor.

F. C. LABERGE,

Provincial Land Surveyor.

The Honorable
The Minister of Lands, Forests and Mines,
Toronto.

(*Appendix No. 47.*)

TOWNSHIP OF SCOLLARD, DISTRICT OF NIPISSING.

SAULT STE. MARIE, ONT., Nov. 15th, 1906.

SIR,—I have the honor to transmit the plan and field notes of my survey of the Township of Scollard, in the District of Nipissing, under instructions from your Department, dated nineteenth of June, nineteen hundred and six.

I left Sault Ste. Marie on the 27th day of June and went in by way of Sturgeon Falls, and found the iron post at the south-east corner of the Township of Mason on Monday, July 2nd, and chained north along the east boundary of Mason 50.80 chains to the line between the second and third concessions of the Township of Mason; and after an astronomical observation I ran the line between the first and second concessions of Scollard due east from that point, running the various lines and planting all posts in accordance with instructions.

This township is very level except for the rocky margins of French River, which extend from five to twenty chains inland. There is a large tract of arable land on the central part of the island, the timber, still in a state of nature, being maple, basswood, birch, elm, etc., on a fine clay loam soil. The north-western part is the same as the central part of the island, but a large portion of the township, which includes the rocky part, has been overrun by fire some thirty years ago and is covered with a dense growth of poplar, white birch, balsam, jack pine and alder, the soil being either good clay loam or flat rocky land.

I planted iron posts at the north-east corner of the township and at French River, concession lines 3 and 4 and the north boundary of lots 12 and 13. I found an iron post at the south-east corner of Mason, marked on the north-west side "Mason, Lot I." On the north-east side I marked it "Scollard, Con. I," on the east side "Lot 24." At the north-west corner of the township I found a good well-graded road and the original iron post buried three feet under the ground, so I left it undisturbed and planted a balsam post at the south-east corner of the road allowance, marked on the south side "Scollard, Con. V," on the west side "R," on the north side "R," on the east side "Scollard, Lot 24." At the north-east corner I planted a one and seven-eighths inch iron post marked on the south "Scollard, Con. I," on the west "Lot I." On the north boundary between lots 12 and 13, I planted an iron post one and one-quarter inches on the south side of a wood post marking the line between the Townships of Falconer and Martland, marked on the south "Scollard, Con. V," on the west "Lot 13," on the east "Lot 12." There was an iron post on the north side of the wood post, and where the said line intersects the line between concessions 3 and 4, I planted a one and one-quarter inch iron post, marked on the north "Con. IV, Scollard," on the east "Lot 12," on the south "Con. IV," on the west "Lot 13." I also planted a one and one-quarter inch iron post where this line intersects the main branch of the French River, marked on the north side "Scollard, Con. I," on the east side "Lot 12," and on the west "Lot 13."

Over 50 per cent. of the township is good arable land, partly well timbered with hardwood. The pine was evidently taken off many years ago. I found only one settler, but several clearings along the north branch.

Although there are several small lakes, there seems to be very few streams and water is scarce on the levels. Both the north and main branches of French River are large streams, with large water power facilities.

The rock exposures are gneissoid, common to that district. I found no indication of valuable minerals.

I have the honor to be,
Sir,
Your obedient servant,
(Signed) THOS. BYRNE,
Ontario Land Surveyor.

The Honorable,
The Minister of Lands, Forests and Mines,
Toronto.

———

(Appendix No. 48).

TOWNSHIP OF MOODY, DISTRICT OF NIPISSING.

TORONTO, ONTARIO, December 14th, 1906.

SIR,—I have the honor to report on the survey of the Township of Moody, in the District of Nipissing, performed during the season of nineteen hundred and five, under instructions bearing date May thirty-first, nineteen hundred and five.

The Township of Moody is situate six miles west of Lake Abitibi and two miles north from the Abitibi River. It is bounded on the south by the Township of Knox, surveyed in nineteen hundred and four by Ontario Land Surveyor J. Cozens; on the east by a meridian line run by Ontario Land Surveyor Galbraith in nineteen hundred and four; and on the north by a base line also run in nineteen hundred and four by Ontario Land Surveyor Galbraith.

My instructions were to adopt the north-west angle of the Township of Knox as the starting point of west boundary of Moody, which was to run north astronomically to its intersection with the base line to the north. This direction was followed and the west boundary of Moody was found to intersect the base line two chains eighty-one links west of the iron post planted by Ontario Land Surveyor Galbraith and marked "XXX M." At the intersection of the line a wooden post and a one and seven-eighth inch iron post were planted to mark the north-west angle of the Township of Moody. These posts are marked on the south "Con. VI," on the east "XIII," on the west "I," on the south-west "Wesley," and on the south-east "Moody."

Iron posts one and seven-eighth inches in diameter, and wooden posts six inches square, are planted at each corner of the township. The posts at the south-east angle of Moody are marked on the south "Con. VI," on the north "Con. I," on the west "I," on the south "Knox," and on the west "Moody." The posts at the north-east angle of Moody are marked on the south "Con. VI" and "LIV M-1c. 15 1," on the west "I and XXXVI M-43c. 12 1," and on the south-west "Moody." The posts at the south-west angle af Moody are marked on the south "Con. VI," on the north "Con. I," on the east "XIII," on the west "I," on the south-east "Knox," on the south-west "Rickard," on the north-west "Wesley," and on the north-east "Moody."

One and one-quarter inch iron posts are also planted alongside of the wooden posts on the line in front of concession four at its intersection with the east and west boundaries, and the intersection of the side line between lots seven and eight. The posts at the east boundary are marked on the south "Con. III," on the north "Con. IV," and on the west "I." The posts at the line between lots seven and eight are marked on the south "Con. III," on the north "Con. IV," on the east "VII," and on the west "VIII." The posts at the west boundary are marked on the south "Con. III," on the north "Con. IV," on the west "I," and on the east "XIII." One and one-quarter inch iron posts are also planted alongside the wooden posts on the line between lots seven and eight at its intersection with the north and south boundaries of Moody. The posts on the south boundary are marked on the south "Con. VI," on the north "Con. I," on the west "VIII," and on the east "VII." The posts at the north boundary are marked on the south "Con. VI," on the east "VII," and on the west "VIII."

My instructions were to run the concession lines west astronomically from the mile posts planted on the east boundary of Moody by Ontario Land Surveyor Galbraith. These instructions were carried out. The instructions also directed me to adopt the mile posts planted on the north boundary of Knox by Ontario Land Surveyor Cozens as the starting points for the several side lines in Moody if the measurements were found to be approximately correct. The measurements were found to be correct, and I accordingly adopted Mr. Cozens' posts as the starting points for the side lines between lots three and four, five and six, seven and eight, nine and ten, and eleven and twelve. These side lines are run north astronomically to the intersection of the north boundary of Moody.

The posts on the south boundary at the several side lines had already been marked with concession number "VI" on the south and the lot numbers on the east and west. I marked the concession number "I" on the north side of each post. On the east boundary I marked the mile posts with the concession numbers on the north and south sides, and the lot number "I" on the west side.

Durable posts, generally six inches square, are planted at each of the concession lines at the intersection with the side lines. These posts are all marked with the concession numbers on the north and south sides, and the lot numbers on the east and west sides.

9 J.M.

On the south boundary, and on each of the concession lines, half-mile or intermediate posts are planted at even distances of forty chains west from the side lines, giving the lots adjoining the side lines on the west a width of forty chains, the width of the other lots being governed by the position of the side lines. These half-mile, or intermediate, posts are marked with the concession number on the north side only, and with the lot numbers on the east and west sides. The intermediate posts are not planted on the north boundary, but the mile posts are planted at each of the side lines and marked "Con. VI" on the south, and with the lot numbers on the east and west sides.

Witness trees are marked for each post planted, their class, size, bearing and distance noted, and are given in the field notes.

The Township of Moody may be described as a plain gently sloping to the water courses, which intersect it in every direction.

The general elevation is from sixty to eighty feet above the level of the Abitibi River. In the immediate vicinity of the larger streams the surface is broken by a number of narrow ravines from twenty to fifty feet deep.

The greater portion of the township will require artificial drainage, but the natural facilities are so well developed that the artificial drainage will be a work comparatively of little cost.

The soil is chiefly clay of varying quality, and joining the streams the land is heavy but grows lighter as you recede from the streams. A sandy ridge with scattered boulders runs through the township in a north-westerly direction, extending from lot one in the second concession to lot eight in the sixth concession. This ridge forms water shed between the Dokis and Misto-Ogo Rivers.

Apart from a small area of muskeg to be found principally in concessions one and two, this township is particularly well adapted for agricultural purposes. The land is fertile and durable. The clearing can be quickly done and at little cost. Good roads can be built at a small cost.

The timber is fairly uniform throughout the township with the exception of the sandy ridges before referred to, on which jack pine is found. On the balance of the township the timber is spruce, balsam and birch. On the heavy clay land adjoining the stream is found a considerable stand of poplar from eight to eighteen inches in diameter, but the quality is not of the best, the larger timber being, as a general rule, decayed at the heart. On this heavy clay is also found the largest growth of spruce, a large percentage of the spruce running up to sixteen inches in diameter. Farther back from the stream on the higher land is found balsam and spruce. The balsam is of little value, but the spruce is good. On the next stretch, as the drainage decreases, is found the spruce swamp. The balsam has disappeared but the quality and quantity of spruce improves. On the next stretch, as the drainage fails, moss-covered land develops. The forest has the appearance of a grove, being free from undergrowth. The spruce is uniform in size from six to ten inches in diameter, very tall and free from limbs. This is the invariable rotation of timber in the country.: poplar, spruce and balsam, spruce swamps and spruce groves. The ideal lands for the agriculturist are the balsam lands and spruce swamp, corresponding to the basswood lands and ash and elm swamps of Southern Ontario. Apart from pulpwood there is not a great quantity of merchantable timber, but when a demand for pulpwood arises the unlimited areas of this timber will make the settlers independent of other sources of revenue.

Small fruits, red and black raspberries, gooseberries and red currants of a fine quality grow in great profusion. If the quality and quantity of

9a L. M.

small fruits can be improved by cultivation, an important industry is assured to this section of the country.

At present the country is handicapped with early frosts, but the forest growth, especially the undergrowth, is so thick the rays of the sun never strike the soil. When the country is cleared and drained the latent heat. in the ground will ward off these troublesome frosts.

The township is fairly well watered. Two small lakes were found, one on lot one in concessions two and three, the other on lots two and three in concession four, and lots three and four in concession five. The Dokis River, a slow stream from two to four feet in depth and from thirty to forty feet in width, is found in the north-east corner of the township. In the north-west corner is found the Misto-Ogo River, also a slow stream about fifty feet wide and varying in depth from one to four feet. In the southern part of the township the natural drainage is not good and a considerable amount of muskeg has developed in concessions one and two. There are no water falls or rapids in the township.

Judging from the tracks seen on every hand, I should say that moose and bear are numerous in this section. We surprised a colony of beaver constructing a dam, and were in turn surprised at the marvelous workmanship of these little animals. The dam was about eight feet in height, four feet thick and a hundred feet long. It is constructed of interlaced branches filled in solidly with clay. The top was brought to a true level so that the water passed slowly over the whole surface.

There is no outcrop of rock in this township, and, of course, mineral indications are lacking.

Frequent observations were taken for azimuth and the variation of the magnetic needle found to be fairly constant at about nine degrees forty minutes west of north.

Accompanying are plans, field notes, etc., prepared in accordance with instructions.

I have the honor to be,

Sir,

Your obedient servant,

(Signed) A. J. HALFORD,

Ontario Land Surveyor.

The Honorable,
    The Minister of Lands, Forests and Mines,
        Toronto.

(Appendix No. 49).

TOWNSHIP OF WESLEY, DISTRICT OF NIPISSING.

TORONTO, ONTARIO, December 14th, 1906.

SIR,—I have the honor to report on the survey of the Township of Wesley, in the District of Nipissing, performed during the season of nineteen hundred and five under instructions from the Honorable the Minister of Lands, Forests and Mines.

The Township of Wesley is situate twelve miles west of Lake Abitibi. and two miles north from the Abitibi River. It is bounded on the south by the Township of Rickard, surveyed in nineteen hundred and four by Ontario Land Surveyor J. Cozens, on the east by the Township of Moody, on the north by a base line run by Ontario Land Surveyor William Galbraith in nineteen hundred and four, and on the west by a meridian run by Ontario Land Surveyor Galbraith in nineteen hundred and four.

This survey was made in conjunction with the survey of the Township of Moody. My instructions directed me to continue the concession lines from the Township of Moody west across Wesley if these concessions were found approximately correct at the west boundary of Moody. The lines in front of the second, third, fourth and sixth concessions were found to be approximately correct and were continued west across the Township of Wesley. The line in front of the fifth concession was found to have varied to the north, leaving concession four two chains sixty links too long. I measured from the front of the fourth concession and gave concession four a depth of eighty chains and ran the line in front of concession five due west from this point.

The instructions directed that I was to accept the mile posts planted by Ontario Land Surveyor Cozens on the north boundary of the Township of Rickard, if his measurements were found to be approximately correct. I found the measurements correct and accordingly adopted his mile posts as the starting points for the several side lines in the Township of Wesley. These side lines are run due north between lots two and three, four and five, six and seven, eight and nine, and between ten and eleven.

The four corners of the township are marked with iron posts one and seven-eighths inches in diameter and wooden posts six inches square. These posts are marked as follows:—At the south-east angle of Wesley the posts are marked on the south "Con. VI," on the north "Con. I," on the east "XIII," on the west "I," on the north-east "Moody," on the south-east "Knox," on the south-west "Rickard," and on the north-west "Wesley." At the north-east angle of Wesley the posts are marked on the east "XIII," on the west "I," on the south "Con. VI," on the south-east "Moody, and on the south-west "Wesley." At the south-west angle of the Township of Wesley the posts are marked on the south "Con. VI, on the north "Con. I," on the east "XII," on the south-east "Rickard," and on the north-east "Wesley." This post is five chains two links north of the south boundary of Edwards. At the north-west angle of Wesley the posts are marked on the south "XII M 4c 11 l," and "Con. VI," on the west "XXIV M 3c," on the east "XII," on the north-west "Mortimer," on the south-west "Edwards," and on the south-east "Wesley."

One and one-quarter inch iron posts are planted on the line in front concession four at the east boundary of Wesley, at the line between lots six and seven and at the west boundary of Wesley. The posts at the east boundary are marked on the south "Con. III," on the north "Con. IV," on the east "XIII," and on the west "I." The posts at the line between lots six and seven are marked on the south "Con. III," on the north "Con. IV," on the east "VI," and on the west "VII." At the west boundary the posts are marked on the south "Con. III," on the north "Con. IV," and on the east "XII."

One and one-quarter inch iron posts are also planted alongside the wooden posts on the side line between lots six and seven at its intersection with the north and south boundaries of Wesley. The posts at the south boundary are marked on the south "Con. VI," on the north "Con. I," on the east "VI," and on the west "VII." The posts on the north boundary are marked on the south "Con. VI," on the east "VI," and on the west "VII."

Durable wooden posts are planted on each of the concession lines at the intersection with each side line. These posts are marked with the concession numbers on the north and south sides and with the lot numbers on the east and west sides.

Wooden posts called half mile or intermediate posts are also planted on the south boundary and each of the concession lines. These posts are planted at even distances of forty chains west from the mile posts. This gives the uneven numbered lots an even width of forty chains, the widths of the other lots being governed by the position of the several side lines. These intermediate or half mile posts are marked with the concession number on the north side only. They are also marked with the lot numbers on the east and west sides.

On the north boundary the half mile posts are not planted, but the mile posts are planted at the intersection of the several side lines. These mile posts are marked with the concession number "VI" on the south and the lot numbers on the east and west sides.

Witness trees are marked for each post and their class, size, bearing and distance noted.

This township may properly be described as an elevated plain considerably cut up with deep narrow ravines. The general elevation I should judge is about sixty feet above the Abitibi River. Natural water courses are numerous and well distributed, furnishing a splendid natural drainage system. As the township is all so flat as to require drainage, these natural facilities are of particular value. The land throughout is clay of varying quality. In the immediate vicinity of the streams the clay is very heavy but the soil becomes lighter as you recede from the streams. What we class as balsam land and spruce swamps, corresponding to our basswood lands and ash swamps of Old Ontario, will prove to be highly productive and durable farm lands.

The timber, apart from the pulpwood, is of small commercial value. On the heavy clay near the streams is found a considerable stand of poplar from eight to eighteen inches in diameter. On this high land is also found spruce of a fair size, that is, large enough for saw logs. Further back from the streams balsam takes the place of poplar and the spruce retains its size from six to sixteen inches in diameter. Further down the slope we encounter the spruce swamp, the balsam has disappeared and dead tamarac replaces it. As the natural drainage fails, moss covered land appears. The only timber found is spruce, uniform in size from six to ten inches in diameter, long and clear. The forest has the appearance of a grove. This is the invariable rotation of timber as you cross the drainage basin. There is an abundance of timber for building purposes. The quantity of merchantable timber is limited, but when a demand for pulpwood arises the unlimited areas of first class timber for this purpose will make the settlers independent of other sources of revenue.

The quality of timber is uniform throughout the township with the exception of a narrow strip of burnt country, extending across the township in a north-westerly direction from lot two in the first concession to west boundary at the rear of concession four and front of concession six. From the size of the second growth timber I should say the burning took place twenty-five years ago. This new growth of timber is particularly dense. It is practically impossible to make way through it without cutting out a passage. The undergrowth of alder is very heavy throughout, the spruce groves excepted.

Although there are no lakes, the township is fairly well watered, the Misto-Ogo River on the east and a large creek on the west furnishing water the year round. Apart from these, the water courses nearly all dry up in the dry season. Through concessions one, two and three the Misto-Ogo River is from a chain to a chain and a half in width, varying in depth from two to six feet. Above concession three it is not navigable for canoes in the dry seasons. The width is about one chain. The creek on the west is from twenty to forty feet in width and from one to two feet in depth. It is not navigable for canoes.

Small fruits, red and black raspberries, gooseberries and red currants grow in great profusion. Judging from the quantity and quality of the wild growth, we may predict an important industry for this country in the cultivation of small fruits.

The only water fall or rapid found in the township is the Misto-Ogo Falls on lot eight, in concession one. This fall has a height of ten feet six inches. The volume of water is so limited in the dry season that the fall is of no commercial value.

The only outcrop of rock encountered is in the immediate vicinity of the Misto-Ogo Falls. It is needless to say that mineral indications are lacking.

Moose and bear tracks are seen on every hand but only two moose were seen during the survey. We had a good view of two timber wolves in pursuit of a moose, cow and calf. A beaver dam in the course of construction was quite a curiosity, but the animals kept out of sight.

Observations for azimuth were taken at frequent intervals. The magnetic variation was found to be fairly constant at about nine degrees and forty minutes west of north.

The area of the township is twenty-three thousand and nine acres. Apart from the streams, there is no water surface to deduct.

I have the honor to be,

Sir,

Your obedient servant,

(Sgd.) A. J. HALFORD,

Ontario Land Surveyor.

The Honorable
    The Minister of Lands, Forests and Mines,
        Toronto.

(Appendix No. 50).

TOWNSHIP OF MARATHON, DISTRICT OF NIPISSING.

WINDSOR, ONT., Dec. 29th, 1906.

SIR,—In compliance with instructions received from your Department, dated May 15th, 1906, I have completed the survey of the Township of Marathon, in the District of Nipissing.

I left Windsor on the morning of June 27th, 1906, via Canadian Pacific Railway and arrived at New Liskeard in the afternoon of June 28th, where I completed my supplies and engaged what men I needed to complete my party, the same evening. I left New Liskeard for Boston June 29th, where I arrived that night. Here I calked my old canoes, fitted out my men and got a work train at noon to take me as far as the end of Steel, at the White River. Thence I travelled by canoes through the White River, Kenogami

Lake, Sucker Creek, White Clay River, Twin Lakes, Black River, Abitibi River and Misto-Ogo River to where the last mentioned river crosses the line between lots numbers 2 and 3, in the fifth concession of the Township of Wesley. Thence I portaged along the last mentioned line to the north boundary of the Township of Wesley, which is also the south boundary of the Township of Sherring, where I arrived on the night of July 13th, and after arranging for my cache and getting my packers, started to move my goods from the river to the cache. I started work on the survey proper on the morning of July 14th.

In surveying this township, I commenced all side lines from the mile posts planted by O. L. S. Galbraith on the south boundary, which posts I found to agree almost exactly with my own chaining, and ran the lines due north from these posts. The lines between concessions 1 and 2, 2 and 3, and 3 and 4, I commenced from posts planted by myself on the boundary line between the Townships of Marathon and Sherring, and ran them due east. The lines between concessions 4 and 5, 5 and 6 and the north boundary I commenced from posts planted by myself on the east boundary of the township and ran them due west. I made a stadia traverse of all the small lakes I saw in this township, and tied on said traverses to principal triangle wherever said lakes were crossed by a line.

Where I commenced my survey at the south-west corner of Marathon I found a one and seventh-eigth inch iron post marked "XXX M" on the west side, and I marked it "Marathon" on north-east, "Con. I" on north, "XIII" on east, "I" on west. This post was set beside a six-inch spruce post marked similarly. Where I commenced my line between lots numbers 7 and 8, I found a one and one-quarter inch post marked "XXXIII M" on west side, and I marked it "VII" on east, "Con. I" on north, "VIII" on west. This post was set beside a six-inch spruce marked similarly.

Where I commenced the east boundary of the township I found a one and seven-eighth inch iron post marked "XXXVI M" plus 43.12 on west, "Galna" on south-east, "Moody" on south-west (LIV M-1.15 Con. VI on south), "XII" on east, "I" on west, and I marked it concession "I" on north, "Marathon" on north-west, "I" on west. This post is set beside a six-inch spruce post marked similarly.

Where the east boundary intersects the line between concessions 3 and 4 I planted a one and one-quarter inch iron post marked "Con. III" on south, "Con. IV" on north, "I" on west. This post was set beside a six-inch spruce post marked similarly.

At the north-east corner of the township I planted a one and seven-eighth inch post marked "Con. VI" on south, "Marathon" on south-west, "I" on west. This post was set beside a five and one-half inch spruce post marked similarly.

Where the line between lots 7 and 8 intersects the line between concessions 3 and 4, I planted a one and one-quarter inch iron post marked "Con. III" on the south, "VII" on east, "Con. IV" on north, "VIII" on west. This post was set beside a six-inch spruce post marked similarly.

Where the line between concessions 3 and 4 intersects the west boundary, I planted a one and one-quarter inch iron post marked "Con. III" on south, "XIII" on east, "Con. IV" on north, and "I" on west. This post was set beside a five-inch spruce post marked similarly.

Where the line between lots 7 and 8 intersects the north boundary, I planted a one and one-quarter inch iron post marked "Con. VI" on south, "VII on east, "VIII" on west. This post was set beside a six-inch spruce post marked similarly.

At the north-west corner of the township I planted a one and seven-eighth inch iron post marked "XIII" on east, "Marathon" on south-east, "Con. VI" on south, "I" on west, "Sherring" on southwest. This post was set beside a six-inch spruce post marked similarly.

All of these iron posts were three feet long, forged at the top, pointed at the bottom and painted red.

Generally speaking the soil of this township is a fertile clay loam with here and there a small cranberry marsh or swamp, sometimes called muskeg, but I think improperly so. There is a small jack pine ridge running through the township in lots 7 and 8, and as a consequence this is the roughest and most broken of any line in the township.

Spruce, white poplar, dead tamarac, birch, balm, jack pine and balsam constitute the forest of the township. The spruce and white poplar are good, clear timber varying from 4 to 24 inches in diameter, of a good quality. The tamarac is nearly all dead. The remaining timbers are not so plentiful and are much smaller.

I did not observe an outcropping of rock in the whole township, although there are quite a lot of boulders in lots 7 and 8, concessions 2 and 3. Hence I did not observe any economic minerals.

As will be seen by the accompanying plan, the Dokis River flows southerly close to the east boundary of the township. The Misto-Ogo River cuts off the south-westerly part, and a creek (which empties into the Low Bush River), cuts off the north-east corner. These main streams, together with the numerous small creeks and water courses, will afford good drainage to the land when it becomes settled and used for agricultural purposes.

Of the larger game, signs of moose and bear were quite plentiful. Rabbits and partridges are fairly numerous, and mink is found along all the streams.

There does not appear to be any fish in the rivers.

The climate during our stay was fine. The rainfall was very small. Light frost was noted on the nights of July 30th and August 13th, the only frosts we had while in the township.

All of which is respectfully submitted.

I have the honor to be,
Sir,
Your obedient servant,
(Signed) J. J. NEWMAN,
Ontario Land Surveyor.

The Honorable,
The Minister of Lands, Forests and Mines,
Toronto.

(Appendix No. 51).

TOWNSHIP OF SHERRING, DISTRICT OF NIPISSING.

WINDSOR. ONT., Dec. 29th, 1906.

SIR,—In compliance with instructions received from your Department dated May 15th, 1906, I have completed the survey of the Township of Sherring, in the District of Nipissing.

The route taken to reach this township is fully set forth in my report of the survey of the Township of Marathon, which bears even date with this.

In surveying this township, I commenced all side lines from the mile posts planted by O. L. S. Galbraith on the south boundary, which posts I found to agree almost exactly with my own chaining, and ran the lines due north from these posts. I ran all the concession lines west from posts planted by me on the boundary line between this township and the Township of Marathon, continuing the concession lines of the latter township, thus there is only one set of posts on the said boundary line.

There were no lakes or large rivers to traverse.

At the south-east corner of this township, which is also the south-west corner of the Township of Marathon, I found a one and seven-eighths inch iron post, which is fully described in my report on the survey of Marathon.

Where the line between concessions 3 and 4 intersects the east boundary of the township, I planted a one and one-quarter inch iron post, which is fully described in my report on the survey of Marathon.

At the north-east corner of the township I found a one and seven-eighths inch iron post marked "Con. I" on north, "Sweatmen" on north-west, "I" on west, and I marked it "Con. VI" on south, "Sherring" on south-west, set beside a six-inch spruce post marked similarly.

Where the line between lots 6 and 7 intersects the south boundary I found a one and one-quarter inch iron post marked "XXVII M" on the west, and I marked it "VI" on east, "Con. I" on north, "VII" on west, set beside a six-inch spruce post marked similarly.

Where the line between lots 6 and 7 intersects the line between concessions 3 and 4, I planted a one and one-quarter inch iron post marked "Con. III" on south, "VI" on east, "Con. IV" on north, "VII" on west, set beside a five-inch spruce post marked similarly.

Where the line between lots 6 and 7 intersects the north boundary I planted a one and one-quarter inch iron post marked "Con. VI" on south, "VI" on east, "VII" on west, set beside a six-inch spruce post marked similarly.

At the south-west corner of the township I found a one and seven-eighths inch iron post marked "Wesley" on the south-east, "XII M plus 14.11 Con. VI" on south, "Edwards" on south-west, "XXIV M-3c., I" on west, "Mortimer" on north-west, "Con. I" on north, and I marked "Sherring" on north-east. set beside a six-inch spruce post marked similarly.

Where the line between concessions 3 and 4 intersects the west boundary I planted a one and one-quarter inch iron post marked "Con. III" on south, "XII" on east, "Con. IV" on north, set beside a five-inch spruce post marked similarly.

At the north-west corner of the township I found a one and seven-eighths inch iron post marked "XVIII M Con. VI" on south, "Mortimer" on south-west, "I" on west, "Stimson" on north-west, "Con. I" on north, "Sweatman" on north-east, "XII" on east, and I marked "Sherring" on south-east. This post was set beside a six-inch spruce post marked similarly.

All of these iron posts were three feet long, forged at the top, pointed at the bottom and painted red.

Generally speaking, the soil of this township is a fertile clay loam with a few cranberry marshes or swamps in the west and north-west parts. These cranberry marshes are sometimes called "muskegs," but I think improperly so.

Spruce, white poplar, dead tamarac, birch, balsam, jack pine and balm constitute the forest of the township. The spruce and white poplar are good clear timber, varying from 4 to 24 inches in diameter, of a good quality. The tamarac is nearly all dead. The remaining timbers are not so plentiful and are much smaller.

I did not observe an outcropping of rock in the whole township, hence I have nothing to report in the way of economic minerals.

As will be seen by the accompanying plan, the Misto-Ogo River enters the township from the north by two branches, both in lot number 6. These two branches join before crossing the line between concessions 5 and 6 in lot 5, and then the said river takes a general southerly or south-easterly direction until it crosses the east boundary in the first concession. There is also another quite large creek flowing southerly through the 5th, 4th, 3rd, 2nd and 1st concessions, generally speaking in lots 10 and 11. These two main creeks, with numerous small creeks and water courses, will form good drainage for the land when it becomes cleared up and tilled.

Of the larger game, signs of moose and bear are quite plentiful. Rabbits and partridges are fairly numerous and mink is found along all the streams. There does not appear to be any fish in the rivers.

The climate during our stay was fine. The rainfall was quite small. A few light frosts were noted before we finished the survey on September 15th.

All of which is respectfully submitted.

I have the honor to be,

Sir,

Your obedient servant,

(Signed)   J. J. NEWMAN,

Ontario Land Surveyor.

The Honorable,
The Minister of Lands, Forests and Mines,
Toronto.

(*Appendix No. 52.*)

TOWNSHIP OF SWEATMAN, DISTRICT OF NIPISSING.

NEW LISKEARD, Ont., Dec. 14, 1906.

SIR,—I beg to submit the following report on the survey of the Township of Sweatman, District of Nipissing, and Province of Ontario, in accordance with instructions dated the twenty-fifth day of May, nineteen hundred and six.

The Township of Sweatman is bounded on the west by the Township of Stimson, the survey of which formed a part of the instructions referred to, on the south by the Township of Sherring, on the east and north by unsurveyed Crown lands.

The survey of the township was commenced in the beginning of August after the completion of the survey of the Township of Stimson. The south boundary being run east from the eighteenth mile post on Ontario Land Surveyor Galbraith's meridian line run in 1904. This boundary was produced eastward until it intersected the production of the westerly boundary of the Township of Marathon, as run by Ontario Land Surveyor Newman in 1906.

Mile posts were planted on the south boundary of the township as thus run, eighty chains apart, the last mile being a distance of seventy-eight chains and eighty-four links to the point of intersection referred to. From these mile posts side lines were run north. Posts were also planted on the south boundary at the end of forty chains in each mile, to mark off the width of the lots not otherwise marked by the mile posts.

The east boundary of the township was run north astronomically from the easterly end of the south boundary (which is the point of intersection referred to above and which is also at the north-west angle of the Township of Marathon) until it intersected the north boundary which was run due east astronomically from the termination of Ontario Land Surveyor Speight's base line run in 1904. The concession lines in the township were run east from the mile posts planted by Ontario Land Surveyor Galbraith on his meridian line run in 1904.

On the iron post one and seven-eighths inches in diameter at the south-west angle of the township was marked "Sweatman" on the north-east, "Con. I" on the north and "XII" on the east. On a similar iron post at the north-west angle of the township was marked "Sweatman" on the south-east, "Con. VI" on the south and "XII" on the east. Wooden posts were found along with the iron posts and were properly marked in each case. An iron post one and seven-eighths inches in diameter marked "Sweatman" on the north-west, "Con. I" on the north and "I" on the west, was planted along with a wooden post similarly marked at the south-east angle of the township, a similar iron post marked "Sweatman" on the north-west, "Con. VI" on the south and "I" on the west, was planted along with a wooden post similarly marked at the north-east angle of the township. An iron post one and one-quarter inches in diameter, along with a wooden post, was planted at the intersection of the line between concessions three and four with the west boundary and was marked "Con. IV" on the north, "Con. III" on the south, and "XII" on the east. One and one-quarter inch iron posts properly marked were planted along with wooden posts at the intersection of the line between concessions three and four with the east boundary; also at the intersection of the line between concessions three and four between lots six and seven; also at the intersection of the line between lots six and seven with north and south boundaries of the township. Wooden posts of the most durable material that could be found were planted at the intersection of the concession lines and side lines throughout the township, and were marked on the north and south sides for the numbers of the concessions, and on the east and west sides for the numbers of the lots. The wooden posts planted at the centre of the mile blocks on the concession lines were marked on the north side for the number of the concession, and on the east and west sides for the number of the lots.

Observations on Polaris at elongation were taken whenever convenient, for the purpose of ascertaining and correcting the course and direction of the various lines being run throughout the township. The variation of the magnetic needle was found to be nine degrees and thirty minutes.

General Features.

The township is situated in the great clay belt of the north, as shown by the accompanying maps. Large creeks flow through the township, being tributaries of the Misto-o-go River. In nearly all cases the valleys of these creeks are deep, with wide ravines adjacent to them, and for a considerable distance back on either side the country is much broken by smaller ravines, many of them containing smaller creeks flowing into larger ones. Stretches of muskeg were found scattered throughout the township, not more than ten per cent. of the whole township being muskeg, and most of this can be drained without much difficulty, as the surface is slightly rolling.

Soil.

A small area of very sandy soil was found in the north-easterly part of the township, which would be of little use for agricultural land. In lot one, concessions two and three, a very steep hill of loose boulders was met with, a little very sandy soil was found on the top, the rest of the hill being entirely boulders of granite rock. In the balance of the township the soil is clay and sandy loam, and most of it is good agricultural land and would require little or no drainage, as the surplus water is easily carried off in the many ravines and small creeks which abound in the country.

Timber.

The township was fairly well timbered throughout, spruce being most prevalent along the banks and slopes of the creeks and ravines; large white spruce were plentiful as well as balsam, poplar, whitewood, balm of gilead and a few white birch. Adjacent to the creeks and ravines the timber was generally large and would be good for building material and lumbering in general. In the south and south-easterly part of the township quite a large area of land was found covered with a thick growth of small balsam and white birch. In the north-easterly part of the township, on the sandy soil already referred to, a thick growth of small spruce and jack pine was encountered. About eighty per cent. of the township was found to be covered with a thick growth of tag-alder and other shrubbery which made our work extremely laborious and slow.

About August 1st, 1906, nearly all of the westerly side of the township was burned over by the fire which swept over it from the south. and is already referred to in the report of the Township of Stimson. Most of the north-easterly part of the township was burnt over in 1906 by a fire which apparently originated in concession three, in lot one or two, and the greater part of concessions four, five and six, in lots one and two, were burnt over.

A number of our party were cut off by this fire from camp while at work, and narrowly escaped with their lives. Brule two or three years old was also met with in lots three and four in concessions three and four.

Water.

As will be seen from the many large and small streams of water on the map accompanying this report, the township is well watered throughout. The water was all found to be very good, many of the creeks and lakes being fed by springs containing clear cold water. The small lake on the line between concessions two and three in lot one might be especially mentioned, as many springs were noticed discharging into it, as well as two spring creeks. The water in all the lakes in the easterly part of the township is especially good, being practically all spring water.

No water powers or economic minerals were met with throughout the whole township.

Fruits.

Wild fruits are very scarce, high and low bush cranberries being the most common.

Game.

Game seemed quite plentiful, though seldom seen; of the larger animals moose, cariboo and bear seemed the most common. Fresh beaver works were plentiful everywhere on the creeks. Creeks and lakes were not large enough to contain many fish. Partridge, mink and marten also seemed to be plentiful.

Survey of the Grand Trunk Pacific Railway Line.

The survey of the Grand Trunk Pacific Raiway line runs through the township, the most probable route being across the south-west corner of the township.

Lake Traverse.

The lakes were traversed by means of a carefully adjusted stadia in the Watt's Transits. This method was also used to obtain or check the distances across some of the lakes along the surveyed lines and was found to be very satisfactory when checked with triangulations.

I have the honor to be,

Sir,

Your obedient servant,

(Sgd.) Jas. H. Smith,

Ontario Land Surveyor.

The Honorable
    The Minister of Lands, Forests and Mines,
        Toronto.

(Appendix No. 53.)

Township of Stimson, District of Nipissing.

New Liskeard, Dec. 17th, 1906.

Sir,—I beg to submit the following report on the survey of the Township of Stimson, in the District of Nipissing, in accordance with instructions dated the 25th day of May, A.D. nineteen hundred and six.

The Township of Stimson is bounded on the west by the Township of Fox, on the south by the Township of Mortimer, on the east by the Township of Sweatman, and on the north by the unsurveyed lands of the Crown.

According to instructions, the side lines were run due north starting at the south boundary, lot number twelve being made thirty-six chains and eighty links; the other lots being respectively forty chains, with the exception of lot number two, which was found to be thirty-nine chains and fifty-four links.

By permission from the Department, the concession lines were commenced at the west boundary and run east; the width of the concessions being eighty chains with the exception of concession number six, which was found to be seventy-nine chains and six links.

On the iron post one and seven-eights inches in diameter at the south-west angle of the township, was marked "Stimson" on the north-east, "Con.

I" on the north and "12" on the east. A similar iron post at the north-west angle was marked "Stimson" on the south-east, "Con. VI" on the south and "12" on the east. Corresponding iron posts at the south-east angle and north-east angle of the township were marked respectively "Stimson" on the north-west, "Con. I" on the north, "I" on the west, "Stimson" on the south-west, "Con. VI" on the south and "I" on the west. In each case wooden posts were similarly marked and planted. One and one-quarter inch posts properly marked were planted along with wooden posts at the intersection of the north and south boundaries of the township with the line between lots six and seven; also at the intersection of the east and west boundaries of the township with the line between concessions three and four; also at the intersection of the line between concessions three and four with the line between lots six and seven.

Wooden posts of the most durable material that could be obtained were planted at the intersections of the side lines and concession lines throughout the township, and properly marked on the north and south sides for the concessions and on the east and west sides for the adjoining lots. The wooden posts planted at the centre of the mile blocks were marked on the east and west sides for the number of the lots, and on the north side only for the number of the concession.

Observations were taken on Polaris at elongation whenever convenient during the progress of the work for the purpose of ascertaining and correcting the course and direction of the lines being run; details of these observations will be found along with the regular field notes. The magnetic variation throughout the township was found to be nine degrees and thirty minutes.

General Features.

The Township of Stimson is situated in the great northern clay belt. About thirty per cent. of the land was found to be muskeg, some of it being sufficiently undulating to enable proper drainage. About four per cent. of the township was sandy jack pine ridges. This was met with chiefly in the north-eastern part of the township in the region of the lakes. The remainder of the township was found to be mostly good agricultural land, the soil being clay and sandy loam. Rock of any kind was only met with in one place in the township, viz., in lot number one, on the line between concessions three and four. This rock was of granite formation with a considerable quantity of mica. It is quite probable that this rock will be utilized by the Grand Trunk Pacific Railway for building bridge abutments.

Timber.

The township was found to be timbered throughout, about seventy per cent. of the timber being spruce, averaging from four to seven inches in diameter. Some large white spruce was found on the banks of the larger creeks. In all parts of the township the timber is sufficient for the settler's needs in the way of fuel and building material. Balsam, poplar, tamarac, a few white birch and jack pine were the other kinds of timber found in the township; the jack pine being found wholly in the north and north-eastern part in the region of the lakes. White or red pine was not found in the township at all.

Water.

The township is well watered by large and small streams shown on the map accompanying this report. In some of these streams there is considerable current, while in others it is quite sluggish. The water was generally good, but especially so in the eastern and north-eastern part of the township; the lakes in this region being mostly fed by springs and spring creeks issuing from the adjacent sandy ridges. A number of large and small lakes were met with which are also shown on the accompanying maps.

No water powers or economic minerals of importance were found in the township.

In July a bush fire originated on the east side of the shore of the lake on the south boundary of the township. An unknown party had been camped there previous to that time. The fire continued with more or less vigor for several days, burning a strip of about three-quarters of a mile in width through concessions one and two. On the first of August the smoke of a bush fire was noticed away to the south of the township. The next day a strong wind was blowing from the south. Shortly after noon the fire was seen to be advancing with great rapidity, sweeping along the east boundary of the Township of Stimson. A strip about a mile and one-half in width, partly in Stimson and partly in Sweatman, was burnt over from one side of the township to the other. A number of our men were cut off by this fire and prevented from returning to camp until the next day. If the wind had shifted to the westward their chance of escape would have been small, as they were on the east side of the fire area.

Summer frosts were experienced several times, but not severe enough to do serious damage.

Fruits.

Wild fruits were very scarce, high bush cranberries being the most plentiful.

Game.

Evidences of moose, caribou, bear and otter were plentiful though the animals were seldom seen. Of the smaller animals the beaver seems to be the most plentiful. A large number of beaver works of recent construction were encountered and plenty of evidence to show that the beavers were still present were seen. Partridges were quite plentiful.

Lake Traverse.

The lakes are traversed by means of carefully adjusted Stadia in the Watt's Transits; this method was also used to obtain or check the distances across some of the lakes along the surveyed lines, and was found to be very satisfactory when checked with triangulations.

Grand Trunk Pacific Survey.

The survey of the Grand Trunk Pacific Railway line runs through the township. The most probable location of the line is shown on the map accompanying this report. When noticeable, the other preliminary lines were noted on the field notes.

I have the honor to be,
Sir,
Your obedient servant,
(Sgd.) JAMES H. SMITH,
Ontario Land Surveyor.

The Honorable
The Minister of Lands, Forests and Mines,
Toronto.

(Appendix No. 54).

TOWNSHIP OF ALLEN, DISTRICT OF NIPISSING.

SUDBURY, ONT., Dec. 18, 1906.

SIR,—I have the honor to submit the following report of the survey of the Township of Allen, in the District of Nipissing, performed under instructions, dated May the twenty-ninth, nineteen hundred and six.

I proceeded to the work by way of Lake Nipissing, Monnetteville, and Cosby Road to the north branch of the French River. At this point we took canoes and went to the Wahnapitae River. This river being filled with logs prevented my going in by all river route from Wahnapitae Village. The survey was commenced at the south-westerly angle of the Township of Cox as per instructions, the post planted by O. L. S. McAree at this point being found. No iron post as described in the notes sent to me being found at this point.

The west boundary of the township was then run south astronomically from this post to the north shore of the north branch of the Wahnapitae River. The east boundary of the township was run south astronomically from a point in the southerly limit of the Township of Cox, six miles measured easterly from the south-westerly angle of the said Township of Cox. The east boundary was run south astronomically to the northerly shore of the main French River, making the depth of the concessions eighty chains, except the First, Second and Third. The concession lines were run due east and west astronomically, and the side lines were run north and south astronomically.

Owing to the French River being closer to the Township of Cox than supposed, concession I had to be left out, except across lots 1 and 2.

Iron posts one and seven-eighths inches in diameter, three feet long, painted red, forged at the top to shed the rain, and pointed at the bottom were planted at the following places:—1st. At the intersection of the west boundary with the north shore of the north branch of the Wahnapitae River. This post was marked with a cold chisel on the north-east side "Allen," on the north side "Con. IV," on the east side "XII." A cedar post was planted alongside and similarly marked except for the word "Allen."

2nd. At the north-east angle of the township, and marked on the south-east side "Allen," on the south-east side "Bigwood," on the north side "Cox," on the south side "Con. VII and Con. VI," on the west side "I," on the east side "XIV." Wooden posts were planted alongside and similarly marked except for the words "Allen," "Bigwood" and "Cox." A substantial stone mound was built around each of the three posts.

3rd. At the intersection of the east boundary with the northerly shore of the Main French River, and marked on the north-west side "Allen," on the north-east side "Bigwood," on the north side "Con. I," on the east side "XIV," on the west side "I." A cedar post was planted alongside and similarly marked except for the words "Allen" and "Bigwood." A stone mound was placed around each of these posts.

Iron posts one and one-quarter inches in diameter and three feet long, painted red, forged at the top to shed the rain and pointed at the bottom were planted at the following places:

1st. At the intersection of side line six and seven with the north boundary of the township and marked with a cold chisel, on the south side "Con. VII," on the east side "VI," on the west side "VII." A wooden post marked similarly was placed alongside, and both mounded with stones.

2nd. At the intersection of side line six and seven with the line between concessions three and four, and marked on the north side "Con. IV," on the south side "Con. III," on the east side "VI," on the west side "VII." A wooden post similarly marked was placed alongside and both mounded with stones.

3rd. At the intersection of side line six and seven with the northerly shore of the Main French River and marked on the north side "Con. II," on the east side "VI," on the west side "VII." A wooden post similarly marked was placed alongside and both mounded with stones.

4th. At the intersection of the line between concessions three and four with the east boundary of the township, and marked on the north side "Con. IV," on the south side "Con. III," on the west side "I." A wooden post similarly marked was placed alongside, and both mounded with stones.

5th. At the intersection of the line between concessions three and four with the easterly shore of Wahnapitae Bay and marked on the north side "Con. IV," on the south side "Con. III," on the east side "X." A wooden post similarly marked was placed alongside and both mounded with stones.

The lines were all clear transit lines well opened out and blazed. Substantial posts of the most durable woods obtainable were placed and carefully mounded with stones where possible. Owing to the small class of timber, very few bearing trees could be marked.

Concession I, part of concession II, and part of concession IV being broken fronted on the French River, Wahnapitae Bay, and the Little Wahnapitae River, posts were planted at the proper places on the shore line for the lines between lots one and two, three and four, five and six, seven and eight, nine and ten, and eleven and twelve, in each case making the odd numbered lot forty chains in width.

After the lines were completed in this township and the Township of Bigwood, I commenced the traverse of the lakes, bays, rivers, and islands. A Lugeol Micrometer and transit were used on this work.

General Features of the Township.

The township as a whole is level except where broken by water, but the surface is very rough and broken by low, narrow rocky ridges. The average level of the land is about fifty feet above Georgian Bay. The rocky ridges run about N. 25 degrees E., are flat on the easterly side and precipitous on the west, and are no doubt due to ancient glacial action. The Main French River, which has an average width of about six chains, runs almost due west, and has rocky shores throughout this township.

Geology.

The only rock found in the township is Laurentian Gneiss of various colors, but usually greyish or reddish.

Soil.

The township as a whole is rocky with very small areas of land between the ridges. The soil in these patches is clay. There are no large areas of clay land in the township suitable for agricultural purposes. A few small areas of clay land occur between Wahnapitae Bay and Wahnapitae River, and to the west of the Wahnapitae River.

10 L.M.

Timber.

That portion of the township north of Hartley's Bay and Wahnapitae Bay is sparsely timbered with small jack pine, birch and poplar. The jack pine occurs on the rocky ridges, and the birch and poplar between the ridges. Large portions of that part of the township lying north of Hartley's Bay and east of Wahnapitae Bay were burned this summer. That part between Hartley's Bay and the Main French River, and several larger islands in Wahnapitae Bay, and the Main French River, is well timbered with large white and red pine, Jack pine, poplar, birch, spruce and balsam.

Islands.

There are seventy-three islands in the township. These were marked with their proper numbers on posts or blazed trees, so situated as to be easily seen from the water. Several of the islands are quite large, and are well timbered with white and red pine. I enclose with the notes a tabulated list of the islands showing the acreage, the markings, timber, soil and the particular use to which they may be put. The majority of these islands would be suitable for pleasure resorts, owing to their close proximity to the James Bay Railway and the Georgian Bay.

Water.

The township is well watered with lakes, rivers and creeks having the Main French River for the entire south boundary, and the Wahnapitae River flowing through the north-west corner. The Main French River has many bays and inlets extending towards the north and east. The only water power of importance in the township occurs at Bear chute, lot 12, concession VI. The details of this water power are given on the traverse plan. This power could be easily developed, and without injuring any appreciable amount of land could have the head raised to double or treble the natural.

Railways and Navigation.

The Canadian Northern Ontario Railway was 'under construction through the township during the progress of the survey. The French River and Wahnapitae Bay are suitable for navigation by steam-boats having a draft of ten feet. The French is navigable as far east as the rapids in lot 1, and Wahnapitae Bay as far north as the little Wahnapitae River, and Hartley's Bay as far east as the narrows at the crossing of the Canadian Northern Ontario Railway. There are several tugs of approximately 150 tons displacement working on these waters.

Game.

Red deer and bear were plentiful, several being seen during the season. Some few signs of moose were seen. Small game, partridges, and duck were comparatively scarce.

Bass, pike, pickerel and white fish appeared to be plentiful.

Accompanying this report are a general plan, a traverse plan. timber plan, field notes and account.

I have the honor to be,
Sir,
Your obedient servant,
(Signed) WM. WALTER STULL,
Ontario Land Surveyor.

The Honorable,
The Minister of Lands, Forests and Mines,
Toronto.

10a L.M.

(Appendix No. 55).

TOWNSHIP OF BIGWOOD, DISTRICT OF NIPISSING.

SUDBURY, ONT., Dec. 18, 1906.

SIR,—I have the honor to submit the following report on the survey of the Township of Bigwood, in the District of Nipissing, performed under instructions, dated May the twenty-ninth, nineteen hundred and six.

I commenced the survey of the Township of Bigwood on the completion of the survey of the Township of Allen, which lies immediately to the west.

I started the survey by running the line between concessions one and two east astronomically from a point in the east boundary of the Township of Allen, five miles due south of the north-east angle of that township. I planted posts on this line every forty chains and made the number of the lots fourteen, thirteen, twelve, etc. That portion of the line between the post marking the line between lots two and three and Dry Pine Bay was made lot two in concession II. The side lines between lots twelve and thirteen, ten and eleven, eight and nine, six and seven, four and five, and two and three were run north astronomically to the south boundary of the Township of Delamere, and south astronomicaly to the north shore of the Main French River, from the corresponding posts on the above mentioned line. Side lines six and seven was run as before stated north and south astronomically, and the concession lines between two and three, three and four, four and five, five and six were started from this line, giving to each concession a depth of eighty chains. The different concession lines were run east astronomically from the six and seven side line to the shore line of Dry Pine Bay and the north branch of the French River, and connected with the corresponding lines in the township of Mason, and west astronomically to the east boundary of the Township of Allen, and connected with the corresponding lines in that township. The chainage between the intersection of the different side lines with the south boundary of the Township of Delamere and the corresponding lines in that township was noted. The north boundary of the township was not chained by me except at places for the purpose of traversing and connecting the railway in respect of my survey.

Concession 1 being broken fronted, posts were planted along the shore of the Main French River to mark the starting points between lots one and two, three and four, five and six, seven and eight, nine and ten, eleven and twelve and thirteen and fourteen. The width of the odd numbered lots, with the exception of lot one, was made forty chains.

Iron posts one and seven-eighths inches in diameter, three feet long, painted red, forged at the top to shed the rain, and pointed at the bottom, were placed at the following points, and all markings were made with the cold chisel.

1st. At the north-westerly angle of the township, and marked on the south-west side "Allen," on the south-east side "Bigwood," on the north side "Cox," on the south side "Con. VII and Con. VI," on the west side "I," on the east side "XIV." A wooden post was planted similarly marked except for the words Allen, Bigwood and Cox, and all mounded with stones.

2nd. At the south-westerly angle of the township at the intersection of the westerly boundary of the township with the north shore of the Main French River, marked on the north-west side "Allen" on the north-east side "Bigwood," on the north side "Con. I," on the east side "XIV," on the west side "I." A cedar post was planted alongside and marked similarly with the exception of the words Bigwood and Allen, and both mounded with stones.

3rd. At the north-east angle of the township alongside of O. L. S. Tyrrel and Ford's post on the shore of the Bay of the French River; marked on the north side "Delamere," on the south-west side "Bigwood," on the south side "Con. VI," on the west side "II." A cedar post similarly marked except for the township names was planted alongside.

Iron posts one and one-quarter inches in diameter, three feet long, painted red, and forged at the top to shed the rain, and pointed at the bottom, were planted at the following places:

1st. At the intersection of side line six and seven with the north shore of the French River marked on the north side "Con. I," on the east side "VI," on the west side "VII." A wooden post similarly marked was placed alongside, and both mounded with stones.

2nd. At the intersection of the side lines six and seven with the line between concessions III and IV, marked on the east side "VI," on the west side "VII," on the north side "Con. VI," on the south side "Con. III," a wooden post was planted alongside.

3rd. At the intersection of side line six and seven with the north boundary of the township. marked on the south side. "Con. VI," on the east side "VI," on the west side "VII." A wooden post similarly marked was placed alongside.

4th. At the intersection of concession line between three and four with the west boundary, marked on the south side "Con. III," on the north side "Con. IV," on the east side "XIV." A wooden post similarly marked was planted alongside.

5th. At the intersection of the line between concessions three and four with the shore of the Bay of French River marked on the north side "Con. IV," on the south side "Con. III," on the west side "III." A wooden post similarly marked was planted alongside.

The lines were all clear transit lines well opened out and blazed. Several observations were taken, the notes of which are included in the field notes.

The traversing of the lakes and rivers was done at the completion of the running of the lines with a Lugeol micrometer and transit.

The magnetic variation in this township remained fairly steady at seven degrees forty-five minutes west.

General Features.

The township as a whole is fairly level no high hills being noted. The surface is much broken with low rocky ridges, particularly in the western. and southern portions of the townships, the north-easterly part, east of the Murdock Creek, is mostly rolling clay land, with rocky ridges near the shore lines of the creek and bays. The shore of the French River is very rocky and precipitous.

Timber.

The western and northern parts of the township are covered with jack pine, birch and poplar of a small size. The part east of the Murdock Creek is mostly poplar and birch of small size. Some large red and white pine is found in a narrow belt bordering on the Main French River and the western shore of Dry Pine Bay. Outside of the white and red pine there is no valuable timber on the township.

Soil and Rock:

The western and southern portions of the township are almost entirely rocky, with a few small narrow belts of clay land between the ridges: The rock being Laurentian Gneiss, corresponds closely with the character of this formation throughout the whole district. The principal colors of the gneiss are reddish and greyish. No minerals of economic value were noticed. There is a fine area of good clay land on the peninsula east of the Murdock Creek. Considerable of this area is already squatted on by settlers. A list of these squatters accompanies this report. The land is this portion of the township appears to be of an excellent quality, and is easily cleared owing to the sparseness of the timber.

The township is well watered with several lakes, rivers and streams.

Water Powers.

There are two water powers in the township, one being on the north branch of the French River, and the other being the Recollet Falls on the Main French River. The former has a head of about eight feet, and at the natural minimum flow would develop about 300 H.P. By damming the eastern channel, which is in the Township of Mason, the power could be increased considerably. The Recollet has a natural head of about seven feet, and would develop naturally about 3,500 H.P. The development of this fall would be comparatively easy were it not for the construction of a dam in the heavy current of the river at this point.

Game.

Red deer were plentiful, bear were very plentiful, and wolves were not met with or heard during the progress of the work. Partridge and small game were scarce. Some fresh beaver work was noticed in the westerly part of the township. Fish of the usual kind were found in the rivers and lakes.

Railway.

The Toronto-Sudbury branch of the Canadian Pacific Railway was constructed through the township, but at the time of the survey the steel had not been laid. The piers for the large steel bridge crossing the Main French River were being built during the progress of the survey. This road when opened for traffic will be of great benefit to the settlers in this township.

Accompanying this report are, a general plan, a traverse plan, timber plan, field notes and account.

I have the honor to be,
Sir,
Your obedient servant,
(Signed) WM. WALTER STULL,
Ontario Land Surveyor.

The Honorable,
The Minister of Lands, Forests and Mines,
Toronto.

(Appendix No. 56).

TOWNSHIP OF LANGTON, DISTRICT OF RAINY RIVER.

SARNIA, Dec., 29th, 1906.

SIR,—I have the honor to report that, in accordance with your instructions dated the 31st of May, 1906, I have surveyed the Township of Langton, in the Rainy River District, and beg to report thereon as follows:—

I left Sarnia on the 13th day of June following, arriving at the Village of Dryden on the 16th, when, after waiting for three weeks for part of my outfit, which had gone astray on the Canadian Pacific Railway, and procuring men and supplies, I was enabled to leave that place on the 3rd day of July following, for Vermilion Bay, Eagle Lake, Township of Langton.

I commenced the survey by running the third and fourth concession line west from Ontario Land Surveyor Stewart's post on the east boundary, marked "III M," to the intersection of location 114 E, planting a wooden post and marking it "114 E" on the west side and "I" on the east side.

I then ran concession lines 4 and 5 due west, starting from Mr. Stewart's post marked "IV M" on the east boundary, taking an observation on this line of Polaris on the evening of the 7th of July, the magnetic variation being 6 degrees 30 minutes E., which gradually increased to 8 degrees 30 minutes at the west boundary of the township. I made this line a base throughout the township, planting posts at intervals of 40 chains, and running the various side lines north and south therefrom. The posts between lots 1 and 2, 3 and 4, 4 and 5, and 5 and 6 on this line are marked on four sides with numbers of lots on the east and west sides, and concessions on the north and south sides. The lines were run to the south and posts planted on the north limit of locations J. D. 3, parcel P. and gravel pits A. & B., the boundaries of which I measured, together with T. T. 16, and surveyed gravel pit B.

I ran concession lines 5 and 6 west from Mr. Stewart's post marked "5 M" on the east boundary, taking an observation of Polaris on the evening of the 21st of July, and planting posts at the intersection of the east and west boundaries of location T. T. 16.

I ran side line 2 and 3 from this line 80 chains north for the purpose of locating the north boundary, which I ran due east to the lake at the north-east corner of the township, planting an iron post alongside a balm of gilead post at the edge of a marsh, at a distance of 6 chains 48 links from the water's edge and distant from the north-east angle of the township 26 chains 44 links. The north boundary was produced west to the lake at the north-west angle of the township, planting a six-inch jack pine post 50 links from the water's edge on the east side of the lake, marked "Langton" on the south-east, "Con. VI" on the south, and "XII" on the east side, distant 35 chains 19 links from the north-west angle of the township.

A portion of the west boundary having been surveyed by Ontario Land Surveyor Bolton in 1905 north from the railway, I retraced and chained this line and produced the same south across the Bay of Eagle Lake and across the peninsula, where I planted an iron post alongside of a spruce post six inches in diameter, 28 links north of the water's edge of Eagle Lake, marked "Langton" on the north-east, "Con. I" on the north, and "XII" on the east side.

The iron post on the east town line on the north shore of Eagle Lake, as shown on projected plan furnished me by the Department, which is the south-east corner of the township on land being lost, I planted another iron post alongside the tamarac post in a cairn of stones 15 links from the water's edge, which is marked "Langton" on the north-west, "Mutrie" on the north-east, "Con. III" on the north, "XII" on the east, and "I" on the west side.

An iron post is planted alongside of a white pine post six and one-half inches in diameter, 20 links north of the water's edge of Eagle Lake on side lines 6 and 7, marked "VI" on the east side, "VII" on the west side, and "Con. I" on the north side.

An iron post is planted alongside a jack pine post five inches in diameter in a cairn of stones where side lines 6 and 7 intersect concession lines 3 and 4, marked "VI" on the east side, "VII" on the west side, "Con. III" on the south side, and "Con. IV" on the north side.

An iron post is planted on side lines 6 and 7 alongside of a jack pine post six inches in diameter 1 chain south of the water's edge, and distant 1 chain 63 links from the north boundary, the corner being in the lake, marked "VI" on the east side, "VII" on the west side, and "Con. VI" on the south side.

An iron post is planted alongside a spruce post six inches in diameter at the intersection of concession line 3 and 4 with the west boundary, marked "Con. III" on the south, "Con. IV" on the north and "XII on the east side.

An iron post is planted on the west town line alongside a wooden post six inches in diameter one chain south of the water's edge, distant 34 chains 82 links from the north-west angle of the township, the same being in the lake, and is marked "Langton" on the south-east. "Con. VI" on south, and "XII" on east side.

All iron posts were marked with a cold chisel.

The balance of the township having been completed by running concession lines east and west, and side lines north and south, I then finished the traverse of the north shore of Eagle Lake, together with the islands therein. Where the corners of lots fall in lakes, posts are planted on the shores where each line enters the lake.

The township throughout is broken and hilly, consisting chiefly of granite ranges lying north-east and south-west, with an occasional muskeg, and where fire has exposed the rock, quartz veins were seen, but no mineral was found, excepting in a highly magnetic range running from lot 3, concession 6, to lot 12, concession 5, carrying red hematite with indications of gold, silver and copper, but of no economic value. This range is from 20 to 30 chains in width, and showed a magnetic variation in places of 15 degrees to 20 degrees. Some development work had been done thereon on location T. T. 16, a shaft having been sunk, but the work has apparently been abandoned. A spring of water, heavily mineralized, was seen on lot 2, concession 6. Posts were planted on the north and south boundaries of T. T. 16, on side line 6 and 7.

The timber is varied, consisting chiefly of jack pine, poplar and birch of small growth, together with a few scattered red and white pine along the shores of Eagle Lake; of the former about thirty trees are standing on lot 2, concession 6, 10 inches to 18 inches in diameter. The most valuable timber has been taken off and fire has destroyed a considerable quantity. Some jack pine and tamarac remains in the western part fit for cordwood, and a considerable quantity of small spruce remains fit for pulpwood.

The soil consists chiefly of white clay loam; some portions in the west is good land. The centre and east part of the township is light and sandy;

some good land is found in the vicinity of alder swamps, creeks and in low places.

The lakes are well supplied with fish, Eagle Lake containing white fish, pike, pickerel and maskinonge, which are shipped to the United States. The water is pure and soft, containing no limestone. The creeks are all small, excepting one emptying into Eagle Lake on concession 3, which is navigable for boats and canoes. There are no waterfalls in the township.

Small game, such as partridge and rabbits, were seen; also larger game, such as moose and deer.

Small fruit, such as blueberries, were plentiful.

The islands in Eagle Lake are not fit for agricultural purposes, but make ideal and valuable summer resorts.

Several windfalls were met with during the progress of the survey, but not to any very great extent.

Location 114 E has no buildings on it. D 113 has a good log house, a small clearing, and is used as a summer resort.

There are two settlers in the township, both on lot 6, concession 4; one a trapper, the other an explorer.

One-third of the township is fit for agricultural purposes.

> I have the honor to be,
>
> > Sir,
>
> > > Your obedient servant,
>
> > > > (Signed) JOHN J. FRANCIS,
>
> > > > > Ontario Land Surveyor.

The Honorable,
> The Minister of Lands, Forests and Mines,
> > Toronto.

(*Appendix No. 57*).

TOWNSHIP OF PELLATT, DISTRICT OF RAINY RIVER.

> KENORA, Feb. 13th, 1906.

SIR,—I have the honor to report that I have surveyed the Township of Pellatt under instructions dated 2nd August, 1905.

I commenced the survey from the south-west corner of the township, having established that point as follows, commencing at the centre of the track of the Canadian Pacific Railway in the west limit of the Ostersund station ground, thence west astronomically one hundred and twenty chains, thence south astronomically forty chains to the said south-west corner of the Township of Pellatt, Boyne Lake preventing me from exactly adhering to instructions.

Iron posts are planted at the following points (with a wooden post at each of the same places), at the south-west corner of the township, marked on the north-east side "Pellatt," north side "Con. I," east side "XVI"; one at the north-west corner marked "Pellatt" on the south east side, "Con. VI" on south side, "XVI" on east side; one at the intersection of north boundary with Winnipeg River, marked on south-west side "Pellatt," on west side "VII." on the south side "Con. VI:" one at the intersection of the south boundary with the west shore of Eagle Lake marked on the north-west side "Pellatt," on the west side "X," on the north side "Con. I;" one at the intersection of the line between lots 8 and 9 with the north boundary marked "Pellatt," "Con. VI" on the south side, "VIII" on the east side, and "IX" on the west side; one at the intersection of the line between the third and fourth concessions with the west boundary marked on the east side "Pellatt," "XVI," on the south side "Con. III," on the north side "Con. IV;" one at the intersection of the line between the third and fourth concessions with the shore of Middle Lake, marked on the west side "III," on the north side "Con. IV," on the south side "Con. III;" one at the intersection of the line between concessions 3 and 4, with the east shore of Sandy Lake marked "Con. III" on the south side, "Con. IV" on the north side, "VIII" on the east side. I found the low-lying lands flooded around Lakes Louise, Middle and Muriel and Locke Bay and their tributary streams, and good hay meadows between Lake Louise and Middle Lake could not be cut, being completely submerged, owing to the stop logs having been removed from the power dam.

Muriel Lake, Lake Louise and Middle Lake are nearly on the same level as Winnipeg River, and there is no rapid water in the outlets from those lakes to the river, and high water in the river means submergence of the lands contiguous to those lakes and their outlets. The rock throughout the township (except the south-east corner between War Eagle Lake and Keewatin) is granitoid gneiss with no appearance of valuable mineral.

The soil north and north-west of Sandy Lake is a rich clay loam impregnated with black vegetable mould, and should prove to be number one for all agricultural purposes. This good land extends from lot 15 in the third concession to lot 7 in the fourth concession, and includes 9, 10, 11 and 12 in the fifth, and parts of 9, 10, 11 and 12 in the sixth. There is also a clay belt between Sandy Lake and Lakes Lulu and Louise, very good in places but of a harder quality and light colored. The sandy soil, called sandy loam in the timber plan, is of good quality and fit for agricultural purposes; the sandy soil round Boyne Lake is of poor quality and covered with jack pine scrub. Concession "I" west of War Eagle Lake is nearly all rock, the only soil being in narrow valleys.

The shores of War Eagle Lake are very rough and rocky, except part of that north of the track, which is low, and submerged, with water-killed trees standing in the water. Boyne Lake is a lake of pure water and on the north shore is a sand beach nearly a quarter of a mile long. The lakes mostly all contain good pure water with high shores, except Sandy Lake, which has a muddy bottom, swampy shore at the west end, and the poorest water in the township, about 20 chains north of the outlet of Muriel, and on Muriel Lake is a fine sand beach. The land all about Muriel Lake is of good quality, and the shores are high and dry.

The north-east portion of the township is very rocky and mostly all unfit for cultivation, the best parts having been previously surveyed and taken up.

The timber in the township has been cut over for ties and stave bolts, and the timber remaining is valuable only for fire wood, and in the north-east and south-west portions of the township there is a great deal of scrub, with intervening patches of good cord wood timber. Fire has been over several portions of the township, some places killing all the timber, in others leaving green patches.

The west boundary passes over some very rocky land. On lots 15 and 16, in the fourth and fifth concessions, is some good level burnt land where the wild grass grows fully six feet high, and if cleared of logs and brush would make good natural meadow land. We saw numerous indications of moose, caribou, red deer, foxes and other animals, and some partridges. Wolves are also to be seen occasionally and are increasing in numbers rapidly.

There is a difference of from six to ten feet between the height of water in Lakes Lulu and Louise, the difference being greatest at low water in the Winnipeg River. The outlet from Lake Lulu to Lake Louise is short and is all rapids. There are also rapids on Culloden Creek.

John Taylor has squatted on lot 10, in the second concession, between Lakes Lulu and Louise. He has five acres cleared, a log house and some outbuildings and keeps cattle, pigs and fowl.

Samuel Palmas, on lot 4 in the third concession, a log house 18 x 20, outbuilding 20 x 24, 5.5 acres cleared. Andrew Anderson, on lot 11 in the second concession, log house hewed, windows, doors and lumber on the ground, small piece underbrushed, no clearing. August Skoglund, on lot 12 in the second concession, half acre cleared, log house 16 x 24. John Johnston, the occupant of D 117, has half an acre and buildings north of his north boundary on lot 13 in the second concession.

The settlers already in the township are asking for a road to Keewatin and for a school, most of them being from seven to nine miles from Keewatin.

I believe the Township of Pellatt to be the best township surveyed in the immediate neighborhood for agricultural purposes. No lot is entirely free from rock, but some will average 70 to 80 per cent. free of rock, and water is plentiful and accessible to most lots, with good winter roads to Keewatin by crossing over the lakes, and hoping for a summer road and a public school in the near future.

I have the honor to be,
Sir,
Your obedient servant,
(Signed)   EDMUND SEAGER,
Ontario Land Surveyor.

The Honorable,
    The Minister of Lands, Forests and Mines,
        Toronto.

(*Appendix No. 58.*)

ALGONQUIN PARK P. O., Feb. 4th, 1907.

To the Honorable,
    The Minister of Lands and Mines,
        Toronto, Ont.

HONORABLE SIR,—I beg to submit a short report on the Algonquin National Park and the work performed here during the past year.

Our staff, as of course you are aware, is composed of twelve rangers, one teamster, chief ranger and superintendent. We have an area of about two thousand square miles, which during the greater part of the year is patrolled by these men to prevent trapping and illegal fishing, to protect the forests from fire, and in every way to look after the interests of this great game preserve. During the season in which there is little or no danger from poachers, their time is taken up cutting out portages, making canoes, snowshoes, etc., cutting wood for the buildings at headquarters, putting in a supply of ice and building shelter houses. This year a large frame shelter house has been built at Brulé Lake, sided log buildings at Opeongo, McDougall, Nipissing and Lindie's Lakes. These buildings are not, as generally supposed, just hunters' camps, but good, substantial, sided log buildings, well finished throughout. New roofs have been put on the houses at Eagle, Rosebery and White Trout Lakes.

There has been very little poaching, and I feel that the staff have done good work. Game of all kinds has very much increased. The numerous visitors last year reported the deer and moose abundant wherever they went, and fishing splendid everywhere. The fur-bearing animals have wonderfully increased, especially the otter and beaver. Large families of the latter are to be found on every stream and lake. The small-mouthed bass introduced into a few of these lakes some years ago have abundantly stocked the streams for fifty miles to the east of the Park, and splendid bass fishing is now had where a few years this gamiest of fish was unknown. I should like very much to see the rainbow trout introduced here. I am confident it would be a success, as so many important rivers flow from the Park and draw their fish supply from the lakes here. I feel that the Government cannot take too great an interest in this question.

We had a great many visitors last year and one and all were delighted with the abundance and tameness of the game and fur-bearing animals.

I have the honor to be,

Sir,

Yours very truly,

(Signed)   G. W. BARTLETT,

Superintendent.

(Appendix No. 59.)

MORPETH P. O., Jan. 8th, 1907.

To the Honorable,
  The Minister of Lands, Forests and Mines,
    Toronto.

SIR,—I have the honor to submit this my report as Caretaker and Ranger of the Rondeau Provincial Park for the year 1906. As my report for 1905 was very lengthy in setting forth the necessity for the several improvements so much needed in the Park, some of which have been carried into effect and add much to the appearance of the Park, I will make this report brief. The improvements made in 1906 are the building of a new refectory, which is much larger and more commodious than the old one that was previously used. The cost of the building was $1,500, and it can be leased to good advantage.

The new Park road was damaged a great deal last spring by drawing heavy loads of ice over it when the roadbed was soft, and this was repaired. First class gravel was secured at a cost of nearly $300, and the road was put into excellent condition.

An excavation was made for the wild geese in the enclosure of about 60 x 15 feet, in which the water at present is nearly three feet deep.

The aviaries for the several kinds of pheasants in the Park enclosure were overhauled and all new cedar posts put in to replace the old oak posts, which were mostly rotten, and new fine mesh wire was used for covering and siding the pens and runways. This secures the birds from their enemies, the weasels, owls, etc., much better than the old coarser mesh wire netting.

At present the water in the Rondeau Bay and in the swales and lagoons on the Park is higher than it has ever been since I came to the Park, and we are looking for heavy floods here towards spring. The root cellar has some water in it now and I expect it will be worse during the balance of the winter.

In regard to the long talked of dock to be built, Mr. Halford, Government Engineer, was here a few weeks ago looking over the situation and figuring on the cost, also Mr. Whitebread, who is in charge of the Government dredge. I think they understand the situation here thoroughly in regard to dredging for the building of the new dock and covering the water weeds and rushes that are such an eyesore in front of the picnic grounds, pavilion and summer cottages. The Government have the details of the reports of Mr. Halford and Mr. Whitebread before them, and I sincerely hope these plans will be carried out, at least in part, so that we may have a dock that will be approachable for reasonable sized crafts, ready for the public use this coming season.

I have strongly urged in my reports for several years the necessity for a public house here, the need for which grows each year, and the Government should make a move in this direction that will result in a large, suitable building being erected at an early date.

I find upon looking through the bush there has been little or no timber blown down this season. The swales are filled with water so that they are impassible for teams. The Government should make a reasonable grant for the extension of the new road into the Park on through the bush to the bar at the other end, for the various reasons stated in my reports for other years. The forty-one church seats bought last spring were scattered around through the pavilion and picnic grounds, and were greatly appreciated by the visitors.

There have been five substantial summer houses erected this season and we expect more than that number in 1907.

I have the honor to be,

Sir,

Your obedient servant,

(Signed) Isaac Gardner.

Appendix No. 60.

List of persons holding Cullers' Licenses issued under the Ontario Cullers Act up to 31st
December, 1905.

Name.	P. O. Address.	Name.	P. O. Address.
Anderson, M. M.	Almonte.	Bromley, Thomas	Pembroke.
Allan, James D.	Bracebridge.	Bremner, John L.	Admaston.
Appleton, Erwin B.	Bracebridge.	Breen, Bernard.	Garden River.
Albert, Andrew	Ottawa.	Buie, Dougal.	Providence Bay.
Adams, J.Q.	Longford Mills.	Baker, Thomas.	Blind River.
Anderson, Patrick J.	Campbellford.	Blais, Felix	Hull, Que.
Anderson, J. C.	Gravenhurst.	Balsdon, George	Keewatin.
Allan, Alfred	Ottawa.	Bromley, W. H	Pembroke.
Allen, R. A.	Bannockburn.	Bowers, Isaac.	Little Current.
Aikens, Geo. M.	French River.	Brown, Thomas.	Barrie.
Appleby, Ridley.	Katrine.	Bass, Walter R.	W. Huntingdon.
Adams, James M.	Sault Ste. Marie.	Bates, Robert.	Rat Portage.
Aylward, James	Peterborough.	Binnie, Thomas.	Port Arthur.
Archibald, John L.	Keewatin.	Blair, William.	Keewatin.
Austin, Wm. G	Renfrew.	Bick, Thomas.	Bobcaygeon.
Anderson, Charles.	Little Current.	Burke, John Thomas.	Midland.
Anderson, John.	Cartier.	Buchan, Sterling.	L'Orignal.
Adair, Thomas Albert.	Gananoque.	Brown, Joseph A.	Spanish.
Anderson, J. G	Alpena, Mich.	Baird. P. C.	Rainy River.
Alexander, Samuel.	Arden.	Brill, J. W	Mine Centre.
Adams, Wm.	Westmeath.	Beattie, Arthur W	Arnprior.
Arkle, George	Rat Portage	Brock, H. S.	Ottawa.
Armstrong, James Theodore.	McKellar.	Benson, John Bird.	Midland.
Armstrong, Thos. J.	Arnprior.	Brennan, Richard Lawrence.	Peterborough.
Acheson, Ira M.	Westmeath.	Brown, Hugh Risside.	Huntsville.
Albert, Alfred E.	Ottawa.	Bryan, Frank.	Keewatin.
Alma, John E.	Hawkesbury.	Bennet. Edward Clinton.	Ahmic Harbor.
Adams, George A	Longford.	Blaine, Harvie Thomas.	Orillia.
Ansley, John Albert.	Thessalon.	Borrett, Thomas.	Barrie.
Ansley, John Jenkins.	Thessalon.	Bickell, James Manuel.	Sault Ste. Marie.
Ainslie, Alexander.	Spanish.	Buisson, William.	Sudbury.
Apleton, E. A.	Kenora.	Borrett, James A.	Sault Ste Marie.
		Bliss, C Lidden.	Sudbury.
Brophy, Michael Patrick.	Massey Station.	Bray, James.	Kinmount.
Boland, Abraham.	Cartier.	Bremner Geo.	Anprior.
Brown, Singleton.	Bracebridge.	Bromley, Samuel.	Pembroke.
Barry, Thomas James.	Hastings.	Brown, A C.	Fitzroy Harbor.
Blanchet, Paul Frederick.	Ottawa.	Berlinquet, Julius.	Opimicon, Que.
Bird, W. S.	Parry Sound.	Blastorah, Fred. L.	Harwood.
Bayley, James T.	Gravenhurst.	Burns, Clifton H.	Little Current.
Bell, Henry.	Ottawa.	Beaumont, Ernest.	Parry Sound.
Beach, Herbert Mahlom.	Ottawa.	Beattie, Alex.	Whitney.
Barry, Thomas.	Millbridge.	Brennan, Reginald.	Gravenhurst.
Beatty, W. R.	Parry Sound.	Boyd, Geo.	Gravenhurst.
Brooks, Frederick William.	Mackay's Station	Bissell, George Thomas.	Trenton.
Brown, Robert D.	Port Sidney.	Baxter, Richard.	Deseronto.
Breed, Arthur G	Penetang'ishene.	Breeaugh, Edward.	Deseronto.
Barnes, Thomas George Lee.	Muskoka Mills.	Boyd, George A.	Thessalon.
Buchanan, Robert.	Coldwater.	Buchan, Frederick.	Arnprior.
Beck, Jacob Frederick.	Penetang'ishene.	Barret, Patrick.	Arnprior.
Bird, Joseph Manly.	Muskoka Mills.	Brundage, Alfred, W.	Pembroke.
Boyd, John F.	Thessalon.	Brougham, Thomas.	Eganville.
Brandin, Martin, W.	Peterborough.	Blair, Robert I.	Arnprior.
Bell, John C.	Peterborough.	Benson, John W.	Sturgeon Bay.
Bartlett, George W.	Warren.	Beck, Charles M., Jr.	Penetang'ishene.
Brown, Silas.	Klock's Mills.	Beatty, W. J.	Coldwater.
Boland, W. G.	Eganville.	Burns, C. W , Jr.	South River.
Baulke, George R.	Aylmer, Que.	Bell, John Henry.	Burk's Falls.

Appendix No. 60.—Continued.

Name.	P. O. Address.	Name.	P. O. Address.
Bettes, John Hiram	Muskoka Mills.	Chalmers, George James	Peterboro.
Brady, John	Renfrew.	Caverly, David Charles	Parry Sound.
Brown, James	Buckingham, Que	Campbell, Archibald J	Little Current.
Brooks, W. J	Blind River.	Close, John L	Arnprior.
Bertrand, Allan	Nairn Centre.	Carmichael, Donald	Arnprior.
Brinkman, Alex. B	Sault Ste. Marie.	Carty, John	Arnprior.
Black, Jacob	Barwick.	Cleary, Patrick M	Arnprior.
Beattie, W. J	Arnprior.	Caldwell, Jas. M	Callander.
Bromley, William	Westmeath.	Cushing, John J	Davidson, Que.
Bissell, Harlie	Trenton.	Crebo, William	Thessalon.
Brown, Robert	Starrat.	Cullen, Michael J	Massey Station.
Beaton, Hugh	Waubaushene.	Cuthbertson, William	Arnprior.
Bailey, Arthur	Parry Sound.	Carss, Percy	Thessalon.
Burd, James Henry	Parry Sound.	Coghlan, Michael	Chapeau, Que.
Bailey, Samuel James	Orillia.	Cameron, Alexander Gordon.	Beauchene, Que.
Burton, Tinswood	Renfrew.	Cassaday, W. W	Emo.
Boyes, James	Huntsville.	Carter, Robert E	Fesserton.
Brown, John	Rockdale.	Coleman, Jos	Baysville.
Brennan, Edward Scott	Sundridge.	Cardiff, George McDougall	Sudbury.
Bell, John Arguey	Klock's Mills.	Cameron, W.D	Rat Portage.
Bromley, Edw. H	Pembroke.	Crandall, F	Port Arthur.
Bliss, Lawrence E	Byng Inlet.	Campbell, James R	Eganville.
Buee, Neil	Spanish Station.	Campbell, John A	Galetta.
Brazziel, Leonard	Spanish Station.	Caillier, Hyacinth	Arnprior.
Bowie, Jas	Bryson, Que.	Chamberlain, Thomas	Bobcaygeon.
Barrie, Nicholas J	Ottawa.	Cooper, David Allan	Millbrook.
Burke, J. D	Rat Portage.	Cox, Henry	Ballerica, Que.
Bowen, Thos	Deseronto.	Currie, James	Ottawa.
Brown, James F	Baysville.	Clarkson, A. E	Midland.
Blastorah, Bernard	Harwood.	Clairmont, E	Gravenhurst.
		Cameron, W. F	Sturgeon Bay.
Campbell, Robt. John	Flinton.	Connolly, David	Gravenhurst.
Carpenter, John A	Arnprior.	Campbell, P. C	Sault Ste. Marie.
Campbell, Alexander J	Trenton.	Cadenhead, Alexander	Midland.
Carson, James	Bracebridge.	Carpenter, R. J	Arnprior.
Campbell, J. M	Bracebridge.	Christie, William Pringle	Severn Bridge.
Campbell, Robert	Bracebridge.	Campbell, C. V	Sault Ste. Marie.
Clairmont, Joseph	Campbellford.	Clegg, Samuel	Peterborough.
Clarkson, Robert. J	Parry Sound.	Clairmont, William. L	Gravenhurst.
Carruthers, Aaron	Hintonburg.	Cook, Sidney P. W	Spanish Station.
Calder, Wm. J	Burk Lake.	Corrigan, John	Baysville.
Chew, Joseph	Gravenhurst.	Chalmers, Alexander M	Peterborough.
Cole, James Colin	Ottawa.	Charlton, George A	Collingwood.
Cameron, William	Collin's, Inlet	Cahill, Thomas	Nosbonsing.
Cain, Robert	Midland.	Chew, Manly	Midland.
Crawford, Stephen W	Thessalon.	Cooper, James Eddly	Saurin.
Cochrane, George	Peterboro.	Cook, Reinhardt	South River.
Coburn, John	Lindsay.	Crowe, Cecil	Bobcaygeon.
Crowe, Nathaniel	Bobcaygeon.	Callaghan, Dennis	Trenton.
Cameron, Alexander	Norman.	Collins, James	Barryville.
Chrysler, Frank R. L	Webbwood.	Campbell, Daniel N	Buckingh'm, Que
Callaghan, Thos., Jr	Campbellford.	Canniff, R. W	Rat Portage.
Carson, Hugh	Rat Portage.	Cassidy, S. C	Dunchurch.
Calder, George	Woodville.	Charleson, John Baptiste	Ottawa.
Callaghan, Dennis	Campbellford.	Comer, Billa F	Tweed.
Corigan, Robert T	Emo.	Carter, George	Sundridge.
Cameron, John H	Rat Portage.	Corrigan, Robt. T	Emo.
Carson, Melvin	Little Current.	Caswell, Grant	Coldwater.
Cameron, John K	Spanish River.	Caswell, Geo	Goldwater.
Cassidy, William	Little Current.	Chemir, David A	Pembroke.
Coons, George Washington	Peterboro.	Clairmont, Philadelp L	Gravenhurst.
Chisholm, George Leopold	Sault Ste. Marie.	Crowe, Edgerton	Bobcaygeon.

Appendix No. 60.—Continued.

Name.	P. O. Address.	Name.	P. O. Address.
Crowe, Leslie	Bobcaygeon.	Eager, James	Parry Sound.
Campbell, Duncan W.	Stewartville.	Elliott, Porter P.	Mine Centre.
Callahan, Thomas N.	Arnprior.	Elliott, William	Cache Bay.
Clements, Albert James	Bent River.	Edgar, J. E.	Rat Portage.
Carney, Albert	Sault Ste. Marie.	Elliott, George E.	Peterborough.
Collins, Arthur	Massey Station.		
Carter, George	Lavallee, Que.	Fraser, John A	Rat Portage.
Chitty, Alfred E.	Kenora.	Ferguson, Wm. H	Red Bay.
		Forbes, Christopher McKay.	McLean's Depot.
Doran, Frank	Barryvale.	Fitzgerald, E. Clair	Parry Sound.
Dunning, E. Percival	Parry Sound.	Farrell, W. H	Ironside, Que.
Duff, R. J.	Arnprior.	French, Lewis William	Byng Inlet.
Durrill, John W.	Ottawa.	Fraser, William A	Mattawa.
Dickeon, John	Sundridge.	Finnerty, Patrick	Rochfort.
Dickson, Jas. L.	Michipic'ten H'r	Farnand, Frank	Diamond.
Dobie, Harry	Sault Ste. Marie.	Fulton, Philip S	Spanish Station.
Deacon, Charles	Sault Ste. Marie.	Fitzgerald, Ullyot C	Parry Sound.
Danter, R. W.	Parry Sound.	Fenn, George	Bracebridge.
Doyle, T. J.	Eau Clair.	Fortune, Owen	Trenton.
Dobie, Alexander R.	Blind River	Fraser, David	Norman.
Darling, J M.	Wisawasa.	France, John	Collins' Inlet.
Dillon, John	Calabogie.	Ferguson, Ernest A	Baysville.
Durrell, Jos. Nelson	P'rt'ge du F'rt, Q	Ferguson, Alpheu	Mattawa.
Durrell, John	Callander.	Ford, John, William B	P'r'tge du F'rt,Q
Donally, Richard S.	Sunbury.	Ford, Charles	Wahnapitae.
Devine, William	Cook's Mills.	Findlay, J. H.	Braeside.
Durrill, William	Nosbonsing.	Fraser, James	Renfrew.
Draper, Patrick	Quyon, Que.	Fairen, Francis	Peterborough.
Davis, J. P.	Bobcaygeon.	Faulkner, Jos	Fesserton.
Dale, John Alexander	Birkendale.	Fraser, Alexander, Jr.	Westmeath.
Dinsmore, Chas. L.	Huntsville.	Fairbairn, William	Calabogie.
Drum, Patrick	Belleville.	Fraser, Wm. A	Pembroke.
Durham, Edgar S.	Rosseau.	Fraser, Foster	Pembroke.
Duquette, Charles	Webbwood.	Fraser, William	Little Current.
Davis, William Albert	Bobcaygeon.	Fraser, Hugh Alexander	Pembroke.
Dickson, Robert Alexander.	Keene.	Flaherty, John	Lindsay.
Dawkins, John	Gravenhurst.	Fisher, William	Trenton.
Doxsee, James E.	Gravenhurst.	Fox, Thomas	Deseronto.
Didier, L. P.	Aylmer, Que.	Fallis, James W	Sturgeon Bay.
Devine, Patrick J.	Sheenboro, Que.	Fairbairn, N. H	Webbwoob.
Dinsmore, Richard	Huntsville.	Friel, John	Trenton.
Dunn, Percy E.	Longford Mills.	Fox, Charles	Trenton.
Duval, Chas.	Halfway.	Featherstonbaugh, William	
Donlevy, James	Calabogie.	Henry.	Penetanguishene
Doris, Patrick	Peterborough.	Friar, Schuyler	Westmeath.
Doris John	Peterborough.	Farren, Joel	Savanne.
Donahoe, Michael.	Erinsville.	Fraser, Duncan	Big Forks.
Doran, W.	Belleville.	Freestone, Walter	Burk's Falls.
Dickson, Robt. R.	Kippewa, Que.	Fraser, John	Bancroft.
Donlevy, Wm. C.	Rockcliffe.	Fitzgerald, D. C	Spanish Station.
Duff, Chas. A.	Stewartville.	Foster, Wm. C	Searchmont.
Dean, James C.	Rat Portage.	Frazer, Jas. C.	Spanish Mills.
Duff, Peter A.	Claybank.	Fremlin, H. P.	Richards Land'g.
Duncan, Downey	Rainy River.	Foster, Ed. G	Sault Ste. Marie,
Dougherty, J M.	Fort Frances.	Farrel, Peter M	Whitefish.
		Fairhall, Edward	Whiteside.
Enlaw, Oliver	Campbellford.	Fraser, Levi	Bracebridge.
Ebert, Andrew P.	Pembroke.	Fiddes, James	Rainy River
Ellis, Alexander	Arnprior.	Frawley, Frank	Orillia.
Ellis, John	Westmeath		
Errington, Joseph	Sundridge.	Griffith, Geo. F	Pembroke.
Eddington, Henry John	Parry Sound.	Graham, John	Arnprior.

Appendix No. 60.—Continued.

Name.	P. O. Address.	Name.	P. O. Address.
Golden, Jno	Gilmour.	Hartt, James	Gilmour.
Gunter, Henry M	Trenton.	Hayes, James	Enterprise.
Goltz, Ernest	Bardsville.	Humphrey, T. W	Gravenhurst.
Green, Forman A	Gilmour.	Huckson, A. H	French River.
Green, Samuel E	Parry Sound.	Handley, Robert	Douglas.
Grant, John	Flinton.	Howe, Alexander	Queensborough.
Green, Arthur	Ottawa.	Hurd, Edwin	Hurdville.
Green, Norman McL	Bancroft.	Huff, J. S. Morris	Arnprior.
Gillis, John J	Whitefish.	Halliday. Robert J	Lindsay.
George, R.	Parry Sound.	Hutton, John	Hutton House.
Gardiner, John	Parry Sound.	Hutchinson. Wm. E	Huntsville.
Golden, Frank J	Trenton.	Hogarth, Joseph Rowan	Pembroke.
Garson, Robert	Thessalon.	Humphrey, John	Gravenhurst.
Gropp, August	Penetanguishene	Hill, Joshua	Midland.
Grozelle, Antoine D	Muskoka Mills.	Hall, David	Lovering.
Goulais, James	Peterborough.	Hartley, Charles	Peterborough.
Grayson, Charles,	Keewatin.	Hawkins. Henry Charles.	Blind River.
Gladstone, Harry E	Cook's Mills.	Hines, Philip Wallace	Huntsville.
Guertin, Oliver.	Biscotasing.	Hudson, John Lewis	Combermere.
Gelinas, Frank	Hull, Que.	Hurdman. William H	Ottawa.
Gwynne, John	Hawkesbury.	Hughes, John	North Bay,
Gray, Frederick M	Brule Lake.	Howie, R. G	New Liskeard.
Graham, Edward G	Wahnapitae.	Helferty, Dennis	Eganville.
Griffin, James	Spanish River.	Hamilton, Robt	Rat Portage.
Gordon, Alexander B	Pembroke.	Hoppins, Abiram	Kingston.
Gareau, Noah J	Pembroke.	Hoppins, Densmore	Kingston.
Gillies, D. A	Carleton Place.	Haystead, John	Parry Sound.
Gilligan, Edward	Mattawa.	Henderson, John Irwin	Bobcaygeon.
Gladman, Charles	Parry Sound.	Hartley, William	Millbridge.
Garrow, John D	Ottawa.	Higgins. John C	Peterborough.
German, William Burton	Wahnapitae.	Harrison, John, Jr	Pembroke.
Gordon, Robert W	Pembroke.	Hawkins, E.	Le Breton Flats.
Guertin, Nelson	Petawawa.	Henderson. Charles	Bracebridge.
Gardener, John	Rat Portage.	Halliday, Frank	Parry Sound.
Gunter, Peter M	Gilmour.	Hammond. W	Orillia.
Glennie, William	Millbridge.	Hall, Charles Asa	Penetanguishene
German, Maurice J	Fenelon Falls.	Hearl. John	Callander.
Gillies, John A	Braeside.	Howe. Isaac	Fort Frances.
Goddin, Edward	Griffith.	Halliday, James	Springtown.
Grant, Joseph	Eganville.	Hurdman, J. A	Ottawa.
Gilmour, James B	Braeside.	Hawkins, Stonewall J	Meldrum Bay.
Gorman, Joseph P	Sault Ste. Marie.	Hinchcliffe, William	Gunter.
Gordon, Thomas A	Hall's Bridge.	Henderson, Arthur.	Baysville.
Gray, Albert H.	Biscotasing.	Hillis, James M	Sutton West.
Gadway, John	Parry Sound.	Harris, William, Jr	Day Mills.
Garrow, Edward	Webbwood.	Hogg. W. J	North Bay.
Golding, William	Dorset.	Hoxie, E. P	Katrine.
Gillies. Harry	White Lake.	Hawkins, Walter	Pembroke.
Gordon, Herbert C	Nelson.	Howard, James	Eganville.
Gillespie, M. H	Cook's Mills.	Howard, William	Baysville.
Griffin, William	Huntsville.	Hogan, Enos W	Savanne.
Ganton, David	Trout Creek.	Horne. John T	Fort William.
Graham, George L	Arnprior.	Hamilton, Chas. E	Rat Portage.
Graham, Frederick S	Arnprior.	Henderson, Leonard	Baysville.
Gill, Cuthbert	Orillia.	Hunter, Thos	Callander.
Graham, James Robert	Rat Portage.	Hamilton, Robert J	Ottawa.
Graham, Thomas Jordan	Byng Inlet.	Hawkins, William A	Pembroke.
Gaudaur, Antoine Daniel	Orillia.	Herring. Edward C	Sebright.
Gorman, Patrick	Eganvil'e.	Hatch, J. W	Dryden.
Guy, Charles	Fort Frances.	Hoard, Wm. Paris	Emo.
Hurd, Cyrus	Parry Sound.	Irving, Thos. H	Parry Sound.

Appendix No. 60.—Continued.

Name.	P. O. Address.	Name.	P. O. Address.
Irwin, Eli.	Rat Portage.	Kehoe, Martin	Huntsville.
Irving, Edward C	Rat Portage.		
		Leannoth, Francis	Arnprior.
Johns, Frank A	Toronto.	Lee, James	Warren.
Jackson, Robert	Brechin.	Lloyd, Alfred	Severn Bridge.
Johnson, Finlay	Bracebridge.	Lawrie, Frank A	Parry Sound.
Jones, Albert	Victoria Harbor.	Latimer, Jas	Frank's Bay.
Johnson, Thomas	Bobcaygeon.	Lemyre, Middey	Campbellford.
Johnston, Archibald M	Norman.	Lutz, Jacob	Parry Sound.
Julien, Charles	Trenton.	Luby, John E	Ottawa.
Junkin, Henry	Marmora.	Law, Wm. J	Markstay.
Johns, Frank	Nipissing Junct'n	Lummis, Daniel	Glanmire.
Jessup, Edward D	Cache Bay.	Lowe, W. C	Port Arthur.
Johnson, Frank N	Ottawa.	Londry, S. C	Sault Ste. Marie.
Johnston, John	Peninsular Lake.	Lochnan, James	Ottawa.
Johnson, S. M	Arnprior.	Link, Henry W	Ottawa.
Jones, Frederick James	Flinton.	Ladarotte, John	Arnprior.
Johnston, William A	Castleford.	Lochnan, John	Aylmer, Que.
Jervis, Henry	Wisawasa.	Lozo, John	Trenton.
Jones, William	Fenelon Falls.	Loughrin, Lawrence	Pembroke.
James, Martin	The Flats.	Linton, J. H	Parry Sound.
Johnston, James	Fort Frances.	Ludgate, James	Peterborough.
Johns, Alexander	Callander.	Lee, Robert	Huntsville.
		Langford, Mark.	Baysville.
Kintree, Stuart	Little Rapids.	Letherby, Edwin	Midland.
Kerby, John	Belleville.	Leahy, Francis M	Chapeau, Que.
Kennedy, Robert	Marmora.	Langford, Henry	Baysville.
Kirby, Louis Russell	Ottawa.	Lessard, Philip	Kenora.
Kennedy, Timothy	Enterprise.	Lovering, William James	Coldwater.
Kirk, Henry	Trenton.	Lane, Maurice	Bobcaygeon.
Knox, Milton	Ottawa.	Lenton, George	Peterborough.
Kinsella, Michael Pierce	Trenton.	Lowe, Thos. A	Renfrew.
Kitchen, D	French River.	Livingston, Robert M	Huntsville.
Kelly, Jeremiah	Sudbury.	Londry, William E	Sault Ste. Marie.
Kelly, Ferdinand	Mattawa.	Labelle, James	Waltham, Que.
Kennedy, T. J	Arnprior.	Labelle, Eli	Waltham, Que.
Kenning, Henry	Pembroke.	Ladurante, J. D	Ottawa.
Kirby, D. F	Belleville.	Ludgate, Theodore	Peterborough.
Kirkpatrick, David	Lindsay.	Lucas, Frank	Sault Ste. Marie.
Kean, John F	Orillia.	Lunam, Duncan	Collfield, Que.
Kellett, Fred	Keewatin.	Lott, George	Trenton
Kelly, Michael J	Baysville.	Lawrie, John D	Parry Sound.
Kirk, William James	Webbwood.	Lovering, George Francis	Coldwater.
Kerr, E. G	Thessalon.	Lucas, R. G	Christina.
King, Napoleon	Mattawa.	LeBlanc, Edmund C. Chapleau	Chapleau.
Kean, B. F	Orillia.	Lavigne, John	Aylmer, Que.
Kemp, Orval Wesley	Trenton.	Landell, Charles S	Huntsville.
Kirk, Charles Barron	Queensborough.	Long, Henry Elisha	Mattawa.
Kingsland, W. P	Ottawa.	Lynch, W. H	Collingwood.
Kerr, John B	Arnprior.	Laplante, Francis	Byng Inlet.
Kennedy, Walter	Arnprior.	Lindsa , Jas	Arnprior.
Kennedy, John	Pembroke.	Labelle, Michael	Arnprior.
Knox, Wm. M	Fesserton.	Legree, John	Dacre.
Kingston, Robert	Wisawasa.	Lagree, James L	Calabogie.
Kearnan, Edward	Blind River.	Leigh, John Chas	Gravenhurst.
Kearney, Michael John	Buckingham, Qu.	Lloyd, Edward L	King.
Kendrick, John	Burk's Falls.	Lemyre, Bruno	Gravenhurst.
Kendrick, John L	Burk's Falls.	Lavelle, Charles H	Canoe Lake.
Kennedy, John W	Ottawa.	Lyons, James	Waltham Sta., Q.
Kelly, James F	Trout Creek.	Ledwood, Chas	Ottawa.
Kauffman, Julius	Blind River.	Lavelle, Emery	Waltham Sta., Q.
Kennedy, Sylvester	Brule Lake.	Little, Theo	Rat Portage.

11 L.M.

Appendix No. 60.—Continued:

Name.	P. O. Address.	Name.	P. O. Address.
Lehman, Joseph	Stratton Station.	Monro, Philip	Braeside.
Lafare, Mark	Cache Bay.	Mangan, Patrick	Arnprior.
Leach, George	Vermilion Bay.	Marcil, Peter	Ottawa.
		Main, Samuel	Spanish Station.
Malloy, Mark	Baysville.	Morley, Charles	Huntsville.
Martin, Hugh	Sault Ste. Marie.	Moore, David Henry	Peterborough.
Miller, R. O.	Gravenhurst.	Murphy, John	Arnprior.
Morrison, James	Toronto.	Mathieson, Daniel	Chelmsford.
Murray, Frederick	Huntsville.	Milne, Wm.	Ethel.
Menzies, Archibald	Burk's Falls.	Mangan, Charles	Burk's Falls.
Manning, James	Trenton.	Mooney, Lincoln	Orillia.
Martin, Philip	Stoco.	Mangan, John	Arnprior.
Malone, Wm. Pat.	Ottawa.	Mooney, Thomas	Kingston.
Marsh, Esli Terril	Trenton.	Mason, Robert T.	Rochesterville.
Millar, John W.	Huntsville.	Moore, Wm. John.	Gravenhurst.
Mutchinbacker, Asa	Rosseau Falls.	Morrison, Donald	Reay.
Morris, George F.	French Bay.	Moore, Wm	Bobcaygeon.
Murray, George, Jr.	Waubaushene.	Mutchenbacker, Herman	Rosseau Falls.
Maughan, Joseph	Fort William.	Moore, Norman	Arnprior.
Margach, Wm. J.	Port Arthur.	Morley, John R.	Rat Portage.
Murray, George, Sr.	Waubaushene.	Mackay, J. A.	Big Forks.
Maniece, Wm	Peterborough.	Miller, Robt.	Montreal.
Murray, Wm.	Rat Portage.		
Morgan, Richard J.	Rat Portage.	McCaw, Joseph E.	Tweed.
Magee, Thomas Arthur	Rat Portage.	McLaren, Peter.	Rat Portage.
Murdoch, James	Cook's Mills.	McGregor, Colin F.	Rat Portage.
Mulvahil, Wm.	Arnprior.	McKenzie, Robert.	Rat Portage.
Murphy, Arthur	Ottawa.	McFadyen, A. J.	Bracebridge.
Mayhew, Jacob	Northcote.	McCauley, Thos. J.	Goulais Bay.
Molyneaux, George	Parry Sound.	McDonald, John C.	Spanish Mills.
Milway, Joseph	Fort William.	McKenzie, Alex. E.	Ansonia.
Mackie, Nathan	Port Arthur.	McIntyre, John.	Arnprior
Milne, Archie	Arnprior.	McDermott Thos.	Orillia.
Murray, James	Peterborough.	McDermott, Jas. E.	North Bay.
Moore, James A. E.	Lakefield.	McCrindle, Jas.	Sudbury.
Merkley, William A.	Ottawa.	McGhie, Chas. S.	Whitestone
Murphy, Hugh R.	Ottawa East.	McGenigal, John H.	Whitby.
Murphy, W. J.	Arnprior.	McCart, Patrick	Arnprior.
Murray, William	Markstay.	McGrath, Thomas B.	Peterborough.
Macfarlane, Robert L.	Warren.	McCormick, James J.	Trenton.
Martin, Edgerton.	Markstay.	McCarthy, Wm.	Fenelon Falls.
Mathieson, Archie.	Fort Frances.	McAvoy, Owen.	Campbellford.
Moore, Henry R.	Lakefield.	McConnell, Lewis	Fesserton.
Mickle, Charles S.	Gravenhurst.	McMullen, George.	Spragge.
Mullen, James.	Webbwood.	McNab, Angus.	Burnstown.
Morley, A. W.	Winnipeg.	McColgan, C. H.	Quyon, Que.
Macdonald, James M.	North Bay.	McCallum, Webster	Arnprior.
Money, Harry	Haileybury.	McCagherty, Robert E.	Westmeath.
Mather, Allan.	Keewatin.	McNab, Archie	Calabogie.
Menzies Alexander	Sault Ste. Marie.	McDonald, Malcolm	Spragge.
Munroe, Peter P.	Commanda.	McIvor, J. A.	Fort Frances.
Mason, Benjamin	Westmeath.	McCulloch, M	Rat Portage.
Monaghan, John B.	Arnprior.	McDonagh, Rod	Callander.
Monaghan, M. J.	Arnprior.	McManus, James	Arnprior.
Mulvihill, John	Arnprior.	McKinley, J. H.	Curran.
Moran, Andrew	Rockingham.	McPherson, Jas. S.	Rama.
Mulvihill, Michael	Arnprior.	McKinley, Edward C.	Toronto.
Mann, John	Manitowaning.	McClelland, John	Parry Sound.
Marrigan, Richard	Deseronto.	McFarlane, J. W.	Cache Bay.
Monaghan, John Dorland	Deseronto.	McDonald, Roderick	Pembroke.
Matheson, Wm	Chelmsford.	McCormack, Wm.	Pembroke.
Munro, Alex. G	Braeside.	McCreary, William	Arnprior.

Appendix No. 60.—Continued.

Name.	P. O. Address.	Name.	P. O. Address.
McCreary, James, Jr	Arnprior.	McNabb, Alexander	Arnprior.
McPhee, Hugh	Byng Inlet.	McFarlane, Alexander	Renfrew.
McCudden, James	Arnprior.	McFarlane, J. D	Stewartsville.
McLachlin, J. A	Arnprior.	McFarlane, Duncan	Renfrew.
Macpherson, John	Ottawa.	McKendry, Wm. B	Arnprior.
McEachren, John A	Gravenhurst W.	McPhee, Hugh	Renfrew.
McLeod, Dugald	Gravenhurst.	McPhee, John	Arnprior.
McClelland, R. H	Parry Sound.	McLachlin, Peter	Arnprior.
McEvoy, Frank	Campbellford.	McLachlin, Alexander	Arnprior.
McDermott, Peter	Orillia.	Mackey, Edward	Arnprior.
McIlroy, John	Madoc.	McEwan, Henry	Trenton.
McNab, Robert J	Parry Sound.	McDonald, Alfred	Peterborough.
McFadden, James	Ottawa.	McGeary, John J	Sundridge.
McIntosh, James G	Carleton Place.	McDonald, Archibald W	Gilmour.
McInnis, Hector D	Bracebridge.	McCaw, John Gillen	Queensborough.
McKinnon, Malcolm	Bracebridge.	McCaulay, Barney	Trenton.
McLean, Daniel	Bracebridge.	McDougall, James T	Klock's Mills.
McKinnon, Archie J	Bracebridge.	McInenly, Thomas	Quebec, Que.
McKay, D. C	Baysville.	McBride, Archibald	Arnprior.
McDonald, James	Parry Sound.	McFarlane, Robert L	Arnprior.
McPherson, Allan	Longford.	McGowan, Wm	Parry Sound.
McDonald, James P	French River.	McLachlin, Norman	Arnprior.
McFarlane, Jos. C	Port Severn.	McDonald, Laughlin	Pendelton.
McNabb, Alexander	Thessalon.	McIvor, William J	Collins Inlet.
McGillivray, Archibald	Port Arthur.	McKee, John P	Sturgeon Falls.
McGrane, Edward	Lindsay.	McGowan, Thomas	Parry Sound.
McLeod, Donald, Jr	Keewatin.	McDermot, Patrick	South River.
McDonald, Hector R	Thessalon.	McKay, Angus	South River.
McDougall, Duncan	Bracebridge.	McDonald, A. J	Longford.
McNabb, Alexander D	Warren.	McInnis, Angus D	Gravenhurst.
McCormack, John C	Sudbury.	MeKendry, Alexander	Waubaushene.
McNamara, John	Byng Inlet.	McGuire, Timothy	North Bay.
McGillivray, Duncan D	Algoma Mills.	McGrath, John	Peterborough.
McIntyre, Daniel A	Klock's Mills.	McWilliams, John Bannon	Peterborough.
McNamara, Lewis	Klock's Mills.	McCagherty, Patrick	Westmeath.
McDonald, Sidney C	Mattawa.	McKendry, Daniel	Arnprior.
McGurn, Jno. J	Buckingham, Que	MacDonald, D. F	Parry Sound.
McKeown, Jno. Joseph	Port Arthur.	McManus, Thomas J	Renfrew.
McNeel, David	Sault Ste. Marie.	Macfarlane, David R	Ottawa.
McEwan, Andrew	Thessalon.	McColgan, Edward	Quyon, Que.
McCool, Christopher L	Cartier.	McKay, John	Emo.
McCollum, Donald	Arnprior.	McKinnon, William	Kenora.
McDowell, Wm	Cache Bay.	McKittrick, Frank R. F	Kenora.
McConachie, Roy Stewart	Huntsville.	McMichael, Charles	North Seguin.
McDonell, J. K	Rat Portage.	McIlroy, Thomas Davis	Madoc.
McDonald, Alex. J	Vermilion Bay.	McDonald, Wm. Henry	Trenton.
McKay, D. A	Rainy Bay.	McGaw, Wm. Thomas	Callander.
McMillan, James	Rat Portage.	McMillan, L	Callander.
McPhee, Ronald	Bracebridge.	McDermott, John L	Orillia.
McKay, George Donner	Dorset.	McDonald, Chas. M	Pembroke.
McWilliams, Maxwell		McPhee, Benjamin	Pembroke.
Theodore	Peterborough.	McGee, John Edward	Parry Sound.
McLeod, John	Keewatin.	Macfarlane, Mack	Arnprior.
McPherson, George	Keewatin.	MacCallum, Alexander	Braeside.
McDougall, John D	Rat Portage.	McRae, Farquhar	Rat Portage.
McGregor, Duncan	Burnstown.	MacCallum, Albert	Arnprior.
McLean, Peter W	Sand Point.	McGonigal, John	Arnprior.
McNichol, John	Sudbury.	McConachie, John	Huntsville.
McInnis, D. E	Cache Bay.	McKay, D. G	Rat Portage.
McLaughlin, Samuel	Waubaushene.	McDonald, James	Peterborough.
McCollman, John	North Bay.	McCulloch, John L	Lonsdale.
McManus, John C	Arnprior.	McConnell, James	Mine Centre.

Appendix No. 60.—Continued.

Name.	P. O. Address.	Name.	P. O. Address.
McNaughton, Daniel	Bracebridge.	Paterson, John	Wannapitae.
McCagherty, William E.	Westmeath.	Paterson, Alexander	Orillia.
McDonald, John D	Mattawa.	Parke, James	Gravenhurst.
McCagherty, Joseph T.	Westmeath.	Parquette, Oliver.	Webbwood.
McAdam, Arch. H	Quyon, Que.	Palmateer, Sherman	Gravenhurst.
McMurphy, Dugald, Jr	Rat Portage.	Paget, George	Huntsville.
McCall, Alfred	Rat Portage.	Pounder, Joseph	Westmeath.
McRitchie, William	Rat Portage.	Pell, Richard D	Arnprior.
McRitchie, Malcolm	Rat Portage.	Perry, Frederick	Port Arthur.
		Paget, Charles Edward	Novar.
Nescott, George	Rat Portage.	Porter, Thomas Robert Mark	Dorset.
Newton, Frank	Gravenhurst.	Ponntey, E. J	Arnprior.
Newburn, Wm	Parry Sound.	Pyburn, David J	Dorset.
Niblett, James	Arnprior.	Purdy, Geo	Hintonburg.
Niblett, Robert	Osceola.	Playfair, Andrew Wm	Sault Ste. Marie.
Newall, John H	Parry Harbor.	Pipe, Taylor.	Haileybury.
Nolan, John	Gravenhurst	Pipher, George E	Mowat.
Newton. Charles W	Victoria Harbor.	Pendee, David	Parry Sound.
Nent, Charles	Vermilion Bay.		
Needham, John G	Pakenham.	Quinn, William	Peterborough.
		Quigley, Hugh	Penetang.
Oullette, Joseph P	Cutler.	Quirk, Thomas J	Petewawa.
O'Neil, Thomas	Bancroft.		
O'Neill, Daniel H. H	Arnprior.	Robertson, D	Rat Portage.
O'Leary, Patrick J	Orillia.	Richardson Frederick George	Trenton.
Oliver, Charles R	Fesserton.	Richards, Richard	Tamworth.
Overend, George J	Longford Mills.	Riddell, Geo. Alexander	Rochesterville.
O'Brien, Andrew	Ottawa.	Robertson, Lewis McLean	Dunchurch.
O'Brien. Frank G	Arnprior.	Robinson, Wm. F	Bobcaygeon.
Oliver, J. A	Fort William.	Reamsbottom, Wm	Mattawa.
Owen, W. J	Wabigoon.	Richey, Evan	Brentwood.
O'Connor, John	Hintonburg.	Randall Lewis G	French River.
Oliver, Darcy	Wahnapitae.	Richardson. Charles Marvyn.	Trenton.
O'Connor, Wm	Nosbonsing.	Rochester, Daniel Baillie	Ottawa.
O'Neill, James W	North Bay.	Riddell, James	Ottawa.
O'Donnell, Wm	Penetanguishene	Rice, Asa A	Hull, Que.
Owens, Richard	Basin Depot.	Roberts, T. A	Huntsville.
O'Reilly. Patrick	Cartier.	Ross, Andrew	Longford Mills.
O'Neill, Mark	Renfrew.	Rose, Donald M	Rat Portage.
Orrill, John	Trenton.	Rawson, Charles Edgar	Coldwater.
O'Neill, Patrick	Bancroft.	Ross, George	Waubaushene.
Orde, Francis W	Rat Portage.	Roberts, Percy T	Keewatin.
O'Driscoll, Joseph	Sault Ste. Marie.	Ritchie, Wm. D	Little Current.
		Ramsay, Robert.	Arnprior.
Pigott, John	Fitzroy Harbor.	Ritchie, J. F	Arnprior.
Paul, Charles A	Sault Ste. Marie.	Ritter, Samuel G	Ahmic Harbour.
Pattison, Thos	Bracebridge.	Rothera, Charles F	Sturgeon Falls.
Price, A. E	Arnprior.	Ryan, Alfred.	Byng Inlet.
Presley, J. F	Ashton.	Rogers, Fred	Sault Ste. Marie.
Power, James	Bobcaygeon.	Reid, George William	Fort Frances.
Patzel, Adolph	Arnprior.	Robertson, John A	Kenora.
Plaunt, William B	Eganville.	Robinson, Wm	Bobcaygeon.
Plaunt, Joseph	Eganville.	Reid, Joseph B	Lindsay.
Porter, Charles C	Longford.	Ross, Walter M	Ottawa.
Preston, R. E	Rat Portage	Ruttle, H. A	Carleton Place.
Petrie, George A	Fergus.	Richards, Benedict	Ottawa.
Pomeroy, Peter	Trenton.	Regan, John	Orillia.
Perry, Pringle K	Bying Inlet, N'th	Russel, Wm	Pembroke
Purcall, W. G	Ottawa.	Ramsay, Charles	Sudbury.
Purvis, John	Parry Sound.	Russell, Corsan L	Pembroke.
Porter, James	Uphill.	Richards, Henry	Dacre.
Pearson, John James	Lindsay.	Ryan, Wm	Killaloe.

Appendix No. 60.—Continued.

Name.	P. O. Address.	Name.	P. O Address.
Rooney, Wm. H	Campbellford.	Scott, Thomas	Parry Sound.
Revell, J. O.	Dryden.	Smith, Lawrence	W.Saginaw,Mich
Rankin, Anthony	Cache Bay.	Shea, Stewart	Campbellford.
Ross, Angus	Orrville.	Sullivan, John	Sault. Ste. Marie.
Robinson, Albert E.	Washago.	Sinclair, Finlay,	Sudbury.
Robinson, Edward	Washago.	Shiels, Henry F.	Cartier.
Robinson, Thomas G.	Washago.	Smith, Gideon Ousley	Burk's Falls.
Raycroft, William T.	Sarnia.	Smith, John Wallis	Thedford.
Roberts, Ivor M.	Garden River.	Smith, Henry G.	Arnprior.
Revell, Lionel Oliver.	W. Gravenhurst.	Story, John A	Ottawa.
Regan, Judd Patrick.	Orillia.	Sweezy, Benjamin	Massey.
Robins, Etna, Rosedale	Orillia.	Sheppard, Charles H	Coldwater.
Regan, John, Jr	Orillia.	Sinclair, Arnon D.	Arnprior.
Ryan, James	Savanne.	Smith, Sidney E.	Ottawa.
Rusk, Oscar W	Cache Bay.	Sleeman, Wm	Rapid River.
Robinson, Thos. Geo	Bracebridge.	Sheeman, Peter F.	Loring.
Rooksby, Wm	Campbellford.	Sleeman, Geo.	Rapid River.
Ramesbottom, Robt.	Byng Inlet.	Sims, William K.	Sault Ste. Marie.
Roy. Lewis	Arnprior.	Skahill, William	Blind River.
Riddell, Horace A.	Galetta.	Shaw, George	Thessalon.
Rowan, A. L.	Sault Ste. Marie.	Sarsfield, George Francis.	Sault Ste. Marie.
Ritchie, James A	Spragge.	Standish, William H	Batchawining
		Simpson, William A	Lakefield. [Bay.
Smith, M. D.	Fort William.	Scollard, Wm	Young's Point.
Scanlan, William	Enterprise.	Shuttleworth, Alma	Trout Creek.
Sutherland, D. H.	Gravenhurst.	Shanacy Wm. J.	Spragge.
Spanner, John.	Huntsville.	Seely, George	Arnprior.
Shier, James D.	Bracebridge.	Stewart, Alex W	Lanark.
Spooner, W. R.	Katrine.	Soreny, William	Braeside.
Simpson, Alfred. E.	Wakefield.	Schneder, Frederick.	Cache Bay.
Souliere, John B.	Ottawa.	Smith, James D.	Rat Portage.
Shields James A,	Carleton Place.	Sullivan, Jas.	Aylmer, Que.
Spargo, George	Ottawa.	Scully, Cornelius	Whitney.
Smyth, W. H.	Byng Inlet North	Savoy, Eutrope	North Ray.
Salmon, R. H.	Baysville.	Smith, Walter J	Campbellford.
Salmon, Alexander C.	Baysville.	Seymour, John J	Whitefish.
Stremer, A.	Ottawa.	Smith, Alex R. C	Burk's Falls.
Shields, Frank A.	Parry Sound.	Stewart. Richard M.	Chelsea, Que.
Stapleton, John J.	Ogidakie.	Souliere, John H.	Canoe Lake.
Sloan, William H.	Fort Frauces.	Smith, Abraim G.	Quyon, Que.
Smyth, Job E.	Cache Bay.	Swallow, C. H.	Day Mills.
Sage, Nelson	Muskoka Mills.	Strave, A. M	Mine Centre.
Seymour, Edward	Whitefish.	Stewart, John	Fort Frances.
Shaw, Thomas B.	Waubaushene.	Sullivan, George L.	Rainy River.
Swanston, James	Peterborough.	Short, James	Kenora.
Simpson, William	Hall's Bridge.		
Sadler, Thomas	Lindsay.	Taylor, Fred L.	Parry Sound.
Smith, Patrick Albert	Norman.	Thomas, Griff J	Thessalon.
Snaith, Wm. J.	Mattawa.	Thomson, R. D.	Biscotasing.
Sinn, William F.	Arnprior.	Tait, Thomas B.	Burk's Falls.
Sheppard, Wm. Joseph	Waubaushene.	Taylor, C. M	Gravenhurst.
Spears, Milton B.	Barry's Bay.	Thornton, W. D.	Longford Mills.
Stevenson, Arthur.	Peterborough.	Trussler, Gilbert.	Trout Creek.
Stein, Paul	Sault Ste. Marie.	Thompson, Geo. S	Lindsay.
Shaw, Alfred	Thessalon.	Thompson, Frederick A. H.	Callander.
Sequin, Napoleon	Spanish Station.	Thompson, Francis Henry	Nosbonsing.
Scrim, Robert	Arnprior.	Train, A. C.	Rowan Mills
Sharp, James A	Sudbury.	Turgeon, George	Cook's Mills.
Shaneay, Harry S.	Cook's Mills.	Thayer, William	Sault Ste. Marie.
Smith, Wm	Ottawa.	Thompson, Alexander W.	Arnprior.
Stewart, Daniel	Braeside.	Taylor, Thomas G.	Gravenhurst.
Sheehan, Michael H.	Waubaushene.	Trowse, A.	Arnprior.

Appendix No. 60.—Continued.

Name.	P. O. Address.	Name.	P. O. Address.
Thompson, Daniel	P'rt'ge duF'rt, Q.	Watson, Wm	North Bay.
Thompson, Richard	Rat Portage	Wagner, Fred	Rat Portage.
Thompson, Joseph H	Bracebridge.	Wainwright, Edward C	Huntsville.
Taylor, Edward A	Westmeath.	Wilson Wm. James	Deseronto.
Tait, Ralph	Arnprior.	Weston, Frank R	Midland.
Train, William	Burk's Falls.	White, James B	Manitowaning.
Turner, Garvin F	North Bay.	Warren, Robt. M	Cache Bay.
Tilson, Joseph	Burk's Falls.	Wilson, Geo. A	Balsam Hill.
Tuffy, John	Cartier.	Welch, Harold	Milberta.
Thorpe, Thos	Pembroke.	Wilson, James A., Jr	Webbwood.
Taylor, Chas. E	Gravenhurst.	Woods, John R	Antrim.
Tench, Arthur	Hekkla.	Wardell, Ernest C. S	Victoria Harbor.
Tulloch, William A	Sault Ste. Marie.	Woods, Joseph F	Roach's Point.
Taylor, Alex. M	Burnstown.	Whaley, Thomas	Huntsville.
Toner, J. A	P'rt'geduF'rt, Q.	Webster, Wm. Alfred	Bracebridge.
Thrasher, Henry G	Pembroke.	Wornsdorf, Frederick Gutlep	Pembroke.
Tooke, Frank	Bala.	Warrell, Wm	Trout Creek.
		Wims, Peter	Blessington.
Udy, Dean	French River.	Wickware, Philip Almonte	Cloyne.
Urquhart, Elias	Gravenhurst.	Wilson, Edward	Deseronto.
Urquhart, Andrew	Barrie.	Whelan, P. J	McDougall.
		Whyte, John Thomas Goth	Ottawa.
Vigrass, Percy J	Dufferin Bridge.	Watterworth, J. A	Sault Ste. Marie.
Vincent, Joseph	Warren.	White, Wm. James	Muskoka Falls.
Vollin, Samuel	Nosbonsing.	Warrell, George	Powassan.
Vannier, Nelson Joseph	Bobcaygeon.	Wells, George W	Little Current.
Vincent, James	Fesserton.	Wilson. Frederick Gould	Rat Portage
Vincent, Henry T	Port Sidney.	Wallace, John Thomas	Thessalon.
Vanderburg, Norman	Wisawasa.	Wilkins, George N	Baysville.
		Wylie, Byrom M	Webbwood.
White, Thomas S	Bracebridge.	White, Allan	Pembroke.
White, A. Thomson	Pembroke.	Warner, Franklin H	Fort Frances.
Watt, R. A	Spanish.	Watts, George	Fort Frances.
Wilkins, Hughes	Blind River.	Wood, Thos	Parry Sound.
Wallace, T. William	Blind River.	White, William	Peterborough.
White, Joseph W	Bracebridge.	Woods, A. L	Rat Portage.
Watson, Wm	Huntsville.	White, John B	Kippewa, Que.
Webb, Geo. W	Parry Sound.	Whelan Peter M	Renfrew.
Wilcox, Thomas	Parry Sound.		
Wheeler, J. A. McL	Tamworth.	Young, R. H	Fort Frances.
Widdifield, C. H	Pine Orchard.	Yuill, John Albert	Braeside.
Whitmore, Edgar	Rosseau Falls.	Young, Wm	Severn Bridge.
Wright, L. B	Sault Ste. Marie.	Young, A. J	Cache Bay.
Ward, Joseph W	Ottawa.	Young, Samuel	Coldwater.
Wilkinson, W	French River.	Young, Patrick P	Young's Point.
Waldie, John E	Victoria Harbor.	Young, Francis G	Young's Point.
Wigg, Thomas G	Thessalon.	Yuill, Thomas	Arnprior.
Wall, Patrick B	Cheboygan, Mich	Yuill, A. D	Braeside.
Wells, John R	Little Current.	Young, C. T	Harvey.
Whiteside, John	Huntsville.	Yuill, John Alex	Arnprior.
Watt, Wm	Peterborough.	Yuill, Archibald	Bracebridge.
Wilson, George	Lindsay.	Yuill, Wm	Braeside.
White, Thomas	Parry Sound.	Total 1188.	

AUBREY WHITE.
Deputy Minister.